SIPRI Yearbook 1992
World Armaments and Disarmament

sipri

Stockholm International Peace Research Institute

SIPRI is an independent international institute for research into problems of peace and conflict, especially those of arms control and disarmament. It was established in 1966 to commemorate Sweden's 150 years of unbroken peace.

The Institute is financed mainly by the Swedish Parliament. The staff, the Governing Board and the Scientific Council are international.

The Governing Board and the Scientific Council are not responsible for the views expressed in the publications of the Institute.

Governing Board

Professor Daniel Tarschys, MP, Chairman (Sweden)
Sir Brian Urquhart, Vice Chairman (United Kingdom)
Dr Oscar Arias Sánchez (Costa Rica)
Professor Francesco Calogero (Italy)
Dr Gyula Horn (Hungary)
Professor Emma Rothschild (United Kingdom)
Dr Lothar Rühl (Germany)
The Director

Director

Dr Adam Daniel Rotfeld (Poland)

sipri

Stockholm International Peace Research Institute
Pipers väg 28, S-170 73 Solna, Sweden
Cable: SIPRI
Telephone: 46 8/655 97 00
Telefax: 46 8/655 97 33

SIPRI Yearbook 1992

World Armaments and Disarmament

sipri

Stockholm International Peace Research Institute

OXFORD UNIVERSITY PRESS
1992

Oxford University Press, Walton Street, Oxford OX2 6DP
Oxford New York Toronto
Delhi Bombay Calcutta Madras Karachi
Petaling Jaya Singapore Hong Kong Tokyo
Nairobi Dar es Salaam Cape Town
Melbourne Auckland
and associated companies in
Berlin Ibadan

Oxford is a trade mark of Oxford University Press

Published in the United States
by Oxford University Press, New York

British Library Cataloguing in Publication Data

Data available
ISSN 0953–0282
ISBN 0–19–829159–0

Library of Congress Cataloging in Publication Data

LC card number 83-643843
ISSN 0347–2205

Typeset and originated by Stockholm International Peace Research Institute
Printed and bound in Great Britain by
Biddles Ltd., Guildford and King's Lynn

Contents

Part I. Weapons, technology and arms control

Part II. Military expenditure, arms trade and production, and armed conflicts

Part III. Conventional arms control in Europe

Part IV. Special features

Annexes

Acknowledgements

This twenty-third edition of the *SIPRI Yearbook* was produced in a period of world changes and transitions, which necessitated an unusual reappraisal of world armaments, disarmament and security matters for the otherwise standard work of the Institute.

As a rule the *Yearbook* is primarily written by the in-house research staff who continuously monitor the data and events. However, we are also proud that a number of chapters are contributed by distinguished outside authors such as, this year, Ambassador Rolf Ekéus, Executive Chairman of the UN Special Commission on Iraq, and several other outstanding contributors who for many years have regularly co-operated in different ways with the Institute. We are also grateful to those who provided us with valuable suggestions in their role as external referees of the *Yearbook* chapters.

Two people deserve special mention and thanks: Connie Wall and Billie Bielckus, whose devotion, great skill, energy, experienced editorial leadership and diligence made it possible to transform fifteen disparate chapters into a unified volume. I would also like to thank Ragnhild Ferm, whose close attention to accuracy extended beyond her own sections of the *Yearbook*.

My appreciation also goes to the other editors—Paul Claesson, Jetta Gilligan Borg and Don Odom—whose mastery of the English language, enthusiasm and experience provided indispensable assistance in preparing this volume in final camera-ready format.

In addition, thanks are due to the secretaries—Felicite Ingrisch, Cynthia Loo, Marianne Lyons, Miyoko Suzuki and Cathy Walsh—and to Gerd Hagmeyer-Gaverus for programming and other computer assistance.

Dr Adam Daniel Rotfeld
Director of SIPRI

GLOSSARY

Acronyms

ABM	Anti-ballistic missile	CBW	Chemical and biological warfare/weapons
ACE	Allied Command Europe (NATO)	CD	Conference on Disarmament
ACM	Advanced cruise missile	CEP	Circular error probable
ACV	Armoured combat vehicle	CFE	Conventional Armed Forces in Europe
ADM	Atomic demolition munition		
AFAP	Artillery-fired atomic projectile	CIS	Commonwealth of Independent States
AIFV	Armed infantry fighting vehicle	CMEA	Council for Mutual Economic Assistance (as COMECON)
ALCM	Air-launched cruise missile	COCOM	Coordinating Committee (on Multilateral Export Controls)
AMF	Allied Mobile Force	COMECON	Council for Mutual Economic Assistance (as CMEA)
ANC	African National Congress		
ASAT	Anti-satellite	CORRTEX	Continuous reflectometry for radius versus time experiments
ASEAN	Association of South-East Asian Nations	CPC	Conflict Prevention Centre
ASLCM	Advanced sea-launched cruise missile	CSBM	Confidence- and security-building measure
ASM	Air-to-surface missile	CSCE	Conference on Security and Co-operation in Europe
ASUW	Anti-surface warfare	CSO	Committee of Senior Officials
ASW	Anti-submarine warfare	CTB(T)	Comprehensive test ban (treaty)
ATBM	Anti-tactical ballistic missile		
ATC	Armoured troop carrier	CTOL	Conventional take-off and landing
ATTU	Atlantic-to-the-Urals (zone)	CW	Chemical warfare/weapons
AWACS	Airborne warning and control system	CWC	Chemical Weapons Convention
BCC	Bilateral Consultation Commission	CWFZ	Chemical weapon-free zone
BMD	Ballistic missile defence	DEW	Directed-energy weapon
BW	Biological warfare/weapons	DST	Defence and Space Talks
BWC	Biological Weapons Convention	EC	European Community
		ECOWAS	Economic Community of West African States
CAS	Committee on Assurances of Supply	ECU	European Currency Unit
CBM	Confidence-building measure	EFA	European Fighter Aircraft

ELINT	Electronic intelligence	INF	Intermediate-range nuclear forces
ELV	Expendable launch vehicle		
EMP	Electromagnetic pulse	IOC	Initial operational capability
EMU	Economic and Monetary Union	IRBM	Intermediate-range ballistic missile
Enmod	Environmental modification	JCC	Joint Consultative Commission
EPU	European Political Union	JCG	Joint Consultative Group
ERW	Enhanced radiation (neutron) weapon	JCIC	Joint Compliance and Inspection Commission
EU	European Union	JSG	Joint Strategy Group
EUCLID	European Cooperative Long-term Initiative on Defence	LDC	Less developed country
FBS	Forward-based system	LDDI	Less developed defence industry
FOC	Full operational capability	MAD	Mutual assured destruction
FOST	Force Océanique Stratégique	MARV	Manœuvrable re-entry vehicle
FOTL	Follow-on to Lance	MD	Military District
FROD	Functionally related observable difference	MIRV	Multiple independently targetable re-entry vehicle
FROG	Free-rocket-over-ground	MLRS	Multiple launcher rocket system
FY	Fiscal year		
GBR	Ground-based radar	MOU	Memorandum of Understanding
GCC	Gulf Co-operation Council		
GDP	Gross domestic product	MRV	Multiple re-entry vehicle
GLCM	Ground-launched cruise missile	MSC	Military Staff Committee
GNP	Gross national product	MTCR	Missile Technology Control Regime
GPALS	Global Protection Against Limited Strikes	MTM	Multinational technical means (of verification)
HACV	Heavy armoured combat vehicle	NACC	North Atlantic Cooperation Council
HLTF	High Level Task Force	NATO	North Atlantic Treaty Organization
HLWG	High Level Working Group		
IAEA	International Atomic Energy Agency	NBC	Nuclear, biological and chemical (weapons)
ICBM	Intercontinental ballistic missile	NMP	Net material product
		NNA	Neutral and non-aligned (states)
IEPG	Independent European Programme Group	NPG	Nuclear Planning Group
IFV	Infantry fighting vehicle	NPT	Non-Proliferation Treaty

NRRC	Nuclear Risk Reduction Centre		SDI	Strategic Defense Initiative
NST	Nuclear and Space Talks		SDIO	SDI Organization
NSWTO	Non-Soviet WTO		SICBM	Small ICBM
NTI	National trial inspection		SLBM	Submarine-launched ballistic missile
NTM	National technical means (of verification)		SLCM	Sea-launched cruise missile
NTS	Nevada test site		SLV	Space launch vehicle
NWFZ	Nuclear weapon-free zone		SNDV	Strategic nuclear delivery vehicle
ODA	Official development assistance		SNF	Short-range nuclear forces
OECD	Organization for Economic Co-operation and Development		SS(M)	Surface-to-surface (missile)
			SRAM	Short-range attack missile
			SRBM	Short-range ballistic missile
OMG	Operational Manœuvre Group		SSBN	Nuclear-powered, ballistic-missile submarine
O&M	Operation and maintenance			
OOV	Object of verification		SSGN	Nuclear-powered, guided-missile submarine
OPANAL	Agency for the Prohibition of Nuclear Weapons in Latin America		SSN	Nuclear-powered attack submarine
OSI	On-site inspection		START	Strategic Arms Reduction Talks
OSIA	On-Site Inspection Agency		SVC	Special Verification Commission
PLO	Palestine Liberation Organization			
			SWS	Strategic weapon system
PNE(T)	Peaceful Nuclear Explosions (Treaty)		TASM	Tactical air-to-surface missile
POMCUS	Prepositioned Organizational Material Configured to Unit Sets		TEL	Transporter–erector–launcher
			TLE	Treaty-limited equipment
PTB(T)	Partial Test Ban (Treaty)		TNF	Theatre nuclear forces
R&D	Research and development		TTB(T)	Threshold Test Ban (Treaty)
RMA	Restricted Military Area		UNIKOM	United Nations Iraq–Kuwait Observation Mission
RPV	Remotely piloted vehicle		UNSCOM	United Nations Special Commission on Iraq
RV	Re-entry vehicle			
SACEUR	Supreme Allied Commander, Europe		VCC	Verification Co-ordinating Committee
SALT	Strategic Arms Limitation Talks		V/STOL	Vertical/short take-off and landing
SAM	Surface-to-air missile		WEU	Western European Union
SCC	Standing Consultative Commission		WTO	Warsaw Treaty Organization (Warsaw Pact)

Glossary

Anti-ballistic missile (ABM) system	Weapon system for intercepting and destroying ballistic missiles and their warheads in flight.
Anti-Ballistic Missile (ABM) Treaty	Treaty signed by the USSR and the USA in 1972 in the SALT I process which prohibits the development, testing and deployment of sea-, air-, space- or mobile land-based ABM systems.
ATTU zone	The Atlantic-to-the-Urals zone of the 1990 Treaty on Conventional Armed Forces in Europe (CFE). Ceilings on NATO and WTO treaty-limited equipment holdings in the ATTU zone are set in the Treaty. *See also:* Conventional Armed Forces in Europe (CFE) Treaty.
Ballistic missile	A missile which follows a ballistic trajectory (part of which may be outside the earth's atmosphere) when thrust is terminated.
Binary chemical weapon	A shell or other device filled with two chemicals of relatively low toxicity which mix and react while the device is being delivered to the target, the reaction product being a supertoxic chemical warfare agent, such as nerve gas.
Biological weapon (BW)	Living organisms, whatever their nature, or infective material derived from them, which are intended for use in warfare to cause disease or death in man, animals or plants, and which for their effect depend on their ability to multiply in the person, animal or plant attacked, as well as the means of their delivery.
Charter of Paris for a New Europe	*See:* Paris Documents.
Chemical weapon (CW)	Chemical substances—whether gaseous, liquid or solid— which might be employed as weapons in combat because of their direct toxic effects on man, animals or plants, and the means of their delivery.
Circular error probable (CEP)	A measure of missile accuracy: the radius of a circle, centred on the target, within which 50 per cent of the weapons aimed at the target are expected to fall.
Commonwealth of Independent States (CIS)	Established by three of the former Soviet republics in the Agreement on the Commonwealth of Independent States signed in Minsk, Belarus, on 8 December 1991 and joined by eight additional republics in Alma-Ata on 21 December 1991. The CIS consists of 11 of the former constituent republics of the USSR: Armenia, Azerbaijan, Belarus, Kazakhstan, Kyrgyzstan, Moldova, the Russian Federation, Tajikistan, Turkmenistan, Ukraine and Uzbekistan.

Conference on
Disarmament (CD)

Multilateral arms control negotiating body, based in Geneva, which is composed of 39 states, including all the permanent members of the UN Security Council. The CD reports to the UN General Assembly. The Russian Federation assumed the seat of the former USSR in December 1991.

Conference on
Confidence- and Security-
Building Measures and
Disarmament in Europe

The Stockholm Conference, part of the CSCE process, was held in 1984–86. The Stockholm Document, in which the confidence-building measures adopted in Helsinki in 1975 are improved and expanded, was signed in 1986. *See also:* Confidence- and Security-Building Measures (CSBM) Negotiations, Vienna Documents on CSBMs.

Conference on Security
and Co-operation in
Europe (CSCE)

A conference which began in 1973 with the participation of all the European states except Albania plus the USA and Canada, and in 1975 adopted a Final Act (also called the Helsinki Declaration), containing, among others, a Document on confidence-building measures and certain aspects of security and disarmament. Follow-up meetings were held in Belgrade (1977–78), Madrid (1980–83), Vienna (1986–89) and Helsinki (1992). A summit meeting of all the CSCE heads of state and government will be held in July 1992. As of 24 March 1992, there are 51 member states: all the European states plus the USA and Canada and the former Soviet republics (including the Asian republics, thereby extending membership outside Europe). The major new CSCE organs created in 1990 are the Council of Foreign Ministers, the Committee of Senior Officials, the Secretariat (seat in Prague), the Conflict Prevention Centre (Vienna), the Office for Democratic Institutions and Human Rights (Warsaw), and the Parliamentary Assembly. *See also:* Conventional Armed Forces in Europe (CFE) Negotiation, Confidence- and Security-Building Measures (CSBM) Negotiations, Paris Documents.

Confidence- and Security-
Building Measures
(CSBM) Negotiations

The CSBM Negotiations, part of the CSCE process and with the participation of all the CSCE states, were held in Vienna in 1989–1990 and built upon the results of the Stockholm Conference. The Vienna Document 1990 was included in the set of Paris Documents. The Negotiations were rejoined in November 1990 and continued until 1992. The Vienna Document 1992 was adopted in March 1992. *See also:* Vienna Documents on CSBMs, Conference on Confidence- and Security-Building Measures and Disarmament in Europe.

Conventional Armed
Forces in Europe (CFE)
Negotiation

A negotiation held in Vienna in 1989–90 between the 23 member states of NATO and the WTO on conventional force reductions in Europe. Part of the CSCE process. The CFE Treaty was signed in Paris in 1990. The object of the follow-up to the CFE Negotiation, CFE 1A, is to work towards an agreement limiting military personnel in the ATTU zone. It resumed in January 1992, with the Russian Federation, Ukraine and Belarus as full-fledged members. The mandate for the CFE II Negotiation will be negotiated and adopted by the CSCE states at the Helsinki CSCE summit meeting of heads of state and government in July 1992.

Conventional Armed Forces in Europe (CFE) Treaty

The CFE Treaty was signed by 22 original signatories in Paris in 1990. It sets ceilings on treaty-limited equipment (TLE) in the ATTU zone. At the Prague CSCE Council of Foreign Ministers meeting on 30–31 January 1992, the former Soviet republics committed themselves to join the CFE Treaty. *See also:* ATTU zone, Treaty-limited equipment (TLE).

Conventional weapon

Weapon not having mass destruction effects. *See also:* Weapon of mass destruction.

Cruise missile

Unmanned, self-propelled, guided weapon-delivery vehicle which sustains flight through aerodynamic lift, generally flying at very low altitudes to avoid radar detection, sometimes following the contours of the terrain. It can be air-, ground- or sea-launched and deliver a conventional, nuclear, chemical or biological warhead.

Defence and Space Talks

Talks conducted from 1985 between the USA and the USSR, under the Geneva Nuclear and Space Talks (NST), on ballistic missile defences and on means of preventing an arms race in space. *See also:* Nuclear and Space Talks.

European Community (EC)

The EC was created in 1951–57 by six governments—Belgium, France, the Federal Republic of Germany, Italy, the Netherlands and Luxembourg—based on the 1951 Treaty of Paris. In December 1991 the texts of draft treaties on an Economic and Monetary Union and a European Political Union were agreed at the EC heads of state and government meeting in Maastricht, the Netherlands, and were signed on 7 February 1992. The Treaty on European Union (EU) is to be ratified by the parliaments of the EC states and to enter into force in early 1993. The 12 EC members in 1991 also included Denmark, Ireland, Greece, Portugal, Spain and the UK.

First-strike capability

Theoretical capability to launch a single attack on an adversary's strategic nuclear forces that nearly eliminates the second-strike capability of the adversary.

Flexible response

The NATO doctrine for reaction to an attack with a full range of military options, including the use of nuclear weapons.

Global Protection Against Limited Strikes (GPALS)

See: Strategic Defense Initiative (SDI).

Helsinki Declaration

See: Conference on Security and Co-operation in Europe (CSCE).

Intercontinental ballistic missile (ICBM)	Ground-launched ballistic missile with a range in excess of 5500 km.
Intermediate-range nuclear forces (INF)	Theatre nuclear forces with a range of from 1000 up to and including 5500 km. *See also*: Theatre nuclear forces.
Intermediate-range nuclear forces (INF) Treaty	The US–Soviet Treaty on the Elimination of Intermediate-Range and Shorter-Range Missiles, negotiated in the Nuclear and Space Talks, signed in 1987 and entered into force in 1988, obliged the USA and the USSR to destroy all land-based missiles with a range of 500–5500 km (intermediate-range, 1000–5500 km, and shorter-range, 500–1000 km) and their launchers by 1 June 1991. *See also* Theatre nuclear forces.
International Atomic Energy Agency (IAEA)	With headquarters in Vienna, the IAEA is endowed by its Statute, which entered into force in 1957, with the twin purposes of promoting the peaceful uses of atomic energy and ensuring that nuclear activities are not used to further any military purpose.
Joint Consultative Group (JCG)	Established by the CFE Treaty to reconcile ambiguities of interpretation and implementation of the CFE Treaty.
Joint Compliance and Inspection Commission (JCIC)	A US–Soviet commission established in the START Treaty as a forum for resolving questions of compliance and for discussing additional procedures to improve implementation of the START provisions. Convenes at the request of either party.
Kiloton (kt)	Measure of the explosive yield of a nuclear weapon equivalent to 1000 tons of trinitrotoluene (TNT) high explosive. (The bomb detonated at Hiroshima in World War II had a yield of about 12–15 kilotons.)
Launcher	Equipment which launches a missile. ICBM launchers are land-based launchers which can be either fixed or mobile. SLBM launchers are missile tubes on submarines.
Launch-weight	Weight of a fully loaded ballistic missile at the time of launch.
Megaton (Mt)	Measure of the explosive yield of a nuclear weapon equivalent to 1 million tons of trinitrotoluene (TNT) high explosive.
Multiple independently targetable re-entry vehicle (MIRV)	Re-entry vehicle, carried by a nuclear missile, which can be directed to separate targets along separate trajectories (as distinct from MRVs). A missile can carry one or several RVs. *See also:* Re-entry vehicle (RV).
Multiple re-entry vehicle (MRV)	Re-entry vehicle, carried by a nuclear missile, directed to the same target as the missile's other RVs. *See also:* Re-entry vehicle (RV).

Mutual assured destruction (MAD)	Concept of reciprocal deterrence which rests on the ability of the nuclear weapon powers to inflict intolerable damage on one another after receiving a nuclear attack. *See also:* Second-strike capability.
National technical means of verification (NTM)	The means used to monitor compliance with treaty provisions which are under the national control of individual signatories to an arms control agreement.
Neutral and non-aligned (NNA) states	The group of 12 European states (Austria, Cyprus, Finland, Holy See [Vatican City], Ireland, Liechtenstein, Malta, Monaco, San Marino, Sweden, Switzerland and Yugoslavia) which worked together in the CSCE process. They ceased to function as a group at the CSCE after the end of the bloc division of Europe.
North Atlantic Cooperation Council (NACC)	Proposed at the NATO North Atlantic Council meeting in Rome on 8 November 1991, NACC was created as an institution for consultation and co-operation on political and security issues between NATO and the countries of Central and Eastern Europe. As of 15 April 1992, the 36 members included the NATO and former WTO states and all the newly independent former Soviet republics.
North Atlantic Treaty Organization (NATO)	Established in 1949 by a treaty between 12 states: Belgium, Canada, Denmark, France, Iceland, Italy, Luxembourg, the Netherlands, Norway, Portugal, the UK and the USA. The 16 member states in 1991 also included the Federal Republic of Germany, Greece, Iceland, Spain and Turkey. (France and Spain are not in the integrated military structures of NATO.)
Nuclear and Space Talks (NST)	Negotiations opened in Geneva in 1985 between the USA and the USSR on intermediate-range nuclear weapons (INF, concluded in 1987), strategic nuclear weapons (START, concluded in 1991), and space weapons (the Defence and Space Talks).
Nuclear Risk Reduction Centres (NRRC)	Established by the 1987 US–Soviet NRRC Agreement. The two centres, which opened in Washington and Moscow in 1988, exchange information by direct satellite link in order to minimize misunderstandings which might carry a risk of nuclear war. Notifications concerning exchange of information about nuclear explosions under the 1974 Threshold Test Ban Treaty, the 1976 Peaceful Nuclear Explosions Treaty and the 1990 Protocols to the two treaties shall also be submitted through the two NRRCs.
Open Skies Talks	In 1989 President Bush revived the idea of an Open Skies regime of aerial inspection put forth by President Eisenhower in 1955, and proposed an agreement permitting flights by

unarmed military or civilian surveillance aircraft from each alliance over the territory of the USA, the USSR and their NATO and WTO allies. Talks were conducted parallel to the CFE and CFE 1A negotiations in Vienna in 1990–91. In 1990 the USA and the USSR agreed on a basic plan for a treaty at the Ottawa Open Skies Conference. The Treaty on Open Skies was signed by 25 NATO and former WTO states in Vienna on 24 March 1992 and provided also for sharing of data.

Organization for Economic Co-operation and Development (OECD)	Established in 1961 to replace the Organization for European Economic Co-operation (OEEC). With the accession of Canada and the USA, it ceased to be a purely European body. OECD objectives are to promote economic and social welfare by co-ordinating policies. The 24 members in 1991 were Australia, Austria, Belgium, Canada, Denmark, Finland, France, Germany, Greece, Iceland, Ireland, Italy, Japan, Luxembourg, the Netherlands, New Zealand, Norway, Portugal, Spain, Sweden, Switzerland, Turkey, the UK and the USA. (Yugoslavia has participated with a special status.)
Paris Documents	A set of five documents adopted at the November 1990 Paris CSCE summit meeting. They include the CFE Treaty, the Joint Declaration of Twenty-Two States, the Charter of Paris for a New Europe, the Supplementary Document to give new effect to certain provisions contained in the Charter, and the Vienna Document 1990. Several new CSCE institutions were set up in the Paris Documents. *See also:* Conference on Security and Co-operation in Europe (CSCE), Conventional Armed Forces in Europe (CFE) Treaty, Vienna Documents on CSBMs.
Peaceful nuclear explosion (PNE)	Application of a nuclear explosion for non-military purposes such as digging canals or harbours or creating underground cavities.
Re-entry vehicle (RV)	That part of a ballistic missile which carries a nuclear warhead and penetration aids to the target, re-enters the earth's atmosphere and is destroyed in the terminal phase of the missile's trajectory. A missile can have one or several RVs; each RV contains a warhead.
Second-strike capability	Ability to receive a nuclear attack and launch a retaliatory blow large enough to inflict intolerable damage on the opponent. *See also:* Mutual assured destruction.
Short-range nuclear forces (SNF)	Nuclear weapons with ranges up to 500 km; not limited by the INF Treaty. *See also*: Theatre nuclear forces.
Special Verification Commission (SVC)	US–Soviet consultative body established in accordance with the 1987 INF Treaty, to promote the objectives and implementation of the Treaty.

Standing Consultative
Commission (SCC)

US–Soviet consultative body established in accordance with the SALT agreements, to promote the objectives and implementation of the agreements.

Stockholm Conference

See: Conference on Confidence- and Security-Building Measures and Disarmament in Europe.

Strategic Arms Limitation
Talks (SALT)

Negotiations between the USSR and the USA which opened in 1969 and sought to limit the strategic nuclear forces, both offensive and defensive, of both sides. The SALT I Interim Agreement and the ABM Treaty were signed in 1972. The negotiations were terminated in 1979, when the SALT II Treaty was signed (it was never ratified). *See also:* Strategic Arms Reduction Talks (START).

Strategic Arms Reduction
Talks (START)

Negotiations initiated in 1982 between the USSR and the USA to reduce the strategic nuclear forces of both sides. Suspended in 1983 but resumed under the Nuclear and Space Talks that opened in Geneva in 1985. The START Treaty was signed in 1991.

Strategic Arms Reduction
Talks (START) Treaty

US–Soviet treaty, signed in Moscow on 31 July 1991, which reduces US and Soviet offensive strategic nuclear weapons to equal aggregate levels over a seven-year period. It sets numerical limits on deployed strategic nuclear delivery vehicles (SNDVs)—ICBMs, SLBMs and heavy bombers—and the nuclear warheads they carry.

Strategic Defense
Initiative (SDI)

The programme announced by President Reagan in his 1983 'Star Wars' speech for research and development of systems capable of intercepting and destroying nuclear weapons in flight and rendering the USA safe from the threat of a nuclear strike by another state. The GPALS (Global Protection Against Limited Strikes) programme was initiated in 1990 and accelerated in 1991 to test and deploy ground- and space-based ABM systems for territorial defence of the continental USA against limited ballistic missile attack, whatever the source.

Strategic nuclear weapons

ICBMs, SLBMs and bomber aircraft carrying nuclear weapons of intercontinental range (over 5500 km), which allows them to reach the territories of the other strategic nuclear weapon powers. *See also* Strategic Arms Reduction Talks (START) Treaty.

Submarine-launched
ballistic missile (SLBM)

A ballistic missile launched from a submarine with a range in excess of 5500 km.

Terminal guidance

Guidance provided in the final, near-target phase of the flight of a missile.

Theatre nuclear forces
(TNF)

Nuclear weapons with ranges of up to and including 5500 km. In the 1987 INF Treaty, nuclear missiles are divided into intermediate-range (1000–5500 km) and shorter-range (500–1000 km). Also called non-strategic nuclear forces. Nuclear weapons with ranges up to 500 km are called short-range nuclear forces. Those with ranges of 150–200 km are often called battlefield nuclear forces.

Throw-weight	The sum of the weight of a ballistic missile's re-entry vehicle(s), dispensing mechanisms, penetration aids, and targeting and separation devices.
Treaty-limited equipment (TLE)	The five categories of NATO and WTO equipment on which numerical limits are established in the 1990 CFE Treaty: battle tanks, armoured personnel carriers, artillery, combat aircraft and attack helicopters.
Toxins	Poisonous substances which are products of organisms but are inanimate and incapable of reproducing themselves as well as chemically induced variants of such substances. Some toxins may also be produced by chemical synthesis.
Vienna Documents on CSBMs	The Vienna Document 1990 on CSBMs, included in the set of Paris Documents, repeats many of the provisions in the 1986 Stockholm Document and expands several others. It established a communications network and the CSCE Conflict Prevention Centre. The Vienna Document 1992 on new CSBMs was adopted in March 1992. It builds on the Vienna Document 1990 and supplements its provisions with new mechanisms and constraining provisions.
Warhead	That part of a weapon which contains the explosive or other material intended to inflict damage plus electronic devices for detonation, etc.
Warsaw Treaty Organization (WTO)	The WTO, or Warsaw Pact, was established in 1955 by a treaty of friendship, co-operation and mutual assistance between eight countries: Albania, Bulgaria, Czechoslovakia, the GDR, Hungary, Poland, Romania and the USSR. Albania ceased to participate in 1961 and formally withdrew from the Treaty in 1968. There were six WTO member states after the October 1990 unification of Germany. On 31 March 1991 the military organs and structures of the WTO were dismantled, and on 1 July 1991 it was dissolved.
Weapon of mass destruction	Nuclear weapon and any other weapon which may produce comparable effects, such as chemical and biological weapons.
Western European Union (WEU)	Established by five West European states in the 1948 Treaty of Brussels of Collaboration and Collective Self-Defence among Western European States and the Protocols signed in Paris in 1954 by seven West European states. In 1950 its defence organization functions were transferred to the NATO

command. In 1991, in connection with discussion of the European Political Union, it was decided to strengthen the European responsibility for defence, with the WEU as a complement to NATO. The nine WEU member states in 1991 were Belgium, France, Germany, Italy, Luxembourg, the Netherlands, Portugal, Spain and the UK.

Yield

Released nuclear explosive energy expressed as the equivalent of the energy produced by a given number of tons of trinitro-toluene (TNT) high explosive. *See also:* Kiloton and Megaton.

Conventions

. .	Data not available or not applicable
—	Nil or a negligible figure
( )	Uncertain data
m.	million
b.	billion (thousand million)
$	US $, unless otherwise indicated

Introduction: The fundamental changes and the new security agenda

ADAM DANIEL ROTFELD

I. The nature of the changes

In 1991 history accelerated. The political map was transformed before our eyes: the Soviet empire broke up, the bipolar division collapsed and other structures which had been considered unchangeable disappeared entirely. The values and notions that determined international stability and security in the wake of World War II lost their meaning. The cold war came to an end in 1991 and an entire era in international relations came to a close. Fifteen new independent states emerged from the ruins of the Soviet Union, and the line which split both Germany and Europe disappeared. The Warsaw Treaty Organization (WTO) ceased to exist, and its former members are urging the North Atlantic Treaty Organization (NATO) to accept them as members. The contours of a new security zone are now being drawn 'from Vancouver to Vladivostok', covering North America and, across the Atlantic, Europe as well as the vast area of Asia to the far eastern borders of Russia.

These changes did not leave the other regions of the world unaffected in 1991. Dialogue was opened between the two Korean states. Radical and important steps were taken to abolish the apartheid system in South Africa. The process of building security in the Middle East between the Arab states and the Palestinians, on the one side, and Israel, on the other, got off to a promising start. With the sanction of the United Nations, an international Coalition forced Iraq not only to leave Kuwait but also to abide by the Security Council resolutions and destroy its weapons of mass destruction and their means of delivery. Several of the arms control negotiations that had been conducted for many years were completed or were nearing completion. A number of significant disarmament agreements were achieved (the 1991 START Treaty and the 1992 Treaty on Open Skies), and landmark unilateral decisions concerning nuclear arms reductions were announced. The unilateral initiatives taken by US President George Bush, Soviet President Mikhail Gorbachev and later Russian President Boris Yeltsin promised reductions in nuclear weapons without prolonged negotiation. These decisions, which exhibited mutual trust between the two former antagonists, were unthinkable as recently as two or three years ago.[1]

---

[1] These agreements and decisions are analysed in the following chapters in this volume: Cowen Karp, R., 'The START Treaty and the future of strategic nuclear arms control' (chapter 1); Fieldhouse, R., with Norris, R. S. and Arkin, W. M., 'Nuclear weapon developments and unilateral reduction initiatives' (chapter 2); Sharp, J. M. O., 'Conventional arms control in Europe: developments and prospects in 1991'

However, it is not only the international political landscape that has changed: even greater changes took place within the states of the former Eastern bloc. These changes are the outcome of the total exhaustion, inefficiency and collapse of the internal driving forces in these states. The end of the cold war is tantamount to the failure of the totalitarian ideology of communism and the centrally planned economy and the repudiation of a concept of power which not only elevates the state above the individual but also ignores the individual's fundamental human rights and freedoms.

While the end of the cold war brought defeat for the East, it does not signal victory for the West. As initial euphoria subsided, the tone of triumph discernible in statements by some US and West European politicians turned out to be premature. The post-cold war political landscape is completely different from that of the past. Although after the breakup of the USSR the threat of global military confrontation and nuclear war vanished, new problems and challenges have come to the fore.[2] In the former security system, based on military alliances that mobilized states against a clearly defined opponent, enemies were known and menaces were recognized. The security systems now sought are intended to organize states not against anything or anyone but rather in the defence of common values. The new system cannot be founded on a balance of power and fear but must be based on prevention of conflicts, the nature and sources of which are different from those in the past and not yet fully understood.

A new and significant phenomenon is that the division between domestic and international security factors is blurred. This phenomenon, inherently related to the implementation of the right of peoples to self-determination, is inalienably bound together with the emergence of new states. The aspirations of the peoples of the multinational states to gain independence are usually treated by their governments as a domestic issue, and the governments consider international recognition of the newly emerging states as interference in their internal affairs.

The course of events in 1991 deepened and consolidated two development tendencies which started in 1989–90: *integration* in the West and *disintegration* in the East. In Eastern Europe the disintegrating trends have got the upper hand, illustrated by the formal dissolution of the Warsaw Pact, the breakup of the Soviet Union[3] and Yugoslavia[4] and by separatist tendencies in other countries of the region. They call into question not only the durability of the

---

(chapter 12); and Lachowski, Z., 'Implementation of the Vienna Document 1990 in 1991' (appendix 12A).

[2] 'The world order which we left was one of high-military threat and high-stability; the order to which we are moving is one of low-military threat, but also low-stability'. Simon, J., 'European (in)security and NATO challenges', ed. J. Simon, *European Security Policy After the Revolutions of 1989* (National Defense UP: Washington, DC, 1991), p. 613.

[3] *After the Soviet Collapse: New Realities, Old Illusions, The Report of a Study Group* (Institute for European Defence and Strategic Studies: London, Jan. 1992).

[4] Vukadinovic, R., *The Break-up of Yugoslavia: The Threats and Challenges* (Netherlands Institute of International Affairs: The Hague, Feb. 1992).

Commonwealth of Independent States (CIS) but also the future existence of the Russian Federation in its present configuration.[5]

The course of events in the East could not but affect the policies of the main actors on the world scene. The policies of the great powers and of the medium- and small-sized states are being profoundly transformed since the perception of the strategic security interests of individual states and groupings has radically changed.[6] Similarly, such multilateral institutions as the United Nations, NATO, the European Community (EC) and the Conference on Security and Co-operation in Europe (CSCE) are undergoing thorough reappraisal. The basic line of division in the world today is no longer between East and West. It is no longer determined by ideology or antagonisms between democratic and totalitarian systems, but rather by the growing economic gap between North and South—between the worlds of the rich and the poor.

Threats have changed, and the substance of national and international security is changing. The major driving force behind the processes taking place in Europe is the need for legitimate governments and democratic states, for human rights and civil freedoms. However, a strong interrelationship exists between the level of economic development and democracy. Poverty, lack of prospects, frustration among many people of all social strata and individual alienation do not help to build democratic systems. On the contrary, they nourish anti-democratic and authoritarian attitudes, populist and xenophobic movements, and a host of other menaces to democracy, many of which can be seen in the world today. The main current threats to global security are the failure of democratic revolutions, the questioning of reform processes and attempts to gain public support by looking for would-be enemies both within and outside the country. The war in Yugoslavia, the 'Lebanonization' of the conflict over Nagorno-Karabakh between Armenia and Azerbaijan, the strife in Moldova, and last but not least the dispute between Russia and Ukraine cannot but confirm US President Bush's view that 'if this democratic revolution is defeated, it could plunge us into a world more dangerous in some respects than the dark years of the Cold War'.[7] Indeed, it remains an open question whether the aid which the USA and other industrialized states have offered as a multilateral package for Russia and other CIS states[8] will halt the continuing slide of post-Soviet states into a further deep political, economic and social crisis, with the possibility of the outbreak of civil war. The complexity of ethnic and national structures, border disputes and the mix of populations resulting both from large-scale forced displacements and natural

[5] See also, Landgren, S., 'Post-Soviet threats to security', chapter 14 in this volume.

[6] See, e.g., Huntington, S. P., 'America's changing strategic interests', *Survival*, Jan.–Feb. 1991, p. 8.

[7] US President George Bush's statement at a 1 Apr. 1992 press conference. *USIS Wireless File*, 2 Apr. 1992, p. 2.

[8] In his 1 Apr. 1992 statement, President Bush announced a $24 billion multilateral aid package. The scale of difficulties is revealed by the money which the Federal Republic of Germany poured into eastern Germany in 1991. It amounted to about $90 billion in various forms of investment. However, it did not stave off the deep depression and the many negative social and economic phenomena in this part of the country.

migration processes all add up to another potentially explosive source of tension.

The most feared threat is a loss of central control or mismanagement of the possibly decentralized vast former Soviet nuclear arsenal.[9] For obvious reasons, it is not conventional weapons but weapons of mass destruction—nuclear, chemical and biological—which are the subject of permanent international concern in the states and institutions established to keep tabs on these weapons (such as the International Atomic Energy Agency—IAEA—and the UN). The inspections of the UN Special Commission on Iraq (UNSCOM) made it possible, for the first time in history, for a group of international observers to prove the violation of international commitments undertaken by a state that had engaged in aggression.[10] More difficult to observe are the transfer and proliferation of most conventional types of light weapon that are the main instruments of local wars and armed conflicts. This problem and other factors determining the changes which have already taken place or are forthcoming necessitate taking a new look at many areas of research. For nearly 48 years, since the end of World War II, the concern of politicians, experts and researchers has focused on the most basic question: how to prevent a nuclear war between the superpowers. No one, whether politician or researcher, envisaged that when the goal was achieved other equally difficult and complex issues and tasks would enter the agenda, catching us unawares.

II. The security research agenda rewritten

A qualitatively new element is that the great world powers no longer threaten each other. This offers an unprecedented opportunity for peace researchers to be self-critical and propose a new security concept.[11] It is clear that the tasks of peace and conflict research have not been accomplished. However, a future-oriented agenda must be carefully thought about. This was the main focus of an international conference held in 1991 on the occasion of SIPRI's 25th anniversary.[12] It is worth noting a few basic questions which were raised at the conference: What will the defence and security policy of states look like, and how should it be shaped in the new circumstances? What criteria should be used to determine threats? Will there be a return to national security

[9] See Campbell, K. M., Carter, A. B., Miller, S. E. and Zraket C. A., 'Soviet nuclear fission: control of the nuclear arsenal in a disintegrating Soviet Union', *CSIA Studies in International Security*, no. 1, Center for Science and International Affairs, Harvard University, Cambridge, Mass., Nov. 1991.

[10] As Rolf Ekéus, Executive Chairman of UNSCOM, writes in the conclusion of his chapter, 'It appears quite obvious that in spite of a continuing lack of full co-operation by Iraq, the greatest part of Iraq's capability with regard to weapons of mass destruction and ballistic missiles has been accounted for and is being disposed of'. Ekéus, R., 'The United Nations Special Commission on Iraq', chapter 13 in this volume.

[11] See Forsberg, R., 'Security through military defense?', ed. E. Boulding, *New Agendas for Peace Research. Conflict and Security Reexamined* (Lynne Rienner Publishers: Boulder, Colo. and London, 1992), p. 67.

[12] SIPRI Conference on Common Security and the Rule of Law: What Have We Learned? Saltsjöbaden, Sweden, 13–14 Nov. 1991. The ideas presented at the conference will be published in Rotfeld, A. D. (ed.), SIPRI, *Global Security and the Rule of Law* (Oxford University Press: Oxford, 1992, forthcoming).

policies, or does the opportunity of building a multilateral co-operative system exist? Many other fundamental questions were also asked. The message addressed to SIPRI was that its research should be problem-oriented, in keeping with the intentions of the founders of the Institute. In addition to SIPRI's main traditional areas of research (military expenditure, the arms trade and arms production, chemical and biological warfare, and nuclear issues) such new subjects of research were suggested as security and technology, peaceful settlement of disputes, peace-keeping activities and regional security-building processes. Serious thought should be given to the questions: What does security after the cold war mean? Should regional or global security be identified with the sum of the national security policies of states members of a system? Is it one of the theoretical paradigms oriented to the future, or should international security be conceived as a process *in statu nascendi*?[13]

Security should be seen in its historical context: the future does not begin today, it started yesterday. In the history of peoples and in international relations there are turning-points and landmarks, but there is no 'zero' hour. The revolutionary changes in Eastern Europe only confirm the extent to which current events have their roots in the past. The security process is multi-dimensional. Reducing the process to military security alone was a mistake in the past; in today's realities this would mean ignoring its essence.[14]

Today, more than ever before, security is based on interdependence: it is being increasingly internationalized. This process is accompanied, particularly in Central and Eastern Europe, by a reversion to national defence policies—a peculiar response to the many years of dependence of the Central European nations on the USSR and the centuries-old subjugation of the former Soviet republics to Russia. This phenomenon should be properly understood; it is part of the history of the region. Conflicts of national interest and sensitivity to maintaining national identity are as natural as the gravitation of these states to partnership, co-operation and the exchange of spiritual and material values. In research terms, one can ponder over whether and how mutual relations can be harmonized among the new states and between them and other participants of the international system. Agreed and accepted principles, norms and rules of procedure in bi- and multilateral relations should help to harmonize often conflicting interests, by seeking compromise solutions or at least warding off the growth of enmity which sooner or later could lead to open armed conflict. To a considerable degree, this depends on the way in which Russia and other

[13] In this context it is worth noting Helga Haftendorn's view: 'I will also criticize the notion of global security as presupposing a common definition of security world-wide and shared sets of values, rules and principles not yet existing. I concede, however, that the world might be moving in the direction of a global security paradigm if institution-building continues and leads to complexes of common practices, shared rules of behaviour, and capabilities for the enforcement of these rules'. Haftendorn, H., 'The security puzzle: theory-building and discipline-building in international security', *International Studies Quarterly. The Journal of the International Studies Association*, no. 35 (1991), p. 4.

[14] 'International security, in contrast to national security, implies that security of one state is closely linked to that of other states, at least of one other state. States are interdependent in their security affairs such that the security of one is strongly affected by the actions of other, and vice versa.' Haftendorn (note 13), p. 9.

post-Soviet states determine their new status—that is, whether they lay claim to the role of world power (Russia) or regional power (Ukraine), and whether they attempt to use military potential, in particular nuclear weapons, as a lever to strengthen their political status or seek solutions within the framework of a new co-operative security system and promote arms reductions.

It is worth considering why neither peace research analyses nor strategic studies envisaged such abrupt changes. While changes, although not so sudden and radical, were expected and action was taken to make them occur smoothly, once they occurred they nevertheless came as a surprise. Why is the prediction of the course of international politics so difficult? Robert Jervis has given eight reasons why this is so.[15] It should be appreciated that he is one of the few eminent scholars who deemed it appropriate to ask why studies on international relations failed to signal the possibility of such fundamental change in the international system, but his answer recalls an ironic depiction of an expert as a person who envisages a given course of events and then explains why they have taken a different course. Jervis' explanation can be complemented with two others: First, the main tasks of social science are cognitive and explanatory functions and not necessarily prognosis. This applies in particular to such a multi-dimensional field as international relations. Second, peace researchers naturally deal with relations among states, whereas the sources of change in the international system as a whole were domestic processes. One conclusion that can be drawn from this experience is that the operation of the international security system is closely connected with the correlation of domestic forces and the potential of states, thereby shaping a given system on a regional or global scale. For many years military strength determined the standing of the Soviet Union as a world power. Retaining this status led to increasing militarization of the Soviet economy, to the growing share of military spending in its budget and consequently to damaging distortions in its development. In effect, it speeded up its economic disaster and the breakup of the USSR as a multinational state.

From the perspective of peace research, it should be said that the judgement that the end of cold war and the emergence of numerous new states mean a return to rules applied in Europe prior to World War I is an oversimplifica-

[15] 'First, social scientists have only a limited stock of knowledge to rely on and there are few laws whose validity is uncontested . . . Second, only rarely does a single factor determine the way politics will work out. Even the best proportions are couched in terms of conditions and probabilities . . . Third, learning about international politics can act as a self-denying prophecy . . . Fourth, unless national behaviour and international outcomes are entirely determined by the external environment, there is significant room for choice by politics and statesman . . . Even if the external environment is dominant, there now is a fifth obstacle to prediction: the current world situation is unprecedented . . . To the extent that the external forces are not only important, but truly constitute a system, there is a sixth difficulty in making predictions . . . The final two arguments as to why prediction is so difficult are more controversial. The flow of international politics is, in significant measure, contingent or path-dependent. History matters. Particular events can send world politics down quite different paths . . . The final reason why prediction is difficult brings me closer to the question of how different the new world will be. Even if we knew what generalizations held in the past and even if they were not sensitive to details and idiosyncrasies, this knowledge would not provide a sure guide for the future if the generalizations themselves are no longer valid . . . If our laws are not timeless—if history resembles an arrow—some of what we have learned will not help us to understand the future.' Jervis, R., 'The future of world politics. Will it resemble the past?', *International Security*, vol. 16, no. 3 (winter 1991/92), pp. 39–45.

tion,[16] as is the conviction that international institutions and the interdependence of states rule out the possibility of war in the future.[17] The present situation is without precedent. Any analogies are misleading and delusive since the similarities are illusory and the causative factors totally different. The political concepts, military doctrines and institutional arrangements in the field of security call for re-definition. It would be illusive to believe that the changes happened fast and according to some grand design for reconstruction of international relations. On the contrary, a long process of search and a clash of interests has just begun. There will be attempts to return to hegemonic politics by one or more powers in a regional or global context. Recourse to a policy of isolationism or neo-isolationism in the USA can also not be ruled out. There will be attempts to regain positions lost as a result of World War II (by Germany and Japan), although not through war but rather through economic and political expansion. A new element in the years to come will be the search by the group of states that emerged from the Soviet Union and Yugoslavia to find their place on the political scene. Finally, a process has started of re-defining the tasks of the UN, NATO, the EC, the Western European Union (WEU), the CSCE and other multilateral organizations and institutions.

It remains to be seen whether a new world order will take shape—a global security system based on 'a universal concept of security with a shared set of norms, principles and practices which [will] result in common patterns of international behaviour'.[18] Many events show that the world has moved much closer than ever towards such a system. The negotiations on a new European Security Forum initiated at the negotiations in Vienna on Conventional Armed Forces in Europe (CFE) and Confidence- and Security-Building Measures (CSBMs) and the 1992 Helsinki CSCE follow-up meeting,[19] the work to make the UN system more effective,[20] and the search for a new strategy and organizational solutions for NATO and West European institutions (the EC and the

---

[16] Only a need for conceptualization of variegated and fast-moving changes as well as a craving for the stable 'old world' can account for such 'realistic' and pessimistic intellectual propositions as those of John Mearsheimer. See Mearsheimer, J., 'Back to the future: instability in Europe after the cold war', *International Security*, vol. 15, no. 1 (summer 1990), pp. 5–56.

[17] Van Evera, S., 'Primed for peace: Europe after the cold war', *International Security*, vol. 15, no. 3 (winter 1990/91), pp. 7–57.

[18] Haftendorn (note 13), p. 11.

[19] Consultations in this regard, recommended in the decision of the CSCE Council of Ministers (at the meeting held in Berlin on 19–20 June 1991, para. 15 of the Summary of Conclusions) were held in Vienna from 17 Sep. 1991 to 19 Mar. 1992. Fifteen drafts were prepared by individual states or groups of states for submission to the Helsinki CSCE follow-up meeting: the UK (draft of 30 Aug. 1991), Finland (16 Sep. 1991), Estonia, Hungary and Poland (16 Oct. 1991), Sweden (22 Nov. 1991), Germany and France (22 Nov. 1991), Belgium, Canada, Italy, Luxembourg and the Netherlands (27 Nov. 1991), Austria (17 Jan. 1992), the Russian Federation (7 Feb. 1992), the Netherlands (28 Feb. 1992), Belgium, Canada, Italy, Luxembourg and the Netherlands (28 Feb. 1992), Norway (18 Mar. 1992), and four texts of 'host's perception' by Finland (7 Feb. 1992), Poland (26 Feb. 1992), Italy (12 Mar. 1992) and Norway (17 Mar. 1992). See also 'New European security architecture', The Finnish Committee for European Security (STETE), Helsinki, 1992.

[20] Childers, E. and Urquhart, B., 'Towards a more effective United Nations', Dag Hammerskjöld Foundation, Uppsala, 1992.

WEU)[21] all show that states are giving international security institutions an increasing role in the decision-making process.

In the field of research on conflict, security and peace, one should consider whether today's definitions, concepts and research areas correspond to the new realities. The dichotomy between peace research and strategic studies is fading away.[22] It seems that future peace research will be increasingly focused on an interdisciplinary approach and non-military discussion of security. In the period of transition from mutual deterrence to a new security system, the outline and nature of which are still unknown, it is wise and justified to keep focusing on arms control in general and weapons of mass destruction in particular. To be sure, there is no threat that these weapons can be used as instruments of aggression by one nuclear power against another, but there are a number of other risks connected with a loss of control and possible proliferation of various types of weapon and their delivery systems. However, one can foresee that global arms control will be boiled down to its true function, and will not play such a significant a role as a substitute for political dialogue as it did in the past. Major decisions will be more technical–military in character and their procedures will be more and more like those agreements which regulate relations among states in other areas. New menaces have come to the fore: economic crises, ethnic conflicts, mass migration, international terrorism and trans-border pollution of the environment. Thus instead of arms control, the main political decisions and international arrangements of the future will address those matters that determine new dimensions of security.

III. *Yearbook* findings and new realities

The cold war did not leave much room for political choice. In the bipolar world choice was, as a rule, illusory since it was a necessity. The lines of division and motivation were quite clear. This facilitated analysis of the situation and formulation of conclusions. The behaviour of the actors on the political scene was roughly predictable. This state of affairs is now a thing of the past, as reflected in the analyses and conclusions of this *Yearbook*.

An analysis of the START Treaty and the future of strategic nuclear arms control leads to the conclusion that its role can become vastly more positive, facilitating a transition to a world in which the place and role of nuclear weapons are marginalized, if not irrelevant.[23] The majority of deterrence scenarios designed to counter perceived Soviet intentions are no longer pertinent, and there is therefore 'no justification to maintain large strategic forces

---

[21] Payne, K. B., *Countering Proliferation: New Criteria for European Security*, Occasional Paper no. 52, and Hartley, A., *The Irrelevance of Maastricht: Redefining the Atlantic Community*, Occasional Paper no. 53, Institute for European Defence and Strategic Studies, London, 1992.

[22] 'International security studies would integrate both. Research and teaching should focus on the various paradigms and problems of security as well as its political, economic, cultural and other implications. Strategic studies, with its emphasis on military aspects of security, is the area of the field'. Haftendorn (note 13), p. 15.

[23] Cowen Karp, R., 'The START Treaty and the future of strategic nuclear arms control' (chapter 1 in this volume).

when reasons for their buildup disappeared'.[24] The only rationale for maintaining nuclear weapons in the future is to deter others from using them. Minimum deterrence is no longer Utopian, and seems to be a real policy option. The intellectual and strategic premises that guided nuclear arms control during the cold war have ceased to exist. However, the threat of the proliferation of weapons of mass destruction and their delivery vehicles is real and ranks high on the international security agenda. One consequence of the revelations presented by the UN Special Commission on Iraq was a considerable momentum to strengthen the IAEA safeguards. Another lesson to be drawn from the Persian Gulf War is that export control and the 1968 Non-Proliferation Treaty (NPT) regime should be strengthened.[25] This seems also to be an excellent basis for efficient negotiation on conversion of the 1963 Partial Test Ban Treaty (PTBT) into a comprehensive test ban.[26]

The Persian Gulf War clearly showed that the concept of chemical and biological weapons as 'the poor man's nuclear weapon' is a myth. Since the two largest possessors of arsenals of chemical weapons agreed to destroy their CW stockpiles, the chances of finalizing a Chemical Weapon Convention (CWC) have significantly increased. The existence of a global CWC would provide international measures to abolish chemical weapons and might facilitate regional approaches to the elimination of these and other weapons of mass destruction. The destruction of CW stockpiles raises a host of challenges for the international community in terms of toxicity problems, health risks, environmental damage and enormous costs.[27]

To what extent are the favourable changes in the sphere of political–military relations reflected in military spending? After more than a decade of rising world military expenditure, and the allocation of huge amounts of financial and human resources for elusive military security, in 1991 it became clear that world defence spending is set on a downward course.[28] Nevertheless, uncertainty surrounds events and relations among countries, and the disarmament dividend is modest compared to expectations and the revolution in world affairs since 1989. Demilitarization will be chaotic for some countries and regions while relatively slow for others, but in the long term it will continue at a steady pace. It will probably be characterized by large reductions in personnel. On the other hand, there could be more volunteer armies with an increase in servicemen's pay and benefits, thus producing a smaller proportional reduction in personnel expenditure. There will be cuts in procurement of major weapon systems but also attempts to increase the efficiency of existing systems. In 1991 world military spending continued to fall—this may have been for economic reasons and is not necessarily a product of arms control.

[24] See note 23.

[25] Müller, H., 'The nuclear non-proliferation regime beyond the Persian Gulf War and the dissolution of the Soviet Union' (chapter 3 in this volume).

[26] Norris, R. S. with Goldblat, J., 'Nuclear explosions and the talks on test limitations' (chapter 4 in this volume).

[27] Lundin, S. J., Stock, T. with Geissler, E., 'Chemical and biological warfare and arms control developments in 1991' (chapter 6 in this volume).

[28] Deger, S. and Sen, S., 'World military expenditure' (chapter 7 in this volume).

Political changes have also affected arms production.[29] Governments are restructuring national armed forces and revising military equipment procurement plans. The changes will certainly affect arms production and sales in the near future and have already had drastic consequences in the former USSR. However, there are developments in the opposite direction in other areas of the world: in contrast to Europe and North America, arms production continues to follow a dynamic path in countries of the Asia–Pacific region. The industrial structure in several countries is in a process of transformation; reduction in size, transnationalization of companies and conversion of non-military production are the most common strategies. Changes in the arms production sector in the CIS states were much more dramatic. Arms procurement was reduced, and production was decelerated or even stopped in places.

Regarding the trade in major conventional weapons, three new factors appeared.[30] First, the USSR—the largest supplier of major conventional weapons for most of the 1980s—ceased to exist. Second, the Persian Gulf War was fought in early 1991. Third, steps to introduce multilateral regulation of arms exports were taken by major arms-exporting countries. While future developments are impossible to predict, it is clear that economic and technological considerations, together with political factors other than US–Soviet competition, will be the primary determinants of arms transfer policy. The global value of the trade in major conventional weapons in 1991 was $22 114 million (expressed in 1990 US dollars). This figure—roughly 25 per cent less than the value recorded for 1990—continues the downward trend in the 1990 aggregate value reported in the SIPRI Yearbook 1991.[31] Among 30 major armed conflicts waged in different parts of the world, three wars broke out in 1991: in the Persian Gulf between the multinational force and Iraq, in Yugoslavia and in Rwanda.[32]

* * *

Dramatic and long-term transformation enhances the sense of uncertainty and unpredictability. By their nature, changes mean destabilization. Former threats have subsided, among which was the possibility of the outbreak of a nuclear war, but the threat of unwanted and unintended wars between neighbouring states has increased. It applies both to the new European states and to African, Asian and Latin American nations. In the current period of transition, as we approach the unknown, the need for intellectual reflection—for conceptualization of international security—is most urgent.

[29] Miggiano, P., Sköns, E., Wulf, H. and Kireyev, A., 'Arms production' (chapter 9 in this volume).
[30] Anthony, I., Courades Allebeck, A., Miggiano, P., Sköns, E. and Wulf, H., 'The trade in major conventional weapons' (chapter 8 in this volume).
[31] See Anthony, I., Courades Allebeck, A., Hagmeyer-Gaverus, G., Miggiano, P. and Wulf, H., SIPRI, SIPRI Yearbook 1991: World Armaments and Disarmament (Oxford University Press: Oxford, 1991), chapter 7.
[32] Heldt, B., Wallensteen, P. and Nordquist, K.-Å., 'Major armed conflicts in 1991' (chapter 10 in this volume).

Part I. Weapons, technology and arms control

Chapter 1. The START Treaty and the future of strategic nuclear arms control

Chapter 2. Nuclear weapon developments and unilateral reduction initiatives

Chapter 3. The nuclear non-proliferation regime beyond the Persian Gulf War and the dissolution of the Soviet Union

Chapter 4. Nuclear explosions and the talks on test limitations

Chapter 5. Military use of outer space

Chapter 6. Chemical and biological warfare and arms control developments in 1991

1. The START Treaty and the future of strategic nuclear arms control

REGINA COWEN KARP

I. Introduction

In 1991, the demise of the Soviet Union was the single most important event for the future of strategic nuclear arms control. While the end of the cold war had already begun to raise questions about the continued utility of traditional approaches to nuclear arms control, the fact that one of the two principal arms control partners ceased to exist has rendered the most basic assumptions of the former US–Soviet strategic relationship irrelevant. The conclusion of the Treaty between the United States and the Soviet Union on the reduction and limitation of strategic offensive arms (the START Treaty) at the Moscow US–Soviet summit meeting on 31 July 1991 marked not only the end of nine years of negotiations but also the end of an era.

What strategic doctrines will emerge from the transformation of the Soviet Union into a Commonwealth of Independent States (CIS)? What will be the function of nuclear weapons in US national security strategy? What role can arms control play in defining new relationships, shaping new security perceptions and strategies, developing new approaches to managing nuclear weapons and creating new opportunities for nuclear disarmament? Will there be a need to devise a new theoretical framework for nuclear arms control to replace the one derived from cold war antagonisms or should arms control come to be seen as a more pragmatic, problem-oriented exercise now that US–CIS relations are unfettered by cold war rivalry? Future nuclear arms control negotiations will have to take these new questions into account.

These profound political changes notwithstanding, it is of more than historical interest to evaluate the 1991 START Treaty. The START process offers important lessons for future negotiations regarding negotiation objectives and approaches. The Treaty provides insights into the complexity of the nuclear arms control problem, and its comprehensive verification provisions contain mechanisms and procedures of lasting value.

The START negotiating process and the Treaty itself can, however, no longer be evaluated within the old cold war frame of reference. While the START Treaty would in any case have been critically examined for strengths, weaknesses and loopholes by the US Senate and the Supreme Soviet, at the end of 1991 so much had changed since it was signed in July that an assessment of the Treaty process and Treaty provisions must be made in light of new conditions that may determine the Treaty's relevance.

This chapter is divided into five parts. Section II explores the reasons that might account for the nine years it took to negotiate the START Treaty. Section III reviews the main provisions of the Treaty and explains their purpose. Section IV provides an assessment of the Treaty in light of political events subsequent to the signing of the Treaty. Section V explores the relevance of the Treaty to future nuclear arms control efforts.

II. Concluding the START Treaty: getting there

The record of US–Soviet nuclear arms control negotiations is dominated by efforts to attain comprehensive agreements encompassing the entire spectrum of strategic offensive nuclear weapon systems.[1] This approach, of which START is the most recent example, was intended to maximize the potential for military and political compromise and trade-offs at the negotiating table. It had been conceived at a time when the two sides were deeply divided ideologically, suspicious of each other's political and strategic motives, and competing for influence world-wide. Retrospectively, it appears that this comprehensive approach to negotiations, coupled with perceptions of a profoundly adversarial relationship, was a prescription for lengthy and laborious negotiations. Indeed, over the course of the 1980s, negotiations became heavily politicized, at times raising hopes of a 'fast track' towards a nuclear weapon-free world while at other times seeming hopelessly deadlocked over the issues of strategic defences and naval arms control.[2]

While strategic arms control negotiators were following an agenda devised in the early 1980s, the security environment of which arms control had been a reflection began to undergo radical change. By the end of 1991, Eastern Europe was no longer part of the Soviet empire, the Warsaw Pact had been disbanded, Germany had been unified and the 1990 Conventional Armed Forces in Europe (CFE) Treaty severely curtailing the potential for a Soviet conventional attack in Europe had been successfully concluded. In short, both the symbols and the realities of the cold war had disappeared; the Soviet threat as the world had come to know it was gone.

The START negotiations proceeded seemingly untouched by the changing political and security context and it was not until June 1991 that negotiations were visibly gathering pace. The reasons for this were, in the first instance, of a practical nature. Much had already been agreed upon by the time the cold war came to an end—so much so, that a shift in negotiation objectives carried real dangers of unravelling the accord. Indeed, many of the Treaty's basic

---

[1] For insightful accounts of strategic arms control negotiations, see Newhouse, J., *Cold Dawn, The Story of SALT* (Holt, Rinehart and Winston: New York, 1973); Smith, G., *Doubletalk: The Story of the First Strategic Arms Limitation Talks* (Doubleday: New York, 1980); Talbott, S., *Endgame: The Inside Story of Salt II* (Harper & Row: New York, 1979); Talbott, S., *Deadly Gambits: The Reagan Administration and the Stalemate in Nuclear Arms Control* (Knopf: New York, 1984); and respective chapters in previous *SIPRI Yearbooks*.

[2] Einhorn, R., 'Revising the START process', *Survival*, vol. 32, no. 6 (Nov./Dec. 1990), pp. 497–505. See also, Cowen Karp, R., 'US–Soviet nuclear arms control', SIPRI, *SIPRI Yearbook 1991: World Armaments and Disarmament* (Oxford University Press: Oxford, 1991), pp. 383–402.

provisions were in place by the end of 1989. The USA and the USSR had begun the START negotiations with different negotiating strategies, agreeing only on the principal objectives of significant nuclear reductions and of strengthening strategic stability. Thus, the agreements that were in place by the end of 1989 reflected hard bargaining and compromise.

At the Reykjavik summit meeting on 11–12 October 1986, the two sides had each agreed to reduce the number of their strategic nuclear delivery vehicles (SNDV) to 1600, carrying no more than 6000 nuclear warheads. During a Foreign Ministers' meeting on 15–17 September 1987, the Soviet Union had agreed to a 50 per cent reduction in heavy intercontinental ballistic missiles (ICBMs) with a warhead ceiling of 1540. At the Washington summit meeting on 7–10 December 1987, agreement was reached to limit the number of warheads on ballistic missiles to 4900 within the overall 6000 warhead limit. Further substantial progress was made at the Wyoming Foreign Ministers' meeting of 22–23 September 1989. The Soviet Union ceased to link an agreement on reduction of strategic offensive nuclear weapons with resolution of the issue of space-based defences against ballistic missiles. The Soviet Union also agreed to dismantle, without preconditions, the phased array radar at Krasnoyarsk which was in violation of the 1972 Anti-Ballistic Missile (ABM) Treaty.[3] The United States had made conclusion of the START Treaty contingent upon the destruction of this radar.[4]

While agreement on these issues was undoubtedly a major achievement, a significant number of other issues still had to be addressed or had previously defied solution at the negotiating table. Most of these issues concerned counting rules for heavy bombers carrying nuclear-armed air-launched cruise missiles (ALCMs), a sub-limit on ICBM warheads, sub-limits on warheads on mobile ICBMs, modernization of heavy ICBMs, how to address the problem of nuclear sea-launched cruise missiles (SLCMs), non-deployed missiles, telemetry encryption, cuts in Soviet missile throw-weight and an effective verification regime to monitor treaty compliance.[5]

Because the START Treaty, unlike the 1987 Treaty between the USA and the USSR on elimination of their intermediate- and shorter-range nuclear missiles (the INF Treaty), did not demand elimination of categories of weapons, agreement on counting rules within agreed sub-limits and verification of adherence to counting rules were crucial issues. Moreover, because START addressed the whole spectrum of strategic nuclear capabilities, it was important to curb the potential for treaty break-out, to find unambiguous language, to close potential loopholes and to assure adequate verification.[6]

---

[3] For a discussion of the ABM Treaty violation issue, see Cowen Karp, R., 'US–Soviet nuclear arms control', SIPRI, *SIPRI Yearbook 1990: World Armaments and Disarmament* (Oxford University Press: Oxford, 1990), pp. 431–32.
[4] 'The Strategic Arms Reduction Treaty, Chronology' (US Information Agency, US Embassy: Stockholm, Aug. 1991), pp. 6–16.
[5] See note 4.
[6] Rühl, L., 'Der START-Vertrag, Eine erste Reduzierung strategischer Angriffswaffen', *Europa Archiv* (25 Oct. 1991), pp. 583–92.

Thus, when the cold war ended, START had an established negotiating format. Negotiations were taking place within that specific format and only secondarily within an evolving political environment. In other words, START was following its own agenda as it had emerged from the basic negotiating approach and from the need to refine agreement on basic treaty provisions.

Although the increasingly close co-operation between the United States and the Soviet Union, especially at the CFE Negotiation, the United Nations and during the Gulf War, would in theory have permitted a revision of arms control objectives, it never was a viable political option. Rather than speeding up negotiations, a decision to go for much deeper cuts in the strategic arsenals than envisioned would, more likely, have unravelled many of the compromises already achieved. Renegotiating the existing treaty draft would most certainly have demanded more time than it took to finalize the present treaty. It is also of interest to note that during the final 18 months of negotiations, the Soviet Union, whose new approach to foreign policy had made a better US–Soviet relationship possible, did not demand a revision of the START process. It was the complexity of the negotiations that defined the details of the agenda, not the state of relations between the negotiating partners.

This is not to suggest a lack of political control over the negotiating process. Rather, it suggests that this type of negotiation is not responsive to quick political redirection. To achieve that degree of political accessibility, the initial agenda would have to be much narrower and far less ambitious. However, it is justified to ask why negotiations during 1990 were proceeding at such a snail's pace. Why was it not possible to conclude the treaty in time for signature at the June 1990 summit meeting in Washington or at the scheduled Moscow summit meeting in February 1991? Was 'the devil' really 'in the detail', or were there other circumstances slowing down the final accord?

There were essentially two developments that reinforced each other and delayed progress. One was the replacement of strategic arms control as the politically most visible link in the superpower relationship by events in Europe and in the Soviet Union itself. The other was that the Geneva negotiations entered the stage of so-called technical issues, a reference to the finer details that had to be worked out. This stage had definitively been reached with agreement in May 1990 on the range threshold for long-range nuclear-armed ALCMs, the sub-limit of deployed warheads on mobile ICBMs, and accords on long-range nuclear-armed SLCMs, the Soviet Tu-22M (Backfire) bomber and nuclear co-operation with third countries.[7] Quite suddenly, strategic nuclear arms control ceased to be the most important (and sometimes only) indicator of the health of US–Soviet relations. For both countries, the political agenda broadened, making strategic nuclear arms control not an unimportant but a less immediate concern. This political marginalization of START was reinforced by the technical nature of the Geneva negotiations

[7] See note 4.

which did not easily lend themselves to front-page coverage. In turn, the lack of high-level political pressure to finalize the agreement gave prominence to minor technical issues that could and should have been averted. At the end of 1990, the START negotiations appeared to be going nowhere.

The year 1991 began with a promise of further delays. The war in the Gulf and Soviet use of force in the Baltic republics led to a postponement of the Moscow summit meeting scheduled for February. Meanwhile, disagreements between the Soviet Union and all other signatories to the 1990 CFE Treaty had emerged. Until the Soviet Union had satisfactorily alleviated these concerns, which was not achieved until a Foreign Ministers' meeting in Lisbon on 1 June, the United States had put the START negotiations on hold.[8] By this time, however, it was apparent that unless US and Soviet leaders themselves became involved, a START treaty would not be ready for signature at a summer summit meeting. President George Bush had previously announced that he would only consent to a US–Soviet summit meeting if a treaty could be concluded during that time. What had also become apparent was that it had simply taken too long to finalize the START Treaty. There would always be another 'technical issue' to be resolved and there would always be another international event diverting top-level attention from ongoing negotiations or making them hostage to resolution of other issues. What the negotiations had needed but were not getting for most of the final year was the unambiguous political message that they should be concluded. When that message did come, it took less than six weeks to agree on outstanding issues.

On 7 June 1991, the two Foreign Ministers met in Geneva and again in Berlin on 20 June. Between 26 June and 2 July, experts from both sides met in Geneva. On 6 July, President Bush urged President Mikhail Gorbachev to push for progress in the negotiations and asked for a high-level Soviet delegation to come to Washington. That delegation, led by Soviet Foreign Minister Alexander Bessmertnykh and Chief of the Soviet General Staff General Mikhail Moiseyev, met US officials on 11–14 July.[9] On 17 July, after a final meeting between Presidents Bush and Gorbachev at the Group of Seven (G7) summit meeting in London, the two leaders announced that the START Treaty was ready and would be signed at a US–Soviet summit meeting in Moscow at

---

[8] See note 4 and chapter 12 in this volume. Also see 'Arms pact problems delay summit', *International Herald Tribune*, 16–17 Mar. 1991, p. 1; 'Arms treaty delay viewed', Foreign Broadcast Information Service, *Daily Report–Soviet Union (FBIS-SOV)*, FBIS-SOV-91-053, 19 Mar. 1991, pp. 9–10, 'Start not ready for signing says chief US negotiator', *International Defense Review*, no. 4, 1991, p. 290, *Wireless File*, no. 119 (United States Information Service, US Embassy: Stockholm, 20 June 1991), p. 11.

[9] See note 4. See also *Wireless File*, no. 110 (United States Information Service, US Embassy: Stockholm, 7 June 1991), p. 1; Friedman, T. L., 'US and Soviets deadlocked on START', *International Herald Tribune*, 8–9 June 1991, p. 1; Hoffman, D., 'Soviet envoy foresees summer summit', *International Herald Tribune*, 4 July 1991, p. 2; *Wireless File*, no. 130, (United States Information Service, US Embassy: Stockholm, 8 July 1991), pp. 3–4; *Wireless File*, no. 132 (United States Information Service, US Embassy: Stockholm, 10 July 1991), pp. 11–12.; 'Baker und Bessmertnych verhandeln', *Frankfurter Allgemeine Zeitung*, 15 July 1991, p. 3; Gordon, M. R., 'Final item: weight of payload', *International Herald Tribune*, 16 July 1991, p. 3; 'Nur noch die künftige Definition neuer Trägersysteme steht dem Abschluss des Start-Abkommens in Wege', *Frankfurter Allgemeine Zeitung*, 16 July 1991, p. 1; and George, L., 'Three issues still impede START agreement', *Defense News*, 15 July 1991, p. 6.

the end of the month.[10] In six weeks, three issues—downloading, new types of missile and data denial—were resolved.

Downloading

Downloading is the term used to describe a process by which the number of nuclear warheads on a deployed ballistic missile with multiple independently targetable re-entry vehicles (MIRVs) is reduced. Under the START sub-limit of 4900 warheads on deployed ballistic missiles, warheads on a downloaded missile would count against the warhead sub-limit with the actual number of warheads on the missile. The problem with downloading was that, because the START Treaty does not demand the destruction of warheads, downloaded warheads could be put in storage and could, in time of crisis, be redeployed. Thus, while each side would normally conform to START sub-limits, unrestricted downloading would not be a reflection of either side's true nuclear capacity. This posed a particular problem for US negotiators who had been trying throughout the START process to reduce the threat of Soviet MIRVed missiles to US silo-based ICBMs. Downloading Soviet missiles would indeed reduce this threat but unrestricted downloading would permit the USSR to stay within START sub-limits and redeploy the warheads. This was unacceptable to the United States. The task was then to agree with the USSR on the number of types of missile that could be downloaded, the total number of warheads that could be downloaded, and the extent to which individual types of missile could be downloaded.

The problem of reaching an agreement was compounded by the fact that the Soviet Union had already downloaded warheads on its SS-N-18 submarine-launched ballistic missiles (SLBMs) from seven to three. The question was whether or not to count the downloaded version of this missile against a quota of permissible downloading. The Soviet Union suggested that since it no longer fielded the seven-warhead version, the SS-N-18 should not count under the quota. The USA, however, felt that the Soviet Union still had the possibility of replacing the three-warhead carrying front end of the missile with one carrying seven warheads and that the downloading status of the missile had therefore not changed.

The downloading issue was finally settled at the Washington Foreign Ministers' meeting on 11–14 July. The two sides agreed on a downloading quota of 1250 warheads. They agreed further that each deployed SS-N-18 missile would count as four warheads towards this downloading quota. The USA is allowed to reduce one or two warheads each from its three-warhead Minuteman III missiles. Both sides are permitted to download two other deployed ballistic missiles types by up to 500 warheads (within the overall 1250 limit), but never by more than four warheads per missile. Should an

[10] Redburn, T., 'G-7 sets mechanism to aid Soviets; Bush to sign START pact in Moscow', *International Herald Tribune*, 18 July 1991, pp. 1 and 6; 'Start—endlich am Ziel', *Neue Züricher Zeitung*, 19 July 1991, p. 3; 'Verschworene Kameraden', *Der Spiegel*, no. 30 (1990), pp. 120–23.

ICBM be downloaded by more than two warheads, the sides pledged to destroy the missile's front section and replace it with one that is only capable of holding the remaining warheads.[11]

New types of missile

Another issue that had raised questions about a break-out from treaty provisions was that of determining what a new type of ballistic missile was and what constituted a modernization of an existing type. The problem was that START permits modernization of existing missiles and that one side could undertake minor missile modernization and call that missile a new type. The USA insisted that to qualify as a new type, a missile needed to be significantly different from those already deployed. In the US view, in the absence of such a provision, the Soviet Union could for instance modify a deployed single-warhead ICBM, test it with multiple warheads and declare it a new type. The crucial problem was that added nuclear capability would be achievable with only minor design changes which could carry the risk that the Soviet Union could refit a START-accountable single-warhead missile type with multiple warheads. Thus, a formula had to be found which would eliminate the problem of new missile types being introduced through small design changes of existing missile types.

The eventual agreement on new types specified that an ICBM or an SLBM will be considered a new type if it shows any of these changes: a change in the number of stages, a change in type of propellant, a 10 per cent change in missile or first-stage length, a 10 per cent change in missile launch weight, a 5 per cent change in diameter, or a 5 per cent change in first-stage length combined with a 21 per cent increase in throw-weight. The USA, however, was still concerned that a 21 per cent increase in throw-weight would still permit the USSR to equip a missile already deployed with a larger number of lighter warheads without significant design changes. In order to forestall this possibility, the sides agreed that in order to be declared a new type, the throw-weight of a new missile must not be smaller than the throw-weight required to carry an ICBM over a distance of 11 000 km and an SLBM over 9500 km.[12]

Data denial

During a flight test, a missile emits engineering data that is either broadcast or recorded for subsequent recovery. For verification purposes it is important for each side to have access to missile flight-test data, either by receiving broadcasts as they are emitted or through later access to the tapes. The USA and the

[11] Starr, B., 'Downloading: key hurdle on the run-up to START', *Jane's Defence Weekly*, 29 June 1991, p. 1173; Lockwood, D., 'START Treaty signed, brings historic cuts in strategic warheads', *Arms Control Today*, vol. 21, no. 7 (Sep. 1991), pp. 25 and 32–33; 'Strategic Arms Reduction Treaty Chronology' (note 4); and Rühl (note 6).

[12] See Lockwood (note 11); and Rühl (note 6). The USA was especially concerned about a follow-on version of the SS-25.

USSR have traditionally used different broadcasting methods and, because of geographic differences, have flight-tested their missiles differently; the USA conducts tests over open waters, the USSR over Siberia. The problem was that if the USSR adopted the US practice of transmitting telemetry at high frequency and low power, how could the USA receive test signals over Soviet territory? Rather than continuing to wrestle with the different test approaches, the issue was eventually settled in the simplest way possible: both sides agreed to exchange telemetry tapes, acceleration profiles and specified information on how to interpret the data. In addition, both sides agreed to broadcast all telemetric information from flight tests of ICBMs and SLBMs and not to engage in encryption, encapsulation or jamming or any other practice that would impede access to data. Limited exception to these rules was agreed but the main focus of the adopted solution rests clearly with the commitment to make data available.[13]

III. The START Treaty: a brief review

With the final three hurdles successfully taken, the START Treaty was signed at the Moscow summit meeting.[14] The START Treaty consists of 19 articles governing basic provisions. The Treaty further contains a series of annexes, protocols, a memorandum of understanding, joint statements, unilateral statements, declarations and an exchange of letters. These documents, which make up the bulk of the Treaty, are intended to amplify basic treaty provisions, define and clarify them and facilitate their implementation to mutual satisfaction.[15]

Article I: the basic commitment[16]

Article I commits both sides to reduce and limit their strategic nuclear weapons in accordance with treaty provisions and to comply with its Annexes, Protocols and Memorandum of Understanding.

---

[13] See Lockwood (note 11); and Rühl (note 6).

[14] Morrocco, J. D., 'START Treaty offers blueprint for future cuts in nuclear arsenals', *Aviation Week & Space Technology*, 29 July 1991, pp. 21–22; 'USA and Soviets agree START cuts', *Jane's Defence Weekly*, 22 July 1991, p. 131; 'Negotiators work late to prepare arms pact', *International Herald Tribune*, 30 July 1991, p. 2; 'START-Vertrag paraphiert', *Süddeutsche Zeitung*, 30 July 1991, p. 1.

[15] For Treaty excerpts, see appendix 1A. See also *START, Treaty Between the United States of America and the Union of Soviet Socialist Republics on the Reduction and Elimination of Strategic Offensive Arms* (US Department of State, Bureau of Public Affairs: Washington, DC, Oct. 1991), Dispatch Supplement, vol. 2, Supplement no. 5; *Wireless File*, no. 145 (United States Information Service, US Embassy: Stockholm, 29 July 1991), pp. 2–5; *Wireless File*, no. 147 (United States Information Service, US Embassy: Stockholm, 31 July 1991), p. 11; Lockwood, D., 'START: an essential step in a new era', in 'Strategic Arms Reduction Treaty (START): analysis, summary, text', *Arms Control Today*, vol. 21, no. 9 (Nov. 1991), pp. 2–3;*Wireless File*, no. 148 (United States Information Service, US Embassy: Stockholm, 1 Aug. 1991), pp. 6–9.

[16] For references to the Treaty text for the Articles reviewed in section V, see note 15.

Article II: general reductions, limits and sub-limits

The START Treaty imposes limits on aggregate numbers of deployed SNDVs and the weapons they carry. These limits must be met over a period of seven years after the Treaty enters into force. Specifically, neither side may exceed a limit of 1600 SNDVs (ICBMs, SLBMs and heavy bombers). These delivery vehicles may carry no more than 6000 accountable warheads according to specified sub-limits. A maximum number of 4900 warheads may be carried by ballistic missiles, and no more than 1100 warheads may be on ICBMs on mobile launchers. No more than 1540 warheads may be carried by heavy ICBMs. Seven years after the Treaty has entered into force, the aggregate ballistic missile throw-weight for deployed ICBMs and SLBMs for both sides may not exceed 3600 tonnes.[17]

These provisions will be implemented in three phases. Implementation 'milestones' are set at 36, 60 and 84 months. At the end of each phase, certain reductions must be completed in order to provide for a structured, verifiable reduction process.

Article III: counting rules

Article III lays out the rules by which SNDVs and their nuclear warheads are counted. Each deployed ICBM and SLBM and their associated launchers count as one SNDV. Each deployed heavy bomber also counts as one SNDV. Each re-entry vehicle (RV) of an ICBM or SLBM counts as one warhead. Each heavy bomber equipped with bombs and short-range attack missiles (SRAMs) counts as one warhead. Different counting rules apply to ALCM-carrying heavy bombers. For the United States, the first 150 ALCM bombers will count as carrying 10 warheads each, although up to 20 ALCMs may be carried. For the Soviet Union, the first 180 ALCM-carrying bombers will count as carrying eight warheads each, but may carry a maximum of 16. US and Soviet bombers equipped with ALCMs above these agreed limits will be counted with the maximum number of ALCMs they are actually equipped to carry.

Since the the START Treaty is concerned with the correct application of counting rules to existing and future types of ICBMs and SLBMs, and aims to prevent undercounting warheads on these missiles, Article III contains specific language on: (a) how warheads on new types of missile are to be counted; (b) downloading existing types of ICBM and SLBM; and (c) the prohibition on downloading ICBM and SLBM of a new type to a warhead number that is greater than the smallest number of warheads on an existing and already downloaded missile.

If a heavy bomber of a certain type is equipped for long-range nuclear-armed ALCMs, all bombers of that type will be regarded as equipped to carry

---

[17] The USA will not have to reduce its aggregate throw-weight, since it is already under the 3600-tonne limit.

long-range nuclear-armed ALCMs, except those that are not so equipped and are distinguishable from those that are. If a heavy bomber of any type has not been tested with ALCMs, no bomber of that type will be considered as having been equipped to carry ALCMs.

Article IV: non-deployed mobile systems

Article IV limits the number of non-deployed mobile missiles and non-deployed mobile launchers, and specifies rules on where and how they may be stored. These provisions are intended to make rapid reload and refire more difficult. Thus, each side is permitted to have only 250 non-deployed ICBMs for mobile launchers of ICBMs. Within this limit, each side may not have more than 125 non-deployed ICBMs for rail-mobile launchers of ICBMs. Non-deployed mobile ICBM launchers are limited to 110, of which no more than 18 may be non-deployed rail-mobile launchers. Non-deployed ICBMs for mobile ICBM launchers must be stored separately from non-deployed mobile launchers located at the same facility.

Article V: basic prohibitions

The START Treaty does not prohibit modernization or replacement of strategic offensive systems except where specifically stated. Article V lists the commitments by both sides: (a) not to produce, test or deploy certain types of weapon; (b) not to convert existing types of weapon which are counted in the treaty as having a specified purpose and capability; and (c) not to base weapons subject to treaty limitations outside either party's national territory. Treaty provisions are especially concerned with preventing production, testing and deployment of heavy ICBMs of a new type, heavy SLBMs, mobile launchers for heavy ICBMs, launchers of heavy SLBM and downloading of heavy ICBMs.

The Treaty further commits both parties: (a) not to produce, test or deploy an ICBM or SLBM with more than 10 RVs; (b) not to flight-test or deploy an ICBM or SLBM with a greater number of warheads attributed to it; (c) not to produce, flight-test or deploy systems for rapid reload (and not to conduct rapid reload); and (d) not to produce, flight-test or deploy long-range nuclear-armed ALCMs with more than one warhead. Each party also undertakes not to locate long-range nuclear ALCMs at air bases where heavy bombers designated as non-long-range nuclear ALCM-carriers are located (i.e., those that are declared as carrying only SRAMs and bombs). Similarly, heavy bombers equipped to carry long-range nuclear ALCMs must not be located at bases where heavy bombers carrying other nuclear or conventional payloads are based.

Article VI: restrictions on basing and movement of deployed mobile systems

Deployed mobile ICBM launchers are difficult to verify, both with regard to numbers of launchers and their associated missiles and their location. In order to facilitate verification, the two sides agreed on specific provisions for road- and rail-mobile launchers. Thus road-mobile launchers can only be based in restricted areas not exceeding five square kilometres and holding no more than 10 deployed road-mobile launchers and associated missiles each. On-site fixed structures for these launchers are restricted, too, in order to facilitate monitoring to assure that launchers cannot be hidden. Restricted basing areas must be located within deployment areas to which launchers can be moved for routine exercises. However, there can only be one restricted area within one deployment area not exceeding 125 000 square kilometres.

Either party may only deploy rail-mobile ICBM launchers and their associated missiles in rail garrisons, of which no more than seven are permitted. With regard to construction of rail garrisons, the parties have agreed on the number of entrances and exits a rail garrison may have, the number of parking sites within each rail garrison and the number of fixed structures at each garrison. Only 50 per cent of rail-mobile launchers and missiles may leave their garrisons for routine movements at a time.

Both sides are allowed to relocate road- and rail-mobile launchers and their associated missiles. However, Treaty provisions regulate the number of systems that can be moved at any one time for purposes of relocation. Thus, only 15 per cent of road-mobile launchers and 20 per cent of rail-mobile launchers and their missiles can leave restricted areas or rail garrisons at any one time for relocation.

Article VII: the verification principle

Article VII establishes the principle of verifying treaty provisions by national technical means (NTM) (satellite monitoring) and on-site inspections in accordance with the Protocol on Conversion or Elimination and the Protocol on Inspections and Continuous Monitoring Activities. Article VII further specifies that only after treaty obligations have been met will weapon systems covered by the Treaty cease to be subject to the Treaty.

Articles VIII–XV: the verification regime[18]

Articles VIII–XV establish the Treaty verification regime; their cumulative effect is to assure mutual confidence that treaty provisions are being complied with. The key to this verification regime is the data base provision (Article VIII) which commits both sides to provide data on the number, loca-

[18] For a useful summary of the START verification regime, see *Verification Technologies; Measures for Monitoring Compliance with the START Treaty* (Office of Technology Assessment, Congress of the United States: Washington, DC, Dec. 1990).

tion and technical characteristics of items (strategic offensive arms, fixed structures and facilities) subject to the Treaty, and to update data regularly. Each side must provide notifications concerning: movement, conversion or elimination of items subject to the Treaty, data on ICBM and SLBM throw-weight, flight tests of ICBMs and SLBMs and telemetric information, and new types of strategic offensive weapons.

Both parties are committed not to interfere with the other's NTM and not to use concealment measures that might interfere with satellite monitoring of treaty compliance (Article IX). Full access to telemetric information obtained from ICBM and SLBM flight tests must be provided; neither party may engage in jamming, encryption or encapsulation of data. An exemption to this rule is limited to 11 ICBM and SLBM flight tests per year (Article X).

The Treaty makes provisions for 12 types of on-site inspection (OSI) and exhibition: baseline data inspections, data update inspections, new facility inspections, suspect site inspections, re-entry vehicle inspections, post-exercise dispersal inspections, conversion or elimination inspections, close-out inspections, formerly declared facility inspections, technical characteristics exhibitions, distinguishability exhibitions and heavy bomber baseline exhibitions. Each party shall also have the right to conduct continuous monitoring activities at the perimeter and portals of the other's production facilities for ICBMs for mobile launchers (Article XI). Procedures for all these inspections and exhibitions are specified in the Inspection Protocol and in the Conversion and Elimination Protocol.

OSI and exhibitions are intended to verify compliance with the Treaty's basic provisions on reduction and elimination of strategic offensive systems and the Treaty's counting rules. Their aim is to minimize the potential for circumventing treaty commitments and for clandestine activities. Thus, each side has the right to verify basic data and updated data on numbers and types of systems and their specified location. New facility inspections serve to confirm that declarations by one side about the facility's purpose and which treaty-limited item it holds are correct. Suspect site inspections are intended to confirm that covert assembly of ICBMs for mobile launchers is not taking place. Re-entry vehicle inspections serve to establish that deployed ICBMs and SLBMs do not carry more RVs than the number of warheads attributed to them.

Post-exercise dispersal inspections of mobile ICBM launchers and missiles are intended to ensure that the number of those returned and those not returned does not exceed the number specified for that base. Article XIII lays out specific rules on the number of exercise dispersals and their duration.

Conversion or elimination inspections allow each side to confirm that conversion or elimination of weapons has actually taken place; close-out inspections will confirm that the elimination of facilities has been completed and that such facilities are not used for purposes inconsistent with the Treaty. Technical characteristics exhibitions are intended to verify that the technical data specified for each type of ICBM, SLBM, mobile ICBM launcher and variants of these correspond to the actual systems in place.

Distinguishability exhibitions for heavy bombers allow the inspecting party to ensure that the counting rules for ALCM-capable bombers and non-ALCM-capable bombers are properly applied and that the technical characteristics of each type of heavy bomber corresponds to those specified. Inspectors will verify that the maximum number of ALCMs an ALCM-capable heavy bomber is actually equipped to carry does not exceed 20 ALCMs each for the USA and 16 ALCMs each for the USSR. Exhibitions of heavy bombers and their variants that do not carry ALCMs and of non-nuclear heavy bombers of the same type, are intended to demonstrate distinguishability. Each party is also obliged to demonstrate the distinguishability of long-range non-nuclear-armed ALCMs from long-range nuclear-armed ALCMs.

Under the agreement on continuous monitoring of mobile ICBM production facilities, the United States has the right to monitor final assembly of SS-25s at Votkinsk and at SS-24s at Pavlograd. The USSR can monitor the Thiokol Strategic Operations plant at Promontory, Utah at which the accountable stage of the MX missile is undergoing final assembly.

In order to enhance satellite verification, a number of co-operative measures are provided for whereby each side can request the other side to display in the open road-mobile launchers of ICBMs, rail-mobile launchers of ICBMs, heavy bombers and former heavy bombers. Such requests can be made up to seven times a year (Article XII).

Article XIV establishes the right of each party to conduct operational dispersal of its strategic nuclear forces in accordance with the Protocol on Notifications. An operational dispersal is an extreme measure and indicates that one side (or both sides) fear an attack on their strategic nuclear forces. Treaty provisions regarding conversion or elimination of strategic nuclear weapons, verification and co-operative measures will be suspended during such a dispersal. The two sides have established procedures to resume compliance with treaty provisions after notification that an operational dispersal has been completed, that is when normal operations have resumed.

Article XV: Joint Compliance and Inspection Commission

The task of the Joint Compliance and Inspection Commission (JCIC) is to resolve compliance questions and to improve the Treaty's effectiveness as may be necessary. Either party may request a meeting of the JCIC.[19]

---

[19] The first meeting of the JCIC took place in Geneva between 18 Nov. and 19 Dec. 1991. US and Soviet delegations discussed data exchanged in accordance with Treaty provisions, and agreed on procedures for initial demonstration of tapes with telemetric data. See *Wireless File*, no. 245 (United States Information Service, US Embassy: Stockholm, 20 Dec. 1991), p. 7.

Article XVI: conflicting international obligations

The Treaty prohibits either side to assume international obligations that would conflict with treaty provisions. Thus, a transfer of strategic offensive systems to a third country is not permitted.[20] Existing patterns of co-operation, such as those that exist between the United States and the United Kingdom, are exempted from this prohibition.

Articles XVII–XIX: entry into force and amendments

The START Treaty will remain in force for a period of 15 years. It can be extended by successive five-year periods or be superseded by another agreement on the reduction and elimination of strategic offensive arms.

Each party has the right to withdraw from the Treaty if it decides that continued adherence to the Treaty would jeopardize its supreme interests. Should one party decide to withdraw from the Treaty, it must give the other six months' notice and declare its reasons for withdrawing.

The Treaty may be amended through proposals from either party and shall be registered persuant to Article 102 of the UN Charter.

IV. Assessing the START Treaty

An assessment of the START Treaty must deal with two basic questions. First, what does the Treaty achieve? And, second, how relevant are these achievements in light of the fundamental political changes that have taken place?

The START Treaty is the first arms control treaty that reduces long-range offensive nuclear weapons by both sides.[21] The exact size of the cuts both sides will have to undertake depends on the kind of force structure each will decide upon. However, it is generally predicted that in order to meet delivery vehicle ceilings and warhead limits (Article II), total US strategic nuclear warheads will decline by 20–25 per cent and by 30–35 per cent for the USSR. Ballistic missile warhead reductions will amount to 35 per cent for the USA and some 50 per cent for the USSR.[22]

The Soviet Union's 308 SS-18 heavy ICBMs will be cut by half, leaving 154 SS-18s with 1540 warheads in place. The Treaty also forecloses options for expanding the Soviet heavy ICBM force by banning new types, mobile missiles and downloading. These measures plus the 4900-warhead limit on ballistic missiles and a cut in Soviet ballistic missile throw-weight by 46 per cent are intended to encourage both sides, but especially the USSR, to reduce reliance on vulnerable MIRVed ICBMs that make attractive targets. In additon, the Treaty promotes a shift to strategic bombers because they are

---

[20] See Article V, section 28 of the START Treaty, reprinted in appendix 1A.

[21] If the 1979 SALT II Treaty had been ratified, the Soviet Union would have had to reduce the number of its SNDVs, although not the number of its warheads.

[22] For a discussion of START mandated cuts, see Cowen Karp (note 2), pp. 395–401.

considered unsuitable for a first strike. The liberal counting rules for bombers with gravity bombs and SRAMs, and the heavy discounts granted for ALCM-carrying bombers, express this desire to limit the growth of ICBM forces. Whether either side will exploit these discounts, however, is doubtful.[23] Although the USA initially had argued for a specific sub-limit on ICBM warheads, the total ballistic missile warhead sub-limit, the cuts in SS-18s and attendant prohibitions on heavy ICBMs are preferable to a strategic environment from which these provisions are absent.[24]

The Treaty makes detailed provisions to limit the potential of Soviet mobile ICBMs. These ICBMs have been of special concern to the USA since the USSR already fields two mobile systems: the rail-mobile SS-24 and the road-mobile SS-25. The USA does not have an ICBM deployed in a mobile mode, although for treaty purposes, the MX missile is regarded as a mobile system.[25] The USA was primarily concerned that while mobility increases survivability, mobile systems are difficult to verify, increasing fears of potential break-out from the Treaty. The Treaty therefore limits the number of warheads on deployed mobile ICBMs to 1100, the number of non-deployed missiles flight-tested from a mobile launcher to 250 of which no more than half may be for rail-mobile launchers, and the number of non-deployed mobile launchers to 110 of which no more than 18 may be for rail-mobile ICBMs. In addition, the Treaty imposes detailed limitations on the movement of deployed mobile ICBMs. Whether these detailed provisions can be verified satisfactorily remains to be seen. It would, of course, have been a much simpler verification task if the two sides had agreed to ban mobile ICBMs altogether, as was initially proposed by the Reagan Administration.[26]

Despite the fact that the START Treaty does not eliminate the threat of Soviet missiles to US ICBM silos, and only imposes limits on numbers and locations of Soviet mobile ICBMs rather than banning them, the Treaty is more of a US- than a Soviet-inspired document. All major treaty provisions, such as the limits on delivery vehicles and warheads, the bomber counting rules and the throw-weight limits were initiated by the United States. Definitions of new types of missiles, limits on missile downloading and access to flight test data, all address primarily US concerns about the potential for

[23] Production and deployment of Tu-160 (Blackjack) strategic bombers has reportedly proceeded more slowly than anticipated. See *Military Forces in Transition* (US Department of Defense: Washington, DC, 1991), p. 34; Starr, B., 'Crisis may freeze force plans', *Jane's Defence Weekly*, 21 Dec. 1991, p. 1206. The Bush Administration has decided to halt production of the B-2 strategic bomber at 20 instead of the originally planned 132. See Healy, M., 'The plug is pulled on the B-2 bomber', *International Herald Tribune*, 9 Jan. 1992, p. 1; 'Some big weapons projects would end', *International Herald Tribune*, 30 Jan. 1992, p. 3; and Graham, G., 'The Pentagon loses its best weapon', *Financial Times*, 14 Jan. 1992, p. 18.

[24] It is not clear when the USA decided to drop its demand for an ICBM sub-ceiling. The START chronology last mentions the sub-limit as an unresolved issue at the end of Round X of the negotiations on 16 Nov. 1988. See note 4, p. 13.

[25] President Bush announced the cancellation of the rail-mobile MX in his uniltateral initiative of 27 Sep. 1991. For the text of the announcement, see appendix 2A.

[26] The Bush Administration withdrew the proposed ban on mobile ICBMs on 19 Sep. 1989 immediately prior to the Wyoming Foreign Ministers' Meeting. However, this decisions was contingent upon congressional approval to fund mobile ICBM programmes. See note 4, p. 13.

treaty circumvention. So does the Soviet statement not to give the Tu-22 bomber the capability to operate at intercontinental range.[27] In addition, the United States has successfully managed to preserve the Strategic Defense Initiative (SDI), despite Soviet concerns about its threat to the ABM Treaty and Soviet attempts to link conclusion of a START agreement to US assurances on the traditional interpretation of the ABM Treaty. The USA has also avoided including in the START Treaty legally binding constraints on long-range nuclear-armed sea-launched cruise missiles, and has safeguarded its conventional SLCM and ALCM options, and its agreement with the UK on the transfer of Trident II SLBMs.

The START Treaty permits the replacement and modernization of strategic offensive arms, except where specifically prohibited. Since both sides have modernization programmes that take account of these prohibitions, none of these programmes will have to be scrapped to comply with START rules. The START Treaty permits both sides to make the required force reductions among older, less capable systems, thus preserving the most modern and accurate ones. The Treaty's impact on offensive nuclear capability is therefore rather limited. Apart from the mandated cuts in SS-18s, the START Treaty does not begin to do more than eliminate redundant nuclear capability. Both sides are left with sufficient numbers of nuclear weapons to cover the targets prescribed by their respective operational plans. Thus, despite the size of nuclear force cuts to be undertaken, the START Treaty cannot be viewed as anything more than a first step towards larger reductions.[28]

The Treaty's most impressive achievement is the creation of a verification regime. Never before in the history of nuclear arms control have compliance verification provisions been as ambitious. While procedures such as those devised for verifying the INF Treaty have been useful in designing the START verification regime, the latter is of an entirely different magnitude. Under the START Treaty, verification is not only about verifying conversion or elimination of nuclear systems as specified in the respective Protocol but also about verifying compliance with treaty provisions governing accountable systems. It is an inherently more difficult task to verify permitted numbers of weapons than it is to establish their absence. If, for example, a particular type of weapon has been banned, discovery of one weapon of such a type would constitute a clear violation of treaty terms. If, however, a specified number of weapons of one type is permitted, the inspecting side will need to verify that: (a) the maximum number permitted has not been exceeded; (b) that these weapons comply with capabilities ascribed to them (numbers of warheads, throw-weight, etc.); (c) that they are located where they should be; and (d) that no other treaty-limited item or treaty-constrained facility is collocated when it

---

[27] For the text of the statement, see appendix 1A.

[28] 'START is a good beginning, arms expert says', *International Herald Tribune*, 29 July 1991, p. 2; Nitze, P., 'Give the strategic disarmers a mandate to keep going', *International Herald Tribune*, 16 Aug. 1991, p. 4.

should not be. The rules that govern these inspections are laid down in the Protocol on Inspections and Continuous Monitoring Activities.[29]

The START Treaty sets a series of major monitoring tasks, such as monitoring by number and type of: (a) deployed silo-based ICBMs; (b) both deployed and non-deployed mobile ICBMs, and their launchers; (c) deployed ballistic missile launching submarines, their launchers and deployed SLBMs; (d) deployed heavy bombers that can and cannot carry ALCMs; (e) previously nuclear-equipped heavy bombers that no longer carry nuclear weapons; and (f) missiles, launchers or bombers eliminated in accordance with treaty limits. In addition, verification includes monitoring the aggregate number of warheads on treaty-limited ballistic and cruise missiles, and their aggregate throw-weight.

The Protocol on Procedures Governing Conversion and Elimination of items subject to the Treaty lays out detailed provisions on what constitutes elimination and procedures on how these items are to be eliminated.[30] These procedures are subject to on-site inspection. The Protocol specifies that conversion or elimination can only take place at facilities designated for these tasks. Most commonly, missiles and their associated launchers will be either cut into pieces, crushed or exploded. Missile silos will be excavated and filled with earth. The process of destroying a silo may not exceed 180 days during which time it must be visible to NTM and an additional 90 days after which it can be filled with earth. Heavy bombers are eliminated by cutting off the tail section, removing the wings and cutting the fuselage into two pieces. Elimination must be completed within 60 days and bomber remains must be visible to NTM for a period of 90 days thereafter. For heavy bombers to be converted to non-nuclear status, bomber weapon bays must be rendered incapable of holding nuclear weapons and all external attachment joints for carrying nuclear weapons must be removed. Completed conversion will be subject to on-site inspection upon notification.

The Protocol on Inspections and Continuous Monitoring Activities governs all activities related to regular inspections, suspect-site inspections and continuous monitoring of mobile ICBM production facilities. It determines the rights of the inspecting party and the duties of the inspecting side. It lays out in great detail and in step-by-step fashion how inspections are to proceed from the point of entry (arrival of the inspecting parties at designated airports) to the site to be inspected, the equipment that may be carried by inspectors for the purposes of inspection, and what inspectors may look at, investigate at close-range, measure and count. The Protocol has 12 annexes further specifying procedures for inspections and continuous monitoring, and the criteria to be applied by the inspecting party when inspecting Treaty items.

Complex verification provisions such as negotiated in the START Treaty will have to prove themselves over time. Only when they are applied can their feasibility and utility be assessed. These reservations notwithstanding, the

---

[29] See START . . . (note 15), pp. 37–102.
[30] See START . . . (note 15), pp. 30–36.

START verification regime is invaluable. It achieves an unprecedented degree of transparency of nuclear forces and their capabilities.[31] Verifiable data exchanges on forces and regular up-dating of data will provide the necessary baseline for Treaty items on which on-site inspections in combination with satellite surveillance can build. The ban on denial of telemetric data and agreed co-operative measures will facilitate verification of compliance. The regulated procedures which guide all verification activity assure that as steps are taken to comply with treaty limits, verification is undertaken to mutual satisfaction.

The START verification regime is not only invaluable for verifying the present treaty. Its provisions can be expanded with relative ease. This would increase the tasks of the inspectors but would not make it more complicated in principle. The benefits of the existing regime are therefore of lasting value. In terms of importance, they clearly outweigh the contribution to strategic stability of the mandated force reductions themselves. And, in light of the profound changes in the international system since the end of the cold war, the START verification regime may well be the key to larger nuclear reductions verifiably undertaken in an otherwise highly uncertain political and military environment.

Should the START Treaty be ratified by the US Senate and the Russian Parliament, with the Russian Federation being the recognized successor state to the former Soviet Union? Have not events since July 1991 invalidated treaty provisions or rendered them irrelevant in resolving security problems in a post-Soviet world? Do not the cuts in nuclear forces envisioned under the START Treaty appear to be puny, and do not its carefully worked out provisions to inhibit cheating appear to be trivial compared to the twin dangers of nuclear proliferation among newly independent republics emerging from the former Soviet Union and nuclear weapons falling into the wrong hands? Finally, can the Treaty be implemented once ratified?

The Treaty achieves what was possible to achieve when it was conceived. There is no doubt that it is a treaty reflecting an era of cold war confrontation in which strategic nuclear arms control was a conservative force in US–Soviet security relations. Its aim was to maintain a military status quo, expressed in terms of strategic parity based on mutual deterrence through strategic offensive nuclear weapons. This military status quo existed since the Soviet Union achieved parity in the early 1970s. Since then, strategic arms control had the task of managing parity (Strategic Arms Limitation Talks I and II agreements) and of preserving it, albeit at a reduced level of forces (the START Treaty). Contrary to widely held popular beliefs, strategic arms control was never intended to transcend the existing force balance. Rather, its aims were to maintain that balance, preserve military options prescribed by nuclear strategy, anticipate and forestall force developments that might endanger the balance, and thus maintain strategic stability. Achieving these objectives was

---

[31] Lockwood, D. 'START: an essential step in a new era', START Supplement, *Arms Control Today*, vol. 21, no. 9 (Nov. 1991), p. 2.

the mandate for the START talks. Underpinning the purposes of this approach to nuclear arms control were particular conceptual assumptions about the nature of the security problem to be addressed through arms control measures and the security condition that generated the security problem.[32]

Like deterrence, from which it is derived, traditional strategic nuclear arms control assumed the existence of a specific threat. This threat was assumed to be constant over time. In order to neutralize the threat, it needed to be deterred. A concomitant assumption was that the threat could indeed be deterred. While theories of deterrence and arms control were primarily of US origin, Soviet nuclear force deployments and arms control behaviour suggested concurrence with the basic tenets of nuclear deterrence and arms control. Differences between the two powers had mainly to do with different assessments of the state of the military balance, the causes of war and the sources of peace, and how to preserve particular force options and promising technologies. Thus, while the two sides used a different strategic vocabulary and differed on how best to redress perceived weaknesses in the military balance, they shared a series of specific assumptions about the bilateral security relationship. This relationship was both adversarial and co-operative. It was adversarial because each side was able to pose a potentially fatal threat to the other. It was co-operative because both sides recognized the need to obviate this mutual threat through deterrence and arms control. Strategic stability then was a function of how well the two sides could co-operate within the deterrence and arms control relationship. Deterrence and arms control were therefore intimately linked. Hence the role of arms control was to enhance mutual deterrence.[33]

The majority of these assumptions are no longer relevant in the post-Soviet era: not merely because the Soviet Union itself has ceased to exist but because the entire intellectual political framework that guided arms control approaches has foundered. The START Treaty is the last cold war strategic nuclear arms control treaty, but if ratified, it will become the first treaty of a new era.

Five rationales are offered in support of this view. First, the START Treaty encapsulates the principle of strategic force reductions. Despite the fact that the START Treaty cuts forces largely considered to be redundant, it does introduce the idea of cutting, rather than limiting strategic forces. With the START Treaty in place, it would be extremely difficult for one side to justify growth in strategic forces in a post-cold war environment. Second, the Treaty provides transparency of existing and predictability of future strategic forces in the former Soviet Union at a time when the new republics are undergoing profound change at all levels. Third, the Treaty can serve as a springboard for larger nuclear reductions. A successor treaty can be quickly negotiated and its provisions accommodated in the START verification regime. Fourth, ratification of the START Treaty by the Russian Parliament and, if necessary, by the

---

[32] For an excellent review of the relationship between deterrence, arms control and strategic stability, see 'Arms control: thirty years on', *Daedalus*, Journal of the American Society of Arts and Sciences, Special issue (winter 1991).

[33] See note 31.

parliaments of those republics on whose territories nuclear weapons are stationed, will create confidence among Western countries that Russia (and other new republics) is a reliable international partner. Fifth, without ratification, it will be very difficult for the former Soviet republics to receive economic aid from Western countries. Indeed, individually and jointly, Western leaders have made it clear that they see a linkage between aid and adherence to international treaty obligations.

A perhaps more important question to ask is: What comes after ratification? The potential for chaos in those former Soviet republics that hold strategic nuclear weapons—Belarus, Kazakhstan, Russia and Ukraine—is still great.[34] Fears of economic reforms failing, of a disgruntled military and of a conservative backlash are still high. With far-reaching transformations going on at all political, economic and military levels, implementing a treaty of the scope and complexity of START might encounter difficulties.

For the time being, the four former republics that hold nuclear weapons are committed to the Agreement on Nuclear Weapons and their Control signed at Alma-Ata on 21 December 1991.[35] The agreement foresees the maintenance of central control over nuclear weapons and commits Ukraine and Belarus to join the 1968 Non-Proliferation Treaty as non-nuclear weapon states. Decisions on nuclear use are to be taken by the President of the Russian Federation in consultation with the heads of the other three former republics. Procedures governing consultations on nuclear use will be drawn up. The eventual nuclear or non-nuclear weapon status of Kazakhstan remains unclear.

Visits by US Secretary of State James Baker in December 1991 and US Undersecretary of State Reginald Bartholomew in January 1992 were intended to impress upon the former republics the need to maintain central command of strategic nuclear forces, take appropriate measures to ensure the safety of nuclear weapons and offer US assistance with eliminating nuclear weapons.[36]

Still, much about the future of the former Soviet nuclear arsenal remains uncertain. Many of the statements issued by leaders of the former republics on nuclear issues since the founding of the Commonwealth have been contradictory. This suggests that issues of nuclear control have not yet been resolved, and that questions regarding where and how and by whom nuclear weapons

[34] In a much noted presentation, US CIA Director Robert Gates told the US House Armed Services Committee's defence policy panel that 'all of the former Soviet republics face enormous economic, social, and political problems that will make the transition to democracy and market economy difficult and potentially dangerous'. See *Wireless File*, no. 237 (United States Information Service, US Embassy: Stockholm, 10 Dec. 1991), pp. 9–13, quoted from p. 9.

[35] FBIS-SOV-91-246, 23 Dec. 1991, pp. 29–32. For the text of the Alma-Ata agreement, see appendix 14A.

[36] *Wireless File*, no. 240 (United States Information Service, US Embassy: Stockholm, 13 Dec. 1991), p. 2; Lockwood, D., '"Commonwealth" leaders pledge arms cuts, central control', *Arms Control Today*, vol. 21, no. 10 (Dec. 1991), pp. 18 and 24–25; *Wireless File*, no. 244 (United States Information Service, US Embassy: Stockholm, 19 Dec. 1991), pp. 9–10; Hoffman, D., 'Breakup poses new questions about nuclear containment', *Washington Post*, 15 Dec. 1991, p. 1; *Wireless File*, no. 10 (United States Information Service, US Embassy: Stockholm, 15 Jan. 1992), p. 1; Freeland, C., 'Ukraine ready to dispose of its nuclear weapons', *Financial Times*, 12 Sep. 1991, p. 2; Hoffman, D., 'Ukraine leader pledges to destroy nuclear arms', *Washington Post*, 19 Dec. 1991, p. 1; Broad, W. J., 'Accord on removal of atom arms from Ukraine', *New York Times*, 19 Dec. 1991, p. 14

should be eliminated are politically sensitive, reflecting as much a struggle for independence from Russia as a genuine desire to become non-nuclear.[37]

The new Commonwealth is still in its infancy and nuclear weapons could easily become entangled in debates of national independence and power-sharing. Its appeal as a viable political body that can equitably represent the interests of its members is untested. Should the CIS become ineffective or even disintegrate, the issue of who controls nuclear weapons could figure prominently and re-nationalization of security policy might appear to be a desirable option.

It would be premature to forecast a resolution of these issues. If, however, Belarus, Kazakhstan and Ukraine should unequivocally decide to become non-nuclear weapon states, this could be accomplished by implementing the START Treaty and transferring tactical nuclear weapons to Russia.

At present, 352 ICBMs are located outside Russia. 46 SS-24s and 130 SS-19s are located in Ukraine. In Kazakhstan, there are 104 SS-18s, while 72 SS-25s are in Belarus. A total of 30 heavy bombers (14 Bear-Hs and 16 Blackjacks) are stationed in Ukraine and 40 are in in Kazakhstan.[38] Since the START Treaty mandates the elimination of 154 SS-18 ICBMs, those based in Kazakhstan could be earmarked for elimination. SS-19 ICBMs are already intended to be destroyed under START (replaced partially by a silo-based version of the SS-24). Road-mobile SS-25s could be driven to Russia. Bomber bases could be built in Russia, and the bombers in Ukraine and Kazakhstan could be relocated.[39] None of these measures could be done quickly. What is important though is that the START Treaty-mandated reductions could be used to undertake these measures in an orderly, verifiable manner and could thus facilitate maintenance of central control of nuclear weapons and the safe disposal of those designated for destruction. With US assistance, such as offered through a congressional appropriation of $400 million, the process of reducing and eliminating nuclear weapons could be advanced.[40]

Thus, there are strong incentives for the new states to ratify and implement the START Treaty. The Treaty offers both security and political benefits. Once in place, it will provide a viable framework for much deeper cuts.

With regard to ratification of the START Treaty by the US Senate, the Treaty is not expected to encounter difficulties as far as its major provisions

[37] For a discussion of evolving relations between former Soviet republics, see chapter 14 in this volume. Also see, Loyd J., 'Struggle for control of Black Sea Fleet intensifies', Financial Times, 10 Jan. 1992, p. 1; Lloyd, J., 'Kazakhs threaten to form their own military', Financial Times, 11–12 Jan. 1992, p. 2; 'Republic feuding concerns Cheney', International Herald Tribune, 11–12 Jan. 1992, p. 5; Loyd, J. and Freeland, C., 'Ukraine believes CIS is "doomed"', Financial Times, 20 Feb. 1992, p. 14; 'Ukraine's rift with Yeltsin deepens', International Herald Tribune, 20 Feb. 1992, pp. 1–2.

[38] 'Factfile: Soviet strategic nuclear weapons outside the Russian Republic', Arms Control Today, vol. 21, no. 10 (Dec. 1991), p. 29.

[39] Bunn, M., 'Soviet coup fails: what impact on arms control?', Arms Control Today, vol. 21, no. 7, (Sep. 1991), pp. 24 and 34; and Campbell, K. M., Carter, A. B., Miller, S. E. and Zraket, C. A., Soviet Nuclear Fission: Control of the Nuclear Arsenal in a Disintegrating Soviet Union, CSIA Studies In International Security no. 1 (Center for Science and International Affairs, Harvard University: Cambridge, Mass., Nov. 1991), pp. 72–75.

[40] Lockwood, D., 'Congress Approves 500 million in Soviet aid', Arms Control Today, vol. 21, no. 10, Dec. 1991, pp. 19 and 25.

are concerned. Although some conservative senators may still fault the Bush Administration for not putting the treaty in place before the collapse of the Soviet Union and for not insisting on deeper cuts of Soviet heavy ICBMs, the Administration and a majority in the Senate share the view that the START Treaty offers an essential degree of stability at a time when the new post-Soviet states are embarked on radical and contentious reforms.[41]

V. The future of strategic nuclear arms control

For more than 40 years, systemic conflict and political rivalry between the United States and the Soviet Union provided the rationale for large nuclear arsenals. Strategic nuclear arms control served the purpose of assuring the two superpowers that the nuclear balance could be maintained and that nuclear weapons could be managed without sacrificing employment options or promising technologies. As a result, arms control became a management tool and offered little prospect for meaningful nuclear reductions.

Now that the cold war is over and the Soviet Union no longer exists, strategic nuclear arms control can play a very different role. It no longer has the task of managing the military status quo because that status quo no longer exists. Its role can become vastly more positive, facilitating a transition to a world in which nuclear weapons are marginalized, if not irrelevant. The post-cold war era thus offers not only opportunities for large reductions in nuclear forces but the opportunity to reassess the role of nuclear weapons generally. As Richard Betts recently observed: 'The ingraining of the principle of deterrence over the course of forty years was so thorough that as euphoria about the end of the cold war and outbreak of peace surged in the late 1980s, scarcely anyone . . . suggested that these happy developments might obviate deterrence'.[42] Indeed, this now appears to be the inescapable consequence of recent events.

With the end of the cold war, the old Soviet threat gone and new non-ideological relations emerging between the West and the new post-Soviet states, force requirements for effective deterrence are sharply reduced. In the past, US leaders believed that the nature of the Soviet Union made it difficult to deter that country and that the deterrent threat of US nuclear weapons had to be credible for every conceivable scenario. Accordingly, US military planning emphasized military options which, at least in theory, could credibly demonstrate to the Soviet Union that the United States had the ability and the resolve to counter Soviet military aggression at any level of engagement.

While deterring an attack on the United States itself was judged to be credible at relatively low nuclear force levels, planning for lesser scenarios, such as deterring conventional attack against US allies, was more difficult. There the task was to devise credible military options and to limit the potential

---

[41] President Bush submitted the START Treaty to the US Senate on 25 Nov. 1991 for its advice and consent to ratification.

[42] Betts, R. K., 'The concept of deterrence in the postwar era', *Security Studies*, vol. 1, no. 1 (autumn 1991), p. 35.

for conflicts to escalate to all-out nuclear retaliation. There existed, of course, a contradiction between credible deterrence at lower levels and the desire to minimize the potential for escalation. This tension in US deterrence strategy was never resolved, nor could it be.[43]

As the new security situation in Europe is unfolding, there is no longer a Warsaw Pact conventional superiority needing to be deterred through US nuclear weapons. Moreover, at the strategic level, there is no longer a USSR that is perceived as inherently aggressive and expansionist. Consequently, the majority of deterrence scenarios designed to counter perceived Soviet intentions are no longer relevant. Equally, it can no longer be argued that in the absence of these sophisticated military scenarios, the USSR, or its successor states, would contemplate an attack on Western Europe or the USA.

There is now no justification to maintain large strategic forces when the reasons for their buildup have disappeared. If the START Treaty was able to cut forces that were considered redundant under prevailing cold war conditions, logic suggests that under post-cold war conditions there is an even greater force redundancy that can be eliminated. Where cuts will be made and how deep they will be depends on the role remaining forces are accorded. What should be the future role of nuclear weapons be?

There is a growing consensus that the only rationale for maintaining nuclear weapons in the future is to deter others from using theirs.[44] Estimates of how many nuclear weapons are required to accomplish this task vary. However, there is agreement on force cuts down to anything between 1000 and 3000 warheads based largely on survivable SLBM-carrying submarines. Adopting the START Treaty framework with its verification regime, these force levels could be achieved relatively quickly. Nuclear targeting doctrines would have to change but if the only role of nuclear weapons were to deter others from using theirs, targeting requirements would be minimal.

No doubt, the world at the beginning of 1992 is nowhere near these goals, but for the first time since the beginning of the cold war, they appear as real policy options and no longer as the utopia of disarmament advocates. By the end of 1991, the world had changed so profoundly that its new realities demand and warrant a reassessment of disarmament options. There are encouraging signs that both the United States and Russia are beginning to grasp these opportunities.

On 27 September 1991, President Bush announced a series of unilateral arms control measures, and proposed that the Soviet Union take joint steps with the USA towards increasing stability and achieving large nuclear reduc-

---

[43] A very useful summary of the USA's search for credible nuclear employment options is provided in Kaplan, F., *The Wizards of Armageddon* (Simon and Schuster: New York, 1983). See also Herken, G., *Counsels of War* (Alfred A. Knopf: New York, 1985); and Bundy, M., *Danger and Survival, Choices about the Bomb in the First Fifty Years* (Random House: New York, 1988).

[44] National Academy of Sciences, Committee on International Security and Arms Control, *The Future of the US–Soviet Relationship* (National Academy Press: Washington, DC, 1991), p. 47; Kaysen, K., McNamara, R. S. and Rathjens, G. W., 'Nuclear weapons after the cold war', *Foreign Affairs*, autumn 1991, p. 102.

tions. On 5 October 1991, President Gorbachev responded with unilateral steps and proposals for further negotiations. While the respective proposals were largely conceived by each in order to address the other side's most threatening systems, the unilateral steps regarding the elimination of tactical land and sea-based nuclear weapons clearly indicated a recognition on both sides that each could freeze programmes and cut nuclear systems without jeopardizing its security.[45]

At the end of January 1992, the United States and Russia announced additional unilateral nuclear arms control measures which, if implemented, will pave the way towards radical disarmament measures. President Bush announced the cancellation of the Midgetman single-warhead ICBM programme, and a production stop for the B-2 strategic bomber and the MX ICBM. These unilateral measures were accompanied by proposals to eliminate land-based ballistic missiles with multiple warheads. In order to make this proposal attractive to the CIS, President Bush pledged to destroy the 50 MX missiles already deployed, to download the 500 three-warhead Minuteman missiles by two warheads and to cut SLBM warheads by one-third below the levels planned under START, if the CIS agrees to eliminate land-based MIRVed ICBMs.[46]

Russian President Boris Yeltsin announced that 130 missile launch silos and missile launch systems of six nuclear submarines had been destroyed, and that the production of the Tu-160 (Blackjack) and the Tu-95MS (Bear-H) heavy bombers would be halted. He also proposed to negotiate a reduction in strategic nuclear warheads to 2000–2500.[47]

The potentially most important step is the promise by President Yeltsin that Russian nuclear ballistic missiles would no longer be directed against US military and civilian targets.[48] For such a promise to be meaningful, the weapons would have to be verifiably dismantled. If the promise is serious, this should not be a problem.

Much of what is happening in the former Soviet republics is, however, still too uncertain to permit accurate predictions about the future course of nuclear arms control. The meaningful survival of the CIS is not assured, nor is the extent of Boris Yeltsin's authority to announce CIS positions and follow them

[45] See appendix 2A. *News Backgrounder* (United States Information Service, US Embassy: Stockholm, 30 Sep. 1991); 'Bush initiative affect on US nuclear inventory', US Department of Defense Fact Sheet, *Wireless File*, no. 200 (United States Information Service, US Embassy: Stockholm, 16 Oct. 1991), pp. 16–19; Bond, D. F., 'Bush's cuts are little threat to US military capabilities', *Aviation Week & Space Technology*, 7 Oct. 1991, pp. 20–22; Schmemann, S., 'Gorbachev matches US on nuclear cuts and goes further on strategic warheads', *New York Times*, 6 Oct. 1991, p. 1; *Wireless File*, no. 194 (United States Information Service, US Embassy: Stockholm, 7 Oct. 1991), p. 1; 'Factfile, Comparison of US and Soviet nuclear cuts', *Arms Control Today*, vol. 21, no. 9 (Nov. 1991), p. 27.

[46] 'The President's State of the Union plans and proposals, White House Fact Sheet', *Wireless File*, no. 19 (United States Information Service, US Embassy: Stockholm, 29 Jan. 1992), pp. 29–30; White, D., 'Sense of urgency prompts Bush to adopt unilateral steps', *Financial Times*, 30 Jan. 1992, p. 7; Fitchett, J., 'Yeltsin arms offer: nuclear cuts to end any threat to US', *International Herald Tribune*, 30 Jan. 1992, pp. 1 and 4; 'Main points of each side's plans', *The Independent*, 30 Jan. 1992, p. 10; Bellamy, C. 'Cuts go further than START Treaty', *The Independent*, 30 Jan. 1992, p. 10.

[47] See note 44.

[48] Lloyd, J. and Barber, L., 'Yeltsin pledge to direct missiles away from US', *Financial Times*, 27 Jan. 1992, p. 1; 'Yeltsin drops US cities as nuclear targets', *International Herald Tribune*, 27 Jan. 1992, p. 1.

through. What is clear though is that the intellectual and strategic premisses that guided nuclear arms control during the cold war have disappeared. Relations between the United States and the new states of the former Soviet Union may not be conflict-free in the future, but there is now no compelling reason to assume that nuclear weapons will play anything but a marginal role in defining these relationships.

The new marginality of nuclear weapons which used to define the traditional context of security and arms control is, however, not a global phenomenon. The threat of the proliferation of weapons of mass destruction and their delivery vehicles is real and ranks high on the international security agenda. This change in the agenda from East–West to more global security concerns ends an era of bifurcation between East–West nuclear issues and problems of proliferation. In the future, stemming the spread of nuclear, chemical and biological weapons will be as strategic a concern as the safe reduction of East–West nuclear arsenals.[49]

---

[49] See the testimony of Ronald Lehman, Director, US Arms Control and Disarmament Agency before the Foreign Affairs Committee, US House of Representatives on 5 Nov. 1991, exerpted in *Wireless File*, no. 214 (United States Information Service, US Embassy: Stockholm, 5 Nov. 1991), pp. 9–10.

Appendix 1A. Excerpts from the 1991 START Treaty and related documents

Treaty Between the United States of America and the Union of Soviet Socialist Republics on the Reduction and Limitation of Strategic Offensive Arms*

The United States of America and the Union of Soviet Socialist Republics, hereinafter referred to as the Parties,

Conscious that nuclear war would have devastating consequences for all humanity, that it cannot be won and must never be fought,

Convinced that the measures for the reduction and limitation of strategic offensive arms and the other obligations set forth in this Treaty will help to reduce the risk of outbreak of nuclear war and strengthen international peace and security,

Recognizing that the interests of the Parties and the interests of international security require the strengthening of strategic stability,

Mindful of their undertakings with regard to strategic offensive arms in Article VI of the Treaty on the Non-Proliferation of Nuclear Weapons of July 1, 1968; Article XI of the Treaty on the Limitation of Anti-Ballistic Missile Systems of May 26, 1972; and the Washington Summit Joint Statement of June 1, 1990,

Have agreed as follows:

Article I

Each Party shall reduce and limit its strategic offensive arms in accordance with the provisions of this Treaty, and shall carry out the other obligations set forth in this Treaty and its Annexes, Protocols, and Memorandum of Understanding.

Article II

1. Each Party shall reduce and limit its ICBMs and ICBM launchers, SLBMs and SLBM launchers, heavy bombers, ICBM warheads, SLBM warheads, and heavy bomber armaments, so that seven years after

---

*The Agreement was signed for the USA by President George Bush and for the USSR by President Mikhail Gorbachev.

entry into force of this Treaty and thereafter, the aggregate numbers, as counted in accordance with Article III of this Treaty, do not exceed:

(*a*) 1600, for deployed ICBMs and their associated launchers, deployed SLBMs and their associated launchers, and deployed heavy bombers, including 154 for deployed heavy ICBMs and their associated launchers;

(*b*) 6000, for warheads attributed to deployed ICBMs, deployed SLBMs, and deployed heavy bombers, including:

(i) 4900, for warheads attributed to deployed ICBMs and deployed SLBMs;

(ii) 1100, for warheads attributed to deployed ICBMs on mobile launchers of ICBMs;

(iii) 1540, for warheads attributed to deployed heavy ICBMs.

2. Each Party shall implement the reductions pursuant to paragraph 1 of this Article in three phases, so that its strategic offensive arms do not exceed:

(*a*) by the end of the first phase, that is, no later than 36 months after entry into force of this Treaty, and thereafter, the following aggregate numbers:

(i) 2100, for deployed ICBMs and their associated launchers, deployed SLBMs and their associated launchers, and deployed heavy bombers;

(ii) 9150, for warheads attributed to deployed ICBMs, deployed SLBMs, and deployed heavy bombers;

(iii) 8050, for warheads attributed to deployed ICBMs and deployed SLBMs;

(*b*) by the end of the second phase, that is, no later than 60 months after entry into force of this Treaty, and thereafter, the following aggregate numbers:

(i) 1900, for deployed ICBMs and their associated launchers, deployed SLBMs and their associated launchers, and deployed heavy bombers;

(ii) 7950, for warheads attributed to deployed ICBMs, deployed SLBMs, and deployed heavy bombers;

(iii) 6750, for warheads attributed to deployed ICBMs and deployed SLBMs;

(*c*) by the end of the third phase, that is, no later than 84 months after entry into force of this Treaty: the aggregate numbers provided for in paragraph 1 of this Article.

3. Each Party shall limit the aggregate throw-weight of its deployed ICBMs and deployed SLBMs so that seven years after entry into force of this Treaty and thereafter such aggregate throw-weight does not exceed 3600 metric tons.

Article III

1. For the purposes of counting toward the maximum aggregate limits provided for in subparagraphs 1(a), 2(a)(i), and 2(b)(i) of Article II of this Treaty:

(a) Each deployed ICBM and its associated launcher shall be counted as one unit; each deployed SLBM and its associated launcher shall be counted as one unit.

(b) Each deployed heavy bomber shall be counted as one unit.

2. For the purposes of counting deployed ICBMs and their associated launchers and deployed SLBMs and their associated launchers:

(a) Each deployed launcher of ICBMs and each deployed launcher of SLBMs shall be considered to contain one deployed ICBM or one deployed SLBM, respectively.

(b) If a deployed ICBM has been removed from its launcher and another missile has not been installed in that launcher, such an ICBM removed from its launcher and located at that ICBM base shall continue to be considered to be contained in that launcher.

(c) If a deployed SLBM has been removed from its launcher and another missile has not been installed in that launcher, such an SLBM removed from its launcher shall be considered to be contained in that launcher. Such an SLBM removed from its launcher shall be located only at a facility at which non-deployed SLBMs may be located pursuant to subparagraph 9(a) of Article IV of this Treaty or be in movement to such a facility.

3. For the purposes of this Treaty, including counting ICBMs and SLBMs:

(a) For ICBMs or SLBMs that are maintained, stored, and transported in stages, the first stage of an ICBM or SLBM of a particular type shall be considered to be an ICBM or SLBM of that type.

(b) For ICBMs or SLBMs that are maintained, stored, and transported as assembled missiles without launch canisters, an assembled missile of a particular type shall be considered to be an ICBM or SLBM of that type.

(c) For ICBMs that are maintained, stored, and transported as assembled missiles in launch canisters, an assembled missile of a particular type, in its launch canister, shall be considered to be an ICBM of that type.

(d) Each launch canister shall be considered to contain an ICBM from the time it first leaves a facility at which an ICBM is installed in it until an ICBM has been launched from it or until an ICBM has been removed from it for elimination. A launch canister shall not be considered to contain an ICBM if it contains a training model of a missile or has been placed on static display. Launch canisters for ICBMs of a particular type shall be distinguishable from launch canisters for ICBMs of a different type.

4. For the purposes of counting warheads:

(a) The number of warheads attributed to an ICBM or SLBM of each existing type shall be the number specified in the Memorandum of Understanding on the Establishment of the Data Base Relating to this Treaty, hereinafter referred to as the Memorandum of Understanding.

(b) The number of warheads that will be attributed to an ICBM or SLBM of a new type shall be the maximum number of reentry vehicles with which an ICBM or SLBM of that type has been flight-tested. The number of warheads that will be attributed to an ICBM or SLBM of a new type with a front section of an existing design with multiple reentry vehicles, or to an ICBM or SLBM of a new type with one reentry vehicle, shall be no less than the nearest integer that is smaller than the result of dividing 40 percent of the accountable throw-weight of the ICBM or SLBM by the weight of the lightest reentry vehicle flight-tested on an ICBM or SLBM of that type. In the case of an ICBM or SLBM of a new type with a front section of a fundamentally new design, the question of the applicability of the 40-percent rule to such an ICBM or SLBM shall be subject to agreement within the framework of the Joint Compliance and Inspection Commission. Until agreement has been reached regarding the rule that will apply to such an ICBM or SLBM, the number of warheads that will be attributed to such an ICBM or SLBM shall be the maximum number of reentry vehicles with which an ICBM or SLBM of that type has been flight-tested. The number of new types of ICBMs or SLBMs with a front section of a fundamentally new design shall not exceed two for each Party as long as this Treaty remains in force.

(c) The number of reentry vehicles with

which an ICBM or SLBM has been flight-tested shall be considered to be the sum of the number of reentry vehicles actually released during the flight test, plus the number of procedures for dispensing reentry vehicles performed during that same flight test when no reentry vehicle was released. A procedure for dispensing penetration aids shall not be considered to be a procedure for dispensing reentry vehicles, provided that the procedure for dispensing penetration aids differs from a procedure for dispensing reentry vehicles.

(d) Each reentry vehicle of an ICBM or SLBM shall be considered to be one warhead.

(e) For the United States of America, each heavy bomber equipped for long-range nuclear ALCMs, up to a total of 150 such heavy bombers, shall be attributed with ten warheads. Each heavy bomber equipped for long-range nuclear ALCMs in excess of 150 such heavy bombers shall be attributed with a number of warheads equal to the number of long-range nuclear ALCMs for which it is actually equipped. The United States of America shall specify the heavy bombers equipped for long-range nuclear ALCMs that are in excess of 150 such heavy bombers by number, type, variant, and the air bases at which they are based. The number of long-range nuclear ALCMs for which each heavy bomber equipped for long-range nuclear ALCMs in excess of 150 such heavy bombers is considered to be actually equipped shall be the maximum number of long-range nuclear ALCMs for which a heavy bomber of the same type and variant is actually equipped.

(f) For the Union of Soviet Socialist Republics, each heavy bomber equipped for long-range nuclear ALCMs, up to a total of 180 such heavy bombers, shall be attributed with eight warheads. Each heavy bomber equipped for long-range nuclear ALCMs in excess of 180 such heavy bombers shall be attributed with a number of warheads equal to the number of long-range nuclear ALCMs for which it is actually equipped. The Union of Soviet Socialist Republics shall specify the heavy bombers equipped for long-range nuclear ALCMs that are in excess of 180 such heavy bombers by number, type, variant, and the air bases at which they are based. The number of long-range nuclear ALCMs for which each heavy bomber equipped for long-range nuclear ALCMs in excess of 180 such heavy bombers is considered to be actually equipped shall be the maximum

number of long-range nuclear ALCMs for which a heavy bomber of the same type and variant is actually equipped.

(g) Each heavy bomber equipped for nuclear armaments other than long-range nuclear ALCMs shall be attributed with one warhead. All heavy bombers not equipped for long-range nuclear ALCMs shall be considered to be heavy bombers equipped for nuclear armaments other than long-range nuclear ALCMs, with the exception of heavy bombers equipped for non-nuclear armaments, test heavy bombers, and training heavy bombers.

5. Each Party shall have the right to reduce the number of warheads attributed to ICBMs and SLBMs only of existing types, up to an aggregate number of 1250 at any one time.

(a) Such aggregate number shall consist of the following:

(i) for the United States of America, the reduction in the number of warheads attributed to the type of ICBM designated by the United States of America as, and known to the Union of Soviet Socialist Republics as, Minuteman III, plus the reduction in the number of warheads attributed to ICBMs and SLBMs of no more than two other existing types;

(ii) for the Union of Soviet Socialist Republics, four multiplied by the number of deployed SLBMs designated by the Union of Soviet Socialist Republics as RSM-50, which is known to the United States of America as SS-N-18, plus the reduction in the number of warheads attributed to ICBMs and SLBMs of no more than two other existing types.

(b) Reductions in the number of warheads attributed to Minuteman III ICBMs shall be carried out subject to the following:

(i) Minuteman III ICBMs to which different numbers of warheads are attributed shall not be deployed at the same ICBM base.

(ii) Any such reductions shall be carried out no later than seven years after entry into force of this Treaty.

(iii) The reentry vehicle platform of each Minuteman III ICBM to which a reduced number of warheads is attributed shall be destroyed and replaced by a new reentry vehicle platform.

(c) Reductions in the number of warheads attributed to ICBMs and SLBMs of types other than Minuteman III shall be carried out subject to the following:

(i) Such reductions shall not exceed 500 warheads at any one time for each Party.

(ii) After a Party has reduced the number of warheads attributed to ICBMs or SLBMs of two existing types, that Party shall not have the right to reduce the number of warheads attributed to ICBMs or SLBMs of any additional type.

(iii) The number of warheads attributed to an ICBM or SLBM shall be reduced by no more than four below the number attributed as of the date of signature of this Treaty.

(iv) ICBMs of the same type, but to which different numbers of warheads are attributed, shall not be deployed at the same ICBM base.

(v) SLBMs of the same type, but to which different numbers of warheads are attributed, shall not be deployed on submarines based at submarine bases adjacent to the waters of the same ocean.

(vi) If the number of warheads attributed to an ICBM or SLBM of a particular type is reduced by more than two, the reentry vehicle platform of each ICBM or SLBM to which such a reduced number of warheads is attributed shall be destroyed and replaced by a new reentry vehicle platform.

(d) A Party shall not have the right to attribute to ICBMs of a new type a number of warheads greater than the smallest number of warheads attributed to any ICBM to which that Party has attributed a reduced number of warheads pursuant to subparagraph (c) of this paragraph. A Party shall not have the right to attribute to SLBMs of a new type a number of warheads greater than the smallest number of warheads attributed to any SLBM to which that Party has attributed a reduced number of warheads pursuant to subparagraph (c) of this paragraph.

6. Newly constructed strategic offensive arms shall begin to be subject to the limitations provided for in this Treaty as follows:

(a) an ICBM, when it first leaves a production facility;

(b) a mobile launcher of ICBMs, when it first leaves a production facility for mobile launchers of ICBMs;

(c) a silo launcher of ICBMs, when excavation for that launcher has been completed and the pouring of concrete for the silo has been completed, or 12 months after the excavation begins, whichever occurs earlier;

(d) for the purpose of counting a deployed ICBM and its associated launcher, a silo launcher of ICBMs shall be considered to contain a deployed ICBM when excavation for that launcher has been completed and the pouring of concrete for the silo has been completed, or 12 months after the excavation begins, whichever occurs earlier, and a mobile launcher of ICBMs shall be considered to contain a deployed ICBM when it arrives at a maintenance facility, except for the non-deployed mobile launchers of ICBMs provided for in subparagraph 2(b) of Article IV of this Treaty, or when it leaves an ICBM loading facility;

(e) an SLBM, when it first leaves a production facility;

(f) an SLBM launcher, when the submarine on which that launcher is installed is first launched;

(g) for the purpose of counting a deployed SLBM and its associated launcher, an SLBM launcher shall be considered to contain a deployed SLBM when the submarine on which that launcher is installed is first launched;

(h) a heavy bomber or former heavy bomber, when its airframe is first brought out of the shop, plant, or building in which components of a heavy bomber or former heavy bomber are assembled to produce complete airframes; or when its airframe is first brought out of the shop, plant, or building in which existing bomber airframes are converted to heavy bomber or former heavy bomber airframes.

7. ICBM launchers and SLBM launchers that have been converted to launch an ICBM or SLBM, respectively, of a different type shall not be capable of launching an ICBM or SLBM of the previous type. Such converted launchers shall be considered to be launchers of ICBMs or SLBMs of that different type as follows:

(a) a silo launcher of ICBMs, when an ICBM of a different type or a training model of a missile of a different type is first installed in that launcher, or when the silo door is reinstalled, whichever occurs first;

(b) a mobile launcher of ICBMs, as agreed within the framework of the Joint Compliance and Inspection Commission;

(c) an SLBM launcher, when all launchers on the submarine on which that launcher is installed have been converted to launch an SLBM of that different type and that submarine begins sea trials, that is, when that submarine first operates under its own power away from the harbor or port in which the conversion of launchers was performed.

8. Heavy bombers that have been converted into heavy bombers of a different category or into former heavy bombers shall be considered to be heavy bombers of that

different category or former heavy bombers as follows:

(*a*) a heavy bomber equipped for nuclear armaments other than long-range nuclear ALCMs converted into a heavy bomber equipped for long-range nuclear ALCMs, when it is first brought out of the shop, plant, or building where it was equipped for long-range nuclear ALCMs;

(*b*) a heavy bomber of one category converted into a heavy bomber of another category provided for in paragraph 9 of Section VI of the Protocol on Procedures Governing the Conversion or Elimination of the Items Subject to this Treaty, hereinafter referred to as the Conversion or Elimination Protocol, or into a former heavy bomber, when the inspection conducted pursuant to paragraph 13 of Section VI of the Conversion or Elimination Protocol is completed or, if such an inspection is not conducted, when the 20-day period provided for in paragraph 13 of Section VI of the Conversion or Elimination Protocol expires.

9. For the purposes of this Treaty:

(*a*) A ballistic missile of a type developed and tested solely to intercept and counter objects not located on the surface of the Earth shall not be considered to be a ballistic missile to which the limitations provided for in this Treaty apply.

(*b*) If a ballistic missile has been flight-tested or deployed for weapon delivery, all ballistic missiles of that type shall be considered to be weapon-delivery vehicles.

(*c*) If a cruise missile has been flight-tested or deployed for weapon delivery, all cruise missiles of that type shall be considered to be weapon-delivery vehicles.

(*d*) If a launcher, other than a soft-site launcher, has contained an ICBM or SLBM of a particular type, it shall be considered to be a launcher of ICBMs or SLBMs of that type. If a launcher, other than a soft-site launcher, has been converted into a launcher of ICBMs or SLBMs of a different type, it shall be considered to be a launcher of ICBMs or SLBMs of the type for which it has been converted.

(*e*) If a heavy bomber is equipped for long-range nuclear ALCMs, all heavy bombers of that type shall be considered to be equipped for long-range nuclear ALCMs, except those that are not so equipped and are distinguishable from heavy bombers of the same type equipped for long-range nuclear ALCMs. If long-range nuclear ALCMs have not been flight-tested from any heavy bomber of a particular type, no heavy bomber of that type shall be considered to be equipped for long-range nuclear ALCMs. Within the same type, a heavy bomber equipped for long-range nuclear ALCMs, a heavy bomber equipped for nuclear armaments other than long-range nuclear ALCMs, a heavy bomber equipped for non-nuclear armaments, a training heavy bomber, and a former heavy bomber shall be distinguishable from one another.

(*f*) Any long-range ALCM of a type, any one of which has been initially flight-tested from a heavy bomber on or before December 31, 1988, shall be considered to be a long-range nuclear ALCM. Any long-range ALCM of a type, any one of which has been initially flight-tested from a heavy bomber after December 31, 1988, shall not be considered to be a long-range nuclear ALCM if it is a long-range non-nuclear ALCM and is distinguishable from long-range nuclear ALCMs. Long-range non-nuclear ALCMs not so distinguishable shall be considered to be long-range nuclear ALCMs.

(*g*) Mobile launchers of ICBMs of each new type of ICBM shall be distinguishable from mobile launchers of ICBMs of existing types of ICBMs and from mobile launchers of ICBMs of other new types of ICBMs. Such new launchers, with their associated missiles installed, shall be distinguishable from mobile launchers of ICBMs of existing types of ICBMs with their associated missiles installed, and from mobile launchers of ICBMs of other new types of ICBMs with their associated missiles installed.

(*h*) Mobile launchers of ICBMs converted into launchers of ICBMs of another type of ICBM shall be distinguishable from mobile launchers of ICBMs of the previous type of ICBM. Such converted launchers, with their associated missiles installed, shall be distinguishable from mobile launchers of ICBMs of the previous type of ICBM with their associated missiles installed. Conversion of mobile launchers of ICBMs shall be carried out in accordance with procedures to be agreed within the framework of the Joint Compliance and Inspection Commission.

10. As of the date of signature of this Treaty:

(*a*) Existing types of ICBMs and SLBMs are:

(i) for the United States of America, the types of missiles designated by the United States of America as Minuteman II, Minuteman III, Peacekeeper, Poseidon,

Trident I, and Trident II, which are known to the Union of Soviet Socialist Republics as Minuteman II, Minuteman III, MX, Poseidon, Trident I, and Trident II, respectively;

(ii) for the Union of Soviet Socialist Republics, the types of missiles designated by the Union of Soviet Socialist Republics as RS-10, RS-12, RS-16, RS-20, RS-18, RS-22, RS-12M, RSM-25, RSM-40, RSM-50, RSM-52, and RSM-54, which are known to the United States of America as SS-11, SS-13, SS-17, SS-18, SS-19, SS-24, SS-25, SS-N-6, SS-N-8, SS-N-18, SS-N-20, and SS-N-23, respectively.

(b) Existing types of ICBMs for mobile launchers of ICBMs are:

(i) for the United States of America, the type of missile designated by the United States of America as Peacekeeper, which is known to the Union of Soviet Socialist Republics as MX;

(ii) for the Union of Soviet Socialist Republics, the types of missiles designated by the Union of Soviet Socialist Republics as RS-22 and RS-12M, which are known to the United States of America as SS-24 and SS-25, respectively.

(c) Former types of ICBMs and SLBMs are the types of missiles designated by the United States of America as, and known to the Union of Soviet Socialist Republics as, Minuteman I and Polaris A-3.

(d) Existing types of heavy bombers are:

(i) for the United States of America, the types of bombers designated by the United States of America as, and known to the Union of Soviet Socialist Republics as, B-52, B-1, and B-2;

(ii) for the Union of Soviet Socialist Republics, the types of bombers designated by the Union of Soviet Socialist Republics as Tu-95 and Tu-160, which are known to the United States of America as Bear and Blackjack, respectively.

(e) Existing types of long-range nuclear ALCMs are:

(i) for the United States of America, the types of long-range nuclear ALCMs designated by the United States of America as, and known to the Union of Soviet Socialist Republics as, AGM-86B and AGM-129;

(ii) for the Union of Soviet Socialist Republics, the types of long-range nuclear ALCMs designated by the Union of Soviet Socialist Republics as RKV-500A and RKV-500B, which are known to the United States of America as AS-15 A and AS-15 B,

respectively.

Article IV

1. For ICBMs and SLBMs:

(a) Each Party shall limit the aggregate number of non-deployed ICBMs for mobile launchers of ICBMs to no more than 250. Within this limit, the number of non-deployed ICBMs for rail-mobile launchers of ICBMs shall not exceed 125.

(b) Each Party shall limit the number of non-deployed ICBMs at a maintenance facility of an ICBM base for mobile launchers of ICBMs to no more than two ICBMs of each type specified for that ICBM base. Non-deployed ICBMs for mobile launchers of ICBMs located at a maintenance facility shall be stored separately from non-deployed mobile launchers of ICBMs located at that maintenance facility.

(c) Each Party shall limit the number of non-deployed ICBMs and sets of ICBM emplacement equipment at an ICBM base for silo launchers of ICBMs to no more than:

(i) two ICBMs of each type specified for that ICBM base and six sets of ICBM emplacement equipment for each type of ICBM specified for that ICBM base; or

(ii) four ICBMs of each type specified for that ICBM base and two sets of ICBM emplacement equipment for each type of ICBM specified for that ICBM base.

(d) Each Party shall limit the aggregate number of ICBMs and SLBMs located at test ranges to no more than 35 during the seven-year period after entry into force of this Treaty. Thereafter, the aggregate number of ICBMs and SLBMs located at test ranges shall not exceed 25.

2. For ICBM launchers and SLBM launchers:

(a) Each Party shall limit the aggregate number of non-deployed mobile launchers of ICBMs to no more than 110. Within this limit, the number of non-deployed rail-mobile launchers of ICBMs shall not exceed 18.

(b) Each Party shall limit the number of non-deployed mobile launchers of ICBMs located at the maintenance facility of each ICBM base for mobile launchers of ICBMs to no more than two such ICBM launchers of each type of ICBM specified for that ICBM base.

(c) Each Party shall limit the number of non-deployed mobile launchers of ICBMs located at training facilities for ICBMs to no more than 40. Each such launcher may contain only a training model of a missile. Non-deployed mobile launchers of ICBMs that contain training models of missiles shall not be located outside a training facility.

(d) Each Party shall limit the aggregate number of test launchers to no more than 45 during the seven-year period after entry into force of this Treaty. Within this limit, the number of fixed test launchers shall not exceed 25, and the number of mobile test launchers shall not exceed 20. Thereafter, the aggregate number of test launchers shall not exceed 40. Within this limit, the number of fixed test launchers shall not exceed 20, and the number of mobile test launchers shall not exceed 20.

(e) Each Party shall limit the aggregate number of silo training launchers and mobile training launchers to no more than 60. ICBMs shall not be launched from training launchers. Each such launcher may contain only a training model of a missile. Mobile training launchers shall not be capable of launching ICBMs, and shall differ from mobile launchers of ICBMs and other road vehicles or railcars on the basis of differences that are observable by national technical means of verification.

3. For heavy bombers and former heavy bombers:

(a) Each Party shall limit the aggregate number of heavy bombers equipped for non-nuclear armaments, former heavy bombers, and training heavy bombers to no more than 75.

(b) Each Party shall limit the number of test heavy bombers to no more than 20.

4. For ICBMs and SLBMs used for delivering objects into the upper atmosphere or space:

(a) Each Party shall limit the number of space launch facilities to no more than five, unless otherwise agreed. Space launch facilities shall not overlap ICBM bases.

(b) Each Party shall limit the aggregate number of ICBM launchers and SLBM launchers located at space launch facilities to no more than 20, unless otherwise agreed. Within this limit, the aggregate number of silo launchers of ICBMs and mobile launchers of ICBMs located at space launch facilities shall not exceed ten, unless otherwise agreed.

(c) Each Party shall limit the aggregate number of ICBMs and SLBMs located at a space launch facility to no more than the number of ICBM launchers and SLBM launchers located at that facility.

5. Each Party shall limit the number of transporter-loaders for ICBMs for road-mobile launchers of ICBMs located at each deployment area or test range to no more than two for each type of ICBM for road-mobile launchers of ICBMs that is attributed with one warhead and that is specified for that deployment area or test range, and shall limit the number of such transporter-loaders located outside deployment areas and test ranges to no more than six. The aggregate number of transporter-loaders for ICBMs for road-mobile launchers of ICBMs shall not exceed 30.

6. Each Party shall limit the number of ballistic missile submarines in dry dock within five kilometers of the boundary of each submarine base to no more than two.

7. For static displays and ground trainers:

(a) Each Party shall limit the number of ICBM launchers and SLBM launchers placed on static display after signature of this Treaty to no more than 20, the number of ICBMs and SLBMs placed on static display after signature of this Treaty to no more than 20, the number of launch canisters placed on static display after signature of this Treaty to no more than 20, and the number of heavy bombers and former heavy bombers placed on static display after signature of this Treaty to no more than 20. Such items placed on static display prior to signature of this Treaty shall be specified in Annex I to the Memorandum of Understanding, but shall not be subject to the limitations provided for in this Treaty.

(b) Each Party shall limit the aggregate number of heavy bombers converted after signature of this Treaty for use as ground trainers and former heavy bombers converted after signature of this Treaty for use as ground trainers to no more than five. Such items converted prior to signature of this Treaty for use as ground trainers shall be specified in Annex I to the Memorandum of Understanding, but shall not be subject to the limitations provided for in this Treaty.

8. Each Party shall limit the aggregate number of storage facilities for ICBMs or SLBMs and repair facilities for ICBMs or SLBMs to no more than 50.

9. With respect to locational and related restrictions on strategic offensive arms:

(a) Each Party shall locate non-deployed ICBMs and non-deployed SLBMs only at maintenance facilities of ICBM bases; submarine bases; ICBM loading facilities; SLBM loading facilities; production facilities for ICBMs or SLBMs; repair facilities for ICBMs or SLBMs; storage facilities for ICBMs or SLBMs; conversion or elimination facilities for ICBMs or SLBMs; test ranges; or space launch facilities. Prototype ICBMs and prototype SLBMs, however, shall not be located at maintenance facilities of ICBM bases or at submarine bases. Non-deployed ICBMs and non-deployed SLBMs may also be in transit. Non-deployed ICBMs for silo launchers of ICBMs may also be transferred within an ICBM base for silo launchers of ICBMs. Non-deployed SLBMs that are located on missile tenders and storage cranes shall be considered to be located at the submarine base at which such missile tenders and storage cranes are specified as based.

(b) Each Party shall locate non-deployed mobile launchers of ICBMs only at maintenance facilities of ICBM bases for mobile launchers of ICBMs, production facilities for mobile launchers of ICBMs, repair facilities for mobile launchers of ICBMs, storage facilities for mobile launchers of ICBMs, ICBM loading facilities, training facilities for ICBMs, conversion or elimination facilities for mobile launchers of ICBMs, test ranges, or space launch facilities. Mobile launchers of prototype ICBMs, however, shall not be located at maintenance facilities of ICBM bases for mobile launchers of ICBMs. Non-deployed mobile launchers of ICBMs may also be in transit.

(c) Each Party shall locate test launchers only at test ranges, except that rail-mobile test launchers may conduct movements for the purpose of testing outside a test range, provided that:

(i) each such movement is completed no later than 30 days after it begins;

(ii) each such movement begins and ends at the same test range and does not involve movement to any other facility;

(iii) movements of no more than six rail-mobile launchers of ICBMs are conducted in each calendar year; and

(iv) no more than one train containing no more than three rail-mobile test launchers is located outside test ranges at any one time.

(d) A deployed mobile launcher of ICBMs and its associated missile that relocates to a test range may, at the discretion of the testing Party, either continue to be counted toward the maximum aggregate limits provided for in Article II of this Treaty, or be counted as a mobile test launcher pursuant to paragraph 2(d) of this Article. If a deployed mobile launcher of ICBMs and its associated missile

that relocates to a test range continues to be counted toward the maximum aggregate limits provided for in Article II of this Treaty, the period of time during which it continuously remains at a test range shall not exceed 45 days. The number of such deployed road-mobile launchers of ICBMs and their associated missiles located at a test range at any one time shall not exceed three, and the number of such deployed rail-mobile launchers of ICBMs and their associated missiles located at a test range at any one time shall not exceed three.

(e) Each Party shall locate silo training launchers only at ICBM bases for silo launchers of ICBMs and training facilities for ICBMs. The number of silo training launchers located at each ICBM base for silo launchers of ICBMs shall not exceed one for each type of ICBM specified for that ICBM base.

(f) Test heavy bombers shall be based only at heavy bomber flight test centers and at production facilities for heavy bombers. Training heavy bombers shall be based only at training facilities for heavy bombers.

10. Each Party shall locate solid rocket motors for first stages of ICBMs for mobile launchers of ICBMs only at locations where production and storage, or testing of such motors occurs and at production facilities for ICBMs for mobile launchers of ICBMs. Such solid rocket motors may also be moved between these locations. Solid rocket motors with nozzles attached for the first stages of ICBMs for mobile launchers of ICBMs shall only be located at production facilities for ICBMs for mobile launchers of ICBMs and at locations where testing of such solid rocket motors occurs. Locations where such solid rocket motors are permitted shall be specified in Annex I to the Memorandum of Understanding.

11. With respect to locational restrictions on facilities:

(a) Each Party shall locate production facilities for ICBMs of a particular type, repair facilities for ICBMs of a particular type, storage facilities for ICBMs of a particular type, ICBM loading facilities for ICBMs of a particular type, and conversion or elimination facilities for ICBMs of a particular type no less than 100 kilometers from any ICBM base for silo launchers of ICBMs of that type of ICBM, any ICBM base for rail-mobile launchers of ICBMs of that type of ICBM, any deployment area for road-mobile launchers of ICBMs of that type of ICBM, any test range from which ICBMs of that type are flight-tested, any production facility for mobile launchers of ICBMs of that type of ICBM, any repair facility for mobile launchers of ICBMs of that type of ICBM, any storage facility for mobile launchers of ICBMs of that type of ICBM, and any training facility for ICBMs at which non-deployed mobile launchers of ICBMs are located. New facilities at which non-deployed ICBMs for silo launchers of ICBMs of any type of ICBM may be located, and new storage facilities for ICBM emplacement equipment, shall be located no less than 100 kilometers from any ICBM base for silo launchers of ICBMs, except that existing storage facilities for intermediate-range missiles, located less than 100 kilometers from an ICBM base for silo launchers of ICBMs or from a test range, may be converted into storage facilities for ICBMs not specified for that ICBM base or that test range.

(b) Each Party shall locate production facilities for mobile launchers of ICBMs of a particular type of ICBM, repair facilities for mobile launchers of ICBMs of a particular type of ICBM, and storage facilities for mobile launchers of ICBMs of a particular type of ICBM no less than 100 kilometers from any ICBM base for mobile launchers of ICBMs of that type of ICBM and any test range from which ICBMs of that type are flight-tested.

(c) Each Party shall locate test ranges and space launch facilities no less than 100 kilometers from any ICBM base for silo launchers of ICBMs, any ICBM base for rail-mobile launchers of ICBMs, and any deployment area.

(d) Each Party shall locate training facilities for ICBMs no less than 100 kilometers from any test range.

(e) Each Party shall locate storage areas for heavy bomber nuclear armaments no less than 100 kilometers from any air base for heavy bombers equipped for non-nuclear armaments and any training facility for heavy bombers. Each Party shall locate storage areas for long-range nuclear ALCMs no less than 100 kilometers from any air base for heavy bombers equipped for nuclear armaments other than long-range nuclear ALCMs, any air base for heavy bombers equipped for non-nuclear armaments, and any training facility for heavy bombers.

12. Each Party shall limit the duration of each transit to no more than 30 days.

Article V

1. Except as prohibited by the provisions of this Treaty, modernization and replacement of strategic offensive arms may be carried out.

2. Each Party undertakes not to:

(a) produce, flight-test, or deploy heavy ICBMs of a new type, or increase the launch weight or throw-weight of heavy ICBMs of an existing type;

(b) produce, flight-test, or deploy heavy SLBMs;

(c) produce, test, or deploy mobile launchers of heavy ICBMs;

(d) produce, test, or deploy additional silo launchers of heavy ICBMs, except for silo launchers of heavy ICBMs that replace silo launchers of heavy ICBMs that have been eliminated in accordance with Section II of the Conversion or Elimination Protocol, provided that the limits provided for in Article II of this Treaty are not exceeded;

(e) convert launchers that are not launchers of heavy ICBMs into launchers of heavy ICBMs;

(f) produce, test, or deploy launchers of heavy SLBMs;

(g) reduce the number of warheads attributed to a heavy ICBM of an existing type.

3. Each Party undertakes not to deploy ICBMs other than in silo launchers of ICBMs, on road-mobile launchers of ICBMs, or on rail-mobile launchers of ICBMs. Each Party undertakes not to produce, test, or deploy ICBM launchers other than silo launchers of ICBMs, road-mobile launchers of ICBMs, or rail-mobile launchers of ICBMs.

4. Each Party undertakes not to deploy on a mobile launcher of ICBMs an ICBM of a type that was not specified as a type of ICBM for mobile launchers of ICBMs in accordance with paragraph 2 of Section VII of the Protocol on Notifications Relating to this Treaty, hereinafter referred to as the Notification Protocol, unless it is an ICBM to which no more than one warhead is attributed and the Parties have agreed within the framework of the Joint Compliance and Inspection Commission to permit deployment of such ICBMs on mobile launchers of ICBMs. A new type of ICBM for mobile launches, of ICBMs may cease to be considered to be a type of ICBM for mobile launchers of ICBMs if no ICBM of that type has been contained on, or flight-tested from, a mobile launcher of ICBMs.

5. Each Party undertakes not to deploy ICBM launchers of a new type of ICBM and not to deploy SLBM launchers of a new type of SLBM if such launchers are capable of launching ICBMs or SLBMs, respectively, of other types. ICBM launchers of existing types of ICBMs and SLBM launchers of existing types of SLBMs shall be incapable, without conversion, of launching ICBMs or SLBMs, respectively, of other types.

6. Each Party undertakes not to convert SLBMs into ICBMs for mobile launchers of ICBMs, or to load SLBMs on, or launch SLBMs from, mobile launchers of ICBMs.

7. Each Party undertakes not to produce, test, or deploy transporter-loaders other than transporter-loaders for ICBMs for road-mobile launchers of ICBMs attributed with one warhead.

8. Each Party undertakes not to locate deployed silo launchers of ICBMs outside ICBM bases for silo launchers of ICBMs.

9. Each Party undertakes not to locate soft-site launchers except at test ranges and space launch facilities. All existing soft-site launchers not at test ranges or space launch facilities shall be eliminated in accordance with the procedures provided for in the Conversion or Elimination Protocol no later than 60 days after entry into force of this Treaty.

10. Each Party undertakes not to:
(a) flight-test ICBMs or SLBMs of a retired or former type from other than test launchers specified for such use or launchers at space launch facilities. Except for soft-site launchers, test launchers specified for such use shall not be used to flight-test ICBMs or SLBMs of a type, any one of which is deployed;
(b) produce ICBMs for mobile launchers of ICBMs of a retired type.

11. Each Party undertakes not to convert silos used as launch control centers into silo launchers of ICBMs.

12. Each Party undertakes not to:
(a) produce, flight-test, or deploy an ICBM or SLBM with more than ten reentry vehicles;
(b) flight-test an ICBM or SLBM with a number of reentry vehicles greater than the number of warheads attributed to it, or, for an ICBM or SLBM of a retired type, with a number of reentry vehicles greater than the largest number of warheads that was attributed to any ICBM or SLBM of that type;
(c) deploy an ICBM or SLBM with a number of reentry vehicles greater than the number of warheads attributed to it;
(d) increase the number of warheads attributed to an ICBM or SLBM of an existing or new

13. Each Party undertakes not to flight-test or deploy an ICBM or SLBM with a number of reentry vehicles greater than the number of warheads attributed to it.

14. Each Party undertakes not to flight-test from space launch facilities ICBMs or SLBMs equipped with reentry vehicles.

15. Each Party undertakes not to use ICBMs or SLBMs for delivering objects into the upper atmosphere or space for purposes inconsistent with existing international obligations undertaken by the Parties.

16. Each Party undertakes not to produce, test, or deploy systems for rapid reload and not to conduct rapid reload.

17. Each Party undertakes not to install SLBM launchers on submarines that were not originally constructed as ballistic missile submarines.

18. Each Party undertakes not to produce, test, or deploy:
(a) ballistic missiles with a range in excess of 600 kilometers, or launchers of such missiles, for installation on waterborne vehicles, including free-floating launchers, other than submarines. This obligation shall not require changes in current ballistic missile storage, transport, loading, or unloading practices;
(b) launchers of ballistic or cruise missiles for emplacement on or for tethering to the ocean floor, the seabed, or the beds of internal waters and inland waters, or for emplacement in or for tethering to the subsoil thereof, or mobile launchers of such missiles that move only in contact with the ocean floor, the seabed, or the beds of internal waters and inland waters, or missiles for such launchers. This obligation shall apply to all areas of the ocean floor and the seabed, including the seabed zone referred to in Articles I and II of the Treaty on the Prohibition of the Emplacement of Nuclear Weapons and Other Weapons of Mass Destruction on the Seabed and the Ocean Floor and in the Subsoil Thereof of February 11, 1971;
(c) systems, including missiles, for placing nuclear weapons or any other kinds of weapons of mass destruction into Earth orbit or a fraction of an Earth orbit;
(d) air-to-surface ballistic missiles (ASBMs);

(e) long-range nuclear ALCMs armed with two or more nuclear weapons.

19. Each Party undertakes not to:

(a) flight-test with nuclear armaments an aircraft that is not an airplane, but that has a range of 8000 kilometers or more; equip such an aircraft for nuclear armaments; or deploy such an aircraft with nuclear armaments;

(b) flight-test with nuclear armaments an airplane that was not initially constructed as a bomber, but that has a range of 8000 kilometers or more, or an integrated platform area in excess of 310 square meters; equip such an airplane for nuclear armaments; or deploy such an airplane with nuclear armaments;

(c) flight-test with long-range nuclear ALCMs an aircraft that is not an airplane, or an airplane that was not initially constructed as a bomber; equip such an aircraft or such an airplane for long-range nuclear ALCMs; or deploy such an aircraft or such an airplane with long-range nuclear ALCMs.

20. The United States of America undertakes not to equip existing or future heavy bombers for more than 20 long-range nuclear ALCMs.

21. The Union of Soviet Socialist Republics undertakes not to equip existing or future heavy bombers for more than 16 long-range nuclear ALCMs.

22. Each Party undertakes not to locate long-range nuclear ALCMs at air bases for heavy bombers equipped for nuclear armaments other than long-range nuclear ALCMs, air bases for heavy bombers equipped for non-nuclear armaments, air bases for former heavy bombers, or training facilities for heavy bombers.

23. Each Party undertakes not to base heavy bombers equipped for long-range nuclear ALCMs, heavy bombers equipped for nuclear armaments other than long-range nuclear ALCMs, or heavy bombers equipped for non-nuclear armaments at air bases at which heavy bombers of either of the other two categories are based.

24. Each Party undertakes not to convert:

(a) heavy bombers equipped for nuclear armaments other than long-range nuclear ALCMs into heavy bombers equipped for long-range nuclear ALCMs, if such heavy bombers were previously equipped for long-range nuclear ALCMs;

(b) heavy bombers equipped for non-nuclear armaments into heavy bombers equipped for long-range nuclear ALCMs or into heavy bombers equipped for nuclear armaments other than long-range nuclear ALCMs;

(c) training heavy bombers into heavy bombers of another category;

(d) former heavy bombers into heavy bombers.

25. Each Party undertakes not to have underground facilities accessible to ballistic missile submarines.

26. Each Party undertakes not to locate railcars at the site of a rail garrison that has been eliminated in accordance with Section IX of the Conversion or Elimination Protocol, unless such railcars have differences, observable by national technical means of verification, in length, width, or height from rail-mobile launchers of ICBMs or launch-associated railcars.

27. Each Party undertakes not to engage in any activities associated with strategic offensive arms at eliminated facilities, notification of the elimination of which has been provided in accordance with paragraph 3 of Section I of the Notification Protocol, unless notification of a new facility at the same location has been provided in accordance with paragraph 3 of Section I of the Notification Protocol. Strategic offensive arms and support equipment shall not be located at eliminated facilities except during their movement through such facilities and during visits of heavy bombers or former heavy bombers at such facilities. Missile tenders may be located at eliminated facilities only for purposes not associated with strategic offensive arms.

28. Each Party undertakes not to base strategic offensive arms subject to the limitations of this Treaty outside its national territory.

29. Each Party undertakes not to use naval vessels that were formerly declared as missile tenders to transport, store, or load SLBMs. Such naval vessels shall not be tied to a ballistic missile submarine for the purpose of supporting such a submarine if such a submarine is located within five kilometers of a submarine base.

30. Each Party undertakes not to remove from production facilities for ICBMs for mobile launchers of ICBMs, solid rocket motors with attached nozzles for the first stages of ICBMs for mobile launchers of ICBMs, except for:

(a) the removal of such motors as part of assembled first stages of ICBMs for mobile launchers of ICBMs that are maintained, stored, and transported in stages;

(b) the removal of such motors as part of assembled ICBMs for mobile launchers of ICBMs that are maintained, stored, and transported as assembled missiles in launch canisters or without launch canisters; and

(c) the removal of such motors as part of assembled first stages of ICBMs for mobile launchers of ICBMs that are maintained, stored, and transported as assembled missiles in launch canisters or without launch canisters, for the purpose of technical characteristics exhibitions.

Article VI

1. Deployed road-mobile launchers of ICBMs and their associated missiles shall be based only in restricted areas. A restricted area shall not exceed five square kilometers in size and shall not overlap another restricted area. No more than ten deployed road-mobile launchers of ICBMs and their associated missiles may be based or located in a restricted area. A restricted area shall not contain deployed ICBMs for road-mobile launchers of ICBMs of more than one type of ICBM.

2. Each Party shall limit the number of fixed structures for road-mobile launchers of ICBMs within each restricted area so that these structures shall not be capable of containing more road-mobile launchers of ICBMs than the number of road-mobile launchers of ICBMs specified for that restricted area.

3. Each restricted area shall be located within a deployment area. A deployment area shall not exceed 125,000 square kilometers in size and shall not overlap another deployment area. A deployment area shall contain no more than one ICBM base for road-mobile launchers of ICBMs.

4. Deployed rail-mobile launchers of ICBMs and their associated missiles shall be based only in rail garrisons. Each Party shall have no more than seven rail garrisons. No point on a portion of track located inside a rail garrison shall be more than 20 kilometers from any entrance/exit for that rail garrison. This distance shall be measured along the tracks. A rail garrison shall not overlap another rail garrison.

5. Each rail garrison shall have no more than two rail entrances/exits. Each such entrance/exit shall have no more than two separate sets of tracks passing through it (a total of four rails).

6. Each Party shall limit the number of parking sites in each rail garrison to no more than the number of trains of standard configuration specified for that rail garrison. Each rail garrison shall have no more than five parking sites.

7. Each Party shall limit the number of fixed structures for rail-mobile launchers of ICBMs in each rail garrison to no more than the number of trains of standard configuration specified for that rail garrison. Each such structure shall contain no more than one train of standard configuration.

8. Each rail garrison shall contain no more than one maintenance facility.

9. Deployed mobile launchers of ICBMs and their associated missiles may leave restricted areas or rail garrisons only for routine movements, relocations, or dispersals. Deployed road-mobile launchers of ICBMs and their associated missiles may leave deployment areas only for relocations or operational dispersals.

10. Relocations shall be completed within 25 days. No more than 15 percent of the total number of deployed road-mobile launchers of ICBMs and their associated missiles or five such launchers and their associated missiles, whichever is greater, may be outside restricted areas at any one time for the purpose of relocation. No more than 20 percent of the total number of deployed rail-mobile launchers of ICBMs and their associated missiles or five such launchers and their associated missiles, whichever is greater, may be outside rail garrisons at any one time for the purpose of relocation.

11. No more than 50 percent of the total number of deployed rail-mobile launchers of ICBMs and their associated missiles may be engaged in routine movements at any one time.

12. All trains with deployed rail-mobile launchers of ICBMs and their associated missiles of a particular type shall be of one standard configuration. All such trains shall conform to that standard configuration except those taking part in routine movements, relocations, or dispersals, and except that portion of a train remaining within a rail garrison after the other portion of such a train has departed for the maintenance facility associated with that rail garrison, has been relocated to another facility, or has departed the rail garrison for routine movement. Except for dispersals, notification of variations from standard configuration shall be provided in accordance with paragraphs 13, 14, and 15 of Section II of the Notification Protocol.

Article VII

1. Conversion and elimination of strategic offensive arms, fixed structures for mobile launchers of ICBMs, and facilities shall be carried out pursuant to this Article and in accordance with procedures provided for in the Conversion or Elimination Protocol. Conversion and elimination shall be verified by national technical means of verification and by inspection as provided for in Articles IX and XI of this Treaty; in the Conversion or Elimination Protocol; and in the Protocol on Inspections and Continuous Monitoring Activities Relating to this Treaty, hereinafter referred to as the Inspection Protocol.

2. ICBMs for mobile launchers of ICBMs, ICBM launchers, SLBM launchers, heavy bombers, former heavy bombers, and support equipment shall be subject to the limitations provided for in this Treaty until they have been eliminated, or otherwise cease to be subject to the limitations provided for in this Treaty, in accordance with procedures provided for in the Conversion or Elimination Protocol.

3. ICBMs for silo launchers of ICBMs and SLBMs shall be subject to the limitations provided for in this Treaty until they have been eliminated by rendering them inoperable, precluding their use for their original purpose, using procedures at the discretion of the Party possessing the ICBMs or SLBMs.

4. The elimination of ICBMs for mobile launchers of ICBMs, mobile launchers of ICBMs, SLBM launchers, heavy bombers, and former heavy bombers shall be carried out at conversion or elimination facilities, except as provided for in Sections VII and VIII of the Conversion or Elimination Protocol. Fixed launchers of ICBMs and fixed structures for mobile launchers of ICBMs subject to elimination shall be eliminated *in situ*. A launch canister remaining at a test range or ICBM base after the flight test of an ICBM for mobile launchers of ICBMs shall be eliminated in the open *in situ,* or at a conversion or elimination facility, in accordance with procedures provided for in the Conversion of Elimination Protocol.

Article VIII

1. A data base pertaining to the obligations under this Treaty is set forth in the Memorandum of Understanding, in which data with respect to items subject to the limitations provided for in this Treaty are listed according to categories of data.

2. In order to ensure the fulfillment of its obligations with respect to this Treaty, each Party shall notify the other Party of changes in data, as provided for in subparagraph 3(a) of this Article, and shall also provide other notifications required by paragraph 3 of this Article, in accordance with the procedures provided for in paragraphs 4, 5, and 6 of this Article, the Notification Protocol, and the Inspection Protocol.

3. Each Party shall provide to the other Party, in accordance with the Notification Protocol, and, for subparagraph (i) of this paragraph, in accordance with Section Ill of the Inspection Protocol:

(*a*) notifications concerning data with respect to items subject to the limitations provided for in this Treaty, according to categories of data contained in the Memorandum of Understanding and other agreed categories of data;

(*b*) notifications concerning movement of items subject to the limitations provided for in this Treaty;

(*c*) notifications concerning data on ICBM and SLBM throw-weight in connection with the Protocol on ICBM and SLBM Throw-weight Relating to this Treaty, hereinafter referred to as the Throw-weight Protocol;

(*d*) notifications concerning conversion or elimination of items subject to the limitations provided for in this Treaty or elimination of facilities subject to this Treaty;

(*e*) notifications concerning cooperative measures to enhance the effectiveness of national technical means of verification;

(*f*) notifications concerning flight tests of ICBMs or SLBMs and notifications concerning telemetric information;

(*g*) notifications concerning strategic offensive arms of new types and new kinds;

(*h*) notifications concerning changes in the content of information provided pursuant to this paragraph, including the rescheduling of activities;

(*i*) notifications concerning inspections and continuous monitoring activities; and

(*j*) notifications concerning operational dispersals.

4. Each Party shall use the Nuclear Risk Reduction Centers, which provide for continuous communication between the Parties, to provide and receive notifications in accordance with the Notification Protocol and the Inspection Protocol, unless otherwise provided for in this Treaty, and to acknowledge receipt of such notifications no later than one hour after receipt.

5. If a time is to be specified in a notification provided pursuant to this Article, that time shall be expressed in Greenwich Mean Time. If only a date is to be specified in a notification, that date shall be specified as the 24-hour period that corresponds to the date in local time, expressed in Greenwich Mean Time.

6. Except as otherwise provided in this Article, each Party shall have the right to release to the public all data current as of September 1, 1990, that are listed in the Memorandum of Understanding, as well as the photographs that are appended thereto. Geographic coordinates and site diagrams that are received pursuant to the Agreement Between the Government of the United States of America and the Government of the Union of Soviet Socialist Republics on Exchange of Geographic Coordinates and Site Diagrams Relating to the Treaty of July 31, 1991, shall not be released to the public unless otherwise agreed. The Parties shall hold consultations on releasing to the public data and other information provided pursuant to this Article or received otherwise in fulfilling the obligations provided for in this Treaty. The provisions of this Article shall not affect the rights and obligations of the Parties with respect to the communication of such data and other information to those individuals who, because of their official responsibilities, require such data or other information to carry out activities related to the fulfillment of the obligations provided for in this Treaty.

Article IX

1. For the purpose of ensuring verification of compliance with the provisions of this Treaty, each Party shall use national technical means of verification at its disposal in a manner consistent with generally recognized principles of international law.

2. Each Party undertakes not to interfere with the national technical means of verification of the other Party operating in accordance with paragraph 1 of this Article.

3. Each Party undertakes not to use concealment measures that impede verification, by national technical means of verification, of compliance with the provisions of this Treaty. In this connection, the obligation not to use concealment measures includes the obligation not to use them at test ranges, including measures that result in the concealment of ICBMs, SLBMs, mobile launchers of ICBMs, or the association between ICBMs or SLBMs and their launchers during testing. The obligation not to use concealment measures shall not apply to cover or concealment practices, at ICBM bases and deployment areas, or to the use of environmental shelters for strategic offensive arms.

4. To aid verification, each ICBM for mobile launchers of ICBMs shall have a unique identifier as provided for in the Inspection Protocol.

Article X

1. During each flight test of an ICBM or SLBM, the Party conducting the flight test shall make on-board technical measurements and shall broadcast all telemetric information obtained from such measurements. The Party conducting the flight test shall determine which technical parameters are to be measured during such flight test, as well as the methods of processing and transmitting telemetric information.

2. During each flight test of an ICBM or SLBM, the Party conducting the flight test undertakes not to engage in any activity that denies full access to telemetric information, including:

(a) the use of encryption;

(b) the use of jamming;

(c) broadcasting telemetric information from an ICBM or SLBM using narrow directional beaming; and

(d) encapsulation of telemetric information, including the use of ejectable capsules or recoverable reentry vehicles.

3. During each flight test of an ICBM or SLBM, the Party conducting the flight test undertakes not to broadcast from a reentry vehicle telemetric information that pertains to the functioning of the stages of the self-contained dispensing mechanism of the ICBM or SLBM.

4. After each flight test of an ICBM or SLBM, the Party conducting the flight test shall provide, in accordance with Section I of the Protocol on Telemetric Information Relating to the Treaty, hereinafter referred to as the Telemetry Protocol, tapes that contain a recording of all telemetric information that is broadcast during the flight test.

5. After each flight test of an ICBM or SLBM, the Party conducting the flight test shall provide, in accordance with Section II of the Telemetry Protocol, data associated with the analysis of the telemetric information.

6. Notwithstanding the provisions of para-

graphs 1 and 2 of this Article, each Party shall have the flight to encapsulate and encrypt on-board technical measurements during no more than a total of eleven flight tests of ICBMs or SLBMs each year. Of these eleven flight tests each year, no more than four shall be flight tests of ICBMs or SLBMs of each type, any missile of which has been flight-tested with a self-contained dispensing mechanism. Such encapsulation shall be carried out in accordance with Section I and paragraph 1 of Section III of the Telemetry Protocol, and such encryption shall be carried out in accordance with paragraph 2 of Section III of the Telemetry Protocol. Encapsulation and encryption that are carried out on the same flight test of an ICBM or SLBM shall count as two flight tests against the quotas specified in this paragraph.

Article XI

1. For the purpose of ensuring verification of compliance with the provisions of this Treaty, each Party shall have the right to conduct inspections and continuous monitoring activities and shall conduct exhibitions pursuant to this Article and the Inspection Protocol. Inspections, continuous monitoring activities, and exhibitions shall be conducted in accordance with the procedures provided for in the Inspection Protocol and the Conversion or Elimination Protocol.

2. Each Party shall have the right to conduct baseline data inspections at facilities to confirm the accuracy of data on the numbers and types of items specified for such facilities in the initial exchange of data provided in accordance with paragraph 1 of Section I of the Notification Protocol.

3. Each Party shall have the right to conduct data update inspections at facilities to confirm the accuracy of data on the numbers and types of items specified for such facilities in the notifications and regular exchanges of updated data provided in accordance with paragraphs 2 and 3 of Section I of the Notification Protocol.

4. Each Party shall have the right to conduct new facility inspections to confirm the accuracy of data on the numbers and types of items specified in the notifications of new facilities provided in accordance with paragraph 3 of Section I of the Notification Protocol.

5. Each Party shall have the right to conduct suspect-site inspections to confirm that covert assembly of ICBMs for mobile launchers of ICBMs or covert assembly of first stages of such ICBMs is not occurring.

6. Each Party shall have the right to conduct reentry vehicle inspections of deployed ICBMs and SLBMs to confirm that such ballistic missiles contain no more reentry vehicles than the number of warheads attributed to them.

7. Each Party shall have the right to conduct post-exercise dispersal inspections of deployed mobile launchers of ICBMs and their associated missiles to confirm that the number of mobile launchers of ICBMs and their associated missiles that are located at the inspected ICBM base and those that have not returned to it after completion of the dispersal does not exceed the number specified for that ICBM base.

8. Each Party shall conduct or shall have the right to conduct conversion or elimination inspections to confirm the conversion or elimination of strategic offensive arms.

9. Each Party shall have the right to conduct close-out inspections to confirm that the elimination of facilities has been completed.

10. Each Party shall have the right to conduct formerly declared facility inspections to confirm that facilities, notification of the elimination of which has been provided in accordance with paragraph 3 of Section I of the Notification Protocol, are not being used for purposes inconsistent with this Treaty.

11. Each Party shall conduct technical characteristics exhibitions, and shall have the right during such exhibitions by the other Party to conduct inspections of an ICBM and an SLBM of each type, and each variant thereof, and of a mobile launcher of ICBMs and each version of such launcher for each type of ICBM for mobile launchers of ICBMs. The purpose of such exhibitions shall be to permit the inspecting Party to confirm that technical characteristics correspond to the data specified for these items.

12. Each Party shall conduct distinguishability exhibitions for heavy bombers, former heavy bombers, and long-range nuclear ALCMs, and shall have the right during such exhibitions by the other Party to conduct inspections, of:

(a) heavy bombers equipped for long-range nuclear ALCMs. The purpose of such exhibitions shall be to permit the inspecting Party to confirm that the technical characteristics of each type and each variant of such heavy bombers correspond to the data specified for these items in Annex G to the

Memorandum of Understanding; to demonstrate the maximum number of long-range nuclear ALCMs for which a heavy bomber of each type and each variant is actually equipped; and to demonstrate that this number does not exceed the number provided for in paragraph 20 or 21 of Article V of this Treaty, as applicable;

(b) for each type of heavy bomber from any one of which a long-range nuclear ALCM has been flight-tested, heavy bombers equipped for nuclear armaments other than long-range nuclear ALCMs, heavy bombers equipped for non-nuclear armaments, training heavy bombers, and former heavy bombers. If, for such a type of heavy bomber, there are no heavy bombers equipped for long-range nuclear ALCMs, a test heavy bomber from which a long-range nuclear ALCM has been flight-tested shall be exhibited. The purpose of such exhibitions shall be to demonstrate to the inspecting Party that, for each exhibited type of heavy bomber, each variant of heavy bombers equipped for nuclear armaments other than long-range nuclear ALCMs, each variant of heavy bombers equipped for non-nuclear armaments, each variant of training heavy bombers, and a former heavy bomber are distinguishable from one another and from each variant of heavy bombers of the same type equipped for long-range nuclear ALCMs; and

(c) long-range nuclear ALCMs. The purpose of such exhibitions shall be to permit the inspecting Party to confirm that the technical characteristics of each type and each variant of such long-range ALCMs correspond to the data specified for these items in Annex H to the Memorandum of Understanding. The further purpose of such exhibitions shall be to demonstrate differences, notification of which has been provided in accordance with paragraph 13, 14, or 15 of Section VII of the Notification Protocol, that make long-range non-nuclear ALCMs distinguishable from long-range nuclear ALCMs.

13. Each Party shall conduct baseline exhibitions, and shall have the right during such exhibitions by the other Party to conduct inspections, of all heavy bombers equipped for non-nuclear armaments, all training heavy bombers, and all former heavy bombers specified in the initial exchange of data provided in accordance with paragraph 1 of Section I of the Notification Protocol. The purpose of these exhibitions

shall be to demonstrate to the inspecting Party that such airplanes satisfy the requirements for conversion in accordance with the Conversion or Elimination Protocol. After a long-range nuclear ALCM has been flight-tested from a heavy bomber of a type, from none of which a long-range nuclear ALCM had previously been flight-tested, the Party conducting the flight test shall conduct baseline exhibitions, and the other Party shall have the right during such exhibitions to conduct inspections, of 30 percent of the heavy bombers of such type equipped for nuclear armaments other than long-range nuclear ALCMs at each air base specified for such heavy bombers. The purpose of these exhibitions shall be to demonstrate to the inspecting Party the presence of specified features that make each exhibited heavy bomber distinguishable from heavy bombers of the same type equipped for long-range nuclear ALCMs.

14. Each Party shall have the right to conduct continuous monitoring activities at production facilities for ICBMs for mobile launchers of ICBMs to confirm the number of ICBMs for mobile launchers of ICBMs produced.

Article XII

1. To enhance the effectiveness of national technical means of verification, each Party shall, if the other Party makes a request in accordance with paragraph 1 of Section V of the Notification Protocol, carry out the following cooperative measures:

(a) a display in the open of the road-mobile launchers of ICBMs located within restricted areas specified by the requesting Party. The number of road-mobile launchers of ICBMs based at the restricted areas specified in each such request shall not exceed ten percent of the total number of deployed road-mobile launchers of ICBMs of the requested Party, and such launchers shall be contained within one ICBM base for road-mobile launchers of ICBMs. For each specified restricted area, the roofs of fixed structures for road-mobile launchers of ICBMs shall be open for the duration of a display. The road-mobile launchers of ICBMs located within the restricted area shall be displayed either located next to or moved half-way out of such fixed structures;

(b) a display in the open of the rail-mobile launchers of ICBMs located at parking sites specified by the requesting Party. Such launchers shall be displayed by removing the entire train from its fixed structure and locating the train within the rail garrison. The number of rail-mobile launchers of ICBMs subject to display pursuant to each such request shall include all such launchers located at no more than eight parking sites, provided that no more than two parking sites may be requested within any one rail garrison in any one request. Requests concerning specific parking sites shall include the designation for each parking site as provided for in Annex A to the Memorandum of Understanding; and

(c) a display in the open of all heavy bombers and former heavy bombers located within one air base specified by the requesting Party, except those heavy bombers and former heavy bombers that are not readily movable due to maintenance or operations. Such heavy bombers and former heavy bombers shall be displayed by removing the entire airplane from its fixed structure, if any, and locating the airplane within the air base. Those heavy bombers and former heavy bombers at the air base specified by the requesting Party that are not readily movable due to maintenance or operations shall be specified by the requested Party in a notification provided in accordance with paragraph 2 of Section V of the Notification Protocol. Such a notification shall be provided no later than 12 hours after the request for display has been made.

2. Road-mobile launchers of ICBMs, rail-mobile launchers of ICBMs, heavy bombers, and former heavy bombers subject to each request pursuant to paragraph 1 of this Article shall be displayed in open view without using concealment measures. Each Party shall have the right to make seven such requests each year, but shall not request a display at any particular ICBM base for road-mobile launchers of ICBMs, any particular parking site, or any particular air base more than two times each year. A Party shall have the right to request, in any single request, only a display of road-mobile launchers of ICBMs, a display of rail-mobile launchers of ICBMs, or a display of heavy bombers and former heavy bombers. A display shall begin no later than 12 hours after the request is made and shall continue until 18 hours have elapsed from the time that the request was made. If the requested Party cannot conduct a display due to circumstances brought about by *force majeure*, it shall provide notification to the requesting Party in accordance with paragraph 3 of Section V of the Notification

Protocol, and the display shall be cancelled. In such a case, the number of requests to which the requesting Party is entitled shall not be reduced.

3. A request for cooperative measures shall not be made for a facility that has been designated for inspection until such an inspection has been completed and the inspectors have departed the facility. A facility for which cooperative measures have been requested shall not be designated for inspection until the cooperative measures have been completed or until notification has been provided in accordance with paragraph 3 of Section V of the Notification Protocol.

Article XIII

1. Each Party shall have the right to conduct exercise dispersals of deployed mobile launchers of ICBMs and their associated missiles from restricted areas or rail garrisons. Such an exercise dispersal may involve either road-mobile launchers of ICBMs or rail-mobile launchers of ICBMs, or both road-mobile launchers of ICBMs and rail-mobile launchers of ICBMs. Exercise dispersals of deployed mobile launchers of ICBMs and their associated missiles shall be conducted as provided for below:

(a) An exercise dispersal shall be considered to have begun as of the date and time specified in the notification provided in accordance with paragraph 11 of Section II of the Notification Protocol,

(b) An exercise dispersal shall be considered to be completed as of the date and time specified in the notification provided in accordance with paragraph 12 of Section II of the Notification Protocol.

(c) Those ICBM bases for mobile launchers of ICBMs specified in the notification provided in accordance with paragraph 11 of Section II of the Notification Protocol shall be considered to be involved in an exercise dispersal.

(d) When an exercise dispersal begins, deployed mobile launchers of ICBMs and their associated missiles engaged in a routine movement from a restricted area or rail garrison of an ICBM base for mobile launchers of ICBMs that is involved in such a dispersal shall be considered to be part of the dispersal.

(e) When an exercise dispersal begins, deployed mobile launchers of ICBMs and their associated missiles engaged in a relocation from a restricted area or rail garrison of an ICBM base for mobile launchers of

ICBMs that is involved in such a dispersal shall continue to be considered to be engaged in a relocation. Notification of the completion of the relocation shall be provided in accordance with paragraph 10 of Section II of the Notification Protocol, unless notification of the completion of the relocation was provided in accordance with paragraph 12 of Section II of the Notification Protocol.

(f) During an exercise dispersal, all deployed mobile launchers of ICBMs and their associated missiles that depart a restricted area or rail garrison of an ICBM base for mobile launchers of ICBMs involved in such a dispersal shall be considered to be part of the dispersal, except for such launchers and missiles that relocate to a facility outside their associated ICBM base during such a dispersal.

(g) An exercise dispersal shall be completed no later than 30 days after it begins.

(h) Exercise dispersals shall not be conducted:

(i) more than two times in any period of two calendar years;

(ii) during the entire period of time provided for baseline data inspections;

(iii) from a new ICBM base for mobile launchers of ICBMs until a new facility inspection has been conducted or until the period of time provided for such an inspection has expired; or

(iv) from an ICBM base for mobile launchers of ICBMs that has been designated for a data update inspection or reentry vehicle inspection, until completion of such an inspection.

(i) If a notification of an exercise dispersal has been provided in accordance with paragraph 11 of Section II of the Notification Protocol, the other Party shall not have the right to designate for data update inspection or reentry vehicle inspection an ICBM base for mobile launchers of ICBMs involved in such a dispersal, or to request cooperative measures for such an ICBM base, until the completion of such a dispersal.

(j) When an exercise dispersal is completed, deployed mobile launchers of ICBMs and their associated missiles involved in such a dispersal shall be located at their restricted areas or rail garrisons, except for those otherwise accounted for in accordance with paragraph 12 of Section II of the Notification Protocol.

2. A major strategic exercise involving heavy bombers, about which a notification has been provided pursuant to the Agreement Between the Government of the United States of America and the Government of the Union of Soviet Socialist Republics on Reciprocal Advance Notification of Major Strategic Exercises Of September 23, 1989, shall be conducted as provided for below:

(a) Such exercise shall be considered to have begun as of the date and time specified in the notification provided in accordance with paragraph 16 of Section II of the Notification Protocol.

(b) Such exercise shall be considered to be completed as of the date and time specified in the notification provided in accordance with paragraph 17 of Section II of the Notification Protocol.

(c) The air bases for heavy bombers and air bases for former heavy bombers specified in the notification provided in accordance with paragraph 16 of Section II of the Notification Protocol shall be considered to be involved in such exercise.

(d) Such exercise shall begin no more than one time in any calendar year, and shall be completed no later than 30 days after it begins.

(e) Such exercise shall not be conducted during the entire period of time provided for baseline data inspections.

(f) During such exercise by a Party, the other Party shall not have the right to conduct inspections of the air bases for heavy bombers and air bases for former heavy bombers involved in the exercise. The right to conduct inspections of such air bases shall resume three days after notification of the completion of a major strategic exercise involving heavy bombers has been provided in accordance with paragraph 17 of Section II of the Notification Protocol.

(g) Within the 30-day period following the receipt of the notification of the completion of such exercise, the receiving Party may make a request for cooperative measures to be carried out in accordance with subparagraph 1(c) of Article XII of this Treaty at one of the air bases involved in the exercise. Such a request shall not be counted toward the quota provided for in paragraph 2 of Article XII of this Treaty.

Article XIV

1. Each Party shall have the right to conduct operational dispersals of deployed mobile launchers of ICBMs and their associated missiles, ballistic missile submarines, and heavy bombers. There shall be no limit on the number and duration of operational dis-

persals, and there shall be no limit on the number of deployed mobile launchers of ICBMs and their associated missiles, ballistic missile submarines, or heavy bombers involved in such dispersals. When an operational dispersal begins, all strategic offensive arms of a Party shall be considered to be part of the dispersal. Operational dispersals shall be conducted as provided for below:

(a) An operational dispersal shall be considered to have begun as of the date and time specified in the notification provided in accordance with paragraph 1 of Section X of the Notification Protocol.

(b) An operational dispersal shall be considered to be completed as of the date and time specified in the notification provided in accordance with paragraph 2 of Section X of the Notification Protocol.

2. During an operational dispersal each Party shall have the right to:

(a) suspend notifications that it would otherwise provide in accordance with the Notification Protocol except for notification of flight tests provided under the Agreement Between the United States of America and the Union of Soviet Socialist Republics on Notifications of Launches of Intercontinental Ballistic Missiles and Submarine-Launched Ballistic Missiles of May 31, 1988; provided that, if any conversion or elimination processes are not suspended pursuant to subparagraph (d) of this paragraph, the relevant notifications shall be provided in accordance with Section IV of the Notification Protocol;

(b) suspend the right of the other Party to conduct inspections;

(c) suspend the right of the other Party to request cooperative measures; and

(d) suspend conversion and elimination processes for its strategic offensive arms. In such case, the number of converted and eliminated items shall correspond to the number that has actually been converted and eliminated as of the date and time of the beginning of the operational dispersal specified in the notification provided in accordance with paragraph 1 of Section X of the Notification Protocol.

3. Notifications suspended pursuant to paragraph 2 of this Article shall resume no later than three days after notification of the completion of the operational dispersal has been provided in accordance with paragraph 2 of Section X of the Notification Protocol. The right to conduct inspections and to request cooperative measures suspended pursuant to paragraph 2 of this Article shall resume four days after notification of the completion of the operational dispersal has been provided in accordance with paragraph 2 of Section X of the Notification Protocol. inspections or cooperative measures being conducted at the time a Party provides notification that it suspends inspections or cooperative measures during an operational dispersal shall not count toward the appropriate annual quotas provided for by this Treaty.

4. When an operational dispersal is completed:

(a) All deployed road-mobile launchers of ICBMs and their associated missiles shall be located within their deployment areas or shall be engaged in relocations.

(b) All deployed rail-mobile launchers of ICBMs and their associated missiles shall be located within their rail garrisons or shall be engaged in routine movements or relocations.

(c) All heavy bombers shall be located within national territory and shall have resumed normal operations. If it is necessary for heavy bombers to be located outside national territory for purposes not inconsistent with this Treaty, the Parties will immediately engage in diplomatic consultations so that appropriate assurances can be provided.

5. Within the 30 day period after the completion of an operational dispersal, the Party not conducting the operational dispersal shall have the right to make no more than two requests for cooperative measures, subject to the provisions of Article XII of this Treaty, for ICBM bases for mobile launchers of ICBMs or air bases. Such requests shall not count toward the quota of requests provided for in paragraph 2 of Article XII of this Treaty.

Article XV

To promote the objectives and implementation of the provisions of this Treaty, the Parties hereby establish the Joint Compliance and Inspection Commission. The Parties agree that, if either Party so requests, they shall meet within the framework of the Joint Compliance and Inspection Commission to:

(a) resolve questions relating to compliance with the obligations assumed;

(b) agree upon such additional measures as may be necessary to improve the viability and effectiveness of this Treaty; and

(c) resolve questions related to the application of relevant provisions of this Treaty to a new kind of strategic offensive arm, after notification has been provided in accordance with paragraph 16 of Section VII of the Notification Protocol.

Article XVI

To ensure the viability and effectiveness of this Treaty, each Party shall not assume any international obligations or undertakings that would conflict with its provisions. The Parties shall hold consultations in accordance with Article XV of this Treaty in order to resolve any ambiguities that may arise in this regard. The Parties agree that this provision does not apply to any patterns of cooperation, including obligations, in the area of strategic offensive arms, existing at the time of signature of this Treaty, between a Party and a third State.

Article XVII

1. This Treaty, including its Annexes, Protocols, and Memorandum of Understanding, all of which form integral parts thereof, shall be subject to ratification in accordance with the constitutional procedures of each Party. This Treaty shall enter into force on the date of the exchange of instruments of ratification.

2. This Treaty shall remain in force for 15 years unless superseded earlier by a subsequent agreement on the reduction and limitation of strategic offensive arms. No later than one year before the expiration of the 15-year period, the Parties shall meet to consider whether this Treaty will be extended. If the Parties so decide, this Treaty will be extended for a period of five years unless it is superseded before the expiration of that period by a subsequent agreement on the reduction and limitation of strategic offensive arms. This Treaty shall be extended for successive five-year periods, if the Parties so decide, in accordance with the procedures governing the initial extension, and it shall remain in force for each agreed five-year period of extension unless it is superseded by a subsequent agreement on the reduction and limitation of strategic offensive arms.

3. Each Party shall, in exercising its national sovereignty, have the right to withdraw from this Treaty if it decides that extraordinary events related to the subject matter of this Treaty have jeopardized its supreme interests. It shall give notice of its decision to the other Party six months prior to withdrawal from this Treaty. Such notice shall include a statement of the extraordinary events the notifying Party regards as having jeopardized its supreme interests.

Article XVIII

Each Party may propose amendments to this Treaty. Agreed amendments shall enter into force in accordance with the procedures governing entry into force of this Treaty.

Article XIX

This Treaty shall be registered pursuant to Article 102 of the Charter of the United Nations.

Done at Moscow on July 31, 1991, in two copies, each in the English and Russian languages, both texts being equally authentic.

Agreed Statements Annex

Excerpts

In connection with the Treaty Between the United States of America and the Union of Soviet Socialist Republics on the Reduction and Limitation of Strategic Offensive Arms, the Parties have agreed as follows:

First Agreed Statement. The Parties agree, in the interest of the viability and effectiveness of the Treaty, not to transfer strategic offensive arms subject to the limitations of the Treaty to third States. The Parties further agree that this Agreed Statement and the provisions of Article XVI of the Treaty do not apply to any patterns of cooperation, including obligations, in the area of strategic offensive arms, existing at the time of signature of the Treaty, between a Party and a third State.

. . .

Fifth Agreed Statement. The Parties agree that the replacement of silo launchers of heavy ICBMs under the provisions of subparagraph 2(d) of Article V of the Treaty shall only take place in the case of silo launchers destroyed by accident or in the case of other exceptional circumstances that require the relocation of existing silo launchers of heavy ICBMs. If such relocation is required, the Party planning to construct the new silo launcher shall provide the other Party with the reasons and plans for such relocation in the Joint Compliance and Inspection Commission prior to carrying out such relocation.

. . .

Definitions Annex

Excerpts

This Annex contains definitions of terms that are used in the Treaty Between the United States of America and the Union of Soviet Socialist Republics on the Reduction and Limitation of Strategic Offensive Arms, and its Annexes, Protocols, and Memorandum of Understanding.

For the purposes of the Treaty and its Annexes, Protocols, and Memorandum of Understanding:

. . .

69. (59) The term 'new type' means, for ICBMs or SLBMs, a type of ICBM or SLBM, the technical characteristics of which differ from those of an ICBM or SLBM, respectively, of each type declared previously in at least one of the following respects:

(a) number of stages;

(b) type of propellant of any stage;

(c) launch weight, by ten percent or more;

(d) length of either the assembled missile without front section or length of the first stage, by ten percent or more;

(e) diameter of the first stage, by five percent or more; or

(f) throw-weight, by an increase of 21 percent or more, in conjunction with a change in the length of the first stage by five percent or more.

. . .

Protocol on ICBM and SLBM Throw-weight Relating to the Treaty Between the United States of America and the Union of Soviet Socialist Republics on the Reduction and Limitation of Strategic Offensive Arms

Pursuant to and in implementation of the Treaty Between the United States of America and the Union of Soviet Socialist Republics on the Reduction and Limitation of Strategic Offensive Arms, hereinafter referred to as the Treaty, the Parties hereby agree upon procedures governing the determination and accountability of ICBM and SLBM throw-weight.

I. Determination and Accountability of ICBM and SLBM Throw-weight

1. The throw-weight demonstrated in a flight test of an ICBM or SLBM shall be:

(a) for an ICBM or SLBM the final stage of which executes a procedure for dispensing reentry vehicles, the aggregate weight of that stage including its propellant and elements not separated from the stage, at the time at which the first release of a reentry vehicle or penetration aid occurs, and its payload;

(b) for an ICBM or SLBM that is not an ICBM or SLBM the final stage of which executes a procedure for dispensing reentry vehicles, the weight of the payload of the final stage or final stages.

2. For each ICBM or SLBM of an existing type, the accountable throw-weight shall be the greatest throw-weight demonstrated in flight tests of an ICBM or SLBM of that type.

3. For each ICBM or SLBM of a new type, the accountable throw-weight shall be the greatest throw-weight demonstrated in flight tests of an ICBM or SLBM of that type, which shall be determined subject to the following provisions:

(a) The greatest throw-weight demonstrated in flight tests of an ICBM or SLBM of a new type shall be no less than the maximum calculated throw-weight that an ICBM or SLBM of that type could deliver to a distance of 11,000 kilometers for ICBMs, or to a distance of 9500 kilometers for SLBMs.

(b) None of the first seven flight tests shall be taken into account in determining the greatest throw-weight demonstrated in flight tests of an ICBM or SLBM of a new type unless the throw-weight demonstrated in such a flight test exceeds the greatest throw-weight demonstrated in subsequent flight tests by more than 20 percent or 250 kilograms, whichever is less, prior to an ICBM or SLBM of that type becoming subject to the limitations provided for in Article II of the Treaty.

4. The maximum calculated throw-weight that an ICBM or SLBM of a new type could deliver to a particular distance shall be calculated by the Party developing such a missile using its own methods of calculation, subject to the following conditions:

(a) the distance to which the throw-weight is delivered shall be measured along the projection of the missile's flight trajectory on the Earth's surface between the launch point and the point that a reentry vehicle that is released immediately after termination of the main engine thrust of the final stage is projected to impact the Earth;

(b) a spherical, non-rotating Earth;

(c) a vacuum ballistic trajectory for the

reentry vehicle;

(d) a full propellant load for each stage, and

(e) the residual propellant in each stage shall not be greater than one percent for solid-propellant ICBMs or SLBMs, or two percent for liquid-propellant ICBMs or SLBMs.

5. Each Party undertakes not to increase the accountable throw-weight of an ICBM or SLBM of an existing type, as determined in accordance with paragraph 2 of this Section, by more than 21 percent of its initial accountable throw-weight.

6. Notifications concerning data on throw-weight of ICBMs or SLBMs in connection with this Protocol shall be provided in accordance with Section III of the Notification Protocol. Throw-weight values, measured in kilograms, shall be specified to the nearest value evenly divisible by 50.

7. In the event of a dispute concerning the initial value of accountable throw-weight of an ICBM of SLBM of a new type, or an increased value of accountable throw-weight of an ICBM or SLBM of an existing or new type, specified in a notification provided in accordance with Section III of the Notification Protocol, the accountable throw-weight shall be the value specified in such notification until such dispute is resolved in the Joint Compliance and Inspection Commission.

II. Verification

1. Verification of compliance with provisions of this Protocol shall be by national technical means of verification.

2. To facilitate verification, for an ICBM and SLBM of each new type, two preannounced flight tests shall be conducted either in the 12-month period prior to an ICBM or SLBM of that type becoming subject to the limitations provided for in Article II of the Treaty, or from among the last five flight tests prior to an ICBM or SLBM of that type becoming subject to the limitations provided for in Article II of the Treaty.

3. No more than one preannounced flight test of an ICBM or SLBM shall be conducted pursuant to paragraph 2 of this Section in any 30-day period.

This Protocol is an integral part of the Treaty and shall enter into force on the date of entry into force of the Treaty and shall remain in force so long as the Treaty remains in force. As provided for in subparagraph (b)

of Article XV of the Treaty, the Parties may agree upon such additional measures as may be necessary to improve the viability and effectiveness of the Treaty. The Parties agree that, if it becomes necessary to make changes in this Protocol that do not affect substantive rights or obligations under the Treaty, they shall use the Joint Compliance and Inspection Commission to reach agreement on such changes, without resorting to the procedure for making amendments set forth in Article XVIII of the Treaty.

Done at Moscow on July 31, 1991, in two copies, each in the English and Russian languages, both texts being equally authentic.

Letters signed by US and Soviet Representatives

Phased Reductions of Heavy ICBMs

Ambassador Linton F. Brooks
Head of Delegation of the
United States of America to the
Negotiations on Nuclear and Space Arms

July 30, 1991

Dear Mr. Ambassador:

On behalf of the Union of Soviet Socialist Republics, I am instructed to state the following:

In connection with the agreement on the phasing of the reductions of strategic offensive arms reached within the framework of the Treaty Between the Union of Soviet Socialist Republics and the United States of America on the Reduction and Limitation of Strategic Offensive Arms, the Soviet Union provides formal assurances to the effect that, in the course of implementing the reductions in accordance with paragraph 2 of Article II of the Treaty, the number of deployed heavy ICBMs and their associated launchers of the Union of Soviet Socialist Republics shall be reduced evenly during all phases. In order to implement this assurance in the most effective manner, it is agreed that deployed heavy ICBMs and their associated launchers shall be reduced by no less than 22 each year until the limits on the aggregate numbers for deployed heavy ICBMs and their associated launchers and for warheads attributed to deployed heavy ICBMs, as provided for in paragraph 1 of Article II of the Treaty, are reached.

Reductions of launchers of heavy ICBMs shall be implemented by means of elimination in accordance with the procedures specified in Section II of the Protocol on Procedures Governing the Conversion or Elimination of the Systems Subject to the Treaty.

If this statement is acceptable, I propose that this letter, together with your response, be included in the official records of the negotiations in the form of statements reflecting the official positions of the Soviet Union and United States.

Mr. Ambassador, please accept the renewed assurances of my highest consideration.

[s]
Ambassador Youri K. Nazarkin
Head of Delegation of the Union of Soviet Socialist Republics to the Negotiations on Nuclear and Space Arms

————

Ambassador Youri K. Nazarkin
Head of Delegation of the Union of Soviet Socialist Republics to the Negotiations on Nuclear and Space Arms

July 30, 1991

Dear Mr. Ambassador:

On behalf of the United States of America. I am authorized to state that the United States accepts the formal assurances set forth in your letter of this date, the substantive portion of which reads as follows:

In connection with the agreement on the phasing of the reductions of strategic offensive arms reached within the framework of the Treaty Between the Union of Soviet Socialist Republics and the United States of America on the Reduction and Limitation of Strategic Offensive Arms, the Soviet Union provides formal assurances to the effect that, in the course of implementing the reductions in accordance with paragraph 2 of Article II of the Treaty, the number of deployed heavy ICBMs and their associated launchers of the Union of Soviet Socialist Republics shall be reduced evenly during all phases. In order to implement this assurance in the most effective manner, it is agreed that deployed heavy ICBMs and their associated launchers shall be reduced by no less than 22 each year until the limits on the aggregate numbers for deployed heavy ICBMs and their associated launchers and for warheads attributed to

deployed heavy ICBMs, as provided for in paragraph 1 of Article II of the Treaty, are reached.

Reductions of launchers of heavy ICBMs shall be implemented by means of elimination in accordance with the procedures specified in Section II of the Protocol on Procedures Governing the Conversion or Elimination of the Systems Subject to the Treaty.

The United States agrees that this response, together with your letter, shall be included in the official records of the negotiations in the form of statements reflecting the official positions of the United States and Soviet Union.

This reply, together with your letter, shall constitute an agreement between the United States of America and the Union of Soviet Socialist Republics, which shall enter into force on the date of entry into force of the Treaty and shall remain in force as long as the Treaty remains in force.

Mr. Ambassador, please accept the renewed assurances of my highest consideration.
Sincerely,

[s]
Ambassador Linton F. Brooks
Head of Delegation of the United States of America to the Negotiations on Nuclear and Space Arms

————

His Excellency
James A. Baker, III
Secretary of State of the US
Moscow

Moscow, July 1991

Dear Mr. Secretary,

On behalf of the Union of Soviet Socialist Republics, I should like to confirm that the provisions set forth in the letter signed on July 30, 1991 by our ambassador concerning the stage-by-stage reduction of deployed heavy ICBMs in connection with the Treaty Between the Union of Soviet Socialist Republics and the United States of America on the Reduction and Limitation of Strategic Offensive Arms are legally binding.
Respectfully,

[s]
Bessmertnykh

Certain Correspondence Related to the Treaty

Third Country Basing

His Excellency
Aleksandr Bessmertnykh,
Minister of Foreign Affairs of the Union of
Soviet Socialist Republics,
Moscow.

July 31, 1991

Dear Mr. Minister:

Our strategic arms control negotiators in Geneva have continued the discussions which Foreign Minister Shevardnadze and I began in New York last year on prohibiting the basing of strategic offensive arms in third countries. I believe a solution to this problem is possible, and would like to offer some concrete thoughts on how this issue could be resolved.

Let me remind you of the many steps that we have already taken to meet your concerns:

First, we have agreed to your proposal to ban the basing of strategic offensive arms outside national territory. That ban will take effect immediately upon entry into force of the START Treaty.

Second, while we do not regard our operations in Holy Loch, Scotland as basing, we are prepared to commit that ballistic missile submarines will be withdrawn from Holy Loch within five months after entry into force of the Treaty.

Third, I can reaffirm our commitment, which I gave to Foreign Minister Shevardnadze orally, that no arrangement involving ballistic missile submarines, such as that currently in Holy Loch, will be carried out in the future.

Finally, I can formally reaffirm that the United States does not base strategic offensive arms outside its national territory.

But, as I explained in New York, we cannot accept a Provision in the START Treaty for inspections outside national territory. At the same time, with respect to our Agreed Statement on this subject, incorporated in the Agreed Statement Annex to the Treaty, I can cite the following paragraph thereof:

The Parties agreed that . . . the Parties have the obligation, if concerns arise under this Agreed Statement, to discuss any ambiguity and, if necessary, to provide each other with information to resolve concerns. Such discussions should occur through diplomatic channels, as well as in the Joint Compliance and Inspection Commission. The Parties do not rule out the possibility that clarifications provided in the Joint Compliance and Inspection Commission might, in certain cases, include inspections or visits.

In this connection, the sides should use, as appropriate, relevant procedures provided for in the Treaty or measures worked out by the Joint Compliance and Inspection Commission under provisions of Article XV of the Treaty.

I believe that, with the clarifications and assurances in this letter and your response, the Agreed Statement and the relevant Treaty provisions, all questions associated with third country basing have been resolved to our mutual satisfaction.

Sincerely,

[s]

James A. Baker, III

Relocation of Heavy ICBM Silos

The Honorable
Richard Cheney
Secretary of Defense
of the United States
Washington, DC

[No Date]

Dear Mr. Secretary,

I received information from the head of our START Delegation in Geneva that the US Delegation had been instructed by Washington to suspend work which involves introducing changes into the Treaty in accordance with the agreement on heavy ICBMs reached in New York. In this context, the US side refers to the fact that allegedly I, in my conversation with you, said that the Soviet side did not intend to construct new silo launchers for heavy missiles.

I believe there is a misunderstanding here. In this connection, I would like to once again set forth the Soviet position, on the basis of which agreement was reached in New York. The essence of the matter is that in modernizing its heavy ICBMs the Soviet Union will construct new silo launchers for heavy ICBMs simultaneously with the elimination of such silo launchers, i.e., staying within the 154 limit. Thus, the Soviet side does not have plans of constructing an additional number (in excess of 154) of heavy ICBM silo launchers.

I wish to emphasize that our position is part of the New York agreement on heavy

ICBMs, which we reaffirm in its entirety.

In conclusion, I would like once again to assure you, Mr. Secretary, that our meetings and discussions have given me a feeling of profound satisfaction, and express confidence that our useful dialogue and contacts will be continued in the interests of our two countries.

Respectfully,

[s]
D. Yazov
Minister of Defense of the USSR
Marshal of the Soviet Union

_____

His Excellency
James A. Baker, III
Secretary of State
United States of America
Washington, DC

His Excellency
Richard B. Cheney
Secretary of Defense
United States of America

Moscow, December 6, 1990

Dear Sirs,

In view of the doubts you had with regard to the issue of constructing new silo launchers for heavy ICBMs—in the context of the broader agreement on heavy ICBMs reached in New York in October 1990—we deem it expedient to provide the following additional clarifications.

First of all, we would like to reiterate with full clarity that under that agreement new silo launchers for heavy ICBMs would be constructed solely for replacing silo launchers of heavy ICBMs eliminated according to the Protocol on Conversion or Elimination Procedures to the START Treaty, which means that their number will remain within the Treaty limits. As we understand it, you may have a question as to what would require such construction. An answer to this question should be sought in situations which might arise in real life.

We hope you agree with us that such accidents unfortunately cannot be fully ruled out, where—in particular, due to long period of operation of silo launchers—their further operation would be impossible. Incidentally, this has been taken into account in the Protocol on Conversion or Elimination Procedures to the START Treaty, which as

the two sides have already agreed upon, provides for a special procedure for notifying and removing from Treaty accountability strategic offensive arms, including ICBM silo launchers, in case of their accidental loss or disablement beyond repair. Naturally each side would have the right in such cases to compensate for the systems removed from accountability—within the appropriate Treaty limits. This of course, applies to heavy ICBMs as well. At least for this reason, the possibility to construct new silo launchers for them should not be precluded.

Also, situations must not be ruled out where it would be necessary to relocate silo launchers, including those for heavy ICBMs, which means that they would be closed in one area of the country and constructed in another, for non-military considerations, particularly in connection with the internal political developments that are taking place in our country. Relocations of silo launchers might be required either during or after the period of reductions under the Treaty. A timely consideration of non-military factors by simply changing our current plans is difficult to realize.

At present we have no plans to relocate silo launchers for heavy ICBMs. Although such relocation, if required in the future, would incur additional great expenses and would be a hard step to take, we cannot, as you may understand, exclude such a possibility.

We hope these additional explanations remove completely the misunderstanding that has arisen and make it possible, at least, to reaffirm the New York agreements on heavy ICBMs and finally close this issue.

Respectfully,

[s]   [s]
E. Shevardnadze   D. Yazov

_____

Statements on the Relationship of START and ABM read at a meeting Between US Ambassador Brooks and Deputy Foreign Minister Obukhov on June 13, 1991.

Statement by the US side at the US–Soviet Negotiations on Nuclear and Space Arms

While the United States cannot circumscribe the Soviet right to withdraw from the START Treaty if the Soviet Union believes its supreme interests are jeopardized, the full exercise by the United States of its legal rights under the ABM Treaty, as we have discussed with the Soviet Union in the past, would not constitute a basis for such withdrawal. The United States will be signing the START Treaty and submitting it to the United States Senate for advice and consent to ratification with this view. In addition, the provisions for withdrawal from the START Treaty based on supreme national interests clearly envision that such withdrawal could only be justified by extraordinary events that have jeopardized a Party's supreme interest. Soviet statements that a future, hypothetical US withdrawal from the ABM Treaty could create such conditions are without legal or military foundation. The ABM Treaty, as signed on May 26, 1972, has already been substantially amended and clarified by subsequent agreements between the Parties. Moreover, current and future negotiations, to which the Soviet Union committed in the June 1990 Summit Joint Statement, could lead to significant additional changes in the ABM Treaty, or its replacement. Changes in the ABM Treaty agreed to by the Parties would not be a basis for questioning the effectiveness or viability of the Treaty on the Reduction and Limitation of Strategic Offensive Arms.

Statement by the Soviet side at the US–Soviet Negotiations on Nuclear and Space Arms Concerning the Interrelationship Between Reductions in Strategic Offensive Arms and Compliance with the Treaty Between the US and the USSR on the Limitation of Anti-Ballistic Missile Systems

In connection with the Treaty Between the United States of America and the Union of Soviet Socialist Republics on the Reduction and Limitation of Strategic Offensive Arms, the Soviet side states the following:

This Treaty may be effective and viable only under conditions of compliance with the Treaty between the U.S and the USSR on the Limitation of Anti-Ballistic Missile Systems, as signed on May 26, 1972.

The extraordinary events referred to in Article XV of this Treaty also include events related to withdrawal by one of the Parties from the Treaty on the Limitation of Anti-Ballistic Missile Systems, or related to its material breach.

Other statements

Declaration by the Union of Soviet Socialist Republics Concerning the Tu-22M Medium Bomber

July 31, 1991

The Union of Soviet Socialist Republics, recognizing the importance of the Treaty on the Reduction and Limitation of Strategic Offensive Arms, and acting in the interest of strengthening stability and enhancing confidence, makes the following declaration concerning its plan with respect to the Tu-22M bomber, which is known to the United States as the Backfire. This declaration will remain in force for the duration of the Treaty and will be politically binding.

The Tu-22M airplane is a medium bomber and is not a strategic offensive arm. At the same time, taking into account the need to remove all concerns standing in the way of the agreements, the Soviet side declares that it will not give the Tu-22M airplane the capability of operating at intercontinental distances in any manner, including by inflight refueling.

The Soviet Union will not have more than 300 Tu-22M airplanes at any one time, not including naval Tu-22M airplanes. The number of naval Tu-22M airplanes will not exceed 200.

In view of the fact that there must be no constraints in the START Treaty on arms that are not strategic offensive arms, Tu-22M airplanes will not be subject to that Treaty.

Source: *START, Treaty Between the United States of America and the Union of Soviet Socialist Republics on the Reduction and Elimination of Strategic Offensive Arms* (US Department of State, Bureau of Public Affairs: Washington, DC, Oct. 1991), Dispatch Supplement, vol. 2, Supplement no. 5.

2. Nuclear weapon developments and unilateral reduction initiatives

RICHARD FIELDHOUSE; tables by ROBERT S. NORRIS
and WILLIAM M. ARKIN

I. Introduction

Nuclear weapon history changed dramatically in 1991: the USA and the USSR ended their 45-year nuclear arms confrontation and began a process of disarmament before the collapse of the USSR at the end of the year.

After the failed coup in the Soviet Union in August 1991, the USA and the USSR each announced unprecedented reductions in their nuclear forces, on a unilateral and reciprocal basis. President George Bush announced his nuclear reduction initiative on 27 September, and President Mikhail Gorbachev responded with a similar initiative on 5 October (for the texts of the announcements of the two initiatives, see appendix 2A). These two initiatives effectively cancelled the bulk of the two nations' respective non-strategic nuclear arsenals and curtailed a portion of their strategic nuclear activities as well.

By early October, the two nations had removed over 4000 strategic nuclear warheads from operational 'alert' duty, had removed all their long-range bomber aircraft from alert duty and had placed the associated nuclear weapons in storage. Although many of these weapon systems were scheduled for retirement under the START Treaty, the 1991 initiatives accelerated the strategic nuclear drawdown considerably, in addition to eliminating several classes of non-strategic weapons and removing others from operational service.

On 17 October 1991, the NATO defence ministers' meeting in Taormina, Italy (Sicily) agreed to reduce NATO's remaining stockpile of nuclear gravity bombs by half, from about 1400 to 700 bombs.[1] The majority of the reductions were to be made by the USA, but the UK agreed to remove about half of its estimated 200 nuclear bombs deployed forward in Germany.[2] With the September Bush initiative and the October NATO decision, NATO's nuclear weapon stockpile was slated to be reduced by some 80 per cent.[3] Along with President Gorbachev's October initiative, the USA and the USSR had agreed within less than a month to rid Europe of all short-range nuclear forces except gravity bombs, all without lengthy arms control negotiations.

[1] Smith, R. J., 'NATO approves 50% cut in tactical A-bombs', *Washington Post*, 18 Oct. 1991, p. A28.
[2] Jacobsen, S., 'NATO agrees to slash nuclear arsenal by 80%', *Washington Times*, 18 Oct. 1991, p. A7; Riding, A., 'NATO to cut aircraft A-bombs by 50%', *New York Times*, 18 Oct. 1991, p. A3.
[3] Jacobsen (note 2).

The USA was motivated largely by the opportunity and the imperative after the failed Soviet coup to secure agreement by the surviving Soviet Government to major reductions in nuclear weapons. It was unclear after the coup attempt how the Soviet Government would evolve, or even whether it would survive, but the possibility of a breakup of the Union and the potential emergence of several independent nuclear-armed republics, or disputes among the republics, spurred the Bush Administration to action. After the attempted coup it was revealed that the plotters had taken President Gorbachev's nuclear war briefcase, raising fears that the massive Soviet nuclear arsenal was either not under strict central control or not under civilian control. This was but the first of many concerns about the fate of some 30 000 nuclear warheads under tumultuous political conditions.[4]

On 28 January 1992 President Bush announced new US unilateral nuclear initiatives and bilateral proposals as part of his annual State of the Union address to Congress. Russian Federation President Boris Yeltsin responded with a set of his own initiatives the next day, thus moving these two nations further in the direction of massive nuclear reductions and co-operative de-nuclearization (see appendix 2A for the texts of these announcements).

US and CIS (Commonwealth of Independent States) officials met several times beginning in late 1991 to exchange ideas on safe, secure and environmentally responsible nuclear warhead transportation, storage and dismantlement. The information exchanged was unprecedented in scope and detail, including US explanations of warhead-disabling techniques and nuclear weapon command and control procedures, and similar Russian details.[5] Barely one year before, these facts were among the nuclear 'crown jewels' of each nation and were some of the most closely guarded atomic secrets of the cold war.

By 1992, the major international concern had shifted from the cold war nuclear confrontation to the proliferation of nuclear weapons and systems.

II. US nuclear weapon programmes and the Bush initiatives

At the start of 1991, the USA was continuing many of its strategic nuclear modernization programmes, including: research and development (R&D) on the MX intercontinental ballistic missile (ICBM) in the rail garrison basing mode; R&D on the Small ICBM (SICBM) in both mobile and silo-based modes; continued production of the Trident II/D5 submarine-launched ballistic missile (SLBM); plans to continue producing the W88 warhead for the Trident II; and plans to build 75 B-2 bombers, continued production of the

---

[4] The precise number of Soviet nuclear warheads is not known publicly, possibly not at all outside a small group of ex-Soviet nuclear officials. The US Government has predominantly used two figures: 27 000 and 30 000 warheads. The CIA figure of 30 000 warheads is used here.
[5] Testimony of Reginald Bartholomew, Under Secretary of State for International Security Affairs, before the Senate Armed Services Committee (SASC), 5 Feb. 1991, (mimeo), p. 3; Statement of Stephen J. Hadley, Assistant Secretary of Defense for International Security Policy, before the SASC, 5 Feb. 1991, (mimeo), p. 5.

Advanced Cruise Missile (ACM), and continued R&D on the Short-Range Attack Missile II (SRAM II) for use with long-range US bombers. The USA planned to continue work on a 'tactical' version of the SRAM II missile known as SRAM-T.

President Bush cancelled several of these programmes in September, and by early 1992 almost all of them had been either curtailed or eliminated. The US strategic modernization programme is over, and Bush proposed cutting strategic forces to half of the START Treaty levels by eliminating major portions of the existing force structure.[6]

During 1991 Congress acted on several of these issues. It denied the Administration's funding request for the SRAM-T tactical air-to-surface missile and came close to terminating the SICBM programme. Congress also reduced the Administration's B-2 bomber request from four to one new plane, with numerous requirements for releasing the funds for the one new bomber. These congressional actions added pressure for President Bush to make significant nuclear cuts, including his 27 September 1991 and 28 January 1992 initiatives.

The Bush initiatives

On 27 September 1991 in a surprise speech President Bush announced a dramatic set of decisions and proposals for US and Soviet nuclear forces.[7] His initiative was a mixture of unilateral decisions concerning US nuclear forces and operations, proposals for reciprocal Soviet and US actions that would permit further reductions in the respective strategic arsenals, and proposals for US–Soviet co-operation on a variety of nuclear control, safety, security and dismantlement issues. President Bush called upon the Soviet leadership to match each of the 10 elements of his initiative and to agree to his proposals for restructuring the remaining strategic forces.

The Bush reductions included: complete elimination of all ground-launched, short-range nuclear weapons (about 1300 artillery shells and 850 Lance missile warheads), including those in Europe and South Korea, and dimantling and destroying all such warheads; withdrawal of all tactical nuclear weapons from US ships and submarines, as well as nuclear depth bombs for land-based naval aircraft, and either storing them at depots in the USA (for the newer systems) or dismantling and destroying the warheads (about one-half); removal of all US long-range bombers (about 40 at 12 bases) from alert operations and moving their weapons (about 640) to separate storage areas;[8] removal of all 450 Minuteman ICBMs from alert operations and accelerating their deactivation and dismantlement before this is required by the START Treaty; cancellation of the mobile rail garrison portion of the

---

[6] For an analysis of the START Treaty, see chapter 1 in this volume.

[7] The speech was first announced earlier the same day by the White House.

[8] Assistant Secretary of Defense for Legislative Affairs, Memorandum for Members of Congress, 'Press initiative to reduce nuclear weapons', 30 Sep. 1991, (mimeo). The estimate of 640 bomber weapons is from Arms Control Association Fact Sheet, 'Impact of the Bush nuclear weapons initiative' (ACA: Washington, DC, Oct. 1991).

MX/Peacekeeper ICBM and the mobile portion of the SICBM; cancellation of the short-range SRAM II missile and its tactical SRAM-T variant; creation of a single nuclear command (Strategic Command) for all US strategic weapons; proposal for the joint elimination of all US and Soviet multiple-warhead ICBMs ('de-MIRVing'); a proposal for co-operation between the USA and the USSR on non-nuclear ballistic missile defences; and a proposal for US–Soviet co-operation on improved nuclear weapon command and control, safety, security, transportation and dismantlement.

The proposal to eliminate all multiple independently targeted re-entry vehicles (MIRVs) from land-based ICBMs used the START Treaty as the basis for either eliminating MIRVed missiles or removing all but one warhead on them, a process known as downloading. In accordance with the START Treaty, President Bush proposed that if the USSR agreed to de-MIRV missiles the USA would eliminate all its MX/Peacekeeper ICBMs and keep the SICBM as a developmental programme. Minuteman III missiles could be downloaded from three warheads each to one, as permitted by the START Treaty, and SICBMs could eventually replace Minuteman III missiles in silos. No US or Commonwealth ICBMs would have more than one warhead each, although warheads on SLBMs would be unaffected.

Under the Bush plan at least 3050 tactical warheads will be eliminated, with an additional but unspecified number of older naval gravity bombs (B57) also to be eliminated. More than 1000 strategic warheads (450 Minuteman II and more than 600 strategic bomber weapons) were removed from alert duty on 28 September 1991.[9] If the USSR were to agree to de-MIRV ICBMs, according to the Bush proposal the USA would remove an additional 1500 ICBM warheads from the US force and the USSR would remove a greater number from the former Soviet Strategic Rocket Forces.

Beyond the numbers, the Bush initiative will completely denuclearize the US Army, for the first time in over 30 years. It establishes the precedent of destroying nuclear warheads that are removed from service. It will remove the great majority of US nuclear weapons on European soil. It eliminates several classes of nuclear weapons altogether: nuclear artillery shells, short-range surface-to-surface missiles (Lance) and nuclear depth bombs for anti-submarine warfare. It effectively ends the nuclear role of the US Marine Corps, which had a limited ground and airborne nuclear capability. It resulted in the complete withdrawal of US nuclear weapons from South Korea, and thus the complete denuclearization of South Korea. It denuclearizes the routine operations of the US Navy, and thus eliminates the problem of the 'neither confirm nor deny' policy regarding nuclear weapons aboard US naval vessels. It ended the practice of 24-hour ground alert for US nuclear bombers, one of the enduring practices of the cold war since 1957.

---

[9] According to a previous plan to accelerate the retirement of strategic weapons under the START Treaty, on 1 Oct. the USA ceased all combat patrols with the last of 10 Poseidon ballistic missile submarines, for a total of 1600 warheads in all. Thus about 2600 warheads were removed from alert duty in less than one week and were not available for rapid use against the USSR.

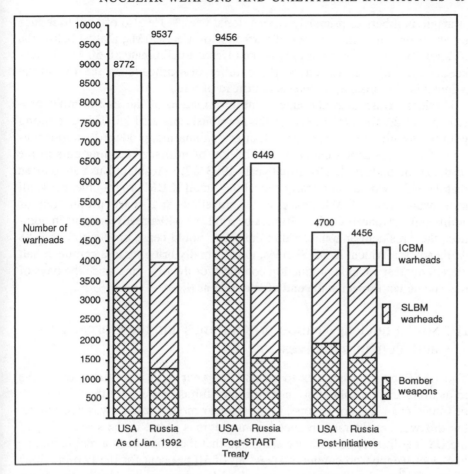

Figure 2.1. US and Russian strategic nuclear warheads: deployed as of January 1992 and after implementation of the START Treaty and the 1991–92 US unilateral initiatives

Notes: The data for the first two bars are taken from tables 2.1 and 2.3 in this chapter and represent *deployed* warheads, not total stockpiles as in the other bars. The data for Russia after the START Treaty and the initiatives are estimates only, based on projections of future Russian force levels made by the Arms Control Association (Washington, DC) and, for US bomber weapons after the START Treaty, from testimony of Gen. Colin L. Powell, Chairman, Joint Chiefs of Staff, on the FY 1993 Defense Budget, before the Senate Armed Services Committee, 31 Jan. 1992. Actual future warhead totals will almost certainly be lower.

On 28 January 1992 President Bush included new nuclear reduction proposals in his State of the Union address. He amplified his earlier proposal for de-MIRVing ICBMs by adding several new ideas designed to make the offer more attractive to Russia and the CIS. He said that if the CIS were willing to de-MIRV their ICBMs the USA would 'convert a substantial portion of [its] strategic bombers to primarily conventional use'.[10] He also offered to reduce by about one-third the number of warheads on US SLBMs, that is, below the START Treaty levels. Additionally, he offered to eliminate all 50 MX/Peace-keeper missiles and to reduce the number of warheads on the remaining Minuteman III missiles to one each, instead of three.

President Bush also announced the termination of the B-2 bomber pro-gramme at 20 aircraft, instead of the previously planned 75. This cut, along with the termination of the Seawolf attack submarine, produced a major por-tion of the President's claim of $50 billion of military spending cuts in the forthcoming budget plan for fiscal years 1993–97.[11] President Bush announced that the USA would unilaterally cancel the Small ICBM programme, cease all new production of MX/Peacekeeper missiles, and cease production of additional Advanced Cruise Missiles beyond the 640 already bought. In addi-tion, the President announced that the USA would cease production of W88 warheads for Trident II/D5 SLBMs, thus formally bringing to a complete halt the US nuclear weapon production complex for the first time since the days of the Manhattan Project at the end of World War II.

III. Soviet nuclear weapon programmes and the Gorbachev and Yeltsin initiatives

The USSR began what was to be its final year with a continuation of the reductions and consolidation of its military forces, especially the withdrawal of forces from Eastern Europe. Some nuclear modernization was continuing, but this was considerably reduced from previous years. In the spring of 1991 the US intelligence community estimated that there had been a real reduction in Soviet weapon procurement spending of 10 per cent for the two previous years.[12] Given the enormous economic difficulties in the USSR, this trend should not have been surprising.

In June 1991 a US Air Force official testified to Congress that there were several Soviet strategic weapon programmes still thought by the USA to be undergoing modernization or development: 'they are developing five or six new strategic ballistic missiles follow-on versions of both the rail and the road-mobile ICBMs, a more accurate version of the SS-18, and two more SLBMs'.[13] This pessimistic testimony did not acknowledge the numerous reductions that had recently taken place and concentrated only on those Soviet programmes for which there was either continuation or no evidence of termi-

---

[10] Text of President Bush's State of the Union Address, reprinted in *Washington Post*, 29 Jan. 1992, p. A14. See also appendix 2A in this volume.

[11] See also chapter 7 in this volume.

[12] CIA/DIA paper 'Beyond *perestroika*: the Soviet economy in crisis', 14 May 1991, presented to the Joint Economic Committee (mimeo), p. 11.

[13] Testimony of Maj. Gen. Stephen B. Croker, US Air Force, before the Senate Armed Services Committee, SASC, *DoD Authorization for Appropriations for Fiscal Years 1992 and 1993*, S. Hrg. 102–255, Part 7 (US Government Printing Office: Washington, DC, 1991), p. 551.

nation. As became apparent during the year, the Soviet military had been continuing only a few of these efforts and in a diminishing way.[14]

The US Defense Intelligence Agency (DIA) and Central Intelligence Agency (CIA) interpret these activities as the last actions of a system that had built up a large store of inertia and had the people, parts and plans in place from previous years. Although modernization of some SS-18 ICBMs continued throughout 1991, the DIA noted that training levels for the SS-25 missile were reduced, no new Soviet ballistic missile submarines were under construction and none are anticipated by the US intelligence community before the year 2000, and the Soviet heavy bomber force modernization programme is basically completed—well short of the level previously anticipated by the United States.[15]

In late 1991, Director of Central Intelligence Robert Gates told a congressional committee that the USA could expect to see a major decline, if not a virtual cessation, of the Soviet nuclear modernization programme: 'It is increasingly hard to see how Russia or other republics with strategic nuclear weapons will be able to continue the modernization effort—or even why they would want to, given the rapid dissipation of tensions with the West.' 'Therefore', he concluded, 'we should not be surprised if most or all Soviet plans for strategic offensive force modernization are abandoned for the foreseeable future.'[16] By early 1992 the US intelligence community agreed that the Soviet military and nuclear threat had diminished tremendously, with huge reductions (approximately 80 per cent) requested in the procurement account of the initial 1991 military budget.[17]

The Gorbachev initiative

On 5 October 1991 Soviet President Mikhail Gorbachev responded to President Bush's 1991 nuclear reduction initiative with his own initiative. Basically, Gorbachev agreed to match the US changes: destroy all Soviet nuclear artillery, short-range missile and land mine warheads, remove all nuclear warheads for air-defence missiles from deployment areas and store or destroy them, remove bombers from alert duty and store their nuclear weapons at storage depots, remove from alert duty those ICBMs slated for retirement under the START Treaty, remove tactical nuclear weapons from naval forces (ships, submarines and land-based aircraft), create a single unified strategic command, and remove 6 SSBNs with 92 SLBMs from operational duty (presumably 5 Yankee I vessels and the only Yankee II submarine).

Gorbachev announced that the USSR would reduce its strategic forces to a level of 5000 START Treaty-accountable warheads—1000 fewer than re-

[14] Before 1992 almost all these programmes had been cancelled by President Gorbachev; shortly after the beginning of 1991 the remainder were terminated by Boris Yeltsin.
[15] Statement for the Record of Lt. Gen. James R. Clapper, Jr, USAF, Director, Defense Intelligence Agency, to the Senate Armed Services Committee, Jan. 1992 (mimeo), p. 8.
[16] Statement of the Director of Central Intelligence before the House Armed Services Committee Defense Policy Panel, 10 Dec. 1991 (mimeo), p. 13.
[17] See note 15, p. 4.

quired by the START Treaty—and challenged the USA to match this additional reduction. He announced that 503 ICBMs, including 137 MIRVed missiles, would be removed from operational alert duty, thus eliminating 1094 warheads from the available force.[18] This includes 366 SS-11 and SS-13 missiles, 47 SS-17s and 90 SS-19 missiles, all of which were slated for retirement under the START Treaty.[19]

President Gorbachev's speech responded nearly item for item to the Bush speech, but went further in several respects. Gorbachev agreed to remove all tactical naval nuclear weapons from ships, submarines and land-based aircraft bases, but suggested eliminating them altogether instead of storing them—as President Bush had announced. Concerning tactical air-delivered bombs and missiles, Gorbachev proposed removing weapons from forward-deployed units and storing the warheads at separate bases. In addition to announcing Soviet strategic cuts to 1000 accountable warheads below the START Treaty limits, he proposed that both nations proceed to negotiate additional cuts of one-half in their strategic weapons. Gorbachev also proposed that the USSR and the USA agree to stop producing fissile material for nuclear weapons. Finally, he announced a one-year moratorium on nuclear testing and proposed that other nations do likewise.[20]

Gorbachev also announced the cancellation of several modernization and deployment programmes. He said that R&D would cease for a new short-range missile for the bomber fleet and for a new mobile SICBM. The rail-mobile SS-24 was frozen at the existing level, and no R&D would continue for a follow-on missile. Gorbachev announced that the SS-24 would be confined to its three permanent garrisons and not deployed in a dispersed manner.

The Yeltsin initiative

On 29 January 1992 President Yeltsin made a major disarmament speech that presented the Russian/Commonwealth proposals for further nuclear reductions after the Bush State of the Union address. He presented a broad programme of cuts and terminations and suggested that the USA and Russia should reduce their strategic nuclear forces to a level of some 2000–2500 warheads each, about half the level proposed by President Bush the night before. Yeltsin provided additional details and an update to the Gorbachev initiative of October 1991.[21]

President Yeltsin offered a 10-point speech covering the full range of arms control and disarmament issues, including strategic and tactical nuclear weapons. The nuclear portions of the speech included the following provisions.

---

[18] 'Nuclear Notebook', *Bulletin of the Atomic Scientists*, Mar. 1992, p. 49. Gorbachev used the figure of 134 MIRVed missiles, but this was later corrected as 137.

[19] 'Nuclear Notebook', *Bulletin of the Atomic Scientists*, Mar. 1992, p. 49.

[20] See also chapter 4 in this volume.

[21] Yeltsin's speech was broadcast on Moscow Television on 29 Jan. 1992 at 9:00 am (GMT). The text was transcribed by the Foreign Broadcast Information Service of the US Department of Commerce and transmitted by wire.

Concerning strategic forces, Yeltsin announced recent reductions: about 600 ballistic missiles (ICBMs and SLBMs) with nearly 1250 warheads had been removed from operational readiness; 130 ICBM launch silos had either been destroyed or prepared for destruction; and six SSBNs had been prepared for their launch tubes to be dismantled. He announced the end of development or modernization programmes for several strategic systems: Tu-160 (Blackjack) and Tu-95M (Bear-H) bombers are no longer being produced; no more AS-15 air-launched cruise missiles (ALCMs) will be produced; he proposed that the USA and Russia agree not to develop new types of ALCM; production of SS-N-21 sea-launched cruise missiles (SLCMs) is ceasing and Russia will not develop any new long-range nuclear SLCMs; and Russia is willing to eliminate nuclear SLCMs on a reciprocal basis with the USA.

President Yeltsin stated several START Treaty-related and operational decisions: strategic forces in Ukraine will be dismantled sooner than planned under the START Treaty; and Russia will accelerate the START Treaty implementation period from seven to three years, and could accelerate this even faster if the USA is willing. Operationally, Russia will not conduct exercises with more than 30 heavy bombers; the number of SSBNs on patrol has been cut by half and further reductions are due; Russia is willing to renounce entirely the practice of submarine combat patrols on a reciprocal basis; and Russia proposes that neither nation (the USA and Russia) target its nuclear weapons at each other. Following on Gorbachev's previous proposal, Yeltsin proposed that the two sides agree to reduce their remaining strategic forces to a level of 2000–2500 weapons—about half of the 5000-weapon level Gorbachev pledged for Soviet START Treaty reductions.

On the tactical side, Yeltsin announced several decisions pursuant to the earlier initiatives: production of warheads for land-based tactical missiles, artillery and land mines has ceased, and stockpiles of these weapons will be eliminated; Russia has begun eliminating one-third of its naval tactical warheads and one-half of its nuclear surface-to-air missile warheads; tactical air force weapons will be reduced by one-half; and Russia proposes removing the remaining weapons from their units and placing them in centralized storage bases on a reciprocal basis with the USA.

President Yeltsin also pledged continued Russian efforts to cease all weapon-grade plutonium production by the year 2000 and announced that several plutonium production reactors would be stopped in 1993, ahead of schedule. He proposed that the USA and Russia agree on a controlled cessation of production of fissile materials for nuclear weapons. This was in addition to a new call for a nuclear testing moratorium, starting with renewed US–Russian talks and possibly a gradual reduction in tests.

These announcements amounted to the end of modernization for Soviet/Russian nuclear forces. While taking a Russian approach, Yeltsin's speech was clearly designed to increase confidence and co-operation between Russia and the USA, especially as Russia claims the mantle of pre-eminent nuclear decision-maker for the Commonwealth of Independent States.

Table 2.1. US strategic nuclear forces, January 1992[a]

Weapon system				Warheads		
Type	No. deployed	Year deployed	Range (km)	Warhead x yield	Type	No. deployed
ICBMs						
Minuteman III (Mk 12)	200	1970	13 000	3 x 170 kt	W62	600
Minuteman III (Mk 12A)	300	1979	13 000	3 x 335 kt	W78	900
MX	50	1986	11 000+	10 x 300 kt	W87-0	500
Total	**550**					**2 000**
SLBMs						
Trident I (20 SSBNs)	384	1979	7 400	8 x 100 kt	W76	3 072
Trident II (4 SSBNs)	96	1990	7 400	4–8 x 475 kt	W88	400[b]
Total	**480**					**3 472**
Bombers[c]						
B-1B	84	1986	19 800	⎧ ALCM[d]	W80-1	1 600
B-52G/H	125	1958/61	16 000	⎨ ACM	W80-1	100
				⎩ Bombs	Various[e]	1 600
Total	**209**					**3 300**
Refuelling aircraft						
KC-135 A/R/E	615	1957	..	..	..	..
KC-10A	59	1981	..	..	..	..

[a] Minuteman II and Poseidon missiles were removed from alert after President Bush's speech of 27 Sep. 1991 and are not considered to be operational.

[b] As a temporary expedient owing to the inability of producing new W88 warheads, the Navy is spreading the 400 already produced over the first 4 Trident II SSBNs, meaning that no submarine will have a full complement.

[c] Numbers reflect Primary Authorized Aircraft. An additional 13 B-1Bs and 10 B-52s are in the total inventory. B-52Gs at Castle AFB, California, and Loring AFB, Maine, some 41 aircraft, have primarily conventional missions. The 1100 SRAM A missiles have been placed in weapon storage areas at SAC bases, are unlikely to be retained, and are not included in the table. Bombers are loaded in a variety of ways, depending on mission. B-1Bs normally carried up to 16 weapons, now either B83 or B61 bombs, but not ALCMs, ACMs or SRAMs. B-52s can carry a mix of 8–24 weapons.

[d] Bomber weapons include ALCMs and ACMs with selectable yields from 5 to 150 kt, three types of bomb (see note *e*) with yields from sub-kiloton to 9 Mt, and the stored SRAMs with a yield of 170 kt.

[e] Bombs are of three types: 650 type B83, 900 type B61-0, -6 and -7, and 50 type B53.

Sources: Cochran, T. B., Arkin, W. M. and Norris, R. S., *Nuclear Weapons Databook, Vol. I: US Forces and Capabilities,* 2nd edn (forthcoming); authors' estimates.

Table 2.2. US non-strategic nuclear forces, January 1992[a]

Weapon system				Warheads		
Type	No. deployed	Year deployed	Range (km)	Warhead x yield	Type	No. in stockpile
Land-based systems						
Aircraft[b]	1 300	..	1 060–2 400	1–3 x bombs	Bombs[b]	1 600
Missiles						
Lance[c]	100	1972	125	1 x 1–100 kt	W70	(850)
Other systems						
Artillery[d]	4 700	1956	30	1 x 0.1–12 kt	[d]	(1 300)
Naval systems						
Carrier aircraft[e]	850	..	1 000–1 800	1–2 x bombs	Bombs[e]	1 100
Tomahawk SLCM	350	1984	2 500	1 x 5–150 kt	W80-0	350
ASW aircraft[f]	500	..	1 160–3 800	1 x bomb < 20 kt	B57	(900)

[a] President Bush's speech of 27 Sep. 1991 and later announcements brought dramatic changes to US non-strategic forces. All 850 Lance warheads and 1300 remaining nuclear artillery shells are to be eliminated. The number of bombs for US and NATO use in Europe will be cut in half and the remainder returned to the USA. By the end of 1991, all US nuclear weapons had been removed from South Korea. All tactical nuclear weapons are to be removed from naval vessels and stored ashore at depots. Currently, this includes bombs aboard aircraft-carriers and Tomahawk cruise missiles. The B57 anti-submarine warfare bombs allocated for carrier-based S-3A/B aircraft and SH-3D/H helicopters will be eliminated, as will some or all of the B57 strike bombs. Some 900 B57 ASW bombs on land for US P-3s, British Nimrods, Italian Atlantics and Netherlands NP-3s will be eliminated.

[b] Aircraft include the US Air Force F-16A/C and F-111A/D/E/F/G. F-15Es are scheduled to be nuclear-certified in 1992. It is believed that the F-117A Stealth fighter is nuclear-certified, although the US Air Force will neither confirm nor deny its nuclear capability. Bombs include B57s and B61s with yields from low kt to 100–200 kt. The last remaining B43 bombs were retired during 1991.

[c] Some Lance systems remain deployed in Germany and Italy, and theoretically are still operational. It is assumed that the missiles and warheads will be removed from Europe in 1992.

[d] President Bush's initiatives include the elimination of all remaining nuclear artillery projectiles. The number of artillery guns is also being significantly reduced as US forces are drawn down, although a precise accounting is not available. Nuclear artillery will be removed from Europe in 1992.

[e] Aircraft include the US Navy A-6E, F/A-18A/C and Marine Corps F-18A/C. Bombs to be stored ashore include B57s and B61s with yields from low kt to 100–200 kt.

[f] Aircraft include the US Navy P-3B/C, S-3A/B and SH-3D/H helicopters. The B57 nuclear depth bomb will be eliminated under the Bush initiatives.

Table 2.2 *cont.*

Sources: Cochran, T. B., Arkin, W. M. and Norris, R. S., *Nuclear Weapons Databook, Vol. 1: US Forces and Capabilities*, 2nd edn (forthcoming); Collins, J. M. and Rennack, D. E., *US Armed Forces*, Library of Congress/Congressional Research Service, Report no. 91-672 RCO, 6 Sep. 1991; International Institute for Strategic Studies, *The Military Balance 1991–1992* (Brassey's: Oxford, 1991); authors' estimates.

Table 2.3. Soviet strategic nuclear forces, January 1992[a]

Weapon system					Warheads	
Type	NATO code-name	No. deployed	Year deployed	Range (km)	Warhead x yield	No. deployed
ICBMs[b]						
SS-18 Mod. 4/5/6	Satan	308	1979	11 000	10 x 550/750 kt (MIRV)	3 080
SS-19 Mod. 3	Stiletto	210	1979	10 000	6 x 550 kt (MIRV)	1 260
SS-24 Mod. 1/2	Scalpel	36/56	1987	10 000	10 x 550 kt (MIRV)	920
SS-25	Sickle	315	1985	10 500	1 x 550 kt	315
Total		**925**				**5 575**
SLBMs[c]						
SS-N-6 Mod. 3	Serb	96	1973	3 000	2 x 500 kt (MRV)	96
SS-N-8 Mod. 1/2	Sawfly	280	1973	9 100	1 x 1.5 Mt	280
SS-N-18 Mod. 1	Stingray	224	1978	6 500	3 x 500 kt (MIRV)	672
SS-N-20	Sturgeon	120	1983	8 300	10 x 200 kt (MIRV)	1 200
SS-N-23	Skiff	112	1986	9 000	4 x 100 kt (MIRV)	448
Total		**832**				**2 696**
Bombers						
Tu-95MS16	Bear H	57	1984	12 800	16 AS-15A ALCMs or bombs	912
Tu-95MS6	Bear H	27	1984	12 800	6 AS-15A ALCMs or bombs	162
Tu-160	Blackjack	16	1988	11 000	12 AS-15B ALCMs, SRAMs or bombs	192
Total		**100**				**1 266**
Refuelling aircraft	..	140–170	..	.. ..		..
SAMs[d]	..	4 000	1970–80	100–300	1 x low kt	2 000
ABMs						
ABM-1B	Galosh Mod.	22	1986	320	1 x unknown	22
ABM-3	Gazelle	68	1985	70	1 x low yield	68
ABM-X[e]	Gorgon	10	1991	?	?	10
Total		**100**				**100**

[a] President Gorbachev's announcement of 5 Oct. 1991 stated that 503 ICBMs, of which 134 were MIRVed, were to be removed from operational duty. On 6 Dec., Gen. Lobov said that this totalled 1094 warheads. Gorbachev also said that 3 SSBNs with 44 launchers had recently been removed and 3 more with 48 launchers would soon be removed. The table reflects

Table 2.3 *cont.*

removal from the operational forces of all remaining SS-11s, SS-13s and SS-17s, 90 SS-19s, 5 Yankee Is and the single Yankee II.

[b] Data in the START Treaty MOU provided ICBM throw-weights: SS-18, 8800 kg; SS-19, 4350 kg; SS-24, 4050 kg; and SS-25, 1000 kg.

[c] Data in the START Treaty MOU provided SLBM throw-weights: SS-N-6, 650 kg; SS-N-8, 1150 kg; SS-N-18, 1650 kg; SS-N-20, 2550 kg; and SS-N-23, 2800 kg.

[d] President Gorbachev announced that all nuclear warheads for SAMs would be withdrawn and centrally stored, and a portion destroyed. The table assumes warheads for SA-2 retired and SA-5 and SA-10 retained.

[e] The Gorgon missile is replacing the Galosh in above-ground launchers around Moscow.

Sources: Cochran, T. B., Arkin, W. M., Norris, R. S. and Sands, J. I., *Nuclear Weapons Databook, Vol. IV: Soviet Nuclear Weapons* (Harper & Row: New York, 1989); US Department of Defense, *Soviet Military Power*, 1st–9th edns; US Department of Defense, *Military Forces in Transition*, 1991; Collins, J. M. and Rennack, D. E., *Soviet Armed Forces*, Library of Congress/Congressional Research Service, Report no. 91-636 RCO, 28 Aug. 1991; authors' estimates.

Table 2.4. Soviet non-strategic nuclear forces, January 1992[a]

Weapon system					Warheads	
Type	NATO code-name	No. deployed	Year first deployed	Range[b] (km)	Warhead x yield	No. deployed
Land-based systems						
Long-range bomber						
Tu-95K/K22	Bear B/G	60	1984	12 800	2 AS-4 or bombs	120
Aircraft						
Tu-26	Backfire A/B/C[c]	145	1974	4 000	1–3 x bombs or ASMs	290
Tu-16	Badger A/G	60	1954	3 100	1–2 x bombs or ASMs	60
Tu-22	Blinder A/B	60	1962	2 400	1–2 x bombs or 1 ASM	60
Tactical aircraft[d]		1 675	..	700–1 300	1–2 x bombs	2 500
Missiles						
SS-1c	Scud B	661	1965	300	1 x 1–10 kt	(1 370)
..	FROG 3/7	370	1965	70	1 x 1–25 kt	(1 450)
SS-21	Scarab	300	1978	70	1 x 10–100 kt	(310)
Other systems						
Artillery[d]	..	7 000	1973–80	10–30	1 x low kt	(2 000)
Atomic land mines	..	?	?	n.a.	?	(?)
Naval systems						
Aircraft						
Tu-22M	Backfire A/B/C	170	1974	4 000	1–3 x bombs or ASMs	340
Tu-16	Badger A/C/G	150	1955	3 100	1–2 x bombs or ASMs	300
Tu-22	Blinder A	10	1962	2 400	1–2 x bombs	20
Su-24	Fencer C/D	100	1989	1 300	2 x bombs	200
Su-17/20	Fitter C/D/H	125	1973	700	1 x bomb	125

Table 2.4 *cont.*

Weapon system					Warheads	
Type	NATO code-name	No. deployed	Year first deployed	Range[b] (km)	Warhead x yield	No. deployed
ASW aircraft[e]	..	265	1963–82	..	1 x depth bombs	300
MiG-27	Flogger J/K	40	1968	850	2 x bombs	80
Anti-ship cruise missiles[h]						
SS-N-9	Siren	248	1969	280	1 x 200 kt	92
SS-N-12	Sandbox	248	1976	550	1 x 350 kt	106
SS-N-19	Shipwreck	180	1980	550	1 x 500 kt	72
SS-N-22	Sunburn	126	1981	100	1 x 200 kt	42
Land-attack cruise missiles						
SS-N-21	Sampson	136	1987	3 000	1 x 200 kt	136
ASW missiles and torpedoes						
SS-N-15	Starfish ⎫	400	1973	37	1 x 10 kt ⎫	400
SS-N-16	Stallion ⎭		1979	120	1 x 10 kt ⎭	
FRAS-1		25	1967	30	1 x 5 kt	25
Torpedoes[g]	Type 65 ⎫	520	1965	16	1 x low kt ⎫	520
	ET-80 ⎭		1980	>16	1 x low kt ⎭	

 [a] On 5 Oct. 1991, President Gorbachev stated that all nuclear artillery projectiles, nuclear land mines and nuclear warheads for non-strategic missiles (FROG, Scud and SS-21) will be destroyed. Those are indicated by parentheses in the table. He also said that tactical naval weapons will be removed from surface ships and submarines and stored ashore with a portion to be destroyed.

 [b] Range for aircraft indicates combat radius, without refuelling.

 [c] The Backfire C can carry up to 10 AS-16 Kickback SRAMs.

 [d] Nuclear-capable tactical aircraft models include 725 MiG-27 Flogger D/J/J2s, 200 Su-17 Fitter C/D/H/Ks and 750 Su-24 Fencer A/B/C/D/Es. There is evidence that some MiG-29 Fulcrum units train to deliver tactical nuclear weapons.

 [e] Nuclear-capable artillery include systems of three calibres: 152-mm (D-20, 2A36/ M-1976, 2S3, 2S5 and possibly a new M1986), 203-mm (M55, 2S7 and M-1980) and 240-mm (2S4 and M-240). Some older systems may also be nuclear-capable.

 [f] It is believed that naval SAMs are no longer nuclear-capable. Numbers of former SAF Su-24 Fencer, MiG-27 Flogger and Su-17 Fitter aircraft have been resubordinated to SNA during 1989–90, resulting in the creation of new air regiments in the ATTU zone.

 [g] Includes 40 Il-38 May and 75 Tu-142 Bear F Mod. 4 patrol aircraft. Land- and sea-based helicopters include 150 Ka-25 Hormone A and Ka-27 Helix A models. The Be-44, the ASW version of the A-40 Albatross jet amphibian, may replace nuclear-capable Il-38 May and Be-12 Mail aircraft.

 [h] Number deployed is total launchers on nuclear-capable ships and submarines. Warheads based on an average of 2 nuclear-armed cruise missiles per nuclear-capable surface ship, except for 4 per Kiev and Kirov Class ships, and 4 per nuclear-capable cruise missile submarine, except for 12 on the Oscar Class.

 [i] The two types of torpedo are the older and new models, respectively, with the ET-80 probably replacing the Type 65.

Table 2.4 *cont.*

Sources: Cochran, T. B., Arkin, W. M., Norris, R. S. and Sands, J. I., *Nuclear Weapons Databook, Vol. IV: Soviet Nuclear Weapons* (Harper & Row: New York, 1989); US Department of Defense, *Soviet Military Power*, 1st–9th edns; US Department of Defense, *Military Forces in Transition*, 1991; Polmar, N., *Guide to the Soviet Navy*, 5th edn (US Naval Institute: Annapolis, Md., 1991); Collins, J. M. and Rennack, D. E., *Soviet Armed Forces*, Library of Congress/Congressional Research Service, Report no. 91-636 RCO, 28 Aug. 1991; International Institute for Strategic Studies, *The Military Balance 1991–1992* (Brassey's: Oxford, 1991); authors' estimates.

Table 2.5. British nuclear forces, January 1992[a]

Weapon system				Warheads		
Type	No. deployed	Year deployed	Range (km)[b]	Warhead x yield	Type	No. in stockpile
Aircraft						
Tornado GR-1	108[c]	1982	1 300	1–2 x 400/200 kt bombs[d]	WE-177A/B ⎫	175[e]
Buccaneer S2B	40	1962	1 700	1 x 400/200 kt bomb	WE-177A/B ⎭	
SLBMs						
Polaris A3-TK	64	1982[f]	4 700	2 x 40 kt	MRV	100[g]
Carrier aircraft						
Sea Harrier FRS.1	42	1980	450	1 x 10 kt bomb	WE-177C ⎫	
						25[h]
ASW helicopters						
Sea King HAS 5/6	46	1976	–	1 x 10 kt depth bomb	WE-177C	
Lynx HAS 2/3	70	1976	–	1 x 10 kt depth bomb	WE-177C ⎭	

[a] The US nuclear weapons for certified British systems, specifically the 11 Nimrod ASW aircraft based at RAF St Mawgan, Cornwall, UK, the 1 Army regiment with 12 Lance launchers and the 4 Army artillery regiments with 120 M109 howitzers in Germany, will be removed and eliminated. Squadron No. 42, the Nimrod maritime patrol squadron, will disband from Oct. 1992, but St Mawgan will remain a forward base for Nimrods and will have other roles.

[b] Range for aircraft indicates combat radius, without refuelling.

[c] The Royal Air Force operated 7 squadrons of dual-capable strike/attack Tornados in Germany (at two bases) and 2 squadrons in the UK at RAF Marham. The 3 squadrons at Laarbruch, Germany (Nos 15, 16, 20), will be disbanded during 1991 and 1992. Approximately 50 British nuclear bombs will be returned to the UK, leaving some 75 for the 4 squadrons at RAF Bruggen (Nos 9, 14, 17, 31). The 2 Tornado squadrons currently at Marham will move to RAF Lossiemouth beginning in early 1993 to replace Buccaneers in the maritime/strike role. The transition will be completed by the end of 1994, and the squadrons will be designated Nos 12 and 617. Total inventory of strike variants, including those for training and spares, is approximately 200.

Table 2.5 *cont.*

[d] The US Defense Intelligence Agency (DIA) has confirmed that the RAF Tornados 'use two types of nuclear weapons, however, exact types are unknown'. The DIA further concludes that each RAF Tornado is capable of carrying two nuclear bombs, on the two outboard fuselage stations.

[e] The total stockpile of WE-177 tactical nuclear gravity bombs is about 200, of which 175 are versions A and B. All three weapons use the same basic 'physics package', and the yield is varied by using different amounts of tritium.

[f] The 2-warhead Polaris A3-TK (Chevaline) was first deployed in 1982 and has now completely replaced the original 3-warhead Polaris A-3 missile (first deployed in 1968).

[g] It is now thought that Britain produced only enough warheads for three full boat-loads of missiles, or 48 missiles, with a total of 96 warheads. In Mar. 1987 French President Mitterrand confirmed that Britain had '90 to 100 [strategic] warheads'.

[h] The C version of the WE-177 bomb is believed to be assigned to selected Royal Navy (RN) Sea Harrier FRS.1 aircraft and ASW helicopters. The WE-177C exists in both a free-fall and depth bomb modification, by varying the fuzing and casing options. There are an estimated 25 WE-177Cs, each with a yield of approximately 10 kt (possible variable yield). Following the Bush and Gorbachev initiatives of 27 Sep. and 5 Oct. 1991, British Secretary of State for Defence Tom King said that 'we will no longer routinely carry nuclear weapons on our ships'. Presumably, they will be stored ashore.

Sources: Cochran, T. B. *et al.*, *Nuclear Weapon Databook, Vol. V: British, French and Chinese Nuclear Weapons* (forthcoming); British Ministry of Defence, *Statement on the Defence Estimates, 1980–91* (Her Majesty's Stationery Office: London, annual).

Table 2.6. French nuclear forces, January 1992

Weapon system				Warheads		
Type	No. deployed	Year deployed	Range (km)[a]	Warhead x yield	Type	No. in stockpile
Aircraft						
Mirage IVP/ASMP	18	1986	1 500	1 x 300 kt	TN 80	18
Mirage 2000N/ASMP[b]	45	1988	1 570	1 x 300 kt	TN-81	45
Refuelling aircraft						
C-135/FR	11	1965	..	..	..	..
Land-based missiles						
S3D	18	1980	3 500	1 x 1 Mt	TN-61	18
Pluton[c]	44	1974	120	1 x 10/25 kt	AN-51	70
Hadès[d]	(15)	1991	480	1 x 80 kt	TN-90	(30)
Submarine-based missiles						
M-20[e]	16	1977	3 000	1 x 1 Mt	TN-61	16
M-4A	16	1985	4 000–5 000	6 x 150 kt (MIRV)	TN-70[f]	96
M-4B	48	1987	6 000	6 x 150 kt (MIRV)	TN-71	288
Carrier-based aircraft						
Super Etendard/ASMP[g]	20	1978	650	1 x 300 kt	TN-81	20

Table 2.6 *cont.*

a Range for aircraft indicates combat radius, without refuelling, and does not include the 90- to 350-km range of the ASMP air-to-surface missile (where applicable).

b 75 Mirage 2000Ns are planned, the last to be delivered in 1992. On 11 Sep. 1991, President Mitterrand announced that as of 1 Sep. the AN-52 gravity bomb, which had been carried by the Jaguar A and Super Etendard, had been withdrawn from service.

c The Pluton will be withdrawn from service in 1993–94.

d Although the first regiment was activated at Suippes, in eastern France, on 1 Sep. 1991, the plan to deploy Hadès was shelved soon after, and the missiles will now be stored. The programme was cut further to 15 launchers and 30 missiles from an original goal of 60 launchers and 120 missiles.

e After completing 58 operational patrols since 1971, *Le Redoutable* was retired during the year, leaving 5 SSBNs in the force. *Le Foudroyant* is the fifth submarine to complete its retrofit to M-4B missiles, and this will be done in 1993.

f The *Inflexible* was the only SSBN to receive the TN-70. All subsequent refits of the M-4 into Redoutable Class SSBNs will incorporate the improved TN-71 warhead.

g The Super Etendard used to carry 1 AN-52 bomb. At full strength the AN-52 equipped 2 squadrons (24 aircraft) of Super Etendard: Flottilles 11F and 17F, based at Landivisiau and Hyères, respectively. From mid-1989 these two squadrons began receiving the ASMP missile. By mid-1990, all 20 aircraft (to be configured to carry the ASMP) were operational. Although originally about 50–55 Super Etendard aircraft were to receive the ASMP, because of budgetary constraints the number of aircraft so configured dropped to 20.

Sources: Cochran, T. B. *et al.*, *Nuclear Weapon Databook*, *Vol. V: British, French and Chinese Nuclear Weapons* (forthcoming).

Table 2.7. Chinese nuclear forces, January 1992

Weapon system				Warheads	
Type	No. deployed	Year deployed	Range (km)	Warhead x yield	No. in stockpile
Aircraft[a]					
H-6 (B-6)	120	1965	3 100	1–3 x bombs[b] ⎱	
H-5 (B-5)	30	1968	1 200	1 x bomb ⎰	200+
Q-5 (A-5)	30–50	1970	400	1 x bomb	
Land-based missiles					
DF-3 (CSS-2)	70–100	1970	2 800	1 x 1–3 Mt	85–125
DF-4 (CSS-3)	15–20	1971	4 800–7 000	1 x 1–3 Mt	20–30
DF-5 (CSS-4)	4–10	1979	13 000	1 x 4–5 Mt	10–20
M-9/SST 600[c]	..	1990	600	1 x ?	..
Submarine-based missiles[d]					
JL-1 (CSS-N-3)	24	1986	2 800–3 300	1 x 0.5–1 Mt	26–38

a All figures for these bomber aircraft refer to nuclear-configured versions only. Hundreds of these aircraft are also deployed in non-nuclear versions.

b Yields of bombs are estimated to range from below 20 kt to 3 Mt.

c The nuclear capability of the M-9 is unconfirmed.

d Two missiles are presumed to be available for rapid deployment on the Golf Class submarine. Additional missiles are being built for new Xia Class submarines.

Table 2.7 *cont.*

Sources: Cochran, T. B. *et al.*, *Nuclear Weapon Databook*, *Vol. V: British, French and Chinese Nuclear Weapons and Nuclear Weapons Proliferation* (forthcoming); Lewis, J. W. and Xue, L., *China Builds the Bomb* (Stanford University Press: Stanford, Calif., 1988).

Table 2.8. Strategic nuclear weapon arsenals of the USA, the USSR, the UK, France and China, 1985–91[a]

	USA		USSR		UK		France		China[c]	
Year[b]	L	W	L	W	L	W	L	W	L	W
1985	1 965	11 974	2 538	10 012	64	96	142	222	331	336
1986	1 957	12 386	2 506	10 108	64	96	138	218	320	325
1987	2 001	13 002	2 535	10 442	64	96	138	298	309	319
1988	1 926	13 000	2 553	10 834	64	96	132	292	313	323
1989	1 903	12 100	2 448	11 320	64	96	132	372	302	317
1990	1 876	11 966	2 354	10 880	64	96	132	452	304	324
1991	1 239	8 772	1 857	9 537	64	96	116	436	304	324

L: Launchers; W: Warheads.

[a] For data for 1946–84, see *SIPRI Yearbook 1991*, table 1.8, p. 25.
[b] Figures are given as at the end of each year.
[c] Figures for China are for deployed systems only.

Sources: Cochran, T. B., Arkin, W. M. and Norris, R. S., *Nuclear Weapons Databook, Vol. I*, forthcoming (for the USA), *Vol. IV*, 1989 (the USSR) and *Vol. V*, forthcoming (the UK, France and China).

IV. Other nuclear weapon programmes

The United Kingdom

Strategic forces

Three of the four Vanguard Class SSBNs have been ordered, and there is some debate in the UK about the need to proceed with the fourth submarine, but opposition does not yet appear strong enough to put the vessel at risk. Besides, long-lead funding for the fourth vessel has been committed, leading some to suggest that the issue is moot.

Even if the UK does build the planned four submarines, there is still a question of whether it is necessary to pursue all the 512 warheads originally planned for the Trident force. Given that the USA and CIS strategic forces are undergoing considerable cuts, Britain might decide to do with fewer than all the 512 warheads. This would be possible by downloading planned missiles to carry fewer than eight warheads each, by purchasing fewer Trident II missiles from the USA and filling a number of launch tubes on the four submarines, or simply by carrying fewer than the maximum number of missiles on some or all submarines.

Tactical forces

Following President Bush's nuclear initiative in September 1991, the UK announced that it would adopt identical measures for its naval nuclear warheads. Accordingly, the Government announced that it would remove its tactical weapons, estimated to number 25, from naval vessels on routine missions. For years the UK had a number of nuclear-certified units for which the USA deployed nuclear weapons. President Bush decided to eliminate most such weapons, including nuclear artillery, Lance missiles and nuclear depth bombs (see table 2.5). Accordingly, these units will either lose their nuclear capability or be disbanded.

As part of the NATO 17 October 1991 decision to further reduce its stockpile of nuclear weapons (gravity bombs), the UK announced that it would withdraw nearly half (50) of its estimated 125 gravity bombs deployed in Germany. The reduction will result in a corresponding reduction and consolidation of British nuclear-capable aircraft deployed in Germany: from seven squadrons at two bases to four squadrons at one base. Three squadrons will be disbanded.

After President Bush cancelled the US SRAM-T nuclear air-to-surface missile for NATO deployment, the UK maintained its 'requirement' for a Tactical Air-to-Surface Missile (TASM), for which NATO had previously stated a requirement as part of its nuclear modernization programme. On 28 September 1991 British Defence Minister Tom King repeated his government's support for the TASM, which is designed to replace the ageing WE177 nuclear bombs.[22] Given economic and political pressures in the UK, resistance from European allies and a lack of conceivable targets in Europe, the future of this missile is uncertain at best. France and Britain are still formally considering nuclear co-operation on a nuclear air-to-surface missile based on a French design.

France

France maintained its major nuclear modernization programme, the acquisition of new ballistic missile submarines to replace the ageing Force Oceanique Strategique (FOST) submarines. Its first SSBN, *Le Redoutable*, was retired during 1991 after 20 years in the fleet.[23] Given French budget constraints and the dissolution of the Soviet Union, it is possible that France may consider acquiring and operating five modern SSBNs, instead of the planned six.

France announced on 10 July 1991 that it had terminated the S45 missile development programme, an adaptation of the M-45 SLBM intended as a replacement for the S3 intermediate-range ballistic missiles (IRBMs) deployed in silos on the Plateau d'Albion.[24] None the less, France continues to

---

[22] De Briganti, G., and Miller, C., 'Allies hail US move to cut nuclear arms from NATO stock', *Defense News*, 7 Oct. 1991, p. 29.
[23] 'Nuclear Notebook', *Bulletin of the Atomic Scientists*, May 1991, p. 48.
[24] 'France drops plans to build new nuclear missile system', *New York Times*, 23 July 1991, p. A6.

develop a follow-on SLBM, the M-5. Some consideration is being given in France to the possibility of adapting a number of M-5 missiles to be used as a replacement for the S3.[25]

On 11 September, French President François Mitterrand announced at a news conference that France had scaled back its plans for the Hadès short-range ballistic missile (SRBM) designed to replace the currently deployed Pluton missile system. Instead of 120 Hadès missiles deployed on 60 mobile launchers, Mitterrand announced that France would build 15 launchers with 30 missiles and would not deploy them but would store them instead. Although a Hadès regiment nominally was established in September, it will not be assigned missiles as an operational unit; it will maintain custody of the weapons in storage.[26]

During the same news conference President Mitterrand announced that the AN-52 nuclear bombs assigned to Jaguar A and Super Etendard aircraft had been withdrawn from service as of 1 September 1991, and that the Pluton missiles would be retired by 1994.[27]

China

Chinese nuclear weapon-related developments in 1991 present a mixed picture. China's nuclear modernization programme is moving ahead slowly and is expected to add improved capabilities and technologies to the ballistic missile forces during the 1990s. Robert Gates, Director of Central Intelligence, testified to this effect before the US Congress in December: 'The Chinese have deployed a small force of nuclear-tipped ICBMs, some of which are aimed at the United States; they plan to deploy additional strategic and regional forces in the 1990s. We expect the Chinese to continue to modernize their missile forces. . . . New Chinese missiles, including a mobile ICBM, will probably be fielded during the 1990s'.[28]

The more pressing international concern is about the proliferation of nuclear weapon systems. Despite encouraging promises from the Chinese leadership on non-proliferation, several actions suggest that these promises are not being fulfilled. Despite the announcement in 1991 that China would accede to the 1968 Non-Proliferation Treaty (it deposited the instruments of accession in March 1992)[29] and verbal assurances that it would adhere to the technology export guidelines of the Missile Technology Control Regime (MTCR), China has continued to market nuclear and missile technology to other nations, including countries with nuclear weapon ambitions.[30]

[25] Lewis, J., 'French bid to give S-45 a Euro role', *Jane's Defence Weekly*, 30 Nov. 1991, p. 1025.

[26] 'France slashes procurement plans for Hades nuclear missile', *Aviation Week & Space Technology*, 23 Sep. 1991, p. 65.

[27] de Briganti, G. and Miller, C., 'Allies hail', *Defense News*, 7 Oct. 1991, p. 29.

[28] Statement of the Director of Central Intelligence Before the House Armed Services Committee Defense Policy Panel, 10 Dec. 1991 (mimeo), p. 19.

[29] See chapter 3 in this volume.

[30] See, for example, statement of Robert Gates, Director of the CIA, before the Senate Armed Services Committee, 22 Jan. 1992, p. 8.

Appendix 2A. The 1991–92 US, Soviet and Russian unilateral nuclear reduction initiatives

**President of the United States
George Bush, announcement from the
White House, 27 September 1991**

Excerpts

. . .

After careful study and consultations with my senior advisers, and after considering valuable counsel from Prime Minister Major, President Mitterrand, Chancellor Kohl, and other allied leaders, I am announcing today a series of sweeping initiatives affecting every aspect of our nuclear forces—on land, on ships, and on aircraft. I met again today with our Joint Chiefs of Staff, and I can tell you they wholeheartedly endorse each of these steps.

I will begin with the category in which we will make the most fundamental change in nuclear forces in over 40 years—non-strategic, or theater, weapons.

Last year, I canceled US plans to modernize our ground-launched theater nuclear weapons. Later, our NATO allies joined us in announcing that the alliance would propose the mutual elimination of all nuclear artillery shells from Europe, as soon as short-range nuclear forces negotiations began with the Soviets. But starting these talks now would only perpetuate these systems, while we engage in lengthy negotiations. Last month's events not only permit, but indeed demand swifter, bolder action.

I am therefore directing that the United States eliminate its entire worldwide inventory of ground-launched short-range, that is, theater nuclear weapons. We will bring home and destroy all of our nuclear artillery shells and short-range ballistic missile warheads. We will, of course, insure that we preserve an effective air-delivered nuclear capability in Europe. That is essential to NATO's security.

In turn, I have asked the Soviets to go down this road with us—to destroy their entire inventory of ground-launched theater nuclear weapons: not only their nuclear artillery and nuclear warheads for short-range ballistic missiles, but also the theater systems the US no longer has—systems like nuclear warheads for air-defense missiles, and nuclear land mines. Recognizing further

the major changes in the international military landscape, the United States will withdraw all tactical nuclear weapons from its surface ships, attack submarines, as well as those nuclear weapons associated with our land-based naval aircraft. This means removing all nuclear Tomahawk cruise missiles from US ships and submarines, as well as nuclear bombs aboard aircraft carriers. The bottom line is that under normal circumstances, our ships will not carry tactical nuclear weapons.

Many of these land- and sea-based warheads will be dismantled and destroyed. Those remaining will be secured in central areas where they would be available if necessary in a future crisis.

Again, there is every reason for the Soviet Union to match our actions—by removing all tactical nuclear weapons from its ships and attack submarines, by withdrawing nuclear weapons for landbased naval aircraft, and by destroying many of them and consolidating what remains at central locations. I urge them to do so.

No category of nuclear weapons has received more attention than those in our strategic arsenals. The Strategic Arms Reduction Treaty (START), which President Gorbachev and I signed last July, was the culmination of almost a decade's work. It calls for substantial stabilizing reductions and effective verification. Prompt ratification by both parties is essential.

But I also believe the time is right to use START as a springboard to achieve additional stabilizing changes.

First, to further reduce tension, I am directing that all US strategic bombers immediately stand down from their alert posture. As a comparable gesture, I call upon the Soviet Union to confine its mobile missiles to their garrisons, where they will be safer and more secure.

Second, the US will immediately stand down from alert all intercontinental ballistic missiles scheduled for deactivation under START. Rather than waiting for the treaty's reduction plan to run its full seven-year course, we will accelerate elimination of these systems, once START is ratified. I call upon the Soviet Union to do the same.

Third, I am terminating the development of the mobile Peacekeeper ICBM as well as the mobile portions of the small ICBM program. The small single-warhead ICBM will be our only remaining ICBM modernization program. I call upon the Soviets to terminate any and all programs for future ICBMs with more than one warhead, and to limit ICBM modernization to one type of single-warhead missile, just as we have done.

Fourth, I am canceling the current program to build a replacement for the nuclear short-range attack missile for our strategic bombers.

Fifth, as a result of the strategic nuclear weapons adjustments I have just outlined, the United States will streamline its command and control procedures, allowing us to more effectively manage our strategic nuclear forces.

As the system works now, the Navy commands the submarine part of our strategic deterrent, while the Air Force commands the bomber and land-based elements. But as we reduce our strategic forces, the operational command structure must be as direct as possible. I have therefore approved the recommendation of Secretary Cheney and the Joint Chiefs to consolidate operational command of these forces into a US Strategic Command, under one commander, with participation from both services.

Since the 1970s, the most vulnerable and unstable part of the US and Soviet nuclear forces has been intercontinental missiles with more than one warhead. Both sides have these ICBMs in fixed silos in the ground where they are more vulnerable than missiles on submarines.

I propose that the US and the Soviet Union seek early agreement to eliminate from their inventories all ICBMs with multiple warheads. After developing a timetable acceptable to both sides, we could rapidly move to modify or eliminate these systems under procedures already established in the START agreement. In short, such an action would take away the single most unstable part of our nuclear arsenals.

But there is more to do. The United States and the Soviet Union are not the only nations with ballistic missiles. Some 15 nations have them now, and in less than a decade that number could grow to 20. The recent conflict in the Persian Gulf demonstrates in no uncertain terms that the time has come for strong action on this growing threat to world peace.

Accordingly, I am calling on the Soviet leadership to join us in taking immediate concrete steps to permit the limited deployment of non-nuclear defenses to protect against limited ballistic missile strikes—whatever their source—without undermining the credibility of existing deterrent forces. And we will intensify our effort to curb nuclear and missile proliferation. These two efforts will be mutually reinforcing. To foster cooperation, the United States soon will propose additional initiatives in the area of ballistic missile early warning.

Finally, let me discuss yet another opportunity for cooperation that can make our world safer.

During last month's attempted coup in Moscow, many Americans asked me if I thought Soviet nuclear weapons were under adequate control. I do not believe that America was at increased risk of nuclear attack during those tense days. But I do believe more can be done to insure the safe handling and dismantling of Soviet nuclear weapons. Therefore, I propose that we begin discussions with the Soviet Union to explore cooperation in three areas. First, we should explore joint technical cooperation on the safe and environmentally responsible storage, transportation, dismantling, and destruction of nuclear warheads. Second, we should discuss existing arrangements for the physical security and safety of nuclear weapons and how these might be enhanced. And third, we should discuss nuclear command and control arrangements, and how these might be improved to provide more protection against the unauthorized or accidental use of nuclear weapons.

My friend, French President Mitterrand, offered a similar idea a short while ago. After further consultations with the alliance, and when the leadership in the USSR is ready, we will begin this effort.

. . .

We can safely afford to take the steps I have announced today, steps that are designed to reduce the dangers of miscalculation in a crisis. But to do so, we must also pursue vigorously those elements of our strategic modernization program that serve the same purpose. We must fully fund the B-2 and SDI program. We can make radical changes in the nuclear postures of both sides to make them smaller, safer, and more stable. But the United States must maintain modern nuclear forces, including the strategic triad and thus insure the credibility of our deterrent.

Some will say these initiatives call for a budget windfall for domestic programs. But the peace dividend I seek is not measured in dollars but in greater security. In the near term, some of these steps may even cost money. Given the ambitious plan I have already proposed to reduce US defense spending by 25 percent, we cannot afford to make any unwise or unwarranted cuts in the defense budget I have submitted to Congress. I am counting on congressional support to ensure we have the funds necessary to restructure our forces prudently and implement the decisions I have outlined tonight.

. . .

Source: *Arms Control Today*, Oct. 1991, pp. 3–5.

**President of the Soviet Union
Mikhail Gorbachev, televised
announcement, 5 October 1991**

Dear compatriots, a week ago US President Bush put forward an important initiative on nuclear weapons. This initiative confirms that a new way of thinking has been widely supported by the world community. George Bush's proposals are a worthy continuation of the drive started in Reykjavik. This is my principled opinion. I know that Boris Yeltsin and leaders of other republics share this opinion. In this statement I will announce our reciprocal steps and countermeasures. First, with respect to tactical nuclear weapons, the Soviet Union will take the following steps:

• All nuclear artillery munitions and nuclear warheads for tactical missiles shall be eliminated.

• Nuclear warheads for air defense missiles shall be withdrawn from the troops and concentrated in central bases, and a portion of them shall be eliminated. All nuclear mines shall be eliminated.

• All tactical nuclear weapons shall be removed from surface ships and multipurpose submarines. These weapons, as well as nuclear weapons on land-based naval aviation, shall be stored in central storage sites and a portion shall be eliminated.

In this fashion, on the basis of reciprocity the Soviet Union and the United States will take essential steps aimed at the elimination of tactical nuclear weapons. [The procedures and timing for carrying out these measures could be agreed on between the sides through consultations.]*

Moreover, we propose that the United States eliminate fully, on the basis of reciprocity, all tactical nuclear weapons of naval forces. In addition, on the basis of reciprocity, it would be possible to withdraw from combat units on frontal (tactical) aviation, all nuclear weapons (gravity bombs and air-launched missiles) and place them in centralized storage bases. The USSR calls upon other nuclear powers to join in these far reaching Soviet–American steps with respect to tactical nuclear weapons.

Second, together with the US, we are in favor of the quickest possible ratification of the historic START treaty, signed in Moscow this summer. As president of the USSR, I intend to present this issue at the first session of the Supreme Soviet in its new composition.

Taking into account the unilateral measures on strategic offensive arms, declared by President Bush, we are undertaking the following actions:

• Our heavy bombers, just as the American ones, shall not be on alert status, while their nuclear arms shall be placed in storage with military units.

• We are stopping the development of the modified nuclear short-range missile for Soviet heavy bombers.

• We are stopping the development in the USSR of the small mobile intercontinental ballistic missile.

• The number of rail-mobile ICBM launchers will not be increased above the current number and such missiles will not be modernized. In this fashion, the number of our mobile MIRVed ICBMs will not be increased.

• All our rail-mobile ICBMs will remain in their permanent basing areas.

• As a reciprocal step, the Soviet Union will remove from alert status 503 ICBMs, including 134 MIRVed ICBMs.

• The Soviet Union has already decommissioned three nuclear missile submarines with 44 launchers of SLBMs and will decommission an additional three submarines with 48 launchers.

---

* The sentence in square brackets was included in the official Soviet proposal text but not in the televised remarks.

Third, we have decided on deeper reductions of strategic offensive arms than provided for in the START treaty. As a result, at the end of the seven-year period of reductions, the number of strategic nuclear warheads on our side will be 5,000, rather than the 6,000 required by the treaty.

We would, of course, welcome a similar approach from the US side.

We propose to the US that immediately after the ratification of the START treaty, we begin intensive negotiations on further radical reductions of strategic offensive arms by approximately one-half.

We are ready to discuss the US proposal on non-nuclear ABM systems.

We also propose to the US side to examine the possibility of developing joint early warning systems of nuclear attacks with land- and space-based elements.

Fourth, with a view to giving new impetus to nuclear disarmament, we announce the introduction, beginning today, of a unilateral moratorium on nuclear testing for one year, hoping to achieve the comprehensive cessation of nuclear testing.

We are for reaching agreement with the United States on the verified cessation of the production of all weapons-grade fissionable materials.

Fifth, we express our readiness to enter into a substantive dialogue with the United States on the development of safe and ecologically sound technologies for the storing and transportation of nuclear warheads, methods of recycling nuclear weapon devices, and enhancing nuclear security.

With the aim of enhancing the reliability of control over nuclear weapons, we will unite under a single operational command all strategic nuclear forces. We will include strategic defensive systems in a single military service.

Sixth, we sincerely hope that, in the final analysis, other nuclear powers will actively join the efforts of the USSR and the United States.

A joint declaration of all nuclear powers on no first use of nuclear weapons could play an exceptionally useful role in the strengthening of stability and mutual trust. The USSR has already firmly adhered to this principle for a long time.

I am convinced that a step of the American side in this direction would be an important milestone on the path toward establishing a durable structure of mutual security.

Seventh, we note with satisfaction the plans of the US administration to reduce the American armed forces by 500,000 men in the next few years. In this connection, we intend to reduce the Soviet armed forces by 700,000 men.

In conclusion, I want to emphasize the following: Acting in this fashion (in one case unilaterally, in a second on a compromise basis, in a third through negotiations), nonetheless we are resolutely furthering the disarmament process, thereby approaching the goal which was proclaimed back at the beginning of 1986: toward a nuclear-free world. There is much work here: for governments, experts, agencies. We have here a new stage of strengthening strategic stability and creating durable, general security.

Evidently, the question also arises of a new USSR–US summit. I have been speaking to US President George Bush. I told him about our countersteps in connection n with his initiative. At the same time, I voiced proposals for a summit meeting. There was a good exchange of views. He gave me a positive assessment of our proposals, and stated his satisfaction with how we are acting and addressing some of the most major issues in world politics.

Source: State Department translation of an official Soviet text of the proposal and Foreign Broadcast Information Service, in *Arms Control Today,* Oct. 1991, p. 6.

President of the United States George Bush, State of the Union Address to Congress, 28 January 1992

Excerpts

. . .

And so, now, for the first time in 35 years, our strategic bombers stand down. No longer are they on 'round-the-clock alert. . . .

. . .

Tonight I can tell you of dramatic changes in our strategic nuclear force. These are actions we are taking on our own—because they are the right thing to do.

After completing 20 planes for which we have begun procurement, we will shut down further production of the B-2 bomber. We will cancel the small ICBM program. We will cease production of new warheads for our sea-based ballistic missiles. We will stop all new production of the Peacekeeper missile. And we will not purchase any more advanced cruise missiles.

This weekend I will meet at Camp David with Boris Yeltsin of the Russian Federation. I have informed President Yeltsin that if the Commonwealth—the former Soviet Union—will eliminate all land-based multiple warhead ballistic missiles, I will do the following:

We will eliminate all Peacekeeper missiles. We will reduce the number of warheads on Minuteman missiles to one, and reduce the number of warheads on our sea-based missiles by about onethird. And we will convert a substantial portion of our strategic bombers to primarily conventional use.

President Yeltsin's early response has been very positive, and I expect our talks at Camp David to be fruitful.

I want you to know that for half a century, American presidents have longed to make such decisions and say such words. But even in the midst of celebration, we must keep caution as a friend.

For the world is still a dangerous place. Only the dead have seen the end of conflict. And though yesterday's challenges are behind us, tomorrow's are being born.

The secretary of defense recommended these cuts after consultation with the Joint Chiefs of Staff. And I make them with confidence. But do not misunderstand me:

The reductions I have approved will save us an additional $50,000 million over the next five years. By 1997 we will have cut defense by 30 percent since I took office. These cuts are deep, and you must know my resolve: This deep, and no deeper.

To do less would be insensible to progress—but to do more would be ignorant of history.

. . .

Source: United States Information Service, USIS Documentation Center, US Embassy, Sweden, 'Bush outlines new world order, economic plans: Text of President's message to Congress', *News Backgrounder*, 29 Jan. 1992.

President of the Russian Federation Boris Yeltsin, record of televised statement, 29 January 1992

Excerpts

. . .

Our fundamental position is the following: Nuclear weapons and other means of mass destruction in the world must be eliminated. Of course, this must be done gradually and on an equal basis. In this vitally important matter we are open to cooperation with all states and international organizations, including within the framework of the United Nations.

The measures I will speak about today have been prepared on the basis of constant interaction among member states of the Commonwealth of Independent States [CIS] and in accordance with the accords reached at the meetings of their leaders in Minsk, Alma-Ata, and Moscow.

Russia considers itself the legal successor to the USSR in terms of responsibility for carrying out international obligations. We confirm all of our obligations with regard to the bilateral and multilateral accords in the sphere of arms limitation and disarmament that were signed by the Soviet Union and are in operation at the current time.

The Russian leadership confirms its adherence to the course of radical reduction of nuclear weapons, guaranteeing the maximum security of nuclear weapons and guaranteeing the security all of the facilities connected with the development, production, and operation of such weapons.

Russia is proposing an initiative on the creation of an international agency to ensure the reduction of nuclear arms. During the subsequent stages this agency could gradually take under its control the whole nuclear cycle from the mining of uranium and the production of deuterium and tritium, to the storage of waste.*

. . .

Conditions are prime today, making it possible to take a number of new, major steps in arms reduction. We are undertaking a proportion of these unilaterally, and others on a reciprocal basis.

---

* [The TASS version reads: '. . . tritium, to the dumping of nuclear waste.']

We have done, and intend first and foremost to do the following: First, in the area of strategic offensive weapons: We will submit for ratification to the Supreme Soviet of the Russian Federation the treaty on strategic offensive weapons. The process of ratifying this treaty has also begun in the United States. I believe that the implementation of this vital document, including its approval by Belarus, Kazakhstan, and the Ukraine, should be carried out as promptly as possible. Even before the treaty on strategic offensive weapons comes into force, Russia will take a whole range of major steps aimed at cutting the strategic arsenal. About 600 land and sea-based strategic ballistic missiles, or almost 1,250 nuclear warheads, have been removed from operational readiness. A total of 130 intercontinental ballistic missile launch silos have been destroyed or are being prepared for destruction. Six nuclear submarines have been prepared for the dismantling of their missile launchers. Programs for the development or modernization of several types of strategic offensive weapons have been halted. Strategic nuclear arms deployed on the territory of the Ukraine are to be dismantled [*razukomplektovany*] sooner than planned. The appropriate accords have been reached.

Let me stress that this is not a case of our unilateral disarmament. Parallel steps are being taken by the United States as a goodwill measure. Now, however, we can and need to advance significantly further along this path.

Recently the following decisions have been made: The production of TU-160 and TU-95MS heavy bombers has ceased.

We are stopping the production of air-launched long-range cruise missiles [*krylatyye rakety*] of the existing types. We are prepared to renounce the creation of new types of such missiles on a reciprocal basis with the United States. The production of the existing types of sea-based long-range nuclear cruise missiles is ceasing. New types of such missiles will not be created.

At the same time we are prepared, on a reciprocal basis, to eliminate all existing sea-based long-range nuclear cruise missiles. We are renouncing the holding of exercises with the participation of large numbers of heavy bombers. This means that not more than 30 of them may be involved in one exercise. The number of atomic submarines with ballistic missiles—submarine-launched nuclear ballistic missiles—which are on combat patrol has been halved and will be reduced further. We are prepared to renounce altogether the practice of combat patrol with the aid of such submarines, on a reciprocal basis. Russia will reduce the number of strategic offensive weapons on operational readiness to the agreed number within a three-year period instead of seven years.

Thus, we will arrive four years earlier at the level that is envisaged by the relevant treaty. Given that there is mutual understanding with the United States, we could proceed in this direction even faster. We are in favor of the strategic offensive weapons retained by the United States and Russia after the reduction not being aimed at Russian and US targets, respectively.

Important talks with leaders of Western countries are to take place in the forthcoming days. Proposals have been prepared on new, in-depth, several-fold cuts in strategic offensive weapons, to the level of 2,000 to 2,500 strategic nuclear weapons on each of the sides.* In doing so we hope that other nuclear powers like China, Britain, and France will join the process of real nuclear disarmament.

Second, tactical nuclear weapons: Major measures concerning their reduction have already been undertaken simultaneously with the United States.

During the recent period, production has been stopped of nuclear warheads for land-based tactical missiles, and also production of nuclear artillery shells and nuclear mines. Stocks of such nuclear devices will be eliminated. Russia is eliminating one-third of sea-based tactical nuclear weapons and one-half of nuclear warheads for anti-aircraft missiles. Measures in this direction have already been taken. We also intend to halve stocks of air-launched tactical nuclear munitions. The remaining tactical air-launched nuclear armaments could, on a reciprocal basis with the United States, be removed from combat units of the frontline tactical air force and placed in centralized storage bases.

Third, antimissile defense and space: Russia confirms its adherence to the ABM Treaty. It is an important factor in maintaining strategic stability in the world. We are

---

* In Russian: *Podgotovleny predlozheniya o novom glubokom sokrashchenii strategicheskikh nastupatelnykh vooruzheniy v neskolko raz do 2,000–2,500 strategicheskikh yadernykh boyezaryadov u kazhdoy storony.*

ready to continue discussion without prejudice of the US proposal for limiting [*ogranicheniye*] non-nuclear ABM systems.*

Our principle is known: If it strengthens strategic stability in the world and Russia's security, we will support this approach. I also announce that Russia is ready, on the basis of reciprocity with the United States, to eliminate the existing antisatellite systems and to work out an accord to ban completely the weapons which have been specially constructed to hit satellites. We are ready jointly to work out and subsequently to create and jointly operate a global system of defense in place of SDI.

Fourth, the testing of nuclear weapons and the manufacture of fissile materials for arms purposes: Russia is resolutely in favor of a ban on all nuclear arms testing. We are faithful to the annual moratorium on nuclear explosions announced in October 1991, and we hope that other nuclear powers will likewise refrain from carrying out nuclear testing. A climate of mutual restraint would facilitate the attainment of accords on not carrying out such tests altogether, possibly curtailing the number of tests gradually.**

In the interests of resolving this task once and for all, we propose to the United States that bilateral talks on further limiting the testing of nuclear arms be resumed.

Russia intends to continue fulfillment of the program for ending the production of weapons grade plutonium. Industrial reactors for making weapons grade plutonium will be stopped before the year 2000, and several of them will be stopped in 1993 under an accelerated timetable.

We confirm the offer to the United States that agreement be reached on a controlled cessation of the production of fissionable materials for weapons.

---

* The TASS version reads: 'We are ready to continue impartial discussion of the US proposal on the limitation of non-nuclear antiballistic missile systems'. The Moscow *Rossiyskaya Gazeta,* in Russian, 1st edn, 30 Jan., pp. 1–2, carries the text of the Yeltsin statement and renders the preceding phrase as follows: '. . . US proposal for limited non-nuclear antiballistic. . .'

** The TASS version reads: 'Fourth, nuclear weapons tests and the production of fissionable materials for military purposes: Russia emphatically favors the banning of all nuclear arms testing.'

Fifth, the non-proliferation of weapons of mass destruction and the means of their delivery: Russia confirms its obligations under the nuclear non-proliferation treaty, including those as a depository. We are counting upon the treaty being joined as quickly as possible as non-nuclear states by Belarus, Kazakhstan, and the Ukraine, and also other CIS member states. Russia states its full support for the activity of the International Atomic Energy Agency [IAEA] and is in favor of the effectiveness of its guarantees being intensified.

We are taking additional steps to prevent our exports leading to the proliferation of weapons of mass destruction. Work is now being conducted aimed at bringing Russia in line with the principle of an all-embracing IAEA guarantee as a condition of our peaceful nuclear exports. Russia, in principle, intends to join the international regime of non-proliferation of missiles and missile technology as an equal participant.

We support the efforts of the so-called [Australia Group] for control over chemical exports. The Russian Federation plans to adopt domestic legislation regulating the export from Russia of dual use materials, equipment, and technology that could be used to create nuclear, chemical, and biological weapons or combat missiles. A government system to control such exports is being established. We are going to establish very close cooperation and coordination between all participating CIS states on these matters. Russia supports the guiding principles on the arms trade approved in London in October 1991.

Sixth, conventional weapons: A motion to ratify the treaty on conventional armed forces in Europe has been tabled in the Russian parliament. The other CIS member states whose territory is covered by this treaty likewise attach importance to its ratification. Russia reaffirms its intention—along with the other members of the Commonwealth—to cut the actual numbers of the former USSR Armed Forces by 700,000.

Russia attaches great significance to the talks currently under way in Vienna on personnel reductions and confidence-building measures, and also to the new talks on security and cooperation in Europe. The latter could become a standing pan-European forum for seeking ways of creating a collective, pan-European security system.

In cooperation with Kazakhstan, Kyrgyzstan, and Tajikistan, Russia will press to reach an accord with China at talks regarding cuts in armed forces and armaments in the border region. A decision has been made not to hold major exercises in 1992 involving more than 13,000 men—and not just on the European part, but also on the Asiatic part of CIS territory.

We also hope that there is a possibility in the near future to sign a treaty on the open skies issue.

Seventh, chemical weapons: We are for the speediest possible conclusion, in 1992, of a global convention banning chemical weapons. This is essential in order to securely close the paths leading to the possession of chemical weapons, without detriment to the legitimate economic interests of the signatories to the convention. Russia adheres to the agreement with the United States on the non-production and elimination of chemical weapons, signed in 1990.

However, the timescale envisaged therein for the destruction of such weapons requires certain amendments. All of the chemical weapons of the former USSR are on the territory of Russia, who takes responsibility for their destruction. We are preparing an appropriate state program. We are open for cooperation in this matter with the United States and other interested countries.

Eighth, biological weapons: Russia favors the rigorous implementation of the 1972 convention banning biological weapons, and the creation of an appropriate mechanism on a multilateral basis for monitoring the implementation of measures for building confidence and openness. Considering that there is a lag in implementing the convention, I can now state that Russia is renouncing that section of provisoes concerning the possibility of the retaliatory use of biological weapons. These provisoes were made by the USSR under the Geneva Protocol of 1925 banning the use of chemical and bacteriological weapons in war.

Ninth, the defense budget: Russia will continue to make substantial reductions in its defense budget, imparting a social orientation to this area. In 1990 and 199 1, defense expenditure was already reduced by 20 percent in terms of comparable prices, including a 30 percent reduction for purchases of weapons and equipment. In 1992, we intend to reduce military expenditure by another 10 percent in terms of 1991 prices. The volume of weapons purchases this year will be re-duced by approximately half compared with last year.

Tenth, conversion: Russia welcomes international cooperation in the area of conversion of military production. Russia favors faster work in this regard. On our part, we will encourage this cooperation by creating a most favored treatment system and by establishing tax benefits for relevant joint projects.*

. . .

Several hours ago, US President Bush addressed the US people and proposed cuts of nuclear potential. We are constantly engaged in mutual consultations on these issues in preliminary terms. We are engaged in a dialogue on the practical implementation of this line and the initiatives that have been proposed. The closeness of the positions of both sides is noteworthy. Therein lies a guarantee of success on the path of reducing offensive nuclear arms.

---

* The TASS version reads: 'On our part, we will encourage such cooperation by giving priority to and providing tax breaks for relevant joint projects.'

Source: Foreign Broadcast Information Service, *Daily Report–Central Eurasia,* FBIS-SOV-92-019, 29 Jan. 1992.

3. The nuclear non-proliferation regime beyond the Persian Gulf War and the dissolution of the Soviet Union

HARALD MÜLLER

I. Introduction

Three decisive events affected the nuclear non-proliferation regime in 1991: the end of the cold war, the Persian Gulf War and the dissolution of the USSR. The position of the United Nations Security Council in dealing with nuclear weapon proliferation was strengthened by the announcements by France and China that they would accede to the 1968 Non-Proliferation Treaty (NPT). However, despite repeated assurances by China that it will follow a restrained nuclear export policy, some Chinese exports have given rise to concern.

II. Violations of the NPT by Iraq

The Persian Gulf War fought between 17 January and 28 February 1991 and the ensuing revelations about Iraq's nuclear weapon programme cast a long shadow over the nuclear non-proliferation regime. The revelations were the result of the work of staff of the International Atomic Energy Agency (IAEA), under the direction of and reinforced by the UN Special Commission on Iraq (UNSCOM) charged with the identification, removal, destruction and long-term guarding of Iraq's weapons of mass production and missiles and the means of their production, as requested in UN Security Council Resolution 687.[1] Eight on-site inspections of Iraq's nuclear weapon programme revealed that:

1. Iraq has experimentally separated a few grams of plutonium from fuel rods produced in a small laboratory fuel fabrication facility, irradiated in the IRT-5000 research reactor and 'reprocessed' in the hot cells supplied by Italy. The laboratory and the hot cells were nominally and the research reactor was factually under IAEA safeguards.[2] Iraq failed to notify that uranium was pro-

---

[1] UN Security Council Resolution S/RES/687, 3 Apr. 1991. The principal findings of the IAEA inspections of Iraqi nuclear capabilities are published in UN Security Council documents S/22788, S/22837, S/22986 (+corr. 1), S/23112, S/23122, S/23215 and S/23283. See chapter 13 in this volume.

[2] The 1971 IAEA model safeguards agreement covers all the nuclear activities of the non-nuclear weapon states parties to the NPT: IAEA document INFCIRC/153 (corrected) (IAEA: Vienna, 1983). IAEA safeguards employ three essential methods of verification: *materials accountancy*, to determine the amount of material unaccounted for over a specific period; *containment*, to restrict access to and prevent or hamper clandestine movement of the material; and *surveillance*, to detect any unreported movement or tampering with safeguarded items.

cessed in the fuel laboratory for insertion in the reactor, and did not inform the Agency that spent fuel was introduced, and plutonium extracted, in the hot cells. Both inactions were breaches of the NPT safeguards agreement, and the IAEA Board of Governors thus condemned Iraq twice for a breach of the Treaty.[3]

2. Iraq was pursuing a comprehensive programme for uranium enrichment. Diffusion enrichment had been studied but abandoned because of its cost and complexity. Chemical separation had also been studied but had not yet reached the experimental stage. By contrast, Iraq had brought the electro-magnetic isotope separation process (EMIS), used in the US Manhattan Project at the end of World War II but later dropped because of inefficiency and high energy consumption, to the threshold of large-scale use. In an 8-calutron pilot facility, a few grams of uranium had been enriched experiment-ally since mid-1990 to low and medium levels and some milligrams reached 45 per cent enrichment. A first full-scale EMIS plant with 90 calutrons at Tarmiyah was about one year from starting operations, and a second facility of the same size at Ash Sharqat was to start up later. While some equipment was imported, much was produced indigenously and the main engineering work also appears to be a domestic achievement. Alongside this, Iraq had also sought to install the much more efficient centrifuge enrichment process. The design, model centrifuges, essential equipment (e.g., flow-turn machines), raw materials (e.g., maraging steel) and parts (e.g., ring magnets, bearings, and caps) were acquired through a well-organized procurement effort abroad. A facility to produce centrifuges was under construction; it is estimated that the plant was intended to yield as many as several thousands of centrifuges per year. Plans foresaw the installation of a first (100-centrifuge) plant by the end of 1993, and a larger (500-centrifuge) facility by the end of 1996. A facility to produce feed material for enrichment—uranium hexafluoride for the centri-fuges and uranium tetrachloride for the calutrons—was in its initial stage near Mosul.[4]

The size of the procurement effort—sales of 25 000 ring magnets were identified by German investigations based on documents seized by inspectors in Iraq—points to the central role of centrifuge enrichment in Iraq's plan. Iraq had access to several design models (Urenco G-1 and G-2), and advanced cen-trifuges made of carbon fibre—of yet unidentified origin—were found. However, these centrifuges are said to have malfunctioned during testing. Iraq had probably not yet managed to mass-produce functioning centrifuges of the required capacity and quality, or all of their parts, let alone full cascades to enrich uranium to high levels.[5]

3. Iraq was also proceeding towards weapon production. Designs for a first device were seized. Experiments on the electronics and metallurgy of essential parts were under way. Conventional chemical explosive had been produced

[3] *Nucleonics Week*, 25 July, p. 11; 26 Sep. 1991, pp. 11–12.

[4] *Nucleonics Week*, 4 July 1991, p. 3; 11 July 1991, pp. 4–5; 25 July 1991, p. 11; 8 Aug. 1991, pp. 9–10; 15 Aug. 1991, pp. 11, 13–14; 22 Aug. 1991, pp. 7–9.

[5] *Nucleonics Week*, 12 Dec. 1991, p. 7; 16 Jan. 1992, p. 7; 23 Jan. 1992, pp. 10–11.

and preformed into the lenses required for an implosion device and Iraq was conducting research into the hydrodynamics of such a device. While progress in the various fields of weapon production was visible, it was uneven. Iraq was not yet at the stage where it could easily turn the weapon blueprint into a real device.[6]

Iraq had blatantly breached its obligations as a state party to the NPT. The IAEA General Conference and the UN Security Council condemned Iraq for its betrayal of legally binding commitments. As part of a plan approved by the Security Council in August for the permanent monitoring of Iraq, IAEA and UN representatives will be granted visa-free, unimpeded movement within the country, overflight rights, short-notice access to nuclear and other sites, and advance information on any addition to Iraq's nuclear knowledge as well as on any new construction 180 days before it starts. Dual-use nuclear equipment shipments to Iraq will be banned, and the right to inspect customs depots in Iraq should be granted.[7]

III. Safeguards reform

One consequence of the revelations about Iraq was considerable momentum to reform IAEA safeguards.[8] *Per se*, safeguards had not 'failed' in Iraq. One might ask whether the IAEA was not following more the letter than the spirit of INFCIRC/153 when it had decided to visit Iraq, a country where more than 40 kg of highly enriched uranium (HEU) were located, only once every six months, on the grounds that the material was located in different material balance areas.[9] Although this material was not diverted by Iraqi authorities, and was secured and removed during the post-war inspection work, the IAEA could not be expected to pick up signs of clandestine production of as little as 3 grammes of plutonium, nor was it supposed to look for clandestine nuclear facilities. Since the NPT and its model safeguards agreement were in force, the prevailing interpretation was that IAEA inspectors only had access to strategic points in facilities that contained fissile material, as notified by the inspected state. Paragraphs 73 and 77 of INFCIRC/153 were read to permit 'special inspections' in places other than strategic points, but only in notified facilities. This interpretation had already been challenged in 1990. The IAEA Secretariat was asked by the General Conference, following a recommendation by the Fourth NPT Review Conference, to review the matter. In February 1991 at a meeting of the IAEA Board of Governors, Director General Hans Blix stated that the IAEA Secretariat had concluded that paragraphs 73 and 77 gave the Agency the right to investigate any location in the state concerned if it had grounds to suspect the existence of unreported material. He also asked exporting and importing states to consider extended reporting obligations for

[6] *Süddeutsche Zeitung*, 30 Sep. 1991; *Nucleonics Week*, 26 Sep. 1991, pp. 11–12.
[7] *Nucleonics Week*, 8 Aug. 1991, p. 9; 19 Sep. 1991, pp. 12–13.
[8] See note 2.
[9] *Nuclear Fuel*, 13 May 1991, pp. 4–8.

nuclear material, plant and equipment, and for exporters to require that safeguards be applied to installations as well as to nuclear materials.[10]

Significantly, some of the countries that had argued strongly against intrusive inspection authority when INFCIRC/153 was negotiated in 1970 now took the position that more intrusion was needed. An unprecedented joint initiative to strengthen IAEA safeguards was submitted by the European Parliamentary Commission (EPC) to the IAEA Board of Governors in June 1991. Their proposal included a provision for challenge inspection based on paragraphs 73 and 77 of INFCIRC/153, and a plea to concentrate efforts to enforce safeguards efforts on 'suspect' countries rather than those with large civilian fuel cycles.[11]

During the June 1991 session of the IAEA Board of Governors, and again before the General Conference, Director General Blix put forward three conditions under which the IAEA would be able to discover operations such as those conducted by Iraq:[12] (a) unlimited access to all 'suspect' facilities in a country; (b) a supply of intelligence on such facilities by member states capable of collecting relevant data (e.g., those which possess observation satellites); and (c) full backing by the UN Security Council. With the support of the industrialized states, the IAEA Secretariat was asked to submit detailed proposals for such reforms. At the December 1991 Board meeting, the Secretariat presented working papers on special inspections and on the use of intelligence. It was proposed that a 'special unit' to collect and evaluate such intelligence submitted by member states be installed, reporting directly to the Director General. Opposition to safeguards reform focused on this proposal. A group of developing countries, including Algeria, Cuba, India, Iran, Mexico, North Korea and Pakistan, objected to the 'intelligence unit', arguing that this might be tantamount to handing over the IAEA to the US Central Intelligence Agency (CIA). Misgivings about a safeguards regime that was much more intrusive into national sovereignty than the established one, and the fear by non-NPT threshold countries of complete exposure once NPT member states were under this stricter regime, motivated the opposition. It was agreed to postpone decision until the February 1992 Board meeting.[13] It might eventually prove preferable to silently assume that the Secretariat can use all the information it can gather, and can claim the right to go 'anywhere' under INFCIRC/153, without a formal vote or position being taken by the Board. That the safeguards issue reopened the North–South divide, with Mexico, the main voice of criticism against the nuclear-weapon states among the NPT developing countries, taking the side of threshold countries, is a serious signal. In their zeal to promote safeguards reform, the industrialized countries have neglected advance consultation with key developing countries. Another source

[10] *IAEA Newsbrief,* vol. 6, no. 2 (Mar./Apr. 1991), p. 1.
[11] *Nucleonics Week,* 19 Sep. 1991, pp. 11–12.
[12] IAEA document GC (XXXV)/999, 16 Sep. 1991.
[13] *Nucleonics Week,* 12 Dec. 1991, pp. 1, 9–10.

of concern is the stubborn refusal of Western countries to enhance the IAEA budget in keeping with enhanced safeguards (and safety) tasks.[14]

IV. Strengthening export controls

The Persian Gulf War also brought to light the weakness of existing export controls. Investigations in Iraq have shown that in most cases a would-be proliferator is still dependent on technological infusions from abroad. The IAEA can only act effectively when it knows what equipment, materials and technology a state is acquiring from abroad. Iraq had made lavish imports of militarily usable goods from industrialized countries for its conventional, missile, chemical, biological and nuclear programmes. With Germany heading the list, practically all technologically advanced countries had contributed to Iraq's concentrated effort to develop imposing arsenals of weapons of mass destruction.[15]

Thus, when, for the first time in 14 years, the Netherlands invited all members of the 'Nuclear Supplier Group', from both East and West, to meet in The Hague in early 1991, the response was positive.[16] The old objections of some suppliers that 'ganging up' by the industrialized exporters would offend and alienate the developing countries had disappeared under the impact of the Gulf War. Germany, one of those states previously reluctant to stiffen restrictions, had become very interested in an international agreement to reinforce export controls. Domestic reforms had already brought in a considerably strengthened and more rigorous system and there were fears in industry of a competitive disadvantage unless these reforms could be turned into internationally agreed standards. France, also traditionally averse to reconvening the Supplier Group, was about to change its policy and was determined to demonstrate its readiness to co-operate internationally for non-proliferation purposes.

The United States submitted a paper on dual-use export controls; this had become a burning issue because of the dismantling of most of the controls of the Co-ordinating Committee on Multilateral Export Controls (COCOM). The US proposals were by and large adopted: the suppliers agreed to work on a list of dual-use items and, in addition, on a list of items of direct use in nuclear weapons but not related to civilian nuclear uses—such as krytrons (electronic switches), tritium (for boosted nuclear weapons) and beryllium (a reflector material enhancing the yield of a given amount of fissile material). This signalled a major change. The meeting agreed to set up a working group to complete these lists before the end of 1991, and another group to prepare guidelines for handling export licences for such items. At the end of 1991, a new dual-use trigger list—containing more than 60 items—was largely com-

---

[14] *Nucleonics Week,* 28 Nov. 1991, pp. 9–10.

[15] *Nucleonics Week,* 12 Dec. 1991, p. 7.

[16] *Nucleonics Week,* 14 Mar. 1991, p. 4. The main suppliers of nuclear plants and materials met in London, 1975–77, and a set of guidelines was agreed by the London Suppliers' Club on 21 Sep. 1977: see IAEA document INFCIRC/254 (IAEA: Vienna, 1978).

pleted. The suppliers had also agreed on a 'Basic Principle' guideline for applying this list; a major difficulty was to find a formulation that would not discriminate in favour of nuclear weapon states.

A German paper pressed the Suppliers to agree that full-scope safeguards should be made a condition for supply of any nuclear material. While they could not yet agree on such an undertaking, there was agreement to pursue the matter further at the next meeting scheduled for the spring of 1992 in Poland. In September 1991 France and Great Britain officially declared that they would apply this condition to their nuclear exports, and Switzerland, Belgium, Spain and Italy followed suit.[17] This left only the Soviet Union without a declared full-scope safeguards policy, and the turmoil in the successor states apparently makes it difficult to reach a decision on a subject that is disputed between various bureaucracies.[18]

The Netherlands, acting as an *ad hoc* secretariat between the meetings (also an innovation), was asked to make approaches to emerging suppliers not yet integrated into the group, such as Argentina, Brazil, South Korea and China, with a view to persuading them to accept the guidelines as their own export policy. These efforts achieved mixed success. Some interest was apparently shown by South Korea and Argentina, but there were still strong reservations about joining what had been seen as a 'rich men's club' for so long. China was giving repeated assurances to the USA that it would follow a restrained export policy, but there still seems to be a difference between words and deeds as far as Chinese exports are concerned. The export of a Chinese research reactor to Algeria, kept secret for five years, has raised suspicion. China also co-operates with Iran and has supplied a calutron for isotope separation—although reportedly incapable of enriching uranium—and a 'micro-reactor' for research. A research reactor of Chinese origin is also under construction in Syria, and this creates some difficulty, as Syria so far refuses to accept the INFCIRC/153 safeguards agreement but rather insists on the INFCIRC/66 agreement that is customary between the IAEA and countries not party to the NPT.[19] Another new supplier, India, has expressed readiness to sell a research reactor to Iran but is under US pressure to abstain from the deal.[20]

While new, small-scale suppliers may prove a distorting force in the future for the international nuclear export regime, old suppliers which have been a source of trouble are turning into strong supporters of this regime.

The most significant group of suppliers, the members of the European Community (EC), took several new actions to strengthen their own non-proliferation policy. The French–German proposal for European security co-operation, made in the winter of 1990, significantly gave non-proliferation a prominent place (as did the Commission's paper on the same subject). In early 1991, the 12 EC member states agreed to consider the possibility of a more

[17] *Nucleonics Week,* 5 Oct. 1991.

[18] *Nucleonics Week,* 24 Oct. 1991, pp. 1, 6; 14 Nov. 1991, p. 11.

[19] *Nucleonics Week,* 12 Dec. 1991, p. 10. Drawn up in 1965, 'The Agency's Safeguards System (1965)' still serves as the framework for all IAEA safeguards agreements with states not parties to the NPT or the 1967 Tlatelolco Treaty: IAEA document INFCIRC/66/Rev. 2 (IAEA: Vienna, 1968).

[20] *Nucleonics Week,* 21 Nov. 1991, p. 2.

sophisticated common policy on nuclear exports, not excluding a further turn to full-scope safeguards by those members (France, Belgium, Britain and Italy) that had not yet subscribed to this principle. The European Commission participated, for the first time, in the Nuclear Supplier Group meeting in The Hague.[21] The EC Council meeting in Luxembourg in June 1991 issued a further statement on proliferation—covering the proliferation of nuclear, chemical, biological and conventional arms. The EC countries called on all states to join the NPT. In the field of export policy it summarized the work done in various EPC working groups, including the group on nuclear non-proliferation, by formulating a list of criteria to be taken into account when export decisions are made. The criteria include, *inter alia*, the human rights and general internal situation in the recipient country, the degree of regional tension or armed conflict, the security of the member states (obviously aimed at the southern flank), the general behaviour of the recipient, including its stance on terrorism and respect for international law, and, finally, an assessment of the diversion risks concerning the items to be transferred. The Council declared its intention to seek harmonization of national export policies on these criteria. This statement went beyond the present criteria governing the export of weapons and militarily-usable technologies and thus presents a genuine initiative of the EC members to improve the existing non-proliferation regimes.[22] The Maastricht agreement of December 1991 again put more emphasis on non-proliferation, which was singled out as one of the foreign–security policy areas in which majority decisions would be taken on procedural issues in the future.

V. New momentum for the NPT

The Persian Gulf War helped to focus attention on the importance of the NPT. Zambia and Tanzania, which had long resisted pressure to join because of the Treaty's discriminatory features and concern about South Africa, announced their accession.[23] In June 1991 the Foreign Minister of South Africa declared that his country had decided to become a party and thus to submit all nuclear materials to full-scope safeguards. By September 1991, the safeguards agreement had already been concluded and brought into force. South Africa handed over an inventory of its nuclear materials and facilities and by the end of the year Agency staff were verifying its authenticity.[24] The South African decision makes the spread of nuclear weapons unlikely in this region of the world and opens the possibility of creating an African nuclear weapon-free zone—a move also supported by the new South African position. Of the remaining front-line states, Angola and Namibia indicated their intention to accede,[25] and Zimbabwe acceded in June.

[21] Informal Meeting of States adhering to the Nuclear Supplier Guidelines, Press Statement, The Hague, 7 Mar. 1992.
[22] *Atlantic News*, no. 2336 (2 July 1991), p. 2.
[23] *PPNN Newsbrief*, no. 14 (summer 1991), p. 1.
[24] *Nucleonics Week*, 19 Sep. 1991, p. 13.
[25] *New York Times*, 28 June 1991; *Nucleonics Week*, 19 Sep. 1991, p. 13.

On 3 June President François Mitterrand announced his far-reaching disarmament plan. Among the measures announced was a commitment to become a party to the NPT, thereby formally subscribing to what—as the President himself declared—had long been in the French interest as well as French policy.[26] This put heavy pressure on China, the last officially declared nuclear weapon state outside the regime. France left no doubt that it was trying hard to draw in China; Foreign Minister Roland Dumas made a well-publicized trip to China to persuade Beijing to follow France's example. The same aim was promoted by a visit of US Undersecretary of State Reginald Bartholomew (who received the assurance that China was 'carefully considering' accession) and relentless Japanese diplomatic pressure. For China, the issue became critical. An additional embarrassment for China was the revelation, first denied and then admitted, that China had secretly collaborated with Algeria for five years in the construction of a large research reactor. China hastened to explain that the reactor would be placed under IAEA safeguards, but distrust in China's sense of responsibility as a nuclear exporter was aroused anew, and the risk of curbs on trade with the West were mounting as a consequence. Isolated as the last major communist state, under sharp criticism because of its human rights record and in great need of infusions of Western capital and technology, China had to make a gesture, and in August 1991 the Chinese Government announced that China would become a party to the NPT.[27] This was formally approved on 29 December at the Standing Committee of the National People's Congress, and China acceded to the Treaty on 9 March 1992.

The fact that all five permanent members of the UN Security Council will now adhere to the Treaty is a most interesting and important development, given the crucial role that the Security Council may be called upon to play in future proliferation emergencies.

VI. Regional developments

From Latin America, the news continued to improve. Civilian controls over nuclear programmes were extended during the year, and the negotiations between Argentina and Brazil on a common system of accounting and control and with the IAEA for an umbrella safeguards agreement were making good progress, although some difficulties appear to have arisen. In December the IAEA Board of Governors accepted the agreement, and it was signed in a solemn ceremony with the Argentinian and Brazilian Presidents present to emphasize the importance of the occasion.[28]

---

[26] Presidence de la Republique, *Plan de Maîtrise des Armements et de Désarmement*, Paris, 3 June 1991.

[27] *Nucleonics Week*, 27 June 1991, p. 10; no. 33 (15 Aug. 1991), pp. 14–16; a comprehensive study of Chinese export policy is contained in *Eye on Supply*, no. 4 (spring 1991), pp. 64–80.

[28] *Nucleonics Week*, 12 Dec. 1991, p. 10; 9 Jan. 1992, p. 12; IAEA Press Release (PR/48), 13 Dec. 1991.

This agreement put the two largest South American threshold states on an equal footing with NPT countries with respect to safeguards coverage and opened the door for bringing the 1967 Tlatelolco Treaty into full force. It seems probable that Chile, the last remaining non-party to the Tlatelolco Treaty in South America, will accede, and Cuba will then find it difficult to remain outside. Cuban participation (by an observer) in most meetings of OPANAL—the Agency for the Prohibition of Nuclear Weapons in Latin America connected to the Tlatelolco Treaty—may indicate a Cuban desire to end its isolation. The elimination of Latin America from the list of areas of nuclear proliferation concern is now in sight.[29]

Over the year pressure grew on North Korea to bring its 30 MW research reactor, and the larger (300 MW) reactor and reprocessing plant still awaiting completion, finally under international safeguards. During high-level visits to Japan and South Korea the USSR declared that it would halt all nuclear assistance as long as the situation was not resolved.[30] Japan refused to agree to a normalization of diplomatic relations, not to speak of economic aid and reparations, as long as North Korea's full-scope safeguards agreement was not in force. Even China indicated in a more veiled manner that it does not favour nuclear proliferation on the peninsula.[31] European countries also expressed concern to the North Korean Government, for example, through a well-briefed German parliamentarian delegation at the meeting of the Inter-parliamentarian Union in April 1991.[32] The announcement on 27 September 1991 by President George Bush that the USA was withdrawing all land-based tactical nuclear weapons, including those in Korea, should put Pyongyang's position to the final test. North Korea took a step by finalizing the negotiations on the agreement and in initialling it in the summer. The agreement was then approved by the IAEA, North Korea signed in January 1992 and ratification is awaited.[33] Long delays would not be altogether unexpected and many observers predict further delays concerning inspection procedures. At the end of 1991, the two Korean states signed a declaration making the peninsula a nuclear-weapon free zone. Each side agreed to renounce not only nuclear weapons, but also reprocessing and enrichment facilities. In addition to IAEA safeguards (North Korea promised to sign the safeguards agreement by end-January 1992), a catch-all safeguards right was conferred on both parties, contingent, however, on procedural agreement.[34] Due adherence to this agreement would remove the Korean peninsula from the list of nuclear proliferation concerns, too.

The end of the East–West conflict has diminished the geopolitical importance of India and Pakistan to their erstwhile allies. In 1990, the US President

[29] Compare *PPNN Newsbrief*, no. 13 (spring 1991), p. 2; no. 14 (summer 1991), p. 1; *Nucleonics Week*, 6 Dec.1990.

[30] *Süddeutsche Zeitung*, 22 Apr. 1991, p. 7.

[31] *Nuclear Fuel*, vol. 32, no. 33 (15 Aug. 1991), pp. 14–16; *PPNN Newsbrief*, no. 14 (summer 1991), p. 6; *Emerging Nuclear Supplier Project Bulletin*, 13 May 1991, details what is known on North Korea's nuclear programme.

[32] *Süddeutsche Zeitung*, 30 Apr.–1 May 1991, p. 9.

[33] IAEA Press Release (92/6), 30 Jan. 1992.

[34] *International Herald Tribune*, 27 Dec. 1991, p. 2; 2 Jan. 1992, pp. 1, 13; *Nucleonics Week*, 9 Jan. 1992, pp. 10–11.

failed for the first time since 1980 to certify that Pakistan did not possess a full-fledged nuclear device. The USA had also changed its definition of possession of such a device from having an assembled bomb to the availability of all materials and components—a hardening of its position. As a consequence, US military assistance for 1991 was suspended. Congress then moved—despite mild objections by the Administration—to apply the same standard to India, to the great dismay of all political parties in that country.[35] The price of pursuing a military nuclear option had risen sharply. Pakistan suffered doubly. The import of a power reactor from France, already beset by uncertainties over financing, was unexpectedly called into question for other reasons. As a further indication of policy change, France now demanded Pakistani concessions on comprehensive safeguards or even that it sign the NPT.[36] The Pakistani Government reacted by displaying a more forthcoming attitude. A high-level Pakistani Senate delegation departed for Washington to convince the USA of the peaceful character of the Pakistani programme. When this mission failed, a message was sent to the five permanent members of the UN Security Council inviting them to take an initiative on nuclear arms control in South Asia. The plan went further than the earlier, largely ritualistic Pakistani proposals for a nuclear weapon-free zone in the area in that it proposed direct action. The Security Council reacted favourably, but Indian responses were mixed. While some government speakers expressed interest, others repeated the well-known Indian position that India's renunciation of nuclear weapons was not in sight unless global nuclear disarmament took place, and that a nuclear weapon-free zone had to include China.[37] Meanwhile, India learned that it would not get the desired reactors from the Russian Federation.[38] Within Pakistan itself, dissenting voices became audible. Opposition politicians publicly warned against selling out Pakistan's nuclear achievements, and public opinion polls showed disturbingly large majorities in favour of a Pakistani bomb. If the Pakistani Government was indeed willing to negotiate the renunciation of its nuclear capability, it would run a risk of losing its domestic support.[39] Both these Asian states are now facing a serious dilemma. Because of the cold war South Asia never really had to pay the full price for its challenge to the non-proliferation regime, but donor states are now on the way to making continued aid (including their votes in international lending institutions) dependent on the non-nuclear status of recipients. Discussions in New Delhi in the summer and autumn of 1991 suggested that India might consider entering a forum with Pakistan and the permanent members of the UN Security Council to discuss ways of defusing the nuclear threat in South Asia, of securing assurances from China, and of reducing the

[35] *PPNN Newsbrief*, no. 12 (winter 1990–91), pp. 8–9; *Nucleonics Week*, 11 Oct. 1990; 1 Nov. 1990; 27 June 1991, pp. 9–10.
[36] *Nucleonics Week*, 2 Jan. 1992, p. 17.
[37] *PPNN Newsbrief*, no. 14 (summer 1991), p. 2; *Nucleonics Week*, 13 June 1991, p. 15.
[38] *Nucleonics Week*, 23 Jan. 1992, p. 3.
[39] *PPNN Newsbrief*, no. 13 (spring 1991), p. 6; no. 14 (summer 1991), p. 2; *Nucleonics Week*, 28 Aug. 1991, p. 13.

presence of US nuclear weapons in the Indian Ocean.[40] As a confidence-building measure, the two countries, pursuant to their agreement not to attack each other's nuclear facilities, exchanged lists of these facilities before the end of 1991.[41]

The Persian Gulf War led naturally to considerations of new arms control initiatives in the Middle East—apart from the special constraints imposed upon Iraq. Both Mitterrand and Bush looked for ways to address the nuclear issue in a broader framework. On 29 May President Bush proposed a total prohibition on the production of weapon-usable fissile material (and the relevant production facilities) in the region. This proposal goes considerably further than the NPT; in fact it would require states in the region to renounce some of their rights under Article IV (which requires states parties to co-operate in the field of peaceful nuclear applications). Even more pertinent is the fact that, for the first time, Bush's plan addresses the ongoing nuclear activities of the USA's closest ally in the region, Israel. So far, Israel has suffered few US sanctions for its nuclear weapon programme other than ritual admonitions, devoid of pressure to accede to the NPT and a refusal of civilian nuclear co-operation that frustrated Israeli plans to acquire nuclear power. Bush's proposal, however, would mean that Israel would stop plutonium pro-duction at its nuclear weapon site at Dimona and would curtail its nuclear arsenal. It can thus be seen as a first step towards a zone free of weapons of mass destruction that might eventually be established in the framework of a far-reaching arms control and dispute settlement plan.[42] The matter may take a more practical shape when the IAEA Secretariat, pursuant to a controversial resolution of the 1991 General Conference, produces a draft model agreement for a special Middle East safeguards regime that will go beyond the require-ments of the NPT (the INFCIRC/153 agreement).[43]

VII. The dissolution of the USSR

The consequences of the dissolution of the Soviet Union have caused much concern for the nuclear non-proliferation regime. At the end of 1991, matters stood as follows:

1. After some hesitation, ambiguity and hard bargaining, the republics appear to be in agreement that, after a period of transition until 1995, Russia will remain as the only nuclear weapon state in the Commonwealth of Independent States (CIS). Large-scale removal of tactical nuclear weapons from the other republics in which they were stationed started in December 1991. The weapons are being brought to depots and weapon manufacturing facilities in Russia for intermediate storage and dismantlement. The storage of

[40] *Nucleonics Week,* 4 July 1991, pp. 14–15; *Arms Control Reporter* (IDDS: Brookline, Mass.), sheet 454.B.144, Nov. 1991.
[41] *Nucleonics Week,* 7 Nov. 1991, p. 10; *Nucleonics Week,* 9 Jan. 1992, p. 10.
[42] Compare *Arms Control Today,* vol. 21, no. 5 (June 1991), pp. 27–28.
[43] *Nucleonics Week,* 26 Sep. 1991, pp. 13–14.

the plutonium and highly enriched uranium emerging from dismantlement is said to cause a major problem, since the required containers and storage buildings are not available in sufficient quantity. Western help is needed, but the spectre of the smaller republics becoming nuclear weapon states, or of individual units or nationalist terrorist groups seizing tactical nuclear weapons, is progressively disappearing.[44]

2. The future of strategic nuclear weapons located in Russia, Belarus, Ukraine and Kazakhstan caused major controversy. Jealously hedging against the supreme position of Russia, and using nuclear weapons as one of the few bargaining chips available, the presidents of Ukraine and Kazakhstan issued contradictory and at times disturbing signals about their nuclear ambitions. As the debate went on, Western pressure, emerging from Washington, Bonn, London, Paris and Brussels grew. The linkage between economic aid, political acceptance and an unequivocally non-nuclear status of all republics but Russia was clearly expressed.[45] As a consequence, commitments to renouncing nuclear weapons became clearer and more credible over time. In October 1991, the Ukrainian Diet passed a resolution promising accession to the NPT as non-nuclear weapon state. In the December 1991 Minsk and Alma-Ata agreements, a joint supreme command for strategic forces was installed for a transition period, and Ukraine and Belarus vowed to get rid of their strategic nuclear weapons and to accede to the NPT.[46] At this point, President Nursultan Nazarbayev of Kazakhstan was not yet ready to take an equally unambiguous position.[47] In early 1992, however, he joined Ukraine and Belarus in committing himself to the removal and dismantlement of all nuclear weapons in the territory under his rule until 1995.[48]

3. As all nuclear weapons are under joint CIS command with CIS Defence Minister Marshal Yevgeniy Shaposhnikov at the helm, the responsibility for the physical security of nuclear weapons is centralized in the hands of special troops, regrouped under the new command. They are reported to enjoy privileged supplies for their daily needs, and attention of the supreme command is highly focused on their discipline and the maintenance of clear lines of command and communication. This provides some hedge against the danger, visible in the Red Army at large, of declining discipline and morale, the perceived need to meet daily needs at the local and regional level, and, consequently, some sort of 'warlordism'. Only if this disintegration progresses fur-

---

[44] This includes tactical nuclear weapons from the three non-Russian republics where strategic nuclear warheads are deployed; *International Herald Tribune*, 21–22 Dec. 1991, p. 2. See chapter 14 in this volume.

[45] For example, *Nucleonics Week*, 5 Dec. 1991, pp. 5–6.

[46] See appendix 14A for the texts of these agreements.

[47] *PPNN Newsbrief*, no. 16 (winter 1991–92), pp. 7–8, 15–16; *International Herald Tribune*, 19 Dec. 1991, p. 2.

[48] *Nucleonics Week*, 24 Oct. 1991, pp. 1, 6; 14 Nov. 1991, p. 1; *International Herald Tribune*, 7 Feb. 1992, p. 5.

ther and reaches the hard core of privileged troops might the physical security of nuclear weapons re-emerge as a serious problem.[49]

4. The civilian and a part of the military nuclear–industrial complex is in a double evolution towards privatization and decentralization. This creates concern about fissile materials, equipment and technology that could be sold for hard currency to proliferating countries or even non-governmental groups. Until the dissolution of the USSR, the Ministry of Heavy Machinery and Atomic Industry (MAPI) and specialized central export agencies (Technsabexport), in co-ordination with the Foreign Ministry, held strict control over the export sector; individual deals of doubtful character (for example, heavy water, lease of a nuclear submarine to India, reactor exports to non-NPT countries) aside, this control appeared to function well. At present, MAPI is making a major effort to decentralize its activities. The creation of Chetek, a semi-private company consisting mainly of nuclear scientists, including nuclear weapon experts, offering a whole spectrum of nuclear and other advanced technologies to the international market, including 'peaceful nuclear explosions' to incinerate and render harmless toxic chemical waste, is one important signal of what might emerge.[50] In the turmoil in Moscow, the orderly process of export controls has largely disappeared.[51] Even MAPI itself will be divided into a governmental and a commercial unit.[52] That the USSR was not able—whether because of lack of funds or inability to decide on the required authorization is unclear—to send a delegation to the Nuclear Suppliers' working meeting at Annapolis in October 1991 was significant. Only recently has President Boris Yeltsin reaffirmed that Russia will shoulder its responsibilities as a nuclear exporter, but it is far from clear whether the administrative capabilities for making good this promise are available. This applies with even greater force to the other republics that harbour relevant capabilities, from nuclear facilities and materials to a capable machine tool and chemical industry, but lack any experience in controlling exports, not to speak about the activities of private economic actors.[53] Small batches of uranium and plutonium, stemming from (former) Soviet, Bulgarian, and Romanian sources are rumoured to have appeared in Switzerland, Italy, and some other places. There is a risk that a 'nuclear black market', so far existing only in the fantasy of creative novelists, will eventually become a reality. So far, however, the amounts of material intercepted were very small.[54]

5. With the partial dissolution of the nuclear–military complex, the fate of the weapon experts has entered the headlines. The complex employs more

---

[49] For the trilateral agreement see *International Herald Tribune*, 9 Dec. 1991, pp. 1–2; *PPNN Newsbrief*, no. 16 (winter 1991–92), pp. 7–8, 15–16; compare also *International Herald Tribune*, 11 Dec. 1991, pp. 1–2.

[50] *Nucleonics Week*, 31 Oct. 1991, pp. 9–10; note also the dissolution of the Kurchatov Institute, *Nucleonics Week*, 19 Dec. 1991, p. 17.

[51] *Nucleonics Week*, 24 Oct. 1991, pp. 1, 6; 14 Nov. 1991, p. 11.

[52] *Nucleonics Week*, 16 Jan. 1992, pp. 3, 12; *PPNN Newsbrief*, no. 16 (winter 1991–92), pp. 7–8, 9.

[53] Milhollin, G. and White, G., 'From the fallen Soviet empire, a rising threat', *International Herald Tribune*, 11 Dec. 1991, p. 8.

[54] *International Herald Tribune*, 1 Jan. 1992, pp. 1–2; *Frankfurter Allgemeine Sonntagszeitung*, 9 Feb. 1992, p. 2.

than 100 000 staff, many of them isolated in whole cities supported solely by the nuclear weapon business. Of these, 1000–2000 persons are said to have relevant knowledge about the design and engineering of nuclear weapons, and another 2000–5000 to have some useful knowledge about the production of weapon-grade fissile material. With the virtual end to nuclear testing and nuclear weapon production, only a few will be employed in maintaining and reworking the arsenal. Most face an uncertain future.[55] In addition, their income and miserable living conditions make foreign offers highly attractive. There are reports of offers from several Middle-Eastern and that a few scientists have already defected to proliferating states; this, however, is denied by CIS authorities.[56] The US Government has promised to use part of the $400 million authorized by the Congress to help with dismantling CIS nuclear weapons for employing these scientists. A 'clearing house' is to find new jobs for them abroad. Germany and Japan plan to set up an international foundation to fund work in the CIS itself, such as setting up a system of material accountancy for fissile material, cleaning up the radioactive contamination at nuclear weapon sites and improving the safety of civilian nuclear facilities.[57] It has also been proposed that Russia, Germany and the USA establish an international scientific centre in Russia, with possible branches in other republics, to match projects with qualified scientists throughout the newly independent states.[58] It will probably be possible to dissuade most but not all experts from lending assistance to undesirable military projects.

VIII. Where do we stand in 1992?

Ironically, the outbreak of violence in the Persian Gulf partially offset the damage created by the failure of the fourth NPT Review Conference,[59] and this, together with a spate of crucial accessions to the NPT and of prospective accessions to the Tlatelolco Treaty, has given the regime an unforeseen boost. The events in the Gulf, the end of the cold war and the break-up of the Soviet Union have alerted more states than ever to the increasing danger that nuclear proliferation poses to national, regional and global security. The five permanent members of the UN Security Council have agreed to devote particular efforts to non-proliferation, as have the EC, NATO and the Group of Seven (G-7). It thus appears that the main consequence of the war was to stimulate a major effort to improve the regime. The success of this effort will hinge on the inclusion, at equal level, of leading developing countries.

[55] Arms Control Reporter, 1991, sheet 611.E-3.23-4; International Herald Tribune, 2 Jan. 1991, pp. 1, 13.

[56] International Herald Tribune, 9 Jan. 1991, p. 1; 1–2 Feb. 1992, p. 2; Frankfurter Allgemeine Sonntagszeitung, 9 Feb. 1992, p. 2.

[57] International Herald Tribune, 25–26 Jan. 1992, pp. 1, 4.

[58] Friedman, T. L., 'Ex-Soviet atom scientists ask Baker for West's help', New York Times, 15 Feb. 1992, p. A1.

[59] For an analysis of the Fourth NPT Review Conference, see Fischer, D. and Müller, H., 'The fourth review of the Non-Proliferation Treaty', SIPRI, SIPRI Yearbook 1991: World Armaments and Disarmament (Oxford University Press: Oxford, 1991), chapter 16.

4. Nuclear explosions and the talks on test limitations

ROBERT S. NORRIS; Section III by JOZEF GOLDBLAT

I. Introduction

The total number of nuclear explosions conducted in 1991 was 14, the lowest since 1954 if the period of the British–US–Soviet moratorium (1959 and 1960) is excluded. The decline continues a trend begun in 1988. Three nations tested during the year: the United States carried out seven tests, France six and the United Kingdom one (conducted jointly, as usual, with the USA at the Nevada Test Site). The USSR and China did not carry out any tests in 1991. As of 11 December 1990, the Soviet Union had planned to conduct two tests during calendar year 1991[1] with a planned yield below 35 kilotons. It was unclear where the USSR had planned to test, becaue of local protests and the turbulent economic and political situation that intensified throughout the year.

The decisive changes that occurred in the USSR during the year will fundamentally alter all aspects of the military relationships among the nuclear weapon states. Testing programmes will no doubt be profoundly affected. Reduced rates of testing are likely to continue because of three factors. First, military budgets in general, and testing budgets in particular, are being reduced in the five declared nuclear weapon states. In the USA, peak budget and underground testing levels were reached in the mid-1980s, when an average of 16 tests per year were conducted. In the 1990s, the average number will probably be around a half dozen or less. However, for the first five years of the 1980s, the Soviet Union averaged more than 26 tests per year, but, for a number of reasons—including the Soviet one-year unilateral moratorium introduced in October 1991—they will most likely conduct many fewer tests per year in the 1990s.

The second reason for a diminished number of tests is the fact that there are very few new nuclear warhead programmes now in research and development. Over the past two or three years, the acknowledged nuclear weapon powers have cancelled several nuclear weapon programmes for one reason or another. Presidents George Bush and Mikhail Gorbachev cancelled several programmes in their initiatives of 27 September and 5 October 1991, respec-

---

[1] Soviet Entry into Force Data, Document no. 3261/UPOVR, 11 Dec. 1990, sent by the Soviet Ministry of Foreign Affairs to the US Embassy. In section 2c it says: 'intends to conduct, during calendar year 1991, two tests with a planned yield below 35 kilotons, to allow the United States to fully exercise its rights, specified in paragraph 2 of Section III of the protocol. More precise information on these tests will be provided immediately after the USSR Supreme Soviet considers the nuclear testing program.' The document also states that no tests above 35 kt were planned.

SIPRI Yearbook 1992: World Armaments and Disarmament

tively,[2] and President François Mitterrand announced that the S45 mobile missile would be cancelled.[3]

The third reason for lower levels of tests is continuing international and domestic pressure to further restrict testing or to ban it completely.

II. Nuclear explosions in 1991

US explosions

The USA carried out seven nuclear explosions in 1991. Six were weapon-related, and one was a weapon-effects test. The fifth test of the year, code-named Hoya and conducted on 14 September, was designated as a 'verification' test under provisions of the new Protocol to the 1974 Threshold Test Ban Treaty (TTBT) which entered into force on 11 December 1990.[4]

In early 1991, as required by the new TTBT Protocol, the two sides exchanged the necessary information about test sites, planned tests with yields of over 35 kilotons, and verification equipment and designated personnel, and established the Bilateral Consultative Commission (BCC) for the TTBT and the Joint Consultative Commission for the Peaceful Nuclear Explosions Treaty (PNET).[5]

On 27 June a group of 23 Soviet scientists arrived at the Nevada Test Site.[6] On 23 July all but five scientists left, as required by the Treaty. Those who remained were involved in scientific measurements of the nuclear device emplacement hole using gamma, neutron and caliper measuring systems. Although the Soviet team observed the emplacement of the canister into the hole, they departed on 10 September and were not present when it was detonated.

There is a wide body of opinion that believes that the entire exercise of the USA pushing for additional verification procedures for the TTBT was a way to divert attention from pressures for a comprehensive test ban (CTB), all the while seeming to be interested in arms control.[7] Advances have been made in seismic verification and they no longer need be an excuse not to have a CTB.[8]

---

[2] See chapter 2 in this volume for an account of the four unilateral nuclear reduction initiatives of late 1991 and early 1992; see appendix 2A for excerpts from the texts of the announcements of the initiatives.

[3] Riding, A., 'France drops plans to build new nuclear missile system', *New York Times*, 25 July 1991, p. A6; 'French halt study work on S45 nuclear missile', *Aviation Week & Space Technology*, 29 July 1991, p. 28.

[4] For excerpts from the Protocol, see SIPRI, *SIPRI Yearbook 1991: World Armaments and Disarmament* (Oxford University Press: Oxford, 1991), appendix 15A.

[5] The first BCC session took place in Geneva on 22 Apr.–24 May 1991. The second session took place on 19 Aug.–18 Sep. 1991, also in Geneva. See Institute for Defense and Disarmament Studies, *Arms Control Reporter* (IDDS: Brookline, Mass.), sheet 605.B.115, 21 Mar. 1991.

[6] Nevada Operations Office News Release, NV-91-76, 14 Sep. 1991; *Arms Control Reporter*, sheet 605.B.119, 14 Sep. 1991.

[7] van der Vink, G. E. and Paine, C. E., 'The politics of verification: limiting the testing of nuclear weapons', *Science & Global Security* (forthcoming, 1992).

[8] Richards, P. G., 'Progress in seismic verification of test ban treaties', *IEEE Technology and Society Magazine*, Dec. 1990/Jan. 1991, pp. 40–52.

In late October 1991, near the end of the congressional session, House Democratic Majority Leader Richard Gephardt introduced the Nuclear Testing Moratorium Act (H.R. 3636) to impose a one-year moratorium on testing. By the beginning of the new session in early 1992, the resolution had 180 co-sponsors. In late November 1991, Senator Mark Hatfield and Senate Majority Leader George Mitchell introduced the same bill in the Senate (S. 2064). After hearings, the plan is to have it come to a vote in 1992.

In the USA, the arguments for continued testing were undermined some-what by the September nuclear reduction initiative announced by President Bush. The cancellation of several future nuclear weapon systems meant that tests are not needed for those warheads. The safety arguments were less per-suasive because the older, less safe weapons were being retired, leaving the new weapons that have more modern safety features. One expert report published during 1991 concluded that the US stockpile can, within a few years, be brought up to modern standards through the retirement of old weapons and conducting, at most, only a small number of tests.[9] Nevertheless, the safety argument is being used as an excuse to continue to test. If safety is the true goal, then a few tests can take care of any outstanding problems and there need not be any others. As a result of the dramatic steps taken in 1991 to retire a wide variety of older weapons and to end deployment of almost all of them in foreign countries, the USA has already gone a long way towards making the US stockpile safer. The question now is to examine the remaining warhead types and assess them. Those that will remain are the most modern types with the newest safety features. It seems unlikely that a convincing case can be made to spend hundreds of millions of dollars to make these modern warheads only marginally more safe than they already are.

French explosions

France carried out six nuclear explosions in 1991, concentrated in a nearly two and a half-month period from early May to mid-July. Five of these tests were held at Mururoa and one at Fangataufa. Because of pressures to reduce the military budget and the fact that there are fewer future warhead programmes, the French nuclear testing programme has been cut back. This would result in the annual number of tests being reduced from six to four.[10] Furthermore, on 8 April 1992, the French Prime Minister announced the suspension of French testing until the end of the year.[11]

[9] Kidder, R. E., *Report to Congress: Assessment of the Safety of US Nuclear Weapons and Related Nuclear Test Requirements,* Lawrence Livermore National Laboratory, 26 July 1991. See also *Toward a Comprehensive Nuclear Warhead Test Ban,* A Report of the International Foundation (Washington, DC, Jan. 1991).

[10] 'Number of annual nuclear tests to be reduced', Foreign Broadcast Information Service, *Daily Report–Soviet Union (FBIS-SOV),* FBIS-WEU-91-196, 9 Oct. 1991, p. 15; 'Reductions in funds for nuclear weapons', FBIS-WEU-91-211, 31 Oct. 1991, p. 16.

[11] *Le Monde,* 10 Apr. 1992, p. 9; *Financial Times,* 9 Apr. 1992.

Soviet developments

A significant development during the year was the formal closing of the Semi-palatinsk test site in Kazakhstan by the President of the republic, Nursultan Nazarbayev, on 29 August, in the aftermath of the failed coup against President Gorbachev.[12] This decision was the culmination of a long period of public pressure, spurred by concerns over the environmental and health hazards of testing at Semipalatinsk.[13]

On 5 October 1991, in response to President Bush's September initiative, President Gorbachev stated that 'as of today we have imposed a unilateral moratorium on nuclear tests for a period of one year. We're hoping that this example will be followed by the other nuclear powers, and in this way a road will be opened up for the earliest and complete cessation of all nuclear tests.'[14] On 15 October, Secretary of Defense Dick Cheney said that the Bush Administration would resist the Gorbachev proposal to halt nuclear testing. 'A nuclear inventory with testing is safer than a nuclear inventory without testing', he said. 'We, I think, will resist the proposition that we ought to go to a comprehensive test ban.'[15]

In a 26 October decree, President of the Russian Federation Boris Yeltsin supported Gorbachev's moratorium by prohibiting tests in Russia. He went further and stated that 'the Novaya Zemlya archipelago testing ground is no longer to be used for nuclear tests'.[16] However, on 27 February 1992 President Yeltsin issued a decree from the Kremlin that preparations for two to four underground nuclear tests will continue on Novaya Zemlya, at the renamed Central Test Site of the Russian Federation, if the existing moratorium is terminated.[17]

Some of the historical record is being filled in as accounts of the early Soviet bomb and testing programmes are published. The most notable contribution came with publication of Andrei Sakharov's memoirs.[18] Other information has come through investigating the environmental consequences of past and present testing practices.[19]

---

[12] 'President's decree closing Semipalatinsk reported', FBIS-SOV-91-169, 30 Aug. 1991, p. 126. See also 'Local meetings follow Semipalatinsk closing', FBIS-SOV-91-170, 3 Sep. 1991, p. 112; and 'Closure of Semipalatinsk testing ground hailed', FBIS-SOV-91-175, 10 Sep. 1991, pp. 24–25.

[13] Reed, S. E., 'Atomic lake', New Republic, 28 Oct. 1991, pp. 12–13.

[14] 'Gorbachev addresses nation on disarmament', FBIS-SOV-91-194, 7 Oct. 1991, p. 1. See also appendix 2A in this volume.

[15] Reuters, 'Cheney rejects call for test ban', International Herald Tribune, 16 Oct. 1991; Smith, R. J., 'Cheney open to bomb storage', Washington Post, 16 Oct. 1992, p. 30.

[16] 'Yeltsin on ending tests on nuclear weapons', FBIS-SOV-91-212, 1 Nov. 1991, p. 43.

[17] 'Decree of the Russian Federation President on the Novaya Zemlya test-site', Moscow, 27 Feb. 1992; see also 'Report on nuclear testing upsets residents', FBIS-SOV-92-055, 20 Mar. 1992, p. 4.

[18] Sakharov, A., Memoirs (Alfred A. Knopf: New York, 1990). See also Cochran, T. B. and Norris, R. S., Soviet Nuclear Warhead Production (Natural Resources Defense Council: Washington, DC, Feb. 1991); 'Novaya Zemlya 1950s H-bomb tests recalled', Joint Publication Research Service, Military History, JPRS-UMA-91-021, pp. 65–67.

[19] International Physicians for the Prevention of Nuclear War International Commission, Radioactive Heaven and Earth: The Health and Environmental Effects of Nuclear Weapons Testings In, On, and Above the Earth (Apex Press: New York, 1991); Ministry for Foreign Affairs of Finland, Group of Experts, Environmental Safety of Underground Nuclear Testing (Helsinki, 1991).

III. Renewed efforts to reach a comprehensive test ban treaty

In the latter part of the 1980s, in view of the deadlock in the consideration of a comprehensive test ban, the UN General Assembly recommended several times that advantage be taken of the amendment provision of the 1963 Partial Test Ban Treaty (PTBT) in order to convert the partial ban into a total ban.

The PTBT Amendment Conference was held in New York in January 1991. The amendment proposed by a group of countries—Indonesia, Mexico, Peru, Sri Lanka, Venezuela and Yugoslavia—consisted of an additional article and two protocols. The new article would state that the protocols constituted an integral part of the Treaty. Parties to Protocol I would undertake, in addition to their obligations under the PTBT, to prohibit, to prevent and not to carry out any nuclear weapon test explosion or any other nuclear explosion under ground or in any other environment. In addition, each party would undertake to refrain from causing, encouraging or in any way participating in carrying out any nuclear explosion anywhere in any of the environments described in Protocol I. Protocol II would deal with the verification of compliance with a comprehensive ban.[20] The proposed amendments were not submitted to a vote, but the Amendment Conference mandated its president to conduct consultations with a view to achieving progress towards a comprehensive ban and resuming the work of the Conference at an 'appropriate time'.

In July 1991, at the Conference on Disarmament in Geneva, Sweden introduced a draft CTB treaty (CTBT),[21] which was an updated version of its proposal made in 1983.[22] The three protocols annexed to the draft deal with the organization to be set up to oversee the functioning of the treaty (Protocol I), with a global monitoring system (Protocol II), and with procedures for on-site inspections and monitoring (Protocol III).

The importance of the proposal to amend the PTBT as well as of the Swedish draft CTB treaty lies in the fact that serious attempts have been made to solve the problem of verification of compliance and thereby to overcome one of the main obstacles barring the way to a CTBT. The following sections review the relevant points of the two documents.

Seismic monitoring

According to the *Swedish draft*, each party would have to undertake to cooperate in an international exchange of seismological data in order to assist all parties in the verification of the projected treaty. These international cooperative measures would include: 50–100 high-quality designated seismological stations in participating countries and in some other territories; efficient systems for the exchange of data; and an international data centre.

---

[20] Document of the Amendment Conference of the States Parties to the Treaty Banning Nuclear Weapon Tests in the Atmosphere, in Outer Space and under Water PTBT/CONF/6 and Conference on Disarmament document CD/1054.

[21] Conference on Disarmament document CD/1089.

[22] Conference on Disarmament document CD/381.

The basic equipment of seismological stations, the ways these stations would be operated, calibrated and maintained, the procedures for reporting seismological data on a regular basis, as well as the procedures for making requests for additional data and for responding to such requests, would be specified in an 'operational manual'. Technical assistance in establishing, operating and maintaining new high-quality seismological stations would be provided in those regions of the world where there are no such stations.

According to the *Amendment Protocol II*, the global seismic monitoring network should have at least the capability to detect, locate and identify a tamped underground explosion[23] of 0.5 kt or more anywhere in the world and of 0.005 kt within the limits of national jurisdiction of any state 'which has conducted more than one nuclear explosion'. This would mean that India, which has exploded a nuclear device only once (in 1974), as well as other nuclear threshold states, which possess the wherewithal to manufacture a nuclear bomb but may not yet have done so, would be subject to less stringent monitoring than the existing nuclear weapon powers.

The appendix to the *Amendment Protocol II* stipulates that 106 non-nuclear weapon states parties to the PTBT would be monitored by one current, 'off-the shelf' high-technology seismological station each. The remaining non-nuclear weapon states would require more than one station each, because of their size and the type of their geophysical terrain: Argentina-2, Australia-3, Brazil-4, Canada-4, India-2, Indonesia-2, Iran-2, Mexico-2. On the territories of the nuclear weapon states parties to the PTBT, higher-quality, state-of-the art stations would have to be installed: 38 in the Soviet Union, 20 in the United States and 1 (or perhaps 1–2 more) in the United Kingdom. (China and France have not signed the PTBT.) Thirty-three stations of the same quality would have to be placed on international territory, primarily to monitor ocean areas. Thus, approximately 219 stations would be needed; their total cost has been estimated at c. $150 million.[24] In addition to the exchange of seismic data, each party would be under the obligation to provide detailed information regarding: every nuclear explosion it has ever conducted; natural events occurring, or activities undertaken, within its territory that might give rise to ambiguity or uncertainty about compliance; large underground cavities created or discovered; vertical shafts and horizontal tunnels drilled in excess of certain agreed dimensions; and chemical explosions exceeding a specified yield. The accuracy of these national data would be subject to corroboration.

The drafters of the *Amendment Protocol II* recognized the value of localized monitoring from obtaining data supplementary to those provided by the global seismic monitoring system. Such additional monitoring would be temporary and would serve to clarify ambiguous situations. The equipment to be utilized

[23] An underground explosion is tamped when it is detonated in close proximity to the surrounding rock.

[24] By comparison, the cost of a single nuclear weapon test explosion, as estimated by the drafters of Protocol II to the PTBT, is US $30–100 million. According to the *Defense Monitor* (vol. 20, no. 3, 1991), tests that require the use of vertical shafts, such as weapon-design and weapon-reliability tests, are less expensive than weapon-effects tests which involve the use of horizontal tunnels and are more complicated.

could be similar to that operated by the global network. Data from the temporary stations would be duplicated on the site and a copy provided to the host country.

Non-seismic monitoring

Under the *Swedish draft*, each party operating an unclassified satellite system providing images with a coverage and resolution relevant to the CTBT would undertake to make the image data available on terms to be agreed. A satellite image-processing centre would store such data and process them at the request of any party.

Moreover, Sweden proposed that international surveillance of radionuclides in the atmosphere be established. A system for such surveillance, designed in the same way as the global seismic monitoring system, would consist of: some 50–100 designated sampling stations properly distributed around the world; national or regional laboratories; a mechanism to exchange the measurements of the samples; and an international data centre. The centre would process the reported measurements in accordance with the procedures laid down in a special operational manual. The results would be rapidly distributed to all participants.[25]

On-site inspection

The *Amendment Protocol II* envisages the possibility of on-site inspection at the request of a party, but the secretariat of the organization to be set up in accordance with this Protocol could decide not to undertake the requested inspection and report its negative decision to all parties. It could also undertake an inspection at its own initiative whenever data from the global permanent monitoring network or the temporary localized monitoring indicated the occurrence of an ambiguous event and suggested that the energy released was over 1 kt. The need for inspection would be rated higher if the event occurred on the territory of a state 'that has conducted more than one nuclear explosion' (that is, on the territory of the generally recognized nuclear weapon powers). If the secretariat decided to carry out an on-site inspection, the host state might appeal the decision to the assembly of the parties. The inspection could then proceed while the assembly was considering the matter; but if the assembly concluded by a two-thirds vote that on-site inspection was not warranted, the inspection would have to be promptly abandoned.

The host state should transport the inspectors to the location of the inspection within 24 hours of their arrival at the point of entry, provide them with immediate and uninhibited access to the entire inspection area, and give them all the necessary logistic support. It may designate personnel to accompany the inspectors during the performance of their duties. Before leaving the inspection area, the inspection team would be under the obligation to complete

[25] Conference on Disarmament documents CD/403 and CD/1089.

a written report summarizing its activities and the collected data. A copy of the report would be provided to the host state which might append to it a commentary.

According to the *Swedish draft*, on-site inspection could be carried out either upon invitation by a party wishing to facilitate the identification of an event observed on its own territory, or upon request by a party wishing to investigate an event observed on the territory of another party. In the latter case, the requesting state would have to explain the reasons for its request, including the available evidence. The requested state would be under the obligation to comply with the request. The inspection team would then begin its duties in the specified area not later than seven days after receipt of a request for inspection. An inspection might last no more than seven days following the arrival of the inspection personnel at the point of entry in the territory of the state to be inspected. Inspectors much be selected on the basis of their competence, and the inspection team must not include a national of the party requesting the inspection. Detailed rules and procedures for on-site inspection would be laid down in an operational manual.

The *Swedish draft* also provides for on-the-spot monitoring of any non-nuclear explosion having a yield in excess of 100 tons TNT, or of a group of such explosions with an aggregate yield exceeding the same limit. The monitoring personnel would be allowed to take pictures and to make measurements of radioactivity in the vicinity of the explosion. It should be entitled to the same privileges and immunities as the personnel conducting on-site investigations of suspicious events. Non-nuclear explosions with a yield of 10–100 tons TNT would be subject only to notification to be given within seven days after the explosion.

Institutions

The *Amendment Protocol II* envisages the establishment of an organization to assist in the verification of compliance with the CTBT. The principal organs of the organization would be the assembly of the parties and the secretariat.

The assembly would meet at least once a year and whenever so requested by the secretary-general or by one-tenth of its membership. It would adopt the budget of the organization and establish its policies and practices, elect the secretary-general and create a technical committee. All decisions of the assembly would be taken by a majority of those voting, unless the assembly adopted a different standard by a majority of two-thirds.

The technical committee, to which each member of the assembly would have the right to designate a representative, would meet at least four times a year to review the technical operations of the secretariat, assess the secretariat's reports and make recommendations regarding possible revisions of the verification measures with a view to enhancing their effectiveness or reducing their cost. The committee would be organized in sub-committees, each of which would be responsible for one branch of the verification technology. The committee's recommendations would be submitted to the assembly which might approve, modify or reject them.

The secretariat would compile and maintain the data gathered by the organization, and would submit an annual report to the assembly as well as periodic reports to the technical committee. It would set up sections responsible for the implementation of verification measures pertinent to the prohibition of nuclear explosions in various environments—in the atmosphere, in outer space, under water and under ground. Each section would develop working descriptions of the phenomena which are observable by global monitoring networks, localized monitoring, on-site inspections or other means and which are associated with nuclear explosions in each of the above specified environments, as well as working descriptions or the phenomena which are associated with natural and legitimate events or activities that might create ambiguity or uncertainty regarding treaty compliance. Each party would designate a competent national body to serve as liaison with the secretariat. The costs of the international organization would be borne by the parties, and the ratio of their contributions would be the same as that established by the annual assessment of UN dues, unless the assembly adopted a different schedule by a majority of two-thirds.

The *Swedish draft* also proposes the establishment of an organization responsible for ensuring the implementation of the CTBT. Following the example set by the draft Chemical Weapons Convention under discussion, the organization would consist of a conference of the parties, an executive council and a technical secretariat.

The conference—the principal organ of the organization—would meet once a year, and its decisions would be taken by a simple majority on questions of procedure and by consensus on matters of substance. Should consensus prove impossible to achieve, decisions of the conference would be taken by a two-thirds majority of those present and voting.

The executive council would be composed of 25 parties elected by the conference for a period of two years in accordance with the principle of equitable political and geographical representation. Its task would be to facilitate consultations among the parties and to help resolve issues related to the treaty, in particular those related to verification. The council would meet annually, or more often if necessary, and its decisions (on questions to be specified) would be taken by a simple majority. An advisory board of international experts would provide scientific expertise on verification measures, and would assist the executive council in assessing the value of new methods which may be suggested for verification of compliance.

The technical secretariat would be headed by a director-general appointed by the executive council for a four-year term. It would co-ordinate the arrangements for the exchange of data as well as the operations of the global seismological network and the network for global surveillance of radio-nuclides in the atmosphere; assist parties in using satellite observations to clarify dubious events, and compile, analyse and report on hydro-acoustic signals in the ocean and other data that may facilitate verification. It would also compile any supplementary information that a party may provide to help interpret a suspicious event which had occurred on its own territory. Such information could include observations from sensitive in-country seismological networks. Moreover, to ascertain the nature of a seismic event, the technical secretariat could conduct on-site inspections on invitation or on request. In addition, it would monitor non-nuclear explosions of an agreed size, and its co-operation with the national authorities of the parties is envisaged to resolve the uncertainties that may arise.

Although the proposed institutional arrangements for a multilateral CTB are, broadly speaking, patterned after existing international institutions, sharp controversies may be expected. One of them regards the composition of the central management authority, such as the executive council. Each country would, quite naturally, defend those formulas which might make its participation in such an authority possible, and there would certainly be opposition to the idea—favoured by some—of establishing two classes of membership—permanent and non-permanent. Another controversy may develop over the voting procedures in the treaty organization. The choice is between decisions taken by a majority—simple or qualified—and decisions taken unanimously or by consensus. The latter procedure seems desirable to the extent that it may guarantee general observance of the adopted resolutions, but its rigid application would be tantamount to introducing the right of veto which could paralyse the operation of the organization.

Conclusion

As can be seen from the above review, the verification schemes comprised in the Amendment Protocol II to the PTBT and the Swedish draft CTBT are far from identical. They nevertheless coincide on many points. Despite some shortcomings, both documents provide an excellent basis for negotiating a CTBT.

Appendix 4A. Nuclear explosions, 1945–91

RAGNHILD FERM

Table 4A.1. Registered nuclear explosions in 1991

Date	Origin time (GMT)	Latitude (deg)		Longitude (deg)		Region	Body wave magnitude[a]
USA							
8 Mar.	210245.0	37.104	N	116.074	W	Nevada	4.7
4 Apr.	190000.0	37.296	N	116.313	W	Nevada	5.6
16 Apr.	153000.0	37.245	N	116.442	W	Nevada	5.5
15 Aug.	160000.0	37.087	N	116.002	W	Nevada	..
14 Sep.	190008.0	37.	N	116.	W	Nevada	5.8
19 Sep.	163000.0	37.	N	116.	W	Nevada	..
18 Oct.	191200.0	37.063	N	116.045	W	Nevada	5.4
UK							
26 Nov.	183504.0	37.7	N	116.3	W	Nevada	4.6
France							
7 May	170000.0	21.	S	138.	W	Mururoa	4.2
18 May	171458.5	21.832	S	139.014	W	Mururoa	5.2
29 May	185958.2	22.256	S	138.794	W	Fangataufa	5.9
14 June	175958.2	21.865	S	139.065	W	Mururoa	5.4
5 July	180000.0	21.	S	138.	W	Mururoa	3.8
15 July	180958.5	21.833	S	138.995	W	Mururoa	5.5

[a] Body wave magnitude (m_b) indicates the size of the event. To be able to give a reasonably correct estimate of yield it is necessary to have detailed information, for example on the geological conditions of the area where the test is conducted. Therefore, to give the m_b figure is an unambiguous way of listing the size of an explosion. m_b data for the US and British tests were provided by the Hagfors Observatory of the Swedish National Defence Research Institute (FOA) and data for the French tests by the New Zealand Department of Scientific and Industrial Research (DSIR), Geology and Geophysics, Wellington.

Table 4A.2. Estimated number of nuclear explosions 16 July 1945–5 August 1963 (the signing of the Partial Test Ban Treaty)

a = atmospheric; u = underground

Year	USA a	USA u	USSR a	USSR u	UK a	UK u	France a	France u	Total
1945	3	0							**3**
1946	2[a]	0							**2**
1947	0	0							**0**
1948	3	0							**3**
1949	0	0	1	0					**1**
1950	0	0	0	0					**0**
1951	15	1	2	0					**18**
1952	10	0	0	0	1	0			**11**
1953	11	0	4	0	2	0			**17**
1954	6	0	7	0	0	0			**13**
1955	17[a]	1	5[a]	0	0	0			**23**
1956	18	0	9	0	6	0			**33**
1957	27	5	15[a]	0	7	0			**54**
1958	62[b]	15	29	0	5	0			**111**
1949–58, exact years not available			18						**18**
1959	0	0	0	0	0	0			**0[d]**
1960	0	0	0	0	0	0	3	0	**3[d]**
1961	0	10	50[a]	1[c]	0	0	1	1	**63[d]**
1962	39[a]	57	43	1[c]	0	2	0	1	**143**
1 Jan.– 5 Aug. 1963	4	25	0	0	0	0	0	2	**31**
Total	**217**	**114**	**183[e] (214)[f]**	**2[c]**	**21**	**2**	**4**	**4**	**547 (576)[f]**

[a] One of these tests was carried out under water.

[b] Two of these tests were carried out under water.

[c] New Soviet information released in Sep. 1990 does not confirm whether these were underground or atmospheric tests.

[d] The UK, the USA and the USSR observed a moratorium on testing, Nov. 1958–Sep. 1961.

[e] The total figure for Soviet atmospheric tests includes the 18 additional tests conducted in the period 1949–58, for which exact years are not available.

[f] The totals in brackets include the (probably atmospheric) explosions revealed by Soviet authorities in Sep. 1990, the exact years for which are not announced. See *SIPRI Yearbook 1991*, p. 41.

Table 4A.3. Estimated number of nuclear explosions 6 August 1963–31 December 1991

a = atmospheric; u = underground

Year	USA[a] a	USA[a] u	USSR a	USSR u	UK[a] a	UK[a] u	France a	France u	China a	China u	India a	India u	Total
6 Aug.–31 Dec. 1963	0	15	0	0	0	0	0	1					**16**
1964	0	38	0	6	0	1	0	3	1	0			**49**
1965	0	36	0	10	0	1	0	4	1	0			**52**
1966	0	43	0	15	0	0	6	1	3	0			**68**
1967	0	34	0	17	0	0	3	0	2	0			**56**
1968	0	45[b]	0	15	0	0	5	0	1	0			**66**
1969	0	38	0	16	0	0	0	0	1	1			**56**

Year	USA[a] a	USA[a] u	USSR a	USSR u	UK[a] a	UK[a] u	France a	France u	China a	China u	India a	India u	Total
1970	0	35	0	17	0	0	8	0	1	0			61
1971	0	17	0	19	0	0	6	0	1	0			43
1972	0	18	0	22	0	0	3	0	2	0			45
1973	0	16[c]	0	14	0	0	5	0	1	0			36
1974	0	14	0	18	0	1	8	0	1	0	0	1	43
1975	0	20	0	15	0	0	0	2	0	1	0	0	38
1976	0	18	0	17	0	1	0	4	3	1	0	0	44
1977	0	19	0	18	0	0	0	8[d]	1	0	0	0	46
1978	0	17	0	27	0	2	0	8	2	1	0	0	57
1979	0	15	0	29	0	1	0	9	1	0	0	0	55
1980	0	14	0	21	0	3	0	13	1	0	0	0	52
1981	0	16	0	22	0	1	0	12	0	0	0	0	51
1982	0	18	0	32	0	1	0	6	0	1	0	0	58
1983	0	17	0	27	0	1	0	9	0	2	0	0	56
1984	0	17	0	29	0	2	0	8	0	2	0	0	58
1985	0	17	0	9[e]	0	1	0	8	0	0	0	0	35
1986	0	14	0	0[e]	0	1	0	8	0	0	0	0	23
1987	0	14	0	23	0	1	0	8	0	1	0	0	47
1988	0	14	0	17	0	0	0	8	0	1	0	0	40
1989	0	11	0	7	0	1	0	8	0	0	0	0	27
1990	0	8	0	1	0	1	0	6	0	2	0	0	18
1991	0	7	0	0	0	1	0	6	0	0	0	0	14
Total	0	605	0	463 (500)[f]	0	21	44	140	23	13	0	1	1 310 (1 347)[f]

[a] See note a, table 4A.4.
[b] Five devices used simultaneously in the same test are counted here as one explosion.
[c] Three devices used simultaneously in the same test are counted here as one explosion.
[d] Two of these tests may have been conducted in 1975 or 1976.
[e] The USSR observed a unilateral moratorium on testing, Aug. 1985–Feb. 1987.
[f] See note f, table 4A.2.

Table 4A.4. Estimated number of nuclear explosions 16 July 1945–31 Dec. 1991

USA[a]	USSR[b]	UK[a]	France	China	India	Total
936	648 (715)	44	192	36	1	1 857 (1 923)[b]

[a] All British tests from 1962 have been conducted jointly with the United States at the Nevada Test Site. Therefore, the number of US tests is actually higher than indicated here.
[b] The figures in brackets include additional tests announced by the Soviet authorities in Sep. 1990 for the period 1949–90. See *SIPRI Yearbook 1991*, p. 41.

Sources for tables 4A.1–4A.4

Swedish National Defence Research Institute (FOA), various estimates; Norris, R. S., Cochran, T. B. and Arkin, W. M., 'Known US nuclear tests July 1945 to 31 December 1988', *Nuclear Weapons Databook*, Working Paper no. 86–2 (Rev. 2C) (Natural Resources Defense Council: Washington, DC, Jan. 1989); Reports from the Australian Seismological Centre, Bureau of Mineral Resources, Geology and Geophysics, Canberra; New Zealand Department of Scientific and Industrial Research (DSIR), Geology and Geophysics, Wellington; Cochran, T. B., Arkin, W. M., Norris, R. S. and Sands, J. I., *Nuclear Weapons Databook, Vol. IV, Soviet Nuclear Weapons* (Harper & Row: New York, 1989), chapter 10; Burrows, A. S., et al., 'French nuclear testing, 1960–88', *Nuclear Weapons Databook*, Working Paper no. 89–1 (NRDC: Washington, DC, Feb. 1989); 'Known Chinese nuclear tests, 1964–1988', *Bulletin of the Atomic Scientists*, vol. 45, no. 8 (Oct. 1989), p. 48, see also vol. 45, no. 9 (Nov. 1989), p. 52; and various estimates.

5. Military use of outer space

JOHN PIKE, SARAH LANG and ERIC STAMBLER

I. Introduction

The events of 1991 dictate that the history of military space activities must now be divided into two epochs. The performance of US military space systems in the war with Iraq, the renewed US commitment to the Strategic Defense Initiative (SDI), and the collapse of the Soviet space programme, all mark the beginning of a fundamentally new era of military space operations.[1]

While it is too soon to fully appreciate the significance of the contribution of US military space systems to the outcome of Operation Desert Storm, it is clear that the disparity in military space capabilities was one of the distinguishing features of that conflict. Whatever the reality, Desert Storm will be regarded as the first 'space war', since it was the first occasion on which the full range of modern military space assets was applied to a terrestrial conflict. And it is equally clear that, while the facts may remain obscure for some time to come, proponents of military space systems will point to the outcome of Desert Storm as a sign of the decisive potential of military space systems.

Taking inspiration from the apparent success of Patriot interceptor missiles against Scud missiles during Desert Storm, and capitalizing on the political disintegration of the USSR, proponents of SDI succeeded in reversing the political fortunes of the programme in 1991. Whereas 1990 had witnessed a major reduction in funding for SDI, the budget approved by Congress in 1991 more than reversed the cutbacks of the prior years. Furthermore, in a major step, the Congress endorsed the eventual deployment of a large ground-based system that would far exceed the limits imposed by the 1972 Anti-Ballistic Missile (ABM) Treaty. The political transformation of the former USSR also led to a major evolution in attitudes towards anti-missile systems.

The least expected but probably most momentous development of 1991 was the political disintegration of the USSR in the wake of the unsuccessful *coup* in August. The resulting devolution of political power from Moscow to the republics has major implications for the future of the Soviet space programme. Since the time of Sputnik and Major Yury Gagarin, the space effort has been the most visible expression of the Soviet assertion of superpower status. Now that this pretence of superpower has been abandoned, a re-evaluation of this effort is inevitable. While the political future of the former USSR remains unclear, a major reduction in the scope and pace of space activities is inevitable.

[1] Many aspects of the treatment of Soviet military space activities are based on discussions with Phillip Clarke. The data in appendix 5A on Soviet satellite launches are based in part on press reports derived from the work of Geoffrey Perry and Saunders Kramer. Useful discussions with Paul Stares and Jeffrey Richelson as well as the support and encouragement of the US Center for Research and Study of Strategy and Technology, in preparation of the analysis of Desert Storm, are gratefully acknowledged.

II. The use of US military space systems in the Persian Gulf War

From the perspective of the 21st century, the use of US military space systems in the Persian Gulf War may be seen as marking a major watershed in the history of military technology and military tactics.

An alternative view would contend that military space systems were of marginal relevance to the outcome of the war. Perhaps Desert Storm was not so much a case of a Coalition victory through superior technology as an Iraqi loss due to political and military incompetence, both strategic and tactical. The relative ineffectiveness of the campaign against Scud launchers was a manifestation of the limited utility of space systems. In fact, by the commencement of the ground campaign, space systems had largely become irrelevant.

It is of course easier to identify the technological input of military space systems in the war than it is to identify the military output resulting from their application, particularly since in most cases there were also non-space systems that provided similar or complementary types of input. However, even though it may be difficult to draw hard and fast lessons about space contribution to terrestrial operations in this conflict, the war underscored the decisive significance of military space systems. From this perspective, the question is not what military space systems accomplished in Desert Storm, but rather what Desert Storm suggested could be accomplished by such systems in future conflicts.

The space segment

The USA entered the conflict with an unprecedented array of operational satellites in orbit (see appendix 5A). These were of higher quality and more numerous than at any time in the past.[2] The range of space systems available to support the US operations Desert Shield and Desert Storm raises an interesting question of timing. If the war had taken place in the mid-1980s, it is unlikely that the contribution of military space systems would have been nearly so great. Some reports notwithstanding, none of the US launches during the operations was in response to the crisis.[3] All had been planned long in advance.

The imaging intelligence order of battle in space included an unusually large number of satellites, including one Lacrosse imaging radar satellite,[4] three of the older KH-11 Kennan digital imaging satellites and three newer Advanced Keyhole photographic reconnaissance satellites (sometimes referred to as the KH-12). This total of seven imaging satellites is the largest number that the USA has ever had in space at one time, in stark contrast to the single KH-11 in orbit as recently as 1986, shortly after the Challenger accident. During the late 1970s and early 1980s the USA normally had two KH-11s and

[2] Kiernan, V., 'War tests satellites prowess', *Space News*, 21 Jan. 1991, pp. 1, 36.

[3] Furnis, T., 'Satellites launched for Desert Shield', *Flight International*, 21 Nov. 1990, p. 11.

[4] Covault, C., 'Atlantis radar satellite payload opens new reconnaissance era', *Aviation Week & Space Technology*, 12 Dec. 1988, pp. 26–28.

one KH-9 Hexagon photographic reconnaissance satellite in orbit, the latter providing film-return during about six months of the year.[5]

The Lacrosse for the first time provided an all-weather capability. The Advanced Keyhole satellites operate in much higher orbits than the older KH-11s, and as a result provide two useful passes per day over a target area, rather than the single pass customary with the KH-11. Together, these satellites provided an average of 12 usable passes over the theatre of operations per day, at average intervals of about two hours. In some cases two satellites were in the sky simultaneously, and at no point did more than five hours elapse without one satellite passing over the theatre. With each satellite producing images at the rate of one every five seconds, hundreds of images were produced daily.

In addition the USA fielded a very robust electronic and signals intelligence order of battle. At least one geostationary Magnum signals intelligence satellite was available for intercepting low-power broadcasts. At least a dozen of the White Cloud Naval Ocean Surveillance Satellites also conducted radio location for higher power transmitters,[6] along with a trio of sub-satellites that were launched with the Advanced Keyhole satellite in June 1990. Altogether there were perhaps 15 or 20 signals intelligence satellites in operation.

At least two Defense Meteorological Support Program (DMSP) weather satellites were operational at the outset of Desert Shield, with a third launched in early January 1991.[7] In addition, 15 or 16 Navstar Global Positioning System (GPS) satellites were in operation during the latter stages of the war,[8] as well as two Fleet Satellite Communications (FLTSATCOM)[9] and at least two Defense Satellite Communications System (DSCS) III communication satellites.[10]. The US Space Command was able to shift the orbit of a DSCS satellite normally over the Pacific Ocean to an orbit over the Indian Ocean to meet the demand for communications.[11] The US military also used images acquired from civilian French SPOT and US Landsat satellites for updating mapping products for the forces in the theatre.[12]

The user segment

The most visible aspect of the use of military space systems in the Persian Gulf War was the proliferation of user equipment to lower-echelon forces.[13] Prior to the 1980s, the primary focus for analysis of overhead imagery as it came down from the satellite was the National Photographic Interpretation

[5] Richelson, J., 'The spies in space', *Air & Space*, Dec. 1991/Jan. 1992, pp. 75–80.
[6] Richelson, J., *The U.S. Intelligence Community* (Ballinger: Cambridge, Mass., 1985), pp. 140–43.
[7] Kiernan, V., 'DMSP satellite launched to aid troops in Middle East', *Space News*, 10 Dec. 1990, p. 6.
[8] 'Sluggers pinch hit for Army GPS', *Military Space*, 24 Sep. 1990, pp. 1, 8.
[9] 'Last FLTSATCOM satellite planned for launch Sep. 22', *Aerospace Daily*, 15 Sep. 1989, p. 466.
[10] 'Satcom gears up for Desert Shield', *Military Space*, 24 Sep. 1990, pp. 3–5.
[11] Kiernan, V., 'War shows military need for space doctrine', *Space News*, 15–21 Apr. 1991, p. 4.
[12] Kiernan, V., 'Satellite data boosts map quality for US troops', *Space News*, 15 Oct. 1990, pp. 3, 28.
[13] Kiernan, V., 'Satellites crucial in countering Iraq', *Space News*, 13 Aug. 1990, pp. 1, 20.

Center,[14] but over the past decade the Tactical Exploitation of National Capabilities Program (TENCAP) has greatly extended the dissemination of satellite imagery.[15] During the seven months of the Gulf crisis most of the Tactical Fighter Wings in the theatre used constant-source terminals to access satellite imagery as soon as it was available. Army Corps commanders also had terminals to receive imagery,[16] Marine Corps commanders at a similar echelon also received such pictures, and each of the aircraft-carriers had a Fleet Imagery Support Terminal (FIST) for receiving satellite pictures.[17]

Another aspect of the user segment was the widespread use of commercial standard equipment. A complete list of satellite terminals used by ground forces would probably show that the bulk were not military, but rather Inmarsat sky phones.[18] An estimated 30 per cent of the Navy's communications traffic went over commercial systems.[19] Similarly, much of the mapping data were derived from commercially operated Landsat and SPOT satellites. In the case of weather satellite support, while two to three DMSP satellites were used,[20] much of the ground segment data were also commercially procured.[21]

Operational applications and limitations

Military space systems were involved in every major aspect of the war. Every component of the effort to deal with Iraqi Scud missile attacks involved the use of one or more satellite systems. Imaging intelligence satellites searched for the transporter erector launchers (TELs), and Defense Support Program (DSP) early-warning satellites were used to detect the missile plumes after launch. All information was relayed back to processing centres in the USA using military communication satellites, and then relayed back to the theatre. Weather satellites were used to try to determine in advance when the Iraqi mobile launcher crews might try to take advantage of cloud cover.[22] Signals intelligence satellites were used to pick up on the meteorological radars the Iraqis utilized to get weather information prior to their launch.

However, despite the generally positive contributions of satellites to terrestrial operations, military space systems demonstrated a variety of failings and shortcomings during the war. Photographic reconnaissance satellite systems were impeded by cloud cover. This was a major problem in the first week of the air campaign, which began with several days of rainy and cloudy weather

[14] Covault, C., 'Recon satellites lead allied intelligence effort', *Aviation Week & Space Technology*, 4 Feb. 1991, pp. 25–26.

[15] Chenard, S., 'Lessons of the first space war', *Interavia Space Markets*, no. 4 (1991), pp. 4–13.

[16] Graves, H., 'Army directions in space', *EASCON 85*, Oct. 1985, pp. 341–44.

[17] US Navy, *FY 1988/89 RDT&E Program Element Descriptive Summaries* (US Department of Defense: Washington, DC, 1988), p. 910.

[18] Klass, P., 'Inmarsat decision pushes GPS to forefront of civ nav-sat field', *Aviation Week & Space Technology*, 14 Jan. 1991, pp. 34–35.

[19] 'Naval space', *Military Space*, 25 Mar. 1991, p. 5.

[20] Kiernan, V., 'DMSP satellite launched to aid troops in Middle East', *Space News*, 10 Dec. 1990, p. 6.

[21] 'Space support', *Military Space*, 24 Sep. 1990, p. 8.

[22] Broad, W., 'Iraqis using clouds to cover Scud firings, meteorologists say', *New York Times*, 25 Jan. 1991, p. A10.

that made it difficult to go after mobile Scud launchers, and extremely difficult to do bomb damage assessment.[23] Cloud cover made the difference between having a total of seven usable imaging satellites providing new pictures on an average of every two hours, and having to rely on a single imaging intelligence satellite, the Lacrosse, which was providing new pictures every 12 hours. The Lacrosse has a significantly lower resolution than the optical satellites, and thus provides less effective damage assessment. In addition, there were difficulties in managing the flow of imagery to combat commanders, with an overload of information 'creating confusion and duplication and consuming scarce lift capability'.[24]

Alternative systems

While some space systems provided services that were not readily duplicated, it is difficult to assess the relative value of satellite *contra* aircraft intelligence collection. Satellite imaging data were supplemented by radar data provided by the Joint Surveillance Target Attack Radar System (JSTARS) and TR-1 surveillance aircraft.[25]

Imaging satellite systems provide intermittent coverage, compared to the continuous coverage possible with airborne platforms. A TR-1 standing back 75 kilometres from the Saudi border was able to look about 150 km into Iraq,[26] giving coverage of the southern two-thirds of the western mobile Scud deployment area, but not of the northern one-third of that area near Syria.[27] A single JSTARS aircraft standing back 75 km from the border was able to survey the entire battle area. During the period of the ground operations, the entire battle field was under continuous surveillance by JSTARS.[28]

This is in sharp contrast to the narrow field of view of imaging intelligence satellites, which have aptly been compared to looking at the world through a soda straw. Depending on whether the satellite is flying directly overhead or looking 1000 km off to the east or west, normally the image from the satellites is on the order of 5–10 km on a side. Encompassing over 30 000 square km, including Kuwait and the surrounding area, it would require 1000–1500 separate images to completely map the immediate theatre of operations. Even

---

[23] Moore, M., 'Cloud and fog over Gulf region knock allied raids off stride', *Washington Post*, 22 Jan. 1991, p. 1.

[24] 'War problems prompt "baseline review" of intelligence imagery', *Aerospace Daily*, 2 Dec. 1991, p. 341.

[25] '"Filtering" helped top military leaders get proper intelligence information', *Aviation Week & Space Technology*, 22 Apr. 1991, pp. 84–85.

[26] 'TR-1 reconnaissance aircraft', *C3I Handbook 1986* (EW Communications: Palo Alto, Calif., 1986), p. 111.

[27] 'Elusive Scuds highlight hardware requirement', *Defense Daily*, 25 Jan. 1991, pp. 121–23. This underscored the reason that the USA requested access to Syrian air space to fly TR-1s in order to allow complete coverage of the Scud deployment area. See Tyler, P., 'Pentagon eyes Syrian airspace but Bush is wary', *New York Times*, 8 Feb. 1991.

[28] Broadbent, S., 'Joint-STARS: force multiplier for Europe', *Jane's Defence Weekly*, 18 Apr. 1987, pp. 729–32. Oddly, it was reported that the US Air Force only managed to get 44 sorties out of the two airplanes over a period of 41 days. This was clearly not the sort of continuous surveillance of the Kuwait theatre of operations that was desired. See 'JSTARS has flown 44 missions in 41 days', *Defense Daily*, 25 Feb. 1991, p. 286.

assuming good weather, this would require two to three days. JSTARS, on the other hand, could refresh the moving target picture of the battlefield every minute or so. Of course the JSTARS moving target indicator could only pick up moving targets and could not perform damage assessment.

In providing Scud missile attack warning, the DSP satellites were supplemented by Airborne Warning and Control System (AWACS) aircraft,[29] and satellite signal intelligence by RC-135 Rivet Joint and U-2R aircraft.

Iraqi capabilities

There was a grotesque disparity between US and Iraqi intelligence collection capabilities. For imaging intelligence the USA had satellites, as well as a wide range of reconnaissance aircraft.[30] In contrast, the only long-range reconnaissance platforms available to Iraq were Soviet-manufactured MiG-25R aircraft, which do not seem to have been used effectively, if at all.[31] Thus, during the ground campaign, Iraqi forces were unable to view the entire theatre of operations[32] and remained unaware of the direction of attack of Coalition forces.[33] The USA could see where the Iraqi troops were and where they were moving.

Similar disparities could be noted in other areas as well. At the same time it is important to understand that there were very different requirements. For instance, US reconnaissance satellites provided data permitting very precise targeting and the ability to plan in advance the exact targets of precision-guided munitions. Iraq did not require this type of targeting information.

Conclusion

Given these considerations, it is difficult to draw a clear picture of the significance of military space systems for the outcome of the conflict. However, US military space commanders have been quick to express their conclusions. According to Lieutenant-General Thomas Moorman, Commander of Air Force Space Command, 'Desert Storm will be an extraordinary learning experience for us . . . Not only is it a watershed, but it is a glimpse into the future . . . For the first time, we have space beginning to become fully integrated into the prosecution of hostilities'.[34] Air Force Chief of Staff Merrill McPeak echoed the view that Desert Storm was the 'first space war', and further indicated the importance of space assets to the military by stating that military space budgets will increase even as the rest of the military budget is reduced. 'Space is a growth business as far as the Air Force is concerned, and it will grow even during this time of decline in many other dimensions of our activity.'[35]

[29] Cody, E., 'Command of the skies eases high-tech hunt for Scud launchers', *Washington Post*, 25 Dec. 1990, p. A44.
[30] Note 25.
[31] Banks, T., 'Techint v. humint: the unseen war', *Jane's Defence Weekly*, 16 Feb. 1991, p. 221.
[32] 'Combat pool report: tank feint deceived Iraqi Army', *Washington Post*, 27 Feb. 1991, p. A28.
[33] Gellman, B., 'Deceptions gave allies fast victory', *Washington Post*, 28 Feb. 1991, p. A1, A30.
[34] 'The JDW interview', *Jane's Defence Weekly*, 9 Feb. 1991, p. 200.
[35] Dudney, R. S., 'The force forms up', *Air Force Magazine*, Feb. 1992, p. 23.

III. Developments in US ballistic missile defence

The Persian Gulf War marked a watershed both in the perception of the threat posed by ballistic missiles and in the perception of the effectiveness of weapons systems designed to counter this threat. President Bush, in his State of the Union address on 29 January 1991, stated that: 'Now, with remarkable technological advances like the Patriot missile, we can defend against ballistic missile attacks aimed at innocent civilians. Looking forward, I have directed that the SDI programme be refocused on providing protection from limited strikes, whatever their source. Let us pursue an SDI programme that can deal with any future threat to the USA, to our forces overseas and to our friends and allies'.[36] Defense Secretary Richard Cheney claimed that:

As Iraq has shown, modern technology can make a third-rate power a first-class military threat. By the year 2000, more than two dozen developing nations will have ballistic missiles . . . Iraq is only one of many countries that now have or will soon acquire these kinds of sophisticated capabilities. The trend is also towards missiles with increased new long ranges. Combined with chemical, biological and nuclear weapons these missile can be vehicles of terror, aggression and intimidation. Who wants to be foolish enough to stake our nation's future on the belief that these weapons will never be used? . . . Because of our global interests, a Third World missile strike can be a danger even when it doesn't reach our shores. Friends, allies, trading partners and strategic resources can all be in range of ballistic missile threats.[37]

The case for the deployment of ABM systems rests on several controversial propositions: that there is a growing threat posed by the proliferation to the Third World of theatre and long-range missiles, as well as the risk of accidental, inadvertent or unauthorized launches from the republics of the former USSR; that these threats cannot be deterred by the threat of retaliation; and that anti-missile weapons will provide an effective response.

The first real world test of anti-missile technology took place in the Persian Gulf War, where the Patriot—which was developed outside of the SDI R&D effort—was used against a conventionally armed missile using 1950s technology. According to the Pentagon, the US Army shot 158 Patriots at 47 Scuds and claimed to have intercepted 45 of them. However, in the wake of the war, subsequent analysis has suggested that, at least over Israel, the Patriot was relatively ineffective. According to a report in the Israeli newspaper *Ha'aretz*, '[t]he tally of the Patriot's performance during the Gulf War shows that the Patriot batteries in Israel did not destroy even one single Scud warhead.'[38]

---

[36] 'Text of President Bush's State of the Union message to the nation', *New York Times*, 30 Jan. 1991, p. A12.

[37] Cheney, R., 'News briefing on FY92 defense budget', 4 Feb. 1991.

[38] Pedatzur, R., ['Failed at time of test: the US Administration and the Patriot's manufacturer presented a deceptive picture of the performance of the Patriot during the war'], *Ha'aretz*, 24 Oct. 1991, p. B1 (in Hebrew).

The Nunn–Warner missile defence proposal

Congressional response to early reports of the success of the Patriot missile was not long in coming. In early March 1991 Republican Senator John Warner offered legislation to immediately abandon the 1972 ABM Treaty and proceed with testing and deployment of both ground-based and space-based systems as part of the Global Protection Against Limited Strikes (GPALS) programme, initiated in late 1990.[39] However, this initial frontal assault was rejected by the Senate.[40]

A compromise approach, the Missile Defense Act of 1991, was proposed in July by Senator Warner and Democratic Senator Sam Nunn, Chairman of the Senate Armed Services Committee. The main feature of this is the accelerated deployment of the ground-based phases of GPALS, moving the proposed target year for initial operational capability forward from 1999 to 1996. Initial deployment of ground-based and exoatmospheric–endoatmospheric interceptors (GBI and E^2I) would be at the old ABM site at Grand Forks, North Dakota, with deployment at other sites to follow. The system is intended as the initial phase of territorial defence of the continental USA, capable of providing an effective defence of the USA against limited ballistic missile attack.

The Nunn–Warner proposal urges the President to negotiate modifications to the ABM Treaty to allow the deployment of these additional ground-based sites. The negotiations would also aim at allowing increased use of space-based sensors, development of other advanced technologies (presumably Brilliant Pebbles[41]), and clarifying the distinction between strategic and tactical anti-missile systems. This measure was adopted after an extensive debate before the full Senate,[42] and was subsequently agreed to by the House.[43]

The $4.15 billion budget approved for fiscal year (FY) 1992 was very close to the $4.6 billion sought by Nunn and Warner, and represents a substantial increase from the $2.9 billion of the previous fiscal year. It would continue the present development and testing schedule of Brilliant Pebbles, the space-based component of SDI, while advancing the deployment of ground-based defences by several years. The level of funding stated in the legislation for Brilliant Pebbles would remain at approximately the same level as in the previous year and would provide adequate funding to remain within its present schedule of research and testing. The legislation also provides funding for advanced

[39] Dewar, H., 'Warner presses for new ABM effort', *Washington Post,* 14 Mar. 1991, p. A5. For a background discussion of GPALS, see Pike, J., 'Military use of outer space', SIPRI, *SIPRI Yearbook 1991: World Armaments and Disarmament* (Oxford University Press: Oxford, 1991), pp. 50–52.

[40] See *Congressional Record,* 13 Mar. 1991, pp. S 3176–89.

[41] The development, function and capabilities of Brilliant Pebbles are discussed in Pike, J., 'Military use of outer space', SIPRI, *SIPRI Yearbook 1990: World Armaments and Disarmament* (Oxford University Press: Oxford, 1990), pp. 62–63.

[42] See *Congressional Record,* 31 July 1991, pp. S 11437–11520, and 1 Aug. 1991, pp. S 11613–12104.

[43] *National Defense Authorization Act for Fiscal Years 1992 and 1993,* Report of the Committee on Armed Services, US House of Representatives, 102nd Congress, 1st Session, Report no. 102–311 (US Government Printing Office: Washington, DC, 13 Nov. 1991), pp. 34–40 and 491–95.

tactical missiles defence (TMD) technologies—systems like the Patriot missile used to defend against short-range missiles.

While these developments represent a significant shift in congressional attitudes towards SDI, ambivalence remains. The Persian Gulf War provided much of the impetus for congressional action in 1991, as some members, notably Senator Nunn, sought to diffuse criticism of their opposition to US military action. Disagreement remains over precisely what was authorized in 1991. Senator Warner claimed that the initial deployment at Grand Forks had received final approval, while Senator Nunn maintained that further congressional action was required prior to deployment. The House of Representatives remains quite sceptical of the desirability of proceeding with the space-based Brilliant Pebbles interceptors, as well as the linkage of strategic and tactical anti-missile efforts.[44] And in September the Senate defeated by only a single vote a proposal to reduce the SDI budget to $3.5 billion.

Threats perceived by GPALS advocates

In contrast to the prior debate over SDI, which primarily focused on costs and technical feasibility,[45] the new SDI debate largely revolves around the reality and significance of the threats the system is intended to counter. Whereas initially SDI was intended to replace—and in later modifications to enhance—deterrence, supporters now see SDI as a tool to cope with its potential failure.

Democratic Representative Les Aspin suggested in September 1991 that deployment of SDI might be needed in the face of the emergence of 'non-deterrable' nuclear threats, noting that 'Saddam Hussein is a case in point . . . It is difficult to say what Saddam would have done if he had completed a nuclear bomb, but his actions in the Gulf War, raise serious doubts about whether he would have been deterred from using it.'[46]

However, the case for the existence of such non-deterrable threats is unclear. While Iraq used both chemical weapons and ballistic missiles extensively in the Iraq–Iran War, the non-use of chemical-armed missiles in the Persian Gulf War may demonstrate the effectiveness of deterrence by the threat of retaliation. The fact that Iraq did fire conventionally armed missiles at Israel stemmed from the unique fact that Hussein was trying to draw Israel into the war in order to split the Coalition. However, even in this effort Iraq observed a threshold that limited its efforts to conventional weapons.[47]

High-ranking US, Israeli and British officials repeatedly gave explicit warning of 'unconventional' retaliation, should Iraq use chemical weapons.[48] Thus, the Iraqi experience demonstrates that even in the midst of war, even the most ruthless dictator was deterred from crossing a threshold that could have

---

[44] 'House zaps Brilliant Pebbles; cuts TMD from SDI', *SDI Monitor*, 24 May 1991, pp. 121–22.

[45] See Pike (note 41), pp. 60–66; Pike (note 39), pp. 50–57.

[46] Aspin, L., 'A new kind of threat: a white paper', 12 Sep. 1991.

[47] See also chapter 6, section II, in this volume.

[48] See Laub, K., 'Israeli official says nation is set to use chemical arms if Iraq attacks', *Philadelphia Inquirer*, 28 July 1990, p. 8; Opall, B., 'Israel debates lasting effects of nonretaliation in Gulf War', *Defense News*, 9 Sep. 1991, p. 38; Arkin, W., 'US nukes in the Gulf', *The Nation*, 31 Dec. 1990, p. 834.

led to massive retaliation. Far from making the case for deploying an anti-missile system, Desert Storm indicates that such a system is not needed.

Tactical and theatre missiles

A total of 26 countries either possess ballistic missiles or may possess them by the year 2000.[49] An examination of the countries on this list should take into account assessments of hostility, current missile deployments, indigenous technical capabilities and the ability to purchase hardware and/or expertise.[50]

With few exceptions, the missiles possessed by developing countries are of very short range, and extremely inaccurate. The motivation for most developing countries to obtain missiles results from regional tensions. Their interest is therefore in acquiring short-range missiles, not ICBMs.

Israel has embarked on a $180 million project (largely funded by the USA) to develop a short-range anti-missile system, the Arrow (Chetz), that could potentially intercept some theatre-range missiles. There is legitimate concern that even a few rockets armed with chemical warheads might temporarily ground the Israeli Air Force, with potentially catastrophic consequences. However, even in this case, there are those in Israel who argue that improved versions of the Patriot would be a more prudent investment than the Arrow missile.[51]

Third World ICBMs

While no Third World state presently possess intercontinental-range missiles, GPALS proponents contend that anti-missile systems should be deployed soon in anticipation of the eventual materialization of such a threat.

Hypothetical future Iraqi, Israeli, Japanese or Libyan missiles could reach portions of Western Europe. Portions of the Commonwealth of Independent States (CIS) can currently be reached by a number of shorter-range missiles, largely Scuds in the hands of neighbouring countries. However, barring the hypothetical threat from Iraq, Israel or Japan, the Russian Federation is safe from attack from any country other than the current nuclear powers.

---

[49] Steven Hadley, Assistant Secretary of Defense for International and Security Policy, stated that 18 countries currently have ballistic missile capability, and that number will rise to about 24 by the year 2000; 'Joint DOD/SDIO briefing on GPALS', unpublished mimeograph, US Department of Defense, 12 Feb. 1991. Thomas Brooks, Chief of Naval Operations, stated that 'By the year 2000, at least 15 Third World countries are expected to have acquired TBMs'; testimony, 'Hearing on Intelligence Issues' Committee on Armed Services, US House of Representatives, 102st Congress, 1st Session, 7 Mar. 1991, mimeo. William Webster, Director of Central Intelligence, stated that by the year 2000, 'as many as 15 countries could be producing their own ballistic missiles'; Webster, W., Speech before a gathering of the Amherst Association of New York, New York, 22 May 1991. Webster's speech writer later clarified that the 15 countries are world-wide, and not just in the Third World; Webster, W., Private communication with the authors, Aug. 1991 For a Russian view, see Kozyakov, V., 'Commentary notes increased SDI funding', Moscow radio, transcript in Foreign Broadcast Information Service *Daily Report–Soviet Union (FBIS-SOV)*, FBIS-SOV-91-215, 6 Nov. 1991, p. 8. Kozyakov states that 'As many as 15 countries are already in possession of delivery vehicles and a number of others will follow in the next few years'.

[50] Lumpe, L., Gronlund, L. and Wright, D., 'Third World missiles fall short', *Bulletin of the Atomic Scientists*, vol. 48, no. 2 (Mar. 1992), pp. 30–37.

[51] 'Arrow ABM may be too late, too costly and off target', *Jane's Defence Weekly*, 1 Feb. 1992, p. 156.

Furthermore, the acquisition of intercontinental-range rockets is a complicated and visible process. The development of relatively advanced missile systems by India and Israel, countries with strong technical infrastructures, was possible only with substantial help from France, Germany, the USA and the USSR. The experience of Brazil, India and Iraq suggests that even a large country with a significant aerospace industry would need more than a decade of readily visible testing to develop a long-range rocket. The world would not be caught by surprise if a country attempted to develop such a missile. The US satellites that tracked Scud launches during the Persian Gulf War would detect missile flight tests, giving unambiguous warning of missile development by any state and providing adequate time to devise an appropriate response.

For those countries that do not have the indigenous capability to develop missiles, buying a missile from another country may be an option. Missile sales and transfers account for most of the missiles in the developing world. However, the longest-range missile sold to a developing country (by China to Saudi Arabia) has a range of 2800 km. China and Russia are the only current potential sources of such intercontinental-range missiles. It is difficult to imagine that they would sell missiles that could be turned against them.[52]

Accidental, inadvertent and unauthorized launch

The anti-missile proponents also stress the risk of *accidental* missile launches due to mechanical failure. However, the USA and the USSR have deployed thousands of strategic missiles for the past three decades without a single incident of accidental launch. Strategic Air Command spokesmen have asserted that 'there is absolutely no way a Minuteman 3 missile could be accidentally launched'.[53] Indeed, the more common problem is the failure of missiles to launch when the count-down reaches zero.[54]

Inadvertent launches are related to accidental launches, but are distinct in the sense that the failure occurs at the level of the command system, rather than the individual missile. There have been a number of instances involving problems with warning sensors or command systems. While these have properly been of concern, in fact these cases did not materially increase the risk of the use of nuclear weapons.

Advocates often suggest that GPALS is needed to protect against nuclear weapons that may be launched against the USA as the result of some crisis during the political disintegration of the USSR.[55] However, the failed *coup* attempt by reactionary factions in the USSR posed the ultimate test of the security of the controls for Soviet nuclear weapons and proved fears to be

---

[52] For a thorough discussion of Third World ballistic missile capabilities, see Pike, J. *et al.*, 'Chicken Little and Darth Vader: is the sky really falling', testimony before the Government Operations Committee, US House of Representatives, 102nd Congress, 1st Session, 1 Oct. 1991, mimeo.

[53] 'Vehicle parked on silo after launch signal', *Washington Post*, 29 Oct. 1987, p.A7

[54] Strobel, W., 'Error made missiles impotent during '86', *Washington Times*, 20 Mar. 1989, p.1

[55] Fialka, J. J., 'Rifts within the military heighten coup's dangers', *Wall Street Journal*, 20 Aug. 1991, p. 10.

groundless.[56] The newly formed CIS has held discussions which resulted in agreement on the unified command of nuclear weapons. Meeting in Minsk on 30 December, the leaders of the republics established that the decision to use nuclear weapons would be made by the president of the Russian Federation 'with the agreement of' the leaders of the other republics in possession of nuclear weapons—Belarus, Kazakhstan and Ukraine—and in 'consultation' with the leadership of the other republics.[57] In any case, should an individual republic wrest control of the nuclear weapons within its territory away from any form of provisional government which evolves, it would still be bound by the same rules of deterrence that are faced by all other nuclear states.[58] A nuclear-armed Kazakhstan would not be any less likely to be exempt from a retaliatory strike than a unified command structure.

Operational problems

As the SDI programme moved out of the laboratory in 1991, the majority of its field tests experienced failures of one form or another.[59] These problems suggest that there are major technical hurdles that SDI must overcome in improving ABM component performance. However, given sufficient time and money (both of which will probably be required in greater quantities than currently estimated), component performance will probably approach SDI requirements. Although significant, these are not the major hurdles to the programme. The experience of the Patriot in the Persian Gulf War demonstrated many of the problems facing more ambitious anti-missile systems.

While advocates pointed to the success of the Patriot, the war also demonstrated some of the frailties of anti-missile systems. Iraqi design flaws in the modification of Scuds to Al-Husseins caused structural weaknesses which led the missiles to disintegrate as they re-entered the atmosphere, inadvertently approximating the effects of deliberate countermeasures. This complicated the intercept task of the Patriots and limited their effectiveness.[60] The availability of countermeasures able to fool sensors, and the unreliability of the computer software running the system, suggest that GPALS could encounter similar difficulties. Effective countermeasures need not be complicated. Balloon decoys can conceal warheads; chaff can distract anti-missile radars; aerosols

[56] See Meyer, S. M., 'Hyping the Soviet nuclear peril', *New York Times*, 12 Dec. 1991; Campbell, K. M., Carter, A. B., Miller, S. E. and Zraket, C. A., 'Soviet nuclear fission: control of the nuclear arsenal in a disintegrating Soviet Union', *CSIA Studies in International Security*, no. 1(Center for Science and International Affairs, Harvard University: Cambridge, Mass., Nov. 1991).

[57] Dobbs, M, 'Unified control set for Soviet a-arms', *Washington Post*, 31 Dec. 1991, p. 1.

[58] Potter, W. C., 'Ukraine as a nuclear power', *Wall Street Journal*, 4 Dec. 1991.

[59] For details, see Neal, S., 'Israel seeks more cash for Arrow', *Jane's Defence Weekly*, 6 Apr. 1991, p. 519; 'SDI testing', *Military Space*, 4 Nov. 1991, p. 6; 'LEAP checkout flight pushed back one to three months', *SDI Monitor*, 30 Aug. 1991, p. 208 Kiernan, V., 'Technician errs, SDI rocket fails', *Space News*, 26 Aug. 1991, p. 1; 'Orbital sciences set to try another SDIO Aries launch Monday', *Aerospace Daily*, 28 Aug. 1991, p. 325; 'Summertime and the testing's tough for SDI', *SDI Monitor*, 30 Aug. 1991, p. 1; 'HEDI telemetry showed on-board electronics enabled warhead', *Aerospace Daily*, 2 Oct. 1991, p. 14; Kiernan, V., 'Interceptor failure deals SDI setback', *Space News*, 30 Sep. 1991, p. 1; 'Arrow delays anticipated', *Flight International*, 13–19 Nov. 1991, p. 6.

[60] Postol, T. A., 'Lessons from the Gulf War experience with Patriot', *International Security*, vol. 16, no. 3 (winter 1991–92), pp. 119–71.

and mists can confuse passive infra-red sensors; and corner reflectors can confuse radars and imaging laser sensors. One of the greatest threats to a theatre defence system comes from missiles dispensing submunitions.[61]

Brilliant Pebbles also appear to be susceptible to countermeasures. A report from the Los Alamos National Laboratory asserts that Russian missiles could be upgraded at a minimal cost by adding decoys and faster-burning boosters. By reducing the burn phase from 300 to 100 seconds, new boosters for the SS-18 would reduced the effectiveness of the interceptors by 50 per cent.[62]

Brilliant Pebbles would also be ineffective against tactical missiles. It seems clear from the operational constraints posed by the earth's atmosphere that theatre missiles could be flown on depressed trajectories so as to be beyond the reach of space-based interceptors.[63] According to US ABM Treaty negotiator Sidney Graybeal, Brilliant Pebbles are 'not capable of defending against ballistic missiles with range under approximately 1000 kilometers'.[64]

Arms control implications

Both the US and Soviet stances towards anti-missile systems and arms control underwent significant evolution in 1991. The Missile Defense Act adopted by the Congress in 1991 calls for deploying an anti-missile system that would be 'cost-effective and operationally effective and [Anti-Ballistic Missile] Treaty compliant.' However, deployment of significant strategic ABM systems would require revision or elimination of the ABM Treaty. Any operationally effective system would violate the terms of the Treaty, and any Treaty-compliant system would not be operationally effective.

While the US negotiating position in the Geneva Defence and Space Talks was previously opposed to any constraints on deployment, the Administration now indicates a willingness to discuss modifications to the Treaty. However, the position put forward as acceptable is the same as the proposed GPALS deployment. President Bush has proposed allowing the deployment of additional ground-based sites. These negotiations would also aim at allowing increased use of space-based sensors, development of other advanced technologies (presumably Brilliant Pebbles), and clarifying the distinction between strategic and tactical anti-missile systems. Also, the US Government failed to include the ABM Treaty on a list of agreements that the newly independent republics are expected to adhere to, causing speculation that the USA seeks to distance itself from its obligations under the Treaty.[65]

The increasing political openness in the former USSR has been accompanied by a growing diversity of attitudes toward ABM deployments. Whereas

[61] Finnegan, P., 'US reviews missile plan; Gulf War exposes effectiveness of countermeasures', *Defense News*, 12 Aug. 1991, p. 1.

[62] Canavan, G., 'Threat modernization in the near term', Los Alamos National Laboratory, as cited in 'Soviets could thwart US missile interceptors', *Military Space*, 9 Sep. 1991, p. 5.

[63] Wright, D. C. and Gronlund, L., 'Underflying Brilliant Pebbles', *Nature*, vol. 350, no. 6320 (25 Apr. 1991), p. 663.

[64] 'Senate Approp. defers $250 million in TMD funding', *SDI Monitor*, 27 Sep. 1991, p. 232.

[65] Smith, R. J., 'US moves away from ABM Treaty', *Washington Post*, 26 Jan. 1992, pp. A1, A22.

the Soviet Government maintained a unified public opposition to SDI, in the post-Soviet era previously hidden viewpoints have come into the open.

Some SDI advocates claim that the Russians have reversed their opposition to the deployment of missile defences.[66] However, at least two approaches to anti-missile issues are now contending for dominance in Moscow. The traditional sceptics at the Foreign Ministry and the Academy of Sciences retain their prior support for the ABM Treaty and scepticism toward anti-satellite weapons, while accepting the possibility of jointly operated warning systems. However, the new enthusiasts at of the General Staff and the aerospace industry are now free to openly advance a more hospitable approach, calling for joint development and operation of space-based interceptor systems.

Although both of these approaches offer a more positive attitude towards anti-missile systems than was to be found in initial Soviet reactions to SDI, neither constitutes an endorsement of the current US approach. In their support for the ABM Treaty and their opposition to large scale anti-missile deployments, the traditional sceptics propose less than the Bush Administration wants. Russian Federation President Boris Yeltsin's response to the nuclear cuts announced by Bush in his 1992 State of the Union address reiterated much of the former Soviet approach to SDI: 'Russia confirms its adherence to the ABM Treaty. It is an important factor in maintaining strategic stability in the world . . . Russia is ready, on the basis of reciprocity with the United States, to eliminate the existing anti-satellite systems and to work out an accord to ban completely the weapons which have been specially constructed to hit satellites . . .'[67] Conversely, the new enthusiasts seek more than the Bush Administration offers, conditioning their support on a new Russian–US condominium.

While there is a significant divergence between the two positions, both approaches are clearly predicated on joint Russian–US development. This would serve to ease the transition for Russian military industry. However, such technical co-operation is highly unlikely. US officials remain hesitant to endorse any collaborative efforts towards missile defences.[68] Congressional supporters of SDI are also sceptical of the prospects of sharing technology.[69] SDI Organization Director Henry Cooper responded: 'I'm not suggesting that we simply share the technology. But there is still a way to cooperate.'[70] Thus far this has largely taken the form of proposals to share data derived from US early-warning satellites, and from the Brilliant Eyes sensors of the SDI

---

[66] Payne, K., 'Debunking the old bromides', *Space News*, 28 Oc.t–3 Nov. 1991, p. 20.

[67] 'Yeltsin delivers statement on disarmament', Moscow television, 29 Jan. 1992, transcript in FBIS-SOV-92-019, 29 Jan. 1992, pp. 1–3. Excerpts of President Bush's adress and of President Yeltsin's reply are given in appendix 2A in this volume.

[68] 'Sawyer, K., 'Cheney dismisses Yeltsin offer on bigger arms cuts', *Washington Post*, 3 Feb. 1992, p. A5.

[69] Riccitiello, R., 'Yeltsin's joint SDI idea draws cautious interest', *Space News*, 10 Feb. 1992, p. 3.

[70] Schoenfeld, B., 'Soviet shift on defenses is turning point in ABM debate', *Defense Week*, 15 Oct. 1991, p. 7.

programme.[71] More recent ideas include spending somewhat less than 1 per cent of the SDI budget to acquire key Russian technology.[72]

The new Soviet approach to SDI is also predicated on a fundamental shift in Russian relations with the rest of the world. Yeltsin has stated: '[T]oday in our military doctrine we no longer consider the US as being our potential opponent. And we want to be allies. And if a global system of protection from outer space is thus set up, and the joint exploitation, there would be no need for nuclear weapons in submarines, based on land, and so on . . .'[73]

Senior US military leaders, including the Chairman of the Joint Chiefs of Staff, General Colin Power, and Air Force General Donald Kutyna, have repeatedly stressed that despite the recent focus on limited anti-missile systems, they still regard the primary requirement for SDI as being the defence of US military forces against a Soviet first strike.[74]

As long as either the USA or the Russian Federation views the other in these terms, as a potential opponent in a full-scale nuclear exchange, negotiating new limits on anti-missile deployments may prove difficult. A treaty that provided each country with equal ceilings on numbers of deployed interceptors would not provide equal protection, and a treaty that provided equal protection would not provide for equal numbers of interceptors. Since neither country would accept a treaty that provided grossly unequal provisions, no replacement treaty is likely to emerge if the ABM Treaty is abandoned.

Open sources estimate the range of the GBI and E^{2}I interceptors that would be used at a single site at Grand Forks at about 1500 km.[75] The most effective Russian interceptors have a range of only about 300 km. Assuming that this range could be extended to 500 km, and that Russia would not choose to defend much of Siberia, it would still require about two dozen deployment sites. Since the missile defence forces of the former USSR rely on less sophisticated nuclear-tipped interceptors, and lag in the development of advanced sensors, they would probably require twice as many interceptors at each site. They would thus have to deploy 10 000 interceptors to match an US deployment of 1 000 interceptors. (The radars used in the former Soviet system would also raise greater concerns about the anti-missile potential of their thousands of anti-aircraft missiles such as the SA-10 and SA-12).

The USA would not accept deployment in the CIS of a system ten times larger than the US system, and the Russians are unlikely to accept US deployment of a system 10 times better than theirs. Thus the prospects for deployment of anti-missile systems within an arms control framework appear bleak at best.

[71] 'Moscow could look to brilliant eyes', *Military Space*, 7 Oct. 1992, pp. 1, 8.

[72] 'SDIO plans to acquire Russian ABM technology, specialists', *Aviation Week & Space Technology*, 10 Feb. 1992, pp. 18–21.

[73] 'News conference by Russian Federation President Boris Yeltsin', transcript (United Nations: New York, 31 Jan. 1992).

[74] *Department of Defense Authorization for Appropriations for Fiscal Years 1992 and 1993*, Hearing before the Committee on Armed Services, US Senate, 101st Congress, 1st Session (US Government Printing Office: Washington, DC, 1991), Part 1, pp. 43, 747.

[75] The George C. Marshall Institute, *U.S. Responses to the Emerging Ballistic Missile Threat*, Report of the Technical Panel (The George C. Marshall Institute: Washington, DC, June 1991), pp. 18–21.

IV. The devolution of the Soviet military space programme

While significant organizational realignments of the Soviet space programme were already under way prior to the establishment of the CIS,[76] the emergence of separate space programmes in the various republics began in earnest in early 1991.[77] More than 2000 enterprises were at the time engaged in space-related work, accounting for 1.5 per cent of the Soviet gross national product.[78] Including support personnel and family members, over 10 million people were in 1991 dependent on the space industry for their livelihood.[79]

The Russian Ministry of Communications, Information Technology and Space launched the first of three of its own communications satellites in early 1991.[80] Bowing to Kazakh interests, plans for launching replacement crews to the Mir space station were changed in July 1991 to accommodate a Kazakh cosmonaut in October.[81] By the end of 1991 various research institutes, including the TsAGI aerospace development centre, the Moscow Aviation Institute, and the Institute for Space Research, were calling for the formation of a Russian Space Agency (RKA) modelled on the US National Aeronautics and Space Administration (NASA).

Kazakhstan formed a Space Research Agency, primarily to operate the Baikonur Cosmodrome. A new joint stock company, International Spaceport, was formed for this purpose, with Kazakhstan holding 80 per cent of the stock and Russian and Ukrainian space groups holding the rest.[82] The intent is to continue Russian and Ukrainian launches from the Cosmodrome on a commercial basis.[83] However, in October 1991 Colonel General Vladimir Ivanov, then chief of the Soviet Ministry of Defence Space Units, announced that Baikonur would remain under military control.[84] The dispute over control of the launch centre found concrete expression on 20 December, when an SS-19 ICBM, reportedly modified to test its potential for commercial applications, was launched without prior notification to the Kazakh Government.[85] Azerbaijan is also formulating its own space programme.[86]

---

[76] Estonia, for instance, set up its own space agency in late 1989. '. . . As Soviet Union develops its commercial image', *New Scientist*, 16 Dec. 1989, p. 12.

[77] 'Shopping the ex-Soviet Union', *Space Business News*, 23 Dec. 1991, pp. 1, 8.

[78] Rebrov, M., Academician opposes space program fragmentation', *Kraznaya Zvezda*, 5 Nov. 1991, p. 4, in FBIS-SOV-91-219, 13 Nov. 1991, pp. 40–41.

[79] Postychov, V., 'NASA, ESA cited as space program models', *Komsomolskaya Pravda*, 8 Oct. 1991, p. 2, in FBIS-SOV-91-203, 21 Oct. 1991, pp. 50–51.

[80] Pomonarev, M. and Rostova, N., 'Continuation of space program discussed, Moscow television, 27 Dec. 1991, transcript in FBIS-SOV-92-001, 2 Jan. 1992, p. 69.

[81] Kiernan, V., 'Soviets cancel fall flight to Mir station', *Space News*, 29 July 1991, pp. 3, 21.

[82] 'Baikonur cosmodrome to go commercial', *RFE Report On the USSR*, 15 Nov. 1991, p. 47.

[83] Rich, V., 'The world turns upside down for Soviet science', *New Scientist*, 14 Sep. 1991, pp. 20–21.

[84] Konovalov, B., 'Future of space complex, program viewed', *Izvestia*, 4 Oct. 1991, p. 4, FBIS-SOV-91-198, 11 Oct. 1991, pp. 25–26.

[85] Nadein, V., 'Further on Kazakhstan missile launch', *Izvestia*, 23 Jan. 1992, FBIS-SOV-92-020, 30 Jan. 1992, p. 6.

[86] Semina, L. 'Colonel addresses deputies on space program', Moscow radio, 2 Oct. 1991, transcript in FBIS-SOV-91-194, 7 Oct. 1991, pp. 60–61.

Soviet military space forces were also reorganized in 1991. A new Strategic Deterrence Forces was created in November 1991, bringing together the Strategic Rocket Forces, the Main Directorate of Space Systems, as well as the nuclear forces of the Air Force and Navy. The new command was placed under the leadership of Marshal Yuri Maximov, commander of the Strategic Rocket Forces.[87] This formation also included control of missile early warning, space surveillance, anti-missile and anti-satellite systems.[88]

The dramatic reduction in the perceived threat, along with the deteriorating economic situation, has led to significant cut-backs in spending. The Russian military budget for the first quarter of 1992 reduced spending on new procurement by about 75 per cent, while research and development spending was cut about 35 per cent.[89] While these reductions apply to the military generally, they are indicative of the pressure on space budgets, since many legislators attribute the recent economic decline to excessive aerospace spending.[90]

Overall funding for space, which stood at 6.9 billion roubles in 1989, dropped by 10 per cent in 1990,[91] and remained at the 6.3 billion rouble level in 1991.[92] Military funding for space, which accounted for 60 per cent of the total in 1991, was reduced by 700 million roubles.[93] Much of this reduction is due to the military's cancellation of its support for the Buran shuttle programme.[94] Thus funding for the Energia production association declined by 40 per cent in 1991, leading to a reported 'six-fold' reduction in personnel.[95] Overall, the budget for civil space programs declined 30 per cent in 1991.[96] The budget of the civilian Institute for Space Research increased 70 per cent from 1990 to 1991, reaching 250 million roubles. However, this was not enough to offset the pace of inflation, which ran 250 per cent in 1991, leading to a funding requirement of nearly 450 million roubles for 1992.[97] The dramatic increase in prices in early 1992 will lead to as much as a five-fold increase in the nominal expense of space projects by the end of the year.[98]

[87] 'Further on plans for new strategic troops', Moscow radio, 19 Nov. 1991, transcript in FBIS-SOV-91-224, 20 Nov. 1991, p. 40.

[88] Litovkin, V., 'Maksimov asserts central claim to missiles', Izvestia, 11 Dec. 1991, FBIS-SOV-91-238, 11 Dec. 1991, pp. 29–31.

[89] 'Russian parliament okays huge cuts in weapons procurement, R&D spending', Inside the Pentagon, 30 Jan. 1992, p. 6.

[90] Romanov, A., 'Collapse of Union threatens space program', Moscow TASS, in FBIS-SOV-91-014, 22 Jan. 1992, p. 25.

[91] Tarasenko, N., 'Shishkin on role of USSR in space market', Ekonomikaizhizn, no. 16 (Apr. 1991), pp. 6–7, in Joint Publications Research Service, USSR–Space (JPRS-USP), JPRS-USP-91-183, 20 Sep. 1991, pp. 43–45.

[92] Chenard, S., 'Budget time in Moscow', Space Markets, no. 5 (1991), p. 10. This is the most comprehensive published review of the history of the Soviet space budget.

[93] 'Former Soviet space industry seen going out of business in months', Aerospace Daily, 9 Jan. 1992, p. 46.

[94] 'Soviet space', Space Business News, 23 Dec. 1991, p. 8.

[95] Covault, C., 'USSR breakup paralyzing advanced Soviet military, space development', Aviation Week & Space Technology, 2 Sep. 1991, pp. 22–23.

[96] Konovalov, B., 'Closer ties to European space program viewed', Izvestia, 8 Oct. 1991, in FBIS-SOV-91-200, 16 Oct. 1991, pp. 43–45.

[97] Socha, E., 'Soviet space science feels pinch', Space News, 21 Oct. 1991, p. 2.

[98] Ponomarev, M. and Rostova, N., 'Continuation of space program discussed', Moscow Television, transcript in FBIS-SOV–92-001, 2 Jan. 1992, p. 69.

These cutbacks have led to growing discontent among space programme personnel. A warning strike occurred at Baikonur in early November 1991.[99] In early January 1992 some employees at the Kaliningrad manned space control centre staged a symbolic strike, threatening more significant action if their salaries of 600 roubles per month were not raised.[100]

The operational tempo of the Soviet space programme had been in decline since the early 1980s. The peak number of launches came in 1982, with 101 launches, gradually declining to 90 launches in 1988. The number declined to 74 in 1989, to 75 in 1990 and to a mere 59 by the end of 1991, the lowest since 1967. The decline in the number of photographic reconnaissance satellites was even more precipitous. The number dropped from a peak of 34 launches in 1985, to 32 in 1987, to 24 in 1989, to 19 in 1990, to a mere 11 in 1991. While some of the drop in launch activity was due to more capable satellites with longer lifetimes, there was also an absolute reduction in level of activity. The total number of days that reconnaissance satellites spent in orbit peaked at over 1100 in 1986, declining to fewer than 900 by 1990, and dropping to fewer than 600 days by 1991.[101]

The Commonwealth of Independent States

The establishment of the CIS has occasioned a number of alterations to the Soviet space programme. With greatly reduced international security interests, the CIS space programme will undoubtedly be significantly smaller than the Soviet effort. In contrast to the peak annual Soviet effort of 100 launches and 120 orbiting satellites, the CIS might achieve 40 launches and a total of 50 spacecraft in orbit each year.

It is also important to keep in mind that the CIS is not co-terminus with the USSR. The Baltic states and Georgia have declined to join the new federation. However, the space-related facilities in these areas are few in number. The Georgian capital of Tblisi hosts a satellite control network tracking station, and a facility for the development of large space-deployable antennae that could be used for radio-astronomy or signals intelligence satellites. Baltic space-related facilities are limited to the Pechora-class and Hen House early-warning radars at Skrunda in Latvia. Along with the other Baltic republics, Latvia has called for the complete withdrawal of Soviet/CIS troops from its territory in the near future, and there has been no public suggestion that these radar facilities would be an exception to this policy.

[99] 'Warning strike at Baykonur cosmodrome', VID, Moscow television, transcript in FBIS-SOV-90-219, 13 Nov. 1990, p. 59.
[100] 'Progress M-11 mission successful, despite threat of strike', *Aerospace Daily*, 28 Jan. 1992, p. 142.
[101] 'CIS ends year with lowest launch total in 25 years', *Soviet Aerospace & Technology*, 13 Jan. 1992, pp. 2–7. This article is based on analysis by Saunders Kramer.

The Russian Federation

In the event of the effective dissolution of the CIS, what would remain is effectively a Russian space effort. The vast bulk of the Soviet space industry is located in Russia, with various estimates placing the Russian share of the total at 75 per cent,[102] 80 per cent[103] and up to 90 per cent.[104] With a few notable exceptions, Russia would have the infrastructure needed to continue a programme of a scope and scale consistent with its national interests. However, retaining access to facilities in Kazakhstan—the Baikonur Cosmodrome and the Sary Sagan and Semipalatinsk test ranges—as well as the various early-warning radars and space facilities in other republics, would clearly be a major issue for Russia.

Outside Russia, space infrastructure is concentrated in Belarus and Ukraine, with a few facilities of note in other republics. These include a laser radar satellite tracking facility near Dushanbe, Tadzhikistan, and spacecraft component production facilities in Dushanbe and in Tashkent, Uzbekistan.

Baikonur is the only launch facility able to support the Proton launch vehicle, the backbone of the Soviet manned space and unmanned planetary programmes, the geostationary communications and signals intelligence efforts and the GLONASS navigation satellite system. Replicating the Proton launch capability at Plesetsk would be both time-consuming and expensive (a billion roubles by one estimate.[105] This more northern location would also result in some loss of payload capability, although this could be offset by upgrades to the launch vehicle. Thus with some difficulty it would be possible to adapt to Plesetsk many programmes currently launched from Baikonur, including the manned space programme.[106]

While the Kazakh launch and test facilities are of considerable (though not overwhelming) value to the Russian Federation, they are of little if any use to Kazakhstan alone. Although the Kazakh Government assumed nominal control of Baikonur in mid-September 1991, the annual operating costs of the facility is probably beyond the means of the Republic (estimates range from over 400 million[107] to 1 billion[108] to nearly 2.5 billion roubles[109]). Thus there would be ample incentive for Kazakhstan to come to terms with Russia.

[102] Dvoyishnikova, N., 'Military dominance of space programs described', *Nezavismaya Gazeta*, 25 Sep. 1991, p. 6, in JPRS-USP, 22 Nov. 1991, p. 50. According to Aleksandr Radionov, Chief of the Space Units press service, of 'space related properties' are 75 per cent located in Russia, 20 per cent in Ukraine 'and as many in the Baltics', 10 per cent in Belarus and 'one-fifteenth' in Uzbekistan. This remarkably precise rendering is marred by two flaws. First, it is unclear what 'space related properties' are measured in—employment, value of output, square meters and total ground area of installations are all possible metrics. Second, the total of these percentages adds up to 132 per cent, rendering the whole exercise meaningless. The percentages cited for the Baltics and Uzbekistan are particularly difficult to reconcile with the known distribution of space facilities, although the relative proportions cited for Russia, Belarus, and Ukraine seem not unreasonable.

[103] 'Former Soviet space industry seen going out of business in months' (note 93). This estimate applies to 'space science and industry', without reference to what is being measured.

[104] Postychov (note 79). This estimate is equally unsatisfactory, since it is denominated in 'enterprises', which range in size from small to very large.

[105] Konovalov (note 84).

[106] Arkhipov, M., 'Problems arising from Kazakhstan's claim to Baykonur cosmodrome emphasized', *Izvestia*, 19 Oct. 1991, p. 10, in JPRS-USP, 22 Nov. 1991, pp. 90–91.

[107] Arkhipov (note 106).

The prospects for co-operation between Russia and Ukraine may not be as promising. Recent political sentiment in Ukraine has favoured a degree of political independence from Moscow that may prove difficult to reconcile with continued close collaboration on space-related programs.

Dniepropetrovsk in Ukraine is the home of the Yuzhnoye industrial complex, which produces the Tsiklon and Zenit launch vehicles and electronic intelligence, early-warning and radar ocean reconnaissance space vehicles.

The Tsiklon booster, derived from the SS-9 and SS-18 family of intercontinental ballistic missiles, is similar in performance to the Soyuz booster, which could probably be used in its stead. The Zenit booster has only been used to launch a new class of large, low-altitude, electronic intelligence satellites, and the future of this programme is questionable. More significantly, the Zenit also serves as the strap-on booster for the Energia heavy lift launch vehicle and the Buran shuttle. However, the future of these projects is quite bleak, even without problems with Ukraine. Difficulties in obtaining components from other republics, as well as the loss of funding from Russia, led to the cancellation of further production of the Zenit in late 1991.[110] The Yuzhnoye plant is being converted to production of Antonov aircraft, which are designed and built in Ukraine. The effective Yuzhnoye monopoly on electronic intelligence satellites, including the naval EORSAT, might prove a more difficult problem.

The status of ballistic missile early-warning satellites and radars is probably the single most significant issue that would be posed by the dissolution of the CIS. Yuzhnoye's early-warning satellites are probably the most important space asset of Ukraine. Such satellites embody relatively specialized technologies that may prove difficult for Russia to replicate until the later part of the 1990s. Given the potential loss of access to peripheral ground-based early-warning radars, the prospective discontinuity of satellite-derived early warning must be a source of concern for Moscow. However, this concern may be tempered by the reduced threat perception. In addition, absent a complete rupture of relations between Russia and Ukraine, it is plausible to expect that these satellites could be made available in the interim on some sort of commercial basis. While negotiating the terms of such an arrangement might prove complicated, it would be in the interest of both parties to come to some mutually beneficial agreement.

The geographical distribution of the industrial infrastructure for the production of early-warning radars is unclear. Some appear to lie in the Moscow region. However, at least one major facility is located in Gomel, in Belarus.

In any event, the demise of the CIS would not necessarily imply the loss of these radars to Russia. The primary interest of some republics in the withdrawal of Russian troops from their territory is the potential threat that these

[108] 'Russian media reports new pessimism about space program', *Aerospace Daily*, 11 Feb. 1992, p. 227.

[109] de Selding, P., 'Republics keep Soviet space machine running', *Space News*, 7 Oct. 1991, pp. 1, 20.

[110] Covault, C., 'Soviet collapse damaging space program infrastructure', *Aviation Week & Space Technology*, 16 Dec. 1991, pp. 18–19.

forces might pose to their new-found independence. The relatively minuscule staff required to operate these radars would pose no such threat. The US experience of operating tracking radars on the territory of other countries, in some cases in conjunction with the personnel of those countries, provides a precedent that may be followed by the Soviet successor states. In any event, the non-Russian republics have neither the means nor the motive to maintain these facilities on their own.

Conclusion

There is no particular reason for anticipating that the process of political disintegration which occasioned the demise of the USSR should stop at the borders of the Russian Federation. The distinction between the Union Republics which were members of the USSR, and the Autonomous Republics and other subsidiary jurisdictions that compose the Russian Federation is as much a product of historical accident and administrative caprice as it is a reflection of more substantial differences in potential for self-government or political viability. Problems such as small population, limited resources or geographical isolation did not impede the march to independence of the former possessions of other European empires, and there is no reason for imagining that these factors would pose barriers to the independence of various national areas in the Russian Federation.

While the independence of these areas might have a significant impact on the political situation in Moscow, it would have relatively little impact on the Russian space programme, over and above the impact of the potential demise of the CIS. Within the Russian Federation, space-related facilities are remarkably absent from autonomous republics and regions. The identifiable exceptions are the telemetry and tracking station at Ulan Ude, in the Buryat Republic (with Russians constituting 70 per cent of the population), and the Pechora-class early-warning radar in the Komi Republic (with Russians constituting nearly 60 per cent of the population).

Appendix 5A. Military satellites launched in 1991

Type/Country/Spacecraft name	Alternative name (Host spacecraft)	Designation	Launch date	Booster	Facility	Mass (kg)	Apogee (km)	Perigee (km)	Inclin. (deg)	Period (min)	Comments
Imaging intelligence											
USSR											
THIRD GENERATION—MEDIUM RESOLUTION											
SU PHOTO 3M-103	Cosmos 2121	1991-004A	17 Jan.	SL-4	PL	6 300	306	325	82.6	90.0	Replaced C-2120
SU PHOTO 3M-104	Cosmos 2136	1991-016A	6 Mar.	SL-4	PL	6 300	256	336	62.8	90.2	..
SU PHOTO 3M-105	Cosmos 2152	1991-048A	9 Jul	SL-4	PL	6 300	237	349	82.3	90.4	Upper stage malfunctioned
FOURTH GENERATION											
SU PHOTO 4-92	Cosmos 2124	1991-008A	7 Feb.	SL-4	PL	6 500	189	317	62.8	89.6	Observed Desert Storm
SU PHOTO 4-93	Cosmos 2134	1991-011A	15 Feb.	SL-4	TT	6 500	235	311	64.9	89.5	Observed Desert Storm
SU PHOTO 4-94	Cosmos 2138	1991-023A	26 Mar.	SL-4	PL	6 500	164	345	67.1	89.6	First at this inclination since C-2052
SU PHOTO 4-95	Cosmos 2156	1991-066A	17 Sep.	SL-4	PL	6 500	185	350	67.1	89.9	..
SU PHOTO 4-96	Cosmos 2163	1991-078A	9 Oct.	SL-4	TT	6 500	214	360	64.8	89.8	Deliberately exploded on 6 Dec.
SU PHOTO 4-97	Cosmos 2171	1991-078A	20 Nov.	SL-4	PL	6 500	186	306	62.8	89.1	..
SU PHOTO 4-98	Cosmos 2174	1991-085A	17 Dec.	SL-4	TT	6 500	204	331	64.9	89.6	..
FIFTH GENERATION											
SU PHOTO 5-13	Cosmos 2153	1991-049A	10 Jul	SL-4	TT	6 800	214	272	64.9	89.0	..
MILITARY MAPPING AND REMOTE SENSING											
Resurs-F1 53	Resurs-F1 10	1991-035A	21 May	SL-4	PL	5 500	166	231	82.3	89.1	..
Resurs-F1 54	Resurs-F1 11	1991-044A	28 June	SL-4	PL	5 500	257	272	82.3	89.8	..
Resurs-F1 55	Resurs-F1 12	1991-052A	23 July	SL-4	PL	5 500	263	285	82.3	89.8	..
Resurs-F1 56	Resurs-F1 13	1991-058A	21 Aug.	SL-4	PL	5 500	226	230	82.3	89.1	..
SU PHOTO 4T-14	Cosmos 2149	1991-036A	24 May	SL-4	TT	6 800	193	383	67.1	90.0	Topographic survey/mapping

USA

Lacrosse P 1	USA-69	1991-017A	8 Mar.	Titan 404A	WTR	14 550	672	679	68.0	98.3	Elements for initial orbit
Lacrosse P 2	USA-72	1991-076A	8 Nov.	Titan 404A	WTR	14 550	1 053	1 165	63.4	107.5	Certainly not White Cloud NOSS

Electronic intelligence

USSR

SU ELINT 3-34	Cosmos 2151	1991-042A	13 June	SL-14	PL	4 375	636	663	82.5	97.8	..
SU ELINT 4-11	..	Failure	30 Aug.	SL-16	TT	12 500	..	..	..	..	Second consecutive failure
SU EORSAT 1-36	Cosmos 2122	1991-005A	18 Jan.	SL-11	TT	4 250	412	427	65.0	92.7	Upper stage mistaken for Iraqi Scud

USA

Lacrosse P2 ESS-1	USA-74	1991-076C	8 Nov.	Titan 404A	WTR	45	1 053	1 165	63.4	107.5	Elint subsatellite
Lacrosse P2 ESS-2	USA-76	1991-076D	8 Nov.	Titan 404A	WTR	45	1 053	1 165	63.4	107.5	Elint subsatellite
Lacrosse P2 ESS-3	USA-77	1991-076E	8 Nov.	Titan 404A	WTR	45	1 053	1 165	63.4	107.5	Elint subsatellite

Military communications

USSR

SU COM 1-345	Cosmos 2125	1991-009A	12 Feb.	SL-8	PL	45	1 458	1 473	74.0	115.3	..
SU COM 1-346	Cosmos 2126	1991-009B	12 Feb.	SL-8	PL	45	1 467	1 497	74.0	115.6	..
SU COM 1-347	Cosmos 2127	1991-009C	12 Feb.	SL-8	PL	45	1 467	1 479	74.0	115.4	..
SU COM 1-348	Cosmos 2128	1991-009D	12 Feb.	SL-8	PL	45	1 446	1 469	74.0	115.1	..
SU COM 1-349	Cosmos 2129	1991-009E	12 Feb.	SL-8	PL	45	1 431	1 469	74.0	114.9	..
SU COM 1-350	Cosmos 2130	1991-009F	12 Feb.	SL-8	PL	45	1 402	1 469	74.0	114.6	..
SU COM 1-351	Cosmos 2131	1991-009G	12 Feb.	SL-8	PL	45	1 388	1 468	74.0	114.4	..
SU COM 1-352	Cosmos 2132	1991-009H	12 Feb.	SL-8	PL	45	1 416	1 469	74.0	114.8	..
SU COM 2-47	Cosmos 2150	1991-041A	11 Jun	SL-8	PL	750	780	806	74.0	97.7	..
SU COM 3-56	Cosmos 2143	1991-033A	16 May	SL-14	PL	400	1 400	1 416	82.6	114.0	Replaced C-2090–C-2095
SU COM 3-57	Cosmos 2144	1991-033B	16 May	SL-14	PL	400	1 413	1 416	82.6	114.2	Replaced C-2090–C-2095
SU COM 3-58	Cosmos 2145	1991-033C	16 May	SL-14	PL	400	1 406	1 416	82.6	114.1	Replaced C-2090–C-2095
SU COM 3-59	Cosmos 2146	1991-033D	16 May	SL-14	PL	400	1 395	1 416	82.6	114.0	Replaced C-2090–C-2095
SU COM 3-60	Cosmos 2147	1991-033E	16 May	SL-14	PL	400	1 390	1 416	82.6	113.9	Replaced C-2090–C-2095
SU COM 3-61	Cosmos 2148	1991-033F	16 May	SL-14	PL	400	1 384	1 416	82.6	113.8	Replaced C-2090–C-2095

Type/Country/ Spacecraft name	Alternative name (Host spacecraft)	Designation	Launch date	Booster	Facility	Mass (kg)	Apogee (km)	Perigee (km)	Inclin. (deg)	Period (min)	Comments
SU COM 3-62	Cosmos 2157	1991-068A	28 Sep.	SL-14	PL	400	1 407	1 415	82.6	114.1	..
SU COM 3-63	Cosmos 2158	1991-068B	28 Sep.	SL-14	PL	400	1 404	1 411	82.6	114.0	..
SU COM 3-64	Cosmos 2159	1991-068C	28 Sep.	SL-14	PL	400	1 389	1 410	82.6	113.8	..
SU COM 3-65	Cosmos 2160	1991-068D	28 Sep.	SL-14	PL	400	1 400	1 410	82.6	114.0	..
SU COM 3-66	Cosmos 2161	1991-068E	28 Sep.	SL-14	PL	400	1 395	1 410	82.6	113.9	..
SU COM 3-67	Cosmos 2162	1991-068F	28 Sep.	SL-14	PL	400	1 408	1 420	82.6	114.2	..
SU COM 3-68	Cosmos 2165	1991-077A	12 Nov.	SL-14	PL	400	1 395	1 413	82.6	113.9	..
SU COM 3-69	Cosmos 2166	1991-077B	12 Nov.	SL-14	PL	400	1 407	1 413	82.6	114.1	..
SU COM 3-70	Cosmos 2167	1991-077C	12 Nov.	SL-14	PL	400	1 400	1 413	82.6	114.0	..
SU COM 3-71	Cosmos 2168	1991-077D	12 Nov.	SL-14	PL	400	1 390	1 413	82.6	113.9	..
SU COM 3-72	Cosmos 2169	1991-077E	12 Nov.	SL-14	PL	400	1 393	1 413	82.6	113.8	..
SU COM 3-73	Cosmos 2170	1991-077F	12 Nov.	SL-14	PL	400	1 412	1 413	82.6	114.1	..
Molniya 1-80	..	1991-012A	15 Feb.	SL-6	PL	1 250	424	39 934	62.8	717.9	..
Molniya 1-81	..	1991-043A	18 June	SL-6	PL	1 250	446	39 903	62.8	735.0	Constellation of 8 satellites
Molniya 1-82	..	1991-053A	2 Aug.	SL-6	PL	1 250	624	40 627	62.8	737.0	..
Potok 8	Cosmos 2133	1991-010A	14 Feb.	SL-12	TT	2 120	35 800	35 800	2.3	1438.0	Not announced; moved twice in 1991
Potok 9	Cosmos 2172	1991-079A	22 Nov.	SL-12	TT	2 120	35 800	35 800	0.0	1436.0	Announced as data relay, 346 East
GALS	Cosmos 2155	1991-064A	13 Sep.	SL-12	TT	2 120	35 762	35 810	1.3	1436.0	Data relay, at 337 East
NATO											
NATO 4A	..	1991-001A	8 Jan.	Delta 7925	ETR	1 433	34 915	35 614	4.2	1409.4	Multiple Access Communications Sat.
USA											
Microsat 1	MACSAT/Multisat	1991-051A	17 July	Pegasus	EAFB	22	358	455	82.0	92.7	1990 launch delayed by spacecraft flaw
Microsat 2	MACSAT/Multisat	1991-051B	17 July	Pegasus	EAFB	22	358	453	82.0	92.7	Bent-Pipe UHF com. satellite
Microsat 3	MACSAT/Multisat	1991-051C	17 July	Pegasus	EAFB	22	357	453	82.0	92.7	In lower orbit due upper stage flaw
Microsat 4	MACSAT/Multisat	1991-051D	17 July	Pegasus	EAFB	22	356	453	82.0	92.7	All re-entered Jan. 1992
Microsat 5	MACSAT/Multisat	1991-051E	17 July	Pegasus	EAFB	22	358	455	82.0	92.7	..
Microsat 6	MACSAT/Multisat	1991-051F	17 July	Pegasus	EAFB	22	360	455	82.0	92.7	..
Microsat 7	MACSAT/Multisat	1991-051G	17 July	Pegasus	EAFB	22	359	456	82.0	92.7	..
AFSATCOM D-11	(on DMSP 5D-2/6)	1991-082A	28 Nov.	Atlas E	WTR	0	840	857	98.9	102.0	..

Ballistic missile early warning

USA

Name		Designation	Date	Vehicle	Site						Comments
DSP-J16 F-16	USA-75	1991-080B	24 Nov.	STS	ETR	2 370	35 780	35 780	1.0	1436.0	Replaced DSP-12 over Indian Ocean

Military navigation

USSR

Nadezhda 3 COSPAS 6	1991-019A	12 Mar.	SL-8	PL	750	938	1 017	82.9	104.7	Replaced C-1727; civil nav.
SU NAV 3-70 Cosmos 2123	1991-007A	5 Feb.	SL-8	PL	750	982	1 019	82.9	104.8	..
SU NAV 3-71 Cosmos 2135	1991-013A	26 Feb.	SL-8	PL	750	922	1 017	82.8	104.5	..
SU NAV 3-72 Cosmos 2142	1991-029A	16 Apr.	SL-8	PL	750	961	1 015	83.0	104.9	..
SU NAV 3-73 Cosmos 2154	1991-059A	22 Aug.	SL-8	PL	750	969	1 004	82.9	104.8	..
SU NAV 3-74 Cosmos 2173	1991-081A	26 Nov.	SL-8	PL	750	971	1 031	82.9	104.8	..
GLONASS 50 Cosmos 2139	1991-025A	4 Apr.	SL-12	TT	900	19 111	19 149	64.8	675.7	..
GLONASS 51 Cosmos 2140	1991-025B	4 Apr.	SL-12	TT	900	19 105	19 154	64.8	675.7	..
GLONASS 52 Cosmos 2141	1991-025C	4 Apr.	SL-12	TT	900	19 108	19 151	64.8	675.7	..

USA

Navstar 2B-22 USA-71	1991-047A	4 July	Delta 7925	ETR	930	20 083	20 278	55.3	717.9	..

Weather

USSR

Meteor 3-4 ..	1991-030A	24 Apr.	SL-14	PL	2 750	1 184	1 210	82.5	109.4	..
Meteor 3-5 ..	1991-056A	15 Aug.	SL-14	PL	2 750	1 197	1 219	82.5	109.4	Carried US ozone mapping instrument

USA

DMSP 5D-2I/6 USA-73 S-11-I	1991-082A	28 Nov.	Atlas E	WTR	755	840	857	98.9	102.0	Replaced DMSP 5D-2 /5

Nuclear explosion detection

USSR Soviet nuclear explosion detection sensors are probably mounted on early warning or navigation satellites.

USA US nuclear explosion detection sensors are mounted on satellites launched for other primary missions.

NDS 15 (On Navstar 2B-22)	1991-047A	4 July	Delta 7925	ETR	135	20 083	20 278	55.3	717.9	Nuclear Detection System

Type/Country/Spacecraft name	Alternative name (Host spacecraft)	Designation	Launch date	Booster	Facility	Mass (kg)	Apogee (km)	Perigee (km)	Inclin. (deg)	Period (min)	Comments
NUDETS DMSP-11	(On DMSP 5D-2 /6)	1991-082A	28 Nov.	Atlas E	WTR	0	840	857	98.9	102.0	..
ARD-1/2 16	(On DSP-I 16)	1991-080B	24 Nov.	STS	ETR	2 370	35 780	35 780	1.0	1436.0	Replaced DSP-12 over Indian Ocean

Other military missions

USSR

RADAR CALIBRATION

SU RADCAL 2-22	Cosmos 2137	1991-021A	19 Mar.	SL-8	PL	950	449	495	65.9	94.0	..
SU RADCAL 2-23	Cosmos 2164	1991-072A	10 Oct.	SL-8	PL	950	295	726	73.9	94.5	..

LAUNCH VEHICLE DEVELOPMENT

SL-17 test	..	Failure	20 Nov.	SL-17	Omsk	..	..	..	..	..	Core stage exploded 20 Nov. 1991

USA

BALLISTIC MISSILE DEFENSE

SDI-S CIRRIS	(On STS-39)	1991-031A	28 Apr.	STS	ETR		253	268	57.0	89.7	Cryogenic IR Radiance Instrum. Shuttle
SDI-S MPEC	..	1991-031F	28 Apr.	STS	ETR		253	268	57.0	89.7	Multi-Purpose Experiment Canister
SDI-S CRO-A	..	1991-031E	28 Apr.	STS	ETR	80	250	270	57.0	89.7	Chemical Release Observation
SDI-S CRO-B	..	1991-031D	28 Apr.	STS	ETR	80	244	256	57.0	89.5	Chemical Release Observation
SDI-S CRO-C	..	1991-031C	28 Apr.	STS	ETR	80	243	261	57.0	89.5	Chemical Release Observation
SDI-S IBSS	SPAS 2-01	1991-031B	28 Apr.	STS	ETR	1 904	242	257	57.0	89.5	IR Background Signature Survey
SDI-E LOSAT-X	..	1991-047B	4 July	Delta 7925	ETR	75	400	414	40.0	92.6	Plume data; re-entered 30 Oct. 1991

TECHNOLOGY DEVELOPMENT

STP-F REX	USA-70? STEP 5	1991-045A	29 June	Scout G-1	WTR	85	773	875	89.6	101.4	Radiation Experiment

LAUNCH VEHICLE DEVELOPMENT

Titan 4 SRMU 1	SRM Upgrade	Failure	28 Mar.	Titan 4 B	EAFB	..	..	..	..	0.1	Rocket motor upgrade test; exploded

Launch facility abbreviations: EAFB = Edwards Air Force Base, California, USA; ETR = Eastern Test Range, Cape Canaveral, Florida, USA; PL = Plesetsk, Russia, USSR; TT = Tyuratam (Baikonur), Kazakhstan, USSR; WTR = Western Test Range, Vandenberg Air Force Base, California, USA

6. Chemical and biological warfare and arms control developments in 1991

S. J. LUNDIN and THOMAS STOCK; Section VI by
ERHARD GEISSLER*

I. Introduction

In 1991 a number of significant developments occurred related to chemical and biological warfare (CBW). Some of these pertained to the Persian Gulf War; others grew out of chemical weapon (CW) and biological weapon (BW) arms control and disarmament efforts; and still others were associated with the proliferation and destruction of these weapons. This chapter focuses on these events. The creation of the United Nations Special Commission (UNSCOM) on Iraq, its work and findings related to chemical and biological weapons are dealt with in chapter 13, but some conclusions which can be drawn from its activities are discussed here. The main events and developments during 1991 were the following:

1. The Gulf War passed without the use of chemical or biological weapons despite widespread fear that these weapons would be employed. Although there has been conjecture, it is not known why they were not used.

2. UNSCOM was established in April 1991 under United Nations Security Council Resolution 687, the cease-fire resolution which outlined the measures to be taken against Iraq after the Gulf War (see appendix 13A). UNSCOM was given unprecedented powers and resources and has been able to reveal the extent of Iraqi efforts to acquire not only chemical and biological weapons but also nuclear weapons. Iraq was able to acquire these weapons because of substantial assistance from a number of industrialized countries.

3. The USA made major policy changes which may accelerate the negotiations on the future Chemical Weapons Convention (CWC). President George Bush announced that the USA now agrees to destroy all of its chemical weapons within 10 years after entry into force of the future CWC, to abandon its position of the right to retaliate with chemical weapons if such weapons are used against it, and to foster efforts to conclude the CWC during 1992. However, another shift from the previous position of support for intrusive challenge verification requirements—the so-called 'any time, anywhere' approach—to support for much less intrusive measures may slow down the

---

* Elisabeth Corell of the SIPRI Chemical and Biological Warfare (CBW) Programme assisted in preparing references and data for this chapter. The references were gathered from the SIPRI CBW Programme Data Base and were also kindly provided by J. P. Perry Robinson, Science Policy Research Unit, University of Sussex, UK, from the Sussex–Harvard Information Bank.

negotiating process. This advocacy of less intrusive inspection procedures is designed to prevent insight into sensitive, secret military installations; some negotiating states have supported this position while others have opposed it. The UNSCOM inspection experience and results may influence verification under the future CWC, since the same degree of authority and resources will not be available under the future convention.

4. In the wake of the Gulf War, new attempts were made to accelerate the Middle East peace process, and efforts continued to institute a zone free from weapons of mass destruction—nuclear, biological and chemical (NBC) weapons. In September, Argentina, Brazil, Chile and Uruguay signed the Mendoza Agreement, which includes a commitment not to acquire biological and chemical weapons.[1] In other developments, discussion about demilitarization began between North and South Korea, while Bolivia, Colombia, Ecuador, Peru and Venezuela signed an agreement renouncing weapons of mass destruction.[2]

5. As always, allegations of BW and CW proliferation continued to be made. Based mainly on US sources, assertions were made that approximately two dozen countries now possess chemical weapons and that approximately 10 countries possess biological weapons. These claims primarily involve countries situated in the Middle East and South-East Asia. If they are true, and in the absence of a regulatory arms control instrument like the CWC, they may provide support for the thesis that in the future CW proliferation will be of particular concern for developing countries.

6. Both the USA and to an even greater extent the former Soviet Union are faced with problems related to their planned destruction of chemical weapons. The USA seems unlikely to meet its goal to destroy the majority of its chemical weapons by the year 2002 as agreed with the former USSR, which has itself not yet begun the destruction process. The extremely high costs which will be incurred in the destruction of these large stockpiles may create additional delays and thereby also delay the entry into force of the CWC. However, recognition of the high cost of destruction may act as a deterrent to acquisition by countries which do not yet possess chemical weapons.

The need to dispose of old and obsolete chemical weapons from World Wars I and II has become an increasingly important and difficult problem not least because of environmental concerns. Several years may be needed to destroy Iraq's CW stockpiles, chemical intermediates and bulk material but valuable information will be obtained about destruction (see also chapter 13).

[1] 'Letter dated 16 September 1991 from the Heads of the Delegations of Argentina, Brazil, Chile and Uruguay to the Secretary-General of the Third Review Conference of the Parties to the Convention on the Prohibition, Development and Stockpiling of Bacteriological (Biological) and Toxin Weapons and on Their Destruction transmitting a message from the Secretary-General of the United Nations welcoming the "Mendoza Agreement" (Declaracion conjunta sobre la Prohibicion de Armas Quimicas y Biologicas: Compromiso de Mendoza), Third Review Conference of the Parties to the Convention on the Prohibition of the Development, Prohibition, Development and Stockpiling of Bacteriological (Biological) and Toxin Weapons and on Their Destruction', BWC/CONF.III/15, 18 Sep. 1991

[2] Institute for Defense and Disarmament Studies, *Arms Control Reporter* (IDDS: Brookline, Mass.), sheet 457.B.81, Dec. 1991; Conference on Disarmament document CD/1114, 9 Jan. 1992.

7. The disintegration of the former USSR has created concern about the possible future proliferation of Soviet chemical weapons and technical know-how to other parts of the world. Information which became available at the end of 1991 indicated that these chemical weapons are probably located in the Russian Federation.

8. Iraq set afire some Kuwaiti oil wells and damaged others so that large quantities of oil leaked out. While these actions were not chemical warfare *per se*, dangerous chemicals were released into the environment on an enormous scale in what could be seen as a violation of the 1977 Environmental Modification (Enmod) Convention.

9. In September 1991 the Third Review Conference of the Convention on the Prohibition of the Development, Production and Stockpiling of Bacteri-ological (Biological) and Toxin Weapons and on Their Destruction (the BWC) was held. The Review Conference reiterated the validity of the language and scope of the BWC and evaluated and strengthened its information exchange measures. A committee of experts was set up to investigate the technical possibilities of instituting verification measures under the BWC. It will report to the next Review Conference in 1996.

II. Iraq and chemical weapons

While the facts regarding Iraq's possession of weapons of mass destruction were largely clarified during the latter part of 1991 by UNSCOM, it is of interest to evaluate how perceptions about chemical and biological weapons influenced both political and military actions during the Gulf War.

The *SIPRI Yearbook 1991*[3] pointed out that before the war the degree of uncertainty about Iraq's CBW capability was large. Assessments about CW agents and stockpiles, BW capability and missile capability differed widely in early 1991 and during the Gulf War. There were doubts about the quantity and quality of Iraqi CW agents,[4] about whether Iraqi Scud missiles were actually armed with chemical warheads[5] and whether chemical weapons would be militarily effective if delivered by missiles.[6] Despite the uncertainty about

---

[3] Lundin, S. J. and Stock, T., 'Chemical and biological warfare: developments in 1990', SIPRI, *SIPRI Yearbook 1991: World Armaments and Disarmament* (Oxford University Press: Oxford, 1991), pp. 85–112.

[4] Schmitt, E., 'Western military aides foresee chemical attack if land battle erupts', *International Herald Tribune*, 24 Jan. 1991, p. 3; 'Die Iraker werden überschätzt', *Der Spiegel*, vol. 45, no. 3 (14 Jan. 1991), pp. 124–25; 'Special ops will dominate Gulf surface conflict', *Defense & Foreign Affairs Weekly*, vol. 17, no. 1 (7 Jan. 1991), p. 1; *Arms Control Reporter*, sheet 704.E-2.31, Mar. 1991.

[5] *Arms Control Reporter*, sheet 704.E-2.31, Mar. 1991; Reuters, 'Trainer of Iraqis doubts capability of chemical war', *International Herald Tribune*, 31 Jan. 1991, p. 3.

[6] The argument was made that the number of missiles was too small for meaningful military use. See Luttwak, E. N., 'The Saddam threat has been grossly exaggerated', *International Herald Tribune*, 14 Jan. 1991, p. 8; 'Engineer says gas attacks with Scud impossible', AU0402175691, Frankfurt/Main, *Frankfurter Allgemeine*, 4 Feb. 91, p. 3, in *Foreign Broadcast Information Service, Daily Report–Near East & South Asia (FBIS-NES)*, FBIS-NES-91-024, 5 Feb. 1991, p. 20; '"No time to fit" gas warheads', *The Guardian*, 31 Jan. 1991, p. 3; 'Iraqi Scuds: gas warfare duds?', *Defense News*, 28 Jan. 1991, p. 2; Slade, A. and Abrahams, P., 'Scuds carry no chemical warheads—so far', *Financial Times*, 24 Jan. 1991, p. 3; James, B., 'The Scud: an unsophisticated weapon capable of sowing mass terror', *International Herald Tribune*, 19 Jan. 1991, p. 5. It was also argued that toxins could also be destroyed

Iraqi possession of biological weapons, US forces in Kuwait were twice inoculated against anthrax and botulism because Iraq was reported to have both anthrax and botulinum in weapons.[7] There were reports that British troops had been inoculated against plague, not only because the disease was said to be present in Kuwait but also out of concern about its possible use as a biological warfare agent.[8]

A compilation of information about alleged Iraqi sites for BW and CW development and production listed facilities at a number of locations.[9] Those for research and development (R&D) were located at the Saad 16 complex (north of Irbil), at Al Kasha and at Salman Pak. CW precursor production was carried out at Baiji, Al Fallujah and Musayyib, and CW production took place at Samarra, Badush and possibly Al Qaim. A munition filling facility was located 2 km from Samarra, and artillery casing production took place at Al Iskandriyah. The United Nations Coalition Command declared that 28 chemical facilities including 11 storage areas were bombed on 17 January 1991, the first day of aerial bombing, but not all of them were destroyed by the bombing.[10] Data about all of the former alleged production sites and estimates of Iraqi capability could later be compared with post-war Iraqi declarations and the findings of UNSCOM (see chapter 13).[11]

There was little new information about CW use in the 1980–88 Iraq–Iran War in 1991 beyond that which was cited in the *SIPRI Yearbook 1991*.[12] However, much has already been written about the Gulf War. In contrast to the Iraq–Iran War, in the Gulf War Iraq risked a nuclear weapon response to CW use. The USA and other UN Coalition members replied ambiguously

---

by heat and that the precision of the missiles was not sufficient for use against Israel since they might land in Jordan. See *Arms Control Reporter*, sheet 704.E-2.26, Feb. 1991.

[7] Boatman, J., 'Biological vaccine for US troops', *Jane's Defence Weekly*, vol. 15, no. 2 (12 Jan. 1991), p. 44; Kolata, G., 'GIs targeted for experimental vaccine', *International Herald Tribune*, 5–6 Jan. 1991, p. 5.

[8] '2 February', *Chemical Weapons Convention Bulletin*, no. 12 (June 1991), p. 7.

[9] *Arms Control Reporter*, sheet 704.E-2.29-30, Feb. 1991.

[10] 'Toxic arms capability is cut, Paris says', *International Herald Tribune*, 18 Jan. 1991, p. 1; Woodward, B., 'At first glance, Iraq seems to weather the raids', *International Herald Tribune*, 29 Jan. 1991, pp. 1, 8.

[11] In accordance with UN Security Council Resolution 687 (3 Apr. 1991), on 18 Apr. Iraq reported on its CW stock to UNSCOM. Iraq declared that chemical weapons were stored at 8 airbases including 1040 mustard gas bombs of various calibres, 105 mustard gas artillery shells and 336 binary-system aerial bombs filled with sarin. At the Al Muthanna State Establishment (70 km west of Baghdad) 5 sites were declared each with 5 R&D laboratories, 6 production sites and 5 sites with workshops for filling munitions. All sites were listed as 'destroyed'. The declaration stated also that in storage at Al Muthanna were: 6920 sarin 120-mm missile warheads, 2500 sarin Saqr-30 missile warheads, 200 DB-2 aerial bombs, 280 tonnes of mustard gas, 150 tonnes of intermediate material for tabun and 500 tonnes of what appears to be phosphoryl chloride, also an intermediate for tabun. The Iraqi declaration also lists 30 chemical warheads for Al Hussein ballistic missiles in storage at Dujayl. See *Arms Control Reporter*, sheet 453.D.6/D.7, May 1991; '18 April', *Chemical Weapons Convention Bulletin*, no. 12 (June 1991), p. 19. This information was probably not intended to be made public by the UN. See *Wireless File*, no. 75, 'Iraq delivers weapons list to UN' (United States Information Service, US Embassy: Stockholm, 18 Apr. 1991), p. 3. On 28 Apr. and 4 May 1991, Iraq forwarded to the Secretary-General additional information relating to its chemical and biological weapons and ballistic missiles.

[12] See, however, Burck, G. M. and Flowerree, C. C, 'Military analysis of the use of chemical weapons', *International Handbook on Chemical Weapons Proliferation* (Greenwood Press: New York, 1991), pp. 85–126; see also SIPRI, *SIPRI Yearbook 1991* (note 3).

when asked whether or not they would retaliate with nuclear weapons,[13] and it is possible that Israel would have done so in the event of Iraqi CW attack.[14]

The war began on 17 January 1991 with heavy bombardment of Iraqi targets by cruise and other missiles and bombs with conventional warheads. Iraq fired 39 Scud missiles at Israel which were armed with conventional warheads, not chemical or biological warheads—the use of which had been feared.[15] Israel was persuaded not to retaliate for political reasons.[16] The Scud attacks initially created more psychological than material damage and aroused fear of a CW attack upon Israel. However, it should be taken into consideration that the Israeli population is comparatively well trained in CW protection. Iraq also attacked Saudi Arabia with Scud missiles.

The ground war began on 24 February and ended on 28 February without any apparent use of chemical or biological weapons. Conflicting reports about chemical weapons were given both during and after the ground war, but no CW use was reported. No large CW frontline stockpiles were found after the war,[17] although allegations were made that there had been leaks from attacked chemical targets.[18] In Kuwait a few CW stockpiles were found (some of them damaged), but no large stockpiles were discovered.[19] After the war US officials were unable to provide an explanation for the failure of Iraq to use chemical weapons,[20] but there was much speculation. One theory was that President Saddam Hussein believed that nuclear weapons would have been used against Iraq in the event of Iraqi use of chemical weapons.[21] However, there are a variety of other reasons which together or singly may have led to the non-use of these weapons including: damage to CW stockpiles and

[13] Conference on Disarmament document CD/PV.574, 16 Aug. 1990, pp. 18–21; Reuters, 'Atomkrieg bleibt Option', *Frankfurter Rundschau*, 2 Feb. 1991, p. 2; Reuters, 'Quayle calls nuclear arms "option" against chemicals', *International Herald Tribune*, 3 Feb. 1991, p. 3. See also 'U.S. decides against use of nuclear weapons', *Guardian Weekly*, vol. 144, no. 2 (13 Jan. 1991), p. 17.

[14] Brinkley, J., 'U.S. stood by as Israel enlarged nuclear arsenal, book says', *International Herald Tribune*, 21 Oct. 1991, pp. 1, 6; 'Gas and nightmares', *The Guardian*, 8 Feb. 1991, p. 2.

[15] See *Jane's Defence Weekly*, vol. 15, no. 9 (2 Mar. 1991), pp. 301–3; Haberman, C., 'Echoes of Iraqi Scuds still a nightmare for Israelis', *International Herald Tribune*, 22 Jan. 1992, pp. 1, 5.

[16] Lucas, E., and Bellamy, C., 'Cheney warns on threat of chemical warheads', *The Independent*, 28 Jan. 1991, p. 1; Diehl, J., 'With battle plan ready, Israel presses U.S. for go-ahead', *International Herald Tribune*, 29 Jan. 1991, pp. 1, 8; Ibrahim, Y. M., 'How to respond to Iraq's attack: Israel ponders the options', *International Herald Tribune*, 2 Jan. 1991, pp. 1, 5.

[17] '26 February', *Chemical Weapons Convention Bulletin*, no. 12 (June 1991), p. 12; Arkin, W. M. *et al.*, 'On impact: modern warfare and the environment, a case study of the Gulf War', A Greenpeace study prepared for a Roundtable Conference jointly organized by the Centre for Defence Studies, King's College, Greenpeace International and the London School of Economics, London, 3 June 1991, pp. 98–99; see, however, 'US-Offizier: Der Irak konnte C-Waffen nicht einsetzen', *Frankfurter Rundschau*, 28 Feb. 1991, p. 7.

[18] 'Panzer fuhr auf Giftgasmine', *Frankfurter Rundschau*, 7 Mar. 1991, p. 2; 'Giftgas-Spuren im Norden Saudi-Arabiens nachgewiesen', *Frankfurter Rundschau*, 31 Jan. 1991, p. 2; 'Iraqi ship destruction: toxic cloud noted', AU0402115191, Paris, AFP, 1114 GMT, Feb. 1991 (in English), in Foreign Broadcast Information Service, *Daily Report–West Europe (FBIS-WEU)*, FBIS-WEU-91-023, 4 Feb. 1991, p. 27; 'Nerve gas said detected after bombing in Iraq', AU0302144191, Paris, AFP, 1431 GMT, 3 Feb 1991 (in English), in FBIS-WEU-91-023, 4 Feb. 1991, p. 26.

[19] '18 August', *Chemical Weapons Convention Bulletin*, no. 14 (Dec. 1991), p. 9; *Arms Control Reporter*, sheet 704.E-2.44, Sep. 1991.

[20] '26 February', *Chemical Weapons Convention Bulletin*, no. 12 (June 1991), p. 12; Reuters, 'Excerpts from Schwarzkopf news conference on Gulf War', *New York Times*, 28 Feb. 1991, p. A8.

[21] See note 13 and Reuters (note 20).

production facilities by Coalition bombing; inability to use chemical weapons because of wind direction; refusal by Iraqi officers to obey Hussein's orders to use chemical weapons; and the possibility that no chemical weapons were in the battle zone either before or during the ground war.[22] It is also conceivable that Coalition bombing prevented Iraq from moving chemical munitions. Additionally, Iraqi nerve gas agents may not have been sufficiently pure or stable to be transported to the front.[23]

A US Department of Defense (DOD) report on the Gulf War included an allegation of BW capability and contested Iraq's assertion that it possessed no biological weapons.[24] Later UNSCOM concluded that Iraq had only a BW military research capability (see chapter 13).

Environmental implications of the Persian Gulf War

Major damage to the environment as well as to buildings and other structures in Iraq and Kuwait was a serious consequence of the Gulf War. The worst damage to the environment resulted from Iraq setting fire to the Kuwaiti oil fields and from the intentional release of oil into the Persian Gulf. The latter acts could be characterized as intentional environmental warfare and thus a possible violation of the Enmod Convention of which, however, Iraq is not a party.[25] Many of the belligerents in the war were not parties to the 1977 additional protocols of the Geneva Convention of 1949, which provide for protection of the civilian population, the environment and 'works and installations containing dangerous forces' during war.[26]

Before the war began warnings were issued about the disastrous outcome of any military action against the Kuwaiti oil fields.[27] The first problem to actually occur was created by an oil spill that developed into an enormous oil slick which threatened to spread throughout the Persian Gulf and destroy the Saudi desalination basins. The US Air Force blew up an oil pipeline complex in Kuwait to stop further crude oil from being pumped into the Gulf. Coalition forces also claimed that Iraq dumped the contents of three tankers and pumped oil directly from an off-shore tanker loading facility into the Gulf. The USA called this 'environmental terrorism' while Iraq blamed the slick on Coalition bombing of Kuwaiti oil storage tanks. US military sources speculated that Iraq had unleashed the oil to foil an amphibious attack to liberate Kuwait.[28]

---

[22] See note 14 and 'Chemicals: bad data or fair wind?', *International Herald Tribune*, 2–3 Mar. 1991, p. 7.

[23] '26 February', *Chemical Weapons Convention Bulletin* (note 20).

[24] See '16 July' and '18 July', *Chemical Weapons Convention Bulletin*, no. 13 (Sep. 1991), p. 15.

[25] Goldblat, J., SIPRI, *Agreement for Arms Control: A Critical Survey* (Taylor & Francis: London, 1982), pp. 228–29; the parties as of 1 Jan. 1992 are listed in annexe A in this volume.

[26] See Goldblat (note 25), pp. 239–44.

[27] Brown, P., 'Scientists warn of Gulf disaster', *The Guardian*, 3 Jan. 1991, p. 24.

[28] 'U.S. planes bomb pipeline complex in an effort to curtail Iraqi oil spill', *International Herald Tribune*, 28 Jan. 1991, p. 1; Pearce, F., 'Wildlife choked by world's worst oil slick', *New Scientist*, vol. 129, no. 1754 (2 Feb. 1991), pp. 24–25; Begley, S. *et al.*, 'Saddam's ecoterror', *Newsweek*, vol. 117, no. 5 (4 Feb. 1991), pp. 22–25.

The potential for ecological damage escalated before the Coalition land offensive started, when explosive charges were used by retreating Iraqi troops to deliberately destroy oil wells or set them ablaze. Initial estimates of the period that these oil fires could burn unchecked ranged from six months to five years. Estimates of the number of oil wells leaking or on fire ranged from 500 to 950. Efforts to extinguish the burning wells began on 22 March 1991 and were completed, well ahead of schedule, on 6 November 1991; between 650 and 750 fires had been put out.[29]

Hydrogen sulphide was emitted from the leaking wells, while carbon dioxide and a number of toxic gases including sulphur dioxide were released from the burning wells. Carbon dioxide is the most important 'greenhouse' gas, and sulphur dioxide is one of the gases responsible for acid rain.[30] Some scientists assessed the potential for environmental damage as minimal; others forecast catastrophe. The more extreme predictions described substantial surface cooling, absence of the Asian monsoons, extensive crop failure and accelerated global warming. Whatever the long-term effects, by March 1991 large quantities of oil had been released into the Persian Gulf; smoke clouds covered Kuwait and were spreading over Iran towards Pakistan; and 'black rain' had fallen over Kuwait, the Persian Gulf and Iran—affecting the population, water supply and agriculture.[31]

III. Negotiations on the Chemical Weapons Convention

Negotiations at the Conference on Disarmament

The 1990 negotiations on the CWC at the Conference on Disarmament (CD) ended with the final session of the *Ad Hoc* Committee on Chemical Weapons on 8–18 January 1991.[32] For 1991 Ambassador Sergey B. Batsanov, head of the then Soviet disarmament delegation, was appointed Chairman of the *Ad Hoc* Committee on Chemical Weapons.[33] This was the first time since the CD began its work in 1980 that a chairman was chosen from a superpower. The chairman organized three working groups dealing with security, verification, and legal and institutional issues including challenge inspection; he also held consultations on a number of issues. Three 'friends of the chair' held consultations on technical issues related to schedules,[34] guidelines, definitions, destruction of CW stockpiles and production facilities, and 'old chemical weapons'. In June a special meeting was held with chemical industry rep-

---

[29] Ibrahim, Y. M., 'Kuwait fires may be costlier than war', *International Herald Tribune*, 14 Mar. 1991, pp. 1, 6; Reuters, 'Fewer than 100 oil wells need capping in Kuwait', *International Herald Tribune*, 17 Oct. 1991, p. 6; *Wireless File*, no. 57, 'Damaged Kuwaiti oil wells are environmental disaster' (United States Information Service, US Embassy: Stockholm, 25 Mar. 1991), pp. 3–4; Associated Press, 'Kuwait caps the last well', *The Independent*, 7 Nov. 1991, p. 12.

[30] Watts, S., 'Kuwait "could burn for a year"', *The Independent*, 3 Jan. 1991, p. 1.

[31] Small, R. D., 'Environmental impact of fires in Kuwait', *Nature*, vol. 350, no. 6313 (7 Mar. 1991), pp. 11–12.

[32] Conference on Disarmament document CD/1046, 18 Jan. 1991.

[33] He completed his chairmanship as the Russian Federation's Ambassador to the CD.

[34] For a discussion of the CWC schedules see SIPRI, *SIPRI Yearbook 1991* (note 3), pp. 522–23.

resentatives. Such meetings have been held annually for several years. Other meetings focused on analytical data bases and laboratories, and CW destruction. The work of the *Ad Hoc* Committee took place at three formal sessions: 22 January–28 March, 14 May–27 June and 23 July–4 September. In addition, work was done in various working groups and consultations during the year except for during the BWC Review Conference on 9–27 September, the meeting of the First Committee of the UN on 14 October–15 November and during the Christmas holidays.[35] The session closed on 20 January 1992.

The 1990 mandate was initially adopted for the negotiations,[36] but in June it was replaced by a new mandate which for the first time included a prohibition on use and requested 'striving to achieve a final agreement on the convention by 1992'.[37] During 1991, 37 states requested observer status to allow them to participate in the work of the *Ad Hoc* Committee.[38] France proposed that a meeting with the *Ad Hoc* Committee be held at the ministerial level in 1991 to finalize the CWC.[39]

The question of verifying that chemical warfare agents are not being produced in the chemical industry has not yet been solved. This is a problem because the chemical industry also produces so-called key precursor and precursor chemicals (i.e., chemicals which could be used in the production of chemical warfare agents but which also have legitimate industrial uses). Sweden presented a working paper aimed at simplifying verification of nonproduction of chemical weapons in the chemical industry by applying a random inspection system for chemicals listed on schedules 2 or 3 of the CWC. The working paper suggested that facilities be selected on the basis of their capability to perform relevant chemical processes rather than on the basis of actual production of the substances, but a clear definition of the term 'capability' was not given. This system would aim to dispense with the need for 'facility agreements', decrease the number of required inspections and increase deterrence against clandestine production of scheduled chemicals in undeclared facilities.[40] The UK issued a working paper on thresholds for the regime regulating those chemicals covered by schedule 2B. The suggested quantitative criterion for a militarily significant quantity of a toxic chemical (which would be subject to verification measures) was set at a billion times the amount of the toxic dose of a substance. Five levels were suggested for different production thresholds to be declared under the CWC.[41] The consultations in the working group on schedules are reflected in an alternative formulation of Article VI (activities not prohibited by the convention), which envisages

[35] Conference on Disarmament document CD/CW/WP.363, 21 Aug. 1991; Conference on Disarmament document CD/1116, 20 Jan. 1992.

[36] Conference on Disarmament document CD/1058, 14 Feb. 1991.

[37] Conference on Disarmament document CD/1085, 20 June 1991.

[38] See Conference on Disarmament document CD/CW/WP.363 (note 35), p. 2; Conference on Disarmament document CD/1108, 27 Aug. 1991; Conference on Disarmament document CD/INF.27, 9 Aug. 1991.

[39] Conference on Disarmament document CD/PV.594, 6 June 1991, pp. 16–20.

[40] Conference on Disarmament document CD/1053, 4 Feb. 1991.

[41] Conference on Disarmament document CD/CW/WP.358, 13 Aug. 1991.

other approaches to the verification problem.[42] A German working paper presented verification options resulting from consultations in the Western Group and suggested definitions related to activity and facility declarations.[43] A final position on verification measures for the chemical industry will probably not be arrived at until there has been adequate discussion of the new US proposal for challenge inspection (or 'inspection on request') described below.

In early 1991 several statements were made that the USA was preparing to abandon its position, which had met with much criticism in the CD and elsewhere, that parties to the CWC should be able to: (a) keep 2 per cent of their CW stockpiles for eight years or longer after entry into force of the CWC, depending on whether or not the convention was considered effective after that time-period,[44] and (b) retain the right to retaliate with chemical weapons during that period. On 13 May 1991, President Bush announced a new US initiative (presented on 16 May in the CD) to abandon the so-called '2 per cent solution' and 'the right of retaliation in kind'. He urged that work on the CWC should be completed by the end of 1991 and that the convention should be ready for signing within a year. He further recommended that the CD remain in continuous session until the CWC was concluded and declared the US intent to be one of the first signatories of the CWC.[45] Bush also stated that a new US position on challenge inspections would be forthcoming, and in fact consultations on this question had been held in the Western Group in the early spring. On 15 July the USA presented a CD working paper on challenge inspections together with Australia, Japan and the UK;[46] the working paper contained a completely new US view. It also differed in some important respects from the widely supported British proposal of 'managed access', which had been presented at the previous session and upon the basis of which several trial inspections had been conducted.[47] As explained in the British working paper, the basic idea is to make it possible for a state party to deny access to sites which it claims contain secret installations and equipment unrelated to the CWC, the disclosure of which could seriously jeopardize the security of the inspected party. For the USA, for example, these include classified military research, development and production sites not related to chemical weapons.[48]

The new joint proposal considerably extends the time-frame within which access to a requested site should be negotiated and accepted, from the previous

[42] Conference on Disarmament document CD/CW/WP.362, 19 Aug. 1991; Conference on Disarmament document CD/CW/WP.363 (note 35), p. 129.

[43] Conference on Disarmament document CD/CW/WP.370, 9 Oct. 1991.

[44] SIPRI, *SIPRI Yearbook 1990: World Armaments and Disarmament* (Oxford University Press: Oxford, 1990), pp. 516–18.

[45] *Arms Control Reporter*, sheet 704.D.159, May 1991; Conference on Disarmament document CD/PV.591, 16 May 1991; Conference on Disarmament document CD/1077, 23 May 1991.

[46] Conference on Disarmament document CD/CW/WP.352, 15 July 1991.

[47] The concept of 'managed access' was presented in Conference on Disarmament document CD/1012, 11 July 1990.

[48] Smithson, A. E., 'Chemical inspectors: on the outside looking in', *Bulletin of the Atomic Scientists*, vol. 47, no. 8 (Oct. 1991), pp. 23–25; Gizewski, P., 'US position on challenge inspection threatens chemical weapon treaty', Canadian Centre for Arms Control and Disarmament, *Arms Control Centre Communique*, no. 82 (17 Oct. 1991).

48 hours up to 168 hours (one week). Four differently defined perimeters of access have been introduced: initial, alternative, provisional and final. The state party to be inspected retains the right to define the 'final perimeter' and is obligated to ensure that 'at least part of the requested perimeter is visible'. The inspected state party is also given the right to deny access completely or to limit access to outside a much larger 'perimeter' border than that which had been requested. Whereas the former US position implied a right to inspect anywhere, the new proposal suggests that alternative inspection sites or information can be offered instead of that which has been requested. In order for the inspection team to confirm that the 'status quo' (i.e., the state of the site prior to notification of the impending inspection) has not been altered, it was proposed that the inspection team be allowed to conduct aerial surveillance of the site in question. The earlier British concept of 'managing' access to a sensitive installation by allowing various concealment measures has been largely abandoned. The challenged party can instead choose to allow access to a suspected site by one of four means: aerial overflight, observation from an 'elevated platform', managed access inside the facility or the use of tamper-proof sensors.

Some negotiating states at the CD appear to support the new proposal, apparently considering it a workable solution to the problem of inspection on challenge.[49] Other countries including some Western states have opposed it, and France is said to have suggested amendments during consultations.[50] There has also been criticism that, under the proposal, the previously accepted obligatory character of the challenge inspections would become voluntary and control of the actual inspection would be shifted from the international inspection team to the inspected state party.

In light of the major changes in Europe, the US agreement with the former USSR on the destruction of chemical weapons and the new power of the UN Secretary-General to investigate accusations of violation of the 1925 Geneva Protocol, the USA in particular seems to have less interest in an 'effectively verifiable' CWC than in preventing potential abuse of the challenge verification mechanism. The USA seems more interested in its own security than in detecting possible violation of the CWC by other countries. In contrast, the chemical industry is willing to accept rather intrusive verification measures under the CWC in order to demonstrate that it is not conducting CW production. The new US position also gives conflicting signals to the chemical industry about the requirement of openness under the CWC.[51] There have been some suggestions that the US Senate may look more favourably upon ratifying a CWC that also protects US security instead of one which may not be completely verifiable as some have claimed.[52] However, the other shifts in US

[49] Among them Argentina and Poland, see Conference on Disarmament document CD/PV.601, 8 Aug. 1991, pp. 3–4, 12–16; see also Pakistan, Conference on Disarmament document CD/PV.600, 1 Aug. 1991, pp. 4–7.
[50] Arms Control Reporter, sheet 704.B.494, Sep. 1991.
[51] Colby, E. and Harris, E. D., 'Look who's barring access to weapons sites', Washington Post, 28 July 1991, p. C7.
[52] Arms Control Reporter, sheet 704.B.496, Sep. 1991.

policy mentioned above—abandoning the 2 per cent solution, agreeing to a prohibition on CW use and giving up the right to retaliate in kind—would make the CWC comprehensive.

By the end of 1991 reports on approximately 60 trial inspections had been presented to the CD;[53] they are outlined in appendix 6A. These trial inspections were for the most part national trial inspections (NTIs) conducted by CD members and observers in their own countries. However, a few international trial inspections of a national facility were performed with the participation of other CD countries.[54] Some of the inspections used routine inspection procedures while others simulated challenge inspections to varying degrees of realism. The inspected facilities included chemical plants, military air fields, nuclear installations and weapon storage sites.[55] Not all of the inspections can be covered here, but a few of them or the criteria used to conduct them deserve special mention.

The British concept of 'managed access', which aims to meet concerns about military security during challenge inspections performed under the CWC, was developed and tested in several NTIs in 1991 and earlier. In Germany, NTIs were performed at air bases with the participation of inspectors from other countries. Realistic inspections were also made at what had been Soviet military bases in Poland and the former German Democratic Republic to certify that no chemical weapons were then stockpiled there. These trial inspections at a number of industrial facilities were intended to work out suitable procedures for routine and challenge inspections. In many cases they were perhaps more intrusive than would have been possible under the CWC, since the risk of leaking commercial and technical secrets could be considered small. Two working papers presented by the US delegation reported on inspections performed using the new US verification approach at an industrial and a military chemical facility.

Both routine and 'any time, anywhere' challenge inspections were endorsed in declarations made by representatives of national chemical industry organizations at a Geneva meeting with representatives of the CD delegations on 24–27 June 1991. The chemical industry agreed to participate fully in such inspections under a future CWC but stressed the need for a qualitative verification system which would make it possible to protect confidential business information and which would concentrate on verification of non-production of

[53] A preliminary discussion of these results was held by the Pugwash Study Group on Chemical Weapons in June 1991; it is reported on in Trapp, R., 'CW technical expert meeting to evaluate experiences from national trial inspections (report)', *Pugwash Newsletter*, vol. 29, no. 1 (July 1991), pp. 28–31.

[54] A SIPRI study evaluating the results of the national and international trial inspections which have been conducted by a majority of the CD negotiating countries is being prepared. See Trapp, R., SIPRI, *Verification under the Projected Chemical Weapons Convention: On-Site Inspection in Chemical Industry Facilities*, SIPRI Chemical & Biological Warfare Studies, no. 14 (Oxford University Press: Oxford, forthcoming).

[55] For a definition of 'facilities' see Conference on Disarmament document CD/1116 (note 35), pp. 17–18.

chemicals listed on schedule 1 of the draft CWC.[56] However, some countries still voiced hesitancy about inspection of the chemical industry.[57]

The technical details of the NTIs are ultimately dependent upon political agreement on the text of the CWC. Also when routine inspection concepts were introduced, the technical limitations of applying certain inspection methods, such as materials balances and singular routine inspections, were not adequately considered. A 1991 SIPRI publication addressed some of these issues in a case study of how the verification provisions of the CWC might be applied to the production of a particular chemical—thiodiglycol, a precursor chemical for mustard gas.[58]

In the context of verification of the future CWC it is important to consider the UNSCOM experience (see chapter 13). UNSCOM's inspections are not directly comparable to verification under the future CWC since it is unlikely that the same level of access could be achieved or that the agreed upon sanctions could be so intrusive or effective under the future CWC.[59] UNSCOM has demonstrated that substantial effort is required to inspect facilities on site, provide logistic support, set up laboratories for analytical investigation, recruit suitable inspection personnel, organize inspections on very short notice and arrange for the destruction of weapon stockpiles. The time aspects are also illustrative; unless an adequate organization exists, it will not be easy to make inspections rapidly enough to obtain crucial evidence. The new US proposal on challenge verification should also be seen in the light of UNSCOM's experiences.[60] The political conditions under which the CWC can be finalized may be such that it will be impossible to obtain information about alleged violation of the convention. It may only be possible to obtain information about alleged violations in situations where the UN Security Council intervenes and applies strong measures.

A number of other issues were also dealt with at the CD negotiations. A solution seems to have been found to the controversial question of how to enforce the provisions of the CWC in all areas under the 'jurisdiction and control' of a party.[61] New language implies that a state party cannot produce chemical weapons on the territory of another country, and that it is responsible for ensuring that its citizens do not engage in illegal activities anywhere in the world. The question of sanctions began to be addressed by the CD but has not

---

[56] The meeting of chemical industry representatives with CD negotiators took place in June 1991. The papers and joint proposals presented by the European Chemical Industry Council (CEFIC), the US Chemical Manufacturers Association (CMA) and the Japanese Chemical Industry Association are reported in *CEFIC and CMA Positions on Chemical Weapons Convention Issues Affecting the Chemical Industry* (Chemical Manufacturers Association: Washington, DC, June 1991).

[57] Conference on Disarmament document CD/1031, 10 Aug. 1990; Conference on Disarmament document CD/PV.600 (note 49); *Arms Control Reporter*, sheet 704. B 494-5, Sep. 1991.

[58] Lundin, S. J. (ed.), SIPRI, *Verification of Dual-use Chemicals under the Chemical Weapons Convention: The Case of Thiodiglycol*, SIPRI Chemical & Biological Warfare Studies, no. 13 (Oxford University Press: Oxford, 1991).

[59] United Nations Security Council Resolution S/RES/687 (1991), 8 Apr. 1991.

[60] Conference on Disarmament document CD/CW/WP.356, 6 Aug. 1991.

[61] Conference on Disarmament document CD/1108 (note 38), pp. 175–76.

yet been resolved.[62] As usual a number of highly technical working papers were presented to the CD, particularly regarding techniques for chemical analysis.[63] The prohibition on use in Article I was discussed in the context of a complete CW ban;[64] this would mean that in the future no reservations to the prohibition on first use of chemical and biological weapons and retaliation in kind under the 1925 Geneva Protocol would be possible. On 13 May, President Bush pledged to withdraw the US reservations to the Geneva Protocol which are related to chemical weapons.[65]

During 1991 work on the CWC took several unexpected turns which may positively affect the rapid conclusion of the convention. However, strong political will to finalize the convention must be demonstrated if the CWC is to be ready for signing in 1992, which President Bush has stated is his goal. If the convention is to be presented to the UN in 1992, the time available for concluding it would therefore be limited to the first half of 1992.

Bilateral and regional negotiations

The bilateral meetings on chemical weapons between the USA and the former USSR continued with a 17th meeting at Geneva in January and February. A US delegation paid a visit to a Soviet CW stockpile site in January,[66] and in February a Soviet Delegation visited the CW storage facility on Johnston Atoll, a Dupont phosgene facility in Deepwater, New Jersey, and the mothballed dichlor facility at Muscle Shoals, Alabama.[67] These visits met the obligations assumed under the 1989 Memorandum of Understanding.[68] Bilateral meetings were not continued during the rest of 1991 due to the unsettled situation in the former USSR and its impact on both political decisions about chemical weapons and the technical capability to begin the CW destruction agreed in the Memorandum of Understanding.

During 1991 a number of attempts were made to obtain regional agreements on chemical weapons and other weapons of mass destruction. The Organization of American States (OAS) sought a ban on chemical and biological weapons for the Americas.[69] In the Mendoza Agreement, Argentina, Brazil, Chile and later Uruguay agreed to stop the development, production and acquisition of chemical weapons and to work for conclusion of the CWC and strengthening of the BWC.[70] India announced that it was interested in entering discussion with Pakistan about chemical weapons following reports

[62] Conference on Disarmament document CD/1075, 14 May, 1991; Conference on Disarmament document CD/PV.592, 23 May 1991, pp. 8–15.

[63] See, for example, the contributions of Finland and the Netherlands, Conference on Disarmament document CD/CW/WP.342, 6 June 1991; Finland, Conference on Disarmament document CD/1112, 9 Oct. 1991; Austria, Conference on Disarmament document CD/1076, 21 May 1991; Norway, Conference on Disarmament documents CD/1078, 30 May 1991 and CD/1084, 14 June 1991.

[64] See Conference on Disarmament document CD/PV.601 (note 49), pp. 7–8.

[65] Arms Control Reporter (note 45); see also table in annexe A, this volume.

[66] See Arms Control Reporter, sheet 704.B.467, Mar. 1991.

[67] See Arms Control Reporter, sheet 704.B.468, July 1991.

[68] SIPRI, SIPRI Yearbook 1990 (note 44), pp. 531–32.

[69] Arms Control Reporter, sheet 704.B.489, July 1991.

[70] See note 1; Arms Control Reporter, sheet 704.B.500, Sep. 1991.

that Pakistan was in the process of acquiring chemical weapons.[71] Talks between India and Pakistan took place in October, and it was agreed that further talks would be held.[72] North Korea and South Korea called for 'phased reductions in armaments, including the elimination of weapons of mass destruction'.[73] In December Bolivia, Colombia, Ecuador, Peru and Venezuela signed a declaration renouncing weapons of mass destruction, including chemical and biological weapons, at Cartagena de India in Colombia.[74]

In the Middle East a number of statements were made during 1991 about establishing a zone free of weapons of mass destruction, including chemical weapons.[75] In his anti-proliferation initiative in May, President Bush expressed support for a chemical weapon-free zone (CWFZ) in the Middle East[76] as did the other leaders of the five permanent members of the UN Security Council during their July meeting in Paris.[77] There is no immediate hope that such a zone will be created in the Middle East. However, despite apprehensions about their use, chemical weapons were not used in the Gulf War and this may provide a basis for negotiations on a CWFZ in the Middle East or, if a CWC is concluded in the near future, make it possible for countries in the Middle East to adhere to the convention.

IV. New developments in CW and BW proliferation

There was intense debate about the proliferation of chemical and to some extent biological weapons during 1991 because of the Gulf War. In addition to Iraq, US officials have identified 14 other developing countries as having CW programmes or possessing an offensive chemical warfare capability.[78] US figures list at least 7 countries as BW possessors or as BW capable.[79] Other figures were given in May 1991 by the departing Director of the US Central

---

[71] *Arms Control Reporter*, sheet 704.B.490, July 1991.

[72] 'Pakistan, India to discuss limiting chemical arms', BK3110155991, Islamabad Radio, Pakistan Network, 15 GMT, 31 Oct. 1991 (in Urdu), in FBIS-NES-91-212, 1 Nov. 1991, p. 86.

[73] See *Arms Control Reporter* (note 2).

[74] See note 2.

[75] *Arms Control Reporter*, sheet 453.B.113, June 1991; sheet 453.B.117, Oct. 1991; sheet 453.B.118, Oct. 1991; sheet 453.B.120, Oct. 1991; sheet 453.B.127, Dec. 1991; Lundin, J. and Stock, T., 'Chemical and biological weapons: proliferation or elimination?', in Rotfeld, A. D., (ed.), SIPRI, *Global Security and the Rule of Law* (Oxford University Press: Oxford, forthcoming)..

[76] See US Department of State, Bureau of Public Affairs, 'Fact sheet: Middle East arms control initiative', *Dispatch*, vol. 2, no. 22 (3 June 1991), pp. 393–94.

[77] Waxman, S., 'Nations draw Mideast arms guidelines', *Washington Post*, 10 July 1991, p. A6; Riding, A., 'Big 5 pledge for Mideast: ban devastating arms', *New York Times*, 10 July 1991, p. A9; Opall, B., 'Big 5 to discuss Mideast arms sale limits', *Defense News*, vol. 6, no. 27 (8 July 1991), p. 11; 'UNSC "Five" committed to Mideast arms control', *Wireless File*, no. 132 (United States Information Service, US Embassy: Stockholm, 10 July 1991), pp. 10–11.

[78] Durbin, R. J. in *Foreign Aid Funding and Chemical Weapons*, Hearing before the Task Force on Defense, Foreign Policy and Space of the Committee on the Budget, House of Representatives, 102nd Congress, 1st session, serial no. 3-1, 30 May 1991(US Government Printing Office: Washington, DC, 1991), p. 2; 'Statement of Harris, Elisa D., Senior Research Analyst, The Brookings Institution' in the same Hearing, p. 4.

[79] 'Statement of Rear Admiral Thomas A. Brooks, USN Director of Naval Intelligence, before the Seapower, Strategic, and Critical Materials Subcommittee of the House Armed Services Committee on Intelligence Issues', Washington, DC, 7 Mar. 1991; Smith, R. J., 'U.S. agencies at odds on who has chemical arms', *International Herald Tribune*, 16–17 Mar. 1991, p. 3.

Intelligence Agency (CIA): 'Twenty years ago, only five countries possessed chemical weapons. By the year 2000, as many as two dozen countries could have chemical and/or biological warfare capabilities'.[80] That CW and to some extent BW proliferation is occurring is no longer disputed, but the only hard evidence relates to Iraq. It is impossible to present more proof of CW acquisition or possession for a number of reasons including: (a) governments are reluctant to openly identify other countries which have chemical weapons or CW programmes; (b) governments do not explain how they acquire information and draw conclusions; and (c) most of the countries about which allegations have been made have not openly deployed chemical or biological weapons.[81] Different factors may influence a country's decision to acquire chemical weapons such as: (a) the geopolitical situation of the country, (b) its military threat perception, (c) its ability to obtain other weapons of mass destruction, (d) its industrial capability, (e) its access to weapons which are capable of delivering chemical agents, and (f) the means of protection against chemical weapons available to it.[82]

CW proliferation in the Middle East

The Gulf War highlighted the proliferation problem in the Middle East. Discussion of the Iraqi chemical and biological acquisition programme and the support from other countries has overshadowed allegations of proliferation which have been made against other countries in the region including Iran, Libya and Syria.

It was alleged that Iran is planning to build a CW plant in Quazvin[83] and has asked Germany to help in the installation of a 'pesticide facility'. Allegations that Libya has a CW programme continued to be made, specifically that a second CW-agent production facility is under construction at Sebha, probably modelled on the German Imhausen-Chemie GmbH project 'Pharma 200' and located underground.[84] In April it was reported that Imhausen's plans for the 'Pharma 150' CW-agent factory at Rabta had been passed on to another unidentified developing country,[85] which would imply that a new stage of CW proliferation has started. Libya denied claims that it is building a large

---

[80] Remarks by William H. Webster, Director of Central Intelligence, at the Amherst Association, New York, N.Y., 22 May 1991, p. 9.

[81] See Lundin and Stock (note 75) and Harris, E. D., 'Stemming the spread of chemical weapons', *Brookings Review*, winter 1989/90, pp. 39-45.

[82] See note 81.

[83] 'Iran plant angeblich Bau einer Giftgasanlage', *Frankfurter Rundschau*, 15 July 1991, p. 5.

[84] Mann, J., 'U.S. says Libya builds bunker for toxic arms', *International Herald Tribune*, 7 Mar. 1991, pp. 1, 4; 'Libye', *Afrique Défense*, June 1991, pp. 7–8; *Hansard*, Written Answers, vol. 189, no. 88 (15 Apr. 1991), p. 110; *Hansard*, Written Answers, vol. 186, no. 6 (26 Feb. 1991), p. 459; 'German TV says weapons arsenal under construction', LD0602110491, Hamburg, DPA, 1023 GMT, 6 Feb. 1991 (in German), in FBIS-NES-91-027, 8 Feb. 1991, p. 9; Associated Press, 'Libya making 2d gas plant, U.S. says', *International Herald Tribune*, 21 Mar. 1991, p. 2. See also 'U.S. concerned about Libyan chemical weapons', *Wireless File*, no. 44 (United States Information Service, US Embassy: Stockholm, 6 Mar. 1991), p. 1.

[85] Scheuer, T. and Rocker, S., 'Immenhausens giftige Kettenreaktionen', *Die Tageszeitung*, 12 Apr. 1991, p. 13; 'Poison gas factory plans reach "Third Party"', LD1104145291, Hamburg, DPA, 1304 GMT, 11 Apr 1991 (in German), in FBIS-NES-91-071, 12 Apr. 1991.

underground storage facility for chemical and nuclear weapons.[86] After a facility at Rabta was allegedly destroyed by fire, Libya also denied that chemical weapons had been produced there[87] and invited the countries of the Maghreb to inspect a new facility at Rabta which will soon begin the production of pharmaceuticals,[88] according to statements made by Libya.

Foreign involvement in the Iraqi CBW programme

It is not possible to make definite judgements concerning all of the allegations made before and during the Gulf War about the assistance provided by other countries to Iraq's CW and BW programme.[89] Before the Gulf War began, at least 20 countries were accused of involvement in building up the technological basis for different Iraqi weapon programmes, particularly the CW programme.[90] Much information came to light about German companies, and officials in the Federal Economics Ministry investigated approximately 110 German firms on suspicion of violation of the embargo against Iraq. Nine of them are under criminal investigation.[91] Other countries, among them the UK and the USA,[92] were also accused of supporting the Iraqi CBW programme by the sale of chemicals and technology. In the UK it was discovered that chemicals on the Australia Group's control list had been sold to Iraq from 1988 to October 1990.[93]

During the second UNSCOM investigation in Iraq in August, a list was compiled of companies which had supplied technology to the Iraqi CBW programme. According to August press reports, 207 companies from 21 countries were involved in the buildup of Iraq's CW capability.[94] The list was not released, but governments can obtain information on the involvement of companies from their own country upon special request to the UN.[95] The Inter-

---

[86] 'Report called "completely false"', LD0602144891, Tripoli, JANA, 1415 GMT, 6 Feb. 1991 (in Arabic), in FBIS-NES-91-027, 8 Feb. 1991, p. 9.

[87] Reuters, 'Giftgas-Produktion bestritten', *Frankfurter Rundschau*, 9 Mar. 1991, p. 2.

[88] Reuters, 'Bald Medikamente aus Rabta?', *Frankfurter Rundschau*, 1 Mar. 1991, p. 2.

[89] SIPRI, *SIPRI Yearbook 1991* (note 3), pp. 88–89.

[90] Cordesman, A. H., *Weapons of Mass Destruction in the Middle East* (Brassey's: London, 1991), pp. 64–65.

[91] Associated Press, 'Crackdown on Germans aiding Iraq', *International Herald Tribune*, 7 Feb. 1991, p. 3; Reuters, 'Germans open embargo inquiry', *International Herald Tribune*, 12 Feb. 1991, p. 4; Donkin, R. *et al.*, 'A country that turned a blind eye', *Financial Times*, 25 Mar. 1991, p. 20.

[92] Wines, M., 'U.S. tells of prewar technology sales to Iraq worth $500 million', *New York Times*, 12 Mar. 1991, p. A6; Friedman, A. *et al.*, 'The sinister alchemy of the Iraqi "doctor"', *Financial Times*, 3 Mar. 1991, p. 4; Friedman, A. and Barber, L., 'US cyanide shipped to Iraq despite warnings to CIA', *Financial Times*, 3 July 1991, p. 1.

[93] The Australia Group is a group which meets semi-annually to discuss which chemicals ought to be subject to various regulatory measures. Mullin, J., 'UK firms sent Iraq chemicals', *The Guardian*, 29 July 1991, p. 1; *Exports to Iraq: Memoranda of Evidence*, House of Commons, Session 1990–91 (Her Majesty's Stationery Office: London, 17 July 1991); Wilkie, T., 'Iraq export row "due to ignorance of statistics"', *The Independent*, 8 Aug. 1991, p. 2.

[94] 'The UN should name names', *The Independent*, 1 Aug 1991, p. 18; Pfäffle, W., 'UNO erstellt Liste westlicher Lieferanten', *Süddeutsche Zeitung*, no. 182 (8 Aug. 1991), p. 6.

[95] DPA, Associated Press, AFP, 'UNO soll deutsche Firmen nennen', *Süddeutsche Zeitung*, 16 Aug. 1991, p. 8.

national Atomic Energy Agency (IAEA) also reported on the support given the Iraqi nuclear programme by foreign companies.[96]

New initiatives to prevent proliferation

In 1991 many countries reconsidered their export regulations and strengthening of regulations on the trade of chemicals and dual-use chemical technology owing to: (a) the current technological, political and economic status of the trade of chemicals and related technology, and (b) the foreign involvement in the Iraqi CBW programme described above.[97]

In December 1990 President Bush approved new unilateral US export control procedures and regulations intended to streamline and clarify export licence processing and to enhance efforts to stem the spread of missile technology and of NBC weapons. One aspect of these new export controls is the Enhanced Proliferation Control Initiative (EPCI), which took effect in February 1991.[98] In connection with the EPCI, the US Department of Commerce issued a draft list of 23 categories of production processes which are to be monitored and which involve sensitive equipment. As a result the chemical and electronic industries embarked upon intensive lobbying to dissuade the Administration from such a large expansion of unilateral export controls.[99] The major problem seemed to be the core list of countries involved, and a compromise was arrived at by listing regions instead of individual countries.[100] A report published by the US National Academy of Sciences advocated inter alia: (a) the use of surprise on-site verification methods to ensure that commercial technology transfer not be used for military purposes, (b) centralization within the Bureau of Export Administration to facilitate enforcement of export controls, and (c) regarding export control of weapons of mass destruction, including chemical agents, as a national security matter.[101]

In February the US Senate passed legislation which requires the President to impose sanctions on countries and companies which develop or use chem-

[96] Reuters, 'Der Irak nutzte deutsche Technik für Atomwaffen-Programm', Süddeutsche Zeitung, 13 Dec. 1991, p. 1.

[97] The following evaluation of initiatives to strengthen export regulations on relevant CBW material and technology is by no means comprehensive; SIPRI plans to address this issue in a future publication.

[98] Davis, Z. S., Non-Proliferation Regimes: A Comparative Analysis of Policies to Control the Spread of Nuclear, Chemical and Biological Weapons and Missiles, CRS Report for Congress, CRS 91-334 ENR (Congressional Research Service, Library of Congress: Washington, DC, 1 Apr. 1991), pp. CRS-24–25; see also SIPRI, SIPRI Yearbook 1991 (note 3), p. 108.

[99] 'War with Iraq spurs new export controls', Science; vol. 251, no. 4993 (1 Feb. 1991), pp. 512–14; 'Neuer Auftrag für die Exportkontrolle', Neue Zürcher Zeitung, 2 Feb. 1991, p. 17.

[100] Auerbach, S., 'U.S. to curb exports of chemicals that can be used for arms', International Herald Tribune, 28 Feb. 1991, p. 2.

[101] Panel on the Future Design and Implementation of U.S. National Security Export Controls, Committee on Science, Engineering, and Public Policy, Finding Common Ground: U.S. Export Controls in a Changed Global Environment (National Academy of Science, National Academy of Engineering, Institute of Medicine: National Academy Press, Washington, DC 1991); Lepkowski, W. and Seltzer R., 'Export controls: high-level panel urges sharp changes', Chemical & Engineering News, vol. 69, no. 5 (4 Feb. 1991); Silverberg, D., 'Science panel calls inspections of commercial exports outdated', Defense News, vol. 6, no. 5 (4 Feb. 1991), p. 40.

ical and biological weapons.[102] In March two new sets of export control regulations were issued. The first makes all 50 chemicals on the Australia Group list subject to export licensing requirements if they are sold to countries which are not members of NATO or the Australia Group; the second regulates equipment and technical data for CW and BW production. Twelve categories of dual-purpose technology are covered, and a list of 28 countries are defined as 'controlled destinations'.[103] An 'inter-agency CBW sanctions working group' was established to work on further development of the US export control policy.[104]

On 29 May President Bush outlined his Middle East arms control initiative on missiles and NBC weapons. As regards chemical weapons, he called for regional states 'to commit to becoming original parties to the convention' and 'to institute confidence-building measures by engaging in pre-signature implementation of appropriate chemical weapons convention provisions'.[105] In a June working paper, the USA officially informed the CD about US export controls on CW-sensitive material and technology and US domestic legislation.[106] Following extensive debate in the USA, another US proposal was tabled at the CD in August; it dealt with the limitation and regulation of the trade of chemicals listed on the schedules of the draft CWC. The proposal recommended that each state party establish and maintain a system to monitor the import and export of listed chemicals, equipment and technology used to produce such chemicals under the provisions of Article VII of the CWC.[107]

Canadian Prime Minister Brian Mulroney and Secretary of State for External Affairs Joe Clark proposed in February that a world summit meeting be held on 'instruments of war and weapons of mass destruction'. The proposal included a call for an 'expansion of the Australia Group's membership and the enhanced enforcement of national controls on the export of chemicals that could be used in the production of chemical weapons'.[108] In March Canada increased the number of chemicals on its restricted export list from 14 to 50 to

---

[102] 'U.S. backs chemical arms' sanctions', *International Herald Tribune*, 22 Feb. 1991, p. 2; Clymer, A., 'New bill mandates sanctions on makers of chemical arms', *New York Times*, 22 Feb. 1991, p. A6.

[103] 'Washington clamps down on chemical exports', *New Scientist*, vol. 129, no. 1759 (9 Mar. 1991), p. 13; 'U.S. sets curbs on arms parts', *International Herald Tribune*, 9–10 Mar. 1991, p. 3; Reuters/DPA, 'USA verschärfen Exportregeln', *Frankfurter Rundschau*, 9 Mar. 1991, p. 2; 'USA erschweren Export von gefährlichen Gütern', *Süddeutsche Zeitung*, 9–10 Mar. 1991, p. 7; Silverberg, D., 'Gulf war highlights new technology export control questions', *Defense News*, vol. 6, no. 12 (25 Mar. 1991), p. 56; Silverberg, D., 'U.S. takes steps to curb chemical arms', *Defense News*, vol 6, no. 1 (11 Mar. 1991), p. 4.

[104] 'Progress seen in curbing weapons proliferation', text of congressional testimony of Richard Clarke, Assistant Secretary of State for Political and Military Affairs, *News Backgrounder* (United States Information Service, US Embassy: Stockholm, 25 Apr 1991).

[105] See note 76.

[106] Conference on Disarmament document CD/1086, 28 June 1991.

[107] Conference on Disarmament document CD/CW/WP.357, 8 Aug. 1991.

[108] 'Gulf War highlights need for better proliferation control', *The Disarmament Bulletin*, no. 16 (spring 1991), pp. 1–3; 'Canada and the challenges of the post-war period in the Gulf', excerpts from a speech by the Right Honourable Joe Clark, Secretary of State for External Affairs, at the Canadian Institute of International Affairs, Quebec City, 8 Feb. 1992, *Disarmament Bulletin*, no. 16 (spring 1991), pp. 3–5.

encourage other countries to restrict the export of arms to unstable regions such as the Persian Gulf.[109]

In February 1991, Australia submitted a working paper to the CD which focused *inter alia* on Australia's increase to 50 of the number of CW precursor chemicals which it subjects to export controls; the list includes chemicals on schedules 1, 2 and 3 of the CWC.[110] The suggestion was also made that certain chemicals be added to schedule 3.

Romania reported to the CD that four of its ministries had issued 'Order no. 40 on the control of exports which could contribute to the proliferation of weapons of mass-destruction and of the missiles carrying such weapons' on 8 July 1991.[111] The legislation covers 50 chemical precursors, equipment, and plants or components that could be used for CW production.

In December 1990, the United Kingdom strengthened its national legislation by increasing the number of chemicals which are covered by export licensing regulations to a total of 37.[112] A seminar for business on the role of export control of NBC and missile technology was organized for the first time in January 1991.[113] In July the UK added 13 potential CW precursors to its export control list, thereby regulating all 50 of the chemicals on the Australia Group list.[114]

In March the Cabinet of the Government of Belgium gave its approval of new legislation regulating the export of military and dual-use equipment.[115]

In June Bulgaria informed the CD that a national commission, which will later become the country's National Authority under Article VII of the CWC, had been established to prepare for the future convention.[116]

Switzerland announced that, as of January 1992, all 50 chemicals on the Australia Group list must meet specific licensing requirements for export from Switzerland.[117]

The Federal Republic of Germany strengthened national export control legislation because of numerous allegations of involvement by German companies in the Iraqi armament programme. In February new proposals were approved that increase penalties for violation of German export control laws or of UN sanctions against Iraq. These proposals give new powers to German customs and security agencies, including the right to tap telephones and intercept mail, and require the Federal Intelligence Service to provide prosecutors with information gained from the interception of mail.[118] The Bundestag (the

[109] Pugliese, D., 'Canada hopes to set pace on exporting', *Defense News*, vol. 6, no. 10 (11 Mar. 1991), pp. 4, 42.

[110] Conference on Disarmament document CD/1055, 5 Feb. 1991.

[111] Conference on Disarmament document CD/CW/WP.365, 23 Aug. 1991.

[112] Montagnon, P., 'Export controls placed on 15 chemicals', *Financial Times*, 21 Dec. 1990, p. 8.

[113] '17 January', *Chemical Weapons Convention Bulletin*, no. 11 (Mar. 1991), p. 11.

[114] '10 July', *Chemical Weapons Convention Bulletin*, no. 13 (Sep. 1991), p. 14.

[115] de Briganti, G., 'European governments take steps to tighten military export controls', *Defense News*, vol. l6, no. 13 (1 Apr. 1991), p. 20.

[116] Conference on Disarmament document CD/PV.595, 13 June 1991.

[117] 'Schweizer Beitrag gegen die C-Waffen-Proliferation', *Neue Zürcher Zeitung*, 30 Nov. 1991, p. 13.

[118] Deupmann, U., 'Zoll soll Telephone abhören und Post überwachen Höhere Strafen für illegale Ausfuhren geplant', *Süddeutsche Zeitung*, 7 Feb. 1991, p. 1; see also Associated Press (note 91); Presse-

lower house of the German Parliament) approved the new legislation in March.[119] However, the Bundesrat (the upper house of the German Parliament) voted against the proposed new export control legislation on the grounds that it would violate civil liberties by invading communications privacy.[120] The bill went back to the Bundestag for further discussion and revision but was once again rejected by the Bundesrat in June.[121] By September the new German Export Regulation Law was still awaiting approval. The German chemical industry was particularly critical of paragraph 5c, which included a list of 54 countries, among them all the states not parties to the 1968 Non-Proliferation Treaty (NPT).[122] Criticism was also levelled against the current rules and procedures for approval of export requests which, according to industry claims, lead to substantial delays for the majority of exports.[123] After long discussion, the country list was reduced to 35 nations, and much easier procedures for approval of export requests are expected to be enacted.[124] Discussion continued about the future effectiveness of the strict German export regulations after establishment of the Single Market of the European Community (EC) in 1993.

Sweden introduced an act 'prohibiting the exportation of certain products which may be used for purposes of mass destruction, and related matters' which entered into force in July 1991.[125] It regulates equipment for chemical production, highly sophisticated bio-technology equipment and 33 precursors and key precursors.

Peru informed the CD that its Foreign Ministry had taken steps to begin the establishment of a National Authority in conformity with Article VII of the draft CWC.[126]

und Informationsamt der Bundesregierung, *Bulletin*, no. 15/S.97 (8 Feb. 1991), pp. 97–98; Der Bundesminister für Wirtschaft, 'Vierzehnte Verordnung zur Änderung der Außenwirtschafts-verordnung', *Runderlaß Außenwirtschaft*, no. 4/91, 11 Mar. 1991; McCartney, R. J., 'Bonn tightens weapon export controls', *International Herald Tribune*, 16 Feb. 1991, p. 2.

[119] See Donkin, R. *et al.* (note 91); Bundesministerium für Wirtschaft, *Dokumentation: Die Reform von Außenwirtschaftsrecht und -kontrolle, Stand: März 1991*, no. 311 (Bundesministerium für Wirtschaft: Bonn, Mar. 1991).

[120] Krause-Brewer, F., 'Bremsen für Rüstungsexporte: Theoretische Forderung und praktische Wirkung', *Europäische Sicherheit/EWK/WWR*, Apr. 1991, pp. 218–21.

[121] 'Rüstungsexportgesetz gescheitert', *Frankfurter Rundschau*, 8 June 1991, p. 6; 'Waffenexport-Gesetz scheitert im Vermittlungsausschuß', *Frankfurter Allgemeine Zeitung*, 4 June 1991; Fisher, M., 'Tougher German law on illegal arms exports stalls on wiretap issue', *International Herald Tribune*, 8–9 June 1991, p. 1.

[122] Hoffmann, W., 'Weichmacher am Werk', *Die Zeit*, no. 39 (19 Sep. 1991), p. 25.

[123] 'Verzögerte Exportgenehmigungen ein Ärgernis', *Frankfurter Allgemeine Zeitung*, 23 Sep. 1991, p. 17.

[124] 'Vereinfachte Verfahren für Exportanträge', *Frankfurter Allgemeine Zeitung*, 10 Dec. 1991, p. 15.

[125] 'Act prohibiting the exportation of certain products which may be used for purposes of mass destrucion, and related matters', *Swedish Code of Statutes*, 1991:341, 16 May 1991, entering into force 1 July 1991.

[126] Conference on Disarmament document CD/PV.592, 23 May 1991, pp. 8–12.

The Australia Group: new initiatives

After a December 1990 meeting in London attended by representatives of 26 countries from the Australia Group and the former Leipzig Group,[127] agreement was reached to produce a collated list of chemicals controlled by various governments.[128] In May 1991 the Australia Group met in Paris, and at that meeting agreement was reached that the 20 participating governments would subject all of the 50 precursor chemicals on the Australia Group list, not just those on the core list, to export licence regulation by the end of 1991.[129] For the first time the Australia Group issued a press communiqué.[130] In December another meeting of the Australia Group took place in Paris in which Finland and Sweden participated for the first time.[131]

Other initiatives

At a July 1991 meeting of the five permanent members of the UN Security Council (China, France, the UK, the USA and the USSR) in Paris a commitment was made to arms control in the Middle East.[132] The participants began work on mechanisms to control the spread of conventional weapons, missile systems and nuclear technology in the Middle East, and advocated the creation of a zone free of weapons of mass destruction in the Middle East. At a July meeting in London the G7 countries (Canada, France, Germany, Italy, Japan, the UK and the USA) agreed on a declaration supporting arms trade restrictions and urging the future prohibition of NBC weapons.[133]

V. Destruction of chemical weapons

Under the June 1990 bilateral agreement between the USA and the former USSR destruction of CW stockpiles was intended to begin at the end of 1992.[134] However, as the Director of the US Arms Control and Disarmament Agency pointed out in May 1991, the bilateral destruction agreement was not submitted for congressional approval because the USSR had not completed its

---

[127] For a discussion of the Leipzig Group, see Lundin, S. J., Perry Robinson, J. P. and Trapp, R., 'Chemical and biological warfare: developments in 1987', SIPRI, *SIPRI Yearbook 1988: World Armaments and Disarmament* (Oxford University Press: Oxford, 1988), p. 103.

[128] Mallet, V., 'Crisis speeds up drive for chemical weapons curb', *Financial Times*, 18 Dec. 1990, p. 4; George, A., 'Weapons control', *The Independent*, 10 Dec. 1990, p. 12.

[129] 'Sources reveal plans to curb chemical exports', OW2202065991, Tokyo, KYODO, 0600 GMT, 22 Feb. 1991 (in English), in Foreign Broadcast Information Service, *Daily Report–East Asia (FBIS-EAS)*, FBIS-EAS-91-036, 22 Feb. 1991, p. 6.

[130] Auerbach, S., '19 nations back U.S. plan for chemical arms curbs', *Washington Post*, 31 May 1991, p. 1; *Wireless File*, no. 105 (United States Information Service, US Embassy: Stockholm, 31 May 1991), pp. 10–11.

[131] *Notes on Arms Control*, no. 9 (Dec. 1991), pp. 4–5.

[132] See note 77.

[133] '"... daß ein solcher Mißbrauch nicht noch einmal vorkommt": Die Londoner Gipfel-Erklärung zum Waffenexport, zur Nichtverbreitung von ABC-Waffen und zur politischen Lage', *Frankfurter Rundschau*, 18 July 1991, p. 14.

[134] For the text of the agreement, see SIPRI, *SIPRI Yearbook 1991* (note 3), appendix 14A, pp. 536–39.

demilitarization plan,[135] while the USA had both a pilot plant and a full-scale destruction plant in operation, and additional facilities under construction. The USSR has not yet been able to open its first destruction plant.[136] In October at a technical expert meeting on CW destruction in Geneva,[137] several CD delegations presented working papers on the destruction of CW stocks and production plants, disposal of old chemical weapons and the effect of such activities on the environment.[138] The USSR introduced a paper describing a mobile destruction facility similar to the one displayed at Shikhany in October 1987 but more technically and technologically advanced.[139]

Destruction efforts in the former USSR

In February in his annual report to Congress on 'Soviet noncompliance with arms control agreements', President Bush noted that the USSR had declared 7 CW storage depots (5 for munitions and 2 for bulk agents) in the information obtained under the bilateral exchange of data required by the Wyoming Memorandum of Understanding.[140]

According to press accounts, the Supreme Soviet had been asked to approve construction of two chemical demilitarization (chemdemil) plants—one at Kambarka (a former CW production site) where the Soviet-developed neutralization technology would probably be used, and another in Russia at an unspecified site. Incineration technology of the type used at the US Johnston Atoll Chemical Agent Disposal System (JACADS) may be employed at the second plant.[141] Kambarka is a CW storage site, known since late 1990, where approximately 6000 tonnes of lewisite from World War II have been stored since the early 1950s.[142] A destruction process for lewisite and a mixture with

[135] '22 May', *Chemical Weapons Convention Bulletin*, no. 12 (June 1991), p. 22; 'Banning chemical weapons', remarks by the Honourable Ambassador Stephen J. Ledogar, US Representative to the Conference on Disarmament, Geneva, Switzerland, before the Senate Foreign Relations Committee, 22 May 1991, pp. 1–9.

[136] 'Chemical weapons destruction program not endorsed', LD1007155591, Moscow, 1200 GMT, 10 July 1991 (in Russian), in Foreign Broadcast Information Service, *Daily Report–Soviet Union (FBIS-SOV)*, FBIS-SOV-91-136, 16 July 1991, p. 2.

[137] The meeting took place on 8–10 Oct. 1991 in Geneva and was reported in Conference on Disarmament document CD/CW/WP.377, 9 Dec. 1991.

[138] Germany, '"Old chemical weapons" disposal', Conference on Disarmament document CD/CW/WP.374, 31 Oct. 1991; UK, 'Destruction of CW stocks, weapons and associated plant', Conference on Disarmament document CD/CW/WP.373, 21 Oct. 1991; USSR, 'Environmental aspects of the destruction of chemical weapons', Conference on Disarmament document CD/CW/WP.368, 7 Oct. 1991; USSR, 'Main technological aspects of the destruction of chemical weapons', Conference on Disarmament document CD/CW/WP.367, 7 Oct. 1991.

[139] USSR, 'Complex for the destruction of faulty chemical munitions (KUASI)', Conference on Disarmament document CD/CW/WP.369, 8 Oct. 1991.

[140] *Text of a Letter from the President to the Speaker of the House of Representatives and the President of the Senate* (Office of the Press Secretary, White House: Washington, DC, 15 Feb. 1991); '15 February', *Chemical Weapons Convention Bulletin*, no. 12 (June 1991), p. 11; *Arms Control Reporter,* sheet 704.E-2.28, Mar. 1991.

[141] Heylin, M., 'Chemical weapons issues aired at AAAS', *Chemical and Engineering News*, vol. 69, no. 8 (25 Feb. 1991), p. 6.

[142] 'Destruction plans for chemical arms store reported', LD1208195291, Moscow, All-Union Radio, First Program, Radio-1 Network, 1200 GMT, 12 Aug. 1991 (in Russian), in FBIS-SOV-91-156, 13 Aug. 1991; 'Prospects for CW destruction examined', PM2711114790, Moscow, *Izvestia,*

mustard gas has been developed in which detoxification is accomplished by using a melt of elemental sulphur which forms a water insoluble polymer that is then buried.[143] Transforming lewisite into arsenic trichloride and then into pure arsenic for commercial use has also been considered. It has also been suggested that another storage site should be located in the Mari Autonomous Republic in Russia.[144]

In April an international CW conference was held in Moscow, focusing on problems of CW destruction and elimination.[145] The International Chetek Corporation stated that it intends to fund development of the use of nuclear weapons for the chemdemil of Soviet chemical weapons.[146] A demonstration using small underground nuclear explosions was planned for mid-1992 on Novaya Zemlya.[147] In July 1991 hearings were held by the Committee for the Issues of Ecology and Expedient Use of Natural Resources of the USSR Supreme Soviet on the programme for destroying chemical weapons in the USSR. When asked about the status of the destruction programme, a member of the Committee answered: 'the program has not been endorsed, draft legislative acts have not been submitted either to the Supreme Soviet or to the country's president . . . not a single one of the new working structures, neither a commission for selecting sites, not a committee or any other structure which could head, as the executive body, the entire work for preparing and implementing the state program for eliminating chemical weapons has been set up'.[148] New non-traditional destruction methods are also being developed using jet propulsion motors for incineration and microbiological techniques.[149]

In October the Chief of the Defence Ministry's chemical troops spoke about the chemical destruction programme, saying that the state programme had been outlined but not yet adopted. He stated that at 1991 prices, over 5.4

26 Nov. 1990, Union Edition, p. 4 (in Russian), in FBIS-SOV-90-229, 28 Nov. 1990, pp. 69–71; 'Concern voiced over chemical weapons' incineration' PM0711094590, Moscow, *Izvestia*, 3 Nov. 1990, Union Edition, p. 6 (in Russian), in FBIS-SOV-90-216, 7 Nov. 1990, pp. 62–63.

[143] See Conference on Disarmament document CD/CW/WP. 367 (note 138).

[144] *Arms Control Reporter,* sheet 704.E-2.41, Sep. 1991; see also '8 May', *Chemical Weapons Convention* Bulletin, no. 12 (June 1991), p. 20.

[145] 'Conference on chemical weapons opens in Moscow', LD0904222191, Moscow, TASS, 2204 GMT, 9 Apr. 1991 (in English), in FBIS-SOV-91-070, 11 Apr. 1991; 'International conference of scientists and experts on the prohibition and elimination of chemical weapons', Papers presented at the Soviet Peace Committee, International Conference of Scientists and Experts on the Prohibition and Elimination of Chemical Weapons, Moscow, 9–10 Apr. 1991.

[146] 'Abrüstung mit der Atombombe', *Frankfurter Rundschau,* 7 May 1991, p. 6; 'Moskau will Chemiewaffen mit Atombomben vernichten', *Frankfurter Allgemeine Zeitung,* 7 July 1991, p. 1; *ASA Newsletter,* 6 June 1991, p. 5.

[147] Dmitriev, V. B. and Trutnev, Y. A., 'Chemical weapons and highly toxic waste industry products destruction by means of an energy of an underground nuclear explosion', Paper presented at International Conference of Scientists and Experts on the Prohibition and Elimination of Chemical Weapons (note 145), pp. 17–21; Potter, C. W., 'Psst, wanna buy a nuclear bomb or two?', *International Herald Tribune,* 8 Nov. 1991, p. 6; 'Da könnten Löcher entstehen', *Der Spiegel,* vol. 45, no. 51 (16 Dec. 1991), p. 138.

[148] 'Chemical weapons destruction program not endorsed', LD1007155591, Moscow, All-Union Radio, Mayak Network, 1200 GMT, 10 July 1991 (in Russian), in FBIS-SOV-91-136, 16 July 1991, p. 2.

[149] See Conference on Disarmament document CD/CW/WP.367 (note 138); 'Prospects for CW destruction examined' (note 142).

billion roubles would be needed to implement the programme but later, because of inflation, a figure of 28 billion roubles was presented for 1992.[150]

In early 1992 information was made public that all of the CW stocks of the former Soviet Union are located in Russia.[151] In November the US Senate voted to allot up to $400 million in fiscal year (FY) 1992 defence funds to provide the former Soviet Union and its republics assistance in dismantling of nuclear or chemical weapons.[152]

Destruction efforts in the USA

In February the US General Accounting Office (GAO) reported that the removal of chemical weapons from Germany had cost $62 million, more than 10 per cent of which had been paid by Germany.[153]

At the Johnston Atoll destruction facility, phase one of the JACADS operation verification test (OVT)—the chemdemil of approximately 7500 GB-filled M55 rockets—was successfully concluded in February.[154] In the JACADS OVT the plant was first shut down in December 1990 for 30 days to boost the rate of destruction from 4 rockets per hour to 11 per hour (the ultimate goal being 24 rockets per hour). The plant was again closed in February and did not resume operation until mid-May; as a result the OVT had to run until March 1992 instead of September 1991.[155] Phase two of the four-phase OVT will involve the destruction of M55 rockets containing the nerve agent VX. An amendment to the appropriations bill for FY 1992 forbade the transfer of any chemicals to Johnston Atoll, except for World War II ammunition discovered in the Pacific region.[156]

In March the USA submitted a working paper to the CD on the destruction of the US stockpile of BZ and BZ-filled ammunition which was completed in June 1990; 1500 cluster bombs and 5 tonnes of bulk agent were destroyed as were several hundred tonnes of contaminated waste. The 13-year project cost $162.9 million.[157]

---

[150] 'No progress in chemical warfare destruction', PM2310091991, Moscow, *Izvestia*, 22 Oct. 1991, Union Edition, p. 4 (in Russian), in FBIS-SOV-91-205, 23 Oct. 1991, pp. 32–33; 'Chemical weapons supply stockpiled in Russia', LD16121333691, Moscow, *Postfactum*, 2213 GMT, 11 Dec. 1991 (in English), in FBIS-SOV-91-241, 16 Dec. 1991, pp. 1–2; 'Officer discusses chemical weapons destruction', PM1612104791, Moscow, *Krasnaya Zvezda*, 13 Dec. 1991, First Edition (in Russian), in FBIS-SOV-91-241, 16 Dec. 1991, pp. 2–3.

[151] 'Alle C-Waffen liegen in Rußland', *Süddeutsche Zeitung*, 10 Jan. 1992, p. 8.

[152] 'US may aid Soviet arms cuts', *International Herald Tribune*, 27 Nov. 1991, p. 2; Fessler, P., 'Sponsors of Soviet packages scramble for support', *Congressional Quarterly*, vol. 49, no. 47 (23 Nov. 1991), pp. 3466–67; 'Congress clears Soviet aid bill in late reversal of sentiment', *Congressional Quarterly*, vol. 49, no. 48 (30 Nov. 1991), p. 3536.

[153] US General Accounting Office, *Chemical Warfare: DOD's Successful Effort to Remove U.S. Chemical Weapons from Germany*, Report to Congressional Requesters, GAO/NSIAD-91-105 (GAO: Washington, DC, Feb. 1991); see also *SIPRI Yearbook 1991* (note 3), pp. 102–6.

[154] 'Statement by Mrs. Susan Livingstone, Assistant Secretary of the Army (Installations, Logistics and Environment) before Subcommittee on Strategic Forces and Nuclear Deterrence, Committee on Armed Services, United States Senate', Washington, DC, 13 June 1991.

[155] *Arms Control Reporter*, sheet 704.E-1.13, June 1991.

[156] See note 155.

[157] Conference on Disarmament document CD/1074, 20 Mar. 1991.

In May the Program Manager for Chemical Demilitarization published a final environmental impact statement on chemdemil activities at the Anniston Army Depot in Anniston, Alabama, where approximately 7 per cent by weight of the US CW stockpile including mustard gas and nerve agent is stored.[158] The statement said that the stockpile of chemical agents and munitions could be destroyed in a safe and environmentally acceptable manner by on-site incineration; actual operations are scheduled to begin in late 1996 and continue through June 1999.

In a study published by Greenpeace, at least 7 different process types (including 28 technologically different processes) were discussed for possible use in the destruction and detoxification of toxic wastes, particularly chemical warfare agents.[159] Most of the processes described are in the early stages of development.

If incineration—the destruction technique employed at the Johnston Atoll, Umatilla, Oregon, and Pine Bluff, Arkansas, facilities—is carried out according to schedule, the USA could meet the December 1999 deadline of 50 per cent destruction required by the bilateral US–Soviet agreement.[160] It was also reported that the overall cost of the US chemdemil programme has increased to $6.5 billion.[161] Another GAO report stated that all US CW storage sites comply with the Army's physical security standards.[162] In FY 1992 the USA was slated to spend approximately $374 million for chemical agent and ammunition destruction.[163] However, the final figure was $362.9 million.[164]

The USA will have difficulty meeting its destruction programme deadline while the major problems which exist in the former Soviet Union may make it impossible to set up a functioning destruction facility there. It may be necessary to reconsider the destruction obligation under the future CWC, which currently requires that all chemical weapons be destroyed within 10 years after entry into force of the convention. This is probably only relevant if the CWC enters into force in the next two to five years.

The problem of old CW ammunition

Problems related to the discovery and destruction of old CW ammunition were often discussed in 1991. A November 1991 conference in Berlin dealt with the

---

[158] Program Manager for Chemical Demilitarization, *Disposal of Chemical Agents and Munitions Stored at Anniston Army Depot, Anniston, Alabama: Final Environmental Impact Statement* (Department of the Army: Aberdeen Proving Ground, Md., May 1991).

[159] Picardi, A., Johnston, P. and Stringer, R., *Alternative Technologies for Detoxification of Chemical Weapons: An Information Document* (Greenpeace International: Washington, DC, 24 May 1991).

[160] *Arms Control Reporter*, sheet 704.E-1.14, June 1991.

[161] 'Serious mechanical problems found in Army's chemical destruction program', *Inside the Army*, vol. 3, no. 17 (29 Apr. 1991), p. 2.

[162] US General Accounting Office, *Chemical Weapons: Physical Security for the US Chemical Stockpile*, GAO/NSIAD-91-200 (General Accounting Office: Washington, DC, May 1991).

[163] Towell, P., 'Where the money goes', *Congressional Quarterly*, vol. 49, supplement to no. 49 (7 Dec. 1991), pp. 55–63.

[164] *Budget of the United States Government, Fiscal Year 1992*, part 4 (US Government Printing Office: Washington, DC, 1991), p. 6.

destruction of toxic ammunition wastes,[165] and several German reports were published on new discoveries of old CW ammunition and contaminated soil from World War II production sites in both the former GDR and the FRG.[166]

In April it was reported that the Austrian Interior Ministry had asked the Bavarian Government for assistance to destroy 29 000 mustard gas shells from World War II stored at Grossmittel-Haschendorf (40 km south of Vienna).[167] At Hallenschlag, Eifel, a former CW production site from World War I is suspected to contain more than 22 000 chemical ammunition shells.[168]

The US Navy transported 109 old 155-mm mustard gas shells—part of 12 0000 US mustard gas rounds sent to the South Pacific during World War II—from the Solomon Islands to the Johnston Atoll destruction facility. The shells were found on Mbanika Island, where they had remained after unsuccessful local chemdemil efforts in 1988.[169]

In 1991 Belgium began construction of a chemdemil facility at Houthulst which will be used to destroy 160 tonnes of World War I CW munitions, at a calculated cost of 145 million Belgian francs.[170] Belgian data also suggested that there may be more than 1100 tonnes of chemical agent in ammunition which was dumped off the Belgian coast by the Allied powers in 1920, at distances of 1.5 km and 3.5 km from the port of Zeebrugge.[171]

There has been increased public concern about World War II CW ammunition which was dumped at sea.[172] Danish fishermen reported 40 incidents of contact with old CW ammunition in 1989, 19 in 1990 and by mid-summer of 1991, 97.[173] German fishermen have also had similar experiences with gas munitions in the Baltic Sea.[174]

New information about the dumping activities of the former Soviet Union became available in 1991. Approximately 5000 chemical explosives were dumped at two sites in the Baltic, 50–60 km west of Palanga and 90 km south-west of the port of Liepaja in 1947.[175] Chemical munitions were also dumped

---

[165] The second Abfall-Wirtschafts-Symposium, special session on Rüstungsaltlasten was held on 27–29 Nov. 1991 in Berlin. See *AbfallwirtschaftsJournal*, vol. 3, no. 11 (1991), pp. 709–17. The proceedings will be published in 1992.

[166] Lohs, Kh., 'Rüstungsaltlasten', *Zeitschrift Umweltchemie Ökotoxikologie*, vol. 3, no. 1 (Jan. 1991), pp. 1–2; Spyra, W., Lohs, Kh., Preussner, M., Rüden, H. and Thomé-Kozmiensky, K. J., *Untersuchung von Rüstungsaltlasten*, (EF-Verlag für Energie und Umwelttechnik: Berlin, 1991); Oberholz, A., *Tödliche Gefahr aus der Tiefe* (Kommunal-Verlag: Düsseldorf, 1991); Kiefer, K.-W., Pfaff-Schley, H. and Schimmelpfeng, L., *Rüstungsaltlasten '91: Untersuchungsmethoden, Sanierungsmöglichkeiten, Verhinderung militärischer 'Neu'-Lasten*, Abfallwirtschaft in Forschung und Praxis, vol. 40 (Erich Schmidt Verlag: Berlin, 1991).

[167] 'Bayern soll Giftgas entsorgen', *Frankfurter Rundschau*, 2 Apr. 1991.

[168] 'Arsen und Spitzenwerte', *Der Spiegel*, vol. 45, no. 26 (8 July 1991), p. 73.

[169] See note 154.

[170] Information Network on CBW, *CBW News*, no. 4 (Apr. 1991).

[171] Zanders, J. P., 'Chemicals were dumped near Belgium, too', letter to the editor, *Bulletin of the Atomic Scientists*, vol. 47, no. 4 (May 1991), p. 47.

[172] Laurin, F., 'Scandinavia's underwater time bomb', *Bulletin of the Atomic Scientists*, vol. 47, no. 2 (Mar. 1991), pp. 11–15; Stock, T., 'Unter Wasser tickt die Bombe', *Deutsches Allgemeines Sonntagsblatt*, no. 22 (31 May 1991), p. 6.

[173] Gurezka, K., 'Ein Fang mit schmerzhaften Folgen', *Der Tagesspiegel*, 17 July 1991, p. 3.

[174] DPA, Reuters, 'Angeblich Gasmunition auf dem Ostseegrund', *Der Tagesspiegel*, 13 July 1991, p. 4.

[175] 'Union allegedly dumped chemical weapons in Baltic', LD1903164191, Vilnius International Service, 2300 GMT, 18 Mar 1991 (in English), in FBIS-SOV-91-056, 22 Mar. 1991, p. 53–54.

in the White Sea in the 1950s as were chemical bombs in the Barents Sea at Pechenga in Murmansk Oblast in 1960–61.[176]

VI. The Third Review Conference of the BWC

The Convention on the Prohibition of the Development, Production and Stockpiling of Bacteriological (Biological) and Toxin Weapons and on Their Destruction (the BWC) was signed in 1972.[177] The Third Review Conference of the parties to the BWC took place on 9–27 September 1991. It was attended by 78 states parties, 6 signatories and 3 states neither party nor signatory to the BWC, among them, for the first time, Israel. Observers to the Conference included a delegation from the World Health Organization (WHO), also for the first time.[178] Preparations for the Conference and the Conference itself were heavily influenced by recent scientific and technological developments, by increasing concern about BW and toxin weapon (TW) proliferation related to the end of the cold war, and by the Gulf War and the results of the work of UNSCOM.

Both governmental and non-governmental organizations contributed to the Conference by evaluating the strength of the BWC, the efficacy of the confidence-building measures (CBMs) agreed upon by the Second Review Conference in 1986 and by elaborating proposals to strengthen the BWC. Several meetings were held before and during the Conference by governmental institutions,[179] by the United Nations Institute for Disarmament Research (UNIDIR)[180] and by non-governmental organizations (NGOs).[181] In addition, several books[182] and numerous articles have been published on the

---

[176] 'Chemical weapons dumped in White Sea in 1950's', PM1406080491, Moscow, *Komsomolskaya Pravda*, 13 Jun. 1991, p. 4 (in Russian), in FBIS-SOV-91-115, 14 June 1991, p. 35.

[177] For the text of the BWC, see Geissler, E. (ed.), SIPRI, *Strengthening the Biological Weapons Convention by Confidence-Building Measures*, SIPRI Chemical & Biological Warfare Studies, no. 10 (Oxford University Press: Oxford, 1990), pp. 155–58.

[178] SIPRI is grateful that S. J. Lundin and E. Geissler were given the possibility to participate in the conference as observers.

[179] 'Symposium on Improving Confidence-Building Measures for the BW Convention', Swedish National Defence Research Establishment (FOA), Umeå, Sweden, 29–30 May 1990; 'Seminar on the Biological Weapons Convention', Noordwijk, the Netherlands, Feb. 1991.

[180] Goldblat, J. and Bernauer, T., *The Third Review of the Biological Weapons Convention: Issues and Proposals*, UNIDIR Research Paper, no. 9 (United Nations: New York, 1991), report on the UNIDIR Workshop held in Moscow, USSR, 29–30 Jan. 1991.

[181] The '12th Kühlungsborn Colloquium, Kühlungsborn, Germany, 14–19 Sep. 1990' is reported in Geissler, E. and Haynes, R. H. (eds), *Prevention of a Biological and Toxin Arms Race and the Responsibility of Scientists* (Akademie Verlag: Berlin, 1991); 'Seminar on CBM Proposals for the Third Review Conference of the BW Convention', Geneva, Switzerland, 9 Apr. 1991; 'Strengthening the Biological Weapons Convention: Proposals for the Third Review Conference', Chateau de Bossy, Céligny, Switzerland, 31 May–2 June 1991; 'Workshop on the BW Convention', Toronto, Canada, 19 June 1991; 'Conference on Chemical and Biological Warfare: History and Present Situation', Tokyo, 6–7 July 1991; 'Briefing for the Delegates to the Third Review Conference of the BW Convention', Geneva, Switzerland, 11 Sep. 1991.

[182] See Geissler (note 177); Geissler and Haynes (note 181); Goldblat and Bernauer (note 180); Lundin, S. J. (ed.), *Views on Possible Verification Measures for the Biological Weapons Convention*, SIPRI Chemical & Biological Warfare Studies, no. 12 (Oxford University Press: Oxford, 1991); Sims, N. A., *Reinforcing Biological Disarmament: Issues in the 1991 Review*, Faraday Discussion Paper no. 16 (Council of Arms Control: London, 1991); ter Haar, B., *The Future of Biological Weapons*, The

BWC including the very detailed recommendations of a working group convened by the Federation of American Scientists (FAS).[183] In their plenary statements many delegations—including Canada, Finland, India, Mexico, Peru, Poland, Romania, Sri Lanka and the United Kingdom—welcomed the preparatory work done by the NGOs, scientific bodies and individual scientists. In his opening statement, the President of the Review Conference mentioned that the activities 'of scholars and members of the public concerned by the subject covered by the Treaty' have multiplied and have 'drawn attention to certain aspects of the Convention, so that this Review Conference may concentrate its analysis on those points'.[184] In its Final Declaration the Review Conference welcomed these activities and appealed to the 'scientific communities to continue to support only activities that have justification under the . . . Convention for prophylactic, protective or other peaceful purposes, and refrain from activities which are in breach of obligations deriving from provisions of the Convention'.[185] A selection of the most important Conference developments are reported on below.

Scientific and technological developments

As early as 1986 participants at the Second Review Conference expressed concern that the broader introduction and rapid progress in genetic engineering and other areas of biotechnology had caused a re-evaluation of the military value of biological and toxin weapons. Numerous delegations to the Third Review Conference shared the Swedish view that these conclusions are still valid and that developments in this field have been at least as rapid during the period now under review. The more so, 'As the techniques of molecular biology have advanced, projects which were previously considered unrealistic have been initiated'.[186]

For example, cells can be manipulated by the insertion of genes and can then be used to produce toxins previously not available to the military.[187] In the view of Australia 'the major impact genetic engineering has had that is

Washington Papers, no. 151 (Praeger: New York, 1991); Wright, S. (ed.), *Preventing a Biological Arms Race* (MIT Press: Cambridge, Mass., 1990).

[183] *Proposals for the Third Review Conference of the Biological Weapons Convention*, Report of the Federation of American Scientists Working Group on Biological and Toxin Weapons Verification, revised Oct. 1990, reprinted in Geissler and Haynes (note 181), pp. 485–505. A more recent version of the proposal was distributed at the above mentioned conferences in Geneva in May–June and Sep. 1991; see note 181.

[184] 'Opening statement by Ambassador Roberto Garcia Moritan (Argentina), President of the Third Review Conference of the Parties to the Convention on the Prohibition of the Development, Production and Stockpiling of Bacteriological (Biological) and Toxin Weapons and on Their Destruction', Geneva, 9–27 Sep. 1991, 9. Sep. 1991.

[185] The references to the final document of the Third Review Conference in this section are to the *Final Document of the Third Review Conference of the Parties to the Convention on the Prohibition of the Development, Production and Stockpiling of Bacteriological (Biological) and Toxin Weapons and on their Destruction, Part II, Final Declaration*, BWC/CONF.III/22, 27 Sep. 1991.

[186] Statement by Ambassador Carl-Magnus Hyltenius, Sweden, at the Third Review Conference, 10 Sep. 1991.

[187] See Geissler (note 177), table 3.1, p. 18 and pp. 27–28.

relevant to the BWC is the possibility of large-scale production of toxins',[188] which according to the USA 'can now be produced in kilogram quantities'.[189] Furthermore, at least some super-toxic toxins are no longer inferior in military terms to classical chemical weapons as was previously the case.[190] New scientific developments could lead to much more efficient dissemination of BW and TW agents. A number of toxins have been proven to be considerably more toxic in aerosol application than with intravenous (IV) injection, have demonstrated an enhanced epidermic activity in comparison to IV injection, and have proved to be more stable in aerosols.[191] In addition toxins and infectious agents can be shielded from inactivation by exposure to air and sunlight or from desiccation by means of micro-encapsulation, including ultraviolet protective pigments.[192]

Participants at the Review Conference also stressed that dramatic improvements in fermentation technology have made BW production more feasible.[193] Hence, 'large quantities of biological products can be produced quickly in small facilities'.[194] The USSR referred to the recent 'introduction of industrial robots to carry out process operations (ranging from preparation of the seed stock to packaging of the final product)'.[195] For these and other reasons, previous assessments that 'development and production of reliable weapons based on infectious agents would be a major undertaking'[196] may no longer hold true. On the contrary, in the view of the USA, 'the confidence derived from the belief that certain technical problems would make biological weapons unattractive for the foreseeable future has eroded'.[197]

Participation in the BWC

The adherence to the BWC has continued to increase: as of 1 January 1992, 118 states were parties to the BWC. As some 50 countries are not yet parties, the Review Conference called upon states to ratify or accede to the BWC 'without delay'. The Conference also welcomed regional measures such as the

[188] *Background Document on New Scientific and Technological Developments Relevant to the Convention on the Prohibition of the Development, Production and Stockpiling of Bacteriological (Biological) and Toxin Weapons and on their Destruction*, BWC/CONF.III/4, 26 Aug. 1991, pp. 2–5.

[189] See note 188, p. 29.

[190] See, for example, the following as quoted in 'Effectiveness of biological weapons', *Arms Control Reporter*, sheet 701.E.2, Sep. 1989. 'No known toxin, at this time rivals the military effectiveness of chemical nerve gas . . . [which] can penetrate the skin as well as the lungs, forcing enemy soldiers to wear cumbersome protective gear. In contrast, most toxins cannot penetrate the skin and are unstable in air.' See also Meselson, M., Kaplan, M. and Mokulsky, M. A., 'Verification of biological and toxin weapons disarmament', *Science & Global Security*, vol. 2, no. 2/3 (1991), pp. 236–38.

[191] *Background Document on New Scientific and Technological Developments Relevant to the Convention on the Prohibition of the Development, Production and Stockpiling of Bacteriological (Biological) and Toxin Weapons and on their Destruction, Addendum*, BWC/CONF.III/4/Add.1, 10 Sep. 1991, p. 10.

[192] See note 188, p. 4.

[193] See note 188, p. 3.

[194] See note 188, p. 29.

[195] See BWC/CONF.III/4/Add.1 (note 191), p. 11.

[196] See Meselson, Kaplan and Mokulsky (note 190), pp. 236–37.

[197] See note 188, p. 33.

Joint Declaration on the Complete Prohibition of Chemical and Biological Weapons, and the Mendoza Agreement signed by Argentina, Brazil and Chile and, subsequently, by Uruguay.[198]

Reservations to the Geneva Protocol

Several states parties to the 1925 Geneva Protocol reserved the right to use chemical and biological weapons in the event of first use by an adversary.[199] Some parties to the BWC have withdrawn their reservations. Only Australia, Barbados, Bulgaria, Canada, the Czech and Slovak Federal Republic, Ireland, Mongolia, New Zealand and Romania have withdrawn their reservations and now renounce the right of retaliatory use of bacteriological methods of warfare.[200] At the Conference these countries were joined by Canada,[201] Chile[202] and the United Kingdom,[203] who withdrew their reservations regarding bacteriological (biological) weapons.

Similar decisions by other states undoubtedly would strengthen the BWC. The Conference therefore stressed 'the importance of the withdrawal of all reservations to the 1925 Geneva Protocol related to the Biological and Toxin Weapons Convention'.

Coverage of the BWC

Several delegations including Argentina, Australia, Brazil, Hungary, Iran, New Zealand, Senegal, Sweden, Ukraine and the USSR called 'for clearer definitions in Article 1'[204] because 'it is necessary to draw a clear borderline . . . between the area where legitimate activities . . . end up and the area of the work to create such weapons begins'.[205] To this end numerous proposals which are more or less identical to corresponding recommendations forwarded by NGOs were made by Conference participants.

First, the Conference explicitly declared that the BWC also covers biological agents or toxins 'harmful to plants and animals', but without defining which organisms are covered by the term 'other biological agents' and without agreeing on a list of putative BW and TW agents. The Conference did not include the suggestion proposed by Chile [206] and several other delegations that

[198] See BWC/CONF.III/15 (note 1).

[199] See Geissler (note 177), pp. 51–52, table 5.2.

[200] Geissler, E., 'Molecular biotechnology and the Third Review of the Biological Weapons Convention', Brauch, H. G., et al., Controlling Military Research & Development and Exports of Dual Use Technologies as a Problem of Disarmament and Arms Control Policy in the 1990s (Free University Press: Amsterdam, and St Martin's Press: New York, 1992).

[201] Statement by Ambassador Peggy Mason, Canada, to the Third Review Conference, 10 Sep. 1991.

[202] Statement by Ambassador Radomiro Tomic, Chile, to the Third Review Conference, 11 Sep. 1991.

[203] Statement by Ambassador Tessa A. H. Solesby, UK, to the Third Review Conference, 27 Sep. 1991.

[204] See note 186.

[205] Statement by Ambassador Sergey B. Batsanov, USSR, to the Third Review Conference, 12 Sep. 1991.

[206] Chile, Panama, Peru and Venezuela, 'Proposals for action by the Third Review Conference of the Biological Weapons Convention', Working Paper, BWC/CONF.III/COW/WP.2, 16 Sep. 1991.

'the creation . . . of biological agents or toxins with altered properties that might increase their usefulness as weapons agents is not justified under the BWC for any military purpose'.

Second, 'the Conference notes that experimentations involving open-air release of pathogens or toxins harmful to man, animals or plants that has no justification for prophylactic, protective or other peaceful purpose is inconsistent with the undertakings contained in Article 1'. The Conference did not accept Australian and Finnish proposals to urge parties 'not to conduct any trials involving the explosive aerosolisation'. In addition, the Conference could not agree 'that they [the parties] will not undertake any trials involving the large-scale aerosolisation without prior notification, approval and provision for the presence of representatives' of an international body of oversight[207] as proposed by several delegations since 'such aerosolisation trials are much more essential to offensive than defensive purposes'.[208]

National implementation

The BWC binds states parties through their governments. Article IV of the BWC imposes an obligation upon parties to pass domestic legislation criminalizing the development, production, acquisition and stockpiling of biological and toxin weapons and to prevent proliferation. Only a minority of parties have thus far considered it necessary to take action to incorporate the commitments of the BWC into national law.[209]

The Review Conference correspondingly reiterated 'its call to any State Party that has not yet taken any necessary measures to do so immediately'. In addition, the Conference agreed that parties are to provide annual Declarations of Legislation, Regulations and other Measures as CBMs.

Confidence-building measures

Other CBMs were instituted by the Second Review Conference. However, they were inadequately implemented.[210] The effectiveness of the five rounds of information exchange which have taken place thus far has been low, both with respect to the level of participation and to the completeness of the information provided. Only 49 states parties (i.e., approximately one-third) have

---

[207] Statement by Ambassador Paul O'Sullivan, Australia, to the Third Review Conference, 12 Sep. 1991.

[208] Statement by Pasi Patokallio, Finland, to the Third Review Conference, 10 Sep. 1991.

[209] Scott, D., 'The concept of treaty-mandated compliance legislation under the Biological Weapons Convention', in Geissler and Haynes (note 181), pp. 345–67; and for states which implemented the obligations of the BWC into national law more recently, the statements made by Austria, Chile, Germany, Italy, Romania, Sweden and Thailand to the Third Review Conference. Selected texts of national measures of implementation are reprinted in Goldblat and Bernauer (note 180), pp. 62–75.

[210] See Geissler, E., 'The first four rounds of information exchange', in Geissler and Haynes (note 181), pp. 267–76; Geissler, E., 'Contribution of confidence-building measures to greater transparency in activities directly related to the Biological Weapons Convention' in Lundin (note 182), pp. 10–25.

participated in the information exchange,[211] including 13 states which participated in 1991 for the first time. The Review Conference, therefore 'urge[d] all States Parties to submit information to future rounds of information exchange' and agreed that implementation of the data-reporting provisions is not voluntary, as held by some states, but that according to the wording in the report of the previous Review Conference, states parties 'are to implement' these as well as a number of additional CBMs.

In order to increase participation in the information exchange, it was decided to add a Declaration form on Nothing to Declare or Nothing New to Declare. In addition to the Declarations of Legislation, Regulations and other Measures mentioned above, the Conference requested declarations of Past Activities in Offensive and/or Defensive Biological Research Development Programmes and of Vaccine Production Facilities. Considering the 'quadruple capability' of vaccines,[212] the latter is of limited value because parties are requested only to provide information on 'facilities . . . producing vaccines licensed by the State Party' and thus to provide information which is usually generally known. However, parties are not obliged to inform on corresponding R&D activities which are carried out before a vaccine is ready for production and licensing, and this may raise concern with respect to the intended use of such vaccines. The Conference did not request a report on military and mass civilian immunization programmes as proposed by Finland[213] and other delegations.

The most substantive decision taken by the Conference was to amend the exchange of data on research centres and to request that detailed information be provided on national biological defence research programmes. This declaration would describe *inter alia* 'the principal research and development activities conducted in the program. Areas to be addressed shall include: prophylaxis, studies on pathogenicity and virulence, diagnostic techniques, aerobiology, . . . and other related research'. If fully implemented, this new measure would not only provide information on military programmes for the development of vaccines, as already proposed by numerous experts, but would also represent a first step towards covering potential misuse of *research* by the BWC. In addition, the Conference developed a set of procedures for the convening of consultative meetings.

Verification

Verification of compliance played a major role at the Review Conference. According to the Finnish delegation, the Conference 'owe[d] it to the world to begin an effort to examine how the Convention could be verified.[214] Although

---

[211] *Implementation of the Confidence-Building Measures Agreed to in the Final Declaration of the Second Review Conference of the Parties to the Convention on the Prohibition of the Development, Production and Stockpiling of Bacteriological (Biological) and Toxin Weapons on Their Destruction*, BWC/CONF.III/2, 20 May 1991; BWC/CONF/III/2/Add.2, 26 Sep. 1991.

[212] See Geissler in Lundin (note 182), p. 12.

[213] See note 208.

[214] See note 208.

most delegations pointed out that verification will be difficult because 'activities necessary for the development of a BW offensive arsenal are virtually identical to most legitimate activities in the field of microbiology'[215] most participants at the Conference did not share the US view that 'the Convention is not effectively verifiable and we do not know any way to make it so'.[216]

In the end the Conference decided 'to establish an *Ad Hoc* Group of Governmental Experts . . . to identify and examine potential verification measures'. The group will meet for the first time in the spring of 1992. It will be able to draw upon an additional set of proposals recommended by the FAS Working Group.[217] The *Ad Hoc* Group 'shall adopt . . . a report . . . on the identification and examination of potential verification measures from a scientific and technical stand-point'. The report is to be provided to states parties, a majority of whom might subsequently ask for convening of a Conference to decide on any further action.

Prevention of proliferation versus peaceful co-operation

As then UN Secretary-General Javier Perez de Cuellar noted in a message to the Conference, 'it is essential . . . to ensure that, on the one hand the Convention is implemented and in a manner that does not hamper the economic and technological development of states parties, as called for in the Convention itself, and that, on the other hand, the Convention is not outpaced or its effectiveness weakened by scientific and technological advances'.[218] Numerous delegations, especially those from developing countries, shared this view and pointed out that strengthening the BWC by prevention of proliferation and by adoption of verification measures 'should not serve as an excuse to build further barriers to prevent access to high technologies'[219] that these countries need for further development and for the welfare of their people.

The problem of proliferation with its inherent difficulties was discussed by many delegations, most explicitly by the US. One cannot but agree with the US evaluation that 'control of proliferation is difficult because many research and development efforts in this field are dual-use in nature. In contrast to the production of chemical weapons, there are no precursors or equipment that can be used solely for the production of biological agents for hostile purposes.

---

[215] Statement by Ambassador Gerard Errera, France, to the Third Review Conference, 12 Sep. 1991.

[216] Statement by Ambassador Ronald F. Lehman, II, USA, to the Third Review Conference, 10 Sep. 1991.

[217] Federation of American Scientists, *Implementation of the Proposals for a Verification Protocol to the Biological Weapons Convention*, Report of the Federation of American Scientists Working Group on Biological and Toxin Weapons Verification (Federation of American Scientists: Washington, DC, Feb. 1991).

[218] UN Information Service, 'Message of the Secretary-General of the United Nations to the Third Review Conference of the Parties to the Biological Weapons Convention', *UN Press Release*, SG/SM/1237, DC/1744, 9 Sep. 1991, Geneva.

[219] Statement by Ambassador Celso L. N. Amorim, Brazil to the Third Review Conference, 12 Sep. 1991.

Actually, any nation with a modestly developed pharmaceutical industry can produce material for biological or toxin weapons, if it so chooses'.[220]

After having considered these problems at length, the Conference agreed that 'transfers [of agents, toxins, weapons, equipment or means of delivery to any recipient whatsoever] should only be authorized when the intended use is for purposes not prohibited under the Convention'. Using language nearly identical to that of the Final Declaration of the Second Review Conference, the Conference stated that these provisions 'should not be used to impose restrictions and/or limitations on the transfer for purposes consistent with the objectives and the provisions of the Convention of scientific knowledge, technology, equipment and materials under Article X'.

The Conference noted 'with concern the increasing gap between the developed and the developing countries in the field of biotechnology, genetic engineering, microbiology and other related areas' and urged all states parties actively to promote international co-operation. The Conference called upon the UN Secretary-General 'to propose for inclusion on the agenda of a relevant UN body, not later than 1993, a discussion and examination of the means for improving institutional mechanisms in order to facilitate the fullest possible exchange of equipment, materials and scientific and technological information for the use of . . . agents and toxins for peaceful purposes'. The Conference requested also that the Secretary-General 'collates on an annual basis, and for the information of States Parties, reports on how this Article is being implemented'.

Further measures

The Conference decided that a Fourth Review Conference should be held at the request of a majority of states parties not later than 1996 and that review conferences should be held at least every five years. In so far as a mechanism for oversight of CBM implementation between review conferences is missing, the USA and many other participants proposed to 'establish a mechanism for facilitating the implementation of the CBMs'[221] (e.g., an 'implementation or oversight committee').[222] These proposals did not meet unanimous approval by the Conference. Both the Netherlands, on behalf of the European Community,[223] and Austria[224] took the floor in the final plenary meeting after adoption of the Final Document to express their regret at the failure of the Conference to decide on establishing such a follow-up institution.

---

[220] See note 216.

[221] See note 216.

[222] Statement by Ambassador Professor Winfried Lang, Austria, to the Third Review Conference, 10 Sep. 1991.

[223] Common statement on behalf of the European Community and its member states at the plenary of the Third Review Conference by Ambassador Hendrik Wagenmakers, The Netherlands, 27 Sep. 1991.

[224] Statement by Ambassador Professor Winfried Lang, Austria, to the Third Review Conference, 27 Sep. 1991.

Concluding remarks

The BWC can and needs to be strengthened. The CBMs agreed upon by the Second Review Conference represented a first step in this direction. Additional measures were decided by the Third Review Conference, both to contribute to a further increase of confidence by requesting more transparency in activities related to the BWC and by agreeing on first measures towards establishment of a verification regime.

VII. Conclusions

Changes in US policy in 1991 regarding a less intrusive challenge inspection mechanism for the CWC and President Bush's aim of achieving a convention in 1992 may have significantly increased the chance of actually finalizing the CWC. This may be true even if there is still strong opposition to making the convention a declaratory rather than a verifiable agreement. The US approach would emphasize demonstrating compliance more so than verifying the occurrence of violations. In a world where the two largest possessors have agreed to destroy their chemical weapons, the US Senate may find it easier and more important to ratify a CWC which protects military secrets rather than one which allows for verification of CW possession in other countries. The inability to obtain information about possession must be weighed against the need to finalize an international convention as soon as possible. A global CWC would serve as the basis for common international measures to abolish chemical weapons and might facilitate regional approaches aimed at eliminating chemical weapons and other weapons of mass destruction.

The fact that chemical weapons were not used in the Gulf War deserves more study. The idea that chemical and biological weapons are 'the poor man's nuclear weapons' is highly questionable. Once again it has been shown that nuclear weapons are in a separate class; any direct comparison with other weapons is not militarily or politically sound. After the Gulf War the UN Secretary-General was given substantial authority to determine which weapons of mass destruction Iraq possessed, to destroy them and to ensure that Iraq would be unable to reacquire such weapons. Thus far the UNSCOM experience has shown that on-site inspection, even where possession is admitted, requires that unquestioned authority be given to the investigating body. The UNSCOM investigation has been an extremely complex and costly undertaking. The CWC negotiations, which have contemplated similar inspection measures, have perhaps not fully appreciated all of the complexities involved.

The UNSCOM investigation in Iraq revealed extensive Iraqi efforts to obtain NBC weapons (see chapter 13), and allegations are continuously being made that a number of other countries are trying to acquire a CW capability. It is very difficult to hinder export of the technology and equipment which are essential to BW and CW programmes, difficulties which are clearly exacerbated by the lack of a CWC. Countries which do acquire chemical weapons are often not adequately aware of the long-term problem of CW destruction.

At some point in the future their CW stockpiles will need to be destroyed, thereby creating toxicity problems, health risks, threats to the environment and enormous cost. The difficulties which the USA and the former USSR and its successor states have had and will continue to have should be instructive. These difficulties also raise questions about safe implementation of the CWC with respect to the currently proposed 10-year destruction period provision. The environmental aspects of a large release of chemicals in war were clearly demonstrated by the enormous fires in the Kuwaiti oil fields and the subsequent effect on the environment.

Attention has been focused on the problem of biological weapons by UNSCOM's findings about Iraq's BW programme and by frequent allegations that other nations are attempting to acquire BW weapons. The Third Review Conference of the BWC stressed that the Convention remains valid despite these developments but that it needs to be strengthened. A number of additional confidence-building measures were therefore agreed upon. No verification measures were established although a group of experts was set up to study the feasibility of such measures. It is conceivable that their work will also be influenced by the results of UNSCOM's inspections, which in turn may affect the CWC, if it is decided that the authority for intrusive verification should be given to the UN Secretary-General rather than entrusted to a particular body under the BWC.

Appendix 6A. National and multinational trial inspections

THOMAS STOCK

Table 6A.1. National trial inspections (NTIs)

The cut-off date for compilation of the data in the table was 31 December 1991.

Country	Document	Date	Routine inspection under schedule 2 regime	Inspection under schedule 1 regime	Challenge inspection at a civilian chemical facility	Challenge inspection at a military installation
Australia	CD/910	5 Apr. 1989	X			
Austria	CD/948[a]	14 Aug. 1989	X			
	CD/999[a]	12 June 1990				
Belgium	CD/917	17 Apr. 1989	X			
Brazil	CD/895/Rev.1	21 Mar. 1989	X			
Canada	CD/987	19 Apr. 1990	X	X		
	CD/1030/Rev.1	10 Aug. 1990	X			
Czechoslovakia[b]	CD/900	15 Mar. 1989	X			
Czech and Slovak	CD/1021	26 July 1990			X	
Federal Republic[b]	CD/1022	26 July 1990				X
Egypt	CD/958	23 Jan. 1990	X			
Finland	CD/CW/WP.233	4 Apr. 1989	X			
Federal Republic	CD/912	7 Apr. 1989	X			
of Germany	CD/950[c]	17 Aug. 1989	X			
	CD/975	9 Mar. 1990				X

Country	Document	Date	Routine inspection under schedule 2 regime	Inspection under schedule 1 regime	Challenge inspection at a civilian chemical facility	Challenge inspection at a military installation
	CD/983	5 Apr. 1990				X
	CD/1101	15 Aug. 1991			X	
France	CD/913	11 Apr. 1989	X			X
	CD/960	1 Feb. 1990	X			X
	CD/1029	8 Aug. 1990				
	CD/1063	21 Feb. 1991				
	CD/CW/WP.351	15 July 1991			X	
German Democratic Republic[b]	CD/899	10 Mar. 1989	X			
	CD/996[c]	12 June 1990			X	
	CD/1020	26 July 1990				X
Hungary	CD/890[d]	20 Feb. 1989	X			
	CD/890/Add.1[d]	20 Mar. 1989				
India	CD/988	20 Apr. 1990	X			
Iran	CD/1040	31 Aug. 1990	X			
Japan	CD/CW/WP.228	13 Mar. 1989	X			
Netherlands	CD/924	23 June 1989	X			
	CD/925[c]	23 June 1989	X			
	CD/1018	19 July 1990				
New Zealand	CD/1057	13 Feb. 1991				X
Norway	CD/CW/WP.285[e]	10 Apr. 1990	X			
Spain	CD/1082	12 June 1991	X			
Sweden	CD/CW/WP.216	9 Dec. 1988	X			
Switzerland	CD/CW/WP.247[f]	16 June 1989	X			

Country	Document	Date			
	CD/CW/WP.309f	25 July 1990			X
	CD/CW/WP.372	11 Oct. 1991			X
UK	CD/921g	14 June 1989			
	CD/CW/WP.249	21 June 1989	X		
	CD/1012h	11 July 1990			X
	CD/1080i	5 June 1991		X	
USA	CD/922	22 June 1989	X		
	CD/CW/WP.301	27 June 1990	X		
	CD/1100	14 Aug. 1991		X	
	CD/1107/Rev.1	23 Aug. 1991		X	
USSRb	CD/894	28 Feb. 1989	X		
	CD/966	14 Feb. 1990	X		
Yugoslavia	CD/982j	30 Mar. 1990			X

a CD/948 and CD/999 report the same inspection.
b The document was submitted to the Conference on Disarmament under this name.
c The inspection was conducted under the proposed format for ad hoc on-site verification.
d CD/890 and CD/890/Add.1 report the same inspection.
e The facility inspected was producing a schedule 3 chemical.
f CD/CW/WP.247 and CD/CW/WP.309 report on the same inspection.
g Two different practice challenge inspections (PCIs) were conducted at conventional ammunition storage facilities.
h Four different PCIs were conducted at governmental military installations.
i Two PCIs were conducted at civilian chemical facilities.
j The facility inspected was producing a schedule 3 chemical. The inspection regime employed was adapted to a schedule 3 regime.

Table 6A.2. Multinational trial inspections (MTIs)

The cut-off date for compilation of the data in the table was 31 December 1991.

Country	Document	Date	Routine inspection under schedule 2 regime	Inspection under schedule 1 regime	Challenge inspection at a civilian chemical facility	Challenge inspection at a military installation
Canada and the Netherlands	CD1052	28 Jan. 1991				X
Federal Republic of Germany	CD/1102[a]	15 Aug. 1991				X
Federal Republic of Germany and the UK	CD/1056[b]	8 Feb. 1991				X
Italy	CD/893[c]	24 Feb. 1989	X			
Poland and the USSR[e]	CD/1093[d]	6 Aug. 1991				X

[a] The inspection was conducted by inspectors from Argentina, Egypt, Iran, Pakistan and the UK.
[b] Two PCIs were conducted at an air force operational base and ammunition storage facility.
[c] Two chemical plants were inspected with the participation of specialists from 11 countries.
[d] Two Soviet military facilities located on Polish territory were inspected.
[e] The document was submitted to the Conference on Disarmament under this name.

Part II. Military expenditure, arms trade and production, and armed conflicts

7. World military expenditure

SAADET DEGER and SOMNATH SEN

I. Introduction

In spite of the 30 wars that raged in various parts of the world in 1991, world military expenditure continued its downward trend in 1991. This was chiefly because both the USA and the former USSR reduced their defence spending and continued the allocation patterns begun in the late 1980s. West European countries, NATO as well as non-NATO members, were more cautious. European NATO military spending remained stable. Countries in Central and Eastern Europe made further cuts, maintaining the trends set in 1989. Military expenditure for the developing world showed significant regional variations, with defence spending increasing in the Far East and decreasing in Africa and Latin America. In the Middle East, the Gulf Co-operation Council (GCC) states increased their military spending, to compensate the US-led multi-national Coalition for costs accrued in the war against Iraq and to cover new arms purchases. At the same time, the UN-sponsored arms embargo and other economic sanctions aimed at halting Iraqi arms procurement effectively contributed to a downward trend in the regional total. In aggregate, the decline in world military expenditure in 1991 did not differ significantly from the annual percentage declines of 1989 and 1990.

The political changes in Europe since 1989 have not had a profound effect on world military expenditure and force levels. The fear of instability has increased while the old threats to security have yet to disappear. Arms control measures, such as the Treaty on Conventional Armed Forces in Europe (CFE), have only had marginal effects on defence spending, since the ceilings imposed on treaty limited equipment (TLE) are rather high, at least for European NATO countries, and can only affect weapons acquisition in the long run. Arms limitations are still a matter of technological and economic structural disarmament (TESD) rather than tuned to the profound transformation taking place in the international political sphere.[1] The substantive reductions that have taken place in 1988–91 have been confined to the USA and the former USSR. However, in both countries (the overwhelmingly largest defence spenders, contributing over 60 per cent of the world total), the reductions have occurred from very high levels, and mainly for economic and technological reasons. In the USA, the huge budget deficit has forced the Administration and Congress to set severe limitations on future discretionary spending, most of it on defence. In the USSR, the economic and systemic crisis implied that the massive share of the gross domestic product (GDP)

---

[1] For a description of TESD, see Deger, S. and Sen, S., SIPRI, *Military Expenditure: The Political Economy of International Security* (Oxford University Press: Oxford, 1990), pp. 5–7.

allocated to defence could not be justified any longer. For regional groupings in the rest of the world, cuts have occurred, mainly when economic constraints forced the relevant countries to reduce expenditure on arms. Political factors, such as the dramatically changed situation in the East–West confrontation in general, and developments in arms control in particular, have had limited impact on military expenditure levels.

This situation could change radically, as a result of the disintegration of the USSR in the early part of 1991 and its ultimate dissolution as a state by the end of the year. Despite its huge weapon stocks, the former USSR no longer constitutes a great military threat to the USA. While broader security issues remain to be resolved, for the first time in the post-World War II period a large-scale war between the major powers can be ruled out with a reasonable degree of certainty. Iraq notwithstanding, the military machine created for a pan-European or a global confrontation has become obsolete. The end of the Soviet state renders such arsenals, requiring high military spending, superfluous. The conflicts of 1991 in the Middle East and the Balkans require altered military structures and doctrines and certainly less expenditures. The reduction of defence spending—and of the forces, procurement and military research that it buys—have moved beyond TESD, and are now subject to the political transformations.

However, it will take a long time for sustained reductions in defence spending to result in a significant build-down of forces. Despite high expectations and a clear need, there is therefore little sign as yet of a 'disarmament dividend' in the coming.[2] To cushion the costs of adjustment in the USA and NATO, the reductions will be slow to appear. Military manpower reductions will require expenditures to cover increased costs for pensions, severance payments and resettlement. Defence industries stand to lose greatly, and there will be costs through unemployment in selective industries as well as specific regions. In the Soviet successor states the cuts will be chaotic and forced by economic constraints. In the developing world, which currently spends about 16–17 per cent of the global total, military expenditure cuts depend very much on the failure or success of national economies as a whole. In the long run, however, conflict resolution and the cessation of wars, as seen in South-East Asia, Central America and Southern and Eastern Africa in 1991, will benefit such economic growth through the elimination of the costs of a war economy.

Section II discusses US military expenditure; section III addresses the former USSR and its successor states; and section IV analyses European military expenditure, under separate headings for NATO, the European Community (EC) and the Central European and Balkan countries. Section V discusses the Asia–Pacific region, with emphasis on the two major regional powers China and Japan; and section VI analyses the developing world, where—aside from the Middle East—overall economic and environmental problems are

---

[2] See Deger, S. and Sen, S., 'Military expenditure, disarmament and security: what are the problems?', ed. A. D. Rotfeld, SIPRI, *Global Security and the Rule of Law* (Oxford University Press: Oxford, forthcoming). For a perceptive discussion on the European dimension of the 'peace dividend', see Kirby, S. and Hooper, N. (eds), *The Cost of Peace: Assessing Europe's Security Options* (Harwood: Chur, Switzerland, 1991).

increasingly becoming more important than military security issues. The costs of the Persian Gulf War are also briefly discussed.

World military expenditure seems to be at a crossroads, reflecting the problems and issues that the international community will face in the future. In one scenario, the major issues will not relate to top-level politics, military structures and doctrines, and the problems of inter-state peace and war, but to more technical matters: how to manage supranational organizations, such as the UN, the EC and the new Commonwealth of Independent States (CIS); how to participate and extend the international economic system; how to maintain effective government; and how to dismantle overgrown military structures. In this scenario military expenditure is bound to fall and to remain low, although the restructuring may take time. Alternatively, the chaotic nature of change, provoked by the instability of the former USSR, developmental failures and insecurity caused by domestic factors, will halt or reverse the current decline.

II. The USA

While the 1980s was characterized by the fastest and largest sustained peace-time expansion of US military expenditure, the 1990s will be characterized by the steady and sustained reduction of US military expenditure and forces. It is still premature to speak of a 50 per cent reduction by the turn of the century, as predicted by some civilian analysts.[3] However, the military share of the US GDP is certain to go down from its late 1980s peak of 6 per cent to around 3 per cent by the late 1990s. The adjustment will be slow, as there are some adjustment costs which will have to be borne in the medium term. The transitional phase to the new equilibrium may be characterized by a relatively rapid reduction in forces, slower cut-backs in procurement, and resilience in military research and development (R&D). However, from the point of view of the military the reduction in US defence capability will be slow and measured, with none of the fundamental structural breaks and systemic shifts that occurred at the end of World War II and, to a more modest degree, the Viet Nam War. There is little euphoria in military circles about the end of the cold war. The mood is rather one of caution, born out of a sense that the insecurity of the past has been traded for the instability of the present. The most complex adjustments will be made in the nuclear field, where the stockpiles of strategic and theatre nuclear weapons clearly far exceed the requirements of the current political situation. Yet, even here drastic changes were not announced until late 1991 after the political collapse of the USSR as an unitary state.[4]

In 1948 the very first Annual Report to the President and the Congress of the Secretary of Defense stated:

We scrapped our war machine, mightiest in the history of the world, in a manifestation of confidence that we should not need it any longer. Our quick and complete

[3] Kaufmann, W. W., 'A plan to cut military spending in half', *Bulletin of the Atomic Scientists*, vol. 46, no. 3 (Mar. 1990), pp. 35–39.
[4] See also chapter 14 in this volume.

demobilization was a testimonial to our good will rather than to our common sense. International frictions which constitute a threat to our national security and to the peace of the world have since compelled us to strengthen our armed forces for self-protection.[5]

Today, the mood is that the dismantling of the US military machine must be done slowly and with care. In his 1991 Annual Report to the President and the Congress, Secretary of Defense Dick Cheney claimed:

[W]e have an opportunity to avoid a similar cycle of mistakes and crises. We must take careful, deliberate action to change the structure of our military without eviscerating our forces and security. We must evaluate, as we build down, whether our hopes for a more peaceful and benign international environment are being realized. This report presents the framework for the task to restructure our defense capabilities. It rests on a superstructure we can rely on—streamlined, effective armed forces that can defend America against the threats and uncertainties of the modern world.[6]

Attention is first given to the US budget, since it reflects the perceptions of the Government and Congress of the security implications of the recent transformations. The discussion also provides a brief analysis of the historical evolution of US military expenditure and the possibilities for the future.

The budget

The intricacies and problems of the US defence budget were less visible in the past fiscal year (FY) of October 1991 to September 1992 than in the previous one. The Administration's 1991 budget agreement with Congress covered multi-year allocations with spending limits on various categories of discretionary spending. The three major categories of such discretionary spending refer to defence, international affairs (including military assistance) and certain parts of domestic spending. The Omnibus Budget Reconciliation Act of 1990 amended and changed the structure of aggregate spending as previously determined by the Balanced Budget and Emergency Deficit Control Act of 1985 (commonly known as the Gramm–Rudman–Hollings Act).[7] Hence many of the major cost decisions and the aggregate caps (upper limits) on discretionary spending (which include national defence) had already been stipulated in 1990 by that year's Budget Enforcement Act.[8] The spending cap on national defence is of the following order for FYs 1991, 1992 and 1993, respectively (in current prices): $288.9 billion, $291.4 billion and $291.5 billion in budget authority (expenditures authorized or obligated in a given fiscal year), and $298.8 billion, $295.8 billion and $292.5 billion for budgetary outlay (actual

[5] Quoted in US Secretary of Defence Dick Cheney, *Annual Report to the President and the Congress* (US Government Printing Office: Washington, DC, Jan. 1991), p. 5.

[6] Cheney (note 5), p. 5.

[7] For a discussion of the Gramm–Rudman–Hollings Act, see Deger, S, 'World military expenditure', SIPRI, *SIPRI Yearbook 1989: World Armaments and Disarmament* (Oxford University Press: Oxford, 1989), pp. 135; Deger and Sen (note 1), pp. 47–49.

[8] See US Congressional Budget Office, *An Analysis of the President's Budgetary Proposals for Fiscal Year 1992* (US Government Printing Office: Washington, DC, Mar. 1991).

Table 7.1. US Department of Defense and 'National Defense' expenditure, budget authority and outlay, FYs 1989–93

Figures are in US $b., current and constant (1992) prices.

	1989	1990	1991	1992	1993
Department of Defense					
Current price					
Budget authority	290.8	293.0	273.0	278.3	277.9
Outlay	294.9	289.8	287.5	283.0	279.1
Constant price					
Budget authority	324.4	316.6	280.9	278.3	267.3
Outlay	330.1	314.3	296.4	283.0	268.4
'National Defense'					
Current price					
Budget authority	299.6	303.3	285.6	290.8	290.9
Outlay	303.6	299.3	298.9	295.2	292.0
Constant price					
Budget authority	334.2	327.7	293.9	290.8	279.8
Outlay	339.8	324.6	308.2	295.2	280.8

Source: US Secretary of Defense Dick Cheney, *Annual Report to the President and the Congress* (US Government Printing Office: Washington, DC, Jan. 1991).

expenditures in that year from current as well as previous appropriations).[9] The actual defence budget aggregates closely follow these limits. However, the allocation pattern and the weapon acquisition programmes in this budget reflect the Government's perception in adjusting US military spending in the post-cold war era to accommodate the waning of the Soviet threat as well as the emergence of the possibility that the USA would again have to fight a war in the developing world. President George Bush's introductory budgetary speech in January 1991 coincided with the start of Operation Desert Storm. By the time final appropriations were passed by Congress, towards the end of 1991, the USSR had ceased to exist. Planning for future US force structures, in the light of the new developments in the former USSR, thus became the new priority in 1992, and the implications of these changes will be more fully reflected in the next budget for FY 1993 (to begin in October 1992).

Table 7.1 compares data for Department of Defense (DOD) and category 'National Defense' budgets for FYs 1991–93 with that for FYs 1989–90. In FY 1991 (ending in September 1991) there was a sharp cut in these budgets, owing to the discretionary caps mentioned above. Thus, in FY 1992 military spending reductions will be modest. The decline in outlays are more spread out, with annual reductions of about 5 per cent for the next two to three years.

The international security environment that influences US defence policy was shaped by developments in the following areas in 1991:

[9] *Congressional Quarterly*, vol. 49, no. 6 (9 Feb. 1991), pp. 336–37.

1. The Middle East, with oil being the dominant concern (two-thirds of the known oil resources of the world lie in the region);

2. The USSR, in particular the disintegration of Soviet central authority and the uncertain future status of its large military capabilities;

3. Eastern Europe, characterized by political unrest and developmental failures and which therefore, despite the demise of the Warsaw Treaty Organization, ranks high on the security agenda;

4. East Asia and the Pacific, where problems may arise as a result of greater economic interdependence and independence, regional security issues (such as the future relationship between the two Korean states and between Viet Nam and Cambodia) and several territorial disputes;

5. Other regional security problems, including tension in South Asia, strains in the US–Chinese relationship, political and economic instability in Latin America and socio-economic upheavals in Africa;

6. Arms proliferation;

7. Narcotics and terrorism.[10]

Military security is closely entwined with economic security, as must be reflected in budgetary priorities. The broader issues of future defence priorities in response to such a changing security environment are discussed below.

The national defence budget for FY 1992, submitted to Congress in February 1991, ignored the financial aspects of the Persian Gulf War, since it was presented at a time when the war was actually in progress and the costs were uncertain. The fundamental imperatives were domestic economic constraints and the rapid waning of the Soviet threat. Even though the response to the latter was cautious, many of the changed programme priorities reflected the view that there was no longer a major enemy. The Persian Gulf War did have some effects on acquisition programmes, particularly in later discussions with Congress. In particular, the success of the Patriot interceptor missiles produced a new rationale for the Strategic Defense Initiative (SDI).[11] The B-2 bomber remained a favourite with the Government, even though in 1990 the House of Representatives had tried to stop it. The argument was made that its 'stealth' properties could be used in wars against less advanced countries, as shown by the success of the F-117 fighter-bomber, which although more primitive than the B-2 had worked well against Iraqi air defences.

Except for the B-2 programme (which in the end received $2.9 billion for four planes and $1.6 billion for development), the strategic forces fared badly. The rail-mobile launcher for the 10-warhead MX intercontinental ballistic missile (ICBM) was effectively abandoned; the small one-warhead Midgetman ICBM received modest funding, although it is relatively better off than the MX, the production of which will be terminated; and the last Trident submarine (number 18, funded in FY 1991) was purchased, while only 28 Trident II missiles will be purchased in FY 1992, compared to 52 in 1991.

---

[10] Cheney (note 5).
[11] See chapter 5 in this volume.

Table 7.2. Budgetary expenditure on the Strategic Defense Initiative and the Tactical Missile Defense Initiative, FYs 1991–93

Figures are in US $b., current prices.

	1991	1992	1993
Strategic Defense Initiative (SDI)			
Near-term nationwide defensive system[a]	870.5	1 612.3	1 593.4
'Thin' nationwide defensive system[b]	395.8	674.4	747.5
Anti-tactical missile defensive system	184.0	279.5	340.7
Future nationwide defensive system	706.6	925.1	1 016.3
Other	744.4	1 089.4	1 235.3
SDI total	**2 901.4**	**4 580.7**	**4 933.2**
Tactical Missile Defense Initiative (TMDI)			
Research and development	218.2	578.0	550.0
Procurement	–	25.0	173.8
TMDI total	**218.2**	**603.0**	**723.8**
Total SDI and TMDI	**3 119.6**	**5 183.7**	**5 657.0**

[a] Near-term nationwide defensive systems include Brilliant Pebbles.
[b] 'Thin' nationwide defensive systems comply with the ABM Treaty.

Source: *Congressional Quarterly*, vol. 49, no. 6 (9 Feb. 1991), pp. 321–96.

The end of the Soviet state by December 1991 made many of these programmes and expenditures redundant. The President's State of the Union address to Congress on 28 January 1992,[12] as well as the 1993 budget, released at the same time, propose more dramatic arms control measures. The Government calls for the termination of the following programmes: (*a*) the B-2 bomber, after 20 aircraft are produced instead of the 75 originally proposed; (*b*) the Midgetman ICBM; (*c*) the W88 nuclear warhead for Trident missiles; and (*d*) the Advanced Cruise Missile, after the procurement of 640 missiles. The long-term impact of these and other continuing cuts will be substantial. Defence outlay as a proportion of gross national product (GNP) is forecasted to fall to 3.4 per cent by 1997—the lowest in 50 years. National defence, which in 1993 will account for an estimated 19 per cent of total federal expenditure, is expected to fall to 16 per cent by 1997.

SDI appropriations and requests for FYs 1991–93 are shown in table 7.2. Both the collapse of the USSR (leaving tactical nuclear missiles spread across several independent states) and Iraq's use of Soviet Scud missiles in the war were used to justify SDI-type programmes. In the FY 1991 budget, Congress reduced the President's request for development funding for Brilliant Pebbles, space-based interceptors that could violate the 1972 Anti-Ballistic Missile (ABM) Treaty. In 1992 the arguments could be more persuasive, particularly for anti-tactical missile programmes. Since 1990 there is a separate Congress-sponsored programme for Tactical Missile Defence (TMD). Funding for

[12] For excerpts of the text, see appendix 2A in this volume.

research in TMD is expected to increase with the rise of missile proliferation and increase in regional instability.[13]

Since a number of Army divisions are to be cut, the budget has no requests for several major weapon acquisitions such as the Bradley armoured personnel carrier (APC) or the Multiple Launcher Rocket System (MLRS). Some modest development funding has been requested for new-generation weapons, such as a new group of armoured combat vehicles and a new tank. The Navy requests five Aegis destroyers, one Seawolf Class submarine and $900 million for components for an aircraft-carrier scheduled for 1995. The Air Force continues development of the Advanced Tactical Fighter (ATF), for production in the late 1990s). Other fighter aircraft, the F-14, the F-16 and the F/A-18, are to be phased out or modernized, but not replaced with new-generation aircraft.

Overall, the budget shows a real decline in many programmes and a general understanding that the military priorities of the past four decades need to be changed. However, a comparison of the past and the proposed future evolution of US defence spending and military capabilities shows that the reduction in armaments is slow relative to the rapid buildup of the early to mid-1980s.

The final authorization bill in November also gives SDI a new lease of life, as it now is seen to be useful against aggressors in the developing world or renegade Soviet states with ICBMs.[14] The Brilliant Pebbles space-based interceptors get developmental funding while ground-based anti-missile systems get the clear for deployment when technology allows. The final budget for SDI in FY 1992 is $4.6 billion, as President Bush requested, far more than the $2.9 billion appropriated in FY 1991. As Representative Ronald V. Dellums, an opponent of SDI, said: 'We have crossed . . . the psychological and political threshold, taking SDI from research to development'.[15]

The past

The 1980s can be characterized by the rise and fall of US military expenditure, with rapid growth in the period 1980–87 and stability and a modest decline thereafter. Both domestic budgetary constraints and the more benign international security environment of the late 1980s contributed to this bell-shaped trend. Table 7.3 gives the real values (in constant prices) of national defence outlays (which closely approximate actual expenditures) for 1980–96. Military spending rose until 1989 before beginning its downward course. Even though the decline will occur it is remarkable how slow it is. The third column shows current defence spending as a proportion of the 1980 level, when the expansion began. Around 1989 US defence expenditure was increased by 50 per cent per year compared to what it was in 1980. Even in 1995, however, after six years of contraction, the level is projected to lie approximately 20 per cent above the 1980 level. It is clear that the reduction of the defence burden is as

[13] See chapter 5 in this volume.

[14] *Congressional Quarterly*, vol. 49, no. 47 (23 Nov. 199), pp. 3468–69.

[15] *Congressional Quarterly* (note 14).

Table 7.3. US national defence outlays, 1980–96

Figures are in US $b., at constant (1982) prices.

Fiscal year	National defence outlay	Increase from 1980 (%)	Year-to-year change (%)
1980	164.0	..	..
1981	171.4	4.5	4.5
1982	185.3	13.0	8.1
1983	201.3	22.7	8.6
1984	211.3	28.8	5.0
1985	230.0	40.2	8.9
1986	244.0	48.8	6.1
1987	251.0	53.1	2.9
1988	252.8	54.2	0.7
1989	256.8	56.6	1.6
1990	247.0	50.6	− 3.8
1991	235.9	43.8	− 4.6
1992	223.3	36.2	− 5.3
1993	212.0	29.3	− 5.1
1994	201.1	22.6	− 5.1
1995	196.0	19.5	− 2.5
1996	192.9	17.6	− 1.6

Source: *Budget of the United States Government* (US Government Printing Office: Washington, DC, 1991)

problematic as was its fast expansion.[16] The final column in table 7.3 gives the year-to-year percentage change in defence outlays.

The historical tables of US defence spending are particularly pertinent at a time of change. More important are the shares of the aggregate of the constituent parts, since these shares reflect threat and security perceptions. Table 7.4 gives data for budget authority. The shares of each major category are also given. The fastest increase occurred in military R&D, followed closely by defence procurement. The shares of each category of military expenditures—personnel, procurement, R&D, atomic energy defence (nuclear weapons programmes) and operations and maintenance (O&M)—changed likewise.

In table 7.4, US defence budget authority is presented in terms of its allocation structure. Both military personnel and O&M shares show a U-shaped curve. The shares of these two categories, broadly representing operating costs, fall until FY 1987 and then begin to rise. The procurement expenditure share, on the other hand, representing major weapon purchases, rises rapidly until FY 1986 and then begins to fall. In FY 1986 the share of procurement is almost one-third of national defence spending; by FY 1991 it falls to almost one-fifth. This bell-shaped curve spells future problems for the defence–industrial complex, since arms producers get smaller shares of a shrinking budget authority. The shares for military R&D and atomic energy defence continue to grow, implying an emphasis on future weapon programmes.

[16] Deger and Sen (note 1), pp. 44–49.

Table 7.4. Allocation of US national defence budget authority, FYs 1982–91

Figures are in US $b., current prices; figures in italics are percentage shares.

	1982	1983	1984	1985	1986	1987	1988	1989	1990	1991
Military personnel	55.7	61.0	64.9	67.8	67.8	74.0	76.6	78.5	78.9	79.0
Percentage share	*25.7*	*24.9*	*24.5*	*23.0*	*23.5*	*25.7*	*26.2*	*26.2*	*26.0*	*27.7*
O&M[a]	62.5	66.6	71.0	77.8	74.9	79.6	81.6	86.2	88.3	86.0
Percentage share	*28.9*	*27.2*	*26.8*	*26.4*	*25.9*	*27.7*	*28.0*	*28.8*	*29.1*	*30.1*
Procurement	64.5	80.4	86.2	96.8	92.5	80.2	80.0	79.4	81.4	64.1
Percentage share	*29.8*	*32.8*	*32.5*	*32.8*	*32.0*	*27.9*	*27.4*	*26.5*	*26.8*	*22.4*
RDT&E[b]	20.0	22.8	26.9	31.3	33.6	35.6	36.5	37.5	36.5	34.5
Percentage share	*9.2*	*9.3*	*10.1*	*10.6*	*11.6*	*12.4*	*12.5*	*12.5*	*12.0*	*12.0*
Energy, defence	4.7	5.7	6.6	7.3	7.3	7.5	7.7	8.1	9.7	11.6
Percentage share	*2.2*	*2.3*	*2.5*	*2.5*	*2.5*	*2.6*	*2.6*	*2.7*	*3.2*	*4.0*
Other	9.1	8.5	9.6	13.7	13.0	10.5	9.6	9.9	8.5	10.4
Percentage share	*4.2*	*3.5*	*3.6*	*4.6*	*4.5*	*3.7*	*3.3*	*3.3*	*2.8*	*3.6*
Total	**216.5**	**245.0**	**265.2**	**294.7**	**289.1**	**287.4**	**292.0**	**299.6**	**303.3**	**285.6**

[a] Operations and maintenance (includes civilian personnel cost).

[b] Research, development, testing and evaluation.

Sources: *Budget of the United States Government* (US Government Printing Office: Washington, DC, 1991); authors' calculations.

Data on defence outlays, approximating actual spendings and their allocations, give a somewhat different picture. Military personnel as well as O&M show a declining trend for shares throughout the 10-year period of study. The procurement share follows a bell-shaped curve, but the adjustments are far less pronounced. The shares of outlays on research and nuclear weapons continue to increase throughout the period. While the fundamental problems remain, the military–industrial complex, which is dependent on actual spending on these three categories, is thus given a longer time to adjust.

The past is no longer a guide to the future, because of the systemic and structural breaks that have taken place in international security. Thus the future will have to see a radical shift in priorities. It is possible that in 1992—an election year in the USA—these priorities will be spelled out. In particular, after the euphoria following the end of the Persian Gulf War, domestic economic issues are becoming more important. Even though rapid cuts in military expenditure will not necessarily translate quickly to economic growth, some transfer of resources are becoming essential. The almost $300 billion defence budget is obviously a large budgetary drain and, being discretionary, will need to be reduced more substantially than as yet envisaged by the DOD.

The future

To understand the current perceptions of US military planners, spending allocations for FYs 1992–96 (the current five-year plan for the military) are

Table 7.5. Projected US national defence outlays, FYs 1992–96

Figures are in US $b., current prices;[a] figures in italics are percentage shares.

	1992	1993	1994	1995	1996
Military personnel	77.8	77.3	76.3	75.7	76.7
Percentage share	*26.4*	*26.5*	*26.6*	*26.2*	*26.2*
O&M[b]	85.7	84.3	84.1	84.9	86.9
Percentage share	*29.0*	*28.9*	*29.3*	*29.4*	*29.6*
Procurement	74.3	68.8	67.2	68.6	71.0
Percentage share	*25.2*	*23.6*	*23.4*	*23.8*	*24.2*
RDT&E[c]	37.8	39.7	40.0	38.4	36.7
Percentage share	*12.8*	*13.6*	*14.0*	*13.3*	*12.5*
Energy, defence	11.4	12.0	12.6	13.2	13.9
Percentage share	*3.9*	*4.1*	*4.4*	*4.6*	*4.7*
Other	8.2	9.9	6.4	7.8	8.0
Percentage share	*2.8*	*3.4*	*2.2*	*2.7*	*2.7*
Total	**295.2**	**292.0**	**286.6**	**288.6**	**293.2**

[a] Then-year price, calculated from projected inflation rate.
[b] Operations and maintenance (includes civilian personnel cost).
[c] Research, development, testing and evaluation.

Sources: Budget of the United States Government (US Government Printing Office: Washington, DC, 1991); authors' calculations.

shown in tables 7.5 and 7.6. It is again necessary to observe both authority and outlays, since the former gives the multi-year planned expenditures while the latter shows how much is actually expected to be spent in each FY.

Table 7.5 gives budget authority requested for FYs 1992–96. Taken together, operating costs (the sum of personnel and O&M) retain their share at around 55 per cent of the total. What is important to note is that procurement cuts are sought to be mitigated, and the procurement share goes up from about one-fifth of total defence spending to around one-fourth. Of course, this does not mean that this share will rise in total terms. It simply shows that the fall will be cushioned, so that the radical reduction of spending authorization in FYs 1991–92 is compensated somewhat in later years. Research expenditures and those for nuclear weapons retain their shares in spite of aggregate cuts. The category 'other', mainly military construction and family housing for service personnel, is slated for large cuts because of base closures.

Tables 7.4–7.6 seem to imply that nuclear weapon research, development and procurement have been expanded and protected in this long cycle of expansion and contraction. Of particular importance, in light of the removal of the Soviet threat, is to analyse the status of the strategic nuclear forces.[17] In a major arms control initiative in September 1991, President Bush announced steps which would: (*a*) direct US strategic bombers to stand down from continuous alert position; (*b*) remove from alert posture all ICBMs scheduled

[17] See also chapters 1, 5 and 14 in this volume.

Table 7.6. Planned allocation of US national defence budget authority, FYs 1992–96
Figures are in US $b., current prices; figures in italics are percentage shares.

	1992	1993	1994	1995	1996
Military personnel	78.0	77.5	76.5	75.9	77.0
Percentage share	*26.8*	*26.6*	*26.2*	*25.7*	*25.9*
O&M[a]	86.5	84.7	84.6	85.7	88.0
Percentage share	*29.7*	*29.1*	*29.0*	*29.0*	*29.6*
Procurement	63.4	66.7	68.8	74.7	74.8
Percentage share	*21.8*	*22.9*	*23.6*	*25.3*	*25.1*
RDT&E[b]	39.9	41.0	40.1	37.5	36.0
Percentage share	*13.7*	*14.0*	*13.7*	*12.7*	*12.1*
Energy, defence	11.8	12.2	12.9	13.6	14.3
Percentage share	*4.0*	*4.2*	*4.4*	*4.6*	*4.8*
Other	11.2	8.8	9.0	7.7	7.7
Percentage share	*3.9*	*3.0*	*3.1*	*2.6*	*2.6*
Total	**290.8**	**290.9**	**291.9**	**295.1**	**297.8**

[a] Operations and maintenance (includes civilian personnel cost).

[b] Research, development, testing and evaluation.

Sources: *Budget of the United States Government* (US Government Printing Office: Washington, DC, 1991); authors' calculations.

for de-activation under the Treaty Between the USA and the USSR on the Reduction and Limitation of Strategic Offensive Arms (START); (*c*) eliminate all ground-launched tactical nuclear weapons; and (*d*) withdraw all naval tactical nuclear forces.[18] The implications could be far-reaching: termination of the development of the MX mobile ICBM and the mobile parts of the Midgetman Small ICBM (SICBM); cancellation of replacements for the short-range attack missile for strategic bombers; and negotiation towards the future elimination of all multi-warhead ICBMs. Although the budgetary implications of these proposals, which have been matched by the USSR, are modest at present,[19] they will eventually lead to long-term reductions in US procurement funding for the strategic forces (which currently account for one-third of all procurement spending). Allocations to the Department of Energy for nuclear weapon production will be cut correspondingly. However, the ecological damage caused by the production and testing of nuclear weapons will require continuously expanding funds to mitigate the adverse ecological impact.[20]

What would the US force structure look like in the mid-1990s? According to current plans, active Army divisions are expected to be cut by one-third, from 18 in 1990 to 12 in 1995. Deployed aircraft-carriers are to be reduced

[18] See also chapter 2 in this volume. Excerpts of President Bush's speech of 27 Sep. 1991 is reproduced in appendix 2A.

[19] *Congressional Quarterly*, vol. 49, no. 40 (5 Oct. 1991), pp. 2878–81.

[20] For an assessment of the adverse environmental impact of military activities, see Sen, S. and Deger, S., 'The re-orientation of military R&D for civilian purposes', eds J. Rotblat and F. Blackaby, *Towards a Secure World in the 21st Century, Annals of Pugwash 1990* (Taylor & Francis: London, 1991), pp. 194–98.

Table 7.7. US active and reserve force and military personnel strengths, FYs 1990 and 1995

Figures in italics show percentage decline.

	1990	1995	Decline (%)
Army divisions	28	18	*36*
Active	18	12	*33*
Reserve	10	6	*40*
Aircraft-carriers, total	16	13	*19*
Deployed	13	12	*8*
Carrier air wings	15	13	*13*
Active	13	11	*16*
Reserve	2	2	*–*
Fighting ships	545	451	*17*
Tactical fighter wings	36	26	*28*
Active	24	15	*38*
Reserve	12	11	*8*
Strategic bombers	268	181	*32*
Military personnel (million)	3.2	2.6	*19*
Active	2.1	1.7	*19*
Reserve	1.1	0.9	*18*

Source: Congressional Budget Office, *An Analysis of the President's Budgetary Proposals for Fiscal Year 1992* (CBO: Washington, DC, 1991).

from 13 to 12, a reduction of only 8 per cent. Active aircraft-carrier air wings are also to fall marginally by 15 per cent. The Air Force's tactical fighter wings are to be cut substantially, while the number of strategic bombers are reduced by one-third. Active duty military manpower is to go down from 1991 levels of about 2.1 million to almost 1.7 million men. The overall effect would be a smaller Army, a leaner but technologically fitter Air Force and a fundamentally unaltered Navy (see table 7.7). The defence of Europe is not an overriding concern, and wars in the developing world are expected to be either technologically sophisticated but short in duration, or low-intensity. The role of the ground forces is thus downgraded. The Persian Gulf War demonstrated the importance of air power, but above all of superior high-technology weapon systems. International obligations require the USA to maintain a relatively large naval force, but technological superiority is less important for the Navy, since its primary task would be power projection.

In spite of these cuts, investment in new-generation weapons continues. In particular, research, development, testing and evaluation (RDT&E) expenditures have proven resilient—when total budgets go down, the RDT&E share rises. A comparison of budgetary requests for current-generation weapons and next-generation weapons in the FY 1992 budget (table 7.8) clearly shows the Administration's preference and conforms with the trend shown in table 7.7. Air Force research rises strongly while naval research falls. Except for the

Table 7.8. US investment in current and next-generation weapon systems, FY 1992

Figures are in US $b., current prices; figures in italics show percentage change.

	President's request	Decline (–)/increase (+) relative to previous year's acquisition cost (%)
Current generation		
Weapon systems		
Bradley fighting vehicles	0.1	*– 84*
F-16 aircraft	1.4	*– 37*
M-1 tanks	0.1	*– 91*
F/A-18 aircraft	2.4	*+ 38*
MX missile	0.2	*– 65*
Aggregate spending		
Air Force aircraft	4.3	*– 7*
Air Force missiles	4.9	*–*
Navy aircraft	5.2	*+ 11*
Navy ships	2.2	*– 36*
Navy weapons	2.9	*– 22*
Total current generation	**49.4**	*– 10ᵃ*
Next generation		
Weapon systems		
SSN-21 submarine	2.4	*– 2*
DDG-51 destroyer	4.5	*+ 35*
Trident II missile	1.3	*– 22*
AMRAAM missile	1.0	*+ 17*
B-2 bomber	4.8	*+ 12*
C-17 transporter	2.8	*+ 165*
Aggregate spending		
Army RDT&Eᵇ	6.1	*+ 13*
Air Force RDT&E	12.6	*+ 32*
Navy RDT&E	7.2	*– 8*
Other RDT&E	10.3	*+ 8*
Total next generation	**54.0**	*+ 13ᵃ*

  ᵃ Percentage average.

  ᵇ Research, development, testing and evaluation.

Source: Congressional Budget Office, *An Analysis of the President's Budgetary Proposals for Fiscal Year 1992* (CBO: Washington, DC, 1991).

Trident II missile, almost all other future-generation weaponry is continued. The greatest cuts occur in current-generation weapons, and this is where the cuts in procurement will impinge.

It is also important to note how each category of military expenditure will fare in the future, compared to the past, and also whether there are significant differences between short-term changes and those occurring on a more long-term basis. Table 7.9 shows the real changes in defence budget authority for military personnel, O&M (which includes civilian pay), procurement (of

Table 7.9. Projected real change in US defence expenditure, budget authority, 1992 and 1995

Figures are percentages; a minus indicates a decrease.

	Real change compared with 1980 levels		Real change compared with 1990 levels	
	1992	1995	1992	1995
Military personnel	– 4	– 18	– 8	– 22
O&M[a]	15	–	– 14	– 26
Procurement	8	14	– 28	– 24
RDT&E[b]	79	49	1	– 16
Energy, defence	139	146	12	15
Total	**16**	**4**	**– 13**	**– 22**

[a] Operations and maintenance (includes civilian personnel cost).
[b] Research, development, testing and evaluation.

Source: Congressional Budget Office, *An Analysis of the President's Budgetary Proposals for Fiscal Year 1992* (CBO: Washington, DC, 1991).

major weapons), RDT&E, military construction, energy defence (nuclear weapons) and total military expenditure (national defence sub-function of the US budget). The changes are shown in terms of the future short term (1990–95) and the more structural changes relative to the past (1980–95).

In the short term, almost every category of spending suffers. In particular procurement falls by a quarter over five years while personnel costs decline by about 20 per cent, matching the fall in active-duty manpower. Even R&D, which has been protected in the recent past, is not immune to the massive reductions of around 4–5 per cent per annum. However, comparing annual data for the 15-year period of FYs 1980–95, it is clear that a long cycle is coming to an end, in a way similar to that at the close of the Viet Nam War. In 1995 R&D expenditure is expected to be almost 50 per cent greater, and procurement expenditure almost 15 per cent greater, than in 1980. Although the sharp cuts in procurement and research budgets cause difficulty for the defence–industrial base, the problems are not insurmountable. Indeed, the long cycle has been characterized by expansion followed by contraction, and the time period of 15 years is sufficient for industrial adjustment to have been completed. Since the markets have been given enough time to adjust, there is little interest in 'conversion' in the USA. In fact, the period after World War II was characterized by a much sharper shock than that witnessed today.

III. The USSR and its successor states

The disintegration of the USSR proceeded rapidly during 1991 and culminated on 25 December, when Soviet President Mikhail Gorbachev resigned, and the Soviet flag was struck from the Kremlin. It is not clear what the future security and economic organizations will look like—in and between the successor states. Since military expenditure is determined by the central Government, and this very entity disintegrated during the year as well, financing of military security needs of the newly independent republics is not clear either. By November, the various military industrial ministries of the USSR, which loosely defined the defence complex, were disbanded. The republics in effect nationalized military properties within their borders. Hence, the allocation of military procurement and research expenditures cannot be evaluated with any precision. In December all central ministries, except for national defence and atomic energy, were shut down and their functions effectively taken over by the Russian Federation.[21] In early 1992 Russia formed its own Ministry of Defence, alhough nominally the armed forces belong to the Commonwealth of Independent States (CIS). Russian President Boris Yeltsin has reportedly claimed that Russia will pay for all personnel costs of the former Union Army in 1992. He has also stated that military salaries will be almost doubled in that year. Press reports also state that in the first quarter of 1992 Russia paid for all the CIS armed forces expenditure except for those incurred in Moldova and Ukraine.[22] Price liberalizations have begun and inflation is high. It is therefore difficult to measure the size of the military sector, especially when it enjoys low pricing structures and subsidies which have become even more distorted as a result of the economic changes taking place. In addition, these subsidies, which have kept the monetary values of procurement low, are paid out from the Union budget, and the republics are refusing to pay their share. Russia opposed payments by the republics of about 90 billion roubles towards central government expenditure (CGE) in the fourth quarter of 1991.[23] Approximately one-third of this sum, 30 billion roubles, was required to pay for military spending. These contradictory influences and arrangements imply that monetary aggregates need to be studied even more carefully.

This *Yearbook* chapter traditionally analyses military, economic, political and geographical factors to determine the level, causes and effects of military spending in the USSR. Much uncertainty surrounds all of these factors today, more so than in the past. Therefore, care is needed to interpret the often conflicting information that is available. The present discussion, based on published facts and on estimates by the authors, concentrates on a few key areas where change will create the maximum impact. To be able to understand the chaotic situation today, some historical analysis is needed.

Defence spending, and the resource cost of maintaining a large military, depends on perceptions regarding national security. In the Soviet successor states, national security is being defined in terms of a very broad set of parameters. Within this broad framework, national defence itself depends on many factors, not all of which are related to strategic considerations or foreign

---

[21] *International Herald Tribune*, 20 Dec. 1991; *Financial Times*, 20 Dec. 1991.

[22] *Guardian Weekly*, 23 Dec. 1991; *Financial Times*, 8 Apr. 1992.

[23] See the discussion by Col. V. Lopatin, Deputy Chairman of the RSFSR State Committee for Defence Questions, in Urban, V., 'What the 1992 military budget will be like', *Krasnaya Zvezda*, 3 Dec. 1991, p. 1, in Foreign Broadcast Information Service, *Daily Report–Soviet Union (FBIS-SOV)*, FBIS-SOV-91-232, 3 Dec. 1991, pp. 50–51.

Table 7.10. Share of the Russian Federation and Ukraine in economic, technological and military variables of the former USSR, 1989–90

Figures are percentages.

Variable	Russia	Ukraine
Population	50.8	15.5
National income	61.1	16.3
State budget revenue retained	55.3	15.9
Value added in industry	63.7	17.2
Value added in agriculture	50.3	17.9
Total fixed capital	61.8	15.2
Oil production	91.0	1.0
Coal production	55.0	24.0
Iron-ore production	44.0	46.0
Military expenditure	61–67	17.0
Defence complex enterprises	75.1	16.7
Research and development establishments	84.3	8.6

Sources: International Monetary Fund, the World Bank, Organization for Economic Co-operation and Development, and the European Bank for Reconstruction and Development, *A Study of the Soviet Economy* (IMF/World Bank/OECD/EBRD: Paris, Feb. 1991), vol. 1; Urban, V., 'What the 1992 military budget will be like', *Krasnaya Zvezda*, 3 Dec. 1991, p. 1, in FBIS-SOV-91-232, 3 Dec. 1991, pp. 50–51; Yermolin, V., 'USSR People's Deputy Col. V. Lobatin: the RSFSR State Committee for Defence Questions exists only on paper', *Kraznaya Zvezda*, 18 Oct. 1991, in FBIS-SOV-91-202, 18 Oct. 1991, pp. 61–63; Cooper, J., Royal Institute of International Affairs, *The Soviet Defence Industry: Conversion and Reform* (RIIA, Pinter: London, 1991).

policy. Internal factors—ethnic unrest and civil disorder—will also affect military-related spending. In the former USSR, military expenditure often reflected increases in military capability, but also the country's perceptions of threat and security. The new states clearly will have a totally different set of priorities. In particular, economic factors will become dominant in determining budgetary trends and the capacity of the state to provide for defence. In addition, economic insecurity will be a far more important factor than threat perceptions of the old type. The level of external debt, or that of foreign aid, could be more critical than new arms procured. In the new group of states the issue of security will become more complicated than in the past. Domestic, foreign and inter-republican influences create a complex web of relationships which will affect the trends in force structure and spending levels. Military spending will no longer be a matter of military security alone.

Since the USSR does not exist as a unitary state, but the Army remains under central command, the relative importance of the former republics has to be studied with care. This applies not only to military costs but also to economic power and control over raw material—all of which will determine the new republics' strategic strength, in the broad sense of the term. The Russian Federation and Ukraine hold the key to the future, given their overwhelming dominance. Table 7.10 gives data on economic, technological and military variables to show the relative dominance of these two republics and their expected importance in the future security structure of the successor states.

This section looks at three features of the military expenditure process of the former USSR and its successor states.[24] The first feature, under the title of *glasnost*, discusses the question 'how much do we know?'. The second, under the title of *perestroika*, discusses the question 'how much has changed?'. The third, under the title of *konversiya*, discusses the question 'how much resources are being transferred from the military to the civilian sectors?'.

Glasnost

It is now well known that, after a slow-down in the late 1970s, Soviet military expenditure rose rapidly in the 1980s, in the process exceeding the growth of the national product which was itself slowing down due to various factors termed 'growth retardation'. The process was the result of a combination of factors: the arms race consequent to the Reagan Administration's spurt in defence spending; modernization, increased R&D, automation, new technologies and a new procurement cycle; and military involvement in and security aid to the developing world. The military burden rose fast, as defence growth exceeded economic growth. The process was halted in 1987 and stabilized in 1988, and the decline in spending began earnestly in 1989. A great 'build-down' characterized 1990 and 1991, and substantial reductions in all categories of forces and expenditures are now being carried out. Particularly evident in 1991 is the chaotic nature of the cuts forced by the dissolution of the state and the inability to acquire funding for most projects, particularly in defence-related research. Statistics on aggregate Soviet military expenditure are more difficult to find, for a number of reasons.

1. The available data, often contradictory, are not organized around a White Paper or defence budget, forcing analysts to search general publications.

2. The level of scrutiny of the budget was more intensive and thorough in 1991. This democratization led to many changes and often conflicting debates about what the amounts actually meant.

3. Price reforms changed radically the price structure but little evidence was available as to the price indices and deflators used by the military or the inflationary assumptions made by the Defence Ministry.

4. The share of military in GDP or aggregate budget was problematic, since even the economic variables were subject to dispute.

5. Actual expenditure almost certainly exceeded the budgetary amounts due to high inflation during 1991, and this nominal rise cannot be ascertained. The discussion below is thus based solely on original requests and authorizations.

---

[24] The discussion is limited to a descriptive analysis of events in 1991. A more general and theoretical perspective can be found in Cooper, J., Royal Intitute of International Affairs, *Defence Industry Conversion in the Soviet Union* (RIIA, Pinter: London, 1991); Sen, S., 'The economics of conversion in the Soviet Union', ed. G. Bird, *Economic Reform in Eastern Europe* (Edward Elgar: Aldershot, 1992).

The military budget for 1991 was publicly scrutinized for the first time by the new Supreme Soviet Committee for Defence and State Security Questions as well as the Supreme Soviet Planning, Finance and Budget Commission. The Defence Ministry originally asked for a budget of 66–67 billion roubles (in 1990 prices), which would amount to a cut of 14 per cent relative to the 1989 level and conform to President Gorbachev's May 1989 announcement of unilateral cuts. The Government reduced the amount to just under 64 billion roubles, including a cut of 20 per cent in procurement and 23 per cent in military R&D. The latter cut was particularly unpalatable to the armed forces. The Supreme Soviet Committee for Defence and State Security Questions raised the budget to a level of 65 billion roubles—a reduction of over 8 per cent from the previous year. However, since major price reforms would increase prices overall, and the rate of inflation could be of the order of 50 per cent on average, the actual figure in 1991 prices was 98.6 billion roubles at this stage.

In a final round of adjustment the Supreme Soviet Planning, Finance and Budget Commission, which is in charge of the aggregate Union budget, reduced the level by around 2 billion roubles. Thus final official military expenditure in 1991, *at current prices*, is of the order of 96.6 billion roubles; the precise figure is 96 562 846 000 roubles.[25] The additional 2 billion roubles reduction would have to come from the procurement and research budgets. This level of aggregate defence spending represents a cut of over 9 per cent in real terms between 1990 and 1991. It also means that between 1989 and 1991 official defence expenditure has been reduced by over 17 per cent exceeding the target set by President Gorbachev two years earlier.

Procurement spending is planned to fall by at least 20 per cent, marking the largest decline in Soviet military hardware acquisition since the 1930s. Military R&D is to be cut by over 20 per cent, also signifying a major change in policy, which, at least in the earlier years of *perestroika*, tried to protect the research base of the defence complex. Expenditure to cover costs of personnel, pensions and housing construction is to increase significantly. A new expenditure category, hitherto unknown in Soviet military budgets, called by Marshal Sergey Akhromeyev 'social security program for servicemen and members of their families',[26] gets 3.3 billion roubles—that is, over 10 per cent of the total spending on personnel pay and O&M. The emphasis clearly is on servicemen and their welfare rather than on extravagant weapons programmes and futuristic research. Space programmes are not detailed separately; if they are left out of the defence budget the level could increase significantly.

For the first time, in 1990 the USSR submitted its official military expenditure budget to the United Nations according to the UN standardized

[25] See 'USSR Law on the Union Budget for 1991, signed by President Mikhail Gorbachev at the Kremlin in Moscow on 11 January', *Izvestia*, 16 Jan. 1991, in FBIS-SOV-91-011, 16 Jan. 1991, pp. 52–55; Litovkin, V., 'The cost of defence', interview with Marshal S. Akromeyev, *Izvestia*, 14 Jan, 1991, in FBIS-SOV-91-009, 14 Jan. 1991, pp. 5–7; Isachenkov, V., 'Defense budget approved', TASS international service, 11 Jan. 1991, in FBIS-SOV-91-008, 11 Jan. 1991, p. 16; 'New defence spending budget reportedly higher', Moscow television service, 13 Dec. 1990, transcript in FBIS-SOV-90-241, 14 Dec. 1990, p. 57; 'Direct discussion on the results of the Fourth Congress of USSR Peoples Deputies', Moscow television service, transcript in FBIS-SOV-90-251, 31 Dec. 1990, pp. 24–28.

[26] Akhromeyev (note 25), p. 7.

information matrix.[27] Table 7.11 gives the data presented in the second Soviet detailed submission of military expenditure to the UN. Although far more comprehensive than in the past, as can be seen from the table, many sections are still blank. Given the disintegration of the Union, in the coming years it may become difficult to get any information at all. What the UN and other multilateral agencies, such as the International Monetary Fund (IMF) and the World Bank, should emphasize and encourage is the publication of White Papers by the newly formed republics. In their absence, misperceptions are bound to increase and confidence- and security-building measures (CSBMs) will fail to achieve their desired aims.

Western—especially US—perceptions of Soviet military strength have often been based on intelligence agency estimates of defence spending. In particular the financial values put forward by the US Central Intelligence Agency (CIA) and the Defense Intelligence Agency (DIA) colour attitudes and portray the USSR as more or less militaristic. The DIA estimate is simplistic, since it tends to take the aggregate state budgetary spending and divide it by three to arrive at a figure of around 150 billion roubles during 1988–89. The CIA has a much more sophisticated methodology and uses a comprehensive set of data to arrive at the defence spending figures. One CIA analyst has claimed that in 1988 the USSR spent about 135–165 billion roubles (current prices) on the military.[28] In 1991, the CIA/DIA report to Congress claimed that in 1989–90 military expenditure fell by 6 per cent per year.[29] Since inflation rates were particularly high during 1990 (retail prices rose by 14 per cent in 1990 according to the same report), the current price level of defence spending would not be substantially different from the level of 135–165 billion roubles given above. The latest NATO figures released at the end of 1990 also give Soviet military expenditure in the range of $130–160 billion for 1989.[30] The same current price value would be applicable in 1990. The lower range is on average about 75 per cent higher than the official figure, while the upper range is more than double the official value. In spite of *glasnost* and the huge volume of information available, there still exists a great difference between Soviet official figures and such Western estimates, and this indirectly affects the perception of a still-powerful Soviet military system. Given the chaotic nature of change currently taking place, and the fact that precise data are still not available, future perceptions of the military power of the larger successor states will also be dependent on intelligence estimates. It

[27] See Deger, S., 'World military expenditure', SIPRI, *SIPRI Yearbook 1991: World Armaments and Disarmament* (Oxford University Press: Oxford, 1991), pp.148–49, table 5.17.

[28] See letter from J. E. Steiner on CIA estimates of Soviet military spending, *International Security*, vol. 14, no. 4 (spring 1990), pp. 185–93, and the reply by F. D. Holzman (same issue, pp. 193–98). Steiner's letter was in response to Holzman's 'Politics and guesswork: CIA and DIA estimates of Soviet military spending', *International Security*, vol. 14, no. 2 (fall 1989), pp. 101–31.

[29] US Central Intelligence Agency and Defense Intelligence Agency, 'Beyond Perestroika: the Soviet economy in crisis', a paper prepared by the CIA and the DIA for the Technology and National Security Subcommittee of the Joint Economic Committee, 103rd Congress, Washington, DC, 14 May 1991.

[30] Wilkinson, C., 'Soviet defence spending: trends, outlook and implications', *NATO Review*, vol. 39, no. 2 (Apr. 1991), pp 16–22.

is therefore important to note the definitions of defence activity that such agencies use while calculating measures of military spending in roubles.

There are three possible definitions. The first is similar to that of US 'national defense', encompassing military-related activities financed by the DOD, the nuclear weapon programme of the Department of Energy (DOE) and selective service and defence-related Coast Guard activities. The second is a broader definition which also includes internal security troops, Defence Ministry railroad and construction troops, civil defence activities performed by uniformed personnel and space programmes, which in the USSR are both run by the Ministry of Defence but which in the USA are conducted by the National Aeronautics and Space Administration (NASA). The third is an impossibly broad one which includes as well other activities of relevance to national security but which are not necessarily defence-related—in broad terms 'efforts to enhance a country's global position', which could mean almost anything from diplomacy to espionage.[31]

Only the first and second definitions are relevant. In practice when the CIA presents Soviet military expenditure figures it uses the second definition, and therefore includes elements which for other countries would not be considered defence-related. In this regard the CIA figures are high, although the Agency claims that the difference is relatively small: 'the quantitative difference in Soviet defence spending . . . when measured by definitions one and two is less than one-half of 1 percent of GNP'.[32] However, it is difficult to believe that the difference will only be marginal. The extra categories of personnel (railroad, construction and civil defence) alone add a further 1.5 million people in defining the armed forces, about one-third more than official figures for military personnel. Soviet space spending at around 7 billion roubles (almost three-fourths of 1 per cent of the GNP) is also very high. The same type of discrepancy arises in evaluating the size of the armed forces. The CIA figure for 1989 was 5.5 million roubles,[33] while the official Soviet figure (now accepted by independent analysts) was about 4 million roubles.

There are many reasons why official Soviet military expenditure, particularly procurement spending, appears low as compared to rouble estimates provided by Western intelligence agencies. The most obvious reason is that prices of weapon systems are kept artificially low to accommodate low budgets. The few prices of individual weapons that are now available clearly demonstrate the wide divergence between Soviet and Western unit prices of weapons. For example, a T-80 tank is claimed to cost around $500 000, about one-quarter of the cost of a Leopard tank.[34] An Su-25 aircraft is costed at 5.8 million roubles and compared to a F-16 which costs around $28 million.[35]

[31] Swain D. D., US Central Intelligence Agency, *A Guide to Monetary Measures of Soviet Defence Activities* (CIA, Directorate of Intelligence: Washington, DC, Nov. 1987).

[32] Steiner (note 28), p. 191.

[33] *Allocation of Resources in the Soviet Union and China*, Hearings before the National Security Economics Committee of the Joint Economic Committee, 101st Congress (US Government Printing Office: Washington, DC, 1989), p. 142.

[34] Zuckerman, M. B. and Trimble, J., 'A chat with Moscow's defence minister', *US News & World Report*, 13 Mar. 1989, p. 28.

[35] *Krasnaya Zvezda*, 23 June 1989, p. 3.

Table 7.11. Soviet military expenditure, detailed submission to the United Nations, 1990

Figures are actual outlays in m. roubles, at 1990 prices.[a]

Resource costs	Land forces	Naval forces	Air forces	Other combat forces	Central support, admin. and command		Para-military forces	Military assistance		UN peace-keeping	Un-distributed	Total milex	Civ. def.
					Support	Command		Home terrritory	Abroad				
Operating costs	9 350	2 580	1 914	2 608	2 399	164	1 280	..	..	..	2 521	22 816	178
Personnel	4 201	1 412	1 342	1 775	..	120	673	..	..	..	2 521	12 044	108
Conscripts	..	..	..	..	..	..	..	..	..	..	..	..	..
Other military, incl. reserves	3 015	944	1 125	1 391	..	58	463	..	..	..	2 521	9 517	36
Civilian	1 186	468	217	384	..	62	210	..	..	..	..	2 527	72
Operations and maintenance	5 149	1 168	572	833	2 399	44	607	..	..	..	..	10 722	70
Materials	2 821	517	149	244	1 226	23	275	..	..	..	..	5 255	29
Maintenance	1 040	502	357	384	200	5	268	..	..	..	..	2 756	22
Purchased services	1 283	149	66	205	973	16	60	..	..	..	..	2 752	17
Rent costs	5	..	..	..	..	..	..	..	..	..	..	5	2
Other	..	..	..	..	..	..	4	..	..	..	..	4	..
Procurement and construction	8 830	7 358	6 552	6 091	4 823	361	758	..	..	..	945	35 718	135
Procurement	8 004	6 776	6 164	4 872	4 318	..	653	..	..	..	945	31 732	16
Aircraft, engines	..	603	2 132	633	..	..	105	..	..	..	..	3 473	..
Missiles (incl. conventional warheads)	951	559	406	1 404	..	..	..	..	..	..	..	3 320	..
Nuclear warheads and bombs	..	..	..	..	..	..	192	..	..	..	945	945	..
Ships and boats	..	3 025	..	..	..	..	37	..	..	..	..	3 217	..
Armoured vehicles	1 791	..	..	..	..	..	..	..	..	..	..	1 828	..
Artillery	380	11	..	..	..	..	..	..	..	..	..	391	..
Other ordnance	684	..	..	..	32	..	10	..	..	..	..	726	..

Ammunition	1 675	411	632	:	:	:	35	:	2 753	:
Electronics, communications	779	608	970	689	2 605	:	224	:	5 875	12
Non-armoured vehicles	:	:	:	:	:	:	33	:	33	4
Other	1 744	1 559	2 024	2 146	1 681	:	17	:	9 171	:
Construction	826	582	388	1 219	505	361	105	:	3 986	119
Airbases, airfields	:	:	:	:	:	:	:	:	:	:
Missile sites	:	:	:	:	:	:	:	:	:	:
Naval bases and facilities	:	:	:	:	:	:	:	:	:	:
Electronics, etc.	:	:	:	:	:	:	:	:	:	:
Personnel facilities	:	:	:	:	:	:	:	:	:	:
Medical facilities	:	:	:	:	:	:	:	:	:	:
Training facilities	:	:	:	:	:	:	:	:	:	:
Warehouses, depots, etc.	:	:	:	:	:	:	:	:	:	:
Command and administration facilities	:	:	:	:	:	:	:	:	:	:
Fortifications	:	:	:	:	:	:	:	:	:	:
Shelters	:	:	:	:	:	:	:	:	:	:
Land	:	:	:	:	:	:	:	:	:	:
Other	:	:	:	:	:	:	:	:	:	:
Research and development	854	1 504	2 488	7 519	129	371	17	:	12 882	17
Basic and applied research	:	:	:	:	:	:	:	:	:	:
Development, testing and evaluation	:	:	:	:	:	:	:	:	:	:
Total	19 034	11 442	10 954	16 218	7 351	896	2 055	574	71 990	313

[a] The UN format has a column for strategic forces. In the Soviet submission, however, it is claimed that the Soviet strategic forces do not have a clearly designated structure, falling as they do within various branches of the armed forces, and that therefore no figures are available for this entry.

Source: United Nations, 'Union of Soviet Socialist Republics, instrument for standardized international reporting of military expenditure, fiscal year 1 January–31 December 1990' (UN: New York, 1991).

This rouble value can be translated into dollars using either the official exchange-rate ($9.3 million) or a purchasing power parity (PPP) conversion rate ($14.5 million). Either way these unit prices are much lower. A Polish source, quoting the Polish Ministry of Defence, compares prices as follows:

Fighters: MiG-29, $18–25 million; F-16, $21–25 million; Mirage 2000, $26–70 million;

Tanks: T-72, $0.4 million; Leopard-2, $2.6 million; Abrams, $3.7 million;

Armoured vehicles: BWP-2 (Czech), $0.5 million; M-2 Bradley, $1.2 million.[36]

Clearly, the Soviet-type weapons cost far less.

However, this cannot be the only difference. Even when Soviet military assets are costed at US prices, using similar technology and dollar prices, the dollar price differential of comparable weapons is vastly different. In 1975 it was estimated that an F-15 cost $15 million, whereas a MiG-23 would cost $5 million, or one-third of the price, if produced in the USA.[37] There is a long history of such startling differences. For example, in the early 1960s it was calculated that a fully manned and mobilized Soviet Army division would cost only one-third of an equivalent US division.[38] The reason may be the qualitative difference in national equipments and strategy: the former USSR fields more basic and rugged designs, does not emphasize C^3I capabilities, restricts systems enhancement equipment, and fails to provide as much Operations and Support (O&S) services as does the USA. The somewhat lower levels of military expenditure, even under PPP comparisons, therefore also reflect less quality, which is sought to be compensated by large quantitative advantages.

There is also the question as to whether the prices paid by the military truly reflect resource cost. This is important in order to know the economic burden of the military on the economy as well as the benefits of conversion. A cost–benefit analysis can be done by comparing similar US weapons, incorporating an efficiency factor to account for qualitative differences, using a conversion rate to change one currency to another and making estimates about inflation to make the prices consistent for a given year. According to a RAND study, while the unit price does indeed reflect resource use within a reasonable margin for tanks and tactical aircraft, for naval ships and helicopters the prices are vastly lower than what any reasonable comparisons would suggest.[39]

Commenting on the wide price differentials between Soviet and US fighting ships of comparable quality, using appropriate conversion rates for unit price (cost), the same analyst notes that:

[36] 'Unwanted weapons', *Warsaw Voice*, 8 Dec. 1991, p. B4.

[37] The figures in 1973 prices are given in *Allocation of Resources in the Soviet Union and China*, Hearings before the Subcommittee on Priorities and Economy in Government, US Joint Economic Committee, 94th Congress (US Government Printing Office: Washington, DC, 1975), Part I, pp. 51–53.

[38] Enthoven A. and Smith, W., *How Much is Enough? Shaping the Defence Burden, 1961–1969* (Harper and Row: New York, 1971).

[39] Alexander, A. A., 'Perestroika and change in Soviet weapons acquisition', RAND Report no. R-3821-USDP (RAND Corp.: Santa Monica, Calif., June 1990).

First, ships take years to construct and require substantial investments in ship-yards, buildings, and equipment; since interest rates are subsidized by the Soviet state and there is no land rent, these 'missing costs' could contribute to the underpricing of Soviet ships. In general, the more capital- and land-intensive the means of production, the more these factors would operate. Another possible explanation is that the Soviets could have been comparing the bare ship cost, unoutfitted, as it was completed at the Nikolaev North shipyard, with a fully equipped *Ticonderoga*. Or the level of technology and complexity is considerably lower than estimated by US naval designers. Or the efficiency of Soviet shipyards and equipment suppliers is many times greater than that of US producers. Or the Soviet navy is stealing the cruiser from the shipyards. Only the first and last explanations are credible. Most likely the price to the shipyard does not cover its costs, and a substantial loss must be covered by the Ministry of Shipbuilding, by the state budget, or by bank loans.[40]

As for the future there is clearly grave uncertainty. More transparency will be difficult to achieve simply because disorderly transition will stop the gathering of proper information. If national armies are formed by the newly independent republics, then data collection and analysis will be made even more complicated. The following questions are potentially important.

1. Will a central Ministry of Defence exist or not, and if so, which part of military expenditure will be spent by it?
2. If a central Ministry exists and a unified army remains, under what constraints will such a system operate and what will the republics' budgetary contributions be? This is the classic burden-sharing problem of 'free riders'.
3. Will each category of defence expenditure be borne by the republics separately? This would increase the confusion even further. Personnel costs could be borne by the budgets of successor states, depending on the number of troops stationed in their territory, as could O&M costs. Procurement costs could be spent centrally. However, since the overwhelming number of defence enterprises are in the Russian Federation and the Ukraine, the prices at which weapons will be 'traded' among the ex-republics could be important. For example, if Russia charges high prices will the other states pay for the arms required for common defence or will they prefer to import in convertible currencies? R&D resources are also concentrated and their expenditure allocation could also be controversial.
4. How are the costs of weapon destruction (the result of arms control agreements) and of safe maintenance of strategic and tactical nuclear weapons (the unresolved legacy of proliferation) to be shared? Any course but an equitable sharing of costs could be catastrophic.

To be resolved, these issues require greater transparency and better quality data than has hitherto been available.

---

[40] Alexander (note 39).

Perestroika

The restructuring of Soviet military expenditure in the period of *perestroika* may be described in terms of six features of change:

1. As mentioned above, Soviet military expenditure was reduced substantially in 1989–91. The decline has almost certainly exceeded the 14 per cent reduction of aggregate Soviet defence spending for 1989–91 proposed by President Gorbachev in his 1989 speech to the Soviet Congress of the Peoples Deputies.[41] In the same speech Gorbachev proposed a cut in procurement spending of 19.5 per cent. This figure has also been exceeded. Military R&D, relatively protected until the late 1980s, was in 1991 slashed by almost 20 per cent in real terms. Table 7.12 gives data for the allocation of official Soviet military expenditure for 1989–91, during which time disarmament proceeded rapidly. While 1989 and 1990 prices are roughly comparable, the 1991 rouble value of aggregate military expenditure represents a real reduction of about 10 per cent from the 1990 value, after inflationary adjustments have been made.

2. Investment costs (procurement, R&D, nuclear defence and military construction) have declined relative to operating costs (personnel, O&M, pensions, social services and housing). From a relative share of 70 per cent in 1989, investment costs declined to about 55 per cent in 1991. If current trends continue, in 1992 the investment share of the budget will account for less than half of total military spending—a level unheard of since World War II.

3. The decline in procurement and R&D spending has significantly altered the scope of major acquisition programmes. It is reported that since 1989 there has been a sharp cut in spending on individual weapons and hardware. By 1991 the acquisition of strategic missiles had been reduced by 40 per cent; sea-launched ballistic missiles by 54 per cent; tanks by 66 per cent; armoured vehicles by 80 per cent; artillery systems by 59 per cent; and combat vehicles by 50 per cent. In addition, a whole class of tactical nuclear missiles has been eliminated. According to Western intelligence, Soviet procurement declined by 10 per cent per annum between 1988–89 and 1989–90. The cuts were almost equally distributed between strategic and conventional forces, with the brunt borne by the Army followed by the Air Force.[42] While naval procurement continues (1991 saw the completion of a new aircraft-carrier, the *Admiral Kuznetsov*[43]), with the breakup of the USSR the future of shipyards (such as the Nikolaev yard in the Ukraine) is uncertain. The control over the Black Sea Fleet is a matter of possible discord between the Russian Federation and the Ukraine. Until early 1991 there were still many reports of weapon modernization and continuing military R&D. However, information gathered in 1991 indicate that these activities are being reduced considerably.

---

[41] 'Report by Mikhail Sergeyevich Gorbachev, General Secretary of the CPSU Central Committee and Chairman of the Supreme Soviet, at the Congress of the Peoples Deputies held in the Kremlin Palace of Congresses', Moscov television service, 30 May 1989, trancript in FBIS-SOV-89-103S, 31 May 1989, pp. 4–62.

[42] Alexander (note 39).

[43] *Jane's Defence Weekly*, 14 Dec. 1991, p. 1150.

Table 7.12. Soviet military expenditure allocation, official figures, 1989–91

Figures are in current b. roubles;[a] figures in italics are percentage shares.

	1989	1990	1991
Procurement	32.6	31.0	39.7
Percentage share	*42.2*	*43.7*	*41.1*
R&D	15.3	13.2	10.4
Percentage share	*19.8*	*18.6*	*10.8*
Personnel and O&M[b]	20.2	19.3	31.0
Percentage share	*26.1*	*27.2*	*32.1*
Construction	4.6	3.8	6.2
Percentage share	*6.0*	*5.4*	*6.4*
Pensions	2.3	2.4	4.1
Percentage share	*3.0*	*3.4*	*4.2*
Social support[c]	..	..	3.3
Percentage share	..	..	*3.4*
Nuclear	2.3	1.4	1.9
Percentage share	*3.0*	*2.0*	*2.0*
Total	**77.3**	**71.0**	**96.6**

[a] See text regarding price changes for 1990 and 1991.
[b] Operations and maintenance.
[c] Allocations for social support were not given as a separate item prior to 1991.

Sources: Litovkin, V., 'The cost of defence', interview with Marshal S. Akhromeyev, *Izvestia*, 14 Jan. 1991, in FBIS-SOV-91-009, 14 Jan. 1991, pp. 5–7; Isachenkov, V., 'Defense budget approved', TASS, 11 Jan. 1991, in FBIS-SOV-91-008, 11 Jan. 1991, p. 16; Novoselov, I., 'The military budget: what form should it take?', *Kraznaya Zvezda*, 13 Dec. 1990, p. 1, in FBIS-SOV-244, 19 Dec. 1990, p. 70; SIPRI data base; authors' estimates.

4. Whether there remains a single armed force or many individual republic armies for the CIS, reductions in manpower are set to continue. At the beginning of 1991 the Soviet armed forces numbered 3 760 000, and the force reductions of half a million men, announced by President Gorbachev in his 1988 UN speech, had been completed. There have been major problems with conscription (accounting for around 60 per cent of Army personnel). Structural decay will likely force the Army to lose more personnel even without disarmament measures. In October 1991 Gorbachev announced a further reduction of 700 000 men, which is likely to be followed by other cuts. There have been press reports that the Army would be cut to 2 million—or even 1.5—million men.[44] However, the 1992 baseline manpower is 3 million men. On the other hand, if the central defence apparatus totally disintegrates, the republic armies will probably not add up to the deployments of the Soviet armed forces in 1991–92. Thus the armed forces of the Soviet successor states could in aggregate have a smaller armed force than the 3 million mentioned above. In terms of the doctrine of reasonable sufficiency, the new armies will not need more than 2 million.

[44] *The Guardian*, 2 Oct. 1991, p. 1; 'Troops to be reduced by 700,000', TASS, 21 Oct. 1991, in FBIS-SOV-91-204, 22 Oct. 1991, p. 43.

5. Grave dissatisfaction has emerged in the armed forces about pay and pensions, which were low in the past, especially for conscripts. Troop withdrawals from Germany and Central Europe have increased the problems, in particular as regards the housing situation. While German foreign aid has alleviated some of the specific problems, the grievances remain and morale is low. The aim of the large increase in pensions and other benefits in 1991 is to reduce tensions in the army which would create problems of law and order. A new budget category, 'social provisions', representing wage protection and social benefits to improve the life of servicemen, was introduced in the official 1991 military expenditure estimates (see table 7.11).

6. The issue of military reform played a prominent role in the debate in the former USSR about the future of the armed forces. Alternative plans have been submitted, but given the controversy over who should control the armed forces, it has proved difficult to analyze the prospects for such reform. At the end of 1990 the Soviet Ministry of Defence released a draft reform plan, which was widely debated at least until the coup attempt in August 1991.[45] After that it seemed to have been shelved. One interesting feature of the plan was the substantial increase in military expenditure planned for the decade 1991–2000 (broken into two phases of five years each). This plan envisaged a total expenditure of 1229.3 billion roubles (in 1991 prices). The annual average of 122.9 billion roubles was about 27 per cent higher than the actual spending budgeted for 1991. In a sense such a high level of expenditures would bring back Soviet military expenditures into line with the official level of 1988, that is, before serious cuts were undertaken. Clearly, the military planners seemed to be unaware of the economic crisis that the country was facing and the fact that the economy simply could not afford the military burden even if it was politically feasible. The Defence Ministry plan is also naive in its attitude to republican control and the problems of a conscripted army. An alternative plan by a commission of the Soviet People's Deputies, under the Chairmanship of Vladimir Lopatin (first deputy chairman of the RSFSR State Committee on Public Security), is more realistic.[46] It clearly recognizes the authority of the republics, and therefore the future successor states, as well as the need to have a professional armed force.

During the past 70-odd years of the Red Army's existence, there have been three other periods in which major demobilization, force reductions, cuts in defence spending and attempts to transfer resources to civilian sectors have been tried. The first two, following the civil war of 1918–20 and at the end of World War II, were essentially post-war reconversions, and as such are difficult to compare with the current phase. The only previous peace-time demilitarization was carried out by Nikita Khrushchev in the early 1960s, and presumably already being implemented in the late 1950s. There were remarkable similarities between Khrushchev's attempts and the current efforts:

[45] Soviet Ministry of Defence, 'Draft military reform plan', *Pravitelstvennyy Vestnik*, Nov. 1990, pp. 5–10, in FBIS-SOV-90-239, 12 Dec. 1990, pp. 62–74.

[46] 'On the preparation and conduct of military reform', *Pravitelstvennyy Vestnik*, Nov. 1990, pp. 10–12, in FBIS-SOV-90-239, 12 Dec. 1990, pp. 75-80.

1. In an unprecedented show of openness, the levels of Soviet armed forces were revealed and proved to be substantially accurate after verification by US intelligence.[47] In early 1948 the Soviet armed forces totalled 2 874 000 men— a reduction through demobilization from the mid-1945 wartime level of 11 365 000 men. The level then rose rapidly to 5 763 000 in 1955, then fell sharply, as a result of Khrushchev's initiatives. In January 1960 the Supreme Soviet was told that the Soviet armed forces stood at 3 623 000 men, and would be reduced by one-third to a level of 2 423 000 men by 1962. This planned massive demobilization of 1.2 million men was one of the largest in modern peacetime history, far exceeding the 500 000 that Gorbachev called for in his UN speech. As is well known, the earlier experiment failed; by the beginning of 1961 almost half of the postulated reductions had taken place, but with the approach of the Berlin crisis the changes were finally stalled and then abandoned. Even if it failed, it is interesting to note that the size of the Soviet armed forces in 1991 would be about similar—indeed slightly larger— than the forces which Khrushchev publicly promised to cut 30 years earlier.

2. The military budget was reduced in the early part of the 1960s, and the savings used to raise pensions substantially, increase construction of residential property and build 100 new factories for the production of pre-fabricated housing.[48] The current resource re-allocation also emphasizes such 'social provisions'. Indeed the most publicized financial saving emanating from the INF Treaty was that used to construct 30 000 flats for servicemen.

3. Military assets were reduced, deactivated and destroyed in the Khrushchev period. The Soviet tactical air forces reduced their aircraft inventories by half; the Navy lost its fighter/interceptor force and about half of its aircraft inventory; older surface ships and submarines were cut significantly; and the number of divisions in the Army was reduced from 175 to 140, with a majority on reduced strength. The Gorbachev defensive doctrine also emphasized large unilateral force reductions, and over the past two years there have been significant reductions in weapon procurement and production.

4. Under Prime Minister Alexei Kosygin, economic reforms followed military reductions in 1965.[49] Decentralization was introduced, price reforms took place, enterprise management was given greater freedom, and more financial incentives were provided to individual enterprises through profit-sharing. The reforms failed, but some of the lessons have been learnt. The most important is that the formation of markets based on a price system obeying the principles of supply and demand is an essential prerequisite for efficiency and incentive-oriented economic actions.

One important difference between the two periods is that the changes in military structures initiated by President Gorbachev took place concurrently

[47] Garthoff R. L., 'Estimating Soviet military force levels: some light from the past', *International Security*, vol. 14, no. 4 (spring 1990), pp. 93–109.

[48] Izyumov, A. I., 'The national experience of the USSR', *Conversion: Economic Adjustments in an Era of Arms Reduction (Volume II)*, Disarmament Topical Papers no. 5 (United Nations: New York, 1991), 61–75.

[49] Desai, P., *Perestroika in Perspective* (L. B. Tauris: London, 1989).

with economic liberalization and increasing marketization and privatization. This poses a challenge as well as an advantage. If the efficiency of the economic system as a whole is enhanced, and the military sector manages to benefit from the increased productivity, the result will be increased defence efficiency, possibly permitting reduced expenditure and increased capability in a framework of reasonable sufficiency. On the other hand, the aggregate systemic restructuring is so fundamental and difficult that there is a possibility of chaos. Instead of a conversion from military to civilian production, there could be a convulsion of the military–industrial system, provoking a reaction from the conservative elements of the military hierarchy.

The most fundamental difference is that the very existence of an unified armed force has now been called into question.[50] In simple terms the issue is whether there will be one armed force or many. In the latter case, a further question is whether the organizational structure would be similar to that of NATO, with national armies, an integrated military command, some joint forces and a flexible structure allowing member nations to opt out of the integrated command structure. The most important doctrinal problem is how to define 'threat' for such a heterogeneous group of countries, extending from Central and Eastern Europe through Central Asia to the Far East. There are also many practical problems associated with the distribution of property and weapons, and the stationing of troops on the territory of other member states.

The breakup of the armed forces met with strong opposition, even from reform-minded members of the Army. In 1991 Soviet Defence Minister Yevgeniy Shaposhnikov argued strongly against such centrifugal tendencies:

I think it is time to examine the possibility of creating a defence union of sovereign states within the framework of a unified economic and military strategic space on the basis of collective security. . . Every republic would assume certain obligations, the centre would also assume certain obligations and, naturally, the people who serve that cause would assume obligations. But I will never reconcile myself to the thought that we should begin to divide up weapons, especially nuclear weapons, and especially people who took an oath to the constitution of the USSR and to the Soviet state as a whole.[51]

Before the August coup attempt the feasibility of republican armies was discussed. After the attempt the speed of disintegration increased, and several republics—including the two largest after the Russian Federation, Ukraine and Kazakhstan—stated their intention to set up their own armies. The Russian Federation was content to have a national guard of 3000–10 000 men by 1993. In an inter-republican conference in November 1991, representatives discussed their contribution to the central defence budget in the light of the possible breakup of the armed forces. The positions taken by the various republics are indicative of the disorder that characterized these efforts: Ukraine will seek to

---

[50] For a lucid discussion of the issues surrounding the feasibility and implications of the devolution of the Soviet armed forces and nuclear weapons among the newly independent republics, see Landgren, S., 'Developments in the Soviet Union', in Rotfeld (note 2).

[51] Barkhatov, A., 'A viewpoint', television interview with Shaposhnikov, Moscow television service, 19 Oct. 1991, transcript in FBIS-SOV-91-203, 21 Oct. 1991, pp. 51–52.

form a national army, but will fund centralized operations of the strategic forces; Moldova, which by decree has nationalized all Soviet army property and armaments in its territory, wishes to create a small armed force (one motorized rifle division), and is willing to fund air defence units of the central command; Georgia wants its own armed force, for which it intends to solicit foreign military aid, but will also contribute to future central military structures; Kazakhstan appears to favour a unified command but wants its 'initial potential' to be considered in determining budget shares, implying a small contribution; Armenia is prepared to contribute to the central defence budget; Belarus enthusiastically supports a unified force; Azerbaijan did not attend. Summing up the meeting, *Krasnaya Zvezda*, organ of the armed forces, wrote:

So let us see what an ambiguous position USSR Defence Minister Marshal of Aviation Ye. Shaposhnikov finds himself in. There is the State Council decision (adopted, however, as is well known, without Ukraine, Moldovia, Georgia, and so forth) on retaining unified Armed Forces. There are no other political decisions. Consequently, the Union Army and Navy are subordinate to the USSR President and the State Council. But at the same time the 'privatization' of military property has begun in several of the republics whose representatives attended the conference. Let us add to that the attempts to enshrine—now by means of a republican conference—the creation of their own armed forces.[52]

The most advanced republic, in terms of announcement of plans, seems to be Ukraine, which has declared its intention to form a national army of its own. It has been claimed that a future force of 420 000 will be created, based on the 1.5 million Soviet Army soldiers already present in the country. The ratio of such an army to the total population would be around 1:100. This is similar to the ratio of the planned Soviet armed force of 3 million men, discussed above, relative to the total population of the former USSR. It has been claimed that the Ukraine wishes to have its own air, ground and naval force, but to share strategic command with the CIS.[53] Major problems will come up about the operation of the Black Sea Fleet, the ownership of the Nikolaev shipyards, and the independent formation of air defence systems.

Whether the armed forces fall under central or republic authority, one thorny issue remains. Although the Soviet Defence Ministry has opposed the idea, all reform plans point to the creation of a professional armed force. The alternative Lopatin draft reform plan stresses: 'A phased transition to professional Armed Forces of lesser size and better quality with a volunteer method of manpower acquisition, an inter-ethnic make-up and the preservation of universal military obligations in wartime is the principal idea of military reform'.[54] What remains unclear is how much this would cost.

Calculations have been made by the Ministry of Defence. Although these are relatively biased, and overstate the expenditures required, they seem to be

[52] Urban (note 23).
[53] *Jane's Defence Weekly*, 16 Nov 1991, p. 939; *International Herald Tribune*, 13 Nov. 1991; *Guardian Weekly*, 13 Nov. 1991.
[54] 'On the preparation and conduct of military reform' (note 46).

Table 7.13. Estimated annual personnel costs of alternative force structures for an all-Union professional armed force

Cost figures are in b. roubles, at constant (1990) prices.

Alternative force structures	Manpower (million)	Cost			
		Wages	Pensions	Housing and social support	Total
Actual					
Conscript force	4.0	5.8	2.4	6.9	15.1
Larger armed force					
Volunteer force with average salary	4.0	31.0	13.2	12.3	56.5
Volunteer force with higher salaries	4.0	36.0	15.3	12.3	63.6
Smaller armed force					
Volunteer force with average salary	2.5	19.4	8.3	7.6	35.3
Volunteer force with higher salaries	2.5	22.6	9.6	7.6	39.8

Source: Soviet Ministry of Defence, 'Draft military reform plan', *Pravitelstvennyy Vestnik*, Nov. 1990, pp. 5–10, in FBIS-SOV-90-239, 12 Dec. 1990, pp. 62–74.

of the correct order of magnitude. The figures are based on the actual costs of the 1990 armed force of about 4 million men, and are compared to a hypothesized future force of 2.5 million men. It is assumed that the volunteer army would also require better facilities, such as housing and pensions, the costs of which would increase commensurately. Two scenarios of volunteer forces are considered: the first has a lower monthly salary structure (ranging from 430 roubles for a private to 950 roubles for a general); the second postulates somewhat better salaries (ranging from 500 to 1100 roubles). Table 7.13 summarizes some of the data for three cases in 1990 prices. Costing is done for personnel alone, and the assumption is that investment costs will remain similar.

It is clear that, under *ceteris paribus* conditions, the cost of volunteer forces will be inordinately high. Even with the reduced—although realistic—size of the army at 2.5 million, the additional personnel-related expenditure is 20–25 billion roubles. As mentioned earlier, these estimates are on the high side given the level of average industrial wages in 1990. The spending on social amenities are also rather luxurious. The changing threat perception in Europe and elsewhere also means that an army of 2 million men would be more than adequate for a defensive military strategy. Recalculating and making adjustments, the personnel-related cost of a professional volunteer armed force would be a *maximum* of 25 billion roubles. This would require additional spending of 10 billion roubles (in 1990 prices). The sum could easily be financed by the type of reductions that the Soviet procurement and weapons acquisition is going through currently. For example, if all procurement-related spending is halved (and current projections make such an option eminently feasible), then the *volunteer army of two million can be financed and the aggregate defence budget reduced by a quarter* (from its 1990 level).

Konversiya

At the end of 1991 it was announced by the Soviet Ministry of Defence that arms procurement had fallen by 23 per cent in real terms during the year. In 1990 prices, the reduction amounted to over 7 billion roubles, that is, over 11 per cent of the aggregate budget, according to SIPRI estimates. There have also been similar cuts in military R&D during the year, although the exact amount is not known. It is also planned that in 1992 the reduction in procurement orders will be of the same percentage size, about 23 per cent. If the cuts are implemented, which is more than likely given the economic chaos, then 1992 figures for arms production in the former USSR will be half the size of those of 1990. Such massive reductions will force the defence complex either to retrench heavily or to focus on the production of civilian goods, which in 1991 accounted for 50–60 per cent of the total industrial output of this sector. Conversion is no longer a luxury but an essential strategy for survival.[55]

Of course, conversion will not be costless.[56] Who bears the cost and how large is it? Many socio-economic costs are as yet unquantifiable: unemployment, loss of privilege, movement of skilled personnel away from productive industry and the possible destruction of the scientific and technological base of the country. From a purely financial point of view, some direct costs will have to be incurred initially to protect wages, re-tool factories and subsidize enterprises requiring more time to adjust. Overall budgetary problems, and the increasing financial autonomy of defence enterprises, mean that some of these expenses have not been paid by the Government, creating problems for the recipients. It should be emphasized that the Soviet defence budget did not include such expenditures. The costs were met by the overall state budget (subsidies), industry's own profits as well as extra-budgetary revenues.

The 1990 budget allocated 4 billion roubles for conversion while the 1991 budget is expected to provide 5 billion roubles from its extra-budgetary stabilization fund. According to the draft State Programme for Conversion, total allocations for investment in the civilian side of the defence complex would be over 40 billion roubles during the 13th Five Year Plan (1991–95). Pure conversion costs, for re-tooling and re-profiling of plants, will amount to almost 9 billion roubles, while the rest will be spent on new investments for civilian production (about 30 billion roubles), as well as for moth-balling military production facilities currently withdrawn but not scrapped. Severance payments (generally six month's salary) will add up to a total of some 500 million

---

[55] For a discussion of the origins of conversion in the USSR, see Deger, S., 'World military expenditure', SIPRI, *SIPRI Yearbooks 1989, 1990* and *1991: World Armaments and Disarmament* (Oxford University Press: Oxford, 1989, 1990 and 1991), pp. 133–94, 143–202 and 115–180, respectively.

[56] Kireyev, A., 'The price of the peace dividend', *International Affairs* (Moscow), no. 8 (Aug. 1991), pp. 8–17.

roubles in 1991. All of these figures are in 1990 prices. How much of these monies will actually be paid is now debatable given the transfer of such enterprises to the republics and the attempt to privatize them.

By 1991 it was clear that the output of the defence–industrial complex (including its civil production) in the USSR was substantial and occupied a major position within the industrial infrastructure. The share of this complex in the national economy had expanded during the period of *perestroika*. A noted Sovietologist estimates that the share of the gross output of the defence complex in total industrial output rose from 15.3 per cent in 1985 to 16.2 per cent in 1987 and to 17.2 per cent in 1990.[57] SIPRI's estimates show that by 1989–90, about 12–13 per cent of GNP emanated from this sector, with an aggregate output of around 120 billion roubles. In 1991 it was estimated that at least half of this output was for civilian production, which was expected to rise to 60 per cent by the end of the year. However, these shares—which are meaningful only if measured in value terms—could be misleading, since the price system is as yet distorted and the 1991 price reforms have affected the military less severely than other sectors.

If one looks at the shares of consumer durables produced by the defence sector then its overwhelming importance becomes clear. This sector produces all cameras, colour televisions, radio receivers, sewing machines and video recorders made in the former USSR. In a period of rising expectations as well as shortages, the role of the defence complex in supplying consumer durables is crucial. Production volumes are also large. SIPRI estimates the annual output of such products by the defence industrial complex as follows: 6.8 million radio receivers; 10.5 million television sets; 1.6 million sewing machines; 3.4 million vacuum cleaners; 4.1 million washing machines. Clearly, the impact of these industries in an excess-demand economy is substantial.

The details of Soviet arms production and conversion are analysed in this *Yearbook* by Alexei Kireyev in chapter 9, section V. Here the focus is on three issues regarding conversion which are indirectly connected with the future evolution of military expenditure in the successor states—most notably the Russian Federation. The first relates to the productivity and efficiency of the defence complex, which will have an impact on future procurement prices and technology. The second concerns military R&D and the resource transfer towards civilian production. The third relates to the 'disarmament dividend' that these countries could hope to enjoy.

The reason for entrusting the defence complex with civilian production is based on the perceived notion of efficiency. There are two differing views on the efficiency of the defence complex in the former USSR and its contribution to the rejuvenation of the economy.[58] The first maintains that the military-industrial complex is inherently more efficient, productive and technologically sophisticated compared to the civilian industrial sector. As the former USSR is

[57] Cooper, J., 'Military cuts and conversion in the defense industry', *Soviet Economy*, vol. 7, no. 2 (1991), pp. 121–42.
[58] For an excellent treatise on the priorities given to the military sector in general within a supply-constrained economy, see Davis, C. M., 'The high-priority military sector in a shortage economy', eds H. S. Rowen and C. Wolf, *The Impoverished Superpower* (ICS Press: San Francisco, 1990), pp. 155–84.

almost as competitive in arms production as the USA, this is the only area where such a comparative advantage exists. Hence, its relative expansion will increase overall growth of the economy. The second view is that efficiency, as measured by lower cost per unit of output, is not necessarily high. The sector is more effective in producing high quality goods simply because its efficiency has been artificially created due to the insulated nature of the sector and the priorities that it has been given in the allocation of resources.

In either case, there is little reason to believe that the defence complex, in its present organizational structure, can cope with the demands of the market economy. These include commercialization of enterprises, reduction of monopoly power and increasing competition. The defence–industrial sector is structured on an industrial organization whose requirements are the exact opposite. Predominantly a producer of merit or public goods (armaments for national security), it has never obeyed the 'rules' of a market economy. It was never subject to commercial considerations or expected to make a profit, relied on the Government to provide extensive subsidies and priorities in receiving scarce inputs, and had an unusually 'soft budget constraint', even by Soviet standards. The monopoly power of individual enterprises increased steadily during the last three decades. Very large design bureaux and enterprises were created, apparently to capture scale economies, so that one or two factory complexes would be able to supply the need for individual items. This monopolization of supply, and the loss of competition that resulted from increasing monopoly power of individual enterprises, are the weakest features of the defence complex in the face of policy reforms currently going on in the former USSR. Burdened with these, it is difficult for the defence complex to participate in the market economy that is expected to be created in the future.

What are the characteristics of an efficient industrial system, within a market economy, for the new states that have succeed the USSR? The experts' team from the International Monetary Fund (IMF), the World Bank, the Organization for Economic Co-operation and Development (OECD) and the European Bank for Reconstruction and Development (EBRD), which wrote a detailed report on the USSR, claimed that for the industrial sector at least:

[T]he principal element of a market economy is the allocation of resources on the basis of market signals. More specifically, the allocation system requires: (1) prices as the primary market signals; (2) profits as a guide to identifying the most effective activities and enterprises and thus to aid capital allocations; and (3) enterprise autonomy which allows adjustments to be made in response to market signals. A second key element is freedom for competition which will allow new entries into profitable activities, and conversely, mechanisms to facilitate the exit of producers who are not competitive. Finally, a market system will not function properly without a wide range of supporting infrastructure and services such as transportation and communications, but also including the free flow of information, a supportive financial system, readily available technical assistance and a coherent legal framework.[59]

[59] International Monetary Fund, the World Bank, Organization for Economic Co-operation and Development, and the European Bank for Reconstruction and Development, *A Study of the Soviet Economy*, vol. 3 (IMF/World Bank/OECD/EBRD: Paris, Feb. 1991), pp. 302–303.

It is clear that such an ideal system does not operate in practice anywhere. However, governments attempt to minimize distortions and prevent market failure, thus producing a market system close to the ideal. In the USSR, where markets are being newly created, rather than simply regulated as elsewhere, there is greater need for preventing such distortions. The defence complex is symptomatic of such distortions. Its planners and administrators had no clear-cut idea of how to price products in a competitive market, and they did not understand the concept of price adjustment as a response to market signals, as they did not have to worry about making profits in any meaningful sense of the term. Budgetary subsidies covered all costs and a desired surplus, and the enterprises sold only to the Government and were required to obey strict quality control but effectively no restriction on cost or input use.

Conversion from below, with greater autonomy of enterprises and respons-iveness to market signals, is necessary. In 1991 there were signs that this lesson has been learnt and that the process of marketization has begun. In 1991 it was planned that 5 per cent of the defence complex, in terms of asset values, will be privatized. The ratio will rise to 75 per cent by the mid-1990s. This is one area where foreign aid and technology transfer will be necessary, but there are only modest signs that the lesson has been learnt in the West. Full-scale assistance programmes for the defence industry are as yet small.

If commercialization of the defence complex succeeds, procurement costs of weapons can be reduced substantially. As distinct from the current arti-ficially low prices, these would reflect the 'true' resource or opportunity costs of arms production. Similarly, increase in civilian sector productivity, particu-larly in research, will bring the benefits of badly needed 'spin-ins'.

Another aspect of the conversion process, important for its long-term implications, is the transfer of resources from military to civilian R&D.[60] For the first half of the 1980s, SIPRI's estimates show that the defence complex spent almost 20 billion roubles on military R&D (including space research). This amounted to almost 80 per cent of industrial R&D. By the late 1980s the figure had fallen to about 15 billion roubles—around half of total industrial R&D.[61] Meanwhile, the civilian R&D share of expenditures has increased fast, indicating that the civilian component of the defence–industrial complex is gaining at the expense of the armament component (see table 7.14).

Finally, there is the broader question of the economic rewards of disarma-ment. At present, mainly because of economic dislocations, these have been few. However, the sheer size of the military sector in the former USSR means that disarmament will have significant developmental returns. SIPRI estimates that direct military expenditures as share of GNP in 1990 was about 11–12 per cent. In addition, there were indirect costs, particularly those related to milit-ary procurement of dual-use technology, space research, non-military employ-ment in the defence sector and others. Finally, if military hardware was costed at a far lower level relative to resource utilization, then procurement expend-

---

[60] See Avduyevskiy, V., 'The problems of changing military industries to civilian production', eds Rotblat and Blackaby (note 20), pp. 212–16.
[61] See Cooper (note 57).

Table 7.14. Civilian and military R&D expenditure in the Soviet defence complex, 1981–85, 1988 and 1991

Figures are in b. roubles, current prices; figures in italics are percentage shares.

	1981–85[a]	1988	1991[b]
Civilian R&D	..	5.8	8.3
Percentage share	..	*28.6*	*40.7*
Military R&D	19.5	14.5	12.1
Percentage share	..	*71.4*	*59.3*

[a] Annual average.

[b] Figures for 1991 are distorted due to high inflation.

Source: Cooper, J. 'Military cuts and conversion in the defense industry', *Soviet Economy*, vol. 7, no. 2 (1991), pp. 121–42.

iture could have been two to three times the sum officially paid. Taking all these factors into account, and assuming that the Soviet GNP is indeed as reported, the military share in GNP was about 20 per cent in 1989–90.

There is also the matter of labour resources in an economy where the natural rate of growth is falling and skilled labour is becoming scarce as a result of the sustained pursuit of the 'extended growth model' in the post-World War II period.[62] The security sector—comprising the military, defence-complex industries, defence-related research establishments, internal security and para-military forces, agencies responsible for the provision of auxiliary services and economic sectors dependent on military spending—account for almost 20 per cent of the labour force. Reducing this sector is considered a problem because of the short-term unemployment this will create. However, the former USSR suffers from labour shortage, with a low labour force growth rate (0.5 per cent per annum, compared to the OECD rate of 1.3 per cent) and a high capital intensity of traditional industries. Thus, in the long run, the decline in the security sector would augment the labour force and could improve its quality.

Whether for the unified armed forces or for the Russian Federation, the way for the future—at least in the medium term—is to: (a) utilize the benign international security climate to re-structure the armed forces on a professional basis; (b) cut back on costly weaponry (some of which is either outdated or in excess of treaty limits); (c) reduce O&M by scrapping ancient systems; (d) re-structure military R&D and skip a generation of modernization; (e) utilize the 'spin-ins' from new civilian research; and (f) begin a new cycle of procurement and modernization, if necessary only after the professional army is completed and political stability achieved.

[62] See Ofer, G., 'Macroeconomic issues of Soviet reforms', Paper presented at the Fifth Annual Conference on Macroeconomics, National Bureau of Economic Research, Cambridge, Mass., 9–10 Mar. 1990.

IV. European NATO[63]

From the point of view of military expenditure allocations, the data for the European NATO countries follow the established trends, except as regards the armed forces, the reduction of which has become essential in the new security environment. In the absence of a specific threat facing NATO in Europe (except for the disintegrating USSR), the political rationale for NATO's military re-structuring is yet to be found. NATO was originally conceived for three major reasons: (a) to counter external threats (from the USSR); (b) to assure stability in Europe (in effect to stop the resurgence of Germany as a military power); and (c) to maintain the involvement of the USA in the defence of Western Europe. The first is now irrelevant; the second guaranteed by other means; and the third is more an issue of burden-sharing than a factor of strict military necessity. In addition, the true nature of European security, and the role of specific organizations such as the EC, the Western European Union (WEU) and the Conference on Security and Co-operation in Europe (CSCE), is yet to be clarified. Where NATO fits in, within this rather messy and overlapping mosaic of structures, was not clear in 1991.

Aggregate military expenditure of European NATO countries remained more or less the same during the year, even though large-scale reductions are increasingly expected. There is little evidence of a short-term financial peace dividend in the form of defence expenditure being diverted to meet other socio-economic needs. In any case, given the budgetary deficits of some of the European NATO countries, any short-term cuts will need to go for deficit reductions rather than re-allocation elsewhere. It is interesting to note that the real reductions in defence spending for 1991 have been in those countries (particularly within the Southern Flank or Mediterranean region) which have the highest budget deficit share in GDP. Economic constraints seem to have been the primary cause for relatively modest spending cuts. Arms control has as yet little impact on defence allocations. This is not surprising, for various reasons: the 'wait and see' attitude which advocates caution at a time of systemic changes; the insurance function, whereby military forces are still maintained at high levels as an insurance, even though the probability of actually using them in war is negligible; the impact of the Persian Gulf War, which necessitated higher spending particularly on personnel and O&M, at least for the United Kingdom and France; the cost of re-structuring where redundancy payments and industrial subsidies require spending to rise during this period of transition; and finally, the need to protect the defence industrial base and sources of technological progress which stop drastic cuts in military R&D.[64]

[63] The discussion on Europe is divided into sections on European NATO, the European Community and the Central European and Balkan states. While this results in some inevitable overlaps, this separation is useful from a politico-economic point of view.

[64] For a analytical discussion of the costs involved in moving towards lower levels of military capability in Europe, see Hartley, K., 'Defence expenditure: budgets and choices'; Hooper, N. and Buck, D., 'Defence industries and weapons procurement options'; and Hartley, K. and Hooper, N., 'Economic adjustments', all in Kirby and Hooper (note 2), pp. 34–54, 107–140 and 199–223, respectively.

In 1991 military expenditures among European NATO countries are estimated to have fallen in Germany, Greece, Italy, the Netherlands, Portugal and Spain. Aggregate expenditure remained almost the same (it fell by 0.4 per cent according to SIPRI's estimates) as between 1990 and 1991. The level has been stable for the past three years. The trend is somewhat distorted since in 1990 German military expenditure was higher than trend forecasts due to the cost of unification of the two armed forces. In 1991 Germany's military expenditure, one of the top three in European NATO, returned to levels consistent with the continuous decline seen since the mid-1980s. Interestingly, if German military spending for 1990 is recalculated according to the trend and correspondingly reduced, then the revised NATO figures for 1990 and 1991 show a rise of the order of 1.5 per cent in constant prices.[65] Overall, it can be concluded that discernible cuts are yet to appear—it is certainly premature to discuss a halving of military expenditure, whether in real terms or as a share of GDP.[66]

Spending on procurement on major weapons and equipment declined by a greater percentage than that of aggregate military expenditure, which as mentioned above showed almost no change. Tables 7.15 and 7.16 give estimates of major weapons procurement of NATO countries as well as the dollar aggregates for European NATO, the EC member states and the nine members of the WEU. Between 1990 and 1991 procurement spending on weapon systems (corresponding to the NATO definition of 'equipment') is estimated to have fallen by 2.2 per cent in European NATO as a whole.[67] However, even this decline is small, and European weapons procurement is still substantial, at around $30 billion (in 1988 prices and exchange rates). Weapons procurement expenditure fell radically in Germany, by about 12.5 per cent, owing to a special circumstance: the prospects for large-scale future reductions of the armed forces according to the terms of unification, and for acquisition of assets from the former GDR such as MiG-29 fighters. Leaving out Germany from the calculations of European NATO, in the remaining countries aggregate spending on weapons acquisition actually rose by 2.2 per cent in 1991.

Expenditures on weapons procurement within the region crucially affect aggregate demand for the West European defence industries. Since this did not fall substantially, it is premature to speak of 'de-industrialization' of the European defence industries. The British and French defence ministries still remain their respective countries' largest industrial customer. France has announced subsidies for defence-related sectors. The major impact on defence industries, as reflected in the structural changes taking place, is more a product of future market anticipations than actual difficulties.[68] The transition to lower long-term levels of defence procurement, which determines the bulk of the demand for defence products in West European countries, will be much

[65] Authors' estimate.

[66] See, for example, Chalmers, M., 'The peace dividend: a European perspective', *European Security: The New Agenda* (Saferworld Foundation: Bristol, Nov. 1990), pp. 87–102.

[67] NATO, 'Financial and economic data relating to NATO defence', Press Release no. 4-DPC-2(91)105 (NATO Press Service: Brussels, 12 Dec. 1991), pp. 3–8; French Ministry of Defence', *Projet de loi de Finances pour 1991* (Government Printer: Paris, 1990).

[68] See also chapter 9 in this volume.

Table 7.15. NATO major weapon procurement expenditure, 1982–91

Figures are in local currency, current prices.

		1982	1983	1984	1985	1986	1987	1988	1989	1990	1991
North America											
Canada	m. dollars	1 332	1 688	1 971	1 941	2 140	2 434	2 486	2 394	2 309	2 263
USA	m. dollars	42 028	50 202	58 328	66 348	72 525	76 362	71 808	76 683	75 512	72 994
Europe											
Belgium	m. francs	17 969	18 853	18 363	18 311	19 618	20 360	18 078	15 139	12 261	12 548
Denmark	m. kronor	1 960	2 075	2 048	1 841	1 867	2 182	2 249	2 091	2 443	2 659
France	m. francs	34 637	39 772	42 216	46 492	49 664	55 943	56 564	60 071	58 094	59 793
FR Germany	m. DM	10 847	11 299	11 455	11 730	12 267	12 332	11 896	12 004	12 100	10 986
Greece	m. drachmas	29 966	30 741	41 604	46 687	53 477	67 605	112 141	110 164	131 042	162 158
Italy	b. lire	2 046	2 664	2 843	3 494	3 693	4 900	5 451	5 605	4 901	5 122
Luxembourg	m. francs	44	36	36	91	74	106	89	114	103	177
Netherlands	m. guilders	2 444	2 794	3 012	3 019	2 661	2 359	2 713	2 388	2 419	2 207
Norway	m. kronor	2 147	2 615	2 297	3 846	3 303	3 784	4 018	5 022	4 803	5 138
Portugal	m. escudos	3 318	3 761	4 416	3 675	8 818	16 088	20 356	27 292	27 532	23 457
Spain	m. pesetas	84 291	116 707	170 745	113 380	168 812	210 633	172 918	168 430	117 197	139 883
Turkey	b. lira	48	56	105	168	334	553	853	1 231	2 773	4 324
UK	m. pounds	3 545	4 122	4 629	4 907	4 762	4 744	4 904	4 731	4 355	4 779

Sources: Financial and Economic Data Relating to NATO Defence, annual publication (NATO: Brussels, various years); authors' calculations. Figures for France are based on national data.

Table 7.16. NATO and EC major weapon procurement expenditure, 1982–91

Figures are in US $m., at constant (1988) prices.

	1982	1983	1984	1985	1986	1987	1988	1989	1990	1991
North America										
Canada	1 405	1 683	1 883	1 784	1 887	2 058	2 020	1 853	1 706	1 579
USA	51 493	59 581	66 359	72 917	78 219	79 396	71 808	73 155	68 359	63 415
Europe										
Belgium	611	595	545	518	548	560	492	400	313	310
Denmark	390	386	359	308	301	339	334	296	337	358
France	7 878	8 255	8 151	8 492	8 850	9 648	9 496	9 744	9 116	9 101
FR Germany	6 533	6 811	6 743	6 760	7 082	7 100	6 773	6 652	6 529	5 715
Greece	583	497	569	535	498	541	790	682	674	704
Italy	2 540	2 883	2 778	3 128	3 122	3 954	4 188	4 052	3 328	3 272
Luxembourg	1.5	1.1	1.0	2.5	2.0	2.9	2.4	3.0	3.0	4.0
Netherlands	1 344	1 494	1 560	1 523	1 346	1 202	1 373	1 195	1 181	1 038
Norway	499	560	463	734	588	620	617	737	677	699
Portugal	59	54	49	34	73	123	141	168	150	115
Spain	1 180	1 456	1 914	1 168	1 593	1 895	1 484	1 353	883	999
Turkey	271	241	304	3 336	496	559	600	530	745	711
UK	8 307	9 240	9 881	9 878	9 270	8 859	8 736	7 818	6 541	6 791
European NATO total	30 197	32 473	33 317	33 417	33 769	35 403	35 026	33 630	30 477	29 817
NATO total	83 095	93 737	101 559	108 118	113 875	116 857	108 854	108 638	102 248	94 811
EC	29 427	31 672	32 550	32 347	32 685	34 224	33 809	32 391	29 083	28 435

Sources: Financial and Economic Data Relating to NATO Defence, annual publication (NATO: Brussels, various years); authors' calculations. Figures for France are based on national data.

Table 7.17. NATO armed forces, total military personnel, 1982–91

Figures are in thousands.

	1982	1983	1984	1985	1986	1987	1988	1989	1990	1991
North America										
Canada	82	81	82	83	85	86	88	88	87	85
USA	2 201	2 222	2 222	2 244	2 269	2 279	2 246	2 241	2 181	2 087
Europe										
Belgium	110	109	107	107	107	109	110	110	106	104
Denmark	30	30	31	29	28	28	30	31	31	30
France	577	578	571	563	558	559	558	554	550	542
FR Germany	490	496	487	493	495	495	495	503	545	521
Greece	188	177	197	201	202	199	199	201	201	204
Italy	517	498	508	504	502	504	506	506	493	474
Luxembourg	1	1	1	1	1	1	1	1	1	1
Netherlands	106	104	103	103	106	106	107	106	104	96
Norway	41	41	39	36	38	38	40	43	51	. .
Portugal	89	93	100	102	101	105	104	104	87	. .
Spain	372	355	342	314	314	314	304	277	263	268
Turkey	769	824	815	814	860	879	847	780	769	845
UK	334	333	336	334	331	328	324	318	308	298
European NATO total	**3 624**	**3 639**	**3 638**	**3 630**	**3 669**	**3 693**	**3 651**	**3 247**	**3 509**	**. .**
NATO total	**5 607**	**5 942**	**5 942**	**5 957**	**6 023**	**6 058**	**5 985**	**5 576**	**5 777**	**. .**

Sources: Financial and Economic Data Relating to NATO Defence, annual publication (NATO: Brussels, various years); authors' calculations. Figures for France are based on national data.

Table 7.18. NATO military and civilian personnel, as share of total labour force, 1982–91

Figures are percentages.

	1982	1983	1984	1985	1986	1987	1988	1989	1990	1991
North America										
Canada	1.0	1.0	1.0	1.0	1.0	1.0	1.0	0.9	0.9	0.9
USA	2.9	2.9	2.9	2.9	2.8	2.8	2.7	2.7	2.6	2.3
Europe										
Belgium	2.8	2.8	2.8	2.7	2.7	2.7	2.8	2.8	2.7	2.7
Denmark	1.5	1.5	1.5	1.4	1.4	1.4	1.4	1.4	1.4	1.4
France	..	..	..	..	2.9	2.9	2.9	2.8	2.8	2.7
FR Germany	2.4	2.4	2.4	2.4	2.4	2.4	2.4	2.3	2.6	..
Greece	5.8	5.2	6.0	6.1	6.0	6.0	6.0	5.8	5.7	5.8
Italy	2.4	2.3	2.3	2.4	2.4	2.3	2.3	2.3	2.3	2.2
Luxembourg	0.8	0.9	0.9	0.9	0.9	0.8	0.8	0.8	0.8	0.8
Netherlands	2.5	2.5	2.2	2.2	2.2	2.1	2.0	2.0	1.9	1.8
Norway	2.6	2.6	2.5	2.3	2.3	2.3	2.3	2.6	2.9	..
Portugal	2.4	2.3	2.5	2.6	2.6	2.6	2.6	2.5	2.1	..
Spain	3.2	3.0	2.9	2.6	2.5	2.4	2.3	2.1	2.0	2.0
Turkey	4.6	4.8	4.7	4.6	4.9	4.9	4.7	4.4	4.2	4.6
UK	2.1	2.0	2.0	2.0	1.9	1.8	1.8	1.7	1.7	1.6
European NATO total	**2.8**	**2.8**	**2.8**	**2.8**	**2.8**	**2.8**	**2.7**	**2.6**	**2.5**	**..**
NATO total	**2.8**	**2.8**	**2.8**	**2.7**	**2.7**	**2.7**	**2.7**	**2.5**	**2.3**	**..**

Sources: Financial and Economic Data Relating to NATO Defence, annual publication (NATO: Brussels, various years); authors' calculations. Figures for France are based on national data.

slower, more stable and orderly than was initially feared by the market. Government intervention by France and other countries, and the sizeable export market that was rejuvenated by the Gulf War, could also help the restructuring of the European defence market. In addition, the political changes arising from the elimination of the threat of war, and the economic change arising out of economic integration, mean that European defence industry will be forced to collaborate and/or specialize. Under that circumstance, substantial cost savings are achievable and estimates of 10–30 per cent have been mentioned in the literature.[69] There is also the possibility (through the EC's increasing role in defence matters, as discussed below) of setting up structural adjustment funds to cushion the impact on unemployment. The procurement expenditure trends in table 7.16 show that the reductions are not yet extravagant and the process of slow-down in European military procurement will be relatively prolonged, allowing sufficient breathing space to industry.

If there is one area of military force structure where changes are dramatic, it is that of personnel reductions. Calculation of force numbers in European NATO is distorted by the size of the Turkish and Greek forces, which are configured on the basis of threat perceptions distinct from those of the rest of NATO. Leaving out these two countries, total military personnel in European NATO declined by only 1.9 per cent over the six-year period 1985–90. The reduction within this category of countries is estimated to be of the order of 3 per cent for 1991 alone. Advances in technology, and changes in political perceptions about the improbability of fighting a prolonged war in Europe, are contributing factors. Tables 7.17 and 7.18 give data for NATO military personnel as well as the share of the armed forces in total labour force—an index which gives an indication of the implications for unemployment.

Of the European NATO countries, Germany will be the most affected by the cuts in manpower required by arms control limits and, above all, the unification of the country. According to the July 1990 discussions between Soviet President Gorbachev and German Chancellor Helmut Kohl, the total strength of the German armed forces will be 370 000 by 1994. No more than 345 000 can be in the Army and the Air Force. The Bundeswehr (which has now integrated the Nationale Volksarmee of the former German Democratic Republic) will have manpower allocations by 1994 of the order of 70 per cent for the Army, 22 per cent for the Air Force and 8 per cent for the Navy.[70] The reduction of the time period for basic military service for conscripts announced in 1990, from 15 to 12 months, effectively cut aggregate personnel numbers by 30 000. From the current level of about 525 000 the Bundeswehr will have to lose 150 000 men—a formidable task in four years. The Army, which is expected to lose 120 000 troops, is to have three major elements, as described by the Chief of Staff of the German Army, Lieutenant General Henning von Ondarza:

---

[69] See Hooper and Buck (note 64).
[70] *Neue Zürcher Zeitung*, 16 Nov. 1990, p. 2; *Frankfurter Allgemeine Zeitung*, 6 Jan. 1992, p. 9. For an overview of the discussions, see FBIS-90-136, 16 July 1990, pp. 28–36.

[T]he army will consist of three elements. In the first place, we will have territorial, national forces, which, in addition to carrying out training and logistical tasks will also continue to liaise with the civilian sector and the allies. In the second place, we will have mobilisation and augmentation-capable troops that would be ready to fight after a certain preparation period, and in the third place, we will have fully present units that could be deployed on short notice in smaller conflicts and outside of the central region—in a crisis management role. The army, as part of the Bundeswehr, is thus organized in keeping with full German sovereignty. It is also oriented to requirements of the alliance, which also distinguishes between the maintenance of highly mobile active armed forces and the capability to re-establish large forces.[71]

The Air Force is to lose 30 per cent of its personnel in this re-organization, leaving a reduced force of about 85 000 men.[72] Clearly, the short period given for such major changes means that the problems of adjustment will be severe.

The *SIPRI Yearbook 1991* chapter on military expenditure discusses in detail the 1990 military expenditure of France, Germany and the UK.[73] The same analysis is carried over to 1991. Steady and slow changes are taking place overall, characterized by large manpower reductions, future procurement cuts and preservation of the technological base through maintaining adequate defence-related R&D and investment in and protection of strategic industries.

V. The European Community

The European Union Treaty, drafted at the EC summit meeting in Maastricht on 9–11 December 1991, was a landmark in terms of a European monetary and political union (EMU and EPU).[74] The Treaty, signed on 7 February 1992, is expected to further the close integration begun with the 1986 Single European Act. Agreement on a monetary union was anticipated, but the advances made in political union, particularly in the area of foreign and security policy, can have more far-reaching long-term implications. Military expenditure, force structure and defence industrialization will be affected indirectly by both EMU and EPU, although more so by the latter. The EMU places ceilings on fiscal deficits and government debt, both as proportions of GDP. The Protocol on Excessive Deficit Procedure gives the upper limit of the planned or actual budget deficit to be 3 per cent of GDP at market prices; in addition, the ratio of government debt to GDP at market price must be less than or equal to 60 per cent. Although such measures are intended to curb total government spending relative to revenue, they will also stop large-scale increases in military expenditure in the absence of major threats. The type of rule that NATO formulated in 1979, regarding 3 per cent annual growth in military spending, would have been infeasible within the EMU even if there was a political consensus behind it. At present, the question of large-scale

[71] 'The goal is a smaller, more professional army', Interview with the Chief of Staff of the German Army, Lt. Gen. Henning von Ondarza, *Military Technology*, vol. 15, no. 2 (Feb. 1991), p. 19.
[72] 'The Luftwaffe faces new challenges'. Interview with Lt. Gen. Horst H. Jungkurth, Chief of Staff of the German Air Force, *Military Technology*, vol. 15, no. 2 (Feb. 1991), pp. 20–24.
[73] Deger (note 27), pp. 128–31.
[74] Lemaitre, P., 'What Maastricht means', *Guardian Weekly*, 22 Dec. 1991, p. 11.

increases in military expenditure in EC countries is academic. However, even in an altered security environment, for example if the USA pulls out of Europe, it will be difficult from a budgetary point of view to raise defence expenditures rapidly in view of the constraints imposed by the EMU. In 1991 military expenditure cuts were made by those countries which had a budget deficit problem. Belgium, Germany, Greece, Ireland, Italy, Netherlands, Portugal and Spain all exceeded the 3 per cent limit.[75] As shown above, even among European NATO countries the military spending cuts in 1991 were made by those governments with the maximum budgetary constraints

The EPU Treaty gives a strong preference for a common security policy, which later could transform itself to a common defence policy. The Treaty states: 'By this Treaty, the High Contracting Parties establish among themselves a European Union . . . to assert its identity on the international scene, in particular through the implementation of a common foreign and security policy, including the eventual framing of a common defence policy'.[76] In a separate declaration, member states are invited to consider common approaches in areas including technological co-operation in defence industries; transfer of arms and technology to non-EC countries; arms control negotiations, in particular the activities of the CSCE; and peace-keeping operations of the UN and other humanitarian intervention programmes. While the limits of defence policy are far reaching, there is a long way to go towards a common European defence system even remotely similar to NATO.

The WEU, consisting of the EC states except Denmark, Greece and Ireland, will be strengthened and activated as the defence arm of the future European Union and will also act as a link to the trans-Atlantic relation. Therefore, there will be a spectrum of military-security organizations linking the EC, the WEU and NATO. The position in this defence-related network of the European neutral and non-aligned countries—Austria, Finland, Sweden and Switzerland—is not clear, but there seems to be scope for a broadly defined common foreign and security policy if and when they join the EC.

The fundamental objective of the EC is economic progress. The 1958 Treaty of Rome sought only to 'promote' economic growth. The EC now sets itself the task of achieving a 'harmonious and balanced development of economic activities, sustainable and non-inflationary growth respecting the environment, a high degree of convergence of economic performance, a high level of employment and of social protection, the raising of the standard and quality of living, and economic and social cohesion and solidarity between member states'.[77] However, these economic goals are dependent on a stable international environment and the absence of security threats both within and outside the EC. Hence, there are close links between economic and security indicators which need to be stressed. Data on economic and military indicators for the EC countries are given in table 7.19 for all the member states as well as

[75] 'A step towards ever closer union', *Financial Times*, 12 Dec. 1991, p. 6.
[76] Conference of the Representatives of the Governments of the Member States, *Treaty on European Union*, document no. CONF-UP-UEM 2002/92 (European Community: Brussels, 1 Feb. 1992), p. 2.
[77] Note 75.

Table 7.19. Comparative economic and military indicators of the European Community countries, the USA and Japan, 1990

Figures are in constant (1988) prices.

Country	GDP (US $b.)	Population (m.)	Per capita GDP (US $)	ODA[a]/GNP (%)	Military expenditure (US $m.)	Armed forces (thou.)	Weapon procurement expenditure (US $m.)
FR Germany	1 296.9	62.50[b]	20 750	0.41	36 890	545	6 529
France	1 016.8	56.40	15 730	0.78	36 463	550	9 116
Italy	887.4	57.60	15 406	0.36	19 024	493	3 328
UK	829.8	57.24	14 497	0.29	32 672	308	6 541
Spain	388.5	38.96	9 972	0.15	6 949	263	883
Netherlands	246.2	14.94	16 479	0.94	6 599	104	1 181
Belgium	166.2	9.85	16 873	0.46	3 959	106	313
Denmark	111.9	5.14	21 770	0.93	2 265	31	337
Greece	54.8	10.03	5 464	0.06	3 151	201	674
Portugal	46.4	10.53	4 407	0.25	1 455	87	150
Ireland	37.1	3.50	10 600	0.16	476	13	28
Luxembourg	7.4	0.39	18 974	0.27	82	1	3.0
EC total	**5 089.4**	**327.08**	**14 243**[c]	**0.50**[c]	**149 985**	**2 702**	**29 083**
USA	5 423.4	249.97	21 696	0.18	277 037	2 181	68 359
Japan	3 134.6	123.64	25 373	0.31	30 340[d]	249	8 466

[a] Official development assistance

[b] The population of Germany was 79.75 million after 3 October 1990 (after unification).

[c] Average figure.

[d] The figure for Japanese military expenditure is not strictly comparable with figures for NATO countries, as it is defined by somewhat different criteria.

Sources: SIPRI data base; authors' calculations.

for the USA and Japan—the two other major economic powers. Aggregates are provided for the EC as a whole. This year, in addition, aggregated data for the WEU are also given, to stress the growing importance of that body.

There are formidable obstacles and practical problems facing the formation of a common defence policy within a future European Union—no less because of its rather ambiguous position with respect to the USA. In addition, there is the whole host of national sovereignty issues, in which defence considerations play an obvious role. The attitudes towards NATO and the USA vary considerably from country to country, with the UK and France likely to take opposite positions. The role of Germany is problematic. After sacrificing its strongly independent monetary policy and having a much reduced military force, it will have to bear the burden of economic leadership without a corresponding political status. The status of the nuclear deterrent is unclear. The economic advantages of a common defence policy, particularly in procurement and joint forces, are considerable.[78] Military expenditure could be reduced if 'European champions' replaced 'national champions' and the externalities of arms production achieved on a European scale. There would also be less incentive for arms exports and a reduction of the adverse selection problem that has plagued governments who profess political objectives for arms sales and then see those objectives undermined by commercial considerations of the manufacturers. But the possibility of an integrated and possibly protectionist European defence industry would create problems with the USA, which would counter by again raising the issue of burden-sharing. US sources claim that 50–60 per cent of US military expenditure is spent on the defence of Europe.[79] Even with the lower figure, US military expenditure on European defence is about the same as EC aggregate defence expenditure. Military expenditure shares of GDP in the EC and WEU countries are still considerably lower than corresponding US shares, even though the opportunity costs (the use of conscript forces who could be used in the civilian sectors of the economy with higher productivity) are high in terms of resource use.[80] Cuts in EC defence budgets have been limited in general, and it is difficult to foresee a simple peace dividend except through structural transformation.[81] If US involvement is reduced in Europe, either because of domestic budgetary pressures or reduced threat perceptions after the dissolution of the USSR, then a European defence union will become a necessity simply because the economics of military security will not allow the luxury of separate armed forces and defence industries. The European Union Treaty could be the first step towards that end and will certainly be an important milestone.

[78] Fontanel, J. and Smith, R., 'A European Defence Union?', *Economic Policy*, Oct. 1991, pp. 394–424.

[79] Maroni, A., 'US perspectives on the economic costs and benefits of a withdrawal of US troops and facilities from Europe', ed. J. Sharp, SIPRI, *Europe After an American Withdrawal: Economic and Military Issues* (Oxford University Press: Oxford, 1990); Deger, S., 'Economic security consequences of the East–West arms control process on the Third World', ed. S. Sur, United Nations Institute for Disarmament Research, *Disarmament Agreements and Negotiations: The Economic Dimension* (UNIDIR/Dartmouth: Aldershot, UK, 1991), pp. 97–113.

[80] See Deger (note 7), p. 141–46.

[81] See Hartley (note 64).

VI. Central Europe and the Balkan states

Central and East European countries continued to reduce military expenditure following the dissolution of the Warsaw Treaty Organization (WTO) in 1991. The process had been initiated even prior to the political changes of 1989, because of systemic economic problems—partly caused by defence spending and distortions. Since 1989 the process has accelerated as a result of the political transformation as well the growing economic crisis. During 1989–90 very large cuts were announced and implemented by all countries in the region. However, the pace of reductions slowed down in 1991. This is partly because minimal military security needs were becoming difficult to meet, particularly in an area of instability. Secondly, the payment of hard currency for arms imports, specially to the USSR, inflated the local currency value of weapons acquisition. In spite of this military spending fell for all countries in the region. For example, Poland reduced its defence spending at a rate of 10 per cent per annum in 1989–90 and 1990–91. In 1991 defence budgets fell by 8 per cent, even though the economic crisis warranted greater cuts.[82] Overall, however, there is rapid demilitarization in the region, with particularly vicious cuts in weapons procurement causing problems for the defence industries. Poland cut its total military expenditure by 32.5 per cent (in current prices) between 1986 and 1991. Correspondingly, the share of defence in GNP has fallen from almost 4 per cent in the mid-1980s to about 3 per cent in 1990.[83]

More information is now available about these countries regarding their defence allocations, procurement budgets and military industries. However, market reforms are still at the initial stages, and price distortions for military hardware continue to exist. Thus, procurement budgets are still priced lower, in relative terms, than warranted by international PPP. In Poland, for example, procurement costs (including R&D) for 1990 amounted to $340 million in official exchange rates but $785 million in PPP prices, which are comparable to international costs. SIPRI has estimated its own PPP rates to convert local currencies into dollars, and will continue to use them until economic reforms are complete. There are also doubts of the authenticity of past data in the light of recent revelations. Trends are therefore more difficult to estimate. For example, from the 1990 defence expenditure data that Romania submitted to the UN in 1991, it is clear that past data contained only spending on personnel and O&M. Other procurement and investment costs had not previously been revealed. Bulgaria's official 1990 data to the UN also show some consistency with SIPRI estimates of past military expenditure, but the level of aggregation is not detailed enough to evaluate hidden categories of expenditure. SIPRI bases its estimates on open sources. Obviously, the quality of the data depends on the original source, which if distorted involves underestimates. The chaotic nature of statistical information gathering in many of these countries makes it

---

[82] *Polish Army: Facts and Figures (In the Transition Period)* (Polish Ministry of National Defence: Warsaw, 1991).
[83] *Guardian Weekly*, 23 Dec. 1991, p. 33.

Table 7.20. Allocation of military expenditure in Czechoslovakia, Poland, Bulgaria and Romania, 1991

Figures are in local currencies; figures in italics are percentage shares.

	Czechoslovakia (m. koruna)	Poland (b. zlotys)	Bulgaria (m. leva)	Romania (m. lei)
Personnel	7 674	4 913	472.1	5 917
Percentage share	*23.8*	*32.9*	*28.9*	*17.5*
O&M*a*	12 214	5 034	498.6	5 749
Percentage share	*37.8*	*33.7*	*30.5*	*17.0*
Procurement	9 989	3 312	593.6	21 151
Percentage share	*31.0*	*22.2*	*36.3*	*62.6*
Construction	1 346	1 320	58.1	527
Percentage share	*4.2*	*8.8*	*3.6*	*1.6*
R&D	1 065	366	12.5	448
Percentage share	*3.3*	*2.4*	*0.8*	*1.3*
Total	**32 288**	**14 945**	**1 635.0**	**33 792**
Percentage share	*100*	*100*	*100*	*100*

a Operations and maintenance (includes civilian personnel cost).

Source: United Nations General Assembly, *Reduction of Military Budgets, Military Expenditure in Standardized Form Reported by States*, Report of the Secretary General, document no. A/46/381 (UN: New York, 18 Sep. 1991).

difficult to construct historical series. Current estimates should be treated with care. Changes will be reported in future *SIPRI Yearbooks*.

Table 7.20 gives data for Bulgaria, Czechoslovakia, Poland and Romania on military expenditure in 1990 and its breakdown into personnel, operating costs, procurement, construction and R&D. More important are the shares allocated to each of these functions. Procurement of arms gets a surprisingly low share in Poland, given the size of its defence industries. Military R&D in Czechoslovakia is relatively high, since it had technologically the most advanced arms industry in the region. The most astonishing figure is that of Romania, which seems to have spent two-thirds of its budget on investment components, including procurement and research.

The civil war in Yugoslavia between the federal armed forces (dominated by Serbia) and the republics of Slovenia and Croatia, continued throughout 1991. It is difficult to forecast the level of military expenditure incurred by the war. It is almost impossible to estimate the economic cost of the war, over and above defence spending, although descriptive accounts give a picture of vast damages. Yugoslav federal procurement expenditure, estimated to be about 40 per cent of the budget, is spent on acquisitions from the domestic defence industry as well as on imports from abroad. While the latter was reduced through arms embargoes, the domestic industry is able to provide the arms needed to fight a civil war. The loss of export markets of the Yugoslav defence industry, due to the conflict, means that more arms output can be

Table 7.21. Economic and military indicators for Yugoslavia, 1989

Dollar figures are in constant (1989) prices.

Indicator	Value[a]
Population	23.7 m.
GDP annual growth rate per capita 1965–80	5.2 %
GDP annual growth rate per capita 1980–89	0.6 %
Annual growth of private consumption 1980–89	– 1.8 %
Annual growth of domestic investment 1980–89	– 0.4 %
Aggregate net transfer	– US $2 017 m.
Per capita	– US $85.1
Official development assistance	US $42.7 m.
As share of GNP	0.1 %
Per capita	US $1.8
Armed forces	180 000
Per 1000 people	7.6
Military expenditure	US $1 900 m.
As share of GDP	3.3 %
As share of CGE[b]	62.3 %

[a] A minus (–) indicates a deficit.

[b] Central government expenditure.

Source: Authors' estimates.

diverted for local use in the war. Since much of the industry is situated in Serbia, the Federal Army has had little difficulty in acquiring armaments. In addition, personnel expenditure and O&M spending has increased. Yugoslavia's military expenditure rose by an estimated 10 per cent in real terms in 1991. This applies only to the Federal budget. The defence expenditure of the two seceded republics cannot be calculated.

Yugoslavia has been troubled with economic insecurity for a time. The combination of developmental failures, the loss of legitimacy of the central government, and the re-kindling of incipient nationalism, have all fuelled the secessionist movement. High military procurement expenditure and accumulation of arms stocks may act as a catalyst to the process, but the fundamental causes that exacerbate the conflict must be sought elsewhere. A much wider vision of security must be considered before one can learn the lessons of the violent disintegration of Yugoslavia. Other countries in Central and Eastern Europe, including the successor states of the USSR, could face similar conflicts if these fundamental causes are not identified. Table 7.21 gives data on economic and security variables for Yugoslavia.

Military expenditure in Yugoslavia in the late 1980s amounted to less than $2 billion. However, if unidentified spending (such as earnings from arms exports) is added, the total could be higher by 10–20 per cent. Thus the defence burden, or the defence share in GDP, is over 3.5 per cent. More important, it is instructive to note that over 60 per cent of CGE was being used to finance the military—an abnormally high level in the industrial world. During the decade of the 1980s, Yugoslavia saw its per capita economic growth plummet from more than 5 per cent per annum to 0.6 per cent (in current prices). The GDP of the country is expected to fall by 30 per cent in 1990, mainly due to the disruption caused by the war. The economy contracted by 10–12 per cent already in 1990. If this level of armed conflict continues in 1992, the aggregate income could be *half* that of the 1988 level. As regards external debt obligations, Yugoslav aggregate net transfer on foreign debt in 1989 was over $2 billion. Thus, it was paying $2 billion more than it received in new loans to service its foreign debt. It is instructive that the EC offered aid of $850 million in 1991 to prevent disintegration and stop the conflict. However, this sum is small compared to the drain in resources that the country has suffered in recent years as a result of the debt crisis alone. In many conflict areas, economic aid and sanctions are often utilized *after* the conflict erupts. Yet the cause of the conflict emanating from developmental failures are not fully realized until and unless war breaks out. Yugoslavia is a classic example that debt and economic problems in general can lead to the type of instability that easily erupts into prolonged military conflict.

Long-term conflict resolution also requires much greater attention to collective agreements and economic re-construction than the relatively short-sighted emphasis on arms embargo and limitations on arms trade, which has characterized most approaches to the Yugoslav problem. Even within the limited diplomatic initiative to get the cease-fire operational, it was by late 1991 clear that overall economic sanctions, particularly the supply embargo on oil, has had more impact than the restrictions put on the arms trade. The black market has provided the republics with channels to acquire weapons. As noted above, the domestic industry is capable of maintaining the procurement needs of the Federal Army. Arms control has limited impact in low-intensity conflicts. Nevertheless, in terms of achieving and preserving peace, economic support is vital. War damage is extensive. Croatia claims that, as a direct consequence of the war, it is paying for 550 000 refugees, 667 000 pensioners and 270 000 unemployed. Almost one-quarter of the Croatian labour force was at the end of 1991, with about 8 per cent serving in the Croatian armed forces. Simply to begin reconstruction will require $1 billion; other expenditures will need to be financed later on.[84] Similar economic problems will be faced by other republics that may secede from the Yugoslav federation.

VII. The Asia–Pacific region

Security and economic issues in the Asia–Pacific region are becoming increasingly interrelated, and are emerging as a major focus of attention in terms of international relations. With high economic growth, developing countries in the region can afford to spend more on defence; indeed the growth of military expenditure in the area has been the highest among all regions in

---

[84] 'Croatia will increase taxes to pay for war', *Financial Times*, 12 Dec. 1991, p. 8.

the mid- to late 1980s. There are a number of unsolved territorial problems—the most important pertaining to the two Korean states, and to the relationship between China and Taiwan. While remarkable progress was made in regional peace settlements in 1991, the potential for conflict remain. One of the most significant developments of the year was the signing of the peace agreement between North and South Korea, which effectively replaced the armistice agreements of 1953.[85] Although nuclear issues are still a matter of concern in North Korea, the agreement is important in normalizing relations between these two major regional powers. These two countries also joined the UN in 1991. However, the two most important powers in the Asia–Pacific region remain China and Japan, which hold the key to security in the region.[86]

Japan

Among its militarily strong neighbours (China and the former USSR), the level and changes of Japanese defence expenditure have been a barometer reflecting its military power. However, the Japanese themselves emphasize their low defence burden as an indicator of their low resource allocation to the military relative to the country's economic strength. Japan's security policy, which affects its military expenditure, came up for close scrutiny during 1991. The Persian Gulf War and the possibility of a Japanese military contribution to the allied war effort called into question the role of the Japanese Self Defense Forces (SDF). The relatively high economic contribution that Japan made to the allied war chest, most of it as financial support for US spending in Operation Desert Storm, defined the parameters of burden-sharing in preserving international security. Japanese efforts to link foreign aid with disarmament in recipient countries in the developing world showed its determination to intervene only in the economic sphere for the cause of world peace. On the other hand, its own military expenditure continued to grow at a rate much higher than that prevalent among industrial countries in general, and new modernization plans for the armed forces were announced.

According to Article 9 of the postwar Japanese Constitution, 'the Japanese people forever renounce war as a sovereign right of the nation and the threat of force as a means of settling international disputes . . . land, sea and air forces, as well as other war potential, will never be maintained. The right of belligerency of the state will not be recognized'.[87] In practice, since the Korean War, and more intensively after the Viet Nam War, the SDF has functioned as a normal army, although with a strictly defined self-defence function. During the 1980s Japanese military capability increased fast, for three reasons: (a) its growing economic power and technological progress helped in expanding defence without a significant adverse impact on the

[85] 'Korean historic accord marks long road to unity' and 'Korean accord eases 40-year tension', *Financial Times*, 13 Dec. 1991, p. 4 and p. 20, respectively.

[86] For a historical analysis of Chinese military expenditure, see Deger and Sen (note 1), pp. 89–90; for Japanese military expenditure, see pp. 105–13.

[87] *The Constitution of Japan*, Chapter 2 ('Renunciation of War'), Article 9. For a discussion, see Delfs, R., 'Acting in self-defence', *Far Eastern Economic Review*, 20 June 1991, pp. 50–52.

Table 7.22. Japanese military expenditure, 1982–91

Figures are in b. yen, current prices; figures in italics are percentage shares

	1982	1983	1984	1985	1986	1987	1988	1989	1990	1991
Operating costs	18.65	19.27	20.20	21.47	22.58	23.3	24.00	25.31	26.90	..
Percentage share	*72.2*	*68.0*	*69.0*	*68.4*	*67.6*	*66.3*	*64.9*	*64.6*	*64.7*	..
Procurement, construction	6.92	7.96	8.78	9.40	10.30	11.20	12.30	13.10	13.80	..
Percentage share	*26.8*	*29.0*	*30.0*	*30.0*	*31.0*	*32.0*	*33.3*	*33.4*	*33.2*	..
Total	**25.86**	**27.54**	**29.35**	**31.40**	**33.43**	**35.20**	**37.00**	**39.20**	**41.60**	**43.86**
Military expenditure as share of CGE[a]	*5.21*	*5.47*	*5.80*	*6.00*	*6.18*	*6.50*	*6.53*	*6.50*	*6.30*	*6.23*

[a] Central govenment expenditure.

Source: Data provided by Japanese Embassy, Stockholm, on the basis of Japanese Defense Agency White Paper, Tokyo, 1991.

budget or on the military burden; (*b*) the USA pressured for greater burden-sharing of costs associated with US forces and bases in the country; and (*c*) the dispute with the USSR over the Northern Territories, the growing capability of the Soviet Far Eastern forces and the modernization of the Chinese Army, increased threat perceptions considerably.

Historical factors were recalled in 1991, which marked the 50th anniversary of the Japanese attack on Pearl Harbour and Japan's entry into World War II. It also marked the 60th anniversary of Japan's invasion of Manchuria and the attempted subjugation of China. Relations with the USA and China, two major powers in the region, are cordial but subject to pressures, which the memory of these aggressions tends to exacerbate. The third major power, formerly the USSR and now the Russian Federation, poses the more direct military threat, given the force modernization of Soviet Far Eastern fleet and other forces carried out in recent years. In 1991 the issue of the South Kurile Islands again surfaced, but no settlement was reached. It remains to be seen whether the new Russian Government is more disposed towards settling this dispute in return for Japanese foreign aid and investment in the Russian far east.

During the 1980s the military expenditure share of GDP remained at or below 1 per cent—the self-imposed limit set by previous governments. At the same time, however, the real value of defence spending rose by over 50 per cent during the decade, matching the growth in national output. The share of defence in CGE rose from around 5.2 per cent in the early 1980s to around 6.2 per cent in FY 1991 (April 1991 to March 1992). More significant has been the allocational changes between investment and operational costs. The share of procurement and construction (the investment component) was around one-quarter of the defence budget in the early 1980s. A decade later this share had gone up to around one-third of aggregate military expenditure.[88] Table 7.22 gives time series data (FYs 1982–91) on total military expenditure, the alloca-

[88] Data are calculated from Japanese Defense Agency, *Defense of Japan* (JDA/Japan Times: Tokyo, various years), the SIPRI data base and information provided by the Japanese Embassy in Stockholm.

tion between investment costs (procurement, R&D and construction) and operating costs (personnel and O&M). The share of defence spending in total CGE is also provided. The trends denote a rising level of military capability.

However, threat and belligerence require a matching of capability and intentions. Japanese foreign policy in general, and security policy in particular, has relied exclusively on peaceful means of settling disputes and a concentration on the non-military aspects of security. Japan ranks first or second (depending on measurement) among the world's major aid donor, and has fulfilled its international responsibilities through economic burden-sharing. In the late 1980s the Japanese share of the total Official Development Assistance (ODA) given by all member countries of the OECD was about 17 per cent. Japan has since promised to double the absolute value of its ODA to countries in the developing world and in Eastern Europe. If this pledge is maintained, the Japanese share could rise to 30 per cent of the OECD total.[89] In 1991 the Government signalled its intention to impose non-economic criteria in evaluating aid donors. Four conditions are reported to be important in determining aggregate aid levels for recipients: (a) military expenditure (as a share of GDP, or in comparison to government social spending); (b) arms imports; (c) human rights violations; and (d) the quality of governance, which may determine the internal security of the country concerned. The use of 'defence conditionality' and other non-economic criterion is a way of imposing sanctions and incentives by which aid policy can promote demilitarization.[90]

Japan's military expenditure rose by 5.5 per cent between FYs 1990 and 1991. Given an inflation rate of 2–3 per cent the real increase is of the order of about 3 per cent. Though not extremely high, such a rise is contrary to the experience of most Western countries, which have reduced their defence spending or kept them stable during the year. Actual spending was in fact reduced by 100 billion yen, to cover the Government's pledged contribution to the allied effort in the Persian Gulf War. Proposals submitted by the Japan Defense Agency (JDA) in the middle of 1991 for the FY 1992 budget asks for a nominal rise of 5.38 per cent for FY 1992. However, the level of procurement expenditure for major weapons has been reduced in this budget request to just over 1 trillion yen, a cut of almost 4.8 per cent in nominal terms.

The Government has also approved the five-year defence plan for the period 1991–95, with a mid-term review in FY 1993. At a total cost of 22.75 trillion yen over five years, the plan envisages modernization of the armed forces but not at an excessive rate.[91] Procurement authorization of major weapon systems has been allowed, but the number of new acquisitions will be less than what was requested by the JDA. Overall, the emphasis is on

[89] Data from Organization for Economic Co-operation and Development, *Development Cooperation*, 1990 Report (OECD: Paris, Dec. 1990). The 30 per cent share is calculated by taking current aid values and projecting Japan's share under hypothesized scenarios for the future.

[90] For a theoretical discussion of the use of 'defence conditionality', see Deger, S and Sen, S., 'Military expenditure, aid, and economic development', Paper prepared for the World Bank Annual Conference on Development Economics, World Bank, Washington, DC, 25–26 Apr. 1991.

[91] *Jane's Defence Weekly*, 12 Jan. 1991 p. 47; *Defense News*, 26 Aug. 1991, pp. 1, 44; *Defense News*, 24 June 1991, p. 46; *Jane's Defence Weekly*, 17 Aug. 1991, p. 250.

personnel benefits as well as on military R&D rather than on procurement of major systems. In this reorientation, the Ground Self Defence Force (GSDF) has fared somewhat better than the Air and Maritime Self Defence Forces (ASDF and MSDF). Nevertheless, the number of Advanced Type 90 main battle tanks to be purchased will be cut to reduce costs, from the planned 150 to 132. An innovation is the introduction of the Multiple Rocket Launch Systems for the GSDF, currently being assembled from kits but which the JDA wishes to produce in Japan under licence.[92] If successful in negotiations, this will be another attempt at self-sufficiency similar to the fighter programmes Japan has already initiated.[93] The ASDF will buy 42 F-15Js (co-produced by McDonnell Douglas and Mitsubishi); and the MSDF will get 8 AEGIS destroyers in the five-year plan. There is also discussion about purchasing the Airborne Warning and Control System (AWACS).

Annual defence spending in Japan is guided by the Mid-Term Defence Plan (MTDP) estimates, which set an upper limit on what the JDA can spend over a five-year period. The previous MTDP ran from 1986 to 1990 and the current one began in 1991. The current MTDP estimate (called the *Chugyo*) allocates 22.75 trillion yen (in 1990 prices), which is almost 23 per cent higher than the previous *Chugyo* of 18.5 trillion yen (in 1985 prices). Even taking into account inflationary adjustments, there seems to be a real increase in military expenditure in the next five years compared to the previous five years. At the same time, military expenditure's share of GDP, currently below the 1 per cent limit, is expected to move towards the 0.9 per cent level, which would leave Japan with one of the lowest military burdens in the industrial world. In addition, the composition of this aggregate spending is planned to change, with procurement expenditure shares (on major weapon systems) expected to fall.[94] In the previous MTDP, the shares were the following: personnel and provisions received about 41 per cent of the total; weapon procurement, called 'front-line equipment', 26 per cent; and OM&S (operations, maintenance and support), called 'rear purpose expenditures' (which includes the payment for Japanese workers in US bases), 33 per cent. The shares for the 1991–95 MTDP change in the following manner: personnel and provisions, 37 per cent; weapons procurement, 22 per cent; OM&S, 40 per cent. The change reflects greater burden-sharing and a stabilizing of procurement expenditures after the rapid rise seen in recent years.

One surprise of the current MTDP is the increasing emphasis on military R&D. Press reports claim that the share of defence-related R&D will rise in the next decade to about 5–6 per cent of the military budget.[95] The 1991 share is around 2.5 per cent—itself a significant rise from the 1.5 per cent level of the mid-1980s. If pursued, Japan's military research spending could go up to $1.5–2 billion per annum (at 1990–91 prices), which would bring it into line with big spenders such as France and the UK—but not the USA or the former

[92] *Mainichi Daily News*, 15 June 1991, cited in *News Review on East Asia*, no. 7 (July 1991), p. 627.

[93] For analysis of Japanese military production, and its relation to the procurement budget, see Deger and Sen (note 1), pp. 108–109.

[94] *Defense News*, 18 Feb. 1991, p. 4.

[95] *Jane's Defence Weekly*, 12 Jan. 1991, p. 47.

USSR. Japanese industry also puts substantial funds into its own research, and if these are added up for major defence companies such as Mitsubishi and Kawasaki Heavy Industries, the total could be very high. Japan's weapon research activities have always been modest compared with other major military spenders. This could change with the rapid growth of civilian research interacting with defence-related production. Japan is the world's second largest spender on civilian R&D, and the possibility of 'spin-ins' means that a greater interaction between military and civilian activities is being sought.

A litmus test of the new Japanese security policy, which requires a more active role in international military affairs without a corresponding rise in the threat perceptions of its neighbours, was provided during the Persian Gulf War. Prime Minister Toshiki Kaifu's attempt to send soldiers in support of the allied forces was a non-starter, given the professed self-defence nature of the Japanese armed forces. After the war ended, mine-sweepers were sent to the Persian Gulf to aid the final clearing of the seas through which a large part of Japan's oil imports need to pass. Yet, even this measure was hotly debated in the Diet as to whether it violated the spirit of the Constitution. The USA was pledged a financial contribution of $9 billion at the outbreak of hostilities in January 1991.[96] It has been claimed that Japan will spend over $13 billion in direct and indirect foreign aid to help the security operations in the Gulf region.[97] The extra $4 billion will go the countries adversely affected by the war, for disaster relief as well as to the UN.

Japanese security policy is at a crossroads. There will be pressure to assume a more interventionist foreign policy role, corresponding to its economic might and growing political stature. On the other hand, its military capabilities might be seen as threatening to the larger regional powers China and the Russian Federation. Foreign economic aid will be used both as an incentive for countries in the developing world but also as an index of burden-sharing with the USA. It will also be necessary, in the future, to bring Japan into the UN Security Council. It will be able to participate in UN peace-keeping forces, but not in any military action authorized by the UN. How these contradictory elements are to be reconciled is yet to be seen.

China

In 1991, for the second successive year, China increased its official defence budget significantly in real terms. However, from 1979 (when military spending peaked) to 1989, Chinese defence spending declined overall.[98] This trend was reversed in 1990. The defence budget in 1991 was 32.5 billion yuan (over $6 billion). However, this official figure is considered to be too low. Alternative estimates indicate that actual military expenditure may be two to four times higher. The trends seem nevertheless to be correct, and reflect the reduction in forces and the military–industrial conversions that took place in

[96] *Financial Times*, 30 Jan. 1991, p. 4.
[97] Delfs (note 87).
[98] Data on past Chinese military expenditure are given in Deger (note 27), p. 157, table 5.21.

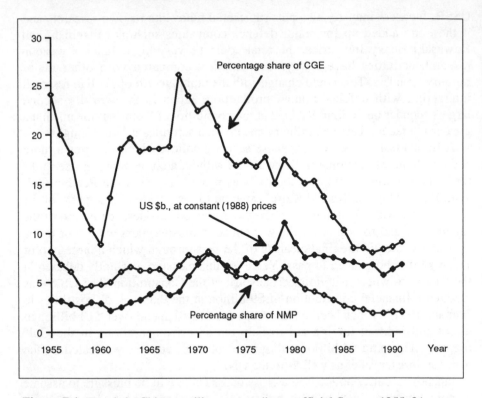

Figure 7.1. Trends in Chinese military expenditure, official figures, 1955–91

Authors' estimates corroborate trends, but orders of magnitude are subject to controversy (see text).

Sources: State Statistical Bureau of the PRC, *Chinese Statistical Yearbook*, various years (China Statistical Information and Consultancy Service Centre: Beijing); authors' estimates.

the 1980s.[99] In 1989 the trend was reversed somewhat, when nominal expenditure was raised to absorb the impact of inflation. However, in 1990 military spending rose by 15.5 per cent, which after allowing for inflation amounted to at least a 10–12 per cent rise in real terms. In 1991 reported defence spending was 12 per cent higher than the previous year's figure. This could imply an 8 per cent increase in real terms if forecasted inflation rates hold.

Figure 7.1 gives the trends of Chinese military spending since 1955, and shows the consistent rise in the 1960s and 1970s as well as the fall in the 1980s. It also shows the trends for the same period in the share of defence in the aggregate state budget as well the share in national income (similar to the net material product). These series are of considerable interest since only recently in the late 1980s have the authorities published such data.

The 1990 increase was clearly intended to allow the People's Liberation Army (PLA) to improve pay and other benefits (such as better family housing)

[99] For a description of Chinese conversion, see Lin, C. Z., 'Employment implications of defence cutbacks in China', Research Working Paper, World Employment Programme, International Labour Organization, Geneva, 1989; Deger and Sen (note 1), pp. 86–89.

Table 7.23. Chinese military expenditure as share of aggregate budgets, 1990 and 1991

Figure are percentages.

	1990	1991
Total state expenditure	8.6	12.0
Central budget	15.1	16.5
Central government expenditure on goods and services	21.8	21.7

Sources: 'Report on the implementation of the state budget for 1990 and on the draft state budget for 1991', excerpts from speech by Wang Bingqian, Fourth Session of the Seventh National People's Congress, Beijing, 26 Mar. 1991, reprinted in *Beijing Review*, 22–28 Apr. 1991, p. 38; authors' estimates.

to soldiers. Although this increase was overdue, after the cuts imposed over a number of years, a more important reason was that the leadership was anxious to secure the allegiance of the armed forces by rewarding them for crushing the 1989 student revolt. The 1991 increases are more explicitly for procurement and force modernization. Presenting the draft state budget, Minister of Finance Wang Bingqian justified the increases, stating that they were 'to be used mainly to modernize our army's weapons and equipment'.[100]

To evaluate the real defence spending it is necessary to analyse total Government expenditure. The share of military expenditure in the total budget is of interest since it also reflects the importance attached by the Government to national security. Chinese statistics are complicated by the fact that the so-called state budget is defined in a different way than the IMF-defined CGE. The state budget includes spending by central as well as local government. Within the more narrowly defined central budget, the actual expenditures on goods and services by the central government needs to be separated out from subsidies and transfers paid by the central to local governments. There are therefore three measures of public sector spending: total State budget; central budget; and actual expenditure on goods and services by the central government. Defence expenditure as a share of each of these aggregates vary enormously. For example, in 1991 official military spending was about 9 per cent of the State budget, over 16 per cent of the central budget (which includes transfers to local authorities) and over 21 per cent of CGE on goods and services. Table 7.23 gives data for 1990 and 1991 for all these three measures of the military burden on the government. Clearly, the impact of defence on CGE of around 21 per cent is quite substantial.

It is well known that revealed or official Chinese military spending is a substantial underestimate. There are hidden elements of the total expenditure which are not found in the official budget. US intelligence agencies identify a number of sources of additional revenues that the PLA could utilize outside

---

[100] *Beijing Review*, vol. 34, no. 16 (22–28 Apr. 1991), p. 38.

the regular published budgetary figures. They also claim that the military share in GDP is around 3.5 per cent rather than the claimed 1.8 per cent.[101]

There are two major sources of additional income or subsidies:

1. There are extra budgetary funds from incomes earned by the PLA or the defence industries. Agricultural production, whereby units of the PLA produce food for the armed forces, reduce expenditure on O&M and subsistence costs for conscripts, which otherwise would have to be incurred by the military. In 1989 such production of foodstuffs had a market value of over $1 billion, or 3.8 billion yuan—around 15 per cent of the regular budget. The PLA also run businesses and commercial enterprises which earn substantial revenues.[102] For example, the five-star Beijing Palace Hotel belongs to the PLA; the Cathay Hotel in Guangzhou is partly owned by the China North Industries Corporation, a semi-autonomous company belonging to the defence-industrial Ministry of Machine Building and Electronics Industry; and the PLA also runs a tourist complex complete with a shooting range outside Beijing. More important, the defence industries which have been converted produce large quantities of civilian goods which can be sold in an expanding market. It has been claimed that in 1989 military establishments produced civilian goods worth 20 billion yuan—80 per cent of the official budget. There is also the foreign exchange earned from arms sales. Even though prices are low and the equipment sold not highly sophisticated, a conservative estimate would put 1988 arms sales revenue at around $1 billion—about 17 per cent of that year's official budget. If all these elements are added up, the total value of expenditures on the PLA would be about double that of the official budget, or over $12 billion in 1991.

2. There are funds allocated to other ministries which are spent on defence-related activities but do not appear in military budgets. This applies in particular to military R&D. Research activities are co-ordinated by the National Defence Science Technology and Industry Commission and the State Science and Technology Commission. Both could be funded from the non-military component of the State budget. There are two major categories of State budget expenditures which have money earmarked for scientific research and product development, 'operating expenses for culture, education, public health and science; tapping the potential of existing enterprises, upgrading technology, and subsidizing trial manufacture of new products'.[103] Further, like in many other countries of the world, pensions of retired military personnel are not paid out of the defence budget, but from the Ministry of Civil Affairs. In addition, it has been claimed that the People's Armed Police expenses have been

[101] Kaufman, R. F., 'Overview'; Harris, J., 'Interpreting trends in Chinese defence spending'; and Kan, S., 'Chinese arms exports', *Report on the Chinese Economy*, Hearings before the Joint Economic Committee, 103rd Congress (US Government Printing Offcie: Washington, DC, 1991), pp. 645–47, pp. 676–84 and pp. 696–711, respectively.

[102] Deger and Sen (note 1), p. 95, table 7.1. On the issue of conversion, see Lin (note 99); 'China: the army that makes money', *The Economist*, vol. 321, no. 7727 (5–11 Oct. 1991), p. 72.

[103] Quote from speech by Chinese Finance Minister Wang Bingqian at the Fourth Session of the Seventh National People's Congress, March 26, 1991, reprinted in *Beijing Review*, vol. 34, no. 16 (22–28 Apr. 1991), pp. 34.

removed from the control of the PLA and hence not accounted for in defence spending. However, this 750 000 strong para-military force should normally be paid for by the military. It is also claimed that military reserves—which are very large indeed—are paid by provincial authorities rather than by the PLA.

The Chinese armed forces continued with reduction in personnel during 1991, although the pace is slowing down. The census of 1990 showed a PLA strength of almost 3.2 million.[104] Since the second half of the 1980s the armed force has been cut by one-quarter, from 4 million to just over 3 million men in active service. Selective conscription keeps costs low. The pay and service conditions of conscripts have deteriorated during budgetary austerity and there is an incessant demand for better pay, housing and benefits.

The immediate effects of procurement cuts since the early 1980s forced the PLA to earn revenues from military industries. This was the beginning of an unprecedented round of conversion, since the Chinese defence industry was very large. The history of Chinese conversion is well documented. It was the first country in the world which made 'swords into ploughshares' an operational and effective concept. It has been successful in this project, even though the costs of conversion were not borne by the PLA. The bloated defence industrial base has been streamlined and its assets utilized for civilian production. Even some of the establishments in the so-called Third Line industries, built in the mountains of South West China, have been physically moved away towards coastal regions—particularly to special economic zones—to promote exports. The revenues from such civilian sales have helped maintain procurement and allowed some force modernization. However, such modernization is still incremental and slow-moving. Chinese weapon systems are dated, and the the Persian Gulf War has produced some soul-searching among the military. However, the political leadership is firm in the belief that economic modernization takes precedence over defence. China will use the relatively benign international climate to further its economic growth and try to double its per capita income in the 1990s (as it has done so remarkably in the 1980s), before embarking on major force modernization. It can afford to skip one generation of weapons technology and catch up later without major security problems.

Nevertheless, steady but slow force improvements continue. In September 1991 the *People's Daily* unveiled reports of naval modernization whereby R&D has produced 'fruitful results' in new naval weaponry, avionics, lasers, electronics, nuclear devices (possibly for a newer planned strategic submarine) and marine engineering.[105] A new naval contingent of helicopter-carrying ships has apparently been formed to complement the shipboard helicopter forces started in early 1991. Standard naval weapons, such as missiles, torpedos and mines, will have higher levels of automation. According to this report, a major new naval base, capable of hosting the next-generation fleet, has been constructed at a classified location. There has been also continued discussion about constructing a 48 000-tonne fixed-wing aircraft-carrier, but

[104] *Asian Security 1991–1992* (Brassey's: London, 1991), p. 94.
[105] Quoted in *China Daily*, 21 Sep. 1991, p.1.

no agreement has been reached on this issue.[106] More modest proposals involve reconfiguring roll on–roll off ships as helicopter carriers.

Such reports show that defence will not be neglected. However, the basic concept of the Four Modernizations remains firm. Defence still has lowest priority among the four (industry, agriculture, science and technology, military). Economic development is the central objective of all Chinese policy, be it security or otherwise. The Ten Year Development Programme (1991–2000) initiated this year by Premier Li Peng maintained the 'strategic' objective that by the year 2000 Chinese GNP will be quadruple that of 1980.[107] According to this type of assessment, military strength will have to come as a product of economic development, not as a substitute to it.

VIII. The developing world

Military expenditure in developing countries has constituted approximately 16–20 per cent of the world total during the 1980s. Given the fact that the two superpowers, the USA and the USSR, alone accounted for around 60 per cent of the world total in this period, the share of the developing countries is small indeed. Nevertheless, relative to their level of poverty this burden is very high. The figures for 1991 show a slow decline in aggregate military expenditure for the developing world, following the firm trend begun in the latter half of the 1980s of a fall from the high levels of the mid-1980s. It is important to note that high military expenditure has historically been concentrated in conflict-prone or rich areas such as the Middle East. The decline or rise of the aggregate is very much a reflection of what happens in those regions.

In 1990, in response to the Iraqi invasion of Kuwait, defence spending in Middle East countries again began to rise. This, coupled with small increases in the Far East, stopped the decline for the developing world in aggregate. It is difficult to apportion the 1991 increases that have taken place in the Middle East, particularly in Saudi Arabia, towards the effort in the Gulf War of the US-led multinational Coalition. If counted, the approximately $25 billion spent by the Gulf Co-operation Council towards the Desert Storm and Desert Shield operations signal a rise in developing world military expenditure of about 6–7 per cent in real terms, relative to the 1990 level. However, defence spending in Latin America, South Asia and Africa fell, while remaining relatively stable in the Far East (except for China, as discussed above).

Both military and economic security affected developing countries during 1991. The total cost of the Persian Gulf War was high,[108] although estimates are still imprecise and it is difficult to say how much of this cost will be attributed to 1991 and how much will be carried over to 1992. Many technical uncertainties make accounting of the direct costs of the war problematic:

---

[106] *Asian Security 1991–1992* (note 104).

[107] The programme was announced by Li Peng at the Seventh National People's Congress. The speech is reprinted in *Asian Recorder*, 6–12 May 1991, pp. 21703–4.

[108] Willett, S., 'The economic implications of the Gulf crisis: who pays the price?', ed. J. Gow, *Iraq: The Gulf Conflict and the World Community* (Brassey's: London, forthcoming).

1. What constitutes the beginning of the war—the Iraqi invasion of Kuwait, the deployment of allied forces in the region under Desert Shield or the allied offensive under Desert Storm? This determines how the expenditures incurred by the combatants break down between the 1990 and 1991 budgets.

2. To what extent is expended equipment and ammunition to be replaced?

3. How long will the restocking take, that is, which years' military expenditure will increase and by how much?

4. What share of the contributions from non-combatants such as Germany and Japan was specifically targeted to finance military budget items, as distinct from general budgetary support?

5. How much of the O&S functions resulted from the war effort and how much were part of routine operations?

6. Should the total or incremental costs of the US troops and the formation of a multinational force be included in the war costs?[109]

7. What are the costs to Iraq of the war and the consequent developments (such as the loss of aircraft to Iran, military operations against the Kurds and the destruction of weapons under the UN resolutions)?

Aside from the direct military-related costs are the whole host of economic, budgetary and financial costs that have been incurred by a vast number of countries in the developing world, as well as in Central and Eastern Europe, as a result of the conflict: falling GDPs as energy use was curtailed and industrial production slowed down consequent to the oil price increases following Iraq's invasion of Kuwait; balance of payments problems of oil importers and increase in international indebtedness; loss of exports to Iraq and Kuwait; loss of migrant worker's remittance from the Gulf region; reduction of international savings used to finance the war; loss of income from tourism; the adverse impact of financial uncertainty caused by war and oil price volatility which reduced international capital flows; and, most important, extensive war damage, including environmental destruction.

Alternative estimates have been made in 1991 about the possible economic implications of the Gulf crisis on developing countries. A report by a major independent development research institute claimed:

[A]t least 40 low- and middle-income countries suffered an impact of more than 1% of GNP; 16 of them over 2%, including countries as distinct from the Gulf as Jamaica and Paraguay. The Indian states of Kerala and Gujarat, with a population over 70 million, would join them, if they were separate countries. The total direct cost for low income countries is at least $3.2 bn, when lower middle income countries are included, it is at least $12 bn.[110]

---

[109] 'Payment of Gulf bills nears $18 billion mark', *Defense News*, 18 Mar. 1991, p. 30; 'The Gulf War and its aftermath: first reflections', *International Affairs*, vol. 67, no. 2 (1991), pp. 223–34; 'Estimated total costs of Operation Desert Storm/Shield', *Operations Desert Storm Briefing Sheet*, no. 8 (Defence Budget Project: Washington, DC, 1 Mar. 1991).

[110] *The Economic Impact of the Gulf Crisis on Third World Countries*, Report of the Overseas Development Institute (Catholic Fund for Overseas Development/Christian Aid/Catholic Institute for International Relations/Oxfam/Save the Children Fund/The World Development Movement: Oxford, Mar. 1991), pp. 21.

Table 7.24. Debt, debt service payments and financial flows to developing countries, 1986–91

Figures are in US $b., current prices.

	1986	1987	1988	1989	1990	1991
Total external debt	1 096.3	1 216.0	1 223.7	1 234.1	1 306.4	1 362.2
Debt service payments	143.3	153.9	171.1	160.7	161.8	175.0
Long-term net resource flows	51.2	46.9	60.9	63.3	71.0	..
Long-term net transfers	– 10.0	– 16.8	– 9.5	– 1.0	9.3	..

Sources: International Monetary Fund, *World Economic Outlook*, May 1991; *The World Bank Annual Report 1991* (World Bank: Washington, DC, 1991).

In its analysis of the costs of the crisis and the impact of post-war reconstruction, the IMF claims: 'Thus, for the world as a whole the combined effect of the war in the Middle East and reconstruction will be a substantial net budgetary cost, thereby reducing the supply of saving that otherwise would have been available to finance investment in new capital goods'.[111]

According to IMF estimates, the Gulf crisis caused a fall in GDP of all net debtor countries taken together, amounting to 1.1 per cent of their GNP. The maximum losses suffered were in the debtor countries of the Middle East (including Egypt, Iraq, Jordan and Yemen), whose GNP in total fell from base line projections by about 23.1 per cent. According to SIPRI estimates, the fall in GDP for the world as a whole would be about $30–35 billion in 1991 alone. For the allied forces the cost of the war would be around $50–$60 billion, most of which was spent on Operation Desert Storm. These are conservative estimates; press reports claim that the cost of financing the war is in the region of $80–$100 billion.[112] Thus, even without costing the re-construction of Kuwait and Iraq or the military spending and value of weapons losses for Iraq, the total cost (economic and military) comes to at least $80 billion. in 1991. If these unidentified elements are included, given the vast destruction of this conflict, the total monetary cost could exceed $100 billion. In many ways this has been one of the most expensive wars ever fought.

The other major problem for the developing world has been that of economic insecurity brought about by the debt crisis. The level of debt and related indicators are given in table 7.24. Although 1991 showed some improvements, the situation for many countries still remained precarious. The problems faced by democratizing countries, with nascent political systems, is particularly vulnerable. One positive impact of the debt problem has been the forced reduction of military expenditure, and possibly arms imports, in the developing world. However, economics should not be an arms controller, and more positive measures are needed. There has been little evidence of regional security systems in the Third World modelled on anything even remotely

[111] International Monetary Fund, 'Economic and budgetary effects of the war', *World Economic Outlook* (IMF: May 1991), p. 25.
[112] *The Guardian*, 28 Jan, 1991, quoted in Willett (note 108).

similar to the CSCE.[113] Thus the fall in regional defence spending could be reversed in the future. However, the current trend in most regions (except the uncertainty in the Middle East) is downward. There are also major signs of conflict resolution in southern Africa, the Horn of Africa, Central America and South East Asia, where major breakthroughs have taken place during this year.[114]

IX. Conclusion

In terms of the evolution of military expenditure, and the many political and economic factors that influence and are influenced by it, 1991 could be characterized as the best of times and the worst of times.

It is the best of times in the sense that the two largest military spenders are permanently committed to a reduction in defence spending which will bring world military expenditure down from the absurd levels of the mid-1980s. Demilitarization will be slow but steady. It will most likely be characterized by large reductions in personnel numbers; increases in servicemen's pay and benefits, thus producing lesser proportional reduction in personnel expenditures; cuts in procurement of major weapons systems and increasing the efficiency of existing systems; decline in procurement spending but less so on O&S; achieving economies of scale through collaboration at the industrial level rather than striving for continuously rising sales; protection of the defence research sector and resilience of military R&D spending, but closer integration with civilian research to acquire the benefits of 'spin-ins'.

It is the worst of times in the sense that uncertainty is great and the possibility of conflict is high. The fall in military expenditure may be due to technological and economic reasons alone and not a product of arms control. This being the case, the reductions are not likely to bring about the structural changes in the politico-economic system which could produce the disarmament dividend in the true sense of the term. Rather current reductions will be spent on curing budget deficits, financing conflicts in 'remote' areas, proliferation of 'minor' weapons and small arms as well as preserving internal security. Thus, although world military expenditure could be less than today, its adverse impact will be much higher.

[113] Deger, S., 'Future approaches to defence and development', Paper presented at the International Conference on 'Defence and Development: Insights from Southeast Asia', organized by the Institute of Southeast Asian Studies (Singapore) and the Institute of Security and International Studies Chulalongkorn University, Bangkok, 29–31 Jan. 1990.
[114] See also chapter 11 in this volume.

Appendix 7A. Tables of world military expenditure

SAADET DEGER, EVAMARIA LOOSE-WEINTRAUB and SOMNATH SEN

Sources and methods are explained in appendix 7B.

Table 7A.1. World military expenditure, in current price figures, 1982–91

Figures are in local currency, current prices.

		1982	1983	1984	1985	1986	1987	1988	1989	1990	1991
NATO											
North America											
Canada	m. dollars	7 655	8 562	9 519	10 187	10 811	11 529	12 180	12 725	13 318	13 868
USA	m. dollars	196 390	218 084	238 136	263 900	282 868	289 391	295 841	304 607	306 026	304 558
Europe											
Belgium	m. francs	132 127	136 615	139 113	144 183	152 079	155 422	150 647	152 917	155 207	162 958
Denmark	m. kroner	11 669	12 574	13 045	13 343	13 333	14 647	15 620	15 963	16 399	16 725
France	m. francs	148 021	165 029	176 638	186 715	197 080	209 525	215 073	224 985	232 376	239 172
FR Germany	m. D. marks	54 234	56 496	57 274	58 649	60 130	61 354	61 638	63 178	68 364	66 182
Greece	m. drachmas	176 270	193 340	271 922	321 981	338 465	393 026	471 820	503 032	612 344	711 221
Italy	b. lire	11 477	13 583	15 616	17 767	19 268	22 872	25 539	27 342	28 007	29 267
Luxembourg	m. francs	1 893	2 104	2 234	2 265	2 390	2 730	3 163	2 995	3 233	3 605
Netherlands	m. guilders	11 921	12 149	12 762	12 901	13 110	13 254	13 300	13 571	13 513	13 542
Norway	m. kroner	10 956	12 395	12 688	15 446	16 033	18 551	18 865	20 248	21 252	22 633
Portugal	m. escudos	63 817	76 765	92 009	111 375	139 972	159 288	194 036	229 344	267 299	289 588
Spain	m. pesetas	465 695	540 311	594 932	674 883	715 306	852 767	835 353	920 381	922 808	938 813
Turkey	b. lira	448	557	803	1 235	1 868	2 477	3 789	7 158	13 866	20 888
UK	m. pounds	14 203	15 605	17 104	18 156	18 581	19 125	19 439	20 748	21 652	23 939
Other Europe											
Albania	m. leks	912	888	986	1 700	978	1 055	1 080	1 075	1 030	900
Austria	m. schillings	13 334	15 362	15 554	16 786	17 940	16 972	16 597	17 850	17 537	18 109

Country	Units										
Bulgaria	m. leva	989	965	1 093	1 127	1 404	1 547	1 751	1 605	1 635	1 439
Czechoslovakia	m. korunas	22 220	23 332	24 387	25 512	26 435	27 362	28 374	28 213	25 089	21 323
Finland	m. markkaa	5 182	5 656	6 082	6 555	7 245	7 636	8 419	9 226	9 672	10 377
German DR	m. marks	11 315	11 970	12 830	13 041	14 045	15 141	15 654	14 871	:	:
Hungary	m. forints	20 050	21 900	22 700	37 700	38 800	41 500	49 200	47 760	44 440	55 440
Ireland	m. pounds	229	222	250	266	292	283	299	303	335	364
Poland	b. zlotys	176	191	251	315	466	576	889	2 154	14 637	23 275
Romania	m. lei	11 340	11 662	11 888	12 113	12 208	11 597	11 552	11 753	11 786	12 000
Sweden	m. kronor	18 500	19 550	21 164	22 762	24 211	25 662	27 215	29 399	32 362	33 518
Switzerland	m. francs	3 727	3 862	4 009	4 576	4 282	4 203	4 458	4 679	5 145	5 235
USSR	m. roubles	:	:	:	:	:	:	:	:	:	:
Yugoslavia	m. new dinars	11.8	15.5	24.7	46	96.8	197.1	524.7	6 112	39 818	61 600
Middle East											
Bahrain	m. dinars	106	62.3	55.6	56.6	60.4	60.3	70.4	70.6	76.6	73.6
Cyprus	m. pounds	17.9	19.1	19.9	18.5	13.7	16.7	20.4	26.8	30	33
Egypt	m. pounds	1 435	1 801	2 173	2 108	2 493	2 742	2 862	3 415	3 640	3 838
Iran	b. rials	341	340	363	455	486	459	505	483	480	644
Iraq	m. dinars	2 400	3 200	4 300	4 000	3 600	4 350	4 000	4 000	4 150	4 000
Israel	m. new shekels	113	309	1 626	4 055	4 936	5 684	6 093	7 373	8 584	10 300
Jordan	m. dinars	179	196	197	219	243	253	256	252	280	291
Kuwait	m. dinars	370	416	434	469	430	380	408	438	450	:
Lebanon	m. pounds	1 215	3 554	2 030	2 448	3 740	:	10 640	:	98 000	100 000
Oman	m. riyals	581	670	728	745	665	584	519	510	520	540
Saudi Arabia	m. riyals	87 695	84 311	77 817	71 992	62 418	60 726	55 750	55 000	57 090	105 775
Syria	m. pounds	10 703	11 309	12 601	13 000	14 440	14 327	16 638	25 881	36 233	50 727
United Arab Emirates	m. dirhams	7 268	7 042	7 093	7 500	6 900	5 800	5 800	5 376	5 824	6 000
Yemen Arab Republic	m. rials	2 933	3 104	2 585	2 616	2 808	3 124	3 660	4 575	4 500	:
Yemen PDR	m. dinars	57.5	65.8	67.0	65.3	68.8	72	76	80	75	:
South Asia											
Bangladesh	m. taka	4 190	5 080	5 325	5 790	7 495	9 080	9 931	11 200	11 400	11 000
India	m. rupees	53 193	61 945	70 834	83 651	105 291	124 965	129 878	142 000	154 375	165 157
Nepal	m. rupees	337	430	493	601	866	1 153	1 304	1 565	1 500	1 617
Pakistan	m. rupees	22 637	26 915	30 689	35 110	38 861	43 995	48 599	54 479	61 548	67 703

		1982	1983	1984	1985	1986	1987	1988	1989	1990	1991
Sri Lanka	m. rupees	1 117	1 653	2 194	5 140	7 926	10 103	9 439	8 435	15 315	17 323
Far East											
Brunei	m. dollars	480	530	534	617	700	568	679	611	..	..
Hong Kong	m. dollars	1 478	1 537	1 523	1 639	1 530	1 645	1 676	1 500	..	..
Indonesia	b. new rupiahs	2 613	2 858	3 106	2 856	3 089	3 058	3 164	3 378	3 204	3 611
Japan	b. yen	2 532	2 712	2 911	3 118	3 296	3 473	3 655	3 865	4 099	4 329
Korea, North	m. won	3 242	3 530	3 819	3 935	3 976	3 971	3 886	4 060	4 466	4 566
Korea, South	b. won	3 163	3 406	3 573	3 957	4 372	4 915	5 753	6 226	6 854	7 202
Malaysia	m. ringgits	4 850	3 888	3 051	2 700	4 075	3 611	3 754	4 007	4 165	3 801
Mongolia	m. tugriks	716	726	764	764	790	837	900	850	800	800
Myanmar (Burma)	m. kyats	1 643	1 630	1 760	1 973	1 858	1 875	2 155	2 371	2 400	5 000
Philippines	m. pesos	7 778	8 530	8 288	7 827	8 662	9 268	10 972	16 447	17 680	18 646
Singapore	m. dollars	1 659	1 640	2 204	2 516	2 403	2 439	2 659	2 845	3 040	3 640
Taiwan	b. dollars	136	139	138	152	158	164	179	186	204	220
Thailand	m. baht	41 250	45 875	49 500	52 275	51 825	53 125	54 655	57 176	64 956	74 811
Oceania											
Australia	m. dollars	4 371	4 992	5 601	6 298	6 932	7 305	7 535	8 079	8 617	9 337
Fiji	m. dollars	14	15	17	16	17	31	35	43	45	50
New Zealand	m. dollars	628	656	724	825	1 017	1 211	1 340	1 382	1 371	1 315
Africa											
Algeria	m. dinars	3 893	4 477	4 631	4 793	5 459	5 805	6 070	6 756	8 419	10 757
Angola	m. kwanzas	15 060	23 295	31 943	34 306	34 572	30 367	26 161	23 438	21 094	16 875
Benin	m. francs	7 821	9 500	9 280	10 190	10 610	9 367	11 420	10 405	10 000	..
Botswana	m. pulas	25.2	28.2	34.9	41.7	64.5	124	90.1	93.0	107	118
Burkina Faso	m. francs	10 800	11 170	11 780	11 810	17 724	15 241	16 003	16 000	16 000	..
Burundi	m. francs	3 300	3 200	3 900	4 200	4 780	3 910	3 198	4 414	4 671	5 003
Cameroon	m. francs	41 015	63 105	73 658	81 920	86 905	83 150	77 889	50 000	57 120	57 000
Central African Rep.	m. francs	5 000	6 500	6 500	6 189	5 892	5 610	5 500	5 500	6 000	..
Chad	m. francs	..	15 000	17 496	17 000	16 850	10 307	20 000	15 517	17 069	18 778
Congo	m. francs	16 500	18 600	21 596	25 000	25 625	26 200	20 440	23 580	25 000	..

Côte d'Ivoire	m. francs	28 400	29 658	30 706	31 320	33 547	35 336	36 250	37 193	37 000	..
Ethiopia	m. birr	802	845	897	923	972	1 182	1 407	1 687	1 856	..
Gabon	m. francs	29 100	33 000	35 100	42 900	47 100	43 407	40 000	40 680	40 000	13 555
Ghana	m. cedis	587	894	1 605	3 432	4 605	6 659	4 603	8 028	11 334	5 251
Kenya	m. shillings	2 662	2 778	2 523	2 395	3 342	3 909	3 945	4 328	4 774	..
Liberia	m. dollars	46.9	25.3	25.2	24.4	23.0	25.8	27.4	28.1	30	36
Libya	m. dinars	1 330	1 107	1 096	1 096	819	549	582	524	525	475
Madagascar	m. francs	27 200	29 600	31 730	33 520	39 830	39 200	39 200	40 000	40 000	..
Malawi	m. kwachas	29.0	26.1	26.6	28.6	46.1	47.8	61.6	71.5	75	..
Mali	m. francs	9 700	10 200	11 100	13 400	13 000	13 300	18 000	20 000	20 000	..
Mauritania	m. ouguiyas	2 931	2 639	..	..	..	..	..	..	..	..
Mauritius	m. rupees	30.8	34.4	36.5	36.1	36.3	38.5	64.9	81.8	80	80
Morocco	m. dirhams	5 814	4 675	4 960	6 453	6 837	7 190	7 630	8 375	9 216	10 134
Mozambique	m. escudos	6 900	8 300	10 300	10 300	11 214	29 600	50 400	80 000	105 000	..
Niger	m. francs	4 232	4 389	4 775	5 075	5 325	5 175	5 365	5 500	5 500	..
Nigeria	m. nairas	1 113	1 179	928	976	957	810	1 270	1 689	2 108	2 325
Rwanda	m. francs	2 622	2 693	2 500	2 760	3 050	2 979	2 800	3 000	3 000	3 150
Senegal	m. francs	23 505	25 110	27 046	28 235	28 490	28 784	29 630	28 476	30 000	30 000
Sierra Leone	m. leones	17.9	18.6	23.3	29.4	64.5	101	125	250	500	..
Somalia	m. shillings	826	1 300	1 786	1 751	2 300	3 800	3 500	7 000	14 000	..
South Africa	m. rands	3 264	3 664	4 314	5 017	6 008	7 389	9 108	10 857	11 278	10 535
Sudan	m. pounds	139	212	361	468	562	723	968	1 831	3 000	4 500
Swaziland	m. emalangeni	16.2	16.0	16.1	15.7	15.9	16.8	21.5	24	25	25
Tanzania	m. shillings	2 433	2 651	3 201	4 277	7 073	11 025	16 250	21 574	22 000	..
Togo	m. francs	6 138	6 328	7 007	8 632	9 200	13 047	13 047	13 000	13 000	..
Tunisia	m. dinars	284	364	296	357	434	413	460	460	350	400
Uganda	m. shillings	82.3	144	327	782	1 157	4 805	8 500	8 000	10 780	16 171
Zaïre	m. zaires	314	345	1 518	5 085	4 046	10 109	12 731	44 283	28 347	30 000
Zambia	m. kwachas	148	161	148	167	480	637	717	896	2 156	..
Zimbabwe	m. dollars	296	353	398	436	554	661	720	804	800	1 000
Central America											
Costa Rica	m. colones	528	928	1 140	1 202	1 426	1 504	1 586	1 660	2 040	2 406
Cuba	m. pesos	1 109	1 133	1 386	1 335	1 307	1 300	1 350	1 377	1 400	1 750

		1982	1983	1984	1985	1986	1987	1988	1989	1990	1991
Dominican Republic	m. pesos	128	129	164	191	202	250	298	346	484	:
El Salvador	m. colones	395	442	534	630	964	885	1 002	1 118	1 200	:
Guatemala	m. quetzales	164	185	205	223	259	259	319	341	412	525
Haiti	m. gourdes	104	102	110	131	138	150	150	165	165	:
Honduras	m. lempiras	160	240	335	445	450	450	500	823	825	:
Jamaica	m. dollars	98.8	97.8	104	124	125	125	156	173	223	328
Mexico	b. pesos	47.4	90.3	181	297	470	894	1 470	1 673	2 024	2 000
Nicaragua	m. cordobas	1.7	3.4	4.9	26.8	91	921	93 827	:	:	:
Panama	m. balboas	55.0	60.0	88.0	92.0	105	105	113	124	125	:
Trinidad and Tobago	m. dollars	563	545	490	465	465	:	:	:	:	:
South America											
Argentina	m. australes	8.9	31.2	236	1 387	2 727	5 863	27 355	834 815	12 482 600	:
Bolivia	t. bolivianos	19.0	58.0	721	94 677	299 374	327 547	400 300	489 214	572 380	686 856
Brazil	m. cruzeiros	0.8	1.4	4.7	16	45	131	1 179	18 662	543 938	:
Chile	m. pesos	117 831	124 901	182 203	194 877	258 675	277 417	385 145	446 768	427 857	504 874
Colombia	m. pesos	44 661	69 531	91 753	105 092	135 712	176 989	265 484	398 226	566 886	:
Ecuador	m. sucres	6 870	8 833	12 086	19 743	25 598	35 442	52 595	83 839	125 759	177 887
Guyana	m. dollars	78	70	83	174	125	109	116	172	196	350
Paraguay	m. guaranies	11 566	11 676	12 826	15 937	20 097	26 885	32 643	57 978	60 000	:
Peru	b. intis	1.5	2.5	3.9	11.9	23.9	37	104	2 254	144 300	:
Uruguay	m. new pesos	5 168	5 877	7 708	12 831	22 828	36 831	59 962	108 275	233 000	:
Venezuela	m. bolivares	9 905	8 488	9 800	9 457	10 520	15 197	17 585	32 404	45 379	:

Table 7A.2. World military expenditure, in constant price figures, 1982–91

Figures are in US $m., at 1988 prices and exchange-rates.

	1982	1983	1984	1985	1986	1987	1988	1989	1990	1991
NATO										
North America										
Canada	8 077	8 534	9 093	9 362	9 535	9 747	9 897	9 852	9 839	9 699
USA	240 616	258 828	270 923	290 026	305 076	300 890	295 841	290 593	277 037	264 383
Europe										
Belgium	4 502	4 323	4 139	4 092	4 261	4 287	4 097	4 035	3 959	4 026
Denmark	2 323	2 342	2 287	2 234	2 153	2 275	2 320	2 263	2 265	2 256
France	33 668	34 252	34 104	34 103	35 118	36 137	36 105	36 494	36 463	36 403
FR Germany	33 786	34 054	33 712	33 796	34 719	35 320	35 097	35 008	36 890	34 268
Greece	3 428	3 128	3 717	3 688	3 152	3 144	3 326	3 116	3 151	3 078
Italy	14 248	14 708	15 262	15 902	16 293	18 463	19 625	19 771	19 024	18 711
Luxembourg	63	64	64	63	66	75	86	79	82	89
Netherlands	6 555	6 497	6 608	6 533	6 633	6 753	6 729	6 791	6 599	6 368
Norway	2 545	2 656	2 558	2 946	2 853	3 037	2 895	2 071	2 994	3 083
Portugal	1 142	1 099	1 021	1 036	1 166	1 212	1 348	1 415	1 455	1 416
Spain	6 518	6 738	6 669	6 952	6 772	7 672	7 171	7 396	6 949	6 674
Turkey	2 528	2 393	2 325	2 467	2 772	2 647	2 664	3 082	3 725	3 870
UK	33 283	34 981	36 511	36 548	36 173	35 713	34 629	34 290	32 672	34 008
EC	142 528	145 004	146 860	147 859	149 748	154 140	153 654	154 185	153 710	151 668
Other Europe										
Albania	152	148	164	283	163	176	180	179	172	150
Austria	1 278	1 426	1 366	1 429	1 501	1 401	1 344	1 409	1 341	1 340
Bulgaria	810	780	877	800	1 071	1 180	1 337	1 122	1 053	842
Czechoslovakia	3 454	3 589	3 716	3 838	3 962	4 097	4 241	4 159	3 363	1 768
Finland	1 714	1 726	1 733	1 765	1 895	1 919	2 013	2 070	2 044	2 107
German DR	5 357	5 667	6 075	6 181	6 656	7 176	7 419	7 048	:	:

	1982	1983	1984	1985	1986	1987	1988	1989	1990	1991
Hungary	1 571	1 599	1 531	2 375	2 321	2 285	2 343	1 944	1 411	1 354
Ireland	484	425	441	445	470	442	457	445	476	501
Poland	4 262	3 796	4 332	4 730	5 945	5 863	5 657	3 904	3 869	3 612
Romania	1 458	1 425	1 437	1 470	1 483	1 407	1 402	1 416	1 373	..
Sweden	4 380	4 253	4 263	4 268	4 357	4 431	4 442	4 508	4 492	4 250
Switzerland	2 907	2 926	2 949	3 255	3 022	2 926	3 047	3 100	3 233	3 109
USSR	..	..	..	..	..	..	..	..	..	..
Yugoslavia	2 137	1 994	2 082	2 249	2 491	2 300	2 082	1 810	1 726	1 376
Middle East										
Bahrain	273	156	139	145	158	161	187	185	199	189
Cyprus	48	49	48	43	31	37	44	55	59	63
Egypt	5 442	5 889	6 070	5 252	5 013	4 607	4 089	4 023	3 672	3 183
Iran	10 230	8 523	8 082	9 705	9 339	7 679	7 353	5 747	5 306	6 125
Iraq	21 952	28 596	31 590	23 506	16 531	17 073	12 868	10 720	9 268	7 414
Israel	7 314	8 000	8 420	5 249	4 318	4 134	3 811	3 830	3 801	3 909
Jordan	557	581	562	607	673	703	689	539	516	502
Kuwait	1 470	1 579	1 629	1 733	1 574	1 382	1 463	1 518	1 523	..
Lebanon	96	262	107	93	97	..	26	..	..	..
Oman	1 016	1 296	1 478	1 517	1 730	1 189	1 350	1 326	1 352	1 404
Saudi Arabia	21 614	20 899	19 513	18 666	16 684	16 384	14 887	14 522	14 798	26 227
Syria	3 526	3 511	3 582	3 152	2 573	1 601	1 482	2 070	2 427	3 134
United Arab Emirates	1 955	1 966	2 091	2 211	2 004	1 587	1 580	1 464	1 586	1 634
Yemen Arab Republic	456	457	339	323	325	340	375	390	..	..
Yemen PDR	234	241	243	225	224	221	220	232	..	..
South Asia										
Bangladesh	235	261	247	243	283	313	313	321	302	273
India	6 325	6 582	6 955	7 778	9 006	9 822	9 332	9 609	9 588	9 033
Nepal	26	29	33	37	45	54	56	62	55	52
Pakistan	1 767	1 974	2 122	2 299	2 459	2 658	2 700	2 805	2 906	2 862
Sri Lanka	63	82	93	214	306	362	297	238	355	357

Far East										
Brunei	265	290	283	319	356	287	314	..	..	..
Hong Kong	271	256	235	245	223	226	215	..	..	..
Indonesia	2 505	2 451	2 410	2 116	2 163	1 960	1 877	1 882	1 661	1 714
Japan	21 291	22 400	23 504	24 672	25 924	27 289	28 521	29 491	30 340	31 083
Korea, North	1 454	1 583	1 713	1 765	1 783	1 781	1 743	1 821	2 003	2 048
Korea, South	5 318	5 535	5 675	6 135	6 593	7 195	7 865	8 057	8 168	7 826
Malaysia	2 075	1 604	1 211	1 068	1 601	1 406	1 434	1 488	1 508	1 316
Mongolia	239	242	255	255	263	279	300	283	267	267
Myanmar (Burma)	481	452	465	488	421	340	337	292	251	429
Philippines	854	851	550	422	463	478	520	705	673	600
Singapore	866	845	1 107	1 258	1 218	1 230	1 321	1 381	1 426	1 648
Taiwan	5 000	5 043	5 007	5 526	5 704	5 891	6 348	6 282	6 562	6 890
Thailand	1 895	2 031	2 174	2 240	2 182	2 181	2 161	2 146	2 301	2 505
Oceania										
Australia	5 309	5 524	5 934	6 272	5 334	6 166	5 910	5 916	5 878	6 158
Fiji	13	13	15	14	14	24	24	26	25	26
New Zealand	756	735	765	754	822	845	879	859	802	749
Africa										
Algeria	1 066	1 138	1 107	1 036	1 050	1 040	1 026	1 045	1 117	1 177
Angola	502	777	1 065	1 144	1 152	..	872	781	703	..
Benin	40	44	41	43	43	35	38	32	..	..
Botswana	24	24	27	30	42	75	50	46	47	47
Burkina Faso	43	41	42	39	60	53	54	54	54	..
Burundi	34	31	33	34	38	29	28	35	34	34
Cameroon	225	296	311	341	336	303	262	168	192	..
Central African Republic	20	23	22	19	18	18	19	18	20	..
Chad	..	61	59	54	62	39	67	55	58	63
Congo	78	81	84	91	91	91	69	76	78	..
Côte d'Ivoire	124	122	121	121	121	127	122	124	125	..
Ethiopia	475	496	486	420	490	611	680	756	790	..
Gabon	114	117	118	134	139	129	134	128	124	..

	1982	1983	1984	1985	1986	1987	1988	1989	1990	1991
Ghana	23	16	20	39	42	44	23	32	33	:
Kenya	247	231	190	160	214	238	222	222	219	212
Liberia	58	30	30	29	26	28	27	20	22	:
Libya	4 650	3 870	3 832	3 832	2 863	1 919	2 035	1 832	1 836	1 661
Madagascar	44	40	39	37	39	33	28	26	23	:
Malawi	33	26	22	21	30	25	24	25	23	:
Mali	42	42	44	51	47	47	60	67	67	:
Mauritania	56	50	:	:	:	:	:	:	:	:
Mauritius	3	3	3	3	3	3	5	5	5	4
Morocco	1 042	788	744	898	876	896	929	989	1 018	1 041
Mozambique	58	55	53	42	36	75	101	107		
Niger	13	14	14	15	16	17	18	19	19	:
Nigeria	717	616	347	346	322	248	280	247	287	275
Rwanda	42	40	35	38	43	40	37	39	37	33
Senegal	111	106	103	95	90	95	100	95	100	99
Sierra Leone	19	12	9	6	8	4	4	5	4	:
Somalia	49	57	41	29	28	36	21	23	25	:
South Africa	3 267	3 266	3 448	3 448	3 481	3 688	4 028	4 187	3 804	3 081
Sudan	163	191	242	216	208	239	215	249	250	:
Swaziland	15	13	12	10	9	8	10	10	10	:
Tanzania	127	109	98	97	121	146	164	170	139	:
Togo	22	21	24	30	31	44	44	44	44	:
Tunisia	509	599	449	502	549	538	536	502	450	407
Uganda	83	116	185	190	104	128	80	40	:	:
Zaire	29	43	51	139	75	99	68	116	41	:
Zambia	120	109	84	69	130	121	87	70	86	:
Zimbabwe	364	353	331	334	371	394	400	395	335	419
Central America										
Costa Rica	19	25	27	25	27	24	21	19	19	18
Cuba	1 429	1 460	1 786	1 721	1 685	1 676	1 740	1 775	1 804	2 255
Dominican Republic	69	66	66	56	54	58	49	39	34	:

El Salvador	241	238	258	249	288	212	200	190	165	:
Guatemala	137	148	158	145	123	110	122	117	100	95
Haiti	26	23	23	25	25	31	30	31	27	:
Honduras	105	145	194	249	241	235	250	375	305	:
Jamaica	43	38	32	30	26	25	28	28	29	29
Mexico	1 015	959	1 161	1 208	1 027	842	647	613	586	473
Nicaragua	292	445	473	810	352	352	348	350	:	:
Panama	58	62	90	93	106	105	113	124	124	:
Trinidad and Tobago	264	222	176	155	144	:	:	:	:	:
South America										
Argentina	4 927	3 897	4 056	3 087	3 194	2 966	3 225	3 000	2 000	:
Bolivia	238	202	182	201	169	162	170	181	181	178
Brazil	4 532	3 276	3 703	3 857	4 428	3 908	3 899	3 874	4 900	:
Chile	1 574	1 313	1 597	1 307	1 451	1 299	1 572	1 557	1 183	1 145
Colombia	483	629	715	660	716	758	887	1 058	1 164	:
Ecuador	143	124	129	165	174	186	174	158	160	152
Guyana	25	20	19	34	23	15	12	12	:	:
Paraguay	71	63	58	57	55	60	59	84	:	:
Peru	785	671	487	568	641	534	806	500	421	:
Uruguay	268	205	173	167	169	166	167	167	169	:
Venezuela	1 678	1 354	1 392	1 207	1 204	1 357	1 213	1 196	1 151	:

Table 7A.3. World military expenditure as a percentage of gross domestic product, 1981–90

	1981	1982	1983	1984	1985	1986	1987	1988	1989	1990
NATO										
North America										
Canada	1.8	2.0	2.1	2.1	2.1	2.1	2.1	2.1	2.0	2.0
USA	5.7	6.3	6.5	6.4	6.6	6.7	6.4	6.1	5.9	5.6
Europe										
Belgium	3.4	3.3	3.2	3.1	3.0	3.0	2.9	2.7	2.5	2.4
Denmark	2.5	2.5	2.5	2.3	2.2	2.0	2.1	2.2	2.1	2.0
France	4.1	4.1	4.1	4.0	4.0	3.9	4.0	3.8	3.7	3.6
FR Germany	3.4	3.4	3.4	3.3	3.2	3.1	3.1	2.9	2.8	2.8
Greece	7.0	6.8	6.3	7.1	7.0	6.2	6.3	6.4	5.7	5.9
Italy	2.1	2.1	2.1	2.2	2.2	2.1	2.3	2.3	2.3	2.1
Luxembourg	1.1	1.0	1.1	1.0	0.9	0.9	1.1	1.1	1.1	1.1
Netherlands	3.2	3.2	3.2	3.2	3.1	3.1	3.1	3.0	2.9	2.7
Norway	2.9	3.0	3.1	2.8	3.1	3.1	3.3	3.2	3.3	3.2
Portugal	3.5	3.5	3.3	3.3	3.1	3.2	3.1	3.2	3.2	3.1
Spain	2.4	2.4	2.4	2.4	2.4	2.2	2.4	2.1	2.0	1.8
Turkey	4.9	5.2	4.8	4.4	4.5	4.8	4.2	3.8	4.3	4.9
UK	4.7	5.1	5.1	5.3	5.1	4.9	4.6	4.3	4.1	3.9
Other Europe										
Austria	1.2	1.2	1.3	1.2	1.2	1.3	1.2	1.1	1.1	1.0
Bulgaria	3.0	3.3	3.1	3.3	3.4	4.0	4.2	4.4	4.0	3.5
Czechoslovakia	3.1	3.1	3.2	3.3	3.3	3.4	3.4	3.4	3.7	3.1
Finland	1.9	2.1	2.1	2.0	1.9	2.0	1.9	1.9	1.9	1.8
German DR	4.4	4.5	4.5	4.7	4.6	4.8	5.0	5.0	5.0	:
Hungary	2.4	2.4	2.4	2.3	3.6	3.6	3.4	3.5	2.8	2.1
Ireland	1.8	1.7	1.5	1.5	1.5	1.6	1.4	1.4	1.3	1.3
Poland	3.1	3.2	2.8	2.9	3.0	3.6	3.4	3.0	2.0	2.9
Romania	1.6	1.5	1.5	1.4	1.4	1.3	1.2	1.2	1.5	1.4
Sweden	3.0	2.9	2.8	2.7	2.6	2.6	2.5	2.4	2.4	2.4

Switzerland	1.6	1.6	1.7	1.7	1.8	2.0	1.9	1.9	1.9	1.9	1.8
USSR	:	2.2	:	:	:	:	:	:	:	:	4.5
Yugoslavia	:	3.4	3.9	4.3	3.9	3.9	3.7	3.8	4.0	3.8	4.0
Middle East											
Bahrain	5.0	5.0	5.0	5.3	5.1	4.2	3.8	4.3	7.5	:	5.9
Cyprus	1.2	1.2	1.0	0.9	0.9	1.2	1.5	1.7	1.7	:	2.0
Egypt	4.6	5.2	4.8	6.2	6.1	5.8	6.9	6.7	6.3	:	6.5
Iran	:	:	:	3.0	3.0	3.0	2.5	2.6	3.4	:	4.3
Iraq	20.0	20.0	23.0	24.3	24.2	26.0	29.1	24.3	18.4	:	12.3
Israel	8.4	8.7	9.1	10.2	11.3	14.4	21.4	20.2	19.0	:	23.5
Jordan	10.9	10.0	15.0	15.0	14.8	13.6	13.1	13.8	13.5	:	13.7
Kuwait	:	6.5	7.3	7.0	8.6	7.9	6.8	6.8	6.0	:	4.4
Lebanon	:	:	:	:	:	:	:	12.0	4.3	:	2.4
Oman	:	15.8	17.8	17.6	23.8	21.6	23.9	24.5	22.2	:	21.0
Saudi Arabia	:	17.7	19.8	22.7	22.4	22.0	20.9	20.3	21.1	:	14.5
Syria	13.0	12.4	9.2	11.3	14.4	15.6	16.7	15.4	15.6	:	14.7
United Arab Emirates	4.7	5.3	6.7	6.7	8.7	7.6	7.0	6.8	6.5	:	6.3
Yemen Arab Republic	:	:	7.0	7.2	7.3	8.4	10.4	14.2	14.7	:	12.6
Yemen PDR	:	:	18.5	18.4	22.2	16.7	17.7	19.1	18.7	:	19.7
South Asia											
Bangladesh	:	1.6	1.6	1.6	1.5	1.3	1.4	1.6	1.5	:	1.3
India	3.3	3.4	3.5	3.9	3.7	3.3	3.2	3.1	3.1	:	3.0
Nepal	:	1.7	1.8	1.8	1.6	1.3	1.2	1.2	1.1	:	0.9
Pakistan	6.6	6.7	6.7	7.1	7.1	6.8	6.8	6.9	6.6	:	5.9
Sri Lanka	4.8	3.3	4.3	5.1	4.4	3.2	1.4	1.4	1.1	:	1.2
Far East											
Brunei	:	:	:	:	:	7.7	6.5	6.5	5.3	:	4.5
Hong Kong	:	:	0.4	0.5	0.5	0.6	0.6	0.7	0.8	:	0.9
Indonesia	1.6	2.1	2.3	2.5	3.0	3.0	3.5	3.7	4.2	:	3.7
Japan	1.0	1.0	1.0	1.0	1.0	1.0	1.0	1.0	0.9	:	0.9
Korea, North	:	:	8.7	9.5	:	:	12.0	12.3	11.8	:	11.5

	1981	1982	1983	1984	1985	1986	1987	1988	1989	1990
Korea, South	6.0	5.8	5.3	4.9	4.9	4.7	4.5	4.6	4.4	4.0
Malaysia	8.1	7.8	5.6	3.8	3.5	5.7	4.5	4.1	4.0	3.6
Mongolia	..	..	..	..	11.2	11.0	11.3	11.7	10.0	10.0
Myanmar (Burma)	4.1	3.6	3.3	3.3	3.6	3.2	3.0	3.1	3.6	3.5
Philippines	2.2	2.3	2.2	1.5	1.3	1.4	1.3	1.3	1.8	1.8
Singapore	5.1	5.1	4.5	5.5	6.5	6.3	5.8	5.5	5.1	5.0
Taiwan	6.7	7.3	6.8	6.1	6.4	5.9	6.3	6.0	6.0	6.0
Thailand	4.8	4.9	5.0	5.0	5.0	4.7	4.3	4.0	3.2	3.2
Oceania										
Australia	2.6	2.7	2.8	2.8	2.8	2.8	2.6	2.2	2.3	2.3
Fiji	1.3	1.3	1.3	1.3	1.2	1.2	2.1	2.3	2.5	..
New Zealand	2.1	2.1	2.0	1.9	1.9	2.0	2.0	2.1	2.1	2.0
Africa										
Algeria	1.8	1.9	1.9	1.8	1.7	1.7	1.7	1.5	1.5	..
Angola	13.8	11.9	16.5	22.0	28.4	28.4	..	21.5	20.0	..
Benin	1.8	1.9	2.2	2.0	2.0	1.9	2.0	2.0	..	..
Botswana	3.7	2.7	2.4	2.4	2.1	2.7	4.1	2.7	2.5	..
Burkina Faso	2.8	3.0	2.9	3.0	2.5	3.5	3.0	2.8	..	..
Burundi	3.0	3.5	3.1	3.2	3.0	3.4	2.7	2.2	..	..
Cameroon	1.1	1.7	2.2	2.1	2.2	2.1	2.1	2.1	..	..
Central African Republic	2.1	2.0	2.6	2.3	2.0	1.8	1.7	1.8	..	..
Chad	..	7.0	7.8	5.7	6.0	4.0	..	..	..	..
Congo	2.1	2.3	2.3	2.3	2.6	4.0	..	3.2	..	..
Côte d'Ivoire	1.1	1.1	1.1	1.1	1.0	1.0	1.2	1.2	..	..
Ethiopia	8.4	8.4	8.4	9.0	8.9	8.9	10.0	12.2	13.5	..
Gabon	2.4	2.4	2.6	2.3	2.6	4.0	4.3	4.5	..	..
Ghana	0.7	0.7	0.5	0.6	1.0	0.9	0.9	0.5	0.6	0.6
Kenya	3.6	3.8	3.6	2.9	2.4	2.9	3.0	2.6	2.5	2.4
Liberia	4.8	4.3	2.3	2.4	2.3	2.2	..	..	..	..
Libya	14.0	15.0	13.0	14.5	15.2	12.7	10.0	8.6	..	..
Madagascar	3.0	2.7	2.4	2.3	2.2	2.2	1.8	1.4	..	..

Malawi	3.3	2.4	1.9	1.6	1.5	1.8	1.6	1.7	1.6	1.5
Mali	2.4	2.4	2.4	2.7	2.3	:	:	3.2	:	:
Mauritania	7.6	6.9	5.7	:	:	:	:	:	:	:
Mauritius	0.4	0.3	0.3	0.2	0.2	0.2	0.2	0.2	0.3	0.2
Morocco	6.6	6.5	4.9	4.7	5.4	5.1	5.0	4.2	4.4	4.5
Mozambique	8.0	10.7	12.1	11.7	10.4					
Niger	0.7	0.6	0.7	0.7	0.7	0.8	0.8	0.8	:	:
Nigeria	2.3	1.8	1.9	1.3	1.2	1.2	0.7	0.9	0.8	0.9
Rwanda	2.0	2.0	1.9	1.6	1.6	1.9	1.8	1.7	0.9	1.7
Senegal	2.8	2.8	2.7	2.7	2.5	2.2	2.0	2.0	1.7	:
Sierra Leone	1.0	0.8	0.7	0.7	0.6	1.1	0.8	0.5	:	0.7
Somalia	4.3	3.4	3.8	2.7	1.8	1.8	1.8	3.0	0.6	:
South Africa	4.0	4.1	4.0	4.0	4.1	4.2	4.5	4.6	4.7	4.3
Sudan	2.0	1.7	2.1	3.9	2.6	2.1	2.0	2.0	:	:
Swaziland	2.2	2.9	2.6	2.3	1.8	1.7	:	:	:	:
Tanzania	4.3	4.2	3.9	3.8	3.8	4.7	4.7	5.2	6.9	:
Togo	2.4	2.3	2.2	2.3	2.6	2.5	2.6	3.2	:	:
Tunisia	2.7	5.9	6.6	4.7	5.2	5.9	5.5	5.3	4.8	3.2
Uganda	3.8	2.7	3.0	5.0	5.9	3.8	3.5	1.7	0.8	:
Zaire	1.3	1.0	1.4	1.5	3.5	2.0	3.1	2.0	3.9	1.2
Zambia	4.4	4.1	3.9	3.0	2.4	3.7	3.2	3.2	:	:
Zimbabwe	6.4	5.7	5.7	6.2	5.7	6.2	6.5	7.3	:	:
Central America										
Costa Rica	0.6	0.5	0.7	0.7	0.6	0.6	0.5	0.4	0.5	0.5
Cuba	8.8	9.1	8.8	10.1	9.6	10.2	10.7	11.3	10.0	:
Dominican Republic	1.7	1.6	1.5	1.6	1.4	1.3	1.3	1.1	0.8	0.8
El Salvador	3.7	4.4	4.4	4.6	4.4	4.9	3.8	3.7	3.5	2.9
Guatemala	1.9	1.9	2.0	2.2	2.0	1.6	1.5	1.6	1.4	1.2
Haiti	1.4	1.3	1.2	1.1	1.2	1.4	1.5	1.5	1.6	1.5
Honduras	2.3	2.8	4.0	5.2	6.4	5.9	5.5	5.6	8.4	6.9
Jamaica	1.6	1.7	1.4	1.1	1.1	0.9	0.8	:	:	:
Mexico	0.6	0.5	0.5	0.6	0.7	0.6	0.5	0.5	0.4	:

	1981	1982	1983	1984	1985	1986	1987	1988	1989	1990
Nicaragua	5.3	6.0	10.3	10.9	23.2	20.9	34.2	28.3	..	..
Panama	1.2	1.3	1.4	1.9	1.9	2.0	2.0	2.5	2.7	2.5
Trinidad and Tobago	2.3	2.9	2.9	2.6	2.6	2.7	..	..	..	..
South America										
Argentina	7.1	6.0	4.6	4.5	3.5	3.7	3.3	3.5	3.3	..
Bolivia	5.3	4.5	3.9	3.4	3.4	2.8	2.9	3.1	3.3	3.2
Brazil	1.3	1.6	1.2	1.2	1.1	1.2	1.1	1.4	1.5	1.7
Chile	7.4	9.5	8.0	9.6	7.6	8.0	6.8	7.8	6.6	5.0
Colombia	1.8	1.8	2.3	2.4	2.1	2.0	2.0	2.3	2.6	2.7
Ecuador	1.7	1.7	1.6	1.5	1.8	1.9	2.0	1.7	1.6	1.5
Guyana	6.0	5.4	4.8	4.9	8.9	5.6	3.2	2.8	2.5	1.9
Paraguay	1.5	1.6	1.4	1.2	1.1	1.1	1.1	1.0	1.3	1.0
Peru	6.0	8.5	8.1	5.6	6.4	6.6	5.0	2.5	2.1	2.1
Uruguay	3.9	4.0	3.2	2.6	2.4	2.3	2.1	2.1	2.1	2.1
Venezuela	3.1	3.4	2.9	2.4	2.0	2.1	2.1	1.9	2.2	2.0

Table 7 A.1: Military expenditure figures are given in local currency at current prices. Figures for recent years are budget estimates.

Table 7 A.2: This series is based on the data given in the local currency series, deflated to 1988 price levels and converted into dollars at 1988 period-average exchange-rates. Local consumer price indices (CPI) are taken as far as possible from *International Financial Statistics* (IFS) (International Monetary Fund: Washington, DC). For the most recent year, the CPI is an estimate based on the first 6–10 months of the year. Period-average exchange-rates are taken as far as possible from the IFS. For WTO countries, purchasing power parities (PPP) are used.

Table 7 A.3: The share of gross domestic product (GDP) is calculated in local currency. GDP data are taken as far as possible from the IFS. For some socialist economies, gross national product (GNP) or net material product (NMP) is used.

Appendix 7B. Sources and methods

I. Methods and definitions

Since the publication of the first *SIPRI Yearbook* (1968/69), SIPRI has provided annual 10-year time series data on world military expenditure. The main purpose of the data is to provide an easily identifiable measure, over time, of the scale of resources absorbed by the military in various countries. Expenditure data are only indirectly related to military strength, although the change in data over time can be utilized to measure the perception of governments towards military capability.

In recent years, the information available on world military expenditure has increased in quantitative terms while there has been a decline in the quality of information provided. Compared to the past there are now many more sources. At the same time, however, the reliability of the available data has gone down. In addition to the primary sources of national budgets and documents published by international organizations, the military expenditure project also studies over 50 specialist journals, annual reference volumes and newspapers.

In 1991 there were major specific problems with respect to the data collection, and all data should be treated as preliminary. The military expenditure costs of the Persian Gulf War, and their allocation among various countries in the region, cannot be dealt with adequately, since information is still unavailable or confusing (see chapter text for estimates). Countries in Eastern and Central Europe are in a state of rapid change which affects the information base of public finance in general and of military spending in particular. New evidence, much of which is still preliminary, makes it more difficult to construct consistent time series data over the relevant 10-year period. In addition, for these countries as well as for many others, distorted prices and high inflation rates can make budgetary data irrelevant.

The NATO definition of military expenditure is utilized as a guideline. Where possible, the following items are included: all current and capital expenditure on the armed forces, in the running of defence departments and other government agencies engaged in defence projects as well as space projects; the cost of paramilitary forces and police when judged to be trained and equipped for military operations; military R&D, tests and evaluation costs; and costs of retirement pensions of service personnel, including pensions of civilian employees. Military aid is included in the expenditure of the donor countries. Excluded are items on civil defence, interest on war debts and veterans' payments. Calendar year figures are calculated from fiscal year data where necessary, on the assumption that expenditure takes place evenly throughout the year.

SIPRI provides current price local currency data as the basic indicator of military expenditure movements. These can then be adjusted according to the user's preference and adapted to other types of economic information as required. The practice of providing all time series data in current prices has proved useful to those who require the basic data alone.

It should be stressed that even though SIPRI provides military expenditure in constant prices, it does not encourage close comparison between individual countries. Priority is given to the choice of providing a uniform definition *over time for each country* to show a correct time trend, rather than to adjusting the figures for single years according to the common definition. In addition, the recent phenomenon of violently fluctuating exchange-rates (and their lack of correlation to inflationary differentials) makes dollar figures more difficult to compare. In the absence of explicit military prices, obeying purchasing power parity, the present system must therefore be kept.[1]

II. Main sources of military expenditure data

Estimates of military expenditure are made on the basis of national sources, including budgets, White Papers and statistical documents published by the government or the central bank of the country concerned. The reference publications listed below are also used. Journals and newspapers are consulted for the most recent figures.

Annual reference publications

Europa Yearbook (Europa Publications: London)
Financial and Economic Data Relating to NATO Defence (NATO: Brussels)
Government Finance Statistics Yearbook (International Monetary Fund: Washington, DC)
Military Balance (Brassey's: Oxford)
Statistical Yearbook (United Nations: New York)
Statistical Yearbook for Asia and the Pacific (United Nations: Bangkok)
Statistik des Auslandes (Federal Statistical Office: Wiesbaden)
World Military Expenditure and Arms Trade (US Government Printing Office: Washington, DC).

Other

'Instrument for standardized international reporting of military expenditure', various countries and years (United Nations Reductions of Military Budgets Programme, UN: New York).

---

[1] For an earlier discussion of methodology, see SIPRI, *World Armaments and Disarmament: SIPRI Yearbook 1984* (Taylor & Francis: London and Philadelphia, 1984), appendix 3B, pp. 132–36.

8. The trade in major conventional weapons

IAN ANTHONY, AGNÈS COURADES ALLEBECK,
PAOLO MIGGIANO, ELISABETH SKÖNS
and HERBERT WULF

I. Major arms trade developments in 1991

The global value of foreign deliveries of major conventional weapons in 1991 is estimated by SIPRI to have been $22 114 million in 1990 US dollars.[1] This figure—roughly 25 per cent less than the value recorded for 1990—continues the downward trend in the aggregate value of the arms trade after 1987 reported in the *SIPRI Yearbook 1991*.[2] The United States accounted for 51 per cent of the total deliveries in 1991.

While the major armed conflict fought in Kuwait and Iraq was a catalyst for discussions of arms trade control, the dissolution of the Soviet Union was the most important event affecting the arms trade in 1991: the acceleration in the downward trend in the value of the arms trade reported in 1990–91 is largely associated with the severing of arms transfer relationships between the former Soviet Union and its allies and clients. Whereas SIPRI data indicate that the USSR accounted for roughly 40 per cent of the global trade in major conventional weapons for most of the 1980s, in 1991 Soviet exports represented less than 20 per cent of the total. The value of Soviet exports of major conventional weapons in 1991 was roughly 22 per cent of the value recorded for 1987. It seems probable that the decline in other forms of Soviet arms trade—in particular transfers of sub-assemblies and components within the former Warsaw Treaty Organization—has also been significant.

In 1991 three entirely new factors appeared in the discussion of the arms trade. First, the USSR—the largest single supplier of major conventional weapons for most of the 1980s—ceased to exist at the end of the year. Second, the implications of the Persian Gulf War fought between 17 January and 28 February 1991 were more fully appreciated. Third, specific steps to introduce multilateral regulations on arms exports were adopted by major arms exporting countries including all five of the permanent members of the United Nations Security Council.

While the Soviet Union had become a constructive participant in the conventional arms control process, including arms transfer control, the

---

[1] Since the SIPRI arms trade value statistics do not reflect actual purchase prices, they are not comparable with economic statistics such as national accounts or foreign trade statistics, nor with the arms sales data reported in chapter 9. The methods used for the valuation of SIPRI arms trade statistics and for the change of base year to 1990 are described in appendix 8D.

[2] Anthony, I. *et al.* 'The trade in major conventional weapons', SIPRI, *SIPRI Yearbook 1991: World Armaments and Disarmament* (Oxford University Press: Oxford, 1991), chapter 7.

Table 8.1. The leading exporters of major conventional weapons, 1987–91

The countries are ranked according to 1987–91 aggregate exports. Figures are in US $m., at constant (1990) prices. Figures may not add up to totals due to rounding.

Exporters	1987	1988	1989	1990	1991	1987–91
To the developing world						
1. USSR	13 420	10 761	10 869	6 845	3 516	45 412
2. USA	6 966	4 609	3 454	4 364	4 224	23 618
3. France	3 403	1 652	2 065	1 617	650	9 028
4. China	2 917	1 866	865	954	1 127	7 729
5. UK	2 006	1 516	1 968	1 261	847	7 599
6. Germany, FR	300	289	173	524	389	1 676
7. Brazil	666	505	287	163	0	1 622
8. Netherlands	313	467	412	83	137	1 412
9. Italy	465	594	127	128	75	1 390
10. Czechoslovakia	309	282	221	85	0	898
11. Israel	318	133	287	37	45	819
12. Spain	169	224	290	74	19	777
13. Sweden	325	259	163	5	5	758
14. Yugoslavia	3	4	0	60	661	728
15. Egypt	234	277	78	42	5	636
Others	706	613	476	475	636	2 908
Total	**32 162**	**24 054**	**21 735**	**16 720**	**12 336**	**107 007**
To the industrialized world						
1. USA	6 725	7 258	8 515	6 870	6 971	36 339
2. USSR	4 324	4 353	4 019	2 817	414	15 927
3. Germany, FR	484	1 020	607	702	1 626	4 439
4. Czechoslovakia	644	644	494	583	0	2 366
5. France	189	721	796	332	154	2 192
6. UK	164	174	693	314	153	1 498
7. Sweden	149	326	139	98	54	766
8. Italy	134	138	98	21	97	448
9. Poland	116	116	116	116	0	463
10. Canada	249	49	57	30	2	387
11. Switzerland	17	37	130	126	52	363
12. Israel	90	22	95	71	74	352
13. Spain	0	7	312	6	27	352
14. Netherlands	4	164	47	59	71	345
15. Romania	46	46	46	46	46	232
Others	372	187	329	92	35	1 015
Total	**13 708**	**15 263**	**16 492**	**12 284**	**9 778**	**67 525**
To all countries						
1. USSR	17 745	15 115	14 887	9 663	3 930	61 339
2. USA	13 691	11 867	11 969	11 234	11 195	59 957
3. France	3 232	2 374	2 861	1 950	804	11 220
4. UK	2 171	1 690	2 661	1 575	999	9 097
5. China	2 917	1 930	929	954	1 127	7 857
6. Germany, FR	784	1 309	780	1 226	2 015	6 115
7. Czechoslovakia	954	927	715	669	0	3 264
8. Italy	599	732	225	149	172	1 878
9. Netherlands	317	631	459	142	208	1 758
10. Brazil	666	507	288	165	2	1 629
11. Sweden	474	585	302	103	59	1 524
12. Israel	408	155	382	108	119	1 172
13. Spain	169	231	602	80	47	1 128
14. Yugoslavia	3	4	0	60	661	728
15. Egypt	234	277	78	42	5	636
Others	1 506	983	1 089	883	771	5 233
Total	**45 870**	**39 317**	**38 228**	**29 004**	**22 114**	**174 532**

Source: SIPRI data base.

Table 8.2. The leading importers of major conventional weapons, 1987–91

The countries are ranked according to 1987–91 aggregate imports. Figures are in US $m., at constant (1990) prices. Figures may not add up to totals due to rounding.

Importers	1987	1988	1989	1990	1991	1987–91
Developing world						
1. India	5 475	4 009	4 461	1 607	2 009	17 561
2. Saudi Arabia	2 617	2 441	1 914	2 487	1 138	10 597
3. Iraq	5 438	2 759	1 526	596	0	10 319
4. Afghanistan	901	1 275	2 615	2 419	1 220	8 430
5. Egypt	2 850	493	248	1 203	667	5 461
6. Korea, North	751	1 734	1 518	612	15	4 631
7. Israel	1 940	604	120	228	1 676	4 567
8. Angola	1 599	1 171	88	748	0	3 606
9. Korea, South	720	1 184	1 101	370	177	3 551
10. Syria	1 392	1 393	395	0	267	3 447
11. Thailand	757	529	530	439	1 115	3 370
12. Iran	823	648	371	832	187	2 862
13. Pakistan	428	331	796	380	364	2 300
14. Taiwan	536	370	368	510	390	2 174
15. United Arab Emirates	69	68	772	740	141	1 790
Others	5 866	5 044	4 912	3 550	2 971	22 606
Total	**32 162**	**24 054**	**21 735**	**16 720**	**12 336**	**107 007**
Industrialized world						
1. Japan	1 644	2 177	2 795	2 094	1 040	9 750
2. Turkey	1 203	1 419	1 138	1 067	1 559	6 384
3. Spain	1 457	1 681	912	674	231	4 955
4. Czechoslovakia	1 167	1 197	1 557	716	47	4 684
5. Greece	92	819	1 471	929	1 081	4 393
6. Poland	1 012	1 247	1 225	334	137	3 954
7. Germany, FR	351	514	1 174	1 333	136	3 509
8. USSR	835	818	656	656	46	3 013
9. Australia	565	690	832	427	442	2 955
10. Canada	846	501	330	329	258	2 263
11. German DR	440	611	610	585	0	2 247
12. Netherlands	420	258	787	282	233	1 980
13. Bulgaria	697	227	53	512	347	1 835
14. France	91	121	232	66	1 191	1 700
15. Norway	428	293	347	313	235	1 616
Others	2 462	2 691	2 373	1 965	2 795	12 286
Total	**13 708**	**15 263**	**16 492**	**12 284**	**9 778**	**67 525**
All countries						
1. India	5 475	4 009	4 461	1 607	2 009	17 561
2. Saudi Arabia	2 617	2 441	1 914	2 487	1 138	10 597
3. Iraq	5 438	2 759	1 526	596	0	10 319
4. Japan	1 644	2 177	2 795	2 094	1 040	9 750
5. Afghanistan	901	1 275	2 615	2 419	1 220	8 430
6. Turkey	1 203	1 419	1 138	1 067	1 559	6 384
7. Egypt	2 850	493	248	1 203	667	5 461
8. Spain	1 457	1 681	912	674	231	4 955
9. Czechoslovakia	1167	1 197	1 557	716	47	4 684
10. Korea, North	751	1 734	1 518	612	15	4 631
11. Israel	1 940	604	120	228	1 676	4 567
12. Greece	92	819	1 471	929	1 081	4 393
13. Poland	1 012	1 247	1 225	334	137	3 954
14. Angola	1 599	1 171	88	748	0	3 606
15. Korea, South	720	1 184	1 101	370	177	3 551
Others	17 005	15 106	15 539	12 919	11 119	71 687
Total	**45 870**	**39 317**	**38 228**	**29 004**	**22 114**	**174 532**

Source: SIPRI data base.

degree of control over arms exports from the country's large arms industry exercised by Moscow during the final stages of the collapse of the Union is in doubt. Little is known about the eventual fate of the massive inventory of equipment owned by the armed forces of the former Soviet Union or the attitudes of government and industry in the successor states towards arms exports. Recent developments are discussed in section II.

With the scale of the reduction in the value of the arms trade, those countries which are significantly increasing either their exports or imports are particularly worthy of note. The value of exports from FR Germany increased in 1990 and again in 1991, making Germany the third largest exporter of major weapons in 1991 and the largest in Europe. In part this reflected sales from the stocks of weapons of the former National Volksarmee inherited by the united Germany. More important, however, have been deliveries of warships—primarily frigates and submarines—contracted in the early 1980s.

Another country whose arms exports increased significantly in 1991 was North Korea, largely reflecting the sale of ballistic missiles to Syria.

Of the importers of major weapons several countries recorded large increases in major conventional weapons delivered in 1991, most notably France, Israel, Thailand, Turkey and India. SIPRI data do not measure the true financial flows associated with arms transfers. Three of the cases where increased arms deliveries were recorded for 1991—France, Israel and Turkey—illustrate how difficult making such a measurement would be. In 1991 France took delivery of four E-3 Sentry Airborne Warning and Control System aircraft. Under the terms of the contract with Boeing the value of the contract—$1258 million—was offset by counter-trade worth $1600 million. This specific deal therefore created a net surplus in Franco-US trade. The increase in Israeli imports was the result of the transfer of German and US arms immediately before the Gulf War, the costs of which were met entirely by German and US economic assistance. The increase in Turkish imports is accounted for, among other things, by the production of US F-16 fighter aircraft in Turkey. However, Turkey will pay $500 million of the costs of the $4 billion programme, the rest being contributed by Egypt, Kuwait, Saudi Arabia, the United Arab Emirates and the USA.[3]

Iraq's use of its imported arsenal of major conventional weapons to invade Kuwait brought the question of arms export regulation and initiatives to restrict the flow of arms to the centre of the conventional arms control debate. The work of the UN Special Commission on Iraq (UNSCOM), established by Security Council Resolution 687, revealed that Iraq had systematically tried to build nuclear, chemical and possibly biological weapons as well as ballistic missiles.[4] The impact of the 1991 Gulf War on the arms trade is discussed in section III. Initiatives to strengthen existing export control mechanisms— including the UN and the European Community (EC)—are discussed in sections V and VI.

---

[3] Enginsov, U., 'Turkey seeks more F-16s with Arab, US funds', *Defense News*, 11 Nov. 1991, p. 12.
[4] See chapter 13 in this volume.

While there is political momentum behind arms export control, economic pressures are working in the opposite direction. Reduced military expenditure and prospects of greater reductions in government spending threaten many arms-producing companies with a severe crisis. Companies whose products are no longer in demand for domestic armed forces have pushed to increase export sales and, asked about prospects for arms export limitation, the President of the US Aerospace Industries Association replied simply 'It's not going to happen'.[5]

II. The major exporters

In 1992 SIPRI decided to report official government data on the value of arms exports to make such information more accessible and to underline the lack of useful data currently published by governments. The available official arms export data are listed in table 8.3.

Countries which disclose information about arms exports remain the exception and not the rule. From a national perspective, in a majority of democracies Parliament does not exercise effective oversight over this aspect of foreign and security policy. From an analytical perspective, cross-country comparisons using official data are impossible because the definition of arms exports is not standard.

Several countries—Australia, Canada, Italy, Germany, Sweden, Switzerland and the United States—have produced country-by-country breakdowns of arms exports showing exactly which countries have received arms and military equipment. Only in this way is it possible for a domestic parliament to hold the government accountable for its export policy.[6] Of these countries, only Canada, Italy, Sweden, Switzerland and the USA produce reports annually. Canada's report omits sales to its largest customer—the USA—for which export licences are not required. In Australia and Germany information was released after a specific request from a member of Parliament (in both cases the member represented the Green Party).

Not all countries which produce export statistics explain the data fully. For Czechoslovakia, the USSR and Poland no explanation of any kind accompanied the release of arms export data. In cases where explanations are given they underline the difficulty of using the data in analysis. Some countries aggregate figures for exports of arms and dual-use equipment; others release only an arms export figure. Some countries release data on the value of items delivered; others on the value of items approved for export.

The USA

In 1991 the USA was the largest single exporter of major conventional weapons. The decline in Soviet arms exports and the delivery of US

---

[5] *Aviation Week & Space Technology*, 4 Mar. 1991, p. 19.

Table 8.3. Official arms export data

Country	Year	Value	Comments
Australia	1990–91	A$168.9 m.	Value of arms export applications approved
	1990–91	A$270.8 m.	Value of dual-use export applications approved under COCOM guidelines
Austria	1984	Sch 164 m.	Unspecified
Belgium	1980s	BF 20 b.	Approximate average value of annual arms exports for the decade of the 1980s
Canada	1990	C$158.8 m.	Value of military goods exported to all destinations except the USA
Czechoslovakia[a]	1990	Kcs 7907 m.	Unspecified
Finland	1988	FIM 34 m.	Unspecified
France	1990	FFr 38 600 m.	Value of deliveries of war *matériel* and associated services
		FFr 33 400 m.	Value of orders of war *matériel* and associated services
Germany	1990	DM 1.5 b.	Value of arms deliveries
	1990	DM 20.6 b.	Value of export applications for dual-use goods approved
Italy	1990	Lire 1 440 b.	Value of export applications approved
	1990	Lire 1 430 b.	Value of licensed goods delivered
Poland	1989	992.5 m. roubles	Unspecified
Soviet Union	1990	9.7 b. roubles	Unspecified
Sweden	1990	SEK 2 980 m.	Value of export licences for war *matériel*
	1990	SEK 3 327 m.	Value of exports of war *matériel*
Switzerland	1990	SFr 320 m.	Value of overseas deliveries of war *matériel*
United Kingdom	1990	£1 980 m.	Value of defence equipment passing through the British Customs barrier
United States	1991	$22 981 m.	Value of Foreign Military Sales accepted in Fiscal Year 1991
	1991	$39 109 m.	Value of licences approved for commercially sold defence articles and services in Fiscal Year 1991

[a] In a February 1992 newspaper interview Minister for Foreign Trade Jozef Baksey stated that arms exports from Czechoslovakia were worth $326 m. in 1990 and $186 m. in 1991. *International Herald Tribune*, 20 Feb. 1992, p. 4.

Sources: All figures taken from reports to Parliament except Canada (*First Annual Report: Export of Military Goods from Canada 1990*, Export Controls Division, External Affairs and International Trade, Mar. 1991); Italy (*Report on Intelligence and Security Policy*, Office of the Prime Minister, Doc. XLVII, no. 9, Oct. 1991). Comments in the table are worded as closely as possible to the details given in the source documents.

weapons to the Middle East partly account for US pre-eminence. However, in spite of the policy focus on the Middle East in particular, it should be remembered that the most important customers for US major weapons are not in the developing world but among US allies in Europe and Asia. Developing

[6] Ideally, a complete list of export licences should be provided stating the recipient and the item licensed as well as the value.

countries accounted for around 40 per cent of total US overseas deliveries in 1991. Middle Eastern countries accounted for 70 per cent of this 40 per cent.

The renewed emphasis on US sales to the Middle East may be temporary. The eventual scale of transfers to the countries located around the Persian Gulf is not yet clear and 1991 sales agreements with Asian countries—in particular with South Korea—may prove more important in the long term. However, at the end of 1991 the Department of Defense completed an assessment of Saudi Arabian equipment requirements. This is likely to be followed by the proposal of a major arms package to include an additional 14 batteries of Patriot surface-to-air missiles and 72 F-15 fighter aircraft.[7]

Systems for air warfare—such as the F-15 and F-16 fighter aircraft and associated weapon systems—have been major US export items since the mid-1970s. In 1991 orders for a total of more than 300 F-16 fighter aircraft were placed by Egypt, Greece, Thailand, Turkey, Portugal and South Korea.[8] Reflecting experience of the war against Iraq, many of these aircraft will be fitted with instrumentation for night fighting and with electronic warfare systems.

Air defence systems—and especially the Patriot system—were given or sold to Israel, Saudi Arabia and Turkey and, in December 1991, the US Congress stated that it would not obstruct a major programme to upgrade Saudi Arabian air defences with up to 24 batteries of Patriot missiles. Airborne early-warning and battle-management platforms—the E-3 Sentry airborne early-warning and control system aircraft—were delivered to France and the UK, while Saudi Arabia contracted for a major retro-fit to upgrade the capabilities of its E-3 fleet.

In Egypt, Saudi Arabia and Thailand the USA is currently integrating a network of ground and airborne radars into a comprehensive air defence network. As part of this programme in Egypt US companies were awarded contracts worth $146 million in 1991 to upgrade 12 batteries of Hawk surface-to-air missiles. In Saudi Arabia separate contracts worth $70 million, $350 million and $919 million were awarded to US companies, to install, among other things, a secure communications network linking air defence headquarters and to upgrade software and computers on board Saudi E-3 aircraft. Within these contracts equipment amounts to a small proportion of the programme cost with construction, installation and software services being more significant.[9]

The shrinkage of the US surface fleet from 203 ships to 167 over the next five years will require the decommission of all Charles F. Adams Class destroyers and all Knox and 16 FFG-7 Class frigates. Many of these ships are likely to be transferred to the navies of friends and allies of the USA, with Brazil and Greece among the most likely customers.[10]

---

[7] Starr, B., 'The United States and arms exports', *International Defense Review*, Defense 92 special edition, pp. 77–80.

[8] *Aviation Week & Space Technology*, 8 Apr. 1991, p. 15; *Interavia Air Letter*, 21 May 1991, p. 4; *Flight International*, 8 Oct. 1991, p. 5; *Defense News*, 1 Apr. 1991, pp. 4, 29.

[9] The Egyptian programme is described in *Aviation Week & Space Technology*, 24 June 1991, p. 62; the Saudi programme is described in *Jane's Defence Weekly*, 19 Jan. 1991, p. 69; and the Thai programme is described in *Asian Defence Journal*, Apr. 1991, pp. 91–92.

[10] *World Weapons Review*, 12 Dec. 1990, p. 2; *World Weapons Review*, 24 Apr. 1991, pp. 5–7.

In the immediate aftermath of the Gulf War, arms exports briefly became the central issue in US politics. During 1991 more than 40 new bills were proposed by congressmen.[11] Few of these were passed and even fewer became law. The most important new legislation relating to arms transfers taken into law in 1991 was PL-102-138, the Foreign Relations Authorization Act. Under the Conventional Forces in Europe Treaty Implementation Act of 1991, PL-102-228, the President is required to keep Congress informed about the progress of equipment transfers carried out as part of the implementation of the Treaty on Conventional Armed Forces in Europe (CFE—discussed in section IV). At the time of writing, legislation introduced at the request of the President to amend the Arms Export Control Act had been passed by the Senate but was awaiting consideration in the House of Representatives. A bill to extend the now expired Export Administration Act was also under discussion after President Bush vetoed the new Act as amended by the Senate. In the absence of any current law, US exports of dual-use items have been licensed under the International Emergency Economic Powers Act.[12]

The clash between politico-military goals and techno-economic considerations in arms export policy has become more apparent as the US economy has become more troubled. Military assistance is still considered a legitimate tool of foreign policy by many, and arms deals are often part of a wider security relationship. In Turkey and in the countries around the Persian Gulf some deals struck in 1991 were linked to the prepositioning of US weapons for future contingencies and access to local military facilities.

At the same time, however, the US Government has to some extent set itself up to compete with US industry. Fighter aircraft delivered to Israel and Saudi Arabia were from the US Air Force inventory. With the reductions of its armed forces, the US Government will not replace this equipment.

Faced with reduced orders from the US Department of Defense, US arms-producing companies have a greater incentive to export than they had in the 1980s, and most F-15 and F-16 fighter aircraft, M-1 Abrams tanks and the §M-2 Bradley armoured personnel carriers (APCs) produced in the future will be for export. Production of the C-130 Hercules, E-3 Sentry and P-3 maritime patrol aircraft is already for foreign customers only.

In order to maintain the defence industrial base there is pressure on the Administration to 'buy American'. At the same time, US companies are developing global supplier networks, often as a consequence of offset and counter-trade agreements with past customers. Consequently, even aircraft whose final assembly takes place in the United States are likely to have a percentage of foreign components.

While US export policy focused on the Middle East, specific decisions were taken in relation to events elsewhere. The arms embargo on Chile was lifted;

---

[11] *Legislative Summary for the 102nd Congress: Bills Relating to Arms Transfers*, Defense Budget Project, Fact Sheet, 12 Aug. 1991. The legislative proposals are also discussed in the *Arms Sales Monitor* compiled by Lora Lumpe of the Federation of American Scientists.

[12] For a discussion of the International Emergency Economic Powers Act, see Heinz, J., *US Strategic Trade: An Export Control System for the 1990s* (Westview Press: Boulder, Colo., 1991), p. 8.

US actions *vis-à-vis* Afghanistan and Yugoslavia are discussed in section V; legislation granting China most-favoured-nation trading status with the USA was amended to make such status contingent on, among other things, Chinese arms export practices; Hungary, Czechoslovakia and Poland were removed from the list of countries automatically excluded from military sales; and military aid (but not the delivery of weapons bought with hard currency) was suspended with Thailand following a coup in February 1991.

The Soviet Union

There is considerable evidence that a serious domestic debate has taken place, at least in the Russian Federation, concerning arms transfer policy. The intention to reduce the level of both arms production and arms exports has been made plain, reflecting the changed international environment and also contributing to further changes in that environment. Given the uncertainties surrounding developments in the successor states to the Soviet Union, however, it is clear that the implementation of policy will not be easy and it is quite conceivable that implementation will not be possible at all.

From January 1991 all Soviet foreign trade, including that in arms, was conducted in hard currency.[13] Deliveries of major conventional weapons to former Warsaw Treaty Organization member states and important customers in the developing world—Ethiopia, Iraq and Syria—fell dramatically after 1989. In 1991 the Soviet Union decided to eliminate arms supplies to three more important clients—Afghanistan, Angola and North Korea.

These decisions reflected US–Soviet discussions of conflicts that played a particularly important role in bilateral relations during the cold war. In 1991 agreements were reached between the Soviet Union and the USA to halt arms supplies to Afghanistan and Angola.[14] In the case of North Korea the decision was made at the request of South Korea, with which the Soviet Union established diplomatic relations at the end of 1990 and with which a $3 billion economic co-operation package has been agreed.[15] At the time of writing it is not known whether the governments of the new states emerging on the territory of the former Soviet Union intend to uphold these decisions.

India—another important customer—has experienced several years of political instability and has a growing balance-of-payments deficit. India may therefore have re-evaluated its arms import policies independently of changes in the Soviet Union. However, the economic and political chaos of the Soviet Union had an immediate impact on the Indian armed forces. Shortages of spare parts, now bought from Yugoslavia and former Soviet allies in Europe, reduced the availability of several weapon systems. A new trade protocol was agreed between India and Russia in January 1992.[16]

[13] Interview with Igor Belousov, Chairman of the Soviet State Commission for Military–Industrial Affairs, reproduced in *Defense Industry Digest*, Mar. 1991, p. 14.
[14] *The Guardian*, 14 Sep. p. 5; *International Herald Tribune*, 20 Sep. 1991, p. 2; *Jane's Defence Weekly*, 15 June 1991, p. 1001.
[15] 'Soviets cut arms flow to North Korea', *International Herald Tribune*, 31 Oct. 1991, p. 2.
[16] *The Guardian*, 21 Jan. 1992, p. 9.

Some arms transfer relationships have been maintained. Although the USA requested a total cut-off of Soviet military assistance to Nicaragua, Soviet Foreign Ministry official Valeri Nikolayenko stated that this 'small-size military–technological co-operation' would continue.[17]

The growing importance of the aerospace industry within Soviet arms exports noted in 1990 was again evident in 1991. A restrictive export policy would damage the aerospace industry since—in an effort to reduce its budget deficit—the Soviet Government reduced new equipment purchases for the Air Force for 1992.[18] The MiG-29 and Su-25 fighter aircraft will be produced only for export from 1992. Soviet aircraft were marketed vigorously at air shows in Paris and Dubai, where several new fighter aircraft versions were unveiled.[19]

Given the current economic and political circumstances in the former USSR it is not clear how effective control can be maintained over the massive inventory of weapons in stock with the armed forces. As part of its economic reform programme, Russia eliminated all custom controls with the other members of the Commonwealth of Independent States (CIS) for the three-month period January–March 1992.[20] Newly emerging states have claimed control over the arms and facilities located on their territory but at the time of writing have no legislative or administrative mechanism for export control. Given greater autonomy, factory managers have tried to prevent economic collapse both by producing non-military goods and by exporting arms.

Although official statements have indicated how export controls will be put in place by Russia, in general there is great uncertainty about the control of arms exports by the new sovereign republics. Russian Vice-President Alexander Rutskoi stated that the Russian Federation would create two bodies to execute arms export policy: a special arms export and import department to make a political evaluation of the prospective customers for arms and war *matériel*; and a directorate for monitoring the export and import of arms to be set up under the Parliamentary Committee for Conversion Affairs. The export–import department—to be called the Commission on Military and Technical Co-operation—will be located in the Ministry for Foreign Affairs but will be headed by Vice-Prime Minister Yegor Gaidar and will include Defence Minister General Pavel Grachev and also civilian advisers appointed by President Yeltsin.[21] It was subsequently announced that an inter-ministerial committee consisting of representatives from the Ministries of Foreign Affairs, Defence and Conversion would decide individual arms sales on a case-by-case basis.[22] On 2 January 1992 an all-Russian agency was established to manage the sale of Russian arms and war *matériel* to members of the new

---

[17] *International Herald Tribune*, 1 Mar. 1991, p. 2; Foreign Broadcast Information Service, *Daily Report–Soviet Union* (FBIS-SOV), FBIS-SOV-91-046, 8 Mar. 1991, p. 35.

[18] *Aviation Week & Space Technology*, 21 Oct. 1991, pp. 94–95.

[19] *International Herald Tribune*, 21 June 1991, p. 2; *Financial Times*, 21 June 1991, p. 4; *The Guardian*, 21 June 1991, p. 4; *Jane's Defence Weekly*, 16 Nov. 1991.

[20] According to Anders Åslund, economic adviser to President Yeltsin, interviewed on Swedish Radio, 2 Feb. 1992.

[21] FBIS-SOV-91-226, 22 Nov. 1991, p. 61; *The Independent*, 4 Feb. 1992, p. 8.

[22] Russian Foreign Minister Andrey Kozyrev quoted in FBIS-SOV-91-233, 4 Dec. 1991, p. 51.

Commonwealth of Independent States and elsewhere. This agency, known as the Commercial Centre and attached to the Ministry of Defence, will be permitted to keep revenues from arms sales to pay for welfare programmes for demobilized soldiers.[23]

The European Community

Sales of major conventional weapons from the EC accounted for 18 per cent of the total trade registered by SIPRI for 1987–91. France, the UK and the FRG accounted for over four-fifths of this share.

In 1991 EC arms export discussions were dominated by the search for a common arms export policy promised as part of a foreign and security policy under the European Political Union; concern about the prospects—especially employment prospects—for national arms industries; and the role that individual countries and companies played in the arming of Iraq.

In most areas of military technology West European producers offer the same types of product in a shrinking market. A rationalization of European arms production appears inevitable in the current market conditions not least because of the similarities in the patterns of European arms exports. Internationally, European companies dominate specific production segments—such as lightweight fighter aircraft, jet trainer aircraft, short-range surface-to-air missiles, light armoured vehicles, diesel-powered submarines, frigates, corvettes, fast attack craft and mine warfare systems.

European companies also derive a major share of their arms export income from the same customers. For example, Saudi Arabia and India together account for 55 per cent of British and 26 per cent of French exports of major conventional weapons. For this reason, European producers are trying to establish themselves as major suppliers in East and South-East Asia. A single EC arms export policy might increase intra-EC competition in world markets by making Germany—which has excluded itself from some markets—better able to compete. European companies face both over-production and market saturation.

France remains a major arms exporter despite a dramatic decline in the value of French arms sales. In 1991 the value of deliveries of French major conventional weapons was estimated to be $804 million—25 per cent of the value recorded in 1987 (see table 8.1). Defence Minister Pierre Joxe reminded the Parliament that the arms industry is of major economic importance in France, being second only to the aerospace industry in the size of its foreign trade surplus. Moreover, military products account for 52 per cent of all French aerospace sales and 44 per cent of aerospace exports.[24]

---

[23] *RFE/RL Research Report* (Radio Free Europe/Radio Liberty), 17 Jan. 1992, p. 53.

[24] *Avis présenté au nom de la commission de la défense nationale et des forces armées sur le projet de loi de finances pour 1991 par M. Jean-Guy Branger*, Tome VI, Défense, recherche et industrie d'armement, Assemblée Nationale, no 2258, 9 Oct. 1991, p. 18; *Air et Cosmos*, 11 Mar. 1991, p. 13.

The decline in the value of arms exports is largely related to the lack of success of current-generation French aircraft in the export market relative to earlier generations. Whereas the Mirage III and V series and the Mirage F-1 were major export items in the 1970s and early 1980s, the Mirage 2000 has lost a series of competitions to the US F-16 fighter.

Public opinion—normally mute concerning arms export policy—expressed discontent over the French contribution to Iraq's military capability, particularly when French weapons were used against French troops. Parliament proposed the creation of a consultative committee to advise the Prime Minister on arms export requests exceeding 20 million francs prior to licence approval. Parliament also sought a commission of enquiry into arms export policy. Neither proposal was adopted.[25]

British exports of major conventional weapons amounted to $999 million in 1991. Saudi Arabia confirmed several orders anticipated under the 1988 Memorandum of Understanding that were considered to be in jeopardy prior to the Gulf War. The Royal Saudi Air Force became the first foreign customer for the ALARM (air-launched anti-radiation missile) system.[26] In addition, Saudi Arabia signed a series of contracts with Racal Electronics for electronic counter-measures and tactical communications systems.[27] These sales suggest that the growing importance of electronic warfare was one lesson derived from the war against Iraq.[28]

The Hawk series of jet trainer aircraft has emerged as a major export item in the 1980s. In 1991 South Korea, Malaysia and Brunei confirmed anticipated orders and Indonesia signed a licensed-production agreement. This will make Indonesia a maintenance and repair hub for Asian operators of the Hawk.[29]

German exports of major conventional weapons in 1991 were valued at $2.0 billion. FR Germany inherited stocks of military equipment maintained by the former German Democratic Republic upon unification including over 2000 tanks, almost 6000 APCs, 700 aircraft, over 2000 artillery pieces and 59 warships.[30] While some obsolete equipment is being destroyed, Germany has retained other equipment—for example, MiG-29 fighter aircraft and some naval vessels—for its armed forces. The Government has sought export markets for surplus weapons. In 1991 equipment and ammunition was sold to Belgium, Denmark, Egypt, Finland, France, Hungary, Israel, the Netherlands,

---

[25] See *Avis présenté au nom de la commission de la défense nationale et des forces armées sur le projet de loi de finances pour 1991 par M. Jean-Guy Branger* (note 24), pp. 57–58. The Minister provided the Parliamentary Commission for National Defense and the Armed Forces with an unprecedented 55-page report documenting French arms exports. The document was not made available to the public and the Ministry of Defence did not commit itself to make such information available to Parliament on a regular basis.

[26] *Aviation Week & Space Technology*, 12 Aug. 1991, p. 42; *Interavia Air Lettter*, 14 Aug. 1991, p. 5.

[27] *Defense Electronics*, Feb. 1991, p. 18.

[28] Shearer, O. V. and Daskal, S. E., 'The desert electronic warfare storm', *Military Technology*, Sep. 1991, pp. 21–27; Klass, P. J., 'Gulf War highlights benefits, future needs of EW systems', *Aviation Week & Space Technology*, 21 Oct. 1991, pp. 34–37.

[29] *Air & Cosmos*, 26 Aug.–8 Sep. 1991, p. 13; *Asian Defence Journal*, Jan. 1991, pp. 67–68; *Milavnews*, Jan. 1991, p. 17; *Financial Times*, 21 June 1991, p. 3; *Milavnews*, July 1991, p. 16.

[30] *Wehrtechnik*, Oct. 1991, pp. 20–23.

Norway, Poland, Spain, Sweden, Turkey, the UK, the USA and Uruguay.[31] In most cases the volume of equipment delivered was small and intended for the purpose of technology evaluation. The value of exports recorded for Germany in 1991 largely reflects deliveries of major warships including submarines to India and Norway, frigates to Argentina and Portugal and corvettes to Poland, Singapore and the United States. Details of these deliveries are contained in appendix 8C, the register of trade in and licensed production of major conventional weapons.

At the end of 1991 it was revealed that the military intelligence service of the FRG had, in the context of a wider co-operative agreement with Israeli intelligence, made 14 shipments to Israel between October 1990 and October 1991, including 82 different types of arms and equipment of Soviet origin. The 15th shipment, declared as agricultural equipment, was intercepted by customs officers.[32] The legitimacy of these transfers and others by the military intelligence services is under investigation in Germany.

III. The impact of the 1991 Persian Gulf War

While it is too soon to predict the long-term impact of the Persian Gulf War, it had not led to a massive increase in the delivery of arms to the region by the end of 1991. In fact, the value of major weapons delivered to the Middle East declined by more than 30 per cent in 1991.

In the period between 2 August 1990 and the start of the allied air offensive against Iraq on 17 January 1991 some arms transfers took place. Most widely publicized was the upgrading of air defences in Israel and Saudi Arabia through the rapid deployment of Patriot surface-to-air missile batteries. These systems were initially operated by US personnel, underlining that in the emergency conditions prevailing before the defeat of Iraq it is difficult to disentangle arms transfers from the massive deployment of US and allied forces to the region.

Deliveries of major conventional weapons to Middle Eastern countries in 1991 are noted in the registers in appendix 8C, while table 8.4 summarizes new agreements identified with Middle Eastern countries in 1991.

In addition to these deals, in which major items of equipment are relatively easily identifiable, there have also been significant agreements to provide military construction and services. For example, US companies will reconstruct two air bases at Ahmed Al Jabar and Ali Al Salem in Kuwait in a deal valued at $350 million. US contracts to develop the air defences of Egypt and Saudi Arabia are discussed above.

[31]*Defense News* 15 Apr. 1991, p. 5; *Defense News*, 27 May 1991, pp. 1, 36; *Military Technology*, Apr. 1991, p. 92; *Interavia Air Letter*, 15 Aug. 1991, p. 5; *Frankfurter Rundschau*, 13 Aug. 1991, p. 2; *Milavnews*, Oct. 1991, p. 360; *International Herald Tribune*, 4–5 Jan. 1992, p. 2; *Dagens Nyheter*, 28 Jan. 1992, p. 7; *Süddeutsche Zeitung*, 13 Dec. 1991, p. 2; *Der Tagesspiegel*, 17 Jan. 1992, p. 4; *Welt am Sonntag*, 19 Jan. 1992.

[32] Schwarz, B., 'BND. Alles sehen, alles hören, nichts wissen', *Die Zeit*, 22 Nov 1991, pp. 15–18; *Frankfurter Allgemeine Zeitung*, 3 Dec. 1991.

Table 8.4. Conventional weapons ordered by Middle Eastern countries in 1991

Buyer	Seller	Designation	Number ordered	Description	Number delivered
Bahrain	USA	AH-64 Apache	8	Helicopter	–
Egypt	Czechoslovakia	L-59	48	Jet trainer	–
	USA	F-16C	46	Fighter	–
		AGM-65D	40	Air-to-surface missile	–
		AGM-65G	40	Air-to-surface missile	–
Iran	Czechoslovakia	T-55	300	Main battle tank	–
Israel	FR Germany	BRDM-2	50	Scout car	50
		Tpz-1	8	APC	8
		Dolphin	2	Submarine	–
	Netherlands	Patriot battery	1	SAM system	1
		MIM-104 Patriot	32	Surface-to-air missile	32
	USA	F-15A Eagle	10	Fighter	–
		AIM-9M	300	Air-to-air missile	–
		Patriot battery	1	SAM system	–
		MIM-104 Patriot	64	Surface-to-air missile	–
Oman	USA	M-60-A3	–	Main battle tank	27
		V-300 Commando	119	APC	–
Qatar	South Africa	G-5 155 mm	12	Towed howitzer	12
Saudi Arabia	USA	AIM-7M Sparrow	770	Air-to-air missile	–
		M-113-A2	207	APC	–
		M-548	50	APC	–
		M-578	43	Recovery vehicle	–
		Patriot Battery	14	SAM system	–
		MIM-104 PAC-2	758	Surface-to-air missile	–
		HMMWV	2 300	Light vehicle	–
Syria	Czechoslovakia	T-72	300	Main battle tank	–
	North Korea	Scud-C launcher	–	SSM launcher	20
		Scud-C	–	SSM	100
United Arab Emirates	USA	AH-64 Apache	20	Helicopter	–
		AGM-114A	620	Air-to-surface missile	–

Note: New agreements in 1991 with Turkey, excluded from the SIPRI definition of the Middle East, are described in appendix 8C.

Source: SIPRI arms trade data base; *Arms Sales Monitor* (various issues) prepared by Lora Lumpe for the Federation of American Scientists.

The massive US–Saudi arms package anticipated before the defeat of Iraq has not yet come about, in part because of anticipated opposition in the US Congress and in part because arms transfers have been a subordinate element of regional security developments in 1991.

Whether or not there will be a major increase in arms flow into the Middle East in the near term depends on four factors: (*a*) the development of the regional security system; (*b*) the nature of commitments to regional countries from extra-regional powers, in particular the United States; (*c*) the outcome of the regional peace process initiated in 1991 in Madrid; and (*d*) the outcome of discussions about arms transfer control among major suppliers. After the end of the cold war these discussions, described in section V, have a better chance of success than earlier attempts to control the arms trade by formal agreement. However, efforts to achieve such agreements after Middle Eastern wars in the 1970s and 1980s failed for reasons not solely connected with cold war antagonisms.

Before the surrender of Iraq on 26 February 1991 Middle Eastern countries discussed a collective security organization aimed at the containment of Iraq. While non-Arab Muslim countries such as Iran, Pakistan and Turkey were mentioned in this context, most discussions focused on the creation of a collective Arab security organization.

In February 1991 foreign ministers of the six Gulf Co-operation Council (GCC) countries, Egypt and Syria met to consider creating an Arab Peace Force including up to 50 000 Egyptian and Syrian troops to be stationed in Saudi Arabia.[33] However, by the end of 1991 the Arab Peace Force existed only on paper. Saudi Arabia was reluctant to permit a permanent foreign troop presence and, with Iraq defeated and subject to continued UN sanctions, the incentives to do so were reduced. On 8 May Egypt announced that its forces would be withdrawn from Saudi Arabia, and Syria did the same shortly afterwards.[34] After the meeting of Foreign Ministers in Kuwait on 16 July 1991, the idea of joint standing forces or command structures for an Arab Peace Force was shelved and it was agreed that military co-operation between the signatories of the 1991 Damascus Declaration would be on an *ad hoc* basis.

Ground forces from the countries which formed the coalition against Iraq will not be based permanently in Saudi Arabia. Future arrangements for air and naval forces from coalition countries remain under discussion. The UK rejected the permanent stationing of British forces in the Persian Gulf area in February 1991. The USA discussed the permanent stationing of a brigade of troops (3000–5000 men) in Saudi Arabia and the pre-positioning of sufficient equipment to allow the rapid entry of a division of troops. Pre-positioning of equipment was still under discussion at the end of the year, but a permanent troop presence appeared to have been ruled out by Saudi Arabia.[35]

From the perspective of the arms trade the importance of the Middle East peace process derives from the possibility that it would include regional arms control. Non-regional governments suggested that arms control should be an important element of the peace process, and the idea was not rejected out of hand by countries in the region. The Egyptian Government put forward a proposal on arms limitation and disarmament in the Middle East which, like

[33] *The Independent*, 15 Feb. 1991; *The Independent*, 6 Mar. 1991; *International Herald Tribune*, 7 Mar. 1991; *International Herald Tribune*, 10 Apr. 1991. An overview of regional security developments in 1991 is contained in Hollis, R., 'Security in the Gulf: no panaceas', *Military Technology*, Oct. 1991. (The Co-operation Council for the Arab States of the Gulf (GCC) was established in 1981 by Bahrain, Kuwait, Oman, Qatar, Saudi Arabia and the United Arab Emirates.)
[34] *Jane's Defence Weekly*, 6 July 1991, p. 14.
[35] *International Herald Tribune*, 26 Mar. 1991; *International Herald Tribune*, 10 May 1991; *International Herald Tribune*, 26–27 Nov. 1991.

most others, focused on the need to address the proliferation of weapons of mass destruction rather than conventional armaments. However, the proposal did call on Middle Eastern states 'to declare their commitment actively and fairly to address measures relating to all forms of delivery systems for weapons of mass destruction'.[36]

The balance of probability is that most regional governments will continue to regard the preparedness of their own armed forces as the most important component of national security policy and that this will lead to new orders for military equipment from foreign suppliers.

Dual-use equipment transfers to Iraq

While the problem of regulating arms transfers was taken up in multilateral discussions in 1991, the problem of defining international regulations for sales of industrial goods with possible military applications to potentially sensitive destinations was not (other than through revisions to COCOM—the Co-ordinating Committee on Multilateral Export Controls—embargo discussed below). While this problem is not confined to Iraq, information published by the Special Commission established by the United Nations under Resolution 687 drew attention to the role of foreign suppliers in developing Iraqi military capabilities.[37]

The USA took some unilateral measures to punish companies and individuals believed to have been supporting Iraqi programmes, and on 1 April 1991 the Office of Foreign Assets Control (OFAC) within the US Department of the Treasury published a list of 'front companies and agents of Iraq'. Of the 100 organizations and agents listed, British companies and residents formed the largest single contingent.[38] US companies are prohibited from trading with companies or individuals on the OFAC's list. The OFAC places the burden of proof on the listed companies and individuals, removing them from the list only if they can prove that their contacts with Iraq were purely non-military in nature.

The list of companies that provided support to Iraq made by the UN Special Commission was not made public, but information was passed to the governments of their countries of origin. The precise role played by these contributors and the degree to which their activities were approved by supplier governments remained unclear.

Before UN Security Council Resolution 661 no country operated a total trade embargo against Iraq. While the USA and most West European countries operated an arms embargo against Iraq during the Iraq–Iran War, interpretations of which goods were subject to embargo differed from country to country. No European country embargoed industrial goods with potential military applications. This observation was made by officials at the British

---

[36] Letter dated 7 Aug. 1991 from the Egyptian Government to the Secretary-General of the United Nations, Conference on Disarmament document CD/1098, 12 Aug. 1991.

[37] See chapter 13 in this volume.

[38] *The Independent*, 28 Mar. 1991; *The Independent*, 2 Apr. 1991, p. 1.

Department of Trade and Industry (DTI) who added that the DTI had no plans to widen its definition of arms and military equipment.[39] With hindsight even the more restrictive US export control list has been criticized as too permissive. In November 1984 renewal of diplomatic relations between the USA and Iraq (suspended since 1967) provided 'a strong impetus to the US business community to explore expanded trade relations with Iraq'.[40] However, a review of export licence applications for sales to Iraq made by the Department of Commerce between 1985 and August 1990 showed that of the approvals were in accordance with regulations then in force.

Authorities in the United Kingdom and Germany continued to grant licences for exports of dual-use goods until 1990. The final licence application granted for the export of listed goods to Iraq from the UK was approved on 5 August 1990, three days after the Iraqi invasion of Kuwait.[41] In Germany, according to the Ministry of Economics, Trade and Industry, export licences worth DM 136 million were granted for Iraq in 1989 and DM 30 million in 1990 under the Foreign Trade Act (Außenwirtschaftsgesetz or AWG).[42] In the British case items licensed included armoured vehicles, spare parts and combat support equipment, and the Government was criticized for continuing to grant licences after the disclosure that British components sold to Iraq were being used in the manufacture of a 1000-mm calibre 'supergun'.

The publication of information relating to British sales to Iraq raised questions in Parliament and in Ministries other than the DTI about export licensing procedures. Members of Parliament regretted the lack of detail given about the circumstances in which specific items—many of which could be for civil use—were approved for export. Foreign Office representatives expressed surprise that some items were given clearance without inter-agency review.[43]

At the beginning of 1991 German Chancellor Helmut Kohl declared that no weapons had been legally exported to Iraq. Several German companies charged in court for illegal exports of equipment used in the Iraqi nuclear, chemical weapon and ballistic missile programmes were acquitted since they had obtained government export licences. Official clearance had been given to German companies to deliver such technology to Iraq between 1982 and 1990.[44]

---

[39] *The Independent*, 3 Apr. 1991.

[40] US export control practice *vis-à-vis* Iraq in the 1980s is described in the Statement of Dennis Kloske, then Under Secretary of Commerce for Export Administration, before the Subcommittee on International Economic Policy and Trade, Committee on Foreign Affairs, House of Representatives, 8 Apr. 1991.

[41] *Financial Times*, 30 July 1991, p. 6; *The Independent*, 27 July 1991, p. 1; *The Guardian*, 7 July 1991, p. 6. A list of all products licenced for export to Iraq from 1 Jan. 1987 to 5 Aug. 1990 is contained in Annexe E of *Exports To Iraq*, Memoranda of Evidence for the Trade and Industry Committee, House of Commons (Her Majesty's Stationery Office: London, 17 July 1991).

[42] Bundesministerium für Wirtschaft, 'Erläuterungen zur statistischen Übersicht über die erteilten Ausfuhrgenehmigung', document no. BMWi V B 4-06 31 02, mimeograph. See also Anthony, I. (ed.), SIPRI, *Arms Export Regulations* (Oxford University Press: Oxford, 1991).

[43] *The Independent*, 7 July 1991, p. 1; *Financial Times*, 2 Aug. 1991, p. 7; *The Guardian*, 4 Aug. 1991, p. 3.

[44] *Der Spiegel*, no. 15, 1991, pp. 28-29; *Financial Times*, 25 Mar. 1991, pp. 1, 20; *Milavnews*, Apr. 1991, p. 354.

As a direct result of these developments German export regulations were amended to strengthen the mechanisms for government oversight of company activity. In November 1991 amendments to the Foreign Trade Act were rejected in the Bundesrat because measures such as telephone tapping by the Customs authorities were considered unacceptable.[45] Revised amendments to the law were accepted in March 1992.

In Italy, in February 1991, the Italian Senate completed its preliminary investigation into the BNL (Banca Nazionale del Lavoro), which had financed Iraqi purchases of military-related equipment. Loans of nearly $3 billion were made by the branch of BNL at Atlanta in the USA, and a list of 240 letters of credit revealed that US and European companies had been supplying technology and equipment for Iraqi weapon programmes. Most of the equipment was for conventional weapons, including ballistic missiles, but some was for nuclear and chemical projects.[46]

IV. The CFE Treaty and its effects on the arms trade

The Treaty on Conventional Armed Forces in Europe (CFE) signed in November 1990 did not enter into force in 1991,[47] but it will have an important impact on the arms trade in that arms exports have become an integral part of its implementation. According to data submitted by mid-1991, the Treaty will require the elimination of about 36 000 pieces of military equipment—about 6100 on the NATO side and 29 900 on the former WTO side[48]—during a three and one-half year period after the Treaty enters into force. The CFE Treaty specifies eight methods of equipment reduction: destruction, conversion to non-military purposes, placement on static display, use for ground instruction purposes, recategorization, use as ground targets, reclassification and modification.[49] Although not stated in the Treaty, the implication is that after ratification it will not be permissable to export surplus quantities of treaty-limited equipment (TLE) as a means of reduction.[50]

[45] Hoffmann, W., 'Quittung für Bombengeschäfte', *Die Zeit*, 22 Nov. 1991, p. 24.

[46] *Mednews*, 18 Feb. 1991, p. 1; *Financial Times*, 14 Oct. 1991, p. 24.

[47] See chapter 12 in this volume.

[48] Forsberg, R. and Lilly-Weber, S., 'CFE and beyond: the need for a global approach to stabilizing reductions and restructuring of conventional armed forces', Paper prepared for the 11th Workshop of the Pugwash Study Group on Conventional Forces, Paris, 11-12 Oct. 1991, tables 1.1 and 2.1.

[49] For more information on these methods, see Koulik, S. and Kokoski, R. (eds), SIPRI, *Verification of the CFE Treaty*, SIPRI Research Report, Stockholm, Oct. 1991, pp. 12–16. As noted in the *SIPRI Yearbook 1991*, the Treaty will not affect exports of newly produced equipment; see Anthony, *et al.*, 'The trade in major conventional weapons', SIPRI, *SIPRI Yearbook 1991: World Armaments and Disarmament* (Oxford University Press: Oxford, 1991), p. 205.

[50] Schäfer, H., 'Conventional arms control and weapons transfer', *Jane's NATO Handbook 1991–92* (Jane's Defence Data: Coulsdon, Surrey, 1991), pp. 130–31. Helmut Schäfer is a Minister of State in the German Foreign Office.

Table 8.5. Planned CFE-related arms transfers within NATO

Recipient	Quantity	Category	Weapon type	Donor(s)
Denmark	140	Tanks	Leopard-1	FR Germany
	12	Artillery	M-110	USA
Greece	75	Tanks	Leopard-1	FR Germany
	170	Tanks	Leopard-1	Netherlands
	359	Tanks	M-60-A1	USA
	312	Tanks	M-60-A3	USA
	200	ACV	M-113	FR Germany
	150	ACV	M-113	USA
	150	Artillery	LARS	FR Germany
	72	Artillery	M-110	USA
	100	Artillery	M-30	USA
Norway	92	Tanks	Leopard-1	FR Germany
	136	ACV	M-113	USA
Portugal	80	Tanks	M-60-A3	USA
	104	ACV	M-113	Netherlands
	24	ACV	YP-408	Netherlands
Spain	160	Tanks	M-60-A1	USA
	260	Tanks	M-60-A3	USA
	100	ACV	M-113	USA
	83	Artillery	M-110	USA
Turkey	100	Tanks	Leopard-1	FR Germany
	164	Tanks	M-60-A1	USA
	658	Tanks	M-60-A3	USA
	550	ACV	M-113	FR Germany
	100	ACV	M-113	Italy
	250	ACV	M-113	USA
	131	Artillery	LARS	FR Germany
	72	Artillery	M-110	USA
USA	70	Tanks	..	FR Germany
	47	Tanks	..	FR Germany
	20	Artillery	..	FR Germany

Note: Quantities are approximate.

Sources: Jane's Defence Weekly, 6 July 1991, p. 18; Hoofdstuk defensie: explanatory Memorandum to the Netherlands Defense Budget 1992, p. 4; *Wehrtechnik*, 1 Dec. 1991, p. 63; information supplied by German Ministry of Foreign Affairs, Bonn, 25 Mar. 1992; information supplied by International Security Policy/NATO Policy, Office of the Assistant Secretary of Defense, Washington, DC, 10 Mar. 1992.

To avoid destroying modern treaty-limited equipment,[51] NATO has planned an Equipment Transfer and Equipment Rationalization Programme—the cascade—between member countries. Recipient countries import TLE more modern than that currently deploy and thereby take on the reduction commitments of donor countries. The major donor countries will be the USA,

[51] TLE include tanks, armoured combat vehicles (ACVs), heavy artillery, combat aircraft and attack helicopters.

Table 8.6. Planned CFE-related arms exports from non-NATO countries

Exporter	Tanks	ACV	Artillery	Aircraft
Bulgaria	446	..	594	156
Czechoslovakia	1 578	1 965	1 898	98
Hungary	..	..	47	..
Poland	..	..	..	53

Source: Vienna Fax, 28 May 1991, p. 2.

Germany, Italy and the Netherlands and the main recipients will be Greece, Spain, Turkey and, to a lesser extent, Denmark, Norway and Portugal. By late 1991 planned CFE-related transfers included over 2600 tanks, 1600 ACVs and 600 artillery pieces (table 8.5). Aircraft and helicopters are not included in the cascade since limits in the CFE Treaty require only minor changes in helicopter holdings and none in aircraft.

For Germany and the USA the aggregate number of ground-force TLE exceeds their respective elimination quotas. Exports will therefore substitute for destruction of military equipment under the Treaty for these countries.[52]

This is thus a major arms transfer programme including almost 5000 pieces of ground-force equipment to be delivered over a relatively short period. The effect will be to speed up the modernization of weapon systems in NATO,[53] and there is a risk that rapid arms modernization in some southern NATO countries might have de-stabilizing effects by changing the balance of forces in the Balkans and the Middle East.

The transportation costs and the costs of repairs to a minimum operational standard will not be paid by the individual countries participating in the cascade programme, but will be financed collectively through the NATO insfrastructure fund. The total costs of the cascade programme have been estimated at around $100 m.[54]

Some former WTO countries announced plans to export TLE outside the European region, but facts are scarce about these transfers. Czechoslovakia has been reported to have plans to export more than 5000 weapons—75 per cent of those that would otherwise have to be destroyed under the Treaty (table 8.6). What is known about policy in Czechoslovakia and Poland suggests that these countries intend to use arms exports as a mechanism to subsidize the restructuring of the arms industry. This is likely to mean that arms production and foreign sales will continue but at a lower level than previously.[55]

[52] Forsberg and Lilly-Weber (note 48).
[53] The advantages to NATO of this approach have been listed by a member of NATO's International Staff; see Lightburn, D. T., 'Enhancing security: arms transfers under CFE ceilings', *NATO's Sixteen Nations,* May/June 1991, p. 60.
[54] Lightburn (note 53); *Jane's Defence Weekly,* 6 July 1991.
[55] Roche, D. C. and Davidson, R., 'Economic significance of Soviet and US defence reductions', in Morgan Stanley International, *Eurostrategy,* no. 13 (11 Oct. 1991), pp. 47–57; Urbanowicz, J., 'Unwanted weapons', *Warsaw Voice,* 8 Dec. 1991, pp. B4–5.

Czechoslovakia, Hungary, Poland and, to a lesser extent, Bulgaria and Romania have examined the reconstruction of arms transfer relationships lost with the dissolution of the Warsaw Treaty Organization.[56] However, the overall intention of all of these countries appears to be to integrate as fully as possible and as quickly as possible into the wider arms market—both as importers and exporters—with industrial joint ventures with West European or North American companies being particularly sought after.

V. Arms transfer control initiatives

At the Third United Nations Special Session on Disarmament in 1988 an initiative was launched to create an arms trade register to be maintained by the United Nations. While this initiative came to fruition in 1991 (see section VI) there is still no multilateral arms trade control process.

The situation was accurately summed up by the Australian Minister for Foreign Affairs and Trade, who said:

It has to be acknowledged that the international community has yet to come to grips with the problem posed by the huge volumes of conventional arms transfers. While agreements are in place or under negotiation to control or eliminate weapons of mass destruction, there is as yet no remotely comparable process for conventional weapons. We need to acknowledge openly the difficulties which stand in the way of conventional arms control: compared with weapons of mass destruction, they are relatively readily available; trade is well established and lucrative; and considerations of national sovereignty, and the legitimate responsibility of any government to ensure national security, mean that countries are reluctant to forgo the right to acquire conventional arms.[57]

A proposal for a multilateral initiative encompassing the arms trade was made on 8 February 1991 by the Canadian Government in simultaneous speeches delivered by Prime Minister Brian Mulroney in Ottawa and Foreign Minister Joe Clark in Quebec.[58]

Preventing the emergence of 'another Iraq' has been the primary objective of arms transfer control initiatives in 1991. However, the difficulty inherent in the process is underlined if it is recalled that Iraq's military capacity was built up during the 1980s largely by the Soviet Union, France and China and in pursuit of what were considered to be valid policy goals. Governments in almost all arms-producing countries consider arms transfers to be legitimate and useful instruments of foreign policy and continue to believe that arms transfers can help create a stable balance of power or deter acts of aggression.

[56] Reisch, A. A., 'New bilateral military agreements', *Report on Eastern Europe*, 8 Nov. 1991, pp. 4–10.

[57] 'Seize the moment', Speech of Senator Gareth Evans to the UN Conference on Disarmament Issues, Kyoto Japan, 27 May 1991. At the same conference former Japanese Prime Minister Toshiki Kaifu made a similar appeal in his address.

[58] The speeches, together with the proposal for a World Summit on the Instruments of War and Weapons of Mass Destruction, are contained in a *Backgrounder* published by the Canadian Department of External Affairs on 8 Feb. 1991.

This belief has not been fundamentally shaken by Iraq's actions. Speaking before the ground war against Iraq began, British Foreign Secretary Douglas Hurd stated:

Countries which are anxious, feel surrounded or threatened are going to exercise their right of self-defence by buying arms—that is for sure. I think one has therefore to try and reduce that anxiety and that sense of alarm. At the same time, we have to concentrate, I think, not on the conventional arms—that is a separate problem—but concentrate on these three, the nuclear, the biological and the chemical, which are causing particular alarm and scare throughout the world. . . . I think we shall all have to look again at the criteria for export of arms but I think the concentration should be on the three that I mentioned—the nuclear, the chemical, biological; there, I think the will to deal with the problem is probably at its strongest.[59]

The approach of coupling regional arms control efforts with efforts to reduce anxiety and the sense of alarm also formed the central strand of United States arms transfer policy to the Middle East.

At the end of May 1991 President Bush unveiled the contents of a Middle Eastern arms control initiative. The President suggested that the five major suppliers of arms—also the five permanent members of the United Nations Security Council—should shoulder a particular responsibility in this regard by committing themselves:

to observe a general code of responsible arms transfers;
to avoid destabilizing transfers; and
to establish effective domestic export controls on the end-use of arms or other items to be transferred . . .
[to] notify one another in advance of certain arms sales;
[to] meet regularly to consult on arms transfers;
[to] consult on an ad hoc basis if a supplier believed guidelines were not being observed; and
[to] provide one another with an annual report on transfers.[60]

This set an agenda for meetings of the five permanent members of the United Nations Security Council in Paris on 8–9 July and in London on 17–18 October 1991.

---

[59] Interview with the British Foreign Secretary, Douglas Hurd, on the BBC Radio 4 programme 'The World this Weekend', 3 Feb. 1991.
[60] *Middle East Arms Control Initiative,* fact sheet issued by The White House, 29 May 1991.

The role of the permanent members of the UN Security Council

The United Nations has been keen to 'promote by all appropriate means a reduction of arms trading'[61] and the major arms exporting countries have chosen to use the UN as a forum for discussion.

At the July meeting of the Security Council France, the United States and the United Kingdom each brought a proposal suggesting how the issue of arms export control could best be approached. The Soviet Union and China seem to have played a more reactive role in the discussions.

The proposals laid out at the meeting by President François Mitterrand, Prime Minister John Major and President George Bush were similar in that each stressed the primary importance of placing effective controls on weapons of mass destruction in enhancing international security, and each recognized the special sensitivity of the Middle East as a potential source of armed conflict. These areas of agreement were reflected in the final communiqué of the July meeting.[62] However, there were differences of approach in dealing with the question of arms export controls.

President Bush presented a supply-side approach in keeping with his 29 May proposal, reflecting US interest in establishing a mechanism for oversight and influence where the export policy and practices of China and the Soviet Union are concerned. It seems probable that proposals for advance notifications of arms export agreements and *ad hoc* consultations on specific prospective agreements were aimed particularly at these countries.

President Mitterrand, by contrast, adopted a demand-side approach, noting that 'with regard to so-called conventional armaments, the goal should be to safeguard or institute a balance of power in each region, and then to bring it down to the lowest level consistent with the right of all states to security.'[63]

Prime Minister Major did not discuss arms export control in any detail, but outlined the proposed United Nations register of arms transfers (a representative of the United Kingdom was chairman of the UN expert group established to design the register during the completion of its work). The register is discussed in more detail in section VI. In his remarks Prime Minister Major argued against a mandatory register and against any veto right for recipient countries in the recording of any given transaction. He argued against expanding the categories of items to be registered—at least in the early years of a register—and also against recording the value of arms transferred.

The communiqué of the July meeting reached general conclusions about arms transfers—the issue was relegated to the end of the document— reflecting the difficulty of reaching substantive agreements in this area. Consequently, the five heads of government agreed that follow-on meetings should continue to work on the question of arms export regulation and that a second plenary meeting would take place in London in October 1991.

---

[61] Speech of Secretary-General Perez de Cuéllar before the European Parliament, *Debates of the European Parliament*, no. 3–44/100, 16 Apr. 1991.
[62] The communiqué is reproduced in appendix 8A.
[63] President F. Mitterrand, 'Plan de maitrise des armements et de desarmement', 3 June 1991, Présidence de la République, Paris (unofficial translation).

At their October meeting the five members produced 'Guidelines for Conventional Arms Transfers' containing more specific undertakings.[64] However, the interpretation of these general undertakings was left to the discretion of the individual exporter. The five permanent members agreed to further consultations early in 1992 in the United States to discuss whether a means of advance notification of arms agreements could be agreed upon. If so, this would allow an informal 'complaints procedure' through which countries could make bilateral representations concerning those potential arms agreements which do not meet the stated criteria.

The London Economic Summit 1991

At the meeting of the heads of government and heads of state of the Group of Seven, the 'G7' in London in July 1991 the issue of arms transfers was also discussed. The G7 is an informal grouping consisting of Canada, France, Germany, Italy, Japan, the United States and the United Kingdom. Since 1977 the President of the Commission of the European Communities has also been present at the meeting as an observer. At the end of the meeting the countries represented released a Declaration on Conventional Arms Transfers and NBC Non-Proliferation on 16 July 1991.[65]

The G7 provided an opportunity to expand the group of countries engaged in the discussion of conventional arms transfer control. The declaration largely repeated the general findings contained in the Paris meeting of the five permanent members of the UN Security Council released only a week before the London Economic Summit. However, two countries not represented in Paris—Japan and Germany—introduced a new element into the discussion which was reflected in the final declaration. This was the belief that 'moderation in the level of military expenditure is a key aspect of sound economic policy and good government.'[66]

The European Community

Three of the constitituent parts of the EC—the Council of Ministers, the European Parliament and the Commission of the EC—have played an active role in the debate on aspects of arms export policy.

Of these bodies, the European Parliament has had the longest and most consistent interest in the issue of arms export regulation. The Parliament expressed its view in favour of an EC arms export policy in March 1989 and July 1990 and, on 18 April 1991, passed another resolution urging action in this area.[67] Governments have paid little attention to the work the Parliament has undertaken on the defence industry and arms exports and, until the

---

[64] The Guidelines are reproduced in appendix 8A.
[65] The Declaration is reproduced as appendix 8A.
[66] This idea is discussed more fully in chapter 7.
[67] European Parliament, *Resolution on the Arms Trade*, PE 150.654, 18 Apr. 1991.

Parliament is given a role in decision making, its resolutions are unlikely to influence the behaviour of EC governments.

The Council of Ministers

The need for a co-ordinated EC approach arms transfer policy has been an important element of the Intergovernmental Conference (IGC) on Political Union which led to the Treaty on European Union agreed in Maastricht on 11 December 1991.[68] Agreement in principle that arms export control and the proliferation of weapons of mass destruction were appropriate components of a joint foreign and security policy was reached at the first meeting of the Conference in Rome on 14–15 December 1990. Subsequently, these issues have appeared in all of the draft treaty texts prepared for the Conference.[69] However, the Treaty on European Union makes no mention of proliferation or export regulation as a specific element of EC common foreign and security policy. Article J.1.3 of the Treaty calls on the Union to establish systematic co-operation in the conduct of policy and gradually to implement joint action 'in the areas in which Member States have important interests in common'. Under Article J.2, the definition of what these important interests might be is left to the Council of Ministers.

At the fourth meeting of the IGC on Political Union in April 1991, Luxembourg—at the time President of the European Council—presented a draft treaty. Annex 1 of the draft listed joint-action priorities, including the control of arms exports, and added as a footnote: 'Possibly to be supplemented by the inclusion of an Article in the EC Treaty reading as follows: "To the extent necessary, Member States shall align their laws, regulations and administrative provisions relating to the export of arms. The Commission shall make all appropriate recommendations to the Member States for this purpose."'[70] At a meeting of the European Council at the end of June a number of criteria were advanced as the basis for a common approach to the implementation of arms export legislation.[71] Seven criteria were to be considered in evaluating a specific arms export, namely:

1. Respect for the international commitments of the member States of the Community, in particular the sanctions decreed by the Security Council of the

---

[68] The Treaty on European Union was signed on 7 February 1992 and is reproduced in *Europe, Document no. 1759/60, 7 Feb. 1992.* This issue is discussed in greater detail in Courades Allebeck, A., 'The European Community and arms export regulations', ed. I. Anthony, SIPRI, *Arms Export Regulations* (Oxford University Press: Oxford, 1991).

[69] Unofficial translation of the *Note des délégations allemande et française en date de février 1991 à la Conférence intergouvernementale sur l'Union politique,* Conference des représentants des gouvernements des Etats Membres–Union Politique, CONF-UP 1718/1/91, pp. 3–4 (in the draft treaty released by France and Germany on 14 Oct. 1991 this language was unamended); *United Kingdom draft treaty text on Common Foreign and Security Policy,* Conference of the Representatives of the Governments of the Member States–Political Union; *Non-paper, Draft Treaty Articles with a View to Achieving Political Union,* presented by Luxembourg on 15 Apr. 1991 to the Conference of the Representatives of the Governments of the Member States–Political Union, CONF-UP 1800/91.

[70] *Non-paper, Draft Treaty Articles with a View to Achieving Political Union,* presented by Luxembourg on 15 Apr. 1991 to the Conference of the Representatives of the Governments of the Member States–Political Union, CONF-UP 1800/91, annex 1, p. 84.

[71] Declaration on Non-Proliferation and Arms Exports, *Europe,* Document no. 5524, 30 June 1991.

United Nations and those decreed by the Community, agreements on non-proliferation and other subjects, as well as other international obligations;

2. Respect for human rights in the country of final destination;

3. The internal situation in the country of final destination, as a function of the existence of tensions or internal armed conflicts;

4. The preservation of regional peace, security and stability;

5. The national security of the member states and of territories whose external relations are the responsibility of a member state, as well as that of friendly and allied countries;

6. The behaviour of the buyer country with regard to the international community, as regards in particular its attitude to terrorism, the nature of its alliances, and respect for international law; and

7. The existence of a risk that the equipment will be diverted within the buyer country or re-exported under undesirable conditions.

The Commission of the European Communities

In 1991 senior officials—including the President of the Commission—began to make explicit references to the issue of arms export policy in their public statements.[72] The primary interest of the Commission has been to stress that the completion of the internal market by 1993 depends to some extent on the successful implementation of joint EC export controls at the perimeter of the Community.

The Commission has noted that member states retain national export controls over goods intended for civilian purposes but with potential military applications destined for Community partners. In the context of the single market, controls on the movement of goods within the Community could not be justified unless there was a risk that items transferred to an EC partner would be re-exported to a third party unacceptable to the country where the goods originated.

In a press release of 29 May 1991 the Commission outlined the view that unless strict extra-Community export controls were in place it would be difficult to eliminate intra-Community controls. Therefore, there was a need for a 'declaration of mutual trust by all the Member States whereby they would undertake to apply effective checks based on common standards for exports of double-use products and technologies to non-member countries.' With this in mind, the Commission instructed its staff 'to determine what measures should be adopted to enable the twelve Member States to apply effective rules on the control of exports to non-member countries' and to define 'the internal and external measures which must be taken to eliminate,

[72] Delors, J., 'European integration and security', 1991 Alastair Buchan Memorial Lecture, International Institute for Strategic Studies, London, 7 Mar. 1991 (mimeo); and Sir Leon Brittan, Vice President of the European Commission, 'International security in a time of change: Europe within NATO', speech to the Royal United Services Institute for Defence Studies, London, 15 Mar. 1991 (mimeo).

by 31 December 1992, checks on intra-Community trade in double-use industrial products covered by the COCOM arrangements.'[73]

Other arms transfer control initiatives in 1991

The United Nations embargo against Iraq

Throughout 1991 the United Nations maintained its trade embargo against Iraq. In addition to the total trade embargo, a mandatory arms embargo against Iraq was originally established in Security Council Resolution 661 of 6 August 1990. In 1991 this mandatory arms embargo was incorporated into Security Council Resolution 687 of 3 April 1991.[74]

In Resolution 687 the Security Council decided that:

until a further decision is taken by the Security Council, all States shall continue to prevent the sale or supply, or the promotion or facilitation of such sale or supply, to Iraq by their nationals, or from their territories or using their flag vessels or aircraft of:

(a) Arms and related matériel of all types, specifically including the sale or transfer through other means of all forms of conventional military equipment, including for paramilitary forces, and spare parts and components and their means of production, of such equipment;

(b) Items specified and defined in paragraphs 8 and 12 above not otherwise covered above;

(c) Technology under licensing or other transfer arrangements used in the production, utilization or stockpiling of items specified in sub-paragraphs a and b above;

(d) Personnel or materials for training or technical support services relating to the design, development, manufacture, use, maintenance or support of items specified in sub-paragraphs a and b above.

The items referred to in sub-paragraph b as being specified and defined in paragraphs 8 and 12 of the Resolution were those associated with biological, chemical and nuclear weapons.

Monitoring the implementation of the United Nations embargo against Iraq has been the responsibility of a Committee which reports direct to the Secretary-General of the United Nations. The Committee, established under Resolution 669 of 24 September 1990, has not released any findings to the public. However, no state actor has been accused by the Committee of violating the embargo. If and when the embargo is modified to permit trade with Iraq other than in arms and military equipment, the problem of monitoring compliance with an arms embargo will be greatly increased.

[73] Commission of the European Communities, *The Single Market of 1993 and Strategic Products and Technologies Which are not Intended Specifically for Military Purposes*, Press Release, Brussels, 29 May 1991.

[74] The text of the resolution is reproduced in appendix 13A of this volume.

Arms embargoes against Yugoslavia

As the civil war in Yugoslavia intensified in 1991 a number of countries embargoed the transfer of arms to any of the warring parties. They were followed by three multilateral bodies: the Conference on Security and Co-operation in Europe (CSCE), the European Community and the United Nations.

On 3 July 1991, after a meeting with representatives of the European Community, United States Secretary of State James Baker indicated that an arms embargo and the cessation of foreign economic assistance to Yugoslavia were two measures under active consideration. The EC countries agreed upon an arms embargo on 5 July 1991 and, from 11 July 1991, the United States suspended licences for direct commercial exports of items on the US munitions list and stated that the State Department would refuse government-to-government sales.[75]

On 7 August Poland introduced an embargo on the supply of arms and military equipment to Yugoslavia, including spare parts, repairs and the transfer of military technologies.[76]

Meeting on 3–4 September 1991 in Prague, Senior Officials of the Consultative Committee at the Conflict Prevention Centre decided that all states participating in the CSCE should stop and refrain from supplying arms to all Yugoslav parties.[77]

On 25 September 1991 UN Security Council Resolution 713 introduced a mandatory embargo on 'all deliveries of weapons and military equipment to Yugoslavia until the Security Council decides otherwise'.[78]

US–Soviet agreement on Afghanistan

Under the agreements signed in Geneva on 14 April 1988 (a series of agreements collectively referred to as the Geneva Accords), Afghanistan and Pakistan agreed to accept mutual restrictions on certain kinds of arms imports.[79] In a Declaration of International Guarantees (also part of the Accords), the United States and the Soviet Union undertook to respect all of the commitments made by Afghanistan and Pakistan. Nevertheless, after the withdrawal of its forces from Afghanistan the Soviet Union continued to supply large quantities of arms and military assistance to the government in Kabul. Similarly, the United States continued to provide financial support to the Afghan Mujahideen and played an important role in co-ordinating arms supplies to anti-government forces.

---

[75] Information contained in a letter of John J. Maresca, US Representative to the Consultative Committee of the Conflict Prevention Centre, to the Director of the CSCE Conflict Prevention Centre, Vienna, 12 Sep. 1991.

[76] *Note Verbale* from the Ministry of Foreign Affairs of the Republic of Poland to the Director of the CSCE Conflict Prevention Centre, 13 Sep. 1991.

[77] Note 76.

[78] Reproduced in the *Department of State Dispatch*, 30 Sep. 1991, pp. 724–25.

[79] The Geneva Accords were reproduced in the Pakistani newspaper *Dawn*, 15 Apr. 1988.

In a joint statement released by US Secretary of State James Baker and Boris Pankin, then Soviet Foreign Minister, the United States and the Soviet Union agreed 'to discontinue their weapons deliveries to all Afghan sides. They also agree that a cease-fire and a cutoff of weapons deliveries from all other sources should follow this step.'[80] According to the agreement reached, arms supplies would not be intensified in the period between 13 September 1991 and 1 January 1992 and would be discontinued from 1 January 1992.

The COCOM embargo

In 1990 and 1991 COCOM has undergone a thorough review in the light of changes in the European security environment. At a high-level meeting of COCOM in May 1991, revisions to the control lists defining items subject to embargo were agreed. The COCOM industrial list was reduced to 'a core list of the most strategic technology and products.'[81]

The changes in the COCOM industrial list were to have been implemented on 1 September 1991. However, following the attempted coup in the USSR in August 1991, the implementation of changes was delayed. The failure of the coup and the changes which subsequently led to the dissolution of the Soviet Union have further undermined the rationale for maintaining an embargo on the trade in non-military items, and additional changes to the COCOM embargo are inevitable.[82]

The May high-level group meeting also agreed to introduce differential treatment of the former WTO members for the first time. Under the new regulations Czechoslovakia, Hungary and Poland were to be allowed access to higher levels of civilian technologies, with potential military applications, than the USSR, once they demonstrated that they had effective national export legislation to prevent the re-export of imported equipment to proscribed recipients. While Czechoslovakia and Poland had previously put in place export control mechanisms, Hungary and Romania introduced national export regulations for the first time in 1991. From 1992 it will probably be necessary for COCOM members to process applications for exemption from the embargo on the basis of the new sovereign states which will replace the Soviet Union, and the dissolution of the USSR will increase pressures from industry for a complete disbandment of the COCOM industrial list.

VI. The United Nations register of arms transfers

On 9 December 1991 the General Assembly of the United Nations voted to establish a register of arms transfers by a vote of 150 to 0 with two

---

[80] Text of US–Soviet Joint Statement on Afghanistan, 13 Sep. 1991, reproduced in *Department of State Dispatch*, 16 Sep. 1991, p. 683.

[81] Allen Wendt, head of the US delegation to the meeting, quoted in Auerbach, S., 'COCOM cuts back its barriers', *International Herald Tribune*, 25–26 May 1991, p. 1.

[82] The revised COCOM industrial list was published in the US *Federal Register* on 30 Aug. 1991.

abstentions.[83] The countries that abstained were Cuba and Iraq. In the resolution the United Nations declared 'its determination to prevent the excessive and destabilizing accumulation of arms, including conventional arms, in order to promote stability and strengthen regional or international peace and security . . . ' and decided to establish and maintain a universal and non-discriminatory Register of Conventional Arms with effect from 1 January 1992.[84]

Member states were invited to provide to the Secretary-General an annual report on imports and exports of arms and the United Nations was to receive two reports—from the exporting and importing government—confirming each transfer.

In the past critics of the idea of a United Nations register have argued that not only arms transfers but also those items produced but not transferred (the bulk of the equipment in the major arms-producing countries) should be monitored. In the initial draft resolution on international arms transfers—drawn up by the members of the EC following the meeting of the European Council on 8 April 1991—the United Nations was asked to keep procedures, input requirements and participation in the Register under review in the appropriate forums with a view to the possibility of progressively supplementing the Register by introducing measures to promote transparency in other military matters such as military holdings and procurements and military doctrines. During the discussion of the draft resolution in the First Committee of the United Nations General Assembly, this paragraph was amended. The final resolution clearly foresees an expansion of the register to include military holdings and procurement through national production.

The resolution 'invites Member States, *pending the expansion of the Register*, also to provide the Secretary-General, with their annual report on imports and exports of arms, available background information regarding their military holdings, procurement through national production and relevant policies'.[85] Moreover, the register will be reviewed in 1994 and a report will be prepared to take a decision on the expansion in the 49th Session (1994) of the General Assembly.

With regard to arms transfers, the first registration shall take place by 30 April 1993 in respect of calendar year 1992 and the data collected will be made available to the public.

The register will not report on the value of transfers. Moreover, it will not report on those areas of the arms trade about which least is known—deliveries of small arms, components, sub-systems and arms-production technologies and dual-use items. The register is voluntary and the governments that voted for its establishment are not obliged to report. Finally, although the register will increase transparency of the arms trade it does not restrict the trade.

---

[83] A Resolution (A/C.1/L.18/Rev.1) was passed by the First Committee of the 46th session of the General Assembly on 13 Nov. 1991 and confirmed (A/RES/46/36L) on 9 Dec. 1991 in the General Assembly.

[84] General Assembly Resolution 46/36 L is reproduced in appendix 8A.

[85] Note 84 (emphasis added).

Nevertheless, the register is an important step forward in the discussion of the arms trade in that it will contribute somewhat to greater transparency. Transparency is an end worth having in itself—as a confidence-building measure—and also a means to further progress on more substantive arms control efforts. Such a register should therefore be judged as a contribution to a wider arms control agenda. More important, it is the first time that governments have agreed on a broad basis to place such information on the arms trade in the public domain.

Appendix 8A. Selected documents relating to arms export control in 1991

Final communiqué of the meeting of the five permanent members of the Security Council in Paris, 9 July 1991

1. Representatives of the United States of America, the People's Republic of China, France, the United Kingdom, and the Union of Soviet Socialist Republics, met in Paris on the 8th and 9th of July to review issues related to conventional arms transfers and to the non-proliferation of weapons of mass destruction.

They noted with concern the dangers associated with the excessive build-up of military capabilities, and confirmed they would not transfer conventional weapons in circumstances which would undermine stability. They also noted the threats to peace and stability posed by the proliferation of nuclear weapons, chemical and biological weapons, and missiles, and undertook to seek effective measures of non-proliferation and arms control in a fair, reasonable, comprehensive and balanced manner on a global as well as on a regional basis.

2. They had a thorough and positive exchange of views on the basis of the arms control initiatives presented in particular by President Bush, President Mitterrand, Prime Minister Major and on other initiatives which address these problems globally and as a matter of urgency in the Middle East. They also agreed to support continued work in the United Nations on an arms transfers register to be established under the aegis of the UN Secretary General, on a non-discriminatory basis, as a step towards increased transparency on arms transfers and in general in military matters.

They stressed that the ultimate response to the threat of proliferation is verifiable arms control and disarmament agreements amongst the parties concerned. They expressed strong support for full implementation of existing arms control regimes. For their part, they will contribute to this objective by developing and maintaining stringent national and, as far as possible, harmonised controls to ensure that weapons of mass-destruction related equipments and materials are transferred for permitted purposes only and are not diverted.

They also strongly supported the objective of establishing a weapons of mass destruction-free zone in the Middle East. They expressed their view that critical steps towards this goal include full implementation of UNSC resolution 687 and adoption by countries in the region of a comprehensive program of arms control for the region, including:

• A freeze and ultimate elimination of ground to ground missiles in the region;
• Submission by all nations in the region of all their nuclear activities to IAEA safeguards;
• A ban on the importation and production of nuclear weapons usable material;
• Agreement by all states in the region to undertake to becoming parties to the CW Convention as soon as it is concluded in 1992.

3. They acknowledged that Article 51 of the UN Charter guarantees every state the right of self-defence. That right implies that states have also the right to acquire means with which to defend themselves. In this respect, the transfer of conventional weapons, conducted in a responsible manner, should contribute to the ability of states to meet their legitimate defence, security and national sovereignty requirements and to participate effectively in collective measures requested by the United Nations for the purpose of maintaining or restoring international peace and security.

They recognized that indiscriminate transfers of military weapons and technology contribute to regional instability. They are fully conscious of the special responsibilities that are incumbent upon them to ensure that such risks be avoided, and of the special role they have to play in prompting greater responsibility, confidence and transparency in this field. They also recognize that a long term solution to this problem should be found in close consultation with recipient countries.

4. They expressed the intention that:

• When considering under their national control procedures conventional weapons transfers, they will observe rules of restraint. They will develop agreed guidelines on this basis.

• Taking into account the special situation of the Middle East as a primary area of tension, they will develop modalities of consultation and of information exchanges concerning arms transfers to this region as a matter of priority.

• A group of experts will meet in September with a view to reaching agreement on this approach.

• Another plenary meeting will be held in October in London.

• Further meetings will be held periodically to review these issues.

5. They expressed the conviction that this process of continuing cooperation will contribute to a worldwide climate of vigilance in this field which other countries will share.

Source: US Department of State Dispatch, 15 July 1991.

Declaration on Conventional Arms Transfers issued at the close of the London Economic Summit, 17 July 1991

1. At our meeting in Houston last year, we, the Heads of State and Government and the representatives of the European Community, underlined the threats to international security posed by the proliferation of nuclear, biological and chemical weapons and of associated missile delivery systems. The Gulf crisis has highlighted the dangers posed by the unchecked spread of these weapons and by excessive holdings of conventional weapons. The responsibility to prevent the re-emergence of such dangers is to be shared by both arms suppliers and recipient countries as well as the international community as a whole. As is clear from the various initiatives which several of us have proposed jointly and individually, we are each determined to tackle, in appropriate fora, these dangers both in the Middle East and elsewhere.

Conventional arms transfers

2. We accept that many states depend on arms imports to assure a reasonable level of security and the inherent right of self-defence is recognized in the UN Charter. Tensions will persist in international relations so long as underlying conflicts of interest are nottackled and resolved. But the Gulf conflict showed the way in which peace and stability can be undermined when a country is able to acquire a massive arsenal that goes far beyond the needs of self defence and threatens its neighbours. We are determined to ensure such abuse should not happen again. We believe that progress can be made if all states apply the three principles of transparency, consultation and action.

3. The principle of *transparency* should be extended to international transfers of conventional weapons and associated military technology. As a step in this direction we support the proposal for a universal register of arms transfers under the auspices of the United Nations, and will work for its early adoption. Such a register would alert the international community to an attempt by a state to build up holdings of conventional weapons beyond a reasonable level. Information should be provided by all states on a regular basis after transfers have taken place. We also urge greater openness about overall holdings of conventional weapons. We believe the provision of such data, and a procedure for seeking clarification, would be a valuable confidence and security building measure.

4. The principle of *consultation* should now be strengthened through the rapid implementation of recent initiatives for discussions among leading arms exporters with the aim of agreeing a common approach to the guidelines which are applied in the transfer of conventional weapons. We welcome the recent opening of discussions on this subject. These include the encouraging talks in Paris among the Permanent Members of the UN Security Council on 8/9 July; as well as ongoing discussions within the framework of the European Community and its Member States. Each of us will continue to play a constructive part in this important process, in these and other appropriate fora.

5. The principle of *action* requires all of us to take steps to prevent the building up of disproportionate arsenals. To that end all countries should refrain from arms transfers which would be destabilising or would exacerbate existing tensions. Special restraint should be exercised in the transfer of advanced technology weapons and in sales to countries and areas of particular concern. A special effort should be made to define sensitive items and production capacity for advanced weapons, to the transfer of which similar restraints could be applied. All states should take steps to ensure that these criteria are strictly enforced. We intend to give these

issues our continuing close attention.

6. Iraqi aggression and the ensuing Gulf war illustrate the huge costs to the international community of military conflict. We believe that moderation in the level of military expenditure is a key aspect of sound economic policy and good government. While all countries are struggling with competing claims on scarce resources, excessive spending on arms of all kinds diverts resources from the overriding need to tackle economic development. It can also build up large debts without creating the means by which these may be serviced. We note with favor the recent report issued by the United Nations Development Programme (UNDP) and the recent decisions by several donor countries to take account of military expenditure where it is disproportionate when setting up aid programmes and encourage all other donor countries to take similar action. We welcome the attention which the managing director of the International Monetary Fund (IMF) and the President of the World Bank have recently given to excessive military spending, in the context of reducing unproductive public expenditure.

Source: US Department of State Dispatch, 22 July 1991.

Guidelines for Conventional Arms Transfers agreed by the five permanent members of the Security Council in London, 18 Oct. 1991

The People's Republic of China, the French Republic, the Union of Soviet Socialist Republics, the United Kingdom of Great Britain and Northern Ireland, and the United States of America,

recalling and reaffirming the principles which they stated as a result of their meeting in Paris on 8 and 9 July 1991,

mindful of the dangers to peace and stability posed by the transfer of conventional weapons beyond levels needed for defensive purposes,

reaffirming the inherent right to individual or collective self-defence recognized in Article 51 of the Charter of the United Nations, which implies that States have the right to acquire means of legitimate self-defense,

recalling that in accordance with the Charter of the United Nations, United Nations Member States have undertaken to promote the establishment and maintenance of international peace and security with the least diversion for armaments of the world's human and economic resources,

seeking to ensure that arms transferred are not used in violation of the purposes and principles of the United Nations Charter,

mindful of their special responsibilities for the maintenance of international peace and security,

reaffirming their commitment to seek effective measures to promote peace, security, stability and arms control on a global and regional basis in a fair, reasonable, comprehensive and balanced manner,

noting the importance of encouraging international commerce for peaceful purposes,

determined to adopt a serious, responsible and prudent attitude of restraint regarding arms transfers,

declare that, when considering under their national control procedures conventional arms transfers, they intend to observe rules of restraint, and to act in accordance with the following guidelines:

1. They will consider carefully whether proposed transfers will:

a) promote the capabilities of the recipient to meet needs for legitimate self-defence;

b) serve as an appropriate and proportionate response to the security and military threats confronting the recipient country;

c) enhance the capability of the recipient to participate in regional or other collective arrangements or other measures consistent with the Charter of the United Nations or requested by the United Nations;

2. They will avoid transfers which would be likely to

a) prolong or aggravate an existing armed conflict;

b) increase tension in a region or contribute to regional instability;

c) introduce destabilizing military capabilities in a region;

d) contravene embargoes or other relevant internationally agreed restraints to which they are parties;

e) be used other than for the legitimate defense and security needs of the recipient State;

f) support or encourage international terrorism;

g) be used to interfere with the internal affairs of sovereign States;

h) seriously undermine the recipient State's economy.

Source: Meeting of the Five on Arms Transfers and Non-Proliferation, London 17–18 Oct. 1991, CD Document CD/113.

Transparency in Armaments: UN General Assembly Resolution 46/36, 9 Dec. 1991

The General Assembly . . .

1. *Recognizes* that an increased level of openness and transparency in the field of armaments would enhance confidence, promote stability, help States to exercise restraint, ease tensions and strengthen regional and international peace and security;

2. *Declares its determination* to prevent the excessive and destabilizing accumulation of arms, including conventional arms, in order to promote stability and strengthen regional or international peace and security, taking into account the legitimate security needs of States and the principle of undiminished security at the lowest possible level of armaments;

3. *Reaffirms* the inherent right to individual or collective self-defence recognized in Article 51 of the Charter of the United Nations, which implies that States also have the right to acquire arms with which to defend themselves;

4. *Reiterates its conviction*, as expressed in its resolution 43/75 I, that arms transfers in all their aspects deserve serious consideration by the international community, *inter alia*, because of:

(a) Their potential effects in further destabilizing areas where tension and regional conflict threaten international peace and security and national security;

(b) Their potentially negative effects on the progress of the peaceful social and economic development of all peoples;

(c) The danger of increasing illicit and covert arms trafficking;

5. *Calls upon* all Member States to exercise due restraint in exports and imports of conventional arms, particularly in situations of tension or conflict, and to ensure that they have in place an adequate body of laws and administrative procedures regarding the transfer of arms and to adopt strict measures for their enforcement;

6. *Expresses its appreciation* to the Secretary-General for his study on ways and means of promoting transparency in international transfers of conventional arms, which also addressed the problem of the illicit arms trade;

7. *Requests* the Secretary-General to establish and maintain at United Nations Headquarters in New York a universal and non-discriminatory Register of Conventional Arms, to include data on international arms transfers as well as information provided by Member States on military holdings, procurement through national production and relevant policies, as set out in paragraph 10 and in accordance with procedures and input requirements initially comprising those set out in the annex to the present resolution and subsequently incorporating any adjustments to the annex decided upon by the General Assembly at its forty-seventh session in the light of the recommendations of the panel referred to in paragraph 8 below;

8. *Also requests* the Secretary-General, with the assistance of a panel of governmental technical experts to be nominated by him on the basis of equitable geographical representation, to elaborate the technical procedures and to make any adjustments to the annex to the present resolution necessary for the effective operation of the Register, and to prepare a report on the modalities for early expansion of the scope of the Register by the addition of further categories of equipment and inclusion of data on military holdings and procurement through national production, and to report to the General Assembly at its forty-seventh session;

9. *Calls upon* all Member States to provide annually for the Register data on imports and exports of arms in accordance with the procedures established by paragraphs 7 and 8 above;

10. *Invites* Member States, pending the expansion of the Register, also to provide to the Secretary-General, with their annual report on imports and exports of arms, available background information regarding their military holdings, procurement through national production and relevant policies; and requests the Secretary-General to record this material and to make it available for consultation by Member States at their request;

11. *Decides*, with a view to future expansion, to keep the scope of and the participation in the Register under review, and, to this end:

(a) *Invites* Member States to provide the

Secretary-General with their views, not later than 30 April 1994, on:

(i) The operation of the Register during its first two years;

(ii) The addition of further categories of equipment and the elaboration of the Register to include military holdings and procurement through national production;

(b) *Requests* the Secretary-General, with the assistance of a group of governmental experts convened in 1994 on the basis of equitable geographical representation, to prepare a report on the continuing operation of the Register and its further development, taking into account the work of the Conference on Disarmament as set forth in paragraphs 12 to 15 below and the views expressed by Member States, for submission to the General Assembly with a view to a decision at its forty-ninth session;

12. *Requests* the Conference on Disarmament to address, as soon as possible, the question of the interrelated aspects of the excessive and destabilizing accumulation of arms, including military holdings and procurement through national production, and to elaborate universal and non-discriminatory practical means to increase openness and transparency in this field;

13. *Also requests* the Conference on Disarmament to address the problems of, and the elaboration of practical means to increase, openness and transparency related to the transfer of high technology with military applications and to weapons of mass destruction, in accordance with existing legal instruments;

14. *Invites* the Secretary-General to provide to the Conference on Disarmament all relevant information, including, *inter alia*, views submitted to him by Member States and information provided under the United Nations system for the standardized reporting of military expenditures, as well as on the work of the Disarmament Commission under its agenda item entitled 'Objective information on military matters';

15. *Further requests* the Conference on Disarmament to include in its annual report to the General Assembly a report on its work in this issue;

16. *Invites* all Member States, in the meantime, to take measures on a national, regional and global basis, including within the appropriate forums, to promote openness and transparency in armaments;

17. *Calls upon* all Member States to cooperate at a regional and subregional level, taking fully into account the specific conditions prevailing in the region or subregion, with a view to enhancing and coordinating international efforts aimed at increased openness and transparency in armaments;

18. *Also invites* all Member States to inform the Secretary-General of their national arms import and export policies, legislation and administrative procedures, both as regards authorization of arms transfers and prevention of illicit transfers;

19. *Requests* the Secretary-General to report to the General Assembly at its forty-seventh session on progress made in implementing the present resolution, including relevant information provided by Member States;

20. *Notes* that effective implementation of the present resolution will require an up-to-date database system in the Department for Disarmament Affairs of the Secretariat;

21. *Decides* to include in the provisional agenda of its forty-seventh session an item entitled 'Transparency in armaments'.

Annex
Register of Conventional Arms

1. The Register of Conventional Arms ('the Register') shall be established with effect from 1 January 1992, and maintained at the Headquarters of the United Nations in New York.

2. Concerning international arms transfers:

(a) Member States are requested to provide data for the Register, addressed to the Secretary-General, on the number of items in the following categories of equipment imported into or exported from their territory:

I. *Battle tanks*

A tracked or wheeled self-propelled armoured fighting vehicle with high cross-country mobility and a high level of self-protection weighing at least 16.5 metric tonnes unladen weight, with a high muzzle velocity direct fire main gun of at least 75 millimetres calibre.

II. *Armoured combat vehicles*

A tracked or wheeled self-propelled vehicle, with armoured protection and cross-country capability, either: (a) designed and equipped to transport a squad of four or more infantrymen, or

(b) armed with an integral or organic weapon of at least 20 millimetres calibre or an anti-tank missile launcher.

III. *Large calibre artillery systems*

A gun, howitzer, artillery piece combining the characteristics of a gun or a howitzer, mortar or multiple-launch rocket system, capable of engaging surface targets by delivering primarily indirect fire, with a calibre of 100 millimetres and above.

IV. *Combat aircraft*

A fixed-wing or variable-geometry wing aircraft armed and equipped to engage targets by employing guided missiles, unguided rockets, bombs, guns, cannons, or other weapons of destruction.

V. *Attack helicopters*

A rotary-wing aircraft equipped to employ anti-armour, air-to-ground, or air-to-air guided weapons and equipped with an integrated fire control and aiming system for these weapons.

VI. *Warships*

A vessel or submarine with a standard displacement of 850 metric tonnes or above, armed or equipped for military use.

VII. *Missiles or missile systems*

A guided rocket, ballistic or cruise missile capable of delivering a payload to a range of at least 25 kilometres, or a vehicle, apparatus or device designed or modified for launching such munitions.

(b) Data on imports provided under the present paragraph shall also specify the supplying State; data on exports shall also specify the recipient State and the State of origin if not the exporting State;

(c) Each Member State is requested to provide data on an annual basis by 30 April each year in respect of imports into and exports from their territory in the previous calendar year;

(d) The first such registration shall take place by 30 April 1993 in respect of the calendar year 1992;

(e) The data so provided shall be recorded in respect of each Member State;

(f) Arms 'exports and imports' represent in the present resolution, including its annex, all forms of arms transfers under terms of grant, credit, barter or cash.

3. Concerning other interrelated information:

(a) Member States are invited also to pro-vide to the Secretary-General available background information regarding their military holdings, procurement through national production, and relevant policies;

(b) The information so provided shall be recorded in respect of each Member State.

4. The Register shall be open for consultation by representatives of Member States at any time.

5. In addition, the Secretary-General shall provide annually a consolidated report to the General Assembly of the data registered, together with an index of the other interrelated information.

Source: UN document A/RES/46/36, 9 Dec. 1991.

Appendix 8B. Tables of the value of the trade in major conventional weapons

IAN ANTHONY, AGNÈS COURADES ALLEBECK, GERD HAGMEYER-GAVERUS, PAOLO MIGGIANO, ELISABETH SKÖNS and HERBERT WULF

Table 8B.1. Values of imports of major conventional weapons, 1982–91

Figures are SIPRI trend-indicator values, as expressed in US $m., at constant (1990) prices.

	1982	1983	1984	1985	1986	1987	1988	1989	1990	1991
World total	43 424	44 026	42 736	39 278	41 874	45 870	39 317	38 228	29 004	22 114
Developing world	28 876	29 705	29 154	25 765	28 265	32 162	24 054	21 735	16 720	12 336
LDCs	1 341	1 038	1 233	1 011	1 638	1 325	2 033	3 126	2 963	1 514
Industrialized world	14 547	14 321	13 582	13 513	13 609	13 708	15 263	16 492	12 284	9 778
Europe	12 558	10 705	10 238	9 899	10 008	10 429	11 848	12 095	9 387	7 863
EC	5 419	3 754	3 775	2 457	3 331	3 102	4 289	5 453	3 863	4 846
Other Europe	7 139	6 952	6 463	7 442	6 676	7 327	7 559	6 642	5 524	3 017
Americas	4 664	5 685	5 413	3 699	3 143	3 485	1 757	2 317	1 636	1 438
North	687	1 096	1 131	1 420	1 077	1 233	782	935	478	572
Central	983	1 168	675	779	694	309	101	217	302	187
South	2 994	3 421	3 607	1 499	1 371	1 943	874	1 165	855	679
Africa	5 596	4 116	4 417	3 925	3 985	3 189	2 367	1 967	1 316	113
Sub-Saharan	1 880	1 915	2 573	2 414	2 167	2 536	1 868	461	1 158	113
Asia	6 716	7 798	7 704	9 568	11 610	12 285	12 769	15 150	9 404	7 507
Middle East	13 712	14 884	14 296	11 780	12 251	15 910	9 833	5 838	6 807	4 721
Oceania	178	837	667	407	878	571	743	861	454	473
OECD	8 794	8 847	8 680	7 892	8 310	8 550	10 094	11 860	8 692	9 100
CSCE	12 819	11 657	11 369	11 314	11 031	11 552	12 487	12 967	9 844	8 435
NATO	6 598	5 496	5 935	4 672	5 033	5 853	6 606	7 809	5 700	7 185
OPEC	10 957	9 946	10 698	10 035	9 617	10 422	7 392	6 292	5 389	2 652
ASEAN	896	1 262	1 393	1 154	1 269	1 451	1 476	961	924	1 547

Note: Despite the breakup of the USSR and Yugoslavia in 1991, these data refer to the old entities.

The following countries are included in each region:

Developing world: Afghanistan, Algeria, Angola, Argentina, Bahamas, Bahrain, Bangladesh, Barbados, Belize, Benin, Bolivia, Botswana, Brazil, Brunei, Burkina Faso, Burundi, Cameroon, Cape Verde, Central African Republic, Chad, Chile, China, Colombia, Comoros, Congo, Costa Rica, Côte d'Ivoire, Cuba, Cyprus, Djibouti, Dominica, Dominican Republic, Ecuador, Egypt, Equatorial Guinea, Ethiopia, Fiji, Gabon, Gambia, Ghana, Guatemala, Guinea, Guinea Bissau, Guyana, Haiti, Honduras, India, Indonesia, Iran, Iraq, Israel, Jamaica, Jordan, Kampuchea, Kenya, North Korea, South Korea, Kuwait, Laos, Lebanon, Lesotho, Liberia, Libya, Madagascar, Malawi, Malaysia, Mali, Mauritania, Mauritius, Mexico, Mongolia, Morocco, Mozambique, Myanmar (formerly Burma), Namibia, Nepal, Nicaragua, Niger, Nigeria, Oman, Pakistan, Panama, Papua New Guinea, Paraguay, Peru, Philippines, Qatar, Rwanda, St Vincent & the Grenadines, E Salvador, Samoa, Saudi Arabia, Senegal, Seychelles, Sierra Leone, Singapore, Solomon Islands, Somalia,

Table 8B.2. Values of exports of major conventional weapons, 1982–91

Figures are SIPRI trend-indicator values, as expressed in US $m., at constant (1990) prices.

	1982	1983	1984	1985	1986	1987	1988	1989	1990	1991
World total	43 424	44 026	42 736	39 278	41 874	45 870	39 317	38 228	29 004	22 114
Developing world	2 631	3 550	3 532	2 598	2 558	4 875	3 413	1 898	1 430	1 750
LDCs	0	0	27	0	3	69	3	0	0	1
Industrialized world	40 793	40 476	39 204	36 680	39 316	40 995	35 904	36 330	27 574	20 365
Europe	25 885	25 967	26 636	26 349	27 263	26 993	23 936	24 277	16 163	9 086
EC	10 455	9 837	11 303	8 650	8 304	7 442	7 004	7 676	5 249	4 253
Other Europe	15 430	16 130	15 333	17 699	18 960	19 551	16 932	16 602	10 913	4 832
Americas	15 214	14 924	12 851	10 522	12 298	14 682	12 504	12 338	11 481	11 218
North	14 884	14 458	12 470	10 276	12 039	13 984	11 960	12 046	11 302	11 210
Central	14	0	0	0	0	1	0	1	3	2
South	315	466	381	246	259	697	544	290	177	7
Africa	281	158	99	109	85	242	125	0	35	37
Sub-Saharan	26	20	52	78	48	149	69	0	7	37
Asia	1 343	1 738	2 289	1 829	1 599	3 128	2 143	1 058	1 063	1 573
Middle East	686	1 212	782	433	625	807	601	548	153	142
Oceania	14	28	79	35	5	18	9	6	110	60
OECD	25 704	24 781	24 159	19 502	20 839	22 116	19 677	20 300	16 960	15 708
CSCE	40 770	40 425	39 106	36 625	39 302	40 977	35 895	36 324	27 464	20 295
NATO	25 427	24 377	23 787	18 969	20 353	21 477	18 983	19 818	16 565	15 473
OPEC	270	245	98	66	98	244	244	35	40	18
ASEAN	21	7	58	65	31	52	33	14	9	0

South Africa, Sri Lanka, Sudan, Suriname, Swaziland, Syria, Tahiti, Taiwan, Tanzania, Thailand, Togo, Tonga, Trinidad & Tobago, Tunisia, Uganda, United Arab Emirates, Uruguay, Vanuatu, Venezuela, Viet Nam, Yemen, North Yemen, South Yemen, Zaire, Zambia, Zimbabwe.

Least developed countries (LDCs): Afghanistan, Bangladesh, Benin, Botswana, Burkina Faso, Burundi, Cape Verde, Central African Republic, Chad, Comoros, Djibouti, Equatorial Guinea, Ethiopia, Gambia, Guinea, Guinea Bissau, Haiti, Laos, Lesotho, Liberia, Malawi, Mali, Mauritania, Mozambique, Myanmar (formerly Burma), Nepal, Niger, Rwanda, Samoa, Sierra Leone, Somalia, Sudan, Tanzania, Togo, Uganda, Vanuatu, Yemen, North Yemen, South Yemen.

Industrialized world: Albania, Australia, Austria, Belgium, Bulgaria, Canada, Czechoslovakia, Denmark, Finland, France, FR Germany, German DR, Greece, Hungary, Iceland, Ireland, Italy, Japan, Liechtenstein, Luxembourg, Monaco, Malta, Netherlands, New Zealand, Norway, Poland, Portugal, Romania, Spain, Sweden, Switzerland, Turkey, UK, USA, USSR, Yugoslavia.

Europe: Albania, Austria, Belgium, Bulgaria, Cyprus, Czechoslovakia, Denmark, Finland, France, FR Germany, German DR, Greece, Hungary, Iceland, Ireland, Italy, Liechtenstein, Luxembourg, Malta, Monaco,

Netherlands, Norway, Poland, Portugal, Romania, Spain, Sweden, Switzerland, Turkey, UK, USSR, Yugoslavia.

European Community (EC): Belgium, Denmark, France, FR Germany, Greece, Ireland, Italy, Luxembourg, Netherlands, Portugal (since 1986), Spain (since 1986), UK.

Other Europe: Albania, Austria, Bulgaria, Cyprus, Czechoslovakia, Finland, German DR, Hungary, Iceland, Liechtenstein, Malta, Monaco, Norway, Poland, Romania, Sweden, Switzerland, Turkey, USSR, Yugoslavia.

Americas: Argentina, Bahamas, Barbados, Belize, Bolivia, Brazil, Canada, Chile, Colombia, Costa Rica, Cuba, Dominica, Dominican Republic, Ecuador, Guatemala, Guyana, Haiti, Honduras, Jamaica, Mexico, Nicaragua, Panama, Paraguay, Peru, St Vincent & the Grenadines, El Salvador, Suriname, Trinidad & Tobago, Uruguay, USA, Venezuela.

North America: Canada, Mexico, USA.

Central America: Bahamas, Barbados, Belize, Costa Rica, Cuba, Dominica, Dominican Republic, Guatemala, Haiti, Honduras, Jamaica, Nicaragua, Panama, St Vincent & the Grenadines, El Salvador, Trinidad & Tobago.

South America: Argentina, Bolivia, Brazil, Chile, Colombia, Ecuador, Guyana, Paraguay, Peru, Suriname, Uruguay, Venezuela.

Africa: Algeria, Angola, Benin, Botswana, Burkina Faso, Burundi, Cameroon, Cape Verde, Central African Republic, Chad, Comoros, Congo, Côte d'Ivoire, Djibouti, Equatorial Guinea, Ethiopia, Gabon, Gambia, Ghana, Guinea, Guinea Bissau, Kenya, Lesotho, Liberia, Libya, Madagascar, Malawi, Mali, Mauritania, Mauritius, Morocco, Mozambique, Namibia, Niger, Nigeria, Rwanda, Senegal, Seychelles, Sierra Leone, Somalia, South Africa, Sudan, Swaziland, Tanzania, Togo, Tunisia, Uganda, Zaire, Zambia, Zimbabwe.

Sub-Saharan Africa: Angola, Benin, Botswana, Burkina Faso, Burundi, Cameroon, Cape Verde, Central African Republic, Chad, Comoros, Congo, Côte d'Ivoire, Djibouti, Equatorial Guinea, Ethiopia, Gabon, Gambia, Ghana, Guinea, Guinea Bissau, Kenya, Lesotho, Liberia, Madagascar, Malawi, Mali, Mauritania, Mauritius, Mozambique, Namibia, Niger, Nigeria, Rwanda, Senegal, Seychelles, Sierra Leone, Somalia, South Africa, Sudan, Swaziland, Tanzania, Togo, Uganda, Zaire, Zambia, Zimbabwe.

Asia: Afghanistan, Bangladesh, Brunei, China, India, Indonesia, Japan, Kampuchea, North Korea, South Korea, Laos, Malaysia, Mongolia, Myanmar (formerly Burma), Nepal, Pakistan, Philippines, Singapore, Sri Lanka, Taiwan, Thailand, Viet Nam.

Middle East: Bahrain, Egypt, Iran, Iraq, Israel, Jordan, Kuwait, Lebanon, Oman, Qatar, Saudi Arabia, Syria, United Arab Emirates, Yemen, North Yemen, South Yemen.

Oceania: Australia, Fiji, New Zealand, Papua New Guinea, Samoa, Solomon Islands, Tahiti, Tonga, Vanuatu.

Organization for Economic Co-operation and Development (OECD): Australia, Austria, Belgium, Canada, Denmark, Finland, France, FR Germany, Greece, Iceland, Ireland, Italy, Japan, Luxembourg, Netherlands, New Zealand, Norway, Portugal, Spain, Sweden, Switzerland, Turkey, UK, USA.

Conference on Security and Co-operation in Europe (CSCE): Albania (since 1991), Austria, Belgium, Bulgaria, Canada, Cyprus, Czechoslovakia, Denmark, Finland, France, FR Germany, German DR, Greece, Hungary, Iceland, Ireland, Italy, Liechtenstein, Luxembourg, Malta, Monaco, Netherlands, Norway, Poland, Portugal, Romania, Spain, Sweden, Switzerland, Turkey, UK, USA, USSR, Yugoslavia.

NATO: Belgium, Canada, Denmark, France, FR Germany, Greece, Iceland, Italy, Luxembourg, Netherlands, Norway, Portugal, Spain (since 1982), Turkey, UK, USA.

Organization of Petroleum Exporting Countries (OPEC): Algeria, Ecuador, Gabon, Indonesia, Iran, Iraq, Kuwait, Libya, Nigeria, Qatar, Saudi Arabia, United Arab Emirates, Venezuela.

Association of South East Asian Nations (ASEAN): Brunei, Indonesia, Malaysia, Philippines, Singapore, Thailand.

Conventions: − = nil, 0 = < 0.5.

Source: SIPRI data base.

Table 8B.3. World trade in major conventional weapon systems, 1987–91

Figures are values of major conventional weapon systems transferred, in US $m., at constant (1990) prices. Figures may not add up to totals due to rounding.

Recipient:	USSR	USA	France	UK	China	FRG	Czech.	Italy	Netherlands	Brazil	Others	Total
									Seller			
Afghanistan	8 125	149	1	43	48	–	22	–	–	–	42	8 430
Algeria	932	–	–	25	64	–	71	–	–	7	0	1 099
Angola	3 544	3	28	–	–	–	–	–	–	7	24	3 606
Argentina	–	–	45	–	–	444	–	52	–	64	80	685
Australia	–	2 727	54	61	–	–	–	10	–	–	104	2 956
Austria	–	29	0	–	–	–	–	–	–	–	189	218
Bahrain	–	570	90	11	–	241	–	–	–	–	0	912
Bangladesh	–	12	–	–	355	–	–	–	–	–	185	552
Belgium	–	738	25	–	–	–	–	18	–	–	104	885
Belize	–	2	–	–	–	–	–	–	–	–	0	2
Benin	–	–	5	–	–	–	–	–	–	–	0	5
Bolivia	–	103	–	–	–	–	–	–	–	3	10	116
Botswana	–	15	–	21	–	–	–	0	–	–	55	91
Brazil	–	591	492	8	–	107	–	–	–	–	50	1 248
Brunei	–	12	18	–	–	–	–	4	–	–	0	34
Bulgaria	1 746	–	–	–	–	–	89	–	–	–	0	1 835
Burma	–	–	–	–	222	–	–	–	–	–	46	268
Cameroon	–	–	19	–	–	–	–	–	–	–	1	20
Canada	3	2 020	–	70	–	21	–	24	–	–	125	2 263
Central African Republic	6	–	–	–	–	–	–	–	–	–	0	6
Chad	–	57	9	–	–	–	–	–	–	–	2	68
Chile	–	80	164	592	1	14	–	–	–	–	208	1 059
China	497	113	163	5	–	–	–	–	–	–	19	797
Colombia	–	186	–	–	–	–	–	–	–	–	215	401
Congo	–	–	2	–	–	–	–	–	–	–	0	2
Cote d'Ivoire	–	3	10	–	–	–	–	–	48	–	0	61
Cuba	510	–	–	–	–	–	–	–	–	–	0	510
Cyprus	–	–	225	–	–	–	–	143	–	38	165	571
Czechoslovakia	4 684	–	–	–	–	–	–	–	–	–	0	4 684
Denmark	–	295	12	299	–	–	–	–	–	–	43	649

Recipient	Seller USSR	USA	France	UK	China	FRG	Czech.	Italy	Netherlands	Brazil	Others	Total
Djibouti	–	–	3	–	–	–	–	–	–	–	0	3
Dominica	–	6	–	–	–	–	–	–	–	–	0	6
Dominican Republic	–	8	–	–	–	–	–	–	–	–	0	8
Ecuador	–	38	–	164	–	–	–	–	–	–	188	390
Egypt	–	4 121	803	3	–	14	–	253	–	149	117	5 460
El Salvador	–	1	–	–	–	–	–	–	–	–	4	5
Ethiopia	239	46	–	–	–	–	259	–	–	–	59	603
Fiji	–	–	1	–	–	–	–	–	–	–	5	6
Finland	232	1	54	35	–	–	–	3	–	–	272	597
France	–	1 633	–	26	–	–	–	–	–	–	42	1 701
Gabon	–	6	151	–	–	–	–	5	–	–	4	166
German DR	2 217	–	–	–	–	–	–	–	–	–	30	2 247
Germany, FR	–	3 309	62	80	–	–	–	–	13	–	46	3 510
Ghana	–	1	–	11	–	–	12	29	–	–	0	53
Greece	–	2 831	962	–	–	295	–	31	59	–	215	4 393
Guatemala	–	–	–	–	–	–	–	43	–	–	0	43
Guinea	22	–	1	–	–	–	–	–	–	–	0	23
Honduras	–	73	–	–	–	–	–	–	–	–	0	73
Hungary	477	–	–	–	–	71	–	–	–	–	0	548
India	13 871	–	882	1 516	–	254	–	–	326	–	713	17 562
Indonesia	–	486	60	375	–	122	–	–	348	–	38	1 429
Iran	715	–	719	–	703	41	125	43	–	25	498	2 862
Iraq	7 049	283	–	–	1 390	–	234	–	–	815	542	10 320
Ireland	–	23	–	30	–	–	–	5	–	–	5	63
Israel	–	4 475	–	–	–	19	–	–	63	–	9	4 566
Italy	–	559	17	–	–	80	–	–	–	–	144	800
Japan	–	9 537	49	164	–	–	–	–	–	–	0	9 750
Jordan	55	75	115	95	–	–	–	–	–	77	199	616
Kampuchea	170	–	–	–	20	–	–	–	–	–	128	318
Kenya	–	–	113	54	–	1	–	–	–	–	48	216
Korea, North	4 217	–	–	–	414	–	–	–	–	–	0	4 631
Korea, South	–	3 273	46	150	–	–	–	69	–	–	14	3 552
Kuwait	211	80	17	28	–	–	–	–	42	–	736	1 114

Laos	125	–	–	–	2	–	–	–	–	–	6	133
Lebanon	–	–	8	–	–	–	–	–	–	–	76	84
Lesotho	–	0	–	–	–	–	–	–	–	–	6	6
Liberia	801	–	–	–	–	–	69	–	–	179	9	9
Libya	–	1	–	–	–	–	–	–	–	–	52	1 101
Malawi	–	–	–	52	–	8	–	28	5	–	0	9
Malaysia	–	11	–	–	–	–	–	–	–	–	9	105
Mali	31	–	–	–	–	–	–	–	–	–	0	31
Malta	–	–	–	–	–	–	–	8	–	–	0	8
Mauritius	–	–	23	16	–	–	–	–	–	17	5	28
Mexico	–	270	25	–	–	–	–	–	–	–	26	337
Morocco	–	86	32	–	–	–	–	–	–	–	416	551
Mozambique	–	6	–	–	–	–	–	–	–	–	14	20
Nepal	–	–	9	3	2	–	–	–	–	–	0	11
Netherlands	–	1 964	–	–	–	–	–	–	–	–	13	1 980
New Zealand	–	23	–	2	–	–	–	24	–	–	57	106
Nicaragua	419	6	–	–	–	4	106	–	–	–	19	444
Nigeria	–	1	81	38	–	524	–	143	–	–	0	373
Norway	–	828	59	10	–	–	–	–	–	–	254	1 616
Oman	–	27	33	510	1 027	–	–	19	–	–	6	602
Pakistan	–	795	–	158	–	–	–	–	–	–	267	2 299
Panama	–	12	–	–	–	–	–	–	–	–	17	29
Papua New Guinea	19	–	–	–	–	–	–	–	–	–	8	27
Paraguay	336	217	284	1	–	–	–	–	–	25	8	33
Peru[a]	–	101	–	4	7	–	–	23	–	33	38	939
Philippines	–	–	–	–	–	5	–	27	–	–	7	144
Poland	3 780	383	–	–	–	172	–	–	–	–	2	3 954
Portugal	–	–	36	25	–	581	–	–	–	–	0	1 025
Qatar	1 278	–	359	–	–	–	–	–	–	–	12	371
Romania	–	–	107	–	–	–	–	–	–	–	0	1 385
Rwanda	–	–	7	–	–	–	–	–	–	–	0	7
Samoa	–	–	–	–	–	–	–	–	–	–	1	–
Saudi Arabia	–	2 855	1 995	3 474	1 715	4	–	295	–	148	111	10 597
Senegal	–	–	2	–	–	–	–	–	–	–	30	32
Seychelles	–	–	–	–	–	–	–	–	–	–	1	1
Sierra Leone	–	–	–	–	10	–	–	–	–	–	0	10
Singapore	–	1 031	101	–	–	144	–	–	–	–	0	1 276

Seller

Recipient	USSR	USA	France	UK	China	FRG	Czech.	Italy	Netherlands	Brazil	Others	Total
Solomon Islands	–	–	–	–	–	–	–	–	–	–	1	1
Somalia	0	–	–	–	–	–	–	–	–	–	13	13
South Africa	–	1	–	–	–	–	–	–	–	–	63	64
Spain	–	4 122	412	29	–	40	–	189	–	–	162	4 954
Sri Lanka	–	12	–	–	158	–	–	3	–	–	101	274
Sudan	–	9	–	0	67	–	–	25	–	–	127	228
Sweden	–	130	91	57	–	35	–	–	–	–	2	315
Switzerland	–	34	81	180	–	846	–	–	–	–	0	1 141
Syria	3 180	–	–	–	–	–	–	–	–	–	267	3 447
Taiwan	–	1 373	–	–	–	–	–	–	476	–	325	2 174
Thailand	–	1 635	132	143	1 290	50	–	58	32	–	30	3 370
Togo	–	–	17	3	–	–	–	–	–	–	4	24
Tonga	–	–	–	–	–	–	–	–	–	–	3	3
Tunisia	–	55	10	–	–	–	–	–	–	–	0	65
Turkey	–	3 953	22	10	–	1 549	–	125	237	–	490	6 386
Uganda	12	–	–	–	–	–	–	19	–	–	11	42
UK	–	1 202	171	–	–	22	–	–	38	7	157	1 597
United Arab Emirates	–	78	188	4	–	188	–	45	8	–	79	1 790
Uruguay	–	22	69	–	–	15	–	–	–	–	3	109
USA	–	–	4	417	128	201	–	50	–	–	599	1 399
USSR	–	–	–	–	–	–	2 277	–	–	–	736	3 013
Vanuatu	–	–	–	–	–	–	–	–	–	–	1	1
Venezuela	–	147	200	54	–	–	–	21	63	35	14	534
Viet Nam	6	–	–	–	–	–	–	–	–	–	0	6
Yemen, North	27	–	–	–	42	–	–	–	–	–	6	75
Yemen, South	292	–	–	–	–	–	–	–	–	–	0	292
Yugoslavia	1 511	–	34	–	–	–	–	–	–	–	7	1 552
Zaire	–	11	–	–	10	–	–	–	–	–	6	27
Zimbabwe	–	–	5	40	182	–	–	44	–	–	20	291
Total	61 339	59 960	11 225	9 096	7 857	6 112	3 264	1 878	1 758	1 629	10 420	174 538

a In 1991 SIPRI reported that Peru exported major conventional weapons worth $62 million in 1987–88. (Anthony, I. (ed.), SIPRI, *Arms Export Regulations* (Oxford University Press: Oxford, 1991), p. 6.) The Government of Peru has brought it to our attention that these were not arms transfers but the return of defective equipment to the USSR.

Appendix 8C. Register of the trade in and licensed production of major conventional weapons in industrialized and developing countries, 1991

IAN ANTHONY, AGNÈS COURADES ALLEBECK, GERD HAGMEYER-GAVERUS, PAOLO MIGGIANO, ELISABETH SKÖNS and HERBERT WULF

This register lists major weapons on order or under delivery, or for which the licence was bought and production was under way or completed during 1991. 'Year(s) of deliveries' includes aggregates of all deliveries and licensed production since the beginning of the contract. Sources and methods for the data collection, and the conventions, abbreviations and acronyms used, are explained in appendix 8D. Entries are alphabetical, by recipient, supplier and licenser.

Recipient/ supplier (S) or licenser (L)	No. ordered	Weapon designation	Weapon description	Year of order/ licence	Year(s) of deliveries	No. delivered/ produced	Comments
I. Industrialized countries							
Australia							
S: Italy	(10)	HSS-1	Surveillance radar	1986	1988–91	(8)	Deal worth $20 m
Papua New Guinea	4	Model 205 UH-1D	Helicopter	1991	1991	4	
Sweden	10	Giraffe	Fire control radar	1991			For Meko-200 Type frigates
USA	4	CH-47C Chinook	Helicopter	(1991)			Order may be for 6
	1	P-3C Orion	Maritime patrol	(1991)			Attrition replacement
	8	SH-60B Seahawk	Helicopter	1986	1990–91	(8)	In addition to 8 ordered 1985
	25	UH-60 Blackhawk	Helicopter	1985	1989–91	25	In addition to previous orders for 14 Blackhawk/Seahawks
	2	RGM-84A Launch	ShShM launcher	1983	1991	1	Arming FFG-7 Class frigates produced under licence; in addition to 4 delivered earlier
	2	RIM-66A Launch	ShAM launcher	1985	1991	1	Arming FFG-7 Class frigates produced under licence; in addition to 4 delivered earlier
	(32)	RGM-84A Harpoon	ShShM	1987	1991	18	Arming FFG-7 Class frigates and Oberon Class submarines

Recipient/ supplier (S) or licenser (L)	No. ordered	Weapon designation	Weapon description	Year of order/ licence	Year(s) of deliveries	No. delivered/ produced	Comments
	(32)	RIM-67C/SM-2	ShAM/ShShM	(1987)	1991	(16)	Deal worth $50 m
L: Germany, FR							
Sweden	10	Meko-200 Class	Frigate	1989			8 for Australia, 2 for New Zealand; option for 2 more
Sweden	6	Type-471	Submarine	1987			Deal worth $2.8 b
Switzerland	65	PC-9	Trainer	1986	1987–91	(58)	In addition to 2 delivered directly; 17 for assembly and 48 for production
UK	105	Hamel 105mm	Towed gun	(1982)	1988–91	(76)	Deal worth $112 m
USA	2	FFG-7 Class	Frigate	1983	1991	(1)	
Austria							
S: Sweden	1	J-35 Draken	Fighter	(1991)	1991	1	Attrition replacement
Sweden	500	RBS-56 Bill	Anti-tank missile	1989	1989–91	(400)	Deal worth $80 m
UK	2	BAe-146	Transport	1991			For Austrian UN relief activities
USA	24	M-109-A2 155mm	SPH	1988	1989–90	(12)	Deal worth $36 m; brings total ordered to 109
Belgium							
S: Burma	8	SF-260M	Trainer	1991	1991	(4)	
France	714	Mistral	Portable SAM	1988			Deal worth $93 m incl 118 launchers; offsets worth 75%
Sweden	28	Helitow	Fire control system	1988	1991	4	To equip A-109 helicopters
USA	545	AIM-9M	Air-to-air missile	1988			Arming F-16 fighters; deal worth $49 m
USA	940	AIM-9M	Air-to-air missile	1989			Deal worth $80 m
USA	(224)	BGM-71A TOW	Anti-tank missile	(1989)	1991	(32)	Arming 28 A-109A Mk-2 helicopters
L: Israel	21	EI/M-2310	Battlefield radar	1989	1990–91	(21)	Refitted to M-113 APCs to create mobile radars
Italy	46	A-109A Mk-2	Helicopter	1988	1991	(8)	Status uncertain; deal worth $317 m incl offsets worth 40%

Supplier	No.	Weapon designation	Weapon description	Year of order	Year of deliveries	No. delivered	Comments
USA	44	F-16A	Fighter	1983	1988–91	(44)	Deal worth $625 m; offsets worth 80%
Bulgaria							
S: USSR	: :	MiG-29	Fighter	1989	1990–91	(18)	
	: :	MT-LB	APC	(1970)	1972–90	(1 140)	
	: :	AA-10 Alamo	Air-to-air missile	1989	1990–91	(72)	Arming MiG-29 fighters
	: :	AA-11 Archer	Air-to-air missile	(1989)	1990–91	(108)	Arming MiG-29 fighters
Canada							
S: France	10 000	Eryx	Anti-tank missile	(1987)		(5)	Programme suspended
Italy	10	Skyguard	Air defence radar	1986	1989–90		Part of ADATS contract
Sweden	12	Giraffe	Fire control radar	(1985)	1988	2	Shipborne version for City Class frigates
Switzerland	28	ADATS	SAM system	1986	1988–90	6	Deal worth $1 b incl SAMs, AA guns and fire control radars
UK	(30)	EH-101	Helicopter	(1991)			Follow-on order for 20 probable
USA	5	C-130H Hercules	Transport	1991	1991	5	Deal worth $190 m
	28	F/A-18 Hornet	Fighter	1989			Attrition replacements
	3	P-3C Update-3	Maritime patrol	1989			
	2	AN/TPS-70	Air defence radar	1990			Deal worth $23 m
	4	Phalanx	CIWS	1987	1989	(1)	Arming Tribal Class frigates
	6	Phalanx	CIWS	1986	1988	(2)	Arming City Class frigates
	6	Phalanx	CIWS	1990			Deal worth $32 m; arming second batch of City Class frigates
	12	RGM-84A Launch	ShShM launcher	1983	1989–90	(2)	Arming City Class frigates
	336	Seasparrow	ShAM	1984	1990–91	(56)	Arming City Class frigates; deal worth $75 m
	12	Seasparrow VLS	ShAM launcher	1983	1990–91	(2)	Arming City Class frigates; deal worth $75 m incl missile modifications
	4	Standard VLS	Fire control radar	1986	1989–91	3	Arming Tribal Class frigates
	3	AGM-84A Harpoon	Anti-ship missile	1991			
	100	AIM-7M Sparrow	Air-to-air missile	(1987)	1990–91	100	Arming F/A-18 fighters; deal worth $31 m incl 24 Mk 48 torpedoes
	: :	RGM-84A Harpoon	ShShM	1988	1989–90	(58)	Arming City Class frigates

Recipient/ supplier (S) or licenser (L)	No. ordered	Weapon designation	Weapon description	Year of order/ licence	Year(s) of deliveries	No. delivered/ produced	Comments
	116	RIM-67C/SM-2	ShAM/ShShM	1986	1989–91	(87)	Arming Tribal Class frigates
L: Germany, FR	..	Bo-105LS	Helicopter	(1981)	1987–89	(17)	
UK	40	L-119 105mm	Towed gun	1990			Further orders expected
China							
S: USA	6	CH-47D Chinook	Helicopter	1989			Deliveries suspended in June 1989
	4	AN/TPQ-37	Tracking radar	(1987)	1988	2	Deliveries suspended in June 1989 along with deliveries of avionics, 4 Mk 46 torpedoes and 155mm howitzer ammunition
USSR	24	Mi-17 Hip-H	Helicopter	1990	1990–91	(24)	
	40	MiG-29	Fighter	1991			
	12	Su-24 Fencer	Fighter/bomber	(1990)			
	24	Su-27 Flanker	Fighter	1991	1991	8	Deal worth $700 m, offsets worth 40%
L: France	50	AS-365N	Helicopter	1980	1982–91	50	Option on 20 more
Israel	..	PL-8H	Air-to-air missile	(1989)	1990–91	100	
Cyprus							
S: France	36	AMX-30-B2	Main battle tank	1989	1989–91	36	Deal worth $115 m
Greece	75	Steyr-4K 7FA	APC	(1990)	1990–91	(32)	Option on 65 more
Yugoslavia	3	Koncar Class	FAC	1991	1991	3	
Czechoslovakia							
S: USSR	..	SA-13 Launcher	AAV(M)	(1984)	1985–89	(25)	
	..	SA-13 Gopher	Landmobile SAM	(1984)	1985–89	(330)	
	..	SA-9 Gaskin	Landmobile SAM	1979	1980–89	(1 600)	

Supplier/recipient	No. ordered	Weapon designation	Weapon description	Year of order	Year(s) of deliveries	No. delivered	Comments
L: USSR	..	T-72	Main battle tank	1978	1981–91	(760)	
Denmark							
S: Germany, FR	140	Leopard-1	Main battle tank	(1991)			CFE cascade
	..	RAM	ShAM	(1985)			Arming 3 Niels Juel Class frigates
Norway	3	Type-207	Submarine	1985	1989–91	3	CFE cascade
USA	12	M-110 203mm	SPH	(1991)			CFE cascade
	1	RGM-84A Launch	ShShM launcher	1991			Coastal defence version incl 2 mobile launchers and 1 fire control vehicle
	162	AGM-65D	ASM	1989			Arming F-16 fighters; deal worth $24 m
	840	FIM-92A Stinger	Portable SAM	1991			
	(24)	RGM-84A Harpoon	ShShM	1991			Arming coastal defence battery
Finland							
S: France	10	TRS-2230/15	3-D radar	1990			Deal worth $200 m
	(360)	Mistral	SAM	1989	1990–91	(180)	Arming Helsinki-2 Class FACs
	(480)	VT-1	SAM	1990	1991	(144)	
	4	Giraffe 100	Surveillance radar	1991			
Sweden	4	RBS-15 Launcher	ShShM launcher	1987	1990–91	(2)	Arming Helsinki-2 Class FACs
	64	RBS-15	ShAM/ShShM	(1987)	1990–91	(32)	Arming Helsinki-2 Class FACs
UK	7	Hawk	Jet trainer	1990	1990–91	(3)	Deal worth $16 m
	..	Marksman	AAV(G)	1988			
L: France	20	VT-1 launcher	SAM system	1990	1991	(6)	Deal worth $230 m
France							
S: Brazil	2	EMB-312 Tucano	Trainer	1991			For evaluation before possible order of 50
Spain	2	CN-235	Transport	1988	1991	2	
Switzerland	5	PC-7	Trainer	1990	1991	5	
USA	2	C-130H-30	Transport	1990	1991	2	Deal worth $58 m
	4	E-3 Sentry	AWACS	1987	1991	4	Deal worth $1258 m; option for 2 more, offsets worth 130%

Recipient/ supplier (S) or licenser (L)	No. ordered	Weapon designation	Weapon description	Year of order/ licence	Year(s) of deliveries	No. delivered/ produced	Comments
L: USA	1 000	VT-1	SAM	1988	1989–91	(1 000)	700 for re-export
	53	MLRS 227mm	MRL	1985	1989–91	(9)	In addition to 2 delivered directly
	..	VT-1	Landmobile SAM	1991			For production by Euromissile
Germany, FR							
S: France	23	TRS-3050	Surveillance radar	1987	1987–91	13	Improved fire control system for Type 148 FACs
Netherlands	3	Goalkeeper	CIWS	1991	1991	3	Arming F-122 Type frigates
	5	Smart	Fire control radar	1989			Fire control radar for Type 123 frigates
Switzerland	10	PC-9	Trainer	1989	1990–91	(10)	Deal worth $46.7 m
USA	3	AN/FPS-117	Air defence radar	1988	1991	(1)	
	28	Patriot battery	SAM system	1984	1989–90	18	
	4	Seasparrow VLS	ShAM launcher	1986			Arming Type 123 Class frigates
	1182	AGM-88 Harm	ARM	1987	1988–91	(720)	Arming Tornado fighters
	175	AIM-120A AMRAAM	Air-to-air missile	1991			Arming F-4F fighters
	804	MIM-104 Patriot	SAM	1984	1989–90	450	
L: USA	204	MLRS 227mm	MRL	1985	1989–91	60	
	..	AIM-120A AMRAAM	Air-to-air missile	1989			
	4 500	FIM-92 Stinger	Portable SAM	1987			
	(10 000)	RAM	ShAM	1985	1989–91	248	
Greece							
S: France	40	Mirage-2000	Fighter	1985	1988–90	28	
	(240)	Magic-2	Air-to-air missile	(1986)	1988–89	(220)	Arming Mirage-2000 fighters
Germany, FR	150	LARS 110mm	MRL	(1991)			CFE cascade
	75	Leopard-1	Main battle tank	(1991)			CFE cascade
	75	Leopard-1-A4	Main battle tank	1988	1991	(75)	Gift as offset for Greek order of 4 Meko-200 Type frigates

Quantity	Country	Designation	Description	Year of order	Year of delivery	No. delivered	Comments
200		M-113	APC	(1991)	1991	2	CFE cascade
(96)		NATO Seasparrow	ShAM	(1988)	1991	12	Arming Meko-200 Type frigates
1		Meko-200 Type	Frigate	1988			Deal worth $1.2 b incl 3 to be built under licence; offsets worth $250 m
5	Netherlands	Thetis Class	Corvette	1989			CFE cascade
12		F-5A	Fighter	1991			
170		Leopard-1-A4	Main battle tank	1991			
4		Smart	Fire control radar	1989			
2	UK	S-723 Martello	3-D radar	1990			For Meko-200 Type frigates
36	USA	A-7E Corsair-2	Fighter	1991			Deal worth $120 m incl overhaul, 14 spare engines and other spares
20		AH-64 Apache	Helicopter	(1991)			Deal worth $505 m incl 3 spare engines, electronic warfare systems, support and spares
(20)		F-16C	Fighter	1991			Deal worth $922 m
28		F-4E Phantom	Fighter	1990	1991	28	
6		P-3A Orion	Maritime patrol	1990			
5		SH-60B Seahawk	Helicopter	1991			Option on 3 more; for Meko-200 Class frigates
72		M-110 203mm	SPH	(1991)			CFE cascade
150		M-113	APC	(1991)			CFE cascade
359		M-60-A1	Main battle tank	1990	1990–91	(359)	CFE cascade
(312)		M-60-A3	Main battle tank	1990	1991	(71)	CFE cascade
26		M-88-A1	ARV	1989	1990–91	(26)	Option on 13 more
4		Phalanx	CIWS	(1987)			Arming Meko-200 Type frigates
(4)		RGM-84A Launch	ShShM launcher	1989	1989		Arming Meko-200 Type frigates
4		RGM-84A Launch	ShShM launcher	1991	1991	2	Arming 4 Charles F. Adams Class destroyers
4		RIM-67A Launch	ShAM launcher	1991	1991	2	Arming 4 Charles F. Adams Class destroyers
(4)		Seasparrow VLS	ShAM launcher	1988	1988		Arming Meko-200 Type frigates
446		AGM-114A	ASM	1991	1991		Arming AH-64 Apache helicopters
1 500		FIM-92A Stinger	Portable SAM	1988	1989–91	(750)	Deal worth $124 m incl 500 launchers
16		RGM-84A Harpoon	ShShM	1989	1989		Arming first of 4 Meko-200 Type frigates; deal worth $19 m
16		RGM-84A Harpoon	ShShM	1991	1991	8	Arming 4 Charles F. Adams Class destroyers; part of deal worth $100 m incl 64 Standard SAMs,

Recipient/ supplier (S) or licenser (L)	No. ordered	Weapon designation	Weapon description	Year of order/ licence	Year(s) of deliveries	No. delivered/ produced	Comments
	64	RIM-67A/SM-1	ShAM/ShShM	1991	1991	32	56 Mk 48 torpedoes, 10 000 rounds 5 in. ammunition and support
	4	Adams Class	Destroyer	1990	1991	2	Arming 4 Charles F. Adams Class destroyers
L: Austria	292	Steyr-4K 7FA	APC	1986	1987–91	242	Follows 300 ordered 1981
Denmark	3	PC-55 Class	Patrol craft	1990			Option on 2 more
Germany, FR	3	Meko-200 Type	Frigate	1988			In addition to 1 delivered directly; deal worth $1.2 b; financial aid from FRG and USA
Hungary							
S: Germany, FR	24	L-39 Albatross	Jet trainer	1991	1991	24	Former GDR equipment
	2	MiG-23MF	Fighter/interceptor	1991	1991	2	Former GDR equipment
	1	MiG-23U	Jet trainer	1991	1991	1	Former GDR equipment
Ireland							
S: Spain	2	CN-235MPA	Maritime patrol	1991			Deal worth $37 m incl 1 transport version
	1	CN-235	Transport	1991	1991	1	
USA	1	Gulfstream-3	Transport	1991	1991	1	
Italy							
S: Germany, FR	8	Do-228-200	Transport	1990	1990	2	Arming Tornado fighters
	..	Kormoran-2	Anti-ship missile	(1986)	1990–91	(30)	
USA	16	AV-8B Harrier-2	Fighter	1990			3 for direct delivery, 13 for assembly in Italy; follow-on order for 18 probable
	2	TAV-8B	Jet trainer	1990	1991	2	
	24	MLRS 227mm	MRL	1985	1989–91	(12)	

	No.	Weapon designation	Weapon description	Year of order	Year(s) of deliveries	No. delivered	Comments
	4	AN/FPS-117	Air defence radar	1990			Arming Animoso Class destroyers
	2	RIM-67A Launch	ShAM launcher	(1987)			Arming Tornado fighter/bomber; option on 30 more
	44	AGM-88 Harm	ARM	1991			Arming A-129 Mangusta helicopters
	(3 900)	BGM-71D TOW-2	Anti-tank missile	1987	1990–91	(360)	Arming Animoso Class destroyers
	(32)	RIM-67C/SM-2	ShAM/ShShM	1987			Arming Animoso Class destroyers
L: France	..	Aster	SAM	1988			To be built by Italmissile consortium
	23 000	Milan	Anti-tank missile	1984	1985–91	9 632	
	5 000	Mistral	SAM	(1988)			
USA	..	AB-206B	Helicopter	1972	1978–91	650	
	..	AB-212	Helicopter	1970	1971–91	180	
	..	AB-212ASW	Helicopter	1975	1975–91	160	
	..	AB-412 Griffon	Helicopter	1980	1982–91	64	Military version of Bell Model 412; Italy holds marketing rights
	..	CH-47C Chinook	Helicopter	1968	1972–91	173	Refit, servicing and maintenance continues
	50	Model 500E	Helicopter	1987	1987–91	30	Refit, servicing and maintenance continues
	..	SH-3D Sea King	Helicopter	1965	1969–91	102	Part of $2.9 b deal incl 1280 missiles
	20	Patriot battery	SAM system	1988			Italy probable supplier of Spanish and Turkish AGM-65 requirements
	(1 100)	AGM-65D	ASM	1988	1991	250	Part of deal worth $2.9 b
	1 280	MIM-104 Patriot	Landmobile SAM	1988			
Japan							
S: UK	3	BAe-125-800	Utility aircraft	1991	1991	1	Follow-on order for up to 24 expected
USA	3	E-2C Hawkeye	AEW	1989			Deal worth $214 m incl spares
	2	E-2C Hawkeye	AEW	1990			Deal worth $170 m
	11	MH-53E	Helicopter	1986	1989–90	(6)	
	80	Model-205 Kai	Helicopter	1991			
	1	AN/SPY-1D	Phased array radar	1988			Part of Aegis system, deal worth $17.7 m
	(28)	Phalanx	CIWS	1985	1987–91	20	Arming Asagiri Class and second batch of Hatsuyuki Class destroyers
	4	Phalanx	CIWS	1988			Part of Aegis air defence system arming Yukikaze Class destroyers

Recipient/ supplier (S) or licenser (L)	No. ordered	Weapon designation	Weapon description	Year of order/ licence	Year(s) of deliveries	No. delivered/ produced	Comments
	4	RGM-84A Launch	ShShM launcher	1988			Part of Aegis air defence system arming Yukikaze Class destroyers
	..	Seasparrow	ShAM	1980	1981–91	(392)	Arming various Japanese frigates and destroyers
	2	Standard VLS	Fire control radar	1988			Part of Aegis air defence system arming Yukikaze Class destroyers
	75	AGM-84A Harpoon	Anti-ship missile	1990	1991	(25)	Deal worth $125 m
	..	FIM-92A Stinger	Portable SAM	(1988)	1990–91	232	
	32	RGM-84A Harpoon	ShShM	1988	1988	(16)	Part of Aegis air defence system arming Yukikaze Class destroyers
	(350)	RIM-66C/SM-2	ShAM/ShShM	1988	1991	24	Part of Aegis air defence system arming Yukikaze Class destroyers
L: UK USA	176	FH-70 155mm	Towed howitzer	1984	1989–91	99	Following direct delivery of 197
	..	CH-47D Chinook	Helicopter	(1984)	1986–91	32	
	2	EP-3C Orion	ELINT	1987	1991	1	Deal worth $91 m; follow-on orders expected
	55	F-15J Eagle	Fighter	1985	1988–91	41	MoU signed Dec. 1984; in addition to 100 on order
	(130)	FS-X	Fighter	1988			Based on F-16C; US firms guaranteed 42% of work
	133	Model 205 UH-1H	Helicopter	1972	1973–91	133	
	88	Model 209 AH-1S	Helicopter	1982	1984–91	61	
	111	OH-6D	Helicopter	1977	1982–91	111	
	70	P-3C Orion	Maritime patrol	1985	1987–91	39	In addition to 45 ordered previously
	41	SH-60J Seahawk	Helicopter	1988	1990–91	17	
	46	UH-60J	Helicopter	1988	1990–91	9	
	36	MLRS 227mm	MRL	(1991)			Deal worth $362 m
	1 330	AIM-7M Sparrow	Air-to-air missile	1990	1990–91	305	Arming F-15 fighters; deal worth $477 m
	..	AIM-9L	Air-to-air missile	(1982)	1983–91	4 288	Arming F-15 fighters
	..	BGM-71C I-TOW	Anti-tank missile	(1983)	1985–91	4 074	Total requirement: up to 10 000
	980	MIM-104 Patriot	Landmobile SAM	1984	1989–91	452	
	..	MIM-23B Hawk	Landmobile SAM	1978	1978–91	3 004	

Netherlands

	No.	Weapon designation	Weapon description	Year of order	Year(s) of deliveries	No. delivered	Comments
S: Germany, FR	25	Buffel	ARV	1990	1990	9	
UK	9	Firefly-160	Trainer	1990	1991		
USA	4	Patriot battery	SAM system	1985			
	8	RGM-84A Launch	ShShM launcher	1988	1991	2	Arming Karel Doorman Class frigates
	(128)	Seasparrow	ShAM	1985	1991	(32)	Arming Karel Doorman Class frigates
	8	Seasparrow VLS	ShAM launcher	1985	1991	2	Arming Karel Doorman Class frigates
	(40)	AGM-84A Harpoon	Anti-ship missile	1988			
	290	AIM-9M	Air-to-air missile	1988	1990–91	(200)	Arming F-16 fighters; deal worth $27 m
	256	MIM-104 Patriot	SAM	1985			
	(88)	RGM-84A Harpoon	ShShM	1988	1991	(8)	
L: USA	57	F-16A	Fighter	1983	1987–91	(50)	Fourth order

New Zealand

	No.	Weapon designation	Weapon description	Year of order	Year(s) of deliveries	No. delivered	Comments
S: Australia	2	Meko-200 Class	Frigate	1989			Option on 2 more; deal worth $554.7 m
Italy	18	MB-339C	Jet trainer	1990	1991	3	Deal worth $206 m

Norway

	No.	Weapon designation	Weapon description	Year of order	Year(s) of deliveries	No. delivered	Comments
S: France	400	Mistral	Portable SAM	1990			Deal worth $60 m; offsets worth 75%
Germany, FR	92	Leopard-1	Main battle tank	1991			CFE cascade
	6	Type-210	Submarine	1983	1989–91	(5)	Norwegian designation: Ula Class
Sweden	(9)	Giraffe	Fire control radar	1989			Deal worth $90 m
	(360)	RBS-70	Portable SAM	1989	1991	(90)	Deal worth $80 m; offsets worth 45%; sixth order
UK	1	SH-3D Sea King	Helicopter	1989			Deal worth $18 m including upgrade of Norwegian Sea King fleet
USA	136	M-113	APC	1991			CFE cascade
	..	AN/TPQ-36	Tracking radar	1990			Part of a fire control for ground-launched AMRAAM
	100	AIM-120A AMRAAM	Air-to-air missile	1989			Deal worth $75 m, arming F-16 fighters
	7 612	BGM-71D TOW-2	Anti-tank missile	1985	1987–91	(4 000)	Deal worth $126 m incl 300 launchers and spares

Recipient/ supplier (S) or licenser (L)	No. ordered	Weapon designation	Weapon description	Year of order/ licence	Year(s) of deliveries	No. delivered/ produced	Comments
Poland							
S: Canada	2	Model 206B	Helicopter	1991	1991	2	Deal worth $4 m
Germany, FR	2	MiG-23U	Jet trainer	1991	1991	2	
	2	Su-22 Fitter-J	Fighter/grd attack	1991	1991	2	
	3	Balcom 10 Class	FAC	1990	1990–91	(3)	Transferred without armament
L: USSR	..	2S1 122mm	SPH	(1980)	1982–91	(490)	Some built for export
Portugal							
S: Germany, FR	3	Seasparrow L	ShAM launcher	1986	1991	2	Deal worth $700 m; 60% from NATO military fund
	3	Meko-200 Type	Frigate	1986	1991	2	CFE cascade
Netherlands	104	M-113	APC	1991			CFE cascade
	24	YP-408	APC	1991			
UK	5	Super Lynx	Helicopter	1989	1991	4	Deal worth $81 m, offsets worth 25%
USA	1	C-130H-30	Transport	1991	1991	1	
	17	F-16A	Fighter	1990			
	3	F-16B	Fighter/trainer	1990			
	..	Model 205 UH-1A	Helicopter.	1989			In exchange for US base in the Azores; ex-USAF; part of a total of 52 helicopters
	..	Model 209 AH-1G	Helicopter	1989			In exchange for US base in the Azores; ex-USAF; part of a total of 52 helicopters
	80	M-60-A3	Main battle tank	1991	1991	80	CFE cascade
	2	AN/MPQ-54	Surveillance radar	1989	1990–91	2	In exchange for US base in the Azores; ex USAF
	1	Hawk SAMS	SAM system	1989			
	3	Phalanx	CIWS	1986	1991	2	Arming 3 Meko-200 Type frigates
	3	RGM-84A Launch	ShShM launcher	1986	1991	2	Arming 3 Meko-200 Type frigates
	24	Seasparrow	ShAM	1986	1991	(16)	Arming 3 Meko-200 Type frigates
	24	RGM-84A Harpoon	ShShM	1986	1991	(16)	Arming 3 Meko-200 Type frigates

		No.	Weapon designation	Weapon description	Year of order	Year(s) of deliveries	No. delivered	Comments
L:	Belgium	100	Jet Squalus	Jet trainer	1989			30 for Portuguese Air Force, 15 for civilian use and 55 for export
Romania								
S:	USSR	40	MiG-29	Fighter	(1989)	1990	16	
L:	France	..	SA-330 Puma	Helicopter	1977	1978–91	155	Attrition replacement
	USSR	..	Ka-126	Helicopter	(1987)	1988–91	16	
Spain								
S:	France	350	Mistral	Portable SAM	1988			Deal worth $336 m; total requirement up to 3000
		720	Mistral	Portable SAM	1991			In addition to 350 ordered in 1989
	USA	5	AV-8B Harrier-2	Fighter	1990	1991	5	
		1	F/A-18 Hornet	Fighter	1990			Attrition replacement
		8	S-76C	Helicopter	1991		2	
		6	SH-60B Seahawk	Helicopter	1991		(2)	Deal worth $251 m; to equip FFG-7 Class frigates
		100	M-113	APC	1991			CFE cascade
		160	M-60-A1	Main battle tank	1991			CFE cascade
		260	M-60-A3	Main battle tank	1991			CFE cascade
		4	RGM-84A Launch	ShShM launcher	1988			Coastal defence version
		2	RGM-84A Launch	ShShM launcher	1989			Arming FFG-7 Class frigates
		2	RIM-67A Launch	ShAM launcher	1989			Arming FFG-7 Class frigates
		250	AGM-65F	Anti-ship missile	1989	1990–91	(200)	Arming F/A-18 Hornet fighters; mix of F and G versions
		(70)	AGM-84A Harpoon	Anti-ship missile	(1987)			Arming F/A-18 Hornet fighters
		200	AIM-120A AMRAAM	Air-to-air missile	1990			Deal worth $132 m
		16	RGM-84A Harpoon	ShShM	1989			Arming coastal defence battery
		(16)	RGM-84A Harpoon	ShShM	1989			Arming FFG-7 Class frigates
		150	RIM-67A/SM-1	ShAM/ShShM	(1989)			Deal worth $88 m; arming FFG-7 Class frigates
L:	UK	5	Sandown Class	Minehunter	(1988)			
	USA	2	FFG-7 Class	Frigate	1990			In addition to 4 ordered previously

Recipient/ supplier (S) or licenser (L)	No. ordered	Weapon designation	Weapon description	Year of order/ licence	Year(s) of deliveries	No. delivered/ produced	Comments
Sweden							
S: France	12	AS-332	Helicopter	1987	1988–90	(10)	Deal worth $106 m; for Navy
	..	TRS-2620	Surveillance radar	1990			
Germany, FR	5	MT-LB	APC	1991	1991	5	Former GDR equipment
	5	T-72	Main battle tank	1991	1991	5	Former GDR equipment; for testing
L: USA	700	AGM-114A	Anti-tank missile	1987	1990–91	300	Deal worth $65 m; Hellfire coastal defence version
Switzerland							
S: France	12	AS-332	Helicopter	1989	1991	6	Deal worth $190 m; offsets worth 100%
UK	3	Watchman	Surveillance radar	1990			
USA	34	F/A-18 Hornet	Fighter	1991			Deal worth $2.5 b incl 26 C versions, 8 D versions and spares; offsets worth 100%
	..	AIM-120A AMRAAM	Air-to-air missile	1988			Arming F/A-18 Hornet fighters
	204	AIM-7M Sparrow	Air-to-air missile	1988			Arming F/A-18 Hornet fighters
	(204)	AIM-9L	Air-to-air missile	(1988)			Arming F/A-18 Hornet fighters
	12 000	BGM-71D TOW-2	Anti-tank missile	(1985)	1988–91	(2 350)	Deal worth $209 m incl 3 000 practice rounds, 400 launchers and night vision sights
	3 500	FIM-92A Stinger	Portable SAM	1988			Licensed production under discussion
L: Germany, FR	345	Leopard-2	Main battle tank	1983	1987–91	290	Deal worth $1400 m incl 35 delivered directly
UK	19	Hawk	Jet trainer	1987	1990–91	19	Deal worth $150 m incl training and logistics
Turkey							
S: France	5	Stentor	Surveillance radar	1987	1988–91	(4)	
	14	TRS-22XX	3-D radar	1987			
Germany, FR	..	Alpha Jet	Jet trainer	1991			
	131	LARS 110mm	MRL	(1991)			
	8	Leopard	ARV	1988	1990	4	CFE cascade

No.	Supplier	Weapon designation	Weapon description		No. delivered	Comments
100		Leopard-1-A1	Main battle tank	(1991)		CFE cascade
150		Leopard-1-A4	Main battle tank	(1987) 1990–91	150	Deal worth $384 m
550		M-113	APC	(1991)		CFE cascade
1		FPB-57	FAC	1991		Prior to licensed production
1	Italy	Meko-200 Type	Frigate	1990		Part of deal worth $465 m incl 1 to be built in Turkey
14		SF-260TP	Trainer	1990 1990–91	12	To be assembled from knock-down kits
100		M-113	APC	(1991)		CFE cascade
2		Seaguard	CIWS	1990		Arming 2 Meko-200 Type frigates
45	Netherlands	F-5A	Fighter	1987 1989–91	45	
2	Spain	CN-235	Transport	1990 1991	2	Followed by licensed production of 50
..	USA	C-130B Hercules	Transport	1991 1991	2	
40		F-4E Phantom	Fighter	1991 1991	40	
5		Model 209 AH-1S	Helicopter	1990 1990–91	(5)	
72		M-110 203mm	SPH	(1991)		CFE cascade
300		M-113	APC	1990		
(250)		M-113	APC	(1991)		CFE cascade
(164)		M-60-A1	Main battle tank	(1991)		CFE cascade
658		M-60-A3	Main battle tank	(1991)		CFE cascade
600		M-60-A3	Main battle tank	(1990) 1991	(300)	Southern Region amendment aid programme
12		MLRS 227mm	MRL	1988 1989–91	12	Part of $1 b deal; 180 more to be co-produced
1		AN/FPS-117	Air defence radar	1991		Deal worth $15 m; option on 2 more
1		Patriot battery	SAM system	1991 1991	1	Follow-on order of 10 expected
2		RGM-84A Launch	ShShM launcher	1990		Arming 2 Meko-200 Type frigates
(32)		Seasparrow	ShAM	1990		Arming 2 Meko-200 Type frigates
2		Seasparrow L	ShAM launcher	1990		Arming 2 Meko-200 Type frigates
350		AGM-65D	ASM	1991		
100		AGM-88 Harm	ARM	1991		Deal worth $29 m incl training missiles and support
80		AIM-7F Sparrow	Air-to-air missile	1987 1990–91	(80)	Arming F-4E fighters from US stockpiles
80		AIM-9E	Air-to-air missile	1987 1990–91	(80)	Arming F-4E fighters
310		AIM-9E	Air-to-air missile	1990		Deal worth $30 m incl training missiles
469		FIM-92A Stinger	Portable SAM	1991		Deal worth $33 m incl 150 launchers
32		MIM-104 Patriot	SAM	1991 1991	32	
(16)		RGM-84A Harpoon	ShShM	(1990)		Arming 2 Meko-200 Type frigates

Recipient/ supplier (S) or licenser (L)	No. ordered	Weapon designation	Weapon description	Year of order/ licence	Year(s) of deliveries	No. delivered/ produced	Comments
L: Germany, FR	1	FPB-57	FAC	1991			Dogan Class; in addition to licensed production of 1
	1	Meko-200 Type	Frigate	1990			Part of deal worth $465 m
	2	Type-209/3	Submarine	1987			Option on 4 more
Italy	26	SF-260D	Trainer	1990			In addition to 14 delivered directly
Spain	50	CN-235M	Transport	1990			Part of deal worth $500 m incl 20 civil versions and 2 delivered directly; initially local assembly only
USA	152	F-16C	Fighter	1984	1987–91	97	Part of deal worth $4 b with direct delivery of 8 C and D versions
	80	F-16C	Fighter	1991			Deal worth $2.8 b incl 12 spare engines
	1 698	AIFV	AIFV	1988	1989–91	100	Deal worth $1 b; offsets worth $700 m
	120	MLRS 227mm	MRL	1988	1991	8	Including 36 000 rockets
	..	FIM-92A Stinger	Portable SAM	1989			Part of NATO Stinger programme

UK

Recipient/ supplier (S) or licenser (L)	No. ordered	Weapon designation	Weapon description	Year of order/ licence	Year(s) of deliveries	No. delivered/ produced	Comments
S: Germany, FR	(3)	Mi-8 Hip	Helicopter	1991	1991	(3)	For combat training prior to Gulf War; former GDR equipment
	1	MiG-23	Fighter/interceptor	(1991)	1991	1	Former GDR equipment
	1	Su-22 Fiter-J	Fighter/grd attack	1991	1991	1	For training purposes; former GDR equipment
USA	6	E-3 Sentry	AWACS	1986	1991	3	130% offsets
	1	E-3 Sentry	AWACS	1987			Deal worth $120 m with offsets of 130%; option on 8th AWACS declined
	(330)	AIM-120A AMRAAM	Air-to-air missile	(1988)			Status uncertain
L: Brazil	128	EMB-312 Tucano	Trainer	1985	1987–91	89	Deal worth $145–150 m; option on 15 more
France	..	Milan	Anti-tank missile	1976	1977–91	75 951	
Switzerland	(1 000)	Piranha	APC	1991			Produced for export to unnamed customer
USA	..	WS-70	Helicopter	1987	1987	1	
	59	MLRS 227mm	MRL	1985	1989–91	14	

Recipient	No.	Weapon designation	Weapon description	Year of order	Year(s) of deliveries	No. delivered	Comments
	223	AIM-120A AMRAAM	Air-to-air missile	1988			Licensed production by Euraam (BAe, MBB, AEG and Marconi)
	..	BGM-71A TOW	Anti-tank missile	1980	1982–91	23 334	
USA							
S: Australia	12	CH-47C Chinook	Helicopter	1988	1991		In exchange for 4 CH-47D
Germany, FR	1	MiG-21F	Fighter	1991	1991	1	Former GDR equipment
	2	MiG-23BN	Fighter/grd attack	1991	1991	2	Former GDR equipment
	5	MiG-23MF	Fighter/interceptor	1991	1991	5	Former GDR equipment
	1	MiG-29	Fighter	(1991)	1991	1	Former GDR equipment
	60	Tpz-1	APC	1989	1989–91	60	Deal worth $31 m
	48	Tpz-1	APC	(1991)	1991	8	Former GDR equipment
	1	Tarantul Class	Corvette	(1991)	1991	1	Former GDR equipment
Italy	10	G-222	Transport	1990	1991	3	Deal worth $157 m; option on 10 more; US designation C-27A
	4	Spada battery	SAM system	1988			For defence of US air bases in Italy
	16	Skyguard	Air defence radar	1990			For defence of US air bases in Italy
	(144)	Aspide	SAM/ShAM	1988			
Norway	64	Penguin-3	Anti-ship missile	1990			Option on 200 more
Spain	(6)	C-212-300	Transport	1989	1990–91	3	Test bed for tactical reconnaissance radar
Switzerland	3	PC-9	Trainer	(1990)	1991	3	
L: Israel	86	Have Nap	ASM	1987	1990–91	54	For co-production with Martin Marietta; US designation AGM-142
Italy	17	Lerici Class	MCM	1986	1989		US designation Osprey Class
Switzerland	160	ADATS	SAM system	1987	1988	3	Deliveries suspended in 1990
	302	T-45 Hawk	Jet trainer	1986	1990–91	2	
UK	436	M-119 105mm	Towed gun	1987	1991	56	Arming US Light Divisions; follows direct purchase of 53
	10	Ramadan Class	Patrol craft	1990		1	
USSR							
S: Romania	..	Yak-52	Trainer	(1979)	1979–91	(1950)	About 200 per year produced for USSR

Recipient/ supplier (S) or licenser (L)	No. ordered	Weapon designation	Weapon description	Year of order/ licence	Year(s) of deliveries	No. delivered/ produced	Comments
Yugoslavia							
S: USSR	48	MiG-29	Fighter	(1987)	1988–89	(16)	
	(216)	AA-7 Apex	Air-to-air missile	(1987)	1988–89	(96)	Arming MiG-29 fighters
	(216)	AA-8 Aphid	Air-to-air missile	(1987)	1988–89	(96)	Arming MiG-29 fighters
L: USSR	..	T-72	Main battle tank	1977	1983–90	(400)	Yugoslavian designation M-84; now produced only for export
II. Developing countries							
Afghanistan							
S: Egypt	..	Sakr-18 122mm	MRL	(1988)	1988–91	(40)	For Mujahideen; with large quantities of artillery rockets
Saudi Arabia	(55)	T-55	Main battle tank	1991	1991	(55)	For Mujahideen; transferred along with artillery captured from Iraq
USSR	..	Mi-24 Hind-D	Helicopter	(1984)	1984–91	(61)	Unknown mix of BMP-1 and 2 versions; may include Czechoslovakian-built BMPs
	..	BMP-1	APC	(1979)	1979–91	(506)	
	..	D-1 152mm	Towed howitzer	(1987)	1988–91	(222)	
	..	D-30 122mm	Towed howitzer	(1978)	1978–91	(508)	
	..	M-46 130mm	Towed gun	(1979)	1979–91	(186)	
	..	T-55	Main battle tank	(1978)	1978–91	(705)	
	..	T-62	Main battle tank	(1979)	1979–91	(155)	
	..	Scud-B	SSM	(1988)	1988–91	(2 300)	
Angola							
S: Spain	(3)	Cormoran Class	FAC	1989	1990		
Switzerland	8	PC-7	Trainer	(1989)	1990	6	

Argentina

	No.	Weapon designation	Weapon description	Year of order	Year(s) of deliveries	No. delivered	Comments
S: Canada	150	Model 212	Helicopter	(1990)			Mix of civil and military versions not clear
L: Germany, FR	6	Meko-140 Type	Frigate	1980	1985–91	5	Armed with MM-40 Exocet ShShMs; last 2 will be available for export
Italy	4	Type TR-1700	Submarine	1977			In addition to 2 delivered directly
	..	A-109 Hirundo	Helicopter	1988			Deal worth $120 m
USA	..	Model-412	Helicopter	1991			Licence authorizes sales to Latin American countries

Bahrain

	No.	Weapon designation	Weapon description	Year of order	Year(s) of deliveries	No. delivered	Comments
S: USA	8	AH-64 Apache	Helicopter	1991			
	43	M-60-A3	Main battle tank	1990	1991	43	Deal worth $50 m
	9	MLRS 227mm	MRL	1990			
	450	AGM-114A	ASM	1990			Arming AH-64 Apache helicopters

Bangladesh

	No.	Weapon designation	Weapon description	Year of order	Year(s) of deliveries	No. delivered	Comments
S: Pakistan	50	F-6	Fighter	1989	1990–91	50	

Bolivia

	No.	Weapon designation	Weapon description	Year of order	Year(s) of deliveries	No. delivered	Comments
S: USA	4	C-130H Hercules	Transport	1990	1991	(2)	Part of $33.2 m aid programme
	1	DC-3	Transport	1991	1991	1	
	6	Model 205 UH-1H	Helicopter	1990			Paid for by US military assistance

Brazil

	No.	Weapon designation	Weapon description	Year of order	Year(s) of deliveries	No. delivered	Comments
S: UK	(5)	Super Lynx	Helicopter	1991			For new class of corvettes, probably to be armed with Sea Skua anti-ship missiles
USA	4	L119 105mm gun	Towed gun	1991			In L118 configuration
	12	AAV-7	APC	1991			
	4	Phalanx	CIWS	1988			Arming 4 Niteroi Class frigates
L: Austria	..	GHN-45 155mm	Towed howitzer	(1985)			Status uncertain
Germany, FR	..	SNAC-1	SSN	1989			

Recipient/ supplier (S) or licenser (L)	No. ordered	Weapon designation	Weapon description	Year of order/ licence	Year(s) of deliveries	No. delivered/ produced	Comments
	3	Type-209/3	Submarine	1982			
Brunei							
S: Germany, FR	(96)	AIM-9L	Air-to-air missile	1989	1991	(12)	Arming Hawk-100 fighters
Indonesia	3	CN-235	Maritime patrol	1989			
UK	16	Hawk-100	Jet trainer	1989			Deal worth $260 m
USA	1	UH-60 Blackhawk	Helicopter	(1989)			VIP version
Burma							
S: China	(12)	F-6	Fighter	1990	1991	(12)	
	..	F-7	Fighter	1990	1990–91	(6)	On lease for 6 months
	1	Y-12	Transport	1991	1991	1	
	..	PL-2A	Air-to-air missile	1990	1990–91	(108)	Arming F-6 and F-7 fighters
	6	Hainan Class	Patrol craft	1990			
Poland	6	W-3 Sokol	Helicopter	1990	1991	6	
Yugoslavia	20	G-4 Super Galeb	Jet trainer	1990	1991	6	Option for 10 more; paid for in teak
Chile							
S: France	4	AS-332	Helicopter	1987	1988	2	Part of a deal worth $77 m incl 4 AS-565 helicopters
	4	AS-565 Panther	Helicopter	1987			To equip County Class frigates; first export of ASW version
Germany, FR	..	Mistral	Portable SAM	(1990)	1991	(50)	
	(30)	Bo-105CB	Helicopter	1985	1986–90	9	
Israel	(6)	Barak Launcher	ShAM launcher	1989			For refit into Chilean frigates
	2	Phalcon	AEW&C radar	(1989)			Deal worth $500 m incl 4 Boeing-707s
	(256)	Barak	ShAM	1989			
UK	2	Leander Class	Frigate	1990	1990–91	2	
L: South Africa	(400)	G-5 155 mm	Towed howitzer	1989	1990	6	

Supplier	Weapon designation	No. ordered	Weapon description	Year of order	Year(s) of deliveries	No. delivered	Comments
Switzerland	Piranha	..	APC	1980	1981–91	251	
USA	Model 206	..	Helicopter	(1988)	1989	1	
Colombia							
S: Israel	Barak Launcher	..	ShAM launcher	1989			Arming F-1500 Type frigate
Spain	C-212-300	3	Transport	1988	1989–91	3	
USA	Citation-2	..	Transport	(1990)	1990	1	
	OV-10A Bronco	16	Trainer/COIN	1991	1991	16	May be up to 18
Cuba							
S: USSR	MiG-29	(36)	Fighter	(1985)	1989–91	(12)	
Ecuador							
S: Canada	Model 206B	12	Helicopter	1991	1991	12	
UK	Jaguar	(3)	Fighter	1991	1991		Withdrawn from RAF service; order may be for 6
	MM-38 Launcher	2	ShShM launcher	1991	1991	2	Arming Leander Class frigates
	MM-38 Exocet	8	ShShM	1991	1991	8	Arming Leander Class frigates
	Leander Class	2	Frigate	1991	1991	2	Deal worth $3.2 m, transferred without Seacat missiles
USA	A-37B Dragonfly	6	Fighter/COIN	1991	1991	6	
Egypt							
S: Czechoslovakia	L-59	48	Jet trainer	1991			Deal worth $204 m
USA	AH-64 Apache	24	Helicopter	1990			Deal worth $488 m incl Hellfire missiles
	E-2C Hawkeye	2	AEW	1989	1990	1	Deal worth $84 m
	F-16C	42	Fighter	1987	1991	(10)	Third order
	F-16C	46	Fighter	1991			From Turkish assembly line; deal worth $1.3 b
	F-16D	4	Fighter/trainer	1987	1991	4	
	M-1 Abrams	15	Main battle tank	1988	1990–91	15	Part of $2 b deal incl 540 to be co-produced
	RGM-84A Launch	4	ShShM launcher	(1990)			Part of Romeo Class submarine modernization programme worth $113.6 m
	Trackstar	(10)	Surveillance radar	(1989)	1990–91	(10)	Deal worth $38 m

Recipient/ supplier (S) or licenser (L)	No. ordered	Weapon designation	Weapon description	Year of order/ licence	Year(s) of deliveries	No. delivered/ produced	Comments
	492	AGM-114A	ASM	1990			Arming AH-64 Apache helicopters
	144	AGM-65D	ASM	1988	1991	80	Arming F-16 fighters; deal worth $27 m incl training missiles, parts and electronic counter measure pods
	40	AGM-65D	ASM	1991			Arming F-16 fighters
	40	AGM-65G	ASM	1991			Arming F-16 fighters
	20	AGM-84A Harpoon	Anti-ship missile	1990			
	282	AIM-7M Sparrow	Air-to-air missile	(1987)			Arming F-16 fighters; deal worth $42 m
	7 511	BGM-71D TOW-2	Anti-tank missile	1988	1989–91	(600)	Includes 180 launchers, 504 night-vision sights and spares
	100	FIM-92A Stinger	Portable SAM	1990	1991	100	Supplied to Egyptian forces in Desert Storm
L: UK							
USA	..	Swingfire	Anti-tank missile	1977	1979–91	7 412	
	540	M-1 Abrams	Main battle tank	1988			Following direct delivery of 15; deal worth $2 b
	34	AN/TPS-63	Surveillance radar	1986	1988–91	25	Deal worth $190 m
	..	AIM-9P	Air-to-air missile	(1988)	1990–91	996	In addition to 37 assembled from kits
Ethiopia							
S: USSR	1	Natya Class	MSO	(1990)			Completed 1991 but not delivered
	2	Sonya Class	MSC	(1990)			Completed 1991 but not delivered
Fiji							
S: France	1	AS-365N	Helicopter	1990			
Israel	4	Dabur Class	Patrol craft	1991	1991	4	
Guatemala							
S: Italy	2	G-222L	Transport	1989	1991	2	Deal worth $36.3 m

India

		No.	Weapon designation	Weapon description	Year of order	Year(s) of deliveries	No. delivered	Comments
S:	UK	10	Sea Harrier	Fighter	1985	1990–91	(10)	Deal worth $230 m incl 1 trainer
	USSR	10	Mi-26 Halo	Helicopter	1988			Second order
		6	SA-N-5 Launcher	ShAM launcher	1987	1987–91	6	Arming Tarantul Class corvettes
		(8)	SA-N-5 Launcher	ShAM launcher	(1983)	1989–91	4	Arming Khukri Class corvettes
		6	SA-N-5 Launcher	ShAM launcher	1987	1991	1	Arming Vibhuti Class corvettes
		8	SSN-2 Styx L	ShShM launcher	1987	1987–91	6	Arming Tarantul Class corvettes
		8	SSN-2 Styx L	ShShM launcher	1983	1989–91	4	Arming Khukri Class corvettes
		6	SSN-2 Styx L	ShShM launcher	1987	1991	1	Arming Vibhuti Class corvettes
		(400)	SA-16	Portable SAM	(1990)	1990–91	(200)	
		(72)	SA-N-5	ShAM	1987	1987–91	(72)	Arming Tarantul Class corvettes
		(96)	SA-N-5	ShAM	(1983)	1989–91	(48)	Arming Khukri Class corvettes
		(72)	SA-N-5	ShAM	1987	1991	(12)	Arming Vibhuti Class corvettes
		(24)	SSN-2 Styx	ShShM	1987	1987–91	(24)	Arming Tarantul Class corvettes
		(32)	SSN-2 Styx	ShShM	1983	1989–91	(16)	Arming Khukri Class corvettes
		(24)	SSN-2 Styx	ShShM	1987	1991	(4)	Arming Vibhuti Class corvettes
		8	Kilo Class	Submarine	(1984)	1986–91	8	
		2	Kilo Class	Submarine	1990			In addition to 8 ordered previously
		5	Pauk Class	Corvette	1983	1989–91	4	
		6	Tarantul Class	Corvette	1987	1987–91	6	Armed with SSN-2 Styx and SA-N-5 missiles
L:	France	(42 000)	SA-316B Chetak	Helicopter	(1962)	1964–91	206	Also produced for civilian use
	Germany, FR	86	Milan	Anti-tank missile	1982	1985–91	24 545	
		2	Do-228	Transport	1983	1987–91	38	
	Korea, South	7	Type-1500	Submarine	1981	1991	1	
		..	Sukanya Class	OPV	1987	1990–91	3	In addition to 2 delivered directly
	Netherlands	212	Flycatcher	Mobile radar	(1987)	1988–91	38	In addition to 3 delivered directly
	USSR	165	MiG-27	Fighter/grd attack	1983	1987–91	100	In addition to direct deliveries
		..	BMP-2	APC	1983	1987–91	184	Indian designation Sarath
		(1 000)	T-72	Main battle tank	(1980)	1987–91	700	Production under way 1987; 10% Indian content
		..	AA-8 Aphid	Air-to-air missile	(1986)			Indian designation Astra
		6	Vibhuti Class	Corvette	1987	1991	1	Order may reach 15

Recipient/ supplier (S) or licenser (L)	No. ordered	Weapon designation	Weapon description	Year of order/ licence	Year(s) of deliveries	No. delivered/ produced	Comments
Indonesia							
S: Netherlands	..	F-27 Mk-100	Transport	1990			
UK	14	AR-325	Surveillance radar	1989	1991	(2)	
	1	Surveiller	Maritime patrol	1991			
USA	2	C-130H-30	Transport	1990	1991	2	
	8	F-16A	Fighter	(1986)	1990–91	(8)	Deal worth $336 m incl 4 F-16Bs; offsets worth $52 m
	(72)	AIM-9P	Air-to-air missile	(1986)	1989–91	(72)	Arming F-16 fighters
L: France	..	AS-332	Helicopter	1983	1985–91	(10)	
Germany, FR	(80)	NBo-105	Helicopter	1987	1988–91	(48)	Licence to produce up to 100
	6	PB-57 Type	Patrol craft	1982	1988–89	(4)	Probably 4 for Coast Guard279
Spain	(80)	CN-212	Transport	1976	1978–91	(36)	
UK	69	Hawk	Jet trainer	1991			Mix of Hawk-100 and 200 versions
Iran							
S: China	(8)	HQ-2B	SAM system	(1989)	1990–91	(4)	Coastal air defence batteries
	(96)	HQ-2B	SAM	1989	1990–91	(48)	For coastal air defence batteries
Czechoslovakia	(300)	T-55	Main battle tank	1991			Order number may be higher
Iraq	47	MiG-21 Bis	Fighter	1991			Flown to Iran and not returned; incl unspecified number of Su-25 fighters
	4	MiG-29	Fighter	1991			Flown to Iran and not returned
	40	Su-20 Fitter-C	Fighter/grd attack	1991			Flown to Iran and not returned
	24	Su-24 Fencer	Fighter/bomber	1991			Flown to Iran and not returned
Pakistan	25	Supporter	Trainer	1989	1989–91	(25)	
USSR	..	T-72	Main battle tank	1989	1990–91	(100)	Order may be up to 500
L: China	..	Oghab	SSM	1985	1986–91	(1 000)	Chinese Type-83 rocket; local production continues

Supplier/recipient	Weapon designation	Weapon description	Year of order	Year(s) of deliveries	No. ordered	No. delivered	Comments
Israel							
S: Germany, FR	BRDM-2	Scout car	1991	1991	50	50	Reconnaissance vehicle with NBC protection
	T-72	Main battle tank	1991	1991	12	12	For technical evaluation
	Tpz-1	APC	1991	1991	8	8	For NBC reconnaissance
	SA-6 SAMS	SAM system	1991		1		For technical evaluation
	AA-10 Alamo	Air-to-air missile	(1990)	1991	(1)	(1)	For technical evaluation
	AA-8 Aphid	Air-to-air missile	(1990)	1991	(1)	(1)	For technical evaluation
	AT-3 Sagger	Anti-tank missile	(1990)	1991	(1)	(1)	For technical evaluation
	AT-4 Spigot	Anti-tank missile	(1990)	1991	(1)	(1)	For technical evaluation
	AT-5 Spandrel	Anti-tank missile	(1990)	1991	(1)	(1)	For technical evaluation
Netherlands	Dolphin	Submarine	1991		2		Deal worth $570 m; financed by US FMS funding
	Patriot battery	SAM system	1991	1991	1	1	
	MIM-104 Patriot	SAM	1991	1991	(32)	(32)	
USA	AH-64 Apache	Helicopter	1989	1990–91	18	18	Deal worth $285 m incl support equipment
	Bonanza A-36	Lightplane	1990		..		
	CH-53E	Helicopter	1990	1990–91	10	10	
	F-15A Eagle	Fighter	1990	1991	15	9	Ex-USAF
	F-15A Eagle	Fighter	1991		10		
	F-16C	Fighter	1988	1991	30	(15)	In addition to 15 leased in 1990
	F-16D	Fighter/trainer	1988	1991	30	(15)	Follow-on order for 60 more under negotiation
	Patriot battery	SAM system	1990	1990–91	4	3	
	Patriot battery	SAM system	(1991)		1		In addition to previous deliveries
	RGM-84A Launch	ShShM launcher	(1988)		3		Arming Saar-5 Class corvettes
	AGM-114A	ASM	1990	1990–91	539	(200)	Arming 18 AH-64 Apache helicopters
	AIM-9M	Air-to-air missile	(1991)		300		Deal worth $32 m incl support
	FIM-92A Stinger	Portable SAM	1990		..		
	MIM-104 PAC-2	ATBM	1990	1991	128	128	
	MIM-104 Patriot	SAM	1991		(64)		
	RGM-84A Harpoon	ShShM	(1988)		(48)		Arming Saar-5 Class corvettes
	Saar-5 Class	Corvette	1988		3		Built in USA to Israeli design; fully financed with FMS credits worth $300 m; some sub-systems to be fitted in Israel

Recipient/ supplier (S) or licenser (L)	No. ordered	Weapon designation	Weapon description	Year of order/ licence	Year(s) of deliveries	No. delivered/ produced	Comments
Jordan							
L: USA	100	Model 300C	Helicopter	1989			Production for civilian and military customers
Kenya							
S: France	100	Mistral	Portable SAM	1990	1990	(20)	
UK	12	EMB-312 Tucano	Trainer	1988	1989–91	12	
Korea, North							
S: USSR	..	BMP-1	APC	(1984)	1985–91	(122)	Locally modified design
L: USSR	..	AT-3 Sagger	Anti-tank missile	1975	1976–91	(1600)	
	..	SA-7 Grail	Portable SAM	(1985)	1986–91	(600)	
Korea, South							
S: Germany, FR	3	Type-209/3	Submarine	1987			Deal worth $600 m
	3	Type-209/3	Submarine	1989			In addition to 3 ordered in 1987
UK	20	Hawk	Jet trainer	1990			Deal worth $140 m
	12	Lynx	Helicopter	1988	1990–91	(12)	Part of deal worth $200 m incl Sea Skua missiles; follow-on order for 20 likely
USA	(48)	Sea Skua	Anti-ship missile	1988	1990–91		Arming Lynx helicopters
	48	F-16C	Fighter	1991	1990–91	48	Deal worth $2.52 b incl 12 delivered directly, 36 assembled locally and 72 licence-produced, 12 spare engines and 20 Lantirn pods
	7	H-76 Eagle	Helicopter	(1988)	1990–91	7	Prior to licensed production of up to 150
	8	P-3C Update-3	Maritime patrol	1990			Deal worth $840 m
	3	AN/FPS-117	Air defence radar	1990			In addition to 5 previously delivered
	21	Seasparrow	ShAM	1990			Arming HDF-3500 Class destroyers; deal worth $33 m incl training rounds and support

Supplier	No.	Weapon designation	Weapon description	Year of order	Year of delivery	No. delivered	Comments
	4	Seasparrow VLS	ShAM launcher	1990			Arming HDF-3500 Class destroyers
	1	AGM-84A Harpoon	Anti-ship missile	1991			
	179	AIM-7M Sparrow	Air-to-air missile	1991			
	704	BGM-71D TOW-2	Anti-tank missile	1987	1990–91	(500)	Deal worth $31 m
L: France	..	Crotale Launch	Landmobile SAM	(1989)	1991	(2)	Based on Crotale missile; developed by Korean consortium
Italy	6	Lerici Class	Minehunter	(1986)	1988–91	(3)	Class may ultimately be of 10 ships
Japan	30	BK-117	Helicopter	1990	1991	(10)	For local assembly
USA	72	F-16C	Fighter	1991			Part of deal worth $2.52 b
	..	H-76 Eagle	Helicopter	1986	1991	(12)	Over 400 civilian versions produced as well
	90	Model 500MD	Helicopter	1976	1978–91	(215)	
		UH-60 Blackhawk	Helicopter	1990	1991		Deal worth $500 m
	242	M-109-A2 155mm	SPH	1990	1991	(50)	Deal worth $260 m
Kuwait							
S: UK	16	EMB-312 Tucano	Trainer	1989	1991	16	Deal worth $1.6 b incl 32 C and 8 D versions, Sidewinder, Harpoon, Sparrow and Maverick missiles
USA	40	F/A-18 Hornet	Fighter	1988	1991	1	
	300	AGM-65G	ASM	1988			Anti-ship version; arming F/A-18 Hornet fighters
	40	AGM-84A Harpoon	Anti-ship missile	1988			Arming F/A-18 Hornet fighters
	200	AIM-7F Sparrow	Air-to-air missile	1988			Arming F/A-18 Hornet fighters
	120	AIM-9L	Air-to-air missile	1988			Arming F/A-18 Hornet fighters
Yugoslavia	200	T-72	Main battle tank	(1989)	1990–91	200	Yugoslavian designation M-84
Malawi							
S: USA	2	C-47	Transport	1991	1991	2	
Malaysia							
S: UK	10	Hawk-100	Jet trainer	1990			Part of deal worth $740 m incl 18 Hawk-200 aircraft, weapons, training and services

Recipient/ supplier (S) or licenser (L)	No. ordered	Weapon designation	Weapon description	Year of order/ licence	Year(s) of deliveries	No. delivered/ produced	Comments
	18	Hawk-200	Fighter	1990			
	6	Wasp	Helicopter	1991	1991	(6)	
	..	Harimau	Scout car	1988	1989–90	30	Version of Ferret scout car
	12	DN-181 Rapier	SAM system	1988			
	2	S-723 Martello	3-D radar	(1988)			Deal worth $190 m
	48	Javelin	Portable SAM	1988			
	576	Improved Rapier	Landmobile SAM	1988			
	1	Bulldog Class	OPV	1989	1991	1	
Morocco							
S: France	(28)	AMX-10RC	Scout car	1990			
	..	HOT-2	Anti-tank missile	1987	1988–90	(84)	
USA	20	F-16A	Fighter	1991			Deal worth $250 m; F-16A and B versions
Nicaragua							
S: El Salvador	(17)	SA-14 Gremlin	Portable SAM	1991	1991	17	FMLN returned 17 of 28 missiles supplied by the Nicaraguan army
Nigeria							
S: Czechoslovakia	30	L-39 Albatross	Jet trainer	1991			
France	12	AS-332	Helicopter	1985	1989–90	6	
UK	(72)	MBT Mk-3	Main battle tank	1990	1991	25	Deal worth $282 m
L: USA	..	Air Beetle	Trainer	1988	1988	1	Version of US RV-6
Oman							
S: UK	4	Hawk-100	Jet trainer	1989			
	12	Hawk-200	Fighter	1990			Deal worth $225 m incl 12 Hawk-200 versions

	No. ordered	Weapon designation	Weapon description	Year of order	Year of delivery	No. delivered	Comments
USA	..	M-60-A3	Main battle tank	1991	1991	27	May be up to 43
	119	V-300 Commando	APC	1991	1991		Deal worth $150 m
	(96)	AIM-9L	Air-to-air missile	1990	1990		Arming 16 Hawk-100/200 aircraft; could be from European production

Pakistan

	No. ordered	Weapon designation	Weapon description	Year of order	Year of delivery	No. delivered	Comments
S: Australia	50	Mirage-3O	Fighter	1990	1990–91	50	Deal worth $28 m
China	98	A-5 Fantan-A	Fighter	1984			Second order
	75	F-7	Fighter	1988			Including 15 trainer versions
	25	Karakoram 8	Jet trainer	1987			
	..	T-69	Main battle tank	1988	1989–91	(275)	Prior to possible licensed production of up to 1 000
	(30)	M-11 launcher	SSM launcher	(1990)	1991	20	
	..	M-11	SSM	(1990)	1991	(55)	
France	6	Rasit-3190B	Surveillance radar	1988	1989–91	(6)	
USA	11	F-16A	Fighter	1988			Second order; deal worth $256 m; attrition replacements
	60	F-16A	Fighter	1989			Third order; deal incl 10 F-100 engines but no air-to-surface armaments; to be funded by Saudi Arabia
	10	Model 209 AH-1S	Helicopter	1990			Deal worth $89 m incl spare engines and support; armed with TOW missiles
	3	P-3C Update-2	Maritime patrol	(1990)			Deal worth $240 m incl spares and support
	6	SH-2F Seasprite	Helicopter	1989	1989	3	3 SH-2F and 3 SH-2G versions
	(20)	M-109-A2 155mm	SPH	1988			Deal worth $40 m incl M-198 howitzers and support equipment
	775	M-113-A2	APC	1989	1990–91	(50)	For assembly in Pakistan
	..	AN/TPQ-36	Tracking radar	(1990)			Deal worth $65 m
	4	AN/TPQ-37	Tracking radar	(1985)	1987–89	(3)	
	44	AGM-84A Harpoon	Anti-ship missile	1990			Arming P-3C Orion aircraft
	200	AIM-7F Sparrow	Air-to-air missile	1988			Arming F-16 fighters
	360	AIM-9L	Air-to-air missile	1988	1989	(60)	Arming F-16 fighters
	(80)	BGM-71A TOW	Anti-tank missile	1990			
	2386	BGM-71D TOW-2	Anti-tank missile	1987			First Pakistani TOW-2 order; with 144 launchers

Recipient/ supplier (S) or licenser (L)	No. ordered	Weapon designation	Weapon description	Year of order/ licence	Year(s) of deliveries	No. delivered/ produced	Comments
L: China	..	Khalid	Main battle tank	(1989)	1991	10	Deal worth $1.2 b; possibly based on T-69 design
	..	HN-5A	Portable SAM	(1988)	1989–90	200	Arming M-113 APCs; may be produced in Pakistan as Anza 2
Sweden	..	Red Arrow-8	Anti-tank missile	1989	1990–91	100	
	..	Supporter	Trainer	1974	1977–91	108	Production to switch to upgraded Shahbaaz from 1992
	(125)	RBS-70	Portable SAM	(1985)	1988–91	125	
Papua New Guinea							
S: Spain	2	CN-235	Transport	1991			May be from Indonesia
Paraguay							
S: Chile	15	T-35 Pillan	Trainer	1991	1991	15	
Taiwan	6	T-33A	Jet trainer	(1991)	1991	6	
Peru							
S: Brazil	10	EMB-312 Tucano	Trainer	1991			
China	6	Y-12	Transport	1991	1991		
Germany, FR	2	BK-117	Helicopter	1989		(6)	Part of deal worth $25–30 m incl 6 Bo-105 helicopters
USSR	18	Mi-17 Hip-H	Helicopter	1989	1990	14	In addition to 15 already delivered
Philippines							
S: Australia	6	PC-57M	Patrol craft	1990			Deal worth $200 m
France	3	MM-38 Launcher	ShShM launcher	1991			Arming Cormoran Class corvettes
	..	MM-38 Exocet	ShShM	1991			Arming Cormoran Class corvettes
Italy	36	S-211	Trainer	1988	1989–91	18	Trainer version
Spain	3	Cormoran Class	FAC	1991			Deal worth $100 m

Supplier	Number	Weapon designation	Weapon description	Year of order	Year of deliveries	No. delivered	Comments
UK	150	FS-100 Simba	Scout car	1990	1990		Deal worth $84 m; offsets worth 110%
USA	28	Model 530MG	Helicopter	(1990)	1991	(6)	
	24	OV-10F Bronco	Trainer/COIN	1991		5	
Qatar							
S: France	6	TRS-2201	Air defence radar	(1986)	1986–91	(6)	
	500	Mistral	Portable SAM	1990	1990–91		
South Africa	12	G-5 155mm	Towed howitzer	1991	1991	(12)	
Saudi Arabia							
S: Canada	1 117	LAV-25	APC	1990	1990		Deal worth $700 m
France	12	AS-332	Helicopter	1988	1990–91	12	6 armed with Exocet missiles; deal worth $430 m incl 20 armed speed boats
	6	Crotale SAMS	SAM system	1990	1991	6	
	3	Crotale Naval L	ShAM launcher	1990			Arming La Fayette Class frigates; part of deal worth $1.2 b
	3	MM-40 Launcher	ShShM launcher	1990			Arming La Fayette Class frigates
	(180)	AS-15TT	Anti-ship missile	1990			Second order
	250	Crotale Naval	ShAM	1990			Arming La Fayette Class frigates
	(1 000)	HOT-2	Anti-tank missile	1990	1991	(350)	
	1 200	Mistral	Portable SAM	1989	1991	(400)	
	(24)	MM-40 Exocet	ShShM	1990			Arming La Fayette Class frigates
	..	R-440 Crotale	Landmobile SAM	1990	1991	(72)	Deal worth $670 m incl logistic support
	4 000	Shahine-2	Landmobile SAM	1984	1986–91	(3800)	Part of 'Al Thakeb' deal worth $4.1 b
	3	La Fayette Cl	Frigate	1989			Deal worth $3.5 b; offsets worth 30%
Germany, FR	10	Tpz-1	APC	(1981)	1991	10	Deal worth $400 m
Switzerland	300	Piranha	APC	1990			
UK	12	BAe-125-800	Utility aircraft	1988	1988–90	6	Part of 1988 Tornado deal; for VIP use
	40	Hawk-100	Jet trainer	1988			Part of 1988 Tornado deal
	20	Hawk-200	Fighter	1988			Part of 1988 Tornado deal
	48	Tornado IDS	MRCA	1988			Part of 1988 Tornado deal
	(40)	WS-70	Helicopter	1988			

Recipient/ supplier (S) or licenser (L)	No. ordered	Weapon designation	Weapon description	Year of order/ licence	Year(s) of deliveries	No. delivered/ produced	Comments
	480	ALARM	ARM	1986	1991	(60)	Arming Tornado IDS fighters
	(480)	Sea Eagle	Anti-ship missile	1985			Arming Tornado IDS fighters
	(560)	Sky Flash	Air-to-air missile	(1986)	1989–91	(560)	Arming Tornado ADV fighters
	6	Sandown Class	Minehunter	1988	1991	1	
USA	12	AH-64 Apache	Helicopter	1990			Deal worth $300 m including 155 Hellfire missiles; follow-on order for 36 probable
	24	F-15C Eagle	Fighter	1990	1991	10	Mix of C and D versions
	7	KC-130H	Tanker/transport	1990			
	8	UH-60 Blackhawk	Helicopter	1990	1991	4	Medivac version, deal worth $121 m
	150	M-1 Abrams	Main battle tank	1990			Second 1990 order
	315	M-1-A2 Abrams	Main battle tank	1990			Deal worth $1.5 b
	207	M-113-A2	APC	(1991)			Part of $3.1 b deal
	27	M-198 155mm	Towed howitzer	1990			
	220	M-2 Bradley	AIFV	1989	1989–91	(200)	Deal worth $550 m incl anti-tank missiles and training
	200	M-2 Bradley	AIFV	1990			In addition to 220 ordered previously
	50	M-548	APC	(1991)			Part of $3.1 b deal
	43	M-578	ARV	(1991)			Part of $3.1 b deal
	12	M-88-A1	ARV	1990			Deal worth $26 m
	9	MLRS 227mm	MRL	1990			
	(6)	AN/TPS-43	3-D radar	1985	1987–91	(5)	
	(6)	AN/TPS-70	Air defence radar	1989	1990–91	(6)	Deal worth $23.5m
	8	Patriot Battery	SAM system	1990			Deal worth $984 m incl 384 missiles, 6 radars and support
	14	Patriot Battery	SAM system	1991			Deal worth $3.1 b incl 758 missiles
	155	AGM-114A	ASM	1990			Arming 12 Apache helicopters
	770	AIM-7M Sparrow	Air-to-air missile	1991			Part of deal worth $365 m incl laser-guided bombs
	671	AIM-9P	Air-to-air missile	1986	1989–91	(671)	
	4 460	BGM-71D TOW-2	Anti-tank missile	1988	1989–91	(1 500)	

	No.	Weapon designation	Weapon description	Year of order	Year of delivery	No. delivered	Comments
Singapore							
S: France	1 750	BGM-71D TOW-2	Anti-tank missile	1990			Deal worth $55 m including 150 launchers
	384	MIM-104 PAC-2	ATBM	1990			
	758	MIM-104 PAC-2	ATBM	1991			
	20	AS-350 Ecureuil	Helicopter	1989	1991	(10)	10 to be armed with anti-tank missiles
	20	AMX-10RC	Scout car	(1990)	1991	(5)	
	36	LG-1 105mm	Towed gun	1990	1991	(12)	
	(200)	Milan	Anti-tank missile	1989	1990–91	(140)	Order may be for 400, deal incl 30 launchers
Netherlands	3	F-50 Enforcer	Maritime patrol	1991	1991		Deal worth $52 m; option on 3 more
Sweden	4	Landsort Class	Minehunter	1991	1991		
USA	5	RGM-84A Launch	ShShM launcher	(1986)	1990–91	5	Arming Type 62-001 corvettes
	6	RGM-84A Launch	ShShM launcher	(1986)	1990–91	6	Arming refitted TNC-45 FACs
	20	AGM-84A Harpoon	Anti-ship missile	1991			
	(240)	BGM-71C I-TOW	Anti-tank missile	1989	1991	(120)	Arming AS-350 Ecureuil helicopters
	48	MIM-23B Hawk	Landmobile SAM	1991			
	(40)	RGM-84A Harpoon	ShShM	(1986)	1990–91	(40)	Arming Type 62-001 corvettes
	(24)	RGM-84A Harpoon	ShShM	(1987)	1990–91	(24)	Arming refitted TNC-45 FACs
L: Germany, FR	5	Type 62-001	Corvette	1986	1990–91	(5)	
South Africa							
S: Switzerland	7	PC-7	Trainer	(1989)	1990–91	7	For Bophuthatswana; follow-on order for up to 14 possible
Sri Lanka							
S: China	4	F-7	Fighter	1990	1991	4	
	2	FT-5	Trainer	(1990)	1991	2	
	3	Y-12	Transport	(1991)	1991	3	
	..	Type 59/1 130mm	Towed gun	(1990)	1991	(18)	
	3	Shanghai Class	Patrol craft	(1990)	1991	3	

Recipient/ supplier (S) or licenser (L)	No. ordered	Weapon designation	Weapon description	Year of order/ licence	Year(s) of deliveries	No. delivered/ produced	Comments
Sudan S: China	2	Y-8	Transport	1991	1991	2	
Syria S: Czechoslovakia	(300)	T-72	Main battle tank	1991			Order may include 90 T-55s
Korea, North	..	Scud-C launcher	Mobile SSM system	1991	1991	(20)	May be up to 20
	..	Scud-C	SSM	(1991)	1991	(100)	
USSR	3	Kilo Class	Submarine	(1987)			
Taiwan S: France	6	La Fayette Cl	Frigate	1991			To be delivered without armament
Germany, FR	4	MCMV 50M	MSO	(1990)			
Israel	34	Kfir-C7	Fighter/bomber	1991			
	6	Kfir-TC7	Fighter/trainer	1991			
USA	1	C-130H Hercules	Transport	1990	1991	1	
	1	E-2C Hawkeye	AEW	1990			Refurbished; option on 5 more for local refurbishment
	10	S-70C	Helicopter	1989	1991	(2)	Deal worth $75 m
	150	M-60-A3	Main battle tank	(1991)			Deal worth $31 m incl overhaul, machine guns, spares and logistics
	7	Phalanx	CIWS	(1989)	1989–91	(3)	Arming 7 ex-US Navy Gearing Class destroyers; deal worth $15 m
	8	RIM-67A Launch	ShAM launcher	1988			Arming FFG-7 Class frigates to be built under licence; deal worth $55 m, incl spares and support
	7	RIM-67A Launch	ShAM launcher	(1989)	1989–91	3	Arming 7 ex-US Navy Gearing Class destroyers
	97	RIM-67A/SM-1	ShAM/ShShM	1991			Arming FFG-7 Class frigates to be built under licence
	70	RIM-67A/SM-1	ShAM/ShShM	(1989)	1989–91	(30)	Arming 7 ex-US Gearing Class destroyers

	No.	Weapon designation	Weapon description	Year of order	Year(s) of deliveries	No. delivered	Comments
L: Israel	..	Gabriel-2	ShShM	(1978)	1980–91	(523)	Taiwanese designation Hsiung Feng
USA	470	Brave Tiger	Main battle tank	1984	1985–91	(448)	M-60 chassis, M-48 turret, advanced fire control system
	8	FFG-7 Class	Frigate	1989			Project management by Bath Iron Works
Thailand							
S: China	(450)	T-69	Main battle tank	1987	1989–91	(300)	Upgraded with 105mm gun
	360	Type 531	APC	1988	1990–91	(360)	Part of deal worth $47 m
	4	C-801 launcher	ShShM launcher	1988	1991	3	Arming 4 Jianghu Class frigates
	..	Type-311B	Fire control radar	1991			Arming 4 Jianghu Class frigates
	32	C-801	ShShM	(1990)	1991	24	Deal worth $40 m; arming 4 Jianghu Class frigates
	(900)	HN-5A	Portable SAM	1991	1991		Deal worth $46 m incl 90 launchers
	4	Jianghu Class	Frigate	1988	1991	3	Part of deal worth $272 m
	2	Jianghu Class	Frigate	1989			In addition to 4 ordered 1988
France	1	A310-324	Transport	(1991)	1991	1	For VIP transport
	20	Crotale New	SAM system	1991			
	(480)	VT-1	SAM	1991			
Germany, FR	3	Do-228-200	Transport	1990	1991	3	Follow-on order likely
	(4)	M-40 Type	MSC/PC	1986			In addition to 2 ordered 1984
Israel	40	Python-3	Air-to-air missile	1989			Status uncertain
Spain	2	C-212-200	Transport	(1990)			In addition to 4 ordered 1981
Switzerland	20	PC-9	Trainer	1990	1991	(10)	Deal worth $90 m incl spares and training
UK	2	743D	3-D radar	1991			
USA	30	A-7E Corsair-2	Fighter	1991			
	3	CH-47D Chinook	Helicopter	1990	1991	3	Deal worth $30 m
	6	F-16A	Fighter	1987	1991	6	Second order
	18	F-16A	Fighter	1991			12 A and 6 B versions; deal worth $547 m incl spare engines, Lantirn pods, spares, logistics and support
	25	Model 212	Helicopter	1990			
	3	P-3B Orion	Maritime patrol	1989			Deal worth $140 m incl Harpoon anti-ship missiles; ex-US Navy
	4	S-70C	Helicopter	1989			

Recipient/ supplier (S) or licenser (L)	No. ordered	Weapon designation	Weapon description	Year of order/ licence	Year(s) of deliveries	No. delivered/ produced	Comments
	2	SH-2F Seasprite	Helicopter	1989			Equipping last 2 of 6 frigates under construction in China
	20	M-109 155mm	SPH	(1991)			Deal worth $63 m
	350	M-48-A5	Main battle tank	1990			
	300	M-60-A1	Main battle tank	1990	1991	(150)	
	20	M-88-A1	ARV	1990	1991	(20)	
	2	AN/FPS-117	Air defence radar	1989	1991	(2)	Deal worth $43 m
	(12)	AGM-65D	ASM	(1987)	1991	(12)	Arming F-16 fighters
	16	AGM-84A Harpoon	Anti-ship missile	1990	1991		Arming P-3 Orion aircraft
	(36)	AIM-9P	Air-to-air missile	(1987)	1991	(36)	Arming F-16 fighters
L: Germany, FR	45	Fantrainer	Trainer	1983	1986–91	(45)	In addition to 2 delivered directly
UK	3	Province Class	FAC	1987	1991	(3)	
	1	Province Class	FAC	1989			
Togo							
S: France	1	Alpha Jet	Jet trainer	1987	1991	1	
Tonga							
S: Australia	3	ASI-315	Patrol craft	1988	1989–91	3	
United Arab Emirates							
S: France	18	Mirage-2000	Fighter	1985	1989–91	18	For Abu Dhabi; modified for US AIM-9 Sidewinder missiles
	1	Mirage-2000	Fighter	1990	1991	1	Attrition replacement
	500	Mistral	SAM	1988	1991	120	Arming 2 Type 62-001 corvettes
	(80)	R-440 Crotale	Landmobile SAM	1988			
South Africa	78	G-6 155mm	SPH	1990	1991	(25)	

Supplier	No.	Weapon designation	Weapon description	Year of order	Year of delivery	No. delivered	Comments
UK	12	Hawk-100	Jet trainer	1989			For Abu Dhabi; part of deal worth $340 m
USA	20	AH-64 Apache	Helicopter	1991			Deal worth $680 m incl Hellfire missiles
	620	AGM-114A	ASM	1991			Arming AH-64 Apache helicopter
Uruguay							
S: Germany, FR	5	Kondor Class	MSC	(1991)	1991	5	
Spain	23	T-34A Mentor	Trainer	1990	1991	23	
Venezuela							
S: Brazil	100	EE-11 Urutu	APC	1988			
France	18	Mirage-5OEV	Fighter	1988	1991	(8)	Arming Mirage-50 fighters
	(50)	AM-39 Exocet	Anti-ship missile	(1988)			Arming Mirage-50 fighters; deal worth approx $30 m
	(100)	Magic-2	Air-to-air missile	1988	1989–90	(40)	
Netherlands	7	F-5A	Fighter	1991	1991	7	
Sweden	70	RBS-70	Portable SAM	1989			
UK	84	Scorpion 90	Light tank	1988	1989–91	(60)	Deal worth $85 m incl support equipment, ammunition and training
USA	18	OV-10A Bronco	Trainer/COIN	1991	1991	18	
	18	OV-10D Bronco	COIN	1991			
	(4)	RGM-84A Launch	ShShM launcher	1989			Coastal defence batteries
	18	RGM-84A Harpoon	ShShM	1989			Deal worth $50 m
Zaire							
S: France	13	AMX-13	Light tank	1989			
Zimbabwe							
S: China	1	Y-12	Transport	1991	1991	1	
UK	5	Hawk	Jet trainer	1990	1991	3	

Abbreviations and acronyms

AA	Anti-aircraft	IDS	Interdictor/strike version
AAV	Anti-aircraft vehicle	Incl	Including/includes
AAV(G)	Anti-aircraft vehicle (gun-armed)	MBB	Messerschmitt-Bölkow-Blohm
AAV(M)	Anti-aircraft vehicle (missile-armed)	MCM	Mine countermeasure (ship)
ADATS	Air defence and anti-tank system	Mk	Mark
ADV	Air defence version	MOU	Memorandum of Understanding
AEW	Airborne early-warning (system)	MRCA	Multi-role combat aircraft
AEW&C	Airborne early warning and control	MRL	Multiple rocket launcher
AIFV	Armoured infantry fighting vehicles	MSC	Minesweeper, coastal
APC	Armoured personnel carrier	MSO	Minesweeper, ocean
ARM	Anti-radar missile	NBC	Nuclear, biological and chemical
ARV	Armoured recovery vehicle	OPV	Offshore patrol vessel
ASM	Air-to-surface missile	PC	Patrol craft (gun-armed/unarmed)
ASW	Anti-submarine warfare	RAF	Royal Air Force
ATBM	Anti-tactical ballistic missile	SAM	Surface-to-air missile
AWACS	Airborne early warning and control system	ShAM	Ship-to-air missile
BAe	British Aerospace	ShShM	Ship-to-ship missile
CIWS	Close-in weapon system	SPH	Self-propelled howitzer
COIN	Counter-insurgency	SSM	Surface-to-surface missile
ELINT	Electronic intelligence	SSN	Nuclear-powered submarine
FAC	Fast attack craft (missile/torpedo-armed)	USAF	US Air Force
FMLN	Farabundo Marti Front for National Liberation	VIP	Very important person
FMS	Foreign Military Sales (USA)	VLS	Vertical launch system
		3-D	Three-dimensional

Appendix 8D. Sources and methods

I. The SIPRI sources

The sources of the data presented in the arms trade registers are of five general types: newspapers; periodicals and journals; books. monographs and annual reference works; official national documents; and documents issued by international and intergovernmental organizations. The registers are largely compiled from information contained in around 200 publications searched regularly.

Published information cannot provide a comprehensive picture because the arms trade is not fully reported in the open literature. Published reports provide partial information, and substantial disagreement among reports is common. Therefore, the exercise of judgement and the making of estimates are important elements in compiling the SIPRI arms trade data base. Order dates and the delivery dates for arms transactions are continuously revised in the light of new information, but where they are not disclosed the dates are estimated. Exact numbers of weapons ordered and delivered may not always be known and are sometimes estimated—particularly with respect to missiles. It is common for reports of arms deals involving large platforms—ships, aircraft and armoured vehicles—to ignore missile armaments classified as major weapons by SIPRI. Unless there is explicit evidence that platforms were disarmed or altered before delivery, it is assumed that a weapons fit specified in one of the major reference works such as the *Jane's* or *Interavia* series is carried.

II. Selection criteria

The SIPRI arms trade data cover five categories of major weapons or systems: aircraft, armour and artillery, guidance and radar systems, missiles, and warships. Statistics presented refer to the value of the trade in these five categories only. The registers and statistics do not include the trade in small arms, artillery under 100-mm calibre, ammunition, support items, services and components or component technology, except for specific items. Publicly available information is inadequate to track these items satisfactorily.

There are two criteria for the selection of major weapon transfers for the registers. The first is that of military application. The aircraft category excludes aerobatic aeroplanes and gliders. Transport aircraft and VIP transports are included only if they bear military insignia or are otherwise confirmed as military registered. Micro-light aircraft, remotely piloted vehicles and drones are not included although these systems are increasingly finding military applications.

The armour and artillery category includes all types of tanks, tank destroyers, armoured cars, armoured personnel carriers, armoured support vehicles, infantry combat vehicles as well as multiple rocket launchers, self-propelled and towed guns and howitzers with a calibre equal to or above 100 mm. Military lorries, jeeps and other unarmoured support vehicles are not included.

The category of guidance and radar systems is a residual category for electronic-tracking, target-acquisition, fire-control, launch and guidance systems that are either (*a*) deployed independently of a weapon system listed under another weapon category (e.g., certain ground-based SAM launch systems) or (*b*) shipborne missile-launch or point-defence (CIWS) systems. The values of acquisition, fire-control, launch and guidance systems on aircraft and armoured vehicles are included in the value of the respective aircraft or armoured vehicle. The reason for treating shipborne systems separately is that a given type of ship is often equipped with numerous combinations of different surveillance, acquisition, launch and guidance systems.

The missile category includes only guided missiles. Unguided artillery rockets and man-portable anti-armour rockets are excluded. Free-fall aerial munitions (such as 'iron bombs') are also excluded. In the naval sphere, anti-submarine rockets and torpedoes are excluded.

The ship category excludes small patrol craft (with a displacement of less than 100 t) unless they carry cannon with a calibre equal to or above 100 mm, missiles or torpedoes, research vessels, tugs and ice-breakers. Combat support vessels such as fleet replenishment ships are included.

The second criterion for selection of items is the identity of the buyer. Items must be destined for the armed forces, paramilitary forces, intelligence agencies or police of another country. Arms supplied to guerrilla forces pose a problem. For example, if weapons are delivered to the Contra rebels they are listed as imports to Nicaragua with a comment in the arms trade register indicating the local recipient. The entry of any arms transfer is made corresponding to the five weapon categories listed above. This means that missiles and their guidance/launch vehicles are often entered separately under their respective category in the arms trade register.

III. The value of the arms trade

The SIPRI system for evaluating the arms trade was designed as a *trend-measuring device*, to enable the measurement of changes in the total flow of major weapons and its geographic pattern. Expressing the evaluation in monetary terms reflects both the quantity and the quality of the weapons transferred. Aggregate values and shares are based only on *actual deliveries* during the year or years covered in the relevant tables and figures.

The SIPRI valuation system is not comparable to official economic statistics such as gross domestic product, public expenditure and export/import figures. The monetary values chosen do not correspond to the actual prices paid, which vary considerably depending on different pricing methods, the length of production runs and the terms involved in individual transactions. For instance, a deal may or may not cover spare parts, training, support equipment, compensation, offset arrangements for the local industries in the buying country, and so on. Furthermore, to use only actual sales prices—even assuming that the information were available for all deals, which it is not—military aid and grants would be excluded, and the total flow of arms would therefore not be measured.

Production under licence is included in the arms trade statistics in such a way that it should reflect the import share embodied in the weapon. In reality, this share is normally high in the beginning, gradually decreasing over time. However, a single estimate of the import share for each weapon produced under licence is made by SIPRI, and therefore the value of arms produced under licence agreements may be slightly overstated.

IV. Review of the SIPRI arms trade valuation system

The arms transfer statistics presented in this Yearbook are based on a revised and updated system of values for the items in the SIPRI arms trade data base. The adjustments shift the value base year from 1985 to 1990.

It has to be emphasized that the SIPRI values are not actual prices of weapons that have been paid in a particular deal. The purpose of the valuation system is to enable the aggregation of data on physical arms transfers. Similar weapon systems require similar values. The SIPRI values are therefore based on average production costs of those weapons for which cost data are available. The values for other weapons are estimated on the basis of technical comparisons (of weight, range, level of technology, year of development and production, etc.) with weapons for which production costs are available. Since the valuation is largely based on estimates the revision and updating of a system of this kind requires the application of basic principles rather than a sophisticated index.

The valuation system for the arms transfer statistics is reviewed at regular intervals, both in order to check that the consistency of the system has been maintained and in order to update the values to the general level of actual weapon costs. The latest previous review of the weapon values was presented in the SIPRI Yearbook 1987[1]—shifting the base year from 1975 to 1985. The main reasons for updating the values are:

1. To facilitate the estimation of new values for weapon systems entering the SIPRI data base.
2. To adjust the values to changing price relations between weapon systems and perhaps even between entire weapon categories.
3. To make them more comprehensible for the reader since the values are closer to current weapon production costs.

However, the presentation of updated arms transfer statistics increases the danger of confusing the SIPRI values with actual prices of weapon systems.

Adjustments in the value system affect the relations of the 4500 weapon systems in the arms trade data base. A re-evaluation of each individual item or group of weapons is a major effort which is required only if major changes (like dramatic price increases for certain categories of weapon systems but average changes for all others) occur that would distort the internal consistency of the valuation system. Such a major revision was undertaken in 1987 and was not required in 1992. This assessment is also supported by the pattern of deflators for US arms procurement in the review period (table 8D.1).

The 1992 review has followed a two-step approach: first values for a selection of individual weapon systems were reviewed and second a general mark-up of the level of values to reflect 1990 weapon cost levels was carried out.

---

[1] SIPRI, *SIPRI Yearbook 1987: World Armaments and Disarmament* (Oxford University Press: Oxford, 1987), appendix 7D, pp. 283–89. 'The SIPRI price system' (appendix 7D) also gives additional information on the SIPRI valuation system and of previous reviews.

Table 8D.1. US deflators for arms procurement, 1985–90

Deflators are US Department of Defense deflators for total obligational authority.

	Weapon category	Percentage change FY 1985–90
Army	Aircraft	20.4
	Missiles	20.6
	Weapons and vehicles	20.6
Navy	Aircraft	20.4
	Weapons	20.5
	Ships	20.9
Air Force	Aircraft	20.9
	Missiles	21.1

Source: US Weapon Systems Costs, 1991, Data Search Associate, Fountain Valley, Calif., Apr. 1991, appendix D.

Review of values of individual weapon systems

This part of the review process was directed at three kinds of item in the SIPRI data base:

1. All of the 100 most traded items in the period since the last valuation review (1986–90) were checked. These items represent approximately 50 per cent of the total trade of major conventional weapon systems recorded by SIPRI.
2. A limited number of 30 weapon systems that have been traded were reviewed where major production cost changes were suspected.
3. The whole category of guidance and radar systems (about 200 items) was reviewed. The reason for including a whole category of equipment is that this category was only introduced into the data base in 1986 and the value estimates were therefore based on less experience than those for the other categories in the data base.

The old (1985) values of the selected systems were compared with available data on actual 1985 unit cost or sales prices. In the absence of relevant cost and price data the above-mentioned comparisons were undertaken on the basis of technical characteristics of similar systems. Including the systems used for comparative purposes the number of individual values reviewed was about 400.

Few adjustments were made in the values of other types of equipment than guidance and radar systems. Those that were made were corrections of previous mis-estimation caused by insufficient cost data. This was the case for systems which were given a value at the outset of their production run. As a general rule—but not in all cases—the unit cost of weapons is high in the early stages of production because of the low quantities being produced and the learning costs involved. During the course of production prices tend to fall, especially for those systems that experience long production runs.

Change of base year

The second step of inflating all values from 1985 to 1990 cost levels was made by using a single inflator—the same mark-up factor for all weapon categories and countries. The inflation factor for the five-year period amounted to 19.1 per cent. The calculation is based on the following principles:

1. The arms trade inflator used is the producer price index (PPI) for the machinery industry in the largest Western exporter countries of major conventional weapons. Since there exist no specific price indexes for arms transfers, a proxy had to be found.

2. A single inflator was used for the entire data base because there was no evidence that price changes were different for different weapon categories. On the contrary, the US Department of Defense deflator shows identical price changes between both weapon categories and services for the period 1986–90.

3. The alternative use of a specific price index for arms procurement was rejected. Specific price indexes for domestic arms procurement do exist in a number of countries. Most of these are, however, not based on price movements of weapons but on price indexes for civil sectors with characteristics similar to the arms industry, for example, machinery production or different segments of that sector, weighted by the pattern of domestic arms procurement.

The only existing price index based entirely on the measurement of actual price changes of military equipment is the US GNP deflator for government purchases of military equipment. It is, however, strongly influenced by the cost profiles of a few high cost weapon programmes, which were not among the major weapons traded during the review period (mainly the B-1 bomber and the C-5 transport aircraft, the M-2 Bradley and the Hummer vehicles). The index is therefore not relevant for a data base on major weapons.[2]

4. The choice of a civil price index as a proxy for inflation in arms production rests on the assumption that inflation is about the same in similar production sectors regardless of the customer. This is a disputed statement. It has been argued that inflation is higher in arms procurement than in the sale of civilian goods.[3] This conclusion rests on the observation that weapon prices often increase dramatically from one generation to the next. It is also claimed that the arms industry is highly inefficient and charges the cost for this inefficiency to the customer.[4] The performance of the US GNP deflator for defence purchases does not support this proposition, however.[5]

These two propositions are not necessarily contradictory. It is possible that the assumption about higher inflation is true when production costs of one generation of a weapon system are compared with those of the next (generational change by design and production of new systems). The production cost then includes both the cost of technological changes and the inflation. The counter-argument is relevant for price changes within generations, including the many weapons with no technological

---

[2] There are also US DOD deflators for procurement, but it is not clear how these are constructed and thus not clear what they measure. These deflators show an increase of around 20 per cent for the period 1985–90 for the aggregate arms procurement of each of the three services—which is close to the inflator we calculated for the SIPRI arms trade data statistics on the basis of different assumptions.

[3] Albrecht, U., 'Armaments and inflation', *Instant Research on Peace and Violence*, vol. 4, no 3 (1974), pp. 157–67.

[4] Melman, S., *Profits Without Production* (Knopf: New York, 1983).

[5] The price index for total military equipment is almost constant for the five-year period 1985–90 (showing a 1% increase), the military aircraft price index declines by 15% in the same period and the price index for missiles increases by only 4%, i.e., far below both the general rate of inflation and inflation in the machinery sector (*Survey of Current Business*, monthly journal, Bureau of Economic Analysis, Washington, DC).

Table 8D.2. Components of the weighted inflator for the SIPRI arms transfer data base year from 1985 to 1990

(1) Exporting country	(2) Percentage share in arms transfers 1986–90[a]	(3) PPI for machinery,[b] % change 1985–90	(4) Exchange rate movement 1986–90, index number (1985=1.000)	(5) Inflator and national components, 1985–90
USA	62	12.6	1.000	7.812
France	15	10.2	1.641	2.511
UK	10	32.7	1.377	4.503
Germany	5	13.0	1.812	1.178
Netherlands	2	9.0	1.813	0.326
Sweden	2	30.1	1.449	0.872
Italy	2	36.4	1.591	1.158
Spain	1	30.5	1.669	0.509
Canada	1	17.7	1.170	0.207
Total/average	**100**	**15.3**	**–**	**19.1**

[a] These nine countries accounted for 51 per cent of total exports of major weapons in the period 1986–90, based on 1985 values.

[b] For France: estimate based on PPI for total manufacturing.

Source: Col. (2) SIPRI data base; col. (3) for France: International Financial Statistics, IMF; for USA: *Survey of Current Business,* US Department of Commerce; for all other countries: OECD, Scientific, Technological and Industrial Indicators Division, Paris, telefax Oct. 1991; col. (4) *International Financial Statistics,* IMF; col. 5 = col. (2) x 0.01 x col. (3) x col. (4)

change and those with intra-generational change by technical improvements and creation of new versions of existing systems. This is especially the case in periods when arms production is dominated by weapon systems which have been in production for a long time and thus experience considerable economies of scale. This is the present situation in the USA.

In the SIPRI data base technological improvements—but not inflationary tendencies—of both intra-generational as well generational changes are integrated by introducing new versions and new systems at higher values. Thus the present mark-up is exclusively intended to represent the inflation for weapons but not the cost for technical improvements.

5. It has not been attempted to include indexes other than those of Western exporters to calculate the SIPRI mark-up factor. This is particularly important to note since Soviet and Chinese exports represent 38 and 4 per cent of global arms exports during the period 1986–90. The reason is that the SIPRI values for Soviet and Chinese weapons are estimates based on the costs of US or other Western weapons of a similar type.[6] Thus, the SIPRI data base, based on Western weapon costs, was shifted according to Western cost or price trends.

[6] In 1991 when the Soviet Union began to market its weapons more aggressively on a commercial basis some prices became available. Apparently the prices quoted for Soviet systems are oriented on comparable Western systems. Mendel, F., "'Jagdflugzeug 90": Eine Dauderdiskussion ohne Ende', *Europeäische Sicherheit,* no. 11 (Nov. 1991), pp. 650–56.

6. The machinery industry resembles and also includes a major part of, the arms industry. So does the production of transportation equipment. The PPI for transportation equipment moves very similarly to the PPI for machinery during this period. The growth rates for the US PPIs, which will dominate the mark-up factor, are identical for the two sectors in the period 1986–90.

7. To arrive at a single inflator the PPIs of the different countries had to be weighted according to each country's share of the arms exports and was corrected for exchange rate movements. (See table 8D.2 for details.)

The inflator based on these principles outlined shows a total growth of 15.3 per cent without and 19.1 per cent with the required exchange rate adjustments for the period from 1986 to 1990. This could be compared to the US DOD deflator for procurement, which shows a growth of 19.9 per cent for the same time period[7], presumably including at least some intra-generational product improvement.

A similarly weighted combination of ordinary all-item consumer price indexes (CPIs) adjusted by exchange-rate movements would amount to a mark-up factor of 25.6 per cent. The CPIs are, however, less representative for the kind of production in the arms industry than the machinery or transportation production sectors.

V. Conventions

The following conventions are used in appendices 8B and 8C:

. .	Data not available or not applicable
–	Negligible figure (<0.5) or none
( )	Uncertain data or SIPRI estimate

---

[7]*National Defense Budget Estimates for FY 1992,* Office of the Comptroller of the Department of Defense, Mar. 1991, table 5-5: Depart of Defense Deflators—TOA; see also table 8D.1.

9. Arms production

PAOLO MIGGIANO, ELISABETH SKÖNS
and HERBERT WULF; Section V by ALEXEI KIREYEV

I. Introduction

Momentous political changes have occurred in the international system that have affected arms production world-wide. Governments are in the process of restructuring national armed forces and revising military equipment procurement plans. These changes were not fully reflected in lower figures for arms sales by the United States and Western Europe in 1990–91, the years reported in this chapter. The changes will certainly have a more profound effect on arms production and arms sales in the near future and have already had drastic consequences in the former USSR. However, there are developments in the opposite direction in other areas of the world: in contrast to Europe (both East and West) and North America, arms production continues to follow a dynamic path in several countries of the Asia–Pacific region.

In 1991 the arms industry continued to be influenced by stagnating or reduced arms procurement, affecting both exports and national production, in many parts of the world. The industrial structure in several countries is in a process of transformation: the most common company strategies are to reduce the size of the firm and lay off employees, to moth-ball production facilities, to 'trans-nationalize' firms, and to convert firms to non-military production. Many companies were engaged in major restructuring programmes, while others compensated for lost domestic orders by expanding exports. Arms-producing companies in the USA and Western Europe still benefited from orders that they acquired before the end of the cold war, but many of these projects will soon be completed. In the future, arms-producing companies will probably have to reduce their production capacities further (see section II).

The changes during 1990–91 in the arms production sector of the former Soviet Union were much more dramatic (see section V). Arms procurement was reduced, and production was decelerated or even stopped in numerous factories. Hundreds of thousands of workers, engineers and scientists were laid off. In the chaotic economic and political situation in the former Soviet Union and the successor republics of the Commonwealth of Independent States (CIS), specialists who have lost their jobs are looking for new employment; thus their skills might become available on the world market to countries with ambitious arms production programmes.

In the Asia–Pacific region, countries such as Australia, China, Japan, South Korea and Taiwan are undertaking major modernization or expansion programmes and in 1991 generally spent more on arms procurement than previously. Investments have been concentrated on naval equipment, but the aircraft industry is also expanding, for example in Japan and South Korea (see sections III and IV for developments in China and Japan, the two largest producers in the region).

II. The SIPRI 100

Developments in the SIPRI list of companies

The data on the 1990 arms sales[1] of the 100 largest arms producers in the OECD (Organization for Economic Co-operation and Development) countries and in the developing countries do not fully reflect the crisis that managers of the arms industry vividly describe in public statements. Although the arms sales of many companies have dropped, a number of other companies increased their arms sales in 1990 (see table 9.2). The value of the combined arms sales of the 100 largest companies increased from $172 billion in 1989 to $182 billion in 1990, a growth of 6 per cent in current prices.[2] However, this should not be interpreted as a sign of recovery in the arms industry. Several factors have influenced the arms sales of the 100 largest companies listed in appendix 9A.

1. The process of concentration of industry has continued. Thus, larger company arms sales figures—which are the combined sales of two or more companies—are not necessarily a reflection of increased business but in a number of cases rather the result of mergers with other arms-producing companies.

2. As mentioned above, the full extent of cuts (or announced reductions) in arms procurement budgets will be experienced in industry after a time lag, since projects often extend over a period of five years or more. However, it can already be seen that investments for new projects are lower than the original plans envisaged.

3. The figures for arms sales by all West European and Japanese companies are influenced by fluctuations in exchange-rates. For example, from 1989 to 1990, the US dollar lost between 5 and 17 per cent in relation to West Euro-

---

[1] Arms sales reported in this chapter are given in current US dollars, based on actual sales as reported by companies, governments, journals, newspapers, etc. For the applied methodology and sources, see appendix 9A. These data cannot be compared with the SIPRI data on the trade in major weapon systems, for which SIPRI applies its own methodology and pricing system, values being trend indicators in 1990 constant US dollars (see appendix 8D).

[2] SIPRI has reported extensively on the arms industry in Western Europe and North America in four publications: *SIPRI Yearbook 1990: World Armaments and Disarmament* (Oxford University Press: Oxford, 1990), chapter 8; *SIPRI Yearbook 1991: World Armaments and Disarmament* (Oxford University Press: Oxford, 1991), chapter 8; Anthony, I., Courades Allebeck, A. and Wulf, H., *West European Arms Production: Structural Changes in the New Political Environment*, SIPRI Research Report, Stockholm, Oct. 1990; and Brzoska, M. and Lock, P. (eds), SIPRI, *Restructuring of Arms Production in Western Europe* (Oxford University Press: Oxford, 1992). The analysis of the arms industry in Western Europe and North America presented in this chapter is therefore limited; basic facts on company development are presented below.

Table 9.1. National shares of arms sales, 1990 compared to 1989, for the 100 largest producers

No. of companies, 1990	Country/region	National/regional % share of total arms sales, 1989	National/regional % share of total arms sales, 1990	Arms sales, 1990 ($b.)
47	USA	62.7	60.5	109.9
41	Total Western Europe[a]	30.5	33.3	60.5
14	UK	9.3	10.6	19.4
10	France	10.3	11.7	21.2
8	Germany, FR	4.4	5.0	9.1
3	Italy	2.9	4.1	5.5
3	Sweden	1.4	1.0	1.9
2	Switzerland	0.9	1.0	1.8
1	Spain	0.8	0.9	1.6
–	Netherlands	0.5	..	..
6	Japan	3.6	3.3	6.1
6	Developing countries	3.2	2.9	5.3
3	Israel	1.2	1.2	2.2
2	India	1.1	1.0	1.8
1	South Africa	0.9	0.7	1.3

[a] West European countries of the OECD.

Source: Appendix 9A.

pean currencies. Thus, changes in sales figures as expressed in US dollars are different than the actual changes as reported by companies in local currencies.

4. Small and medium-sized arms-producing companies have been more affected than the large companies among the 100 top companies in the SIPRI list. Large companies have apparently been able to increase their share in a shrinking arms market.

In 1989 corporations from 14 different countries were represented in the SIPRI list of the 100 largest companies;[3] as table 9.1 illustrates, 13 countries are represented in the current list for 1990. The Netherlands does not appear in this list because of the sale in 1990 of large parts of the Philips arms-production sector to Thomson in France, because of economic difficulties. Other changes were marginal, with one fewer French and Swedish company, replaced in the list by an additional German and two US companies. These changes are the result of acquisitions of companies or increased arms sales. The country distribution has therefore shifted only marginally.

With 47 of the 100 largest companies and a share of 60 per cent of the total arms sales by these companies, the USA continues to dominate arms production. As in 1989, the total of 41 West European companies form the second

[3] See *SIPRI Yearbook 1991* (note 2), table 8A, pp. 310–16.

Table 9.2. Companies which lost and won the most in arms sales in 1990

Rank	Company	Country	Arms sales, 1990 ($m.)	Change in arms sales, 1990 compared to 1989 ($m.)
Companies which lost arms sales				
100	Honeywell	USA	360	– 1 040
65	Ford Motor	USA	700	– 400
14	Rockwell International	USA	4 100	– 400
Companies which won arms sales				
12	GEC	UK	4 280	+ 1 400
3	British Aerospace	UK	7 520	+ 1 220
46	Alliant Tech Systems	USA	1 150	+ 1 150
8	Thomson S.A.	France	5 250	+ 930
50	Bremer Vulkan	Germany, FR	1 050	+ 910
16	DCN	France	3 830	+ 830
29	Loral	USA	1 920	+ 770
21	Aérospatiale	France	2 860	+ 670
31	Rolls Royce	UK	1 830	+ 610
30	Textron	USA	1 900	+ 500
22	IRI	Italy	2 670	+ 440
27	GIAT	France	1 430	+ 410
17	Mitsubishi Heavy Industries	Japan	3 040	+ 400

Source: Appendix 9A.

largest group in the SIPRI 100 list for 1990: they account for one-third of total arms sales. Six companies from Japan and only 6 companies from non-OECD countries (Israel, India and South Africa) are among the SIPRI 100.

Table 9.2 lists the companies that lost or won the most in arms procurement, ranked according to their total dollar value loss or gain in arms sales in 1990 compared to 1989; all companies with changes in arms sales of $400 million or more are included. Far more companies gained than lost in arms sales, and 13 companies increased their arms sales by $400 million or more in 1990. Several of the arms sale increases are a result of company mergers or acquisitions. GEC, British Aerospace, GIAT, Thomson, Bremer Vulkan, Loral and Aérospatiale have all bought up other arms-producing facilities or entire companies, while Alliant Tech Systems is a newly formed company. Larger companies appear in the SIPRI 100 list and smaller companies disappear from the list entirely as a result of these mergers and acquisitions. The reductions in arms sales by both Honeywell and Ford are partly the result of sales of arms-production facilities. This is an indication of the international restructuring taking place in industry.

The ownership restructuring strategies currently applied by arms-producing companies to avoid declining profitability are of three general types: *(a)* the complete sell-off of arms production divisions or subsidiaries; *(b)* partial sales of units or divisions—in civilian as well as military production—in order to raise the working capital; and *(c)* the merger or acquisition of complete arms-producing companies or units in the same product area in order to exploit economies of scale and to reduce competition in the shrinking market.[4] The two leading arms manufacturers in the world, McDonnell Douglas and General Dynamics, have chosen different strategies. McDonnell Douglas, with about half of its sales in arms, is attempting to strengthen the non-military part of its activities. In contrast, General Dynamics, with over 80 per cent dependence on arms sales, has decided to increase the performance of its defence market operations by focusing on certain segments of the market and by selling some of its non-military production facilities.

Crisis in industry: employment cuts

The impact of the procurement of fewer weapons and of falling arms exports is now clearly visible in arms industry employment. The simultaneous deterioration of the commercial aircraft market is adding to the difficulties, at least temporarily, since weapon systems and civil aircraft and space systems are often produced by the same company. A study of the stock prices of major US defence contractor firms showed that they performed far worse than the market average. Surplus capacity and lack of capital are now common features of these companies.[5]

The arms industry is unable to maintain previous employment levels. Employment cuts are being implemented in most major arms-producing companies, either as regular lay-offs or through normal staff attrition. Some of these reductions are the consequences of planned structural adjustment programmes over a longer period. Other cuts are the immediate effects of the cancellation of specific weapon procurement programmes, resulting in the closure of production lines.

The major new employment reduction schemes announced in 1991 are shown in table 9.3.

---

[4] A systematization of company strategies in reaction to falling orders is made in Anthony, I. and Wulf, H., 'The economics of the West European arms industry', in eds Brzoska and Lock (note 2); Taylor, T., 'The future of European defence industries: problems and responses', paper presented at the British International Studies Association Annual Conference, London, Dec. 1989; Huffschmid, J. and Voss, W., *Militärische Beschaffungen-Waffenhandel-Rüstungskonversion in der EG. Ansätze koordinerter Steuerung*, PIW-Studien no. 7 (Progress-Institut für Wirtschaftsforschung: Bremen, 1991). For an overview of strategies used in the French arms industry, see *Avis présenté au nom de la commission de la défense nationale et des forces armées sur le projet de loi de finances pour 1991 par M. Jean-Guy Branger*, Tome VI, Défense, recherche et industrie d'armement, Assemblée Nationale, no. 2258 (9 Oct. 1991), pp. 25–37. International mergers and acquisitions have been described and analysed in *SIPRI Yearbook 1990* (note 2), chapter 8, pp. 335–38 and *SIPRI Yearbook 1991* (note 2), chapter 8, pp. 288–91.

[5] US Congress, Office of Technology Assessment, *Redesigning Defense: Planning the Transition to the Future US Defense Industrial Base*, OTA-ISC-500 (US Government Printing Office: Washington, DC, July 1991), pp. 65–67.

Table 9.3. Large employment cuts in arms production announced in 1991

Company	Reduction[a]	Comments[b]
France		
Aérospatiale	1 100	By 1994; due to cancellation of S-45 missile programme
CEA	400	By end-1993
Dassault Aviation	730	By 1994; in addition to 4000 jobs cut in military and civil production since 1988
Dassault Electronique	370	In 1991–92
Direction des Construc-tions Navales	> 250	May be up to 400
Snecma Groupe	1 337	Of which 837 in 1991, including in subsidiaries
SNEP	675	In 1992
Thomson-Brandt Armements	120	Of which 70 in R&D; in addition to 130 announced in 1990; mainly due to cuts in the ACED missile programme
Thomson-CSF	3 000	In 1991–93
Germany		
Diehl	< 1 000	In 1992
FMW	100	In 1992
Heckler & Koch	450	In addition to 200 already cut in 1991
Krauss-Maffei	100	..
Mainz Industries	300	In addition to 2400 jobs cut since 1987
MBB	300	In addition to 700 jobs cut in aerospace
MTU	200	In military and civil production; military share falling
Rheinmetall	840	..
Italy		
Alenia	3 100	By end-1993
EFIM	> 700	Restructuring plan due to defence budget cuts
Piaggio	400	By end-1992; due to fall in military and civil orders
UK		
BAe	2 200	In 1991 in missile division; in addition to 2500 in civil production and 5500 announced in 1990 in military production
British Nuclear Fuels	400	..
Dowty	1 305	In addition to 1200 announced in 1990
GEC Ferranti	1 150	Due to fall in defence systems orders
Link-Miles Ltd	325	Due to anticipated drop in defence-related business
Rediffusion Simulation	600	Due to decline in military orders and in aircraft industry
Rolls Royce	1 500	In 1991; 1991 total job cuts of 7000 (military and civil)
Royal Ordnance	860	Due to decline in military orders

Company	Reduction[a]	Comments[b]
Shorts	250	..
VSEL (Vickers)	> 3 000	May be up to 5500; by 1995; in addition to 1500 since 1989
Westland Group	700	350 in Westland Helicopters and 300 in Normalair Garret
Yarrow shipyards	645	By end-1991
Other Europe		
FN Moteurs, Belgium	530	..
Saab Aircraft, Sweden	1 000	By 1993
Swedish Ordnance, Sweden	2 485	By end-1993
Eidgenössische Rüstungs- betriebe, Switzerland	100– 200	Annually until 1994 ..
Oerlikon-Bührle, Switzerland	6 000	Of which 1900 in 1991 and 980 in 1992
USA		
Boeing	2 500	In Defense & Space Group; due to nuclear arms cuts
General Dynamics	5 800	In 1991–92; due to cancellation of A-12, cuts in air defence division and in cruise missile development; plan to cut c. 27 000 jobs over 4 years (military and civil)
General Electric	1 000	Due to loss of ATF contract
GE Aerospace	1 400	By mid-1992
Grumman	1 900	In 1991; due to termination of A-6 and F-14 line
GTE	500	In telecommunications; due to defence cuts
McDonnell Douglas	4 650	Due to cancellation of A-12 and cuts in helicopter and missile units
Martin Marietta	400	In the Information Systems Group
Newport News	< 3 000	In the Tidewater area
Lockheed	> 2 000	In missile division
Texas Instruments	725	In addition to 1500 in 1990, of which 1000 in defence units
TRW	2 650	In 1991; about half as lay-offs in defence and space units
United Technologies	13 900	By 1995; in military and civil units
Westinghouse Electric	1 200	Due to cancellation of A-12

[a] Unless otherwise stated in the next column, employment cuts are in military production only.

[b] Information given by the company.

Sources: SIPRI company data base.

The magnitude of total future employment cuts in the arms and aerospace industries is likely to be extensive, as confirmed by the available forecasts. It has been predicted that US arms industry employment will shrink by 814 000 jobs, from a total of 3 million, by the year 1996.[6] Employment in the French defence industry has declined from 270 000 in 1988 to 255 000 in 1991.[7] Ongoing restructuring activities will result in further cuts of 12 000–18 000 jobs in 1992 and an estimated 100 000 jobs in arms production and related industries by 1995.[8] Arms industry employment in the UK is forecasted to fall from 618 000 in 1990 to about 495 000 in the mid-1990s, according to one estimate.[9] The combined arms industry employment in the European NATO countries is estimated to decline by 485 000–650 000 in the period 1989–95 to less than 1 million people in 1995,[10] and even higher unemployment estimates have been made.[11] Thus, the employment impact of the contraction of the arms industry may become comparable to recent large industrial crises, such as that in the steel industry—with reductions of about 440 000 jobs between 1975 and 1985 in the European Community (EC) countries—and in shipbuilding—with about 230 000 jobs lost in the same area during the same period.[12]

In many countries arms industries are rather strongly concentrated in certain areas,[13] which means that the impact on employment will also be most strongly felt there. Regions with a heavy dependence on arms production are potential constituencies for opposition against arms reductions, unless the impact of arms industry employment cuts is softened.

[6] The Defense Budget Project, *Potential Impact of Defense Spending Reductions on the Defense Labour Force by State* (DBP: Washington, DC, Aug. 1991). The US aerospace industry has forecasted a 13% decline in its employment during the period 1990–94, of which 112 600 jobs in military activities and 126 000 in civil activities. In 1990 US aerospace employment declined by 61 000 jobs, in 1991 by 78 000, of which 45 000 in military aircraft production; *Aviation Week & Space Technology*, 20 Jan. 1992.

[7] *Avis* (note 4), p. 14; *Interavia Air Letter*, 10 Sep. 1991, p. 6.

[8] 'L'industrie de l'armement va supprimer 18000 emplois', *Le Monde*, 14 Jan. 1992, p. 24; *Defense News*, 9 Sep. 1991, p. 42.

[9] According to the director-general of the British Defence Manufacturers' Association, in *Defence Industry Digest*, Mar. 1991, p. 7.

[10] The details of this estimate can be found in Anthony and Wulf (note 4).

[11] In the European Parliament cuts have been mentioned, amounting to 800 000–1 million jobs in the arms industry in the EC region during the next 5-year period. *Financial Times*, 12 Sep. 1991, p. 3.

[12] *Industry Statistical Yearbook 1988*, Eurostat, Theme 4, Series A, Luxembourg, 1989.

[13] In the USA the biggest losers in the defence budget cuts are the states of Alaska and Hawaii (each losing 2.8% of total production), Virginia (2.7%), California (2.3%), Washington (2.2%) and Maryland (1.9%), according to a forthcoming study by the US Congressional Budget Office (CBO) (*Defense News*, 26 Aug. 1991). California has already lost 175 000 jobs in the aerospace industry since 1986 (*Aviation Week & Space Technology*, 20 Jan 1992). In the UK, the direct impact of reduced military expenditure on employment in the south-western region has been estimated at 40 000 lost jobs in the arms industry by the year 2000 plus an indirect impact of 12 000 jobs lost in related industrial branches. See *Defense News*, 27 May 1991, p. 27, which cites the report *The Impact of Reduced Military Expenditure on the Economy of South West England* (Research Unit in Defense Economics, Bristol Polytechnic: Avon, UK, May 1991). In France arms industry employment accounts for more than 10% of industrial employment in several regions: Ile de France, Bretagne, Aquitaine and Provence-Alpes-Cote d'Azur; *Avis* (note 4), p. 14. In Germany the arms industry is concentrated around Munich, in south-western Germany and along the northern coastline. However, more important than the cuts in the arms industry are job losses in the armed forces, both with the Bundeswehr and foreign troops.

Within the EC there is an ongoing debate on the nature and extent of possible EC-funded support programmes for the arms industry. While there is strong support in the European Parliament for the formation of a structural fund comparable to previous EC funds for the shipbuilding and steel industries, the EC Council and the majority in the EC Commission are reluctant to agree to any large support programmes. The limited regional aid programme Perifra, initiated in 1990, has more of a symbolic than a real value.[14] According to Article 223 of the Treaty of Rome, the EC should not become involved in national security policies but should deal with industry purely in industrial–economic terms. This article was not deleted from the Treaty in the December 1991 Maastricht EC meeting, despite the long debates on such a possible revision of the Treaty.

Most governments have in the past insisted that the process of restructuring industry should take place in a free market competition without government interference. However, the French Government considers that there is a need to plan current restructuring activities. In the late summer of 1991, the Ministry of Defence appointed two bodies for the preparation and planning of structural changes in the arms industries: a high-level committee for 'restructuring the military and industry' and a delegation for collaboration with regional and local organizations as well as trade unions and interest groups.[15] As part of this strategy, the Government is actively promoting mergers of the industry which would affect Thomson-CSF, CEA, SNECMA and Aérospatiale.

The US Government is primarily interested in maintaining a viable defence industrial base. Specific mention was made in the Secretary of Defense's *Annual Report* for 1991. It was requested that 'the U.S. defense industrial base must be prepared to respond to a broad range of military contingencies that may emerge in the future'.[16]

Arms-producing companies are confronted with a situation in which their business is likely to be further reduced. Companies have already reacted to the apparent political changes, but it is fair to predict that the process of adjustment to smaller procurement budgets is far from complete.

---

[14] *Communiqué de presse de Communautés Européennes,* Affectation des crédits, IP (91) 816, Brussels, 9 Sep. 1991. The Perifra special scheme was allocated 40 million ECUs ($33 million) for each of the years 1990 and 1991 for financing regional pilot schemes to counteract the impact of not only reduced arms production and military base closings but also trade concessions to Central and Eastern Europe, the integration of the former German Democratic Republic and the Persian Gulf War.

[15] *Le Monde,* 31 Aug. 1991, p. 12; *Damoclès,* no. 51 (Dec. 1991/Jan. 1992), p. 13.

[16] Dick Cheney, Secretary of Defense, *Annual Report to the President and the Congress* (US Government Printing Office: Washington, DC, 1991), p. 43. A special report, studying different alternatives, was prepared for Congress by the Office of Technology Assessment (note 5).

III. China

Mixed signals

The Chinese Government is sending mixed signals to the international community about its arms production: military expenditures have been substantially increased since 1988, after a period of drastic reductions during the early 1980s and moderate growth during the mid-1980s. The Government announced with great satisfaction the success of the process of conversion from military to civil production during the 1980s.[17] However, for China, conversion is not only intended to reduce the quantity of military production or—as is often proclaimed by the leadership—to contribute to world peace; it is also a policy to modernize the Chinese defence industrial base through imports of modern technology. In 1991 China began to participate in international arms trade control forums but remains an important exporter of major conventional weapons, including ballistic missiles.

The modernization drive during the 1980s is a result of the general weakness of industry. The arms industry—which could not be debated until the end of the 1970s—was reformed when Chinese international relations improved and threat perceptions changed.[18] Economic factors were given priority over political ideology. The new objectives were: significant down-sizing and modernization of the industry, technological improvement, economic efficiency in production and efficient use of resources, military–civil integration of industry, and priority for military products only if this was not damaging for the economy. The methods used were decentralization of the decision-making process, new management procedures (that is, more autonomy for military industry managers) and utilization of arms industry facilities for non-military production. The emphasis was on moving from quantity to quality, for both personnel and weapon systems.[19] Improved international relations allowed the proposed changes to be made.

Arms production: less quantity, more quality

Chinese arms factories produce a complete range of weapon systems, from small arms to heavy ordnance, from anti-tank missiles to intercontinental ballistic missiles, from munitions to nuclear warheads, from small patrol craft

---

[17] Papers presented at the International Conference on International Cooperation in Peaceful Use of Military Industrial Technology, Beijing, 22–26 Oct. 1991, which will be available in a forthcoming publication.

[18] According to Huai Guomo, Vice Minister in charge of the Commission of Science, Technology and Industry for National Defence (COSTIND), the policy was first formulated in the 1979 with an intention to 'combining military and civilian production'. According to Huai '[I]ts central implication is to integrate organically the defence construction with the development of national economy and to apply military–industrial technologies in the cause of peace and for the benefit of mankind.' Huai Guomo, 'Peace, development and cooperation', address to the International Conference on International Cooperation in Peaceful Use of Military Industrial Technology, Beijing, 22–26 Oct. 1991, p. 4.

[19] Copley, G. R. (ed.), *Defence and Foreign Affairs Handbook 1989* (International Media Corp.: Alexandria, Va. and London, 1989), pp. 206–20.

to destroyers, from utility planes to bombers, and from jeeps and trucks to main battle tanks. China is one of the major arms producers of the world. In 1991 the total inventory of the different branches of the armed forces included 7500–8000 main battle tanks, 5000 fighter aircraft, 94 submarines of different classes and 56 principal surface combat ships.[20]

In technological terms, most Chinese equipment is not comparable to weapons produced in the former USSR and the NATO countries. The fast rate of generational change in weapon systems, fuelled for several decades by the cold war, could not be matched by the Chinese arms industry. For example, most fighter planes are F-6s, the Chinese version of the Soviet MiG-19, which has been produced since 1958. Main battle tanks consist mainly of the T-59 (a modernized version of the Soviet T-54 of the 1950s) and the T-69 which began to be produced in the late 1960s. The Chinese arms industry is not only based on Soviet designs but also modelled according to the Soviet bureaucratic system, with many economic inefficiencies. According to Western observers, Chinese arms development appears to involve incremental and evolutionary changes rather than major design breakthroughs.[21]

However, since the changed policy at the end of the 1970s there has also been an emphasis on quality. For a small number of weapons, China has successfully sought international collaboration to upgrade and modernize its equipment. The pattern of collaboration seems based on some distinctive features: orders for a small number of advanced weapons as a means to obtain a large transfer of technology and parallel development of collaboration with many countries, sometimes on the same technology, perhaps to avoid dependence on a single country.

Until the early 1980s the Chinese arms industry, an autonomous sector with no connections to the rest of industry, was almost entirely geared to weapon design and production. It was concerned with supplying the armed forces and not with economy.[22] Chinese military industry managers conclude today that 'the enterprises merely paid attention to production rather than management, causing productive capacity to be insufficiently developed and poor economic efficiency'.[23] Low productivity, poor management, underutilized capacity and utilization of a large proportion of scarce resources characterized the industry.

[20] International Institute for Strategic Studies (IISS), *The Military Balance 1991–1992* (Brassey's: London, 1991), pp. 150–53.

[21] Frankenstein, J., 'People's Republic of China: defense industry, diplomacy, and trade', ed. J. E. Katz, *Arms Production in Developing Countries* (Lexington Books: Lexington, Mass., 1984), pp. 89–102.

[22] Latham, R. J., 'China's defense industrial policy: looking toward the year 2000', in ed. R. H. Yang, *SCPS PLA Yearbook 1988/89*, Sun Yat-sen Center for Policy Studies, National Sun Yat-sen University: Kaohsing, Taiwan (Lynne Rienner Publishers: Boulder, Colo., 1989), pp. 79–93. For the structure of the industry and the decision-making process, see Latham, R. J., 'People's Republic of China: the restructuring of defense–industrial policies', in ed. Katz (note 21), pp. 103–22. For a more recent description, see Lewis, J. W., Hua Di and Xue Litai, 'Beijing's defense establishment', *International Security*, vol. 15, no. 4 (spring 1991), pp. 87–109.

[23] Li Baozhen, 'Brief introduction on conversion from military to civilian and domestic to overseas production in aviation enterprises', paper delivered at the International Conference on International Cooperation in Peaceful Use of Military Industrial Technology, Beijing, 22–26 Oct. 1991, p. 7.

Table 9.4. Current products of the Chinese aircraft industry

Company	Work-force	Military products	Civilian products
Chengdu Aircraft Corp. (CAC)	20 000	F-7 fighter; FT-5 trainer	Nosecones for McDonnell Douglas MD-80 and MD-82
Changhe Aircraft Factory (CAF)	6 000	Z-8 transport helicopter	Coaches, commercial road vehicles
Guizhou Aviation Industry Corp. (GAIC)	>18 000	F-7 fighter; FT-7 trainer	Unidentified
Guanzhou Orlando Helicopters LTD (GOHL)	..	None/..	OHA-S-55 helicopter for crop and forest spraying
Harbin Aircraft Manufacturing Co. (HAMC)	15 000	H-5 light bomber; PS-5 maritime patrol; Z-9 helicopter	Y-11 and Y-12 utility transport; PS-5 water-bomber version
Nanchang Aircraft Manufacturing Co. (NAMC)	>20 000	A-5A Fantan fighter; CJ-6A basic trainer	N-5A farming and forestry; CJ-6 Haynan agricultural and forestry
Shaanxi Aircraft Co. (SAC)	10 000	Y-8 Cub transport; Y-8MPA maritime patrol	Y-8 Cub for civil transport, Y-8MPA for fishery patrol, pollution monitoring, oil exploration
Shenyang Aircraft Corp. (SAC)	>20 000	F-8B Finback multi-role; F-6	Cargo door for Boeing 757 and Dash 8; rudders for British Aerospace; wing ribs for Airbus 320
Shangai Aircraft Manufacturing Factory (SAMF)	7 000	Y-10 for troop transport	Y-10 transport; assembling MD-82; producing landing gear doors, other components and complete tailplanes for McDonnell Douglas
Shijiazhuang Aircraft Plant (SAP)	>4 000	None/..	Y-5 small transport
Xian Aircraft Manufacturing Co. (XAC)	15 000	B-6 Badger and B-7 multi-role bombers; Y-7-100 and Y-7-500 transport	Same Y-7 models for civilian transport

Source : *Jane's All the World's Aircraft 1990–91* (Jane's Publishing Co.: Coulsdon, Surrey, 1990), pp. 32–37.

The two-pronged strategy of conversion is reflected in table 9.4, which lists both the civilian products of the aircraft industry and some of the co-operation agreements with aircraft companies from the West, and in table 9.5, which gives an overview of all five sectors of the arms industry.

Conversion: guns and butter

The objectives of the reform programme in the 1980s, now considered in China as a decade of fairly successful conversion, and the challenge posed to industry by these reforms were encapsulated in the flowery slogan that the arms industry should no longer 'wait for the rice to cook' but 'look for the rice to cook'.[24] Conversion and diversification[25] were as much a modernization of the arms industry as they were a reduction of arms production in quantitative terms.

During the decade of conversion experience, industry passed through several stages.

1. In the first stage, non-military products, mainly durable consumer goods, were 'more or less blindly developed',[26] but the emphasis was not only on production of non-military products. At the same time commercialization of arms production had priority. It was intended to improve the availability of technology through increased weapon sales—the profits of which could be used for importing military technology.[27] However, import of technology was not realized on any large scale during this phase.

China was able to seize the opportunity provided by the Iraq–Iran War, selling directly and through North Korea to both sides. The loss of orders from North Viet Nam was more than compensated for by sales not only to Iran and Iraq, but also to Egypt, Bangladesh and Zimbabwe. By 1985 China had become the seventh major exporter of weapons in the SIPRI ranking.

2. During the second stage of conversion an attempt was made to tap military technology by integrating the non–military product range into existing plans. The domestic sale of non-military products increased. At the same time China was more successful in importing foreign technology for military products on a large scale than during the earlier stage. Numerous co-operation agreements with Western countries were signed.[28]

During the second half of the 1980s, Chinese companies pursued a forceful marketing effort, being continuously present at all the arms exhibitions organized in Asia and the Middle East. With this strategy, China was able to

---

[24] Quoted in Latham, R. J., 'People's Republic of China: the restructuring of defense–industrial policies,' in Katz (note 21), p. 107.

[25] The term 'conversion' is used in China not only for the process of changing arms-producing facilities to non-military production—civilian production at the expense of military production. Changes made in industry—as described in this section—could at least partly be termed 'diversification', e.g., expanding the range of products into areas of non-military production.

[26] Wang Jinchen, 'Strengthen international cooperation and bring into play the technical superiority of the military electronics in the drive to stimulate social and economic development', paper delivered at the International Conference on International Cooperation in Peaceful Use of Military Industrial Technology, Beijing, 22–26 Oct. 1991, p. 4.

[27] In 1980, six new import–export companies specializing in weapons were created: CATIC (China Aero-Technology Import–Export Corporation), NORINCO (China North Industries Corporation), CPMIEC (China Precision Machinery Import–Export Corporation, now subordinate to China Shipbuilding Corporations CSC), CGWIC (China Great Wall Industrial Corporation), CEIEC (China National Electronics Import–Export Corporation) and CNEIC (China Nuclear Engineering Import and Export Corporation).

[28] See *SIPRI Yearbook 1991* (note 2), pp. 206–7; and *Jane's Fighting Ships 1991–92* (Jane's Information Group: Coulsdon, Surrey, 1991), pp. 112–14; *Asian Defence Journal*, no. 4 (1991), pp. 6–7.

add another big client to its list, Thailand. According to SIPRI statistics, during this period China sold as many major conventional arms as the UK.[29]

3. In the third stage, which very few factories have reached so far, it is intended to produce military and civil products complementary to each other, such that military production should benefit from civil production and vice versa. While holding on to the priority of self-reliance, the import of foreign technology is actively promoted.[30] The 1989 Tiananmen Square massacre has delayed but not stopped this process. The arms embargo imposed on China by the Western countries has been of short duration, and is now given up or circumvented. Several of the previously embargoed projects have been taken up again. New projects have been agreed upon.[31]

The 1991 Persian Gulf War influenced the last adjustment of the modernization programme, and high priority was given to electronics in the 1991–95 Five Year Plan. At the same time a new import–export company specializing in electronics, the Military Equipment Corporation, was created.[32]

The gradual introduction of market mechanisms in the Chinese economy is also touching the arms industry. In a critical article on the performance of the arms industry the defence economist Wang Liguo requests the arms industry 'to play a more important role in the areas of "high-tech, high risk, and high profit"'. He suggests introducing the rule of cost–profit and of competition in the defence enterprises.[33]

The extent to which conversion and diversification were successful in the 1980s is difficult to conclude. According to official Chinese information it has been a rapid process, as illustrated in table 9.5. According to Chinese sources, annual growth rates of civil production within the arms industry are impressively high—although the growth rates relate to a low level in the 1980 base year. Thus, the share of civil production within the arms industry has been growing to high levels: the figures given officially range between almost 50 per cent for the nuclear industry and 97 per cent for electronics. However, these official figures should be treated with caution, since there is no means to verify the information. Annual growth rates of up to 43 per cent of civil production in the arms industry are phenomenally large and should thus be questioned until further empirical evidence is available.

[29] For details, see chapter 8 in this volume, especially table 8.1.

[30] Zhou Sili, 'Step towards the world by introducing foreign investment and combining with interior', and Chen Quinjie, 'An approach to the subject of developing economy and moving to the world for China's inland defence industrial enterprises by making use of foreign financing', papers delivered at International Conference on International Cooperation in Peaceful Use of Military Industrial Technology, Beijing 22–26 Oct. 1991.

[31] *Interavia Air Letter*, 28 Feb. 1991, p. 4; *Defence*, July 1990, p. 422; *La Tribune de L'Expansion*, 2 July 1991, p. 9; *Jane's Defence Weekly*, 24 Feb. 1990, p. 367; *Defence Industry Digest*, May 1991, p. 12.

[32] *Asian Defence Journal*, no. 6 (1991), p. 117; *Pacific Defence Reporter*, Feb. 1991, p. 29.

[33] Wang Liguo, 'The readjustment of the defense industrial enterprises in turning to the civil market', paper delivered at the International Conference on International Cooperation in Peaceful Use of Military Industrial Technology, Beijing, 22–26 Oct. 1991, pp. 6–7.

Table 9.5. Conversion of the Chinese arms industry, 1980–90

Sector	1980–90 annual growth rate of civil production, %	Civil share of total production, % 1980	Civil share of total production, % 1990	No. of civil products developed 1990	Type of products
Aerospace	30	10	67	>7 000	Civil aircraft, consumer goods
Ordnance (North China Industries)	19.8	10	63.8	nearly 1 000	Motorcycles, buses, trucks, refrigerators, sports pistols; exports 1990: $130 m.
Shipbuilding	..	40[a]	81	>1 000 non-marine products	Railway rolling stocks, coal mining equipment, containers, gasometers, exports 1990: $2 b.
Nuclear industry	21.3[d]	4.9	48	..	Nuclear power plants, isotope and radiation technology
Electronics	..	70[b]	97	>1000	Products for energy, communication, agriculture, textile machinery, chemistry, mining, food, computers
Total arms industry	43[c]	8.1[b]	65[e]	nearly 10 000	See above

[a] End of the 1970s.
[b] 1979.
[c] 1980–88.
[d] 1986–90.
[e] 1991.

Sources: Ministry of Aero-Space Industry of China, 'Peacefully utilizing aerospace technology, strengthening international co-operation and promoting further development of the shift from military production to civil production' (this and the following sources are papers delivered at the International Conference on International Cooperation in Peaceful Use of Military Industrial Technology, Beijing, 22–26 Oct. 1991, to be published); Wang Ligua, 'The readjustment of the defence industrial enterprises in turning to the civil market'; speech made by the senior executive of China North Industries Group; Zhao Zhongyi and Zhon Xingfu, 'Shipbuilding industry in transferring military industrial technologies to civilian purposes'; Wang Jincheng, 'Strengthen international co-operation and bring into play the technical superiority of the military electronics in the drive to stimulate social and economic development'; Wang Xipeng and Li Zhenchen, 'Bring advantage of military industry into full play to serve the construction of national economy'; Jin Zhude and Chai Benliang, 'Strategic thinking of China's conversion in the 1990's'.

The difficulties experienced in conversion and differences in comparison to civil production were not so different in China from the experience in other planned economies. They can be summarized as follows:

1. Military enterprises, long accustomed to government planning, need marketing practices, particularly if they want to export their civil products.

2. Civil production lines have often been taken up at the discretion of company managers without integration into the overall economic plan.

3. Military enterprises are still not fully integrated into the Chinese economy.

4. Funding for the conversion process has not been sufficient.

5. Difficulties in attracting international collaborators have been experienced.

6. Military enterprises employ larger numbers of qualified scientists and engineers and invest more in R&D.

7. The quality control system in the military enterprises is more elaborate than in non-military production facilities.

Chinese defence economists stress the importance of conversion for future economic development in China by underlining the broader economic and political aims.[34] The basic aims for the 1990s remain emphasizing high technology in arms production, reducing quantities in exchange for higher quality, and supporting the economy through non-military production in the arms industry.

IV. Japan

Growing arms production

The corner-stones of Japanese security policy and arms production are:[35]

1. The so-called 'no war clause' of Article 9 of the Constitution that renounces the use of force in the settlement of international conflicts.

2. Quantitative limitations of military expenditures that the Government laid out in 1976, limiting the military budget to 1 per cent of the gross national product (GNP).[36]

3. Limitations on weapon exports.

4. Prohibitions to possess, introduce or manufacture nuclear weapons.

5. Provisions to use space exclusively for peaceful purposes.

[34] Jin Zhude and Chai Benliang, 'Strategic thinking of China's conversion in the 1990's', paper delivered at the International Conference on International Cooperation in Peaceful Use of Military Industrial Technology, Beijing, 22–26 Oct. 1991, p. 9.

[35] See Japanese Defense Agency (JDA), *Defense of Japan* (JDA: Tokyo, several editions); and a summary in US Congress, Office of Technology Assessment, *Arming our Allies: Cooperation and Competition in Defense Technology*, OTA-ISC-449 (US Government Printing Office: Washington, DC, May 1990), pp. 61–72.

[36] This provision was replaced in 1986 by a quantitative 5-year procurement plan. In practice the 1% GNP limit still exists.

In addition the Japanese Government is not allowed to enter any collective security treaty and has restricted its military arrangements to a bilateral treaty with the USA.

In contrast to the general trend in the USA, the former USSR and most of Europe (East and West), Japan is still increasing its investment in military production, and Japanese firms are increasing their involvement in arms production. The budget for the Japanese Self Defense Forces grew continuously during the 1980s and is planned to continue to grow.[37] The increase of 5.5 per cent for fiscal year 1991[38] represents a substantial increase in line with the increases of previous years at a time when most other defence ministries and arms-producing firms are faced with cuts. Domestic arms procurement has grown at similar rates during the 1980s and is planned to increase further.[39] The 1991 budget initiates an average 3 per cent annual growth in real terms for a five-year period. Of the total 1991 military budget, approximately 45 per cent (R&D, maintenance and equipment and material purchases) is of direct importance to the arms-producing companies in Japan.[40]

Arms-producing companies

Over the past decade arms production has become more important in Japan. Although the percentage of arms production in the large and expanding Japanese economy is small—still below 1 per cent of total industrial production—this share is growing.[41]

Parallel to the budget, contracts to arms-producing companies grew at nominal annual rates of 7 per cent from 1986 to 1990. Although arms production in Japan is highly concentrated, with roughly three-quarters of the procurement orders going to only 20 companies (see table 9.6), most Japanese companies do not depend heavily on arms sales. This is because most Japanese arms-producing companies are large concerns, with a wide variety of different civilian product lines. Of the top 20 contractors, only Nippon Koki, a small arms- and ordnance-producing company which during the past three years ranked between 17 and 20 on the list of the largest Japanese arms producers, depended for more than half of its sales on Defense Agency contracts. Many contractors report single-digit percentage shares of dependence. For the aircraft sector and some companies, the government-sponsored arms industry buildup is important. Japan's aircraft producers are trying to develop an integrated, highly sophisticated aircraft industry. Japan's aerospace industry employs 28 600 persons according to the Society of Japanese Aerospace Companies;[42] its sales depend to 75 per cent on Defense Agency orders.[43]

[37] Japanese Defense Agency, *Defense of Japan* (JDA: Tokyo, several editions).
[38] Aviation Advisory Services, *Milavnews*, Sep. 1991, p. 17.
[39] Japanese Defense Agency, *Defense of Japan 1990* (JDA: Tokyo, 1991), p. 319; and Japanese Defense Agency, *Defense of Japan 1991* (JDA: Tokyo, 1992), p. 99.
[40] Baker, C., 'Japanese defense firms expect robust decade', *Defense News*, 18 Feb. 1991, pp. 16, 30.
[41] The percentage grew from 0.36% in 1980 to 0.54% in 1989 according to JDA (note 39), p. 263.
[42] Quoted in *Aviation Week & Space Technology*, 29 July 1991, p. 43.
[43] *Financial Times*, 11 June 1991, p. 13.

Table 9.6. The top arms contractors and value of defence contracts in Japan, 1986–90

Figures are in b. yen.

Rank	Company	Industry[a]	1986	1987	1988	1989	1990 Military contracts as % of total sales
1	Mitsubishi Heavy Industries	Ac, Mi, MV, Sh	291	262	364	364	441 _17_
2	Kawasaki Heavy Industries	Ac, Sh	145	171	150	175	146 _14_
3	Mitsubishi Electric	El, Mi	81	87	101	112	100 _3_
4	Ishikawajima–Harima	Eng, Sh	78	75	77	63	79 _8_
5	Toshiba	El, Mi	67	72	83	68	60 _1_
6	NEC	El	49	61	74	71	54 _1_
7	Japan Steel Works	A	22	24	31	31	35 _26_
8	Komatsu	MV, SA/O	16	21	24	24	22 _2_
9	Fuji Heavy Industries	Ac	18	20	22	22	22 _3_
10	Hitachi	El, MV	13	11	16	19	21 _>1_
11–20 ..		..		117	138	115	153	139 ..
Total top 20 companies		..		897	942	1 057	1 102	1 119 ..
Total no. of contracts		..		1 190	1 272	1 398	1 499	1 569 ..
Share of top 20 companies in total contracts (%)		..		75	74	76	74	71 ..

[a] Ac = aircraft, El = electronics, Eng = engines, Mi = missiles, MV = military vehicles, SA/O = small arms/ordinance, and Sh = ships.

Source: Office of Defense Production Committee, Keidanren (Federation of Economic Organizations), communication to SIPRI; annual reports.

Three of the major producers, Mitsubishi Heavy Industries, by far the largest arms manufacturer, Kawasaki Heavy Industries, the second largest, and Ishikawajima–Harima Heavy Industries Co., usually between rank 4 and 6 of the top arms producers, have greatly profited in their sales from military contracts and record 17, 14 and 8 per cent, respectively, of total sales as military contracts.

Besides the ambitions to forge a viable and highly sophisticated commercial and military aerospace industry, capable eventually of designing and producing modern commercial aircraft as well as military fighters, helicopters, aircraft engines and missiles, investments are made in a wide range of conventional weapon systems: submarines are built by Mitsubishi Heavy Industries and Kawasaki Heavy Industries; and destroyers and frigates by Ishikawajima–Harima, Mitsubishi Heavy Industries, Mitsui and Sumitomo. Mitsubishi Heavy Industries develops and produces main battle tanks and other combat vehicles. Six of the top 20 Defense Agency contractors develop and produce military electronics. Komatsu, Daikin Industries and Nippon Koki produce small arms and ordnance.

Japanese arms manufacturers produce most weapon systems in short production runs compared particularly to the United States but also to the production runs in Western Europe, which results in higher unit production costs. This is partly due to the fact that Japanese companies are not allowed to export weapons.[44]

The situation is different in military electronics production. Companies such as Mitsubishi Electric, NEC, Hitachi and Fujitsu benefit from the growing importance of electronics in the Japanese procurement programme. Part of the difference of the military electronic and other arms-producing sectors can be explained by the fact that the development of military electronics depends much less on funds from the Japanese Defense Agency. It is more common to integrate commercial electronic products into weapon systems. This is the area in which Japanese producers have been successful at selling to US weapon producers.

Technology flow

Although key sectors of Japanese weapon development continue to depend on imported technology (almost entirely from the United States), Japan's declared goal has been to produce its weapons domestically since it resumed arms production in the early 1950s.[45] The extent to which Japan has been successful in indigenous production can be seen by the high share of domestic procurement. As early as the end of the 1960s, a level of 90 per cent domestic procurement had been reached. Since then it has usually fluctuated around this percentage.[46] The remaining 10 per cent are important technology imports for high-technology weapon systems, accounted for by commercial imports from different countries and by the United States foreign military sales.[47]

Licensed production of US weapon systems in Japan during the past few years include several versions of helicopters from Bell, Boeing, McDonnell Douglas and Sikorsky; the Lockheed P-3C Orion patrol airplane; the McDonnell Douglas F-4E Phantom, F-15DJ and F-15D jet fighters; the Lockheed EP-3 electronic warfare aircraft; the Raytheon Patriot anti-aircraft

---

[44] Hummel, H., *The Policy of Arms Export Restrictions in Japan*, PRIME Occasional Paper no. 4 (Peace Research Institute, Meiji Gakuin University (PRIME): Yokohama, Dec. 1988); Anthony, I., 'Japan', in ed. I. Anthony, SIPRI, *Arms Export Regulations* (Oxford University Press: Oxford, 1991), pp. 103–9. SIPRI records negligible Japanese arms exports since the definition of arms exports is wider than the Japanese Government's. There have been reports of Japanese companies violating COCOM rules; these cases were not arms exports in the strict sense but related to the export of dual-use technology.

[45] Drifte, R., *Arms Production in Japan* (Westview Press: Boulder, Colo. and London, 1986).

[46] This statement does not contradict the fact that Japan is recorded in the SIPRI arms trade statistics as one of the major importers of major conventional weapons. Licence-produced weapons in Japan are considered as imports of Japan in the SIPRI statistics. For the methodology applied, see appendix 8D in this volume.

[47] See Drifte (note 45), p. 22 for earlier years; for the 1980s, see Japanese Defense Agency (note 39), p. 262.

system; and several types of ship-, air- and surface-launched missiles. The most ambitious and also most controversial collaboration is the Fighter Support Experimental aircraft (FSX), a derivate and remodelled version of the General Dynamics F-16C Fighting Falcon, co-developed by Mitsubishi Heavy Industries and General Dynamics and to be produced eventually by Mitsubishi Heavy Industries, with approximately 40 per cent of the work subcontracted to US companies.

Collaboration in military technology between Japan and the United States has been a one-way street for many decades. Critique of the massive technology transfers from the United States to Japan culminated in congressional debates over the FSX programme. According to US interpretations, the failure to establish a two-way technology flow has led to questioning the value of the co-operation.[48] While Japanese arms-production planners want to continue to invest in major projects and the Japanese industry would like to continue to expand, the debate over the FSX fighter has affected other major licensed production programmes as well, particularly the Multiple Launch Rocket System (MLRS) and the Airborne Warning and Control System (AWACS), whose rationale was questioned in the United States. It is probably safe to predict that the intensive co-operation between the United States and Japan in arms production is not likely to be interrupted abruptly, since many security and economic interests on both sides are involved. However, Japan is considered as the main competitor in many non-military industrial areas, especially in high technology. If the disturbances in the trade relations in these areas continue, this might affect arms production collaboration as well, particularly if the Japanese industry achieves more and more technological competence in manufacturing weapons.

V. The former Soviet Union

At the turn of the year 1991–92, the USSR ceased to exist as a subject of international law. Eleven of the newly independent republics of the former Soviet Union formed the Commonwealth of Independent States. The process of the dissolution of the Soviet Union also led during 1991 to the disintegration of the Union structures of the defence complex[49] into national entities in the new republics.

---

[48] This conclusion is drawn by US Congress, Office of Technology Assessment, *Global Arms Trade*, OTA-ISC-460 (US Government Printing Office: Washington, DC, 1991), p. 107.

[49] Soviet analysts of arms production make a distinction between a broad and a narrow interpretation of the concept 'defence complex'. In a broad sense, it includes the State Military and Industrial Commission of the USSR (prior to Apr. 1991 called the State Military and Industrial Commission of the Council of Ministers of the USSR), the Defence Ministry of the USSR, the Committee of State Security of the USSR, the Ministry of the Interior of the USSR, defence subdivisions of the State Planning Committee of the USSR (in Apr. 1991 transformed into the Ministry of Economics and Forecast of the USSR), 9 ministries of defence branches and the subdivisions of non-military ministries working for defence needs. In a narrow sense, the defence complex was understood to be the State Military and Industrial Commission of the USSR and the enterprises of the following 9 ministries of this Commission: the Ministry of Aircraft Industry, the Ministry of Atomic Energy and Industry, the Ministry of Defence Industry, the Ministry of General Engineering, the Ministry of Radio Industry, the Ministry of

Soviet arms production in 1991 can be divided into two phases, with the attempted military coup of 19–21 August as the turning-point. The first phase was characterized by slow reforms of the military economy. The second phase, after the failure of the coup, was characterized by the rapid disintegration of the Union and dissolution of government structures of both the military–industrial complex and the defence ministries themselves by the end of the year.[50] The majority of the republics which formerly constituted the USSR declared state sovereignty, that is, they nationalized the enterprises subordinated to the Union, including the arms production plants located on their territories. The central government authorities were replaced by authorities in the republics. The enterprises they governed began to make their own decisions on the forms of interaction and co-ordination.[51]

Thus in 1991 a radical reform of the entire system of management of the Soviet defence complex took place. Military enterprises acquired more freedom and independence. Decisions on production began thereafter to be taken independently by the former Soviet republics. In the near future, the main directions of the development of the defence industry will be determined by the decisions of these independent states.

Military production

In 1991 analysts still did not have access to full official information about the quantities and values of goods produced by the Soviet military industry, although democratization and *glasnost* made this delicate sphere increasingly more transparent.[52]

In late 1991 there were 1100 defence enterprises in the entire area of the former USSR; the value of the fixed capital of these enterprises was 108 billion roubles,[53] or about 15 per cent of the value of fixed capital in the economy as a whole.[54]

About 2000 enterprises and organizations—both military and non-military branches, 90 per cent of which are located in the Russian Federation—work

Communication, the Ministry of Shipbuilding Industry, the Ministry of Electronics, and the Ministry of Electrotechnical and Instrument Making Industry. 'Decree of the Cabinet of Ministers of the USSR', no. 176 (13 Apr. 1991, 'On the list of Ministries and other central organs of State government of the USSR'), *Government Vestni*, no. 17 (Apr. 1991). See also *SIPRI Yearbook 1990* (note 2), chapter 8; and *SIPRI Yearbook 1991* (note 2), chapter 8.

[50] Cooper, J., *The Soviet Defence Industry: Conversion and Reform* (Pinter: London, 1991); Åslund, A. 'Gorbachev, perestroika and economic crisis', *Problems of Communism*, Jan.–Apr. 1991, pp. 30–41.

[51] In Oct. 1991 it was declared that the Ministry of Aircraft Industry would stop its activity. The directors of the 300 largest enterprises took the decision to create an association for the aircraft industry, which was voluntarily joined by the enterprises situated in Russia and Ukraine. Georgia has also shown interest in the work of this association. A Department of Aircraft Industry was set up in the Industrial Ministry to provide communication between the enterprises and the government. *Izvestia*, 19 Oct. 1991.

[52] Given the difficulties of gathering reliable information, all figures in this section are to be treated as rough estimates only.

[53] Protasov, V., member of the Committee on an Operative Management of the National Economy (an organ formed to replace the Cabinet of Ministers of the USSR after the failure of the Aug. coup), Associate Member of the Academy of Sciences of the USSR, in *Krasnaya Zvezda*, 17 Oct. 1991.

[54] 'Business', Economic Review of *Moscow News*, no. 10 (Oct. 1991), p. 11.

on highly defence-related space projects. Production in the space programme constituted about 1.5 per cent of the Soviet GNP in 1990.[55]

It is not possible to assign a precise value to the volume of Soviet military production. Professor Vladimir Felzman of the Institute of Economy of the Academy of Sciences of the USSR describes this problem as follows:

In 1990 the value of civil production in the defence complex was 63 billion roubles, a share of 49 per cent of total production, while military production totalled approximately 55 billion roubles. The arms procurement budget was 31 billion roubles, or 44 per cent lower than the value of arms production. However, the military sector also buys much technology from civil enterprises. Where in this case is the other half of military production—was it for export or was it transferred to stocks?[56]

A substantial share of Soviet economic resources has been absorbed by the defence complex (see table 9.7). This has also been the case for the consumption of certain types of materials. However, the arms production sector of the defence complex has used a relatively small share of materials. The reason for this is that defence enterprises have traditionally produced a wide range of civil goods. The share of non-military goods in the output of the defence complex was 42.6 per cent in 1988; it increased to 50.2 per cent in 1990, to 54 per cent in October 1991 and was expected to rise to 60 per cent by the end of 1991.[57] In reality, however, the non-military share may have been larger due to the fact that a considerable amount of goods and services produced by the civil enterprises of the defence complex traditionally has been used also for military and quasi-military purposes. Statistics on the share of military and civil goods in total defence complex output can in general be nothing more than an approximation, because in many cases the attribution of dual-use equipment and materials to the military or civil sectors actually proves impossible.

The volume and dynamics of Soviet military production were entirely dependent on the scale of state financing. The reduction of military expenditure from 77 billion to 72 billion roubles from 1988 to 1991[58] influenced the volume of the output of military equipment.

---

[55] Postishev, V., *Komsomolskaja Pravda*, 8 Oct. 1991.

[56] Felzman, V., *Nezavisimaja Gazeta*, 9 Oct. 1991 (author's translation).

[57] *Izvestia*, 17 Oct. 1991.

[58] Estimates mentioned in the order of magnitude of 90 billion roubles were in current prices. *Izvestia*, 23 Oct. 1991. The allocation for purchases of military equipment was 29% lower in 1991 than in 1988, and 22% lower for NIOKR (R&D); *Pravda*, 22 Mar. 1989, and 12 Jan., 21 Feb., 30 May 1991.

Table 9.7. The defence complex in the structure of the Soviet economy, 1 January 1991

Figures in italics are percentage shares.

Share of capital assets of the defence complex

In the economy as a whole	*6.4*
In industry	*12.6*

Share of actually utilized production equipment

In the defence complex	*59.0*
In the civil engineering industry	*61.0*

Share of imported equipment in the utilized part of capital assets

In the country as a whole	*22.2*
In the defence complex	*17.9*
In the civil engineering industry	*27.2*
In the chemical and timber complex	*35.0*

Share of defence complex consumption of select materials in total national production

	Total defence complex, mil. and civil	Military sector
Ferrous metal rolling	*9.8*	*5.6*
Construction cold-rolled sheet metal	*20.5*	*5.6*
Steel pipes	*5.6*	*2.2*
Rolled aluminium	*53.3*	*23.6*
Polystyrene and styrol copolymers	*38.1*	*2.7*
Polyethylene	*7.1*	*1.8*
Polypropylene	*15.7*	*1.6*

Average wages	Roubles per month
In the country as a whole	268.0
In the defence complex	294.6
In civil mechanical engineering	278.3

Source: Scherbakov, V., *Economy and Life*, no. 34 (Aug. 1991), p. 3.

In the period 1988–91, the production of aircraft declined by 44 per cent, tanks by 52 per cent, strategic missiles by 58 per cent, ammunition by 64 per cent, self-propelled and towed artillery by 66 per cent, and fighting landing craft and armoured carriers by 76 per cent. Production of all medium- and short-range missiles was completely stopped.[59]

The reduction of military expenditure was not supported by the leadership of the defence branches. Thus, Mikhail Zakharov, Deputy Minister of the Defence Industry of the USSR, stated that 'if allocations continue to be reduced at the same rate as now we will completely ruin the defence industry'.[60]

[59]Scherbakov, V., *Economy and Life*, no. 34 (Aug. 1991), p. 2.
[60] Zakharov, M., *Krasnaya Zvezda*, 18 Apr. 1991 (author's translation).

The reduction in the volume of arms production led to a fall in the rate of profits in the defence complex enterprises from 16.9 to 11.8 per cent between 1989 and 1991. Unfinished products, surplus materials and stocks with a combined value of 3.1 billion roubles in 1990 became a heavy burden for the enterprises. More than 450 enterprises in the defence complex became unprofitable.[61] For 1991 it was expected that reduced military orders would result in the release of 4.5 per cent of the fixed capital. However, only 40 per cent of the released plant capacity and equipment can be used for civil production; the rest must be transferred to the civil branches or prematurely written off.[62]

It was believed that the solution to the problems of the defence industry would be found in partial privatization. Only those enterprises which had been converted to civil production would be subject to privatization. According to laws which were introduced in 1991, individuals and commercial enterprises as well as foreign investors could buy stocks and assets. Although several stock exchanges were opened, they were not sufficiently developed in 1991 to guarantee sales and purchases in the course of privatization. The share of joint-stock companies (private/state-owned enterprises) in the fixed capital of military enterprises was planned to reach 50–70 per cent by 1995, and the total volume of privatized capital to amount to 72 billion roubles during 1991–95 (see table 9.8) according to the Law of the USSR 'On the basic ways of denationalization and privatization of enterprises'.

Replying to the question of who will determine the development strategy of the defence branches, Ivan Silaev, Chairman of Inter-State Economic Committee, said:

I'd like to know if any defence branches as we see them today will exist in future? I think that they will not exist. I think that the strategy of development for defence production will perhaps be determined by the programmes of armament, which will be worked out by the Ministry of Defence of the USSR proceeding from the adopted defence doctrine but with due regard and within the limits of the allocations assigned for these purposes by the republics.[63]

The possibility for some of the then Soviet republics to have their own defence industries was discussed in 1991. The prevailing opinion even before the dissolution of the USSR was the following. The scale of militarization of the country was possible only because of the availability and low prices of natural resources and labour. It has been estimated that it was four to six times cheaper to produce a military product of a given quality in the Soviet Union than in the United States because of the very low prices for raw materials set only for military enterprises.[64] In the transition to market prices, fuel and energy resources will become much more expensive, which will become an

---

[61] The enterprises of the Shipbuilding Ministry in 1991 received 250 million roubles less in profits. *Kraznaja Zvezda*, 24 Oct. 1991.

[62] Bukatov, V. and Matsak, Y., 'Conversion in the defence complex of the USSR', *Problems of Economy and Conversion*, no. 3 (1991), pp. 10–11.

[63] Silaev, I., *Government Vestnik*, no. 22 (Oct. 1991), p. 3 (author's translation).

[64] Felzman (note 56).

objective limitation to the development of defence industries in the republics. This also applies to the Russian Federation, on whose territory 82 per cent of the former Soviet defence industry is located and which is the only republic with its own oil reserves. Iron-ore, coking coal and other mineral resources, which are still sufficient in Russia, Kazakhstan and Ukraine, will soon become more expensive owing to the worsening geological conditions for their extraction and concentration. This means that the basic materials of the military economy—oil and metal—will be more expensive. Hence not all the republics will be able to afford a defence industry.[65]

The response to the question of whether the newly formed states will prefer to produce arms themselves rather than purchasing from Russia will depend on the terms of political agreements between them and on their economic situation. So far only Russia has the necessary prerequisites to develop a wide range of weapon systems and to compete internationally. No matter what role the armed forces of Ukraine will play, this state will hardly be able to sustain the powerful missile production and military shipbuilding facilities which exist on its territory; and Kazakhstan will not need its vast nuclear, missile and space test sites. Consequently, these problems will most likely be solved on the basis of inter-state co-operation programmes of arms production and conversion of defence enterprises.

The military industry and the entire economy of the USSR were in a state of crisis at the time of its dissolution at the end of 1991. This situation will be aggravated in the near future by the need to reduce armaments and, consequently, arms production on the basis of unilateral decisions and international treaties. Future inter-state co-operation in the production of armaments is still an open question.

Employment

Official arms industry employment data for the former USSR were for the first time made public in 1991. One official figure for total defence complex employment (in both civil and military production) was 7.3 million in 1991, with possibly half this figure for employment in military production.[66] According to other information given by Vassily Schlykov, Deputy Chairman of the State Defence Committee of Russia, 9 million people worked in the former Soviet defence industry.[67] Over 10 million people (including service staff and families) were employed in space activities (research, development and production).[68]

As a result of the reduction in military orders, the arms industry had to reduce its staff—both production employees and scientists and engineers. Of the 300 000 people who lost their jobs in 1990, only 76 per cent were re-employed at the same enterprises for production of civil products. In 1991,

[65] Felzman (note 56).
[66] Protasov (note 53).
[67] *Izvestia*, 17 Oct. 1991.
[68] Postishev (note 55).

about 380 000 additional people were to be released, 70 000 of whom, as estimated, may remain unemployed and 80 000 of whom would have to leave the defence industry. In 1990–91, a number of military enterprises lost 25 per cent of their most highly qualified workers.[69] The loss of highly qualified staff from the defence complex is mainly caused by the level of payment. The salary level of the defence complex ranked in eleventh place among all the branches of the economy in 1990.[70]

As a result of reduced allocations for the military sphere, scientific staff also tended to leave the defence complex: in 1990 it lost 39 000 scientists and in 1991 over 240 000. In 1990 the average monthly wage in defence scientific centres was 15 per cent lower than in civil scientific organizations. In order to maintain the payment fund, over 300 defence scientific centres requested central financial support in 1991.[71] However, this was not granted.[72]

This 'brain drain' from the defence complex is likely to continue as a result of economic reforms, the liberalization of prices and the difficulties associated with the market orientation of the arms industry. With a reduced volume of military production, attempts to centralize financing of the defence sectors in order to maintain wage levels will not be effective. In the period 1989–90, 570 million roubles were allocated from the state budget to maintain wage levels and to lessen social tension among workers.[73] This could not be done in 1991 because of the increasing budget deficit.

Conversion

In 1990–91 there was an understanding in the USSR that the transition to a market economy was not possible without radical conversion of the defence industry.[74] According to the decision of the First Congress of the People's Deputies of the USSR, the state programme for conversion of the defence industry was worked out and adopted on 15 December 1990. However, practical realization of the goals of the programme had begun earlier—in late 1989. Still earlier, in 1988 the defence complex was entrusted with the task of producing equipment for the processing of agricultural products, light industry and trade, in addition to the existing non-military production lines. These civil activities of the defence complex were later integrated into the Programme of Conversion for 1989–95.

[69] *Krasnaya Zvezda*, 25 June 1991.
[70] Scherbakov (note 59), p. 2.
[71] Bukatov and Matsak (note 62), pp. 11–12.
[72] Professor E. Potemkin, Director of the Scientific Research Institute, who deals with the problems of tank production, underlines: 'The people who develop such technologies are forced to leave because the level of their wages is lower than that of construction workers. Entire construction bureaus break up. The same situation prevails in specialized institutes, technical schools which prepare specialists for the defence industry'. A. M. Zakharov, Deputy Minister of the Defence Industry of the USSR, adds: 'If this situation continues, in two years there will no longer be any scientists in the defence scientific research institutes'. *Krasnaya Zvezda*, 18 Apr. 1991.
[73] Bukatov and Matsak (note 62).
[74] The term 'conversion' is used in the USSR and the successor republics to describe both the process of introducing additional civil production lines in the arms industry (which could be called diversification) and switching to civil production at the expense of arms production.

Table 9.8. Task force programmes under the state programme for defence industry conversion, 1991–95

| Programme | Expenditure in 1991–95 (b. roubles) | | | Main directions |
	Invest-ments	R&D	Imports	
1. Aircraft	4.2	8.0	0.45	Using aircraft technology of planes such as Il-96-300, Tu-204, Il-114, construction of commercial planes, designing a new plane for agricultural purposes
2. Shipbuilding	0.7	1.8	–	Development of new navigation and communications, energy and electro-technical equipment
3. Space	0.7	11.0	0.14	Space communication, TV, navigation, semi-conductors, forest and land inventory, weather forecast
4. Means of communication	4.4	4.6	–	Improvement of all types of communication, fibre-optic, digital, mobile communication, high-definition TV equipment
5. New materials	6.1	1.8	–	Highly accurate materials, micro-electronics, computers and fibre-optics

Sources: Compiled on the basis of the data given by Scherbakov, V., *Economy and Life*, no. 34 (Aug. 1991), pp. 2–3; and Bukatov, V. and Matsak, Y., 'Conversion in the defence complex of the USSR', *Problems of Economy and Conversion*, no. 3 (1991), pp. 7–8.

In 1991, 616 defence enterprises were engaged in conversion: 460 were located in Russia, 94 in the Ukraine, 19 in Byelorussia (Belarus) and 11 in Kazakhstan. The majority (118) of enterprises engaged in conversion belonged to the Ministry of Aircraft Industry, 115 belonged to the Ministry of Defence Industry, 113 to the Ministry of Radio Industry and 93 to the Ship-building Ministry.[75]

The conversion programme was concentrated on such priority branches as the production of consumer goods, equipment for the processing branches of the agro-industrial complex, medical computers, means of communication, civil aviation, shipbuilding and space technology for economic purposes. To this end, the project included five task force programmes (see table 9.8).

In 1989–90, conversion contributed to an increase in the annual growth rate of consumer goods production in the defence sector from 7–8 per cent to an interval of 13–30 per cent. The absolute increase in the volume of civil production in the defence complex from 1989 to 1990 was 8.1 billion roubles,

[75] Scherbakov (note 59), p. 2.

more than 40 per cent of which was achieved through conversion: for example, 134 defence plants and 135 scientific and research institutes and construction bureaus were engaged in activities for support of the agro-industrial complex, and 102 defence plants and 83 scientific and research institutes took part in the modernization of light industry.

The state conversion programme, based on directives which are characteristic for the period of totalitarianism, was severely criticized in scientific and industrial circles. This was primarily due to the fact that, in spite of a considerable increase in civil production in the defence enterprises, the majority of the population did not derive any 'peace dividend' from conversion.[76] In the first half of 1991 the defence enterprises fulfilled the state directives on civil production: they produced civil goods worth 25.9 billion roubles, including 4.4 million radio sets, 3.3 million tape recorders, 5.1 million refrigerators, 3.1 million freezers, 1.4 million bicycles and 1.6 million cameras.[77]

While administration of the conversion programme was initially highly centralized on the Union level, after the failure of the coup in August 1991 it was carried out mainly at the branch and regional levels in the republics. These programmes were closer to the direct producer and thus more viable.

Russia, for instance, has developed an extensive programme, for which a special committee was created.[78] In the defence complex of the Moscow region, the production of consumer goods is planned to increase by 165 per cent in 1990–95.[79] In the St Petersburg region, defence enterprises planned in the same period to increase the value of civil production, including equipment for the agro-industrial complex, from 175 million to 301 million roubles.[80] In the region of the Urals, production of civil goods by some branches of the defence enterprises will increase 15–20 times.[81]

The defence enterprises located in Ukraine carried out conversion within the limits of the Union plan until August 1991. For the period 1990–95, this plan included an increase in the production of consumer goods in the military aircraft enterprises from 253 million to 436 million roubles, in the enterprises of general engineering from 1.1 billion to 2.5 billion roubles, and in the radio industry from 8.9 billion to 12.9 billion roubles.[82] However, the declaration by Ukraine of state sovereignty, including sovereignty over the defence industry, will probably lead to a Ukrainian national plan for conversion.

---

[76] For a review of the discussion on this question in 1991, see Kireyev, A., 'The price of "peaceful dividend"', *International Affairs*, no. 7 (1991), pp. 11–12.

[77] Bukatov and Matsak (note 62), p. 8.

[78] Speaking at the Congress of people's deputies in Oct. 1991, Russian President Boris Yeltsin, announcing the next plan of economic reforms, said: 'The Program of conversion stipulates the transition to the system of orders directly from the Defence Ministry. They are already defined for 1992. The division of military and civil production will be carried out. It is supposed to close some enterprises as well as to switch a number of military works to the output of civil products and consumer goods'. *Izvestia*, 28 Oct. 1991.

[79] *Konversia*, no. 5 (1991), pp. 4–5.

[80] *Konversia*, no. 4 (1991), p. 4.

[81] *Konversia*, no. 2 (1991), p. 4.

[82] *Konversia*, no. 1 (1991), pp. 4–7.

In 1991, management of the conversion strategy was increasingly centred on the company level, whose authorities, under the conditions of management confusion, were forced either to make independent decisions or to resign. The role of the state organs (whether Union, republic or local) increasingly became the following: to inform producers in advance about the reduction of military orders and, in the case of cancellation of orders already made, to compensate for losses; to promote privatization of the defence industry by passing laws and regulations establishing social security funds and financing retraining of military enterprise personnel; and to overcome obstacles to the development of business activity in the defence sector.

New commercial structures

In the process of the development of the defence complex and its conversion as a result of privatization and demonopolization, new commercial structures have appeared, such as commodity exchanges, commercial banks, inter-branch concerns and funds. In the majority of cases they are very different in character from corresponding structures in the West. Nevertheless, they constitute the first steps of the defence complex towards a market economy.

The largest structure of this kind is the Military Industrial Investment Company—an open joint-stock company with a declared regulated capital of 1 billion roubles and a minimum value of shareholdings of 100 000 roubles. The aim of the company's activity was annulment of the money of individual investors and the financing of highly profitable enterprises in the former USSR and abroad, mainly joint-stock enterprises of defence branches. The structure of the company includes military and industrial commercial and investment banks, a specialized insurance company, a foreign trade firm, an integrated network of commercial relations and a number of joint-stock companies (for operations with real estate, information resources and securities).[83]

In 1989, 11 organizations and enterprises of the Ministry of Atomic Energy and Industry of the USSR created the commercial Conversion Bank, with a declared capital of 200 million roubles and a licence from the State Bank of the USSR to make all types of bank operations. The Conversion Bank specialized in financing programmes in the field of defence conversion and in oil and gas-extraction enterprises, construction and the industries producing consumer goods, medical equipment and communication systems.[84]

The Military and Industrial Exchange and the Conversion Exchange,[85] which sell surplus material stocks of the defence enterprises and a wide range of other products, actively operate on the commodity market.

---

[83] *Izvestia*, 30 Sep. 1991.

[84] Konversbank, Advertising sheet M, 1991, pp. 2–3.

[85] The Conversion Exchange is a joint-stock company of the open type, with a regulated capital of 30 million roubles divided into 300 inscribed shares of 100 000 roubles each. Among its founders are 179 enterprises and organizations, 60% of which are defence complex enterprises. *Round Table of the Russian–American University on Conversion and the Market* (RAU Press, 1991).

The International Conversion Fund, an independent, non-governmental, non-profit organization, has functioned since 1990. The Fund has an office in Italy and strong ties with the USA, Belgium, Brazil, Australia and China. Enterprises within the structure of the Fund carry out commercial activities.

Under the conditions of the disintegration of the USSR and the liberalization of prices, market structures increasingly influence the processes of conversion. The democratic leadership of the country and the former republics declare their support for such structures because they see in them the possibility of setting real prices on defence products, of demonopolization and rationalization of arms production and of an increase in competitiveness. During the realization of decisive measures for the transition to market conditions, the task of introducing competition principles into defence production and the process of conversion assumes not only economic but also political importance.

Conclusion

The member states of the CIS decided to co-operate 'in safeguarding international peace and security and in implementing effective measures for reducing armaments and military spending', according to Article 6 of the Minsk Declaration of 8 December 1991 (for the full text, see appendix 14A).[86] The Agreement does not contain any provisions on the military industry, employment or conversion. Through the declaration of independence of the former Soviet republics, the new governments assumed control over all industries on their territories—including the defence industry. Consequently, defence enterprises are divided among the republics—mainly the Russian Federation, Ukraine and Belarus.

Obviously it would be inappropriate and uneconomical to break existing relations between military enterprises involved in the manufacture of military hardware. Although Russia possesses the largest part of the military–industrial complex, it is also dependent on supplies of components and spare parts from other CIS states. Thus the CIS member states will have to establish some form of co-ordination of military production and conversion.

It is possible that CIS states in search of hard currency will try to sell military equipment abroad, but the prospects for the military industry are still gloomy. Because of budgetary constraints, all the republics are doomed to reduce military orders and military production and to look for reasonable ways of economic conversion.

Will the existing chaos and disorder continue in the future and the economy of the former USSR collapse? Will the military–industrial complex also be affected since it is an integral part of the manufacturing sector? Will the republics in a joint effort or each one separately be able to overcome the crisis? At present there are more open questions and speculations about the outcome of this process than definite answers.

---

[86] *Financial and Business News*, no. 25 (Dec. 1991), p. 2.

Appendix 9A. The 100 largest arms-producing companies, 1990

IAN ANTHONY, AGNÈS COURADES ALLEBECK,
GERD HAGMEYER-GAVERUS, PAOLO MIGGIANO,
ELISABETH SKÖNS and HERBERT WULF

Table 9A contains information on the 100 largest arms-producing companies in the OECD and the developing countries in 1990.[1] Companies with the designation S in the column for rank in 1990 are subsidiaries; their arms sales are included in the figure in column 6 for the holding company. Subsidiaries are listed in the position where they would appear if they were independent companies. In order to facilitate comparison with data for the previous year, the rank order and arms sales figures for 1989 are also given. Where new data for 1989 have become available, this information is included in the table; thus the 1989 rank order and the arms sales figures for some companies which appeared in table 8A in the *SIPRI Yearbook 1991* have been revised.

Sources and methods

Sources of data. The data in the table are based on the following sources: company reports, a questionnaire sent to over 400 companies, and corporation news published in the business sections of newspapers and military journals. Company archives, marketing reports, government publication of prime contracts and country surveys were also consulted. In many cases exact figures were not available, mainly because companies often do not report their arms sales or lump them together with other activities. Estimates were therefore made.

Arms sales. The criterion for the rank order of companies is their arms sales in 1990 (column 6). The arms sales figures are based on the sources mentioned above and thus not comparable to the SIPRI arms transfer figures given in chapter 8.

Coverage. The data are for 1990; data in columns 2 and 7 are for 1989. The fiscal year for companies is not always the calendar year. No calculations have been made to adjust fiscal to calendar years.

Exchange-rates. Most figures collected were given in local currencies. To convert figures into US dollars, the period-average of market exchange-rates of the International Monetary Fund, *International Financial Statistics,* was used.

Profit. Profit after taxes is shown for the entire company, not for the arms-producing sector alone. For figures taken from journals and periodicals, it was not always clear whether profit was given before or after taxes.

Employment. The figure shown is either a year-end or yearly average figure for the entire company, as published in the sources used.

Key to abbreviations in column 5. A = artillery, Ac = aircraft, El = electronics, Eng = engines, Mi = missiles, MV = military vehicles, SA/O = small arms/ordinance, Sh = ships, and Oth = other.

---

[1] The 24 member countries of the Organization for Economic Co-operation and Development are: Australia, Austria, Belgium, Canada, Denmark, Germany, Finland, France, Greece, Iceland, Ireland, Italy, Japan, Luxembourg, the Netherlands, New Zealand, Norway, Portugal, Spain, Sweden, Switzerland, Turkey, the UK and the USA (Yugoslavia participates with special status). For the countries in the developing world, see appendix 8B.

Table 9A. The 100 largest arms-producing companies in the OECD and the developing countries, 1990[a]

Figures in columns 6, 7, 8 and 10 are in US $ million.

1	2	3	4	5	6	7	8	9	10	11
Rank					Arms sales			Col. 6 as	Profit	Employment
1990	1989[b]	Company[c]	Country	Industry	1990	1989[d]	Total sales 1990	% of col. 8	1990	1990
1	1	McDonnell Douglas	USA	Ac El Mi	9 020	8 890	16 255	55	306	121 200
2	2	General Dynamics	USA	Ac MV El Mi Sh	8 300	8 400	10 182	82	–578	98 100
3	5	British Aerospace	UK	Ac A El Mi SA/O	7 520	6 300	18 811	40	496	127 900
4	3	Lockheed	USA	Ac	7 500	7 400	9 958	75	335	73 000
5	4	General Motors	USA	Ac Eng El Mi	7 380	7 050	126 017	6	–1 986	761 400
S	S	Hughes Electronics (General Motors)	USA	Ac El	6 700	6 380	11 723	57	726	96 000
6	6	General Electric	USA	Ac Eng	6 450	6 250	58 414	11	4 303	298 000
7	7	Raytheon	USA	El Mi	5 500	5 330	9 632	57	557	76 700
S	S	Thomson-CSF (Thomson S.A.)	France	El Mi	5 250	4 120	6 799	77	399	46 900
8	12	Thomson S.A.	France	El Mi	5 250	4 320	13 811	38	–454	105 500
9	8	Boeing	USA	Ac El Mi	5 100	4 900	27 595	18	1 385	161 700
10	9	Northrop	USA	Ac	4 700	4 700	5 493	86	210	38 200
11	11	Martin Marietta	USA	Mi	4 600	4 350	6 143	75	328	62 000
12	18	GEC	UK	El	4 280	2 880	16 923	25	1 460	118 529
13	14	United Technologies	USA	Ac El Mi	4 100	4 100	21 442	19	751	192 600
14	10	Rockwell International	USA	Ac El Mi	4 100	4 500	12 443	33	624	101 900
15	13	Daimler Benz	FRG	Ac Eng MV El Sh	4 020	4 260	52 918	8	1 111	376 800
16	16	Direction des Constructions Navales	France	Sh	3 830	3 000	3 831	100	..	30 500
S	S	DASA (Daimler Benz)	FRG	Ac Eng El Mi	3 720	3 930	7 752	48	–84	61 276

17	20	Mitsubishi Heavy Industries	Japan	Ac MV Mi Sh	3 040	2 640	17 718	17	669	44 272
18	15	Litton Industries	USA	El Sh	3 000	3 000	5 156	58	179	50 600
19	17	TRW	USA	MV Oth	3 000	2 900	8 170	37	208	75 600
20	19	Grumman	USA	AcEl	2 900	2 850	4 014	72	86	26 100
21	25	Aérospatiale	France	Ac Mi	2 860	2 190	6 464	44	−73	37 691
22	23	IRI	Italy	Ac Eng El Sh	2 670	2 230	7 413	36	1	366 697
S	S	Pratt & Whitney (United Technologies)	USA	Eng	2 500	2 500	7 300	34	..	41 300
23	22	Westinghouse Electric	USA	El	2 330	2 270	12 915	18	268	115 774
24	24	Dassault Aviation	France	Ac	2 260	2 200	3 454	65	52	14 900
25	26	Texas Instruments	USA	El Mi Oth	2 120	2 160	6 567	32	−26	70 300
26	27	Tenneco	USA	Sh	2 110	1 950	14 511	15	561	92 000
S	S	Newport News (Tenneco)	USA	Sh	2 110	1 950	2 113	100	225	29 000
27	21	Unisys	USA	El	2 000	2 300	10 111	20	−437	75 000
28	45	Loral	USA	El	1 920	1 150	2 127	90	90	12 700
29	35	Textron	USA	Ac Eng MV	1 900	1 400	7 918	24	283	54 000
S	–	Alenia (IRI)	Italy	Ac El Mi	1 840	0	3 069	60	25	21 981
30	44	Rolls Royce	UK	Eng	1 830	1 220	6 550	28	314	65 900
31	31	CEA Industrie	France	Oth	1 810	1 560	5 456	33	312	37 800
32	32	EFIM	Italy	Ac MV El	1 710	1 510	2 178	79	−0	37 097
33	30	ITT	USA	El	1 610	1 580	20 604	8	958	114 000
34	28	IBM	USA	El Oth	1 600	1 600	69 018	2	6 020	373 816
35	38	INI	Spain	Ac A MV El Sh SA/O	1 560	1 290	18 101	9	98	146 625
36	29	LTV	USA	Ac MV El	1 490	1 580	6 138	24	71	35 300
37	41	SNECMA Groupe	France	Eng	1 490	1 260	4 322	34	38	27 616
38	49	GIAT Industries	France	A MV SA/O	1 430	1 020	1 469	97	..	15 000
39	37	Ordnance Factories	India	A SA/O Oth	1 430	1 400	1 468	97	..	..
S	S	MBB (DASA)	FRG	Ac El Mi	1 420	1 840	2 853	50	37	23 229
40	42	E-Systems	USA	El	1 350	1 250	1 810	75	86	18 435

Rank 1990	Rank 1989[b]	Company[c]	Country	Industry	Arms sales 1990	1989[d]	Total sales 1990	Col. 6 as % of col. 8	Profit 1990	Employment 1990
					6	7	8	9	10	11
41	34	Armscor	S. Africa	Ac A MV El SA/O	1 330	1 460	1 663	80	..	18 900
42	33	Allied Signal	USA	Ac El Oth	1 300	1 500	12 343	11	462	105 800
43	43	GTE	USA	El	1 250	1 250	18 374	7	1 541	154 000
44	39	FIAT	Italy	Eng	1 180	1 280	7 145	17	2	303 238
45	54	Matra Groupe	France	Mi El Oth	1 180	870	4 471	26	111	24 348
46	–	Alliant Tech Systems	USA	SA/O	1 150	0	1 248	92	24	8 000
47	48	Israel Aircraft Industries	Israel	Ac El Mi	1 120	1 030	1 400	80	13	16 650
S	S	MTU (DASA)	FRG	Eng	1 110	780	2 229	50	93	17 524
48	47	Oerlikon-Bührle	Switzerl.	Ac A El SA/O	1 080	1 040	3 375	32	–66	26 437
49	53	FMC	USA	MV Sh Oth	1 060	900	3 743	28	211	23 882
50	133	Bremer Vulkan	FRG	Sh	1 050	140	2 369	44	22	10 922
51	40	Kawasaki Heavy Industries	Japan	Ac Eng Sh	1 010	1 270	7 052	14	107	20 690
52	52	Siemens	FRG	El	990	900	39 107	3	1 032	373 000
53	50	Nobel Industries	Sweden	El Mi SA/O	930	950	4 606	20	199	26 654
54	55	VSEL Consortium	UK	MV Sh	930	870	933	100	–112	15 464
S	S	Matra Défense (Matra)	France	El, Mi, Oth	920	710	925	99	::	::
55	65	Diehl	FRG	A MV El SA/O	860	620	1 779	48	::	15 108
56	58	Hercules	USA	Ac Mi SA/O Oth	800	800	3 200	25	96	19 867
57	59	Harris	USA	El	790	800	3 052	26	131	33 400
58	51	Gencorp	USA	Ac Eng El Mi SA/O Oth	790	930	1 775	45	63	13 900
S	S	CASA (INI)	Spain	Ac	780	480	961	81	–39	10 050
S	S	Oto Melara (EFIM)	Italy	AMV Mi	780	580	783	100	4	2 245
59	80	Rheinmetall	FRG	A SA/O	750	510	1 838	41	58	14 062

60	73	Thyssen	FRG	Ac El SA/O Oth	710	540	22 396	3	427	149 644
61	66	Olin	USA	El	700	600	2 592	27	84	15 200
62	67	AT&T	USA	Eng El Oth	700	600	37 300	2	2 700	273 700
63	60	Sequa	USA	Ac MV El Mi	700	700	2 211	32	33	18 500
64	46	Ford Motor	USA	Ac Eng A SA/O	700	1 100	97 650	1	860	370 400
65	72	Eidgenössische Rüstungsbetriebe	Switzerl.		700	550	738	95	..	4 672
66	56	Mitsubishi Electric	Japan	El Mi	690	810	22 904	3	551	97 002
S	S	Telefunken System Technik (DASA)	FRG	El	680	730	1 045	65	44	9 372
S	S	SNECMA (SNECMA Groupe)	France	Eng	650	530	2 595	25	14	14 083
67	64	Motorola	USA	El	650	650	10 885	6	499	105 000
68	70	Israel Military Industries	Israel	A SA/O	640	590	655	98	-46	12 000
69	87	Lucas Industries	UK	Ac	630	490	4 221	15	149	54 942
70	52	Thiokol	USA	Eng Mi SA/O Oth	620	660	1 181	52	41	11 500
S	S	Bofors (Nobel industries)	Sweden	A El Mi SA/O	620	740	657	94	..	4 549
71	61	Emerson Electric	USA	El	610	680	7 573	8	613	73 700
72	91	SAGEM Groupe	France	El	570	410	2 018	28	55	16 162
73	69	Science Applications Intl	USA	Ac Eng El	570	590	1 163	49	33	12 000
S	S	Agusta (EFIM)	Italy	Ac	560	610	927	60	-33	8 117
74	75	Computer Sciences	USA	El	560	530	1 738	32	65	23 000
75	71	Avondale Industries	USA	Sh	550	550	752	73	-26	8 500
S	S	AVCO (Textron)	USA	Ac	550	450	..	..	..	..
76	89	Ishikawajima-Harima	Japan	Eng Sh	540	460	6 677	8	137	15 280
77	82	Dassault Electronique	France	El	530	500	736	72	-8	4 331
78	95	Westland Group	UK	Ac	510	390	734	69	76	9 800
79	79	FFV	Sweden	A El SA/O Oth	500	510	1 055	47	..	9 709
S	S	Dornier (DASA)	FRG	Ac El Mi	500	590	1 787	28	-23	10 931
80	84	Teledyne	USA	Eng El Mi	500	500	3 446	15	95	33 200

1	2	3	4	5	6	7	8	9	10	11
Rank					Arms sales					
1990	1989[b]	Company[c]	Country	Industry	1990	1989[d]	Total sales 1990	Col. 6 as % of col. 8	Profit 1990	Employment 1990
81	77	Hindustan Aeronautics	India	Ac Mi	500	520	515	97	23	43 000
82	68	Smiths Industries	UK	El	490	590	1 201	41	161	13 100
S	S	Hollandse Signaal (Thomson-CSF)	Netherl.	El	490	330	515	95	–46	4 522
83	85	Racal Electronics	UK	El	480	490	3 719	13	257	38 461
84	100	Hawker Siddeley	UK	El	480	350	3 887	12	145	44 600
S	–	Systemtechnik Nord (Bremer Vulkan)	FRG	El	470	0	629	75	–1	2 397
85	92	Devonport Management	UK	Sh	470	410	500	94	15	7 942
S	S	EN Bazan (INI)	Spain	Sh	460	300	530	87	29	9 613
S	S	FIAT Aviazione (FIAT)	Italy	Ac Eng	460	410	841	55	21	4 666
86	76	SAAB-SCANIA	Sweden	Ac Eng	450	530	5 339	8	60	32 536
87	93	Dowty Group	UK	Ac El	450	400	1 372	33	1	15 022
88	74	Thorn EMI	UK	El	450	540	6 532	7	462	57 932
89	88	Ferranti-International Signal	UK	El	440	470	817	54	–175	10 325
90	63	Hunting	UK	SA/O	420	650	1 377	31	69	6 918
91	78	Rafael	Israel	SA/O Oth	420	510	420	100	–17	5 960
92	99	Mannesmann	FRG	MV	410	360	14 819	3	287	124 000
S	S	Krauss-Maffei (Mannesmann)	FRG	MV	410	360	873	47	14	5 408
93	83	Toshiba	Japan	El Mi	410	500	32 429	1	835	162 000
S	S	Sextant Avion (Thomson-CSF/ Aérospatiale)	France	El	400	350	1 119	36	35	9 152
S	S	Collins International (Rockwell International)	USA	El	400	300	..	..	..	..

S	S	CFM Intern (General Electric & SNECMA)	USA	Ac Eng	400	500	..	..	..	1 080
94	105	Lürssen	FRG	Sh	400	320	495	81	..	6 100
S	–	Esco Electronics (Emerson Electric)	USA	El	400	0	..	..	..	..
S	S	SAGEM (SAGEM Groupe)	France	El	390	280	946	41	27	6 392
95	90	Sundstrand	USA	Ac	390	430	1 600	24	114	13 000
96	81	NEC	Japan	El	380	510	25 546	1	376	117 994
97	97	Morrison Knudsen	USA	MV Oth	380	380	1 653	23	35	..
98	101	Mitre	USA	El	370	350	..	..	..	..
99	102	Dyncorp	USA	Ac El	360	350	717	50	..	18 000
100	36	Honeywell	USA	El Mi	360	1 400	6 309	6	382	60 300

.. Data not available.

[a] Both the rank designation and the arms sales figures for 1989 are also given, in columns 2 and 7, respectively, for comparison with the data for 1990 in columns 1 and 6.

[b] The rank designation in this column may not correspond to that given in table 8A in the *SIPRI Yearbook 1991*. A dash (–) in this column indicates either that the company did not produce arms in 1989, in which case there is a zero (0) in column 7, or that it did not rank among the 100 largest companies in table 8A in the *SIPRI Yearbook 1991*, in which case figures for arms sales in 1989 do appear in column 7. A figure above 100 in this column shows the actual rank order in 1989, although the company was not included in the SIPRI 100 table in the *SIPRI Yearbook 1991*.

[c] Company names in parentheses after the name of the ranked company are the names of the holding companies. The parent companies, with data pertaining to them, appear in their rank order for 1990.

[d] A zero (0) in this column indicates that the company did not produce arms in 1989, but began arms production in 1990, or that in 1989 the company did not exist as it was structured in 1990.

Note: The authors acknowledge financial assistance to operate the SIPRI arms production data bank from The John D. and Catherine T. MacArthur Foundation and assistance in the data collection provided by Anthony Bartzokas (Athens), Defence Research & Analysis (London), Ken Epps (Ontario), Ernst Gülcher (Antwerp), Peter Hug (Bern), Keidanren (Tokyo), Rudi Leo (Vienna), Arcadi Olivares i Boadella (Barcelona), Reuven Padhatzur (Tel Aviv), Giulio Perani (Rome), Paul Rusman (Haarlem), Gülay Günlük-Senesen (Istanbul) and Werner Voß (Bremen).

10. The effects of arms transfers on wars and peace negotiations

FREDERIC S. PEARSON, MICHAEL BRZOSKA
and CHRISTER CRANTZ

I. Introduction

Arms transfers have both precipitant and deterrent effects on armed conflicts; they are also a factor in the conduct and the cessation of wars. Often heard categorical statements—either that arms transfers are inherently conflict-enhancing or that, properly managed, they are a trustworthy instrument for stability—ignore the complex record. Despite the obvious relevance of these factors, the literature contains little systematic evidence of the actual effects of arms transfers on conflicts.[1] A historical study of 10 inter-state wars confirmed the complexity of the issue (see table 10.1).[2] Several general conclusions could be drawn.

1. Arms deliveries are a factor in decisions to go to war because of considerations of military superiority, perceptions of changes in the balance of power and the interest in establishing links with supporting states. Arms transfers may also condition decision makers' perceptions about external recognition of their justifications for waging war.

2. Another major conclusion is something of a 'non-conclusion': on the whole, supplying states have little leverage in conditioning or even determining the outcome of hostilities. The possibility to use arms transfers as an instrument of power declined from the 1960s to the 1980s. An exception are some long wars in which arms transfers contributed to the end of hostilities either by enabling one side to win or by exhausting one side's resources.

3. Although the effect of arms supply on the level of hostility and on the occurrence of negotiated settlement varied across the cases, the third major conclusion was that arms transfers generally prolonged and escalated wars, resulting in more suffering and destruction.

4. The fourth conclusion is a combination of the first three with respect to arms embargoes. Embargoes, whether partial or total, in and of themselves had little chance of compelling warring parties to stop wars or come to the

[1] The major exceptions are Harkavy, R., 'Arms resupply during conflict: a framework for analysis', *Jerusalem Journal of International Relations*, vol. 7, no. 3 (1985), pp. 5–41; and Neuman, S., *Military Assistance in Recent Wars: The Dominance of the Superpowers*, Washington Papers, no. 122 (Center for Strategic and International Studies, Georgetown University with Praeger Publishers: Washington, DC, 1986).

[2] The conclusions of this study were presented in Pearson, F. S., Brzoska, M. and Crantz, C., 'The effects of arms transfers on the course of war and peace negotiations', paper presented to the 25th North American meeting of the Peace Science Society (International), Ann Arbor, Mich., Nov. 1991.

Table 10.1. The impact of arms resupply on military and diplomatic outcomes of war

War/ Resupply[a]	Embargo[b]	Outcome[c]	Pre-war advantage[d]	Negotiations during war
1965 India–Pakistan				
Symmetric[e]	Symmetric: USA, UK	Stalemate: India	Pakistan (qualitative)	Growing major power pressure to restrain parties
1969 El Salvador–Honduras				
None	Symmetric: USA	Stalemate: El Salvador	El Salvador (qualitative)	High pressure (OAS); delayed effect
1971 India–Pakistan				
Symmetric	Asymmetric: USA against Pakistan	India (mil.)	India (qualitative)	Major power pressure to restrain parties
1973 Arab states–Israel				
Symmetric	Threat: USA, USSR	Advantage: Israel	None	Pressed by major powers; delayed effect
1976–91 Morocco–Polisario				
Asymmetric: Morocco	Asymmetric: (only partial) USA, France against Morocco	Morocco (mil.) Polisario (pol.)	Morocco	Major and regional power pressure; delayed effect; UN mediation
1977–78 Ethiopia–Somalia				
Asymmetric: Ethiopia	Asymmetric: (informal) USSR against Somalia	Ethiopia	Somalia	Failed (OAU/ Cuba/USSR); military intervention (Cuba)
1978–79 Tanzania–Uganda				
Asymmetric:[f] Tanzania	Asymmetric: (informal) USSR against Uganda	Tanzania	Uganda	Failed (OAU); military intervention (Libya)
1980–88 Iraq–Iran				
Asymmetric: Iraq	Asymmetric: USA, EC against Iran	Stalemate	Iraq (just before war)	Failed attempts (Gulf states, UN); delayed effect
1982 Argentina–UK				
Asymmetric: UK	Asymmetric: EC, USA against Argentina	UK	UK (qualitative) Argentina (geographical)	Failed attempts (USA, Peru, UN)

War/ Resupply	Embargo	Outcome	Pre-war advantage	Negotiations during war
1982 Israel–Lebanon				
Symmetric	Asymmetric: (only partial) USA against Israel	Israel (mil.) Syria (pol.)	Israel	Multilateral/bilateral pressures; delayed effects; Western intervention

[a] In the column *resupply*, 'symmetric' indicates that no combatant was favoured; 'asymmetric' indicates that the named party received substantially more arms.

[b] In the column *embargo*, arms embargoes were either threatened or actually put into effect (sometimes only partially, informally or with insignificant results) by the suppliers named, either against all warring parties ('symmetric') or against the party mentioned ('asymmetric').

[c] In the column *outcome*, the wars ended with the victory of the named combatant or with a 'stalemate', in which the named party had an advantage in military and/or political terms.

[d] In the column *pre-war advantage*, the named combatants had an advantage before the war in the ability to fight, either with respect to all indicators or with respect to the quality or the quantity of arms.

[e] However, the USA tried to keep the Pakistani capability comparable to the Indian capability.

[f] Late in the war, Uganda received substantial arms supplies from Libya.

negotiation table. While they had only a limited effect on the outcome of the war, they helped to contain the actual fighting. Embargoes were undermined by arms importers' supplier-diversification strategies, domestic arms production, the unwillingness of decision-makers to submit to external pressures and the dynamics of 'the heat of war'. The effectiveness of embargoes improved with high war attrition rates, the technological level of the war and the inability of the arms recipient to diversify weapon sources. The ability to find such sources generally increased with the economic means available to warring parties—El Salvador, Honduras, Uganda and Somalia were more vulnerable to decreased weapon deliveries from their former patrons than were India, Pakistan or the Arab states.

5. The fifth and final general conclusion is that the two superpowers were more prone to use arms transfers as a means to influence warring parties than were other suppliers, even taking into account their quantitative lead in the arms market. It is therefore not surprising that during wars the superpowers' share in deliveries generally declines—a central finding in an earlier study of the subject by Stephanie Neuman.[3] In the view of the present authors, diversification to more economically motivated suppliers, such as France or the 'new' suppliers in Southern Europe, East Asia and Latin America, is a way to undercut great-power leverage via arms supplies. The USA had this experience with India and Pakistan between the wars of 1965 and 1971 and with Morocco in the late 1970s, and the Soviet Union had similar experiences after

---

[3] Neuman, S. G., 'Arms, aid and the superpowers', *Foreign Affairs*, vol. 66, no. 5 (summer 1988), pp. 1064–65.

the 1973 war in the Middle East and with both warring states in the Iraq–Iran War.

Short summaries of the 10 historical case studies must suffice here to illustrate some of the points made above. In three of the wars there were no formal arms embargoes, although there were informal supply restraints. The 1973 Arab–Israeli War was characterized by massive resupply on both sides, in a situation in which the parties depended very heavily on single major arms partners. The military attrition rate was extremely high, so replenished supplies proved militarily if not politically crucial. Yet superpower efforts to 'manage' the fighting and produce a stalemate through the rate of arms supplies fell short. Supplies tended to strengthen the weaker party and keep it in the war. Finally, the implied US threat to withhold further supplies compelled Israel to accept the second proposed cease-fire, although not against Israel's own battlefield interests. The US supply policy therefore had a somewhat dampening effect and laid the foundation for Israeli participation in the negotiations.

In the war between Ethiopia and Somalia, as in that between Tanzania and Uganda, restrictions on arms supplies to the aggressor proved crucial in leading to its military defeat; yet both Somalia and Uganda collapsed as much because of internal organizational deficiencies as because of arms scarcity. Similarly, the 1965 India–Pakistan War ended as much because of Pakistani tactical disadvantages as because of the effective US–British arms embargo. In the India–Pakistan War of 1971, marked by the decisive thrust of India's military action, Pakistan was again technically embargoed by the USA, although small amounts of arms got through. The 1965 war had the attributes of the model embargo case, but the embargo did not appear to be solely responsible for the cease-fire. In the El Salvador–Honduras War, the effect of the embargo was unequivocal; the US embargo of arms to both highly dependent combatants greatly enhanced US and OAS (Organization of American States) leverage and helped to shorten the combat.

In the war between Argentina and the United Kingdom, the European Community (EC) embargo against Argentina did not have a decisive effect: the more diversified arms supply and superior military capability (augmented by US satellite intelligence and resupply commitments) of the British expeditionary force brought a swift end to the war before lack of arms or the embargo had had time to do so. Resupplies for Britain had the twin effects of intensifying and shortening the conflict.

Against the background of these conclusions, sections II and III turn to the two wars of 1991 that have received most international attention.[4] The studies of the Persian Gulf and Yugoslavia wars seek to find support for or refutation of the conclusions of the larger historical study, using the same methodology. The two sections describe the patterns of arms supplies prior to the wars; the military conduct of the wars; the arrival, if any, of arms resupply; and the

---

[4] For descriptions of the major armed conflicts of 1991, see chapter 11 in this volume.

effects of arms resupply on the process of escalation, de-escalation and negotiation. Three strands of events are compared for each conflict—arms supplies, war fighting and diplomacy to end fighting—in order to show the impact of arms supplies on all aspects of these wars.

II. The Persian Gulf War

Arms transfers

In the period 1987–91, Iraq was the world's third largest importer of arms, acquiring major weapons valued at $10.3 billion. Iraq's war with Iran fuelled its demand for and increased its leverage to acquire weapons. During the war with Iran, Iraq took deliveries from some 30 supplier states, with the USSR and France being the most important suppliers.[5] One-third of the major weapons bought by Iraq in the period 1980–90 came from countries which ultimately joined the military alliance against Iraq.

The 1988 cease-fire with Iran enabled the Iraqi leadership to consolidate its military apparatus. Iraqi imports of major weapons declined year-by-year because of difficulties in financing further arms imports, a shift in emphasis towards domestic production and, from August 1990, a United Nations-enforced arms embargo.[6] In the two years before the invasion of Kuwait, the USSR, France as well as other major European powers, Brazil and the USA supplied additional weapons.

Ambitious arms production projects were launched in Iraq, all with outside technical assistance. The most threatening to world peace was the attempt to attain the capability to produce nuclear weapons. Even before the Iraqi invasion of Kuwait, German experts and firms were implicated in supplying machines for enriching uranium and providing nuclear know-how.[7] The production of chemical weapons, originally with West German assistance,[8] continued at a high level. Another spectacular project concerned superguns of 350-mm and 1000-mm calibre. The designer of these weapons, Gerald Bull, operated from Brussels. Parts came from all over Western Europe.[9]

Iraqi weapon acquisition patterns reflected the preoccupation with the regional security complex. The emphasis was on weapons suited for warfare against less sophisticated forces such as those of Iran. Iraqi forces, despite all the money spent, had gaps in some more advanced types of weaponry, such as electronic warfare systems, surveillance, command and control equipment, and night-fighting capabilities.

---

[5] SIPRI, 'Fact sheet on military expenditure and Iraqi arms imports', Stockholm, 8 Aug. 1990 (mimeo).

[6] The arms embargo against Iraq was established in UN Security Council Resolution 661 of 6 Aug. 1990; see also chapter 8 in this volume.

[7] Der Spiegel, Apr. 1990, p. 81.

[8] Leyendecker, H. and Rickelmann, R., Exporteure des Todes [Exporters of Death] (Steidl: Göttingen, 1990).

[9] Jane's Defence Weekly, 14 Sep. 1991, pp. 458–59.

Arms and the course of the war

Early on 2 August 1990, on the pretext of oil and debt disputes, Iraqi tanks and troops crossed into Kuwait. The forces encountered little resistance from Kuwait's 15 000 troops and reached Kuwait City within hours.

Kuwait's arms policy aimed at a deterrent effect in threatening high costs to invaders, and as such resembled that of numerous other small states. Yet in reality the deployed military force was deficient. The moderate defensive ambitions of the Kuwaiti leadership were illustrated in January 1990 when they cancelled a deal to acquire 30 Mirage 2000 aircraft. The Kuwaiti Deputy Chief of Staff, Jabar Khaled al Sabah, explained that, instead, the 'purchase of [the] F-18 is sufficient to meet [Kuwait's] air force needs'.[10]

The day after the invasion, US Secretary of Defense Dick Cheney announced the decision to dispatch ground units and combat aircraft to Saudi Arabia as the first step in building a multinational force. The USA contributed F-15 fighter-bombers and airborne warning and control system (AWACS) radar aircraft.[11]

On 6 August the UN imposed a sweeping trade embargo against Iraq, in Resolution 661.[12] The embargo stopped open arms deliveries and Iraq lost its major supplier, the Soviet Union. The Soviet denunciation of Iraq's action may have taken President Saddam Hussein by surprise, but with large stockpiles available and low arms attrition as Iraq overran Kuwait, Iraq was still in a seemingly strong military position in the autumn of 1990.

While the embargo was effective, some arms probably leaked through to Iraq via clandestine suppliers. The actual routes of arms transfers are, of course, notoriously difficult to track. One clandestine route might have taken Chinese munitions to Iraq via Pakistan. Chinese officials acknowledged that discussions about delivery had taken place.[13.] None the less, the Chinese Foreign Ministry maintained that, since it had declared an embargo, sales of arms to Iraq would be stopped.[14] Israeli sources claimed that five ships carrying Soviet and Polish arms also headed for Iraq within a fortnight of the invasion, while the USA and Britain scrambled to interdict ships carrying goods destined for Iraq. Turkish authorities also stopped ships with food and other cargo.[15] The embargo was circumvented by Armscor, the South African state-owned arms manufacturing company. Until December 1990, the company supplied Iraq with long-range artillery ammunition, designed by Gerald Bull, the man who had also designed the Iraqi 'supergun'. The shells

[10] *Defense Electronics*, Jan. 1990, p. 14.

[11] *Keesing's Record of World Events,* Aug. 1990, p. 37638. For a description of the forces employed in the Gulf conflict in Aug. 1990–Jan. 1991, see Posen, B., 'Military mobilization in the Persian Gulf conflict', SIPRI, *SIPRI Yearbook 1991: World Armaments and Disarmament* (Oxford University Press: Oxford, 1991), chapter 19.

[12] See also Resolution 660 of 2 Aug. 1990, the text of which is reprinted in *SIPRI Yearbook 1991: World Armaments and Disarmament* (Oxford University Press: Oxford, 1991), appendix 18A, p. 627.

[13] *Far Eastern Economic Review*, 13 Sep. 1990, p. 6.

[14] *Defence*, Oct. 1990, p. 615.

[15] *International Herald Tribune*, 16 Aug. 1990, p. 1.

were shipped via Jordan.[16] A large number of German firms were accused of being associated with Iraqi arms projects during the second half of 1990.[17]

In the various diplomatic attempts to avoid the initiation of hostilities, Iraq's two major weapon suppliers were seemingly more conciliatory than Iraq's major opponent, the United States. Throughout the autumn of 1990, France sought to formulate a diplomatic proposal which would lead to an Iraqi withdrawal from Kuwait without recourse to war. An eleventh-hour proposal was formulated in January 1991. Put before the UN Security Council, it called for Iraqi withdrawal from Kuwait, after which a conference on the Middle East would be convened. While it won the backing of the Soviet Union, Germany and Italy, it was opposed by the USA—which rejected the Arab–Israeli linkage—and Britain. More importantly, the proposal was ignored by Iraq. Soviet President Mikhail Gorbachev also tried to throw in his weight to stop the war, repeatedly sending special envoy Yevgeniy Primakov to Iraq. In the week prior to the UN-set final date for an Iraqi withdrawal, Gorbachev personally tried to mediate but was rebuked from both Baghdad and Washington.

Both the French and the Soviet governments had voted in favour of UN Security Council Resolution 678, authorizing the allies 'to use all the necessary means' from 15 January, and stood by this position when their mediation attempts failed. There are no detailed reports on how the French or the Soviet governments used their prior arms relationships to influence Iraqi behaviour, but it seems fair to assume that they tried to use it as an argument of their good will; ostensibly, both failed. Given Saddam Hussein's intransigence, it seems unlikely that he would have been susceptible to power broking even if the two major suppliers had not implemented an arms embargo early on in the conflict.

Two days after the UN deadline expired, the US-led offensive, Operation Desert Storm, began. This first phase of the war was fought from the air. Early damage was inflicted on Iraqi command structures, airfields, missile sites, chemical and nuclear facilities, and elements of civilian infrastructure such as electrical power plants. Later the bombing was shifted to troop concentrations—particularly the élite Republican Guard—and supply lines in both Iraq and Kuwait. Efforts to knock out the politically troublesome Scud missiles were also stepped up. The allies employed carrier-based and land-based aircraft, including US B-52 bombers and British Tornados as well as US sea-launched Tomahawk cruise missiles.[18] One of the high-technology weapons, the F-117A Stealth fighter, successfully evaded Iraqi radar and hit ground targets.[19] The Patriot missile was first used operationally as an anti-missile

---

[16] *The Independent*, 28 Jan. 1991, p. 4.

[17] The West German Government received more than 150 allegations from British and US sources concerning violations of the embargo against Iraq. After initial screening, German authorities decided to open criminal procedures in 16 cases. *Unterrichtung durch die Bundesregierung, Bericht der Bundesregierung über legale und illegale Waffenexporte in den Irak und die Aufrüstung des Irak durch Firmen der Bundesrepublik Deutschland*, Deutscher Bundestag, Drucksache 12/487, 8 May 1991.

[18] *Keesing's Record of World Events*, Jan. 1991, p. 37936.

[19] *Facts on File*, 17 Jan. 1991, p. 27.

missile system on 18 January. Not developed for this role, there were numerous failures to hit incoming missiles.[20]

The one-sided character of the air war was a stark demonstration of the effectiveness of weapon systems at the highest level of development, with one side enjoying a monopoly of satellite and airborne surveillance.[21] There was also an apparent imbalance in training and tactics, despite the Iraqis' experience in the long war with Iran. Together, these factors rendered the Iraqi Air Force impotent. Instead of attempting attacks on allied positions, the Air Force concentrated on preserving their aircraft. Many of Iraq's 700 planes survived the war in British-designed, fortified underground hangars[22] or in the north of the country, and about 100 aircraft were moved into Iran.

Despite its conventional military might, Iraq could not respond to the highly computerized air war that the Coalition launched. Iraq's modern, high-technology weapons, which would have been effective against most regional opponents, proved inadequate in the night skies. Allied commanders were puzzled as to why Iraq's Exocet-armed Mirage aircraft were not deployed against allied ships and why the Iraqi Air Force fled to Iran. As in the other wars studied, including the Falklands/Malvinas and India–Pakistan conflicts, Iraqi leaders possibly realized the futility of using these weapons and opted for preserving them for the future.

The effects of arms supply on diplomacy and negotiation

The Gulf War ended in an unequivocal military victory for the Coalition. Both the swiftness of the campaign and the lop-sided distribution of war fatalities and damage upset most predictions. While the actual numbers of Iraqi deaths may never be precisely known, common estimates are 100 000 or more. The allies lost about 111 lives in combat.[23] Iraq suffered colossal damage to its infrastructure and industry. Damage to the allies was negligible, except for occupied Kuwait and related Scud attacks on Israeli cities.

Iraq also operated under a comprehensive trade embargo. As noted, some war *matériel* got through the embargo but was of only minor importance to the war effort. Because of the brevity of the war, sanctions did not appear to affect supplies and ammunition to the Iraqi troops. Iraqi troop supplies were subject to a problem of distribution rather than source. Any additional supply probably would not have helped, especially as the Air Force withdrew existing planes from battle. It is possible that with a larger inventory of fighters the Air

[20] *Defense News*, 2 Dec. 1991, p. 24.

[21] See section II of chapter 5 in this volume.

[22] *Facts on File*, 24 Jan. 1991, p. 42.

[23] This is the Pentagon figure for deaths by enemy fire. See also figure of 216 battle-related deaths in appendix 11A, table 11A in this volume. The US, Iraqi and Saudi Arabian governments all later gave higher estimates, in the range of 85 000–100 000 casualties; *Facts on File*, 28 Feb. 1991, p. 125. Greenpeace estimated a total of over 150 000 deaths; Arkin, W., Durrant, D. and Cherni, M., 'On impact: modern warfare and the environment, a case study of the Gulf War' (Greenpeace: London, May 1991), mimeo. Included in this estimate are civilian casualties up to the beginning of May 1991 and deaths that occurred during the civil war. See also Moser, T., 'Ein Versuch, die Toten der Golfkrise zu zählen', *Tageszeitung*, 26 July 1991, p. 6.

Force would have been willing to risk more of them, but the Iraqi fleet was not small, at 700 aircraft.

Resupplies had an important political impact, involving non-combatant Israel. US deliveries of Patriot missiles, F-15 fighter aircraft and cargo helicopters helped to attain the Israeli pledge to stay out of the conflict. This assurance was given in August 1990 and again in January 1991, as Iraqi Scuds hit Israel. In January, in addition to rushing more Patriot missiles to Israel, the USA also provided US personnel to operate them as well as satellite reconnaissance and battle reports.[24] At the end of January Germany also delivered a Patriot missile battery with eight launchers, along with nuclear–biological–chemical (NBC) tracking vehicles. It also announced that two submarines would be built for Israel, for delivery in the mid-1990s. This was controversial in light of German arms export restraints regarding areas of tension. In the heat of the war, Israeli political pressure proved especially effective. If Israel had entered the conflict, the Coalition might have split, and some Arab member states might even have switched sides. This would have widened the conflict, creating a second battlefield, and would perhaps have delayed its conclusion. More difficult post-war relations among the states involved would have resulted.

The Coalition ended in a position to dictate cease-fire terms. The USA had set a deadline for Iraqi withdrawal from Kuwait of 8 p.m. on 23 February. Iraq defiantly delayed its withdrawal until 26 February, after the USA pledged to continue the war. On 27 February, Iraq informed the UN that it agreed to comply fully with all the 12 UN resolutions. Baghdad had been brought to this position by the superiority of allied arms and continued prosecution of the war. After the cease-fire, the lifting of sanctions—enabling Iraq to earn oil revenue—was contingent upon Baghdad fully implementing the requirements of the resolutions. International regimes to examine the Iraqi armaments potential also were strengthened. In addition, the resounding US victory may also have subtly shifted Washington's strategic calculations about the need for Israeli power, a shift reflected in growing US–Israeli bickering over the subsequent Arab–Israeli peace conference.

III. War in Europe: the disintegration of Yugoslavia

Arms transfers

Although the fighting at least began as a civil war, the external supply of arms to the opposing forces made this conflict similar to an inter-state war. The flow of arms clearly fuelled the fighting. Before the armed hostilities, the central authorities—the Yugoslav National Army (YNA)—had a near monopoly on battle weapons and the quite sizeable domestic arms industry, which is predominantly situated in Serbia. As the Yugoslav state disintegrated in the fighting, the army progressively came to resemble a Serbian national army. As

---

[24] *Keesing's Record of World Events*, Jan. 1991, p. 37939.

a result of defections from the Yugoslav forces and a flow of arms from external sources, Slovenia and Croatia could sustain a moderate level of fighting. The Slovenians especially owed their fighting capability initially to the considerable quantities of arms, including infantry and air defence weapons, they retained as the Yugoslav Army tried to disarm the territorial defence forces. The Slovenians kept 40 per cent of their weapons, and the Croats considerably less, but enough to mount campaigns against the YNA.

Croatia and Slovenia proclaimed independence on 25 June 1991. The declarations were greeted by an escalation of the ongoing clashes between Serbs and Croats. Unlike the Slovenian Defence Force, the Croatian National Resistance (CNR) had not been preparing for possible military action in the years just before fighting broke out. The Croatian Army still numbered 150 000 former federal army conscripts and in June and July was strengthened by federal army deserters who often carried personal weapons.[25] Raids on government weapon stores were another important source of arms.

Weapons are said to have reached the separatists in Slovenia and Croatia from a number of diverse sources. The now stilled Lebanese civil war has released artillery, rocket launchers, machine-guns and ammunition to the arms market. The Lebanese Forces, the largest Christian group, reportedly sold most of its $100 million worth of these weapons in secret during the spring of 1991.[26] Much of the weapons and ammunition bound for the break-away republics reportedly also came from the Soviet Union, where in common with Lebanon, not all arms are under central control. The USA also is an important source for small arms which can be bought openly because of permissive gun laws. Guns and rifles from the USA were found in numerous seizures of arms by German and Austrian border control forces.[27] Additional attempts to export $12 million worth of US-produced infantry weapons to Croatia were stopped by US customs. The Croatians also were interested in more expensive items, including the General Dynamics FIM-92 Stinger low-altitude SAM missile system.[28] The Hungarian firearms manufacturer FEG was threatened by bankruptcy in late 1991 when the Hungarian Government enforced stringent export restrictions following the discovery that a large number of Kalashnikov-type rifles had been sold to Croatia.[29] Croatian and Slovenian officials talked openly of buying weapons from German, Austrian and Singaporean sources. Slovenia reportedly spent $50 million on imports from these countries and from the Soviet Union and Eastern Europe.[30] Arms also were shipped from South Africa using a Boeing 707 plane chartered from Uganda Airlines Corporation flying from Mambastho (Bobhutatswana) airport via Entebbe to Zagreb.[31] Because of the notorious difficulty in tracking flows of small arms and ammunition, it is probable that there were many more ship-

---

[25] Jane's Defence Weekly, 24 Aug. 1991, p. 311.
[26] International Herald Tribune, 2 July 1991, p. 3.
[27] Frankfurter Rundschau, 16 Nov. 1991, p. 2, and 19/20 Nov. 1991, p. 4.
[28] Jane's Defence Weekly, 24 Aug. 1991, p. 311.
[29] Jane's Defence Weekly, 30 Nov. 1991, p. 1073.
[30] International Herald Tribune, 9 July 1991, p. 1.
[31] New African, Nov 1991, p. 31.

ments. However, it emerges that there was a predominance of deliveries from countries without effective arms transfer controls because of a lack of legal instruments or because of a breakdown of authority.

Unlike Croatia, Slovenia had prepared for its declaration of independence for two years. Within weeks of independence, the Slovene Territorial Defence Force (STDF) clashed with federal forces. The Slovenians used M56 submachine guns produced in Yugoslavia, derived from the German MP 40, as basic equipment. They also carried Romanian AK-47 and Hungarian AMD-65 assault rifles. The farthest travelled weapon used was the Armbrust, a short-range anti-armour weapon designed in Germany and marketed from Singapore.[32] The Slovenians claimed to have destroyed eight federal army battle tanks in the summer of 1991. Until independence, the Slovenians had had no armoured personnel carriers (APCs) but quickly captured a number of them from deserting troops. Slovenian officials asserted that they had captured more federal weapons than they could possibly use.

The most recent major arms purchase by the debt-ridden Yugoslav Government was of AA-11 Archer air-to-air missiles from the Soviet Union in 1990 to arm MiG-29 fighter aircraft. These weapons are inappropriate for this type of warfare since neither Slovenia nor Croatia possesses an air force. Somewhat more appropriate for civil warfare were the three Hercules transport planes that were ordered from the USA in 1989 but not delivered by the end of 1991. The Serbian-controlled forces could rely on a diversified arms industry producing a wide range of ammunitions and weapons including light aircraft and tanks. Prior to the outbreak of hostilities, this arms industry was a major source of export earnings.[33] Later it was geared to supplying the Serbian fighting forces; but as is often the case in civil wars, it also became a major source of supply for the opposing forces.

Arms and the course of the war

Ethnic tensions had been rising noticeably from around the Serbian and Croatian referenda for independence, in December 1990 and May 1991, respectively.

Serbian separatists had engaged Croatian police in gun battles. After such an incident in April 1991, when Serbs in Croatia had proclaimed the Serbian Autonomous Region of Krajina, the YNA went in with the proclaimed aim to reduce tensions. Tanks and armoured vehicles were deployed in the Plivice National Park, a tourist attraction incorporated by the Serbs into their 'Autonomous Region'. While the Croatian police complied with a YNA order to withdraw from the park, the inter-communal violence nevertheless continued with shootings and bombings. The YNA faced increasing attacks and retorted with force.[34] Despite assurances that the YNA would not interfere in

[32] *Jane's Defence Weekly*, 13 July 1991, p. 49.
[33] Brzoska, M. and Ohlson, T., SIPRI, *Arms Transfers to the Third World 1971–85* (Oxford University Press: Oxford, 1987), pp. 110–12.
[34] *Keesing's Record of World Events*, Apr. 1991, pp. 38163–64.

the settlement of the political crisis and limit itself to peace-keeping, the YNA's growing presence heightened fears among Croats of a creeping military takeover. Misgivings about the YNA prompted the formation of a *de facto* republican army in the form of the Croatian National Guard Corps.

By early May, Croats and Serbs were engaged in their bloodiest clashes since World War II. The YNA moved tanks into Borovo Selo and occupied villages near Knin, the main town in the 'Autonomous Region'. Croatia's President Franjo Tudjman blamed Serbian nationalists and fascists for trying to provoke military intervention in order to set up a Greater Serbia. He declared that open warfare had begun against Croatia. The eight-member Yugoslav Collective State Presidency met on 4 May and condemned the Borovo Selo incidents but ordered a reinforcement of the YNA's role. On 6 May the Defence Secretariat placed the army in a full state of combat alert, ordered the Croatian Government to stop its attacks against the YNA, and threatened to settle accounts with those who set the people against the YNA. On 9 May the Collective State Presidency gave the YNA wider powers in Croatia but stopped short of invoking a state of emergency. Ironically, the presence of the YNA had contributed to the heightened tensions.[35]

Declarations of independence by Croatia and Slovenia in June 1991 further intensified the crisis. On 27 June, 1900 members of the YNA were mobilized, and troops headed for Slovenia's three international borders. They met heavy, well-organized armed resistance. In Yugoslavia's ethnically homogeneous province, the separatists enjoyed the support of nearly the entire population. Fighting and air attacks continued until the afternoon of 28 June. Both sides claimed to have gained control of Slovenia's border crossings after battles that claimed 100 lives.[36]

By the summer the Croatian separatists were beginning to face difficulties in their struggle with the army. Supply problems might have been the major factor in forcing the Croats to retreat. They had entered the hostilities less well equipped than the Slovenians in their prior struggle, but by August the Croats reportedly were receiving new arms deliveries and were ready for continued combat.[37]

On 25 August the YNA bombarded the Croatian town of Vukovar with artillery and aircraft. The Croats claimed to have knocked out 30 tanks, a boast the YNA called nonsense. Bits of Croatia began to fall to Serbian forces which by summer 1991 had gained at least one-fifth of the republic.[38] By the autumn, inadequate supplies appeared to be a factor as the Croats were out-gunned. Retreating, they tried to organize a defence, and Croatian troops were ordered to surround federal bases in Zagreb. Oil lines to Serbia had been cut and atrocities on both sides mounted.[39] The late October siege of Dubrovnik was a disaster for the defending Croatian forces. Lack of arms was clearly one

[35] *Keesing's Record of World Events*, May 1991, p. 38203.
[36] *Keesing's Record of World Events*, May 1991, p. 38275.
[37] *The Economist*, 10 Aug. 1991, p. 38.
[38] *The Economist*, 31 Aug. 1991, p. 44.
[39] *The Economist*, 21 Sep. 1991, p. 57.

culpable factor, letting down Croatian fighting morale. The only large weapons the Croats had with which to fend off the Montenegrin troop encirclement of the city were one heavy machine-gun and two 40-year-old artillery pieces. Clandestine blockade-running provided insufficient supplies.[40] Late in November followed the fall of Vukovar—Serbia's first set piece victory.

The effects of arms supply on diplomacy and negotiation

On 24 June the EC offered $850 million to Yugoslavia if it did not disintegrate.[41] Secret talks reportedly took place in July between Serbian and Croatian government representatives about carving up Bosnia and Herzegovina between them, with a Muslim buffer territory in between.[42] The fact that the parties engaged in these talks suggests that either side might have been adequately equipped and supplied to fight for the territory. However, the Serbs were stronger, as the Croatian retreat indicates, and as the Croatian offer of 'political autonomy' for Serbian areas also suggests. At this time the Serbs had little incentive to accept, as they were still gaining territory.

There was widespread diplomatic activity to contain the war and find a political settlement. Under EC auspices, a number of cease-fires were negotiated during the summer and autumn of 1991. The EC also sent observers. For the Conference on Security and Co-operation in Europe (CSCE), the Yugoslav War provided an instant test of its crisis-management mechanism. When Europe proved unable to solve the crisis, from the autumn of 1991, the UN Security Council also got involved. On 1 January 1992 UN special envoy Cyrus Vance announced that Serbia and Croatia had agreed to accept UN peace-keeping forces to oversee a cease-fire put into effect as of 3 January. The UN decided to send peace-keeping troops on the condition that all sides observed the cease-fire, the fifteenth since the summer of 1990.[43]

The question of arms transfers played an important role in the deliberations and actions in the diplomatic sphere. The EC decided to ban all weapon deliveries to Yugoslavia on 5 July 1991, and the USA followed on 11 July. In early August the EC approached more than 20 governments suspected of delivering arms to the warring parties in order to ask their support for the arms embargo and received favourable answers, according to the Chairman of the EC Council, Netherlands Foreign Minister Hans van den Broek.[44] On 25 September 1991 the UN Security Council voted for a voluntary arms embargo in Resolution 713.[45] These decisions to invoke arms embargoes against all the parties were seen mostly as symbolic, aimed at stressing the significance attributed to the fighting by the major powers. Ironically, if they

[40] *The Economist*, 2 Nov. 1991, p. 45.
[41] *The Economist*, 29 June 1991, p. 41. With this 'carrot' had come the 'stick' of threatened sanctions against the central government if force were used.
[42] *The Economist*, 20 July 1991, p. 49.
[43] *Financial Times*, 7 Jan. 1992, p. 2.
[44] *Frankfurter Rundschau*, 14 Aug 1991, p. 2.
[45] See chapter 8, section V, for a full account of the arms embargoes against Yugoslavia.

had any effect at all, they reduced the flow of arms to the Slovenian and Croatian forces at a time when public opinion in several of the states prominently involved in diplomatic activity swung towards official recognition of Slovenia and Croatia.[46] Because of the domestic arms industry, the Serbian forces were not vulnerable to an arms embargo per se, although an embargo on fuel, components and materials used in the arms industry would be felt. Arms resupply problems might have motivated acceptance of some of the many unsuccessful cease-fires. Reportedly, the combatants used these pauses to get more food and ammunition.[47]

The EC used the embargo threats in August and September 1991 to influence decision making. The EC warned Serbia that, unless it signed the EC's peace initiative, it would face economic sanctions and political isolation. Serbia relented and let foreign observers monitor the next cease-fire.[48] After a number of unsuccessful cease-fires, the EC finally imposed economic sanctions on 8 November, at the NATO summit meeting in Rome, after having debated and threatened to do so for much of the conflict. The sanctions were imposed on all combatants, but since the aim was to punish Serbia, and not Croatia, ways were drawn up to compensate friendly republics.

Economic sanctions were one factor in bringing the warring parties back to serious negotiations. All the sides, but especially the YNA which relies on state revenues for its existence, felt the growing economic deterioration throughout the disintegrating Yugoslavia. It is instructive that economic and supply embargoes had a somewhat greater impact on negotiations than arms embargoes per se, at least when strategic fuel were involved and while clandestine arms sources were available. Strategic victories in Croatia and growing international condemnation also conditioned Serbian acceptance of the cease-fire terms and UN peace-keeping.

IV. Findings

In the Persian Gulf War, *arms technology levels* were crucial to the conduct and outcome of the war. At the point of initiating hostilities, the aggressor, Iraq, enjoyed a military advantage over Kuwait by virtue of its larger war machine. Previous large-scale arms deliveries from many suppliers tempted the Iraqi leadership to try to change the balance in the Gulf. When the Coalition had been assembled—a development that the Iraqi leaders had probably not envisioned—the advantage shifted to the allies. Still, before the war Iraq remained impervious to diplomatic initiatives, including a UN arms embargo and only belatedly accepted them after fighting had begun.

In Yugoslavia, *arms supply* was a determinant of the level of hostilities. The Croatian and Slovenian forces obtained their initial arms from domestic sources: the territorial units of the Yugoslav Army. The Slovenians retained a

---

[46] The Croatian Government is the only party involved that has openly attacked the arms embargo. *Financial Times*, 21 Aug. 1991, p. 12.

[47] *The Economist*, 10 Aug. 1991, p. 38.

[48] *The Economist*, 7 Sep. 1991, p. 48.

Table 10.2. The impact of arms resupply on military and diplomatic outcomes of selected wars in 1991

War/ Resupply	Embargo	Outcome	Pre-war advantage	Negotiations during war
Iraq–Kuwait and Coalition				
Asymmetric: Coalition (via weapon deployment)	Asymmetric: UN against Iraq	Coalition	Iraq (summer 1990) Coalition (from autumn 1990)	Failed UN, French, Soviet efforts
Yugoslavia				
Asymmetric: Serbia (domestic arms production)	Symmetric: EC, USA, UN	Stalemate: Serbia	Serbia	EC, Soviet, UN mediation with little success; UN peacekeeping agreed
Sri Lanka				
Asymmetric: Government	None	Stalemate: Government	Government	Failed direct negotiations; aborted Indian intervention
Myanmar				
Asymmetric: Government	None	Stalemate: Government	None	..
Sudan				
Symmetric	Asymmetric: USA (informal) against Government	Stalemate	Government	Failed OAU attempts

Note: See notes *a–d* to table 10.1.

considerably larger share of these weapons than the Croats. They also fared better in the fighting with the central authorities, in which their geographic position and ethnic homogeneity also aided them. The Croats appeared to run out of arms and parts by the autumn. This appears to account in large measure for the setbacks that their forces suffered. The secret talks between the Croats and Serbs were broken off by the latter at about the time when the Croats were beginning to have resupply problems.

Table 10.2 summarizes the findings from these and three additional selected armed conflicts of 1991—the conflicts in Sri Lanka, Myanmar and Sudan—only briefly summarized here.

Sri Lanka provided a clear case of arms acquisitions and their timing prompted by developments in the conflict. Sri Lanka received large consignments of weapons appropriate for the anti-guerrilla campaign from China in 1991, including F-7 and F-5 fighters, HY-2 transport planes, Shanghai Class patrol craft, landing ships and 130-mm type 59-1 artillery pieces. Resupply of the armed forces was instrumental in successful operations against the insurgents in 1991. The Sri Lankan armed forces were able to put the Jaffna peninsula under siege, the main stronghold of the LTTE (Liberation Tigers of Tamil Eelam) guerrilla. Sri Lankan arms acquisitions followed almost exclusively from the Government's needs to deal with insurgents and the resupplies aided that struggle. The supplies enabled the army to maintain the upper hand and weakened pressures to submit to cease-fires and negotiations.[49] However, the insurgency persists.

The escalation of a conflict, fuelled by arms supplies, emerged in Myanmar, where the military government was fighting unarmed and armed popular groups. Government forces received large amounts of weapons from China in the summer of 1991, including F-7 combat aircraft, armoured vehicles, rocket launchers and small arms. This enabled government forces to move into areas that had earlier been controlled by regional guerrilla forces, such as the Western region of Arakan. In response, militant groups, mostly Muslim, asked for and received financial assistance from Middle Eastern sources. The money was used to buy weapons along the Cambodia–Thailand and Afghanistan–Pakistan borders.[50]

In another long-run communal war, in Sudan, government forces were unable to improve their position, although the opposing SPLA (Sudan People's Liberation Army) was weakened. Its major ally and arms supplier, the Mengistu regime in Ethiopia, was toppled in May 1991. The Government promptly rejected a US peace initiative and launched a military offensive against the group. The campaign was a failure. In a counter-offensive in November, the government stronghold of Juba was surrounded by the SPLA and shelled.[51] Economic exhaustion made it difficult for the Sudanese Government to order new weapons.

These findings verify several conclusions of the previous historical study. Arms embargoes had a weak impact on the course and outcome of hostilities. In the Persian Gulf and Falklands/Malvinas wars, one side's weapon superiority ended the conflict before the other side developed a resupply problem. Supplier leverage tended to be parried by the engagement of new, albeit apparently inferior, weapon sources. Arms supply did affect the level of hostilities and the ability of combatants to forego negotiations, as in Yugoslavia, Sri Lanka and Sudan. The Gulf War demonstrated the decisive importance of the quality of the arms supplied, although some advanced US systems had persistent technological problems.[52] Access to high-technology exporters may continue to prove crucial in future conflicts.

In the end, the possibilities of arms transfer relationships and arms transfers containing wars are limited to specific circumstances involving attrition rates,

---

[49] From BBC World Service interview with Rev. Michael Taylor, director of Christian Aid, 30 Nov. 1991.
[50] *Jane's Defence Weekly*, 15 June 1991, pp. 1053–54; and 19 Oct. 1991, pp. 717–18.
[51] BBC World Service, 23 Nov. 1991.
[52] See also chapter 5 in this volume.

technological levels of fighting and alternatives in supply. While there is in some states a tendency to raise the technological level of domestic armed forces—thus improving the chances for an embargo to work—the number of alternative suppliers, including those ready to supply high-technology arms, has grown. On balance and over time, the diplomatic impact of arms transfers seems to have weakened. The case studies provide some support for the position that it is best not to deliver any weapons during conflict, unless the supplier favours one side to win. This is not because a halt in deliveries can stop the fighting, but because more weapons tend to make conflicts longer and bloodier.

Two conclusions may be drawn from the analysis.

1. Support is found for the policy not to supply to combatants or states close to war, a policy formally adopted by several countries,[53] unless one wants one side to win. Arms transfers to belligerents have predominantly negative consequences. Even if one side is clearly favoured in the post-cold war era, it makes more sense to seek to engage the UN Security Council in peace-making efforts rather than to send weapons unilaterally. In this sense, the handling of the Yugoslav crisis, with all its tragic consequences, was an improvement over what happened in other, earlier cases, or in Myanmar and Sri Lanka.

2. Multilateral activities to control the arms trade, that greatly increased after the end of the Gulf War in 1991, can only be judged a modest step in the right direction. While it certainly makes sense to focus on weapons of mass destruction and their delivery systems, as did US President George Bush and French President François Mitterrand in their proposals for arms transfer control that were later discussed and approved in the framework of the Group of Seven (G7) largest Western economic powers and the five permanent members of the UN Security Council, efforts should not stop there. People suffering in wars mostly suffer from the destruction wrought by conventional weapons. An important element in alleviating the dangers from arms transfers is the elimination of the black market, which unfortunately is in danger of growing because of the collapse of the Soviet Union. In the longer run, arms transfers to belligerents have to be tightly controlled. Now that the cold war is over, this should be easier than during the past decades. In September 1991, an important agreement on Afghanistan was struck between US Foreign Minister James Baker and then Soviet Foreign Minister Boris Pankin that points in the direction the international community might want to move: they agreed to stop deliveries to all combatants from 1 January 1992.

---

[53] Anthony, I. (ed.), SIPRI, *Arms Export Regulations* (Oxford University Press: Oxford, 1991).

11. Major armed conflicts in 1991

BIRGER HELDT, PETER WALLENSTEEN and KJELL-ÅKE
NORDQUIST*

I. Introduction

In 1991, major armed conflicts were waged in 30 locations. There has been a gradual reduction of the number of locations of major armed conflicts since 1987, documenting a slow but noticeable downward trend.[1]

In four of the 31 locations of conflict in 1990, no major armed conflict was waged in 1991—Laos, Lebanon, Nicaragua and India–Pakistan—in some instances the result of a peace process. Three new major armed conflicts emerged in 1991: the international conflict between Iraq and Kuwait and its allies, the state-formation conflict in Yugoslavia and the internal conflict in Rwanda. These conflicts may be seen as examples of a shift in conflict patterns following the end of the cold war. During the year settlements were recorded in five conflict locations: Angola, Cambodia, El Salvador, Liberia and Western Sahara. As in previous years, internal conflicts, that is, conflicts over government, were the most frequent, followed by state-formation conflicts, that is, conflicts over territory, where a rise in the number was recorded. In 1991 the United Nations was activated: in the Persian Gulf War and in new peace-keeping operations.

II. Definitions and criteria

The conflict data for 1991 are presented in appendix 11A, which gives brief comments on the development of the 30 conflict locations up to 31 December 1991, from information available as of 31 January 1992. A *major armed conflict* is characterized by prolonged combat between the military forces of two or more governments or of one government and at least one organized armed group, involving the use of weapons and incurring battle-related deaths of at least 1000 persons.[2]

---

[1] In 1990, major armed conflicts were waged in 31 locations; in 1989, 33; 1988, 34; and 1987, 36. A revised and updated presentation of all major armed conflicts in 1986–91, more comprehensive descriptions of the major armed conflicts in 1990 and 1991, all minor conflicts (below 1000 battle-related deaths) for 1990 and 1991 as well as a revised list of minor conflicts in 1989 are found in Heldt, B. (ed.), *States in Armed Conflict 1990, 1991* (Department of Peace and Conflict Research, Uppsala University: Uppsala, Sweden, 1992).

[2] The definition is presented in Heldt (note 1).

* The Department of Peace and Conflict Research, Uppsala University, Sweden. This chapter constitutes part of a project at the Department of Peace and Conflict Research.

By applying the same definition since 1986, the *SIPRI Yearbook* has been able to present comparable statistics on the development of conflict patterns over this period. The data are revised each year as new information becomes available.[3] One element in the definition requires further explanation: the criterion of 1000 battle-related deaths. This criterion is set in order for the table of conflicts to include what normally is perceived as a 'war' or *major* armed conflict, that is, a military conflagration of a certain magnitude and human impact.[4] Sometimes there are conflicts which require close scrutiny to determine whether they meet this criterion or not. For instance, by late 1991 the conflict in Nagorno-Karabakh, Azerbaijan, had resulted in some 850 battle-related deaths.[5] This conflict has involved not only the Armenian majority population in the Nagorno-Karabakh enclave in Azerbaijan but also the relations between these republics and the central Soviet Government. The Soviet Government acted for a time as an 'armed arbitrator'. Following the dissolution of the Soviet Union in December 1991 and the establishment of sovereign states, the conflict has become an international conflict. It is undoubtedly the most acute armed conflict in the newly formed Commonwealth of Independent States (CIS). Another armed conflict of significance during the year was that in the former Soviet republic of Georgia, escalating at the end of 1991 and early 1992. There were also other conflicts which were active during 1991, for instance, in Burundi, Djibouti, Mali and Spain, which for reasons of the criteria do not appear in the table in appendix 11A.

It is important to note that the criterion of 1000 battle-related deaths concerns the accumulated number of deaths from the start of the conflict. Rwanda is included in the table of major armed conflicts for the first time because accumulated deaths passed 1000 in 1991, although the conflict was joined in 1990.[6]

Some states are the location of several different conflicts, none of which alone approaches the threshold of 1000 deaths. These conflict locations are consequently not reported in the table.

III. Conflicts in 1990 that were not active in 1991

There were four locations in which major armed conflicts recorded for 1990 were no longer active in 1991. All but one were internal conflicts concerning control of government. In two of the internal conflicts, a process for settle-

---

[3] Information available after the publication of the *SIPRI Yearbooks* may lead to revisions in the annual table. For example, the conflict in Ecuador included in the table for 1986 is no longer considered as a major armed conflict since new data put the death toll below 1000. Furthermore, new information shows that the conflict in Turkey should have been included in the table for 1988 since the threshold of 1000 deaths was crossed in that year. Additional information showed that the conflict in Laos was active in 1989, while the international conflict between Laos and Thailand is not considered as a major armed conflict in 1988.

[4] The 1000 battle-related deaths threshold has also been used in other international scholarly work, although in different ways.

[5] Information suggests that this conflict may have passed this threshold for deaths by the end of Feb. 1992.

[6] See note 1.

ment was agreed upon. One of these was the internationally supervised electoral process in Nicaragua, resulting in the loss of power for the Sandinista National Liberation Front in February 1990. The peace process continued throughout 1991.[7] In this case, a civil war which lasted over 10 years was brought to an end. In the case of Lebanon, an arrangement was worked out in October 1990 and was implemented in 1991. In this case, the role of Syria was particularly significant. In the third location, Laos, no fighting was recorded in 1991.

A change was recorded in the international conflict between India and Pakistan. A set of confidence-building measures was instituted between the two countries. The issue of Kashmir remained contentious between the parties, but there were apparently no ordered attacks between the regular forces of the two sides. Although some shelling took place during 1991, it was not regarded as a major armed conflict. According to some reports, the shelling aimed at drawing attention away from the infiltration of militants into the Indian-controlled part of Kashmir. Thus, this case was not entered as a major armed conflict in 1991.[8]

IV. New conflicts in 1991 and the end of the cold war

Three new major armed conflicts emerged in 1991, two of which, in different ways, bore testimony to the post-cold war period: the Gulf War between Iraq and Kuwait and its allies, and the conflict in Yugoslavia. The third is the conflict in Rwanda.

In the Gulf War, fought between 17 January and 28 February 1991, the UN for the second time in its existence had an extraordinary role in an international war. In the previous case, the Korean War, troops were placed under UN command and carried UN emblems.[9] In UN Security Council Resolution 678 (29 November 1990), the UN authorized the multinational Coalition allied with Kuwait to use all necessary means to make Iraq comply with all the UN Security Council resolutions relevant to the conflict.

The Gulf War had features which would have been impossible during the cold war. First, there was the intimate, although not complete, co-operation between the United States and the Soviet Union, in a long and severe international crisis preceding the outbreak of large-scale military operations.[10] Second, and related to this, was the ability to find a common ground between major and minor states on a principle of international law as given in the UN

---

[7] Some fighting occurred in 1991 but concerned other issues and parties than before (e.g., between the re-contras and the UNO Government, rather than with the Sandinistas).

[8] A similar case was the situation between Iran and Iraq during 1989: some shelling took place, possibly due to unruly troops. Iran–Iraq was subsequently not recorded as a major armed conflict in 1989.

[9] The UN was also a party to the internal conflict in Congo, where UN troops repulsed the attempt by Katanga to secede from the Congo.

[10] The Soviet Union tried to find solutions in various instances, most notably in the period 12–24 Feb. 1991, before the ground war, reportedly to the dissatisfaction of the US leadership.

Charter.[11] Many countries, including the superpowers, may have had their own agenda, but international law provisions became a platform for joint action.

The end of the cold war opened prospects for a common position by the former superpower rivals towards a severe international crisis. It also enabled them to collaborate in the settlement of some conflicts which had long been stalemated, for example, the conflicts in Afghanistan, Angola and South Africa. However, it also removed various restraints exercised over parties to ethnic conflicts during the cold war. Issues of ethnicity and nationalism came to the forefront in the dissolution of Yugoslavia and the Soviet Union, resulting in 18 new sovereign states.[12]

The conflict in Yugoslavia followed the end of the Communist regimes in Eastern and Central Europe. It brought to light old and unresolved animosities between, in particular, Serbs and Croats. The Communist regime had kept these animosities under control through repression. In Croatia in particular, the Serbian minority demanded a close link to Serbia and proclaimed an autonomous region in a period when Croatia was moving towards independence. On 25 June 1991 Croatia and Slovenia proclaimed independence, resulting in practice in wars with the federal government, parts of the Yugoslav National Army, Serbia and armed members of the Serbian minority in Croatia. Fighting was concentrated in Croatia, and only after 15 cease-fire agreements was the conflict brought to a standstill in January 1992.

The third new conflict which emerged in 1991 was that in Rwanda, which concerned control of government. An organization building on refugees from the dominated group (Tutsi, the former ruling group) initiated an armed attack, demanding democracy, repatriation of refugees who had fled the country in previous upheavals and the elimination of ethnic ID cards. It set in motion mediation attempts by neighbouring states and the Organization of African Unity (OAU).

V. Three types of conflict in 1991

As noted in section I, the bulk of the major armed conflicts in 1990 continued throughout 1991. As in previous years, most conflicts in 1991 were within rather than between states. Only one *international* (inter-state) major armed conflict was recorded, the Gulf War.[13] The other conflicts concerned control over either government or territory.

The majority of the major armed conflicts were *internal*, that is, they concerned control over the government. Typically, an incumbent government was faced with non-governmental opposition forces desiring to take control of the

[11] The war was fought to uphold the principle of non-aggression, although Iraq was not formally described as the 'aggressor' in UN Security Council Resolution 660, 2 Aug. 1990.

[12] This was more than the number of new states created in one year as part of the decolonization process, when 17 new states were formed in 1960 and admitted to the UN. Three former Soviet republics became members of the UN in 1991 (the Baltic states), two were already members (Belarus and Ukraine) and one succeeded an earlier member (the Russian Federation, replacing the USSR).

[13] For the work of the UN Special Commission on Iraq conducted after the war, see chapter 13 in this volume.

state, for the pursuit of a fundamentally different policy. The record for 1991 shows that incumbent governments were forced out in two cases (Ethiopia and Somalia), resulting in peaceful transformation in one of these (Ethiopia). In one case, the government clearly won militarily (the Iraqi Government *vs* the Shiite opposition). In some other cases, the government had the upper hand, without being able to militarily defeat the opponents (in Chad, Peru, the Philippines and Uganda). In four cases, settlements were concluded between the government and guerrillas aiming at reuniting the warring parties into a national framework (Angola, the Bicesse Peace Accord, May 1991; Cambodia, the Paris Agreement, October 1991; El Salvador, concluded in principle at UN headquarters in New York on 31 December 1991; and Liberia, the Yamoussoukro Accord, October 1991). Such processes were seemingly also under way in some other cases (Colombia and South Africa). In some conflicts, no direct contacts between the parties were recorded (Chad, Iran and Uganda). In all these cases of settlement, international parties in general, and the UN in particular, were actively involved, resulting in UN verification or other forms of presence in three of these conflicts.

There was also international involvement in conflict settlement in a number of other internal conflicts. The UN had a role in Afghanistan, and there were regional processes to contain conflict and promote solution: in Colombia, Guatemala and Rwanda. The talks on Mozambique took place in Rome, with Italy chairing.

A third set of conflicts concerned the issue of *state formation:* non-governmental opposition forces were in favour of changing the constitutional status of a territory, either by seceding or by gaining autonomy. Such issues were important in the conflicts of the late 1980s. However, the dissolution of the Soviet empire in 1991 might, to some, have set an example for the peaceful attainment of independence. There was one case of settlement (Western Sahara, formalized in UN Security Council Resolution 690, April 1991), several cease-fire agreements (the Iraqi–Kurdish conflict, Somalia and Yugoslavia) and a few cases of open negotiations (Ethiopia–Eritrea and Israel–Palestine). In a number of conflicts of this type there were no direct contacts between the fighting sides (Bangladesh, India, Indonesia, Northern Ireland and Sudan). A question that arises is whether these conflicts are to be seen as entirely domestic or as international, that is, part of the birth process of new nations that will eventually become independent.

The intricacies of these types of conflict can be seen in the few cases of open negotiations that were recorded. In the Middle East Peace Conference on future negotiations on the Israel–Palestine conflict, a very difficult issue concerned the composition of the Palestinian delegation. Eventually a solution was found, by having the Palestinians as part of a Jordanian delegation, but with its own identity and with a supporting delegation outside the negotiation room. In the Iraqi–Kurdish conflict there were fewer difficulties regarding the negotiation process itself, as the Kurdish demands were directed to autonomy within the existing Iraqi state. However, the issue of the territorial extension of the autonomous area (to include the oil city Kirkuk or not), for example, proved problematic, and no agreement was reached. In this case, in an unprecedented way, an international armed contingent on Iraqi territory temporarily assured the security of the Kurdish population against the Iraqi Army.

A serious challenge to the international community was posed by the conflict in Yugoslavia. Several international organizations became engaged in settlement processes, with a mixed record of success. Persistent efforts were made by the European Community (EC), resulting after almost six months of fighting in a cease-fire between Croatian and Serbian/Yugoslav forces. Some of the actions of the EC were made in connection with the Conference on Security and Co-operation in Europe (CSCE), meaning that cease-fire observers were also drawn from non-EC member states in Europe. In addition, the UN became an actor through the assignment of the UN special envoy, former US Secretary of State Cyrus Vance. Preparations were under way for a major UN peace-keeping operation in Yugoslavia. Other actors were also engaged at different times (including Soviet President Mikhail Gorbachev). A debate emerged whether diplomatic recognition of Croatia and Slovenia would result in escalation or de-escalation of the conflict. Also, the issue of an economic boycott came to the forefront: whether a boycott would be provocative or containing.

Several locations of major armed conflict contained issues of control over government as well as territory. During 1991 there were important developments in four such cases: Ethiopia, Somalia, Sudan and Iraq. The military victory over the Ethiopian central government by the EPRDF (Ethiopian People's Revolutionary Democratic Front), a front of several guerrilla movements, also resulted in the EPLF (Eritrean People's Liberation Front) taking control over Eritrea, a conflict that had raged for 30 years. An agreement was worked out giving Ethiopia access to Eritrean ports and providing for an internationally supervised referendum on the independence of Eritrea. Somaliland, the northern part of Somalia, being a former British colony, proclaimed independence in May 1991. In this case, the conflict had begun with the ambition to remove the central government, under Siad Barre. Once this was achieved in January 1991, the goals changed for the SNM (Somali National Movement), which was in control of northern Somalia. In southern Sudan a split occurred within the SPLA (Sudanese People's Liberation Army), the organization battling the central government. Hitherto the SPLA had argued for the continued existence of Sudan. However, in August a group challenged the leadership of John Garang, the chief commander of the SPLA, and argued instead for secession. Battles occurred between the two factions, and by the end of the year the outcome for the SPLA was still unclear. Finally, in Iraq, the Gulf War was followed by an anti-government rebellion in the south of the country which was subdued in two weeks.

The lack of early action to prevent major armed conflicts was evident in the new conflicts during the year. In the case of Yugoslavia, very little action was taken outside of Yugoslavia before the fighting started. The same seems to be true in the case of Rwanda. In the case of the Gulf War, on the other hand, early warnings and threats were part of the strategy employed by the multinational coalition against Iraq. The onset of the war on 17 January 1991 thus did not come as a surprise. A debate emerged on the early-warning signals that were received before Iraq entered Kuwait in August 1990.

The end of the cold war increased the possibilities for conflict settlement in one particular respect: international organizations could work more effectively when they were no longer paralysed by the US–Soviet rivalry. This can be seen to have resulted in a more determined pursuit of solution to some old cold war-inflamed conflicts. A set of new peace-keeping operations was instituted during the year: UNIKOM (the UN Iraq–Kuwait Observation Mission, supervising the border between Iraq and Kuwait), MINURSU (the UN Mission for the Referendum in Western Sahara), UNAMIC (the UN Advance Mission in Cambodia) and UNAVEM 2 (the Second UN Angola Verification Mission). There were also decisions on UN observer missions and peace-keeping operations, setting up ONUSAL (the UN Observers Mission for El Salvador) dissolving UNOCA (the United Nations Observer Group in Central America), and dispatching UNMLO (the UN Military Liaison Officer's force) to Yugoslavia in 1992. The financing of all these operations had not been solved by the end of 1991. A special operation during the year was the dispatch of UN guards to supervise the safe return of Kurdish refugees to Iraq. For the first time, the UN involved itself in an internal conflict in a member state against the wishes of the government of that state.

Some other international organizations were also activated as part of the new opportunities created after the cold war. Most notable was the EC and its involvement in Yugoslavia, as a mediator, cease-fire supervisor and actor, pursuing the recognition of the former republics of Yugoslavia. The EC also had a minor role in the Middle East Peace Conference that began in Madrid in late October 1991. Some of these activities were in conjunction with the CSCE which, however, was not as active as some might have expected. In Africa, ECOWAS (the Economic Community of West African States) handled a peace-keeping operation in Liberia, and the OAU had a diplomatic role in some conflicts (e.g., in Mozambique, Rwanda, Somalia, Sudan and Western Sahara), sometimes in co-ordination with the UN. In 1991, to many warring parties the United Nations was the preferred peace-keeping organization.

Appendix 11A. Major armed conflicts in the world, 1991

BIRGER HELDT, PETER WALLENSTEEN and KJELL-ÅKE NORDQUIST*

The following notes and sources apply to table 11A in this appendix:

a 'Year formed' is the year in which the two or more warring parties last formed their conflicting policies or the year in which a new party, state or alliance involved in the conflict came into being. 'Year joined' is the year in which the armed fighting last began or the year(s) in which armed fighting recommenced after a period for which no armed combat was recorded.

b In the list of warring parties, note that one side is always a government. The non-governmental warring parties are listed by the name of the organization conducting armed operations. Only those parties which were active during 1991 are listed in this column.

c The figures for 'No. of troops in 1991' are for total armed forces (rather than for army forces, as in the *SIPRI Yearbooks 1988–90*), unless otherwise indicated by a note (*).

d The figures for deaths refer to total battle-related deaths during the conflict. *'Mil.'* and *'civ.'* refer to estimates, where available, of *military* and *civilian* deaths; where there is no such indication, the figure refers to total military and civilian battle-related deaths in the period or year given. Information which covers a calendar year is by necessity more tentative for the last months of the year. Experience has also shown that the reliability of figures is improved over time; they are therefore revised each year.

e The 'change from 1990' is measured as the increase or decrease in battle-related deaths in 1991 compared with deaths in 1990. Although based on data that cannot be considered totally reliable, the symbols represent the following changes:

+ +	increase in battle deaths of > 100%
+	increase in battle deaths of 10–100%
0	stable rate of battle deaths (+ or – 10%)
–	decrease in battle deaths of > 10% to < 50%
– –	decrease in battle deaths of > 50%
n.a.	not applicable since conflict not recorded for 1990

Sources: For additional information on these conflicts, see chapters in previous editions of the *SIPRI Yearbook*—Lindgren, K., Heldt, B., Nordquist, K-Å. and Wallensteen, P., 'Major armed conflicts in 1990', *SIPRI Yearbook 1991: World Armaments and Disarmament* (Oxford University Press: Oxford, 1991), chapter 10; Lindgren, K., Wilson, G. K., Wallensteen, P. and Nordquist, K.-Å., 'Major armed conflicts in 1989', *SIPRI Yearbook 1990* (OUP: Oxford, 1990), chapter 10; Lindgren, K., Wilson, G. K. and Wallensteen, P., 'Major armed conflicts in 1988', *SIPRI Yearbook 1989* (OUP: Oxford, 1989), chapter 9; Wilson, G. K. and Wallensteen, P., 'Major armed conflicts in 1987', *SIPRI Yearbook 1988* (OUP: Oxford, 1988), chapter 9; and Goose, S., 'Armed conflicts in 1986, and the Iraq–Iran War', *SIPRI Yearbook 1987* (OUP: Oxford, 1987), chapter 8.

---

* Several of the conflict descriptions were prepared by Thomas Ohlson, Masako Ikegami-Andersson, Christer Ahlström, Ramses Amer and Karin Lindgren. Magnus Marklund, Karin Axell and Ylva Nordlander provided assistance in the collection of data and preparation of a few conflict descriptions in the table.

The following reference books were used: *Amnesty International Årsrapport 1990 [Annual report 1990]* (Amnesty International: Stockholm, Sweden); Brogan, P., *World Conflicts* (Bloomsbury: London, 1989); Gantzel, K.-J. and Meyer-Stamer, J. (eds), *Die Kriege nach dem Zweiten Weltkrieg bis 1984* (Weltforum: Munich, 1986); Gunson, P., Thompson, A. and Chamberlain, G., *The Dictionary of Contemporary Politics of South America* (Routledge: London, 1989); International Institute for Strategic Studies, *The Military Balance 1991–1992* (Brassey's: London, 1990); Janke, P., *Guerrilla and Terrorist Organisations: A World Directory and Bibliography* (Harvester Press: Hemel Hempstead, UK, 1983); Jongman, B., *War, Armed Conflict and Political Violence* (Polemological Institute, National University: Groningen, the Netherlands, 1982); Kaye, G. D., Grant, D. A. and Emond, E. J., *Major Armed Conflict, A Compendium of Interstate and Intrastate Conflict 1720 to 1985*, report R95 (Operational Research and Analysis Establishment [ORAE], Canadian Department of National Defence: Ottawa, 1985); Keesing's, *Political Dissent* (Longman: Harlow, Essex, 1983); Lindgren, K. (ed.), *States in Armed Conflict 1989* (Department of Peace and Conflict Research, Uppsala University: Uppsala, 1991); Minority Rights Group, *World Directory of Minorities* (Longman: Harlow, Essex, 1989); Munro, D. and Day, A. J., *A World Record of Major Conflict Areas* (Edward Arnold: London, 1990); *The Statesman's Yearbook* (Macmillan: London, annual); Small, M. and Singer, J. D., *Resort to Arms: International and Civil Wars, 1816–1980* (Sage: Beverly Hills, Calif., 1982); Wallensteen, P. (ed.) *States in Armed Conflict 1988* (Department of Peace and Conflict Research: Uppsala, Sweden, 1989); research reports on particular conflicts; and information available at the Department of Peace and Conflict Research, Uppsala University, in the continuous research project on armed conflicts.

The following journals, newspapers and news agencies were consulted: *ACEN–SIAG* (Guatemala); *Africa Confidential* (London); *Africa Events* (London); *Africa News* (Durham); *Africa Research Bulletin* (Oxford); *Africa Reporter* (New York); *African Defense* (Paris); *AIM Mozambique File* (Maputo); *Amnesty Press* (Stockholm); *Asian Defence Journal* (Kuala Lumpur); BBC World Service News (London); *Central America Report* (Guatemala City); *Centroamérica Hoy, CSUCA Pax* (San Jose, Costa Rica); *Christian Science Monitor* (Boston, Mass.); *Dagens Nyheter* (Stockholm); Dialog Information Services Inc. (Palo Alto); *The Economist* (London); *Facts and Reports* (Amsterdam); *Far Eastern Economic Review* (Hong Kong); *Financial Times* (London and Frankfurt); *The Guardian* (London); *Horn of Africa Bulletin* (Uppsala); *India Today* (New Delhi); *Jane's Defence Weekly* (Coulsdon, Surrey); *IDSA Journal* (New Delhi); *The Independent* (London); *International Defence Review* (Geneva); *International Herald Tribune* (Paris); *Kayhan International* (Teheran); *Keesing's Contemporary Archives* (Harlow, Essex); *Latin America Weekly Report* (London); *Mexico and Central America Report* (London); *The Middle East* (London); *MIO Mozambique News Review* (London); *New Statesman & Society* (London); *Newsweek* (New York); *New York Times* (New York); *Panorama Centroamericano* (INCEP, Guatemala); *S.A. Barometer* (Johannesburg); *Selections from Regional Press* (Institute of Regional Studies: Islamabad); *South Scan* (London); *Der Spiegel* (Hamburg); *Sri Lanka Monitor* (London); *The Statesman* (Calcutta); *Svenska Dagbladet* (Stockholm); *Teheran Times* (Teheran); *Time* (New York); *The Times* (London); *Upsala Nya Tidning* (Uppsala); *US News & World Report* (Washington, DC); *Washington Post* (Washington, DC); and *Weekly Mail* (Johannesburg).

Table 11A. Major armed conflicts in 1991

Location	Year formed/ year joined[a]	Warring parties[b]	No. of troops in 1991[c]	Deaths[d] Total (incl. 1991)	Deaths[d] During 1991	Change from 1990[e]
Europe						
United Kingdom/ Northern Ireland	1969/1969	British Govt vs. IRA	300 100 200–400	2 900*	94	0

Comments: In 1921 the Catholic Irish Free State was formed, while the mainly Protestant Northern Ireland was retained as a part of the UK. The IRA, formed during the Irish civil war and bent on the reunification of all of Ireland, was only sporadically active until 1969, when the organization split into the Provisional IRA and the Official IRA. The Official IRA declared a unilateral cease-fire in 1972. In 1985 the Hillsborough Agreement was signed, stipulating Ireland's right to be consulted on matters concerning Northern Ireland and increased rights for Ulster Catholics (the election system was working to their disadvantage). During the 1960s several militant Protestant groups were formed: e.g. the Ulster Defence Association (UDA, with its armed wing the Ulster Freedom Fighters, UFF) and the Ulster Voluntary Force (UVF). There are also several militant Catholic groups (e.g. the Irish People's Liberation Organization and the Irish National Liberation Army). In 1990 the Provisional IRA increased its attacks on the UK mainland to a level not seen since 1974. In 1990 preparatory talks with the 4 main political parties of Northern Ireland began, led by British Northern Ireland Secretary Peter Brooke and aimed at paving the way for formal talks on new arrangements on the exercise of political power. However, these talks do not address the incompatibility between the Provisional IRA and the British Govt. The talks were planned to be held in 3 phases: between the 4 main constitutional political parties in Northern Ireland on devolution and power sharing; between these political parties and the Irish Govt; and between the Irish and British Govts. The first phase of the talks was opened on 17 June 1991. The talks were halted on 3 July. The level of sectarian violence increased in Aug. with killings of Catholics and persons with alleged Provisional IRA contacts (e.g. members of the Sinn Fein political party) by the UFF and the UVF. Several of the most noticed actions by the Provisional IRA during 1991 were a mortar attack on the British Prime Minister's residence at Downing Street (Feb.), bombings in the London underground (Dec.) and the use of 'human bombs' against security forces. British troops on Northern Ireland were reinforced with 1500 soldiers during 1991, bringing the total number to 11 000.

* The IRA is claimed to be responsible for half of these deaths.

| Yugoslavia | Yugoslav Govt,
Serbian Govt,
YNA,
Serbian irregulars
vs. Slovenia
vs. Croatia
vs. Croatian irregulars | 1991/1991
1990/1990
1991/1991 | ..
..
169 000
..
30 000–68 000
30 000–42 000
.. | .. | .. | n.a. |

Comments: The multi-ethnic Socialist Federal Republic of Yugoslavia (SFRY), initially called the Kingdom of Serbs, Croats and Slovenes, had for much of its existence seen disagreement between Serbs (desiring a centralized state) and Croats (and later on Slovenes, desiring autonomy/decentralization). During the 1980s the country worked less and less as a political and economic unit, with deteriorating relations between the republics. In Jan. 1990 talks on the future of Yugoslavia began, in which Serbia and Montenegro supported a reworked but centralized federal structure while Croatia and Slovenia supported a confederation of independent states. In Mar. Slovenia adopted amendments to its constitution, stipulating sovereignty, and in early July declared sovereignty. In Aug. Serbs in Croatia organized a referendum on political and cultural autonomy. Clashes took place with Croatian Govt forces in late Sep. In early Oct. the Serbian Autonomous Region of Krajina was proclaimed and further clashes took place. The Serbian Govt called on the federal Govt to 'defend Serbs from repression in Croatia'. In late Dec. Croatia promulgated a new constitution, stipulating sovereignty and the right to secede from Yugoslavia. A referendum on independence was held in Slovenia, ending in favour of declaring independence if no agreement on a new structure for Yugoslavia was reached within 6 months. By late 1990, multi-party elections had been held in all republics. Talks on the future of Yugoslavia took place in Jan. and Feb. 1991. On 20 Feb. Slovenia adopted a resolution stipulating concrete steps towards secession, arguing that they had abandoned the hope that a new formula on the structure of Yugoslavia could be reached. Croatia adopted similar resolutions the following day. On 28 Feb. the Serbian Autonomous Region of Krajina declared its wish to unite with Serbia and Montenegro. Sporadic clashes in the region took place from late Feb. to late May. Further talks on the future of Yugoslavia took place in late Mar. and Apr. It was agreed that separate referenda on the future of Yugoslavia would be held in each republic. Croatia announced that it would proclaim independence if agreement on the future of Yugoslavia had not been reached by the end of June. In early June the republics agreed to consider a plan to transform Yugoslavia into a loose alliance of sovereign states. However, Slovenia and Croatia continued to take steps towards independence and on 25 June declared independence. Fighting between the Serb-dominated YNA (Yugoslav National Army) and Slovenian forces broke out 2 days later. A meeting on 28 June between a European Community (EC) delegation and federal and republic leaders resulted in an agreement on a cease-fire, the YNA's return to military barracks and a 3-month suspension of Slovenia's declarations of independence. However, the agreement was rejected by the Slovenian Assembly. Another attempt at a cease-fire by the EC delegation on 30 June failed. On 7 July, at talks at Brioni between the EC delegation and representatives from Croatia, Slovenia and the Federal Collective State Presidency, Croatia and Slovenia agreed to suspend their declarations of independence for 3 months, during which talks on the future of Yugoslavia would be held. A monitored cease-fire would also enter into force, the YNA would return to barracks, and the

Location	Year formed/ year joined[a]	Warring parties[b]	No. of troops in 1991[c]	Deaths[d] Total (incl. 1991)	Change from 1990[e]

Slovenian forces would be demobilized. On 18 July it was decided that the YNA would begin immediate withdrawal from Slovenia, to be completed within 3 months. The fighting in Slovenia is estimated to have resulted in c. 50 persons killed, 15 of whom were civilians. Clashes in Croatia between ethnic Serbs and the Croatian National Guard escalated after 26 June and further intensified in July. Further talks on the future of Yugoslavia, begun on 22 July, resulted in a call for the EC to monitor demobilization of paramilitary groups after which the YNA would return to barracks. However, the call was rejected by Croatia. On 31 July Croatia offered autonomy to the Serbian Autonomous Region of Krajina. By mid-August Croatia had lost control of one-fifth of its territory and a Serbian Autonomous Region of Western Slavonia was proclaimed. An EC-mediated agreement on a cease-fire monitored by the EC, the CSCE and representatives of the parties; the military withdrawal of forces from each other's range; and the formation of an arbitration committee was agreed on 2 Sep. but broke down in hours. EC and CSCE cease-fire monitors started to arrive in Croatia on 5 Sep. The first session of a Peace Conference on Yugoslavia opened in The Hague on 7 Sep., chaired by Lord Carrington, with the foreign ministers of all EC countries, the Yugoslav Federal Collective Presidency, Prime Minister and the Presidents of all republics, resulted in a declaration on 12 Sep. establishing that as a basis for negotiations internal borders could not be changed by means of force and that the rights of minorities must be guaranteed. By mid-Sep. the YNA openly fought on the side of the Croat Serbs, acted independently and rejected a call from the federal Pres. to withdraw. A cease-fire (the 5th in order) agreed on 17 Sep., mediated by Lord Carrington, with provisions similar to the 2 Sep. agreement, failed in hours. After the 4th session of the Hague Peace Conference in late Sep., working groups to study constitutional solutions, economic relations between the republics and the position of ethnic minorities were established. On 1 Oct. attacks by YNA naval units against towns on the Adriatic coast began and navy blockades were reimposed 2 days later. On 8 Oct. Croatia and Slovenia implemented their declarations of independence. On 13 Oct. UN special envoy Cyrus Vance arrived in Yugoslavia. On 18 Oct. in The Hague, the EC proposed a confederation of sovereign states for the future structure of Yugoslavia. Serbia rejected the proposal. The 8th session of the Hague Peace Conference opened on 5 Nov. The first UN-brokered cease-fire (the 14th) came into force on 23 Nov. On 27 Nov. the UN Security Council adopted Resolution 721, e.g. requesting a report on the feasibility of sending a peace-keeping force to Yugoslavia, conditioned on observance of the cease-fire. Croatia agreed on 28 Nov. to allow UN peace-keeping forces to be deployed in the Serb-inhabited battle zones rather than at the republics border. The cease-fire of 23 Nov. was broken in early Dec. Lord Carrington and Cyrus Vance continued their diplomatic efforts during Dec. The Hague Peace Conference reopened on 9 Dec. An advance team of UN observers arrived and an ICRC (International Committee of the Red Cross)-supervised exchange of captured troops was made in mid-Dec. On 1 Jan. 1992 Serbia (but not some of the Serbian irregulars) and Croatia accepted a UN peace plan, providing for demilitarization of battle zones after which a UN peace-keeping force would be deployed. A UN-mediated cease-fire (the 15th) was imposed 2 days later.

Iran   1970/1991   Iranian Govt   504 000*   60–300   +
                     vs. Khalq   4 500

Comments: The Mujahideen Khalq is an underground movement formed in 1970. Although it took part in the 1979 Islamic revolution, it was forced in exile and during the Iran–Iraq War fought alongside Iraq. In July 1988 the Mujahideen Khalq and the Iraqi Army launched heavy offensives, resulting in deep penetration of Iranian territory. Some fighting took place late Mar.–early Apr. 1991 in Iran–Iraq border areas (Qasr-e-Shirin) between the Revolutionary Guard and the NLA (National Liberation Army), the military wing of the Mujahideen Khalq.

* Total armed forces, incl. the Revolutionary Guard.

Iraq   ../..   Iraqi Govt   150 000–200 000   ..   ++
        ../1991 vs. Kurdistan Front* 30 000–200 000**
                 vs. SAIRI   ..

Comments: A rebellion under the leadership of the DPK (Democratic Party of Kurdistan) was launched in northern Iraq in 1961. Negotiations during 1970 resulted in an accord of Kurdish autonomy but a final settlement was delayed by the Govt's refusal to install a Kurd as Vice Pres. and to include the oil city of Kirkuk in the autonomous Kurdish region. The fighting, at a low level in 1990, increased dramatically in Mar. 1991 when an unco-ordinated Kurdish revolt (dominated by the PUK, Patriotic Union of Kurdistan, and the DKP) in the north and a Shiia Muslim revolt (led by SAIRI, the Supreme Assembly of the Islamic Revolution in Iraq) in the south took place against a weakened Iraq. The southern revolt, which spread to several southern cities, was crushed in 2 weeks. The northern revolt, which initially ousted Iraqi forces from most of Iraqi Kurdistan incl. Kirkuk, was subdued in c. 4 weeks, with the Govt retaking half of Iraqi Kurdistan. Some fighting took place until mid-Apr. The failure of the 2 revolts resulted in large numbers of Kurdish and Shiia Muslim refugees, both inside Iraq and at the borders with Turkey and Iran. After the failure of the Kurdish revolt, talks were initiated between the Kurdistan Front (an umbrella organization of 8 Kurdish opposition groups, formed in 1987) and the Govt. On 19 Apr. the existence of an informal cease-fire was reported, and on 24 Apr. Jalal Talablani (leader of the PUK and the Kurdistan Front delegation) announced that the Govt had in principle agreed to grant Kurds autonomy based on the 1970 agreement and to install democracy. However, he claimed a few days later that the status of Kirkuk was contested, as in 1970, as was the degree of self-rule and right to have contacts with foreign governments. A 2nd round of talks, with a Kurdistan Front delegation led by Masoud Barzani (leader of the DKP), was held from early May to late June: the Kurdistan Front's demands (free elections and the inclusion of Kirkuk in the autonomous Kurdish region) were rejected by the Govt, which demanded that the Kurds sever ties with Western states and co-operate against internal and external enemies of the Iraqi state. However, there were also differences between the KDP and the PUK on what an agreement should include. Clashes between Govt forces and Kurdish groups were reported in early June and the second half of July. A 3rd round of talks took place from early July to mid-Aug., after which the Kurdistan Front decided to suspend further talks. Further fighting took place in early Sep. and Oct.

* Consists of 8 groups, mainly PUK and DPK, of which at least 7 are reported as militarily active during 1991.
** Different assessments during 1991.

Location	Year formed/ year joined[a]	Warring parties[b]	No. of troops in 1991[c]	Deaths[d] Total (incl. 1991)	During 1991	Change from 1990[e]
Iraq–Kuwait	1990/1991	Iraqi Govt vs. Kuwait Govt, Multinational Force***	1 035 000* 705 000****	..	..**	n.a.

Comments: In June 1963 Iraq, repeating the assertion that Kuwait had been a part of Iraq during Ottoman rule, claimed sovereignty over Kuwait. Kuwait responded with a request to the UK for assistance. The UK sent military forces, which arrived within a week, left Kuwait by Oct. and were replaced by a pan-Arab force. Iraq recognized Kuwait in 1963 and the pan-Arab force left. In Mar. 1973 Iraq occupied areas close to the Kuwaiti islands of Bubiyan and Warba, leading to minor clashes. Iraq left the occupied areas in Apr. In negotiations Iraq proposed to recognize Kuwaiti land borders if the status of the islands were changed. On 17 July 1990 Iraq accused Kuwait and the United Arab Emirates of a conspiracy aimed at weakening Iraq by reducing Iraq's oil revenues through over-production. The next day Iraq accused Kuwait of having advanced into and occupied Iraqi territory during the Iran–Iraq War, established oil installations and stolen large amounts of oil. On 19 July, in a letter to the League of Arab States, Kuwait denied Iraq's allegations and called for mediation on disputed sections of the Kuwaiti–Iraqi border. Mediation efforts were made the following days by several Arab countries. On 25 July President Mubarak of Egypt announced Iraqi assurances of no intentions of attacking Kuwait and that delegations from Kuwait and Iraq had agreed to meet in late July. The meeting between Kuwaiti and Iraqi delegations on 31 July collapsed in a few hours. On 2 Aug. Iraq invaded Kuwait. The Amir of Kuwait, Sheikh Jabir al Ahmed al Jabir al Sabah, fled to Saudi Arabia where a Govt-in-exile was formed. Iraq claimed that the invasion—which had caused a few hundred deaths—was a response to a request by 'Kuwaiti revolutionaries' and said that it hoped to withdraw from Kuwait within a few days. On 2 Aug. the UN Security Council (UNSC) passed Resolution 660, which condemned the invasion and demanded Iraq's immediate, unconditional withdrawal. The rest of 1990 saw the buildup of a multinational military force in Saudi Arabia—Operation Desert Shield, led by the USA—issuing of UNSC resolutions and diplomatic initiatives. On 29 Nov. UNSC Resolution 678 was issued, authorizing states co-operating with the Govt of Kuwait, unless Iraq on or before 15 Jan. 1991 fully complied with all previous resolutions, to use all means necessary to uphold and implement Resolution 660 and all subsequent resolutions and to restore international peace and security in the area. On 30 Nov. the USA proposed talks between the US and Iraqi Foreign Ministers in mid-Dec. The talks did not take place: the USA considered Iraq's proposal for talks on 12 Jan. as too close to 15 Jan. A meeting was held in Geneva on 9 Jan. between the US and Iraqi Foreign Ministers and another meeting between UN Secretary-General Pérez de Cuéllar and Iraqi President Saddam Hussein was held in Baghdad on 13 Jan., both of which failed to produce an Iraqi withdrawal from Kuwait. On 17 Jan. the multinational military force launched a massive air offensive—Operation Desert Storm—against strategic targets in Iraq and Kuwait. Iraq retaliated by launching missiles against Israel and Saudi Arabia (a total of 57 by 31 Jan.). The air offensive, which quickly achieved air superiority, stepped up attacks against Iraqi ground forces and supply lines after 20 Jan. Attacks between 23 Jan. and 11 Feb. nearly destroyed the Iraqi Navy. The first major ground battle took place 29 Jan.–1 Feb., when an Iraqi attack on the Saudi Arabian coastal town Khafji was repulsed. Artillery bombardments as well as probing attacks on Iraqi positions began on 12 Feb. An Iranian proposal in Feb. (reportedly calling for an immediate cease-fire, an end to the embargo on necessities, mutual withdrawal of foreign troops from the region, replacement of Iraq's troops in Kuwait and ending of emigration by Soviet Jews to Israel) was dismissed by Iraq. The Soviet President's special envoy, Yevgeny Primakov, held talks with Pres. Hussein on 12–13 Feb. On 15 Feb. Iraq offered to withdraw from Kuwait in accordance with UNSC Resolution 660, provided certain conditions were met (e.g. annulment of all other UNSC resolutions on Kuwait, cancellation of Iraq's debts to countries of the multi-national military Coalition and reparations for war damage). On 18 Feb., at talks in Moscow with Iraqi Foreign Minister Aziz, Soviet Pres. Gorbachev presented an 8-point peace plan. The plan (which called for Iraq's compliance with UNSC Resolution 660 and Iraqi withdrawal from Kuwait in accordance with a timetable after which all UNSC resolutions would be annulled) was reportedly accepted by Iraq on 21 Feb. The plan was rejected by the USA, which the following day issued an ultimatum calling for Iraq's unconditional and immediate withdrawal from Kuwait to be completed within 7 days and Iraqi compliance with all UNSC resolutions. If Iraq had not agreed within 24 hours a ground offensive would be launched. On 24 Feb. the multinational military forces, after having flown c. 100 000 sorties, launched a full-scale land assault—Operation Desert Sabre—on Kuwait and Iraq. On 26 Feb. Iraq announced its military withdrawal from Kuwait. The land assault, which met little resistance and resulted in the defeat of the Iraqi Army and the taking of a large number of Iraqi POWs, were together with all other military actions suspended on 28 Feb., after 100 hours of fighting, shortly after Iraq had accepted all UNSC resolutions on the conflict. UNSC Resolution 687, spelling out terms for a full cease-fire and a comprehensive resolution of the conflict, was issued on 3 Apr. The resolution also required that Iraq's non-conventional weapons and ballistic missiles with a range exceeding 150 km should be destroyed, required payment of war reparations and lifted the embargo on food exports to Iraq. Other sanctions (imposed during the autumn of 1990) were to be reviewed bi-monthly taking regard of Iraq's 'policies and practices'. On 9 Apr. UNSC Resolution 689 was issued, establishing a demilitarized zone between Iraq and Kuwait to be monitored by the UN Iraq–Kuwait Observation Mission (UNIKOM).

*   Total armed forces, incl. reserves.

**   US and Saudi forces reportedly buried 16 000–17 000 Iraqi soldiers. The multinational force lost 216 soldiers.

***   Includes forces or teams from Argentina, Australia, Bahrain, Bangladesh, Belgium, Canada, Czechoslovakia, Denmark, Egypt, France, Greece, Honduras, Italy, Kuwait, Morocco, Netherlands, Niger, Norway, Oman, Pakistan, Portugal, Qatar, Saudi Arabia, Senegal, Spain, Syria, United Arab Emirates, the UK and the USA.

****   The figure is for late Jan. 1991.

Location	Year formed/ year joined[a]	Warring parties[b]	No. of troops in 1991[c]	Deaths[d] Total (incl. 1991)	During 1991	Change from 1990[e]
Israel/Palestine	1964/1964 ./..	Israeli Govt vs. PLO* vs. Non-PLO groups**	141 000	1948–91: >11 000	..	..

Comments: The current warring parties were formed in 1948 and 1964, with the formation of the State of Israel and the PLO (Palestine Liberation Organization, an umbrella organization for Palestinian groups, some of which existed before 1964), respectively. The Arab–Israeli Wars of 1967 and 1973 resulted in Israeli occupation of the West Bank (incl. East Jerusalem), the Gaza Strip and the Golan Heights (1973). Following the War of 1967, Israel extended legal jurisdiction over Jerusalem which together with the Golan Heights were formally annexed in 1980 and 1981, respectively. Since Dec. 1987 a popular uprising, the *intifada*, has taken place in the Occupied Territories, increasingly led by Hamas and the UNLU (Unified National Leadership of the Uprising). The PLO Central Council, at its 22–23 Apr. 1991 meeting in Tunis, renewed the proposal for an international conference under UN auspices, while rejecting a proposal from the USA and Israel for a regional peace conference. Gradually, a demand for changes in the PLO position was expressed from within the movement. At the 20th session of the PNC (Palestine National Council) in Algiers on 23–28 Sep., the PLO welcomed the initiative of a Middle East peace conference. Following a US-orchestrated diplomatic process the Israeli Govt and a Palestinian delegation as part of the Jordanian delegation met at the opening of a peace conference co-sponsored by the USA and the USSR, in Madrid, on 30 Oct. Also participating were delegations from Egypt, Lebanon and Syria, an observer from the GCC (Gulf Co-operation Council) and a representative from the EC. At the conference, the Israeli position *vs.* the Palestinian issue was formulated by Israeli Prime Minister Shamir as 'to reach an agreement on interim self-government arrangements with the Palestinian Arabs' while the Palestinian position, presented by Mr Abdel-Shafi, was a 'confederation between the 2 states of Palestine and Jordan'. The conference was a starting-point for a process including bilateral negotiations between Israel and the delegations as well as regional issues involving more parties. Violent confrontations took place in the Occupied Territories, in pre-1967 Israel and in the Israel/SLA (Southern Lebanese Army)-controlled zone in southern Lebanon, where the Israeli Air Force attacked bases/camps of PFLP (Popular Front for the Liberation of Palestine), DFLP (Democratic Front for the Liberation of Palestine), FRC (Fatah Revolutionary Council) and Hezbollah. The *intifada* in the Occupied Territories had by mid-1991 claimed 876 Palestinian and 76 Israeli lives. In addition, 478 lives had been lost through intra-Palestinian violence. An important factor in the conflict in 1991 was the sharply increasing immigration of Jews into Israel, mainly from the USSR, creating a stronger pressure for building of settlements in the Occupied Territories—i.e. in areas proposed as a Palestinian state—and tensions with the USA as well as during the peace conference.

* The main PLO factions are Al-Fatah (Yassir Arafat), PFLP (Popular Front for the Liberation of Palestine; George Habash), DFLP (Democratic Front for the Liberation of Palestine; Nayef Hawatmeh), ALF (Arab Liberation Front), PPSF (Palestine Popular Struggle Front; Samir Ghosheh), PCP (Palestinian Communist Party; Bashir al-Barghuti)

and PLP (Palestinian Liberation Front; Mahmoud Abul Abbas). In September there was a split within the DFLP. Mr Abed Rabbo, formerly deputy leader and DFLP representative in the PLO Executive Committee, announced that the new wing should drop its 'commitment to the comprehensive ideology—Marxism and Leninism and central democracy—that was implemented in the past'.
** Examples of such groups are the Muslim 'fundamentalist' Hamas, active in the Occupied Territories, the PNSF (Palestine National Salvation Front), and PFLP-GC (Popular Front for the Liberation of Palestine—General Command) and the FRC (Fatah Revolutionary Council).

Turkey	1974/1984	Turkish Govt	579 200	1984–91: 2 500–3 100	250	0
		vs. PKK	3 400*			
	1978/1978	vs. Devrimci Sol	100			

Comments: Kurdish rebellions during the 1920s and 1930s were suppressed by the Govt. In 1974 the PKK (Kurdish Worker's Party) was created with a separate Kurdish state as a goal. Since the start of the PKK (through its armed wing, the People's Army for the Liberation of Kurdistan) insurgency in 1984 the death toll is estimated at 2500–3000 people. Insurgency operations are reportedly controlled from Damascus and Syrian-supported training camps in Bekaa Valley, Lebanon. The fighting escalated in late 1989 and early 1990, with a marked increase in urban insurgency in major Turkish cities (over 20 assassinations in 1990). New emergency measures were announced by the Govt in Apr. 1990. In July 1991 tensions escalated in Kurdish areas following the killing of a Kurdish human rights activist and a chairman of the People's Labour Party (HEP). The Govt launched raids against alleged PKK camps in northern Iraq in Aug.–Oct. Following the 20 Oct. general election, the new Govt stated that Kurdish cultural rights were to be recognized and that Kurdish regions would enjoy increased autonomy, while strong measures would continue to be taken against the PKK. Besides the PKK insurgency, there were bombings and shootings by the left-wing groups of Devrimci Sol (Revolutionary Left). Devrimci Sol split from Devrimci Yol (Revolutionary Way) in 1978 and have since then committed a number of assassinations and bombings (over 30 during 1991). Ten of its members were killed and 12 were arrested in a police raid in July. There is speculation of co-operation between Devrimci Sol and the PKK.

* Of these, 1500 are under training.

Location	Year formed/ year joined[a]	Warring parties[b]	No. of troops in 1991[c]	Deaths[d] Total (incl. 1991)	During 1991	Change from 1990[e]
South Asia						
Afghanistan	1978/1978	Afghan Govt vs. Mujahideen based in Afghanistan, Iran, Pakistan	45 000 .. 115 000 40 000	1978–90: 1 000 000*	..	..

Comments: The Afghan civil war began in Apr. 1978 after the Govt take-over by the PDPA (People's Democratic Party of Afghanistan). The armed opposition consists of Muslim groups—the Mujahideen, or Holy Islamic Warriors. The USSR intervened militarily on a large scale in late Dec. 1979. In 1988, after 6 years of UN-mediated talks between Afghanistan and Pakistan, an accord regulating the conflict was signed between the 2 countries. The accord, whose adherence was to be monitored by UN observers, pledged non-interference in each other's internal affairs, provisions for the voluntary return of refugees and the complete withdrawal of Soviet troops by 15 Feb. 1989. A Govt-in-exile, the Islamic Interim Afghan Govt (IIAG), was formed late Feb. 1989 by the 7-party Pakistan-based Mujahideen. Efforts during 1989 and 1990 to broaden the IIAG collapsed on the question of degree of representation of the Iran-based Mujahideen. During talks in Nov. 1990 a proposal on a cease-fire, an interim Govt and UN-supervised elections was dismissed by the Mujahideen groups who rejected inclusion of then Pres. Najibullah in the interim Govt. In late Mar. 1991 the heavily defended eastern city of Khost fell to Mujahideen forces after having been under intensified attacks since mid-Mar. The battle for the city is estimated to have resulted in the death of 1000 Mujahideen, 600 Govt soldiers/militia wounded and the surrender of 2500 Govt soldiers (according to the Mujahideen). On 21 May a 5-point UN peace plan was presented, envisaging a cease-fire, cessation of arms supplies, an end to all external interference, the establishment of a broad-based interim Govt and the right of Afghans to choose their Govt. The plan received support from the Govt and the main secondary parties to the conflict (the USSR, the USA, Iran, Saudi Arabia and Pakistan). Efforts towards co-operation between Iran-based and Pakistan-based Mujahideen groups continued in 1991. A meeting in Islamabad on 28–30 July with representatives from the Govts of Pakistan and Iran, the 9 Iran-based Mujahideen, 4 groups from the Pakistan-based IIAG and 3 independent Mujahideen groups also based i Pakistan resulted in a declaration supporting the UN peace plan as 'a possible basis for a settlement' of the conflict. However, some Mujahideen groups reportedly had objections to the inclusion of representatives from the present Govt in the proposed interim Govt (Pres. Najibullah had refused to step down) while other Mujahideen groups opposed greater representation of Iran-based Mujahideen in future negotiations. A 2nd meeting was held on 28–29 Aug. in Teheran, resulting in an agreement to form a joint delegation to seek clarifications on the UN peace plan. In mid-Sep. 1991 the USA and the

USSR declared their intentions to halt arms deliveries by 1 Jan. 1992, to encourage other countries to act likewise, and not to step up arms deliveries in the meantime. Mujahideen attacks intensified in July in northern Afghanistan and had by early Sep. resulted in the fall of 5 Govt-held towns. Further attacks, most notably against the city of Gardez in late Sep., had by early Oct. resulted in several hundred deaths. Talks in early Oct. in New York between some Mujahideen leaders, the USSR and UN officials resulted in the USSR dropping its demand that Pres. Najibullah remain in office during the UN-proposed interim period, provided Fazal Haq Khaleqiar remain Prime Minister (Pres. Najibullah had since Sep. offered to step down, provided his resignation was part of a peace deal and that the presently ruling party would have a role in the interim Govt). However, the Mujahideen shortly afterwards withdrew from the agreement, resulting in a Soviet announcement of continued support for Pres. Najibullah. A further meeting in mid-Nov. in Moscow with 4 of the 7 Pakistan-based and all 9 Iran-based Mujahideen resulted once again in the USSR dropping support for Pres. Najibullah.

* The figure is likely to include all deaths in connection with the conflict, that is, not only battle-related deaths. According to Soviet sources, the total number of Soviet troops killed in the period 1979 to 15 Feb. 1989 was 15 000.

Bangladesh	1971/1982	Bangladesh Govt vs. JSS/SB	106 500 5 000	1975–91: >2 200	100	–

Comments: The ethnically distinct Chakma (Buddhist Mongol) people of the Chittagong Hill Tracts (CHT) in south-eastern Bangladesh enjoyed autonomy under British rule. However, the Bangladesh Govt created in 1971 proposed to make way for settlers to move into the region. In 1971 Buddhist tribes formed the Parbattya Chattagram Jana Sanghati Samiti (JSS, or the Chittagong Hill Tracts People's Coordination Association) and a JSS military wing, the Shanti Bahini (SB, or Peace Fighters). Guerrilla warfare erupted in 1974–75 after demands for regional autonomy for south-eastern CHT met no response. Six rounds of talks were held between the Govt and the JSS/SB from Oct. 1985 to Dec. 1988. On 1 Mar. 1989 the Bangladesh National Assembly passed 4 laws aimed at resolving the conflict; the legislation provided for the establishment of local Govt councils in the 3 major CHT districts (Rangamati, Khagrachari and Bandarban) with limited autonomy such as the power to regulate transfer or sale of land rights in the territory, thus regulating the influx of settlers. However, the SB thought the councils were powerless. In May 1989, a month before district council elections, insurgency intensified but did not stop the planned election. Since the election, both the Army and the SB have stepped up their operations. In mid-June 1991, the Govt announced that it would grant limited autonomy to the CHT and hand over all local Govt powers to 3 CHT councils. Since then the insurgency has decreased.

Location	Year formed/ year joined[a]	Warring parties[b]	No. of troops in 1991[c]	Deaths[d] Total (incl. 1991)	During 1991	Change from 1990[e]
India	1947/1981	Indian Govt	1 265 000	..	>7 000	0
	./..	vs. Sikh militants	..			
	1982/1988	vs. Kashmir militants	3 000–5 000			
	1967/1967	vs. ULFA	..			
	./..	vs. Naxalites, PWG	..			
		vs. People's Liberation Army	..			

Comments: In Punjab several Sikh groups are waging an armed struggle for an independent Sikh state of Khalistan. In late Dec. 1990 a new militant Sikh organization was formed, the International Liberation Tigers (ILT). The Akali leader, Simranjit Singh Mann, sought to bring various Akali and Sikh factions together in negotiations with the Central Govt. However, in Mar. it became evident that these talks would not lead to any substantial results. The same month, presidential rule over Punjab was extended for a period of 6 months. Violence in Punjab escalated prior to the general elections, which were postponed for security reasons. The deputy chief of the Khalistan Commando Force (KCF), Balwinder Singh, was killed in a shoot-out with security forces in Dec. It is estimated that *c.* 5700 people were killed in Punjab in 1991, 2000 more than in 1990. The secessionist insurgency in the Muslim majority state of Jammu and Kashmir (J&K), which erupted in early 1990, escalated during the spring and summer of 1991. In early Mar. the Jammu and Kashmir Liberation Front (JKLF), Jammu and Kashmir Student's Liberation Front (JKLSF), Hizb-ul-Mujahedeen and Dukhteranimilat reportedly sought to frame a joint strategy. However, in late Mar. clashes between Hizb-ul-Mujahideen and JKLF were reported: the Hizb-ul-Mujahedeen wants to incorporate J&K into Pakistan, while the JKLF is striving for an independent state of Kashmir, including the Azad-Kashmir province in Pakistan, and the areas occupied by China in the 1962 India–China War. In May, 73 people were killed close to the Line of Control in fighting between border forces and militants entering J&K from the Pakistani side. In May it was reported that some 3000–5000 militants were waiting on the Pakistani side to cross into J&K. Some 140 militant groups are claimed by the Govt to exist as of July 1991, amounting to *c.* 3000 men. In Oct. it was reported that 1000 militants and 290 members of the security forces had been killed during 1991. However, journalists contend that many of the killed 'militants' were in fact civilian bystanders. Over 6000 people have been killed since early 1990. In Nov. 1990 the Indian Army launched 'Operation Bajrang', involving *c.* 30 000 army personnel, in 6 districts of Upper Assam against the United Liberation Front of Assam (ULFA, formed in 1982), seeking secession from India. In Feb. 1991 the ULFA agreed to negotiate. Presidential rule over Assam imposed in late Nov. 1990 was extended for an additional 6 months in mid-Mar. 1991. 'Operation Bajrang' was called off in Apr. as a part of a truce before the May/June elections. However, in Sep. the Army resumed military operations against the ULFA which in Dec. declared a unilateral cease-fire. In mid-Jan. 1992 leaders of the

ULFA agreed to end the rebellion. In Manipur the central Govt is faced with an insurgency by the People's Liberation Army (PLA) and in Andra Pradesh, with Naxalites (People's War Group). Both conflicts were on a low level of activity during 1991.

Myanmar (formerly Burma)	1948/1949	Myanmar Govt	280 000–300 000	1948–51: 8 000
	1948/1948	vs. KNU	5 0000–20 000	1950: 5 000
	1949/1949	vs. KIA	8 000**	1981–84: 400–600 yearly
	../1991	vs. NMSP	3 000**	1985–87: >1 000 yearly
		vs. All-Burma Students Democratic Front	..	1988: 500–3 000
	../1991	vs. RSO	..	

Comments: The Burma Socialist Party (BSPP) came to power through a military coup in 1962. BSPP changed its name to the National Unity Party in 1988 after pro-democracy demonstrations, which were quelled in Aug.–Sep. with up to 3000 persons reported killed (500 according to Govt sources). A military take-over followed, and the State Law and Order Restoration Council (SLORC) seized power. The Burma Communist Party (BCP), after a mutiny in 1989, split into at least 4 groups organized along ethnic lines (see SIPRI Yearbook 1991) and some BCP troops of Kachin origin joined the Kachin Independence Army (KAI). The Govt reportedly used a new strategy, first towards the BCP but later also towards other groups dependent on the BCP for military support, offering development schemes and political concessions in exchange for pledges not to attack Govt forces and sever ties with other groups. The BCP and, subsequently, other opposition groups, i.e. Shan State Army (SSA), the 4th Brigade of KIA, the Palaung State Liberation Army as well as the Pa-O National Army (all operating in the Shan State), signed agreements with the Govt. The Govt has intensified its military operation against remaining groups along the Thai border. Reportedly only 4 major insurgent groups remain, all operating in the Kachin State along the Thai border: the main KIA, the Karen National Union (KNU), the New Moon State Party (NMSP) and the All-Burma Students Democratic Front (consisting of persons who took part in the 1988 uprising). Several clashes were reported during the the dry-season Govt offensive. Fighting over Kawmoora, one of the last KNU strongholds, took place in Jan. 1991. Heavy fighting between the combined forces of KNU and student groups and Govt troops took place in Mar.–Apr. over the town of Phaw Hta. Reportedly, the Govt used the same strategy as towards the groups in Shan Sate, offering negotiations and development schemes. In late Dec. fighting between Govt forces and the RSO (Rohingya Solidarity Organization, fighting for an independent state in the western part of Myanmar and inactive since the early 1980s) took place, spilling over into Bangladesh and causing tension between the 2 countries.

* Information on battle-related deaths has been scarce since the military take-over.
** Reported number of troops 1990. Figures for 1991 not available.

Location	Year formed/ year joined[a]	Warring parties[b]	No. of troops in 1991[c]	Deaths[d]		Change from 1990[e]
				Total (incl. 1991)	During 1991	
Sri Lanka	1976/1983	Sri Lankan Govt vs. Tamil Tigers (LTTE)	77 000 8 000	..	6 000	+

Comments: The constitution of Sri Lanka was amended in 1972, stipulating the primacy of the Sinahala and Buddhism, the language and religion of the Sinhalese majority. In 1976 the Tamil United Front (TUF) announced the goal of establishing, preferably with peaceful means, an independent state of Tamil Eelam in the northern part (predominantly Tamil) and the eastern part (where Tamils are in minority) of Sri Lanka. During the late 1970s several armed Tamil separatist organizations were created and some attacks by the LTTE (Liberation Tigers of Tamil Eelam) occurred. Regular fighting between Tamil groups, mostly LTTE (which received refuge and military training in the Indian state of Tamil Nadu), and the Govt erupted July 1983. Talks held in 1985 between the Govt and the LTTE collapsed. In July 1987 the Indo-Sri Lanka Accord was signed, stipulating e.g. the merger of the Northern and Eastern Provinces into 1 administrative unit, in which elections to a Provincial Council would be held. An Indian Peace-Keeping Force (IPKF) would be deployed to disarm Tamil groups, and Govt troops would withdraw to barracks. Several Tamil groups agreed to disarm and cease demanding a separate state, e.g. the EPRLF (Eelam People's Revolutionary Liberation Front). However, the LTTE attacked these groups. In Oct. the IPKF launched a successful offensive against the LTTE. In Mar. 1988 the LTTE offered unconditional talks. Talks started in May and continued throughout June. In early Oct. the Northern and Eastern Provinces were merged and elections to a provincial Council were held in Nov. The EPLRF won a majority of the votes. In June 1989 a permanent cease-fire was announced. In Sep. India and Sri Lanka reached an agreement on the withdrawal of the IPKF. India reportedly arranged, together with the Tamil groups which had disarmed in 1987, for the formation of a small Citizen's Voluntary Force (CVF) against the LTTE after the withdrawal of the IPKF. Later a larger force, the Auxiliary CVF, was formed, later known as the Tamil National Army (TNA), which disintegrated as the IPKF withdrew. Many members of the North-Eastern Provincial Council, fearing reprisals from the LTTE, fled to India, which caused the council more or less to cease functioning. In Dec. the LTTE formed the political party the People's Front of Liberation Tigers, saying it would contest in elections. However, the Govt conditioned elections on the LTTE disarming. In late Mar. 1990 India completed its withdrawal. The cease-fire agreed in 1989 was broken in June, reportedly by the LTTE. The fighting continued throughout 1990, with the Govt increasingly gaining control in the eastern part of the North-Eastern Province. The fighting escalated in late Mar. 1991. On 11 June the LTTE, expressing willingness to settle for a separate state within a federal Sri Lanka, offered unconditional talks. However, the Govt had presented several conditions for talks: agreement that the armed struggle be abandoned after a political solution; participation by other Tamil groups in the talks; and acknowledgement of the indivisibility of Sri Lanka. In mid-July the LTTE, using 5000 troops, attacked a heavily fortified army camp by Elephant Pass, strategically located controlling access to the northern Jaffna peninsula, leading to the biggest battle so far in the conflict. The Govt sent 8000–10 000 men as reinforcements. The LTTE had lost the battle by mid-Aug., according to observers after having lost 1000 troops. The army launched further attacks on the LTTE strongholds in early Sep., leading to heavy fighting. The LTTE offered unconditional talks monitored by the international community for early Sep. However, the army launched further offensives in late Sep. and mid-Oct., resulting in Govt control of all land routes to the Jaffna peninsula and the capture of several LTTE bases. Sri Lanka's Minister of Tourism presented a peace proposal in mid-Dec. envisaging federal autonomy for the Tamil northern parts of Sri Lanka. The proposal was not accepted by the Govt, which a few days later launched another offensive. It is estimated that over 1500 soldiers, 3500 LTTE troops and 6000 civilians were killed in June 1990–Dec. 1991.

Pacific Asia

Cambodia	1975/1979	Cambodian Govt	50 000–70 000	1979–89: >25 300*	--
	1979/1979	vs. DK (KR)	30 000–45 000	..	
	1979/1979	vs. KPNLF	10 000–15 000		
		vs. FUNCINPEC/ANS	15 000–20 000		

Comments: Border clashes between Kampuchea and Viet Nam during 1977–78 ended with a Vietnamese military intervention (Dec. 1978) which ousted Democratic Kampuchea (DK), i.e. the Khmer Rouge (KR), from power (Jan. 1979). Armed opposition to the Govt is made up of a coalition of DK, Khmer People's National Liberation Front (KPNLF) and Front Uni National pour un Cambodge Indépendant, Neutre, Pacific et Coopératif/Armée Nationale Sihanoukiste (FUNCINPEC/ANS), forming the Coalition Government of Democratic Kampuchea (CGDK) in 1982, which changed its name to the National Government of Cambodia (NGC) in Feb. 1990. The 5 permanent members of the UNSC agreed on a 'peace plan' for Cambodia in Aug. 1990. The plan, which e.g. include a cease-fire, disarmament, UN administration of Cambodia during an interim period and the formation of a Supreme National Council (SNC) to represent Cambodia in the UN, was accepted in Sep. 1990 by the 4 Cambodian parties as a framework for a comprehensive solution to the Cambodian conflict. In Nov. the UNSC presented a new 'peace plan' which would give the UN more influence over Cambodian administration during the interim period. Most military activities in 1991 took place during Jan.–Apr. A cease-fire was enforced in early May, although violations were reported. The dialogue was deadlocked during the first 5 months of 1991 due to divergent views on the Nov. plan: the Govt demanded revisions of the plan, whereas the NGC insisted on it being implemented without alteration. A meeting was held in Pattaya in June. At preparatory discussions the 4 Cambodian parties agreed on an unconditional and indefinite cease-fire as well as on 3 other issues: the NGC and the Govt were to be preserved and continue to function in the zones which they controlled pending general elections to be held; the SNC would set up its headquarters in Phnom Penh and represent the Cambodian State at the UN; and the Cambodian parties would stop receiving foreign military assistance. At a meeting of the SNC in Beijing (July), Prince Sihanouk resigned as leader of the NGC and officially became the chairman of the SNC. It was decided that the SNC would begin to function normally in Phnom Penh in Nov. 1991.

Furthermore, the SNC requested the Secretary-General to determine the number of UN personnel needed to monitor the cease-fire and the cessation of foreign military assistance. The SNC held a further meeting in Pattaya in late Aug. which resulted in an agreement to cut military forces by 70%: the remaining troops would hand over their weapons to UN supervisors and enter cantonments. According to Prince Sihanouk, the demobilization and handing over of weapons would begin at the arrival of the planned UN Transitional Authority in Cambodia (UNTAC). The Cambodian parties did not initially reach an agreement regarding the mode for conducting general elections in the country: the Govt wanted a system based on majority elections in each constituency for representation in the National Assembly, whereas the NGC wanted proportional representation. The question of the electoral system was solved in Sep. when a proportional system within each of the provinces of Cambodia but not at the national level was agreed upon. The UNSC unanimously adopted Resolution 717 on 15 Oct., deciding to create a UN Advance Mission in Cambodia (UNAMIC) to be dispatched after a peace agreement. The Paris Conference on Cambodia (arranged in Aug. 1989) was reconvened and a 'peace agreement' was signed on 23 Oct. In mid-Nov. Prince Sihanouk returned to Cambodia as chairman of the SNC. The first meeting of the SNC in Phnom Penh opened on 30 Dec.

* For figures for battle-related deaths in this conflict before 1979, see *SIPRI Yearbook 1990*, page 405, and note *p*, page 418. Regarding battle-related deaths during 1979–89, the only figure available is from official Vietnamese sources, indicating that 25 300 Vietnamese soldiers died in Cambodia. An estimated figure for the period 1979–89, based on various sources, is >50 000, and for 1989, >1000.

Location	Year formed/ year joined[a]	Warring parties[b]	No. of troops in 1991[c]	Deaths[d] Total (incl. 1991)	During 1991	Change from 1990[e]
Indonesia	1975/1975	Indonesian Govt	278 000	1975–91: 16 500– 17 500 (mil.)*	..	– –
	1977/1989	*vs.* Fretelin	200–400			
	.. /1984	*vs.* Aceh Merdeka	100			
		vs. OPM	100			

Comments: As a part of the dissolution of the Portuguese colonial empire, East Timor was to be granted independence. The Revolutionary Front for an Independent East Timor (Fretelin) proclaimed the independent state of the Democratic Republic of East Timor in Nov. 1975. Indonesia invaded the following month and annexed the area in 1976. Fretelin put up armed resistance through its military wing, FALANTIL (Armed Forces for the Liberation of East Timor), but by late 1978 most armed resistance had been quelled. Negotiations took place but were broken off in 1983, and low-level warfare has continued since the mid-1980s. In late 1990 Indonesia launched a military operation aiming at eliminating the remaining armed forces of Fretelin. The military operations were called off in May 1991 by the Govt, claiming the strength of Fretelin to be around 200 and no longer posing a military threat. The issue of East Timor was brought to international attention in early Nov. following the killing by Indonesian forces of at least 50 civilians participating in a funeral. There were reports of intensified fighting between the Army and Fretelin in Nov. The UN General Assembly has continued to regard Portugal as the administrative power. Aceh, the northern tip of Sumatra, gained a special province status in 1959 following a 6-year-long uprising. In 1977 Aceh Merdeka (also known as the Free Aceh Movement, Gerakan Aceh Merdeka, or National Liberation Front of Aceh) was formed and staged an armed uprising which was quickly suppressed by the Govt. In 1989 the movement re-emerged, leading to some fighting, with escalation in 1990. The armed opposition was by mid-1991 seen to be suppressed. Summary executions of rebels were reported during the first half of 1991. Fighting continued at a low level during the second half of 1991. A total of 1500 people are estimated at least 2300 killed, of whom one-third were civilians. Aceh Merdeka demands independence for the province and in particular attacks the transmigration policy of the Govt. Attacks on Javanese immigrants are reported. The Free Papua Movement (OPM, Organisasi Papua Merdeka) was created in the mid-1960s with the aim of resisting the incorporation of the Dutch colony of West Irian into Indonesia. After a period of inactivity, the OPM re-emerged in the 1980s. In 1990 an OPM attack, possibly launched from Papua New Guinea, led to a large-scale incursion by the Indonesian Army into Papua New Guinea. Since then Papua New Guinea has co-operated with Indonesia against the OPM, resulting in OPM attacks in Papua New Guinea. During 1991 very little was reported but some low-level armed activity evidently continued. An issue in this conflict, as in other conflicts in Indonesia, is the transmigration policy, leading to an influx of people from other parts of Indonesia.

Editor's note: The reported figures for people are estimated. Reuter news agency gave the figure of at least 1500 people are estimated.

* 15 000–16 000 of these refer to the East Timor conflict.

| Philippines | 1968/1986 | Philippine Govt vs. NPA | 106 500 16 000 | 1972–91: >38 500 | 1 200 | ++ |

Comments: The conflict between the Govt and the New People's Army (NPA), connected to the Communist Party of the Philippines (CPP) has concerned land distribution and political power. In 1986–87 the Govt and the NPA entered short-lived talks. In 1990 and 1991 there were reports of severe divisions of opinion on armed strategies within the NPA, e.g. between those preferring an urban strategy and those preferring a people's war. In Feb.–Apr. 1991 fighting took place, particularly in the north, reportedly leading to the death of over 560 soldiers. The fighting seems to be part of the Aquino Govt commitment to end the rebellion before the elections of 1992. In May 1991 the Govt initiated a new offensive north of Manila. In June a cease-fire was declared in areas affected by the eruptions of Mount Pinatubo. In July and Aug. several top NPA leaders were captured by the Army and the Police. In Sep. a temporary cease-fire was announced by the NPA following the Philippine Senate decision to reject renewal of the US base lease. However, new fighting was reported by the end of Sep. A special feature is the local cease-fires (in the Negros, Quezon and Laguna areas) which were negotiated between the Army, the NPA and non-governmental organizations.

| Location | Year formed/ year joined[a] | Warring parties[b] | No. of troops in 1991[c] | Deaths[d] | | Change from 1990[e] |
				Total (incl. 1991)	During 1991	
Africa						
Angola	1975/1975 1975/1975	Angolan Govt vs. UNITA vs. FLEC	100 000 60 000 ..	1975–91: 100 000*	..	..

Comments: The Angolan Govt (MPLA–PT, Popular Liberation Movement of Angola–Worker's Party) faced armed opposition by UNITA (National Union for the Total Independence of Angola) until 31 May 1991. The conflict was formed in 1975, when the power-sharing agreement between 3 liberation movements (MPLA, UNITA and FNLA, Angolan National Liberation Front) collapsed. The Govt received military aid from the USSR (equipment) and Cuba (personnel); UNITA from S. Africa, the USA and Zaire (supply routes). S. African forces fought alongside UNITA, much of the time up to mid-1988. In Dec. 1988 Cuba, Angola and S. Africa agreed on S. African troop withdrawal from Angola, an end to S. African support for UNITA and Cuban withdrawal from Angola (to be monitored by a UN Angola Verification Mission, UNAVEM). After several military offensives by both parties, especially during early 1990, an agreement was reached to hold direct talks. At the fourth round of talks in Sep. 1990, US and Soviet observers participated alongside Portuguese mediators. An agreement on monitoring procedures for an eventual cease-fire was reached. In Jan. 1991 Portugal, the USA and the USSR outlined the framework of a peace plan, which was broadly approved by the Govt and UNITA. Negotiations in Portugal followed during Mar.–Apr., accompanied by fierce fighting. UNITA sought to take a province capital in central Angola and, after a failed attempt to take Kuito, Bié Province, UNITA amassed 7000 men around Luena, Moxico Province. Heavy artillery bombardment took place throughout Apr. On 1 May a Principle Agreement of Peace was signed, stipulating a cease-fire on 15 May and a formal peace accord at the end of the month. The Cuban troop withdrawal was completed late May. On 31 May the Bicesse Peace Accord was signed, stipulating a complete cease-fire, the creation of a unified defence force, and the holding of multi-party elections in the autumn of 1992. The task of overseeing the political and cease-fire process was given to a Joint Politico-Military Commission (CCPM), including various sub-groups, members of the Govt, UNITA, and representatives of Portugal, the USA and the USSR. A UN verification operation (UNAVEM-2, the Second UN Angola Verification Mission) will be deployed until 31 Oct. 1992. The re-grouping of more than 150 000 troops from the 2 armies at assembly points was slow and, according to a UN official, in late Oct. threatened to delay the creation of a unified army and the general elections. UN sources reported mid-Dec. that about 65% of Govt and UNITA troops were by then confined to assembly points. Another problem concerned the release of captured troops. 10–20% of all captured troops had been released in time for the deadline of 1 Aug. The situation improved after the Govt decided to unilaterally release all its captured troops in late Oct. Despite these problems and sporadic fighting, the cease-fire held throughout 1991. A minor conflict in Angola concerns the oil-rich Cabinda enclave. FLEC (Front for the Liberation of the Enclave of Cabinda) was formed in 1963 and later split into 5 groups, the most dominant of which is FLEC-R (Removado), supported by right-wing organizations. The Govt and UNITA are opposed to independence. The Govt agreed in Oct. to negotiate autonomy and a greater share of oil revenues for Cabinda. In Nov. the Govt asked the Portuguese Govt for assistance in negotiating a resolution to the conflict.

* Total battle deaths, of which 1/3 mil. and 2/3 civ.; total war casualties, including indirect deaths, estimated at 300 000–500 000.

Chad	1989/1989	Chad Govt vs. Forces of Habre	17 200 3 000	..	200	– –

Comments: Chad has been the location of conflicts between numerous factions in changing alliances since the mid-1960s. Hissene Habre siezed de facto power in 1982 and became Pres. the same year. In Apr. 1989 Idriss Deby fled to Sudan after a failed coup attempt. He formed Revolutionary Forces of April 1, joined MOSANAT (Mouvement pour la Salvation Nationale Tchadienne; Movement for the Salvation of Chad) in 1989 and later formed MPS (Mouvement Patriotique du Salut: Patriotic Salvation Movement). Fighting in 1990 resulted in Deby, with support from Islamic Legion, seizing power in Dec. (see SIPRI Yearbook 1991). Habre was granted aylum in Senegal. The conflict reemerged in Sep. and Oct. 1991 as forces reportedly loyal to former Pres. Habre mounted attacks, resulting in almost 100 persons killed. A more serious attack was launched on 31 Dec., involving 3000 men. The attack was reportedly subdued after three days fighting, with, according to the Govt, 425 rebels killed. Another source claimed the number of persons killed as over 100.

Ethiopia	1972/1972 1974/1975 1975/1989 1975/1975 1977/1977	Ethiopian Govt vs. EPLF vs. EPRP vs. EPRDF vs. ALF vs. OLF	300 000–400 000 60 000 .. 65 000 .. 7 000	1962–91: 150 000– 200 000 (mil.)	20 000– 30 000 (mil.)	+ +

Comments: In a UN decision of 1952, a union was created between Eritrea and Ethiopia. In 1961 Eritrea was made a province of Ethiopia. The main guerrilla movement fighting for Eritrea's independence since the 1970s has been the EPLF (Eritrean People's Liberation Front). Attempts at peaceful solutions were tried, particularly in the mid-1970s and the latter part of the 1980s. During this time the EPLF gained territorial control over parts of Eritrea. In 1990 the EPLF increased territorial control, including, for the first time, a major harbour (Massawa). Attempts at negotiations, for instance led by former US Pres. Jimmy Carter (1989) and US envoy Herman Cohen (Feb. 1991), did not produce results. Earlier negotiations had broken down over the question of UN participation.

Location	Year formed/ year joined[a]	Warring parties[b]	No. of troops in 1991[c]	Deaths[d] Total (incl. 1991)	During 1991	Change from 1990[e]

In Feb. 1991 this issue was settled, but another issue, the EPLF's demand for a referendum on the status of Eritrea, proved problematic. In late Feb. the EPLF launched a new offensive, in co-ordination with the EPRDF (see below). In Mar. and Apr. an additional harbour town was captured by the EPLF, and Asmara, the capital of Eritrea, and Assab, Ethiopia's major port, were sealed off. The TPLF (Tigray People's Liberation Front), in conflict with the Govt since 1975, demanded a change of Govt and was willing to give Eritrea the right to secede. In 1989 the TPLF and the EPDM (Ethiopian People's Democratic Movement) merged as the EPRDF (Ethiopian People's Revolutionary Democratic Front). The first attempts at public negotiations between the Govt and the EPRDF were made in 1990. An offensive was launched late Feb. 1991, quickly resulting in the EPRDF gaining control over the provinces of Gojjam and Gondar by Mar., and the capture of Nekemte, capital of the Wollega province, in Apr. In late Apr.–early May fighting took place around Ambo, c. 100 km from Addis Ababa. The Ethiopian Govt ordered further mobilization and proposed a cease-fire and the formation of a Govt of national unity. Peace talks were scheduled for London, led by US envoy H. Cohen. Before they took place, the head of the Ethiopian Govt, Mengistu Haile Mariam, facing a military defeat, fled the country on 21 May. Effective resistance from the Ethiopian armed forces ceased, and Asmara and Assab were captured by the EPLF. In early June, the EPRDF established control in the rest of the country, except Eritrea which was under the control of the EPLF with its own provisional Govt headed by Isaias Afewerki, the EPLF leader. An interim Govt of Ethiopia was created, headed by the EPRDF leader Meles Zenawi. During these conflicts other armed opposition groups emerged, most important being the OLF, the Oromo Liberation Front, demanding the creation of an independent state of Oromia, militarily active in the Western parts of the country. Its significance was primarily political, the Oromos being the largest ethnic group in the country. Another Oromo organization, the OPDO (Oromo People's Democratic Organization), had joined closely with the EPRDF and the EPLF. An Afar movement, AFL (Afar Liberation Front), had also been formed. The EPRP (Ethiopia's People's Revolutionary Party, a Marxist organization active in the mid-1970s) showed some activity and in May clashes with the EPRDF were reported. However, in early July a Charter for Ethiopia's development was agreed upon at a National Conference on Peace and Democracy, involving most of the armed opposition groups active during the Mengistu era. The Charter outlined the future of Ethiopia, including the right of Eritrea to vote on its independence, and Assab was made a free port for Ethiopia. In Aug. and Sep. local clashes were reported between the EPRDF and the OLF, but resolution attempts were quickly undertaken from both sides. In Eritrea, in June, July and Sep., attacks occurred along the road from Assab to Addis Ababa, allegedly carried out by Afars opposed to the EPLF. In Oct. fighting occurred between EPRDF forces and groups of the Issa and Gugura Liberation Front in Dire Dawa and along railway lines. There were also clashes between Oromo and Amahara in Dire Dawa (Nov.).

| Liberia | 1991/1991 | RUF, | .. | 10 000–13 000 | | – – |
| | 1989/1989 | NPLF, | 7 000 | | .. | |

1989/1990	Burkina Faso Govt	500
1991/1991	LUDF,	1 200
1991/1991	ULIMO,	..
1991/1991	MOJA	..
1990/1990	INPLF	..
1990/1990	ECOMOG	7 000
1989/1989	AFL	..
1991/1991	Forces of Kromah	..

Comments: In late Dec. 1989 the National Patriotic Forces of Liberia (NPFL), led by Charles Taylor, crossed into Liberia to topple Pres. Samuel Doe. The NPFL and its adversary the Independent NPFL (INPFL), formed by an NPFL commander (Prince Johnson) who had parted with the NPFL in Feb.–Mar. 1990, controlled two-thirds of Liberia by late May. By early July heavy fighting reached the capital, Monrovia. A peace formula by ECOWAS (Economic Community of West African States), which included the sending of a peace-keeping force to establish a cease-fire, an interim Govt and preparations for free elections, was rejected by the NPFL. Taylor proclaimed himself Pres. in late July. An ECOWAS peace-keeping force ECOMOG (ECOWAS Monitoring Group) arrived late Aug. The NPFL immediately attacked ECOMOG, while Burkina Faso reportedly sent troops in support of the NPFL. At an ECOWAS meeting on 30 Aug. Amos Sawyer was declared head of an interim Govt until elections, due in Oct. 1991. Pres. Doe was captured by the INPFL on 9 Sep. The same day Johnson proclaimed himself Pres., while forces loyal to Doe, the AFL (Armed Forces of Liberia, the Liberian Army) appointed Gen. David Nimley as constitutional successor. Doe was killed by the INPFL the following day. On 1 Oct. ECOMOG, alongside INPFL and AFL, launched an offensive, forcing the NPFL to retreat. In late Nov. the NPFL agreed to a cease-fire. On 21 Dec. the parties agreed to work for the establishment of an interim Govt. In mid-Jan. 1991 the INPFL and the NPFL announced that they would co-operate and demanded the resignation of the interim Govt. Talks in Nigeria a few days later between the INPFL, NPFL and AFL resulted in agreements on the creation of buffer zones, halt of imports of arms and the release of prisoners and hostages. However, the NPFL refused to sign an agreement on the confinement and disarmament of troops. Two days of talks in Togo mid-Feb., convened by the ECOWAS mediation committee, resulted in an agreement on the monitoring of cease-fire and the confinement and disarmament of troops under ECOMOG supervision after the holding of a national conference 'with a view to establishing an interim Govt', planned to take place in Mar. The conference, held in Liberia between mid-Mar. and mid-Apr. and attended by the 3 factions and e.g. Liberian political parties, failed to produce any significant results: Sawyer was re-elected as Pres., the INPFL received a chair as Vice Pres., while the second chair of Vice Pres. was reserved for the NPFL. The NPFL, who walked out on 27 Mar., had criticized the composition of the conference: the NPFL demanded the inclusion of representatives from Liberia's 13 counties, of which 12 were under their control, and that only the warring parties should be included in the talks. A few days later forces from the NPFL and, reportedly, the RUF (Revolutionary United Front, consisting of Sierra Leonean dissidents) attacked Sierra Leone, a member of ECOMOG. Amid intense fighting, Nigeria and

Location	Year formed/ year joined[a]	Warring parties[b]	No. of troops in 1991[c]	Deaths[d] Total (incl. 1991)	During 1991	Change from 1990[e]
		Guinea sent troops to Sierra Leone in late Apr. There were also reports that a group calling itself the LUDF (Liberian United Defence Force, consisting of irregulars from former President Doe's ethnic group) joined the fighting in Sierra Leone against the NPFL. By mid-May the forces (estimated at 1000) from the NPFL and the RUF were reported to have penetrated up to 100 miles (160 km) inside Sierra Leone. In late May the LUDF combined forces with ULIMO (United Liberation Movement of Liberia for Democracy) consisting of different Liberian groups and reportedly enjoyed support from a Libya-trained group called MOJA (Movement for Justice in Africa). On 21 June the NPFL and the RUF lost the Sierra Leonean city of Pjehen, one of their main bases. The Govt described the fighting as over by Nov., although further fighting took place in early Dec. The fighting in Liberia was reported as sporadic in Mar., late May and much of June. The NPFL and Sawyer met for talks in late June in Yamaoussoukru, Ivory Coast. The talks resulted in an agreement to confine and disarm troops of all Liberian groups and to hold elections within 6 months. However, it was reported that the NPFL as well as the INPFL had not disarmed during July and Aug. In mid-Aug. the INPFL withdrew from the Govt, accusing it of economic mismanagement and protesting against appointments to top posts. The INPFL simultaneously expressed willingness for a dialogue with the AFL and the NPFL 'to settle differences'. Talks mid-Sep. in Yamoussoukro, with members of ECOWAS, the NPFL and Pres. Sawyer resulted in the NPFL agreeing to disarm and confine troops to designated areas under the supervision of a restructured ECOMOG force. It was also agreed to establish an electoral commission for the organization and supervision of elections. However, ULIMO, which had attacked the NPFL early Sep., rejected the agreement. The NPFL had also been attacked by forces of Alhaji Kromah (former Pres. Doe's Minister of Information) from Guinean territory early Sep. A further meeting in Yamoussoukro in late Oct. resulted in the NPFL agreeing to surrender control of territory to ECOMOG and disarm within 60 days from 15 Nov. It was also agreed that elections would be held within 6 months. The INPFL rejoined the Govt in early Nov., and in mid-Nov. ULIMO pledged willingness to confine and disarm its troops. By mid-Jan. 1992 none of the warring parties had disarmed.			
Morocco/ Western Sahara	1975/1976	Moroccan Govt *vs.* Polisario	195 500 4 000	10 000–13 000	. .	. .

Comments: Western Sahara became a Spanish protectorate in 1884 and a Spanish province in 1958. In 1974 Spain indicated willingness to hold a referendum in 1975 under UN supervision to enable the inhabitants to decide the future of the area. The proposal was opposed by Morocco and Mauritania, claiming the northern and southern parts of the territory, respectively. In Nov. 1975 the Madrid Agreement was signed by Spain, Morocco and Mauritania, stipulating a joint provisional administration of Western Sahara until Spain's final withdrawal in late Feb. 1976. Polisario (People's Front for the Liberation of Saguiet El Hamra and Rio Oro) was formed in 1973 with an independent state as goal. On 27 Feb. 1976, a day after Spain's completed withdrawal, Polisario proclaimed the independent Sahara Arab Democratic Republic (SADR) and a Govt-in-exile was formed. In Aug. 1979, after fighting with Polisario, Mauritania renounced all territorial claims to Western Sahara. By early 1980, 36 countries had recognized the SADR and the same year the UN General Assembly called on Morocco to end its occupation of Western Sahara. In 1981 Morocco agreed to a referendum according to OAU recommendations to be carried out under the auspices of an OAU/UN peace-keeping force but the conditions of the referendum were never agreed upon by Polisario and Morocco. By late 1980, when Morocco only controlled the northern twelfth of Western Sahara, an effort to build a defended 'wall' of sand was initiated. This strategy had by Apr. 1987 left c. 90% of Western Sahara under Moroccan control. After separate talks with the UN Secretary-General and an OAU special envoy, in late Aug. 1988 Polisario and Morocco accepted (with some reservations) settlement proposals (including a cease-fire to be followed by a referendum under UN monitoring, offering West Saharans a choice between independence and integration with Morocco). The first direct talks took place in Jan. 1989. Calls in Apr. and May by Polisario for the resumption of talks were rejected by Morocco. In June 1990, tribal leaders met in Geneva under UN auspices to set out details for the referendum and validate electoral lists, reaching consensus to use a Spanish census from 1974 as a starting-point to determine voter eligibility. In late June the UNSC approved the full text of the preliminary plans to establish a UN Mission for the Referendum in Western Sahara (MINURSO). According to the plan (further detailed and authorized by the UNSC in late Apr. 1991) a cease-fire would come into effect, monitored by MINURSO (2800 personnel strong), after which a transitional period (lasting 20 weeks) towards the referendum (scheduled for 26 Jan. 1992) would begin. During the transitional period, Morocco would undertake troop reductions and the parties would be confined to locations monitored by MINURSO. All captured troops would be released and the administration during the transitional period as well as the referendum would be monitored and conducted by the UN. Polisario and Morocco agreed on 28 June to lay down arms from 6 Sep., but in early Aug., just a week before the planned arrival of the first MINURSO personnel, fighting erupted, reportedly initiated by Morocco. Morocco refused to let MINURSO into Western Sahara and on 21 Aug. called for postponement of the referendum, claiming that the UN had 'not adhered to the agreed terms' and demanded expansion of the list of eligible voters from 74 000 to c. 200 000 persons. The fighting, which was the first serious combat since late 1989, ended early Sep. By early Sep. fewer than 300 of the MINURSO personnel had arrived. The referendum was postponed in late Dec. after disagreement on the list of eligible voters.

Mozambique	Mozambican Govt,	36 000	10 000–12 000 (mil.)
	Zimbabwe Govt,	6 000	110 000 (civ.)
1975/1976	vs. Renamo	10 000–20 000	

Comments: Renamo (or Mozambican National Resistance, MNR), originally created by Rhodesia as a strike force against ZANU (Zimbabwe African National Union) guerrillas based in Mozambique, was inherited by the S. African Defence Force (SADF) on Zimbabwean independence. Large-scale military destabilization of Mozambique began in 1981. Renamo still receives clandestine material support and military training in bases inside S. Africa and is supported from Kenyan and Malawian territory. Money and material support arrive from non-Govt organizations (e.g. right-wing and/or religious organizations) and individuals. Renamo's main recruitment method is press-ganging youths captured in attacks. Military co-operation has taken place between the Govt and Zimbabwe since 1985, and many Western governments grant military aid to the Govt. Other military units include the Napramas (spiritualist peasant militia groups fighting both Renamo and Govt) and Unamo (a Renamo defector force fighting both Renamo and Govt). Renamo concentrates on non-military targets such as civilians, production units and bridges. In the 1984 Nkomati Non-Aggression Accord between the Govt and S. Africa, the latter promised to terminate its involvement with Renamo. Preliminary mediation efforts were initiated in Aug. 1988. The first direct talks were held in Rome in July 1990. At the 3rd round of talks in Rome Nov.–Dec. 1990 a partial cease-fire in 2 transport corridors was agreed and implemented on 15 Dec. The agreement also stipulated a reduction of Zimbabwean troops by about half and confined them to the corridors. A 46-member strong Joint Verification Committee (JVC) to monitor the cease-fire was constituted at the 4th round of talks in Dec. 1990.* The Zimbabwean troop reduction was completed by late Dec. About 30 violations of the cease-fire were reported Jan.–Mar. 1991, the vast majority ascribed to Renamo by the JVC. The 5th round of talks was blocked by Renamo in late Jan., accusing the Govt of having Zimbabwean troops stationed outside the corridors. However, the JVC found no evidence of this. In Feb. 1991 Renamo resumed attacks in the 2 corridors. The 6th round of talks took place in May. An agenda for negotiations was agreed upon. The 7th round started but broke down in early Aug., as Renamo introduced new demands. In the 8th round of talks in Oct.–Nov., a Protocol on Fundamental Principles was signed where Renamo recognized the legitimacy of the Govt during a transition period between a formal cease-fire and elections, thus dropping an earlier demand that the UN take over 5 key ministries during this period. The Govt committed itself not to pass laws on items relevant for the agenda. The Protocol confirmed the May agenda and cleared the ground for a general peace accord, once a protocol is negotiated for each agenda item. On 13 Nov. a second Protocol, dealing with criteria for and registration of political parties, was signed. The 9th round of talks began on 18 Dec. On 20 Dec. a joint communiqué was issued, confirming consensus on simultaneous presidential and parliamentary elections supervised by the UN and the OAU to be held within a year of the signing of a general peace agreement. The 9th round was scheduled to resume on 15 Jan. 1992. Renamo military activities were evenly distributed throughout 1991 and covered all 10 provinces.

* The JVC consists of members of the Govt, Renamo and 10 countries: Italy (chair), Congo, France, Kenya, Portugal, the UK, the USA, the USSR, Zambia and Zimbabwe.

Location	Year formed/ year joined[a]	Warring parties[b]	No. of troops in 1991[c]	Deaths[d] Total (incl. 1991)	During 1991	Change from 1990[e]
Rwanda	1987/1990	Rwandan Govt, vs. RPF/A	5 200	..	..	n.a.

Comments: The area that forms present Rwanda has a history of societal stratification on ethnic lines with the Hutu ethnic group (in 1991, *c.* 86% of the population) dominating the Twa ethnic group (*c.* 1% of the population) until the 17th century, when the Tutsi ethnic group (*c.* 12% of the population) became dominant. This system of societal stratification was kept during the colonial era. In 1959 Rwanda's first 2 political parties were formed: the predominantly Tutsi UNAR (Union National Rwandaise) and the all-Hutu PARMEHUTU (Parti du Mouvement de l'Emancipation Hutu). Local elections held in mid-1960 resulted in victory for PARMEHUTU, whose leader was given the task of forming a new Govt. In 1962 Rwanda became formally independent. Militant members of UNAR, calling themselves Inyenzi ('Cockroaches'), had initiated armed struggle in 1961. Attacks led to large-scale reprisal killings of Tutsis, causing flows of refugees to neighbouring countries. In 1966 Inyenzi ceased its activity, having launched 10 major attacks. In 1980 the Govt initiated a policy of 'regional equilibrium' and 'ethnic balance', where allocation of social and economic opportunities was based on ethnicity and region of origin. One of the countries that had received refugees from Rwanda is Uganda. Talks between Uganda and Rwanda (Rwanda had resisted repatriation of refugees) on repatriation of refugees began in 1988 and led to an agreement in 1989 that UNHCR (United Nations High Commissioner for Refugees) would survey the exiles to determine if they desired to return to Rwanda. The survey was to begin in Oct. 1990. The Rwandan Alliance for National Unity (RANU) changed its name to the Rwandan Patriotic Front (RPF) in 1987 which presented a programme, e.g. calling for democracy in Rwanda, national union and repatriation of refugees. On 1 Oct. 1990 the RPF (a predominantly Tutsi organization), with its armed wing the RPA (Rwandan Patriotic Army), invaded Rwanda from Ugandan territory with the confessed goals of establishing democracy, ending corruption and the unconditional return of refugees. However, the Govt accused RPF/A of aiming to reinstate Tutsi dominance and Uganda of e.g. supplying the RPA (the invasion force was to a large extent comprised of deserters from the Ugandan National Army). The RPF/A had by 3 Oct. managed to penetrate *c.* 75 km into Rwanda. On 5 Oct. the Govt offered unconditional peace talks and on 5–7 Oct. Zaire sent troops to aid the Govt. On 16 Oct. it was reported that the Govt had agreed to a cease-fire to be followed by negotiations on refugees. The offer was rejected by the RPF/A, demanding e.g. the resignation of Rwanda's Pres. Habyarimana. On 17 Oct. the Govt agreed to a unconditional cease-fire to be monitored by an intervention force followed by talks with the RPF/A, promised 'political dialogue' and 'accepted in principle' the repatriation of refugees. The same day Zaire announced withdrawal of its troops from Rwanda. On 22 Oct. it was reported that the RPF/A had accepted the cease-fire. The same day, however, the Govt issued demands that the RPF/A also must lay down arms and withdraw before talks can be held. The demands were rejected by the RPF/A. Following a meeting in Gbadolite (Zaire) on 26 Oct. between the Presidents of Zaire, Rwanda, Burundi and Uganda, the Presidents reiterated support for the 17 Oct. agreement, decided to set up a cease-fire monitoring force with participants from the RPF/A and appointed Zaire's President Mobuto as mediator. The RPF/A, having suffered military set-backs, had by early Nov. been dispersed/regrouped in smaller units. Meetings between the leaders of Zaire, Rwanda and Uganda during Nov. were followed by further talks in Zaire on 22 Nov. It was agreed that President Mobuto would continue as mediator, take steps towards a regional refugee conference and give specific directives to military observers. The fighting intensified periodically in mid- and late Dec. In late Dec. Pres. Habyarimana announced that the multi-party system would be based on a referendum to be held before mid-June 1991. In 1991 there was continued, although mostly rather sporadic, fighting in the border areas of Uganda and Rwanda. Talks in Tanzania in mid-Feb. sponsored by its President between the Presidents of Uganda and Rwanda resulted in a unilateral cease-fire, which was not respected by the RPF/A. A regional conference on Rwandan refugees was held 2 days later in Tanzania. It was agreed that refugees would be allowed to return or be granted citizenship in the countries they resided in. The OAU and UNHCR were requested to draw up plans to implement the decision. A draft cease-fire agreement was signed on 18 Mar., due to enter into force on 23 Mar., to be followed by a general amnesty and direct talks. The cease-fire was signed on 29 Mar. and was to be monitored by neutral military observers. The cease-fire was broken the next day. On 10 June a multi-party constitution was adopted. No timetable was set for elections. The RPF/A rejected the constitutional changes as diversion: the parties were only allowed to operate under the patronage and guidance of the current ruling party. An early Sep. meeting in Zaire under the aegis of the OAU between Rwanda, Burundi, Zaire, Uganda, Nigeria led to the restructuring of the cease-fire monitoring group under Nigerian and Zairean officers, placed under direct OAU supervision. The first direct talks ended (after 3 days) on 17 Sep. in Zaire, with the 2 parties 'expressing commitment' to the cease-fire agreement of 29 Mar.

Location	Year formed/ year joined[a]	Warring parties[b]	No. of troops in 1991[c]	Deaths[d] Total (incl. 1991)	Deaths[d] During 1991	Change from 1990[e]
Somalia		Somalian (Barre) Govt	30 000	1988–91: 60 000 (civ. and mil.)	10 000–25 000	++
	1981/1981	SNM	5 000–10 000			
	1989/1989	SPM	5 000–10 000			
	1979/1991	SSDF	..			
	1989/1990	USC (Madhi)	..			
	1991/1991	USC (Aidid)	..			

Comments: The Somali National Movement (SNM, drawn largely from the Isaaq clan) in the north of Somalia began armed struggle in 1981 against the Govt of Pres. Siad Barre. In 1988 the conflict escalated as the SNM attempted to create military bases inside Somalia in order to replace bases held on Ethiopian territory, which, following an agreement between Ethiopia and Somalia, were to be dismantled. Emerging from a military mutiny in the south in 1989 the Somali Patriotic Movement (SPM, drawn from the Ogadeen clan) became an important armed opposition group. A third armed opposition group was formed in 1990, the United Somalia Congress (USC, drawn from the Hawiye clan). In Aug. 1990 the 3 groups began to co-operate. In late Dec. 1990 fighting in the capital Mogadishu, with USC forces gradually gaining control resulted in an estimated 5000–10 000 people killed. On 26 Jan. 1991, facing a military defeat, Pres. Barre left the capital and established a HQ in the south from which he was militarily active during the rest of the year. He formed the Somalia National Front (SNF), but reportedly later split with this organization. USC leader Ali Madhi Mohamed was declared interim Pres. of Somalia by a faction within the USC, but was not accepted by the other faction, the SPM or the SNM. In Feb. 1991 the SNM gained control over northern Somalia and demanded the revision of the Union Act of 1960 which joined British Somalia with the rest of the country. Fighting between the SPM combined with the Somali Salvation Democratic Front (SSDF) against USC forces was reported in Mar. There were also reports of fighting between USC factions. Talks in Apr. resulted in a cease-fire. Also in Apr., the SNM established a Govt in Northern Somalia and on 16 May unilaterally declared the independent Somaliland Republic (corresponding in area to the former British Somaliland), headed by the leader of the SNM, Ahmed Ali. The declaration was rejected by the interim Govt and other groups. Nevertheless a Govt was formed in June and in Nov. elections were announced for 1993. In July a conference was arranged in neighbouring Djibouti, with participation of all parties opposing Barre, except the SNM. Ali Madhi was confirmed as interim Pres. for 2 years on 18 Aug. In fighting in Sep. between the President and opponents, 500 people were killed. In Oct an Ethiopian–Eritrean delegation attempted to mediate between the factions. The fighting intensified in Nov. in Mogadishu between forces loyal to the interim President and those of Farrah Aidid, heading a faction of the USC and also a member of the Hawiiye clan. Aidid claimed to have replaced Ali Madhi and to control some 7000 USC soldiers. The fighting continued throughout 1991, resulting in at least 4000 deaths.

South Africa	South African Govt vs. ANC	1948/1961	158 700* 6 000–10 000	1984–91: 11 000**	2 600**	–

Comment: The declared overall goal of the African National Congress (ANC) since its foundation in 1912 is the creation of a non-racial, democratic and unitary S. Africa. The ANC declared armed struggle in 1961. Since then ANC's declared strategy rested on 4 pillars: mass organization and mobilization, underground activities (after 1960 Govt ban), armed struggle (at a low scale) and international support. In connection with the 'talks about negotiations' process under way since 1990, the ANC suspended the armed struggle in Aug. 1990. The Govt tried to isolate the ANC and co-opt parts of the black majority into a process of what was called 'constitutional reform'. This failed, and the Govt now openly recognizes that credible negotiations are impossible unless organizations representative of the majority are involved. In the first part of 1990 events indicated that the Govt followed a dual agenda of negotiation and violence. First, the unfolding of the 'Inkhata-gate' scandal, revealing secret Govt and Police funding for Zulu Chief Buthelezi's Natal-based Inkhata movement and other anti-ANC groups. This led to additional revelations about security forces co-operating with Inkhata. Second, evidence was presented by several 'defectors' from within the security forces. A former major in the SADF (South African Defence Forces) military intelligence claimed that current Govt and SADF strategy centred on securing white influence in a post-apartheid S. Africa. He also claimed that the violence instigated by the security forces aimed to weaken the morale and organizational capacity of the ANC; boost Inkhata; and split blacks along tribal lines. The South African Institute for Race Relations (SAIRR) claimed 3699 killed in political violence during 1990. The SAIRR estimate for 1991 was just over 2500. Research by CASE (Community Agency for Social Inquiry) into township violence in the Reef from Aug. 1990 to May 1991 listed 146 acts of political violence, killing 1805 people. Inkhata was identified as aggressor in the majority of cases. Because of the violence, the ANC decided in July 1991 to maintain its military wing Umkhonto we Sizwe (MK) until the advent of a democratic constitution and continue to recruit soldiers and operate self-defence units in townships. Following bi- and multilateral

Location	Year formed/ year joined[a]	Warring parties[b]	No. of troops in 1991[c]	Deaths[d]		Change from 1990[e]
				Total (incl. 1991)	During 1991	
Sudan	1980/1983 1991/1991	Sudanese Govt vs. SPLA/SPLM (Garang) vs. SPLA/SPLM (Nazir-based faction)	65 000	>36 000 (mil.)	3 000– 5 000 (mil.)*	+ +

talks earlier in 1991, 31 organizations, including the Govt, the ANC, Inkhata and all parties represented in Parliament except the Conservative Party (CP), signed a National Peace Accord in Sep. 1991 which seeks to end violence and establish a background for all-party constitutional talks. The Accord stipulates the formation of a multi-party commission to investigate the nature and causes of violence. It also places obligations on the parties to prevent members from engaging in violence and on the security forces to act with political impartiality. This—as claimed by the ANC, trade unions, civic associations, the press and others—has led to selective, targeted killings increasingly replacing more indiscriminate actions, with responsibility for the violence shifting to well-organized groups, a so-called 'third force'. The stipulations of the peace accord remained unfulfilled by the end of 1991. On 20–21 Dec. the all-party conference, referred to as Codesa (Convention for a Democratic South Africa), on a new constitutional dispensation held its first session. 18 political organizations participated, including the Govt and the ANC. The Declaration of Intent signed after the meeting pledges allegiance to the notion of a democratic, non-racial S. Africa and gives Codesa decisions the status of law. Codesa working committees will resume work in Feb. 1992.

*   Total security forces, expressed as active duty SADF and SAP (South African Police) personnel.
** Victims of 'political violence'.

Comments: Since 1983 the SPLA/SPLM (Sudanese People's Liberation Army/Movement) has been fighting the central Govt to increase autonomy of southern Sudan and to repeal Islamic Law (Sharia). A major war over the same issues, but with different parties, ended with the Addis Ababa Agreement in 1972. However, according to the SPLA, in 1983 the central Govt broke this agreement by reintroducing Sharia laws. The SPLA has consistently controlled large parts of the countryside in the south. Talks have been attempted between the warring parties, notably in 1989, but without result. SPLA made military advances in the western Equatoria province in Nov. 1990. On 1 Feb. 1991 the Govt proposed a peace plan consisting of devolution, reconstruction and a peace agreement with the SPLA. Also in Feb. the Govt signed a law making the Sharia code applicable only to the predominantly Arabic north of the country. Later in Feb. the Govt divided Sudan into 9 states, as part of its peace effort. However, the SPLA argued that the real power in the southern states was extended to Muslim deputy governors. During Feb. Govt forces opened roads to besieged towns, notably Yei, and also maintained control of Juba. In Mar. the SPLA claimed to have captured Maridi, another besieged town in Equatoria. Throughout Apr. and May fighting continued, without fundamental changes in the military situation. In May the SPLA suggested that peace talks could be held in any neutral country, with the Govt responding positively. In June efforts were made to involve Nigeria's President Ibrahim Babangida, Chairman of the OAU, as mediator and contacts were made with the warring parties. Talks, scheduled for late Oct. were repeatedly postponed. Govt blamed the delay on a split in the SPLA, which was announced on 31 Aug. The leader of the SPLA, John Garang, was accused of being a 'dictator' by 3 of the 13 SPLA commanders. A leader of the dissident group said in Nov. that secession was the best option for the people in southern Sudan while Garang argued for a solution within a united Sudan. Also, the dissidents wanted to turn the SPLA into a political organization with a proper constitution and to respect human rights within the organization. The dissidents have a base in Nasir, Upper Nile region. Incidents and local clashes were reported in Sep. and Oct. Battles occurred in Nov., and the dissidents were reported to have captured the town of Bor in the south. A cease-fire was concluded in Nairobi on 27 Nov. between the SPLA factions, and negotiations took place in Dec., when procedures for negotiations were agreed. Continued talks were scheduled for Feb. 1992. In Dec. heavy fighting took place around Juba, involving the 2 factions as well as Govt forces. The developments in Sudan were affected by the ending of the internal conflict in Ethiopia (May). In June, the new Ethiopian Govt gave the SPLA a deadline to leave the country or become ordinary refugees and in Oct. supported Govt efforts for finding a solution to the conflict.

* Most of these deaths refer to the intra-SPLA conflict.

Uganda	Uganda Govt vs. UPA vs. UPDCA	1987/1987 1987/1987	70 000	1986–90: >12 000 (mil.) >1 000 ..

Comments: The NRM (National Resistance Movement) Govt seized power in Jan. 1986 and was immediately confronted with several armed opposition movements, the number of which decreased the following years (see SIPRI Yearbook 1991). Of the 3 groups active during 1990—the UPDM (Uganda People's Democratic Movement) with its armed wing the UPDA (UPD Army), the UPA (Uganda People's Army) and the UDCM (United Democratic Christian Movement, until 1990 named the Holy Spirit Resistance Movement)—the UDCM and to a small extent the UPA were reported to be active in 1991. Some fighting between the Govt and the UPA took place in Feb. In Mar. the UPA expressed willingness to enter talks. The UDCM, which apparently by Feb. 1991 had changed its name to the UPDCA (Uganda People's Christian Democratic Army), had reportedly been involved in 5 major battles against the Govt between Dec. 1990 and Feb. 1991. The Govt, in a professed goal of routing out the resistance group once and for all, launched military operations in mid-Mar. in northern Uganda. According to the Govt, more than 400 rebels had been killed in the military operations by late Apr. Military operations continued during the following months and had by late July (when the operations were called off), according to the Govt, resulted in the deaths of 85 soldiers and 1500 rebels. Further military operations against the UPA and the UPDCA were launched in early Dec.

Location	Year formed/ year joined[a]	Warring parties[b]	No. of troops in 1991[c]	Deaths[d] Total (incl. 1991)	During 1991	Change from 1990[e]
Central and South America						
Colombia		Colombian Govt	134 000	..	..	—
	1949/1978	vs. FARC	5 000–6 000			
	1965/1978	vs. ELN	1 500–2 000			
	1968/1977	vs. EPL	800–1 500			
	1991/1991	vs. Faction of FARC	..			
	1991/1991	vs. Faction of ELN	..			

Comments: Since 1970s, bombings, kidnappings and armed attacks have been staged by a number of groups. The Simón Bolívar Guerilla Co-ordinating Committee (CNGSB) was formed in 1987, then consisting of the Fuerzas Armadas Revolucionarias de Colombia (FARC), the Apr. 19 Movement (M-19), the Partido Revolucionario de los Trabajadores (PRT), the Ejército Popular de Liberación (EPL), Quintín Lame and Camilista Union (representing the Ejército de Liberación Nacional, ELN). Between 1988 and 1991 a return to civil political life was the main trend. Peace talks in 1987 were in 1988 followed by a Govt peace plan, proposing a 3-phase transition process, including stop of terrorist attacks, a Bill of Pardon, relocation of guerrillas into certain regions and participation of former guerrillas in civil political life. The then largest guerrilla group, M-19, declared in 1989 a unilateral cease-fire as part of its transition to civil political life. In the 1990 presidential elections the M-19 won strong support. The M-19 transition had followers in 1991: on 25 Jan., the PRT surrendered their weapons in an act of transition to civil political life followed on 1 Mar. by the EPL and on 31 May, by the 130 members of the guerrilla group Quintin Lame. In Jan. 1991 a 4-month offensive was initiated by FARC and the EPL as a response to a Govt attack in Dec. 1990 against the FARC HQ ('Casa Verde') in La Uribe. A joint FARC–ELN offensive was launched on 5 Feb. In early May the Govt and the 2 groups agreed to hold talks in the city of Cabo Norte. Following the talks, an offensive was launched late June. However, FARC and the ELN announced suspension of all hostilities (mainly against oil and electricity installations) on 1 Aug. following several days of public mass protest. After the 1990 presidential elections, a constitutional reform process was initiated under Pres. Cesar Gaviria, where all guerrilla groups were participating (except FARC and the ELN), leading to the adoption of a new constitution on 4 July. In late 1991, peace-talks between the Govt and FARC and ELN as well as with dissident groups within these groups were repeatedly initiated and broken. By the end of the year, the peace talks between the Govt and FARC and the ELN respectively had broken down because of Govt demands for a cease-fire before further talks.

Location	Year formed/joined	Warring parties			
El Salvador	1976/1979	Salvadorean Govt vs. FMLN	63 000 6 000–7 000	1979–91: 77 000–82 000	.. ..
Guatemala	1967/1968	Guatemalan Govt vs. URNG	46 000 1 000	<2 500 (mil.) 43 000 (civ.)	<1 000 ++

Comments: The FMLN (Farabundo Martí Front for National Liberation) is a coalition of 5 armed opposition groups (People's Revolutionary Army, ERP; Popular Liberation Forces, FPL; Armed Forces of National Resistance, FARN; Revolutionary Party of Central American Workers, PRTC; and Armed Forces of Liberation, FAL) formed in Oct. 1980. The 1990 peace process, under UN auspices, continued in 1991, but with numerous interruptions. A cease-fire, a major goal, was never reached. An FMLN cease-fire for 3 days made the parliamentary elections on 10 Mar. the calmest for a decade. The results included loss of the absolute majority for the ruling Arena Party and, for the first time during the conflict, seats in the assembly for leftist politicians. During talks between the Govt and the FMLN in Mexico City, in Apr., constitutional reforms (making Public Security Corps a civilian body, requiring two-thirds majority for Supreme Court elections, establishing guaranteed funding for the judiciary and allowing the Democratic Left representation in the national electoral tribunal) were agreed upon, requiring approval by 2 consecutive legislative assemblies. On 29–30 Apr. (i.e. on the eve of its dissolution) the Assembly voted for changes in the constitution. On 20 May, the UNSC approved the creation of the ONUSAL (UN Observe Mission to El Salvador) with the task of monitoring agreements on human rights between the FMLN and the Govt. The monitoring team began working on 26 July in 6 regional centres of El Salvador. Talks in New York ended on 25 Sep. in a major agreement, to be implemented after a permanent cease-fire. The agreement included dissolution of the Treasury Police and the National Guard, a 'purge' of the armed forces, the establishment of a Commission supervising future accords incl. the cease-fire and the restructuring of the armed forces, an agrarian reform programme, and the creation of a forum (representing the Govt, the business sector and trade unions) for the settlement of socio-economic problems. Further talks were held mid-Dec. at the UN, New York. Mediated by UN Secretary-General Perez de Cuellar, an agreement was reached on 31 Dec. on all 'technical–military aspects of an end to the armed confrontation'. A formal cease-fire was scheduled to begin on 1 Feb. 1992.

Comments: Armed opposition against right-wing, often military Govts dates back to the 1960s when remnants of reformist army officers formed rebel groups, aimed at breaking the military's intervention in politics. In 1982 the Guatemalan National Revolutionary Unity (URNG) was formed, co-ordinating 4 groups (Ejercito Guerrillero de los Pobres, EGP; Partido Guatemalteco del Trabajo, PGT; Fuerzas Armadas Rebeldes, FAR; and Organizacion del Pueblo en Armas, ORPA). A counter-insurgency campaign in 1982–83 by Govt forces cut the strength of the armed opposition. In 1985 the military handed over power. A reduction of political violence (e.g. deaths of local political and trade union leaders) followed but again reached high levels in 1990 and 1991. A peace process was initiated in a meeting in Mar. 1990 in Oslo (between the Guatemalan National Commission for Reconciliation, CNR, established under the Esquipulas II

Location	Year formed/ year joined[a]	Warring parties[b]	No. of troops in 1991[c]	Deaths[d] Total (incl. 1991)	During 1991	Change from 1990[e]

Agreement, and the URNG) with an agreement on a series of 5 meetings between different sectors of Guatemalan society. In Mar. 1991, 1 meeting remained: between the Govt and the URNG. On 24–25 Apr. the Govt and the URNG met in Mexico, resulting in an agreement on an agenda for further talks. Talks in Cuernavaca on 16–22 July ended without any agreement, but a meeting in Mexico on 22–23 July produced a 4-point framework, which included the need for institutional democracy, an effective judicial system, the elimination of political repression, respect for human rights, subordination of the armed forces under civilian authorities, and respect for the rights of indigenous peoples. A 6th round of talks between the Govt and the URNG was aborted early Dec. In all talks, the CNR played a crucial role. Throughout the year, widespread clashes between the URNG and the military took place. A human rights organization reported 616 politically motivated deaths (incl. insurgency) and 96 disappearances in 1991.

| Peru | 1980/1981 /1984 | Peruvian Govt vs. Sendero Luminoso vs. MRTA | 105 000 4 200 500 | >24 000 | 2 700 | – |

Comments: The armed conflict between the Govt and Sendero Luminoso (i.e. Communist Party of Peru—for the Shining Path of José Carlos Mariategui) dates from 1980. Following a split in 1970 in the Peruvian Communist Party, one group based in the Ayacucho area developed a Maoist ideology in which Indian rebel leaders serve as important exemplary models. Sendero Luminoso claims the goal of returning Indian governance to Peru through peasant-based armed struggle. The movement is influencing, if not controlling, about one-third of Peruvian territory with Ayacucho as the centre. Reports in Lima in early 1991 highlighted the possibility of an 'independent state' being set up by the Senderistas in the Huallaga valley, the key Peruvian coca trade area. In 1991 the conflict displayed 2 new features: foreign aid workers were kidnapped and killed by the Sendero Luminoso, and the Govt created urban-based self-defence patrols ('Rondas Urbanas Civiles'), a complement to previously organized peasant-based civilian patrols ('Rondas Campesinas'), both of which were involved in numerous clashes with the Sendero Luminoso during 1991. An announced and expected offensive (on the 18 June 5-year anniversary of a massacre in a prison uprising) by the Senderistas was warded off in an early phase. Movimiento Revolucionario Tupac Amaru (MRTA), a left-wing revolutionary group active since 1986 but with a low profile for most of 1991, staged a bombing campaign during Nov. on the seventh anniversary of the 'insurgency'. Between Jan. and Oct., Sendero Luminoso reportedly caused 379 deaths and the MRTA 116 in Lima. The killing of 100 people in the first 5 days of Nov. marked a new peak in political violence. By Aug. 1606 politically motivated deaths (incl. clashes between the Govt and Sendero Luminoso) and disappearances were reported. In Oct. a Senate Commission reported 23 916 deaths as a result of political violence between May 1980 and Sep. 1991.

Part III. Conventional arms control in Europe

Chapter 12. Conventional arms control in Europe: developments and prospects in 1991

12. Conventional arms control in Europe: developments and prospects in 1991

JANE M. O. SHARP

I. Introduction

This chapter traces the progress of the Treaty on Conventional Armed Forces in Europe (CFE) since its signature in November 1990. It reviews the process of ratification in the signatory states and explores the obstacles to ratification and implementation posed by the dissolution of the Soviet Union, including the difficulties of establishing relations between the republics and the prospect of re-allocating CFE ceilings between the former Soviet Union and the non-Soviet states that formerly belonged to the Warsaw Treaty Organization (WTO). Finally the chapter assesses the progress made in the next phase of the CFE process: the CFE 1A Negotiations, that seek to establish limits on manpower, and the Open Skies talks, that sought agreement on aerial inspection and resulted in the 1992 Treaty on Open Skies.

II. The CFE Treaty ratification process

As signed in November 1990, the CFE Treaty codified a balance in five categories of military equipment between the member states of the North Atlantic Treaty Organization (NATO) and the Warsaw Treaty Organization. The agreement was remarkable for the speed with which it was negotiated (less than two years) and the co-operative attitude displayed to the West by the former Soviet Union. Never was a treaty more overtaken by events, however: first, the two German states unified and Germany elected to remain in the NATO alliance; second, the WTO collapsed, rendering meaningless the balance between NATO and WTO states codified by the Treaty; and third, the USSR began to devolve into its constituent republics, raising the question of whether President Mikhail Gorbachev's November 1990 signature could bind the 10 former Soviet republics with territories in the CFE Treaty zone of application (Armenia, Azerbaijan, Belarus, Estonia, Georgia, Latvia, Lithuania, Moldova, Russia and Ukraine).

The compliance mechanism that provided for regular exchanges of information and a schedule of hundreds of on-site inspections annually was considered by military and foreign policy experts alike to be the most important feature of the 1990 CFE Treaty. At the time of writing (March 1992), the Treaty had not been ratified by all the signatories and was not yet in force. Even if the Treaty itself never enters into force, budget restrictions and the new security environment in Europe could achieve the CFE ceilings unilaterally. Without formal codification, however, it is unlikely that the signatory states will submit to the intrusive inspection regime laid out in the Treaty.[1]

The Joint Consultative Group (JCG) established to reconcile ambiguities of interpretation and implementation of the Treaty was in almost continuous session during 1991. Most delegates favoured early ratification without amendment, to lock in agreed cuts and establish an inspection regime that would facilitate transparency of military planning in Europe. Some argued that ratification should await clarification by the newly independent (former Soviet) republics of their CFE Treaty obligations, but others countered that if governments delayed they risked losing a treaty that would seem increasingly irrelevant to their legislators.[2] The dissolution of the USSR raised difficult questions of international law and, in the USA, sensitive constitutional questions about the treaty-making process. An accepted rule of international law (*rebus sic stantibus*) holds that when circumstances change from those under which a treaty was negotiated and signed, the new circumstances provide grounds for a change in the rights and obligations of the parties.[3] In the USA, senators have been especially sensitive to their prerogatives to give advice and consent to treaty ratification after the Reagan Administration's unilateral reinterpretation of the 1972 Anti-Ballistic Missile (ABM) Treaty in 1985.[4]

By the end of December 1991, nine of the original 22 signatories had deposited instruments of ratification with the depositary government, the Netherlands. In order of the date of deposit these were: Czechoslovakia, Hungary, the Netherlands, Bulgaria, the UK, Canada, Poland, Norway and Belgium.[5] The parliaments of seven other signatory states had ratified, but not deposited the instruments of ratification: Denmark, France, Italy, Luxembourg, Iceland, Germany and the USA. Among the remaining six signatories (Greece, Portugal, Romania, Spain, Turkey and 10 of the successor states to the USSR), for various reasons the agreement had not been submitted for ratification.

Portugal and Turkey initially delayed because of pending national elections, but when these were over the situation in the former Soviet Union made the Treaty appear less relevant and harder to present to sceptical legislatures. Greece continued to resent the way in which the CFE Treaty area of application between the Atlantic and the Urals (the ATTU zone) leaves vague the inclusion of the Turkish port of Mersin from which Turkey invaded Cyprus in

---

[1] For details of the verification provisions in the CFE Treaty see Koulik, S. and Kokoski, R., *Verification of the CFE Treaty*, SIPRI Research Report (SIPRI: Stockholm, 1991); Lewis, P. M., 'The Conventional Armed Forces in Europe Treaty', ed. J. B. Poole, *Verification Report 1991* (Apex Press: New York, 1991), pp. 55–66; Dunay, P., 'Verifying conventional arms limitations: the case of the November 19, 1990 Treaty on Conventional Armed Forces in Europe', Bochumer Schriften no. 6, Bochum, Germany, 1991.

[2] In Washington, Senator Jesse Helms claimed that the Treaty was so meaningless that it was not worth either opposing or supporting; *Arms Control Today*, vol. 21, no. 7 (Sep. 1991), p. 34.

[3] Vienna Convention on the Law of Treaties, 1969, Article 62.

[4] Rhinelander, J. B. and Bunn, G., 'Who's bound by the former Soviet Union's arms control treaties?', *Arms Control Today*, vol. 21, no. 10 (Dec. 1991), pp. 3–7.

[5] Information provided to the author by the Foreign Ministry of the Netherlands.

1974.[6] The French Parliament ratified the CFE Treaty in December 1991, but Netherlands officials were told that Foreign Minister Roland Dumas would not deposit the instruments of ratification until the 10 former Soviet republics with territory in the ATTU zone clarified their positions on ratification and implementation. In late 1991 and early 1992, seven of the relevant states (Armenia, Azerbaijan, Belarus, Georgia, Moldova, Russia and Ukraine) repeatedly declared their intention to implement the Treaty: for example, at the end of January 1992 in identical letters to Jiri Dienstbier, Foreign Minister of Czechoslovakia, who was Chairman-in-Office of the CSCE Council of Foreign Ministers meeting on the occasion of the entry of the CIS states into the CSCE as full participants.[7] Despite these expressions of good intentions, however, it was clear that a precondition for ratification would be a political–military settlement among the CIS states, especially between Russia and Ukraine, and between Armenia and Azerbaijan.

Clarification of Soviet data before the August 1991 attempted coup

In February 1991, in Washington, a bipartisan group of senators on the Senate Armed Services Committee told Secretary of State James Baker that they would consider ratifying the CFE Treaty only if there was a legally binding provision demanding Soviet acceptance of the US interpretation that counted the treaty-limited equipment (TLE) of Soviet land-based naval forces.[8] When Baker went to Moscow in mid-March he found Foreign Minister Alexander Bessmertnykh and President Mikhail Gorbachev uncompromising on the principle of exempting naval TLE, but anxious to deal with the problem by other means.[9] At the Joint Consultative Group in Vienna and in a series of letters exchanged between Presidents Bush and Gorbachev in early 1991, the Soviet Union initially offered a no-increase commitment for land-based naval forces, such as it had already made with respect to land-based naval aviation.[10] Non-Soviet delegates repeated their earlier insistence that land-based treaty-limited equipment, whether nominally assigned to naval- or ground-force units, must be subject to Treaty limits and emphasized that the conditions under which the items of treaty-limited equipment are exempt are

---

[6] Article II of the Treaty defines the ATTU zone. The CFE Treaty is reprinted in SIPRI, *SIPRI Yearbook 1991: World Armaments and Disarmament* (Oxford University Press: Oxford, 1991), pp. 461–74.

[7] The relevant language in the letters reads 'recognizes the requirement for prompt entry into force of the Treaty on Conventional Armed Forces in Europe. To that end, the Government of the Republic of . . . underlines the need to move forward promptly with the ratification of the CFE Treaty and to assume in co-operation with other relevant newly independent states, all CFE obligations of the former Soviet Union.' Text supplied to the author by the Canadian delegation to the CFE Negotiation.

[8] Smith, R. J., 'Senators balk at arms treaty: panel wants Soviets to back down on European forces', *International Herald Tribune*, 16–17 Mar. 1991.

[9] AP, 'Arms pact problems delay summit', *International Herald Tribune*, 16–17 Mar. 1991.

[10] Three declarations are annexed to the CFE Treaty; the first states that the 22 CFE signatories will not exceed 430 land-based naval aircraft for each alliance group of states, with a single-country limit of 400.

Table 12.1. Revised data on disputed Soviet TLE deployments

Unit type	Tanks		ACVs		Artillery		Total	
	Old	Revised	Old	Revised	Old	Revised	Old	Revised
Coastal defence	813	813	972	1 672	846	846	2 631	3 331
Naval infantry	120	120	753	903	234	234	1 107	1 257
SRF	0	0	1 701	1 701	0	0	1 701	1 701
Civil defence	0	0	18	0	0	0	18	0
Total	**933**	**933**	**3 444**	**4 276**	**1 080**	**1 080**	**5 457**	**6 289**

Source: Institute for Defense and Disarmament Studies, *Arms Control Reporter* (IDDS: Brookline, Mass.), sheet 407.B.443, 1 May 1991.

unambiguously listed in Article III of the Treaty and do not include assignment to naval infantry.[11]

On 1 May 1991, after some judicious leaks by Western intelligence agencies, the Soviet delegation in Vienna submitted revised data on TLE deployed with naval infantry, coastal defence, strategic rocket force (SRF) and civil defence units that they claimed should be exempt from CFE Treaty limits (see table 12.1). In late May, Chief of the Soviet General Staff Mikhail Moiseyev visited Washington, still insisting that if equipment with naval forces was included in CFE limits then the ceiling for Soviet TLE in active units elsewhere in the zone of application should be raised. The USA rejected this but did accept face-saving language in the unilateral Soviet statements that allowed separate accounting and inspection provisions for naval and non-naval TLE. In early June 1991, however, parallel to the Soviet effort to garner economic aid and an invitation to the Group of Seven (G7) meeting in London in July, Mikhail Gorbachev apparently insisted that the Soviet General Staff accept the terms of the CFE Treaty. This was confirmed when Alexander Bessmertnykh met James Baker in Lisbon during the first weekend of June.[12]

On 14 June, at a separate meeting of the JCG, the Soviet delegate clarified new obligations with respect to equipment transferred east of the Urals that would be politically rather than legally binding.[13] Strictly speaking, the transfer of thousands of pieces of equipment outside the CFE Treaty area of

[11] Towards the end of round VII of the CFE Negotiation, US delegate James Woolsey insisted, and Soviet delegate Oleg Grinevskiy agreed, on language in paragraph 2 of section III of the Protocol on Information Exchange that became known in Vienna as the Naval Infantry Article. The paragraph does not mention naval infantry explicitly but is designed to include naval infantry in the information exchange by including 'conventional armaments and equipment in service with its conventional armed forces but not held by its land forces, or air or air defence aviation forces'. To counter the inclusion of naval infantry in the data exchange, however, Grinevskiy insisted on language in the Protocol on Inspection that excludes naval infantry from the Soviet objects of verification (OOVs). Thus section 1J, para. 1, includes all that TLE mentioned in section III, para. 1 of the Protocol on Information Exchange, but not that mentioned in section III, para. 2, (i.e. not naval infantry).

[12] 'Nailed at last' and 'Let's make a deal', *The Economist*, 8 June 1991, pp. 28 and 30.

[13] Statement of the Representative of the USSR in the Joint Consultative Group, 14 June 1991, reprinted in *BASIC Reports on European Arms Control*, no. 16 (20 Aug. 1991), p. 3.

Table 12.2. Soviet pledge on TLE east of the Urals, 14 June 1991

TLE	Destroy/convert	Deploy	Store	Replace
Battle tanks	6 000	8 000	8 400	..
ACVs	1 500	11 200	4 700	..
Artillery	7 000	1 600	16 400	7 000
Total	14 500	20 800	29 500	7 000

Source: Statement of the Representative of the USSR in the Joint Consultative Group, 14 June 1991, in *BASIC Reports on European Arms Control*, no. 16 (20 Aug. 1991).

application did not abrogate any agreement with the West, but it certainly eroded confidence and trust by suggesting a deliberate effort to evade an obligation to destroy excess TLE that remained in the ATTU zone. In the 14 June statement, the Soviet Union pledged to destroy some TLE with units in the Asian part of the country, to use some to replace and repair old equipment, and to store the rest, but not in unit sets: in other words not to create a strategic reserve (see table 12.2).

Although thoroughly debated at the Joint Consultative Group, final resolution of the problems raised by Article III of the Treaty required a series of bilateral deals between Moscow and Washington which in turn undermined the confidence of the smaller powers in the multilateral compliance mechanism. The other 20 CFE Treaty signatories were distressed that the USA and the USSR chose to resolve discrepancies in Soviet data bilaterally rather than through the JCG. Delegates from several countries, including France and Canada, complained.[14] Czechoslovakia, Hungary and Poland also expressed concern that the Soviet proposals might affect the WTO agreement on storage of TLE reached at Budapest on 3 November 1990.[15]

In mid-June the Foreign Relations Committee of the US Senate recommended ratification of the CFE Treaty but on condition that the USSR offered clarification of three issues: compliance by republics leaning towards independence from Moscow, interpretation of Article III, and the fate of equipment transferred east of the Urals. These conditions were also attached to the documents of ratification when the full Senate voted 90–4 in favour of the Treaty on 25 November 1991.[16]

Problems associated with the collapse of the USSR

The CFE Treaty was to some extent already out of date when it was signed in November 1990 because by then the two German states had united in NATO and the WTO was manifestly about to collapse; but the collapse of

[14] *Arms Control Reporter*, sheets 407.B.444–45, 7–8 May 1991.
[15] *Arms Control Reporter*, sheet 407.B.451, 14 June 1991.
[16] See the ratification debate in *United States Congressional Record*, vol. 137, no. 176 (25 Nov. 1991), pp. S18018–69.

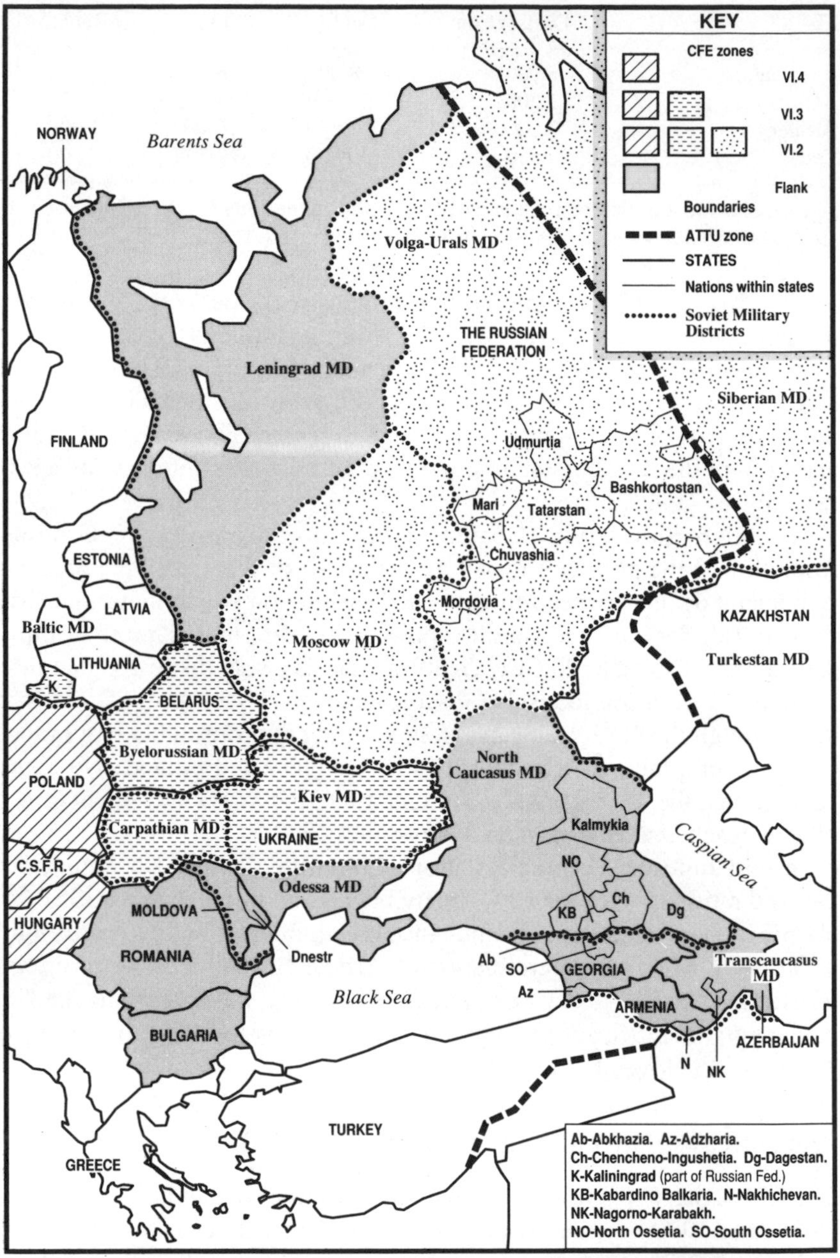

Greece, Turkey and Norway are in the NATO flank zone. On 18 October 1991 the CFE signatories agreed that Estonia, Latvia and Lithuania were no longer part of the Baltic MD.

Figure 12.1. Former Soviet military districts and republics in the ATTU zone

Source: Based on a map prepared by Sarah Hooker for *Verification Report 1992* (VERTIC: London, 1992).

the USSR in late 1991 rendered the CFE ceilings and inspection quotas highly impracticable. Not only were the ceilings based on old Soviet military districts (MDs), that were for the most part not coincident with the old republic boundaries, but also in several cases the newly independent Soviet successor states had moved from friendly to adversarial relationships.

Of the 10 former Soviet republics with territory west of the Urals in the ATTU zone, Estonia, Latvia and Lithuania achieved independence in September 1991 and in October 1991 dissociated themselves from any CFE Treaty obligations undertaken by the Soviet Union in November 1990. Of the other seven, Russia and Ukraine were increasingly at odds over control of the Crimea and the Black Sea Fleet, as well as former Soviet armed forces deployed on Ukrainian territory; Russia and Moldova were troubled by independence movements within the ATTU zone that if successful could create yet more states parties to the CFE Treaty. Armenia and Azerbaijan were frequently at war with each other over the control of Nagorno-Karabakh and, for some months in late 1991, Georgia was wracked by civil war.

CFE sub-zones and former Soviet borders

The three Baltic states (Estonia, Latvia and Lithuania), all of which are located in the CFE Treaty expanded central zone (defined in Article IV.3), comprised the former Baltic MD. Belarus coincides with the former Byelorussian MD, which was in the same sub-zone IV.3 as the Baltic states. Ukraine stretches over the area of the Carpathian and Kiev MDs which were also in sub-zone IV.3, as well as the Odessa MD, which belonged to the outer flank of the CFE Treaty zone of application, subject to different ceilings and different inspection quotas. The Russian Federation west of the Urals is subject to CFE limits, that is, the area of the former Leningrad and North Caucasus MDs that belong to the CFE flank zone (Article V.1), as well as that of the Moscow and Volga-Urals MDs, belonging to the extended central zone (Article IV.2). Moldova lies between Ukraine and Romania, wholly within the Odessa MD. Armenia, Azerbaijan and Georgia together formed the Transcaucasus MD in the flank zone, together with the North Caucasus and the Leningrad and Odessa MDs. Finally, the north-western tip of Kazakhstan, not normally considered part of the CFE Treaty area of application, lies 'west of the Urals and the Caspian Sea'—the definition given of Soviet territory in the ATTU zone (Article II, para. B). Figure 12.1 shows the borders of former military districts and former Soviet republics in the ATTU zone.

Baltic states take the neutral and non-aligned route

At the JCG meeting in Vienna on 18 October 1991, the 22 delegations agreed that the territory of the three independent Baltic states would no longer be considered part of the Baltic MD and thus no longer part of the ATTU zone. However, the treaty-limited equipment deployed there by the former Soviet Union (600 main battle tanks, 800 armoured combat vehicles and 400 artillery pieces) would be included in Soviet ceilings and remain subject to inspections under the CFE Treaty.[17] In effect all that remains of the Baltic MD is the Russian enclave of Kaliningrad between Lithuania and Poland. On 15 November 1991 Mikhail Gorbachev resolved that the Soviet forces in the Baltic states be renamed the North-Western Group of Forces (NWG).[18] Soviet equipment with the NWG would be subject to CFE inspection until withdrawn, but any national forces created by the three independent Baltic states would presumably not be subject to CFE Treaty limits. In effect, the Baltic states were treated in much the same way as the neutral and non-aligned (NNA) states of the Conference on Security and Co-operation in Europe (CSCE).

Although all 22 CFE Treaty signatories went along with this solution for the Baltic states, several of the former non-Soviet WTO (NSWTO) states, notably Czechoslovakia, Hungary and Poland, were dissatisfied for several reasons. In the first place, the early October proposal by some Baltic state officials that Soviet troops should leave their equipment behind for use by the new national armies suggested that any new national armed forces among the Baltic states would be well equipped and as much in need of CFE Treaty controls as any other small states in the ATTU zone.[19] Second, letting the Baltic states off the hook with respect to CFE Treaty obligations set an unfortunate precedent for other Soviet successor states, especially Ukraine, whose Parliament authorized the establishment of a 450 000-man national army in October 1991.[20] Finally, because of the strategic importance of the three Baltic states and their proximity to the three Central European states, Poland in particular would have preferred that Estonia, Latvia and Lithuania be subject to the same arms control regime as their neighbours.[21]

Who inherits the obligation to ratify?

At the JCG meeting on 18 October 1991 all 22 CFE signatory states agreed that the USSR could ratify the agreement on behalf of all those republics that had not yet been recognized as independent. In early November, Lieutenant-General Fyodor Ladygin, Director of the Legal Affairs Division of the Soviet General Staff, announced that the USSR would ratify the CFE Treaty, but on 8 December the USSR collapsed and was replaced by a loose Commonwealth

---

[17] For the 18 Oct. agreement see *Arms Control Reporter*, sheet 407.D-83, 18 Oct. 1991; see also *Congressional Record*, vol. 137, no. 176 (25 Nov. 1991), p. S18037; and *Atlantic News*, no. 2362 (23 Oct. 1991), p. 2.

[18] *Krasnaya Zvezda*, 26 Nov. 1991, in Foreign Broadcast Information Service, *Daily Report–Soviet Union (FBIS-SOV)*, FBIS-SOV-91-228, 26 Nov. 1991, p. 45.

[19] Tett, G., 'Army of pre-occupation in Baltics', *Financial Times*, 8 Oct. 1991.

[20] This target was modified to an army of 200 000 to 250 000 by President Leonid Kravchuk in Nov. 1991, see *Krasnaya Zvezda*, 2 Nov. 1991, in FBIS-SOV-91, 4 Nov. 1991.

[21] In a statement by Ambassador Jerzy M. Nowak at a CFE plenary meeting on 10 Oct. 1991, the Polish delegate urged that the CFE area of application not be changed, that the three Baltic states be invited to join the Treaty as independent states, and that the proposed solution for the Baltic states should not serve as a precedent for other Soviet republics that might not achieve independence.

of Independent States (CIS).[22] The international community accepted the Russian Federation as the successor state to the USSR and as a permanent member of the UN Security Council and recognized Russia's assumption of control of Soviet embassies throughout the world. Clearly Russia could not take on all the obligations of the USSR alone, and certainly not its CFE Treaty obligations, since all the former Soviet states in the ATTU zone would have to clarify and accept specific national obligations.

On 8 November 1991, in order to offer the newly independent states a measure of stability and to help clarify their positions with respect to the CFE Treaty, NATO invited the former NSWTO states, the Baltic states and the USSR to join in the North Atlantic Co-operation Council (NACC).[23] Since the CSCE also extended an invitation to these same political entities, some observers considered the NACC to represent an excessive interlocking of institutions.[24] At the inaugural meeting of the NACC on 20 December 1991 a High Level Working Group (HLWG) was formed, comprising all the NATO and non-NATO CFE signatories including the Soviet successor states with territory in the zone of application. The purpose of the Group was to clarify the rights and obligations of the new republics under the CFE Treaty.[25] The HLWG met in Brussels on 10 January 1992 and agreed on the nine points summarized below:[26]

1. The CFE Treaty should enter into force without re-negotiation.

2. CFE Treaty obligations should be apportioned between the former states in a manner acceptable to all Treaty signatories.

3. The former Soviet republics should first agree on these matters collectively in accordance with the provisions laid down for each group of states defined in the Treaty.[27]

4. The allocation of responsibilities should preferably be achieved before ratification, or at least coincident with it.

5. All newly independent states in the area of application should ratify the Treaty.[28]

6. The Treaty would need updating after its entry into force, and any amendments would need to be formalized by all states parties.[29]

---

[22] Georgia did not join the CIS. For the text of the Minsk Agreement Establishing a Commonwealth of Independent States, 8 Dec. 1991, see appendix 14A in this volume.

[23] Para. 11 of the Rome Declaration on Peace and Co-operation issued by the Heads of State and Government participating in the meeting of the North Atlantic Council in Rome on 7–8 Nov. 1991, reprinted in *NATO Review*, vol. 39, no. 6 (Dec. 1991), pp. 19–22.

[24] Mortimer, E., 'Europe's security surplus', *Financial Times*, 4 Mar. 1992.

[25] The first HLWG meeting on 10 Jan. was attended by all 16 NATO states, plus Bulgaria, Czechoslovakia, Hungary, Poland, Romania, Armenia, Azerbaijan, Belarus, Estonia, Georgia, Latvia, Lithuania, Moldova, Russia and Ukraine. Kazakhstan was invited but did not participate.

[26] From the 'Points for press coverage' issued after the HLWG meeting on 10 Jan. 1992, reprinted in *BASIC Reports on European Arms Control,* no. 19 (21 Jan. 1992), p. 3.

[27] The CFE Protocol on Notification and Exchange of Information, Section VIII, requires states parties to the Treaty to exchange information on changes in organizational structures or force levels.

[28] This appears to contradict the 18 Oct. decision that the three independent Baltic states were no longer part of the Baltic MD and were thus defined out of the area of application; see note 17.

[29] Article XX of the CFE Treaty states that amendments must be approved by all states parties before they can enter into force.

7. The deadline for completion of the ratification process should be as soon as possible, bearing in mind the CSCE follow-up meeting in Helsinki from March to July 1992.

8. The CFE Treaty is the basis for further progress in fostering a common security forum in which all CSCE states should participate.

9. The HLWG would meet again on 14 February 1992 to discuss points 3, 4 and 5.

In fact the HLWG did not meet again until 21 February 1992. The CIS states met in Minsk on 14 February but made no headway on military issues or allocation of CFE Treaty obligations.[30] For example, on a vote as to whether to set up a council of CIS defence ministers, Azerbaijan, Moldova and Ukraine voted against, and Belarus, Kyrgyzstan and Turkmenistan abstained.[31] On 21 February the HLWG agreed on a two-phase 'road map' for bringing the CFE Treaty into force. In the preliminary phase, to be concluded by the end of May 1992, there would be an 'informal mode' in which 'the states successors to the Soviet Union with regard to the CFE would keep the HLWG informed of their progress in discussions designed to come to an agreement'.[32] This would be followed by a 'formal mode' in the form of an 'extraordinary conference', the final document of which would record agreements reached in the informal phase and provide the basis for the entry into force of the Treaty. The HLWG participants assumed that immediately after entry into force of the Treaty certain minor changes to the Treaty would be necessary.

The second phase anticipated the bringing into force of the Treaty 10 days after the last signatory had deposited its instruments of ratification with the Netherlands Government. A meeting of the JCG was envisaged shortly after the entry into force to deal with any necessary changes and discuss the possibility of an amendment conference.

Re-allocating the TLE ceilings in the former WTO member states

Table 12.3 shows the essential features of the CFE Treaty. As the Treaty was being negotiated it was clear that the WTO was not likely to survive and the NSWTO states wanted to differentiate between long-term membership in that group of states for the duration of the Treaty and membership in the WTO, that was about to end. Specifically, the NSWTO states wanted to be sure that this grouping did not imply continued membership in the WTO.[33] Their interests thus coincided with those of France in negotiating not as a member of

[30] The documents signed in Minsk on 14 Feb. 1992 are reprinted in FBIS-SOV-92-032, 18 Feb. 1992, pp. 18–29.

[31] *Krasnaya Zvezda*, 18 Feb. 1992.

[32] NATO communiqué, Chairman's summary, HLWG Meeting, NATO Press Service, Brussels, 21 Feb. 1992.

[33] For a Hungarian view, see Dunay, P., 'The CFE Treaty: history, achievements and shortcomings', PRIF Reports, no. 24, Frankfurt, Oct. 1991, pp. 90–91.

Table 12.3. Sub-zonal ceilings of the 1990 CFE Treaty

Zone[a]	TLE Battle tanks	Artillery	ACVs	AIFVs	HACVs	Combat aircraft	Attack helicopters
Active TLE							
Sub-zone IV.4	7 500	5 000	11 250	..	..	..	..
Sub-zone IV.3	10 300	9 100	19 260	..	..	..	..
Sub-zone IV.2	11 800	11 000	21 400	..	..	..	..
Flank zone	4 700	6 000	5 900	..	..	..	..
Total in ATTU zone	**16 500**	**17 000**	**27 300**	..	..	..	..
Stored TLE	3 500	3 000	2 700	..	..	..	..
Odessa MD	400	500	..	..	..	..	..
S. Leningrad MD	600	400	800	..	..	..	..
Sub-zone IV.2	2 500	2 100	1 900	..	..	..	..
Active and stored TLE in ATTU zone	**20 000**	**20 000**	**30 000**	**18 000**	**1 500**	**6 800**	**2 000**
Single-country limits	13 300	13 700	20 000	16 800	1 000	5 150	1 500
Kiev MD	2 250	1 500	2 500	..	..	..	..

[a] Sub-zones IV.4 and IV.3 nest inside sub-zone IV.2; the flank zone is outside sub-zone IV.2. Ceilings for the entire ATTU zone (IV.1) equal the sum of IV.2 plus the flank states.

| Sub-zone IV.4 | NATO: | Belgium, Germany, Luxembourg, the Netherlands |
| | WTO: | Czechoslovakia, Hungary, Poland |

Sub-zone IV.3	Sub-zone IV.4, plus	
	NATO:	Denmark, France, Italy, the UK
	WTO:	USSR (Baltic, Byelorussian, Carpathian, Kiev MDs)

Sub-zone IV.2	Sub-zone IV.3, plus	
	NATO:	Portugal, Spain
	WTO:	USSR (Moscow and Volga-Ural MDs)

| Flank zone | NATO: | Greece, Iceland, Norway, Turkey |
| | WTO: | Bulgaria, Romania, USSR (Leningrad, North Caucasus, Odessa, Transcaucasus MDs) |

Note: ACV: armoured combat vehicle; AIFV: armed infantry fighting vehicle; HACV: heavy armoured combat vehicle.

Source: Sharp, J. M. O., 'Conventional arms control in Europe', SIPRI, *SIPRI Yearbook 1991: World Armaments and Disarmament* (Oxford University Press: Oxford, 1991), p. 408.

an alliance but rather as an individual state. National TLE ceilings were difficult to negotiate within the WTO 'group of six' states in late 1990 as the interests of the USSR and the NSWTO states drifted further apart. Table 12.4. shows the intra-WTO allocations negotiated on 3 November 1990 and adjusted after the 14 June statement by the USSR in the Joint Consultative Group. Whether these reallocations will continue to be acceptable to the former NSWTO states, and to the non-Russian republics, remains to be seen. A number of potential problems could arise.

Table 12.4. WTO agreement on TLE entitlements, 3 November 1990

Figures are adjusted after the Soviet statement of 14 June 1991.

State	Battle tanks	ACVs	Artillery	Combat aircraft	Attack helicopters
WTO 'group of six'	20 000	20 000	30 000	6 800	2 000
USSR	12 217[a]	11 450[b]	18 920[c]	5 150	1 500
Bulgaria	1 457	1 750	2 000	235	67
Czechoslovakia	1 435	1 150	2 050	345	75
Hungary	835	840	1 700	180	108
Poland	1 730	1 610	2 150	460	130
Romania	1 375	1 475	2 100	430	120

[a] Adjusted down from 13 150 by the 933 tanks redeployed with naval infantry (120) and coastal defence (813) units.

[b] Adjusted down from 13 175 by 1 725 ACVs redeployed with naval infantry (753) and coastal defence (972) units.

[c] Adjusted down from 20 000 by 1080 artillery pieces redeployed with naval infantry (234) and coastal defence (846) units.

Source: Based on the Statement by the Government of the USSR, 14 June 1991, reprinted in *Arms Control Reporter*, sheet 407.D.80–8, 14 June 1992; and *BASIC Reports on European Arms Control*, no. 15 (17 June 1991), pp. 3–4.

Re-allocating the TLE ceilings in the former Soviet republics

Redistribution of the TLE from the Baltic states

Until the CIS states reorganize their military districts, Kaliningrad is all that remains of the Baltic MD and treaty-limited equipment permitted in the Baltic MD under the CFE Treaty could be concentrated there for the duration of the Treaty. Estonia, Latvia and Lithuania obviously wanted all Soviet forces to be withdrawn, although not westwards to Kaliningrad but eastwards into Russia or the neighbouring CIS republics. Negotiations to schedule Soviet withdrawals were conducted between the three Baltic states and the former Soviet Government in late 1991 and renewed with the Government of the Russian Federation in early 1992. The Baltic leaders tried to insist on complete withdrawals by the end of 1991, but the Russian Government refused to agree, pleading lack of housing for the the returning troops and their families.[34] In late 1991, in an effort to accelerate the process, the Baltic leaders asked Sweden and other Nordic neighbours to follow the German example and earmark economic aid to Russia to provide housing for returning troops. These requests for Nordic aid were repeated in early March 1992 at a meeting of all the states bordering the Baltic Sea, including Russia, Estonia, Latvia, Lithuania, Poland and the Scandinavian countries. Estonia and Latvia also

[34] Tett, G., 'Army of pre-occupation in Baltics', *Financial Times*, 8 Oct. 1991.

Table 12.5. Declared Soviet TLE by republics, February 1991

Republic	Battle tanks	ACVs	Artillery	Attack helicopters	Combat aircraft
Armenia	258	641	357	7	0
Azerbaijan	391	1 285	463	24	124
Belarus	2 263	2 776	1 384	82	650
Estonia	184	201	29	10	153
Georgia	850	1 054	363	48	245
Latvia	138	100	81	23	183
Lithuania	184	1 591	253	0	46
Moldova	155	402	248	0	0
Russia	5 017	6 279	3 480	570	2 750
Ukraine	6 204	6 394	3 052	285	1 431
Total USSR	15 644	20 723	9 710	1 049	5 582
Non-Soviet group of forces	5 081	9 167	4 228	432	1 029
Total in the ATTU zone	20 725	29 890	13 938	1 481	6 611

Source: *BASIC Reports on European Arms Control*, no. 19 (21 Jan. 1992).

complained to the Russian Foreign Minister about the delays in Soviet withdrawals.[35]

An issue separate from that of the schedule of Soviet troop withdrawals was whether the amount of TLE which the Soviet Union was permitted in CFE Treaty sub-zone IV.3 would remain the same as that agreed in November 1990. If so, the TLE currently deployed in the Baltic states could presumably be reallocated elsewhere in sub-zone IV.3 (i.e., to neighbouring Ukraine and Belarus). Alternatively, the allocations could be cut by the numbers that would have remained in the Baltic MD had the three states not left the Soviet Union.

Ukraine's ceilings too high?

During the CFE Negotiation the Soviet General Staff insisted on moving the Kiev MD from the outer flank to the central zone, to allow higher TLE ceilings and thereby incorporate in the Kiev MD some of the equipment being withdrawn from Afghanistan and Eastern Europe. Russians on the General Staff were thus 'hoist with their own petard' as the CFE Treaty could be interpreted to permit the Ukraine to have more tanks west of the Urals than Russia is allowed.[36] Table 12.5 shows the TLE deployed in each Soviet republic as of February 1991. In mid-February 1992, General Konstantin Kobets, Russian Army General and adviser on defence matters to President Boris Yeltsin, suggested certain criteria (e.g., population size and length of border to defend) by which the former Soviet republics west of the Urals might reallocate the

---

[35] Mauthner, R., 'Baltic states list troop pullout snag', *Financial Times*, 7–8 Mar. 1992.

[36] CFE Treaty sub-zones are nested within each other so there is flexibility here to readjust within the zones.

Table 12.6. Possible 1992 allocation of tank ceilings by republic

	Total	Stored	Active
Total in the ATTU zone	**12 217**	**2 650**	**9 567**
Ukraine and Moldova	4 450	450	4 000
(Carpathian, Kiev and Odessa MDs)			
Russia plus the Baltic states	3 780	600	3 180
(Leningrad, Baltic, N. Caucasus, Moscow, Volga-Urals MDs)			
Belarus	1 880	..	1 880
(Byelorussian MD)			
Georgia, Armenia and Azerbaijan	480	0	480
(Transcaucasus MD			
Tanks stored in unspecified republics in ATTU zone	1 627	1 600	27
Total in Asia east of the ATTU zone	**30 820**	**15 709**	**15 111**
Russia	22 335	10 400	11 935
(Far East, Siberia, Transbaykal MDs)			
Kazakhstan, Kyrgyzstan, Tajikistan	1 856	..	1 856
(Central Asian MD)			
Turkmenistan, Uzbekistan	1 320	..	1 320
(Turkestan MD)			
Tanks stored in Asia	5 309	5 309	..
Global total:	**43 037**	**18 359**	**24 678**
Russia and the Baltic states	26 115	11 000	15 115
Ukraine and Moldova	4 450	450	4 000
Belarus	1 880	..	1 880
Georgia, Armenia, Azerbaijan	480	..	480
Storage in Europe	1 627	1 600	27
Kazakhstan, Kyrgyzstan, Tajikistan	1 856	..	1 856
Turkmenistan and Uzbekistan	1 320	..	1 320
Storage in Asia	5 309	5 309	..

Source: Based on Institute for Defence and Disarmament Studies (IDDS), 'Analysis of possible USSR tanks and divisions by republic after CFE', *Vienna Fax*, vol. 2, nos 10 and 11 (20 Dec. 1991), p. 8.

CFE Treaty ceilings allotted to the USSR. He proposed new percentages: 54.17 per cent for Russia, 21.8 per cent for Ukraine and 6.6 per cent for Belarus. The 1991 percentages were 30 per cent for Ukraine, 28 per cent for Russia and 18 per cent for Belarus, respectively.[37]

Ukraine and Belarus seem unlikely to find the Kobets proposal acceptable, but others would be distressed if Ukraine retained a high proportion of tanks, especially neighbouring Hungary and Poland, which are interested in cutting down the military potential of Ukraine. Potential Ukrainian tank holdings of 4450 dwarf those allowed Poland (1730) and Hungary (835) (see table 12.6).

[37] 'Kobets intervewed on division of armed forces', *Izvestia*, 13 Feb. 1992, in FBIS-SOV-92-031, 14 Feb. 1992, pp. 20–22.

Transcaucasus ceilings too low?

Given the tensions in this region between Armenia and Azerbaijan over the disputed enclave of Nagorno-Karabakh, and the civil war in Georgia, it seems likely that the governments in these three states will argue for higher ceilings to be able adequately to defend their borders.

Creation of more republics in the ATTU zone?

In late March 1992, most republics in Russia signed a new treaty of federation. Among those republics wanting sovereignty, however, were the fiercely independent Tartarstan, and Checheno-Ingushetia, both of which lie west of the Urals and could thus become additional states parties to the CFE Treaty.

Allocation of new inspection quotas?

Based on the number of military sites, or objects of verification (OOVs), states parties to the CFE Treaty must accept a specific number of annual inspections: some passive, of previously declared sites with advance notice, and a smaller number of challenge inspections, of undeclared military sites at short notice.[38] Table 12.7 shows the inspections each state must accept, based on revised data submitted by all states in February 1991.

At issue in the new political situation in early 1992 was the extent to which the Soviet inspection quotas would be reallocated to the seven Soviet successor states west of the Urals bound by the Treaty (i.e., excluding the Baltic states). In the Stockholm Document agreed at the CSCE Conference on Confidence- and Security-Building Measures and Disarmament in Europe in 1986, each state was obliged to accept only three on-site inspections annually. To avoid exhaustion of these small quotas, states belonging to the same alliance agreed not to inspect each other.[39] During the 1989–90 CFE Negotiation, however, Hungary insisted (and the other NSWTO states concurred as and when their communist governments were toppled) that members of the two groups of states should be allowed to inspect each other.[40] Thus the CFE Treaty permits each state five inspections annually of other states within the same group. NATO states indicated that they would maintain the Stockholm Document formula and not exercise rights to inspect each other (not least to prevent Greece and Turkey getting into a conflict over inspections); but the former NSWTO states are likely to exercise their rights, especially to inspect the Soviet successor states. With the breakup of the USSR there are now seven separate former Soviet republics west of the

---

[38] Details of the inspection procedures are laid out in the Protocol on Inspection attached to the CFE Treaty.

[39] Borawski, J., *From the Atlantic to the Urals: Negotiating Arms Control at the Stockholm Conference* (Pergamon–Brassey's: Washington, DC, 1988), pp. 242–43.

[40] For details on the position of Hungary, see Dunay (note 1), especially pp. 89–106.

Table 12.7. Passive and challenge inspection quotas in the CFE reduction period

Figures are adjusted for February 1991 corrections.

State	Declared objects of verification	Inspections each state must accept			
		Phase I	Phase II	Phase III	Phase IV
Belgium	50	10 (2)	5 (1)	10 (2)	8 (2)
Canada	13	3 (1)	1 (1)	3 (1)	2 (1)
Denmark	64	13 (2)	6 (1)	13 (2)	10 (2)
France	257	51 (8)	26 (4)	51 (8)	39 (9)
Germany	470	94 (14)	47 (7)	94 (14)	70 (16)
Greece	60	12 (2)	6 (1)	12 (2)	9 (2)
Iceland	–	– (1)	– (1)	– (1)	– (1)
Italy	190	38 (6)	19 (3)	38 (6)	28 (6)
Luxembourg	2	– (1)	– (1)	– (1)	– (1)
Netherlands	88	18 (3)	9 (1)	18 (3)	13 (3)
Norway	59	12 (2)	6 (1)	12 (2)	9 (2)
Portugal	28	6 (1)	3 (1)	6 (1)	4 (1)
Spain	93	19 (3)	9 (1)	19 (3)	14 (3)
Turkey	150	30 (4)	15 (2)	30 (4)	22 (5)
UK	226	45 (7)	23 (3)	45 (7)	34 (8)
USA	169	34 (5)	17 (3)	34 (5)	25 (6)
Total	**1 919**	**385 (62)**	**192 (32)**	**385 (62)**	**287 (68)**
Bulgaria	93	19 (3)	9 (1)	19 (3)	14 (3)
Czechoslovakia	179	36 (5)	18 (3)	36 (5)	27 (6)
Hungary	59	12 (2)	6 (1)	12 (2)	9 (2)
Poland	134	27 (4)	13 (2)	27 (4)	20 (5)
Romania	127	25 (4)	13 (2)	25 (4)	19 (4)
USSR	910	182 (27)	91 (14)	182 (27)	136 (31)
Total	**1 502**	**301 (45)**	**150 (23)**	**301 (45)**	**225 (51)**

[a] Taking the declared number of objects of verification after corrections have been provided to all other states parties within 90 days after signature of the Treaty (Protocol on Notification and Exchange of Information, section VII, para. 1, subpara. A). Challenge inspections are in parentheses.

Source: Dunay, P., 'Verifying conventional arms limitations: the case of the November 19, 1990 Treaty on Conventional Armed Forces in Europe', Bochumer Schriften no. 6, Bochum, FRG, 1991, table 6, p. 139.

Urals—the former WTO group of six is now a group of 12 separate states.[41] It is not clear, however, how to divide up the inspections among the newly independent states. For example, will Russia be willing to accept inspectors from Azerbaijan, Georgia and Ukraine?

During 1991, even though the CFE Treaty was not yet in force, several CFE signatory states put their national verification teams into action, and NATO set

[41] The 12 countries are the five former NSWTO states (Bulgaria, Czechoslovakia, Hungary, Poland and Romania), and the seven former Soviet republics (Armenia, Azerbaijan, Belarus, Georgia, Moldova, Russia and Ukraine). Two oblasts (Guryev and Uralsk) of Kazakhstan are also in the ATTU zone but at the end of Mar. 1992 Kazakhstan had declined all invitations to attend HLWG or NACC meetings.

up a Verification Co-ordinating Committee (VCC) in the Netherlands. Together with the Supreme Headquarters Allied Powers Europe (SHAPE) and the NATO international military staff, the VCC devised a common training course for inspectors, encouraged common reporting procedures and developed a schedule to avoid unnecessary duplication while at the same time covering the entire ATTU zone. Several states conducted test inspections. The USA inspected Czechoslovakia and Hungary, the USSR inspected Germany, and the UK inspected Czechoslovakia.[42] Some of these test inspections were bilateral: Canada and Hungary inspected Germany together, for example, and this could become the model for future inspections, both to share technology as well as to prevent the exhaustion of quotas by intra-group inspections. One possibility would be for NATO states to invite observers from former NSWTO states (mostly lacking modern surveillance equipment) to accompany their inspections of the members of the group of 12 states. Another possibility would be to renegotiate a new quota of inspections after the Treaty enters into force.

III. Prospects for ratification of the CFE Treaty in 1992

In late January 1992 the CIS states expressed their willingness to comply with the CFE Treaty when they joined the CSCE. The other CSCE states did not insist on Treaty ratification as a condition for their participation, however, since it was considered in the general interest to embrace the whole of the former Soviet Union in the CSCE process. With the best of intentions, the CIS states will find ratification and implementation of the CFE Treaty impossible until they have resolved differences among themselves. In early 1992, the main issues disputed among the CIS states were the command, control and disposition of Soviet nuclear weapons, the reorganization of the armed forces and the general sharing out of former Soviet resources.[43] Additional problems between Ukraine and Russia centred around which state should control the Crimea and how to share command and control of the Black Sea Fleet. Between Armenia and Azerbaijan there were recurrent bouts of conflict over the disputed enclave of Nagorno-Karabakh. Within states, there was serious unrest in Georgia and problems of secession could be seen in the Russian Federation, especially in the independent republics of Tartarstan and Checheno-Ingushetia.

In general, while all the other CSCE states wanted the CIS to ratify and implement the CFE Treaty, not least to achieve and maintain military transparency in Europe, little effort was made to impose solutions or to resolve disputes between and within the Soviet successor states. Middle-level NATO officials were anxious to offer various TLE reallocation schemes to the CIS

---

[42] Bellamy, C., 'European armies stand ready to bury each other's hatchets', *The Independent*, 17 Feb. 1992.
[43] See chapter 14 in this volume.

states, but NATO capitals were wary of appearing to take sides, for example, to intercede between Russian and Ukrainian interests.

Various targets were set and missed, for example, 14 February 1992 and 20 March 1992, for the CIS states to reallocate their TLE ceilings for the CFE Treaty. As this chapter went to press the hope was to complete the CFE Treaty ratification by the close of the CSCE follow-up meeting in Helsinki in July 1992.

IV. Prospects for manpower reductions in the CFE 1A Negotiations

Despite uncertainties about whether the 1990 CFE Treaty would enter into force, the 22 signatories began negotiations in Vienna on 26 November 1990 towards a follow-up agreement to limit military personnel. The USA and some other Western delegates refused to negotiate seriously or to participate in plenary meetings until the Soviet General Staff had resolved the disputes over Soviet data in the JCG in mid-June 1991 (see table 12.4). France, Germany and the former NSWTO states, however, were anxious not to break off the CFE 1A talks altogether. Germany was especially anxious not to undermine the possibility that the USSR would ratify the 'Two-plus-Four' agreement on German unification.[44] The Supreme Soviet did so on 3 March 1991. Work proceeded informally in the absence of plenary sessions for several months.

The main difference between the CFE 1A Negotiations and the 1989–90 CFE Negotiation was that there was no longer any semblance of a WTO caucus. The former WTO states negotiated independently or closely with individual NATO states, as did Canada and Hungary, for example, at the Open Skies negotiations. Czechoslovakia, Hungary and Poland frequently formed a caucus on security issues, including arms control positions at the CFE 1A Negotiations as well as in the CFE Joint Consultative Group.[45]

Once the Soviet data problems were settled NATO's High Level Task Force (HLTF) submitted a document via Luxembourg in early July 1991. This draft proposed national rather than group-of-state ceilings and included limits on personnel in all branches of the armed services (land, sea and air) as well as on reservists.

Working groups were formed on 5 July 1991. Group A dealt with manpower definition questions and Group B with stabilization measures. Germany took the lead as the only one of the 22 CFE Treaty signatories with limits on its manpower and the most anxious to impose limits on others. In mid-July Germany presented a 'playground' chart of 11 categories of military manpower: (a) commands, headquarters, agencies, central training establishments;

---

[44] The Treaty on the Final Settlement with Respect to Germany, 12 Sep. 1990, is reprinted in Rotfeld, A. D. and Stützle, W. (eds), SIPRI, *Germany and Europe in Transition* (Oxford University Press: Oxford, 1991), pp. 183–86.

[45] For a schedule of meetings between Czechoslovakia, Hungary and Poland (sometimes referred to as the Visegrad Triangle after a meeting in Feb. 1991), see Clarke, D. L., 'Central Europe: military cooperation in the triangle', *RFE/RL Research Report*, 10 Jan. 1992, pp. 42–45.

(*b*) centrally controlled units; (*c*) land forces; (*d*) air forces; (*e*) air defence forces; (*f*) land-based naval forces; (*g*) internal security forces; (*h*) strategic rocket forces; (*i*) other forces; (*j*) UN forces; and (*k*) reservists.[46] The Soviet delegate wanted an additional category of rear forces or strategic reserves. Data submitted in 1991 showed NATO military personnel at 5.4 million, Soviet at 3.15 million and former NSWTO forces at 1.19 million. These levels could all be considerably reduced before conclusion of a CFE-1A treaty in 1992.[47]

By the end of the year the 22 CFE Treaty signatories were working on a German draft treaty, submitted on 21 November, that built on earlier proposals by Czechoslovakia, Hungary, Poland and the UK and was supported by 10 other states. States that had withheld support were troubled by provisions that allowed for upward revision of manpower limits, which they saw as built-in instability.[48]

After the collapse of the Soviet Union at the end of 1991, the CFE 1A forum spent several sessions debating how to incorporate the newly independent former sovereign states.

V. The Treaty on Open Skies

The idea of an 'Open Skies' regime of aerial inspection was first proposed by President Dwight Eisenhower in July 1955, but made little progress during the cold war years. The idea was resurrected by President Bush in May 1989, and talks were conducted parallel to the CFE and CFE 1A negotiations in Vienna during 1990 and 1991. Hungary and Romania signed a bilateral treaty in May 1991 and a multilateral Open Skies Treaty was signed by 25 states in March 1992: the 16 NATO countries, the five former NSWTO states and four former Soviet republics. Russia, Belarus and Ukraine all participated in the negotiations during early 1992 and, on the day of signature, Georgia also signed up as a 'founder member', even though it was not listed as such on the first copies of the Treaty document. The non-Soviet states parties agreed that all the former Soviet republics could adhere automatically but adherence may not be automatic for other applicants; for example, Turkey has apparently threatened to block the adherence of Cyprus.[49]

Issues in the negotiations

The main issues to be resolved were: the territory to be covered, the sophistication of the surveillance technology and the sharing of gathered data, the number of flights, and the ownership of the aircraft used. In common with the CFE Negotiation, the Open Skies talks were characterized by an increasingly

[46] *Arms Control Reporter*, sheet 410.B.10, 12 July 1991.
[47] *Focus on Vienna*, no. 25 (Nov. 1991), p. 2.
[48] *Focus on Vienna*, no. 26 (Dec. 1991).
[49] 'Opening the skies', *The Economist*, 28 Mar. 1992, p. 58.

co-operative attitude on the part of the Soviet delegation, especially after the appointment of Ambassador Yevgeniy Golovko as Head of Delegation in November 1991.

Hungary was particularly active in this forum, not only in pursuing a bilateral agreement with Romania but also in pioneering test flights with Canada.

Territory to be inspected

Unlike the CFE Treaty, that applies only to territory between the Atlantic Ocean and the Ural Mountains, the Open Skies Treaty covers all the territory of the signatory states, that is, currently from Vancouver to Vladivostok. For several months the Soviet delegation insisted that certain militarily sensitive areas should be exempt from military overflights. This was rejected by all the other participants, however. The Treaty only exempts areas in which overflights would be hazardous, for example, in the vicinity of nuclear energy installations and chemical plants emitting dangerous waste gases.

Surveillance technology

The US position during the negotiations was that any types of sensor could be used except those used for signals intelligence (SIGINT). Initially the former USSR adopted a more restrictive attitude, wanting only sensors with image resolution considered inadequate by Western standards. The Soviet delegates in Vienna gave no specific reason for these restrictions but non-Soviet delegates assumed it to be mainly paranoia about inferior technology.[50] Eventually all delegates agreed to choose sensors and flight parameters so as to achieve a resolution of no better than 30 cm with their optical and infra-red sensors and no more than 3 m with the radar.[51] Four categories of sensor are permitted: optical panoramic and framing cameras, video cameras with real-time display, infra-red line-scanning devices, and sideways looking synthetic aperture radar.

Data sharing

The Soviet delegation wanted to have maximum sharing of data and shared data processing, with the results available to all states parties and perhaps distributed via the CSCE Conflict Prevention Centre. The USA was unenthusiastic about sharing data, being unwilling to share its more sophisticated technology. In the end the Open Skies Treaty provided for the sharing of raw data but made no provision for assistance with analysis of the data gathered.[52]

---

[50] Jones, P., 'Open Skies, a review of events at Ottawa and Budapest', in Poole (note 1), pp. 73–82.
[51] Treaty on Open Skies, 25 Mar. 1992, Article IV, para. 2.
[52] Treaty on Open Skies, 25 Mar. 1992, Article IV, para. 1.

Flight quotas and advance notice requirements

Negotiations about the number and frequency of overflights was complicated by the growing number of Soviet successor states and by the wide range of national capabilities to conduct such flights. To make the Treaty more equitable the parties formed groups of states that would be treated as single states parties for the purpose of setting quotas; for example Russia with Belarus, and the three Benelux countries together. Both active and passive quotas are set for different groups of states so that no state party may conduct more inspections than it accepts over its own territory. The USA and Russia will each accept up to 42 flights per annum; medium European powers—France, Germany, Italy, Ukraine and the UK—will each accept 12 per annum; smaller countries will accept proportionately fewer. Far more states want to overfly Ukraine than Ukraine is obliged to accept under the terms of the Treaty so Canada, for example, plans to share its flights over Ukraine with the USA. Article VI ensures that overflights truly are short-notice inspections by establishing the advance notice that must be given: 72 hours notice for a planned flight and 24 hours for the exact flightpath.

Ownership of aircraft

The most contentious issue during the negotiations was that of whether the observed or observing state should provide the aircraft. The USA argued that each party should have the choice of using its own aircraft or asking the host state to provide one. The USSR, however, insisted that all flights over its territory be in Soviet aircraft. Non-Soviet delegates acquiesced in this so long as Western sensors could be used on the flights over Russian territory. It remains to be seen whether Russia will be able to keep sufficient observation aircraft on standby throughout its territory as the notice required for observation flights is so short.

Appendix 12A. Implementation of the Vienna Document 1990 in 1991

ZDZISLAW LACHOWSKI

I. Introduction

On 17 November 1990 the Vienna Document 1990 of the Negotiations on Confidence- and Security-Building Measures, incorporating traditional and new confidence- and security-building measures (CSBMs), was adopted in Vienna by the Conference on Security and Co-operation in Europe (CSCE). CSBMs and the other co-operative arrangements in this agreement have acquired new significance in the post-cold war era. With the threat of massive surprise attack in Europe gone, CSBMs are obtaining a new function in this period of transition. Now they are to create co-operative, positive relationships on the one hand, and prevent, defuse and manage new threats, emerging no longer from the East–West confrontation but within individual states or across borders—mainly along ethnic and national lines—on the other. In this sense, the Vienna Document is rather an extension of the classical confidence-building measures than a thorough innovation. At the same time, however, it called into being new institutions of the CSCE process to address more effectively the new security challenges and problems arising in the European context. During 1991, the CSCE states made efforts to cope with the new developments, both inside and outside the pan-European framework.

This appendix reviews developments in the field of CSBMs since the entry into force of the Vienna Document 1990[1] and details the notifiable military activities for 1992 as planned by the then 38 CSCE states.[2] The new CSBM agreement incorporated measures contained in the 1986 Stockholm Document[3] with a number of new categories—risk reduction, transparency of military organization, contacts and communications.

The measures adopted in the Vienna Document 1990 were, in line with the CSCE rule, politically rather than legally binding and came into force on 1 January 1991. The new measures were as follows:

Note: As of 27 Mar. 1992 the following CSCE participating states had failed to respond positively to SIPRI's request for information on the implementation of the Vienna Document 1990: Albania, Austria, Estonia, France, Greece, Latvia, Lithuania, Luxembourg, Monaco, San Marino, Spain, the UK and Yugoslavia.

[1] Vienna Document 1990 of the Negotiations on Confidence- and Security-Building Measures Convened in Accordance with the Relevant Provisions of the Concluding Document of the Vienna Meeting of the Conference on Security and Co-operation in Europe, Vienna, 17 Nov. 1990, reprinted in SIPRI, *SIPRI Yearbook 1991: World Armaments and Disarmament* (Oxford University Press: Oxford, 1991), appendix 13B, pp. 475–88.

[2] With the accessions of Albania (19 June 199), Estonia, Latvia and Lithuania (10 Sep. 1991) the CSCE consisted of 38 states during 1991. This number rose to 48 on 29 Jan. 1992 when 10 former Soviet republics were admitted to the CSCE, and to 51 on 24 Mar. 1992 when Georgia, Slovenia and Croatia joined the Helsinki process.

[3] For the text of the 1986 Stockholm Document see SIPRI, *SIPRI Yearbook 1987: World Armaments and Disarmament* (Oxford University Press: Oxford, 1987), appendix 10A, pp. 353–69. The implementation of the Stockholm Document is discussed in all subsequent *SIPRI Yearbooks*.

1. Under the heading *annual exchange of military information*: (*a*) information exchange on military forces down to brigade/regiment for land and amphibious forces and to wing/air regiment for air forces and naval aviation permanently based on land, including normal peacetime location; (*b*) information exchange on the deployment of major weapon and equipment systems; and (*c*) information exchange on military budgets in accordance with the UN format.

2. Under *risk reduction*: (*a*) the mechanism for consultation and co-operation as regards unusual military activities; and (*b*) co-operation as regards hazardous incidents of a military nature.

3. Under *contacts*: (*a*) visits to normal peacetime air bases; and (*b*) military-to-military contacts between senior and defence ministry representatives and other military experts.

4. Under *prior notification of certain military activities* the measures in the 1986 Stockholm Document are enhanced by the requirement for a more detailed information exchange on the designation, subordination, number and type of formations and units down to and including brigade/regiment or equivalent level.

5. Under *observation of certain military activities* it is envisaged that host states will provide detailed information regarding the exercises to facilitate close observation; furnish or allow the use of better maps and observation equipment; be encouraged to provide aerial surveys; facilitate discussion between host state officials and observers on the course of the observed activity; provide for the invitation of media representatives, and so on.

6. Under *constraining provisions* it is specified that military activities involving more than 40 000 troops require special notification procedures.

7. Under *verification and compliance* another new measure, evaluation, is introduced.

8. Establishment of a direct communications network between CSCE capitals is envisaged for the transmission of messages relating to agreed measures.

9. Under the auspices of the Conflict Prevention Centre, established by the 1990 CSCE Summit Meeting in Paris,[4] an annual meeting is to review present and future implementation of CSBMs.

The Vienna Document 1990 not only developed and extended the scope of the Stockholm Document CSBMs but also institutionalized the process of providing information and developing co-operation about the military activities of CSCE participating states. Among various CSCE institutions the Conflict Prevention Centre (CPC) plays a central role in giving support to the implementation of CSBMs: it covers such arrangements as the mechanism for consultation and co-operation as regards unusual military activities; an annual exchange of military information; the communications network; annual implementation assessment meetings; and co-operation as regards hazardous incidents of a military nature. The first session of the CSCE Council of Foreign Ministers in Berlin on 19–20 June 1991 set up the mechanism for consultation and co-operation with regard to emergency situations.[5]

---

[4] For a more detailed discussion of the provisions of the Vienna Document, see Borawski, J., 'The Negotiations on Confidence- and Security-Building Measures: The Vienna agreement and beyond', *Jane's NATO Handbook 1991–92* (Jane's Publishing Co.: Coulsdon, UK, 1991), pp. 125–30.

[5] Institutionalizing CSBM information has, however, had a paradoxical effect as regards its public availability. In requesting such information according to the Vienna provisions, SIPRI encountered a good deal of reluctance on the part of some CSCE states, across Europe, to furnish the data to a public institution. A number of governments, such as those of the USA, Germany and Central and East

On 4 March 1992 a new CSBM document, the Vienna Document 1992, was agreed in Vienna by the then 48 CSCE participants.[6]

II. Implementation

As of 1 January 1992, all CSCE participating states have generally complied with the terms of the Vienna Document 1990 concerning the exchange of annual calendars, forecasts, and notifications and as regards observations and inspections. Some problems arose with implementing provisions concerning the exchange of military information, mainly because of the innovative and complex nature of this requirement. The most serious concern arose over the failure of Yugoslavia to provide its military data at the end of 1991, which bears witness to the fact that CSBMs tailored to work in peacetime are of little use in time of war.[7] Similarly, the risk reduction mechanisms failed in the case of Yugoslavia because of their inherent drawbacks (the consensus rule and the lack of peace-keeping capabilities). There was also one case of non-compliance in the area of evaluation.

Calendars

The developments of 1991 in Eastern and Central Europe, and especially events in the USSR, have profoundly affected military activities in Europe. In 1990, 21 notifiable activities were included in the annual calendars for 1991, of which 12 were notified and conducted.[8] Six of the 10 activities originally announced in the annual calendars were scaled down below the notifiable or observable levels or cancelled altogether. Of the four remaining activities only two were observed by representatives of other CSCE states: one in Sweden in March and the other in Germany in September. The provisions of the Vienna Document 1990 on transparency, openness and confidence-building are poorly relevant in responding to the developments and trends of the new European politico-military reality. With less insight into the military activities of other states a 'transparency gap' has been felt.

On 31 March, the military structures of the WTO ceased to exist. The economic crisis and the consequent budgetary constraints painfully felt by all former WTO countries have had a considerable effect on limiting the military activities of the individual states. The abortive August coup in the USSR ushered in the final phase of dismantling that state and, in the military realm, led to reducing the magnitude of or cancelling the planned notifiable manoeuvres.[9] Of the four exercises foreseen

---

European states, were very co-operative in delivering the information requested, but some others considered that military information, and in particular information about military forces, should be made available only to the other CSCE governments and not to the general public. The problem of public access to CSBM information deserves careful scrutiny, because an across-the-board restriction is bound to contradict and depreciate the very concept of confidence-building.

[6] Vienna Document 1992 of the Negotiations on Confidence- and Security-Building Measures Convened in Accordance with the Relevant Provisions of the Concluding Document of the Vienna Meeting of the Conference on Security and Co-operation in Europe, Vienna, 4 Mar. 1992.

[7] The USSR's restrictive approach to provision of information in the first half of 1991 also added to the complications.

[8] Krohn, A., 'Implementation of the Stockholm Document and calendar of planned notifiable military activities in 1991', SIPRI, *SIPRI Yearbook 1991: World Armaments and Disarmament* (Oxford University Press: Oxford, 1991), p. 495.

[9] Russia's defence expenditures for 1992 will be reduced by about 30 per cent; *Izvestia*, 27 Jan. 1992. According to CIA estimates, the Russian military budget in 1992 will be about one-third that of the

Table 12A.1. Military activities at or above the notifiable threshold which were scaled down or cancelled in 1991

State(s)/Location	No. of troops reduced from—to	Exercise no. in *SIPRI Yearbook 1991*[a]
UK and Netherlands in Norway ('Adger 91')	4 000 –*c.* 900 (below notifiable level)	1
USA, UK, Belgium, Netherlands, France and FRG in FRG ('Certain Shield 91')	42 850–28 400	4
Denmark, FRG, Netherlands, UK, USA, Belgium, Luxembourg, Italy and Canada in Denmark ('Action Express 91')	20 000–14 500 (below observable level)	5
USSR in USSR (Leningrad MD)	17 000–*c.* 7 800 (below notifiable level)	6
USSR in USSR (Odessa MD)	*c.* 9 000–*c.* 5 000 (below notifiable level)	8
USSR in USSR (Byelorussian MD)	*c.* 10 000–*c.* 7 000 (below notifiable level)	9
USSR in USSR (Carpathian MD)	Cancelled	10

[a] See Krohn, A., 'Implementation of the Stockholm Document and calendar of planned notifiable military activities in 1991', SIPRI, *SIPRI Yearbook 1991: World Armaments and Disarmament* (Oxford University Press: Oxford, 1991), table 13C.1, pp. 490–92.

by the USSR for the period September–October 1991, three were reduced in size to below the notifiable level and the fourth was cancelled.

Of the neutral and non-aligned (NNA) states, which previously conducted a rather constant number of two to three military exercises annually, only Sweden conducted a notifiable activity in 1991.

The new climate and developments in international relations in Europe also affected the size and character of NATO exercises. The Atlantic Alliance has had to come to grips with budgetary constraints on military expenditures. The largest NATO exercise, 'Certain Shield 91', was reduced in scope and involved only 28 400 troops (instead of the planned 42 850) including 4500 (instead of 15 500) from the USA in the 'Reforger 91' deployment. The 'Certain Shield' manœuvre was primarily a command post exercise using computers to simulate and generate a realistic battle picture for tactically deployed brigade and higher-level headquarters. Moreover, NATO's new Multinational Airmobile Division (MNAD), a key component of the Allied Command Europe Rapid Reaction Corps, was given its first trial since its

Soviet Union in 1991, see *International Herald Tribune*, 26 Feb. 1992. The military expenditure of the former USSR and its successor states is addressed in chapter 7 in this volume.

establishment in May 1991 during this type of exercise. The deployment of the multinational division resulted in the largest helicopter operation in the history of NATO.[10] Unlike previous exercises of this type, no tanks or any other heavy ACVs were used nor were any low-flying aircraft allowed. For the first time the 'Certain Shield' exercise scenario did not include a real enemy. Another major NATO exercise, 'Action Express 91', was also scaled down and employed 14 500 troops as against a planned 20 000.

Annual exchange of military information

By 15 April 1991 information on military forces and plans for the deployment of major weapons, valid as of 1 May 1991, were provided by the participating states, as envisaged in the Vienna Document 1990.[11] The information exchanged is to be standardized and presented, together with other data on CSBMs, in a CPC Yearbook by the Conflict Prevention Centre in Vienna. However in April 1991, during the meeting of the CPC Consultative Committee, it emerged that the participants were far from agreement on the guidelines for the yearbook: what it should contain and whether it ought to go beyond purely statistical information.[12] Later in the year, the CSCE participating states managed to reach near consensus on the yearbook, with the exception of two issues: the language in which it should be published and the level of public availability it should have. Publication was also overtaken by the breakup of the Soviet Union which contributed to further delay.

In the debates in April–May in the CPC Consultative Committee, and in statements made during the CSBM Negotiations, the military information exchange was repeatedly welcomed as a highly important measure enhancing openness in military matters. Most military information exchanged previously concerned top military secrets. Moreover, for states not signatory to the 1990 Treaty on Conventional Armed Forces in Europe (CFE) this was the first thorough military information available, and even the CFE Treaty signatories found the exchange to contain important new elements of the military situation in Europe.

The favourable assessment of the first annual exchange notwithstanding, the restrictive approach to and even manipulation in interpretation of the Vienna Document by the USSR was pointed out and criticized. In another case, a state was denounced for behaving as if certain areas were outside the area of application despite the clear mandate for the Conference on Confidence- and Security-Building Measures and Disarmament in Europe agreed upon in the 1983 concluding document of the second CSCE follow-up meeting in Madrid.[13] All in all, however, participants withheld

[10] The 8000-strong MNAD consisted of the British 24th Airmobile Brigade, the German 27th Airborne Brigade and the Belgian Para-Commando Brigade supported by British, German and Netherlands helicopters. The MNAD will not become operational before 1993. Hallerbach, R., 'Manöver "Certain Shield 91", Nachweis von Mängeln der Luftbeweglichkeit', *Europäische Sicherheit*, no. 11 (1991), pp. 618–19. In 1992, a newly established Netherlands air-mobile brigade will join the MNAD which is eventually expected to number about 15 000. See 'Debut for MNAD in "Certain Shield"', *Jane's Defence Weekly*, 21 Sep. 1991.

[11] The Vienna Document 1990 requires that the annual information be provided to all other participating states not later than 15 Dec. of each year (para. 10).

[12] Among other things, a technical problem has arisen since the quantity of information exchanged is quite considerable; it amounts to about 500 pages. See an interview with CPC Director, Bent Rosenthal in *Focus on Vienna*, no. 23 (May 1991), pp. 6–7.

[13] In the first annual exchange of military data, Turkey did not provide information on its forces in northern Cyprus. Later, in Nov. 1991, it disseminated this information to CSCE participants at the annual implementation assessment meeting, stating at the same time that it did that without prejudice to its

individual criticism and rather pointed to general drawbacks of information provided while seeking to clear up misunderstandings and discrepancies. Concerns were also voiced about inconsistencies likely to emerge in the process of restructuring armies in years to come—between information received during evaluation visits and the annually exchanged information, on the basis of which such visits are to take place.

At the Berlin CSCE Council of Foreign Ministers meeting in June 1991 a dialogue on arms sales and transfers was recommended. This question was picked up at the CSBM negotiations and a Polish proposal was submitted suggesting extending the information exchange to those areas. It gained considerable support among other delegations, but because of the complexity of the subject it seems unlikely to be agreed before the CSCE follow-up meeting in Helsinki (March–July 1992) ends.[14]

The significance of information on military budgets lies in the fact that all CSCE states undertook to exchange information on the basis of the categories set out in the UN 'Instrument for Standardised International Reporting of Military Expenditures' adopted on 12 December 1980. However, comparing military budgets constitutes a very complex question, and a number of CSCE states have never participated in the UN data exchange before. At the implementation assessment meeting in November 1991 the complexity of the problem was taken note of, and it was considered to be too early to come to any conclusion. Hope was expressed that, with further transparency and time, it will be possible to draw conclusions about the direction that each country is taking.

In this light it seems that many of the problems that have arisen in the field of military information exchange stem from or are related to the novelty of the subject matter and to the political changes in Europe. Many states, and not only those that have little experience in these matters, had difficulties with providing appropriate information regarding armed forces and military budgets.

In the run-up to the CSCE follow-up meeting in Helsinki a number of suggestions and proposals regarding exchange of military information were made: to hold yearly meetings on military information exchange as part of a 'common defence review' (based on NATO defence planning experience); to harmonize information exchanged at the CFE and CSBM negotiations; to provide broader information about reallocation of units and weapon systems during the reorganization of formations, with a brief explanation of their origin; to streamline budget information to make it comparable both among the states and within them; to extend periods for notifying plans for the deployment of major weapons and equipment systems and make more details available, including the destination of equipment; to complete information by a count of the total number of units in order to have quotas correctly calculated; and to explain terminology not generally used while providing information.[15] A later proposal concerned the 'notification of upgrading of low-strength formations and combat units'.[16]

reservation regarding the issue of the status of northern Cyprus. The accuracy of Turkish information was, on the other hand, called into question by the Greek and Cypriot representatives.

[14] *Focus on Vienna*, no. 25 (Oct.–Nov. 1991), p. 3. The Prague CSCE Council of Foreign Ministers meeting in Jan. 1992 adopted a declaration calling for inclusion of international armaments transfers as a matter of priority in the programme for the post-Helsinki arms control process. See Declaration of the CSCE Council on Non-Proliferation and Arms Transfers, Prague, 30 Jan. 1992.

[15] Non-paper: 'Suggestions for improvement in the provisions of the Vienna Document', Annual Implementation Assessment Meeting, 1991, Vienna, 19 Nov. 1991.

[16] Institute for Defense and Disarmament Studies, *Arms Control Reporter* (IDDS: Brookline, Mass.), sheet 402.B.293, 21 Nov. 1991. This proposal, submitted by the UK on 21 Nov. 1991, found reflection in the Vienna Document 1992, para. 11.3.

The successive annual military information exchange had taken place by the end of 1991 in accordance with the Vienna Document. One CSCE state, Yugoslavia, did not provide any military data.

Risk reduction

The CSCE mechanism for consultation and co-operation which allows each participant to seek an explanation from another country when an unusual military activity takes place was invoked for the first time in the case of the crisis in Yugoslavia.[17] After Slovenia and Croatia had declared their independence on 25 June 1991, the Yugoslav Government outlawed their declarations and ordered the federal army to take control of Yugoslavia's international borders in those two republics.[18] On 27 June, Austria, supported by Italy, requested the convening of a meeting of the CPC Consultative Committee to examine 'unusual military activities on the part of the Yugoslav army'. On the same day, the Western European Union (WEU) asked the CSCE to convene a meeting of the Committee of Senior Officials (CSO) under another CSCE emergency procedure—the mechanism for consultation and co-operation with regard to emergency situations, established one week before at the Berlin CSCE Council of Foreign Ministers meeting.[19] From then on, the Yugoslav crisis was dealt with in parallel by those two bodies.

Two days later Yugoslavia responded to the request by Austria and Italy for information in accordance with the required 48-hour deadline. The next day, Austria, not satisfied with Yugoslavia's response, called for a full meeting of the CSCE at the Vienna CPC. The meeting took place on 1 July and called for an immediate cease-fire and the return of all troops to their barracks. Meanwhile the European Community (EC) was displaying diplomatic initiative and dispatching a peace mission to Belgrade. On 3–4 July 1991 the CSO meeting in Prague called for a cease-fire and offered the 'good offices' of the CSCE to promote the peace process in Yugoslavia. It also backed up the EC monitoring mission to observe the Slovenian cease-fire.

After the failure of cease-fire efforts Germany called for a second CSCE emergency meeting in Prague on 8–9 August, at which it was agreed to expand the international observer force in Yugoslavia into Croatia and to include non-CSCE countries. On 4 September the CSCE crisis management session in Prague called on all states to 'refrain, for the duration of the crisis in Yugoslavia, from supplying arms and military equipment to all Yugoslav parties.'

On 20 August, the mechanism for consultation and co-operation as regards unusual military activities was triggered once again, and this time delegations of Hungary and Yugoslavia met at the Secretariat of the CPC to settle the growing tension between the two states. When on 27 October Yugoslav aircraft bombarded the Hungarian town of Barcs, the Hungarian Government circulated a *note verbale* on 30 October to protest against the incident and referred to the Vienna provision on co-operation as regards hazardous incidents of a military nature.

---

[17] Some states had considered calling an emergency meeting of the CPC in early 1991 to help prevent Soviet moves against the Baltic states. The USSR opposed this, claiming that the measures applied only to a 'threat to security in international relations', for which they were rebuked by the US representative. *Arms Control Reporter,* sheet 402.B.282, 26 Feb. 1991.

[18] For more details of the conflict see chapter 11 in this volume.

[19] 'Mechanism for consultation and co-operation with regard to emergency situations', Annex 2 to the Summary of Conclusions adopted at the Berlin Meeting of the CSCE Council of Foreign Ministers, 19–20 June 1991; and chapter 15 in this volume.

In the late summer of 1991 it seemed that the European Community was better equipped to deal with the crisis than the cumbersome CSCE consensus mechanisms, so the latter soon virtually ceded efforts to resolve the Yugoslav crisis to the EC political co-operation mechanism. This fact made many participants of the CSCE Conference on the Human Dimension in Moscow, which opened on 10 September, criticize Europe-related security structures as inadequate to handle qualitatively new situations like that in Yugoslavia. With the EC unable to solve the question of its security identity and NATO paralysed by the resistance of several of its members (the USA and Britain) to get militarily involved in Yugoslavia, some European countries, especially Germany, would like to see the CSCE entrusted with the authority to intervene militarily in ethnic and nationality conflicts in individual states and across national borders.[20] However, this idea has also been strongly resisted, and in 1991 Europe was left still unable to define its role in defusing and resolving the existing disputes and those to come. The CSCE crisis management emergency mechanism held five meetings during the year, the last one in late November when it endorsed UN efforts to deploy a peace-keeping mission in Yugoslavia. The failure of the CSCE clearly demonstrated that its mechanisms were ill-equipped to handle the Yugoslav civil war: each time the federal government was in a position to block CSCE resolutions contrary to its interests.[21]

Visits to air bases

In line with the Vienna Document 1990, each participating state with air combat units, as reported in the annual exchange of military information, will arrange visits for representatives of all other participating states to one of its normal peacetime air bases and provide the visitors with the opportunity to view activity at the base. No participating state is obliged to arrange more than one such visit in any five-year period.

The first two visits, which took place in 1991, were paid to Swedish and Netherlands air bases, respectively. On 19–20 September 1991, the first CSBM-related visit to an air base was arranged by Sweden. The then 48 CSCE representatives from 26 countries were flown to the Norrköping air base where fighter and reconnaissance wings are stationed. The observers inspected various types of aircraft, including the modern Viggen, and the manœuvrability of the aircraft was demonstrated. The other visit was paid to the Netherlands Twenthe air base on 7–8 October, when 42 observers from 23 CSCE countries were briefed on the forthcoming restructuring of the Netherlands Air Force and on the organization and role of the base. The CSCE representatives were able to visit logistics and operational facilities and were shown various demonstrations, for example, of air defence and

---

[20] In the wake of the Aug. coup in the USSR, German Foreign Minister Hans-Dietrich Genscher stated in the Bundestag on 4 Sep. 1991 that the CPC should be enlarged to become a 'security council' capable of taking action (e.g., by setting up its own peace-keeping force), see *Der Bundesminister für Auswärtigen informiert, Mitteilung für die Presse*, no. 1192/91, Bonn, 4 Sep. 1991.

[21] In response to mounting criticism of the unwieldy CSCE conflict prevention and crisis management capabilities, the CSCE Council meeting in Prague on 30–31 Jan. 1992 decided to amend the consensus rule and consider 'appropriate action', if necessary in the absence of the consent of the state concerned, whenever 'clear, gross and uncorrected violations' of CSCE commitments take place. See Prague Document on Further Development of CSCE Institutions and Structures, Prague, 30 Jan. 1992. At the CSBM assessment meeting in Vienna in Nov. 1991, a proposal was made to hold CPC meetings at shorter notice than the envisaged 48 hours if the Chairman of the Consultative Committee deems it necessary.

radar systems. The visitors were also allowed to photograph the base. These events were a first experience in implementing the new confidence-building measures (Swedish and Netherlands organizers tried to synchronize their approaches before-hand, but there were still some differences in how they handled the visits[22]), and served as a point of departure for organizing successive ones.

Finland has announced that it will organize a visit to one of its air bases in September 1992, and Italy expressed its intention to organize such a visit to one of its air bases in the course of 1992.

Military contacts

In the CSCE area of military contacts, apart from a flurry of mutual visits of NATO and former WTO high-ranking defence officials and officers in Brussels and other European capitals, and other contacts on lower levels, one of the most significant events in 1991was the second military doctrine seminar held on 8–18 October in Vienna as a follow-up to the first held more than one year earlier. It provided a new opportunity to meet and discuss at the highest military level various aspects of military concepts, activities, postures, training, and so on.[23]

Another significant event was NATO's invitation for officers from CSCE states to attend special courses at the Alliance's Defence College in Rome, Italy, and the NATO school in Oberammergau, FRG, in line with the North Atlantic Council's decision taken in Copenhagen on 6–7 June 1991.[24] The courses started in October 1991; their aim is to 'promote greater awareness of NATO and how it is responding to the changing politico-military situation in Europe'.

In the light of experience gained from the military contacts accomplished, sug-gestions were made to draw up and distribute written reports after all such visits as well as to forward information on contacts to the CPC Secretariat for circulation to the participating states.

Notification and observation

Prior notifications for 1992 demonstrate a further steep decrease in planned exercises at or above the notifiable level. According to data obtained by SIPRI, NATO countries intend to carry out five major military exercises in 1992, the largest one not exceeding 22 000 troops. The neutral and non-aligned countries are not planning any notifiable military activities for 1992. The Russian Federation and other CIS members were unable as of 30 January 1992 to provide information on their planned military activities; however, in view of their military and economic problems, as well as a host of other problems, these military activities, combined or separate, will certainly be considerably scaled down.[25] On the whole, the military activities of the former WTO states no longer reach the Vienna prior notification thresholds.

---

[22] The Netherlands proposed to make the visits less formalized, allowing for an open discussion of the results.

[23] See appendix 12B in this volume.

[24] See statement by the NATO spokesman in *NATO Review*, no. 4 (Aug. 1991), p. 14. For more details, see Watt, A., 'The hand of friendship—the military contacts programme', *NATO Review*, no. 1 (Feb. 1992), pp. 19–21.

[25] In mid-Nov. 1991 the USSR let other CSCE governments know that it did not intend to carry out military activities subject to notification in 1992, nor would it envisage manœuvres exceeding 40 000 troops for 1993.

At the CSBM Negotiations in Vienna, it was suggested by the UK on 21 November 1991 that the threshold for notification of military activities be lowered to 9000 troops or 250 tanks, and the thresholds at which observers from other CSCE states have to be invited to the exercises be lowered to 13 000 troops and 3500 amphibious or airborne troops.[26] Such a lowering of thresholds seems desirable in the light of the considerable reduction in the number and magnitude of manoeuvres in recent years, particularly in 1991. The virtual application of those measures has become sporadic, and a need was voiced by many CSCE delegations to further decrease or establish supplementary parameters for those activities (e.g., new measures for activation of units or the right to observe command-post exercises).[27] Furthermore, smaller-scale exercises involving elements of highly mobile troops and requiring a shorter preparation time can now also be considered 'militarily significant', so the criterion of the large scale of an activity no longer seems exclusively valid, especially in view of the future character of military conflict on the continent marked by 'regionalism' rather than globalism. Consequently, a regional differentiation in notification and observation levels for military activities has been proposed. Other delegations, however, found the further lowering of thresholds and/or making them flexible burdensome and lacking in military relevance. Nevertheless, new criteria for military significance of military activities have been strongly called for by most participants, and new parameters on notification and observation were agreed in the Vienna Document 1992.

Constraining provisions

The Vienna Document 1990 states that military activities subject to prior notification involving more than 40 000 troops (the threshold was lowered from the 75 000 troops provided for in the 1986 Stockholm Document) may not be conducted unless they have been communicated more than a year in advance (by 15 November each year for the second subsequent calendar year). No such activities are to be carried out in 1992 nor are any planned for 1993. Constraining provisions were a major issue at the Vienna CSBM Negotiations, and the Vienna Document 1992 states *inter alia* that a participating state may conduct a military manoeuvre involving more than 40 000 troops or 900 battle tanks only once every two years; and that six exercises involving more than 13 000 troops or 300 battle tanks, but less than 40 000 troops or 900 battle tanks, can be carried out yearly. Of these six manoeuvres, only three may involve more than 25 000 troops or 400 battle tanks; there may be only three simultaneous military activities, each involving more than 13 000 troops or 300 battle tanks.[28]

Inspection and evaluation

This section in the Vienna Document 1990 on compliance and verification covers inspection and a new measure—evaluation. The significant element marking the new post-cold war era was the interpretative statement by Czechoslovakia, Hungary and Poland, made at the end of the CSBM Negotiations, indirectly retracting their

---

[26] *Arms Control Reporter*, sheet 402.B.293, 21 Nov. 1991. These parameters were agreed in the Vienna Document 1992 (paras 38 and 45), the tank threshold of 300 being added for exercises subject to observation.
[27] See note 16.
[28] The Vienna Document 1992 (note 6), paras 71–74.

statement at the Stockholm Conference in 1986 to the effect that the three countries would not inspect each other. The new statement declares that each of the three countries 'has the right to carry out inspections and evaluation visits on the territory of any other participating states and is ready to accept on its territory such inspections and evaluation visits' under the Vienna Document 1990.[29]

As noted by many observers at the annual assessment meeting in November 1991 inspections have become a widely accepted routine instrument for verification and for gaining insight into military activities, and not only in cases of doubt about other states' compliance with the agreed CSBMs. With the number of notifiable military activities systematically decreasing, there is a feeling that increasing the quota of inspections would help maintain the standard of openness achieved so far; also, by forming larger and multinational inspection teams, more countries would be given the opportunity to take part in compliance and verification activities.[30]

According to information acquired by SIPRI, all inspections and evaluation visits made in 1991 confirmed that the states concerned complied with the relevant Vienna Document 1990 provisions and that their military activities or deployments conformed to information given to other participating states. For the most part, inspections and evaluation visits were valuable in promoting confidence among CSCE states, and on some occasions the host states permitted examination way beyond the requirements of the Vienna provisions. However there was one complaint (by Greece, on the grounds of Turkey's failure to communicate the request to all CSCE states, including the Republic of Cyprus) in connection with the refusal to a request for an evaluation visit. It was found by CSCE states to be done, as one delegate stated, for 'reasons that have nothing to do with the aims and objectives of the Vienna Document itself'.[31]

During 1991, NATO countries (Canada, France and the USA) conducted three inspections on Soviet territory, and the USSR demanded four inspections on NATO territory (France, Italy, Norway and Turkey).

The number of evaluation visits known to SIPRI was 24 in 1991. The Soviet Union itself paid seven evaluation visits to NATO countries (three to Germany, including those to British and US troops—one each to France, Greece, Spain and the UK). The USSR was requested to accept seven evaluation teams from six states— Finland, France, Germany, Sweden, the UK (twice) and the USA. As far as other evaluation requests are concerned, the United Kingdom sent its teams to three countries (Poland, Romania and Sweden), French observers paid two visits (to Bulgaria and Romania) and Germany requested such visits to Bulgaria and Finland. There were also requests for evaluation visits from: Bulgaria (to Germany), the Netherlands (to Austria), Yugoslavia (to Greece) and Turkey (to Greece—refused).

The evaluation measure applies only to active units; however, Annex V to the Vienna Document 1990 provides that 'an adequate solution will be found to evaluate non-active[32] formations and units which are activated for routine training purposes'.

[29] CSCE Negotiations on Confidence- and Security-Building Measures, Vienna, 1989, *Journal*, no. 241/Rev. 1, Plenary Meeting, 17 Nov. 1990.

[30] Other suggestions concern the language preferred in inspections, the 'appropriate telecommunication equipment' for inspectors and defining provision of inspection reports in number of days. See note 16.

[31] Statement by the Netherlands Ambassador Veenendaal at the annual implementation assessment meeting, Vienna, 11 Nov. 1991.

[32] According to the Vienna Document 1990 definition, 'non-active units' have less than 15 per cent of combat strength.

At the CSBM Negotiations a proposal concerning evaluation visits to non-active and temporarily activated units was tabled on 15 March 1991 by Bulgaria, Hungary and Norway. The proposal would make temporarily activated or mobilized units with over 15 per cent of their staff subject to reporting and notification at least 42 days before activation. When units and formations were moved to a new normal location more than 50 km from the previous one, 42 days' prior notification would also be given. Some countries, however, particularly those whose strategies rely largely on mobilization (the USSR, Sweden, Switzerland), have felt that the new provisions will put them at a disadvantage as regards freedom of defence operations and burden them with the requirement of constantly providing information.[33]

Among other suggestions regarding evaluation visits are the following: the introduction of a homogenous verification procedure regime; an increase in the minimum number of quotas and balancing distribution of such visits, taking into account the circumstances of different countries; re-definition of the evaluation period; and provision for the use of cameras and plans of barracks.[34]

Communications

The Vienna Document 1990 provided for the establishment of 'a network of direct communications between CSCE capitals for the transmission of messages relating to agreed measures' to complement the existing use of normal diplomatic channels. The joint statement of 10 May 1991 by US Secretary of State James Baker and German Foreign Minister Hans-Dietrich Genscher recommended endorsement of the CPC communications facilities as a 'hotline' for emergency communications between CSCE capitals.[35] However this suggestion was not picked up and supported explicitly by the North Atlantic Council at its Copenhagen ministerial session on 6–7 June 1991. In the light of the impending Yugoslav crisis, however, the CSCE foreign ministers agreed two weeks later at their Berlin meeting that the communications network be used for all communications foreseen in the procedures for emergency situations; in this connection the CSCE Secretariat was to be integrated into the network.

The Netherlands was entrusted with the task of setting up and managing the communications network. It should have become operational by 15 April 1991, but because of financial problems the communications issue was not settled until September, and the system was put into operation on 1 November. None the less, by mid-November only 10 end-user stations were connected,[36] and the system is still far from satisfactory regarding efficient and fast communications among CSCE governments in all matters concerning CSBMs. The problem of communication among states was raised repeatedly in the CSBM implementation assessment debate in Vienna in November 1991.

An important question is how to provide Vienna-based delegations with copies of various communications transmitted through the communications network—either

---

[33] For example, Switzerland has a force structure predominantly based on non-active units, with relatively frequent call-ups for training.

[34] See note 16.

[35] *Dispatch*, vol. 2, no. 19 (13 May 1991), pp. 345–47.

[36] The Netherlands delegate at the annual implementation assessment meeting complained that of the 34 original signatories of the Paris Charter only 30 ordered the necessary equipment, and some states indicated explicitly that they did not intend to connect their capitals to the network.

this will be left to the national communications between capitals and their respective delegations or the role of the CPC Secretariat ought to be enhanced in this respect. This problem and that of how to supply messages to states not connected to the network were not solved in 1991. However, the intermediary role of the CPC seems to be gaining the upper hand, particularly in the view of states that, for various reasons, are not connected to the CSCE network.

The annual implementation assessment meeting

The first implementation assessment meeting was held by the Consultative Committee of the CPC in Vienna on 11–15 November 1991. Its agenda was broad and consisted of the following two main items:

1. Discussion on the operation of agreed measures and clarification of questions arising from their implementation in 1991 in the fields of: (a) military information (military forces, plans for deployment, military budgets and evaluation); and (b) military activities (risk reduction, contacts, notification, observation, annual calendars and constraining provisions, inspection and communications).
2. Discussion on the implications of all information originating from the implementation of any agreed measures for the process of confidence- and security-building in the framework of the CSCE in the future, including envisaged changes in the annual exchange of information, trends in military activities, indications of forthcoming schedules for visits to air bases.[37]

The meeting provided an opportunity to discuss virtually all matters of concern to participating states. The propitious political climate enabled a frank debate and the resolution of most differences in interpretation of the Vienna Document. On the other hand, there were no major discrepancies, which led to the comment that it was a 'fair-weather' meeting—an assessment not shared by all delegations. Particularly useful explanations were given by the Soviet delegation regarding information supplied under the provisions of the Vienna Document section on annual exchange of military information. Supplementary military information given by the Turkish representatives was also welcomed as a *signum temporis* reflecting the new climate in European relations. There were many proposals and ideas, and it was decided that the suggestions and conclusions submitted at the meeting be discussed in the Consultative Committee, which is also to consider the working programme and the date of the 1992 annual implementation assessment meeting. After the November meeting, the CPC submitted a list (non-paper) of suggested improvements to the Vienna Document.

III. Assessment and outlook

The 1990 Charter of Paris for a new Europe[38] provided for the continuation of the CSBM Negotiations under the same mandate and sought to conclude them not later than the CSCE follow-up meeting to be held in Helsinki, March–July 1992. The

---

[37] CSCE Conflict Prevention Centre, *Journal,* nos 10, 11 and 12, Vienna, 11, 12 and 13 Nov. 1991.
[38] The 1990 Charter of Paris for a New Europe is reprinted in Rotfeld, A. D. and Stützle, W. (eds), SIPRI, *Germany and Europe in Transition* (Oxford University Press: Oxford, 1991), pp. 603–10.

participating states also undertook to seek more structured co-operation among themselves aimed at merging the CSBM and CFE negotiations in 1992, after the Helsinki meeting, in the form of 'new negotiations on disarmament and confidence and security building open to all participating States'. Accordingly, the CSBM Negotiations reconvened on 26 November 1990 and were conducted throughout 1991.[39]

In the arms control process of the 1990s CSBMs and other co-operative security measures are becoming equally or even more important than further arms reductions. Since the adoption of the Vienna Document 1990, Europe has fortunately not been affected by major conflicts affecting the continent as a whole. The propitious political climate notwithstanding, mindful of the miserable events in Yugoslavia, the participating states have striven to prepare for contingencies. In the emerging 'European security architecture' the CSCE was equipped with a network of institutions, mechanisms and procedures which have been further developed in 1991.[40] However, the one-year experience of implementing the Vienna Document 1990 clearly shows that its 'classic' instruments, which were relevant to the cold war period, have become unsuitable for the new times. In the sphere of military activity and openness a set of new measures and parameters must be worked out to fill the growing 'transparency gap'; the risk reduction mechanisms are badly in need of improvement to handle new contingencies which have more to do with domestic than interstate relations; communications among the participants should also be further developed, and so on. In the run-up to the Helsinki follow-up meeting in 1992, some new steps were taken to catch up with the events, and the need for new measures and commitments to enhance security and co-operation in the CSCE area is under discussion.

On the other hand, the implementation of the Vienna Document was made easier by the continuing co-operative atmosphere. It could be said that the Vienna CSBMs enjoyed the benefit of 'good weather' and did not face (except in the case of Yugoslavia) a real test of their effectiveness. Exchanging military information, for instance, encounters objective obstacles; many participating states proved to be not familiar with with drawing up and providing such information. Again, thanks to the improved political climate, the implementation of this measure has not given rise to any major concerns. The failure by some CFE Treaty signatories to ratify the Treaty in 1991 threw the role of CSBMs into starker relief (particularly as regards verification provisions). The developments in Yugoslavia and the Soviet Union, and later, the emergence of independent Soviet successor states, also had a stimulating effect on the CSCE participants to speed up work on new security arrangements.

The Vienna Document 1992 agreed in March 1992, just prior to the CSCE Helsinki follow-up meeting, builds on existing CSBMs, supplementing them with more detailed parameters, and introduces a set of new measures integrated with the former. Under annual exchange of military information, the states undertook to provide additional information on planned personnel increases or activation of units and formations. Similarly, states will provide detailed data relating to major weapon and equipment systems to all other CSCE states once by the end of 1992. The risk

---

[39] However, it was only on 10 Apr. that the states agreed to form a Committee of the Whole to discuss additional CSBMs because of discrepancies that had prevailed as to whether to do any work on new measures. For this reason the less formal Committee, instead of a plenary, started its work, but no working groups were set up. *Arms Control Reporter*, sheet 402.B.284, 10 Apr. 1991.

[40] See also chapter 15 in this volume.

reduction provisions were strengthened by encouragement of states to host visits to dispel concerns about military activities. Under military contacts, demonstration of new types of major weapons and equipment systems was envisaged. Parameters for prior notification and observation of military exercises were changed and supplemented to meet new circumstances. In the area of constraining measures, most visible progress was made in further limiting the carrying out of major manœuvres. As regards verification, the main novelty is making non-active formations and units temporarily activated subject to evaluation; inspections may now be carried out by multinational teams. Like the preceding document, the Vienna CSBM Document 1992 is politically binding and comes into force as of 1 May 1992.

Discussion on further CSBMs and stabilizing measures is characterized by the search for stronger constraints on military activities and deployments; early notification of transfers; lower thresholds and limits on the size of military exercises; restrictions on the deployment of certain kinds of troops or equipment into specified areas; information on and possible limits on ground and air transport capacities; and better communication between states. Research and development, military planning, and information on military budgets, purchases and weapon production are also important for transparency.[41] A number of these subjects have already found reflection in the CFE and CSBM talks, but they are still in need of further elaboration and harmonization. Another important area is 'force generation': restrictions on the readiness level of active-duty manpower and limitation or regulation of the readiness of forces and of the call-up of reservists would certainly enhance crisis stability.

At the Berlin CSCE Council of Foreign Ministers meeting in June 1991 it was decided that informal preparatory consultations on the mandate for the post-Helsinki negotiations would start soon among the representatives to the CPC Consultative Committee. From mid-September 1991 until March 1992 a series of meetings were held and several proposals were made as regards the future structure of the negotiations. A new 'CSCE forum for security co-operation' is envisaged to be charged with the task of starting new negotiations on measures of arms control and disarmament, enhancing regular consultations and co-operation as well as furthering the process of reducing the risk of conflict among the participating states.[42]

---

[41] Torstila, P., 'New negotiations on disarmament and confidence and security building in Europe'. *Yearbook of Finnish Foreign Policy 1991* (The Finnish Institute of International Affairs, Helsinki, 1991), pp. 13-16.

[42] Compare Norway's 'host perception' summary of conclusions of the informal consultations carried out in Vienna from 17 Sep. 1991 to 19 Mar. 1992, circulated on 18 Mar. 1992 to all CSCE participants.

Table 12A.2. Calendar of planned notifiable military activities in 1992, as required by the Vienna Document 1990

States/Location	Dates/Start window	Type/Name of activity	Area	Level of command	No. of troops	Type of forces or equipment	No. and type of divisions	Comments
1. FRG, Netherlands, Norway, UK, USA in Norway	5 days, 17–27 Mar.	FTX 'Teamwork 92'	Andørja–Finnsnes–Lenvik–Tromsø–Karlsøya–Rotsund–Kåfjord–Mandalen–Bardu	Norwegian regional command	21 400[a]	Ground and air forces	1 light inf. div. and 2 brigs	Land operations and practice co-operation and interoperability between Norwegian and allied formations
2. Denmark, Netherlands, UK, USA, Norway in Norway	1–2 days, 19–22 Mar.	Amphibious landing exercise 'Teamwork 92'	Lenvik–Tromsø–Karlsøya–Rotsund–Kåfjord–Mandalen–Tomokdalen	Brigade	8 000[b]	Amphibious, air and ground forces	2 brigs	Involves landing craft and support helicopters. In conjunction with and precedes FTX 'Teamwork 92'
3. Italy, USA, UK, Spain, Neths, France, Portugal, Greece in Italy	6–19 May	Amphibious exercise 'Dragon Hammer 92'	SW Sardinia	Air command of amphibious operations	4 840[c]	Air and amphibious forces		Training the allied nations' troops for amphibious landing
4. USA, Germany, Canada and France in Germany	67 days, 10 Sep.–15 Nov.	FTX/CFX 'Certain Caravan 92'	Schweinfurth–Manheim–Köln–Kassel	NATO Central Army Group	21 100[d]	Ground and air forces	3 arm. divs (–) 5 mech. inf. divs (–) 1 light inf. div.	In conjunction with 'Reforger 92'; about 8 000 US troops to be transferred to Eur.; activity notifiable after transfer; active exercise—26 Sep.–9 Oct.
5. Germany, USA, France in Germany	16–25 Sep.	CFX 'Wackerer Schwabe'	Neckarhausen–Freudenbach–Friesenhofen–Ibach	Corps	15 000[e]	Ground and air forces	2 tank divs (–) 2 arm. inf. divs (–) 1 mtn div. (–)	Preparatory phase 6–19 Sep; French–German brig. will take part

[a] 12 000 Norway, 4 300 UK, 3 700 USA, 800 Netherlands, 600 Germany.

[b] 3 700 USA, 3 500 UK, 800 Netherlands.

[c] 1 800 USA, 800 UK, 800 Spain, 500 Greece, 400 France, 250 Italy, 150 Netherlands, 140 Portugal.

[d] 18 700 USA, 2 200 Germany, 300 Canada, 200 France.

[e] 3 500 FRG, 1 000 USA, 500 France.

Note: (–) means that the division is below full strength or not comprised of all its component parts; abbreviations: arm: armoured; brig: brigade; CFX: command field exercise; div: division; FTX: field training exercise; mech: mechanized; mtn: mountain.

Appendix 12B. The Second Vienna Seminar on Military Doctrine

ZDZISLAW LACHOWSKI

I. Introduction

The Second Seminar on Military Doctrine, held in Vienna on 8–18 October 1991, was organized within the institutional framework of the Conference on Security and Co-operation in Europe (CSCE)—the Confidence- and Security-Building Measure (CSBM) Negotiations and the Conflict Prevention Centre (CPC) and its Consultative Committee—according to the provisions of the Vienna Document 1990 of the CSBM Negotiations and the documents of the Paris summit meeting of the CSCE, 19–21 November 1990.[1] The CPC served as a forum for the seminar, which was initially scheduled for June–July 1991. However, since NATO was still in the process of reassessing its doctrine and many aspects of military strategy and policy, the Western delegates strongly insisted that it would make little sense to talk about the doctrines before the Atlantic Alliance itself had reached agreement. The Persian Gulf War fought between 17 January and 28 February also contributed to the decision to hold the seminar in October 1991.[2]

Anxiety was voiced in the spring and summer of 1991 that the seminar could fall victim to the success of the first such meeting, held 16 January–5 February 1990 in Vienna.[3] The 1991 seminar was to be organized along the same lines, gathering high-ranking military men to discuss detailed aspects of their states' military doctrines, but the same level of military representation was not assured. It was clear that the USA was unwilling to have the Chairman of the Joint Chiefs of Staff attend,[4] which was bound to lower the rank of other delegations sent to Vienna. In view of this, some

---

Note: This appendix is based mainly on an analysis of presentations delivered during the Vienna military doctrine debate. All quotations, except for those cited otherwise, derive from the official seminar materials. Statements made at the seminar are collected in National Defense Academy, *Second Seminar on Military Doctrine*, Vienna, Nov. 1991.

[1] Vienna Document 1990 of the Negotiations on Confidence- and Security-Building Measures convened in accordance with the Relevant Provisions of the Concluding Document of the Vienna Meeting of the Conference on Security and Co-operation in Europe, Vienna, 17 Nov. 1990. Reprinted in SIPRI, *SIPRI Yearbook 1991: World Armaments and Disarmament* (Oxford University Press: Oxford, 1991), appendix 13 B, pp. 475–88. The supplementary document to give effect to certain provisions contained in the Charter of Paris for a New Europe, Paris, 21 Nov. 1990 is reprinted in Rotfeld, A. D. and Stützle, W. (eds), SIPRI, *Germany and Europe in Transition* (Oxford University Press: Oxford, 1991), pp. 226–30.

[2] As one Western delegate in Vienna commented, 'You don't want officials guessing at what the new doctrine might be, nor do you want them defending a doctrine that's out of date'; *Vienna Fax*, vol. 2, no. 4 (6 May 1991), p. 2. Eventually, the decision to hold the seminar on 8–18 Oct. 1991 was adopted at the CSBM plenary session on 15 May 1991. See CSCE document CSCE/WV/Dec.3, Vienna, 15 May 1991.

[3] See Krohn, A., 'The Vienna Military Doctrine Seminar', SIPRI, *SIPRI Yearbook 1991: World Armaments and Disarmament* (Oxford University Press: Oxford, 1991), appendix 13D, pp. 501–11.

[4] Nevertheless, the US Government was anxious to assure that it supports CSCE-related institutional-ization of openness and transparency and envisages 'a regular dialogue about military forces, budgets, defense plans and doctrines'. See James Baker's Aspen Institute address on 'The Euro-Atlantic Archi-tecture: From East to West', Berlin, 18 June 1991, *Dispatch*, vol. 2, no. 25 (24 June 1991), pp. 439–43.

officials in the CSBM Negotiations insisted that the Second Seminar on Military Doctrine be better prepared and more structured than its predecessor. Eventually, however, a mandate was agreed upon, providing an agenda and rules of procedure similar to those of the 1990 meeting.

II. The seminar

The agenda

The purpose of the seminar was 'to allow for a discussion on military doctrine in relation to posture, structure and activities of conventional forces in the zone in particular with a view to current and prospective restructuring of forces and other developments in Europe and their implications for the military doctrines of the participating States.'[5] All meetings of the seminar were closed to the public.

The main points on the agenda were as follows:

1. Presentation and discussion by the participating states of their military doctrines or similar concepts against the background of their security policy in accordance with the purpose of the seminar.

2. Discussion of military doctrine or similar concepts as regards: (a) posture and structures of armed forces (including organization, command structures, deployment, support systems, personnel, armament, equipment, state of preparedness and procurement plans); and (b) military activities and military training (including exercises, training of military personnel, and use of relevant military manuals).

A major difference from the first seminar was the absence of discussion on military budgeting and planning. In line with the Vienna Document 1990, the participating states had already undertaken to exchange annual information on their military budgets for the forthcoming fiscal year, itemizing defence expenditures on the basis of the categories set out in the United Nations 'Instrument for Standardised International Reporting of Military Expenditures' adopted on 12 December 1980.[6]

The seminar did not arouse great public excitement or expectation. It was held in the shadow of the NATO summit meeting in Rome in November, which was to agree on a new Allied policy and doctrine. Delegations of 37 CSCE states (Latvia did not attend the seminar)[7] were headed by high-ranking political representatives and military officers. However, the NATO countries delegated representatives of lower ranks (except for France which sent its Chief of Staff) compared to those sent to the previous seminar. There were at least three reasons for this: the Vienna seminar took place during a period of transition, in which military thinking was still to be crystallized; new military doctrines in the East and the West were not yet fully elaborated; although flexible and open-ended, the mandate drawn up for this meeting by the first Vienna seminar was no longer felt to correspond to the new situation and the challenges European nations now face.

---

[5] CSCE document CSCE/WV/Dec. 3, Vienna, 15 May 1991. The agenda and modalities of the seminar were based on the proposals submitted by Austria, Finland, Ireland and Poland (CSCE document, WV.17, 21 Mar. 1991), and Canada (WV.17/Amend. 1, 8 May 1991). In Feb. the USSR proposed a seminar on naval doctrines (concepts) but this was not accepted by the USA.

[6] Vienna Document 1990 in SIPRI (note 1), p. 476. See also appendix 12A of this volume.

[7] After Albania (June 1991) and the three Baltic republics (Sep. 1991) joined the CSCE, the number of participating states rose to 38.

Political change

The meeting took place in a security environment quite different from that of the first military doctrine seminar. Such momentous developments in the period between the two seminars as the reunification of Germany, the signing of the CSCE Charter of Paris putting a formal end to the East–West confrontation, the dissolution of the Warsaw Pact in April 1991, the withdrawal of Soviet troops from Central Europe, the abortive August *coup d'état* in the Soviet Union, the accession of Albania and the Baltic states to the CSCE caucus, the developing conflict in Yugoslavia as well as fresh US and Soviet initiatives on nuclear forces all had a considerable bearing on the content and character of the debate and the scope of openness among the discussants.

The course of political events strongly affected the debate on military doctrines and made it more politically than militarily oriented. However, the presentations delivered during the seminar showed much greater openness and transparency, and simultaneously demonstrated that the process of military adaptation to new circumstances has not yet been completed.

The participants shared the view that future military operations are less likely to be the consequence of a threat, but rather the result of conflicts arising in relatively unexpected places, at unpredictable times and with an unforeseeable intensity. For the most part participants stressed the defensive nature of their national doctrines, now based on the principle of sufficient defence. Paradoxically, whenever the national character of defence posture was emphasized, anxiety was expressed (by former WTO states) that it be structurally integrated into a multilateral security framework.

All NATO countries were anxious to reiterate their commitment to the Atlantic Alliance as a stabilizing and balancing factor on the European scene. For the United States, Britain, Germany, Italy and other member-states, NATO will continue to be the central and essential element, the 'backbone' of the European security structure. At the same time, however, other elements of a European security architecture were stressed by the European NATO states—the CSCE security-related mechanisms and institutions, the European Community (EC), with its future responsibilities in the security and defence fields, and the Western European Union (WEU).

Much has changed, particularly for Central and East European states. The former WTO states were proud to completely repudiate the Soviet-imposed WTO doctrine and make progress in developing their own national military thinking. As the hosting Austrian Foreign Minister, Alois Mock, observed at the opening of the seminar, the changes in security concepts in Central and Eastern Europe have embraced: (*a*) the disappearance of the image of 'ideological enemy' and 'inimical alliance'; (*b*) the clear directing of the military doctrines and force structures towards the defence of a country's own territory; (*c*) the removal of offensive structures; and (*d*) a dramatic reduction of military potentials, budgets and exercise activities.[8]

Assessments of the situation by the three 'Visegrad triangle' states— Czechoslovakia, Hungary and Poland—had much in common. Prior to the seminar in early October 1991, facing the disintegration of the USSR and the civil war in Yugoslavia, central European leaders at the Cracow summit meeting renewed their call for a treaty-based relationship with NATO as a reassurance in an increasingly

---

[8] Eröffnung des zweiten Seminars über Militärdoktrinen durch den Bundesminister für Auswärtige Angelegenheiten, Alois Mock, Austrian Minister for Foreign Affairs, at the Second Seminar on Military Doctrine, Vienna, 8 Oct. 1991.

unstable Europe.[9] This also found expression in speeches at the seminar by representatives of those states. They stressed the need for closer, all-European co-operation, including close links with NATO. While appreciating the CSCE framework, especially the CPC, as a basis for a future co-operative security regime, these states showed a degree of disappointment that their appeals to be directly included in the activities of the Atlantic Alliance had not yet been appropriately answered. At the same time these countries rejected the idea of building a sub-regional military bloc and, partly as a result of their infamous 'internationalist' past experiences, put more pronounced stress on the national character of their military policy, doctrine and defence.

Newly independent Lithuania and Estonia primarily expressed their concern about the continuing presence of the Soviet Army on their territories and Soviet military capabilities in the areas adjacent to their borders. Accordingly, they emphasized the importance of the earliest pull-out of Soviet troops from their territories, implementation of the 1990 Conventional Armed Forces in Europe (CFE) Treaty and confidence-building elements of a future European security regime.

In assessing the changing European scene, attitudes of the neutral and non-aligned (NNA) states varied. Sweden's Supreme Commander, while favourably assessing the developments in the continent, stressed that uncertainty remained, especially in view of continuing Soviet strategic interest in the Kola peninsula and surrounding sea areas, and the fact that Soviet military capabilities in the northern region would largely remain at their earlier strength or even increase, with quantitative reductions of the land forces being compensated by qualitative improvements; consequently, the main elements of Sweden's military doctrine are likely to prevail for some years to come.[10] Finland also expressed concern over the increase of the relative importance of the north-western part of Europe as a result of the CFE Treaty. On the other hand, Switzerland declared that in the face of new developments in Europe it has started to study the value and future advantage of its neutrality for security policy co-operation in Europe. A number of NNA countries (Austria, Finland, Ireland and Sweden) have strongly supported the upgrading of CSCE structures and institutions to deal with new challenges, and especially its crisis management and peace-keeping capabilities.

New strategies

To some extent the presentations delivered at the seminar expressed the strategy requirements facing the CSCE states. Beyond the above generalizations, a survey of individual interventions shows a variety of approaches in addressing existing and emerging threats.

---

[9] See Cracow Declaration adopted at the meeting of the leaders of the Republic of Poland, the Czech and Slovak Federal Republic and the Republic of Hungary, Cracow, 6 Oct. 1991.

[10] Statement by General Bengt Gustafsson, Supreme Commander, Swedish Armed Forces, at the Second Seminar on Military Doctrine, Vienna, 8 Oct. 1991. In late Feb. 1992 Sweden announced that in face of the growing risks of local conflicts in Eastern Europe, it was going to increase annual military expenditure to 2.4 per cent of its GNP with an additional rise every year until 1997 equivalent to 1.5 per cent of the appropriation for military equipment; *Financial Times*, 26 Feb. 1992. In contrast, in Mar. 1992, another Scandinavian state, NATO member Norway, expressed no concern with developments on the Kola peninsula, pointing out that the Soviet fleet did not seem to have global ambitions; *Atlantic News*, no. 2407 (20 Mar. 1992).

The United States and most NATO members demonstrated rather traditional attitudes to new challenges. Although the Soviet threat has faded away, it often seemed still to lurk somewhere in the background of the debate.[11]

The US representative extensively outlined US military strategy, which is supposed to 'move from a strategy based on containing communism and deterring global conflict to a more diverse, flexible strategy that responds decisively to regional threats to peace and stability'. The four foundations of this strategy are: (a) deterrence; (b) forward presence replacing forward-basing of US troops with smaller military forces; (c) reconstitution of forces in the event of a global threat; and (d) crisis-response capability to deal with regional crises arising on short notice.

These foundations have been supplemented by a set of strategic concepts designed to carry out US military strategy, which were worked out as a decisive measure in the light of the Persian Gulf War experience. They include: (a) readiness to provide capabilities for rapid deployment; (b) collective security (i.e., multinational operations under the auspices of international security organizations, with combined doctrines, interoperability and integrated command structures); (c) arms control to 'inject greater predictability into military relationships and channel force postures in more stabilizing directions while retaining vital military capabilities'; and (d) security assistance for allied and friendly nations to enhance their ability to 'resist coercion or aggression'.

In the case of a crisis where major military forces are to be invoked, the new US doctrine envisages the following concepts: (a) maritime and aerospace superiority, (b) power projection, (c) overwhelming force and strategic agility, and (d) technological superiority.

The US strategic concepts hardly seem to be a satisfactory or adequate response to the new requirements of European security, particularly in the face of dramatic changes occurring after the Moscow August *putsch* and the breakup of the Soviet Union. Similarly the British, Italian and other NATO delegates presented positions which seemed to have little to do with the nature of developments and contingencies on the European scene. The French delegate stated that France would hold firm to principles which 'retained value and relevance in the new situation.'[12] The declaration that France would build a second component of its nuclear submarine force by 2000 was a striking example of this line of thinking. Characteristically, almost all NATO member states emphasized manpower reductions, but at the same time they stressed compensating these reductions by raising combat readiness, mobility, and other qualitative improvements in weapons and military technologies.[13]

---

[11] The US delegate stated that: 'The evolving security environment requires that we contend with the continuing Soviet reality ... '. 'New directions in United States military strategy', General James McCarthy, Deputy Commander in Chief, US European Command, at the Second Seminar on Military Doctrine, Vienna, 8 Oct. 1991. The French Chief of Staff, Admiral Lanxade, stated that '(t)he threat of sudden aggression has disappeared ... [however] a considerable [Soviet] arsenal, nuclear and conventional, will remain for a long time. . . '. Admiral J. Lanxade at the Second Seminar on Military Doctrine, Vienna, 8 Oct. 1991

[12] '[T]his continuity of doctrine is explained by the fact that a number of factors to be taken into account in working out our military strategy have basically not changed', concluded the French representative, see Lanxade (note 11).

[13] These and other US/NATO steps met with criticism from the Soviet delegates who found them hardly reconcilable with the spirit of co-operativeness and non-offensiveness postures. See statement by Soviet delegate Ambassador K. F. Mikhailov at the Second Seminar on Military Doctrine, Vienna, 18 Oct. 1991.

Central and East European presentations were less militarily sophisticated and used a different vocabulary from the Western ones. They put more stress on political–military aspects and problems encountered in the process of their force restructuring. Emphasizing the defensive and 'no enemy' character of their doctrines, the Eastern participants drew Western delegates' attention to the idea of building a co-operative security environment in Europe, to include former WTO members.

The discussion on nuclear weapons was carried out in the aftermath of the sweeping new US and Soviet proposals presented by Presidents Bush and Gorbachev. Both delegations addressed these problems; however, it was too early to grasp and take into account all implications of those steps.[14]

Sufficient defence and force structure

Most states declared their commitment to sufficient defence, irrespective of the various names given to this principle, and provided details of how they were chang-ing their force structures to meet this goal. However, there was no common understand-ing or definition of the meaning and contents of a defensive posture. Instead, all countries repudiated the relevance of offensive-oriented postures. The USA, while announcing major changes in its military doctrine, forces and posture, declared its preparedness for future challenges as a leader with world-wide interests and com-mitments in an era marked by uncertainty, instability and unpredictability. All US interventions at the seminar referred extensively to the Persian Gulf War experience. While US forces are to be scaled back they are still to demonstrate US commitment to its allies and to 'contribute to regional stability and provide an initial crisis-response capability' through forward presence and power projection.[15]

British restructuring of forces is connected with an 'all-weather strategy' under the Alliance's new military policy. Although focused overwhelmingly on 'good weather', the strategy is nevertheless designed to ensure an inherent versatility of smaller British armed forces in order efficiently to confront the unpredictable chal-lenges of the 1990s. Here, the British interest is in provision of ready reaction forces 'for the defence of NATO territory', as well as playing a part in UN and international peace-keeping forces.[16]

The German statements put strong emphasis on the political aspects rather than defensive capabilities while discussing the problems connected with the defensive posture. The FRG force structure is undergoing a deep transformation connected with the complex process of integrating the former East German Nationale Volksarmee into the Bundeswehr, its obligations under international agreements and in accor-dance with its co-operative security aims. This embraces three requirements: (a) a basic military infrastructure, that is, forces to safeguard German sovereignty and ter-ritorial forces; (b) mobilizable, reconstitutable forces to perform defence operations after prolonged preparations (mostly fully or partially skeletonized Army units); and (c) quickly available forces for minor conflicts and for crisis management after short warning (in Central Europe and as a German contribution for employment at

---

[14] For a more detailed discussion of the US and Soviet initiatives, see chapter 2 of this volume.

[15] McCarthy (note 11).

[16] 'The need for balanced appropriate forces during a time of unprecedented change', Vice Chief of the Defence Staff (UK) at the Second Seminar on Military Doctrine, Vienna, 8 Oct. 1991. See also the British delegation paper, 'Second CSCE Military Doctrine Seminar—Presentation by ACDS (Programmes)', 11 Oct. 1991.

Europe's borders). Generally, the readiness and availability of German forces will be graduated. The Air Force will have its defence component strengthened at the expense of its offensive capabilities, and the smaller Navy will shift its emphasis towards the North Sea and concentrate the necessary cuts on forces and facilities in the Baltic. Germany's forces of those categories will meet requirements of collective security requirements within the Atlantic Alliance, the United Nations and/or the CSCE.

The structure of German armed forces, and especially of the Bundeswehr, in a 'post-disarmament environment', will be characterized by: (a) quick-reaction command and control and electronic warfare means (also as part of verification systems); (b) a maximum degree of operational flexibility and mobility; (c) a defence posture with predominantly blocking forces and a high degree of firepower; (d) a quick-reaction, strong air defence; and (e) a maritime presence in crisis areas. These requirements are to be met with an unchanged budget in 1991 and 1992, and within gradually declining budgets for the period 1993–95.[17]

The French Chief of Staff declared that the main aim for France's conventional forces is to be able to detect, manage and deal with crises 'with rapidity and precision'. To this end, three areas will have priority: obtaining information, information systems that enable the command to act swiftly, and forces structured so as to be employable 'whenever and wherever needed'. The armies will be smaller and of higher quality. Rapid reaction forces will be the preferred instrument for dealing with crises. However, unlike the British concept for a NATO rapid reaction force, the French concept is European-oriented and associated with Western European institutions (the EC and the WEU). The Western concepts of rapid reaction force gave rise at the seminar to concerns that this could provide a new route to an offensive potential.

Representatives of the Soviet Army strongly emphasized their defensive sufficiency doctrine, and indicated developments proving their sincerity in this regard, such as the ongoing reorganization of Soviet armed forces, the reduction of personnel by 500 000, the withdrawal of Soviet troops from Central Europe, the change of emphasis from offensive to defensive troops, the elimination of the so-called 'armoured fists', that is, operational manœuvre groups, and the establishment of a coastal defence for defending major naval bases.[18] The significance of Soviet statements consisted in their being the first military presentations of the planned changes after the August *putsch*, signalling a desire to embark upon the road towards depoliticizing and de-ideologizing the armed forces. However, the Soviet commitments were soon to be overtaken by events with the situation dramatically changed after the dissolution of the Soviet Union and the official proclamation of the Commonwealth of Independent States (CIS), in December 1991.

Central and East European participants were anxious to stress that qualitative changes were being made in their force structures in line with the declared principles of defensiveness, sufficiency, co-operativeness and peaceful solution of international disputes. Hungary presented a 'home defence concept', Poland announced a 'no a priori enemy' defence concept, and Romania presented a concept of 'adequate sufficiency of defence and optimum gradual response'. The other East European countries

---

[17] 'Armed forces for a co-operative security structure as shown by the example of the Bundeswehr', Remarks by Captain Ulrich Weisser, German Navy, Chief Force Planning Branch, Armed Forces Staff, Federal Ministry of Defence at the Second Seminar on Military Doctrine, Vienna, 11 Oct. 1991.

[18] Statement by the Deputy Head of the Main Administration, Soviet Armed Forces General Staff, Col.-Gen. F. M. Markovskiy at the Second Seminar on Military Doctrine, Vienna, 11 Oct. 1991.

also emphasized the transformations in their armed forces aimed at reaching the same goals. Although processes of reorganization in Central and Eastern Europe are not yet completed, a number of steps have been taken, such as the considerable reductions in forces and manpower, the establishment of new command and control structures and their separation from the political and administrative levels in the army, the reduction of military presence in western parts of the states' territories, and transfer of forces to central and eastern parts in order to achieve a more even and balanced military deployment. The states undertook to make budget cuts and maintain a reasonable ratio between their economic potential and military structure and defence preparations. Generally, the intention was declared to give the armies in the region a more and more professional character.

The northern NNA countries saw no pressing need to make additional changes in their defensive (or 'non-offensive') force structures, and declared that the process of rationalizing command and administrative systems of military defence would proceed according to earlier plans (Finland and Sweden). Changes are more the result of military–technical considerations and economic realities than of European developments. Other NNA states, located in the central part of Europe, announced their readiness to review and/or restructure their armed forces in order to meet new challenges emerging in the continent. Austria will put more emphasis on the versatility of its army—thus stressing mobile forces and aerial surveillance. As events in Yugoslavia have demonstrated, rapid deployment forces, available without mobilization, are needed more than ever in order to protect borders and permit swift reaction. Switzerland, while reducing its forces, is moving from a doctrine of comprehensive area coverage to one of local rapid deployment force concentrations ('dynamic area defence').

Training and military activity

Recent developments have also had an impact on military activities and the training of forces. Countries that are making changes in their force structures are also declaring their readiness to introduce changes in the operational and tactical training of their armed forces, and to modify their military activities.

NATO countries were in general agreement that recent experience, particularly that of the Persian Gulf War, has proved the wisdom of changes they have made over the past few years. Military budget restrictions and force restructuring call for smaller exercises both in scale and scope. Germany is coping with the problem of expanding the Bundeswehr into an all-German force. The underlying idea of this process is a 'leadership and civic education concept' tailored to bringing the armed forces under full parliamentary and governmental control. Its aim is, among others, to convey the basic ideas and values of democracy to the former communist German Democratic Republic, and to strike a balance between 'the tensions and burdens that on the one hand derive from the rights of a citizen and on the other from the legally founded duties of a soldier and what is asked of him by military service'.[19]

More changes have been introduced by the Central and East European states, since they are in the process of departing from WTO offensive capabilities, postures and

---

[19] See Weisser (note 17). See also the statement by Admiral Ulrich Hunolt, 'Democratie und Streitkräfte durch Demokratie', at the Second Seminar on Military Doctrine in Vienna, 16 Oct. 1991.

training procedures. Those countries are also squeezed by budgetary constraints[20] and seek more cost-effective solutions to maintain military training (e.g., use of computer technology in operational training). The main effort in the planned training of forces is focused on the level of the company and battalion. New solutions are being sought for co-operation of the armed forces with paramilitary forces and civil defence. The military educational system is also undergoing defence-oriented transformation, including the search for more co-operation among the armed forces in the region, particularly between the three Central European states—Czechoslovakia, Hungary and Poland (tactical and firing exercises, staff exchanges for officers of various specialities at the tactical and operational levels, training centres for operations in urban areas and mountainous regions, etc.), and extensive training of East European career soldiers in Western military schools.

III. Conclusion

The Second Vienna Seminar on Military Doctrine reflected recent changes in military thinking, how far military *rapprochement* in Europe has gone, and what is common to and divergent among the participants of European security dialogue. Because of the prevailing circumstances, it was a seminar on doctrines in transition, thus no definite answers were expected but rather indications of trends and directions in their development. As one observer noted, the following areas of consensus emerged at the seminar: offensive postures and doctrines are no longer desirable or fail-safe, although how to define and carry out the defensive orientation of the armed forces still remains unclear; arms control should be continued and promoted; openness and transparency has taken root for good in military matters; all participants share common problems stemming from lower military budgets, personnel reductions, base closures, political constraints on military activity, the conversion of the defence industry, and so on; and last but not least, with the exception of the USSR, all delegations recognized the relevance of NATO to European security.[21]

Many participants felt that the Second Seminar on Military Doctrine did not abound in ideas which could serve as the basis for new proposals in the European military dialogue. Analysis of the presentations in Vienna confirms the fears voiced beforehand that the timing was not particularly fortunate. The Atlantic Alliance was still in the process of elaborating on and streamlining its military policy and strategy, and the EC and the WEU also lacked a clear military security identity. Western military thinking was greatly influenced by the Persian Gulf War experience and Western countries are building up rapid reaction forces with 'high-tech' weaponry to be stationed in Western Europe ready for contingency tasks in other regions of the world. Along with the claimed striving for a defensive character of their structures, postures and doctrines, the military restructuring within the Atlantic Alliance leads to the development of some potential for offensive action. The swollen threat perceptions discernible on the part of some NATO states could lead to military efforts easily exceeding the real needs. Other participating states, however, saw a greater need for standing rather than mobilizable forces.

---

[20] The tight defence budget led Poland to cancel reserve training for 1992 university graduates. The funds would be used for the upkeep of conscript forces. *Rzeczpospolita*, 9 Jan. 1992.

[21] Silverman, W., 'Talking "sufficiency" in the Hofburg Palace: the second seminar on Military Doctrine', *Arms Control Today*, vol. 21, no. 10 (Dec. 1991), p 17.

The process of dividing up and restructuring the former Soviet armed forces by the newly independent states is experiencing ups and downs as they strive to determine and reshape their national identity, political, social, economic and, last but not least, military lives. Both Russia and Ukraine announced their intentions to change their respective military doctrines to make them less aggressive-looking and more defence-oriented, but at the same time it is the 'military dimension' on which the CIS has seemed to founder in early 1992.

In Eastern Europe, countries are striving to 'return to Europe' as quickly as possible, not least in terms of their military postures. Therefore, they are eagerly taking bold steps to take advantage of the favourable international premises, abandon the remnants of WTO military postures and deployments, and change the image and character of their armed forces. However, the declarations by these states are more of a political character and, compared with Western statements, have addressed technical–military issues to a lesser degree.

A number of interesting suggestions were put forward during the meeting. A proposal was made to identify certain common elements of doctrines which could constitute a code of military security conduct. Furthermore, as a consequence of the long duration and the very formal conduct of the seminar with the rather disappointing outcome, in-depth studies of individual topics—'mini-seminars'—were proposed as a follow-up to the military doctrine seminars.[22] In view of the not always compatible terminology used by states, it was proposed that the CPC develop a comparative list of terms and notions regarding doctrines, pointing to the need to standardize the nomenclature both for the sake of formulation of military doctrines and of future discussions of this type.

The Vienna seminar was actually a new attempt to speak a common language and find common ground among all European participants regarding co-operative military thinking. It showed a good deal of prevailing conservatism in military thinking in the process of adapting to new circumstances, but at the same time the will was demonstrated to attempt to understand each other's concerns and problems. Its deficiencies notwithstanding, it was a useful confidence-building event as a platform for military-to-military contacts, helping to overcome stereotypes and psychological barriers still lingering among former adversaries.

[22] In line with this two specialized seminars were held in early 1992; the first, sponsored by Czechoslovakia, concerned 'Conversion of military industry to civilian production' (Bratislava, 19–21 Feb.) and the second, proposed by Poland and Hungary, dealt with 'The armies in democratic societies' (Vienna, 4–6 Mar.). Both seminars were convened by the CPC and, as a novelty in the CSCE process, NATO was invited to send its representatives to these forums.

Part IV. Special features

13. The United Nations Special Commission on Iraq

ROLF EKÉUS

I. Introduction: UN Security Council Resolution 687

The adoption by the United Nations Security Council of Resolution 687 (the so-called cease-fire resolution) on 3 April 1991 signified the conclusion of the Gulf War.[1] On 6 April 1991, when Iraq notified the Secretary-General and the Security Council of its official acceptance of the provisions of the resolution, a formal cease-fire took effect between Iraq and Kuwait and the UN member states co-operating with Kuwait in the multinational Coalition force.

Part C of Resolution 687 (paragraphs 7–14) addresses Iraq's weapons of mass destruction: their declaration, identification, location and disposal, and the establishment of a monitoring system to ensure that they not be reintroduced to Iraq, either internally or from abroad. Resolution 687 required Iraq to declare the location, amount and type of all items specified under paragraphs 8 and 12 within 15 days of adoption of the resolution. The items thus to be eliminated are all of Iraq's chemical weapons (CW), biological weapons (BW), stocks of agents, related subsystems and components, and all research, development, support and manufacturing facilities. Also included are all ballistic missiles with a range greater than 150 km and related major parts, as well as repair and production facilities. Disposal is to be carried out under international supervision through destruction, rendering harmless or removal of the proscribed items. As regards Iraq's nuclear capability, the cease-fire resolution provides that nuclear weapons, 'nuclear-weapons-usable material', any subsystems or components and any research, development, support and manufacturing facilities related to nuclear weapons and 'nuclear-weapons-usable material' shall be subject to destruction, removal or rendering harmless.

These provisions in part C of the resolution are linked to the economic sanctions against Iraq which are outlined in paragraphs 21 and 22, and the Security Council will make its decision to lift its embargo 'against the import of commodities and products originating in Iraq and the prohibitions against financial transactions related thereto contained in resolution 661'[2] dependent upon Iraq's completion of the actions defined in part C of Resolution 687.

The resolution provides for two plans, one for nuclear weapons and one for non-nuclear weapons, for future monitoring and verification that Iraq does not use, develop, construct or acquire anew any items specified for elimination.

[1] United Nations Security Council document S/RES/687 (1991), 8 Apr. 1991; see appendix 13A.
[2] See note 1; see also United Nations Security Council document S/RES/661 (1990), 6 Aug. 1990.

On 11 October 1991, the Security Council adopted Resolution 715 which approved two plans for compliance monitoring: one for non-nuclear items submitted by the UN Secretary-General and one for nuclear items submitted by the Director-General of the International Atomic Energy Agency (IAEA).[3]

II. Organization and functioning of UNSCOM

The United Nations Special Commission on Iraq (UNSCOM) was established in early May 1991 in accordance with paragraph 9(b) of Resolution 687 to carry out immediate on-site inspection of Iraq's biological, chemical and missile capabilities, to provide for the elimination of these capabilities and to perform other functions assigned to it in part C of the resolution.[4] With the assistance and co-operation of UNSCOM, the Director-General of the IAEA was requested to carry out the corresponding tasks regarding Iraq's nuclear capability.

While the Special Commission is fully responsible for matters related to Iraq's chemical and biological weapons and ballistic missiles, the IAEA has primary responsibility for Iraq's nuclear capability, a responsibility which it discharges with the assistance and co-operation of UNSCOM. UNSCOM provides the IAEA with facilities for transportation and communication and logistic support; information and surveillance services are also furnished. Under the supervision of the IAEA Director-General, an IAEA Action Group carries out the tasks which Resolution 687 entrusts to the IAEA.

After extensive negotiation, an agreement was concluded on 14 May 1991 with the Government of Iraq concerning the status, privileges and immunities of both UNSCOM and the IAEA.[5] These provisions are recapitulated, elaborated upon and reinforced in the UNSCOM plan for future monitoring and verification of Iraq's compliance with part C of Resolution 687.[6] An agreement has also been concluded with the Government of Bahrain about the field office at Manama (see below).

The Special Commission, which is a subsidiary organ of the Security Council, consists of 21 individuals appointed by the Secretary-General, each of a different nationality and drawn from all regions of the world, who are experts in nuclear, chemical and biological weapons and ballistic missiles. The Executive Chairman and Deputy Executive Chairman are vested with responsibility for directing the operations of UNSCOM. They are assisted by a secretariat with headquarters in New York, a field operations office in Bahrain and a support office in Baghdad. In addition to the executive office, the New York headquarters include an Information Assessment Unit and an Operational Planning and Operations Unit. The field offices are provided with administrative, transportation, communication and medical personnel, and appropriate equipment. The UNSCOM members are organized in four groups—nuclear,

---

[3] United Nations Security Council document S/RES/715 (1991), 11 Oct. 1991.
[4] United Nation Security Council document S/22614, 17 May 1991.
[5] See note 4, paragraph 6, p. 2.
[6] United Nations Security Council document S/22871/Rev.1, 2 Oct. 1991.

chemical/biological, ballistic missiles and future compliance monitoring—which meet regularly to assess progress and to assist the Executive Chairman in the planning of activities. A Destruction Advisory Panel was also established to deal with investigation and recommendation of destruction undertakings as outlined in Resolution 687.

UNSCOM has at its disposal advanced communication systems such as satellite global-positioning system units. The Special Commission is also able to gather information about sites it deems of interest through high-altitude aerial surveys of Iraq by a U-2 reconnaissance aircraft with crew and support personnel provided by the United States. From an airbase in Baghdad, the Special Commission operates its own helicopter service for transportation of its inspection teams and for close-range surveillance of designated targets. Three helicopters with crews and support personnel have been put at the disposal of the Special Commission by the German Government as have two heavy transport aircraft (C-160s) operating between the field offices and based in Bahrain and Iraq. In addition, UNSCOM commands a large fleet of land transport equipment, various analysis instruments, detection devices, medical equipment and explosive ordnance equipment.[7]

The nuclear and non-nuclear sites to be inspected are those which were declared by Iraq[8] under the provisions of paragraphs 8, 12 and 13 of Resolution 687 and additional locations which have been designated by UNSCOM.

For inspection purposes the UNSCOM and IAEA inspection teams are allowed unconditional and unrestricted access to any and all areas, facilities, equipment, records and means of transport. Iraq is also required to provide full and complete disclosure of all aspects of its programmes to develop weapons of mass destruction and ballistic missiles. No movement or destruction by Iraq of material or equipment relating to the weapon categories under the resolution is supposed to take place without notification to and prior consent of the Special Commission. Furthermore, Resolution 687 provides for the halting of all nuclear activities of any kind except for the use of isotopes for limited purposes. The Security Council explicitly allowed UNSCOM and the IAEA to conduct flights throughout Iraq for all relevant purposes including inspection, surveillance, aerial survey, transportation and logistics on conditions to be determined by the Special Commission, and to make full use of UNSCOM aircraft and those Iraqi airfields deemed most appropriate for the work of the Special Commission.

As a subsidiary body of the Security Council, UNSCOM has the responsibility to designate sites for nuclear as well as non-nuclear inspection. Such designations are aimed at sites which have not been declared by Iraq; declared sites can be inspected without designation. As any designation must be based

---

[7] United Nations Security Council document S/23165, 25 Oct. 1991, pp. 34–35.

[8] On 18 and 28 Apr. and 4 May 1991, the Government of Iraq forwarded to the Secretary-General information relating to its chemical and biological weapons and ballistic missiles. On 18 and 27 Apr., information was forwarded to the Director-General of the IAEA regarding the nuclear items (see note 4, paragraph 7, p. 2). As a result of findings during inspections, Iraq declared on 7 July 1991 a large number of activities and facilities related to the nuclear programme (see note 7, p. 21).

upon a judgement of probability and feasibility, the Special Commission needs to have full access to all available and relevant information when carrying out its mandate. The information system and organizational structure of the Special Commission were set up with this requirement in mind. In the nuclear field, where the IAEA leads the inspection activities, UNSCOM assists and advises about scheduling inspections, proposes the composition of teams, recruits some experts not normally available to the IAEA—notably nuclear weapon and document research experts—and provides data and information on designated sites.

For non-nuclear missions (CW, BW and missile inspections) the Chairman of the Special Commission decides the sites to be inspected. This is done on the basis of information provided (*a*) by Iraq in its declarations, (*b*) by other governments providing special information, and (*c*) most importantly by data produced within UNSCOM in earlier inspection reports—all of which have been analysed and assessed by the Information Assessment Unit together with imagery obtained by the U-2 reconnaissance aircraft. In the case of non-declared sites, the Chairman has to make a special designation.

When it has been decided that a site should be inspected, the Operational and Planning Unit develops an operational plan which covers the objectives and chronology of the inspection, names a chief inspector and composes an inspection team. The Chief Inspector is called to the headquarters in New York to be briefed in detail on the mission and to participate in fine-tuning the operational plan that outlines administration, logistics and communication arrangements for the inspection team. The individual inspectors are recruited from various governments, and UN documents and certificates are issued for the inspectors. The team members are assembled at the field office in Bahrain for training, final briefing, preparation and planning. The team is then flown on the Special Commission's C-160 aircraft to Baghdad, where it is supported by the field office with communication, medical, transport and interpretation services. The inspectors use either land or helicopter transport to the sites to be visited, depending upon the distance from Baghdad. Helicopters can also support inspection with parallel aerial surveillance. Non-declared designated sites are normally visited with very short notice or no notice to the Iraqi authorities. The length of missions varies from one to six weeks; the inspection team reports from the field on a daily basis to headquarters in New York about the development of the mission. After the mission is concluded, the inspection team returns to Bahrain for debriefing and the drafting of a report. The inspectors thereafter return to their home countries. The Chief Inspector travels to the New York headquarters to finalize the report to the Special Commission or for a full debriefing. An Executive Summary of the report is sent to the members of the Security Council.

A similar routine has been established for the IAEA-led nuclear inspections. Briefing, debriefing, operational planning and reporting are carried out in the IAEA headquarters in Vienna. As a rule the Director-General of the IAEA sends a concentrated report of each inspection to the UN Secretary-

General for the information of the Security Council. During 1991 the Special Commission and the IAEA were primarily engaged in carrying out the first two stages of their mission—inspection and disposal—and routines were developed for sending teams for inspection or destruction missions to Iraq and for their functioning in Iraq. Table 13.1 lists the nuclear and other inspections carried out in 1991.

As a consequence of continuing Iraqi obstruction of implementation the mandate of the Special Commission defined in the cease-fire resolution was amplified by UN Security Council Resolution 707.[9]

Table 13.1. UNSCOM missions in Iraq, as of 31 December 1991

Team	Type of inspection	Date
IAEA 1/UNSCOM 1	Nuclear	14–22 May
UNSCOM 2	Chemical	9–15 June
UNSCOM 3	Ballistic missile	30 June–7 July
IAEA 2/UNSCOM 4	Nuclear	22 June–3 July
IAEA 3/UNSCOM 5	Nuclear	6–19 July
IAEA 4/UNSCOM 6	Nuclear	27 July–10 Aug.
UNSCOM 7	Biological	2–8 Aug.
UNSCOM 8	Ballistic missile[a]	8–15 Aug.
UNSCOM 9	Chemical	15–22 Aug.
UNSCOM 10	Ballistic missile	18–20 July
UNSCOM 11	Chemical	31 Aug.–9 Sep.
UNSCOM 12	Chemical	31 Aug.–5 Sep.
UNSCOM 13	Ballistic missile	6–13 Sep.
IAEA 5/UNSCOM 14	Nuclear	14–20 Sep.
UNSCOM 15	Biological	20 Sep.–3 Oct.
IAEA 6/UNSCOM 16	Nuclear	21–30 Sep.
UNSCOM 17	Chemical	6 Oct.–9 Nov.
UNSCOM 18	Ballistic missile[a]	1–14 Oct.
IAEA 7/UNSCOM 19	Nuclear	11–22 Oct.
UNSCOM 20	Chemical	22 Oct.–2 Nov.
UNSCOM 21	Chemical and biological	18 Nov.–1 Dec.
IAEA 8/UNSCOM 22	Nuclear	11–18 Nov.
UNSCOM 23	Ballistic missile	1–9 Dec.
UNSCOM 24	Ballistic missile	9–17 Dec.

[a] UNSCOM 8 and UNSCOM 18 also surveyed and rendered harmless superguns with ranges of 350 mm and 1000 mm and related components.

III. Nuclear inspections

The IAEA-led inspections of Iraq's nuclear programme have disclosed three clandestine uranium enrichment programmes for nuclear weapon purposes. The major discovery was Iraq's electromagnetic isotope separation (EMIS) programme.[10] Considerable efforts were made by Iraq to conceal the pro-

[9] United Nations Security Council document S/RES/707 (1991), 15 Aug. 1991.
[10] EMIS is accomplished by creating a high-current beam (tens to thousands of milliamps) of low energy (tens of KeV) ions and allowing them to pass through a magnetic field (typically 3000–7000

gramme, with equipment being dispersed and in many cases buried in remote areas. With the help of overhead photography, it was possible in late June 1991 to locate some of the equipment—the calutrons.[11] An inspection team found the calutrons but was denied control of the equipment when Iraqi security personnel threatened the inspectors with firearms and fired warning shots.[12] Subsequently, despite extensive deception efforts by Iraq, an EMIS facility under construction at Tarmiya was identified as capable of industrial-scale production of highly enriched uranium.[13] On the basis of the design data provided by Iraq, it was estimated that if the Tarmiya facility were fully operational with 90 separators running at design capacity, it could produce up to 15 kg of highly enriched (93 per cent) uranium per year.[14] The Iraqi authorities were also forced to admit the existence of an identical facility at Ash Sharqat, a replica of the one at Tarmiya, which was 85 per cent complete when it was destroyed during the war.

Confronted with irrefutable evidence, Iraq admitted a research and development (R&D) programme for gas centrifuge enrichment aiming at production of gas centrifuges so that a 100-machine cascade[15] would be in operation by 1993 and a 500-machine cascade by 1996.[16] In the opinion of the inspectors, an identified centrifuge production facility could have manufactured thousands of centrifuges per year, and evidence obtained in January 1992 indicated that Iraq had procured key components sufficient for several thousand centrifuges. When presented with this information, Iraq stated that these supplies had been destroyed. Some but not all of the destroyed components and equipment were verified by inspectors. A chemical exchange enrichment facility which was shown to inspectors had been thoroughly cleaned, leaving no evidence of the extent of the chemical enrichment programme.[17]

In September 1991 an inspection team found a large number of documents relating to Iraq's nuclear programme. The team was initially denied access and later subjected to serious harassment by four days of confinement in a parking lot at Iraq's document centre.[18] Furthermore, some documents collected by the inspectors in the course of the inspection were forcibly confiscated by Iraqi authorities, and some of them were not returned. Conclusive documentary evidence was found that Iraq had had a well-funded programme for developing an implosion-type nuclear weapon linked to a surface-to-surface missile project. An extensive weaponization programme had been carried out

Gauss or 0.3–0.7 Tesis). The heavier ions bend in a larger radius than the lighter ions, and suitably placed collector pockets capture the different isotopes. EMIS is the process originally used by most of the nuclear weapon states to prepare their first highly enriched uranium for nuclear explosives (see United Nations Security Council document S/22788, 15 July 1991, p. 9).

[11] Calutron (from *California University* + *Electron*): an electromagnetic apparatus for separating isotopes according to their masses on the principle of the mass spectrograph.

[12] These incidents were reported to the Security Council; see United Nations Security Council documents S/22739, 26 June 1991 and S/22743, 28 June 1991.

[13] United Nations Security Council document S/22788, 15 July 1991.

[14] United Nations Security Council document S/22837, 25 July 1991.

[15] Identical gas centrifuges arranged in a specific way for the uranium enrichment process.

[16] United Nations Security Council document S/22986, 28 Aug. 1991.

[17] United Nations Security Council document S/23112, 4 Oct. 1991.

[18] United Nations Security Council document S/23122, 8 Oct. 1991.

at the Al Tuwaitha nuclear research centre and at the Al Atheer site, including work with neutron initiators, high-explosive components, exploding bridge wire detonators and firing sets for multiple detonator systems.[19] Until October 1991 Iraq consistently denied any work related to nuclear weapons and went to great lengths to conceal and destroy any evidence of such a programme. Facing overwhelming proof, Iraq thereafter acknowledged that a research programme existed and that Al Atheer had been built to serve the weaponization programme.

According to a number of statements made by Iraq, components, equipment and material related to the clandestine nuclear programme were dismantled or destroyed prior to the inspection activities under the cease-fire resolution. With the assistance of Iraqi personnel, the IAEA has destroyed components of the EMIS programme together with centrifuges and related equipment items. Unirradiated highly enriched fuel was removed from Iraq as were two streak video cameras and equipment suitable for nuclear weapon development. Remaining radiated highly enriched fuel is scheduled to be removed during 1992.

At the end of June 1991, as a consequence of the access refusal and the shooting incident, the Security Council dispatched a high-level mission composed of the Executive Chairman of the Special Commission, the Director-General of the IAEA and the United Nations Under-Secretary-General for Disarmament Affairs to meet with the highest levels of the Iraqi Government.[20] This mission received various assurances of full co-operation from Iraq, but as the mission reported to the Security Council 'in spite of their unambiguous character, the general assurances given and the specific measures promised can only be evaluated in the light of present and future implementation by the Iraqi authorities'.[21]

As Iraq has so far refused to provide full disclosure of its nuclear programme, the IAEA has to continue its inspection activities of declared sites and of suspected sites designated by the Special Commission.

IV. Chemical weapon inspections

Thus far Iraq has acknowledged possession of 46 000 pieces of filled chemical munitions.[22] The Special Commission inspections have provided evidence which tends to increase this number by several thousand. By the end of 1991, nearly 12 000 unfilled chemical munitions of an estimated amount of 75 000 had been destroyed by Iraqi personnel under the supervision of UNSCOM inspectors. Iraq's facilities include the substantial CW production complex of the Al Muthanna State Establishment—also known as the State Enterprise for Pesticide Production (SEFP)—and three planned precursor production plants in the Al Fallujah area. In addition to the central storage of filled chemical

---

[19] See note 7, p. 23.
[20] United Nations Security Council document S/22746, 28 June 1991.
[21] United Nations Security Council document S/22761, 5 July 1991.
[22] See note 7.

munitions, warfare agents and precursor chemicals in bulk at Al Muthanna, filled chemical munitions, often damaged and leaking, are stored at various sites throughout the country.[23]

The filled munitions consist of different types of aerial bombs, artillery rockets and shells. Twelve types of weapon have been found in the Iraqi CW arsenal which, Iraq maintains, were manufactured locally or modified in Iraq for CW fill. So far only equipment and facilities for production of aerial bombs have been disclosed. Iraq has been unwilling to account for the location of equipment for the fabrication of the remaining types of chemical weapon or for the acquisition of weapons which have not been produced in the country. Thirty chemical-filled ballistic missile warheads have been found by the Special Commission. Various chemical warfare agents, mostly mustard and nerve agents, have been declared and found in bulk and in the filled munitions. A number of weapons, including grenades, containing the riot control agent CS have also been found.[24] The Muthanna State Establishment is in a highly dangerous condition, with many facilities damaged during the war and a large number of munitions leaking and in unstable condition. However, the site is deemed to provide a suitable location for the centralized destruction of Iraq's CW agents and munitions. Destruction is planned to start in 1992 but will not be completed until 1993 because of the technical problems involved in carrying out such destruction. The Destruction Advisory Panel of the Special Commission is continuously developing methods and technical approaches to be proposed to the Executive Chairman regarding the destruction of the chemical weapons and facilities.

Although the Iraqi authorities have been co-operative in the preparation of the destruction of their declared chemical stockpile, they have as yet failed to disclose fully all the information required under the Security Council resolutions on the development, support and manufacturing components of their CW programmes despite repeated requests from UNSCOM. Iraq has likewise not been forthcoming as regards information about the pattern and the details of its international procurement activities.

V. Biological weapon inspections

Paragraph 7 of the cease-fire resolution notes that Iraq became a party to the Convention on the Prohibition of the Development, Production and Stockpiling of Bacteriological (Biological) and Toxin Weapons and on Their Destruction (the BWC) when it deposited its instrument of ratification in Moscow on 8 April 1991.[25] In the area of BW capability, UNSCOM has

---

[23] At Tammuz (Al Taqqadum) Air Base at Habbaniyah 200 mustard-filled aerial bombs were stored; 30 chemical-filled ballistic missile warheads in the Dujayl area were declared; at Al Bakr Air Base 25 type 250 gauge aerial bombs and 135 type 500 gauge aerial bombs were stored; at Al Fallujah Proving Ground 6394 mustard-filled 155-mm artillery shells were stored; also 6120 sarin-filled 122-mm rocket warheads were declared by Iraq (see note 7).

[24] A variety of grenades containing CS were found in a depot at Al Fallujah General Headquarters (see note 7, p. 27).

[25] See note 4, p. 5; see also annexe A in this volume.

focused its activities on the major R&D site at Salman Pak, but a large number of other sites have also been inspected.[26] Iraq initially denied possession of biological weapons and related items. However, in the course of its inspection activities UNSCOM has collected conclusive evidence that Iraq was engaged in an advanced military biological research programme. The micro-organisms involved were *Clostridium botulinum*, *Clostridium perfringens* and *Bacillus anthracis*. Inspectors also found indications that Iraq has possessed other micro-organisms which are considered biological warfare agents,[27] but no evidence of actual weaponization was found.

During 1991 the Special Commission inspected 90 different sites to map out Iraq's CW and BW programmes. In the absence of a full, complete and final disclosure by Iraq of these programmes, UNSCOM continues its efforts to identify these programmes through first-phase inspections and the designation of further suspected sites in order to uncover the full scope of the programmes. The inspections have provided a sound data base for future monitoring of Iraq's BW capability.

VI. Missile inspections

Iraq has declared the possession of 62 ballistic missiles, primarily Scud or Scud variants.[28] In 1991 the UNSCOM inspection teams supervised the destruction of all of these missiles and, in addition, found and destroyed *inter alia* 18 fixed Scud missile launch pads, 10 launchers, 32 ballistic missile warheads, 127 missile support vehicles and a substantial amount of rocket fuel. Furthermore, UNSCOM supervised the destruction of an assembled 350-mm supergun, components for 350-mm and 1000-mm superguns and one tonne of supergun propellent.[29] A large number of production, repair and test equipment and machinery associated with the Scud, Al Hussein and Badr 2000 missiles have been identified for destruction at five declared and seven undeclared sites.

During 1991 UNSCOM inspected 71 different sites—some on more than one occasion—which had been declared by Iraq or designated by the Special Commission under Iraq's ballistic missile programme. While the declared missiles were destroyed, substantial uncertainty remains as to whether all of the missiles subject to Security Council Resolution 687 (primarily Scud and Scud variants) have been declared as required. Information was obtained that various significant components for indigenously produced Scud missiles have been contracted for and received by Iraq. Confronted with evidence of the existence of additional proscribed material, on 9 March 1992 Iraq declared possession of an additional 89 Scud or Scud variant missiles and 3 training missiles, 8 mobile launchers, 45 missile warheads designed for chemical war-

[26] See note 7.
[27] They were the following: *Brucellus abortus*, *Brucella melitensis*, *Francisella tularensis* and various strains of *Clostridium botulinum*. In addition, three simulants of biological warfare agents were provided by Iraq: *Bacillus subtillis*, *Bacillus cereus* and *Bacillus megaterium* (see note 7).
[28] See note 7.
[29] United Nations Security Council document S/23268, 4 Dec. 1991.

fare and a large number of other items, all of which were said to have been destroyed in late summer 1991. Subsequent UNSCOM inspections are in the process of verifying the data. In addition to continued inspection and surveillance activities, the Special Commission endeavours by means of an exchange of information with governments and by various interactions with Iraq to resolve conclusively the existing uncertainties.

VII. Destruction of dual-purpose items

In the matter of the destruction, rendering harmless or removal of Iraq's capability as regards weapons of mass destruction, plans are well developed for destroying Iraq's chemical weapons. However, complex and contentious issues have to be addressed with regard to dual-purpose items, especially in relation to those missiles and CW production facilities which have both military and non-military uses. Iraq seeks as far as possible permission to divert these items from its military to its civilian programmes. UNSCOM has therefore faced difficult decisions about the extent to which the cease-fire resolution requires destruction of such items or permits their diversion to civilian use—subject to future monitoring to ensure that they are not again diverted to military programmes. A major consideration in this context must be whether the items can be reconverted to prohibited use or not. Refusal by Iraq in February 1992 to go along with destruction of missile production facilities, including buildings and equipment, led to strong reactions by the Security Council, condemning Iraq's failure in this regard and to a statement on 28 February by the Council that Iraq's behaviour constituted a material breach of Resolution 687.[30] After special Security Council meetings on 11 and 12 March 1992,[31] at which Iraq's Deputy Prime Minister presented the position of the Iraqi Government, Iraq acquiesced and destruction of Iraq's missile production capability could be initiated, followed later by uncontested destruction of essential installations related to Iraq's nuclear weapon development programme.

VIII. Monitoring and verification of compliance

With Resolution 715, adopted on 11 October 1991, the Security Council approved the two plans for future monitoring and verification of non-nuclear and nuclear weapons which had been requested under the cease-fire resolution.[32] Under Resolution 715, Iraq is required to meet unconditionally all its obligations under the two plans and to co-operate fully with the Special Commission and the IAEA. The non-nuclear weapon plan was developed by

[30] United Nations Security Council document S/23663, 28 Feb. 1992.
[31] United Nations Security Council document S/PV.3059; S/PV.3059 (Resumption 1); and S/PV.3059 (Resumption 2).
[32] See note 3.

the Special Commission[33] and the nuclear weapon plan by the IAEA.[34] The two plans, although not identical, have been closely co-ordinated.

Monitoring and verification of non-nuclear weapons

The obligations for the non-nuclear weapon categories includes the requirement to provide UNSCOM with full details of all items, equipment and facilities (both military and civilian) that could be used for purposes related to chemical and biological weapons, or for purposes related to ballistic missiles with a range greater than 150 km. More specifically, the plan is designed so as to ensure that Iraq does not reacquire any proscribed weapons. Since the items and facilities involved could have a dual use (i.e., be used for both prohibited and non-prohibited purposes), the monitoring and verification activities must cover not only military but also civilian facilities, material and items in order to preclude the creation of any new prohibited weapon capabilities. The plan has a set of general provisions that are applicable irrespective of weapon category. To this are added three specific parts and annexes which address each particular weapon category and which contain provisions related to chemical and biological items and missiles. For specific components of all weapons, clear distinctions have been made between prohibited items and activities, on the one hand, and items and activities which will be permitted but subject to monitoring because of a dual-use potential on the other hand. The plan is flexible so as to make it suitable even if the situation changes; technical or procedural modifications of detailed annexes can be made in the light of experience and developments. The state of affairs in the negotiations on a global ban on chemical weapons, the Chemical Weapons Convention (CWC), and the provisions of the BWC have been taken into account. From this starting-point the plan has been developed particularly bearing in mind that (a) Resolution 687 was adopted under Chapter VII ('Action with respect to threats to the peace, breaches of the peace, and acts of aggression') of the UN Charter,[35] and (b) the experience gained during 1991 about Iraq's compliance with its obligations under Resolution 687. The plan is prepared specifically for Iraq and in no way prejudges any existing international agreement or any agreement under negotiation. The main instruments of the plan are the right of UNSCOM to inspect any facility, item or activity, whether declared or undeclared, to use aerial overflights and to request extensive data-reporting by Iraq.

For verification and monitoring purposes Iraq is required to declare: (a) all chemicals that could be used for the development, production or acquisition of chemical weapons but which also have significant uses for purposes not prohibited by Resolution 687, and (b) all chemicals that have little or no use except as chemical warfare agents or for the development, production or

[33] See note 6.
[34] United Nations Security Council document S/22872/Rev.1, 20 Sep. 1991 and S/22872/Rev. 1/Corr.1, 10 Oct. 1991.
[35] For the text, see SIPRI, *SIPRI Yearbook 1991: World Armaments and Disarmament* (Oxford University Press: Oxford, 1991), appendix 18B, pp. 636–37.

acquisition of chemical weapons, or which have been used by Iraq as essential precursors for chemical weapons. These chemicals are specified in lists included in the annexes to the plan. Iraq must also declare equipment and facilities which could be used for purposes related to chemical weapons.

Biological items to be declared by Iraq for verification and monitoring include *inter alia* facilities where work is carried out with toxins or micro-organisms meeting criteria for risk groups II, III or IV according to the classification in the 1983 World Health Organization (WHO) *Laboratory Biosafety Manual*,[36] or with genetic material coding for toxins or genes derived from such micro-organisms. Maximum containment or containment laboratories designated as bio-safety level BL4 (P4)[37] or BL3 (P3)[38] and sites or facilities at which fermentation or other means for the production of micro-organisms or toxins using vessels larger than 10 litres individually, or 40 litres in the aggregate, should also be declared. Furthermore, Iraq is prohibited to carry out within its military organization any activities involving micro-organisms or toxins without prior permission from UNSCOM or to conduct activities related to diseases other than those indigenous or immediately expected to break out in its environment. Unless given permission by UNSCOM, Iraq may not conduct any breeding of vectors of human, animal or plant diseases or import certain micro-organisms, toxins and vaccines and related items as specified in the annex to the plan, nor may Iraq possess at any one time more than one BL4 laboratory and two BL3 laboratories.

In order for UNSCOM to verify and monitor ballistic missiles, Iraq must declare *inter alia* all of its missiles which are designed for use, or capable of being modified for use, in a surface-to-surface role with a range greater than 50 km, and provide information on any project and on any facility for production, repair, maintenance, and storage as well as on any project or facility for missile research, development, modification or testing. Iraq is furthermore obliged to provide information on the development, production or other acquisition of equipment and technologies related to ballistic missiles with a range greater than 150 km including: subsystems which can be used in missile systems, propulsion components, guidance and control equipment, pyrolytic deposition and densification equipment, launch and ground support equipment, analogue computers, digital computers and digital differential analysers, specially designed software or components for missile design and

---

[36] World Health Organization, *Laboratory Biosafety Manual* (World Health Organization: Geneva, 1983).

[37] Biosafety level 4, BL4 (formerly P4), designates maximum-containment laboratories and facilities with highly specialized architectural, sterilization and ventilation features for work with dangerous and/or exotic biological agents including recombinants that pose a high individual risk of life-threatening disease both for the laboratory worker, the community and the environment (risk group IV agents). In addition, BL4 laboratories are usually equipped with safety cabinets to further minimize the risk that the laboratory worker or the environment becomes contaminated by the biological agent studied.

[38] Biosafety level 3, BL3 (formerly P3), designates containment laboratories and facilities with special architectural and ventilation features for work with indigenous or exotic biological agents that present a high risk to laboratory workers (risk group III agents) or recombinant DNA molecules and recombinant organisms, where the potential for infection is real and the disease may have serious or lethal consequences.

material, and devices for reduced observables in missile systems as well as for protecting missile systems against nuclear effects.[39]

The monitoring plan entered into force on the date of its approval, 11 October 1991, which meant that for a limited period elimination of existing weapons, items and facilities continues parallel to the monitoring of future compliance. Since the substantive matters involved in the different phases are closely interrelated, such an approach makes it possible to fully and directly utilize the expertise, knowledge and experience gained since the outset of the Special Commission's operations.

The sanctions under UN Security Council Resolution 661 prohibit the sale or supply to Iraq of any weapons or related items.[40] Should the Security Council at some date decide to lift the sanctions on any relevant dual-use items, the plan provides for monitoring of such imports from within Iraq. Moreover, in order for the regime to be comprehensive, the plan foresees that a mechanism needs to be developed for transparency and information as regards export to Iraq of relevant dual-use items. Such a mechanism is to be developed in close co-operation between UNSCOM and the Sanctions Committee which was established by Resolution 661.[41]

According to the plan, Iraq was required to submit an initial declaration on the specific dual-purpose activities, facilities and items outlined in the plans and their annexes by 10 November 1991. In late November the Special Commission received from Iraq a document referring to Resolution 687 which restated and repeated earlier declarations on specific weapons. Iraq did not recognize that it had any obligations under Resolution 715 or under the plan approved under that resolution. Instead Iraq insisted on the right to decide what information it would provide to UNSCOM, stating that the plan 'aimed at objectives incompatible with the letter and the spirit of the United Nations Charter, [and] the norms of international and humanitarian pacts and covenants'. Iraq also declared that the plan causes the gravest damage to the credibility of the United Nations and its fundamental role in the protection of the independence and territorial sovereignty of member states. In spite of serious representations by the Special Commission, Iraq has continued its policy of non-compliance by not fulfilling its obligations to make continuous declarations on specific dates. In a special report on 18 February 1992 to the Security Council, the Commission outlined the serious shortcomings of Iraq with regard to its obligations under the plans.[42] In a statement on 19 February which condemned the failure by Iraq to implement Resolution 707, the Security Council requested that the Chairman of the Commission be sent on a special mission to present to the highest political level in Iraq the Council's stand on the issue. This mission was carried out on 21–24 February and the

---

[39] Annex IV of United Nations Security Council document S/22871/Rev.1 (note 6) contains a detailed list.

[40] See note 2.

[41] See note 2.

[42] United Nations Security Council document S/23606, 18 Feb. 1992.

outcome was reported to the Security Council on 26 February 1992.[43] The matter was also dealt with by the Security Council on later occasions in 1992.[44]

Monitoring and verification of nuclear weapons

The IAEA plan for monitoring and verification of nuclear weapons takes into account the safeguards agreement concluded with Iraq pursuant to the Non-Proliferation Treaty (NPT).[45] The IAEA has the responsibility of carrying out its plan with the co-operation and assistance of the Special Commission. In this context UNSCOM performs such functions as may be necessary to co-ordinate activities under the two plans, including providing the IAEA with special expertise, logistical assistance, informational and other operational support. UNSCOM also continues its activities related to site designation and aerial surveillance in support of the IAEA inspections.[46]

The nuclear weapon compliance-monitoring plan gives the IAEA the right to conduct inspections in Iraq anywhere at any time and to install continuous containment and surveillance equipment. Furthermore, a complete inventory of items and activities in the nuclear field which are relevant to the development of nuclear weapons and the acquisition of nuclear-weapons-usable material is required to be completed. Iraq is obliged to provide advance information on the construction of nuclear facilities and the import of nuclear items that might be relevant to the production of nuclear weapons or nuclear-weapons-usable material. Under the IAEA plan, other states are barred from supplying Iraq with proliferation-sensitive equipment and technology.

It must, however, be recalled that under Resolutions 687 and 707 Iraq's engagement in any nuclear activity is regulated by the requirement that Iraq is obliged to halt all nuclear activities of any kind, except for the use of isotopes for medical, agricultural and industrial purposes until the Security Council determines that Iraq is in full compliance with Resolution 707 and paragraphs 12 and 13 of Resolution 687, and until the IAEA determines that Iraq is in full compliance with its safeguards agreement with the IAEA.

IX. Conclusions

The two plans for monitoring compliance which were adopted in Resolution 715 were implemented because of Iraqi obstruction of UNSCOM's investigation. On 31 January 1992, the Security Council, on the level of Heads of State and Government, stated that all of the resolutions adopted by the Security Council on this matter must be fully implemented.[47] The matter of non-

---

[43] United Nations Security Council document S/23643, 26 Feb. 1992.
[44] See note 30.
[45] See note 29.
[46] See note 3.
[47] United Nations Security Council document S/PV.3046.

implementation of the plans by Iraq was subsequently subject to Security Council action.

The first two phases of the task which was given to UNSCOM and the IAEA were the disclosure and disposal of prohibited items. As can be seen from the preceding sections, while Iraq has made a number of declarations relating to proscribed weapon capabilities, these declarations have been far from complete. The Special Commission has therefore had no alternative but to make numerous designations of undeclared sites. In the absence of full and complete disclosure as called for in Resolution 707, designations and inspections of sites will continue with no advance notice. Since its initial declarations, Iraq has consistently maintained that it has no further declarations to make except when confronted with evidence of the inadequacy of its prior declarations. Iraq has repeatedly stated that it has no further declarations to make and has merely responded to information provided by UNSCOM, the IAEA and its inspection teams. Iraq presented its position and views in detail in a 24 January 1992 letter from the Iraqi Foreign Minister to the President of the Security Council.[48] In the letter Iraq maintained that it has complied with a very large part of the conditions, restrictions and measures imposed upon it by Resolution 687. A further detailed elaboration of Iraq's position was given by Iraq's Deputy Prime Minister at the Security Council meetings on 11 and 12 March 1992.[49] Both the Director-General of the IAEA and the Chairman of the Special Commission outlined their assessment of Iraq's implementation on the same occasion.

It appears quite obvious that in spite of a continuing lack of full co-operation by Iraq, the greatest part of Iraq's capability with regard to weapons of mass destruction and ballistic missiles has been accounted for and is being disposed of. However, in order to arrive at full disclosure and especially as the result of inspection activities, UNSCOM and the IAEA have on a number of occasions posed specific questions about particular capabilities to Iraqi authorities. Many of these questions remain unanswered. Consequently and despite inspection efforts by UNSCOM and the IAEA, some important lacunae remain which preclude full knowledge of the weapon programmes concerned. The Special Commission must therefore continue and intensify its aerial surveillance activity and expand its information-gathering capability, while making full use of the analytical capability vested in its Information Assessment Unit; it will also, with the support of the Security Council, seek further information from Iraq.

In co-operation with the governments of UN member states, it would be possible to establish the pattern and methods of procurement of Iraq's weapon programme so that a comprehensive understanding of the issues involved may be achieved. Only then will the Special Commission be in a position to report with confidence on any assessment of Iraq's compliance with the cease-fire resolution and related resolutions. This is also of considerable economic

---

[48] United Nations Security Council document S/23472, 24 Jan. 1992.
[49] See note 31.

significance for Iraq: paragraph 22 of Resolution 687 provides that only upon agreement by the Security Council that Iraq has completed all of its obligations with regard to weapons under the resolution will it be possible to remove the embargo on exports from Iraq.

In paragraph 14 of the cease-fire resolution the Security Council notes that the actions Iraq must take as regards its weapons of mass destruction and the missiles for their delivery represent steps towards the goal of establishing in the Middle East a zone free from such weapons. In this perspective, the current process acquires added importance as something of a prerequisite for such a zone, namely, an Iraq freed from weapons of mass destruction. The full and complete implementation of the cease-fire resolution in this respect could therefore also constitute an important contribution to the peace process in the Middle East.

The unique experience of the implementation of Resolutions 687, 707 and 715 ought to foster broader understanding of the complexities, difficulties and opportunities linked to creating methods, procedures, techniques and institutions for future arrangements for the non-proliferation of weapons of mass destruction and their means of delivery.

Appendix 13A. UN Security Council Resolution 687, the cease-fire resolution

Resolution 687 (3 April 1991)

The Security Council,

Recalling its resolutions 660 (1990) of 2 August 1990, 661 (1990) of 6 August 1990, 662 (1990) of 9 August 1990, 664 (1990) of 18 August 1990, 665 (1990) of 25 August 1990, 666 (1990) of 13 September 1990, 667 (1990) of 16 September 1990, 669 (1990) of 24 September 1990, 670 (1990) of 25 September 1990, 674 (1990) of 29 October 1990, 677 (1990) of 28 November 1990, 678 (1990) of 29 November 1990 and 686 (1991) of 2 March 1991,

Welcoming the restoration to Kuwait of its sovereignty, independence and territorial integrity and the return of its legitimate Government,

Affirming the commitment of all Member States to the sovereignty, territorial integrity and political independence of Kuwait and Iraq, and noting the intention expressed by the Member States cooperating with Kuwait under paragraph 2 of resolution 678 (1990) to bring their military presence in Iraq to an end as soon as possible consistent with paragraph 8 of resolution 686 (1991),

Reaffirming the need to be assured of Iraq's peaceful intentions in the light of its unlawful invasion and occupation of Kuwait,

Taking note of the letter sent by the Minister for Foreign Affairs of Iraq on 27 February 1991[1] and those sent pursuant to resolution 686 (1991), [2]

Noting that Iraq and Kuwait, as independent sovereign States, signed at Baghdad on 4 October 1963 'Agreed Minutes Between the State of Kuwait and the Republic of Iraq Regarding the Restoration of Friendly Relations, Recognition and Related Matters', thereby recognizing formally the boundary between Iraq and Kuwait and the allocation of islands, which were registered with the United Nations in accordance with Article 102 of the Charter of the United Nations and in which Iraq recognized the independence and complete sovereignty of the State of Kuwait within its borders as specified and accepted in the letter of the Prime Minister of Iraq dated 21 July 1932, and as accepted by the Ruler of Kuwait in his letter dated 10 August 1932,

Conscious of the need for demarcation of the said boundary,

Conscious also of the statements by Iraq threatening to use weapons in violation of its obligations under the Geneva Protocol for the Prohibition of the Use in War of Asphyxiating, Poisonous or Other Gases, and of Bacteriological Methods of Warfare, signed at Geneva on 17 June 1925,[3] and of its prior use of chemical weapons and affirming that grave consequences would follow any further use by Iraq of such weapons,

Recalling that Iraq has subscribed to the Declaration adopted by all States participating in the Conference of States Parties to the 1925 Geneva Protocol and Other Interested States, held in Paris from 7 to 11 January 1989, establishing the objective of universal elimination of chemical and biological weapons,

Recalling also that Iraq has signed the Convention on the Prohibition of the Development, Production and Stockpiling of Bacteriological (Biological) and Toxin Weapons and on Their Destruction, of 10 April 1972,[4]

Noting the importance of Iraq ratifying this Convention,

Noting moreover the importance of all States adhering to this Convention and encouraging its forthcoming Review Conference to reinforce the authority, efficiency and universal scope of the convention,

Stressing the importance of an early conclusion by the Conference on Disarmament of its work on a Convention on the Universal Prohibition of Chemical Weapons and of universal adherence thereto,

Aware of the use by Iraq of ballistic missiles in unprovoked attacks and therefore of the need to take specific measures in regard to such missiles located in Iraq,

Concerned by the reports in the hands of Member States that Iraq has attempted to acquire materials for a nuclear-weapons programme contrary to its obligations under the Treaty on the Non-Proliferation of Nuclear Weapons of 1 July 1968, [5]

Recalling the objective of the establishment of a nuclear-weapons-free zone in the region of the Middle East,

Conscious of the threat that all weapons of mass destruction pose to peace and security in the area and of the need to work towards the establishment in the Middle East of a zone free of such weapons,

Conscious also of the objective of achieving balanced and comprehensive control of armaments in the region,

Conscious further of the importance of achieving the objectives noted above using all available means, including a dialogue among the States of the region,

Noting that resolution 686 (1991) marked the lifting of the measures imposed by resolution 661 (1990) in so far as they applied to Kuwait,

Noting that despite the progress being made in fulfilling the obligations of resolution 686 (1991), many Kuwaiti and third country nationals are still not accounted for and property remains unreturned,

Recalling the International Convention against the Taking of Hostages,[6] opened for signature at New York on 18 December 1979, which categorizes all acts of taking hostages as manifestations of international terrorism,

Deploring threats made by Iraq during the recent conflict to make use of terrorism against targets outside Iraq and the taking of hostages by Iraq,

Taking note with grave concern of the reports of the Secretary-General of 20 March 1991[7] and 28 March 1991,[8] and conscious of the necessity to meet urgently the humanitarian needs in Kuwait and Iraq,

Bearing in mind its objective of restoring international peace and security in the area as set out in recent resolutions of the Security Council,

Conscious of the need to take the following measures acting under Chapter VII of the Charter,

1. *Affirms* all thirteen resolutions noted above, except as expressly changed below to achieve the goals of this resolution, including a formal cease-fire;

A

2. *Demands* that Iraq and Kuwait respect the inviolability of the international boundary and the allocation of islands set out in the 'Agreed Minutes Between the State of Kuwait and the Republic of Iraq Regarding the Restoration of Friendly Relations, Recognition and Related Matters', signed by them in the exercise of their sovereignty at Baghdad on 4 October 1963 and registered with the United Nations and published by the United Nations in document 7063, United Nations, *Treaty Series*, 1964;

3. *Calls upon* the Secretary-General to lend his assistance to make arrangements with Iraq and Kuwait to demarcate the boundary between Iraq and Kuwait, drawing on appropriate material, including the map transmitted by Security Council document S/22412 and to report back to the Security Council within one month;

4. *Decides* to guarantee the inviolability of the above-mentioned international boundary and to take as appropriate all necessary measures to that end in accordance with the Charter of the United Nations;

B

5. *Requests* the Secretary-General, after consulting with Iraq and Kuwait, to submit within three days to the Security Council for its approval a plan for the immediate deployment of a United Nations observer unit to monitor the Khor Abdullah and a demilitarized zone, which is hereby established, extending ten kilometres into Iraq and five kilometres into Kuwait from the boundary referred to in the 'Agreed Minutes Between the State of Kuwait and the Republic of Iraq Regarding the Restoration of Friendly Relations, Recognition and Related Matters' of 4 October 1963; to deter violations of the boundary through its presence in and surveillance of the demilitarized zone; to observe any hostile or potentially hostile action mounted from the territory of one State to the other; and for the Secretary-General to report regularly to the Security Council on the operations of the unit, and immediately if there are serious violations of the zone or potential threats to peace;

6. *Notes* that as soon as the Secretary-General notifies the Security Council of the completion of the deployment of the United Nations observer unit, the conditions will be established for the Member States cooperating with Kuwait in accordance with resolution 678 (1990) to bring their military presence in Iraq to an end consistent with resolution 686 (1991);

C

7. *Invites* Iraq to reaffirm unconditionally its obligations under the Geneva Protocol for the Prohibition of the Use in War of Asphyxiating, Poisonous or Other Gases, and of Bacteriological Methods of Warfare, signed at Geneva on 17 June 1925, and to

ratify the Convention on the Prohibition of the Development, Production and Stockpiling of Bacteriological (Biological) and Toxin Weapons and on Their Destruction, of 10 April 1972;

8. *Decides* that Iraq shall unconditionally accept the destruction, removal, or rendering harmless, under international supervision, of:

(*a*) All chemical and biological weapons and all stocks of agents and all related subsystems and components and all research, development, support and manufacturing facilities;

(*b*) All ballistic missiles with a range greater than 150 kilometres and related major parts, and repair and production facilities;

9. *Decides*, for the implementation of paragraph 8 above, the following:

(*a*) Iraq shall submit to the Secretary-General, within fifteen days of the adoption of the present resolution, a declaration of the locations, amounts and types of all items specified in paragraph 8 and agree to urgent, on-site inspection as specified below;

(*b*) The Secretary-General, in consultation with the appropriate Governments and, where appropriate, with the Director-General of the World Health Organization, within forty-five days of the passage of the present resolution, shall develop, and submit to the Council for approval, a plan calling for the completion of the following acts within forty-five days of such approval:

(i) The forming of a Special Commission, which shall carry out immediate on-site inspection of Iraq's biological, chemical and missile capabilities, based on Iraq's declarations and the designation of any additional locations by the Special Commission itself;

(ii) The yielding by Iraq of possession to the Special Commission for destruction, removal or rendering harmless, taking into account the requirements of public safety, of all items specified under paragraph 8(*a*) above, including items at the additional locations designated by the Special Commission under paragraph 9(*b*)(i) above and the destruction by Iraq, under the supervision of the Special Commission, of all its missile capabilities, including launchers, as specified under paragraph 8(*b*) above;

(iii) The provision by the Special Commission of the assistance and cooperation to the Director-General of the International Atomic Energy Agency required in paragraphs 12 and 13 below;

10. *Decides* that Iraq shall unconditionally undertake not to use, develop, construct or acquire any of the items specified in paragraphs 8 and 9 above and requests the Secretary-General, in consultation with the Special Commission, to develop a plan for the future ongoing monitoring and verification of Iraq's compliance with this paragraph, to be submitted to the Security Council for approval within one hundred and twenty days of the passage of this resolution;

11. *Invites* Iraq to reaffirm unconditionally its obligations under the Treaty on the Non-Proliferation of Nuclear Weapons of 1 July 1968;

12. *Decides* that Iraq shall unconditionally agree not to acquire or develop nuclear weapons or nuclear-weapons-usable material or any subsystems or components or any research, development, support or manufacturing facilities related to the above; to submit to the Secretary-General and the Director-General of the International Atomic Energy Agency within fifteen days of the adoption of the present resolution a declaration of the locations, amounts, and types of all items specified above; to place all of its nuclear-weapons-usable materials under the exclusive control, for custody and removal, of the International Atomic Energy Agency, with the assistance and cooperation of the Special Commission as provided for in the plan of the Secretary-General discussed in paragraph 9(*b*) above; to accept, in accordance with the arrangements provided for in paragraph 13 below, urgent on-site inspection and the destruction, removal or rendering harmless as appropriate of all items specified above; and to accept the plan discussed in paragraph 13 below for the future ongoing monitoring and verification of its compliance with these undertakings;

13. *Requests* the Director-General of the International Atomic Energy Agency, through the Secretary-General, with the assistance and cooperation of the Special Commission as provided for in the plan of the Secretary-General in paragraph 9(*b*) above, to carry out immediate on-site inspection of Iraq's nuclear capabilities based on Iraq's declarations and the designation of any additional locations by the Special Commission; to develop a plan for submission to the Security Council within forty-five days calling for the destruction, removal, or rendering harmless as appropriate of all items listed in paragraph 12 above; to carry out the plan within forty-five days following

approval by the Security Council; and to develop a plan, taking into account the rights and obligations of Iraq under the Treaty on the Non-Proliferation of Nuclear Weapons of 1 July 1968, for the future ongoing monitoring and verification of Iraq's compliance with paragraph 12 above, including an inventory of all nuclear material in Iraq subject to the Agency's verification and inspections to confirm that Agency safeguards cover all relevant nuclear activities in Iraq, to be submitted to the Security Council for approval within one hundred and twenty days of the passage of the present resolution;

14. *Takes note* that the actions to be taken by Iraq in paragraphs 8, 9, 10, 11, 12 and 13 of the present resolution represent steps towards the goal of establishing in the Middle East a zone free from weapons of mass destruction and all missiles for their delivery and the objective of a global ban on chemical weapons;

D

15. *Requests* the Secretary-General to report to the Security Council on the steps taken to facilitate the return of all Kuwaiti property seized by Iraq, including a list of any property that Kuwait claims has not been returned or which has not been returned intact;

E

16. *Reaffirms* that Iraq, without prejudice to the debts and obligations of Iraq arising prior to 2 August 1990, which will be addressed through the normal mechanisms, is liable under international law for any direct loss, damage, including environmental damage and the depletion of natural resources, or injury to foreign Governments, nationals and corporations, as a result of Iraq's unlawful invasion and occupation of Kuwait;

17. *Decides* that all Iraqi statements made since 2 August 1990 repudiating its foreign debt are null and void, and demands that Iraq adhere scrupulously to all of its obligations concerning servicing and repayment of its foreign debt;

18. *Decides also* to create a fund to pay compensation for claims that fall within paragraph 16 above and to establish a Commission that will administer the fund;

19. *Directs* the Secretary-General to develop and present to the Security Council for decision, no later than thirty days following the adoption of the present resolution,

recommendations for the fund to meet the requirement for the payment of claims established in accordance with paragraph 18 above and for a programme to implement the decisions in paragraphs 16, 17 and 18 above, including: administration of the fund; mechanisms for determining the appropriate level of Iraq's contribution to the fund based on a percentage of the value of the exports of petroleum and petroleum products from Iraq not to exceed a figure to be suggested to the Council by the Secretary-General, taking into account the requirements of the people of Iraq, Iraq's payment capacity as assessed in conjunction with the international financial institutions taking into consideration external debt service, and the needs of the Iraqi economy; arrangements for ensuring that payments are made to the fund; the process by which funds will be allocated and claims paid; appropriate procedures for evaluating losses, listing claims and verifying their validity and resolving disputed claims in respect of Iraq's liability as specified in paragraph 16 above; and the composition of the Commission designated above;

F

20. *Decides*, effective immediately, that the prohibitions against the sale or supply to Iraq of commodities or products, other than medicine and health supplies, and prohibitions against financial transactions related thereto contained in resolution 661 (1990) shall not apply to foodstuffs notified to the Security Council Committee established by resolution 661 (1990) concerning the situation between Iraq and Kuwait or, with the approval of that Committee, under the simplified and accelerated 'no-objection' procedure, to materials and supplies for essential civilian needs as identified in the report of the Secretary-General dated 20 March 1991,[9] and in any further findings of humanitarian need by the Committee;

21. *Decides* that the Security Council shall review the provisions of paragraph 20 above every sixty days in the light of the policies and practices of the Government of Iraq, including the implementation of all relevant resolutions of the Security Council, for the purpose of determining whether to reduce or lift the prohibitions referred to therein;

22. *Decides* that upon the approval by the Security Council of the programme called for in paragraph 19 above and upon Council agreement that Iraq has completed all actions contemplated in paragraphs 8, 9, 10, 11, 12

and 13 above, the prohibitions against the import of commodities and products originating in Iraq and the prohibitions against financial transactions related thereto contained in resolution 661 (1990) shall have no further force or effect;

23. *Decides* that, pending action by the Security Council under paragraph 22 above, the Security Council Committee established by resolution 661 (1990) shall be empowered to approve, when required to assure adequate financial resources on the part of Iraq to carry out the activities under paragraph 20 above, exceptions to the prohibition against the import of commodities and products originating in Iraq;

24. *Decides* that, in accordance with resolution 661 (1990) and subsequent related resolutions and until a further decision is taken by the Security Council, all States shall continue to prevent the sale or supply, or the promotion or facilitation of such sale or supply, to Iraq by their nationals, or from their territories or using their flag vessels or aircraft, of:

(a) Arms and related *matériel* of all types, specifically including the sale or transfer through other means of all forms of conventional military equipment, including for paramilitary forces, and spare parts and components and their means of production, for such equipment;

(b) Items specified and defined in paragraphs 8 and 12 above not otherwise covered above;

(c) Technology under licensing or other transfer arrangements used in the production, utilization or stockpiling of items specified in subparagraphs (a) and (b) above;

(d) Personnel or materials for training or technical support services relating to the design, development, manufacture, use, maintenance or support of items specified in subparagraphs (a) and (b) above;

25. *Calls upon* all States and international organizations to act strictly in accordance with paragraph 24 above, notwithstanding the existence of any contracts, agreements, licences or any other arrangements;

26. *Requests* the Secretary-General, in consultation with appropriate Governments, to develop within sixty days, for the approval of the Security Council, guidelines to facilitate full international implementation of paragraphs 24 and 25 above and paragraph 27 below, and to make them available to all

States and to establish a procedure for updating these guidelines periodically;

27. *Calls upon* all States to maintain such national controls and procedures and to take such other actions consistent with the guidelines to be established by the Security Council under paragraph 26 above as may be necessary to ensure compliance with the terms of paragraph 24 above, and calls upon international organizations to take all appropriate steps to assist in ensuring such full compliance;

28. *Agrees* to review its decisions in paragraphs 22, 23, 24 and 25 above, except for the items specified and defined in paragraphs 8 and 12 above, on a regular basis and in any case one hundred and twenty days following passage of the present resolution, taking into account Iraq's compliance with the resolution and general progress towards the control of armaments in the region;

29. *Decides* that all States, including Iraq, shall take the necessary measures to ensure that no claim shall lie at the instance of the Government of Iraq, or of any person or body in Iraq, or of any person claiming through or for the benefit of any such person or body, in connection with any contract or other transaction where its performance was affected by reason of the measures taken by the Security Council in resolution 661 (1990) and related resolutions;

G

30. *Decides* that, in furtherance of its commitment to facilitate the repatriation of all Kuwaiti and third country nationals, Iraq shall extend all necessary cooperation to the International Committee of the Red Cross, providing lists of such persons, facilitating the access of the International Committee of the Red Cross to all such persons wherever located or detained and facilitating the search by the International Committee of the Red Cross for those Kuwaiti and third country nationals still unaccounted for;

31. *Invites* the International Committee of the Red Cross to keep the Secretary-General apprised as appropriate of all activities undertaken in connection with facilitating the repatriation or return of all Kuwaiti and third country nationals or their remains present in Iraq on or after 2 August 1990;

H

32. *Requires* Iraq to inform the Security Council that it will not commit or support

any act of international terrorism or allow any organization directed towards commission of such acts to operate within its territory and to condemn unequivocally and renounce all acts, methods and practices of terrorism;

I

33. *Declares* that, upon official notification by Iraq to the Secretary-General and to the Security Council of its acceptance of the provisions above, a formal cease-fire is effective between Iraq and Kuwait and the Member States cooperating with Kuwait in accordance with resolution 678 (1990);

34. *Decides* to remain seized of the matter and to take such further steps as may be required for the implementation of the present resolution and to secure peace and security in the area.

[1] S/22275, annex.

[2] S/22273, S/22276, S/22320, S/22321 and S/22330.

[3] League of Nations, *Treaty Series*, vol. 94 (1929), no. 2138.

[4] General Assembly Resolution 2826 (26), annex.

[5] General Assembly Resolution 2373 (22).

[6] General Assembly Resolution 34/146.

[7] S/22366.

[8] S/22409.

[9] S/22366.

Source: UN document A/RES/46/36, 9 Dec. 1991.

14. Post-Soviet threats to security

SIGNE LANDGREN

I. Introduction

The Soviet Union did not come to an end in a nuclear war, a conventional war or a civil war. It was formally ended by three signatures on a piece of paper—the Minsk Agreement of 8 December 1991, in which the presidents of the Russian Federation, Ukraine and Belarus announced the abolition of the Soviet Union and the formation of a new association, the Commonwealth of Independent States (CIS).[1] The announcement of the CIS took not only the Soviet leadership and the outside world by surprise but also the leadership of the Union republics. On 13 December 1991, the presidents of the five Central Asian republics (Kazakhstan, Kyrgyzstan, Tajikistan, Turkmenistan and Uzbekistan) met in Ashkhabad, Turkmenistan, and issued a declaration of support of and participation in the CIS, but only on condition that they were accepted as co-founders.[2] From the text of this document it is clear that the Central Asian representatives resented this surprise and in particular the fact that they had not in any way been prepared for the move undertaken by the presidents of the three Slavic republics (Belarus, Russia and Ukraine) in Minsk. The final formation of the new Commonwealth took place in Alma-Ata, the capital of Kazakhstan, on 21 December 1991, and included all the former Soviet republics except the three Baltic states (Estonia, Latvia and Lithuania) and Georgia.[3]

The demise of the Soviet Union and the creation of the CIS could have marked the beginning of a new era of peaceful evolution of a European security system and a smooth continuation of nuclear and conventional arms reductions, particularly since it is generally agreed that the cold war is over, and that there is no direct military threat from the former Soviet Union towards the West or other areas.

Instead, the realities of the post-Soviet world involve a whole range of new dangers that could jeopardize both international security and the European security process, thereby illustrating the general insight that the solution to one problem invariably creates new problems demanding new solutions. The new threats to stability and security that have surfaced are all connected to the dissolution of the Soviet Union but not necessarily directly caused by it: that

---

[1] For the text of the Minsk Agreement of 8 Dec. 1991, see appendix 14A. The CIS member states are: Armenia, Azerbaijan, Belarus, Kazakhstan, Kyrgyzstan, Moldova, the Russian Federation, Tajikistan, Turkmenistan, Ukraine and Uzbekistan.

[2] See the text of the Ashkhabad Declaration of 13 Dec. 1991 in appendix 14A.

[3] See the text of the Alma-Ata Declaration on the CIS of 21 Dec. 1991 in appendix 14A. Estonia, Latvia and Lithuania gained independence in Sep. 1991.

is, some security threats would presumably have arisen even if it had been possible to preserve a reformed Soviet Union.

The most immediate dangers to stability and security after the breakup of the former superpower are connected with the fate of the nuclear arsenal and the risk of a spread of nuclear arms, the risk of abuse of the nuclear arms still present on the territories of the former republics, the risk of accidents or terrorist take-over of nuclear arms stocks and the risk of complications of the internationally agreed processes of destruction of these armaments.

Related to these dangers, the fate of the former Soviet armed forces that were in effect left over with no state to serve creates a potential for future conflicts within the newly created nation-states and perhaps in the outside world. The plans for a smooth transition of the unitary Soviet forces into a unitary CIS force have failed so far; and with continued uncertainty, the position of the military *per se* involves the dangers of new state coups and an entirely new role for the military. In December 1990, President Mikhail Gorbachev warned that a breakup of the Soviet Union would mean world-wide catastrophe, saying that 'if we split up the Army and the nuclear arms, this will mean a catastrophe not only for the USSR but for the entire world'.[4] The ominous prospect of a Yugoslav-style development on a Soviet scale involving nuclear weapons in conflicts has been looming large also in the minds of Western actors.[5] The military heritage of the former superpower clearly makes up a threat category that arose as a direct result of the breakup of the Soviet Union.

Other important dangers to security concern the mounting opposition to the central government in Moscow and the explosion of demands for more independence and sovereignty on the part of former republics creates the prospects of inter- and intra-republic conflicts. In some areas the former Soviet Union is already at war, as in the case of the Caucasus and Moldova. The conflict heritage makes up a risk category that existed historically long before communist rule. In retrospect it seems clear enough that the international support voiced throughout 1991 for preserving a central Soviet power by definition underrated the centrifugal forces that eventually made the recreation of any sort of union impossible.[6] In contrast to President Gorbachev, Russian Foreign Minister Andrey V. Kozyrev declared in December 1991 that the successful formation of the new Commonwealth of Independent States 'has averted the danger of a Yugoslav development' politically as well as militarily, and that the CIS has created viable and

---

[4] See the text of the speech by President Gorbachev at a Moscow meeting of scientists and artists, broadcast on Soviet television, in *Frankfurter Rundschau*, 1 Dec. 1990, p. 1.

[5] See, for example, the excerpt from a television interview with US Secretary of State James A. Baker on 8 Dec. 1991, quoted in *International Herald Tribune*, 9 Dec. 1991, p. 1.

[6] In early Sep. 1991, the USA, the UK and Germany had already taken the position that the Soviet Union must preserve a common foreign policy and a united military command, if Western economic aid should be extended. See, for example, 'Kohl warns Soviet Union must retain unified policies', *Financial Times*, 5 Sep. 1991, p. 1.

'understandable' structures as compared to the past attempts at reorganizing the Soviet Union.[7]

In this chapter, the new threats to security are thus divided under two main headings: the military heritage and the conflict heritage of the former Soviet Union. The justification for this is that although they are interrelated they are not necessarily interdependent. The nuclear weapon issue may eventually be solved while the issue of the armed forces may develop for the worse. Conflicts have already broken out and demand negotiated solutions regardless of military power.

Finally, the painstaking efforts to democratize the former Soviet states and to initiate co-operation with the Western powers in security matters are taking place against the background of the declining economy. The outcome of the ongoing transition to a market economy defies prediction and may end in disaster. In the event of a total collapse of civil society in the former Soviet territory, civil strife and civil war may follow, and the negotiated arms reduction treaties may be transformed into insignificant pieces of paper.

II. The military heritage of a superpower

The nuclear arsenal

The Soviet Union was one of the two nuclear superpowers, possessing a vast arsenal of strategic nuclear weapons located in four of its former republics—Belarus, Kazakhstan, Russia and Ukraine (see figure 14.1). No scenario by Western military planners, by politicians, by disarmament negotiators or by the scientific community prior to September 1991 predicted the immediate disappearance of this superpower, leaving the nuclear arsenal behind as a most precarious heritage.

The Agreement on Joint Measures on Nuclear Weapons signed by Russia, Ukraine, Belarus and Kazakhstan in Alma-Ata on 21 December 1991 most importantly confirms that the strategic and tactical nuclear weapon forces will be kept as a unitary CIS force: 'Until nuclear weapons have been completely eliminated on the territory of the Republic of Belarus and the Ukraine, decisions on the need to use them are taken, by agreement with the heads of the member states of the agreement, by the RSFSR president, on the basis of procedures drawn up jointly by the member states'.[8] This agreement also provides for continued central control of the nuclear arms based in Belarus, Kazakhstan and Ukraine until removed to Russia for destruction. The new force comprises the former Strategic Rocket Forces and the strategic units of the Air Force and Navy, the central directorate of the Early Warning System, the Missile Space Defence and the Space Systems Control.[9] In order to launch

---

[7] See the interview with A. V. Kozyrev by R. Mustafin in *Krasnaya Zvezda*, 20 Dec. 1991, p. 1.

[8] See the text of the Agreement on Joint Measures on Nuclear Weapons of 21 Dec. 1991 in appendix 14A.

[9] See *Izvestia*, 10 Dec. 1991, p. 7. The newly formalized strategic force under central CIS command is named *Strategicheskiye Sily Sderzhivaniya* (Strategic Deterrent Forces).

strategic nuclear weapons, this entire network has to be put into operation, and may be initiated only by the central command in Moscow.[10] However, the governments in Ukraine and Kazakhstan are objecting with a growing furore to Russian hegemony as a nuclear successor state and to being excluded from future international nuclear weapon contexts. Ukraine has, for example, independently requested US assistance to handle the arms destructions under the 1991 START Treaty. President Nursultan Nazarbayev of Kazakhstan declared at the meeting in Alma-Ata in January 1992 with Foreign Minister Roland Dumas of France that the nuclear arms in Kazakhstan will remain there until the year 2000, and that their mere presence will serve to obtain both recognition and reimbursement to the country for damages caused by the nuclear weapon testing at the Semipalatinsk site since 1949. Nazarbayev also repeated his claim for a real veto over the use of nuclear weapons, which was expressed as the capacity to interrupt the chain of command needed to launch them.[11]

Strategic and tactical weapons

The *strategic* nuclear arsenal totals 12 500 nuclear missiles on land, on heavy bomber aircraft and on nuclear submarines. The overall total is generally estimated as 27 000, which includes the unknown tactical missile stocks. Seventy-five per cent of the strategic missiles are based on Russian territory, as is shown in figure 14.1.[12] This accounts for the Russian Federation's internationally accepted status as the nuclear weapon successor state to the Soviet Union. With central control firmly in Moscow, the other republics have little chance to use the nuclear card militarily. The mere possession of strategic missiles would be militarily meaningless. What remains would be a political use which in the end might not yield much result, however. The risk of proliferation of strategic missiles under present circumstances must be regarded as nil.

Tactical nuclear weapons may total 15 000 nuclear warheads and in some respects make up a separate risk category. First, the total number of these weapons has never been officially disclosed, nor has their exact location. Second, these weapons could at least theoretically be taken over by a national

---

[10] Reportedly, the central command in this case means solely Marshal Shaposhnikov, appointed as temporary Defence Minster of CIS forces, and President Yeltsin of the Russian Federation. Concrete details about the operating line of command and control over the nuclear arsenal remain undisclosed, as is indeed the case with the other nuclear forces in the world.

[11] See Amalric, J., 'Le Kazakhstan conteste le monopole nucléaire de la Russie', *Le Monde*, 28 Jan. 1992, p. 4.

[12] These figures were presented by analysts Alexander Pikayev and Alexander Savelyev of the Institute of World Economy and International Relations (IMEMO) of the USSR Academy of Sciences in response to a call by NATO leaders on the USSR to provide data on the nuclear weapon locations in Russia, Ukraine, Belarus and Kazakhstan. This is the first information from the Soviet side on the breakdown and location of its nuclear arsenal. The figures differ somewhat from the previously commonly used estimates from the US Department of Defense (DOD) and the International Institute of Strategic Studies (IISS), but the order of magnitude remains roughly the same, in particular the proportions between Russia and the other new countries with nuclear weapon bases—Belarus, Kazakhstan and Ukraine. See *Nezavisimaya Gazeta*, no. 137 (2 Nov. 1991), pp. 1 and 4.

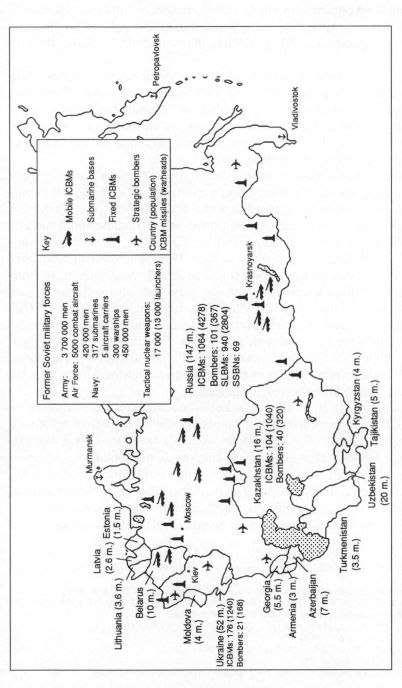

Figure 14.1. The former Soviet military forces

Sources: For Army, Air Force and Navy data see International Institute for Strategic Studies, *The Military Balance 1991–1992* (Brassey's: London, 1992); for strategic nuclear weapons see Pikayev, A. and Savelyev, A., *Nevavisimaya Gazeta*, no. 137 (2 Nov. 1991), pp. 1–4.

force since they are relatively small, transportable and do not present the same technical challenge as do the large ICBMs. For the same reason, this type of nuclear weapon might fall into the hands of terrorist or dissident groups for use in bargaining and/or nuclear blackmail. However, tactical weapons, like strategic nuclear weapons, are connected to a central line of operational control, and warheads are reportedly stored separately from their launchers. As with strategic weapons, the mere possession of tactical nuclear weapons without the capacity to add or launch the warheads is also militarily meaningless.[13]

Tactical nuclear weapons consist of some 3000 short-range missiles (the most well-known being the Scud)[14] and 2000 nuclear shells on 6700 nuclear-capable artillery systems.[15] Also included are air-launched bombs, naval bombs and torpedoes. Tactical nuclear weapons are in service within the different branches of the armed forces. Western estimates credit the former Soviet Army with some 4700 tactical arms.[16]

According to recent Russian information, by 1991 Ukraine had 2605 tactical nuclear weapons on its territory, and it rather seems as if dispersion outside Russia was not as widespread as sometimes feared in the West.[17] By 1989, these weapons were already being taken out of such potential conflict areas as the Baltic states, Moldova and the Caucasus. Marshal Yevgeniy Shaposhnikov confirmed this when in January 1992 he told Foreign Minister Dumas of France that all tactical weapons had already been withdrawn from Central Asia and the Caucasus. Reportedly, they were also withdrawn from outside the Soviet Union before 1989.[18] According to the plans of the CIS central command, the remainder, located in Belarus and Ukraine, were to be removed by July 1992 for destruction in Russia.[19] In fact, the removal began in January 1992, with the full adherence of both these countries.[20] The possibility of the sale or proliferation of tactical *weapons* outside Russia must be regarded as unlikely under present conditions.

The risk of proliferation of nuclear know-how and raw materials may be more immediate, in particular against the background of the agreed reductions and ensuing shut-down of plants and test sites. Many reports have circulated about former Soviet nuclear scientists seeking employment on nuclear weapon programmes in certain developing countries, and of plutonium and uranium finding its way onto the international market. President Boris Yeltsin assured US Secretary of State James Baker during their meeting on 16 December 1991 that strict export control would be enforced on all nuclear equipment and

[13] Meyer, S. M., 'The post-Soviet nuclear menace is being hyped', *International Herald Tribune*, 16 Dec. 1991, p. 8.

[14] US Department of Defense, *Soviet Military Power* (DOD: Washington, DC, Sep. 1991).

[15] Cochran, T. B., Arkin, W. M., Norris, R. S. and Sands, J. I., *Nuclear Weapons Databook, Vol. IV: Soviet Nuclear Weapons* (Harper & Row: New York, 1989), p. 198.

[16] Steele, J., 'An embarrassment of missiles', *Guardian Weekly*, 15 Dec. 1991, p. 2.

[17] *Krasnaya Zvezda*, 14 Jan. 1992, p. 1

[18] *Komsomolskaya Pravda*, 4 Sep. 1991, p. 2.

[19] *Le Monde*, 25 Jan. 1992, p. 20.

[20] Swedish Radio, Programme 1, 27 Jan. 1992, quoting international news agencies.

know-how.[21] President Nazarbayev emphatically denied the reports of nuclear exports from Kazakhstan during his meeting with French Foreign Minister Dumas in January 1992, reportedly saying: 'We are not Arabs, and all rumours about our readiness to transfer nuclear technology to them amount to slander'.[22]

Finally, the dissolution of the Soviet Union into its constituent republics may complicate, if not endanger, the ratification and implementation of the international nuclear arms control and reduction treaties concluded by the Soviet Union—that is, the multilateral 1968 Non-Proliferation Treaty (NPT), and the bilateral 1972 Anti-Ballistic Missile Treaty and 1991 START Treaty.[23] The formal inclusion of Russia, Ukraine, Belarus and Kazakhstan as parties to the treaties and the ratification procedures are by no means incompatible with international law—all of these countries have consistently assured their adherence to the international agreements concluded by the former Soviet Union. How this adherence will be effectuated is another matter, and the controversy between Ukraine and Kazakhstan on one hand and Russia on the other seems to concern matters of procedure rather than the issue of reductions. The two former parties object to Russia acting as the sole representative of the CIS in the context of international treaty negotiations. In the four-power Agreement on Joint Measures on Nuclear Weapons signed in connection with the Alma-Ata Declaration of 21 December 1991, Article 5.1 stipulates that Ukraine and Belarus undertake to accede to the NPT as non-nuclear weapon states and to enter safeguards agreements with the International Atomic Energy Agency.[24] The position of Kazakhstan remains more unsettled: at the end of January 1992, President Nazarbayev told French Foreign Minister Dumas that if Kazakhstan ever becomes a party to the NPT this will be in its capacity as a 'nuclear-weapon country like France'.[25]

On 10 February 1992, the Russian Federation's Ministry of Foreign Affairs declared in a note to all foreign embassies that Russia has assumed the responsibilities of the former USSR with regard to all international treaties, including that of depositary government where applicable. Simultaneously, the Russian Government took over the obligations under the NPT Treaty.[26]

The early-warning system comprising a chain of radar stations now located in independent states might cause a jurisdictional problem related to the ABM

---

[21] The Western nuclear weapon states will have to cope with the same kind of problem as nuclear programmes are cut down and unemployment of high-techology specialists increases, in which case the potential customers remain limited to largely the same as those mentioned in the context of the former Soviet Union. The majority of countries have after all agreed to accede to the NPT and are not intending to become nuclear weapon states.

[22] See note 11.

[23] See chapter 1 in this volume for an analysis of the START Treaty and the post-Soviet arms reduction situation.

[24] See note 8.

[25] See note 11. The NPT permits only five nuclear weapon powers—the USA, the USSR, the UK, France and China—and prohibits the transfer of nuclear weapons to other states.

[26] Telefax message by the Russian Embassy in Stockholm to Sweden's Foreign Ministry, 10 Feb. 1992.

Treaty. This comes at a time when the entire problem area related to ABM defence may be fading away in the new international context.

The post-Soviet armed forces

The Soviet Union possessed the world's largest armed forces, with an army numbering nearly five million men. The future of this massive force, which was sometimes called the 'sixteenth Soviet republic', may determine the survival of the CIS as well as of Russia and the other former Soviet republics. One bizarre result of the dissolution of the Soviet Union into its 15 union republics is that this 'sixteenth state' was left over without a nation to serve. Officially, the planned CIS unitary military forces will still come into being, but perhaps a new unitary force was already rendered obsolete in October 1991 when Ukraine decided to establish its own national force. The Minsk Agreement of 30 December 1992 expressly notes that each independent state decides on how to solve the defence issue, and that Azerbaijan, Moldova and Ukraine decided to have national forces. The same decision was also announced soon after the meeting by Belarus, Turkmenistan and Uzbekistan. In January 1992, Marshal Shaposhnikov toured the countries which still may become the members of a unitary force being, in addition to the Russian Federation, Armenia, Kazakhstan, Kyrgyzstan and Tajikistan. The CIS summit meeting on 14 February 1992 in Minsk failed to solve the problem concerning the future organization of the defence forces. Marshal Shaposhnikov advocated a step-by-step moderate reorganization and reform under the CIS central direction during a two-year transition period, but Ukraine and Azerbaijan refused participation. Thus, there is a parallel development which might result in a hybrid version in which the former Soviet armed forces in practice are nationalized in all of the western republics except Armenia, while the CIS force involves Russia and some of the Central Asian republics. There is also the additional option that some of the new nation-states will first set up their national forces and then eventually join a CIS force.

Meanwhile, however, serious problems arise that demand speedy solutions or they will multiply the risk factors related to the fate of the armed forces and the military–industrial complex as a whole. Parts of the military establishment even advocate the re-establishment of the Soviet Union, by force if necessary. During 1991, Soviet forces were increasingly dragged into the armed conflicts in progress, in Nagorno-Karabakh and elsewhere. Outright attacks on these forces by local armed groups may ultimately provoke Russian intervention in other republics or in the autonomies.

Social problems faced by demobilized officers and troops returning from Eastern Europe and the Baltic states are mounting, and a social explosion is feared that might provoke the military to actively interfere with politics. Military representatives demand a solution to their status, the establishment of a new central command structure and the offer of social guarantees.[27] The conflict potential may eventually turn out to be greater than the nuclear weapon issue. In addition, the prospect of dividing the military–industrial complex between the republics is an integral part of one and the same threat to stability and security.[28] The conversion of military industries and rising unemployment resulting from cuts in arms production programmes present risk factors of a dimension other than strictly military. Uncontrolled exports of high-technology weapons and know-how may collide with the Russian Government's avowed policy of erecting strict export controls, and contribute to destabilization in conflict areas both within the former Soviet territory and internationally.[29]

The question of financing and social security for the military, in particular the hundreds of thousands of soldiers being demobilized after the unilateral force reductions over the past few years or after returning from Eastern Europe, has to be solved irrespective of the CIS outcome. The official military budget for 1992 would, according to a presentation based on the option of a single joint defence force for the 11 Commonwealth states, be calculated on the basis of the number of troops stationed on each state's territory, the size of population, volume of national income and GNP.[30] By February 1992, no joint military budget had been agreed. The current financing of the strategic military forces has meanwhile been taken over by Russia alone in the name of the CIS, pending final agreement on the composition of the joint CIS forces and final agreement on the participants. Russia also finances the forces that are not nationalized by the other republics. The picture remains very unclear, however, and information on national military budgets is almost non-existent. Presumably, former Soviet forces transferred under national authority, such as interior troops, border troops and, from January 1992, all the conventional forces in Ukraine, are being financed locally.

[27] As formulated at the meeting in the Kremlin of 4839 CIS military officers representing the armed forces. See for example, 'The problems of the army are the problems of peace in our country', *Izvestia*, 17 Jan. 1992, pp. 1–2; and 'The army does not want to become an independent political force', *Krasnaya Zvezda*, 22 Jan. 1992, pp. 1–2.

[28] See section V, chapter 9 in this volume for an analysis of the defence industry complex of the former Soviet Union.

[29] See chapter 8 in this volume. For example, President Yeltsin declared that Russia will adhere to the principles for exports of conventional armaments agreed to in London in Oct. 1991. See *Izvestia*, 22 Feb. 1992, p. 3.

[30] See Orlov, A., 'The Army: financial cross-section', *Moscow News*, no. 52 (Dec. 1991), p. 8 (Dr Alexander Orlov was chairman of the USSR Control Board). The respective shares would have been: Russia: 61.2%; Ukraine: 17%; Azerbaijan: 1.9%; Moldova:1.2%; Kyrgyzstan: 0.9%; Tajikistan: 0.8%; Armenia: 1.1%; Turkmenistan: 1.0%. For an analysis of developments in Soviet military spending during 1991, see chapter 7 in this volume.

III. The conflict heritage of a superpower: new nation-states with new national forces

The Soviet Union was the world's largest multinational state. The 15 former republics are inhabited by over 100 ethnically different peoples.[31] A meticulous count results in over 800 ethnic peoples, including all the very small remnants of various nomad populations usually described as being at the point of extinction. Aggregate population figures are given in figure 14.1. Russians make up the obvious majority and over the centuries have spread into the other republics where they now make up considerable minorities.

The Soviet regional administration of its vast empire was a complex division of ethnic areas which were given differing degrees of autonomy under the central government of the Russian Federation, or under a republican government. The Russian Federation thus encompasses the former 16 Autonomous Soviet Socialist Republics and 15 other autonomous areas, as shown in figure 14.2. In addition, there are autonomies under the jurisdiction of other republics, in Georgia and Moldova. Both the total number and status of these minorities were uncertain at the end of 1991. Some of these smaller nations actively challenged the previous order during 1991 by demanding a change of status to full sovereignty, leading to a situation in which the Russian Federation has to face a process of dissolution similar to the dissolution of the Soviet Union into its constituent states.

Soviet geographers and demographers have identified 72 current territorial claims concerning ethnic minorities within larger regions or states, of which many are incompatible.[32] Of these 72 conflict issues, 40 are considered as having reached an acute stage. The origins of these conflicts are diverse, but all may be considered as based on some historical violation of human rights such as forced resettlement, a change of borders, a negative change of administrative status, a division of a former ethnic unity, or the suppression of national identity. There are also conflicts with a social and economic background, such as the outburst of violence in the city of Osh in Kyrgyzstan in 1990 between Uzbeks and Kyrgyzians.

In fact, the dissolution of the Soviet Union into its republics and the creation of the CIS proceeded surprisingly quietly and as of 1991 have not provoked armed conflicts between the member states. The controversy between the largest and most powerful former republics, Ukraine, Russia and Kazakhstan, amounts to a war of words as yet. However, other former Soviet republics are at war, as exemplified by the situation in Georgia and the Nagorno-Karabakh conflict. The prospect that the new national armies will be used in civil wars is very realistic in some cases, for example in Azerbaijan and Moldova. In other cases the establishment of national armed forces

---

[31] For a thorough analysis of the nationalities issue in the Soviet Union, see, for example, Carrère d'Encausse, H., *Decline of an Empire: The Soviet Socialist Republics in Revolt* (Harper & Row: New York, 1980).

[32] See 'A map of unrest in the USSR', *Moscow News*, no. 11 (1991), pp. 8–9.

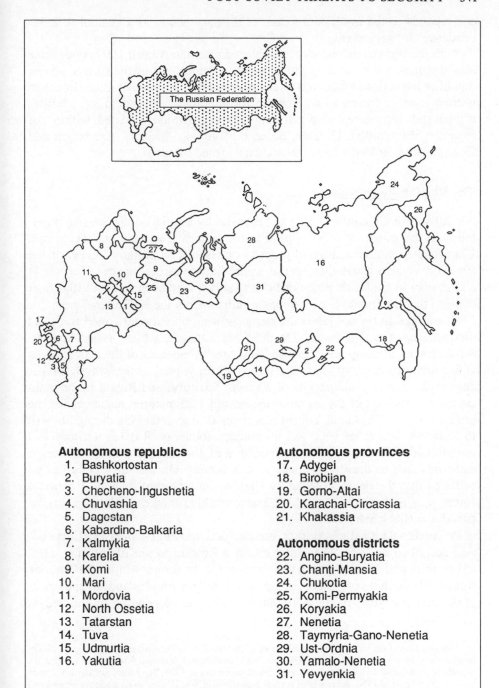

Figure 14.2. The Russian Federation and its ethnic autonomies

Autonomous republics
1. Bashkortostan
2. Buryatia
3. Checheno-Ingushetia
4. Chuvashia
5. Dagestan
6. Kabardino-Balkaria
7. Kalmykia
8. Karelia
9. Komi
10. Mari
11. Mordovia
12. North Ossetia
13. Tatarstan
14. Tuva
15. Udmurtia
16. Yakutia

Autonomous provinces
17. Adygei
18. Birobijan
19. Gorno-Altai
20. Karachai-Circassia
21. Khakassia

Autonomous districts
22. Angino-Buryatia
23. Chanti-Mansia
24. Chukotia
25. Komi-Permyakia
26. Koryakia
27. Nenetia
28. Taymyria-Gano-Nenetia
29. Ust-Ordnia
30. Yamalo-Nenetia
31. Yevyenkia

corresponds to the traditional axiom of military power as a symbol of independence and sovereignty.[33]

With the right to independence, achieved after the August 1991 coup, came also the principal right to organize defence forces. All of the former Soviet republics have since embarked on the organization of national guard forces or special interior forces to replace the former Soviet interior troops, border troops and sometimes also railway troops previously located within the republics. In addition, Ukraine, Belarus, Moldova, Armenia, Azerbaijan and Georgia have decided to establish national armed forces.

The Russian Federation

For Russia, future conflicts may be provoked by attacks on the Russian population in the other republics similar to the riots in Tatarstan and Tajikistan. Unnegotiated nationalization of property or assaults on military forces outside Russia may also cause intervention under certain circumstances. Territorial claims may in the future prove difficult to solve, such as the recent Lithuanian demand that the former Soviet troops withdraw from the Kaliningrad area.

Russia has so far not taken the step of setting up national armed forces as distinct from the CIS forces. On the other hand, it is often stated that the Soviet forces in many respects were Russian: '90 per cent of the officer corps is Russian, two thirds of the military expenditure is paid by the RSFSR, 80 per cent of the military industry is on Russian territory, and Russia is the main supplier to the rest of the union of technology and material resources for the armed forces'.[34] President Yeltsin reconfirmed in an interview during his visit to Rome in December 1991 that all military forces on Russian territory will remain under the unified CIS command, and also that each other sovereign state was free to decide for itself on this issue.[35] On the same occasion he declared that the decision taken by Ukraine on its establishment of national forces was 'no problem', and that Ukraine could also take control of a smaller part of the Black Sea Fleet.[36]

A Russian national guard force was decided upon in October 1991. Its task was described by Vice-President Alexander Rutskoi as one of ensuring internal security and of serving as a replacement for the former Ministry of Interior troops. The initial cost was planned at 3–4 billion roubles and manpower at 3000 after one year, rising to 10 000 by 1993 and, depending on the budget

[33] Varennikov, (Gen.) V. I., ['From the history of the creation and organization of national military formations'], *Voennaya Mysl*, no. 2 (1990), pp. 3–13 [in Russian]. National forces existed during the Bolsehvik Revolution and were placed under central command in 1923. They were not abolished until the military reform of 1938. After a brief revival during World War II, they were gradually phased out. These forces existed in Armenia, Azerbaijan, Bashkortostan, Belarus, Buryat-Mongolia, Central Asia, Georgia, Karelia, Kazakhstan, Tatarstan, the Volga district, Transcaucasus, Ukraine and Yakutia.

[34] See the interview with Colonel V. N. Lopatin, Chairman of the RSFSR State Committee on Defence Affairs, in *Krasnaya Zvezda*, 18 Oct. 1991, p. 1.

[35] In Mar. 1992, Russia decided to set up its own Defence Ministry, which may signal the future establishment of Russian national forces.

[36] *Krasnaya Zvezda*, 19 Dec. 1991, p. 3.

situation, to an upper limit of 66 000 men.[37] The first international task for this force was to guard the southern border of Georgia from early 1992.

The first presentation of Russia's military budget for 1992 appeared only in February 1992, giving the total as 50.4 billion roubles of which as much as 70 per cent was allocated for pensions.[38] Of this total, 42.4 billion roubles was for the Russian Federation while the remaining 8 billion roubles in the future are supposed to be paid by the other CIS members. Russia is thus financing the majority of all the military forces of the former Soviet Union, strategic as well as conventional.

Ukraine

Ukraine has appeared on the world map as a new and potentially powerful state in its own right. It may actually hold the key to future conflict escalation in the CIS. Its controversy with Russia may escalate with unknown consequences. There may occur disputes over territory acquired by the Soviet Union in 1939 from Poland, Czechoslovakia, Hungary and Romania which in a European context will demand negotiated solutions.

On 22 October 1991, the Ukrainian Parliament decided to set up armed forces including an army, an air force and a naval force. The planned combined strength was initially quoted at 420 000 men, in addition to the planned national guard of 30 000. This declaration provoked adverse if not violent reactions not only from Russia but also from the West: the United States issued a warning the day after the Ukrainian decision. The Conference on Security and Co-operation in Europe (CSCE) and NATO also objected. It was pointed out that this would give Ukraine the largest army in Europe, and violate the 1990 Conventional Armed Forces in Europe (CFE) Treaty limiting tank and artillery forces on Ukrainian territory. Later it was clarified that the basis for an estimated army of 420 000 men was an arithmetic calculation— rather than the result of military planning—of how to employ the approximately 600 000 Ukrainian troops serving in the former Soviet forces.[39] Other arithmetical explanations followed, for example that the total figure would make up only 0.8 per cent of the 52 million population, or that the total figure should be seen in comparison to the present 1.2 million former Soviet forces based in Ukraine.[40]

Smaller numbers have also been quoted. In his pre-election campaign in November 1991, President Leonid Kravchuk mentioned a total of 200 000– 250 000, including a republican guard, border troops and internal troops, and reaffirmed at the same time that the strategic forces in Ukraine would remain under unified CIS control and could consist of 700 000–800 000 troops.[41] First

[37] *Argumenty i Fakty*, no. 40 (Oct. 1991), p. 2.

[38] *Krasnaya Zvezda*, 4 Feb. 1992, p. 2.

[39] Information as reported by Zbigniew Brzezinski after his visit with officials of the Ukrainian Government. See *International Herald Tribune*, 12 Nov. 1991, p. 4.

[40] *The Guardian*, 8 Dec. 1991, p. 5.

[41] *Krasnaya Zvezda*, 2 Nov. 1991, p. 1; *Izvestia*, 5 Nov. 1991, p. 2.

Deputy Foreign Minister Nikolay Makarevich stated during a visit to Czechoslovakia in November 1991 that: 'The Ukrainian Army will be 100 000 strong at most. It will be a small, mobile, professional army, ready to protect interests of the Ukrainian state and the people. . . . I wish to assure Czechoslovak citizens that no powerful military force will threaten them on the part of the Ukraine'.[42]

Ukraine also set up a National Guard, the press service of which informed in early January 1992 that about 8000 servicemen had entered the force, and that the planned number by the end of 1992 was 18 000–20 000 men.[43]

The controversy with Russia over the division of the Black Sea Fleet broke out in early January 1992 and sharply worsened relations between the two countries. The fleet is based in the port of Sevastopol in the Crimea and has over 45 major warships, 300 smaller ships and over 100 aircraft, with a total manpower of 70 000. It remains under the central CIS command, although conscripts and officers from January 1992 began to swear allegiance to Ukraine.[44] On 12 January 1992, a joint Russian–Ukrainian communiqué was published, declaring that Ukraine will receive part of the fleet and that a joint CIS expert commission was set up to sort out which ships can be transferred, with the understanding that ships included in the Strategic Forces will stay under unified CIS command. The planned transfer should take place in July 1992. The conflict is fomented by excessive demands from more nationalistic groups in the parliaments in both countries as well as by economic considerations focusing on the export value of the warships.[45]

The total national budget as well as the total military expenditure allocations are not yet known, but the Ukrainian Finance Ministry in October 1991 estimated a cost of 8 billion roubles for the upkeep of the Army alone.[46] Ukrainian Minister of State Security Evhen Marchuk declared in November that from 1 January 1992 Ukraine will fulfil its financial obligations to the CIS central military budget for the Strategic Forces on its territory, which will amount to perhaps 17 per cent of the overall CIS military budget as mentioned above. From the same date, Ukraine will also take over the financing of border, interior and railway troops transferred to Ukrainian jurisdiction by agreement with Russia in October 1991.[47] By 20 January 1992, 6400 servicemen including 200 officers had been sworn in under the new national military oath.[48] These include the personnel of the Defence Ministry of Ukraine, the railway troops and air force maintenance units in Kiev. The ministerial cabinet also informed in January that, in the context of new legislation on social security for the military staff, an allocation had been made for the first quarter

[42] TASS report from Prague, 28 Nov. 1991, in Foreign Broadcast Information Service, Daily Report— Soviet Union (FBIS-SOV), FBIS-SOV-91-230, 29 Nov. 1991, pp. 45–46.

[43] Interfax report of 8 Jan. 1992, as transmitted by Kyodo, FBIS-SOV-92-006, p. 61.

[44] See Dagens Nyheter (Stockholm, Sweden), 13 Jan. 1992, p. A6.

[45] In Feb. 1992 there were reports of Russian sales of several of the Black Sea Fleet warships not only to India but also to 'private companies' in Moscow.

[46] Ukrainian Minister for State Security Evhen Marchuk, as reported in a statement after Ukraine's declaration of independence, in Financial Times 12–13 Oct. 1991, p. 2.

[47] Izvestia, 5 Nov. 1992, p. 2.

[48] Radio Kiev report of 8 Jan. 1992, in FBIS-SOV-92-006, pp. 60–61.

of 1992 in the amount of 350 million roubles to be used entirely for the Black Sea Fleet's personnel costs.[49]

The international arms reduction programmes under the CFE and START treaties are generally assumed to involve financing on a scale beyond the means of Ukraine. Discussions have already been held with NATO and US representatives on the possibility of economic aid for these programmes. Military conversion programmes have to be financed as well, reflecting industrial, economic and military disarray on a scale impossible to calculate in the absence of reliable data.

Belarus

After independence, Belarus declared its aspiration to create a neutral and nuclear weapon-free state, with its own independent military policy. Belarus eventually opted for the creation of national military forces but holds the door open for participation in a joint CIS force at a later stage. The most immediate problem after independence concerns the overdeployment of former Soviet forces in the country, which by October 1991 amounted to a total of 160 000 men in 14 tank and artillery divisions. According to President Stanislav Shushkevich, 'troop density in our republic is three times greater than the average for the former Union'.[50] In November, the Parliament agreed in principle to create national armed forces. Later in the month, the commander of the then Soviet Byelorussian Military District, Colonel-General A. Kostenko, announced a planned cut of the military forces by one-third.[51]

On 11 January 1992, after a two-day debate described as 'furious', the Belarus Parliament resolved to place all armed forces on Belarussian territory (except the strategic CIS troops and weapons) under the jurisdiction of its government, ratified the text of a new military oath and transformed the Ministry for Defence Affairs into a Defence Ministry. After the decision on the armed forces was taken, President Shushkevich in an interview issued a firm protest against the ongoing campaign in the Russian press and elsewhere not to split up the former Soviet forces, denouncing this as 'illegal gambling' and 'pseudo-patriotism'.[52] He went on to say that Belarus is looking for a way to make the armed forces serve the country, and not the other way around.

President Shushkevich later outlined a possibility of participating in a CIS joint force in the future, illustrating the eventual third option for a unitary force:

---

[49] See report of the press conference by Defence Minister K. Morozov and Conversion Minister V. Antonov in Kiev after Black Sea Fleet talks with Russia, in *Izvestia*, 15 Jan. 1992, p. 2.

[50] Interview with S. Shushkevich by S. Vaganov, in *Trud*, 14 Jan. 1992, p. 3; in FBIS-SOV-92-009, p. 59. Another report claims that the troop ratio is 1 soldier to every 43 civilians (1:43) compared to 1:64 in Russia and 1:528 in Tajikistan. See *Le Monde,* 22 Feb. 1992, p. 6.

[51] Information from Moscow Interfax quoting 'circles close to the Belarussian government', as transmitted via Kyodo, with the statement that one-third equalled 120 000 troops which would give an initial total of 360 000 Soviet forces. See FBIS-SOV-91-225, 21 Nov. 1991, p.-76.

[52] Interview with S. Shushkevich in *Krasnaya Zvezda*, 17 Jan. 1991, pp. 1–2.

At the last Minsk meeting we reaffirmed each Commonwealth state's right to set up its own army. It is another matter that at the time only three of them—Azerbaijan, Moldova and Ukraine—had enshrined this right in decisions passed by their parliaments. Our parliament was some way from passing such a decision. In principle the decisions can be different. For instance, we could allow our—and I stress 'our'—troops to be part of a unified command. A decision on this score is being adopted.[53]

The size of the future Belarussian armed forces has not yet been decided upon. A preliminary figure of 90 000 received wide publication, but Defence Minister Peter Chaus explained the figure as being based on a calculated relationship between conscripts and the size of the population:

This figure cannot be rigidly adhered to today. The date when we will approach it has not been determined either. However, why should it be 90 000? As the experience of civilized countries shows, 0.8–0.9 per cent of the adult population usually serves in the army. The figure was arithmetically computed on this basis. But in determining the strength of the armed forces, you need not just arithmetic, but algebra, so to speak, and even geometry. In short, for the moment this is a guide figure, which has no political or economic basis as yet.[54]

The economic basis for supporting a large conscript army is clearly not at hand, and a probable option would be a smaller professional force in the future. Plans for 1992 call for considerable troop reductions and the allocation of 30 per cent of the budget for weapons procurement to be switched to welfare programmes for the military, in particular for the construction of housing.[55]

Moldova

The Republic of Moldova, like the other westernmost former Soviet republics, has declared its intention to participate in the CSCE, and its adherence to the CFE Treaty and other international treaties concluded by the USSR. Moldova decided in October 1991 to organize national military forces and refuses to participate in any unitary military force. Its government may eventually opt for reunification with Romania, which already caused revolt by the Russian population in the country and in the future may bring a conflict with Ukraine as well as Russia.

Moldova (except for the Dnestr area) was incorporated into the Soviet Union in 1940 as a result of the 1939 Molotov–Ribbentrop Pact. It is largely made up of the former Romanian province of Bessarabia, and the majority of the population are of Romanian origin. A large Russian population lives in the Dnestr area, and in the south there is an autonomy of the Gagauz people, who are Christians of Turkish origin. The Moldovan Government challenged Soviet power by demanding independence at the same time as the Baltic

[53] Interview with S. Shushkevich by *Trud* correspondent S. Vaganov in Minsk, 10 Jan. 1991, in *Trud*, 14 Jan. 1991, p. 3, in FBIS-SOV-92-009, p. 59.
[54] Interview with Defence Minister P. Chaus by P. Chernenko, in *Krasnaya Zvezda*, 3 Jan. 1992, p. 1.
[55] Moscow Television, quoting Defence Minister P. Chaus, 13 Jan. 1992, in FBIS-SOV-92-008, p. 52.

states, and Moldova became a crisis area and the scene of armed fighting. The National Guard was set up in 1990 specifically for action in Gagauzia and in the Dnestr area. A civil war situation also arose when government forces in November 1990 attacked the town of Dubasari in the Dnestr area. The Russian population subsequently set up a breakaway republic called the Dnestr Moldavian Republic and demanded transfer to the Russian Federation. The Gagauz minority also declared independence of its autonomous area under the name of the Gagauz Moldavian Republic, and also demands transfer to the Russian Federation (see figure 14.3). Small armed forces exist in both areas and armed clashes continue.

The size of the future army is at the planning stage and will be set up from the former Soviet contingent of 30 000 troops in the country. According to the Director of the Moldovan Department for Military Affairs, Nikolae Kirtoake, the manpower potential in Moldova would allow for an army of 100 000 men. However, this would mean: 'militarization of the state and enormous spending. It has been decided therefore, to set the limit at a 12 000–15 000-strong professional army. . . . The Army will keep out of politics and will protect the constitutional order and territorial integrity of the republic'.[56] In November 1991, President Mircea Snegur decreed the nationalization of former Soviet military property in the country. In accordance with the Minsk Agreement on the Armed Forces of 30 December 1991, the first military unit was sworn in to Moldova on 5 January 1992—an interior troops battalion located in the Dnestr area, formerly under the authority of the Soviet Interior Ministry. Reacting to the central government's military policy, on 9 January the parliament of the breakaway Dnestr Republic announced *its* take-over of the former Soviet military forces promising a threefold salary increase to officers loyal to Dnestr and introduced compulsory military service.[57]

The Caucasus

The Caucasus region is the most conflict-ridden area and provides ample warning of the complexity of inherited political and ethnic grievances as well as their potential for escalation (see figure 14.4). In the Caucasus, there are three newly independent states in addition to the Russian Federation— Armenia, Azerbaijan and Georgia—seven Autonomous Republics and four Autonomous Regions, populated by 60 indigenous nationalities. There are some 30 current territorial disputes over borders that were changed in the 1920s, 1930s and 1950s. The Russian Federation issued new legislation in

[56] See TASS report from Moscow of 19 Nov. 1991, in FBIS-SOV-91-224, 20 Nov. 1991, p. 73; and FBIS-SOV-91-225, 21 Nov. 1991, p. 77.
[57] *Dagens Nyheter* (Stockholm, Sweden), 10 Jan. 1992, p. A8.

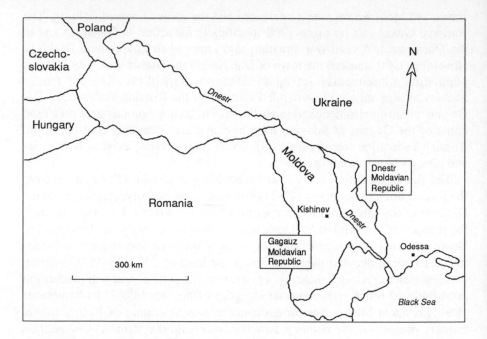

Figure 14.3. The Moldovan conflict area

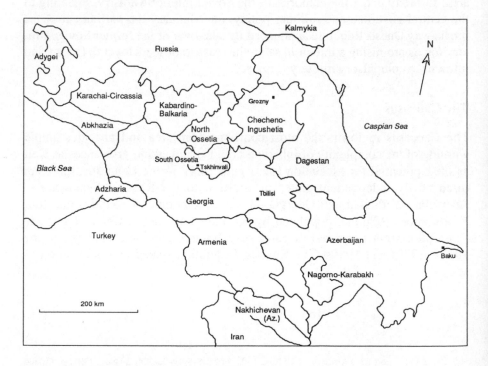

Figure 14.4. The Caucasus conflict area

1990 to remedy past violations against ethnic peoples and has since demonstrated a non-provocative policy in the face of upheavals in the Caucasian autonomies.[58]

Chechnia

The Chechnian crisis in November 1991 provides an exception to this cautious policy demonstrated by the Yeltsin Government and nearly resulted in Russian military intervention. It also presented the first example of the use of nuclear blackmail of sorts. The autonomy of Checheno-Ingushetia was set up only in 1990, as the rehabilitation of two formerly oppressed minorities. However, opposition to Moscow continued to grow, involving mass demonstrations and attacks on Soviet forces and military stocks in the country. President Dzhokhar Dudayev, elected on 9 November 1991, announced the Republic of Chechnia as an independent state, put the already formed national guard units on alert and also announced general mobilization of the male population. These events provoked President Yeltsin into declaring a state of emergency in the area and to dispatch special riot troops to the capital Grozniy. The troops were held captive in the airport by local forces, and General Dudayev threatened in a telephone interview with Agence France Presse to strike back with terrorist acts against nuclear power stations and other strategic targets in Russia.[59] Eventually, however, the Russian Parliament stopped the action and withdrew the Soviet troops. Subsequently, the Russian Ministry of Interior presented the following judgement of the Chechnian incident: 'The use of troops 8–9 November in the actual situation that arose in Grozniy could have led to unpredictably serious consequences, the scale of which would have been many times worse than in the tragic events in Tbilisi, Baku and Vilnius'.[60]

By the end of November 1991, the Chechnian National Guard was reported to number 62 000 men, and the President demanded a right to take over Soviet military equipment in the territory. Legislation was passed in January 1992 on the set-up of a national army and the terms of service. Meanwhile, the status of the former Soviet forces in Chechnia has not been clarified and local attacks on these forces continue.

The Ingushetian autonomy is on the brink of war with the North Ossetian autonomy in the area in a conflict that also demands its solution. Further, there are plans to revive the Caucasus republic that existed in the 1920s and create a federal state fully independent from the Russian Federation.

[58] Russia has so far not reacted adversely to the split-up of Karachai-Circassia into two sovereign 'states', to the split-up of the Checheno-Ingushetian autonomy or to the dividing of Kabardino-Balkaria into two parts, which all happened in late 1991.

[59] See *Expressen* (Stockholm, Sweden), 10 Nov. 1991, p. 17.

[60] USSR Ministry of Interior press service, in *Krasnaya Zvezda*, 13 Nov. 1991, p. 2.

The Nagorno-Karabakh conflict

The most serious conflict to date in the Caucasus is the war between Armenia and Azerbaijan which has been going on since 1988 over the largely Armenian-populated enclave of Nagorno-Karabakh. The Karabakh demand for the area's transition to Armenia led to massacres of Armenians in Sumgait and Kirovabad in 1988 and in Baku in 1990. A cycle of violence erupted causing a great number of casualties and streams of refugees in both directions. The efforts of the Soviet Government to mediate by using the interior troops served to aggravate the situation. Ensuing efforts at mediation by the Russian and Ukrainian leaders have failed, as well as the efforts by the CSCE mission sent to the area. The Russian Government decided to withdraw all former Soviet forces from the area where they increasingly were being brought into the conflict. In early 1992, both Iran and Turkey offered mediating assistance, and the Karabakh Government appealed to the United Nations for peace-keeping forces. Meanwhile, the conflict is escalating and seems to be growing into an all-out inter-republic war.

Both Armenia and Azerbaijan adhere to the 1990 CFE Treaty. Armenia is willing to participate under a CIS unified command. Azerbaijan advocates a defence option similar to the position taken by Belarus: it wants to set up national forces and to keep an option to participate in a unitary CIS force at a later stage.[61]

In Armenia, militia forces were set up after the massacres in Baku in 1990. By 1991 it was estimated that Armenia might have some 10 000 such troops but the number of armed men might be 140 000.[62] In early 1992, the decision was taken to set up national armed forces. Azerbaijan decided in October 1991, after Armenian military advances in Karabakh, to nationalize all Soviet military property on its territory and to create a national army. According to the opposition Popular Front, the army is expected to number some 35 000 troops, and it will be organized from a core of the 10 000 Azerbaijanis in the former Soviet forces outside the country.[63] The same source said that the army might turn to Iraq and Turkey to acquire weapons. President Ayaz Mutalibov signed a decree on 16 December 1991 on the transfer of all former Soviet armed forces—with the exception of the Strategic Forces—in the territory under national authority.

---

[61] This policy was outlined by president Ayaz Mutalibov: 'As to the solutions on how to establish military forces within the CIS framework, I am convinced that they will be found and regulated. Only after the creation of national military forces can the common military and strategic defence space of the CIS emerge, and it will emerge very rapidly. Also a joint command of the military forces will then be created, by mutual agreement and after the model of the Nato countries for example'. See *Izvestia*, 23 Jan. 1992, p. 2.

[62] See International Institute of Strategic Studies, *The Military Balance 1991–1992* (Brassey's: London, 1992).

[63] See *International Herald Tribune*, 12 Oct. 1991, p. 4.

Georgia

Like Armenia and Azerbaijan, Georgia has become a country devastated by war and unsolved minority conflicts. Violent anti-Soviet demonstrations brought the intervention of Interior Ministry troops in 1990 which led to shootings of civilians in Tbilisi, later subject to an investigation by the Soviet authorities. Since then the country has been heavily burdened and torn apart both by the minority conflicts and by the armed opposition to President Zviad Gamsakhurdia who eventually fled the country in January 1992. Up to that time, Georgia opted to stay out of the CIS agreement and to refuse participation in any joint structures with the former Soviet states. The autonomy of South Ossetia demands secession from Georgia and new status as a sovereign republic within the Russian Federation. South Ossetia's capital Tskhinvali has been the scene of armed clashes and massacres of civilians. The autonomy of Abkhazia in the northern part of the country also demands secession from Georgia and status as an independent republic within Russia.

Georgia set up a national guard in December 1990, which was planned to number 13 000 troops. By 1991, it was estimated to number 5000 men.[64] In May 1991, a riot police force was created with modern equipment and special vehicles, to function under the authority of the President and the Ministry of Interior as an anti-terrorist force. At the beginning of 1992, the former Soviet troops were being evacuated in order not to be further involved in the fighting, and it was also decided that national armed forces should be created.

In March 1992, Georgia became the final former Soviet republic to join the CSCE.[65]

Soviet Asia

The former Soviet republics of Kazakhstan, Kyrgyzstan, Tajikistan, Turkmenistan and Uzbekistan are often referred to as the five Central Asian countries. They are, however, not identical, although they certainly possess common characteristics. Their populations are largely of Turkish origin, and they are Sunni Muslims, so culturally these nations have little in common with the Orthodox Slavic nations to the west and with Russia. They are important suppliers of raw materials with very low per capita incomes and low levels of industrialization compared to the western parts of the former Soviet empire. The Islàmic renaissance in Soviet Central Asia, which occurred as a result of the new policy of freedom of religion instigated by President Gorbachev, may

---

[64] See note 62.
[65] In Mar. 1992, Eduard Shevardnadze was called back to Georgia to take over the position as Head of State. Shortly thereafter it was declared that Georgia will remain continue to remain outside of the CIS.

in the future become a politically destabilizing factor. All five former Soviet Central Asian republics plus Azerbaijan will become members of the regional economic organization established in 1985 by Iran, Turkey and Pakistan. To regard this newly emerging economic association as leading to the development of an Islamic great power is premature, but this development is a clear break with the past and represents a new policy for Soviet Central Asia.

After the CIS summit meeting in Minsk on 30 December 1991, all five Central Asian states decided on some form of national guard forces to replace the former Soviet interior and border troops. But their attitude towards a future joint CIS military force begins to differ, illustrating that these countries may not be so monolithic as earlier assumed. Kazakhstan, Kyrgyzstan and Tajikistan remained firm in their support for joint forces at the CIS summit meeting on military matters in February 1992, while Turkmenistan and Uzbekistan began to show some variation in their future plans for national defence.

Through their inclusion in the CSCE in February 1992, all of these countries have undertaken to adhere to the confidence-building measures already agreed within that body and to observe the Helsinki Final Act of 1975. The also recognized the requirement for prompt entry into force of the 1990 CFE Treaty. For the Central Asian countries, this involves a commitment to limit military forces in the future, as they have no tank forces to reduce. Their incorporation into the CSCE process means that the conventional arms control process is advancing towards the goal of covering the entire area from Vancouver to Vladivostok.[66]

In the Soviet Far East, there are as yet no new nation-states in addition to Russia, and autonomous areas there have not developed into breakaway republics along the pattern illustrated in the Caucasus.[67]

Kazakhstan

In Central Asia, the republic of Kazakhstan is rising out of anonymity and will play a new role in its own right strategically as well as politically. During the Gorbachev era, the Nazarbayev Government was characterized by loyalty to the central Soviet power, followed by initial co-operation with Russia and the CIS process. This co-operation on military forces is in stark contrast to Kazakhstan's posture regarding nuclear weapons, where its government emphasizes the country's right to be treated as a sovereign actor. President Nazarbayev announced the formation of a National Guard immediately after the August 1991 coup attempt, saying this was 'indispensable in view of the tragic August events' to protect the country's sovereignty.[68] A state committee for defence affairs was set up. In January 1992, the number of the National

---

[66] See chapters 12 and 15 in this volume.

[67] Although there is talk of a 'Far Eastern Republic', a 'Siberian Republic', a 'Urals Republic', a 'Yenisei Republic' and a 'Sakhalin-Kuriles Republic', it is certainly premature to judge if any of these republics will come into being and, if so, whether it could cause conflict within the Russian Federation.

[68] *Krasnaya Zvezda*, 12 Oct. 1991, p. 2.

Guard force was planned to be 2000 men. At the same time, President Nazarbayev signed a decree to form interior troops based on the former Soviet interior forces in the country.[69] From 1 January 1992, these interior troops are financed out of the national budget.

In early 1992, Kazakhstan still stands out as the single most firm ally of Russia on the issue of a future unitary CIS military force: 'whatever the situation, we will continue efforts to preserve our army in one piece, even if Russia remains our single ally. . . . We will maintain a single army under dual control'.[70] President Nazarbayev also sharply criticized Ukraine's defence policy and called upon the Central Asian republics to work out a single defence concept.

Kyrgyzstan

President Askar Akayev in January 1992 issued a decree to form Interior Ministry troops, on the basis of existing former Soviet Interior Ministry troops in the country. The new national troops are to take orders directly from the President, and be composed of special mechanized police units and one special unit in charge of prisons and prisoner escorting. A state committee for defence will be set up as well as a National Guard. According to presidential adviser Colonel Z. Nogoybayev, the guard will be multinational and will total 800 men.[71]

Tajikistan

Tajikistan so far has co-operated with Russia and Kazakhstan for a joint CIS military force. Marshal Shaposhnikov visited the country in January 1992 with the task of co-ordinating the position of Tajikistan regarding future CIS Armed Forces including border troops.

Turkmenistan

Turkmenistan diverged from a pattern of co-operation when the Government declared interest in national armed forces after the December 1991 Minsk summit meeting. According to a statement by President Saparmurad Niyazov of 6 January 1992, Turkmenistan will not set up its own armed forces during the next five years. Instead, the Government hopes for an agreement with the Russian Federation to help Turkmenistan by supporting the former Soviet troops stationed there, specifically the border troops. President Niyazov expressed hope that Turkmenistan's economy would improve within two to three years and be able to provide for the army units in the country. In the

---

[69] Interfax report from Moscow of 11 Jan. 1992, as transmitted via Kyodo, in *Postfactum Moscow*, 11 Jan. 1992, in FBIS-SOV-92-009, p. 64.

[70] Interfax report from Moscow, 13 Jan. 1992, in FBIS-SOV-92-009, p. 64.

[71] Interfax report from Moscow, 17 Jan. 1992, in FBIS-SOV-92-009, p. 3.

immediate future, a meeting was planned in Ashkhabad with CIS Commander-in-Chief Marshal Shaposhnikov and Ukrainian President Leonid Kravchuk, to discuss military questions. Plans also call for a national defence ministry to be set up.

The Commander of the Central Asian Border District, and member of the Presidential Council of Turkmenistan, Alexander Bogdanov, reportedly suggested in January 1992 that the future of the former Soviet Caspian Sea Fleet could be discussed at the next military CIS meeting. In the event of a division of the Caspian Fleet, one of its bases near Krasnovodsk could be handed over to Turkmenistan, which would provide the border district with sufficient naval equipment.[72]

Uzbekistan

Uzbekistan opted in principle for the creation of national military forces after the Minsk summit meeting in December 1991. President Islam Karimov by decree of 13 January 1992 decided, like the other Central Asian nations, to transfer the interior troops under national authority. The Tashkent military high school was also transferred to the Uzbek Ministry of the Interior.

IV. Concluding assessment

The Commonwealth of Independent States is a fragile construction. Its future rests basically upon the capacity to co-operate on the part of its largest and strategically most important members, Russia, Ukraine and Kazakhstan. It is currently first of all an economic association of countries that in the future may diverge sharply from each other. Alternatively, they may revert to a firmer association after a certain period. Thus, at present the CIS exists solely in terms of those agreements that have been reached, including the decision to keep the nuclear arms and the Strategic Forces under joint command.[73] The structures of the CIS remain to be worked out. If political controversies grow, for example between Russia and Ukraine, the present CIS arrangement could collapse with unknown military and political consequences. How the

---

[72] See Interfax report from Moscow of 13 Jan. 1992, in FBIS-SOV-92-010, p. 74. By Mar. 1992, Nazarbayev had become frustrated by the lack of progress on a joint CIS force and announced that Kazakhstan too will create its own armed forces.

[73] At the summit meeting in Minsk on 30 Dec. 1991, nine documents were signed by the 11 participants: (a) a temporary agreement on the establishment of a council including the heads of state and the prime ministers of all CIS member states; (b) an agreement on the CIS unitary strategic force; (c) an agreement of all heads of state of the CIS on armed forces and border troops; (d) agreement on joint research and utilization in space; (e) an agreement by the heads of state concerning ownership of former USSR property abroad; (f) an agreement on preparation of joint measures to deal with the problems of the Aral lake, and the problems resulting from the earthquake in Spitak; (g) an agreement on preparation of special measures to preserve fishing resources in the Caspian Sea; (h) an agreement on measures to liquidate dangers ensuing from the Chernobyl accident, to be undertaken in 1992, including their financing and scale; and (i) a joint decision to work out the title, structure and financing of the working group that shall plan and organize CIS summit meetings. See *Krasnaya Zvezda*, 31 Dec. 1991, p. 1.

management of new post-Soviet threats to security can be incorporated into a new concept of global security remains an open question.

As of March 1992, concluded arms agreements have not been violated. All 11 member states have continued the arms reduction policy and the non-confrontational foreign policy inherited from the Gorbachev era. None of the new CIS states has declared any non-adherence to previous arms control and reduction agreements. President Boris Yeltsin has responded positively to US proposals for further arms reductions and in addition made new proposals, seemingly intent to continue the 'disarmament race'.[74] Russia and other CIS states have expressed interest in a joint participation in the US space defence system known as 'GPALS' (Global Protection Against Limited Strikes).[75] What constitutes a 'reasonable sufficiency' in the level of nuclear arms has yet to be determined. There are signs, however, that Russian thinking on the issue is becoming more similar to the Western position than was the case during the Gorbachev era. However, it is clear that there is no drive for nuclear rearmament, even among supporters of the attempted coup in the Soviet Union in August 1991.

If military reform can be made to work, reducing the size of the armed forces and at the same time providing social security for demobilized troops, the envisaged risk for a military-led coup will diminish. According to the reform plans a professional army will be created during a period of seven years, making up the core of a new jointly commanded CIS defence force. The size of this force may be 2–2.5 million men, and first steps to recruit to a professional force should begin from January 1992. The military reform plans also incorporate many innovative ideas, for example for the re-employment of the chemical weapon troops, otherwise to be dismantled, as 'ecological troops'.

The danger of actual use of the strategic nuclear arsenal, even in hypothetical large-scale conflicts within the former Soviet empire, must be deemed as slight in spite of the various demands for 'control' by Ukraine and Kazakhstan. Neither country has demanded the capacity to launch nuclear weapons. On the contrary, the demands voiced consistently since September 1991 concern the issues of a veto over the launch of nuclear weapons and the right to participate in international processes involving future reductions and destruction of nuclear weapons. The granting of a launch veto, as demanded by both Ukraine and Kazakhstan, would not violate the Non-Proliferation Treaty, and could actually be agreed based on the precedent of West Germany.[76] Further, under international law, the mere existence of nuclear weapons on a country's territory without ownership or control neither violates the NPT nor confers the status of nuclear weapon state regardless of statements by the leadership of Kazakhstan. In any event, both Ukraine

---

[74] See chapter 2 and appendix 2A in this volume.

[75] See chapter 5 in this volume.

[76] See the arguments presented in Rhinelander, J. B. and Bunn, G., 'Who's bound by the former Soviet Union's arms control treaties?', *Arms Control Today*, vol. 21, no. 10 (Dec. 1991) pp. 3–7.

and Kazakhstan persistently declare their intention to become non-nuclear weapon states and never to set up their own nuclear weapon forces, a possibility already precluded by their declared intention to accede to the NPT. It may of course be argued that governments change and new political leaderships may take a radically different stance.

Meanwhile, both the Russian Federation and the Western powers could incorporate the Kazakhstan and Ukraine to a greater extent in the arms reduction and negotiating processes. Russia might need to work out a solution to conflicting policies in which, on the one hand, the remaining nuclear arsenal inherited from the Soviet Union is ostensibly not Russian property but handled under CIS joint command, and, on the other hand, Russia is accepted and treated as the sole successor to the Soviet Union as a nuclear weapon power. If Ukraine and Kazakhstan are to finance part of the CIS Strategic Force, clearly they may want to participate in or inspect destruction processes, for example, or attend international negotiations, at least as observers. These are new nations that had no say on military matters during the Soviet era (whether concerning the launch of a nuclear war or the entry into Afghanistan). Of course, the same can be said for the Russian Federation. Hence a speedy and determined policy to implement the START reductions, as well as continued reductions of the nuclear arsenals, will also improve the internal balance of power within the former Soviet territory.

One factor not to be overlooked is the fierce local opposition to nuclear weapons, nuclear power and nuclear tests in Kazakhstan, Ukraine and Belarus alike. Public opinion may not have mattered much during the Soviet era but must be taken into account in the new democratic states. Ecological damage is a reality in Kazakhstan, where President Nazarbayev closed down the Semipalatinsk nuclear testing range at the end of 1991. Similarly, Russia has closed the nuclear testing site at Novaya Zemlya, although preparations have been made for a resumption of underground tests if necessary. The 1986 Chernobyl nuclear reactor accident severely damaged both Ukraine and Belarus.

Tactical nuclear weapons have been rapidly withdrawn to Russian territory, and by February 1992 it appears that only Ukraine still has them. The greatest risk connected with the existing stocks of tactical weapons may lie in the doubtful security of the destruction programmes, if they exist at all, for these weapons, and the storing of plutonium and handling of radioactive waste. Given the numerous problems with chemical and radioactive waste as well as other environmental destruction in the Soviet territory, these dangers associated with the nuclear weapons have spread over into the general category of ecological security which also calls for international co-operation. International inspection and international aid are still not at hand. Accidents and terrorist use of tactical nuclear weapons at least for bargaining or blackmail are also possibilities with unimaginable consequences.

The Russian Federation will have to continue to try to solve the many inherited conflict issues with measures short of war if it wants to retain its position as an important actor in the European and international peace processes. The emerging new policy seems to recognize that, behind what used to be denounced as 'zoological nationalism', there is in principle a violation of human rights at some point in history and the sole alternative lies in compromise solutions. The uncertainty that the Russian Government will remain in power may be greater than the uncertainty of its military intentions within its territory. Conflict resolution will be a formidable task also for other nations such as Georgia, Armenia and Azerbaijan. International help has been requested but may be too slow in coming.

Appendix 14A. Selected documents relating to the Commonwealth of Independent States

Text of the Minsk Agreement Establishing a Commonwealth of Independent States, 8 December 1991

We, the Republic of Belarus, the Russian Federation, and the Ukraine, as founder states of the USSR which signed the Union Treaty of 1922, henceforth described as the high-contracting parties, conclude that the USSR has ceased to exist as a subject of international law and as a geopolitical reality.

Taking as our basis the historic community of our peoples and the ties that have been established between them, taking into account the bilateral treaties concluded between the contracting parties;

Striving to build democratic law-governed states;

Intending to develop our relations on the basis of mutual recognition and respect for state sovereignty, the inalienable right to self-determination, the principles of equality and non-interference in internal affairs, repudiation of the use of force and of economic or any other methods of coercion, settlement of contentious problems by means of mediation, and other generally recognized principles and norms of international law;

Considering that further development and strengthening of relations of friendship, good-neighborliness, and mutually beneficial cooperation between our states correspond to the vital national interest of their peoples and serve the cause of peace and security;

Confirming our adherence to the goals and principles of the United Nations Charter, the Helsinki Final Act, and other documents of the Conference on Security and Cooperation in Europe;

And committing ourselves to observe the generally recognized internal norms on human rights and the rights of peoples,

We have agreed the following:

Article 1

The high-contracting parties form the Commonwealth of Independent States.

Article 2

The high-contracting parties guarantee their citizens equal rights and freedoms, regardless of nationality or other distinctions. Each of the high-contracting parties guarantees the citizens of the other parties, as well as persons without citizenship who live on its territory, civil, political, social, economic, and cultural rights and freedoms in accordance with generally recognized international norms of human rights, regardless of national allegiance or other distinctions.

Article 3

The high-contracting parties, desiring to promote the expression, preservation, and development of the ethnic, cultural, linguistic, and religious individuality of the national minorities resident on their territories and that of the unique ethnocultural regions that have come into being, take them under their protection.

Article 4

The high-contracting parties will develop the equal and mutually beneficial cooperation of their peoples and states in the spheres of politics, the economy, culture, education, public health, protection of the environment, science, trade, and in the humanitarian and other fields; they will promote broad exchange of information, and will conscientiously and unconditionally observe reciprocal obligations.

The parties consider it a necessity to conclude agreements on cooperation in these spheres.

Article 5

The high-contracting parties recognize and respect one another's territorial integrity and the inviolability of existing borders within the Commonwealth. They guarantee openness of borders and freedom of movement for citizens and of transmission of information within the Commonwealth.

Article 6

The member states of the Commonwealth will cooperate in safeguarding international peace and security and in implementing effective measures for reducing armaments and military spending. They seek the elimination of all nuclear weapons and universal, total disarmament under strict international control. The parties will respect one another's aspiration to attain the status of a non-nuclear zone and a neutral state. The member states of the community will preserve and maintain under united command a common military–strategic space, including unified control over nuclear weapons, the procedure for implementing which is regulated by a special agreement. They also jointly guarantee the necessary conditions for the stationing and functioning of the strategic armed forces and for their material and social provision. The parties contract to pursue a harmonized policy on questions of social protection and pension provision for servicemen and their families.

Article 7

The high-contracting parties recognize that within the sphere of their activities, the following will be implemented on an equal basis through the common coordinating institutions of the commonwealth:
 – Cooperation in the sphere of foreign policy;
 – Cooperation in forming and developing the united economic area and the common European and Eurasian markets, and in the area of customs policy;
 – Cooperation in developing transport and communication systems;
 – Cooperation in preservation of the environment and participation in the creation of a comprehensive international system of ecological safety;
 – Migration policy issues;
 – Fighting organized crime.

Article 8

The parties realize the global character of the Chernobyl catastrophe and pledge themselves to unite and coordinate their efforts in minimizing and overcoming its consequences.
 To this purpose they have decided to conclude a special agreement that will take into consideration the gravity of the consequences of this catastrophe.

Article 9

Disputes regarding the interpretation and application of the norms of this agreement are to be solved through negotiations between the appropriate organs and when necessary at the level of heads of governments and states.

Article 10

Each of the high-contracting parties reserves the right to suspend the validity of the present agreement or its individual articles after informing the parties to the agreement of this fact one year in advance.
 The clauses of the present agreement may be added or amended by common consent of the contracting parties.

Article 11

From the moment the present agreement is signed, the norms of third states, including the former USSR, are not permitted to be implemented on the territories of the signatory states.

Article 12

The high-contracting parties guarantee the fulfillment of the international obligations binding upon them from the treaties and agreements of the former USSR.

Article 13

The present agreement does not affect the obligations of the high-contracting parties with regard to third states.
 The present agreement is open to all member states of the former USSR to join, as well as to other states that share the goals and principles of the present agreement.
 The city of Minsk is the official location of the coordinating bodies of the Commonwealth.
 The activities of bodies of the former USSR are discontinued on the territories of the member states of the Commonwealth.
 Executed in the city of Minsk on 8 December 1991 in three copies each in the Belarussian, Russian, and Ukrainian languages, the three texts being of equal validity.

[Signed]

For the Republic of Belarus: S. Shushkevich, V. Kebich
For the RSFSR: B. Yeltsin, G. Burbulis
For the Ukraine: L. Kravchuk, V. Fokin

Source: Moscow TASS International Service, 9 Dec. 1991 [in Russian], cited in FBIS-SOV-91-237, 10 Dec. 1991, pp. 56–57.

Text of the Ashkhabad Declaration, 13 December 1991

Declaration of the heads of states of the Republic of Kazakhstan, the Republic of Kyrgyzstan, the Republic of Tajikistan, Turkmenia, and the Republic of Uzbekistan:

In accordance with the accords reached at the meetings in Alma-Ata (1990) and in Tashkent (1991), heads of states N. A. Nazarbayev, A. A. Akayev, R. N. Nabiyev, S. A. Niyazov, and I. A. Karimov gathered for a routine consultative meeting in Ashkhabad. They discussed the situation that has taken shape since the signing in Minsk of the agreement setting up a Commonwealth of Independent States. Following a comprehensive exchange of views and an analysis of the political situation, those attending the meeting declared the following:

We view with understanding the desire of the leaders of the Republic of Belarus, the Russian Soviet Federated Socialist Republic, and Ukraine to create, in place of the republics that previously had no rights, independent law-governed states united to form a commonwealth. The Minsk initiative on the creation of a Commonwealth of Independent States, with the participation of Ukraine, is positive. However, this agreement came as a surprise to us.

The participants in the conference agree with the assertion that the process of new integration of the subjects of the former USSR on the basis of the decisions of the Fifth USSR Congress of People's Deputies has reached a dead end. The center's short-sighted policy has led to a profound economic and political crisis, the breakdown of production, and a catastrophic decline in the living standards of virtually all strata of society.

The participants in the meeting believe that:

– It is necessary to coordinate efforts to shape the Commonwealth of Independent States.

– The establishment of the Commonwealth of Independent States must be implemented on a lawful basis.

– There must be a guarantee of equal participation by the subjects of the former Union in the process of elaborating decisions and documents on the Commonwealth of Independent States. All the states forming the commonwealth must be recognized as founders and referred to in the text of the agreement as high contracting parties.

– One should take into account in these documents, decisions, and agreements, the historic and socioeconomic realities of the republics of Central Asia and Kazakhstan, who were not considered, unfortunately, during the preparation of the agreement on a commonwealth.

– The Commonwealth of Independent States should guarantee the equality of rights of all nations and ethnic groups, and the protection of their rights and interests.

– The Commonwealth of Independent States cannot take shape on an ethnic, religious, or any other basis infringing on the rights of individuals or peoples.

– The Commonwealth of Independent States recognizes and respects the territorial integrity and inviolability of presently existing borders.

– In the interests of preserving strategic stability in the world, it is expedient to ensure common control [*yedinyy kontrol*] of nuclear weapons and a unified command [*obyedinennoye komandovaniye*] for strategic restraint troops and naval forces.

– It is essential to endorse the treaty concluded earlier on an economic community and to complete work on it in full.

Proceeding from the aforementioned, we declare our readiness to become equal co-founders of the Commonwealth of Independent States, which takes the interests of all its subjects into account. Issues involved in the Commonwealth of Independent States coming into being should be examined at a conference of the heads of the sovereign states.

The participants in the consultative meeting regard with understanding the fact that the Republic of Uzbekistan will determine its final position with regard to participation in the Commonwealth of Independent States after nationwide presidential elections are held on 29 December 1991.

The preliminary amendments and proposals agreed upon at the meeting and concerning the Minsk Commonwealth of Independent States agreement are appended to this statement.

[Signed]

N. A. Nazarbayev, President of the Republic of Kazakhstan

A. A. Akayev, President of the Republic of Kyrgyzstan

I. A. Karimov, President of Turkmenistan

S. A. Niyazov, President of the Republic of Uzbekistan

Source: Moscow TASS International Service, 13 Dec. 1991 [in Russian], cited in FBIS-SOV-91-240, 13 Dec. 1991, pp. 84–85.

Text of the Alma-Ata Declaration, 21 December 1991

The independent states–

The Azerbaijani Republic, the Republic of Armenia, the Republic of Belarus, the Republic of Kazakhstan, the Republic of Kyrgyzia, the Republic of Moldova, the Russian Federation, the Republic of Tajikistan, Turkmenistan, the Republic of Uzbekistan and Ukraine,

Seeking to build democratic law-governed states, the relations between which will develop on the basis of mutual recognition and respect for state sovereignty and sovereign equality, the inalienable right to self-determination, principles of equality and non-interference in the internal affairs, the rejection of the use of force, the threat of force and economic and any other methods of pressure, a peaceful settlement of disputes, respect for human rights and freedoms, including the rights of national minorities, a conscientious fulfillment of commitments and other generally recognised principles and standards of international law,

Recognising and respecting each other's territorial integrity and the inviolability of the existing borders,

Believing that the strengthening of the relations of friendship, good neighbourliness and mutually advantageous cooperation, which has deep historic roots, meets the basic interests of nations and promotes the cause of peace and security,

Being aware of their responsibility for the preservation of civilian peace and inter-ethnic accord,

Being loyal to the objectives and principles of the agreement on the creation of the Commonwealth of Independent States,

Are making the following statement:

Cooperation between members of the Commonwealth will be carried out in accordance with the principle of equality through coordinating institutions formed on a parity basis and operating in the way established by the agreements between members of the Commonwealth, which is neither a state, nor a super-state structure.

In order to ensure international strategic stability and security, allied [*obyediennoye*] command of the military–strategic forces and a single control over nuclear weapons will be preserved, [and] the sides will respect each other's desire to attain the status of a non-nuclear and (or) neutral state.

The Commonwealth of Independent States is open, with the agreement of all its participants, to the states–members of the former Soviet Union, as well as other states sharing the goals and principles of the Commonwealth, which may join it.

The allegiance to cooperation in the formation and development of the common economic space, and all-European and Eurasian markets is being confirmed.

With the formation of the Commonwealth of Independent States the Union of the Soviet Socialist Republics ceases to exist.

Member states of the Commonwealth guarantee, in accordance with their constitutional procedures, the fulfillment of international obligations, stemming from the treaties and agreements of the former USSR.

Member states of the Commonwealth pledge to observe strictly the principles of this declaration.

[Signed]

For the Azerbaijani Republic – A. Mutalibov
For the Republic of Armenia –
    L. Ter-Petrosyan
For the Republic of Belarus –
    S. Shushkevich
For the Republic of Kazakhstan –
    N. Nazarbayev
For the Republic of Kyrgyzia – A. Akayev
For the Republic of Moldova – M. Snegur
For the Russian Federation – B. Yeltsin
For the Republic of Tajikistan – R. Nabiyev
For Turkmenistan – S. Niyazov
For the Republic of Uzbekistan – I. Karimov
For Ukraine – L. Kravchuk

Source: Moscow TASS International Service, 21 Dec. 1991 [in English], cited in FBIS-SOV-91-246, 23 Dec. 1991, pp. 29–30.

Agreement on Joint Measures on Nuclear Weapons, Alma-Ata, 21 December 1991

Belarus, Kazakhstan, the Russian Federation and the Ukraine, called henceforth member states, confirming their adherence to the non-proliferation of nuclear armaments, striving for the elimination of all nuclear armaments, and wishing to act to strengthen international stability, have agreed on the following:

Article 1

The nuclear armaments which are part of the joint [*obyedinennykh*] strategic armed forces ensure the collective security of all members of the Commonwealth of Independent States.

Article 2

The members states of the present agreement confirm the obligation not to be the first to use nuclear weapons.

Article 3

The member states of the present agreement are jointly drawing up a policy on nuclear matters.

Article 4

Until nuclear weapons have been completely eliminated on the territory of the Republic of Belarus and the Ukraine, decisions on the need to use them are taken, by agreement with the heads of the member states of the agreement, by the RSFSR president, on the basis of procedures drawn up jointly by the member states.

Article 5

1. The Republic of Belarus and the Ukraine undertake to join the 1968 Nuclear Nonproliferation Treaty as non-nuclear states and to conclude with the International Atomic Energy Agency the appropriate agreements–guarantees.

2. The member states of the present agreement undertake not to transfer to any-one nuclear weapons or other explosive devices [*yadernyye vzryvnyye ustroystva*] and technologies, or control over such nuclear and explosive devices, either directly or indirectly; and equally not in any way to help, encourage, or prompt any state not pos-sessing nuclear weapons or to acquire by any other means nuclear weapons or other nuclear explosive devices, and also control over such weapons or explosive devices.

3. The provisions of Paragraph 2 of this article do not stand in the way of transferring nuclear weapons from Belarus, Kazakhstan and Ukraine to RSFSR territory with a view to destroying them.

Article 6

The member states of this agreement, in accordance with the international treaty, will assist in the eliminating of nuclear weapons. By July 1, 1992 Belarus, Kazakhstan and Ukraine will ensure the withdrawal of tacti-cal nuclear weapons to central factory premises for dismantling under joint supervi-sion.

Article 7

The Governments of Belarus, Kazakhstan, the Russian Federation and the Ukraine undertake to submit a treaty on strategic offensive arms for ratification to the Supreme Soviets of their states.

Article 8

The present agreement requires ratification. It will come into force on the 30th day after the handing over of all ratification papers to the Government of the RSFSR for safe keeping.

Done in Alma-Ata in one certified copy in Belarussian, Kazakh, Russian and the Ukrainian languages, all texts being equally authentic.

[Signed]

For Belarus, S. Shushkevich;
For Kazakhstan, N. Nazarbayev;
For the Russian Federation, B. Yeltsin;
For Ukraine, L. Kravchuk.

Source: *Pravda*, 23 Dec. 1991, p. 2, cited in FBIS-SOV-91-246, 23 Dec. 1991, pp. 30–31.

15. European security structures in transition

ADAM DANIEL ROTFELD

I. Introduction

The documents adopted at the Paris summit meeting of 19–20 November 1990 were intended to adapt European security structures to new political and military realities.[1] As a result of rapid developments and changes, however, the institutions established on the basis of the Paris documents have played only a limited role in strengthening European security. The tasks that were drawn up in Paris to address the problem of new structures and institutions created within the Conference on Security and Co-operation in Europe (CSCE) framework have far exceeded the means, procedures and mechanisms to carry them out.[2] On the one hand, the Paris documents were unquestionably unprecedented and gave expression to a qualitatively new approach by participating states to the future place and role of the CSCE process. On the other hand, the furious pace of unanticipated developments has given rise to an urgent need to re-think concepts, tasks, organizational structures and mutual links among the European multilateral security institutions.

Any critical assessment of new structures must focus on their effectiveness, rather than on their intended activities. Indeed, a number of mechanisms and procedures outlined in the Paris documents have already been set in motion: (a) two meetings of the CSCE Council of Foreign Ministers have been held (in Berlin on 19–20 June 1991 and in Prague on 30–31 January 1992); (b) the CSCE Committee of Senior Officials (CSO) has met repeatedly as recommended, and a mechanism of holding CSO meetings in emergency situations was launched; (c) the CSCE Secretariat in Prague was set up; (d) the Conflict Prevention Centre (CPC) in Vienna began operation; (e) the CSCE Parliamentary Assembly was established; and (f) in Warsaw, the Office for Democratic Institutions and Human Rights was launched.

In addition, a number of CSCE expert meetings, seminars and symposia were held during 1991. However, some of these meetings addressed not issues of military security *per se* but mainly the sphere of human rights and the human dimension of security. These meetings included: (a) the Cracow Symposium on the Cultural Heritage of the CSCE Participating States (28 May–7 June 1991); (b) the Geneva Meeting of Experts on National Minorities (1–19 July 1991); (c) the third Meeting on the Human Dimension

---

[1] See 'The Charter of Paris for a New Europe', in SIPRI, *SIPRI Yearbook 1991: World Armaments and Disarmament* (Oxford University Press: Oxford, 1991), appendix 17B, pp. 603–10. See especially the section of the Charter: 'New structures and institutions of the CSCE process', pp. 609–10.

[2] This was partly to be expected. See Rotfeld, A. D., 'New security structures in Europe: concepts, proposals and decisions', in SIPRI (note 1), pp. 612–15.

of the CSCE held in Moscow (10 September–4 October 1991),[3] at which a new multilateral monitoring mechanism for human rights was agreed;[4] and (d) the Oslo Seminar of Experts on Democratic Institutions (4–15 November 1991).

Businesslike negotiations were conducted in Vienna on an agreement on new confidence- and security-building measures (CSBMs), and were crowned with the conclusion of the Vienna Document 1992.[5] Quite unexpectedly, basic agreement was quickly reached in March 1992 on the Treaty on Open Skies.[6]

Progress was made in several other areas in 1991. The CSCE communications network established after the Paris summit meeting began operation, and the Second Seminar on Military Doctrine within the framework of the CPC was held.[7] Never before had the CSCE engaged in such widespread activity. Negotiating dynamics were intense in 1991, both in their pace and in the variety of accords reached. Nevertheless, in the face of new realities, the new structures and procedures came unglued. The test case was the crisis in Yugoslavia.[8] The Yugoslav crisis was kept under permanent review by the CSO, and two CSCE special missions—a monitor mission and a human rights rapporteur mission—visited Yugoslavia and reported back on their findings. The emergency mechanism of the CPC and its efforts could not prevent the outbreak of war, nor did the hostilities cease when arrangements on peaceful settlement of disputes, established by the Berlin Meeting of the Council of Foreign Ministers, were put in motion.[9]

War in Yugoslavia was not averted by other security organizations either: equally ineffective were the mechanisms of the North Atlantic Treaty Organization (NATO), the European Community (EC), the Western European Union (WEU), the Council of Europe and other organizations. As a consequence of this failure, a need has arisen to reassess the whole political and military architecture of European security.

---

[3] The first meeting of the CSCE Conference on Human Rights was held in Paris (30 May–23 June 1989); the second meeting took place in Copenhagen (5–29 June 1990).

[4] Under new mechanisms adopted in Moscow, a written response to a request for information is to be provided 'in the shortest possible time, but not later than 10 days'. Bilateral meetings are to take place 'as soon as possible and as a rule within one week of the date of request'. A CSCE participating state may now request the assistance of a CSCE mission of experts to address or contribute to the resolution of questions on its territory. The task of a mission of experts will be the resolution of a particular problem relating to the human dimension of security. See *Focus on Vienna*, no. 25 (Oct.–Nov. 1991), p. 16.

[5] The text of the Vienna Document 1992 of the Negotiations on CSBMs was agreed on 4 Mar. 1992 in Vienna (before the opening of the Helsinki follow-up meeting) and signed in Helsinki on 25 Mar. 1992.

[6] The negotiations on the text were finalized with the draft submitted by the Polish delegation. See CSCE/WV.31/Rev. 1, Vienna, 28 Feb. 1992. See also chapter 12 in this volume.

[7] See appendix 12B in this volume.

[8] For more on the Yugoslavian crisis, see Vukadinovic, R., *The Break-up of Yugoslavia: Threats and Challenges* (Netherlands Institute of International Relations: Amsterdam, Feb. 1992), pp. 20–34.

[9] See Peaceful settlement of disputes, Annex 3 to the Summary of Conclusions adopted at the Berlin Meeting of the CSCE Council, 19–20 June 1991.

II. The new architecture

In 1991, the CSCE agenda addressed a new item: that of the new European security architecture. This concept was outlined for the first time by US Secretary of State James Baker in 1989, soon after the Berlin Wall came down:

This new architecture must have a place for old foundations and structures that remain very valuable—like NATO—while recognizing that they can also serve new collective purposes. The new architecture must continue the construction of institutions—like the European Community—that can help draw together the West while also serving as an open door to the East. And the new architecture must build up frameworks like the CSCE process—that can overcome the division of Europe and, at the same time, can bridge the Atlantic Ocean.[10]

In Baker's view, this new architecture had two special purposes:

First, as a part of overcoming the division of Europe, there must be an opportunity to overcome through peace and freedom the division of Berlin and of Germany. The United States and NATO have stood for unification for forty years, and we will not waiver from that goal.
    Second, the architecture should reflect that America's security—politically, militarily and economically—remains linked to Europe's security.[11]

In just two years, the tables have turned: Europe is no longer divided; and whether the United States—as in the past—will continue to identify its security with European security remains an open question. The CSCE principles and provisions, established with a view towards the future, now require certain changes and corrections. On the one hand, they partly fulfilled their task by stimulating the processes that helped to overcome the division of Europe. On the other hand, some provisions of some CSCE accords are no longer of importance or relevance.

Just prior to the first meeting of the CSCE Council of Foreign Ministers, Secretary Baker presented the main proposals of a new Euro-Atlantic security architecture.[12] He referred back to the goals formulated in the 1967 Harmel Report of achieving 'a just and lasting peaceful order in Europe'.[13] New structures—according to US political philosophy—should be based on such Enlightenment ideals of universal applicability as individual political rights and economic liberty. As Secretary Baker noted: 'They need to establish the components of cooperative security for a Europe whole and free . . .'.[14] While drawing up the concept of a new European architecture of security and co-

---

[10] See 'A new Europe, a new Atlanticism: architecture for a new era, address by James A. Baker, III, US Secretary of State, to the Berlin Press Club, 12 December 1989', in Rotfeld, A. D. and Stützle, W. (eds), SIPRI, *Germany and Europe in Transition*. (Oxford University Press: Oxford, 1991), p. 96.
[11] See note 10.
[12] 'The Euro-Atlantic architecture: from West to East, James Baker's address to the Aspen Institute, Berlin, 18 June 1991', *US Department of State Dispatch*, 24 June 1991, pp. 439–45.
[13] See note 12.
[14] See note 12, p. 439.

operation, certain complex and often opposing tendencies should be taken into account: namely, the *devolution* of the European nation-state in the West and the accelerated *evolution* of nation-states in the East. At the same time, in the context of West European integration, some of the functions of the nation-state are being delegated 'upwards' and others 'downwards'. In effect, in Western Europe, the relinquishing of many competencies to local communities is, paradoxically, accompanied by a considerable transfer of government functions from the national to the supranational level. This trend is also increasingly apparent in the area of defence.

In Central and Eastern Europe, including the territory of the former Soviet Union, the reverse tendency can be observed: namely, the rapid re-emergence of the nation-state idea, and the avoidance of any forms of integration and institutionalized co-operation (out of the fear that something akin to the former government should take over in Russia). In fact, the interest now is in political initiatives inspired by the West or leading to membership in Western institutions. A case in point is the establishment of the 'triangle' of co-operation (the Visegrad Triangle) among Czechoslovakia, Hungary and Poland. Its participants do not conceal the fact that their main intention is 'a full-range integration into the European political, economic and juridical as well as security system'.[15] Similar motives guided the participants of the 'pentagonale' group (Austria, Czechoslovakia, Hungary, Italy and Yugoslavia). Eventually, with the addition of Poland, the group was expanded to the 'hexagonale'.[16] However, the conflict in Yugoslavia swept the structure into insignificance before it managed to take root. It seems that prospects for subregional co-operation above former divisions among Baltic or Black Sea countries are now considerably improved.

Among Central and East European states, a determination to join Western structures (mainly NATO and the EC), rather than to create new organizations, is evident. Among NATO and EC members, however, there is a prevalent conviction that the admission of Central European states into the two structures would weaken them or even change their character. In this connection, the concept of establishing a Euro-Atlantic community has emerged, with a particular role for the CSCE to play. Still, the CSCE structures are seen as a framework—and not as a unitary body—for the Euro-Atlantic agenda. As James Baker stated in Berlin: 'Indeed, as we extend the Euro-Atlantic architecture to the East, we need to be creative about employing multiple methods and institutions—including NATO, the EC, the Organization for Economic Co-operation and Development (OECD), the Council of Europe, and others—to address common concerns'.[17] Thus, the foundations of a new, evolving co-

---

[15] The Cracow Declaration of 6 Oct. 1991, adopted at the end of the meeting between Lech Walesa (Poland), Vaclav Havel (Czechoslovakia) and Jozsef Antall (Hungary), was preceded by similar declarations of intention issued in Bratislava (1990) and Visegrad (1991).

[16] For more on this, see Neuhold, H. P. (ed.), *The Pentagonal/Hexagonal Experiment: New Forces of Cooperation in a Changing Europe*, The Laxenburg Papers, no. LP10, Austrian Institute for International Affairs (Braumüller: Vienna, 1991).

[17] See note 12, p. 442.

operative security system would consist of a variety of structures and institutions, and involve new and expanded goals for the CSCE:

1. The CSCE, in Baker's view, would contribute to a new security system by creating the political, economic and security conditions that may defuse conflict. The CSCE would also have systems to warn of potential dangers, mechanisms to attempt to mediate them and ways to engage other countries to help resolve them. The aim is to prevent a course of developments that could get out of control and lead to a war, as was the case in 1914.

2. NATO would provide a complementary role. As the US Secretary of State declared: 'A strong defensive alliance allows for lower levels of military forces and provides a foundation of stability within Europe as a whole'.[18]

3. Such institutions of the Euro-Atlantic community as the EC, the Council of Europe and the OECD would create a network of political and economic support.

4. The United States defined some new goals for the CSCE process 'beyond the concept of balance . . . to establish the basis for cooperative security'.[19] Several aims for future CSCE activities in the arms control and security area were enumerated: (a) to institutionalize openness and transparency in military affairs; (b) to establish conflict prevention mechanisms; and (c) to address the challenge of proliferation.

Openness and transparency in military affairs should be enhanced through the Treaty on Open Skies, and a regular dialogue about military forces, budgets, defence plans and doctrines. In addition, there is also a need 'to address the possible regeneration of forces within the Atlantic to the Urals region'.[20]

Conflict prevention mechanisms must be established. The 1990 Treaty on Conventional Armed Forces in Europe (CFE) and the new agreement on CSBMs will all but eliminate the threat of a short-warning, massive conventional war in Europe. The new challenge is 'to address more discrete localized problems within the CSCE area with the potential to lead to conflict between CSCE members'.[21] These mechanisms might include new measures such as fact-finding, mediation and peace-keeping capabilities and address some of the security concerns of particular regions (such as in 'the Balkans or other areas where stability could be at risk').[22]

The challenge of proliferation—stopping the spread of chemical, biological and nuclear weapons, as well as missiles—must be addressed. In addition, cooperation in the development of national policies to exercise restraint in the sale of conventional weapons is necessary.

The programme drawn up in mid-1991 could be carried out because the former East–West dichotomy prevailing in the CSCE process was replaced not only by a declared system of common values but also by a convergence of

[18] See note 12, p. 442.
[19] See note 12, p. 442.
[20] See note 12, p. 442.
[21] See note 12, p. 442.
[22] See note 12, p. 442.

political interests. Central and East European perceptions regarding Western aims and institutions have changed. There has also been a change in the approach of EC and NATO member states with regard to their neighbours in the East. The Copenhagen Statement on Partnership with the Countries of Central and Eastern Europe proclaimed that the security of NATO member states 'is inseparably linked to that of all other states in Europe' and 'the consolidation and preservation throughout the continent of democratic societies and their freedom from any form of coercion or intimidation are therefore of direct and material concern to the NATO'.[23] For the first time in the history of the Helsinki process, the aims of NATO and the CSCE were compatible, which resulted in a qualitative and beneficial change in shaping a system of interrelated and complementary security institutions. It concerns not only the interrelationship between NATO, the European Community and the CSCE, but also the new role and place of the Council of Europe in the process of security and co-operation in Europe.[24]

The desirability of making use of and adapting the existing organizations and structures in addressing new realities cannot be denied.[25] It would be a misunderstanding, however, to look upon what is called 'security architecture' as a remedy for present and future challenges. The key question is the political will of states and the corresponding security concepts, as well as new principles and norms. Some of them have already been rendered unimportant or irrelevant, while others call for reinterpretation.

III. Principles and realities

The CSCE created institutions and formulated principles that embrace all European states,[26] which is the basis for creating 'a true community of values'.[27] The Charter of Paris for a New Europe adopted by the CSCE heads of state or government in November 1990 announced new principles for the post-cold war European system: (a) steadfast commitment to democracy based on human rights and fundamental freedoms; (b) prosperity through economic liberty and social justice; and (c) equal security for all countries.[28]

One can ask the following questions: To what extent are these principles being realized? What are the new risks? In what measure are the Paris docu-

---

[23] See *NATO Review*, no. 3 (June 1991), p. 28.

[24] During the June 1991 CSCE debate in Berlin on a new European peace order, Foreign Minister Sten Andersson, the Swedish representative who also served as the Chairman of the Committee of Ministers of the Council of Europe, stated: 'The Council of Europe, too, is an essential component in the new European architecture'. See Statement by Sten Andersson, Minister of Foreign Affairs of Sweden, at the meeting of the CSCE Council of Foreign Ministers in Berlin, 19 June 1991.

[25] For an instructive comparison of the aims, tasks and structures of the four Europe-related security institutions (NATO, the WEU, the EC and the CSCE), see d'Armaillé, B., 'L'architecture européenne de sécurite: Aide-memoire à l'usage du chercheur', *Le Cahiers du Crest*, 5 Dec. 1991, p. 193.

[26] Albania joined the CSCE in June 1991. The Baltic states (Estonia, Latvia and Lithuania) joined in Sep. 1991, followed by the rest of the post-Soviet states (except Georgia) in Jan. 1992.

[27] See note 12, p. 441.

[28] See note 1, p. 603.

ments and the new security structures set up on the basis of these documents adequate to meet new challenges?

The authors of the CSCE documents negotiated in Vienna in 1989–90 and signed in Paris in 1990 were guided by the assumptions and political philosophy that breathed life into the European multilateral process initiated almost 20 years before in Helsinki during 1972–75.[29] Europe at that time was part of a world divided by two political, economic, military and ideological blocs. Relations between the two groupings were marked by mutual mistrust and suspicion, tension and confrontation.

The Helsinki Final Act of 1975 formulated aims for the states signatories in the sphere of security so as to gradually reduce tensions and overcome divisions. It postulated *inter alia*: (*a*) the need to continue efforts to make *détente* a lasting, continuing, all-embracing and universal process (of which implementation of CSCE results was to be a significant contribution); (*b*) that solidarity among nations and the common pursuit of goals set out in the CSCE documents were to lead to developing better and closer relations between them in all fields, and thus 'overcom[e] the confrontation stemming from the character of their past relations, and to better mutual understanding';[30] and (*c*) the search—fully taking account of the diversity of individual positions and views—for possibilities of joining efforts with a view to overcoming distrust and increasing confidence, solving the problems that separate them, and co-operating in the interest of mankind.

The list of tasks agreed in Helsinki was naturally much longer. It should be remembered that the predominant conviction at the time—expressed both in documents and in declarations by the participants of the negotiations—was that the bipolar world and the separate socio-political systems were of a durable character. This view applied not only to the Helsinki Final Act but also to subsequent documents of the CSCE follow-up meetings in Madrid (1983) and in Vienna (1989).

The division of Europe was also a reference point for agreeing the mandate on negotiating the 1990 CFE Treaty,[31] at a time time when the aim was to liberalize the communist system rather than to overthrow it. Certainly, the possibility of a radical transformation of the autocratic and one-party system into a democratic and pluralist one was not anticipated by the governments of the communist-ruled states. The form of rule could at most undergo some favourable evolution: in return for an expansion of limited individual freedoms and an enhancement of the rule of law in the East, Western states consented to a recognition of the post-war political and territorial status quo.

Of key importance for East European governments in the CSCE process were the principles of inviolability of frontiers and territorial integrity, and non-intervention in domestic affairs, thus legitimizing one-party rule. East

[29] Lehne, S., *The CSCE in the 1990s: Common European House or Potemkin Village?*, The Laxenburg Papers, no. LP9, Austrian Institute for International Affairs (Braumüller: Vienna, 1991).
[30] See Final Act of the CSCE Helsinki 1975, p. 77.
[31] For an account of the status of the 1990 CFE Treaty at the end of 1991, see chapter 12 in this volume.

European states considered the principle of sovereign equality as the commitment to 'respect each other's right freely to choose and develop its political, social, economic and cultural systems as well as its right to determine its laws and regulations'.[32] The sovereign rights, then, were interpreted as if the CSCE commitments were addressed to governments, not to nations. A similar weight was attached to the principle of equal rights of peoples and their right to self-determination, while stressing the necessity to respect the norms regarding the territorial integrity of states. In this context, for example, how could Croatia and Slovenia have taken advantage of their right to self-determination, including secession, while respecting the territorial integrity of Yugoslavia? The same sort of question applies to all multinational states.

As far as Western policies were concerned, the process initiated in Helsinki, and continued at follow-up meetings in Belgrade, Madrid and Vienna, was supposed to contribute to a *sui generis* humanization of totalitarian, one-party and undemocratic governments in Central and Eastern Europe. Hence, the standing and significance of human rights and individual freedoms, as well as the provisions concerning Basket 3 issues—human contacts, information, culture and education—have increased. In the West, the CSCE process was perceived as a tool to legitimize the emphasis upon domestic developments in communist-ruled states. Relevant demands contained in CSCE documents were, in essence, addressed to the states of the then Warsaw Pact. They were aimed at securing free movement of people, information and ideas. With time, the provisions of the concluding documents of the Madrid and Vienna follow-up meetings took on the character of very detailed instructions on how to safeguard freedoms of conscience and belief, speech and association; the right to emigrate; and respect for individual liberties.[33] In this regard, the 1990 Charter of Paris for a New Europe represents the crowning moment of the process of including in the catalogue of international commitments political provisions regarding respect for individual freedoms, the democratization of internal systems and the rule of law.

Thus, international recognition was given to the internal changes which—starting with the establishment of the Solidarity popular movement in Poland in 1980—led almost 10 years later, through peaceful transformation, to the relinquishment of power by communist parties across Central and Eastern Europe. The adoption of the Charter of Paris closed a specific chapter in the history of the CSCE process but did not change the essence of the process itself: 'The era of confrontation and division of Europe has ended', reads the Charter. The signatories further declared: 'The Ten Principles of the [Helsinki] Final Act will guide us towards this ambitious future, just as they have lighted our way towards better relations for the past fifteen years'.[34] The new commitments covered human rights, consolidation of the rule of law and democratic institutions.

[32] See note 30.
[33] For more on this, see Rotfeld, A. D., *Europejski system bezpieczeństwa in statu nascendi* [European security system in *statu nascendi*] (Polish Institute of International Affairs: Warsaw, 1990), *passim.*
[34] See note 1, p. 603.

In the past, one of the main features of the CSCE process concerned decision-making by consensus,[35] which meant the absence of *any* objection by *any* representative. This 'golden rule' was taken advantage of chiefly by small states (such as Malta and Liechtenstein)[36] and governments (such as Romania and the Soviet Union) in order to prevent the adoption of recommendations or specific actions aimed at them.[37] The first case of a departure from consensus decision-making involved the mechanism for consultation and co-operation during emergency situations.[38] The change consisted of a provision under which the Chairman-in-Office of the CSO might hold a meeting in an emergency on the demand of a state concerned, if this request was supported by at least 12 participating states (formerly the consent of all the CSCE member states would be required). The other equally important step is that security issues and the human dimension of the CSCE are now given equal weight. Thus, a new phase has been given a good beginning in shaping a multilateral security system, although these are only the first steps.

Numerous meetings, conferences, institutions and offices were intended to adjust the CSCE process to new conditions.[39] As recently as 1989, these activities would have meant a revolutionary change. However, in light of the transformations that have since taken place in Europe, particularly after the breakup of the Soviet Union and the demise of the Soviet Communist Party, it seems that a thorough rethinking and reassessment are needed not only of specific solutions and institutions but also, first and foremost, of the basic premises of the whole political philosophy that undergird the multilateral CSCE process. It is worthwhile to consider whether if, in the new situation, the European process will still define the rules and determine the framework within which the processes of domestic transformation in individual countries and relations between states should take place. If the repressive systems and violations of human rights on a massive scale gave way to governments that declare their readiness to abide by the universal values of the democratic world, then one should consider whether the principles and norms negotiated in the antagonistically divided Europe can fulfil their task in an entirely different environment. Furthermore, the old formula is repeated in the new documents to the extent that a departure from consensus does not entitle a

[35] See Final Recommendations of the Helsinki Consultations, Helsinki, 8 June 1973, para. 69, point 4.

[36] Malta used the requirement of consensus as an instrument to block progress in negotiations when its demands were not taken into consideration. Liechtenstein opposed the establishment of the Secretariat in Prague because of a bilateral dispute with Czechoslovakia.

[37] Romania often blocked recommendations regarding human rights under the pretext that they constituted a violation of the principle of non-intervention in internal affairs. In Jan. 1991, the USSR was opposed to the Conflict Prevention Centre addressing the question of armed intervention in the Baltic republics.

[38] See Annex 2, Summary of Conclusions, Berlin Meeting of the CSCE Council, 19–20 June 1991.

[39] For a general review of the CSCE activities in 1991, see Summary of Conclusions, Berlin Meeting of the CSCE Council (19–20 June 1991); and Summary of Conclusions, Prague Meeting CSCE Council of Ministers (30–31 Jan. 1992). Excerpts from these documents are included in appendix 15A of this volume.

state, even in emergency situations, to ignore the principle of non-intervention in internal affairs.[40]

It should be noted that it is the post-communist states themselves which demand that this resilient principle of non-interference be ignored or reinterpreted, whereas the firm adherents to the principle are some of the democratic states of the West. As British Foreign Secretary Douglas Hurd stated: 'We cannot go into action in another country without the consent of that country. This is not a mechanism for overruling governments on internal affairs'.[41] A similar position was expressed by the Italian Foreign Minister.[42] Illustrative of the measure of change that has taken place in Europe is the fact that, on the eve of the Moscow Meeting on the CSCE Human Dimension, Russian Foreign Minister Andrey Kozyrev stated: 'It is of particular importance that the meeting succeeded in . . . shaping the new mechanisms of "intervention" on the part of the CSCE in domestic affairs of states. . . . It is worthwhile considering, for example, a matter of CSCE inspection—without the right to refuse—on information provided on the request for human rights or of an attempt at legal organs of government'.[43] The reason for this radical change was the situation in the aftermath of the failed *coup d'état* and the search for instruments to block a possible restoration of the status quo ante in Russia.

IV. The new security environment

Europe from the Atlantic to the Urals is still being torn by conflicts. However, they are quite different from past conflicts in that they are not based upon ideological antagonisms nor rivalries between two military blocs. The new tensions result from the economic collapse of East European countries, differences in development and associated disintegration, and growing ethnic and national conflicts in post-communist Europe. To the West of the former line of division—the Oder River—integration processes are accelerating. In a nutshell, Europe is still divided *de facto*, although less and less formally, into the group of affluent and prosperous states with assured external security, and a group of post-communist states, including the post-Soviet ones, in which the economic, social and security situation is in a shambles. In fact, the latter group of states have lost their former security guarantees and have not obtained new ones.

The new international environment and radical changes have brought to the forefront of the political agenda not only the past question of respecting provisions in this or another sphere (for example, Basket 3) but also a more fundamental need to rethink the whole concept of the multilateral CSCE process. In other words, the tasks of the conference referred to as 'Helsinki 2' do not amount to a streamlining of the existing mechanisms but rather an elaboration

[40] See note 39, p. 6. See also Weitz, R., 'The CSCE's new look', *Radio Free Europe/Radio Liberty Research Report*, 7 Feb. 1992, p. 30.

[41] See *Los Angeles Times*, 21 June 1991.

[42] See *Washington Post*, 21 June 1991.

[43] See *Komsomolskaya Pravda*, 5 Sep. 1991.

of new principles, norms and procedures. They should reflect the challenges and needs of the future, and not of the past. For this reason, today's search for a European co-operative security system should begin from a different point of departure, based on the following premises.

1. The end of the cold war means that a new system shall not organize one group of states against another, nor will it, as in the 1970s and the 1980s, determine the framework of rivalry between antagonistic blocs.

2. The need for and the role of mediating actors played thus far by the neutral and non-aligned countries (NNA) is fading away.

3. The need to create a new co-operative security system is now a part of the European agenda. What is important is that the non-NATO member CSCE participating states no longer consider NATO to be incompatible with new structures.

4. The preservation of the present security disorder over the long term could lead to menacing developments getting out of control. The conflict in Yugoslavia has highlighted the fact that in a world of interdependence the border is blurred between what was formerly considered a domestic conflict and today constitutes a matter of warranted concern and intervention on the part of the international community. The Yugoslav conflict has also revealed the inadequacy of existing structures to handle new tasks in the prevention and settlement of such conflicts.[44] A paradoxical situation has arisen: the Yugoslav conflict was discussed within the CSCE and the EC; concrete action was taken under the auspices of the WEU, but it was actually NATO that took the un-written decisions.

5. Membership in NATO for such Central and Eastern European states as Czechoslovakia, Hungary and Poland would be tantamount to a thorough change of character of the organization. Intense efforts to join NATO by former Warsaw Pact states led to the establishment of a new structure—the North Atlantic Co-operation Council (NACC).[45]

6. The new architecture of European security consists of: (*a*) the CSCE process and institutions;[46] (*b*) NATO and the NACC; (*c*) the WEU and its links with the European Union and NATO;[47] (*d*) the 'European security iden-

---

[44] The resolutions adopted by the CSO on the situation in Yugoslavia are reminiscent of many UN resolutions both in their spirit and content as well as terminology: one can find such empty and non-operational verbs as 'welcomes', 'commends', 'supports', 'condemns', 'takes note', 'insists', 'urges', etc. The last sentence of the resolution adopted in Prague (10 Oct. 1991) contains the promise that the CSO 'will examine ways in which the institutions of the CSCE, including the CPC, could further assist in the implementation of the provisions of this resolution'. Agreeing on this type of document is a new practice in the CSCE process and hardly enhances the credibility of the new institutions which were to ensure that the decisions adopted would be effective.

[45] See 'Final Communiqué issued by the North Atlantic Council Meeting in Ministerial Session, 19th December 1991', *Atlantic News*, no. 2382 (21 Dec. 1991), Annex I; and 'North Atlantic Cooperation Council Statement on dialogue, partnership and cooperation, 20th December 1991', *Atlantic News*, no. 2382 (21 Dec. 1991), Annex II. Excerpts of these documents are reproduced in appendix 15A of this volume.

[46] See note 2, pp. 585–615.

[47] See *Declaration of the Member States of Western European Union which are also members of the European Union on the role of WEU and its relations with the European Union and with the Atlantic*

tity' ('which might in time lead to a common defence');[48] and (e) various attempts to establish new structures east of the Oder River.

7. The institutions mentioned above (and others, such the Council of Europe in Strasbourg) proved to be inefficient or even helpless in face of the growing wave of new conflicts, tension and threats. One possible explanation for this phenomenon is that these threats do not result from an upsetting of a balance of forces between military blocs or one of the world powers getting the upper hand; rather it was the downright collapse of the one-party totalitarian system which constituted a component part of and point of reference for constructing the security mechanisms of Western democracies. Considering the lack of democratic institutions and deeply rooted rules of the game in post-communist states, the economic collapse in those countries (the scope of which is already much greater than that of the Great Depression of 1929) could trigger social, national and religious conflicts. The existing international institutions and mechanisms are unable in their present form to fulfil their preventive function *vis-à-vis* uncontrollable domestic conflicts. Nor are they suitable for defusing crisis situations when they have spilled over to open conflicts.

Moves being taken within the CSCE and the EC aimed at ending the war in Yugoslavia are illustrative of the thesis that existing structures and procedures for preventing and resolving conflicts are ineffective. In part, these moves stem from past experience when any action taken *vis-à-vis* the parties to the Yugoslav conflict would have been considered tantamount to intervention in domestic affairs; in part, they are a product of abstract thinking, whereas each internal conflict has a different historical background and specific political roots.[49]

Still, it is hard to accept the following reasoning:

The West must expect to face long periods in which it remains unclear who is shooting whom and for what purpose. It is doubtful that it can do anything to contain the fissiparous tendencies that are structurally inherent in all post-communist regimes. It is more questionable still whether violence can be managed where it is endemic, where it is structured into East European states that still fall short of developing a civil society.[50]

Alliance. Annex V. European Council. Maastricht, 9 and 10 Dec. 1991. Presidency Conclusions (European Council: Maastricht, 11 Dec. 1991), pp. 29–33.

[48] See 'Final Communiqué issued by the North Atlantic Council Meeting in Ministerial Session, 19th December 1991' (note 45), p. 3.

[49] Not insignificant is the widespread tendency for countries in the West to separate themselves from negative and, for them, often unintelligible phenomena in the East. It leads sometimes to the following conclusion: 'Often the consequences of unrest are grossly exaggerated. Frequently, the measures for dealing with it are politically unrealistic, or undesirable or both'. See Institute for European Defence and Strategic Studies, 'Security agenda for Eastern Europe', *After the Soviet Collapse: New Realities, Old Illusions*, The Report of a Study Group (IEDSS: London, Jan. 1992).

[50] See note 49.

Such long-standing simmering conflicts as those in Northern Ireland or in the Basque region of Spain, as well as growing problems in relations between Flamands and Walloons in Belgium, call this reasoning into question.

In Europe and the world, a new landscape of political and military security thoroughly different from that which dominated during the cold war is taking shape. However, even if changes take place, no matter how violent and revolutionary, some elements of the old reality still persist. It is, for instance, easier to change organizational forms than ways of thinking. The new élites in the post-communist countries involuntarily have recourse to revolutionary (i.e., undemocratic) methods of solving the difficult problems they are facing. The experience of underground activism against the structures of a totalitarian system are of little use in building a democratic system. Hence, the search for quick, simple solutions, such as the proposals immediately to join NATO, the WEU or the EC. These organizations are seen as a cure-all for economic ills and a guarantee against external threats. In the West, the whole of post-communist Europe is perceived as a source of potential, and barely comprehensible, conflicts and challenges; it accounts, at least partly, for NATO's unusual restraint in addressing the demands to include a few Central European states in this organization, and its desire to stay out of conflicts and tensions to the east of the Oder River. NATO's response to problems haunting this region is to act as a 'security forum' operating within the CSCE.

IV. New challenges

The main threats to European security after the cold war are usually associated with the following factors:

1. Discredited communist ideology has been replaced in all post-communist countries with aggressive nationalism and chauvinism. This *sui generis* reaction to an ideological vacuum creates a real threat that the former leftist totalitarian regimes will assume—after a period of populist government—a rightist character, and power will be seized by neo-fascist forces.

2. The collapse of such multinational states as Yugoslavia and the Soviet Union is resulting in a new configuration in the security sphere. The fading away of one of the global powers from the international scene may have removed one source of old threats but at the same time new problems have entered the global security agenda. Often they are reduced, mainly if not exclusively, to non-proliferation of nuclear weapons, missiles and conventional arms. In fact, military threats are not, for the most part, of a technical nature (for example, how to ensure control over the process of arms reductions and the remaining weapons) although this aspect should certainly not be played down. In particular, the consequences of weapons of mass destruction falling into the hands of terrorist organizations, or some ambitious and

aggressive leaders aspiring to the role of global power for their countries in the developing world, should not be underestimated.[51]

In this connection, two other problems of a political nature have also emerged. First, the breakup of the Soviet Union is not yet over. The Commonwealth of Independent States (CIS) is not subject to international law and does not have a centre of power. Its very existence continues to be questionable. Many nations within the Russian Federation want independence.[52] In Russia itself a deep structural transformation is bound to take place, including recognition of far-reaching autonomy for other nationalities in the country; otherwise Russia would break apart and other new states (such as Checheno-Ingushetia, Tatarstan and Yakutia) would emerge. Second, there is a real danger that in view of growing social unrest and tension an 'unholy alliance' will appear: that the army, which has ambitions to play an independent political role in Russia, will develop closer ties to conservative groups descending from the former communist party and new pro-fascist and chauvinist organizations (often of the same social origin). Bandying slogans on restoring law and order, retaining the unity of the state and engaging in populist demagoguery, this sort of alliance can seize power in many, if not in all, post-Soviet states. Whether power is seized with the participation of the army or not, we can already witness the process of pushing the forces weilding power towards extremist nationalism.

3. The next serious threat to European security are territorial claims both stemming from and linked to the threats described above. Frequently, these claims are centuries-old. However, it was the return to public life of forces that were not in a position to express their views under communist rule that gave rise to the re-emergence of historical disputes among neighbours. Nevertheless, the main cause is that the power élites are unable to solve social and economic problems, and attempt instead to divert societal attention from them and to gain support. It does not mean that all borders between the new states are just. Some of them were arbitrarily demarcated by dictatorship, or are the legacy of Russia's colonial past or the outcome of invasions.

4. The economic situation in all the post-communist countries is going from bad to worse. The causes are of a structural nature: the cumbersome militarized economy requires an enormous injection of capital in order to convert to a civilian one. The example of difficulties encountered by the economy of eastern Germany—subsidized to an unprecedented degree by western Germany—in the process of adjusting to the requirements of the world market economy illustrates the unwillingness and the inability of the industrialized world (the EC, Japan and the USA) to meet the challenges facing post-communist economies. The process of the transformation and inclusion of post-communist economies in the global free market will be much longer and more complicated than was envisaged by politicians and experts both in the East and in the West. The slow transitional period and diminishing living stan-

[51] See, for example, Payne, K. B., *Countering Proliferation: New Criteria for European Security* (IEDSS: London, 1992), pp. 36–38.
[52] For more on this, see chapter 14 in this volume.

dards, as well as growing unemployment and inflation, are bound to compound the sense of insecurity and corresponding social frustrations. As a consequence, there is a risk of massive migration movements, political instability, and the increased appeal of authoritarian, nationalist and populist slogans and solutions. The outcome can be attempts to define and forge nationally oriented policies of security directed against neighbours instead of seeking guarantees within the multilateral structures designed to build co-operative or collective security.[53]

V. New institutions

The CSCE structures created in 1990–91 illustrate the desire to adapt available instruments to meet new challenges.[54] However, these structures were overtaken by events. The major change concerns the fact that in the area addressed by CSCE provisions a dozen or so new actors have emerged. The Baltic states were soon joined by the remaining former Soviet republics which—having declared their independence—gained international recognition. By decision of the Second Meeting of the CSCE Council of Foreign Ministers (at Prague on 30–31 January 1992),[55] following Estonia, Latvia and Lithuania, which had already been accepted, the status of participating states was accorded to: Armenia, Azerbaijan, Belarus, Kazakhstan, Kyrgyzstan, Moldova, Tajikistan, Turkmenistan, Ukraine and Uzbekistan.[56] Immediately after the dissolution of the Soviet Union and proclamation of the CIS, the Ministry of Foreign Affairs of the Russian Federation announced that the USSR's membership in the United Nations and all its institutions and organizations, as well as its participation in all treaties, conventions and negotiations, would be continued by the Russian Federation as the successor state.[57] This move was not contested by any state.

Enlarging the number of participants of the CSCE process was also accompanied by a considerable expansion of tasks. The new CSCE concept of security and stability includes human rights, political, military, economic and

[53] For more on this, see Kupchan, Ch. A. and Kupchan C. A., 'Concerts, collective security and the future of Europe', *International Security*, vol. 16, no. 1 (summer 1991), pp. 117–61.

[54] See note 2.

[55] The decision was preceded by the recommendation of the Sixth Meeting of the CSCE Committee of Senior Officials that the states interested in accession to the CSCE forward a letter in which they state that they would undertake to adopt the Helsinki Final Act, the Charter of Paris for a New Europe and all other documents of the CSCE. See *Journal*, no. 1 (Prague, 27 Jan. 1992). They also agreed to: (*a*) apply all the provisions of the Vienna Document on CSBMs; and (*b*) to 'an understanding that the geographic scope of its application should be revised as soon as possible in order to ensure full effect of the rules of transparency, predictability and conflict prevention' on their territories. The specific provisions will be included in the Vienna Document 1992. The governments of the new states also recognized the requirement for 'prompt entry into force of the Treaty on Conventional Armed Forces in Europe'. See 'Draft letter of accession to the CSCE', *Journal*, no. 1 (Prague, 27 Jan. 1992), annex 2. The letters of accession are published in 'Second Meeting of the CSCE Council of Ministers, Prague', *Journal*, no. 1 (30 Jan. 1992).

[56] Georgia, the last post-Soviet state to join the CSCE, joined on 24 Mar. 1992 during the follow-up meeting in Helsinki. See chapter 12 in this volume.

[57] Russia sent notes to this effect to the UN and the Conference on Disarmament on 24 and 27 Dec. 1991, respectively, and to all diplomatic missions in Moscow (12 Jan. 1992).

environmental components. The important new role of the Helsinki process consists in fostering democratic development and fully integrating participating states into the network of shared CSCE values.

The Document on Further Development of CSCE Institutions and Structures defined new guidelines for the Helsinki follow-up meeting set for March 1992.[58] It was agreed that the efficiency of the institutions established in 1991 should be enhanced. To this end, the CSO will act as the agent of the Council of Foreign Ministers in taking appropriate decisions (between meetings of the CSCE Council). Therefore, the CSO will meet more regularly, at least once every three months. The facilities of the CSCE communications network will be made available to the Chairman-in-Office of the CSO 'for transmission of urgent messages related to the work of the Committee'.[59]

The tasks in the human dimension of security, which 'remains a key function of the CSCE', were also broadly expanded.[60] Regarding the task of crisis management, the intentions resemble academic parlance (i.e., 'to study possibilities for improving') more than concrete political and organizational decisions. Hopefully, actions will be backed by instruments tested both in theory and practice: fact-finding and rapporteur missions, monitoring, good services, counselling and conciliation, dispute settlement and also peacekeeping activities in Europe. The tasks entrusted to the CPC remain in blatant disproportion to the means and capabilities available to it.

The meeting of the CSCE Council of Foreign Ministers in Prague was attended by representatives of the UN and the UN Economic Commission, and by official representatives of the heads of a number of international institutions and organizations: NATO, the WEU, the Council of Europe, the OECD and the European Bank for Reconstruction and Development (EBRD). Until 1991, all conferences and meetings were held in accordance with the Helsinki Final Recommendations of 1973, outside military alliances.[61] Hence, the participation of NATO and WEU representatives means a substantial change of and a new approach to the role of these institutions in the pan-European process. What is important is that the Prague Document determined for the first time the rules of co-operation with such organizations as NATO, the EC, the WEU, Council of Europe, the OECD, the EBRD, the European Investment Bank, and other European and transatlantic organizations. As a result, these institutions and organizations are seen as compatible and not competitive with the CSCE. There is no doubt that the area in which the CSCE role is not challenged is the human dimension of relations among states. The meetings in Copenhagen, Moscow, Geneva and Oslo gave the human dimension of security an institutional shape.

The same cannot yet be said about military aspects of security. The decisions contained in the Vienna documents concerning CSBMs and those in the

[58] See Prague Document on Further Development of CSCE Institutions and Structures, CSCE/2-C/2 Dec. (30 Jan. 1992).

[59] See note 58.

[60] See note 58.

[61] Recommendation 65, Final Recommendation of the Helsinki Consultations, Helsinki, 8 June 1973.

1990 CFE Treaty concerning conventional force reductions reflect significant progress; however, they are not adequate to new politico-military realities.

A qualitatively new approach is also required in the areas of crisis management and conflict prevention. The Prague Document asserts only 'the need to strengthen the capacity of the CSCE to contribute . . . to a peaceful solution of problems involving national minorities which could lead to tensions and conflict—both within and between States—including possibilities for "early warning"' and the 'need for further development of the CSCE's capability for conflict prevention, crisis management and peaceful settlement of disputes'.[62] This is how the tasks and the mandate of the Helsinki follow-up meeting have been formulated.

The CSCE's admission of all of the former Soviet republics gives institutional scope to a new security area from Vancouver to Vladivostok. The CSCE decisions already apply not only to Europe ('from the Atlantic to the Urals') and North America (the United States and Canada) but also to the states of Central Asia and the Far East. Such a significant expansion of geographic scope and the inclusion of new participating states necessitates a differentiation of tasks and expectations connected with the implementation of the provisions already adopted and those yet to be negotiated. States that have emerged as a result of the collapse of the Soviet Union are at a crossroads— facing difficult choices about how to proceed with their development. Their acceptance as participating states in the CSCE process was contingent upon the commitment of each of them to accept 'in their entirety all commitments and responsibilities' contained in the CSCE documents.[63] Indeed, they declared their determination to act in accordance with these provisions. Specific commitments were made regarding the Vienna Document 1990 requirements on CSBMs and the prompt ratification of the 1990 CFE Treaty.

To implement these commitments, it was agreed in Prague that the governments of the newly admitted states will invite a rapporteur mission (arranged by the Chairman of the Council of Foreign Ministers of the CSCE) to visit and will fully facilitate its activities.[64] This mission will report back to the CSCE on progress towards full implementation of CSCE commitments in those states and will provide assistance towards that objective. The procedures adopted within the CSCE, and the established institutions and structures, ought, on the one hand, to facilitate a stabilization of democracy and the rule of law in the post-totalitarian states, and, on the other hand, help prevent the Central Asian participants from sliding into political Islamic fundamentalism. It is also envisaged that informal consultations under the direction of the CSO Chairman should take place at Helsinki during the follow-up meeting in order to establish the modalities for a programme of co-ordinated support to recently admitted states, through which appropriate diplomatic, academic, legal and

---

[62] Summary of Conclusions, Prague Meeting of the CSCE Council, 30–31 Jan. 1992.

[63] See 'Second meeting of the CSCE Council of Ministers, Prague' (note 55).

[64] A relevant identical formula is contained in the letters of all foreign ministers of the newly admitted states addressed to the Chairman-in-Office of the CSCE Council of Ministers, Jiri Dienstbier, Foreign Minister of the Czech and Slovak Federal Republic. See 'Second meeting of the CSCE Council of Ministers, Prague' (note 55).

administrative expertise and advice on CSCE matters could be made available.[65]

A clear tendency has developed in the CSCE process to make specific and binding decisions, as well as general recommendations, and to apply multilateral mechanisms and procedures to monitor implementation of those decisions. Thus, the possibility exists to shape a common system based on both declared and implemented values. An important step along the road towards making the system more viable is the understanding reached in Prague which makes possible a departure from consensus decision-making in cases of clear and gross violations of CSCE commitments regarding human rights, democracy and the rule of law.[66]

VI. The agenda ahead

The changes in Europe confirm the fact that menaces today are of an utterly different character compared to those of the cold war period. They no longer arise from the supremacy of one bloc or from the aggressive policies pursued by one of the great powers. The new threats result from the domestic plight which was bequeathed to new democratic states in Central Europe and Asia, both in economic terms and in terms of national and inter-ethnic conflict. The main challenge for the future is uncertainty and its related risks.[67]

The search for a new security system in Europe must take account of mechanisms for preventing both external aggression and aggression directed by a state against its own society. Consequently, a new catalogue of principles should embrace—along with CSCE Principle VI (non-intervention in internal affairs)—a principle of legitimized interventionism to fend off a threat to common values. Proposals for a new political and legal regulation in this area deserve careful attention on the part of not only experts in international law but also political decision-makers.[68] It is of utmost importance to match the words in the declaration on equal security with concrete actions: to reduce in equal measure the levels of armaments in both East and West to diminished external threats, and to establish common institutions in the area of military security. The shaping of these institutions should by no means be subject to

[65] See Summary of Conclusions, Prague Meeting of the CSCE Council, 30–31 Jan. 1992, para. 19, p. 8.

[66] See Prague Document on Further Development of CSCE Institutions and Structures, CSCE/2-C/2 Dec. (30 Jan. 1992), especially section IV, para 16. The Romanian delegation made an interpretative statement to the effect that 'the conditions and modalities of implementing this procedure . . . should try to prevent the risks that resorting to it might become a stimulus for those who may be tempted to use the issues of human rights, including in particular the rights of persons belonging to minorities, as a substitute for promoting a revisionist policy, through incitation from outside of tensions, unrest and even conflicts in another country'. See note 63, point 8.

[67] In NATO documents the term 'threats' is being replaced by 'risks' and 'uncertainties'. See 'The Alliance's New Strategic Concept. Agreed by the Heads of the State and Government participating in the Meeting of the North Atlantic Council in Rome on 7–8 Nov. 1991', NATO Review, no. 6 (Dec. 1991), pp. 25–32.

[68] Damrosch, L. F., 'Politics across borders: nonintervention and non-forcible influence over domestic affairs', American Journal of International Law, no. 1 (1989); Bierzanek R., 'Ingerencja w sprawy wewnetrzne innych panstw', Sprawy Miedzynarodowe, no. 12 (1991).

ready-made blueprints or theoretical concepts but, as a starting-point, must take into account the different and heterogeneous situations in various parts of Europe, and the territory stretching from Vancouver to Vladivostok. This pre-supposes a need for a thorough transformation of not only the CSCE but also NATO and other Western institutions, and the possibility of co-operation between the new democratic states and the Western organizations with a view to future full membership for them in these structures.

NATO, the WEU, the EC, the Council of Europe and other multinational organizations should get involved to an increasing degree in the multilateral CSCE process initiated. One cannot exclude the possibility of membership of some Central European states in Western organizations such as the EC and NATO. An improvement in mutual relations between NATO and the CSCE was heralded by the Rome decisions of the NATO summit meeting on 7–8 November 1991. It was agreed that, as a result of the Paris summit meeting, the CSCE process now included new institutional arrangements and 'provide[d] a contractual framework for consultation and co-operation that can play a constructive role, complementary to that of NATO and the process of European integration, in preserving peace'.[69] The Rome NATO document clearly staked out the role of the CSCE process in 'the Alliance's new strategic concept':

The potential of dialogue and co-operation within all of Europe must be fully developed in order to help to defuse crises and to prevent conflicts since the Allies' security is inseparably linked to that of all other states in Europe. To this end, the Allies will support the role of the CSCE process and its institutions. Other bodies including the European Community, Western European Union and United Nations may also have an important role to play.[70]

What are the main tasks and expectations related to the CSCE follow-up meeting in Helsinki of March–July 1992 and the CSCE Summit Meeting of Heads of State and Government which is set to begin on 9 July 1992? The main result will probably be the establishment of a CSCE Forum for Security Co-operation. For East European states, the significance of such a body consists chiefly in handling the problems of preventing and resolving conflicts; for West European states, which abound in these types of institution, the new forum will likely be a useful instrument to deal with developments in Europe.

Political rather than military factors will play an increasing role in maintaining security. Clearly, the threat of armed aggression has substantially diminished. Whereas the sources of instability are of a political and economic, and not military, character, new means and mechanisms must focus on political, ethnic and economic problems, rather than on military ones. This applies

---

[69] See note 67, para. 5, p. 25.
[70] See note 67, para. 34, p. 29.

both to the CSCE and NATO,[71] as well as other organizations. The aim is not to form one, all-embracing security institution but the effective operation of the 'interlocking system of institutions'.[72] The starting-points in building a new system in the military field are multilateral agreements (on CSBMs, the CFE Treaty, on the CPC and its emergency mechanisms, the Treaty on Open Skies, and the regulations concerning arms transfers and non-proliferation). The foundation of the new system will be, among others, the already agreed principles: openness and transparency of military activities; restraint from threatening activities; limitation of armed forces; and a permanent dialogue on security. One of the ways of consolidating the new security order might be the conclusion of a General Treaty on Security and Co-operation in Europe.

The formation of a new co-operative security system calls not only for adapting existing procedures and mechanisms to a completely new situation but also, above all, for agreeing upon new principles of collaboration for those states. It requires a departure from the classical academic interpretation of sovereignty and a new definition of matters which fall within the discretionary internal competencies of states. It also presupposes—perhaps above all—the repudiation of the view that the CSCE is mainly a debating club or a forum of never-ending negotiations and the adoption of decisions backed by sanctions (i.e., collective actions to ensure the effectiveness of the decisions). The solutions should be tailored to the requirements of the great transformation which the European system is now experiencing.

---

[71] 'The Alliance stands ready to make its own collective experience available to CSCE and will seek to establish an appropriate relationship with the CSCE'. See 'Final Communiqué issued by the North Atlantic Council Meeting in Ministerial Session, 19th December 1991' (note 46), p. 3.

[72] See Statement by Mr Krzysztof Skubiszewski, Minister of Foreign Affairs of the Republic of Poland at the meeting of the CSCE Council of Ministers in Prague, 30 Jan. 1992.

Appendix 15A. Selected documents relating to the CSCE

Meeting of the CSCE Council in Berlin, 20 June 1991

Summary of conclusions

I

1. The Council of the CSCE held its first Meeting in Berlin on 19 and 20 June 1991.

2. The Ministers welcomed the Republic of Albania as a participating State of the CSCE following receipt of a letter accepting all CSCE commitments and responsibilities from the Minister for Foreign Affairs of the Republic of Albania, Mr. Kapllani, to the Chairman-in-Office of the Council, Federal Minister of Foreign Affairs, Mr. Genscher (Annex 1).

II

3. The Ministers had political consultations on the European architecture and the strengthening of security in Europe as well as the consolidation of human rights, democracy and the rule of law, on prospects for economic transition and social change in Europe, on current issues and on the future work of the CSCE.

In the framework of these consultations the Ministers came to the following conclusions:

4. They reaffirmed the importance of continued political and economic transformation in the democratic countries in transition towards a market economy. They stressed the necessity to continue support to these countries in their efforts to consolidate democracy and transform their economies.

5. They reaffirmed that co-operation in the fields of economy, science, technology and the environment remains an important pillar of the CSCE.

6. They adopted a mechanism for consultation and co-operation with regard to emergency situations (Annex 2).

7. They decided that the communication network, to be established under the provisions of the Vienna CSBM Document 1990, will be preferably used for all communications foreseen in the procedures in emergency situations. In this connection the CSCE Secretariat will be integrated into this communication network.

8. They endorsed the report of the Valletta Meeting on Peaceful Settlement of Disputes and agreed to designate the Conflict Prevention Centre as the nominating institution for the CSCE Dispute Settlement Mechanism under the provisions of the recommendations thereto of the Committee of Senior Officials (Annex 3).

9. They welcomed the establishment of the CSCE Parliamentary Assembly (Annex 4).

10. They noted with satisfaction the results of the Cracow Symposium on the Cultural Heritage of the CSCE participating States.

11. They invited the United Nations Centre for Human Rights to contribute to the Geneva Meeting of Experts on National Minorities.

12. They decided to invite the Council of Europe to make a contribution at the Moscow Meeting of the Conference on the Human Dimension.

13. They encouraged the exchange of information and relevant documents among CSCE and the main European and transatlantic institutions, such as the European Community, Council of Europe, ECE, NATO and WEU. The procedure concerning the CSCE's participation in this exchange should be considered at the next Meeting of the Committee of Senior Officials and reviewed after six months.

14. They requested the Committee of Senior Officials to prepare recommendations for the next Meeting of the Council on the further development of the CSCE institutions and structures, taking into account the debate at this First Council Meeting. The Consultative Committee of the Conflict Prevention Centre would contribute those sections of the recommendations which concern the enhancement of the role of the Conflict Prevention Centre.

15. They looked forward to a range of informal discussions and consultations on new negotiations on disarmament and confidence an security building open to all CSCE participating States. In this context they requested their representatives in Vienna, as a rule their representatives to the Consultative Committee of the Conflict Prevention Centre, to start informal preparatory consultations in September this year

aimed at establishing by 1992, from the conclusion of the Helsinki Follow-up Meeting, new negotiations on disarmament and confidence and security building open to all participating States as set out in the Charter of Paris. They decided that formal preparatory negotiations for the new forum will be carried out at the Helsinki Follow-up Meeting.

16. They welcomed the fact that a further seminar on military doctrine would be held within the context of the Conflict Prevention Centre in Vienna, from 8 to 18 October 1991, and also welcomed the possibility of future seminars as may be agreed by the participating States.

17. In the light of the recent experience in the Gulf region, the Ministers see a need to halt the spread of weapons on mass destruction and for restraint and transparency in the transfer of conventional weapons and weapons technologies, particularly to regions of tension. This should be a priority of CSCE governments, and Ministers agreed to maintain a dialogue on these issues among CSCE countries.

18. They recalled the links of solidarity and of co-operation that unite their countries with the developing countries as well as the importance they attach, in this context, to respect for human rights and to the promotion of the fundamental values of the CSCE. They underlined the usefulness of an increasing co-operation among their countries on these questions in the appropriate fora.

19. They stressed that the CSCE must remain open to dialogue and co-operation with the rest of the world and noted the interest of other countries in the CSCE. In this regard, they requested the CSO to explore this idea and to report to a future meeting of the Council.

20. They agreed that the next Meeting of the Council will be held in Prague on 30 and 31 January 1992.*

---

* This document also includes four annexes not reproduced here: (a) letter from the Government of the Republic of Albania; (b) statement on the mechanism for consultation and co-operation in emergency situations; (c) statement on the peaceful settlement of disputes; and (d) a concluding note.

Source: Summary of Conclusions, Meeting of the CSCE Council in Berlin, 20 June 1991.

Second Meeting of the CSCE Council in Prague, 30–31 January 1992

Summary of Conclusions

Excerpts

I

1. The Council of the CSCE held its second Meeting in Prague on 30 and 31 January 1992.

2. The Ministers welcomed Armenia, Azerbaijan, Belarus, Kazakhstan, Kirgistan, Moldova, Tajikistan, Turkmenistan, Ukraine and Uzbekistan as participating States, following receipt of letters accepting CSCE commitments and responsibilities from each of them (Annex).*

3. The Ministers granted observer status to Croatia and Slovenia in the CSCE process.

4. They welcomed as guests of honour the representatives of the heads of the following international institutions and organizations: United Nations; United Nations Economic Commission for Europe; Council of Europe; Western European Union; North Atlantic Treaty Organization; Organisation for Economic Co-operation and Development; European Bank for Reconstruction and Development.

II

5. The Ministers had political consultations on the transformation in Europe—the role of the CSCE and the contribution of European and other institutions, and on the strengthening of CSCE institutions and structures and orientations for the Helsinki Follow-up Meeting. They adopted with immediate effect the Prague Document on the further development of the CSCE institutions and structures.

III

6. The Ministers agreed that the Helsinki Follow-up Meeting should be an important milestone in the development of the CSCE process and should provide a clear vision for its future course. Representatives to the Follow-up Meeting should, in particular, be guided by:
– the CSCE's comprehensive concept of security and stability, which includes human rights, political, military, economic and environmental components;

---

* See chapter 15, footnote 55 in this volume.

– the important role of the CSCE in fostering democratic development and fully integrating participating States into the network of shared CSCE values, principles and norms and its role in promoting a stable security environment in Europe;

– the importance of a thorough implementation review, particularly in the area of human rights and fundamental freedoms, which will take account of the new situation in Europe and the enlarged number of CSCE participating States;

– the objective of the CSCE to prevent conflict and consolidate peace through eliminating the root causes of tensions, by attaining in particular full respect for human rights, including those inscribed in the CSCE provisions on national minorities, by building democratic institutions and by fostering economic and social progress;

– the need to strengthen the capacity of the CSCE to contribute, in accordance with CSCE principles, to a peaceful solution of problems involving national minorities which could lead to tensions and conflict both within and between States—including possibilities for 'early warning';

– the need for further development of the CSCE's capability for conflict prevention, crisis management and peaceful settlement of disputes;

– the need to strengthen the effectiveness of CSCE institutions by matching their functions more closely to the achievement of these objectives.

. . .

Source: CSCE/2–C/Dec. 3/30 Jan. 1992.

Second Meeting of the CSCE Council in Prague, 30–31 January 1992

Prague Document on Further Development of CSCE Institutions and Structures

Excerpts

1. The Ministers reaffirmed their commitment to pursue actively all the objectives set out in the Charter of Paris for a New Europe, and their determination to further strengthen CSCE institutions and structures for this purpose. To this end they took the following decisions and established certain guidelines for the discussions at the Helsinki Follow-up Meeting.

. . .

VI

Crisis management and conflict prevention instruments

21. The Council agreed that the capabilities of the CSCE to engage in crisis management and conflict prevention and resolution should be improved.

22. To this end, the Council requested the Helsinki Follow-up Meeting to study possibilities for improving the following instruments:

– fact finding and rapporteur missions;
– monitor missions;
– good offices;
– counselling and conciliation;
– dispute settlement.

23. In this context the Helsinki Follow-up Meeting should also give careful consideration to possibilities for CSCE peace-keeping or a CSCE role in peacekeeping.

24. Provision should be made for the further operational implementation within the CSCE of decisions by the Council or the Committee of Senior Officials.

25. Tasks may be delegated to the Chairman-in-Office of the Committee of Senior Officials, to the Consultative Committee of the Conflict Prevention Centre or to open-ended groups of participating States of an *ad hoc* character. In each case a precise mandate and arrangements for reporting back should be established.

Conflict Prevention Centre

26. In addition to the tasks already given to the Conflict Prevention Centre in the Supplementary Document of the Paris Charter and in the Summary of Conclusions of the Berlin Meeting of the CSCE Council, the functions and working methods of the CPC are enhanced as follows:

27. The Consultative Committee will serve as a forum in the security field wherein the CSCE participating States will conduct comprehensive and regular consultations on security issues with politico-military implications. In this context, any participating State may, in order to reduce the risk of conflict, promptly raise an issue which in its view has such implications. This is without prejudice to later decisions on the structure of a new security/arms control forum and the relationship it may have to the CPC.

28. The Consultative Committee will serve as a forum for consultation and cooperation in conflict prevention and for co-

operation in the implementation of decisions on crisis management taken by the Council or by the CSO acting as its agent.

29. The Consultative Committee has the authority to initiate and, with the assistance of the CPC Secretariat, execute fact-finding and monitor missions in connection with paragraph 17 of the Vienna Document 1990 (Mechanism for Consultation and Co-operation as regards Unusual Military Activities).

30. The Consultative Committee, with the assistance of the CPC Secretariat, will execute any additional tasks assigned to it by the Council, or by the Committee of Senior Officials acting as its agent. This will include full responsibility in the implementation of such tasks. The Consultative Committee will report in an appropriate manner on the implementation of these tasks to the Committee of Senior Officials.

31. The Consultative Committee will develop general guidelines for the implementation of its operational tasks including, in due time, those that may be assigned to it by the Helsinki Follow-up Meeting and in the future.

32. In addition to the existing support to the implementation of CSBMs, the CPC will fulfil other functions as regards the implementation and verification of agreements in the field of disarmament and arms control, if so requested by the parties to those agreements and agreed upon by the Consultative Committee.

33. The Consultative Committee may at any time draw the attention of the Committee of Senior Officials to a situation which it considers requires the consideration of the Committee of Senior Officials.

34. The Consultative Committee will meet regularly, as a rule at least once a month. Working schedules should be flexible and additional meetings may be held, in the light of circumstances and future requirements.

35. The Consultative Committee may establish subsidiary working bodies, including open-ended ad hoc groups entrusted with specific tasks.

36. The regular meetings of the Consultative Committee will be chaired in alphabetical rotation. The Chairmanship will rotate immediately after the last regular meeting in every month.

37. The Chairman of the Consultative Committee and the Chairman of the Committee of Senior Officials will maintain contact with each other.

38. The Chairman of the Consultative Committee or his representative will attend meetings of the Committee of Senior Officials which are relevant to the tasks of the CPC.

39. In accordance with the paragraph on 'CSCE Relationship with International Organizations', European, Transatlantic and other international organizations, such as the North Atlantic Treaty Organization (NATO), the Western European Union (WEU) and relevant United Nations bodies, will be invited to make appropriate contributions to future seminars organized by the CPC.

40. The Helsinki Follow-up Meeting should also examine further how the CSCE could co-operate with other international organizations in these fields.

VII

Parliamentary Assembly

41. In the interest of encouraging an active dialogue with the CSCE Parliamentary Assembly, the Chairman-in-Office of the Council will be in contact with the Chairman of the Committee of Heads of Delegation of the Assembly in order to explore possible interest in the presence of the Chairman of the Council at the Budapest Meeting of the Assembly in July 1992. The Chairman of the Council will be prepared to make himself available to report on the work of the CSCE; to answer parliamentarians' questions in this regard; and to take note of parliamentarians' views for subsequent transmission to the Council.

VIII

Non-Governmental Organizations

42. The Council requests the Helsinki Follow-up Meeting to strengthen relations between the CSCE and non-governmental organizations, in order to increase the role of non-governmental organizations in implementing CSCE goals and commitments. In particular, the Follow-up Meeting will develop opportunities and procedures for meaningful non-governmental organization involvement in the CSCE and possibilities for non-governmental organizations to communicate with CSCE structures and institutions, recalling *inter alia* the texts on non-governmental organizations agreed by the Sofia and Moscow Meetings and by the Oslo Seminar.

CSCE relationship with international organizations

43. The Council of Europe, ECE, NATO, the Western European Union, OECD, EBRD, EIB and other European and transatlantic organizations which may be agreed will be invited to make contributions on the basis of CSCE precedent and practice to specialized CSCE Meetings where they have relevant expertise.

44. To ensure full co-ordination, the Ministers would welcome it if the above organizations would inform the CSCE Secretariat annually of their current work programme and of the facilities available for work relevant to the CSCE.

Relations with non-Participating States

45. The Council requests the Helsinki Follow-up Meeting to recommend practical ways to establish a flexible dialogue between the CSCE and interested non-participating States or groups of States, for example through contacts between the said States and the Chairman-in-Office of the Council or of the Committee of Senior Officials.

Financial arrangements of the CSCE and cost-effectiveness

46. The Council requested the Helsinki Follow-up Meeting to develop procedures which would ensure greater predictability and transparency of the costs of CSCE meetings and other activities. Measures to provide for increased cost-effectiveness should also be examined.

47. States proposing to host future CSCE meetings will present draft budgets along with their proposals. Detailed provisions in this respect will be developed at the Helsinki Follow-up Meeting.

Source: CSCE/2–C/Dec. 2/30 Jan. 1992.

Final Communique issued by the North Atlantic Council Meeting in Ministerial Session

Brussels, 19 December 1991

1. We, the Foreign Ministers of the Atlantic Alliance have met at a time when dramatic developments are taking place in Europe. The Soviet Union and the republics are undergoing fundamental changes. Leaders there, like those in the other countries of Central and Eastern Europe, are pursuing far-reaching political and economic reforms. In this endeavour, they expect support and cooperation from us. Against this background, the decisions taken by our Heads of State and Government at their Summit in Rome, which emphasise NATO's role as a source of stability for the whole of Europe, assume a special importance by adding the dimension of cooperation to the Alliance's traditional approach of dialogue and collective defence. At the same time, the member states of the European Community have taken decisive steps at the European Council meeting in Maastricht to deepen their integration and to establish their common foreign and security policy in order to assume greater responsibility in Europe. As all countries of Europe and North America draw more closely together in a community of shared values, and their relationship becomes increasingly one of partnership, we will be able to realise in full the new and broad approach to security which was set out in the Rome Declaration and the Alliance's new Strategic Concept.

Relations with the Soviet Union and the other countries of Central and Eastern Europe

2. The inaugural meeting tomorrow of the North Atlantic Cooperation Council will enhance our liaison relationship with the countries of Central and Eastern Europe and launch a new era of partnership. Our consultations and cooperation will focus on security and related issues where Allies can offer their experience and expertise. They are designed to aid in fostering a sense of security and confidence among these countries and to help them transform their societies and economies, making democratic change irreversible.

3. We have consulted closely on developments in the Soviet Union and the republics. In the interest of peace and security, we look to all the leaders to take matters forward in an orderly and democratic manner, as they develop towards a common ground of cooperation. We will lend our individual and collective support to help the Soviet Union and the republics move towards these objectives. The Allies have a legitimate interest in seeing viable arrangements established between the republics for implementing the Soviet Union's international arms control and disarmament obligations. We urge the leaders of the

Union and the republics to respect the Soviet Union's commitments under the Helsinki Final Act, the Charter of Paris and other CSCE documents. We call on them to comply fully with the provisions of arms control agreements to which the Soviet Union is a signatory.

4. We expect the leaders of the Union and the republics to ensure the safe, responsible and reliable control of nuclear weapons and actively to prevent the proliferation of those weapons or other means of mass destruction. We are ready to respond as fully as possible to requests for practical assistance in achieving these objectives. In this context, we have discussed efforts and proposals made by individual Allies. We will monitor the situation in the Soviet Union and the republics, coordinate our efforts and contribute to the international effort to prevent the proliferation of nuclear weapons or other weapons of mass destruction. In particular, we will actively encourage the Soviet Union and the republics to take firm measures to prevent the unauthorised export of nuclear or other destabilising equipment and technology. We will continue to consult actively on these and on other developments in the Soviet Union and the republics, with a view to harmonising our approach to these rapidly unfolding events.

5. We agreed upon the gravity of the problems being experienced by the peoples of the Soviet Union and the republics, as they grapple with the difficult transition to democracy and a market economy, in obtaining food, medicine and other basic necessities. We agreed that these problems pose a serious threat to the reform process, and to stability in Europe. We recognise the urgent nature of the humanitarian needs and stand ready to support peace as effectively as we have deterred aggression. In that spirit, the relevant bodies of the Alliance will now draw up plans to make its unique expertise and capabilities, such as the coordination capabilities in the Senior Civil Emergency Planning Committee, available to assist in the urgent transportation and distribution of humanitarian assistance. Also, the efforts of the militaries of those NATO members participating in this enterprise, working jointly and with others, including the Soviet military, to alleviate human suffering in the Soviet Union and the republics, can help demonstrate again that the Cold War is behind us, and that a new community of shared values and interests is taking root.

6. We have also consulted closely on developments in the other nations of Central and Eastern Europe. We welcome the continuing progress towards democratic pluralism, respect for human rights and market economies. We encourage these nations to continue their reforms and contribute to the further implementation of CSCE commitments and arms control agreements.

Yugoslavia

7. We condemn the continuing violence and deplore the loss of life in Yugoslavia. We strongly urge all parties to respect ceasefire agreements in order to allow the prompt deployment of a UN peacekeeping force. We also urge all parties actively to pursue the peace process through UN efforts and the Hague Conference called by the EC on the mandate of the CSCE to find a negotiated solution to this crisis. We will continue to consult closely on the situation in Yugoslavia.

A security architecture for Europe

8. The peace and security of Europe will increasingly depend on a framework of interlocking institutions which complement each other, since the challenges we face cannot be comprehensively addressed by one institution alone. We are determined to ensure that our Alliance will play its full part in this framework.

CSCE

9. We are actively pursuing the initiatives taken by our Heads of State and Government in Rome to strengthen the CSCE process. We are determined to contribute towards decisions to be taken at the CSCE Council in Prague in January to develop the political structures and the institutions of the CSCE and to provide guidelines for the further pursuit of this work at the Helsinki Follow-Up Meeting in March. We intend to ensure that the Helsinki Summit next summer marks an important step in consolidating the new European architecture and in strengthening CSCE's institutions and mechanisms. We are convinced that the CSCE must develop the means to promote the implementation of existing commitments. We further believe that the CSCE should fulfil its increasingly important role in furthering cooperation and

security in Europe by fostering democratic change, securing freedom, and developing and applying effective instruments for conflict prevention, the peaceful settlement of disputes and crisis management.

10. The CSCE has frequently sought contributions to meetings from various international organisations within their spheres of competence. The Alliance stands ready to make its own collective experience available to CSCE and will seek to establish an appropriate relationship with the CSCE. Following the conclusions of the meeting of the CSCE Council in Berlin, we look forward to exchanging information and relevant documents and to the Alliance contributing as such, on the same basis as other international organisations, other than the European Community, and in a manner consistent with CSCE precedent and practice, to future CSCE meetings on subjects in which it has relevant expertise.

European security identity and defence role

11. In the spirit of our Alliance's Rome Declaration, we welcome the decisions taken at Maastricht by the European Council on the common foreign and security policy of the European Union which shall include all questions related to the security of the European Union, including the eventual framing of a common defence policy, which might in time lead to a common defence, and by the member states of the Western European Union on the role of WEU and its relations with the European Union and with the Atlantic Alliance. We note with satisfaction the European Council's agreement that the common foreign and security policy of the European Union shall be compatible with the common security and defence policy established within the framework of the North Atlantic Treaty. Enhancing European responsibility on defence matters while strengthening the solidarity and cohesion of the transatlantic partnership will greatly contribute to our common security.

12. We support the objective of developing WEU as the defence component of the European Union and as a means of strengthening the European pillar of the Atlantic Alliance. We welcome the fact that in stating their aim of introducing joint positions into the process of consultation in the Alliance, the WEU member states have affirmed that the Alliance will remain the essential forum for consultation among its members and the venue for agreement on policies bearing on the security and defence commitments of Allies under the Washington Treaty. We are appreciative of WEU's stated intention to strengthen the role, responsibilities and contributions of the WEU member states in the Alliance and to act in conformity with the positions adopted in the Alliance. We welcome the invitation to member states of the European Union to accede to the WEU, or to become observers if they so wish, and the simultaneous offer to other European member states of NATO to become associate members of WEU, giving them the possibility of fully participating in its activities. This will help ensure the necessary transparency and complementarity between the emerging European security identity and defence role and the Alliance.

13. We reciprocate WEU's preparedness to develop further close working links between WEU and the Alliance. We stand ready to implement practical arrangements to this end, including close cooperation between the two organisations and, where necessary, the synchronisation of dates and venues of meetings and the harmonisation of working methods. We have today tasked the Council in permanent session to develop as soon as possible with the WEU proposals for the appropriate arrangements.

Arms control

14. Stability and security on the European continent require the full implementation of all arms control agreements, in particular the CFE Treaty. We urge all CFE signatories which have not already done so to move forward promptly with the Treaty's ratification. It is critical that all relevant political authorities assume their responsibility in the new architecture of cooperative security in Europe and take all necessary actions to ensure that the CFE Treaty is respected, ratified and implemented.

15. We are hopeful that the new proposals introduced by the Allies in Vienna will enable us to conclude successfully the CFE 1A and the CSBM negotiations by the time of the Helsinki Follow-Up Meeting. We urge our negotiating partners to work constructively with us towards this goal. We welcome the progress made in Vienna in the Open Skies negotiations and express our strong hope that agreement can be achieved in time for the Helsinki Follow-Up meeting.

16. The Helsinki meeting will mark a turning point in the arms control and disarmament process in Europe, and we are actively engaged in developing a common approach. The CSCE Council of Ministers on 19th–20th June 1991 launched informal preparatory consultations aimed at establishing at the Helsinki Follow-Up Meeting new negotiations on disarmament and confidence and security-building. They decided that formal preparatory negotiations for the new forum would take place at the Helsinki Follow-Up Meeting. We have followed closely and participated in these informal preparatory consultations, carefully noting the views of CSCE partners. A broad measure of consensus is already apparent. In the period leading up to the meeting and at the meeting itself, we propose that our negotiators and those of our CSCE partners should be guided by the following broad policy objectives:

– in order to achieve our goal of a new cooperative order in which no country need harbour fears for its security, we should establish a European security forum in a manner which preserves the autonomy and distinct character of the various different elements in the process, but which also ensures coherence between them;

– we should strengthen security and stability through the negotiation of concrete measures aimed at keeping the levels of armed forces in Europe to the minimum commensurate with common and individual legitimate security needs, within Europe and beyond: these may entail further reductions of armed forces;

– we should institute a permanent security dialogue, in which participants will be able to address legitimate security concerns, and which will foster a new quality of transparency and cooperation about armed forces and defence policies. This dialogue should contribute to the strengthening of the achievements of the Helsinki process in the field of security; and

– we should enhance the ability of CSCE institutions, including the Conflict Prevention Centre, to reduce the risk of conflict, through the full and open implementation of agreed measures in the security field, and through the elaboration of relevant conflict prevention and crisis management techniques.

We consider it important that, in addition to setting the broad objectives for the new process, the Helsinki Follow-Up Meeting should establish a concrete work programme for the first phase of the process. In our view, early attention should be given to:

– appropriate harmonisation of arms control obligations in Europe, which will provide a basis for consideration of further limitations and, to the extent possible, reductions of armed forces;

– negotiated confidence-building and cooperative measures, designed to ensure greater transparency and predictability in military affairs;

– cooperation to support and enhance existing multilateral non-proliferation regimes, including in the field of transfer of conventional weapons; and

– enhancement of mechanisms and instruments for conflict prevention and crisis management.

We envisage that some measures may appropriately be devised on a selective or regional basis.

17. We will continue to work for security at minimum levels of nuclear arms sufficient to preserve peace and stability. Ratification of the START agreement and its early implementation together with the implementation of the decisions of President Bush and President Gorbachev to reduce unilaterally nuclear weapons are of fundamental importance to future security and stability.

The proliferation of weapons of mass destruction and of their means of delivery undermines international security. It will be our priority task to enhance the authority of the Treaty on Non-Proliferation of Nuclear Neapons (NPT), and to further its worldwide adherence. We also deem it essential to complete a global, comprehensive and effectively verifiable ban on chemical weapons next year. We reaffirm our belief that transfers of conventional armaments beyond legitimate defensive needs to regions of tension make the peaceful settlement of disputes less likely. In this context we welcome the decision to establish a universal register of conventional arms transfers under United Nations auspices.

18. The Spring 1992 meeting of the North Atlantic Council in Ministerial Session will be held in Oslo in June.

Source: *Atlantic News*, no. 2382 (Annex I) 21 Dec. 1991.

North Atlantic Cooperation Council Statement on Dialogue, Partnership and Cooperation

Brussels, 20 December 1991

Excerpts

1. We, the Foreign Ministers of the North Atlantic Alliance consisting of Belgium, Canada, Denmark, France, Germany, Greece, Iceland, Italy, Luxembourg, Netherlands, Norway, Portugal, Spain, Turkey, United Kingdom and the United States, and the Foreign Ministers of Bulgaria, the Czech and Slovak Federal Republic, Estonia, Hungary, Latvia, Lithuania, Poland and Romania, and the Representative of the Soviet Union have gathered in Brussels to develop further the process of regular diplomatic liaison and to build genuine partnership among the North Atlantic Alliance and the countries of Central and Eastern Europe. This inaugural meeting of the North Atlantic Cooperation Council marks an historic step forward in our relationship.

. . .

3. We are determined to make another substantial contribution to our shared goal: a Europe whole and free. Our new joint undertaking will contribute to strengthening the role of the CSCE and to the achievement of its objectives without prejudice to its competence and mechanisms. We seek an architecture for the new Europe that is firmly based on the principles and provisions of the Helsinki Final Act and the Charter of Paris. Security is today based on a broad concept that encompasses more than ever political, economic, social and environmental aspects as well as defence. For this reason an interlocking network in which institutions such as the CSCE, the Atlantic Alliance, the European Community, the WEU and the Council of Europe complement each other, can best safeguard the freedom, security, and prosperity of all European and North American states. Frameworks of regional cooperation will also be an important part of this comprehensive security architecture.

. . .

4. Following the proposal of the Alliance Summit in Rome, we have agreed to build on our existing liaison and to develop a more institutional relationship of consultation and cooperation on political and security issues, and in particular to:
– hold annual meetings with the North Atlantic Council at Ministerial level in a North Atlantic Cooperation Council;
– hold bi-monthly meetings of the North Atlantic Council with liaison partners at the Ambassadorial level, beginning in February 1992;
– hold additional meetings of the North Atlantic Cooperation Council at Ministerial level, or of the North Atlantic Council in permanent session with Ambassadors of liaison partners, as circumstances warrant;
– hold meetings at regular intervals of NATO subordinate committees with representatives of liaison partners. This will include *inter alia* meetings with the Political and Economic Committees, as well as with the Military Committee and under its direction other NATO Military Authorities, and NATO's Atlantic Policy Advisory Group.

5. The focus of our consultations and cooperation will be on security and related issues, such as defence planning, conceptual approaches to arms control, democratic concepts of civilian–military relations, civil–military coordination of air traffic management and the conversion of defence production to civilian purposes. We will enhance participation of liaison partners in NATO's 'Third Dimension' scientific and environmental programmes. We will cooperate actively in disseminating as widely as possible information about NATO in the countries of Central and Eastern Europe, *inter alia* through diplomatic liaison channels and embassies of NATO member countries.

6. The implementation of the process described above and in particular the practical arrangements for meetings with the North Atlantic Council at Ambassadorial level and with NATO committees will be determined by Ambassadors who will prepare a workplan.

7. The annual meetings of the North Atlantic Cooperation Council will, as a rule, take place in Brussels in conjunction with the Autumn Ministerial of the North Atlantic Council. Exceptions are not excluded. Our next annual meeting will take place in Oslo in June at the invitation of the Norwegian government.

Source: *Atlantic News*, no. 2382 (Annex II) 21 Dec. 1991.

Address by President of the Russian Federation Boris Yeltsin to the participants of the session of the North Atlantic Cooperation Council

Brussels, 20 December 1991

On behalf of the leadership of Russia I would like to greet the participants of the session of the North Atlantic Cooperation Council and express my conviction that the functions of this newly created institution of international cooperation will contribute to creating a climate of mutual understanding and trust, strengthening stability and co-operation on the European continent.

These processes are undoubtedly promoted by profound changes going on in my country, which open up unprecedented opportunities for productive cooperation between Russia and the international community. Today these relations can be based on the recognition of common values and a comprehensive approach to promoting international security. It is from this standpoint that we view the future of our relations with the North Atlantic Treaty Organization.

We consider these relations to be very serious and wish to develop this dialogue in each and every direction, as well as contacts with the North-Atlantic Alliance both on the political and military levels. Today we are raising a question of Russia's membership in the NATO, however regarding it as a longterm political aim.

The leadership of Russia welcomed the results of the Rome session of NATO Council and its decisions. We fully support the efforts to create a new system of security 'from Vancouver to Vladivostok'. Today it is important to rapidly overcome the heritage of confrontation, to take resolute measures for reciprocal cuts in military potentials and at the same time foster mutual understanding and predictability.

Russia and other members of the Commonwealth of Independent States, now undergoing the process of formation, intend to pursue a policy of strengthening international peace and security. They guarantee their adherence to the implementation of all international commitments, stemming for them from treaties and agreements, signed by the former USSR. Special attention will be paid to ensuring single control over nuclear armaments and their non-proliferation. All this, in our conviction, creates prerequisites for building a reliable system of collective security in Europe with the participation of the members of the Commonwealth of Independent States, as well as, naturally, the United States and Canada. We believe that Russia, as well as other member-states of the Commonwealth, will be able to make their significant contribution to the work of the North Atlantic Cooperation Council and is prepared to take part in its follow-up sessions.

Source: *Atlantic News*, No. 2382 (Annex II) 21 Dec. 1991.

Annexes

Annexe A. Major multilateral arms control agreements

Annexe B. Chronology 1991

Annexe A. Major multilateral arms control agreements

RAGNHILD FERM

For the texts of the arms control agreements, see Goldblat, J., SIPRI, *Agreements for Arms Control: A Critical Survey* (Taylor & Francis: London, 1982); for the Treaty of Rarotonga, see SIPRI, *World Armaments and Disarmament: SIPRI Yearbook 1986* (Oxford University Press: Oxford, 1986), pp. 509–19.

I. Summaries of the agreements

Protocol for the prohibition of the use in war of asphyxiating, poisonous or other gases, and of bacteriological methods of warfare (Geneva Protocol)

Signed at Geneva on 17 June 1925; entered into force on 8 February 1928.

Declares that the parties agree to be bound by the above prohibition, which should be universally accepted as part of international law, binding alike the conscience and the practice of nations.

Antarctic Treaty

Signed at Washington on 1 December 1959; entered into force on 23 June 1961.

Declares the Antarctic an area to be used exclusively for peaceful purposes. Prohibits any measure of a military nature in the Antarctic, such as the establishment of military bases and fortifications, and the carrying out of military manœuvres or the testing of any type of weapon. Bans any nuclear explosion as well as the disposal of radioactive waste material in Antarctica, subject to possible future international agreements on these subjects.

At regular intervals consultative meetings are convened to exchange information and hold consultations on matters pertaining to Antarctica, as well as to recommend to the governments measures in furtherance of the principles and objectives of the Treaty. A Protocol on the protection of the Antarctic environment was signed on 4 October 1991.

Treaty banning nuclear weapon tests in the atmosphere, in outer space and under water (Partial Test Ban Treaty—PTBT)

Signed at Moscow on 5 August 1963; entered into force on 10 October 1963.

Prohibits the carrying out of any nuclear weapon test explosion or any other nuclear explosion: (*a*) in the atmosphere, beyond its limits, including outer space, or under water, including territorial waters or high seas; (*b*) in any other environment if such explosion causes radioactive debris to be present outside the territorial limits of the state under whose jurisdiction or control the explosion is conducted.

Treaty on principles governing the activities of states in the exploration and use of outer space, including the moon and other celestial bodies (Outer Space Treaty)

Signed at London, Moscow and Washington on 27 January 1967; entered into force on 10 October 1967.

Prohibits the placing into orbit around the earth of any objects carrying nuclear weapons or any other kinds of weapons of mass destruction, the installation of such weapons on celestial bodies, or the stationing of them in outer space in any other manner. The establishment of military bases, installations and fortifications, the testing of any type of weapons and the conduct of military manœuvres on celestial bodies are also forbidden.

Treaty for the prohibition of nuclear weapons in Latin America (Treaty of Tlatelolco)

Signed at Mexico City on 14 February 1967; entered into force on 22 April 1968.

Prohibits the testing, use, manufacture, production or acquisition by any means, as well as the receipt, storage, installation, deployment and any form of possession of any nuclear weapons by Latin American countries.

The parties should conclude agreements with the IAEA for the application of safeguards to their nuclear activities.

Under *Additional Protocol I* the extra-continental or continental states which, *de jure* or *de facto*, are internationally responsible for territories lying within the limits of the geographical zone established by the Treaty (France, the Netherlands, the UK and the USA) undertake to apply the statute of military denuclearization, as defined in the Treaty, to such territories.

Under *Additional Protocol II* the nuclear weapon states undertake to respect the statute of military denuclearization of Latin America, as defined and delimited in the Treaty, and not to contribute to acts involving a violation of the Treaty, nor to use or threaten to use nuclear weapons against the parties to the Treaty.

In 1990 the General Conference of the Agency for the Prohibition of Nuclear Weapons in Latin America proposed a change in the official name of the Treaty by adding the words 'and the Caribbean'. In 1991 a proposal was made to modify paragraph 2 of Article 25 that determines which states may not become parties to the Treaty. By January 1992 the amendments had not entered into force.

Treaty on the non-proliferation of nuclear weapons (NPT)

Signed at London, Moscow and Washington on 1 July 1968; entered into force on 5 March 1970.

Prohibits the transfer by nuclear weapon states, to any recipient whatsoever, of nuclear weapons or other nuclear explosive devices or of control over them, as well as the assistance, encouragement or inducement of any non-nuclear weapon state to manufacture or otherwise acquire such weapons or devices. Prohibits the receipt by non-nuclear weapon states from any transferor whatsoever, as well as the manufacture or other acquisition by those states of nuclear weapons or other nuclear explosive devices.

Non-nuclear weapon states undertake to conclude safeguard agreements with the International Atomic Energy Agency (IAEA) with a view to preventing diversion of nuclear energy from peaceful uses to nuclear weapons or other nuclear explosive devices.

The parties undertake to facilitate the exchange of equipment, materials and scientific and technological information for the peaceful uses of nuclear energy and to ensure that potential benefits from peaceful applications of nuclear explosions will be made available to non-nuclear weapon parties to the Treaty. They also undertake to pursue negotiations in good faith on effective measures relating to cessation of the nuclear arms race at an early date and to nuclear disarmament, and on a treaty on general and complete disarmament.

Twenty-five years after the entry into force of the Treaty (1995), a conference shall be convened to decide whether the Treaty shall continue in force indefinitely or shall be extended for an additional fixed period or periods.

Treaty on the prohibition of the emplacement of nuclear weapons and other weapons of mass destruction on the seabed and the ocean floor and in the subsoil thereof (Seabed Treaty)

Signed at London, Moscow and Washington on 11 February 1971; entered into force on 18 May 1972.

Prohibits emplanting or emplacing on the seabed and the ocean floor and in the subsoil thereof beyond the outer limit of a 12-mile seabed zone any nuclear weapons or any other types of weapons of mass destruction as well as structures, launching installations or any other facilities specifically designed for storing, testing or using such weapons.

Convention on the prohibition of the development, production and stockpiling of bacteriological (biological) and toxin weapons and on their destruction (BW Convention)

Signed at London, Moscow and Washington on 10 April 1972; entered into force on 26 March 1975.

Prohibits the development, production, stockpiling or acquisition by other means or retention of microbial or other biological agents, or toxins whatever their origin or method of production, of types and in quantities that have no justification of prophylactic, protective or other peaceful purposes, as well as weapons, equipment or means of delivery designed to use such agents or toxins for hostile purposes or in armed conflict. The destruction of the agents, toxins, weapons, equipment and means of delivery in the possession of the parties, or their diversion to peaceful purposes, should be effected not later than nine months after the entry into force of the Convention.

Convention on the prohibition of military or any other hostile use of environmental modification techniques (Enmod Convention)

Signed at Geneva on 18 May 1977; entered into force on 5 October 1978.

Prohibits military or any other hostile use of environmental modification techniques having widespread, long-lasting or severe effects as the means of destruction, damage or injury to states party to the Convention. The term 'environmental modification techniques' refers to any technique for changing—through the deliberate manipulation of natural processes—the dynamics, composition or structure of the Earth, including its biota, lithosphere, hydrosphere and atmosphere, or of outer space.

The understandings reached during the negotiations, but not written into the Convention, define the terms 'widespread', 'long-lasting' and 'severe'.

Convention on the prohibitions or restrictions on the use of certain conventional weapons which may be deemed to be excessively injurious or to have indiscriminate effects ('Inhumane Weapons' Convention)

Signed at New York on 10 April 1981; entered into force on 2 December 1983.

The Convention is an 'umbrella treaty', under which specific agreements can be concluded in the form of protocols.

Protocol I prohibits the use of weapons intended to injure by fragments which are not detectable in the human body by X-rays.

Protocol II prohibits or restricts the use of mines, booby-traps and similar devices.

Protocol III restricts the use of incendiary weapons.

South Pacific Nuclear Free Zone Treaty (Treaty of Rarotonga)

Signed at Rarotonga, Cook Islands, on 6 August 1985; entered into force on 11 December 1986.

Prohibits the manufacture or acquisition by other means of any nuclear explosive device, as well as possession or control over such device by the parties anywhere inside or outside the zone area described in an annex. The parties also undertake not to supply nuclear material or equipment, unless subject to IAEA safeguards, and to prevent in their territories the stationing as well as the testing of any nuclear explosive device. Each party remains free to allow visits, as well as transit, by foreign ships and aircraft.

Under Protocol 1, France, the UK and the USA would undertake to apply the treaty prohibitions relating to the manufacture, stationing and testing of nuclear explosive devices in the territories situated within the zone, for which they are internationally responsible.

Under Protocol 2, China, France, the UK, the USA and the USSR would undertake not to use or threaten to use a nuclear explosive device against the parties to the Treaty or against any territory within the zone for which a party to Protocol 1 is internationally responsible.

Under Protocol 3, China, France, the UK, the USA and the USSR would undertake not to test any nuclear explosive device anywhere within the zone.

II. Status of the implementation of the major multilateral arms control agreements, as of 1 January 1992

Number of parties

1925 Geneva Protocol	130	Seabed Treaty	85
Antarctic Treaty	40	BW Convention	118
Partial Test Ban Treaty	119	Enmod Convention	54
Outer Space Treaty	92	'Inhumane Weapons' Convention	31
Treaty of Tlatelolco	23	Treaty of Rarotonga	11
Additional Protocol I	3	Protocol 1	0
Additional Protocol II	5	Protocol 2	2
Non-Proliferation Treaty	146	Protocol 3	2
NPT safeguards agreements (non-nuclear weapon states)	88		

Notes

1. The Russian Federation, constituted in 1991 as an independent sovereign state, has confirmed the continuity of international obligations assumed by the Union of Soviet Socialist Republics (USSR).

2. The Federal Republic of Germany and the German Democratic Republic merged into one state in 1990. The dates of entry into force of the treaties listed in the table for the united Germany are the dates previously given for the FR Germany.

3. The Yemen Arab Republic and the People's Democratic Republic of Yemen merged into one state in 1990. According to a statement by the united Yemen state, all agreements which either state has entered into are in force for Yemen. The dates of entry into force of the treaties listed in the table for Yemen are the earliest dates previously given for either of the former Yemen states.

4. The table records year of ratification, accession or succession.

5. The Partial Test Ban Treaty, the Outer Space Treaty, the Non-Proliferation Treaty, the Seabed Treaty and the BW Convention provide for three depositaries—the governments of the UK, the USA and the USSR. For these agreements, the dates indicated are the earliest dates on which countries deposited their instruments of ratification, accession or succession—whether in London, Washington or Moscow. The dates given for other agreements (for which there is only one depositary) are the dates of the deposit of the instruments of ratification, accession or succession with the relevant depositary, except in the case of the 1925 Geneva Protocol, where the dates refer to the date of notification by the depositary.

6. The 1925 Geneva Protocol, the Partial Test Ban Treaty, the Outer Space Treaty, the Non-Proliferation Treaty, the Seabed Treaty, the BW Convention, the Enmod Convention and the 'Inhumane Weapons' Convention are open to all states for signature.

The Antarctic Treaty is subject to ratification by the signatories and is open for accession by UN members or by other states invited to accede with the consent of all the contracting parties whose representatives are entitled to participate in the consultative meetings provided for in Article IX.

The Treaty of Tlatelolco is open for signature by all the Latin American republics; all other sovereign states situated in their entirety south of latitude 35° north in the western hemisphere; and (except for a political entity the territory of which is the subject of an international dispute) all such states which become sovereign, when they have been admitted by the General Conference; Additional Protocol I—by 'all extra-continental or continental states having *de jure* or *de facto* international responsibility for territories situated in the zone of application of the Treaty'; Additional Protocol II—by 'all powers possessing nuclear weapons', that is, the USA, the USSR, the UK, France and China.

The Treaty of Rarotonga is open for signature by members of the South Pacific Forum; Protocol 1—by France, the UK and the USA; Protocol 2—by France, China, the USSR, the UK and the USA; Protocol 3—by France, China, the USSR, the UK and the USA.

7. Key to abbreviations used in the table:

S	Signature without further action
PI, PII	Additional Protocols to the Treaty of Tlatelolco
P1, P2, P3	Protocols to the Treaty of Rarotonga
CP	Party entitled to participate in the consultative meetings provided for in Article IX of the Antarctic Treaty
SA	Nuclear safeguards agreement in force with the International Atomic Energy Agency as required by the Non-Proliferation Treaty or the Treaty of Tlatelolco, or concluded by a nuclear weapon state on a voluntary basis.

8. The footnotes are listed at the end of the table and are grouped separately under the heading for each agreement. The texts of the statements contained in the footnotes have been abridged, but the wording is close to the original version.

9. A complete list of UN member states and year of membership appears in section III.

State	Geneva Protocol	Antarctic Treaty	Partial Test Ban Treaty	Outer Space Treaty	Treaty of Tlatelolco	Non-Proliferation Treaty	Seabed Treaty	BW Convention	Enmod Convention	'Inhumane Weapons' Convention	Treaty of Rarotonga
Afghanistan	1986		1964	1988		1970 SA	1971	1975	1985	S	
Albania	1989					1990					
Algeria	1992		S								
Angola	1990[1]										
Antigua and Barbuda	1988[2]		1988[1]	1988[1]	1983[1]	1985[1]	1988[1]		1988[7]		
Argentina	1969	1961 CP	1986	1969	S[3]		1983[2]	1979	1987[2]	S	
Australia	1930[1]	1961 CP	1963	1967		1973 SA	1973	1977	1984	1983	1986
Austria	1928	1987	1964	1968		1969 SA	1972	1973[1]	1990[3]	1983	
Bahamas			1976[1]	1976[1]	1977[1]	1976[1]	1989	1986			
Bahrain	1988[1, 3]					1988[2]		1988[2]			
Bangladesh	1989[1]		1985	1986		1979 SA	1979	1985	1979		

Country										
Barbados	1976[4]			1968	1969[1]	1980		1973		
Belarus (Byelorussia)	1970[5]		1963[2]	1967[2]			1971	1975	1978	1982
Belgium	1928[1]	1960 CP	1966	1973		1975 SA	1972	1979	1982	S
Belize						1985[1]		1986[3]		1989[1]
Benin	1986		1964	1986		1972	1986	1975	1986	
Bhutan	1979		1978			1985 SA		1978		
Bolivia	1985		1965	S	1969[1]	1970	S	1975	S	
Botswana			1968[1]	S		1969	1972	1991		
Brazil	1970	1975 CP	1964	1969[3]	1968[3]		1988[3]	1973	1984	
Brunel Darussalam						1985 SA		1991		
Bulgaria	1934[1]	1978	1963	1957		1969 SA	1971	1972	1978	1982
Burkina Faso	1971		S	1968		1970		1991		

State	Geneva Protocol	Antarctic Treaty	Partial Test Ban Treaty	Outer Space Treaty	Treaty of Tlatelolco	Non-Proliferation Treaty	Seabed Treaty	BW Convention	Enmod Convention	'Inhumane Weapons' Convention	Treaty of Rarotonga
Burma see: Myanmar											
Burundi			S	S		1971	S	S			
Cambodia (Kampuchea)	1983[6]					1972	S	1983			
Cameroon	1989		S	S		1969	S				
Canada	1930[1]	1988	1964	1967		1969 SA	1972[4]	1972	1981	S	
Cape Verde	1992		1979			1979	1979	1977	1979		
Central African Republic	1970		1964	S		1970	1981	S			
Chad			1965			1971					
Chile	1935[5]	1961 CP	1965	1981	1974[4]			1980			
China	1952[7]	1983 CP		1983	PII: 1974[5]	1992	1991[5]	1984[4]		1982[2]	P2: 1989[1] P3: 1989[1]
Colombia		1989	1985	S	1972[1] SA	1986	S	1983			

Country											
Congo	1970					1978	1978	1978			
Cook Islands											1985
Costa Rica	1970		1967		1969¹ SA¹⁶	1970 SA		1973			
Côte d'Ivoire	1970		1965			1973 SA	1972	S			
Cuba	1966	1984		1977⁴			1977⁶	1976	1978	1987	
Cyprus	1966²		1965	1972		1970 SA	1971	1973	1978	1988³	
Czechoslovakia	1938⁸	1962	1963	1967		1969 SA	1972	1973	1978	1982	
Denmark	1930	1965	1964	1967		1969 SA	1971	1973	1978	1982	
Dominica					S	1984¹					
Dominican Republic	1970		1964	1968	1968¹ SA¹⁶	1971 SA	1972	1973			
Ecuador	1970	1987 CP	1964	1969	1969¹ SA¹⁶	1969 SA		1975		1982	

State	Geneva Protocol	Antarctic Treaty	Partial Test Ban Treaty	Outer Space Treaty	Treaty of Tlatelolco	Non-Proliferation Treaty	Seabed Treaty	BW Convention	Enmod Convention	'Inhumane Weapons' Convention	Treaty of Rarotonga
Egypt	1928		1964	1967		1981[3] SA		S	1982	S	
El Salvador	S		1964	1969	1968[1] SA[16]	1972 SA		S			
Estonia	1931[9]					1992					
Equatorial Guinea	1989		1989	1989		1984	S	1989			
Ethiopia	1935		S	S		1970 SA	1977	1975	S		
Fiji	1973[1,2]		1972[1]	1972[1]		1972[1] SA		1973			1985
Finland	1929	1984 CP	1964	1967		1969 SA	1971	1974	1978	1982	
France	1926[1]	1960 CP		1970	PI: S[5] PII: 1974[7]	[4]		1984		1988[4]	
Gabon			1964			1974		S			
Gambia	1966[2]		1965[1]	S		1975 SA	S	S			

Germany	1929	1979 CP	1964	1971		1975[5] SA	1975	1983[5]	1983	S
Ghana	1967		1963	S		1970 SA	1972	1975	1978	
Greece	1931	1987	1963	1971		1970 SA	1985	1975	1983	S
Grenada	1989[2]				1975[1]	1975[1]		1986		
Guatemala	1983	1991	1964[3]		1970[1] SA[16]	1970 SA	S	1973	1988[4]	1983
Guinea						1985	S			
Guinea-Bissau	1989		1976	1976		1976	1976	1976		
Guyana				S			S	S		
Haiti			S	S	1969[1]	1970	S	S		
Holy See (Vatican City)	1966			S		1971[6] SA			S	
Honduras			1964	S	1968[1] SA[16]	1973 SA	S	1979		

State	Geneva Protocol	Antarctic Treaty	Partial Test Ban Treaty	Outer Space Treaty	Treaty of Tlatelolco	Non-Proliferation Treaty	Seabed Treaty	BW Convention	Enmod Convention	'Inhumane Weapons' Convention	Treaty of Rarotonga
Hungary	1952	1984	1963	1967		1969 SA	1971	1972	1978	1982	
Iceland	1967		1964	1968		1969 SA	1972	1973	S	S	
India	1930[1]	1983 CP	1963	1982			1973[7]	1974[6]	1978	1984	
Indonesia	1971[2]		1964	S		1979[7] SA		S	S		
Iran	1929		1964	S		1970 SA	1971	1973	S		
Iraq	1931[1]		1964	1968		1969 SA	1972[6]	1991	S		
Ireland	1930[10]		1963	1968		1968 SA	1971	1972[7]	1982		
Israel	1969[11]		1964	1977							
Italy	1928	1981 CP	1964	1972		1975[8] SA	1974[8]	1975	1981	S[5]	
Jamaica	1970[2]		1991	1970	1969[1] SA[16]	1970 SA	1986	1975			

Japan	1970		1960 CP	1964	1967		1976[9] SA	1971	1982	1982	1982	
Jordan	1977[12]			1964	S		1970 SA	1971	1975			
Kampuchea see Cambodia												
Kenya	1970			1965	1984		1970		1976			
Kiribati							1985[1] SA					1986
Korea, Dem. People's Rep. of (North)	1989[4,13]		1987				1985			1984		
Korea, Republic of (South)	1989[1]		1986 CP	1964[3]	1967[4]		1975[10,11] SA	1987	1987[8]	1986[5]		
Kuwait	1971[14]			1965[4]	1972[5]		1989[12]	1971	1972[9]	1980[6]		
Lao People's Dem. Republic	1989			1965	1972		1970		1973	1978	1983	
Latvia	1931[9]						1992					
Lebanon	1969			1965	1969		1970 SA	S	1975	S		

State	Geneva Protocol	Antarctic Treaty	Partial Test Ban Treaty	Outer Space Treaty	Treaty of Tlatelolco	Non-Proliferation Treaty	Seabed Treaty	BW Convention	Enmod Convention	'Inhumane Weapons' Convention	Treaty of Rarotonga
Lesotho	1972[2]			S		1970 SA	1973	1977			
Liberia	1927		1964			1970	S	S	S		
Libya	1971[15]		1968	1968		1975 SA	1990	1982			
Liechtenstein	1991					1978[13] SA	1991	1991		1989	
Lithuania	1932[9]					1991					
Luxembourg	1936		1965	S		1975 SA	1982	1976	S	S	
Madagascar	1967		1965	1968[6]		1970 SA	S	S			
Malawi	1970		1964[1]			1986		S	1978		
Malaysia	1970		1964	S		1970 SA	1972	1991[10]			
Maldives	1966[2]					1970 SA					
Mali			S	1968		1970	S	S			

Country										
Malta	1964[2]	1964[1]			1970 SA	1971	1975			
Mauritania		1964								
Mauritius	1970[2]	1969[1]	1969[1]		1969 SA	1971	1972			
Mexico	1932	1963	1968	1967[1,8] SA	1969[14] SA	1984[9]	1974[11]		1982	
Monaco	1967									
Mongolia	1968[16]	1963	1967		1969 SA	1971	1972	1978	1982	
Morocco	1970	1966	1967		1970 SA	1971	S	S	S	
Mozambique					1990	S	S			
Myanmar (formerly Burma)		1963	1970			S	S			
Nauru					1982 SA					1987
Nepal	1969	1964	1957		1970 SA	1971	S			

State	Geneva Protocol	Antarctic Treaty	Partial Test Ban Treaty	Outer Space Treaty	Treaty of Tlatelolco	Non-Proliferation Treaty	Seabed Treaty	BW Convention	Enmod Convention	'Inhumane Weapons' Convention	Treaty of Rarotonga
Netherlands	1930[7]	1967 CP	1964	1969	PI: 1971[9] SA[17]	1975 SA	1976	1981	1983[7]	1987[6]	
New Zealand	1930[1]	1960 CP	1963	1968		1969 SA	1972	1972	1984[8]	S	1986
Nicaragua	1990		1965	S	1968[1, 10] SA[16]	1973 SA	1973	1975	S	S	
Niger	1967[2]		1964	1967			1971	1972			
Nigeria	1968[1]		1967	1967		1968 SA		1973		S	
Niue											1986
Norway	1932	1960 CP	1963	1969		1969 SA	1971	1973	1979	1983	
Pakistan	1960[2]		1988	1968				1974	1986	1985	
Panama	1970		1966	S	1971[1] SA	1977	1974	1974			
Papua New Guinea	1981[1, 2]	1981	1980[1]	1980[1]		1982 SA		1980	1980		1989

Paraguay	1933[18]		S		1969[1] SA[16]	1970 SA	S	1976			
Peru	1985	1981 CP	1964	1979	1969[1] SA[16]	1970 SA		1985			
Philippines	1973		1965[3]	S		1972 SA		1973	S	S	
Poland	1929	1961 CP	1963	1968		1969 SA	1971	1973	1978	1983	
Portugal	1930[1]		S			1977 SA	1975	1975	S	S	
Qatar	1976					1989	1974	1975			
Romania	1929[1]	1971[1]	1963	1968		1970 SA	1972	1979	1983	S[7]	
Russian Federation	1928[19]	1960 CP	1963	1967	PII: 1979[11]	1970 SA[15]	1972	1975	1978	1982	P2: 1988[2] P3: 1988[2]
Rwanda	1964[2]		1963	S		1975	1975	1975			
Saint Christopher and Nevis	1989[2]										
Saint Lucia	1988					1979[1] SA		1986[3]			

State	Geneva Protocol	Antarctic Treaty	Partial Test Ban Treaty	Outer Space Treaty	Treaty of Tlatelolco	Non-Proliferation Treaty	Seabed Treaty	BW Convention	Enmod Convention	'Inhumane Weapons' Convention	Treaty of Rarotonga
Saint Vincent and the Grenadines						1984[1]					
Samoa, Western			1965			1975 SA					1986
San Marino			1964	1968				1975			
Sao Tome and Principe						1983	1979	1979	1979		
Saudi Arabia	1971			1976		1988	1972	1972			
Senegal	1977		1964			1970 SA	S	1975			
Seychelles			1985	1978		1985	1985	1979			
Sierra Leone	1967		1964	1967		1975	S	1976	S	S	
Singapore			1968[1]	1976		1976 SA	1976	1975			
Solomon Islands	1981[2]					1981[1]	1981[1]	1981[3]	1981[1]		1989
Somalia			S	S		1970		S			

South Africa	1930[1]	1960 CP	1963	1968		1991 SA	1973	1975		
Spain	1929[20]	1982 CP	1964	1968		1987 SA	1987	1979	1978	S
Sri Lanka	1954		1964	1986		1979 SA		1986	1978	
Sudan	1980		1966			1973 SA	S			S
Suriname					1977[1] SA[16]	1976[1] SA				
Swaziland	1991		1969			1969 SA	1971			
Sweden	1930	1984 CP	1963	1967		1970 SA	1972	1976	1984	1982
Switzerland	1932	1990	1964	1969		1977[13] SA	1976	1976[12]	1988[9]	1982
Syria	1968[21]		1964	1968[7]		1969[10]		S	S	
Taiwan	1929[22]		1964	1970[8]		1970	1972[10]	1973[13]		
Tanzania	1963		1964			1991	S	S		

State	Geneva Protocol 1931	Antarctic Treaty	Partial Test Ban Treaty	Outer Space Treaty	Treaty of Tlatelolco	Non-Proliferation Treaty	Seabed Treaty	BW Convention	Enmod Convention	'Inhumane Weapons' Convention	Treaty of Rarotonga
Thailand	1931		1963	1968		1972 SA		1975			
Togo	1971		1964	1989		1970	1971	1976		S	
Tonga	1971[2]		1971[1]	1971[1]		1971[1]		1976			
Trinidad and Tobago	1962[2]		1964	S	1970[1]	1986					
Tunisia	1967		1965	1968		1970 SA	1971	1973	1978	1987	
Turkey	1929		1965	1968		1980[16] SA	1972	1974	S[10]	S	
Tuvalu						1979[1] SA					1986
Uganda	1965		1964	1968		1982			S		
UK	1930[1]	1960 CP	1963[5]	1967	PI: 1969[12] PII: 1969[12]	1968[17] SA[18]	1972[11]	1975[14]	1978	S	
Ukraine			1963[2]	1967[2]			1971	1975	1978	1982	
United Arab Emirates								S			

Country	1	2	3	4	5	6	7	8	9	10
Uruguay	1977	1980[2] CP	1969	1970	1968[1] SA[16]	1970 SA	S	S		
USA	1975[23]	1960 CP	1963	1967	PI: 1981[13] PII: 1971[14] SA[17]	1970 SA[19]	1972	1981	1980	S[8]
Venezuela	1928		1965	1970	1970[1,15] SA[16]	1975 SA		1975		
Viet Nam	1980[1]			1980		1982 SA	1980[12]	1978	1980	S
Yemen	1971[24]		1979	1979		1979	1979	1980	1977	
Yugoslavia	1929[25]		1964	S		1970[20] SA	1973[13]	1979		1983
Zaire			1965	S		1970 SA		1973	S	
Zambia			1965[1]	1973		1991	1972	1977		
Zimbabwe						1991		1990		

The 1925 Geneva Protocol

[1] The Protocol is binding on this state only as regards states which have signed and ratified or acceded to it. The Protocol will cease to be binding on this state in regard to any enemy state whose armed forces or whose allies fail to respect the prohibitions laid down in it.

Australia withdrew its reservation in 1986, New Zealand in 1989, and Romania, Bulgaria and Chile in 1991. In 1991, Canada and the UK withdrew their reservations concerning the right to retaliate in case of an attack by bacteriological weapons.

[2] Notification of succession.

[3] The accession of Bahrain to the Protocol shall in no way constitute recognition of Israel or be a cause for the establishment of any relations with it.

[4] In notifying its succession to the obligations contracted in 1930 by the UK, Barbados stated that as far as it was concerned the reservation made by the UK was to be considered as withdrawn.

[5] In a note of 2 Mar. 1970, submitted at the UN, Byelorussia stated that 'it recognizes itself to be a party' to the Protocol. However, it has not notified the depositary.

[6] The accession was made on behalf of the exiled coalition government of Democratic Kampuchea with a statement that the Protocol will cease to be binding on it in regard to any enemy state whose armed forces or whose allies fail to respect the prohibitions laid down in the Protocol. France declared that as a party to the Geneva Protocol (but not as the depositary) it considers this accession to have no effect. A similar statement was made by Austria, Bulgaria, Cuba, Czechoslovakia, GDR, Hungary, Mauritius, Netherlands, Poland, Romania, USSR and Viet Nam, which did not recognize the coalition government of Kampuchea. In Feb. 1990 the country was officially renamed Cambodia.

[7] On 13 July 1952 the People's Republic of China issued a statement recognizing as binding upon it the 1929 accession to the Protocol in the name of China. China considers itself bound by the Protocol on condition of reciprocity on the part of all the other contracting and acceding powers.

[8] Czechoslovakia shall cease to be bound by this Protocol towards any state whose armed forces, or the armed forces of whose allies, fail to respect the prohibitions laid down in the Protocol. This reservation was withdrawn in 1990.

[9] None of the Baltic states (Estonia, Latvia and Lithuania) has yet reconfirmed its adherance to the Protocol upon attaining independence in 1991. (In this table, they are included in the total number of parties.)

[10] Ireland does not intend to assume, by this accession, any obligation except towards the states having signed and ratified this Protocol or which shall have finally acceded thereto, and should the armed forces or the allies of an enemy state fail to respect the Protocol, the government of Ireland would cease to be bound by the said Protocol in regard to such state. In 1972, Ireland declared that it had decided to withdraw the above reservations made at the time of accession to the Protocol.

[11] The Protocol is binding on Israel only as regards states which have signed and ratified or acceded to it. The Protocol shall cease to be binding on Israel as regards any enemy state whose armed forces, or the armed forces of whose allies, or the regular or irregular forces, or groups or individuals operating from its territory, fail to respect the prohibitions which are the object of the Protocol.

[12] The accession by Jordan to the Protocol does not in any way imply recognition of Israel. Jordan undertakes to respect the obligations contained in the Protocol with regard to states which have undertaken similar commitments. It is not bound by the Protocol as regards states whose armed forces, regular or irregular, do not respect the provisions of the Protocol.

[13] The Dem. People's Rep. of Korea does not exclude the right to exercise its sovereignty vis-à-vis a contracting party which violates the Protocol in its implementation.

[14] The accession of Kuwait to the Protocol does not in any way imply recognition of Israel or the establishment of relations with the latter on the basis of the present Protocol. In case of breach of the prohibition laid down in this Protocol by any of the parties, Kuwait will not be bound, with regard to the party committing the breach, to apply the provisions of this Protocol.

[15] The accession to the Protocol does not imply recognition of Israel. The Protocol is binding on Libya only as regards states which are effectively bound by it and will cease to be binding on Libya as regards states whose armed forces, or the armed forces of whose allies, fail to respect the prohibitions which are the object of this Protocol.

[16] In the case of violation of this prohibition by any state in relation to Mongolia or its allies, Mongolia shall not consider itself bound by the obligations of the Protocol towards that state. This reservation was withdrawn in 1990.

[17] As regards the use in war of asphyxiating, poisonous or other gases and of all analogous liquids, materials or devices, this Protocol shall cease to be binding on the Netherlands with regard to any enemy state whose armed forces or whose allies fail to respect the prohibitions laid down in the Protocol.

[18] This is the date of receipt of Paraguay's instrument of accession. The date of the notification by the depositary government 'for the purpose of regularization' is 1969.

[19] The Protocol only binds the USSR in relation to the states which have signed and ratified or which have definitely acceded to the Protocol. The Protocol shall cease to be binding on the USSR in regard to any enemy state whose armed forces or whose allies *de jure* or *de facto* do not respect the prohibitions which are the object of this Protocol.

[20] For Spain the Protocol is binding ipso facto, without special agreement with respect to any other state accepting and observing the same obligation, that is, on condition of reciprocity.

[21] The accession by Syria to the Protocol does not in any case imply recognition of Israel or lead to the establishment of relations with the latter concerning the provisions laid down in the Protocol.

[22] The Protocol, signed in 1929 in the name of China, is taken to be valid for Taiwan (the Republic of China, which is part of China). However, unlike the People's Republic of China, Taiwan has not reconfirmed its accession to the Protocol. (Therefore, it is not included in the total number of parties in this table.)

[23] The Protocol shall cease to be binding on the USA with respect to use in war of asphyxiating, poisonous or other gases, and of all analogous liquids, materials, or devices, in regard to an enemy state if such state or any of its allies fail to respect the prohibitions laid down in the Protocol.

[24] In case any party fails to observe the prohibition under the Protocol, the People's Democratic Republic of Yemen will consider itself free of its obligation. This reservation appears to be valid for the united state of Yemen, unless stated otherwise by the Government of Yemen.

[25] The Protocol shall cease to be binding on Yugoslavia in regard to any enemy state whose armed forces or whose allies fail to respect the prohibitions which are the object of the Protocol.

The Antarctic Treaty

[1] Romania stated that the provisions of Article XIII, para. 1 of the Treaty were not in accordance with the principle according to which multilateral treaties whose object and purposes concern the international community, as a whole, should be open for universal participation.

[2] In acceding to the Treaty, Uruguay proposed the establishment of a general and definitive statute on Antarctica in which the interests of all states involved and of the international community as a whole would be considered equitably. It also declared that it reserved its rights in Antarctica in accordance with international law.

The Partial Test Ban Treaty

[1] Notification of succession.

[2] The USA considers that Byelorussia and Ukraine are already covered by the signature and ratification by the USSR.

[3] With a statement that this does not imply the recognition of any territory or regime not recognized by this state.

[4] Kuwait stated that its signature and ratification of the Treaty do not in any way imply its recognition of Israel nor oblige it to apply the provisions of the Treaty in respect of the said country.

[5] The UK stated its view that if a regime is not recognized as the government of a state, neither signature nor the deposit of any instrument by it, nor notification of any of those acts, will bring about recognition of that regime by any other state.

The Outer Space Treaty

[1] Notification of succession.

[2] The USA considers that Byelorussia and Ukraine are already covered by the signature and ratification by the USSR.

[3] Brazil interprets Article X of the Treaty as a specific recognition that the granting of tracking facilities by the parties to the Treaty shall be subject to agreement between the states concerned.

[4] This does not imply the recognition of any territory or regime not recognized by this state.

[5] Kuwait acceded to the Treaty with the understanding that this does not in any way imply its recognition of Israel and does not oblige it to apply the provisions of the Treaty in respect of the said country.

[6] Madagascar acceded to the Treaty with the understanding that under Article X of the Treaty the state shall retain its freedom of decision with respect to the possible installation of foreign observation bases in its territory and shall continue to possess the right to fix, in each case, the conditions for such installation.

[7] Syria acceded to the Treaty with the understanding that this should not mean in any way the recognition of Israel, nor should it lead to any relationship with Israel that could arise from the Treaty.

[8] China declared as illegal and null and void the signature and ratification of the Outer Space Treaty by the Taiwan authorities.

The Treaty of Tlatelolco

[1] The Treaty is in force for this country due to a declaration, annexed to the instrument of ratification in accordance with Article 28, para. 2, which waived the requirements for the entry into force of the Treaty, specified in para. 1 of that Article: namely, that all states in the region deposit the instruments of ratification; that Protocol I and Protocol II be signed and ratified by those states to which they apply; and that agreements on safeguards be concluded with the IAEA. (Colombia made this declaration subsequent to the deposit of ratification, as did Nicaragua and Trinidad and Tobago.)

[2] On signing the Treaty, Argentina stated that it understands Article 18 as recognizing the rights of parties to carry out, by their own means or in association with third parties, explosions of nuclear devices for peaceful purposes, including explosions which involve devices similar to those used in nuclear weapons. On 18 July 1991 the Presidents of Argentina and Brazil signed an agreement pledging to abstain from using nuclear explosive devices for any purpose.

[3] On signing the Treaty, Brazil stated that, according to its interpretation, Article 18 of the Treaty gives the signatories the right to carry out, by their own means or in association with third parties, nuclear explosions for peaceful purposes, including explosions which involve devices similar to those used in nuclear weapons. This statement was reiterated at the ratification. On 18 July 1991 the Presidents of Argentina and Brazil signed an agreement pledging to abstain from using nuclear explosive devices for any purpose. Brazil has not waived the requirements for the entry into force of the Treaty laid down in Article 28. The Treaty is therefore not yet in force for Brazil.

[4] Chile has not waived the requirements for the entry into force of the Treaty laid down in Article 28. The Treaty is therefore not yet in force for Chile.

[5] On signing Protocol II, China stated, *inter alia*: China will never use or threaten to use nuclear weapons against non-nuclear Latin American countries and the Latin American nuclear weapon-free zone; nor will China test, manufacture, produce, stockpile, install or deploy nuclear weapons in these countries or in this zone, or send its means of transportation and delivery carrying nuclear weapons to cross the territory, territorial sea or airspace of Latin American countries. The signing of the Protocol does not imply any change whatsoever in China's stand on the disarmament and nuclear weapons issue and, in particular, does not affect its stand against the Non-Proliferation Treaty and the Partial Test Ban Treaty.

China holds that, in order that Latin America may truly become a nuclear weapon-free zone, all nuclear countries, and particularly the superpowers, must undertake not to use or threaten to use nuclear weapons against the Latin American countries and the Latin American nuclear weapon-free zone, and implement the following undertakings: (1) dismantle all foreign military bases in Latin America and refrain from establishing new bases there, and (2) prohibit the passage of any means of transportation and delivery carrying nuclear weapons through Latin American territory, territorial sea or airspace.

[6] On signing Protocol I, France made the following reservations and interpretative statements: The Protocol, as well as the provisions of the Treaty to which it refers, will not affect the right of self-defence under Article 51 of the UN Charter; the application of the legislation referred to in Article 3 of the Treaty relates to legislation which is consistent with international law; the obligations under the Protocol shall not apply to transit across the territories of the French Republic situated in the zone of the Treaty, and destined to other territories of the French Republic; the Protocol shall not limit, in any way, the participation of the populations of the French territories in the activities mentioned in Article 1 of the Treaty, and in efforts connected with the national defence of France; the provisions of Articles 1 and 2 of the Protocol apply to the text of the Treaty as it stands at the time when the Protocol is signed by France, and consequently no amendment to the Treaty that might come into force under Article 29 thereof would be binding on the government of France without the latter's express consent.

[7] On signing Protocol II, France stated that it interprets the undertaking contained in Article 3 of the Protocol to mean that it presents no obstacle to the full exercise of the right of self-defence enshrined in Article 51 of the UN Charter; it takes note of the interpretation of the Treaty given by the Preparatory Commission for the Denuclearization of Latin America and reproduced in the Final Act, according to which the Treaty does not apply to transit, the granting or denying of which lies within the exclusive competence of each state party in accordance with the pertinent principles and rules of international law; it considers that the application of the legislation referred to in Article 3 of the Treaty relates to legislation which is consistent with international law. The provisions of Articles 1 and 2 of the Protocol apply to the text of the Treaty as it stands at the time when the Protocol is signed by France. Consequently, no amendment to the Treaty that might come into force under the provision of Article 29 would be binding on the government of France without the latter's express consent. If this declaration of interpretation is contested in part or in whole by one or more contracting parties to the Treaty or to Protocol II, these instruments would be null and void as far as relations between France and the contesting state or states are concerned. On depositing its instrument of ratification of Protocol II, France stated that it did so subject to the statement made on signing the Protocol. On 15 Apr. 1974, France made a supplementary

statement to the effect that it was prepared to consider its obligations under Protocol II as applying not only to the signatories of the Treaty, but also to the territories for which the statute of denuclearization was in force in conformity with Article 1 of Protocol I.

8 On signing the Treaty, Mexico said that if technological progress makes it possible to differentiate between nuclear weapons and nuclear devices for peaceful purposes, it will be necessary to amend the relevant provisions of the Treaty, according to the procedures established therein.

9 The Netherlands stated that Protocol I shall not be interpreted as prejudicing the position of the Netherlands as regards its recognition or non-recognition of the rights or of claims to sovereignty of the parties to the Treaty, or of the grounds on which such claims are made.

10 Nicaragua stated that it reserved the right to use nuclear energy for peaceful purposes such as the removal of earth for the construction of canals, irrigation works, power plants, and so on, as well as to allow the transit of atomic material through its territory.

11 The USSR signed and ratified Protocol II with the following statement:

The USSR proceeds from the assumption that the effect of Article 1 of the Treaty extends, as specified in Article 5 of the Treaty, to any nuclear explosive device and that, accordingly, the carrying out by any party to the Treaty of explosions of nuclear devices for peaceful purposes would be a violation of its obligations under Article 1 and would be incompatible with its non-nuclear status. For states parties to the Treaty, a solution to the problem of peaceful nuclear explosions can be found in accordance with the provisions of Article V of the Non-Proliferation Treaty and within the framework of the international procedures of the IAEA. The signing of the Protocol by the USSR does not in any way signify recognition of the possibility of the force of the Treaty being extended beyond the territories of the states parties to the Treaty, including airspace and territorial waters as defined in accordance with international law. With regard to the reference in Article 3 of the Treaty to 'its own legislation' in connection with the territorial waters, airspace and any other space over which the states parties to the Treaty exercise sovereignty, the signing of the Protocol by the USSR does not signify recognition of their claims to the exercise of sovereignty which are contrary to generally accepted standards of international law. The USSR takes note of the interpretation of the Treaty given in the Final Act of the Preparatory Commission for the Denuclearization of Latin America to the effect that the transport of nuclear weapons by the parties to the Treaty is covered by the prohibitions in Article 1 of the Treaty. The USSR reaffirms its position that authorizing the transit of nuclear weapons in any form would be contrary to the objectives of the Treaty, according to which, as specially mentioned in the preamble, Latin America must be completely free from nuclear weapons, and that it would be incompatible with the non-nuclear status of the states parties to the Treaty and with their obligations as laid down in Article 1 thereof.

Any actions undertaken by a state or states parties to the Treaty which are not compatible with their non-nuclear status, and also the commission by one or more states parties to the Treaty of an act of aggression with the support of a state which is in possession of nuclear weapons or together with such a state, will be regarded by the USSR as incompatible with the obligations of those countries under the Treaty. In such cases the USSR reserves the right to reconsider its obligations under Protocol II. It further reserves the right to reconsider its attitude to this Protocol in the event of any actions on the part of other states possessing nuclear weapons which are incompatible with their obligations under the said Protocol. The provisions of the articles of Protocol II are applicable to the text of the Treaty of Tlatelolco in the wording of the Treaty at the time of the signing of the Protocol by the Soviet Union, due account being taken of the position of the USSR as set out in the present statement. Any amendment to the Treaty entering into force in accordance with the provisions of Articles 29 and 6 of the Treaty without the clearly expressed approval of the USSR shall have no force as far as the USSR is concerned.

In addition, the USSR proceeds from the assumption that the obligations under Protocol II also apply to the territories for which the status of the denuclearized zone is in force in conformity with Protocol I of the Treaty.

12 When signing and ratifying Protocol I and Protocol II, the UK made the following declarations of understanding: In connection with Article 3 of the Treaty, defining the term 'territory' as including the territorial sea, airspace and any other space over which the state exercises sovereignty in accordance with 'its own legislation', the UK does not regard its signing or ratification of the Protocols as implying recognition of any legislation which does not, in its view, comply with the relevant rules of international law.

The Treaty does not permit the parties to carry out explosions of nuclear devices for peaceful purposes unless and until advances in technology have made possible the development of devices for such explosions which are not capable of being used for weapon purposes.

The signing and ratification by the UK could not be regarded as affecting in any way the legal status of any territory for the international relations of which the UK is responsible, lying within the limits of the geographical zone established by the Treaty.

Should any party to the Treaty carry out any act of aggression with the support of a nuclear weapon state, the UK would be free to reconsider the extent to which it could be regarded as committed by the provisions of Protocol II.

In addition, the UK declared that its undertaking under Article 3 of Protocol II not to use or threaten to use nuclear weapons against the parties to the Treaty extends also to territories in respect of which the undertaking under Article I of Protocol I becomes effective.

[13] The USA ratified Protocol I with the following understandings: The provisions of the Treaty made applicable by this Protocol do not affect the exclusive power and legal competence under international law of a state adhering to this Protocol to grant or deny transit and transport privileges to its own or any other vessels or aircraft irrespective of cargo or armaments; the provisions of the Treaty made applicable by this Protocol do not affect rights under international law of a state adhering to this Protocol regarding the exercise of the freedom of the seas, or regarding passage through or over waters subject to the sovereignty of a state, and the declarations attached by the United States to its ratification of Protocol II apply also to its ratification of Protocol I.

[14] The USA signed and ratified Protocol II with the following declarations and understandings: In connection with Article 3 of the Treaty, defining the term 'territory' as including the territorial sea, airspace and any other space over which the state exercises sovereignty in accordance with 'its own legislation', the ratification of the Protocol could not be regarded as implying recognition of any legislation which does not, in the view of the USA, comply with the relevant rules of international law.

Each of the parties retains exclusive power and legal competence, unaffected by the terms of the Treaty, to grant or deny non-parties transit and transport privileges.

As regards the undertaking not to use or threaten to use nuclear weapons against the parties, the USA would consider that an armed attack by a party, in which it was assisted by a nuclear weapon state, would be incompatible with the party's obligations under Article 1 of the Treaty.

The definition contained in Article 5 of the Treaty is understood as encompassing all nuclear explosive devices; Articles 1 and 5 of the Treaty restrict accordingly the activities of the parties under para. 1 of Article 18.

Article 18, para. 4 permits, and US adherence to Protocol II will not prevent, collaboration by the USA with the parties to the Treaty for the purpose of carrying out explosions of nuclear devices for peaceful purposes in a manner consistent with a policy of not contributing to the proliferation of nuclear weapon capabilities.

The USA will act with respect to such territories of Protocol I adherents, as are within the geographical area defined in Article 4, para. 2 of the Treaty, in the same manner as Protocol II requires it to act with respect to the territories of the Parties.

[15] Venezuela stated that in view of the existing controversy between Venezuela on the one hand and the UK and Guyana on the other, Article 25, para. 2 of the Treaty should apply to Guyana. This paragraph provides that no political entity should be admitted, part or all of whose territory is the subject of a dispute or claim between an extra-continental country and one or more Latin American states, so long as the dispute has not been settled by peaceful means. The relevant provision is about to be amended.

[16] Safeguards agreements under the Non-Proliferation Treaty cover the Treaty of Tlatelolco.

[17] Safeguards agreements under Protocol I.

The Non-Proliferation Treaty

[1] Notification of succession.

[2] Bahrain declared that its accession to the Treaty shall in no way constitute recognition of Israel or be a cause of establishment of any relations of any kind therewith.

[3] On the occasion of the deposit of the instrument of ratification, Egypt stated that since it was embarking on the construction of nuclear power reactors, it expected assistance and support from industrialized nations with a developed nuclear industry. It called upon nuclear weapon states to promote research and development of peaceful applications of nuclear explosions in order to overcome all the difficulties at present involved therein. Egypt also appealed to these states to exert their efforts to conclude an agreement prohibiting the use or threat of use of nuclear weapons against any state, and expressed the view that the Middle East should remain completely free of nuclear weapons.

[4] In June 1991 France announced that it had taken the decision to accede to the Treaty. An agreement between France, the European Atomic Energy Community (Euratom) and the IAEA for the application of safeguards in France had entered into force in 1981. The agreement covers nuclear material and facilities notified to the IAEA by France.

[5] On depositing the instrument of ratification, FR Germany reiterated the declaration made at the time of signing: it reaffirmed its expectation that the nuclear weapon states would intensify their efforts in accordance with the undertakings under Article VI of the Treaty, as well as its understanding that the security of FR Germany continued to be ensured by NATO; it stated that no provision of the Treaty may

be interpreted in such a way as to hamper further development of European unification; that research, development and use of nuclear energy for peaceful purposes, as well as international and multinational co-operation in this field, must not be prejudiced by the Treaty; that the application of the Treaty, including the implementation of safeguards, must not lead to discrimination of the nuclear industry of FR Germany in international competition; and that it attached vital importance to the undertaking given by the USA and the UK concerning the application of safeguards to their peaceful nuclear facilities, hoping that other nuclear weapon states would assume similar obligations.

[6] On acceding to the Treaty, the Holy See stated, *inter alia*, that the Treaty will attain in full the objectives of security and peace and justify the limitations to which the states party to the Treaty submit, only if it is fully executed in every clause and with all its implications. This concerns not only the obligations to be applied immediately but also those which envisage a process of ulterior commitments. Among the latter, the Holy See considers it suitable to point out the following: (a) The adoption of appropriate measures to ensure, on a basis of equality, that all non-nuclear weapon states party to the Treaty will have available to them the benefits deriving from peaceful applications of nuclear technology. (b) The pursuit of negotiations in good faith of effective measures relating to cessation of the nuclear arms race at an early date and to nuclear disarmament, and on a treaty on general and complete disarmament under strict and effective control.

[7] On signing the Treaty, Indonesia stated, *inter alia*, that it attaches great importance to the declarations of the USA, the UK and the USSR affirming their intention to provide immediate assistance to any non-nuclear weapon state party to the Treaty that is a victim of an act of aggression in which nuclear weapons are used. Of utmost importance, however, is not the action *after* a nuclear attack has been committed but the guarantees to prevent such an attack. Indonesia trusts that the nuclear weapon states will study further this question of effective measures to ensure the security of the non-nuclear weapon states. On depositing the instrument of ratification, Indonesia expressed the hope that the nuclear countries would be prepared to co-operate with non-nuclear countries in the use of nuclear energy for peaceful purposes and implement the provisions of Article IV of the Treaty without discrimination. It also stated the view that the nuclear weapon states would observe the provisions of Article VI of the Treaty relating to the cessation of the nuclear arms race.

[8] Italy stated that in its belief nothing in the Treaty was an obstacle to the unification of the countries of Western Europe; it noted full compatibility of the Treaty with the existing security agreements; it noted further that when technological progress would allow the development of peaceful explosive devices different from nuclear weapons, the prohibition relating to their manufacture and use shall no longer apply; it interpreted the provisions of Article IX, para. 3 of the Treaty, concerning the definition of a nuclear weapon state, in the sense that it referred exclusively to the five countries which had manufactured and exploded a nuclear weapon or other nuclear explosive device prior to 1 Jan. 1967, and stressed that under no circumstance would a claim of pertaining to such category be recognized by Italy for any other state.

[9] On depositing the instrument of ratification, Japan expressed the hope that France and China would accede to the Treaty; it urged a reduction of nuclear armaments and a comprehensive ban on nuclear testing; appealed to all states to refrain from the threat or use of force involving either nuclear or non-nuclear weapons; expressed the view that peaceful nuclear activities in non-nuclear weapon states party to the Treaty should not be hampered and that Japan should not be discriminated against in favour of other parties in any aspect of such activities. It also urged all nuclear weapon states to accept IAEA safeguards on their peaceful nuclear activities.

[10] A statement was made containing a disclaimer regarding the recognition of states party to the Treaty.

[11] On depositing the instrument of ratification, the Republic of Korea took note of the fact that the depositary governments of the three nuclear weapon states had made declarations in June 1968 to take immediate and effective measures to safeguard any non-nuclear weapon state which is a victim of an act or an object of a threat of aggression in which nuclear weapons are used. It recalled that the UN Security Council adopted a resolution to the same effect on 19 June 1968.

[12] On depositing the instruments of ratification, Kuwait declared that the ratification of the Treaty does not mean in any way a recognition of Israel. No treaty relation will arise between Kuwait and Israel.

[13] On depositing the instruments of accession and ratification, Liechtenstein and Switzerland stated that activities not prohibited under Articles I and II of the Treaty include, in particular, the whole field of energy production and related operations, research and technology concerning future generations of nuclear reactors based on fission or fusion, as well as production of isotopes. Liechtenstein and Switzerland define the term 'source or special fissionable material' in Article III of the Treaty as being in accordance with Article XX of the IAEA Statute, and a modification of this interpretation requires their formal consent; they will accept only such interpretations and definitions of the terms 'equipment or material especially designed or prepared for the processing, use or production of special fissionable

material', as mentioned in Article III of the Treaty, that they will expressly approve; and they understand that the application of the Treaty, especially of the control measures, will not lead to discrimination of their industry in international competition.

[14] On signing the Treaty, Mexico stated, *inter alia*, that none of the provisions of the Treaty shall be interpreted as affecting in any way whatsoever the rights and obligations of Mexico as a state party to the Treaty of Tlatelolco.

It is the understanding of Mexico that at the present time any nuclear explosive device is capable of being used as a nuclear weapon and that there is no indication that in the near future it will be possible to manufacture nuclear explosive devices that are not potentially nuclear weapons. However, if technological advances modify this situation, it will be necessary to amend the relevant provisions of the Treaty in accordance with the procedure established therein.

[15] The agreement provides for the application of IAEA safeguards in Soviet peaceful nuclear facilities designated by the USSR.

[16] The ratification was accompanied by a statement in which Turkey underlined the non-proliferation obligations of the nuclear weapon states, adding that measures must be taken to meet adequately the security requirements of non-nuclear weapon states. Turkey also stated that measures developed or to be developed at national and international levels to ensure the non-proliferation of nuclear weapons should in no case restrict the non-nuclear weapon states in their option for the application of nuclear energy for peaceful purposes.

[17] The UK recalled its view that if a regime is not recognized as the government of a state, neither signature nor the deposit of any instrument by it, nor notification of any of those acts, will bring about recognition of that regime by any other state.

[18] This agreement, signed by the UK, Euratom and the IAEA, provides for the submission of British non-military nuclear installations to safeguards under IAEA supervision.

[19] This agreement provides for safeguards on fissionable material in all facilities within the USA, excluding those associated with activities of direct national security significance.

[20] In connection with the ratification of the Treaty, Yugoslavia stated, *inter alia*, that it considered a ban on the development, manufacture and use of nuclear weapons and the destruction of all stockpiles of these weapons to be indispensable for the maintenance of a stable peace and international security; it held the view that the chief responsibility for progress in this direction rested with the nuclear weapon powers, and expected these powers to undertake not to use nuclear weapons against the countries which have renounced them as well as against non-nuclear weapon states in general, and to refrain from the threat to use them. It also emphasized the significance it attached to the universality of the efforts relating to the realization of the Non-Proliferation Treaty.

The Seabed Treaty

[1] Notification of succession.

[2] On signing and ratifying the Treaty, Argentina stated that it interprets the references to the freedom of the high seas as in no way implying a pronouncement of judgement on the different positions relating to questions connected with international maritime law. It understands that the reference to the rights of exploration and exploitation by coastal states over their continental shelves was included solely because those could be the rights most frequently affected by verification procedures. Argentina precludes any possibility of strengthening, through this Treaty, certain positions concerning continental shelves to the detriment of others based on different criteria.

[3] On signing the Treaty, Brazil stated that nothing in the Treaty shall be interpreted as prejudicing in any way the sovereign rights of Brazil in the area of the sea, the sea-bed and the subsoil thereof adjacent to its coasts. It is the understanding of Brazil that the word 'observation', as it appears in para. 1 of Article III of the Treaty, refers only to observation that is incidental to the normal course of navigation in accordance with international law. This statement was repeated at the time of ratification. The USA declared, in 1989, that under customary international law and Article III of the Treaty, these observations may be undertaken whether or not they are incidental to a so-called 'normal course of navigation,' and that such activity is not subject to unilateral coastal state restriction. The USSR and the FRG also stated that they did not agree with Brazil's interpretation of the term 'observation'.

[4] In depositing the instrument of ratification, Canada declared: Article I, para. 1, cannot be interpreted as indicating that any state has a right to implant or emplace any weapons not prohibited under Article I, para. 1, on the sea-bed and ocean floor, and in the subsoil thereof, beyond the limits of national jurisdiction, or as constituting any limitation on the principle that this area of the sea-bed and ocean floor and the subsoil thereof shall be reserved for exclusively peaceful purposes. Articles I, II and III cannot be interpreted as indicating that any state but the coastal state has any right to implant or emplace any weapon not prohibited under Article I, para. 1 on the continental shelf, or the subsoil thereof, appertaining to that coastal state, beyond the outer limit of the sea-bed zone referred to in Article I and defined in Article II. Article III cannot be interpreted as indicating any restrictions or limitation upon the rights

of the coastal state, consistent with its exclusive sovereign rights with respect to the continental shelf, to verify, inspect or effect the removal of any weapon, structure, installation, facility or device implanted or emplaced on the continental shelf, or the subsoil thereof, appertaining to that coastal state, beyond the outer limit of the sea-bed zone referred to in Article I and defined in Article II. On 12 Apr. 1976, FR Germany stated that the declaration by Canada is not of a nature to confer on the government of this country more far-reaching rights than those to which it is entitled under current international law, and that all rights existing under current international law which are not covered by the prohibitions are left intact by the Treaty.

[5] The Chinese Government reaffirms that nothing in this Treaty shall be interpreted as prejudicing in any way the sovereign rights and the other rights of the People's Republic of China over its territorial sea, as well as the sea area, the seabed and subsoil thereof adjacent to its territorial sea.

[6] A statement was made containing a disclaimer regarding recognition of states party to the Treaty.

[7] On the occasion of its accession to the Treaty, the government of India stated that as a coastal state, India has, and always has had, full and exclusive rights over the continental shelf adjoining its territory and beyond its territorial waters and the subsoil thereof. It is the considered view of India that other countries cannot use its continental shelf for military purposes. There cannot, therefore, be any restriction on, or limitation of, the sovereign right of India as a coastal state to verify, inspect, remove or destroy any weapon, device, structure, installation or facility, which might be implanted or emplaced on or beneath its continental shelf by any other country, or to take such other steps as may be considered necessary to safeguard its security. The accession by the government of India to the Treaty is based on this position. In response to the Indian statement, the USA expressed the view that, under existing international law, the rights of coastal states over their continental shelves are exclusive only for the purposes of exploration and exploitation of natural resources, and are otherwise limited by the 1958 Convention on the Continental Shelf and other principles of international law. On 12 Apr. 1976, FR Germany stated that the declaration by India is not of a nature to confer on the government of this country more far-reaching rights than those to which it is entitled under current international law, and that all rights existing under current law which are not covered by the prohibitions are left intact by the Treaty.

[8] On signing the Treaty, Italy stated, *inter alia*, that in the case of agreements on further measures in the field of disarmament to prevent an arms race on the sea-bed and ocean floor and in their subsoil, the question of the delimitation of the area within which these measures would find application shall have to be examined and solved in each instance in accordance with the nature of the measures to be adopted. The statement was repeated at the time of ratification.

[9] Mexico declared that in its view no provision of the Treaty can be interpreted to mean that a state has the right to emplace nuclear weapons or other weapons of mass destruction, or arms or military equipment of any type, on the continental shelf of Mexico. It reserves the right to verify, inspect, remove or destroy any weapon, structure, installation, device or equipment placed on its continental shelf, including nuclear weapons or other weapons of mass destruction.

[10] Ratification of the Treaty by Taiwan is considered by Romania as null and void.

[11] The UK recalled its view that if a regime is not recognized as the government of a state neither signature nor the deposit of any instrument by it, nor notification of any of those acts, will bring about recognition of that regime by any other state.

[12] Viet Nam stated that no provision of the Treaty should be interpreted in a way that would contradict the rights of the coastal states with regard to their continental shelf, including the right to take measures to ensure their security.

[13] On 25 Feb. 1974, the Ambassador of Yugoslavia transmitted to the US Secretary of State a note stating that in the view of the Yugoslav Government, Article III, para. 1, of the Treaty should be interpreted in such a way that a state exercising its right under this Article shall be obliged to notify in advance the coastal state, in so far as its observations are to be carried out 'within the stretch of the sea extending above the continental shelf of the said state'. On 16 Jan. 1975 the US Secretary of State presented the view of the USA concerning the Yugoslav note, as follows: In so far as the note is intended to be interpretative of the Treaty, the USA cannot accept it as a valid interpretation. In addition, the USA does not consider that it can have any effect on the existing law of the sea. In so far as the note was intended to be a reservation to the Treaty, the USA placed on record its formal objection to it on the grounds that it was incompatible with the object and purpose of the Treaty. The USA also drew attention to the fact that the note was submitted too late to be legally effective as a reservation. A similar exchange of notes took place between Yugoslavia and the UK on 12 Apr. 1976. FR Germany stated that the declaration by Yugoslavia is not of a nature to confer on the government of this country more far-reaching rights than those to which it is entitled under current international law, and that all rights existing under current international law which are not covered by the prohibitions are left intact by the Treaty.

The BW Convention

[1] Considering the obligations resulting from its status as a permanently neutral state, Austria declares a reservation to the effect that its co-operation within the framework of this Convention cannot exceed the limits determined by the status of permanent neutrality and membership of the UN.

[2] Bahrain declared that its accession to the Convention shall in no way constitute recognition of Israel or be a cause of establishment of any relations of any kind with it.

[3] Notification of succession.

[4] China stated that the BW Convention has the following defects: it fails explicitly to prohibit the use of biological weapons; it does not provide for 'concrete and effective' measures of supervision and verification; and it lacks measures of sanctions in case of violation of the Convention. China hopes that these defects will be corrected at an appropriate time, and also that a convention for complete prohibition of chemical weapons will soon be concluded. The signature and ratification of the Convention by the Taiwan authorities in the name of China are considered illegal and null and void.

[5] On depositing its instrument of ratification, FR Germany stated that a major shortcoming of the BW Convention is that it does not contain any provisions for verifying compliance with its essential obligations. The Federal Government considers the right to lodge a complaint with the UN Security Council to be an inadequate arrangement. It would welcome the establishment of an independent international committee of experts able to carry out impartial investigations when doubts arise as to whether the Convention is being complied with.

[6] In a statement made on the occasion of the signature of the Convention, India reiterated its understanding that the objective of the Convention is to eliminate biological and toxin weapons, thereby excluding completely the possibility of their use, and that the exemption with regard to biological agents or toxins, which would be permitted for prophylactic, protective or other peaceful purposes, would not in any way create a loophole in regard to the production or retention of biological and toxin weapons. Also any assistance which might be furnished under the terms of the Convention would be of a medical or humanitarian nature and in conformity with the UN Charter. The statement was repeated at the time of the deposit of the instrument of ratification.

[7] Ireland considers that the Convention could be undermined if the reservations made by the parties to the 1925 Geneva Protocol were allowed to stand, as the prohibition of possession is incompatible with the right to retaliate, and that there should be an absolute and universal prohibition of the use of the weapons in question. Ireland notified the depositary government for the Geneva Protocol of the withdrawal of its reservations to the Protocol, made at the time of accession in 1930. The withdrawal applies to chemical as well as to bacteriological (biological) and toxin agents of warfare.

[8] The Republic of Korea stated that the signing and ratification of the Convention does not in any way mean or imply the recognition of any territory or regime which has not been recognized by the Republic of Korea as a state or government.

[9] In the understanding of Kuwait, its ratification of the Convention does not in any way imply its recognition of Israel, nor does it oblige it to apply the provisions of the Convention in respect of the said country.

[10] Malaysia's ratification of this convention does not in any way constitute recognition of the states of Israel and South Africa nor does it consider itself duty bound by Article VII to provide assistance to those two states.

[11] Mexico considers that the Convention is only a first step towards an agreement prohibiting also the development, production and stockpiling of all chemical weapons, and notes the fact that the Convention contains an express commitment to continue negotiations in good faith with the aim of arriving at such an agreement.

[12] The ratification by Switzerland contains the following reservations:

1. Owing to the fact that the Convention also applies to weapons, equipment or means of delivery designed to use biological agents or toxins, the delimitation of its scope of application can cause difficulties since there are scarcely any weapons, equipment or means of delivery peculiar to such use; therefore, Switzerland reserves the right to decide for itself what auxiliary means fall within that definition.

2. By reason of the obligations resulting from its status as a perpetually neutral state, Switzerland is bound to make the general reservation that its collaboration within the framework of this Convention cannot go beyond the terms prescribed by that status. This reservation refers especially to Article VII of the Convention as well as to any similar clause that could replace or supplement that provision of the Convention.

In a note of 18 Aug. 1976, addressed to the Swiss Ambassador, the US Secretary of State stated the following view of the USA with regard to the first reservation: The prohibition would apply only to (*a*) weapons, equipment and means of delivery, the design of which indicated that they could have no other use than that specified, and (*b*) weapons, equipment and means of delivery, the design of which indicated that they were specifically intended to be capable of the use specified. The USA shares the view of

Switzerland that there are few weapons, equipment or means of delivery peculiar to the uses referred to. It does not, however, believe that it would be appropriate, on this ground alone, for states to reserve unilaterally the right to decide which weapons, equipment or means of delivery fell within the definition. Therefore, while acknowledging the entry into force of the Convention between itself and Switzerland, the USA enters its objection to this reservation.

[13] The deposit of the instrument of ratification by Taiwan is considered by the Soviet Union as an illegal act because the government of the People's Republic of China is regarded by the USSR as the sole representative of China.

[14] The UK recalled its view that if a regime is not recognized as the government of a state, neither signature nor the deposit of any instrument by it nor notification of any of those acts will bring about recognition of that regime by any other state.

The Enmod Convention

[1] Notification of succession.

[2] Argentina interprets the terms 'widespread, long-lasting or severe effects' in Article I, para. 1, of the Convention in accordance with the definition agreed upon in the Understanding on that article. It likewise interprets Articles II, III and VIII in accordance with the relevant Understandings.

[3] Austria's instrument of accession contains the following reservation: 'Considering the obligations resulting from its status as a permanently neutral state, the Republic of Austria declares a reservation to the effect that its co-operation within the framework of this Convention cannot exceed the limits determined by the status of permanent neutrality and membership of the United Nations'.

[4] Guatemala accepts the text of Article III on condition that the use of environmental techniques for peaceful purposes does not adversely affect its territory or the use of its natural resources.

[5] It is the understanding of the Republic of Korea that any technique for deliberately changing the natural state of rivers falls within the meaning of the term 'environmental modification techniques' as defined in Article II of the Convention. It is further understood that military or any other hostile use of such techniques, which could cause flooding, inundation, reduction in the water-level, drying up, destruction of hydrotechnical installations or other harmful consequences, comes within the scope of the Convention, provided it meets the criteria set out in Article I thereof.

[6] Kuwait made the following reservations and understanding: This Convention binds Kuwait only towards states parties thereto; its obligatory character shall *ipso facto* terminate with respect to any hostile state which does not abide by the prohibition contained therein. It is understood that accession to this Convention does not mean in any way recognition of Israel by Kuwait; furthermore, no treaty relation will arise between Kuwait and Israel.

On 23 June 1980, the UN Secretary-General, the depositary of the Convention, received from the government of Israel a communication stating that Israel would adopt towards Kuwait an attitude of complete reciprocity.

[7] The Netherlands accepts the obligation laid down in Article I of the Enmod Convention as extending to states which are not party to the Convention and which act in conformity with Article I of this Convention.

[8] In the interpretation of New Zealand, nothing in the Convention detracts from or limits the obligations of states to refrain from military or any other hostile use of environmental modification techniques.

[9] Because of its obligation incumbent upon it by virtue of its status of perpetual neutrality, Switzerland made a general reservation specifying that its co-operation in the framework of this Convention cannot go beyond the limits imposed by this status. This reservation refers, in particular, to article V, para. 5, of the Convention, and to any similar clause which may replace or supplement this provision in the Convention.

[10] On signing the Convention, Turkey declared that the terms 'widespread', 'long-lasting' and 'severe effects' contained in the Convention need to be more clearly defined, and that so long as this clarification was not made, Turkey would be compelled to interpret for itself the terms in question and, consequently, reserved the right to do so as and when required. Turkey also stated its belief that the difference between 'military or any other hostile purposes' and 'peaceful purposes' should be more clearly defined so as to prevent subjective evaluations.

The 'Inhumane Weapons' Convention

[1] The accession of Benin refers only to Protocols I and III of the Convention.

[2] Upon signature, China stated that the Convention fails to provide for supervision or verification of any violation of its clauses, thus weakening its binding force. The Protocol on mines, booby traps and other devices fails to lay down strict restrictions on the use of such weapons by the aggressor on the territory of the victim and to provide adequately for the right of a state victim of an aggression to defend

itself by all necessary means. The Protocol on incendiary weapons does not stipulate restrictions on the use of such weapons against combat personnel.

[3] Cyprus declared that the provisions of Article 7, para. 3b, and Article 8 of Protocol II of the Convention will be interpreted in such a way that neither the status of peace-keeping forces or missions of the UN in Cyprus will be affected nor will additional rights be, *ipso jure*, granted to them.

[4] France ratified only Protocols I and II. On signing the Convention France stated that it regretted that it had not been possible to reach agreement on the provisions concerning the verification of facts which might be alleged and which might constitute violations of the undertakings subscribed to. It therefore reserved the right to submit, possibly in association with other states, proposals aimed at filling that gap at the first conference to be held pursuant to Article 8 of the Convention and to utilize, as appropriate, procedures that would make it possible to bring before the international community facts and information which, if verified, could constitute violations of the provisions of the Convention and the Protocols annexed thereto. Reservation: Not being bound by the 1977 Additional Protocol I to the Geneva Conventions of 1949, France considers that para. 4 of the preamble to the Convention on prohibitions or restrictions on the use of certain conventional weapons, which reproduces the provisions of Article 35, para. 3, of Additional Protocol I, applies only to states parties to that Protocol. France will apply the provisions of the Convention and its three Protocols to all the armed conflicts referred to in Articles 2 and 3 common to the Geneva Conventions of 1949.

[5] Italy stated its regret that no agreement had been reached on provisions that would ensure respect for the obligations under the Convention. Italy intends to undertake efforts to ensure that the problem of the establishment of a mechanism that would make it possible to fill this gap in the Convention is taken up again at the earliest opportunity in every competent forum.

[6] The Netherlands made the following statements of understanding: A specific area of land may also be a military objective if, because of its location or other reasons specified in Article 2, para. 4, of Protocol II and in Article I, para. 3, of Protocol III, its total or partial destruction, capture, or neutralization in the prevailing circumstances offers a definitive military advantage; military advantage mentioned in Article 3, para. 3 under c, of Protocol II, refers to the advantage anticipated from the attack considered as a whole and not only from isolated or particular parts of the attack; in Article 8, para. 1, of Protocol II, the words 'as far as it is able' mean 'as far as it is technically able'.

[7] Romania stated that the provisions of the Convention and its Protocols have a restricted character and do not ensure adequate protection either to the civilian population or to the combatants as the fundamental principles of international humanitarian law require.

[8] The USA stated that it had strongly supported proposals by other countries to include special procedures for dealing with compliance matters, and reserved the right to propose at a later date additional procedures and remedies, should this prove necessary, to deal with such problems.

The Treaty of Rarotonga

[1] In signing Protocols 2 and 3 China declared that it respected the status of the South Pacific nuclear-free zone and would neither use nor threaten to use nuclear weapons against the zone nor test nuclear weapons in the region. However, China reserved its right to reconsider its obligations under the Protocols if other nuclear weapon states or the contracting Parties to the Treaty took any action in 'gross' violation of the Treaty and the Protocols, thus changing the status of the zone and endangering the security interests of China. This reservation was not referred to at the time of ratification.

[2] In signing Protocols 2 and 3 the USSR stated the view that admission of transit of nuclear weapons or other nuclear explosive devices by any means, as well as of visits by foreign military ships and aircraft with nuclear explosive devices on board, to the ports and airfields within the nuclear-free zone would contradict the aims of the Treaty of Rarotonga and would be inconsistent with the status of the zone. It also warned that in case of action taken by a party or parties violating their major commitments connected with the nuclear-free status of the zone, as well as in case of aggression committed by one or several parties to the Treaty, supported by a nuclear-weapon state, or together with it, with the use by such a state of the territory, airspace, territorial sea or archipelagic waters of the parties for visits by nuclear weapon-carrying ships and aircraft or for transit of nuclear weapons, the USSR will have the right to consider itself free of its non-use commitments assumed under Protocol 2.

The Soviet Union ratified Protocols 2 and 3 to the Treaty without reference to the conditions included in its statement made at the time of signature. It expressed the hope that all states members of the South Pacific Forum would join the Treaty, and called upon the nuclear powers, which had not done so, to sign and ratify the relevant Protocols.

III. UN member states and year of membership

In the following list of the 175 UN member states as of 1 April 1992, the countries marked with an asterisk are also members of the Geneva-based Conference on Disarmament (CD).

Afghanistan, 1946
Albania, 1955
*Algeria, 1962
Angola, 1976
Antigua and Barbuda, 1981
*Argentina, 1945
Armenia, 1992
*Australia, 1945
Austria, 1955
Azerbaijan, 1992
Bahamas, 1973
Bahrain, 1971
Bangladesh, 1974
Barbados, 1966
Belarus, 1945
*Belgium, 1945
Belize, 1981
Benin, 1960
Bhutan, 1971
Bolivia, 1945
Botswana, 1966
*Brazil, 1945
Brunei Darussalam, 1984
*Bulgaria, 1955
Burkina Faso, 1960
Burma (see Myanmar)
Burundi, 1962
Byelorussia (see Belarus)
Cambodia (Kampuchea), 1955
Cameroon, 1960
*Canada, 1945
Cape Verde, 1975
Central African Republic, 1960
Chad, 1960
Chile, 1945
*China, 1945
Colombia, 1945
Comoros, 1975
Congo, 1960
Costa Rica, 1945
Côte d'Ivoire, 1960
*Cuba, 1945
Cyprus, 1960
*Czechoslovakia, 1945
Denmark, 1945
Djibouti, 1977
Dominica, 1978
Dominican Republic, 1945
Ecuador, 1945
*Egypt, 1945
El Salvador, 1945
Equatorial Guinea, 1968
Estonia, 1991
*Ethiopia, 1945
Fiji, 1970
Finland, 1955

*France, 1945
Gabon, 1960
Gambia, 1965
*Germany, 1973
Ghana, 1957
Greece, 1945
Grenada, 1974
Guatemala, 1945
Guinea, 1958
Guinea-Bissau, 1974
Guyana, 1966
Haiti, 1945
Honduras, 1945
*Hungary, 1955
Iceland, 1946
*India, 1945
*Indonesia, 1950
*Iran, 1945
Iraq, 1945
Ireland, 1955
Israel, 1949
*Italy, 1955
Ivory Coast (see Côte d'Ivoire)
Jamaica, 1962
*Japan, 1956
Jordan, 1955
Kazakhstan, 1992
*Kenya, 1963
Korea, Dem. People's Rep. of (North Korea), 1991
Korea, Rep. of (South Korea), 1991
Kuwait, 1963
Kyrgyzstan, 1992
Lao People's Democratic Republic, 1955
Latvia, 1991
Lebanon, 1945
Lesotho, 1966
Liberia, 1945
Libya, 1955
Liechtenstein, 1990
Lithuania, 1991
Luxembourg, 1945
Madagascar, 1960
Malawi, 1964
Malaysia, 1957
Maldives, 1965
Mali, 1960
Malta, 1964
Marshall Islands, 1991
Mauritania, 1961
Mauritius, 1968
*Mexico, 1945
Micronesia, 1991
Moldova, 1992

*Mongolia, 1961
*Morocco, 1956
Mozambique, 1975
*Myanmar (formerly Burma), 1948
Namibia, 1990
Nepal, 1955
*Netherlands, 1945
New Zealand, 1945
Nicaragua, 1945
Niger, 1960
*Nigeria, 1960
Norway, 1945
Oman, 1971
*Pakistan, 1947
Panama, 1945
Papua New Guinea, 1975
Paraguay, 1945
*Peru, 1945
Philippines, 1945
*Poland, 1945
Portugal, 1955
Qatar, 1971
*Romania, 1955
Rwanda, 1962
Saint Christopher (Kitts) and Nevis, 1983
Saint Lucia, 1979
Saint Vincent and the Grenadines, 1980
Samoa, Western, 1976
San Marino, 1992
Sao Tome and Principe, 1975
Saudi Arabia, 1945
Senegal, 1960
Seychelles, 1976
Sierra Leone, 1961
Singapore, 1965
Solomon Islands, 1978
Somalia, 1960
South Africa, 1945
Spain, 1955
*Sri Lanka, 1955
Sudan, 1956
Suriname, 1975
Swaziland, 1968
*Sweden, 1946
Syria, 1945
Tajikistan, 1992
Tanzania, 1961
Thailand, 1946
Togo, 1960
Trinidad and Tobago, 1962
Tunisia, 1956
Turkey, 1945
Turkmenistan, 1992
Uganda, 1962

*UK, 1945
  Ukraine, 1945
  United Arab Emirates, 1971
  Uruguay, 1945
*USA, 1945
*USSR, 1945
  Uzbekistan, 1992
  Vanuatu, 1981
*Venezuela, 1945
  Viet Nam, 1977
  Yemen, 1947[a]
*Yugoslavia, 1945
*Zaire, 1960
  Zambia, 1964
  Zimbabwe, 1980

---

[a] Yemen Arab Republic, 1947;
People's Democratic Republic of
Yemen, 1967.

Annexe B. Chronology 1991

RAGNHILD FERM

For the convenience of the reader, key words are indicated in the right-hand column, opposite each entry. They refer to the subject-areas covered in the entry. Definitions of the acronyms can be found on page xiv.

7–18 Jan.	The parties to the 1963 Partial Test Ban Treaty (PTBT) meet in New York at an Amendment Conference. A decision is adopted, stating that further work needs to be undertaken towards a comprehensive test ban. (74 parties vote in favour of the decision, the USA and the UK vote against, and 19 parties abstain.)	Nuclear tests
12 Jan.	The Council of Ministers of the USSR decides to implement a unilateral moratorium on nuclear tests in the following four months.	USSR; Nuclear tests
12 Jan.	The US Congress authorizes the Administration to use force against Iraq.	Iraq/Kuwait; USA
17 Jan. (GMT)	US-led multinational Coalition forces begin an air offensive against Iraq. Iraqi targets in Kuwait and Iraq are attacked.	Iraq/Kuwait; UN; USA
17 Jan.	The first Iraqi Scud missiles hit Israel.	Iraq/Kuwait; Israel
21 Jan.	At a foreign ministers meeting in Budapest, Czechoslovakia, Hungary and Poland agree to withdraw all cooperation with the WTO with effect from 1 July 1991. On the same day the defence ministers of Hungary and Czechoslovakia sign a five-year bilateral defence treaty.	Czechoslovakia, Hungary, Poland/WTO
27 Jan.	The Indian–Pakistani agreement prohibiting attack on each other's nuclear installations (signed on 31 Dec. 1988) enters into force, as the two countries exchange instruments of ratification.	India/Pakistan
29 Jan.	In his State of the Union address, President Bush says that the SDI programme will now be refocused on global protection against limited strikes (GPALS), whatever their source. The new programme should be able to deal with any threat to the USA, its overseas forces or its friends and allies, whatever the source.	USA; GPALS; SDI; ABM
1 Feb.	Speaking to the Parliament, the President of South Africa declares that all remaining apartheid legislation will be abolished.	South Africa

9 Feb.	A referendum on independence is held in Lithuania. Over 90% of the voters vote in favour. (On 11 Feb. the Supreme Council of Lithuania adopts a law proposing independence.)	Lithuania/USSR
15 Feb.	Iraq offers to withdraw from Kuwait, provided that Israel withdraws from Palestine and Arab territories, the multinational Coalition forces withdraw from the Gulf region within one month after a cease-fire is declared, all UN Security Council resolutions on the conflict are annulled and economic sanctions lifted, Iraq is paid for reparation of the damage caused by the Coalition forces, and all Iraqi debts are cancelled. The offer is immediately dismissed by the Coalition.	Iraq/Kuwait; UN
21 Feb.	A Soviet plan for peace in the Gulf area is accepted by Iraq. It includes a full and unconditional withdrawal of Iraqi forces from Kuwait beginning on the second day after the cessation of hostilities. UN sanctions would cease to apply when two-thirds of Iraqi forces are withdrawn, and the withdrawal is to be completed within 21 days.	Iraq/Kuwait; USSR
22 Feb.	The USA gives an ultimatum that, unless Iraq starts to withdraw from Kuwait on 23 Feb. and complete the withdrawal within seven days, the Coalition will start a ground offensive.	Iraq/Kuwait; USA
24 Feb.	As Iraq does not observe the ultimatum of 22 Feb., the Coalition forces begin a ground offensive against Iraq.	Iraq/Kuwait; UN
25 Feb.	Iraqi President Saddam Hussein orders Iraqi armed forces to withdraw from Kuwait.	Iraq/Kuwait
25 Feb.	The member countries of the WTO, meeting in Budapest, sign a protocol on terminating the military agreements within the WTO and abolishing its military structures as of 31 Mar. 1991.	WTO
26 Feb.	Iraqi forces begin to withdraw from Kuwait.	Iraq/Kuwait
27 Feb.	The Iraqi Government informs the UN that it unconditionally accepts all 12 UN Security Council resolutions on Kuwait.	Iraq/Kuwait; UN
27 Feb.	Poland and Czechoslovakia sign a military co-operation agreement.	Poland/ Czechoslovakia
28 Feb. (GMT)	President Bush announces that Kuwait is liberated and allied military action suspended.	Iraq/Kuwait; UN; USA
2 Mar.	The UN Security Council adopts Resolution 686, calling on Iraq to take the necessary measures which would permit a definitive end to the hostilities in the Gulf region. (Cuba votes against; China, India and Yemen abstain.)	Iraq/Kuwait; UN

3 Mar.	Referendums on independence are held in Estonia and Latvia. In both states over 70% of the voters vote in favour.	Estonia; Latvia/ USSR
6 Mar.	The USA expands its system of export controls to prevent proliferation to Third World countries of CBW and ballistic missiles.	USA; CBW; Ballistic missiles
17 Mar.	An all-Union referendum on the preservation of the Soviet Union is held. Six republics (Armenia, Georgia, Estonia, Latvia, Lithuania and Moldova) refuse to participate, for different reasons. The results of the referendum in the nine remaining republics vary.	USSR
31 Mar.	The military structures of the WTO are formally dissolved.	WTO
31 Mar.	A referendum on independence is held in Georgia (USSR). Nearly 99% of the voters vote in favour. (On 9 Apr. 1991 the Supreme Soviet of Georgia adopts a declaration on independence.)	Georgia/USSR
3 Apr.	The UN Security Council adopts Resolution 687 declaring that a cease-fire would be effective between Iraq and Kuwait and the states co-operating with Kuwait in accordance with UN Security Resolution 678 of 29 Nov. 1990. The UN Secretary-General is requested to submit a plan for the immediate deployment of UN observers to monitor a demilitarized zone on both sides of the Kuwait–Iraq border. Iraq should unconditionally accept the destruction, removal or rendering harmless of all its CBW and its ballistic missiles with a range of over 150 km and should submit within 15 days a declaration of all such weapons possessed by Iraq as well as Iraqi nuclear-weapons usable material and related facilities. A UN Special Commission (UNSCOM) should be established to carry out on-site inspections of the above items. The IAEA is requested to carry out, in co-operation with UNSCOM, immediate on-site inspection of Iraqi nuclear capabilities. (Cuba votes against; Yemen and Ecuador abstain from voting.)	Iraq/Kuwait; NBC; UN; IAEA
6 Apr.	Iraq notifies the UN Secretary-General and the Security Council of its official acceptance of the provisions of Resolution 687, and a formal cease-fire thereby takes effect between Iraq and Kuwait and the UN member states co-operating with Kuwait in the Coalition force.	Iraq/Kuwait; UN
9 Apr.	The UN Security Council unanimously adopts Resolution 689 providing for the establishment of a UN Iraq–Kuwait Observation Mission (UNIKOM). (See *3 Apr.*)	Iraq/Kuwait; UN

18 Apr.	In accordance with UN Security Council Resolution 687, Iraq reports that all its nuclear material remains under IAEA control. It submits reports listing its stock of ballistic missiles and CW and states that it does not possess binary CW nor BW. It informs that it has now ratified the BW Convention. (UNSCOM decides that the list is not complete. A declaration, admitting the possession of some nuclear material and facilities in addition to those known to the IAEA, is submitted on 27 Apr. On 16 May Iraq submits an expanded list of items listed in Resolution 687.)	Iraq; UN; CBW; IAEA
23 Apr.	President Gorbachev signs a pact with nine of the Soviet republics (Azerbaijan, Belarus, Kazakhstan, Kyrgyzstan, Russia, Tajikistan, Turkmenistan, Uzbekistan and Ukraine), aimed at achieving stable relations between the central and republican governments.	USSR
12 May	The last Soviet SS-20 missiles are destroyed, completing the elimination of all missiles covered by the INF Treaty ahead of the 1 June 1991 deadline. (The last US ground-launched cruise missile was destroyed on 1 May, and the last US Pershing II missile on 6 May.)	INF Treaty
13 May	President Bush states that when a CW convention enters into force the USA forswears the use of CW for any reason, including retaliation. All US CW will be destroyed within 10 years of that date. (He thereby drops the previous US position that the USA and certain other states must be allowed to keep at least 2% of their CW stockpile until all CW-capable states have joined the convention.) This initiative is presented to the CD on 16 May.	USA; CW; CD
20 May	The UN Security Council adopts Resolution 692 approving the establishment of a compensation fund to be financed by Iraq's oil exports to pay damages incurred by foreign governments, nationals and corporations during the Gulf War. (Cuba abstains from voting.)	Iraq; UN
28–29 May	The NATO Defence Planning Committee and Nuclear Planning Group, meeting in ministerial session in Brussels, agree on a new force structure, including rapid reaction forces, of which the Rapid Reaction Corps should be under British command.	NATO; UK
29 May	Addressing the US Air Force Academy in Colorado Springs, USA, President Bush announces a proposal to ban weapons of mass destruction in the Middle East, to regulate sales of conventional weapons to the region, and to freeze the production and testing of surface-to-surface missiles by states in the region.	USA; Middle East; NBC; Arms transfers

31 May	A peace agreement for Angola is signed in Lisbon by the MPLA–PT (Popular Liberation Movement of Angola–Worker's Party) and UNITA (National Union for the Total Independence of Angola), witnessed by the UN Secretary-General, the US Secretary of State, the Soviet Foreign Minister and the Chairman of the OAU (Organization of African Unity).	Angola
3 June	France presents an arms control and disarmament plan, covering conventional weapons as well as weapons of mass destruction. The plan calls for the prohibition and elimination of CW and BW. It states that France already applies all the terms of the NPT and has taken the decision to accede to the Treaty. France supports the 1987 Guidelines for a Missile Technology Control Regime and suggests a more extensive, better verifiable agreement, applicable to all states.	France; NBC; NPT; MTCR
6–7 June	The North Atlantic Council, meeting in Copenhagen, declares that the development of a European security identity and defence role will reinforce the integrity and effectiveness of NATO. In a separate statement on Partnership with the Countries of Central and Eastern Europe, the Council suggests initiatives for expanded contacts in security questions.	NATO
12 June	As the first democratically elected Russian head of state, Boris Yeltsin is elected President of Russia.	Russia
14 June	At the CFE 1A talks the Soviet Union presents a legally binding document showing how it will comply with the limits on equipment laid down in the CFE Treaty. The other CFE signatories submit binding declarations accepting the Soviet pledges.	CFE Treaty; USSR
17 June	The UN Security Council adopts Resolution 699, approving the IAEA plan for the destruction, removal or rendering harmless of Iraq's nuclear-weapon usable material and related facilities. (See *3 Apr.*)	Iraq; IAEA; UN
17 June	Germany and Poland sign a 10-year Treaty of Good Neighbourliness and Friendly Co-operation.	Germany/ Poland
18 June	Addressing the Aspen Institute, Berlin, the US Secretary of State says that the CSCE should be seen as a framework, not a unitary body, for the Euro-Atlantic agenda and should contribute to create the political, economic and security conditions that may defuse conflict. As a strong defensive alliance, NATO would provide a foundation of stability within Europe as a whole, and its arms control agenda would augment this security. The EC, the Council of Europe and the OECD should create a network of political and economic support.	USA/Europe

19 June	The USSR completes its withdrawal of troops from Czechoslovakia and Hungary.	USSR/ Czechoslovakia, Hungary
19 June	The CSCE Council of Foreign Ministers, meeting in Berlin, issues a statement on the situation in Yugoslavia. It expresses support for the unity and territorial integrity of Yugoslavia and stresses that only the peoples of Yugoslavia can decide on the country's future.	Yugoslavia; CSCE
19–20 June	At the first session of the CSCE Council of Foreign Ministers, held in Berlin, a mechanism for consultation and co-operation with regard to emergency situations is adopted. A detailed mandate for the Conflict Prevention Centre suspends the CSCE unanimity rule, allowing a minimum of 13 members to convene emergency meetings. Albania is admitted as a member state of the CSCE.	CSCE; Albania
20 June	The CD adopts a new mandate which includes the prohibition of the use of CW as well as a request to strive to achieve final agreement on a CW convention by 1992.	CD; CW
25 June	The Croatian and Slovenian parliaments adopt declarations of independence. At an emergency session, the Yugoslav Parliament calls on the national forces to intervene and protect Yugoslavia's border. The next day troop movements and military overflights are reported.	Croatia, Slovenia/ Yugoslavia
30 June–3 July	The UN Security Council dispatches a high-level mission, including the Chairman of the Special Commission (UNSCOM), the Director-General of the IAEA and the UN Under Secretary-General for Disarmament Affairs, to Baghdad to discuss Iraq's non-compliance with Resolution 687 and refusal of access during inspections.	Iraq; UN; IAEA
1 July	The member states of the Warsaw Treaty Organization sign a protocol on terminating the validity of the 1955 Treaty of Friendship, Co-operation and Mutual Assistance.	WTO
1–2 July	The CSCE Conflict Prevention Centre, meeting for the first time, in Vienna, calls for an immediate cease-fire in Yugoslavia but fails to reach agreement on sending a CSCE observation mission.	Yugoslavia/ CSCE
3–4 July	The first emergency meeting of the CSCE Committee of Senior Officials is convened in Prague, at the instigation of the EC, to discuss the situation in Yugoslavia. The Committee recommends the dispatch of an EC-based mission to Yugoslavia.	Yugoslavia/ CSCE; EC
7 July	Iraq submits information to the IAEA indicating that it has violated the Non-Proliferation Treaty by engaging in unsafeguarded nuclear activities, specifically uranium enrichment with calutrons.	Iraq; NPT; IAEA

9 July	Representatives of the five permanent members of the UN Security Council, meeting in Paris, state that they would not transfer conventional weapons in circumstances which would undermine stability and undertake to seek effective measures to stop proliferation of weapons of mass destruction. They strongly support the objective of establishing a weapons of mass destruction-free zone in the Middle East and the implementation of UN Security Council Resolution 687. (See *3 Apr.*)	UN; NBC; Middle East; Arms transfers
10 July	South Africa accedes to the Non-Proliferation Treaty. (The safeguards agreement with the IAEA enters into force on 16 Sep. 1991.)	South Africa; NPT
16 July	The heads of government of the Group of Seven Western industrialized countries (the G7), meeting in London, issue a statement on arms control, calling for a universal register of transfers of conventional weapons under the auspices of the UN.	G7; Arms transfers; UN
17 July	Presidents Bush and Gorbachev, meeting in London at the G7 meeting, agree on the final details of a START Treaty.	G7; USA/USSR; START
18 July	An agreement between Argentina and Brazil for the exclusively peaceful use of nuclear energy is signed at Guadalajara, Mexico, by the two states' presidents. The parties agree to abstain from carrying out the testing, use, manufacture, production or acquisition by any means of any nuclear explosive device and to submit all the nuclear materials in all their nuclear activities to a common system of accounting and control. An Argentinian–Brazilian Agency for Accounting and Control of Nuclear Materials (ABACC) shall administer and implement the system.	Argentina/ Brazil; NPT; Treaty of Tlatelolco
18 July	The IAEA declares that Iraq has violated its safeguards agreements with the Agency under the Non-Proliferation Treaty by not submitting nuclear material and relevant facilities in its uranium enrichment programme to IAEA inspection.	Iraq; IAEA; NPT
25 July	At the CD Sweden presents a draft Comprehensive Test Ban Treaty.	CD; Sweden; CTB
30 July	The US Department of Defense announces a plan to close nearly 80 of the US military bases in Europe.	USA; Military bases
31 July	The US Senate adopts a plan, the Missile Defense Act, calling for the construction of a single treaty-compliant ABM site by 1996 as the initial step towards a nation-wide missile defence incorporating 'one or an adequate additional number' of ABM sites and ABM interceptors,	USA/USSR; ABM Treaty

space-based battle-management sensors, and an unspecified relaxation of limits on ABM testing. If the USSR does not agree, the USA could 'consider the options available', including withdrawal from the ABM Treaty. The US President is urged to negotiate with the USSR to modify the ABM Treaty.

31 July–1 Aug.   At a summit meeting held in Moscow the US and Soviet Presidents sign (on 31 July) the START Treaty, reducing US and Soviet strategic offensive weapons to equal aggregate levels over a seven-year period and setting numerical limits on deployed strategic nuclear delivery vehicles (ICBMs, SLBMs and heavy bombers) and their nuclear warheads. The two Presidents agree that an international Middle East conference should be held in Oct. 1991.   USA/USSR; START; Middle East

10 Aug.   At a meeting held in Beijing between the Chinese and Japanese Prime Ministers, China announces that it has decided to accede to the Non-Proliferation Treaty.   China; NPT

15 Aug.   The UN Security Council unanimously adopts Resolution 707, demanding that Iraq provide full disclosure of its programmes to develop weapons of mass destruction and their missiles and to halt all nuclear activities except those for isotopes for medical and agricultural purposes, until it has complied with UN Security Council Resolution 687 and its IAEA safeguards agreement.   UN; Iraq; IAEA; NBC

19 Aug.   In a military coup, Soviet Vice President Yanayev assumes power from President Gorbachev and declares a six-month state of emergency in the USSR. All power in the country is transferred to the State Committee for the State of Emergency in the USSR.   USSR

21 Aug.   The coup in the USSR collapses. In a broadcast statement, President Gorbachev declares that he is again in control of the USSR. A State Council will be responsible for foreign affairs, the military, law enforcement and security.   USSR

24 Aug.   President Gorbachev resigns as the head of the Soviet Communist Party and disbands its leadership.   USSR

24 Aug.   The Supreme Soviet of Ukraine adopts a resolution proclaiming Ukraine an independent state. (On 1 Dec. 1991 a referendum on independence is held in Ukraine. Over 90% of the voters vote in favour.)   Ukraine/ USSR

25 Aug.   The Supreme Soviet of Byelorussia (Belarus) adopts a declaration of independence.   Belarus/ USSR

27 Aug.   The Supreme Soviet of Moldova adopts a declaration of independence.   Moldova / USSR

29 Aug.	The Supreme Soviet of the USSR votes to suspend all activities of the Soviet Communist Party. (283 members vote in favour, 29 against and 52 abstain from voting.)	USSR
29 Aug.	The President of Kazakhstan issues a decree closing the nuclear test site at Semipalatinsk.	USSR; Kazakhstan; Nuclear tests
30 Aug.	Azerbaijan declares independence. (On 18 Oct. 1991 the Supreme Soviet of Azerbaijan adopts a constitutional act of independence.)	Azerbaijan/ USSR
31 Aug.	The Supreme Soviet of Uzbekistan adopts a declaration of independence.	Uzbekistan/ USSR
31 Aug.	The Supreme Soviet of Kyrgyzstan adopts a declaration of independence.	Kyrgyzstan/ USSR
5 Sep.	The Foreign Ministers of Argentina, Brazil and Chile, meeting in Mendoza, Argentina, sign a joint declaration (the Mendoza Agreement) on the complete prohibition of chemical and biological weapons. Their countries will proclaim the region a peace zone and refrain from the development, production and purchase of chemical weapons. (Uruguay accedes to the Agreement.)	CBW; Argentina/ Brazil/Chile/ Uruguay
6 Sep.	The State Council of the USSR unanimously votes to recognize the independence of Estonia, Latvia and Lithuania.	Estonia, Latvia, Lithuania/USSR
7 Sep.	An EC peace conference on Yugoslavia is opened in The Hague.	Yugoslavia; EC
8 Sep.	In a referendum held in Macedonia, 95% vote in favour of a 'sovereign and independent Macedonia with a right to enter a union of sovereign states of Yugoslavia'.	Macedonia/ Yugoslavia
9 Sep.	The Supreme Soviet of Tajikistan adopts a declaration of independence.	Tajikistan/ USSR
9–27 Sep.	The Third Review Conference of the 1972 Biological Weapons Convention is held in Geneva. The meeting agrees to strengthen measures to enforce the Treaty and delegates a working group to study the feasibility of monitoring mechanisms.	BW
10 Sep.–4 Oct.	The third Meeting on the Human Dimension of the CSCE is held in Moscow. On the opening day, Estonia, Latvia and Lithuania are admitted as members of the CSCE.	CSCE; Baltic states
11 Sep.	President Gorbachev informs the US Secretary of State that the USSR intends to withdraw its military forces from Cuba.	USSR/Cuba

13 Sep.	The US Secretary of State and the Soviet Foreign Minister, meeting in Moscow, announce that their governments have agreed to stop weapon deliveries to Afghanistan. Other countries are also encouraged to stop arms exports to Afghanistan. The UN is requested to supervise a transition to free elections for a new Afghan government.	Afghanistan; USA/USSR; UN
14 Sep.	A peace agreement is signed in Johannesburg by the South African Government and a number of political parties and organizations, among them the ANC (African National Congress) and the Inkatha Freedom Party.	South Africa
17 Sep.	The UN General Assembly accepts the former Soviet republics of Estonia, Latvia and Lithuania, and North Korea and South Korea as well as the federal states of the Marshall Islands and Micronesia as members of the UN, bringing the total number of member states to 166.	UN
20 Sep.	The IAEA adopts a resolution on strengthening the effectiveness and efficiency of the Agency's safeguards system.	IAEA
21 Sep.	A referendum is held in Armenia on independence. Nearly 95% of the voters vote in favour. (The Supreme Soviet of Armenia proclaims Armenia an independent state on 23 Sep.)	Armenia/USSR
24 Sep.	A cease-fire agreement is reached between Azerbaijan and Armenia in the armed conflict over the Armenian enclave of Nagorno-Karabakh in Azerbaijan.	Azerbaijan/ Armenia
25 Sep.	The UN Security Council unanimously adopts Resolution 713, imposing an embargo on all deliveries of weapons and military equipment to Yugoslavia.	Yugoslavia; UN
27 Sep.	President Bush presents an initiative for unilateral US arms reductions: withdrawal and destruction of all land-based nuclear artillery shells and nuclear warheads for short-range ballistic missiles; removal of all tactical nuclear weapons, from surface ships and attack submarines as well as nuclear weapons associated with land-based naval aircraft; removal of strategic bombers from alert status as well as ICBMs scheduled for deactivation under the START Treaty; and termination of the development of the mobile versions of the MX and Midgetman missile systems and new short-range missiles.	USA; SNF
3 Oct.	At the US–Soviet Defence and Space Talks in Geneva, the USA presents its proposal for 'a new legal regime' to permit limited deployment of strategic ballistic missile defence systems (Global Protection Against Limited Strikes, GPALS).	USA/USSR; Outer space: GPALS; SDI; ABM

4 Oct.	A Protocol to the 1959 Antarctic Treaty on environmental protection, banning mineral and ore exploration in Antarctica for 50 years, is signed in Madrid.	Antarctic Treaty
4 Oct.	The UK and Italy issue a joint declaration proposing the creation of a rapid reaction force for operations outside the NATO area of operations under the Western European Union (WEU).	UK; Italy; WEU
5 Oct.	In response to President Bush's nuclear reduction initiative of 27 Sep., President Gorbachev announces that the USSR will destroy all its nuclear artillery shells, nuclear mines and tactical missile nuclear warheads. All nuclear surface-to-air missiles and tactical nuclear weapons on surface ships and multi-purpose submarines will be withdrawn or destroyed. Strategic bombers and some 500 ICBMs will no longer be on alert. The programmes for mobile small ICBMs and a modified short-range nuclear missile will be halted. A further 50% cut in strategic weapons should be negotiated as soon as the START Treaty is ratified. The USSR announces a unilateral one-year moratorium on nuclear weapon tests and urges the USA to do the same. (On 15 Oct. the US Defense Secretary rejects the moratorium proposal.)	USSR; SNF; Strategic weapons; Nuclear tests
5 Oct.	At a meeting of the Baltic Council in Vilnius, Estonia, Latvia and Lithuania demand the withdrawal of the Soviet Army from their territories by the beginning of Dec. 1991 and that nuclear weapons be immediately removed.	Baltics; Nuclear weapons
8 Oct.	The IAEA director informs the UN Security Council that the sixth UN inspection team to Iraq has found documents showing that a programme to produce lithium 6 has been conducted by Iraq. A small quantity of lithium has already been produced, and large-scale production was planned.	Iraq; IAEA; UN
11 Oct.	The UN Security Council unanimously adopts Resolution 715, approving plans aimed at eliminating Iraq's nuclear, chemical and biological weapons and monitoring Iraq's compliance with Resolutions 687 and 707. (See *3 Apr.* and *15 Aug.*)	UN; Iraq; NBC
16 Oct.	France and Germany announce their joint initiative for a European Political Union (first presented in Apr. 1990). The Union should include the implementation of a common foreign and security policy which, in the long term, would include a common defence and a step-by-step buildup of the WEU as a component of the Union's defence. Franco-German co-operation will be reinforced beyond the existing brigade (4200 men) in order to form the nucleus of a European corps (of some 35 000 men) which could include forces from other WEU member states.	France/Germany/EC; WEU

17–18 Oct.	The five permanent members of the UN Security Council, meeting in London, agree to avoid weapon transfers that could prolong or aggravate an existing armed conflict, increase tension in a region, contribute to regional instability or seriously undermine the recipient state's economy. They pledge to inform each other about transfers of major conventional weapon systems to the Middle East.	UN; Arms transfers
18 Oct.	The NATO Nuclear Planning Group, meeting in Taormina, Italy, endorses President Bush's nuclear reduction initiative of 27 Sep. and confirms that NATO nuclear weapons stationed in Europe will thereby be reduced by 80%. The remaining NATO nuclear forces in Europe will consist of dual-capable aircraft with widespread participation in nuclear roles and peacetime basing by allies.	NATO; Nuclear weapons
18 Oct.	A Protocol is signed in Rome between the Mozambican Government and the MNR (National Resistance Movement) rebels laying out political guarantees for a peaceful settlement of the conflict in Mozambique.	Mozambique
18 Oct.	The CFE Joint Consultative Group, meeting in Vienna, states that it acknowledges that the area of application of the Treaty no longer includes the territories of the Baltic states. It declares that the treaty-limited equipment (TLE) in the area will be included in the Soviet ceilings and subject to CFE inspections.	CFE; Baltics
22 Oct.	The Ukrainian Supreme Soviet adopts a draft law on the creation of Ukrainian armed forces of some 450 000 troops. (On 24 Oct. a statement is made demanding a veto right over the use of nuclear weapons on Ukrainian territory. Ukraine will pursue a policy aimed at the complete annihilation of nuclear weapons.)	Ukraine; Nuclear weapons
23 Oct.	An Agreement on a comprehensive political settlement of the Cambodia conflict, ending 13 years of civil war, is signed in Paris by the warring factions in Cambodia and 19 states, including the five permanent members of the UN Security Council. Cambodia's neutrality shall be proclaimed and enshrined in the constitution which will be adopted after free and fair elections. The UN undertakes to administer the peace-keeping operations.	Cambodia; UN
23 Oct.	The UN Special Commission (UNSCOM) presents its report to the UN Security Council. The inspections carried out in Iraq have uncovered a vast amount of data and material indicating one of the largest military production programmes in the developing world.	UN; Iraq
26 Oct.	Supporting President Gorbachev's decision on a one-year test moratorium, Russian President Yeltsin issues a decree stating that the Novaya Zemlya archipelago will no longer be used for nuclear tests.	USSR; Nuclear tests

26 Oct.	An agreement is initialled in Moscow between Poland and the USSR on withdrawal of Soviet combat units from Poland by 15 Nov. 1992 and support units by the end of 1993. (The USSR began to withdraw its troops from Poland on 9 Apr.)	Poland/USSR
26 Oct.	A referendum on independence is held in Turkmenistan. Over 90% of the voters vote in favour. (On 27 Oct. the Turkmenian Supreme Soviet adopts a law on independence.)	Turkmenistan/ USSR
30 Oct.–1 Nov.	The opening session of a Peace Conference on the Middle East is held in Madrid. Delegations from Israel, Lebanon, Syria and a joint Jordanian–Palestinian delegation participate. The USA and the USSR are co-sponsors; a special UN representative is present as an observer.	Middle East; USA; USSR; UN
5 Nov.	At the Open Skies talks, held in Vienna, the USSR presents a proposal which implies that it is now prepared to allow aerial surveillance of all its territory.	Open Skies; USSR
8 Nov.	The NATO heads of state and government participating in the North Atlantic Council meeting, held in Rome, issue a New Strategic Concept which, while reaffirming NATO's core functions, allows NATO within a radically changed situation in Europe to pursue a broad approach to stability and security, encompassing political, economic, social and environmental aspects along with the defence dimension. It was agreed that the European defence role can be seen as a contribution in developing a strong new trans-Atlantic partnership by strengthening the European component in a transformed alliance. The establishment of a North Atlantic Co-operation Council (NACC) is proposed, and the foreign ministers of Bulgaria, Czechoslovakia, Estonia, Hungary, Latvia, Lithuania, Poland, Romania and the USSR are invited to participate in the next meeting of the North Atlantic Council to issue a joint declaration to launch this initiative. (See *20 Dec.*)	NATO; NACC; Europe
8 Nov.	The EC Council of Ministers, meeting at the NATO summit meeting in Rome, agree on imposing trade sanctions on Yugoslavia and propose a UN Security Council oil embargo.	Yugoslavia; EC; UN
8 Nov.	The South Korean President declares that South Korea will not manufacture, possess, store, deploy or use nuclear weapons nor develop nuclear enrichment facilities. It calls upon North Korea to make a similar pledge. South Korea also pledged to implement a policy of not possessing CBW.	South Korea; NBC
15 Nov.	China informs the IAEA that it will in the future provide the Agency with information on its exports and imports of nuclear material.	China; NPT, IAEA

21 Nov.	A broad coalition of senior US senators present a plan (based on a Harvard study) to provide funds to assist the USSR in dismantling its nuclear arsenal and to prevent nuclear weapons outside the Russian Republic from falling into unauthorized hands. The Congress authorizes $400 million.	USA; USSR; Nuclear weapons
25 Nov.	The US Senate ratifies the CFE Treaty. (The instruments of ratification are deposited on 29 Jan. 1992.)	USA; CFE
25 Nov.	The US Administration submits the START Treaty to the Senate for ratification.	START; USA
4 Dec.	The heads of state of the member states of the Andean Group (Bolivia, Colombia, Ecuador, Peru and Venezuela), meeting in Cartagena de Indias, Colombia, sign a declaration on the renunciation of weapons of mass destruction. They also consider it necessary to halt all nuclear tests.	Andean Group; NBC; Nuclear tests
8 Dec.	At a meeting in Minsk, Belarus, the leaders of Russia, Ukraine and Belarus sign an Agreement establishing the Commonwealth of Independent States (CIS). They declare that the USSR has ceased to exist as a subject of international law and as a geopolitical reality. The new Commonwealth will preserve and maintain under united command 'a common military–strategic space', including unified control of nuclear weapons, the procedure for implementing which is regulated by a special agreement. The parties guarantee the fulfilment of the international obligations binding upon them from the treaties and agreements of the former USSR. Membership in the CIS is open to all republics of the former USSR and to any other state which shares its aims.	Russia, Ukraine, Belarus/USSR; CIS
9–11 Dec.	The EC heads of state and government, meeting in Maastricht, the Netherlands, agree on the text of a draft Treaty on an Economic and Monetary Union (EMU) and a draft Treaty on a European Political Union (EPU). Together these treaties make up the Treaty on European Union (EU). Under the EPU Treaty they pledge to work towards the framing of a common defence policy which might in time lead to a common defence, compatible with that of the Atlantic Alliance.	EC
9 Dec.	The UN General Assembly adopts Resolution 46/36L on 'Transparency in armaments'. It calls for the establishment of a register of conventional arms and urges all member states to provide annually for this register data on their imports and exports of arms.	UN; Arms transfers

11 Dec.	The South Korean President announces that all US nuclear weapons have been removed from South Korean territory. He offers to open US military bases to inspection by North Korea on condition that the North permit simultaneous inspection of its nuclear facilities.	South Korea; Nuclear weapons; Military bases
13 Dec.	The heads of states of Kazakhstan, Kyrgyzstan, Tajikistan, Turkmenistan, and Uzbekistan, meeting in Ashkhabad, Turkmenistan, declare that they wish to become equal co-founders of the Commonwealth of Independent States.	CIS
13 Dec.	The Prime Ministers of North and South Korea sign, in Seoul, an agreement on reconciliation, non-aggression, exchange and co-operation.	North Korea/ South Korea
13 Dec.	A safeguards agreement, covering all Argentinian and Brazilian nuclear activities, is signed between Argentina, Brazil, the joint Argentinian–Brazilian Agency for Accounting and Control of Nuclear Materials (ABACC) and the IAEA. (See *18 July.*)	Argentina/ Brazil/ABACC/ IAEA
15 Dec.	The UN Security Council unanimously adopts Resolution 724, endorsing a proposal by the UN Secretary-General to send a small group of personnel, including military personnel, to prepare for a possible deployment of a UN peace-keeping operation in Yugoslavia.	Yugoslavia; UN
16 Dec.	The Supreme Soviet of Kazakhstan declares independence.	Kazakhstan/ USSR
17 Dec.	The EC states, debating extending diplomatic recognition to Croatia and Slovenia, agree on the conditions which the new states wanting recognition will have to fulfil.	EC/Croatia, Slovenia
17 Dec.	Soviet President Gorbachev and Russian President Yeltsin agree that the USSR will cease to exist by the end of 1991.	USSR
19 Dec.	The North Atlantic Council, meeting in Brussels, supports the objective of developing the WEU as the defence component of the European Union and as a means of strengthening the European pillar of the Atlantic Alliance.	NATO; WEU
20 Dec.	The North Atlantic Cooperation Council (NACC) (see *8 Nov.*), holding its inaugural meeting in Brussels, issues a statement that it will undertake to contribute to strengthening the role of the CSCE and achieve full implementation of the CFE and the START treaties. It mandates an informal working group to discuss the ratification and implementation of the CFE Treaty.	NACC
21 Dec.	A Protocol to the Agreement on the Commonwealth of Independent States (CIS) (see *8 Dec.*) is signed in Alma-Ata, Kazakhstan, by the heads of state of Armenia, Azerbaijan, Belarus, Kazakhstan, Kyrgyzstan, Moldova,	CIS; UN; Russia; Nuclear weapons

Russia, Tajikistan, Turkmenistan, Uzbekistan and Ukraine. The Protocol makes the 8 Dec. Agreement valid for each of the states as soon as it is ratified. The CIS Council of Heads of State adopts a resolution supporting Russia in continuing the Soviet UN membership, including the permanent membership of the USSR in the UN Security Council and other international organizations. In a Declaration signed the same day, the states state that allied command of the military–strategic forces and single control over nuclear weapons will be preserved.

21 Dec.	Belarus, Kazakhstan, Russia and Ukraine sign, in Alma-Ata, Kazakhstan, an Agreement on joint measures with regard to nuclear weapons. They reaffirm their renunciation of the first use of nuclear weapons. Until those on the territory of Belarus and Ukraine have been completely eliminated, the decision to use them will be taken by the Russian President upon consulting with the heads of states, members of the Agreement. Belarus and Ukraine undertake to accede to the NPT as non-nuclear states. By 1 July 1992 Belarus, Kazakhstan and Ukraine will ensure the withdrawal of tactical nuclear weapons to central factory premises for dismantling under joint supervision. All four republics undertake to submit the START Treaty to their Supreme Soviets for ratification.	Nuclear weapons; Belarus, Kazakhstan, Russia, Ukraine
25 Dec.	President Gorbachev announces his resignation and reports to President Bush that he is handing over the nuclear launch codes to the President of Russia. The Soviet flag is lowered from the Kremlin.	USSR/Russia; Nuclear weapons
25 Dec.	The Yugoslav Federal Government calls for the introduction of UN peace-keeping forces.	Yugoslavia; UN
26 Dec.	The Soviet of the Republics of the USSR Supreme Soviet adopts a declaration stating that, with the establishment of the CIS, the USSR ceases its existence as a state and subject of international law.	USSR
27 Dec.	The Soviet representative to the CD delivers a letter to the CD in which the Ministry of Foreign Affairs of Russia announces that the membership of the USSR in the UN and the CD as well as its participation in all treaties and conventions negotiated in the CD are continued by the Russian Federation.	USSR/Russia
30 Dec.	At a meeting held in Minsk, the member states of the CIS sign an Agreement stating that they will observe the international treaties of the USSR and pursue a co-ordinated policy in the area of international security and arms control. They authorize the President of the Russian Federation to decide on the use of the strategic forces in agreement with the heads of Belarus, Kazakhstan and	CIS; Nuclear weapons

Ukraine and in consultation with the other CIS member states. Until their destruction, strategic nuclear weapons in Ukraine shall be under the control of an allied command, with the aim that they not be used, and be dismantled by the end of 1994. Tactical nuclear weapons should be dismantled by 1 July 1992. The destruction of nuclear weapons in Belarus and Ukraine shall take place in Russia with the participation of Belarus, Russia and Ukraine under the joint control of the CIS. In an Agreement on armed forces and border troops, signed on the same day, the CIS states confirm their legitimate right to set up their own armed forces.

31 Dec.   North and South Korea announce that they have signed a Declaration for a non-nuclear Korean peninsula in Panmunjom. The two states pledge not to test, produce, receive, possess, store, deploy or use nuclear weapons and not to possess facilities for nuclear reprocessing or uranium enrichment. Inspections will be conducted of objects chosen by the other side and agreed by both parties, according to the procedure and methods prescribed by a South–North Joint Control Committee.

North Korea/ South Korea; Nuclear weapons

About the contributors

Dr Ian Anthony (United Kingdom) is a Researcher on the SIPRI arms transfers and arms production project. He is the author of several chapters in and editor of the SIPRI volume *Arms Export Regulations* (1991) and author of the monograph *The Arms Trade and Medium Powers: Case Studies of India and Pakistan 1947–90* (1991). He has written chapters in the *SIPRI Yearbooks 1988–91*.

William M. Arkin (United States) is Director of Military Research of Greenpeace International. In 1981–89 he was Director of the National Security Program of the Institute for Policy Studies, Washington, DC. He is co-editor of the Natural Resources Defense Council *Nuclear Weapons Databook* series, and co-author of *Volume IV, Soviet Nuclear Weapons* (1989) and chapters in the *SIPRI Yearbooks* since 1985. He is a co-author of *Encyclopedia of the US Military* (1990) and a contributing editor of the *Bulletin of the Atomic Scientists*.

Dr Michael Brzoska (Germany) is a Researcher at the University of Hamburg Unit for the Study of Armaments, Wars and Development (1986–) and a Lecturer at the Institute for Political Science (1988–). He was formerly Researcher at the University of Hamburg Institute for Peace Research and Security Studies (1980–83) and Researcher at SIPRI on the arms trade project (1983–86). He is co-editor (with P. Lock) of the SIPRI volume *Restructuring of Arms Production in Western Europe* (1992). He co-authored chapters in the *SIPRI Yearbooks 1984–87*.

Agnès Courades Allebeck (France) is a Research Assistant on the SIPRI arms transfers and arms production project. She was formerly a Research Assistant at the European Parliament Luxembourg (1985) and has done research on the external relations of the European Community. She is a co-author of the SIPRI Research Report *West European Arms Production: Structural Changes in the New Political Environment* (1990), the author of a chapter in the *SIPRI Yearbook 1989* and co-author of chapters in the *SIPRI Yearbooks 1990* and *1991* and several chapters in the SIPRI volume *Arms Export Regulations* (1991).

Dr Regina Cowen Karp (Germany) is Senior Researcher and Leader of the SIPRI project on stability and instability in Central Europe and the new independent states. She is the editor of the SIPRI volumes *Security Without Nuclear Weapons* (1992) and *Security with Nuclear Weapons? Different Perspectives on National Security* (1991), and co-editor (with W. Stützle and B. Jasani) of *The ABM Treaty: To Defend or Not to Defend?* (1987). She is the author of chapters in the *SIPRI Yearbooks 1988–91*.

Christer Crantz (Sweden) is a Doctoral Candidate in Political Science at Wayne State University, Detroit, USA. He is a graduate research assistant at the Center for Peace and Conflict Studies at Wayne State University (1990–) and a former instructor at the Henry Ford Community College in Dearborn, Michigan (1987–88).

Dr Saadet Deger (Turkey) is Senior Researcher and Leader of the SIPRI world military expenditure project. She was formerly Research Fellow at Birkbeck College, University of London (1977–87). She is a member of the UNIDIR Working Group of Experts for the Economics of Disarmament, an expert adviser to the United Nations, consultant to the World Bank, and member of the Executive Board of the International Defence Economics Association and the Editorial Board of the journal *Defence Economics: The Political Economy of Defence Disarmament and Peace.* She is co-author (with S. Sen) of the SIPRI volume *Military Expenditure: The Political Economy of International Security* (1990), a co-editor of *Defence, Security and Development* (1987) and author of *Military Expenditure in Third World Countries: The Economic Effects* (1986). She has published many articles on disarmament and development, the economics of security in the Third World and the arms trade, and is the author of chapters in the *SIPRI Yearbooks 1988–91.*

Ambassador Rolf Ekéus (Sweden) is Executive Chairman of the United Nations Special Commission for overseeing the elimination of weapons of mass destruction in Iraq. Since 1989, he is the chief of the Swedish Delegation to the CSCE negotiations in Vienna. In 1983–88, he was the Permanent Representative of Sweden to the Conference on Disarmament and *inter alia* served in 1984 and 1987 as Chairman for the negotiations on the global convention to ban chemical weapons, the CWC.

Ragnhild Ferm (Sweden) is a Researcher on the SIPRI arms control and disarmament project. She has published chapters on nuclear explosions, a comprehensive test ban and arms control agreements, and the annual chronologies of arms control and political events in the *SIPRI Yearbooks* since 1982. She is the author of the serial SIPRI publication *Rustning eller nedrustning?* (in Swedish) [*Armaments or Disarmament?*].

Richard Fieldhouse (United States) is a US Senate legislative assistant on military and arms control affairs. He was previously Senior Research Associate at the Natural Resources Defense Council, Washington, DC, and is co-author of the forthcoming NRDC publication *Nuclear Weapons Databook, Volume V, British, French and Chinese Nuclear Weapons.* In 1985–89 he was a Researcher at SIPRI and leader of the project on naval forces and arms control. He is the editor of the SIPRI volume *Security at Sea: Naval Forces and Arms Control* (1990) and co-author (with S. Taoka) of *Superpowers at Sea: An Assessment of the Naval Arms Race* (1989). He is co-author or author of chapters in the *SIPRI Yearbooks* since 1985.

Professor Erhard Geissler (Germany) is Professor of Genetics at the Max Delbrück Centre for Molecular Medicine (Berlin), and has conducted research in the fields of biophysics, microbial genetics and tumour virology. He is editor of the SIPRI volumes *Biological and Toxin Weapons Today* (1986) and *Strengthening the Biological Weapons Convention by Confidence-Building Measures* (1990), and author of a chapter in *Views on Possible Verification Measures for the Biological Weapons Convention* (1991) and a chapter in the *SIPRI Yearbook 1984.* He co-edited *Prevention of a Biological and Toxin Arms Race and the Responsibility of Scientists* (1991). Over the past 20 years he has published extensively on the subject of biological weapons, the social impact of genetics and other biosciences and the responsibility of scientists.

Jozef Goldblat (Sweden) is a Senior Lecturer at the Geneva Institute of International Studies and Consultant to UNIDIR. He was formerly head of the arms control and disarmament programme of studies at SIPRI (1968–88). He is the author or editor of several SIPRI volumes as well as *Twenty Years of the Non-Proliferation Treaty: Implementation and Prospects* (1990) and *The Third Review of the Biological Weapons Convention: Issues and Proposals* (1991) and editor of *Confidence-Building Measures for Maritime Security*, (a forthcoming UNIDIR publication).

Gerd Hagmeyer-Gaverus (Germany) is a Researcher on the SIPRI arms transfers and arms production project. He was formerly a Researcher at the Centre for Social Science Research at the Free University, Berlin, where he co-authored several research reports. He is a co-author of chapters on world military expenditure in the *SIPRI Yearbooks 1985, 1987* and *1988* and on arms production in the *SIPRI Yearbooks 1990* and *1991*.

Birger Heldt (Sweden) is a Research Associate and responsible for the armed conflicts data project at the Department of Peace and Conflict Research, Uppsala University, Sweden. He is co-author of a chapter in *States in Armed Conflict 1989* (1991) and a chapter in the *SIPRI Yearbook 1991*, and author of *States in Armed Conflict 1990, 1991* (1992).

Professor Alexei Kireyev (Russian Federation) is economic adviser to the Moscow Office of the World Bank. He was in 1982–89 Associate Professor at the Moscow State Institute of International Relations, and in 1989–91 senior economic adviser on the staff of the President of the USSR. He is the author of *Who Will Pay for 'Star Wars'?* (1989) and the booklet *Conversion: disarmament for development* (1990). He has written over 100 articles on military economy and the economics of disarmament.

Dr Zdzislaw Lachowski (Poland) is a Research Associate on the SIPRI project on building a co-operative security system in and for Europe. He has been a Researcher at the Polish Institute of International Affairs since 1980, where he dealt with problems of European security and the CSCE process in particular, as well as Western European political integration. He has written extensively on these subjects. He is the co-editor of *Visions of Europe* (in Polish, 1989).

Signe Landgren (Sweden) is a Researcher on the SIPRI Soviet arms control programme. She is the author of the SIPRI volumes *Embargo Disimplemented: South Africa's Military Industry* (1989), *Southern Africa: The Escalation of a Conflict* (1976) and *Sufficient Defence: The Post-Soviet States, New Conflicts and New Armed Forces* (1992).

Sarah Lang, (United States) a graduate of Amherst College, is a Research Associate of the Space Policy Project at the Federation of American Scientists in Washington,

DC, specializing in issues related to the Commonwealth of Independent States and the Baltic nations.

Evamaria Loose-Weintraub (Germany) is a Research Assistant on the SIPRI military expenditure project. She has published chapters on Spanish and Austrian arms trade and production in the *SIPRI Yearbooks 1984–86*. She is currently doing post-graduate research on Latin America's economic development.

Dr S. J. Lundin (Sweden) is a Senior Director of Research at the Swedish Defence Research Institute (FOA) and was in 1987–92 Senior Researcher and Head of the SIPRI chemical and biological warfare programme and editor of the SIPRI CBW Studies. He was formerly Scientific Adviser to the Swedish Disarmament Delegation (1969–85) and adviser on NBC questions to the Swedish Supreme Commander (1985–87). He is the author of chapters in the *SIPRI Yearbooks 1988–91* and has written extensively in the field of chemical and biological weapons.

Paolo Miggiano (Italy) is a Research Assistant on the SIPRI arms transfers and arms production project. He was formerly Researcher at the Istituto Ricerche Disarmo Sviluppo e Pace (IRDISP) in Rome (1985–89). In 1989–90 he was Senior Visiting Fellow at the Pugwash Office, Rome. He is the author of chapters on civil defence and the defence postures of Italy and the neutral states, and on Italian military policy in the yearbook of the Istituto Affari Internazionali. He is a co-editor of *L'Italia e la corse al riarmo* (1987).

Dr Harald Müller (Germany) is Senior Researcher and Director of International Programs at the Peace Research Institute Frankfurt (PRIF). His most recent publications include *Falling into Line? France and the NPT* (1990) and *Germany and the Bomb: Nuclear Policies in the Two German States, and the United Germany's Non-proliferation Commitments* (1990). He is editor of *Deciding on the Atom: How West ern European Nuclear Policy is Made* (1990), co-author (with R. Kokoski) of the SIPRI Research Report *The Non-Proliferation Treaty: Political and Technological Prospects and Dangers in 1990* (1990), author of a chapter in the *SIPRI Yearbook 1990*, and co-author of a chapter in the *SIPRI Yearbook 1991*.

Kjell-Åke Nordquist (Sweden) is a Research Associate at the Department of Peace and Conflict Research, Uppsala University, Sweden. He is co-author (with C. Ahlström) of *Casualties of Conflict* (1991), prepared for the Red Cross/Red Crescent Movements' World Campaign for the Protection of Victims of War, and author of *Conflicting Peace Proposals: Four Peace Proposals in the Palestine Conflict Appraised* (1985) and of a contribution in C. Alger and M. Stohl (eds), *A Just Peace Through Transformation* (1988). He is a co-author of chapters in the *SIPRI Year-books 1990* and *1991*.

Dr Robert S. Norris (United States) is Senior Staff Analyst at the Natural Resources Defense Council, Washington, DC. He was formerly Senior Research analyst for the Center for Defense Information, Washington, DC. He is co-author of the 1987 and 1989 volumes of the NRDC *Nuclear Weapons Databook*, and *Volume V, British,*

French and Chinese Nuclear Weapons and Nuclear Weapons Proliferation (forthcoming). He is co-author of chapters in the *SIPRI Yearbooks* since 1985 and a column for the *Bulletin of the Atomic Scientists*. With an NRDC colleague he wrote the entry on nuclear weapons for the *Encyclopedia Britannica* (1990 printing).

Dr Frederic S. Pearson (United States) is a Professor of Political Science and Director at the Center for Peace and Conflict Studies at Wayne State University, Detroit, USA. He was formerly Professor of Political Science and Fellow at the Center for International Studies, University of Missouri, St Louis. Recent publications include *International Relations: The Global Condition in the Late Twentieth Century* (1991) with J. M. Rochester and *The Spread of Arms in the International System* (forthcoming) and 'Foreign military intervention and realpolitik' in *The Changing Nature of Realpolitik*, edited by P. Diehl with R. A. Baumann and J. Pickering (forthcoming).

John Pike (United States) is Director of the Space Policy Project at the Federation of American Scientists in Washington, DC. He directs FAS research and public education on military and civilian space policy. A former political consultant and science writer, he is the author of over 170 studies and articles on space and national security chapters in the *SIPRI Yearbooks 1989–91* on the military uses of outer space.

Dr Adam Daniel Rotfeld (Poland) is the Director of SIPRI and leader of the project on building a co-operative security system in and for Europe. He has been head of the European Security Department in the Polish Institute of International Affairs, Warsaw since 1978. He was a member of the Polish Delegation to the Conference on Security and Co-operation in Europe (Geneva, 1973–75) and to the CSCE Follow-up Meetings (Belgrade 1977–78, Madrid 1980–83 and Vienna, 1986–88). He is the author or editor of over 20 studies on European security and the CSCE process, most recently (co-edited with W. Stützle) the SIPRI volume *Germany and Europe in Transition* (1991).

Dr Somnath Sen (India) is a Reader in Development Economics at the University of Birmingham, UK. He was Senior Researcher on the SIPRI world military expenditure project (1989–92). He is a co-author (with S. Deger) of the SIPRI volume *Military Expenditure: The Political Economy of International Security* (1990). His other publications include *Protectionism, Exchange Rates and the Macroeconomy* (1985), many articles on disarmament and development and macroeconomics, as well as chapters in the *SIPRI Yearbooks 1990* and *1991*.

Jane M. O. Sharp (United Kingdom) is a Senior Research Fellow at King's College and the Institute for Public Policy Research (IPPR), both in London. In 1987–91 she was Senior Researcher at SIPRI and before that held teaching and research fellowships at Harvard and Cornell Universities. She has written extensively on arms control and the security dilemmas of military alliances, with a current focus on security options available to the former members of the Warsaw Treaty Organization following the collapse of the WTO and dissolution of the USSR. She is the editor of the

SIPRI volume *Europe After an American Withdrawal* (1990) and author of *Negotiations on Conventional Armed Forces in Europe: 1989–91* (forthcoming).

Elisabeth Sköns (Sweden) is a Researcher on the SIPRI arms transfers and arms production project. She was previously Researcher at the Research Service of the Swedish Parliament (1987–91) and Research Assistant on the SIPRI military expenditure and arms transfers projects (1978–87). She is co-author of chapters in the *SIPRI Yearbooks 1984, 1985* and *1987*, and author of chapters in the *SIPRI Yearbooks 1983* and *1986*.

Eric Stambler (United States) is a Research Analyst with the Space Policy Project of the Federation of American Scientists. He is a graduate of Dartmouth College and has previously held research positions at the Committee for National Security and the Institute for Peace and International Security.

Dr Thomas Stock (Germany) is a Researcher on the SIPRI chemical and biological warfare programme. He is an analytical chemist and was formerly a researcher at the Research Unit for Chemical Toxicology of the former Academy of Sciences of the GDR. He is a co-author of chapters in the SIPRI volumes *Verification of Conventional Arms Control in Europe* (1990) and *Non-Production by Industry of Chemical Warfare Agents: Technical Verification under a Chemical Weapons Convention* (1988) and co-editor of *National Implementation of the Future Chemical Weapons Convention* (1990). He is also co-author of the CBW chapter in the *SIPRI Yearbook 1991* and has written several articles in the field of verification of chemical disarmament.

Professor Peter Wallensteen (Sweden) holds the Dag Hammarskjöld Chair in Peace and Conflict Research and is the Head of the Department of Peace and Conflict Research, Uppsala University, Sweden. He is the author of a chapter in *Behaviour, Society and Nuclear War, vol. II* (in ed. Tetlock *et al.*, 1991), and co-author of *Environmental Destruction and Serious Social Conflict* (1991). He is a co-author of chapters in the *SIPRI Yearbooks 1988–91*.

Dr Herbert Wulf (Germany) is Senior Researcher and Leader of the SIPRI project on arms transfers and arms production. He is on leave of absence from the University of Hamburg Institute for Peace Research and Security Policy. Prior to his work in peace research, he was Director of the German Volunteer Service in India. He is co-author of the SIPRI Research Report *West European Arms Production: Structural Changes in the New Political Environment* (1990), author of chapters in *Arms Export Regulations* (1991) and *Alternative Produktion statt Rüstung* (1987), and the author of *Rüstungsexport aus Deutschland* (1989). He has published books and articles on security policy, arms production, arms transfers, conversion, and disarmament and development. He is the author of a chapter in the *SIPRI Yearbook 1985* and co-author of two chapters in the *SIPRI Yearbooks 1990* and *1991*.

SIPRI Yearbook 1992: World Armaments and Disarmament

Oxford University Press, Oxford, 1992, 670 pp.
(Stockholm International Peace Research Institute)
ISBN 0-19-829159-0

ABSTRACTS

ROTFELD, A. D., 'Introduction: The fundamental changes and the new security agenda', in *SIPRI Yearbook 1992*, pp. 1–10.

The cold war ended in 1991: the 1991 START Treaty and the 1992 Treaty on Open Skies were agreed upon and landmark unilateral nuclear arms reductions were announced. After the breakup of the USSR the threat of global military confrontation vanished and new problems and challenges emerged. UN Special Commission inspections proved the violation of international commitments by Iraq. Discussions on a new European Security Forum at the Vienna CFE and CSBM talks and the 1992 CSCE follow-up meeting in Helsinki, work to improve the UN system, and the search for new strategy and organizational solutions for NATO, the EC and the WEU all show the growing role of international security institutions.

COWEN KARP, R., 'The START Treaty and the future of strategic nuclear arms control', in *SIPRI Yearbook 1992*, pp. 13–64.

Signature of the START Treaty in July 1991 and the breakup of the USSR signalled the end of an era of bilateral nuclear arms control negotiations. The START Treaty requires both sides to make significant cuts in offensive nuclear forces although some provisions have been superseded by radical change in the former USSR, unilateral reduction initiatives and the prospect of far-reaching reductions in negotiations. The verification provisions provide transparency, predictability and an orderly transition to a new post-cold war and post-Soviet arms control environment. The future of strategic nuclear arms control will be very different. Policy rationales that created and sustained the traditional approach will have to be revised in the new international situation. Nuclear arms control is becoming an exercise of safely disposing of cold war arsenals while the proliferation of weapons of mass destruction has begun to govern the new international security agenda.

FIELDHOUSE, R., 'Nuclear weapon developments and unilateral reduction initiatives', in *SIPRI Yearbook 1992*, pp. 65–92.

Nuclear weapon history changed dramatically in 1991. The USA and the USSR, and then Russia, announced nuclear reduction initiatives in late 1991 and early 1992 which effectively cancelled the bulk of their respective non-strategic nuclear arsenals and curtailed a portion of their strategic nuclear activities. NATO agreed to reduce its remaining stockpile of nuclear gravity bombs by half, most to be cut by the USA, but the UK would cut about half of its nuclear bombs deployed in Germany. By 1992 international concern had shifted from the cold war nuclear confrontation to proliferation of nuclear weapons and systems. The activities of China were of great concern in this regard.

MÜLLER, H., 'The nuclear non-proliferation regime beyond the Persian Gulf War and the dissolution of the Soviet Union', in *SIPRI Yearbook 1992*, pp. 93–106.

An unprecedented number of events in nuclear proliferation and non-proliferation took place in 1991. After findings by the UN Special Commission and the IAEA, Iraq was condemned for breaching the NPT. Major initiatives were taken to reform nuclear safeguards and export controls and all EC member states adopted full-scope safeguards as a condition for nuclear exports. South Africa acceded to the NPT; France and China announced intentions to do so, and Argentina and Brazil each signed a full-scope safeguards agreement with the IAEA. Increasing international pressure about North Korea's unsafeguarded nuclear activities led the two Korean states to agree on a nuclear-weapon free zone on the peninsula and on renouncing enrichment and reprocessing. There was also concern, but with less evidence, about Algeria and Iran. No real progress in non-proliferation policies was reported from South Asia or the Near East.

NORRIS, R. S. and GOLDBLAT, J., 'Nuclear explosions and the talks on test limitations', in *SIPRI Yearbook 1992*, pp. 107–19.

In 1991, 14 nuclear tests were conducted, 4 fewer than in 1990 and the lowest number since the early 1950s. The USA conducted 7, the French 6 and the UK 1 test. The USSR and China did not conduct any tests in 1991. The decline continues a trend begun in 1988 and is likely to continue due to reduced military budgets, fewer warhead programmes, and international and domestic pressures to restrict or ban testing. Other developments included Kazakhstan's President Nazarbayev ordering the closure of the Semipalatinsk test site and Soviet President Gorbachev imposing a one-year moratorium on testing on 5 October. At the 1991 Partial Test Ban Treaty Amendment Conference, a group of 6 states proposed a new article and two protocols in which parties would prohibit, prevent and not carry out any explosions underground or in any other environment. At the Conference on Disarmament, Sweden introduced a draft comprehensive test ban treaty. Both were serious attempts to solve problems of verification and pave the way to a CTBT.

PIKE, J., LANG, S. and STAMBLER, E., 'Military use of outer space', in *SIPRI Yearbook 1992*, pp. 121–46.

Interest in military space and strategic defence systems in 1991 focused on the battlefield role of US space assets in the Persian Gulf War, reorientation of parts of the US strategic defence programmes to meet global tactical missile threats and the devolution of the Soviet space programme after the disintegration of the Soviet Union. The disparity in military space capabilities was a distinguishing feature of the Persian Gulf War, the first 'space war' in which modern military space assets were applied to a terrestrial conflict. US proponents of the Strategic Defense Initiative succeeded in reversing the political fortunes of the programme in 1991. The budget approved by Congress more than reversed the cutbacks of prior years. Congress endorsed the eventual deployment of a large ground-based system that would far exceed limits imposed by the Anti-Ballistic Missile Treaty. The political transformation of the Soviet Union led to an evolution in US attitudes towards antimissile systems.

LUNDIN, S. J., STOCK, T. and GEISSLER, E., 'Chemical and biological warfare and arms control developments in 1991', in *SIPRI Yearbook 1992*, pp. 147–86.

Chemical weapons (CW) and biological weapons (BW) were not used in the Gulf War, but the setting afire of Kuwaiti oil wells created environmental damage. Allegations of BW and CW proliferation continued. The question of how Iraq acquired its huge chemical arsenal was investigated. Problems arose in US and Soviet CW destruction efforts and related to the discovery of old CW. The USA urged that the Chemical Weapons Convention (CWC) be finalized in 1992, agreed not to retain a small CW stockpile during the CWC's 10-year destruction period, pledged not to retaliate in kind to CW attack and advocated less intrusive verification measures. Efforts to create zones free of weapons of mass destruction continued in South America and on the Korean peninsula. The Third Review Conference of the BWC reinforced its validity and coverage, instituted new information exchange measures and set up an expert committee to study verification measures.

DEGER, S. and SEN, S., 'World military expenditure', in *SIPRI Yearbook 1992*, pp. 189–270.

World military expenditure fell in 1991 for the third successive year. In spite of 30 wars, the downward trend is established, owing to the fact that the USA and the former Soviet Union, accounting for more than 60% of the world total, cut spending considerably. European NATO was more cautious, but plans for re-structuring and reductions are being made. Third World military spending also fell, although the Middle East showed an increase. In the USSR, where procurement and military R&D were being drastically pruned, military personnel spending remained stable. Economic constraints and arms control have forced defence cuts in the former Soviet Union, although the pace of de-militarization is still slow. Personnel numbers are expected to fall, while spending on manpower will show less decline because of increases in pay and benefits. Procurement in major weapons systems will fall but increased efficiency of existing systems will be sought. Military R&D will also decline but there will be greater integration with civilian research to get the benefits of technological 'spin-ins'.

ANTHONY, I., COURADES ALLEBECK, A., MIGGIANO, P., SKÖNS, E. and WULF, H., 'The trade in major conventional weapons', in *SIPRI Yearbook 1992*, pp. 271–359.

The dissolution of the USSR, the Gulf War and steps by major exporting countries to introduce multilateral arms export regulations were new factors in the arms trade discussion in 1991. Post-cold war economic, technological and political factors are the new determinants of arms transfer policy. The global value of the trade in major conventional weapons in 1991 is estimated at $22 114 million—continuing the downward trend after 1987. The USA was the dominant supplier, and the value of Soviet arms transfers declined dramatically. Collectively, EC countries increased their market share. Countries whose imports fell most dramatically—Angola, Czechoslovakia, Iraq and North Korea—were all major clients of the USSR in the 1980s. Iraq was removed from the arms market by the 1990 UN trade embargo, but other Middle Eastern countries evaluated new equipment and large contracts are likely in 1992. In 1991 many governments accepted the need for arms transfer control, but the nature and extent of an appropriate regime were not determined.

MIGGIANO, P., SKÖNS, E., WULF. H. and KIREYEV, A., 'Arms production', in *SIPRI Yearbook 1992*, pp. 361–97.

The political changes of 1991 have affected arms production world-wide. Governments are in the process of restructuring national armed forces and revising military equipment procurement plans. Many companies in North America and Western Europe were engaged in down-scaling, although many of them still benefit from orders that they acquired before the end of the cold war. In the Asia–Pacific region, in contrast, a number of governments are undertaking major modernization projects. Arms production in China and Japan—the two largest producers in that region—exemplify this trend. The changes in the arms production sector in the Commonwealth of Independent States were much more dramatic than in other parts of the world. In the chaotic economic and political situation in the former Soviet Union arms procurement was reduced and the conversion programme was in jeopardy.

PEARSON, F. S., BRZOSKA, M. and CRANTZ, C., 'The effects of arms transfers on wars and peace negotiations', in *SIPRI Yearbook 1992*, pp. 399–415.

Relationships between two major armed conflicts in 1991, in the Persian Gulf and Yugoslavia, and arms transfers immediately before and during these wars are analysed in detail. The method used is adapted from a larger historical study. The complexity of individual cases found in that study is confirmed again, as are a few general conclusions. The leverage of arms suppliers on warring parties—before and during wars as well as in peace negotiations—is small. Arms transfers before wars can enhance stability and deterrence but often will not because assessments of the situation, and risk calculations differ between suppliers and recipients. The behaviour of Iraq's leadership illustrates the latter point. Arms transfers during wars often prolong and escalate suffering and destruction, a lesson fortunately soon learned during the war in Yugoslavia. These conclusions lend analytical support to policies aiming at cutting arms transfers to conflict areas.

HELDT, B., WALLENSTEEN, P. and NORDQUIST, K.-Å., 'Major armed conflicts in 1991', in *SIPRI Yearbook 1992*, pp. 417–56.

Major armed conflicts were waged in 30 locations in 1991. There is a gradual reduction of the number of conflicts since the mid-1980s. During 1991 there were settlements in five conflict locations (Angola, Cambodia, El Salvador, Liberia and Western Sahara). In four locations, no major armed conflict was recorded for 1991 (Laos, Lebanon, India–Pakistan and Nicaragua). Major armed conflicts emerged in three new locations (Iraq–Kuwait, Rwanda and Yugoslavia). As in previous years, most major armed conflicts were internal and an important proportion dealt with territorial issues. The end of the cold war was apparent in the global patterns of conflict, for instance, in the termination of some conflicts with a marked cold war dimension (Cambodia, El Salvador). This was also reflected in the emergence of new conflict patterns, the most notable of which was the collaboration between the USA and the USSR during the Iraq–Kuwait conflict, the most publicized conflict of the year.

SHARP, J. M. O., 'Conventional arms control in Europe: developments and prospects in 1991', in *SIPRI Yearbook 1992*, pp. 459–505.

The dissolution of the USSR presented obstacles to the ratification and implementation of the 1990 Treaty on Conventional Armed Forces in Europe (CFE), and by the end of 1991 only 9 of the original 22 signatories had ratified the Treaty. The North Atlantic Co-operation Council (NACC) formed a High Level Working Group (HLWG) of all signatories and former Soviet republics within the area of application to help bring the Treaty into force. Separate negotiations on military personnel (CFE 1A) and aerial surveillance (Open Skies) continued in Vienna, and a Treaty on Open Skies was signed in March 1992. Appendices to the chapter examine the implementation of the confidence- and security-building measures of the Vienna Document 1990 and report on the Second Vienna Seminar on Military Doctrine.

EKÉUS, R., 'The United Nations Special Commission on Iraq', in *SIPRI Yearbook 1992*, pp. 509–30.

UN Security Council Resolution 687 signified the conclusion of the Persian Gulf War. It established the UN Special Commission (UNSCOM) and empowered it to carry out on-site inspection of Iraq's biological, chemical, nuclear and missile capabilities and to provide for their elimination. Two plans provide for future monitoring and verification that Iraq does not use, develop, construct or reacquire any items specified for elimination. UNSCOM is responsible for chemical and biological weapons and ballistic missiles while the IAEA has primary responsibility for Iraq's nuclear capability with the assistance and co-operation of UNSCOM. The inspection teams are to have unrestricted access, and Iraq is required to disclose all information about its programmes to develop weapons of mass destruction and ballistic missiles. Iraq has not fully complied with these provisions and it has not been possible to acquire full knowledge of the weapon programmes. UNSCOM must therefore continue its investigation and expand its information-gathering capability. Only when UNSCOM can adequately assess Iraqi compliance with Resolution 687 and related resolutions could the embargo imposed by the UN Security Council on Iraq be lifted.

LANDGREN, S., 'Post-Soviet threats to security', in *SIPRI Yearbook 1992*, pp. 531–62.

The dissolution of the USSR brought new dangers to security both in the context of the European peace process and internationally. These dangers are presented under the headings of the military heritage of a superpower and the conflict heritage of a superpower. Foremost among the emerging security risks is the fate of the former Soviet nuclear arsenal and the fate of the huge armed forces including the risk of a political take-over by conservative military forces. Second, the unsolved and during the Soviet era artificially pacified national and ethnic conflicts within the vast empire are now coming to the surface and demanding their solution. The escalating and increasingly violent conflict over Nagorno-Karabakh stands out as a disheartening example, so far defying all attempts at mediation. Against the background of a hazardous transformation of the economic system, the prospects of civil strife and social disaster, the situation in the post-Soviet countries presents a formidable challenge to the rest of the world.

ROTFELD, A. D., 'European security structures in transition', in *SIPRI Yearbook 1992*, pp. 563–92.

Rapid developments and dramatic changes made the new security institutions established by decisions of the 1990 Paris CSCE summit meeting play only a limited role in strengthening security among European states. These new structures must be critically examined, focusing on the new architecture of European security, in order to show how CSCE principles have stood the test of confronting new realities and challenges. Enlarging the number of CSCE members was accompanied by expanding the tasks. The new CSCE security concept includes political, economic and human rights components and more military aspects, such as new CSBMs, the 1990 CFE Treaty and a European Security Forum. The main tasks related to the 1992 CSCE summit meeting in Helsinki are not so much connected with the question of how to form the new structures but with how to make operation of the 'interlocking system' of existing institutions more efficient. The conclusion of a General Treaty on Security and Co-operation in Europe may be considered.

Errata

SIPRI Yearbook 1991: World Armaments and Disarmament

Page 107, line 11:

'Australia Group, a group of 21 countries' should read 'Australia Group, a group of 21 members (20 countries and the European Community)'.

Page 228–29, table 7A.1:

In the row South Asia, A, figures in the last nine columns, for 1982–90, should read: 11 434, 12 339, 11 677, 10 150, 10 401, 13 522, 8 087, 4 469, 4 838. In the row Central America, A, figures for the entire row, 1971–90, should read: 135, 261, 309, 299, 201, 234, 557, 263, 295, 181, 753, 1 188, 1 092, 574, 658, 618, 376, 203, 248, 368. In the row North Africa, A, figures for the entire row, 1971–90, should read: 224, 373, 340, 591, 2 343, 2 282, 2 619, 3 936, 5 749, 3 341, 3 008, 3 059, 1 707, 1 522, 1 136, 1 398, 538, 409, 1 281, 133.

Page 371, line 5, in the conflict description for Liberia:

'On 21 Dec. the parties agreed to form an interim Govt.' should read 'On 21 Dec. the parties agreed to work for the establishment of an interim Govt.'.

INDEX